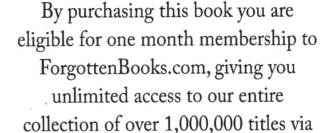

ISBN 978-0-266-97984-5
PIBN 10918759

FB &c Ltd, Dalton House, 60 Windsor Avenue, London, SW19 2RR.
Company number 08720141. Registered in England and Wales.

U. S. DEPARTMENT OF AGRICULTURE.

Department Bulletins

Nos. 201-225,

WITH CONTENTS
AND INDEX.

Prepared in the Division of Publications.

WASHINGTON:
GOVERNMENT PRINTING OFFICE.
1916.

CONTENTS.

INDEX.

○

UNITED STATES DEPARTMENT OF AGRICULTURE

BULLETIN No. 201

Contribution from the Bureau of Plant Industry, WM. A. TAYLOR, Chief, and the Bureau of Chemistry, CARL L. ALSBERG, Chief

NATIVE PASTURE GRASSES OF THE UNITED STATES

By

DAVID GRIFFITHS, Agriculturist, Office of Farm Management, Bureau of Plant Industry, and GEORGE L. BIDWELL, Chief of the Cattle-Food and Grain Investigation Laboratory, and CHARLES E. GOODRICH, Assistant Chemist, Bureau of Chemistry

CONTENTS

WASHINGTON
GOVERNMENT PRINTING OFFICE
1915

BULLETIN OF THE
US DEPARTMENT OF AGRICULTURE

No. 201

Contribution from the Bureau of Plant Industry, Wm. A. Taylor, Chief, and the Bureau of Chemistry, Carl L. Alsberg, Chief.
May 26, 1915.

(PROFESSIONAL PAPER.)

NATIVE PASTURE GRASSES OF THE UNITED STATES.

By DAVID GRIFFITHS, *Agriculturist, Office of Farm Management, Bureau of Plant Industry*, and GEORGE L. BIDWELL, *Chief of the Cattle-Food and Grain Investigation Laboratory*, and CHARLES E. GOODRICH, *Assistant Chemist, Bureau of Chemistry*.

CONTENTS.

INTRODUCTION.

On account of the widely varying conditions, the meagerness, or often absence, of information relative to the economic value of the numerous range forage plants entering into the beef, mutton, and wool producing rations of the range animals of this country, it has become desirable that a great deal of original investigation and much compilation should be made. In order that this information may be available, it is highly desirable that it be brought together and made sufficiently comprehensive to furnish a general reference.

It was with these ideas in mind that these investigations were begun several years ago. A large part of the work has been done on the saltbushes, the legumes, the browse plants, sedges, and rushes, the nonlegume and nongrass herbaceous forages, and the miscellaneous plants from all groups.

The field work is done in connection with other investigations in the Office of Farm Management of the Bureau of Plant Industry and the laboratory work by the Cattle-Food and Grain Laboratory of the Bureau of Chemistry.

This installment of the work, dealing with a part of the grasses, treats of the most important group of native forages, but of course only a fraction of that group is included.

NOTE.—This bulletin contains the results of investigations and compilations, mainly of experiment-station literature, that will be of value to chemists, agricultural writers, and ranchmen.

In the analyses, the methods of the Association of Official Agricultural Chemists, as published in Bulletin No. 107 of the Bureau of Chemistry, U. S. Department of Agriculture, have been employed. The analytical work in large measure was done by Mr. C. E. Goodrich, assistant chemist, Cattle-Food and Grain Laboratory. About one-fourth of the determinations were made by various other analysts in the same office.

The work is confined to the continental United States, and the references cited are mainly from departmental and experiment-station literature. Discretion has been constantly exercised in the admission of data from all sources. Many analyses found in the literature have been omitted from our compilations on account of incompleteness, doubt as to the identity of the species dealt with, evident errors, and other reasons. To obviate such uncertainties in connection with our own work, museum specimens have been preserved. These, in all cases, can be located by the aid of the serial collection number of the senior writer of this paper, given in each table as "Our sample No."

It appears that nothing is to be gained by attempting any scientific arrangement of the species discussed, and few botanical data are given. It is considered that an alphabetical arrangement will be more convenient, and that the indices to the different parts will be much more serviceable to the one using the paper than an arrangement in conformity with botanical usage.

Chemical analyses of feeds are used by all feeders in calculating rations and by investigators in performing digestion experiments. Nearly all experiment stations maintain a laboratory to make analyses of feeds in connection with their experiments on the feeding value of various farm products.

It has been shown by numerous experiments that a plant varies in composition with age. On this account care has been exercised to indicate definitely the condition of growth of the samples analyzed by us. This fact must be considered in any comparisons made. Failure to record such data is a fertile source of irregularity in much chemical work done on natural feeds.

While these analyses do not show all that is desirable, they do show relative values, when taken in connection with the notes, and they enable a comparison of the species here enumerated to be made with better known feeds. The compilations of other analyses will simplify the labors of agronomists, agriculturists, and agricultural writers generally who have occasion to employ such data.

GENERAL CONSIDERATIONS.

It has been quite conclusively shown that the range question in this country is preeminently one of management. The greater part of our range land capable of economical improvement through seeding with any plants whose seed can be secured successfully is worth more for farming purposes than for uncultivated pastures. Land capable of being farmed is called for; consequently, pastures capable of artificial improvement by easy displacement of native vegetation are rapidly decreasing.

The more moist situations, usually small in extent, where the use of certain seed, such as that of timothy, redtop, and bluegrass, without thorough cultivation, will produce economic results are, however, in the aggregate extensive. (Pl. II, fig. 1.) These moist mountain and other meadows can be improved greatly, and they constitute the main areas where the use of seed upon land, without placing that land under thorough cultivation, has been productive of economic results.

It is true that many introduced plants are of very great importance upon some of the western ranges to-day, but those intentionally introduced have as yet become of only minor importance, with the exception of possibly some of the bur clovers, and even these can scarcely be expected to become of greater importance than the common accidental introduction of very early date. The Australian saltbush (*Atriplex semibaccata*), from which so much was once expected, is now known to be very much restricted in importance. This is not saying that plants may not yet be found which will increase the feed upon some of the western uncultivated pastures. Every effort should be made to introduce such crops. But it is evident from past experience that over most of the native pastures of our country we must depend mostly, if not entirely, upon the native forage plants indigenous to the different regions (Pl. VII, fig. 2). It is, therefore, highly important that these natives, which are manifestly to furnish in the future, as in the past, the most important part of the feed supply of the stock ranges, should receive continuous and careful study. This paper is intended as a contribution toward a better knowledge of the problems of these feeds.

The immediate problem, as in agriculture generally, is one of production. The copious literature on the subject of native pastures which has been issued by the Department of Agriculture and the State agricultural experiment stations clearly shows that the production of feed has decreased and has been so modified upon accessible lands as to furnish a poor indication of the production and the aspect which once obtained. At present, it is only in areas where ingenuity has not yet devised adequate water supply, or where areas have been protected, that present feed production resembles the original either in quality or quantity (Pl. I, figs. 1 and 2).

DISCUSSION OF SPECIES.

AGROPYRON SMITHII Rydb.

Agropyron smithii is an important species, familiarly known as Colorado bluestem. All in all, it is undoubtedly the most important native hay grass of the western Plains region, extending into the mountains of northern Arizona. It is closely related to the quack-grass of the cultivated East, to which its habits are very comparable; like quack-grass, it is benefited by partial cultivation. For this reason throughout the Dakotas it is a familiar thing to see this species making a very decided increase in growth in the edges of cultivated fields. Here it comes in contact with the undisturbed prairies, where it once grew in abundance, either pure or mixed with the gramas and buffalo grass. In some situations, where water is available for irrigation, especially along the eastern slope of the Black Hills of South Dakota, meadows have been cut for 10 years, yielding an excellent quality of hay from this grass, to the extent of 1½ tons to the acre. Although its seed habits are good and the seed production abundant, it is seldom that it reproduces from seed under natural conditions, although under cultivation it is readily grown in this way. Indeed, upon the native prairies it is common for it not even to head out, seed production taking place only in favorable years. Its reproduction is almost entirely by running rootstocks. In 1897 crops of it were excellent throughout the Dakotas and Montana, many areas of uncultivated lowland prairies having a perfect stand and resembling fields of grain more than native hay. It certainly could be easily domesticated and might prove a valuable grass for cultivation. It has already been extensively grown in small plats by the State experiment stations and reports of it are generally favorable.

No. 8810 was collected near Fargo, N. Dak., August 10, 1907.

Material analyzed.	Percentage of moisture.	Water-free basis (per cent).					
		Ash.	Ether extract.	Crude fiber.	Nitrogen-free extract.	Protein.	Pentosans.
Our sample No. 8810	7.88	11.58	2.32	32.27	43.73	10.10	24.13
Average of 19 others [1]	....	8.05	2.93	34.41	44.98	9.63	....
Average of all	....	8.23	2.90	34.30	44.92	9.65	....

[1] Canada Central Experiment Farm Bul. 19, pp. 28, 32. Colorado Bul. 12, p. 130. Iowa: Bul. 11, p. 464; Bul. 56, p. 465. Montana Report, 1902, p. 66. South Dakota: Bul. 40, p. 150; Bul. 114, p. 551. Wyoming: Bul. 65, pp. 10, 11; Bul. 70, pp. 11; Bul. 76, p. 11; Bul. 87, p. 14.

AGROPYRON SPICATUM (Pursh) Rydb.

Agropyron spicatum is the famous "bunch-grass" of the Columbia Basin, and in many sections of that general region it covers the ground in big bunches. When undisturbed it often resembles a field of grain at a distance. Considerable work has been done by the Department of Agriculture and some of the State experiment stations in securing seed of this native species and attempting to introduce it in other situations, but with indifferent success. The difficulty has been largely one of germinating the seed. The regions in which it grows are somewhat arid, and the plant in its natural habitat is accustomed to get along without the use of seeds; in other words, it is perennial and seldom has occasion to renew from seed. Under favorable conditions of cultivation it reproduces readily. On account of greater ease in handling, selections from the awnless forms are best adapted to cultivation.

No. 8850 was collected near Summit, Mont., August 15, 1907. The sample represents the plant when the seed is in the early milk. It was cut 3 inches from the ground.

Material analyzed.	Percentage of moisture.	Water-free basis (per cent).					
		Ash.	Ether extract.	Crude fiber.	Nitrogen-free extract.	Protein.	Pentosans.
Our sample No. 8850	6.26	4.49	2.26	31.73	55.42	6.10	24.96
Average of 7 others [1]	....	10.67	3.13	30.71	49.33	6.16	....
Average of all	....	9.90	3.02	30.84	50.09	6.15	....

[1] Colorado Bul. 12, p. 65; Oregon Report, 1903, p. 47; Washington Bul. 72, p. 15; Wyoming Bul. 76, p. 16.

AGROPYRON TENERUM Vasey.

Agropyron tenerum is generally known as slender wheat-grass in experiment-station and departmental literature. It has been given considerable prominence as a promising grass for cultivation, and its seed has been placed on the market by seed firms. It has good habits, makes a good quality of hay, and is palatable to stock. There are many varieties of it, some of the natives from the Rocky Mountain region being much ranker and taller in their habits of growth than the forms which have been upon the market.

No. 8791 was collected near Fargo, N. Dak., August 8, 1907. No. 8837 was collected at Havre, Mont., August 13, 1907. This sample was a tall, rank, robust form, growing in large bunches; it was mature, but all green except the heads.

Material analyzed.	Percentage of moisture.	Water-free basis (per cent).					
		Ash.	Ether extract.	Crude fiber.	Nitrogen-free extract.	Protein.	Pentosans.
Our sample No. 8791	6.64	6.65	2.62	33.73	50.10	6.90	25.88
Our sample No. 8837	5.41	6.64	3.24	37.49	46.49	6.14	26.49
Average of 9 others [1]	....	7.17	2.07	34.79	47.73	8.24	....
Average of all	....	7.08	2.23	34.94	47.82	7.93	....

[1] Canada Central Experiment Farm Bul. 19, pp. 28–29. Colorado Bul. 12, p. 64. Montana Report, 1902, p. 66. South Dakota: Bul. 40, p. 147; Bul. 69, p. 27. Wyoming: Bul. 65, p. 14; Bul. 87, p. 15.

AGROSTIS ASPERIFOLIA Trin.

Agrostis asperifolia (rough-leaved bent-grass) is especially common in moist situations from the Mississippi River westward. It is readily grazed by all classes of live stock, but is never abundant enough to receive serious consideration. It inhabits the edges of running streams or fresh-water pools, where the ground may be covered with water for some little time. In such situations small patches of it grow, but the areas are never extensive.

No. 8867 was collected near Summit, Mont., August 15, 1907. This sample was collected in blossom and cut close to the ground. No. 8890 was collected at Hood River, Oreg., August 23, 1907. The seeds in the sample were all ripe, and half of the leaves were dry. This sample was cut 2 inches high.

Material analyzed.	Percentage of moisture.	Water-free basis (per cent).					
		Ash.	Ether extract.	Crude fiber.	Nitrogen-free extract.	Protein.	Pentosans.
Our sample No. 8867	5.86	6.55	2.33	32.60	45.93	12.59	23.51
Our sample No. 8890	5.56	15.03	1.97	30.26	47.71	5.03	22.18
Average of 4 others [1]	....	8.11	2.64	24.89	53.95	10.41	....
Average of all	....	9.01	2.47	27.07	51.57	9.88	....

[1] Colorado Bul. 12, p. 40; Connecticut Report, 1879, p. 155; Montana Report, 1902, p. 66; U. S. Department of Agriculture Report No. 32, 1884, p. 127.

AGROSTIS HIEMALIS (Walt.) B. S. P.

Agrostis hiemalis (bent-grass) is very likely to take possession of situations in the mountains which for some reason have become completely denuded of other vegetation. Its extensive purplish panicles make it very conspicuous in such places, for it often grows almost pure. It is a species of comparatively little value, although often grazed in close pastures.

No. 8847 was collected at Summit, Mont., August 15, 1907. The sample was collected in late blossom and cut close to the ground.

Material analyzed.	Percentage of moisture.	Water-free basis (per cent).					
		Ash.	Ether extract.	Crude fiber.	Nitrogen-free extract.	Protein.	Pentosans.
Our sample No. 8847	5.62	7.31	4.85	30.03	51.85	5.96	24.70
Average of 4 others [1]		7.18	2.96	32.30	48.96	8.60	
Average of all		7.21	3.34	31.84	49.54	8.07	

[1] South Dakota Bul. 40, p. 81. Wyoming: Bul. 70, p. 18; Bul. 87, p. 19.

ALOPECURUS FULVUS Sm.

Alopecurus fulvus is a much smaller species of foxtail than the one that follows and is of much less importance. It inhabits low, wet, loose soils of high mountain meadows, and, like the other species, it sheds its seeds from the top downward immediately after they ripen. It may often be found growing in the water, but not in stagnant pools. While furnishing considerable feed in limited areas, it is not nearly as important as the other species. (Pl. II, fig. 2.)

No. 8864 was collected at Summit, Mont., August 15, 1907. The sample was perfectly green and succulent, although half of the seeds had dropped off. It was cut close to the ground.

Material analyzed.	Percentage of moisture.	Water-free basis (per cent).					
		Ash.	Ether extract.	Crude fiber.	Nitrogen-free extract.	Protein.	Pentosans.
Our sample No. 8864	7.87	6.90	2.89	29.51	52.39	8.31	20.39
Average of 2 others [1]		12.12	3.75	27.19	46.64	10.30	
Average of all		10.38	3.46	27.97	48.55	9.64	

[1] South Dakota Bul. 40, p. 72; Wyoming Bul. 70, p. 23.

ALOPECURUS OCCIDENTALIS Scribn.

Alopecurus occidentalis (mountain foxtail) is an important grass in high mountain meadows of the Rocky Mountain region. It resembles more closely than any other common grass the cultivated timothy. It frequently makes practically pure crops of considerable extent in wet situations. It commonly attains a height of 2½ feet and will often yield 2 tons of hay to the acre. The areas where it grows most satisfactorily are usually too wet to be either grazed or cut in early summer, but by August, when the grass matures, these are often so well dried up that they can be harvested. It is probably more valuable for hay than for grazing.

No. 8862 was collected at Summit, Mont., August 15, 1907. The specimen was overripe, about half of the seeds had fallen, but the culms and leaves were still green. It was cut about 2 inches above the ground.

Material analyzed.	Percentage of moisture.	Water-free basis (per cent).					
		Ash.	Ether extract.	Crude fiber.	Nitrogen-free extract.	Protein.	Pentosans.
Our sample No. 8862	5.04	6.29	2.15	29.91	54.08	7.57	23.53
One other sample [1]		7.06	2.57	28.41	54.37	7.59	
Average of both		6.68	2.36	29.16	54.22	7.58	

[1] Montana Report, 1902, p. 66.

ANDROPOGON FURCATUS Muhl.

Andropogon furcatus (big bluestem) is very characteristic of the grass flora of the prairie region of the Great Plains, but its distribution is much wider than this. It is particularly abundant in the edges of bottom lands in the Dakotas and Montana, but farther south and east, where the rainfall is more abundant, it inhabits the open prairies and uplands. Very good pasture is produced by it early in the season, but after the stems begin to stretch it is not particularly relished by stock. It is one of the important ingredients of prairie hay from the Dakota-Oklahoma region and is considered of fair quality. The species withstands burning better than almost any other grass. While mowing to rid the ground of the old dead stems would undoubtedly be conducive to better growth, it has withstood repeated burnings throughout central Kansas and Nebraska for a great many years and still produces well.

No. 8827 was collected at Williston, N. Dak., August 11, 1907. The sample was in early maturity and was cut close to the ground. It contained, therefore, the entire culm and all the root leaves, which are abundant.

Material analyzed.	Percentage of moisture.	Water-free basis (per cent).					
		Ash.	Ether extract.	Crude fiber.	Nitrogen-free extract.	Protein.	Pentosans.
Our sample No. 8827	4.73	5.83	1.89	33.87	54.15	4.26	28.24
Average of 19 others [1]		6.70	3.26	33.81	49.09	7.14	
Average of all		6.66	3.19	33.81	49.35	6.99	

[1] Canada Central Experiment Farm Bul. 19, p. 32. Colorado Bul. 12, p. 96. Connecticut Report, 1887, p. 103. Iowa: Bul. 11, p. 458; Bul. 56, p. 474. Mississippi Report, 1895, p. 90. South Dakota Bul. 40, p. 28. U. S. Department of Agriculture Report No. 32, 1884, p. 126. West Virginia Report, 1890–91, p. 36.

ANDROPOGON SCOPARIUS Michx.

Andropogon scoparius is a species of bluestem easily distinguished from the preceding by its greater tendency to grow in bunches and its smaller stature throughout. Its distribution is not essentially different from the larger species; likewise, it has a purplish color early in the season. While grazed readily before it begins to head, it gets woody even earlier than *A. furcatus* and then is not relished. It is not large enough to amount to much as a hay crop.

No. 8825 was collected at Williston, N. Dak., August 11, 1907. The sample was cut close to the ground and represents the plant in early maturity.

Material analyzed.	Percentage of moisture.	Water-free basis (per cent).					
		Ash.	Ether extract.	Crude fiber.	Nitrogen-free extract.	Protein.	Pentosans.
Our sample No. 8825	5.48	6.19	2.36	32.95	53.87	4.63	26.69
Average of 18 others [1]		6.05	2.29	34.47	51.15	6.04	
Average of all		6.05	2.29	34.39	51.31	5.96	

[1] Canada Central Experiment Farm Bul. 19, p. 32. Connecticut Report, 1879, p. 153; 1887, p. 103. Iowa: Bul. 11, p. 460; Bul. 56, p. 476. Mississippi Report, 1895, p. 90. South Dakota Bul. 40, p. 26. U. S. Department of Agriculture Report No. 32, 1884, p. 126. Wyoming Bul. 87, p. 24.

ANDROPOGON SCRIBNERIANUS Nash.

Andropogon scribnerianus, the beautiful bluestem of the dry pine regions of Florida and adjacent States, furnishes considerable feed early in the season, but, like the remainder of the bluestems, the feed is of second quality.

No. 8725 was collected near Jacksonville, Fla., June 8, 1907. The sample was secured in full blossom, the plants being cut at the surface of the ground. Its percentage of moisture was 5.66. Other constituents (on a water-free basis) were as follows: Ash, 3.02; ether extract, 2.11; crude fiber, 39.38; nitrogen-free extract, 51.87; protein, 3.62; pentosans, 28.44.

ANDROPOGON TORREYANUS Steud.

Andropogon torreyanus (white-topped beard-grass) is conspicuous upon prairies, in the edges of swales, upon railroad embankments, and along roadsides where the ground has been stirred or there is an accumulation of moisture, from Arizona to eastern Texas and northward to Kansas and Nevada. It furnishes a large amount of grazing, and in some situations, even in the valleys of southern Arizona, it furnishes at times considerable crops of hay. While common upon the prairies in the eastern limit of its range, in more arid regions it grows mainly in depressions or in places which receive an accumulation of water from the nature of the surface drainage. In the desert regions it is strictly a summer grass, starting to grow about the first of July and maturing its seed in late September or early October, corresponding with the rainy season. Farther east, in Texas, its period of development is entirely different. There it may mature as early as June.

Under proper conditions it grows readily from seed, and were it not for the fact that its seed habits are poor (that is, the seeds are difficult to gather) it would be a promising grass for cultivation. Like many other valuable native species, however, its seed habits are such that it would be very difficult indeed to thrash the plants after they are harvested, although the seed itself is produced in good quantity and is unusually fertile. The grass is peculiar in having a distinctly characteristic and pleasing aroma. (Pl. IV, fig. 1.)

No. 8394 was collected near Green, Tex., August 14, 1906. The sample was a trifle overripe; about half of the seed had fallen, but the plant was still green. A few dead leaves were attached to the lower part of the clump, which was cut 2 or 3 inches above the ground. Its percentage of moisture was 8.37. Other constituents (on a water-free basis) were as follows: Ash, 7.16; ether extract, 1.64; crude fiber, 36.78; nitrogen-free extract, 48; protein, 6.42; pentosans, 23.51.

ANDROPOGON VIRGINICUS L.

Andropogon virginicus, the broom sedge of the East and South, is commonly looked upon as a pernicious weed which gradually works into permanent pastures and neglected places, driving out more valuable plants. Still it is persistent and furnishes a great deal of fairly good pasture early in the season, and it often enters into the composition of hay upon long-established meadows.

No. 8727 was collected near St. Petersburg, Fla., June, 1907. The sample consisted of root leaves only from burned-over ground; consequently, the analysis represents a most favorable composition.

Material analyzed.	Percentage of moisture.	Water-free basis (per cent).					
		Ash.	Ether extract.	Crude fiber.	Nitrogen-free extract.	Protein.	Pentosans.
Our sample No. 8727	8.29	8.40	3.70	33.57	44.48	9.85	23.89
Average of 6 others [1]		6.80	2.11	37.04	47.82	6.23	
Average of all		7.03	2.33	36.54	47.35	6.75	

[1] Connecticut Report, 1879, p. 153; 1887, p. 103. Mississippi Report, 1895, p. 90. North Carolina Bul. 90b, p. 5. U. S. Department of Agriculture Report No. 32, 1884, p. 126. Virginia Bul. 180, p. 96.

FIG. 1.—A PRIMITIVE WAY OF PUMPING WATER FOR STOCK ON THE MEXICAN BORDER.

FIG. 2.—A COMMON WAY OF IMPOUNDING THE RUN-OFF WATER FOR STOCK PURPOSES.

FIG. 1.—A WEEDY MOUNTAIN MEADOW IN CALIFORNIA, WHERE THE SEEDING OF TIMOTHY AND REDTOP WOULD BE HIGHLY ADVANTAGEOUS.

FIG. 2.—ALOPECURUS FULVUS IN A POCKET-LIKE DEPRESSION IN THE GRAND COULEE, WASH.

ARISTIDA CALIFORNICA Thurber.

In southern Arizona *Aristida californica*, a species of needle grass, is of some value, occupying, as it does, gravelly ridges of the foothills. It is closely grazed by cattle and commonly makes two appreciable crops during the year. The main growth, of course, is in the summer rainy season, but there is usually a considerable development of root leaves in the spring, which is not true of many of the perennial species of this region. Its perennial culms add decidedly to its value.

No. 9588 was collected in the Santa Rita Mountains of Arizona, September 16, 1908. Its percentage of moisture was 3.27. Other constituents (on a water-free basis) were as follows: Ash, 8.05; ether extract, 0.90; crude fiber, 34.50; nitrogen-free extract, 50.54; protein, 6.01; pentosans, 25.67.

ARISTIDA LONGISETA Steud.

Aristida longiseta, a species of poverty grass, is very conspicuous on dry hills and rolling prairies of the western Plains and Rocky Mountain region, extending southward to northern Arizona. Very often large areas may be seen, but it seldom grows pure. While it sometimes reaches a foot in height, it is commonly only about 6 inches. This, however, depends upon the season and the character of the locality in which it grows, the drier situations producing, of course, much smaller plants. It is readily grazed with other vegetation in both dry and green conditions, except for a short period after the plant approaches maturity, when the awns are troublesome.

Nos. 7089 and 7090 (Wooton) were collected near Las Cruces, N. Mex., October 4, 1912. No. 8873 was collected near Kalispell, Mont., August 16, 1907. This sample was in late blossom; some old leaves were included, and it was cut close to the ground.

Material analyzed.	Percentage of moisture.	Water-free basis (per cent).					
		Ash.	Ether extract.	Crude fiber.	Nitrogen-free extract.	Protein.	Pentosans.
Our sample No. 7089 (E. O. W.)	3.55	9.71	1.56	35.40	44.32	9.01	26.63
Our sample No. 7090 (E. O. W.)	2.60	8.40	1.32	36.79	45.47	8.02	27.39
Our sample No. 8873	5.73	5.82	1.51	33.73	52.70	6.24	28.54
One other sample[1]	....	8.47	1.31	41.55	42.21	6.46	....
Average of all	....	8.10	1.42	36.87	46.18	7.43	....

[1] Wyoming Bul. 87, p. 26.

ARISTIDA MICRANTHA (Vasey) Nash.

In southern and southwestern Texas *Aristida micrantha* furnishes half of the grazing over large areas and is a persistent palatable species, growing in large tufts about 15 inches high. Generally it grows best in open brushy regions and in reasonably fertile loamy soils. This is one of the few grasses of the Southwest which has perennial stems; for this reason its value on a previously unstocked range is apt to be overestimated.

No. 8387 was collected at Encinal, Tex., August 12, 1906. The sample was fully mature, was cut at the surface of the ground, and contained about 5 per cent of old growth.

Material analyzed.	Percentage of moisture.	Water-free basis (per cent).					
		Ash.	Ether extract.	Crude fiber.	Nitrogen-free extract.	Protein.	Pentosans.
Our sample No. 8387	8.88	11.37	1.43	31.60	49.36	6.24	24.90
One other sample[1]	....	6.85	2.59	24.88	61.36	4.32	....
Average of both	....	9.11	2.01	28.24	55.36	5.28	....

[1] U. S. Department of Agriculture Report No. 32, 1884, p. 126.

ARISTIDA SCABRA Kth.

Aristida scabra is closely related to *A. scheidiana*, but is a larger, coarser plant, commonly inhabiting the 4,500 to 5,000 foot levels of the mountains of southern Arizona, where it grows mostly in large, isolated bunches. Inhabiting as it does rough, rocky hill and mountain sides, it is not usually grazed as closely as the other species and probably is not quite as good feed.

No. 8590 was collected in the Santa Rita Mountains, Ariz., September 27, 1906. The specimen was completely dried up with the exception of a small portion near the base. It was harvested about 3 inches high. Its percentage of moisture was 4.62. Other constituents (on a water-free basis) were as follows: Ash, 7.15; ether extract, 1.54; crude fiber, 31.59; nitrogen-free extract, 53.37; protein, 6.35; pentosans, 25.49.

ARISTIDA SCHEIDIANA (T. and R.) Vasey.

Aristida scheidiana, a species of needle grass, is abundant from western Texas to Arizona. It inhabits, in Arizona especially, the upper foothill regions and extends in many instances into the mountains to an altitude of about 6,000 feet. Often the amount of feed produced by it is unequaled in quantity by any other species over considerable areas. It is at present invariably closely grazed, and in situations where the ground is not too rough it could be made into hay of fair quality at the rate of a ton to the acre. It is most abundant in the open foothills of the isolated mountain ranges at an altitude of about 4,000 feet. It is now seldom conspicuous upon the open range, because it appears to be quite easily injured by trampling and close grazing. In the large inclosure made by the Department of Agriculture in the Santa Rita Mountains several years ago it is exceedingly abundant and productive over considerable areas, and it produces probably as heavily to the acre as any other species which grows in as pure stands as this does.

Although the whole genus Aristida is commonly referred to as poverty grass and consists usually of species which produce a poor quality of feed, this one is a decided exception. It is perennial in character, produces a good quantity of leaves, and, although quite rigid and hard, is evidently relished by stock. However, it is not grazed nearly as readily as the gramas with which it is commonly associated.

No. 9521 was collected at Prescott, Ariz., August 31, 1908. The sample was in blossom, and cut between 2 and 3 inches high. Its percentage of moisture was 6.93. Other constituents (on a water-free basis) were as follows: Ash, 7.20; ether extract, 2.55; crude fiber, 34.89; nitrogen-free extract, 49.71; protein, 5.65; pentosans, 24.59.

AVENA BARBATA Brot.

Avena barbata is botanically a different species of wild oats from the one that follows, but to the rancher this is unimportant, since no distinction is popularly made between them in the California region. Both are known under the same name. This differs in having a little stricter and narrower panicle and a smaller and narrower seed, while the brown hairs with which both are clothed are somewhat less prominent and lighter in color.

No. 8264 was collected at Colton, Cal., May 8, 1906, when the entire plant was green and most of the seed in the milk condition. The plants were pulled up and the roots then cut off below the lower leaves, which were all preserved. The sample grew in a rather favorable situation; consequently, it was greener than most of the plants upon the native ranges. No. 8313 was collected at Garvanza, Cal., May 19, 1906. The sample was cut about 3 inches high and was in about the same stage of maturity as No. 8264.

Material analyzed.	Percentage of moisture.	Water-free basis (per cent).					
		Ash.	Ether extract.	Crude fiber.	Nitrogen-free extract.	Protein.	Pentosans.
Our sample No. 8264	5.26	7.26	2.69	36.56	44.78	8.71	24.58
Our sample No. 8313	6.45	8.06	2.68	36.27	47.38	5.61	25.16
Average of both	5.86	7.66	2.69	36.41	46.08	7.16	24.87

AVENA FATUA L.

Avena fatua, commonly known as wild oats, is a weedy grass introduced from European countries. It is rather common in cultivated fields in all of the small-grain regions of the West. In California it is especially abundant, having found conditions favorable for its spread and development upon uncultivated lands, where it often forms an almost pure stand. There it is made into hay, often yielding 1 to 1½ tons to the acre of excellent forage, if cut in season. It is an annual, reproducing from seed each season. This limits its value as a range plant to the regions which are turfless, for the seed could not become sufficiently covered or, if covered, could not gain a foothold and thrive in competition with perennial grasses which form a turf. In California, where it attains its best growth, it is a winter annual, maturing its seed about May. Without doubt it should be classed as one of the most important wild forage plants of California from both a grazing and a hay standpoint. The curing of the hay to produce the best quality is considered to be more difficult than with many crops. However, in a region like the one in which it grows this is not a serious matter, for the atmosphere is dry and rains have usually ceased before the crop is ready to cut.

The plant is found rather frequently in the mountains of southern Arizona, especially in the Huachucas, where it was doubtless introduced by the military operations conducted there, but it does not find conditions suitable to its becoming sufficiently abundant to produce any appreciable quantity of feed. The mountains receive only sufficient rainfall for it to grow at all, and they are too cold for its winter development; consequently, only a few plants in favored localities are able to thrive. Upon the open lands of the foothills and deserts the rainfall is insufficient and occurs in too hot a season for it to thrive. Experiments conducted in the Santa Rita Mountains in the introduction of this grass upon native pastures have yielded only negative results. In occasional seasons a few stray plants mature in favored situations, but around cabins and in small irrigated gardens plants are frequently seen. It is also abundant in the Pacific Northwest.

No. 8301 was collected near Banning, Cal., May 15, 1906; in early maturity, but straw still green; cut about 3 inches above ground.

Material analyzed.	Percentage of moisture.	Water-free basis (per cent).					
		Ash.	Ether extract.	Crude fiber.	Nitrogen-free extract.	Protein.	Pentosans.
Our sample No. 8301	8.79	11.23	3.60	29.86	47.42	7.89	25.09
Average of 11 others [1]		7.98	3.14	30.61	51.28	6.99	
Average of all		8.25	3.18	30.55	50.95	7.07	

[1] California Bul. 132, p. 5. Oregon Report, 1904–5, p. 70. Washington: Bul. 72, p. 17; Bul. 82, p. 10.

BOUTELOUA ARISTIDOIDES (H. B. K.) Thurber.

Bouteloua aristidoides is one of the "six weeks' grasses" of the Southwest and has a wide distribution from Texas to California and south to South America. It is an annual with seed habits perfectly adapted to make it an aggressive plant in an unsodded region. Being an annual, its forage is of low value, but its seed production is large. It occupies the lower foothills and mesas in the southwestern United States, and when the season is favorable it makes nearly a ground cover over extensive areas and reaches the higher altitudes of 6,000 feet or more. Like many annuals, it pulls up readily; consequently, it is not relished by stock even in the green stage, although extensively grazed then and in the dry condition when other feed is scarce. During its maturity it is especially annoying to sheep on account of the spikes, which fall readily and penetrate the fleece and feet of the animals, sometimes disabling them. In spite of these drawbacks, however, it is extensively grazed, and in many situations, where the more valuable grasses have been exterminated, it constitutes the main feed, aside from that furnished by the shrubs. (Pl. III, fig. 2.)

No. 9618 was collected in the Santa Rita Mountains of Arizona, September 22, 1908. The sample was mature, but only a few spikes had fallen off. It was cut close to the ground. Its percentage of moisture was 2.44. Other constituents (on a water-free basis) were as follows: Ash, 6.84; ether extract, 2.12; crude fiber, 35.11; nitrogen-free extract, 46.96; protein, 8.97; pentosans, 23.16.

BOUTELOUA BURKII Scribn.

Bouteloua burkii, a species of grama, is one of the most abundant of the pasture grasses of central to southern Texas. It is a perennial, seldom growing over 10 inches high, and usually only about 6 inches, but it produces an abundance of root leaves and furnishes a very large percentage of the forage of the native pastures of the region. It never gets large enough to be considered as a hay crop. Like the vast majority of gramas its seed habits render it useless for cultivation.

No. 8398 was collected near Green, Tex., August 14, 1906. The sample was overripe, the seed having all fallen, and half of the plant was dead and dry. It was cut close to the ground. Its percentage of moisture was 6.81. Other constituents (on a water-free basis) were as follows: Ash, 12.89; ether extract, 1.82; crude fiber, 30.54; nitrogen-free extract, 46.70; protein, 8.05; pentosans, 22.13.

BOUTELOUA CURTIPENDULA (Michx.) Torr.

Bouteloua curtipendula, the side-oat grama, as it is popularly called, is the most promising of the gramas for cultivation. It makes a taller, ranker growth than any of the other species, but like the others has poor seed habits for an agricultural grass. It has a wider distribution in the United States than any of the other gramas except, possibly, *B. hirsuta*, which is of much less value. Some efforts have been made to domesticate it, and this species is one that was always included in the tests made during the grass-garden period of experimentation of 12 to 15 years ago. A stand of it is not difficult to obtain from seed, but in all cases of cultivation whole spikes, as they were stripped from the plant, were invariably sown or drilled in. The separation of pure, clean seed is not to be considered.

The species is conspicuous and is an important pasture plant mainly upon the rougher portions of the Plains region. In southern Arizona it inhabits similar situations at altitudes mainly between 3,000 and 5,000 feet. However, when sown and furnished sufficient water, it thrives upon the desert mesas at 2,000 feet or less. The controlling factor in its growth is moisture. When this is properly supplied, it adapts itself to almost all other conditions.

No. 8589 was collected on the north slope of the Santa Rita Mountains of Arizona September 27, 1906. The straw in this sample was ripe and dry; some of the seed had fallen.

Material analyzed.	Percentage of moisture.	Water-free basis (per cent).					
		Ash.	Ether extract.	Crude fiber.	Nitrogen-free extract.	Protein.	Pentosans.
Our sample No. 8589	4.60	8.31	1.59	32.49	53.28	4.33	25.88
Average of 5 others [1]	....	9.76	1.85	37.76	45.05	5.58	....
Average of all	....	9.63	1.94	32.86	49.23	6.34	....

[1] Colorado Bul. 8, p. 11; Iowa Bul. 56, p. 461; New Mexico Bul. 17, p. 36; Wyoming Bul. 87, p. 28.

BOUTELOUA ERIOPODA Torr.

Bouteloua eriopoda, the black grama of New Mexico and the woolly-foot of other regions, is a species of varying importance from Colorado south and from Texas to California. Over the greater portion of its range it is strictly a pasture grass, but in portions of southern New Mexico it is frequently cut for hay in almost pure stands from the upper, open grassy mesa slopes just below and extending to the foothills of the mountains. In southern Arizona it is also limited to gravelly ridges, the better soils of the gently sloping mesas being occupied by other species. However, the present distribution may be largely the result of artificial conditions of grazing. There are indications that the species will occupy greater areas when stock is kept off, probably simulating conditions which once existed. Where it grows in sufficient abundance, it is very valuable during long droughts, on account of the perennial character of its culms. On this account, also, it is more likely to be injured during the dry season by close grazing.

No. 8946 was collected in the Santa Rita Mountains of southern Arizona, September 24, 1907. The sample was nearly mature and was cut 2 inches high.

Material analyzed.	Percentage of moisture.	Water-free basis (per cent).					
		Ash.	Ether extract.	Crude fiber.	Nitrogen-free extract.	Protein.	Pentosans.
Our sample No. 8946	7.38	9.20	1.68	34.22	49.84	5.06	23.96
One other sample[1]	....	11.34	1.79	33.61	47.69	5.57	....
Average of both	....	10.27	1.74	33.92	48.76	5.31	....

[1] New Mexico Bul. 17, p. 36.

BOUTELOUA FILIFORMIS (Fourn.) Griff.

Bouteloua filiformis is another grama of good quality which furnishes a large amount of feed in about the same situations as *B. rothrockii*, but at rather higher elevations. Next to *B. gracilis* it is probably the most important pasture species of this important genus, furnishing a large quantity of most palatable grazing, and at times it is cut for hay. It is one of the important species of southern Texas and extends from there to Arizona and southward far into Mexico. Along the entire Mexican border, from Laredo to Quitovaquito, it is one of the most important pasture grasses. It stands trampling a little better than *B. rothrockii*, but not nearly as well as *B. gracilis*.

No. 8591 was collected in the northern foothills of the Santa Rita Mountains of Arizona, September 21, 1906. The sample was completely dried up when gathered and was cut close enough to include all the root leaves. Its percentage of moisture was 4.48. Other constitutents (on a water-free basis) were as follows: Ash, 7.64; ether extract, 1.87; crude fiber, 30.94; nitrogen-free extract, 54.84; protein, 4.71; pentosans, 26.07.

BOUTELOUA HIRSUTA Lag.

Bouteloua hirsuta (rough grama) occurs between the Mississippi and the Rockies from British Columbia southward, reaching its highest perfection and importance from the southern Plains region southward far into Mexico. It also occurs in many places east of the Mississippi and is abundant in some parts of the prairie regions of Florida. The habits of the species render it of much less value than its close relative, the blue grama, but on account of its very wide distribution and abundance as a filler over large areas it is a very important species. It is not a well-rooted species, and consequently does not withstand trampling by stock very well.

No. 8951 was collected in the Santa Rita Mountains, Ariz., September 23, 1907. The sample was cut close, in nearly mature condition.

Material analyzed.	Percentage of moisture.	Water-free basis (per cent).					
		Ash.	Ether extract.	Crude fiber.	Nitrogen-free extract.	Protein.	Pentosans.
Our sample No. 8951	5.97	12.01	2.62	37.10	41.62	6.65	23.75
One other sample[1]	....	10.14	2.55	32.84	48.59	5.88	....
Average of both	....	11.07	2.59	34.97	45.10	6.27	....

[1] South Dakota Bul. 40, p. 97.

BOUTELOUA PARRYI (Fourn.) Griff.

Bouteloua parryi (hairy grama) never occurs in sufficient abundance to be a first-quality grass, but it often furnishes half or more of the feed on small areas. It has several more or less distinct habits, like many other species of the genus. In favorable situations it may become 2 feet high, while in barren situations the whole plant may not be over 2 or 3 inches tall. It is one of the most handsome grasses of the genus, of good grazing quality, but of minor economic importance on account of its sparse growth.

No. 7095 (E. O. W.) was collected in the northern foothills of the Santa Rita Mountains of Arizona, October 9, 1912. Its percentage of moisture was 3.49. Other constituents (on a water-free basis) were as follows: Ash, 7.96; ether extract, 1.90; crude fiber, 35.56; nitrogen-free extract, 48.58; protein, 6.00; pentosans, 26.13.

BOUTELOUA ROTHROCKII Vasey.

In some situations in southern Arizoza *Bouteloua rothrockii* (mesa grama) makes almost pure stands over large areas of the gently sloping upper mesas, just below the mountain foothills. It is especially abundant on the northern slopes of the Santa Rita and Santa Catalina mountains. In favorable seasons it often yields a ton of hay to the acre. It is a very handsome, tall species, growing rather thinly, but under protection from overgrazing—as has been done in the Santa Rita Mountains—it has thickened up wonderfully and crowded out the less valuable *Bouteloua aristidoides* and *Aristida bromides*, which had gained ascendency. It does not stand trampling as well as some of the other species of the genus and as a consequence does not yield abundantly today in many situations where it formerly predominated. (Pl. III, fig. 1.)

No. 8592 was collected on the northern slope of the Santa Rita Mountains, Ariz., September 27, 1906. The sample was taken after the plant had completely dried up, but the seed had not yet shattered. Its percentage of moisture was 3.55. Other constituents (on a water-free basis) were as follows: Ash, 6.53; ether extract, 1.58; crude fiber, 36.67; nitrogen-free extract, 50.55; protein, 4.67; pentosans, 25.68.

BROMUS CARINATUS HOOKERIANUS (Thurb.) Shear.

Bromus carinatus hookerianus is rather coarse, tall brome-grass, which adds a great deal to the feed in the region where the sample was collected. It grows scatteringly and also often inhabits very limited areas to the exclusion of practically everything else. It is regularly grazed by cattle in this section, even when old, and probably does not differ materially in pasture value from some of the cultivated species, but it has a decided advantage over the weedy introduced annuals which occupy the greater part of the land in this region.

No. 8302 was collected near Banning, Cal., May 15, 1906. The seed of the sample was nearly mature. The culms were cut about 2 inches from the ground. Its percentage of moisture was 7.01. Other constituents (on a water-free basis) were as follows: Ash, 9.36; ether extract, 2.52; crude fiber, 29.20; nitrogen-free extract, 53.62; protein, 5.30; pentosans, 24.28.

BROMUS HORDEACEUS L.

Bromus hordeaceus, a species of cheat, cultivated as a hay grass in some sections, is an important introduced annual weed of California west of the Sierras. It makes a fair quality of feed and is adapted for either pasture or hay. It does not possess the disadvantageous characteristics of the tucolote and some of the other species.

No. 7107 (Wooton) was collected at Red Bluff, Cal., April 7, 1913. No. 8315 was collected near Santa Barbara, Cal., May 21, 1906. The sample was taken when the seed was in the milk. It was cut close to the ground.

Material analyzed.	Percentage of moisture.	Water-free basis (per cent).					
		Ash.	Ether extract.	Crude fiber.	Nitrogen-free extract.	Protein.	Pentosans.
Our sample No. 7107 (E. O. W.).	6.30	8.37	2.86	27.60	50.83	10.34	21.78
Our sample No. 8315	6.70	9.46	1.66	36.81	42.99	9.08	25.18
Average of 5 others [1]	....	11.49	5.60	28.53	37.34	17.04	....
Average of all	....	11.15	4.95	29.91	38.28	15.71	....

[1] Iowa Bul. 56, p. 443.

BROMUS MARGINATUS Nees.

The distribution of *Bromus marginatus*, a native species of brome-grass, is not remarkably different from that of *B. richardsoni*, and the quality of the feed produced by the two is somewhat similar, but this species is much coarser than the other.

No. 8846 was collected near Summit, Mont., August 15, 1907. The seed was in early dough and the plant was cut 2 inches high. No. 8887 was collected near Dee, Oreg., August 23, 1907. The sample was fully mature, the upper part of the culm being dead and dry, but the leaves were all green. It was cut about 3 inches above the ground.

Material analyzed.	Percentage of moisture.	Water-free basis (per cent).					
		Ash.	Ether extract.	Crude fiber.	Ntrogein-free extract.	Protein.	Pentosans.
Our sample No. 8846	6.23	6.89	1.91	35.10	49.91	6.19	23.97
Our sample No. 8887	7.34	10.55	2.07	40.11	42.99	4.28	21.22
Average of 14 others [1]	....	10.65	3.61	29.93	40.05	15.76	....
Average of all	....	10.41	3.41	30.89	40.85	14.44	....

[1] Iowa: Bul. 11, pp. 465, 474; Bul. 56, p. 440. Montana Report, 1902, p. 66. Nevada Bul. 71, p. 23. South Dakota Bul. 69, p. 13. Wyoming: Bul. 70, p. 28; Bul. 76, p. 22.

BROMUS POLYANTHUS Scribn.

Bromus polyanthus is a valuable tufted perennial species of brome-grass, inhabiting the open wooded areas of the Rocky Mountains. It has a wide distribution in the West, extending northward to Saskatchewan. So far as known, it never forms anything like a complete stand, but on the contrary is found in isolated patches scattered among other species. It is, however, an important component of the pasture lands, mountain meadows, and dry hillsides throughout the region. In the San Francisco highlands it has been practically killed out by grazing except where protected.

No. 8860 was collected near Summit, Mont., August 15, 1907. The seed of this sample was in milk, and the plants were harvested about 3 inches high. No. 9536 was collected in Prescott, Ariz., September 1, 1908. This sample was in late blossom and was cut 2 inches high.

Material analyzed.	Percentage of moisture.	Water-free basis (per cent).					
		Ash.	Ether extract.	Crude fiber.	Nitrogen-free extract.	Protein.	Pentosans.
Our sample No. 8860	4.22	4.12	2.04	34.01	53.24	6.59	25.00
Our sample No. 9536	6.39	10.88	1.59	37.56	41.89	8.08	19.38
One other sample [1]	....	5.57	1.71	35.09	47.22	10.41	....
Average of all	....	6.86	1.78	35.55	47.45	8.36	....

[1] Wyoming Bul. 87, p. 32.

BROMUS RUBENS L.

While not possessing the deleterious characteristics described under *Bromus villosus* to quite as serious a degree, *B. rubens* nevertheless causes considerable injury in the same way. On the whole, it is a grass of very little value. It is not as good feed as *B. villosus* in either its early or its mature stages. The injuries caused by it are not quite so pronounced, but the ranges would undoubtedly be better off without it.

No. 8263 was collected near Colton, Cal., May 8, 1906. The sample was mature and harvested about 1 inch high. Its percentage of moisture was 5.02. Other constituents (on a water-free basis) were as follows: Ash, 4.16; ether extract, 2.07; crude fiber, 33.24; nitrogen-free extract, 55; protein, 5.53; pentosans, 28.20.

BROMUS VILLOSUS Forsk.

Bromus villosus, a weedy annual, popularly known as tucolote, is one of the many species of Bromus introduced into the western United States. It is more abundant and conspicuous in California than anywhere else, and its presence in such quantity is undoubtedly a detriment to the California ranges. The feed produced by it when young, before it is headed out, is equal to that produced by any of the other weedy brome-grasses which have been introduced throughout the region, but as soon as the seed has ripened it is of very little value as feed, and in many cases it is positively detrimental to stock which happen to graze upon an area where it occurs abundantly. It is an aggressive grass and has a tendency to drive out the other annuals that compete with it. The injury done is mainly to the sheep industry. The sharp-pointed seeds work into the fleece, the feet, and even the eyes of the animals, often causing them to lose the eyesight entirely. On this account the herdsman considers it imperative that his flocks be removed from the tucolote areas of the valleys and foothills before this plant ripens its seed. The seeds also work their way into the feet of the animals, causing them to become lame and in some cases unable to travel. This is the very characteristic which enables the plant to obtain the mastery over other species. The seeds are rather sharp-pointed and slightly barbed, so that they will work their way into the ground. The sharp-pointed seeds are even more injurious to stock than the awns. (Pl. IV, fig. 2.)

No. 8262 was collected near Colton, Cal., May 8, 1906, and the sample was then practically ripe. The seed was mostly in late dough, with the leaves fast turning color, but by no means dry. The stems had turned color also, but were still full of sap. The culms were cut off 1 to 2 inches above the ground.

Material analyzed.	Percentage of moisture.	Water-free basis (per cent).					
		Ash.	Ether extract.	Crude fiber.	Nitrogen-free extract.	Protein.	Pentosans.
Our sample No. 8262	6.22	5.20	1.79	29.14	59.51	4.36	26.60
One other sample [1]	....	13.82	3.99	28.18	40.24	13.77	....
Average of both	....	9.51	2.89	28.66	49.88	9.06	....

[1] South Dakota Bul. 69, p. 16.

BULBILIS DACTYLOIDES (Nutt.) Raf.

Bulbilis dactyloides (buffalo grass) is strictly a pasture species, distributed from the Dakotas to the Rocky Mountains and south into Mexico. Popularly, several other species are confused with this one. *Bouteloua gracilis*, especially when not in head, is very similar and frequently mistaken for it. On this account the true buffalo grass is very much overestimated in importance, because there are so many things included with it in the popular mind. Much of the credit given this species is due to the gramas, which in age especially look very much like it. On the other hand, the species is an important one throughout its range. Upon the Plains it is a very short grass, seldom getting over 2 to 4 inches high, but in southern Texas, where conditions

FIG. 1.—BOUTELOUA ROTHROCKII UNDER PROTECTION JUST BELOW THE NORTHERN FOOTHILLS OF THE SANTA RITA MOUNTAINS, ARIZ.

FIG. 2.—BOUTELOUA ARISTIDOIDES IN A FAVORABLE SEASON ON DESERT MESAS, SOUTH OF TUCSON, ARIZ.

FIG. 1.—ANDROPOGON TORREYANUS FROM SEED SOWN THE PREVIOUS SEASON ABOVE A LOW EARTHEN DAM, THROWN UP ON DESERT MESAS NEAR TUCSON, ARIZ.

FIG. 2.—NATIVE PASTURE LANDS IN THE FOOTHILLS, FRESNO COUNTY, CAL., SHOWING INTRODUCED BROME-GRASSES THAT ARE ALMOST ENTIRELY WEEDY.

of heat and moisture are more favorable, it may become a foot high. In spite of this, however, its importance upon the Plains is greater than in southern Texas, for two reasons. Upon the Plains it dry-cures and furnishes excellent winter grazing. In south Texas the rainfall is more irregular, making the use of dry-grass pasture of shorter duration and much less importance. There is probably very little difference in the value of this species and *Bouteloua gracilis* for dry grazing.

No. 9315 was collected near Bellevue, Tex., June 26, 1908. The sample consisted of the staminate plant mostly and was cut close to the ground. It was a little out of blossom.

Material analyzed.	Percentage of moisture.	Water-free basis (per cent).					
		Ash.	Ether extract.	Crude fiber.	Nitrogen-free extract.	Protein.	Pentosans.
Our sample No. 9315	6.18	10.25	1.23	25.74	57.08	5.70	20.56
Average of 6 others[1]		10.55	2.26	25.22	54.35	7.62	
Average of all		10.51	2.11	25.29	54.74	7.35	

[1] Canada Central Experiment Farm Bul. 19, pp. 28-29. Colorado Bul. 12, p. 130. North Dakota Report, 1904, p. 35. South Dakota Bul. 40, p. 102. Wyoming: Bul. 76, p. 28; Bul. 87, p. 36.

CALAMAGROSTIS CANADENSIS (Michx.) Beauv.

Calamagrostis canadensis is a species that inhabits moist meadows of the northern United States. It has some differences in the floral structure and on the whole is somewhat less stout than *C. langsdorfii*. It is more erect, but of approximately equal feeding value.

No. 8863 was collected at Summit, Mont., August 15, 1907. The specimen was cut before blossoming and at a height of 2 inches. Its percentage of moisture was 5.44. Other constituents (on a water-free basis) were as follows: Ash, 6.92; ether extract, 2.15; crude fiber, 34.92; nitrogen-free extract, 46.88; protein, 9.13; pentosans, 26.29.

CALAMAGROSTIS CANADENSIS ACUMINATA Vasey.

Calamagrostis canadensis acuminata, the familiar purple-panicled reed-grass, has a wide range of distribution in the United States, extending from Maine to California and southward to North Carolina. It is one of the most important of the mountain grasses in moist cool situations, along streams and lakes, and in mountain meadows. It produces a fairly good quality of both hay and pasture, and its habit of growth is such as to well adapt it to being cut for hay in places where it is sufficiently abundant for this purpose.

No. 8854 was collected at Summit, Mont., August 15, 1907. The specimen was rather immature and a little under blossom. It was cut 2 inches high.

Material analyzed.	Percentage of moisture.	Water-free basis (per cent).					
		Ash.	Ether extract.	Crude fiber.	Nitrogen-free extract.	Protein.	Pentosans.
Calamagrostis canadensis: 14 samples[1]		7.47	2.86	35.37	45.71	8.59	
Calamagrostis canadensis acuminata:							
Our sample No. 8854	5.98	6.29	2.70	35.01	46.82	9.18	22.96
Average of 3 others[2]		9.44	2.57	34.44	45.02	8.53	
Average of the 4 samples		8.65	2.61	34.59	45.46	8.69	
Average of the 18 samples		7.73	2.81	35.20	45.66	8.60	

[1] Connecticut Report, 1879, p. 153. Iowa: Bul. 11, p. 462; Bul. 56, p. 512. Maine Report, 1888, p. 86; 1889, p. 38. Massachusetts Report, 1885, p. 97. South Dakota Bul. 40, p. 86. Wyoming: Bul. 70, p. 21; Bul. 87, p. 36.
[2] Montana Report, 1902, p. 66. Wyoming: Bul. 70, p. 22; Bul. 76, p. 35.

CALAMAGROSTIS MONTANENSIS Scribn.

Upon the prairies of the Dakotas and eastern Montana, *Calamagrostis montanensis* is a plant of low stature, inhabiting high prairies entirely. It attains a maximum height of 7 or 8 inches. In favorable situations, however, it may be 1½ feet in height and can contribute very decidedly to the pasturage of the region. It is a tough, wiry species, but readily grazed by all kinds of live stock. It never forms a turf or anything approaching a complete stand. It is found scattering among species of Agropyron, Bouteloua, and Sporobolus.

No. 8818 was collected at Devils Lake, N. Dak., August 11, 1907. The specimen was a robust one, 15 to 18 inches high, and was cut close to the ground. It was overmature, but the whole plant was still in a green condition, with the exception of the lower leaves. The seeds were very badly ergoted.

Material analyzed.	Percentage of moisture.	Water-free basis (per cent).					
		Ash.	Ether extract.	Crude fiber.	Nitrogen-free extract.	Protein.	Pentosans.
Our sample No. 8818	6.21	11.10	2.78	32.68	48.77	4.67	27.53
One other sample [1]		10.01	1.99	33.08	49.09	5.83	
Average of both		10.55	2.39	32.88	48.93	5.25	

[1] South Dakota Bul. 69, p. 19.

CALAMOVILFA LONGIFOLIA (Hook.) Hack.

Calamovilfa longifolia (big sand-grass) is a species conspicuous in sandy regions from British Columbia to central Arizona and eastward to Indiana. It is especially at home upon sandy lands of the Plains regions and is common in many situations in northern Arizona. Its rapid spread by running rootstocks renders it of some value in holding sands and makes it quite a persistent grass for sandy regions. It is coarse and harsh; consequently, it is not relished by stock while finer feeds are available. In portions of western Nebraska and the Dakotas it forms a large part of the winter grazing, and on this account is, of course, very important. When cut in season it makes a fair quality of coarse hay.

No. 8828 was collected at Williston, N. Dak., August 11, 1907. The specimen was in late blossom and was cut at the surface of the ground.

Material analyzed.	Percentage of moisture.	Water-free basis (per cent).					
		Ash.	Ether extract.	Crude fiber.	Nitrogen-free extract.	Protein.	Pentosans.
Our sample No. 8828	6.79	4.80	2.08	37.64	50.18	5.30	25.18
Average of 3 others [1]		6.93	1.73	40.24	44.79	6.31	
Average of all		6.39	1.82	39.59	46.14	6.06	

[1] Montana Report, 1902, p. 66; South Dakota Bul. 40, p. 88; Wyoming Bul. 87, p. 38.

CHAETOCHLOA GRIESBACHII (Fourn.) Scribn.

Chaetochloa griesbachii is an upright, smooth, rank, perennial native millet, distributed from Texas to Arizona. It is especially abundant upon dry, sandy situations in southern Texas. While frequent in southern Arizona, it is not of nearly as much importance. It is an important grass in Texas, furnishing a large amount of palatable grazing. Nothing is known of it as a hay grass.

No. 8384 was collected at Encinal, Tex., August 12, 1906. The sample represents the plant when fully matured, but before any of the seed had fallen. It was cut about 2 inches high. Its percentage of moisture was 10.58. Other constituents (on a water-free basis) were at follows: Ash, 11.58; ether extract, 1.70; crude fiber, 11.49; nitrogen-free extract, 65.51; protein, 9.72; pentosans, 22.05.

CHAETOCHLOA VERTICILLATA (L.) Scribn.

Chaetochloa verticillata (foxtail) is a common, introduced weed in waste places and cultivated fields in many parts of the United States. It often furnishes some grazing and is sometimes included with hay.

No. 8792 was collected near Fargo, N. Dak., August 8, 1907. The sample was in late blossom and cut close to the surface of the ground.

Material analyzed.	Percentage of moisture.	Water-free basis (per cent).					
		Ash.	Ether extract.	Crude fiber.	Nitrogen-free extract.	Protein.	Pentosans.
Our sample No. 8792	7.47	11.98	2.38	30.40	41.86	13.38	24.27
One other sample [1]		13.43	2.32	35.15	31.91	17.19	
Average of both		12.70	2.35	32.77	36.89	15.29	

[1] South Dakota Bul. 40, p. 41.

CHLORIS CUCULLATA Bisch.

Chloris cucullata is distinctly a sandy-land perennial, extending from Texas northeastward. It is a valuable species, producing a large quantity of root leaves of good forage value.

No. 8401 was collected near Green, Tex., August 14, 1906. The sample represents the plant in a state of overmaturity, two-thirds of the seed having shattered, the culms being nearly all dead. The root leaves, however, were all green. It was cut close to the surface of the ground. Its percentage of moisture was 6.11. Other constituents (on a water-free basis) were as follows: Ash, 12.37; ether extract, 1.89; crude fiber, 29.12; nitrogen-free extract, 45.77; protein, 10.85; pentosans, 23.81.

CHLORIS ELEGANS H. B. K.

Chloris elegans is an annual plant growing 1 or 2 feet high, depending upon the situation in which it develops. It is a grass of great importance throughout the Southwest, oftentimes taking up spaces which were formerly occupied by perennials and making considerable of a volunteer crop of good pasture or hay in neglected places and along irrigated fields. It produces an abundance of fertile seed and is consequently easily established whenever the season is sufficiently moist, often upon lands which were formerly stocked with perennials that have been largely killed out by overstocking. In some situations the six-weeks grama and an annual species of Aristida occupy such areas. In other places this grass goes in. Quite frequently, in portions of the Sulphur Spring Valley in Arizona, over limited areas in favorable situations, 1½ tons of hay to the acre of this grass may be cut. It adapts itself well to cultivation and were it not for the awns upon the seeds it would be much more promising for domestication. Of course, it does not cure up as well when drought strikes it as the perennial gramas. (Pl. V, fig. 2.)

No. 8578 was collected at Green, Tex., September 24, 1906. The sample represents a very rank growth of the species in early maturity. It was cut close to the ground.

Material analyzed.	Percentage of moisture.	Water-free basis (per cent).					
		Ash.	Ether extract.	Crude fiber.	Nitrogen-free extract.	Protein.	Pentosans.
Our sample No. 8578	4.22	13.13	2.18	27.99	45.34	11.36	24.59
One other sample [1]		12.73	1.74	36.39	39.53	9.61	
Average of both		12.93	1.96	32.19	42.44	10.48	

[1] Arizona Report, 1902-3, p. 349.

COTTEA PAPPOPHOROIDES Kunth.

Cottea pappophoroides is a handsome species, growing in bunches of moderate size, 12 to 18 inches high, from western Texas to Arizona. It is not abundant enough to be seriously considered, except as a filler which adds an occasional palatable morsel in the general forage supply. At the present time it is much more abundant where protected by shrubbery than elsewhere, owing probably to the fact that it has been largely killed out by overgrazing.

No. 9617 was collected in the Santa Rita Mountains, Ariz., September 22, 1908. The sample was nearly mature and was cut 1½ inches high. Its percentage of moisture was 2.54. Other constituents (on a water-free basis) were as follows: Ash, 5.90; ether extract, 1.66; crude fiber, 33.21; nitrogen-free extract, 51.76; protein, 7.47; pentosans, 20.17.

DESCHAMPSIA CAESPITOSA (L.) Beauv.

Deschampsia caespitosa (tussock grass) is common in the wet meadows of all the Northern States, and extends in the mountainous regions even into central California and northern Arizona. While producing tussocky formations in some of the Northeastern States, its habit is usually very different in the western moist mountain regions. There tussocks are seldom formed, the grass growing scatteringly among other species with no semblance of tussock formation. It is a handsome silvery-topped species, which enters very largely into the composition of both hay and pasture meadows. Its quality is good, and it is relished by stock.

No. 8859 was collected at Summit, Mont., August 15, 1907. The sample was in blossom and was cut 3 inches high.

Material analyzed.	Percentage of moisture.	Water-free basis (per cent).					
		Ash.	Ether extract.	Crude fiber.	Nitrogen-free extract.	Protein.	Pentosans.
Our sample No. 8859	7.70	7.29	1.67	32.31	52.63	6.10	25.57
Average of 9 others[1]		7.20	1.56	36.12	47.31	7.81	
Average of all		7.21	1.57	35.75	47.84	7.63	

[1] Canada Central Experiment Farm Bul. 19, pp. 28, 32. Colorado Bul. 12, p. 72. Wyoming: Bul. 65, p. 34; Bul. 70, pp. 54, 57; Bul. 87, p. 44.

DISTICHLIS SPICATA L. Greene.

In some portions of the country, *Distichlis spicata* (salt-grass) is considered of no value as a forage plant. However, upon large areas of alkaline soils throughout the arid West it is the principal grass and furnishes continuous pasturage to thousands of stock through the entire summer season. It is true that it is a tough, wiry species, but cattle eat it readily and apparently thrive where they have no other feed. It is also grazed in the dry condition, that is, after it is dry-cured upon the ground. What its value is in this condition, as compared with other grasses which mature in the same way upon the western prairies, no one has investigated. In spite of the fact that it is often tabooed as of no value it must be considered as one of the important native grasses of the arid West, and especially is it important, since it often inhabits soils upon which very few other plants would live. This is one of several species of grass which has been noted in recent years as secreting a gummy acid substance. This is very noticeable in some situations in the arid West, and it is so abundant as to gum the clothing of a person walking through it.

No. 8725a was collected near Tampa, Fla., June 12, 1907. The sample was in full blossom and was cut at the surface of the water in which it grew, about 3 inches above the ground.

Material analyzed.	Percentage of moisture.	Water-free basis (per cent).					
		Ash.	Ether extract.	Crude fiber.	Nitrogen-free extract.	Protein.	Pentosans.
Western samples:							
Our sample No. 8725a	4.27	7.60	1.43	31.66	51.71	7.60	28.12
Average of 7 others[1]	....	11.10	2.25	28.69	49.18	8.78	....
Average of 8 samples	....	10.66	2.15	29.06	49.50	8.63	....
Eastern samples:							
Average of 3 samples[2]	....	8.61	2.61	27.33	54.07	7.38	....
Average of 11 eastern and western samples	....	10.11	2.27	28.59	50.74	8.29	....

[1] Colorado Bul. 12, p. 105. Montana Report, 1902, p. 66. New Mexico Bul. 17, p. 36. South Dakota Bul. 40, p. 118. Washington Bul. 72, p. 15. Wyoming: Bul. 76, p. 38; Bul. 87, p. 45.
[2] Hatch Station Report, 1903, pp. 15, 87; Connecticut Report, 1889, p. 244.

ECHINOCHLOA COLONA Link.

Echinochloa colona is a common weedy species introduced throughout the warmer sections of this country, but it reaches its best development in the irrigated Southwest, where it often enters in an important way into the composition of both hay and pasturage. It is a smaller plant and produces a much finer feed than the coarse barnyard grass.

No. 8567 was collected near Phoenix, Ariz., September 24, 1906. The sample represented the plant in early maturity. Its percentage of moisture was 4.16. Other constituents (on a water-free basis) were as follows: Ash, 15.33; ether extract, 1.92; crude fiber, 30.84; nitrogen-free extract, 44.08; protein, 7.83; pentosans, 20.51.

ECHINOCHLOA CRUS-GALLI (L.) Beauv. (*Panicum crus-galli*).

Echinochloa crus-galli (barnyard grass, or barnyard millet) is an introduced weed common throughout the country. It furnishes considerable quite palatable grazing in waste places, and in moist, rich, loose, soils it commonly forms an important ingredient of hay. In some sections of the irrigated West, where water is used injudiciously upon newly planted alfalfa and other forage crops, this grass volunteers for several years to the detriment of the crop seeded. Often it persists to some extent continuously. The hay produced by it, if cut in season, is of very fair quality, although rather light. In exceptional cases, where conditions are proper, it has been known to make a yield of 1½ or 2 tons to the acre. (Pl. VIII, fig. 2.)

No. 8396 was collected near Green, Tex., August 14, 1906. The sample was a robust form growing in waste places. It was fully 4 feet high. The plants were considerably under maturity and were cut about 4 inches above the ground.

Material analyzed	Percentage of moisture.	Water-free basis (per cent).					
		Ash.	Ether extract.	Crude fiber.	Nitrogen-free extract.	Protein.	Pentosans.
Our sample No. 8396	5.15	15.06	2.28	37.86	36.30	8.50	19.41
Average of 29 others[1]	....	9.79	2.28	30.85	47.49	9.59	....
Average of all	....	9.96	2.28	31.08	47.12	9.56	....

[1] Canada Central Experiment Farm Bul. 19, pp. 28, 29. Connecticut Report, 1879, p. 155; 1887, p. 103. Hatch Station Report, 1901, p. 35; 1903, p. 91. Iowa Bul. 56, p. 483. Kentucky: Bul. 87, p. 116; Bul. 104, p. 302. Massachusetts Report, 1884, p. 110; 1893, p. 326. New Jersey Report, 1906, p. 37. New Mexico Bul. 17, p. 36. South Dakota: Bul. 40, p. 38; Bul. 69, p. 21. Storrs Report, 1896, p. 280. U. S. Department of Agriculture Report No. 32, 1884, p. 125. Vermont Report, 1893, p. 115; 1895, p. 195; 1896–7, p. 188.

ELYMUS CANADENSIS L.

Elymus canadensis is a familiar drooping, awned rye-grass which, like *E. condensatus*, has a very wide distribution and is an important forage plant, especially throughout the Plains region. It inhabits commonly the moist situations of the river valleys, where it forms an important ingredient in both hay and pasture meadows. In pastures it is relished only while young, and to make the best quality of hay it must be cut before it is woody. Its general habits are favorable for cultivation. Its seeds are abundantly produced, but the long, persistent awns would be difficult to thrash out. It is, at best, a rather hard, coarse grass for either pasture or hay.

No. 8801 was collected near Fargo, N. Dak., August 10, 1907.

Material analyzed.	Percentage of moisture.	Water-free basis (per cent).					
		Ash.	Ether extract.	Crude fiber.	Nitrogen-free extract.	Protein.	Pentosans.
Our sample No. 8801	5.61	9.28	2.28	31.94	48.95	7.55	24.61
Average of 10 others [1]	....	8.81	2.22	34.77	45.97	8.23	....
Average of all	....	8.85	2.23	34.51	46.24	8.17	....

[1] Canada Central Experiment Farm Bul. 19, p. 32; Colorado Bul. 12, p. 58; Iowa Bul. 11, p. 467; Montana Report, 1902, p. 66; South Dakota Bul. 40, p. 158; Tennessee Bul. 3, vol. 9, p. 111; U. S. Department of Agriculture Report No. 32, 1884, p. 128; Wyoming Bul. 87, p. 48.

ELYMUS CONDENSATUS Presl.

Elymus condensatus is the giant rye-grass which extends from Montana to Arizona and has a very wide altitudinal distribution. Like many other species it has two distinct habits of growth. In some situations it grows in scattered, large bunches, often 7 or 8 feet high. In other places it is scattered uniformly over the area in which it grows and frequently makes almost a complete stand. It is a very coarse, rank, smooth species, which, if used for hay, must be cut before it gets too woody. Like many other species, the estimate placed upon it varies with the locality in which it is found and with the general quality of the feed of that locality. In portions of Montana and Wyoming it is pronounced absolutely worthless, and while it is not used nearly so widely in those States as it is in the Great Basin, where extensive areas of it are cut for hay, it is, nevertheless, usually considered of very good quality. Its seed habits are very good, and it is quite probable that something could be made of it under cultivation. It ergots very badly, however, and sometimes deleterious effects upon stock are said to be produced on this account. Horses running in pastures of it are very partial to the ripe seeds. It is a common thing to see them graze off the heads and pay little attention to any other feed when the plant is mature. These heads are commonly 6 inches in length and are almost a solid mass of seeds, which, of course, are practically the same as grain. (Pl. VI, fig. 2.)

No. 8830 was collected near Havre, Mont., August 13, 1907. The sample was mature, but was all green with the exception of the head. It was harvested about 4 inches high.

Material analyzed.	Percentage of moisture.	Water-free basis (per cent).					
		Ash.	Ether extract.	Crude fiber.	Nitrogen-free extract.	Protein.	Pentosans.
Our sample No. 8830	8.29	6.41	2.40	34.95	48.40	7.84	25.45
Average of 4 others [1]	....	8.34	2.91	38.48	40.31	9.96	....
Average of all	....	7.96	2.81	37.77	41.93	9.53	....

[1] Montana Report, 1902, p. 66. Nevada Bul. 62, p. 28. Wyoming: Bul. 70, p. 38; Bul. 87, p. 50.

ELYMUS GLAUCUS Buckl.

Elymus glaucus is a species of rye-grass, common and important, especially in the edges of open mountain meadows and among shrubbery, from Michigan to California. Its habit of growth depends upon the environment. It is always a comparatively tall, coarse grass, with a fairly good leafage. In some situations it may grow scatteringly among species of Poa, Danthonia, etc. In other situations it has been seen fully 6 feet high growing in large clumps. It is seldom that it makes a pure growth. The seed is produced in abundance, and it is usually of very good quality, but the awns are a drawback. In the locality in which one of the specimens was collected it is commonly very badly attacked by smut (Tilletia). This, however, has not been observed elsewhere.

No. 8851 was collected near Summit, Mont., August 15, 1907. The seed was in the milk stage and this sample was cut 2 inches high. No. 8893 was collected near Albany, Oreg., August 25, 1907. In this sample the upper portion of the culm and many of the leaves were dead and dry. The specimens were 6 feet high and were cut 6 inches above the ground.

Material analyzed.	Percentage of moisture.	Water-free basis (per cent).					
		Ash.	Ether extract.	Crude fiber.	Nitrogen-free extract.	Protein.	Pentosans.
Our sample No. 8851	7.60	4.59	2.16	32.59	53.18	7.48	23.70
Our sample No. 8893	4.17	8.47	1.97	35.22	50.89	3.45	21.69
One other sample [1]	....	9.61	2.79	36.36	43.62	7.62	....
Average of all	....	7.56	2.31	34.72	49.23	6.18	....

[1] Montana Report, 1902, p. 66.

ELYMUS TRITICOIDES Buckl.

Elymus triticoides resembles in many ways the Colorado bluestem. It has underground stems and very similar seed habits and appearance, although placed by botanists in a different genus. It prefers to grow in alluvial, nonsaline edges of sinks and along river courses. It reaches its best development in the Great Basin and is of less importance in the interior valleys of California. It is an excellent hay grass, often cutting two tons of hay of good quality, which resembles that of the Colorado bluestem, but, unlike that grass, this species grows where the lands overflow once or twice in a season. There is no more promising grass for domestication, as the seed habits are excellent and both the quality and the quantity of seed produced are first class.

No. 8322 was collected near Bakersfield, Cal., May 27, 1906. The sample was in full blossom and was harvested about 2 inches high. Its percentage of moisture was 6.72. Other constituents (on a water-free basis) were as follows: Ash, 6.33; ether extract, 1.97; crude fiber, 39.55; nitrogen-free extract, 46.32; protein, 5.83; pentosans, 25.61.

ELYMUS VIRGINICUS L.

Elymus virginicus is a species of wild rye, widely distributed throughout the United States. It never becomes important except in moist woodlands and in nonalkaline situations along river banks. In such situations patches of small extent are commonly found growing to the exclusion of practically everything else. In the natural condition, however, it is of secondary importance on account of the limited areas in which it grows. It produces a good leafage, its seed habits are first class, and it is well adapted to cultivation. Like nearly all of the rye-grasses, it is somewhat coarse, but not so coarse as many of the species.

No. 8794 was collected near Fargo, N. Dak., August 8, 1907. The specimen was in late blossom and was cut close to the ground.

Material analyzed.	Percentage of moisture.	Water-free basis (per cent).					
		Ash.	Ether extract.	Crude fiber.	Nitrogen-free extract.	Protein.	Pentosans.
Our sample No. 8794[1]	6.40	11.10	2.55	28.08	46.52	11.75	20.52
Average of 8 others	....	7.15	2.89	32.37	48.97	8.62	....
Average of all	....	7.59	2.85	31.89	48.71	8.96	....

[1] Canada Central Experiment Farm Bul. 19, p. 28; Connecticut Report, 1889, p. 245; Iowa Bul. 56, p. 498; Mississippi Report, 1895, p. 91; South Dakota Bul. 40, p. 157.

ERAGROSTIS LUGENS Nees.

Eragrostis lugens is a tall, hard, perennial species, strictly a filler only and of secondary quality. It occurs mostly on rocky, exposed situations and produces feed that remains green quite late in the season. It is not eaten until other more palatable feed has been used.

No. 7091 (E. O. W.) was collected in the San Andreas Mountains near Las Cruces, N. Mex., October 6, 1912. Its percentage of moisture was 5.79. Other constituents (on a water-free basis) were as follows: Ash, 9.03; ether extract, 1.77; crude fiber, 32.58; nitrogen-free extract, 49.82; protein, 6.80; pentosans, 25.46.

ERAGROSTIS SECUNDIFLORA Presl.

Eragrostis secundiflora is distinctively a sand-grass, being characteristic of dry, sandy areas from Florida to the Pacific coast. While extensively grazed, it is not of first quality, either in abundance or palatability. It is wiry in its nature and rejected by live stock until more palatable feeds fail.

No. 8390 was collected at Encinal, Tex., August 12, 1906. The sample was a little underripe, but contained considerable old dead leaves, although nothing was included but this year's growth. It was cut off about half an inch above the ground. Its percentage of moisture was 5.87. Other constituents (on a water-free basis) were as follows: Ash, 15.15; ether extract, 2.12; crude fiber, 30.39; nitrogen-free extract, 45.70; protein, 6.64; pentosans, 23.96.

ERAGROSTIS SPICATA Vasey.

Eragrostis spicata is a tall, conspicuous grass, not abundant enough in the United States to be seriously considered as a native forage. It is a hard, rank species, not particularly relished by stock, although grazed in close pastures.

No. 8402 was collected at Green, Tex., August 14, 1906. The seed was ripe, but not fallen, and all herbage was green and fresh. It was cut 4 inches high. Its percentage of moisture was 10.30. Other constituents (on a water-free basis) were as follows: Ash, 8.77; ether extract, 1.20; crude fiber, 36.31; nitrogen-free extract, 47.44; protein, 6.28; pentosans, 23.28.

ERIOCOMA CUSPIDATA Nutt.[1]

Eriocoma cuspidata (Indian millet) is a grass peculiarly adapted to the loose, sandy soils of the arid West. Although not particularly confined to such situations, it is here that it reaches its most striking development. It is distinctively a bunch grass, growing scatteringly and often in very large bunches in the most sterile of soils, often upon unstable sands. It is a highly prized and valuable species, the only objection to it being that it does not grow abundantly enough. Nowhere is it found forming anything like a ground cover. Sometimes in the edges of cultivated fields, upon railroad embankments, beside roadways, and in other situations where the ground is loosened up, its growth is very much facilitated. It is not a grass that bears grazing very well, being easily pulled up by the roots or tramped out by stock.

No. 8340 was collected near Ashfork, Ariz., May 30, 1906. This sample represents the plant in early maturity. This is true, however, of not over half of the plants,

[1] More recently written *Oryzopsis hymenoides* (R. and S.) Ricker.

FIG. 1.—HORDEUM JUBATUM, WALLA WALLA, WASH.

FIG. 2.—CHLORIS ELEGANS IN SOUTHERN ARIZONA.

FIG. 1.—MUHLENBERGIA EMERSLEYI IN THE MOUNTAINS OF SOUTHERN ARIZONA.

FIG. 2.—ELYMUS CONDENSATUS CUT FOR HAY IN NORTHERN NEVADA.

most of them being still green. They were harvested 2 to 2½ inches high, and all dead herbage was excluded. No. 8834 was collected near Havre, Mont., August 13, 1907. This sample was cut 2 inches high and consisted of large mature plants growing in a favored locality where they had received some cultivation.

Material analyzed.	Percentage of moisture.	Water-free basis (per cent).					
		Ash.	Ether extract.	Crude fiber.	Nitrogen-free extract.	Protein.	Pentosans.
Our sample No. 8340	6.72	14.72	1.31	32.25	45.16	6.56	10.59
Our sample No. 8834	5.51	4.47	2.35	36.52	52.66	4.00	29.03
Average of 9 others[1]	....	7.76	2.31	31.69	48.17	10.07	....
Average of all	....	8.09	2.22	32.19	48.30	9.20	....

[1] Colorado Bul. 12, p. 92. Montana Report, 1902, p. 66. Nevada: Bul. 62, p. 19; Bul. 66, p. 46. Wyoming: Bul. 65, p. 18; Bul. 76, p. 11, 40; Bul. 87, p. 50.

FESTUCA CONFINIS Vasey (*Festuca kingii*).

Festuca confinis is a characteristic and valuable species of fescue of the Rocky Mountain and Sierra Nevada regions. It seldom, if ever, makes pure growths over any extended areas, but, on the other hand, grows in large bunches scattered among other species of Festuca and Agropyron. It is a rather coarse grass—indeed, one of the coarsest of the genus—of about the same texture and stature as the common cultivated English bluegrass. It is readily grazed and constitutes a valuable adjunct of the pasturage, especially of the Rocky Mountain region.

No. 8849 was collected at Summit, Mont., August 15, 1907. The sample was cut 4 inches high when the seed was in stiff dough.

Material analyzed.	Percentage of moisture.	Water-free basis (per cent).					
		Ash.	Ether extract.	Crude fiber.	Nitrogen-free extract.	Protein.	Pentosans.
Our sample No. 8849	6.51	7.48	2.79	34.69	47.65	7.39	24.28
Average of 4 others[1]	....	6.13	2.80	36.81	45.91	8.35	....
Average of all	....	6.40	2.79	36.39	46.26	8.16	....

[1] Nevada Bul. 62, p. 14. Wyoming: Bul. 70, p. 40; Bul. 87, p. 51.

FESTUCA MEGALURA Nutt.

Festuca megalura, sometimes called squirreltail fescue, is one of the characteristic introduced weedy annuals of the California region and may be found at altitudes of 6,000 or 7,000 feet in the mountains. As a filler in the native pastures it is of some importance early in the season. Like all other annual species of this group, it pulls up readily by the roots and is consequently objectionable to stock. After the seeds become mature it is not relished, and it never gets large enough to be cut for hay.

No. 8700 was collected at El Toro, Cal., April 16, 1907. The sample was in blossom and was cut off at the surface of the ground. No. 7108 (Wooton) was collected at Willows, Cal., April 8, 1913. Sometimes known here as poverty grass.

Material analyzed.	Percentage of moisture.	Water-free basis (per cent).					
		Ash.	Ether extract.	Crude fiber.	Nitrogen-free extract.	Protein.	Pentosans.
Our sample No. 8700	6.53	6.82	1.33	35.23	50.34	6.28	27.79
Our sample No. 7108 (E. O. W.)	5.69	5.66	2.01	27.12	56.66	8.55	24.84
Average of both	6.11	6.23	1.67	31.17	53.50	7.42	26.32

FESTUCA OVINA INGRATA Hack.

Throughout the entire Rocky Mountain region, from the San Francisco highlands in Arizona northward, there are large numbers of closely related forms of fescue, of which *Festuca ovina ingrata* may be considered economically typical. In the southernmost portion of this highland region they grow at an altitude of about 7,000 feet. Farther north they come down to the 4,000-foot level and may spread out to the adjoining bare foothills and mesas. They are characteristic grasses of bare hills and mountain sides, where they often grow to the exclusion of practically everything else. They constitute an exceedingly important group of native forage plants which will stand trampling by stock very well, although they have been killed in many sections by excessive stocking. Some very closely related forms are now in cultivation, and it would doubtless be a comparatively easy matter to domesticate some of the forms whose seed habits are just as good as those now under cultivation. They are all popularly known as sheep fescue. (Pl. VII, fig. 1.)

No. 8848 was collected at Summit, Mont., August 15, 1907. The seed of the sample was in the dough. It was cut close to the ground.

Material analyzed.	Percentage of moisture.	Water-free basis (per cent).					
		Ash.	Ether extract.	Crude fiber.	Nitrogen-free extract.	Protein.	Pentosans.
Our sample No. 8848	5.11	4.89	3.13	34.33	52.12	5.53	26.68
One other sample [1]	....	7.72	1.04	37.30	49.19	4.75	....
Average of both	....	6.30	2.09	35.81	50.66	5.14	....

[1] Washington Bul. 82, p. 11.

HETEROPOGON CONTORTUS Beauv.

Heteropogon contortus, a beard-grass with long, twisted, dark-brown to black awns, is very characteristic of the native grass flora of many situations from central Texas to Arizona and southward into Mexico. It produces a quality of feed very similar to that of some of the larger species of Andropogon. On the whole, it is probably not grazed so extensively as those species. Some sheep growers in southern Texas especially deplore its presence on account of the injury which the awns do in working into the fleece and flesh of their flocks. Anyone who has walked through a patch of this grass when mature will readily recognize the injury that it may do to sheep. However, cattle in southern Arizona graze it to the ground very frequently. In some situations, in the sandy arid mountains, it grows thick over small areas, but usually it is distinctively a bunch grass, growing only in scattered bunches among other vegetation.

No. 8397 was collected at Green, Tex., August 14, 1906. The plants were in early maturity and were cut about 3 inches above the ground. Many of the lower culm leaves were dead. No. 9589 was collected in the foothills of the Santa Rita Mountains, Ariz., September 16, 1908. The sample was duplicated on account of the viscid, sweet, gummy secretion which appeared upon the inflorescence of the plants. This is a very common phenomenon in this section.

Material analyzed.	Percentage of moisture.	Water-free basis (per cent).					
		Ash.	Ether extract.	Crude fiber.	Nitrogen-free extract.	Protein.	Pentosans.
Our sample No. 8397	9.06	7.44	1.34	34.47	51.93	4.82	27.46
Our sample No. 9589	1.73	4.58	1.54	32.10	57.65	4.13	24.00
Average of both	5.40	6.01	1.44	33.28	54.79	4.48	25.73

HILARIA CENCHROIDES H. B. K.

Hilaria cenchroides (curly mesquite) is one of the characteristic grasses of the Southwestern United States and of Mexico. In habit it simulates very closely the buffalo grass (*Bulbilis dactyloides*), spreading by slender, creeping rootstocks. It never grows large enough to be cut for hay, but is a very important pasture grass in many situations from Texas to Arizona. It seldom attains a height of 12 inches; more often it is only about 6 inches tall. It produces, however, an abundance of root leaves and grows whenever the rainfall is sufficient. In southern Arizona the species grows only during the rainy season of summer, maturing in late September. In many situations west of central Texas there are large areas where this species forms the main pasturage.

No. 9200 was collected at San Antonio, Tex., April 18, 1908. The sample was mature, but still perfectly green. It was cut close to the ground; hence it included the root leaves, creeping stocks, and upright stems, as well as a few old dead leaves. Its percentage of moisture was 8.16. Other constituents (on a water-free basis) were as follows: Ash, 9.37; ether extract, 2.09; crude fiber, 24.51; nitrogen-free extract, 55.26; protein, 8.77; pentosans, 21.13.

HOLCUS LANATUS L.[1]

Holcus lanatus (velvet grass), like many other aggressive species, has many warm friends, and it has bitter enemies. It is widely introduced throughout the United States as far south as the Carolinas. While commonly considered to produce a feed of low grade, many ranchers in the Pacific Northwest, the only place in which it is abundant, find it a very valuable grass. It inhabits moist meadows and furnishes both hay and pasturage of medium quality.

No. 8891 was collected near Hood River, Oreg., August 23, 1907. The sample was mature, one-half of the culm dry, but the leaves were all green. It was cut 3 inches high.

Material analyzed.	Percentage of moisture.	Water-free basis (per cent).					
		Ash.	Ether extract.	Crude fiber.	Nitrogen-free extract.	Protein.	Pentosans.
Our sample No. 8891	4.89	12.24	2.83	27.42	51.47	6.04	21.63
Average of 8 others [2]	....	9.42	2.97	29.68	47.98	9.95	....
Average of all	....	9.73	2.95	29.43	48.38	9.51	....

[1] More recently written *Notholcus lanatus* (L.) Nash.
[2] Canada Central Experiment Farm Bul. 19, p. 28; Kentucky Report, 1902, p. 302; Louisiana Bul. 19, series 2, p. 553; Mississippi Report, 1895, p. 91; U. S. Department of Agriculture Report No. 32, 1884, pp. 127, 136; Virginia Bul. 180, p. 96; West Virginia Bul. 23, p. 36.

HOMALACENCHRUS ORYZOIDES (L.) Poll.

Homalacenchrus oryzoides, the cut-grass with which every boy is disagreeably acquainted, is commonly pastured by cattle along streams and fresh-water lakes throughout its range. It never grows abundantly enough or pure enough to enter appreciably into the composition of hay.

No. 8793 was collected at Fargo, N. Dak., August 8, 1907. The sample was 2 to 2½ feet high, but had not quite headed out. It was cut close to the ground.

Material analyzed.	Percentage of moisture.	Water-free basis (per cent).					
		Ash.	Ether extract.	Crude fiber.	Nitrogen-free extract.	Protein.	Pentosans.
Our sample No. 8793	10.24	17.35	2.71	32.17	37.04	10.73	21.11
Average of 4 others [1]	....	13.73	2.23	29.90	44.87	9.27	....
Average of all	....	14.45	2.33	30.35	43.31	9.56	....

[1] Kentucky: Bul. 87, p. 116; Bul. 104, p. 302. Mississippi Report, 1888, p. 33. South Dakota Bul. 40, p. 52.

HORDEUM GUSSONEANUM Parl. (*Hordeum maritimum* With.).

Hordeum gussoneanum, like *H. jubatum*, is an introduced weed, but it inhabits lower, moister situations and is not so abundant and widely distributed in this country. The situations in which it is found are mostly low, moist places where water stands for a portion of the year, thus killing out other plants. Its feeding value is approximately the same as *H. jubatum*.

No. 8319 was collected near Stockton, Cal., May 26, 1906. The sample represents the plant in the milk state. It was cut close to the ground. Its percentage of moisture was 6.35. Other constituents (on a water-free basis) were as follows: Ash, 11.77 ether extract, 1.96; crude fiber, 33.02; nitrogen-free extract, 44.65; protein, 8.60; pentosans, 26.19.

HORDEUM JUBATUM L.

Hordeum jubatum is the common squirreltail grass which inhabits saline, moist situations as far west as the valley of the Little Colorado in Arizona. West of this it gives place to *H. murinum*, or wall barley, discussed elsewhere. The quality of the feed produced by *H. jubatum* is about the same as that produced by the other species and approximately the same remarks apply to it. It is often a troublesome weed in meadows in situations best adapted for its development. (Pl. V, fig.1.)

No. 8356 was collected in cultivated irrigated fields and meadows on the bottoms along the Little Colorado River near Winslow, Ariz., June 1, 1906. Here this grass appears to gain a foothold in the lower, poorer tilled portions of alfalfa fields and gradually spreads from here to occupy more and more of the field. The sample was in early blossom and was cut 1½ inches high. No. 8799 was collected near Fargo, N. Dak., August 10, 1907. The sample was somewhat rusty and the seed nearly ripe. It was cut close to the ground.

Material analyzed.	Percentage of moisture.	Water-free basis (per cent).					
		Ash.	Ether extract.	Crude fiber.	Nitrogen-free extract.	Protein.	Pentosans.
Our sample No. 8356	7.24	15.08	1.96	28.23	47.26	7.47	12.60
Our sample No. 8799	5.21	12.11	2.67	32.49	42.77	9.96	25.58
Average of 13 others [1]		10.41	3.56	32.13	41.99	11.91	
Average of all		10.83	3.39	31.90	42.40	11.48	

[1] Colorado Bul. 12, p. 118. Iowa: Bul. 30, p. 320; Bul. 56, p. 533. Montana Report, 1902, p. 66. South Dakota Bul. 40, p. 156. Wyoming: Bul. 65, p. 25; Bul. 87, p. 56.

HORDEUM MURINUM L.

Hordeum murinum is a very persistent and pernicious annual weed, introduced from the Mediterranean region. It grows in the most favorable places on uplands, as well as lowlands, throughout California and extends eastward into Arizona. In California it has found congenial conditions upon uncultivated lands. In Arizona, however, where conditions are less favorable, it inhabits cultivated and irrigated areas, being especially troublesome in alfalfa fields. On this account, it is a common practice of the renter to require that the first crop of alfalfa be cut, in order to get rid of as much as possible of this weed. While it may be classed among the weeds, it nevertheless furnishes a large amount of quite valuable forage. It is readily grazed up to the time that it heads out; after that time the awns are very annoying to stock. When it occurs in hay, these work in between the teeth of horses and cattle and often cause considerable injury. Reports show that there is a way to feed it successfully, however. Some have chopped it up with a hay cutter and moistened it for 12 or 24 hours, when the awns are so softened that they produce no deleterious effects. Pasture meadows having very much of this grass in them should be mowed about the time that it begins to head out, thus getting rid of the awns and sharp fruit.

No. 8300 was collected near Banning, Cal., May 15, 1906. The sample was in early maturity and was harvested 1 inch above the ground. Its percentage of moisture was 6.70. Other constituents (on a water-free basis) were as follows: Ash, 6.86; ether extract, 2; crude fiber, 35.99; nitrogen-free extract, 47.72; protein, 7.43; pentosans, 26.84.

KOELERIA CRISTATA (L.) Pres.

Koeleria cristata (June-grass) furnishes very important grazing throughout the Plains regions; it extends from British Columbia to Arizona and from the Alleghanies to the Sierra Nevadas, according to the common acceptance of the species. It is very doubtful, however, whether the prairie forms of the Dakotas and Montana should be considered under the same name as the ones which grow in the mountains of the Southwest. Upon the Plains, from the Dakotas to the Panhandle of Texas, it grows in scattering bunches among other prairie grasses, forming often one-fourth to one-eighth of the vegetation, mostly upon the rolling hillsides. In the mountains of the Southwest it grows in scattering bunches, mostly in thin-growing scattering timber, and matures its seeds in late September and early October; upon the prairies of the Dakotas its seed ripens in early June. Its abundant root leaves, 5 to 10 or 12 inches in length, and its early maturity upon the prairies are characteristics which render it a valuable pasture grass. As a hay plant it is of only medium quality, because the culms are mostly bare and many of the root leaves are lost in the cutting.

No. 7120 (Wooton) was collected at Moorpark, Cal., April 18, 1913. The specimen was just forming the panicle. No. 8839 was collected at Havre, Mont., August 13, 1907. This sample was cut close to the ground and represents the composition of the plant when the culms are well dried up and only about half of the root leaves are green.

Material analyzed.	Percentage of moisture.	Water-free basis (per cent).					
		Ash.	Ether extract.	Crude fiber.	Nitrogen-free extract.	Protein.	Pentosans.
Our sample No. 7120 (E. O. W.)	4.96	9.26	2.46	34.45	44.69	9.14	26.80
Our sample No. 8839	4.47	9.65	2.99	34.32	48.56	4.48	24.91
Average of 8 others [1]	....	7.18	3.03	33.90	46.77	9.12	....
Average of all	....	7.45	3.03	33.94	46.98	8.60	....

[1] Canada Central Experiment Farm Bul. 19, p. 28. Colorado Bul. 12, p. 110. South Dakota Bul. 40, p. 116. Wyoming: Bul. 70, p. 44; Bul. 76, p. 48.

LAMARCKIA AUREA (Dalech) Moench.[1]

Lamarckia aurea (golden-top grass) is a handsome species that is native to the Mediterranean region of the Old World. It is widely introduced in southern California where, together with wild oats, the brome-grasses, and other introduced weedy annuals, it furnishes a large amount of grazing. It can not be considered a first-quality grass, because, in the first place, it is an annual and, in the second place, it is low in stature, seldom becoming a foot in height. It is, however, probably fully as valuable as many of the brome-grasses, but is not to be compared with wild oats.

No. 8314 was collected at Garvanza, Cal., May 19, 1906. The sample was at nearly full maturity and was pulled up, the roots being then cut off close. Its percentage of moisture was 7.40. Other constituents (on a water-free basis) were as follows: Ash, 25.79; ether extract, 3.17; crude fiber, 29.90; nitrogen-free extract, 36.21; protein, 4.93; pentosans, 23.94.

[1] More recently written *Achyrodes aureum* (L.) Kunze.

LEPTOCHLOA DUBIA (H. B. K.) Nees.

Leptochloa dubia is a species said to be distributed within the limits of the United States from Florida to Arizona, and it extends southward far into Mexico. In the Southwest, where it reaches the greatest perfection, it inhabits the higher valleys and lower mountain areas, making a very striking and favorable growth, often 3 feet in height. It never produces a perfect stand, but grows scatteringly among the gramas, muhlenbergias, and similar species. Its seed habits are good, and it is considered a promising species for cultivation. It is rather coarse, but the leafage and habit are both good, and really it is but little coarser than timothy or English bluegrass.

No. 8950 was collected in the Santa Rita Mountains, Ariz., September 25, 1907. The specimen was nearly mature. It was cut 3 inches high. Its percentage of moisture was 6.57. Other constituents (on a water-free basis) were as follows: Ash, 10.23; ether extract, 1.74; crude fiber, 33.36; nitrogen-free extract, 47.98; protein, 6.69; pentosans, 22.62.

LEPTOCHLOA FILIFORMIS (Lam.) Beauv. (*Leptochloa mucronata*).

Leptochloa filiformis is a common and conspicuous species in the edges of streams, ponds, and neglected irrigating ditches throughout the Southwest. It is especially partial to alkaline soils; and, in some situations in the San Joaquin Valley of California, upon lands which have been abandoned for ordinary crops on account of the accumulation of soluble salts in the surface soils, so long as the ground is irrigated and not invaded by Bermuda grass and other perennials which choke it out, this grass is known to yield a large amount of forage. It seems to make a fair quality of feed, but its annual habit and its being adapted to peculiar special conditions make it of only secondary importance.

No. 8577 was collected near Tempe, Ariz., September 24, 1906. The specimen was in early maturity and was harvested close to the ground.

Material analyzed.	Percentage of moisture.	Water-free basis (per cent).					
		Ash.	Ether extract.	Crude fiber.	Nitrogen-free extract.	Protein.	Pentosans.
Our sample No. 8577	2.26	14.79	1.88	22.36	52.27	8.70	15.43
Average of 4 others[1]	....	10.95	2.28	30.94	43.82	12.51	....
Average of all	....	11.72	2.20	29.22	45.11	11.75	....

[1] Connecticut Report, 1879, p. 155; Mississippi Report, 1895, p. 91; U. S. Department of Agriculture Report No. 32, 1884, p. 127.

LIMNODEA ARKANSANA (Nutt.) Dewey.

Limnodea arkansana ranges from Texas to Florida and enters largely into the composition of dry upland pastures in southern Texas. It appears to be a valuable species, which when in the vegetative condition is grazed by stock as readily as the gramas. When dried, however, it seems to lose substance. In some seasons in southern Texas (and this was true especially in 1908) it grows large enough to be cut for hay in ungrazed upland pastures.

No. 9204 was collected at San Antonio, Tex., April 20, 1908. The specimen was in late blossom and was cut 2 inches above the ground. Its percentage of moisture was 8.47. Other constituents (on a water-free basis) were as follows: Ash, 9.56; ether extract, 2.18; crude fiber, 34.48; nitrogen-free extract, 46.10; protein, 7.68; pentosans, 20.86.

LYCURUS PHLEOIDES H. B. K.

Lycurus phleoides is a species of the arid Southwest which has been popularly called "Texan timothy," and it really does have a faint superficial resemblance to timothy, the cultivated hay plant. It is a common species from Colorado to Texas and westward to Arizona. In southern Arizona, where we are most familiar with it, this grass inhabits gravelly ridges of the foothills region midway between the desert mesas and the moister mountains. Nowhere does it form a complete ground cover, but it is commonly found in bunches scattered among other grasses and is consequently not a grass of the first importance, although readily eaten by stock in both dry field-cured and green conditions.

No. 9518 was collected near Prescott, Ariz., August 31, 1908. The sample was in late blossom and was harvested by being cut close to the ground.

Material analyzed.	Percentage of moisture.	Water-free basis (per cent).					
		Ash.	Ether extract.	Crude fiber.	Nitrogen-free extract.	Protein.	Pentosans.
Our sample No. 9518	7.07	7.25	2.00	34.08	50.06	6.61	19.74
One other sample[1]	....	7.55	2.28	34.16	49.80	6.21	....
Average of both	....	7.40	2.14	34.12	49.93	6.41	....

[1] New Mexico Bul. 17, p. 37.

MELICA BULBOSA Geyer.

Melica bulbosa (melic grass) is a Pacific coast species of importance only as a filler. It is a tall, coarse species with bare, hard culms, growing scatteringly among other grasses and shrubbery, but it is always grazed where opportunity offers. This is one of the native bunch grasses which have been almost exterminated. The fact that it is to be found rather abundantly along the railroad right of way in some places indicates that it might come back on much of the range country if given a chance.

No. 7106 (E. O. W.) was collected at Red Bluff, Cal., April 6, 1913. Its percentage of moisture was 4.65. Other constituents (on a water-free basis) were as follows: Ash, 8.76; ether extract, 2.94; crude fiber, 30.36; nitrogen-free extract, 45.16; protein, 12.78; pentosans, 24.74.

MELICA IMPERFECTA Trin.

Melica imperfecta is one of the original perennial bunch grasses of California which was no doubt much more abundant formerly than it is now. At present it is found mostly in the protection of shrubbery. It is relished by stock and is therefore always closely grazed.

No. 7118 (E. O. W.) was collected at Moorpark, Cal., April 18, 1913. Its percentage of moisture was 4.93. Other constituents (on a water-free basis) were as follows: Ash, 8.70; ether extract, 1.94; crude fiber, 36.95; nitrogen-free extract, 43.60; protein, 8.81; pentosans, 27.

MUHLENBERGIA ARENICOLA Buckl.

Muhlenbergia arenicola is strictly a sandy-land species, at times very conspicuous because it follows up other species which have been grazed out. Although at times abundant over considerable areas, it is not relished by stock.

No. 7084 (E. O. W.) was collected on sand hills northeast of Las Cruces, N. Mex., October 3, 1912. Its percentage of moisture was 4.52. Other constituents (on a water-free basis) were as follows: Ash, 9.03; ether extract, 2.05; crude fiber, 33.80; nitrogen-free extract, 48.31; protein, 6.81; pentosans, 26.58.

MUHLENBERGIA EMERSLEYI Vasey.

Muhlenbergia emersleyi is a typical Mexican species which extends into the mountains of the southwestern United States, forming a coarse, harsh forage resorted to by cattle when other more palatable feeds fail. It grows in large bunches, often 2½ feet high and having a spread of similar dimensions. In southern Arizona it invariably inhabits the oak belt in the mountains, from the open, gently sloping, upper mesas to an altitude of approximately 5,000 feet. It never gets down to the desert mesas. It is a very handsome grass and, were it possible to cultivate it, might make a valuable ornamental. The first number listed below is considered to be typical of the species, However, the group has not been carefully worked out. Segregations in the future may separate the second number as a distinct species from the first. (Pl. VI, fig. 1.)

No. 8952 was collected in the upper foothills of the Santa Rita Mountains, Ariz., September 25, 1907. The sample was in late blossom and was cut 3 inches high; hence it included all of the material that could possibly be eaten by stock. Indeed, the stubble of the sample collected would represent conditions under very close grazing. No. 9600 was collected in the northern foothills of the Santa Rita Mountains, September 18, 1908. The sample was in early blossom and prepared about the same as the previous number.

Material analyzed.	Percentage of moisture.	Water-free basis (per cent).					
		Ash.	Ether extract.	Crude fiber.	Nitrogen-free extract.	Protein.	Pentosans.
Our sample No. 8952	5.72	7.19	1.79	30.72	55.46	4.84	25.95
Our sample No. 9600	3.01	9.05	1.05	41.34	43.56	5.00	24.92
Average of both	4.37	8.12	1.42	36.03	49.51	4.92	25.43

MUHLENBERGIA GRACILIMA Torr.

Muhlenbergia gracilima is a dry-land species extending from western Texas to California and northward to Colorado and Nevada. It is a conspicuous plant upon the semisodded mesas and foothills of the region. It occupies neither the moister nor the drier situations, but rather the medium lands on the dividing line between sodded and unsodded conditions. Where it occurs it usually forms a mat of tangled stems and leaves upon the surface of the ground, thus producing a semblance at least of a turf. While of a great deal of importance on account of its wide distribution and abundance, it is not a first-quality grass. It seldom gets over 3 inches high before the bare culms stretch up a foot or less beyond this. The culms invariably break off easily and are seldom grazed by live stock. Associated with the species are usually found buffalo grass, the gramas, and the bluestems, all of which are more palatable to stock. In spite of this, however, the species is grazed to extermination in many situations and is more or less relished by stock when other feeds become scarce.

No. 9515 was collected near Prescott, Ariz., August 30, 1908. The sample was in early fruit and was cut close to the ground, some old dry leaves being unavoidably included. Its percentage of moisture was 8.57. Other constituents (on a water-free basis) were as follows: Ash, 12.36; ether extract, 2.53; crude fiber, 31.03; nitrogen-free extract, 46.31; protein, 7.77; pentosans, 18.41.

MUHLENBERGIA NEOMEXICANA Vasey.

Muhlenbergia neomexicana is a low, tufted, hard, wiry perennial, at times of considerable value on account of its abundance, but it is a filler only. In limited localities in the Southwest, however, it is abundant enough to give character to the pasturage. It usually occurs on rocky exposed ridges in the mountains of southern Arizona, New Mexico, and western Texas in the woodlands or open coniferous forests up to about 7,000 feet elevation.

No. 7094 (E. O. W.) was collected in the San Andreas Mountains near Las Cruces, N. Mex., October 6, 1912. Its percentage of moisture was 5.61. Other constituents (on a water-free basis) were as follows: Ash, 5.65; ether extract, 2.39; crude fiber, 37.55; nitrogen-free extract, 48.28; protein, 6.13; pentosans, 26.90.

MUHLENBERGIA PORTERI Scribn.

Muhlenbergia porteri (black grama) although of less importance by far than many other southwestern grasses, is in many ways most interesting. At the same time it is so important that it never should be omitted from a list of forage grasses of the region from western Texas to California and northward to Colorado and Utah. In the Santa Rita Mountains of southern Arizona it always grows in tangled masses in bunches of

FIG. 1.—FESTUCA ARIZONICA IN OPEN PARKS IN THE WHITE MOUNTAINS OF ARIZONA.

FIG. 2.—A GOOD MOUNTAIN PASTURE IN SOUTHERN ARIZONA, CONSISTING OF SPECIES OF BOUTELOUA, ANDROPOGON, LYCURUS, ETC.

FIG. 1.—SPOROBOLUS WRIGHTII ON THE VALLEY FLOOR, ERODED INTO TUSSOCKS, SOUTHWESTERN ARIZONA.

FIG. 2.—ECHINOCHLOA CRUS-GALLI, A VOLUNTEER CROP, NEAR WESTFALL, OREG.

shrubbery, cat's-claw, hackberry, mesquite, etc., where it remains unmolested by stock as long as other feeds are available with less annoyance from the shrubby spiny protectors. In the Organ Mountains of New Mexico it grows in clumps of shrubbery also, but more often in the open.

Eight or nine years ago, when a large tract of range land was fenced by the United States Department of Agriculture in the northwestern foothills of the Santa Rita Mountains in southern Arizona, this grass was nowhere conspicuous. It was invariably closely cropped except where it was impossible for stock to get at it. Now tangled clumps 3 feet high and 6 or 8 feet in diameter are not uncommon, generally produced since the field was inclosed. In times past it was a common thing for the Mexican people to cut large quantities of this grass in the upper foothills along the Mexican border, packing it to villages and mining camps on burros.

The species is in reality a shrub. It makes a growth approximately equal each year to some of the other grasses, but instead of dying to the ground each winter, only the leaves, flowers, and smaller branches die, the older hardened culms remaining alive. In time, therefore, a tangled mass, such as that described above, representing portions of the growths of several years, is formed. Although several years old the stems are not so woody as one might expect. Indeed, they are not so woody but that cattle will eat them even if they are 3 or 4 years old. It can be easily imagined how fond stock are of these green clumps in winter when other vegetation is dead and dried up.

No. 8940 was collected in the foothills of the Santa Rita Mountains, Ariz., September 23, 1907. The sample represents the nearly mature plant of the current year's development. This season's growth, about 10 to 12 inches, was taken with very little of the older culms. Its percentage of moisture was 5.76. Other constituents (on a water-free basis) were as follows: Ash, 6.53; ether extract, 2.28; crude fiber, 35.63; nitrogen-free extract, 49.59; protein, 5.97; pentosans, 26.25.

MUHLENBERGIA WRIGHTII Vasey.

Muhlenbergia wrightii grows in large bunches upon the second bottoms of mountain streams and dry washes of northern Arizona. Its affinities are with *Sporobolus brevifolius*. The leaves are a little more abundant, and the plant throughout is less wiry than that species. In this region it adds considerable to the pasturage, since it is resorted to by stock and readily grazed when more palatable feeds fail.

No. 9554 was collected at Prescott, Ariz., September 7, 1908. Its percentage of moisture was 6.58. Other constituents (on a water-free basis) were as follows: Ash, 8.39; ether extract, 1.91; crude fiber, 32.14; nitrogen-free extract, 50.50; protein, 7.06; pentosans, 27.39.

PANICULARIA GRANDIS (Wats.) Nash.

Panicularia grandis is a soft, spongy stemmed, sprangle-topped reed-grass, inhabiting low, moist, alluvial grounds in the edges of swamps and streams from Labrador to California. It never grows abundant enough to be of any great economic importance, but furnishes very acceptable grazing wherever it occurs. Usually it is more or less pure in small patches, but it may also be found scattered among sedges, rushes, and other water-loving plants.

No. 8795 was collected at Fargo, N. Dak., August 8, 1907. The sample was cut close to the ground when in late fruit.

Material analyzed.	Percentage of moisture.	Water-free basis (per cent).					
		Ash.	Ether extract.	Crude fiber.	Nitrogen-free extract.	Protein.	Pentosans.
Our sample No. 8795	7.19	17.31	2.22	26.71	43.38	10.38	17.79
Average of 5 others [1]	....	9.48	1.74	33.39	45.42	9.97	....
Average of all	....	10.78	1.82	32.28	45.08	10.04	....

[1] South Dakota Bul. 40, p. 134. Wyoming: Bul. 70, p. 35; Bul. 87, p. 64.

PANICULARIA PAUCIFLORA (Presl.) Kuntze.

Panicularia pauciflora is a soft, water-loving species of smaller stature than *P. grandis*. It also never becomes abundant, but commonly makes almost pure stands in the edges of fresh-water ponds, streams, and marshes, especially in the high altitudes of the Rocky Mountain regions. The areas are all small, however, being seldom over a few rods in extent, and usually they are much smaller in area than this. What there is of it is readily grazed by all classes of live stock.

No. 8868 was collected at Summit, Mont., August 15, 1907. The sample was cut close to the ground when the seed was in early maturity. Its percentage of moisture was 6.34. Other constituents (on a water-free basis) were as follows: Ash, 10.01; ether extract, 5.27; crude fiber, 25; nitrogen-free extract, 46.23; protein, 13.49; pentosans, 20.37.

PANICUM FASCICULATUM Swartz.

The main economic interest in *Panicum fasciculatum* is derived from the fact that it often produces a heavy aftermath of good quality in grain fields or in waste places in our irrigated Southwest.

No. 8568 was collected near Phoenix, Ariz., September 24, 1906. The sample represents the plant when the seeds are fully mature. Its percentage of moisture was 4.68. Other constituents (on a water-free basis) were as follows: Ash, 15.19; ether extract, 2.01; crude fiber, 25.91; nitrogen-free extract, 46.99; protein, 9.90; pentosans, 19.44.

PANICUM FILIPES Scribn.

Panicum filipes resembles more closely than anything else a somewhat dwarf-leaved form of switch-grass (*P. virgatum*). It grows abundantly in dry situations in southern Texas and forms a valuable part of the pasturage, growing in scattered bunches. It can not be considered of much consequence in native hays, but its delicate panicle, abundant leafage, and rather small culms render it of considerable importance as a pasture grass.

No. 8403 was collected near Green, Tex., August 14, 1906. The sample represents the plant with the seed fully mature and half of the leaves dead and dry. It was harvested about 2 inches high. Its percentage of moisture was 5.44. Other constituents (on a water-free basis) were as follows: Ash, 9.66; ether extract, 1.89; crude fiber, 32.57; nitrogen-free extract, 50; protein, 5.88; pentosans, 26.09.

PANICUM HALLII Vasey.

Panicum hallii (panic-grass) is of a great deal of importance as a filler on the open mesas and rocky hills, as well as in poorly cultivated fields from Texas to Arizona. It is a species of secondary quality.

No. 7087 (E. O. W.) was collected on the mesas near Las Cruces, N. Mex., October 4, 1912. Its percentage of moisture was 3.42. Other constituents (on a water-free basis) were as follows: Ash, 10.77; ether extract, 1.56; crude fiber, 31.93; nitrogen-free extract, 50.29; protein, 5.45; pentosans, 25.05.

PANICUM OBTUSUM H. B. K.

Panicum obtusum is a common and familiar grass, sometimes known as vine mesquite, extending from Colorado to the Gulf of Mexico and westward through Arizona. It usually inhabits waste places, alluvial bottoms, and other moist situations, commonly to the exclusion of everything else wherever it gains a good foothold. Its ability to develop by long overground stems, which root at every joint, gives it a great advantage in soils which are comparatively loose. It seldom is in condition to be cut for hay, but in a few situations it has been seen making a growth which would yield, if cut with the mower, fully 1 ton to the acre. Near Seligman, Ariz., during the autumn of 1908 there were considerable areas of it, in one place 5 or 6 acres which would make 1 to 1½ tons to the acre. This situation, however, was an exceptional one. A large quantity of earth had been washed down from a dam which broke in the early summer, depositing from 1 to 6 inches of loose earth over the entire area. It is in situations where the soil is of this nature that the plant shows to best advantage. It makes but a fair quality of hay and is not usually grazed where other palatable feeds occur. (Pl. IX, fig. 1.)

No. 9551 was collected near Seligman, Ariz., September 6, 1908. The sample was in full blossom and was harvested close to the ground.

Material analyzed.	Percentage of moisture.	Water-free basis (per cent).					
		Ash.	Ether extract.	Crude fiber.	Nitrogen-free extract.	Protein.	Pentosans.
Our sample No. 9551	6.43	9.44	4.45	35.27	39.32	11.52	21.21
Average of 3 others [1]	....	9.49	2.38	32.74	47.45	7.94	....
Average of all	....	9.48	2.90	33.37	45.42	8.83	....

[1] Connecticut Report, 1879, p. 155; New Mexico Bul. 17, p. 37; U. S. Department of Agriculture Report No. 32, 1884, p. 125.

PANICUM VIRGATUM L.

The common switch-grass (*Panicum virgatum*) is familiar and conspicuous on account of its large stature. It extends from the East to the Middle West. In the Plains region it mostly inhabits the moist situations. It seldom forms a pure growth over any extended areas, but is commonly found in large bunches several feet across and 3 to 4 feet high. It is a coarse, rank, smooth species, with good seed habits, and it adapts itself to cultivation very well. It has been considered by some as rather promising for domestication.

No. 9337 was collected near Henrietta, Tex., July 1, 1908. The sample was just beginning to head out and was cut 4 inches high.

Material analyzed.	Percentage of moisture.	Water-free basis (per cent).					
		Ash.	Ether extract.	Crude fiber.	Nitrogen-free extract.	Protein.	Pentosans.
Our sample No. 9337	5.95	5.64	2.05	37.20	50.44	4.67	21.63
Average of 16 others [1]	....	6.30	2.26	33.28	51.60	6.56	....
Average of all	....	6.26	2.25	33.52	51.52	6.45	....

[1] Canada Central Experiment Farm Bul. 19, p. 28. Colorado Bul. 12, p. 30. Connecticut Report, 1879, p. 155; 1887, p. 103. Iowa Bul. 56, p. 480. Mississippi Report, 1895, p. 92. North Carolina Bul. 90b, p. 4. South Dakota Bul. 40, p. 36. Tennessee Bul. 3, vol. 9, p. 112. U. S. Department of Agriculture Report No. 32, 1884, p. 125. West Virginia Report, 1891, p. 35. Wyoming Bul. 87, p. 68.

PAPPOPHORUM APERTUM Munro.

Pappophorum apertum is a perennial bunch grass with a long, white, spikelike head, common in the moister situations from western Texas to Arizona. It is never very abundant and almost never forms a continuous growth. On the other hand, it is found scatteringly among other species, thus simply adding to the sum total of the feed and not imparting any distinctive character to it.

No. 8393 was collected near Green, Tex., August 14, 1906. The sample was overripe, the seed having very largely dropped off, and there were some dry leaves at the base. It was harvested about 3 inches above the ground. Its percentage of moisture was 8.29. Other constituents (on a water-free basis) were as follows: Ash, 8.85; ether extract, 1.68; crude fiber, 34.87; nitrogen-free extract, 48.26; protein, 6.34; pentosans, 24.11.

PASPALUM DILATATUM Poir.

Paspalum dilatatum is a coarse, wide-leaved, perennial species, widely distributed from Virginia to Florida and westward to the arid portion of western Texas. It is partial to low, moist grounds and produces in such situations a valuable part of the pasturage. Like other species of the genus, however, the forage produced is of secondary quality.

No. 8726 was collected near Tampa, Fla., June 12, 1907. The sample was in full-blossom and was cut at the surface of the ground.

Material analyzed.	Percentage of moisture.	Water-free basis (per cent).					
		Ash.	Ether extract.	Crude fiber.	Nitrogen-free extract.	Protein.	Pentosans.
Our sample No. 8726	7.07	7.49	2.42	35.72	45.60	8.77	22.83
Average of 4 others [1]	....	10.40	2.77	30.82	48.11	7.90	....
Average of all	....	9.82	2.70	31.80	47.61	8.07	....

[1] Louisiana Bul. 114, p. 23; Mississippi Report, 1895, p. 92; Texas Report, 1888, p. 30.

PASPALUM STRAMINEUM Nash.

Paspalum stramineum is a low, ascending, spreading species, of a great deal of importance in some localities upon sandy lands. It has some value as a sand binder and furnishes very early feed. It is found upon loose sands in circumscribed areas from Nebraska to New Mexico and southward.

No. 7078 (E. O. W.) was collected in the San Andreas Mountains, N. Mex., September 23, 1912. Its percentage of moisture was 4.72. Other constituents (on a water-free basis) were as follows: Ash, 7.17; ether extract, 1.37; crude fiber, 34.31; nitrogen-free extract, 52.73; protein, 4.42; pentosans, 24.83.

PHALARIS ARUNDINACEA L.

Reed canary grass (*Phalaris arundinacea*) is a common, stout, rank, smooth, leafy, perennial grass, widely distributed from Nova Scotia to Tennessee and westward to California. It inhabits marshes and low, wet meadows in general, often growing in a foot of water for a considerable period. It is seldom that it forms pure growths, usually being found scatteringly among other grasses and sedges in river bottoms and other moist situations, where it is a valuable adjunct to the native hay and pasture crops.

It adapts itself well to cultivation and, although growing in moist situations naturally, develops well on dry cultivated uplands. The serious objection to it as a cultivated plant is its seed habits. It produces an abundance of fertile seeds, and they are free from any wool, lint, or chaff which would make them objectionable in gathering, but they are very loosely attached to the plant and drop off immediately when ripe, Maturing as they do from the top downward, the upper seeds are often shed before the lower ones are fit to harvest.

No. 8323 was collected at Bakersville, Cal., May 27, 1906, when the seed was mature but the entire plant was still green. It was cut 3 inches above the ground.

Material analyzed.	Percentage of moisture.	Water-free basis (per cent).					
		Ash.	Ether extract.	Crude fiber.	Nitrogen-free extract.	Protein.	Pentosans.
Our sample No. 8323	6.05	8.04	1.41	31.09	55.73	3.73	20.39
Average of 17 others [1]	....	8.34	3.06	30.20	47.67	10.73	....
Average of all	....	8.32	2.97	30.25	48.12	10.34	....

[1] Canada Central Experiment Farm Bul. 19, pp. 28, 32. Colorado Bul. 12, p. 88. Connecticut Report, 1879, p. 153. Iowa Bul. 11, p. 457. Kentucky Bul. 87, p. 116; Report, 1902, p. 302. Montana Report, 1902, p. 66. North Carolina Bul. 90b, p. 4. New York Report, 1886, p. 342; 1887, p. 407. South Dakota Bul. 40, p. 54. Vermont Report, 1889, p. 86. Washington Bul. 72, p. 15.

PHLEUM ALPINUM L.

Mountain timothy (*Phleum alpinum*), native to both hemispheres and to both the North American and South American continents, resembles very closely the cultivated timothy. It can be easily distinguished, however, by its shorter, stouter heads and smaller stature throughout. It usually inhabits the drier portions of moist mountain meadows. Growing scatteringly among other grasses, it can not be considered as a forage plant of prime importance in these situations, because it is never sufficiently abundant to impart its own character to the vegetation. So far as it goes, however, it is probably as valuable as the common cultivated timothy, which is widely introduced throughout the mountain ranges of this country, furnishing in many places vastly more feed than this smaller native.

No. 8845 was collected at Summit, Mont., August 15, 1907, when the upper florets were in early maturity. It was cut 1 inch above the ground.

Material analyzed.	Percentage of moisture.	Water-free basis (per cent).					
		Ash.	Ether extract.	Crude fiber.	Nitrogen-free extract.	Protein.	Pentosans.
Our sample No. 8845	6.51	4.19	2.50	32.55	54.64	6.12	24.94
Average of 7 others [1]		4.92	2.31	32.15	51.26	9.36	
Average of all		4.83	2.33	32.20	51.69	8.95	

[1] Colorado Bul. 12, p. 113. Nevada Bul. 62, p. 24. Wyoming: Bul. 70, p. 48; Bul. 76, p. 50; Bul. 87, p. 70.

PHRAGMITES COMMUNIS Trin.

Phragmites communis, commonly distributed in the United States, and indeed throughout the entire Northern Hemisphere, is a characteristic species of reedlike grass, inhabiting marshes and edges of ponds and streams. It is not usually considered much of a forage plant, but in closely grazed regions it is frequently resorted to in times of scarcity and furnishes really a great deal of supplemental feed. In some situations, where the soils are wet in spring and dry in midsummer, the grass is cut for hay and makes a fair quality of very coarse roughage.

No. 8808 was collected at Fargo, N. Dak., August 10, 1907. The specimen was in full blossom and was cut 1 foot high.

Material analyzed.	Percentage of moisture.	Water-free basis (per cent).					
		Ash.	Ether extract.	Crude fiber.	Nitrogen-free extract.	Protein.	Pentosans.
Our sample No. 8808	5.27	8.48	2.97	32.91	46.93	8.71	24.70
One other sample [1]		7.14	2.87	39.02	41.86	9.11	
Average of both		7.80	2.92	35.97	44.40	8.91	

[1] South Dakota Bul. 40, p. 106.

PLEURAPHIS MUTICA Buckl.

Pleuraphis mutica is the galleta of the southwestern United States and is in many respects a very valuable species. Like the closely related tabosa (*Hilaria jamesii*) of regions a little farther north, it comes into prominence during seasons of excessive drought. It is peculiarly adapted to shallow swales, which catch or retard a portion of the run-off of the desert during the rainy season. In such situations in southern Arizona, often upon desert mesas, small crops of this grass are sometimes harvested as hay. The prime importance, however, of this and closely related species is from a pasture standpoint. It is a hard, brittle-stemmed, brash species, but the stems are perennial, remaining green from year to year, the new growth springing from near the base. On this account it furnishes a feed that is often more palatable to stock after long periods of drought than even the gramas. Taking it all in all, it is not to be compared as a feed with blue grama or with *Hilaria cenchroides*, but the perennial character of the stems renders it exceptionally valuable after other feeds have become desiccated so as to be of little value.

No. 7014 (Wooton) was collected near Congress Junction, Ariz., February 18, 1912. This sample represents the grass in its winter condition and was prepared by taking the lower 4 or 5 inches of the stems and leaves, cut about 1 inch above the ground. No. 8600 was collected near Deming, N. Mex., September 29, 1906. The specimen was overripe, but all excepting the upper portion of the culm was still green. It was so harvested as to include nothing but this year's growth.

Material analyzed.	Percentage of moisture.	Water-free basis (per cent).					
		Ash.	Ether extract.	Crude fiber.	Nitrogen-free extract.	Protein.	Pentosans.
Our sample No. 7014 (E. O. W.).	5.96	7.27	1.17	34.68	52.68	4.20	26.72
Our sample No. 8600	4.37	8.55	2.06	29.70	52.17	7.52	24.52
One other sample[1]	....	7.80	1.26	35.83	48.47	6.64	....
Average of all	....	8.17	1.66	32.77	50.32	7.08	....

[1] New Mexico Bul. 17, p. 37.

POA ARIDA Vasey.

In many respects *Poa arida* is one of the most remarkable species of this genus. It has methods of propagation exactly comparable to the common cultivated Kentucky bluegrass, but its rootstocks are much longer and it is a salt-loving species of excellent quality. In many situations in the Rio Grande Valley, especially north of El Paso, and in the Pecos Valley, in the vicinity of Roswell, it is found abundantly mixed with *Distichlis spicata* and *Sporobolus airoides*. It never makes a perfect stand, but grows scatteringly, as indicated above, among other salt-loving grasses, and it is certainly relished by stock. It grows large enough to be cut for hay, and its seed habits are as good as those of Kentucky bluegrass.

No. 8363 was collected near Albuquerque, N. Mex., June 2, 1906. The specimen was in a rather overripe condition and was cut off close to the ground.

Material analyzed.	Percentage of moisture.	Water-free basis (per cent).					
		Ash.	Ether extract.	Crude fiber.	Nitrogen-free extract.	Protein.	Pentosans.
Our sample No. 8363	4.02	7.02	1.99	33.51	51.88	5.60	25.43
Average of 2 others[1]	....	7.20	2.87	38.38	45.92	5.63	....
Average of all	....	7.14	2.58	36.76	47.90	5.62	....

[1] Montana Report, 1902, p. 60; South Dakota Bul. 40, p. 28.

POA BIGELOVII Vasey & Scribn.

Poa bigelovii is a typical species of the Mexican-boundary region of Arizona. What its habits were originally we do not know, but at the present day it grows almost invariably in the protection of shrubbery in the foothills at an altitude of 3,500 to 5,000 feet. It seems to desire protection from the sun as well as from live stock. In these situations it furnishes a small quantity of grazing of a fairly good quality. It undoubtedly is not as good feed as the perennial species of Poa, but it grows in this region as a winter and early-spring annual when the stock feed is made up almost entirely of weedy, nongrass forage plants.

No. 9167 was collected in the foothills of the Santa Rita Mountains, Arizona, April 10, 1908. The sample was nearly mature and was cut close to the ground. Its percentage of moisture was 9.30. Other constituents (on a water-free basis) were as follows: Ash, 7.35; ether extract, 2.93; crude fiber, 24.39; nitrogen-free extract, 58.26; protein, 7.07; pentosans, 16.37.

POA LAEVIGATA Scribn.

Poa laevigata, although somewhat distantly related to the common cultivated bluegrass, is quite wiry, but it is still a very important pasture and hay grass in the edges of moist bottoms of the interior Great Basin and Rocky Mountain regions. The situations most suitable for its development are those which receive one or possibly two good floodings during the year. This is characteristic of the heavy, hard, adobe soils between the lower moist bottoms and the surrounding ridges in the eastern part of this range and of the sinks and swales of the Great Basin. In such situations, this species often grows luxuriantly, in almost perfect stand, and will sometimes cut 1½ tons of hay to the acre. It makes a good quality of hay and, when properly handled, a good grade of pasture. Its seed habits are as good as those of Kentucky bluegrass.

No. 8840 was collected at Virdon, Mont., August 14, 1907. The specimen was overmature. It was cut about 1 inch above the ground.

Material analyzed.	Percentage of moisture.	Water-free basis (per cent).					
		Ash.	Ether extract.	Crude fiber.	Nitrogen-free extract.	Protein.	Pentosans.
Our sample No. 8840	4.36	5.04	2.56	33.96	55.11	3.33	27.32
One other sample[1]	....	10.96	2.17	38.27	42.87	5.73	....
Average of both	....	8.00	2.37	36.11	48.99	4.53	....

[1] Montana Report, 1902, p. 66.

POA NEMORALIS L.

Poa nemoralis is a valuable species which reaches its characteristic development in woodland meadows and has a wide distribution in both the North American and Eurasian continents. There are few species that possess such an altitudinal variation of distribution. It ranges from 2 or 3 inches in height at the snow line to 2 feet or more in favored situations at the base of the mountain. While it is an important grass and one relished by all kinds of live stock, it is never abundant enough to be of first importance. It commonly grows in large isolated bunches in favorable situations at lower levels; higher up in the mountains the bunches are smaller and the plants more dwarfed. In palatability to stock and general characteristics of value it stands very close to Kentucky bluegrass. Its habits of growth, however, are not as good. Its seed habits are just as desirable for a cultivated species as those of Kentucky bluegrass.

No. 8869 was collected at Summit, Mont., August 15, 1907. The specimen was in early blossom and was cut close to the ground.

Material analyzed.	Percentage of moisture.	Water-free basis (per cent).					
		Ash.	Ether extract.	Crude fiber.	Nitrogen-free extract.	Protein.	Pentosans.
Our sample No. 8869	7.52	5.89	1.69	31.06	52.84	8.52	22.84
Average of 9 others [1]		6.30	2.69	32.01	51.47	7.53	
Average of all		6.26	2.59	31.92	51.60	7.63	

[1] Connecticut Report, 1888, p. 101; 1889, p. 248. Mississippi Report, 1895, p. 92. Montana Report, 1902, p. 66. New York Report, 1886, p. 365. South Dakota Bul. 40, p. 130. Wyoming Bul. 87, p. 82.

POA ORCUTTIANA Vasey.

Poa orcuttiana is a species which is characteristic of the western slope of the southern Sierras. It is a highly prized, important pasture grass. Like some of the other species of the *P. buckleyana* group, it grows in large bunches. At the present time the weedy bromes and fescues are the most conspicuous grasses in the upper foothills, where this species grows, and are much less palatable to live stock. This grass is, therefore, closely cropped upon all the pasture lands of the section. In the localities where the specimen cited below was secured, it grew in almost pure stands on steep, bare, northern slopes of the mountains.

No. 9103 was collected at Caliente, Cal., March 24, 1908. The sample was in very early blossom and was cut as close to the ground as practicable. Its percentage of moisture was 1.65. Other constituents (on a water-free basis) were as follows: Ash, 7.96; ether extract, 3.21; crude fiber, 31.72; nitrogen-free extract, 48.02; protein, 9.09; pentosans, 24.29.

POA SCABRELLA Benth.

Poa scabrella is a palatable species of bluegrass, but strictly of secondary importance, because it never occurs abundantly. It is found in open gravelly ground and also in partial shade of timber throughout the Pacific States from Oregon southward. It was doubtless formerly of much more importance before the native plants were replaced by the introduced annuals now everywhere dominant in the region.

No. 7116 (E. O. W.) was collected at Moorpark, Cal., April 18, 1913. The specimen was just coming into flower. Its percentage of moisture was 6.59. Other constituents (on a water-free basis) were as follows: Ash, 5.30; ether extract, 2.24; crude fiber, 35.22; nitrogen-free extract, 50.68; protein, 6.56; pentosans, 26.50.

POLYPOGON MONSPELIENSIS (L.) Desf.

Polypogon monspeliensis is a foreign, annual, short-bearded grass, widely introduced in this country from Maine to California. It is especially abundant in moist alluvial soils of the Great Basin and California regions. Its best growth is attained in the edges of fresh-water ponds and streams where the warm waters are but 2 or 3 inches in depth. In such small areas it often forms a pure growth and attains a height of 12 to 24 inches. It is readily eaten in the green condition by stock.

No. 8879 was collected near The Dalles, Oreg., August 22, 1907. The sample was completely dried up and was cut close to the ground.

Material analyzed.	Percentage of moisture.	Water-free basis (per cent).					
		Ash.	Ether extract.	Crude fiber.	Nitrogen-free extract.	Protein.	Pentosans.
Our sample No. 8879	6.99	11.26	2.21	26.93	53.39	6.21	21.99
One other sample [1]		11.88	2.95	21.89	50.95	12.33	
Average of both		11.57	2.58	24.41	52.17	9.27	

[1] Colorado Bul. 12, p. 99.

FIG. 1.—A GENERAL VALLEY PASTURE, MADE UP OF PANICUM OBTUSUM, CHLORIS ELEGANS, SPECIES OF BOUTELOUA, AND VARIOUS WEEDY PLANTS.

FIG. 2.—VALOTA SACCHARATA IN MOUNTAIN FOOTHILLS, SOUTHERN ARIZONA.

PUCCINELLIA AIROIDES (Nutt.) Wats. and Coult.

Puccinellia airoides is distinctly a salt-grass, and it is much more palatable to stock than most grasses which inhabit salt marshes. It is not only able to withstand large amounts of soluble salts in the soil, but will grow in situations where water holding a large amount of the same ingredients in solution stands on the ground for a month or more at a time. Indeed, it is in the edge of salt waters of this kind that the species appears to be at home. When found, it is usually growing almost to the exclusion of everything else, but commonly in very restricted areas, from northern Arizona northward through the Great Basin and Great Plains regions.

No. 8814 was collected at Devils Lake, N. Dak., August 11, 1907. The sample was from overripe specimens growing in the edge of brackish waters. It was cut at the surface of the water 2 inches above the ground.

Material analyzed.	Percentage of moisture.	Water-free basis (per cent).					
		Ash.	Ether extract.	Crude fiber.	Nitrogen-free extract.	Protein.	Pentosans.
Our sample No. 8814	4.58	7.86	2.67	31.72	49.20	8.55	25.89
Average of 2 others [1]		7.50	2.44	33.46	51.19	5.41	
Average of all		7.62	2.52	32.88	50.53	6.45	

[1] Montana Report, 1902, p. 66; Wyoming Bul. 65, p. 30.

SCLEROPOGON BREVIFOLIUS Philippi.

Schleropogon brevifolius is a peculiar-awned, stoloniferous, rigid-leaved species, inhabiting the drier situations of the arid Southwest. Sometimes it is the only vegetation over considerable areas, and it makes almost a continuous cover only in rare instances. It is difficult to conceive of stock being driven to such an extremity as to eat this species. Such, however, sometimes is the case, but it is only rarely observed to be touched.

No. 8601 was collected near Deming, N. Mex., September 29, 1906. The sample was all green with the exception of the spike, which was entirely dead and dry. Many old leaves were attached to the base of the culm and consequently were included in the sample, which was cut close to the ground. Its percentage of moisture was 3.56. Other constituents (on a water-free basis) were as as follows: Ash, 8.59; ether extract, 2.02; crude fiber, 30.41; nitrogen-free extract, 51.20; protein, 7.78; pentosans, 26.94.

SITANION BREVIFOLIUM J. G. S.

As a filler in barren places, among rocks, and in the shade of bushes *Sitanion brevifolium* is of secondary importance only. It extends throughout the highland region from Wyoming into northern Mexico.

No. 7142 (E. O. W.) was collected in the San Andreas Mountains, N. Mex., May 23, 1913. The specimen was in full head, but not yet in blossom.

Material analyzed.	Percentage of moisture.	Water-free basis (per cent).					
		Ash.	Ether extract.	Crude fiber.	Nitrogen-free extract.	Protein.	Pentosans.
Our sample No. 7142 (E. O. W.)	4.48	9.52	2.24	34.50	45.56	8.18	27.70
One other sample [1]		10.68	2.31	36.72	40.84	9.45	
Average of both		10.10	2.27	35.61	43.21	8.81	

[1] Wyoming Bul. 87, p. 86.

SITANION LONGIFOLIUM J. G. S.

The genus Sitanion in general does not contain grasses which are considered to be of much value for either pasture or hay. *Sitanion longifolium*, however, grows in large clumps and furnishes a small amount of very valuable grazing up to the time it heads out. After this the awns and brittle spikes are very annoying, but when these have disappeared, in late maturity, it is again relished by stock. The feed produced by it appears to be of very fair quality early in the season, but it is small in amount.

No. 9555 was collected near Prescott, Ariz., Sept. 7, 1908. Its percentage of moisture was 7.08. Other constituents (on a water-free basis) were as follows: Ash, 7.02; ether extract, 2.18; crude fiber, 35.08; nitrogen-free extract, 47.89; protein, 7.83; pentosans, 26.69.

SITANION PUBIFLORUM J. G. S.

So far as forage value is concerned, the remarks under *Sitanion longifolium* apply equally well to *S. pubiflorum.*

No. 8341 was collected near Ashfork, Ariz., May 30, 1906. The specimen was completely headed out, but was mostly under blossom. It was cut 1½ to 2 inches high. Its percentage of moisture was 8.13. Other constituents (on a water-free basis) were as follows: Ash, 19.51; ether extract, 1.55; crude fiber, 31.64; nitrogen-free extract, 38.59; protein, 8.71; pentosans, 12.18.

SPARTINA CYNOSUROIDES (L.) Willd.

The giant cord-grass (*Spartina cynosuroides*) is a familiar species in lowland pastures and meadows of the States as far west as Colorado and Texas. Like the other two species of this genus discussed in this report, it is rank, tough, and wiry, but in spite of this it makes a very fair quality of hay and is readily grazed by stock, especially when young. The hay it produces, if cut in proper season and when not too rank, is of very good quality and weighs heavily. Its natural habitat is in moist bottoms and swales, where it may often be found growing almost pure, but never forming tussocks. On the other hand, like *S. gracilis*, the culms are isolated, and it propagates almost entirely by running rootstocks.

No. 8796 was collected near Fargo, N. Dak., August 10, 1907. The sample was in late blossom in an entirely green and fresh condition, but coarser than is usually cut for hay. It was harvested 3 inches above the ground.

Material analyzed.	Percentage of moisture.	Water-free basis (per cent).					
		Ash.	Ether extract.	Crude fiber.	Nitrogen-free extract.	Protein.	Pentosans.
Our sample No. 8796	5.03	7.20	1.77	37.50	46.16	7.37	26.04
Average of 19 others [1]	....	6.10	2.27	36.75	47.22	7.66	....
Average of all	....	6.16	2.25	36.79	47.16	7.64	....

[1] Canada Central Experiment Farm Bul. 19, p. 32. Connecticut Report, 1889, p. 245. Iowa: Bul. 11, pp. 456, 478; Bul. 56, pp. 506, 507. Montana Report, 1902, p. 67. South Dakota: Bul. 40, p. 94; Bul. 114, p. 546. U. S. Department of Agriculture Report No. 32, 1884, p. 125.

SPARTINA GRACILIS Trin.

Spartina gracilis is the species commonly known as the small cord-grass, in contradistinction to the giant cord-grass (*S. cynosuroides*). Unlike the larger species, this one seldom, if ever, grows in pure stands. On the other hand, it is found in scattering individuals among other vegetation, from the Dakotas and Kansas westward to California. It is almost invariably found in somewhat alkaline soils, in moist situations in river and lake bottoms, and other places of a similar nature. It is a tough, wiry species, but in spite of this it is a valuable adjunct to the hay crops where it is included and is readily grazed by cattle.

No. 8881 was collected at The Dalles, Oreg., August 22, 1907. The sample represents the plant in a state of early maturity, cut 2 inches high.

Material analyzed.	Percentage of moisture.	Water-free basis (per cent).					
		Ash.	Ether extract.	Crude fiber.	Nitrogen-free extract.	Protein.	Pentosans.
Our sample No. 8881	6.05	9.58	1.92	31.95	51.79	4.76	23.80
Average of 3 others [1]	....	7.00	2.02	36.30	46.39	8.29	....
Average of all	....	7.65	2.00	35.21	47.74	7.40	....

[1] South Dakota Bul. 69, p. 9. Wyoming: Bul. 76, p. 58; Bul. 87, p. 88.

SPARTINA JUNCIFORMIS Engelm. and Gray.

Spartina junciformis is also a salt-loving plant, being found along the Gulf coast from Texas to Florida. It is usually accepted by stockmen as an indication of the presence of common salt in the soils. Among the Mexican population of southwest Texas the grass is universally known as sacahuiste, and this is the common popular designation of the plant even among the Americans. It is an exceedingly important and useful grass from many points of view. It is largely grazed along the coast and is often the mainstay during long periods of drought, and some herds live on it continuously. Cattle and horses will eat the old growth when driven to it, but the common way of handling it is to burn the old grass off in small areas at intervals of two or three weeks, thus covering the entire pasture and furnishing fresh growth during the entire season. Stock appear to be fond of this young growth.

This species has been in the past, and is to some extent yet, extensively used as a thatch plant, and it appears to the casual observer much better adapted for this purpose than for forage. Its durability is certainly remarkable when properly laid upon roofs. Buildings have been seen which were thatched with this grass over 30 years ago and are still in fairly good condition.

Like *Sporobolus airoides*, which inhabits alkaline soils in more interior situations, *Spartina junciformis* has two distinct habits of growth. About the inland limit of its development it is likely to be found in very large, compact bunches, while closer to the coast, where conditions are more favorable and its growth is consequently more abundant, its bunch character is to a large extent obliterated.

No. 9064 was collected near Cactus, Tex., March 12, 1908. The sample consists of young growth, 4 to 6 inches high, and probably none of it was over three weeks old. Its percentage of moisture was 3.67. Other constituents (on a water-free basis) were as follows: Ash, 12.33; ether extract, 1.97; crude fiber, 31.05; nitrogen-free extract, 46.28; protein, 8.37; pentosans, 23.59.

SPOROBOLUS AIROIDES Torr.

Sporobolus airoides, to which the name alkali saccaton has been applied by some, is one of the most important native pasture and hay grasses of the alkaline river and lake bottoms from South Dakota to Texas and westward. In some sections it is known as salt-grass. It has two distinct habits of growth. In portions of the valley of the Rio Grande and its tributaries, particularly the Pecos, it forms a continuous, smooth, quite uniform growth, approaching a turf. In other situations it grows in bunches. On the whole, the latter is the more common and characteristic aspect. While able to withstand large amounts of soluble salts in the soil, such conditions do not appear to be necessary for its perfect development. Upon the saline bottoms of the valley of the Little Colorado in Arizona, for instance, it may make a uniform growth, or it may grow in bunches 2 feet high; and upon the sandy bluffs and hillsides, under still more arid conditions, the plants, although scattering, may be fully as tall, although bearing fewer culms. It withstands much abuse in the shape of close grazing and trampling by stock, especially upon the bottom lands where soils are heavy and hard. In sandy areas, of course, it is easier to kill out. In the Pecos Valley in New Mexico, injury has been done to cattle by allowing them to graze upon this grass at certain seasons of the year. It is the opinion of close observers, however, that the grass was not at fault, but that the injury was done by the soluble salts in the soil, these salts, by creeping up the grass stems during moist weather and by being eaten along with the grass, produce the deleterious effects.

There are very extensive areas of this grass in the Cheno Valley of northern Arizona, which, owing to overgrazing, resemble the tussocky condition of *Sporobolus wrightii*, described later. It is evident that the condition produced by overgrazing, if continued, will gully out the valley to such an extent that the bottom lands will be as unproductive as the hills surrounding. In the year 1908, 1 to 1½ tons of hay to the acre of this grass could be cut upon the lands which had not become tussocky.

No. 8324 was collected at Bakersfield, Cal., May 27, 1906. The specimen grew on apparently nonalkaline, well-drained, sandy-loam soil, where the ground had been disturbed somewhat, producing magnificent large bunches of the plant. The sample was cut when the seed was in the dough, 2 to 3 inches above the ground, care being taken to include all of the root leaves. No. 8575 was collected at Tempe, Ariz., September 24, 1906. The sample grew in what appeared to be strongly alkaline soil. It was a much smaller sample than No. 8324 and was cut close to the ground when the seed was nearly mature.

Material analyzed.	Percentage of moisture.	Water-free basis (per cent).					
		Ash.	Ether extract.	Crude fiber.	Nitrogen-free extract.	Protein.	Pentosans.
Our sample No. 8324	6.10	9.62	1.63	32.56	48.20	7.99	25.92
Our sample No. 8575	2.79	12.48	1.62	33.04	46.17	6.69	24.04
Average of 7 others[1]		7.63	1.83	32.02	49.41	9.11	
Average of all		8.39	1.78	32.19	48.92	8.72	

[1] Colorado Bul. 12, p. 74. New Mexico Bul. 17, p. 36. Wyoming: Bul. 76, p. 60; Bul. 87, p. 89.

SPOROBOLUS ASPERIFOLIUS Thurber.

Sporobolus asperifolius is a species that can be justly considered one of the salt-grasses of this country. It is almost invariably found in salty bottom lands from the Mississippi westward. Its habit of growth, by creeping rootstocks, and its partiality for heavy adobe soils make it one of the most persistent grasses under heavy grazing. It is not as much relished by stock as many species, but it probably is about equal to the familiar salt-grass *Distichlis spicata*. It never gets tall enough, excepting when growing among other grasses, to be cut for hay, and when in pure stands it is almost impossible to cut it with a mower.

No. 8819 was collected at Devils Lake, N. Dak., August 11, 1907. The sample was cut close to the ground and represents the species in early blossom.

Material analyzed.	Percentage of moisture.	Water-free basis (per cent).					
		Ash.	Ether extract.	Crude fiber.	Nitrogen-free extract.	Protein.	Pentosans.
Our sample No. 8819	7.43	9.69	2.92	27.83	52.84	6.72	28.94
Average of 2 others[1]		6.80	2.00	36.64	49.04	5.52	
Average of all		7.76	2.31	33.70	50.31	5.92	

[1] Mississippi Report, 1888, p. 33; South Dakota Bul. 40, p. 80.

SPOROBOLUS AURICULATUS Vasey.

Such species as *Sporobolus auriculatus* are in the aggregate of considerable importance, as they add a great deal to the sum total of the pasturage. This one is never abundant enough to give character to the vegetation. It is apparently of limited distribution in southwestern Texas and southern New Mexico. It commonly occurs on more or less alkaline soils.

No. 7083 (E. O. W.) was collected on the mesas near Las Cruces, N. Mex., October 3, 1912. Its percentage of moisture was 3.85. Other constituents (on a water-free basis) were as follows: Ash, 10.46; ether extract, 2.26; crude fiber, 33.42; nitrogen-free extract, 48.11; protein, 5.75; pentosans, 25.72.

SPOROBOLUS BREVIFOLIUS (Nutt.) Scribn.

Sporobolus brevifolius is a short-leaved, tough, wiry, low, drop-seeded grass, a common and even conspicuous species upon dry second bottoms, hillsides, and upland prairies, especially of the Great Plains region. It forms a complete ground cover in only very limited areas, but is commonly scattered among other grasses and is an important ingredient of the make-up of the forage cover of the rolling prairies. The quality of feed produced by it, whether hay or pasture, is low, probably largely on account of its tough, wiry nature. Under conditions of short pasturage, however, it is always closely grazed.

No. 8829 was collected at Williston, N. Dak., August 11, 1907. The sample represents the plant in early maturity, cut at the surface of the ground.

Material analyzed.	Percentage of moisture.	Water-free basis (per cent).					
		Ash.	Ether extract.	Crude fiber.	Nitrogen-free extract.	Protein.	Pentosans.
Our sample No. 8829	5.76	9.94	2.83	30.88	50.87	5.48	26.83
Average of 4 others [1]	....	6.47	2.29	33.90	50.24	7.10	....
Average of all	....	7.16	2.40	33.30	50.37	6.77	....

[1] Montana Report, 1902, p. 66. Wyoming: Bul. 70, p. 32; Bul. 87, p. 88.

SPOROBOLUS CRYPTANDRUS (Torr.) Gray.

Although tough and wiry, like the other species of the genus, *Sporobolus cryptandrus* is of great importance, along with some of the closely related forms, especially upon the sandy bench and mesa lands of Arizona and New Mexico. Its distribution, however, is very wide, extending from here to New England. It furnishes a great deal of feed in the Southwestern States.

No. 8395 was collected near Green, Tex., August 14, 1906. The sample was fully mature, but only a little of the seed had shattered. It was cut about 2 inches high. No. 9553 was collected at Prescott, Ariz., September 7, 1908. The plant was ripe, but still green, and it was cut close to the ground.

Material analyzed.	Percentage of moisture.	Water-free basis (per cent).					
		Ash.	Ether extract.	Crude fiber.	Nitrogen-free extract.	Protein.	Pentosans.
Our sample No. 8395	6.59	7.48	1.38	34.71	47.66	8.77	23.07
Our sample No. 9553	6.43	6.36	1.30	31.30	54.09	6.95	20.09
Average of 2 others [1]	....	7.19	1.80	33.98	49.17	7.86	....
Average of all	....	7.05	1.57	33.49	50.03	7.86	....

[1] Montana Report, 1902, p. 66; Wyoming Bul. 87, p. 90.

SPOROBOLUS FLEXUOSUS (Thurber) Rydb.

Sporobolus flexuosus is a familiar species of rather wiry but palatable grass, inhabiting sandy lands from southwestern Texas to Nevada. It grows in scattering small bunches, 2 feet or more high. In some situations it grows almost pure, but it never makes a thick stand. Commonly on the looser sands it is found only in scattering bunches among other species. It is palatable to stock in all stages and is consequently closely grazed.

No. 7073 (E. O. W.) was collected near Las Cruces, N. Mex., September 21, 1912. No. 8602 was collected at Deming, N. Mex., September 29, 1906. It was fully mature, but still green. It was harvested about 1 inch high.

Material analyzed.	Percentage of moisture.	Water-free basis (per cent).					
		Ash.	Ether extract.	Crude fiber.	Nitrogen-free extract.	Protein.	Pentosans.
Our sample No. 7073 (E. O. W.)	3.57	6.00	1.23	35.94	51.29	5.54	24.64
Our sample No. 8602	4.57	6.99	1.39	32.07	50.97	8.58	22.86
Average of both	4.07	6.49	1.31	34.01	51.13	7.06	23.75

SPOROBOLUS GIGANTEUS Nash.

Sporobolus giganteus is one of the most striking of the species of "dropseed," growing invariably in sandy, loose lands, especially in New Mexico and western Texas. It grows scatteringly in large clumps with culms 3 or 4 feet high and furnishes a large amount of pasturage.

No. 7068 (E. O. W.) was collected on the sand hills northeast of Las Cruces, N. Mex., September 8, 1912. Its percentage of moisture was 4.32. Other constituents (on a water-free basis) were as follows: Ash, 5.77; ether extract, 0.98; crude fiber, 43.47; nitrogen-free extract, 45.46; protein, 4.32; pentosans, 25.63.

SPOROBOLUS INDICUS (Trin.) R. Br.

Sporobolus indicus, a characteristic species of the Southern States, is said to have been introduced from tropical regions, although it often has all the appearance of a native species. Being coarse and early becoming woody, it is a grass of secondary importance, but where feed is scarce, and especially in waste places and partially disturbed ground, i toften makes a good growth and furnishes considerable grazing.

No. 8724 was collected at Jacksonville, Fla., June 8, 1907. The sample represents plants in full fruit, but perfectly green. They were cut at the surface of the ground.

Material analyzed.	Percentage of moisture.	Water-free basis (per cent).					
		Ash.	Ether extract.	Crude fiber.	Nitrogen-free extract.	Protein.	Pentosans.
Our sample No. 8724	5.50	8.18	1.94	29.88	54.43	5.57	27.68
Average of 3 others[1]	....	6.99	3.80	23.87	53.05	12.29	....
Average of all	....	7.29	3.33	25.37	53.40	10.61	....

[1] Connecticut Report, 1879, p. 153; South Carolina Report, 1888, p. 132; U. S. Department of Agriculture Report No. 32, 1884, p. 126.

SPOROBOLUS GRACILIS (Trin.) Merrill.

Sporobolus gracilis is a tough, wiry species to which some have applied the name rush-grass. Indeed, it resembles in texture some of the wiry rushes and produces a feed not unlike them in texture. So far as our experience goes, it is not a grass relished by stock. It inhabits dry, sandy areas from Virginia southward. It is especially common in open pine woods.

No. 8731 was collected at Sutherland, Fla., June 14, 1907. The sample was collected in full blossom by being cut close to the ground. Its percentage of moisture was 6.55. Other constituents (on a water-free basis) were as follows: Ash, 3.43; ether extract, 2.05; crude fiber, 35.35; nitrogen-free extract, 53.88; protein, 5.29; pentosans, 30.29.

SPOROBOLUS NEALLEYI Vasey.

Nealley's rush-grass is a hard, wiry species, inhabiting the gypsum soils of western Texas and eastern New Mexico. It and *Bouteloua breviseta* grow thriftily upon stable "gyp" soils, containing as high as 95 per cent of calcium sulphate. It is of value only because it is one of the few grasses which will grow in such situations and so produce a forage crop where otherwise none would be possible.

No. 7099 (E. O. W.) was collected upon the white sands west of Alamogordo, N. Mex., October 21, 1912. Its percentage of moisture was 6.16. Other constituents (on a water-free basis) were as follows: Ash, 9.27; ether extract, 1.61; crude fiber, 36.26; nitrogen-free extract, 43.60; protein, 9.26; pentosans, 21.79.

SPOROBOLUS RAMULOSUS Kunth.

Sporobolus ramulosus is one of the annual species of drop-seeded grass of very little value, although it is grazed to some extent by sheep. It grows only in loose temporary sand washes and depressions. It is small, light, delicate, and not of much value.

No. 9538 was collected at Prescott, Ariz., September 1, 1908. Its percentage of moisture was 6.88. Other constituents (on a water-free basis) were as follows: Ash, 7.35; ether extract, 2.22; crude fiber, 30.56; nitrogen-free extract, 50.08; protein, 9.79; pentosans, 23.93.

SPOROBOLUS STRICTUS (Scribn.) Merrill.

Although rather tough and hard, *Sporobolus strictus* is a very important pasture grass in many of the sandy regions of Arizona, New Mexico, and western Texas. It is well adapted to dry, sandy soils, where it grows scatteringly to a height of 2 to 2½ feet, producing for the region a large quantity of apparently nutritious feed. It is readily grazed by stock, and where close pasturing occurs it is invariably closely cropped.

No. 8947 was collected in the foothills of the Santa Rita Mountains, Ariz., September 24, 1907. The sample, although green, had fully matured its seed. It was a rank specimen and was cut 3 inches high. Its percentage of moisture was 7.14. Other constituents (on a water-free basis) were as follows: Ash, 6.87; ether extract, 1.13; crude fiber, 35.42; nitrogen-free extract, 50.93; protein, 5.65; pentosans, 21.59.

SPOROBOLUS VIRGINICUS (L.) Kunth.

Sporobolus virginicus is a familiar grass of the Southern States that grows mostly in medium-sized bunches and propagates by running rootstocks. Like most species of this genus, it is tough and wiry, but it appears to be quite extensively grazed where the specimen was collected. It is of especial interest, inasmuch as it secretes a salty substance with which the entire vegetative portion may be covered, much like *Distichlis spicata*, *Leptochloa viscida*, and some other western grasses.

No. 8732 was collected at Sutherland, Fla., June 14, 1907. The sample was collected when the plant was in full blossom, and was harvested close to the ground. Its percentage of moisture was 8.46. Other constituents (on a water-free basis) were as follows: Ash, 13.27; ether extract, 2.28; crude fiber, 29.41; nitrogen-free extract, 46.44; protein, 8.60; pentosans, 25.88.

SPOROBOLUS WRIGHTII Scribn.

Sporobolus wrightii is the "sacaton" of the Mexicans, and it is confined to the southwestern United States and Mexico. In former times it was a beautiful, characteristic species of the river bottoms of the Southwest, forming dense growths 6 and even 8 feet in height, through which it was difficult to ride on horseback. At the present time there are but faint traces of this magnificent growth left. Some notion of its habit of growth can be obtained from Plate I in Bulletin No. 4 of the Bureau of Plant Industry, United States Department of Agriculture. Like *Sporobolus airoides*, it has two distinct habits of growth, depending upon the location in which it is found and the treatment which it receives. As near as can be judged, it made a quite uniform stand over portions of the Santa Cruz bottoms in southern Arizona in early days, but of late years it grows almost invariably in large tussocks and at present there is very little of it left. In the valley east of the Baboquivari Mountains in Arizona, we have a fine illustration of the effect of overgrazing on this grass; likewise, a good illustration of its importance in preventing erosion. There are here pastures which were formerly covered with a tall, smooth, uniform growth of saccaton. The grass is now in huge bunches and this bunched condition is directly traceable to paths cut in every direction by cattle. Invariably, when this species is grazed this condition is produced, until the tussocks are often a foot in height. Of course, when the grazing is carried to sufficient excess, one or more of these paths become cut to a sufficient depth in the center of the valley to carry off the water very rapidly. Side branches form and the tussocks are left high in the air, receiving but scant moisture. Under this condition they soon die, and a great deal of the bottom land in southern Arizona is to-day in this condition. In many places the tussocks have disintegrated and disappeared altogether. (Pl. VIII, fig. 1.)

No. 8400 was collected near Green, Tex., August 14, 1906. The sample was collected in full blossom, the entire plant being green except the lower leaves, which were dead and dry. It was cut 4 inches high. Its percentage of moisture was 8.59. Other constituents (on a water-free basis) were as follows: Ash, 8.53; ether extract, 1.70; crude fiber, 32.27; nitrogen-free extract, 47.93; protein, 9.57; pentosans, 25.89.

STIPA COMATA T. and R.

Stipa comata is a coarse species of needle grass of the western Plains region, where it replaces the more eastern *S. spartea*. The pasturage and hay produced by it are both of medium quality, but when found in hay meadows it is difficult to cut the grass at exactly the proper time for the best quality of hay. The sharp-pointed fruits of this grass sometimes injure stock to some extent. On this account, cutting the grass after the seeds have fallen has been recommended. At this stage, however, it has deteriorated somewhat in value and, inasmuch as it matures earlier than the other prairie grasses, it can not be cut before the seeds have become old enough to be injurious. Sheep grazing upon the prairies are sometimes injured by having the seeds of this grass work into the fleece. Mowing, close grazing, or the removal of the flocks from the localities where the plant grows at the time it is maturing its seed are the remedies which have been suggested. Fortunately, the seeds drop to the ground very soon after they mature and cause no further annoyance.

No. 8824 was collected at Williston, N. Dak., August 11, 1907. The culms of the sample were all dead and dry and the seeds had fallen, with the exception of those included in the expanded sheath. It was cut at the surface of the ground.

Material analyzed.	Percentage of moisture.	Water-free basis (per cent).					
		Ash.	Ether extract.	Crude fiber.	Nitrogen-free extract.	Protein.	Pentosans.
Our sample No. 8824	5.83	6.62	3.65	33.09	50.66	5.98	29.67
Average of 8 others [1]		6.71	2.15	34.56	49.61	6.97	
Average of all		6.70	2.31	34.40	49.73	6.86	

[1] Colorado Bul. 12, p. 70. Montana Report, 1902, pp. 60, 66. Nevada Bul. 62, p. 22. South Dakota Bul. 69, p. 17. Wyoming: Bul. 76, p. 62; Bul. 87, p. 93.

STIPA EMINENS Cav.

Stipa eminens (needle grass) is one of the original valuable perennials of California, which is found as far east as Texas and south into Mexico. It is a valuable, palatable species, but has been so much reduced in quantity by close grazing that it is now of very secondary importance. It occurs commonly as a filler in rocky, broken country, and is of some use as a spring feed.

No. 7069 (E. O. W.) was collected upon limestone hills in the foothills of the San Andreas Mountains, near Las Cruces, N. Mex., September 8, 1912. Its percentage of moisture was 4.82. Other constituents (on a water-free basis) were as follows: Ash, 6.53; ether extract, 2.37; crude fiber, 38.57; nitrogen-free extract, 45.38; protein, 7.15; pentosans, 28.19.

STIPA RICHARDSONII Link.

Although it always grows scatteringly upon dry hillsides and in open pine timber, *Stipa richardsonii* furnishes many a relished morsel of feed to cattle throughout the region in which it thrives. It always grows in scattering large bunches and is invariably closely grazed.

No. 8878 was collected at Columbia Falls, Mont., August 17, 1907. The sample was mature and was cut close to the ground. Its percentage of moisture was 6.06. Other constituents (on a water-free basis) were as follows: Ash, 6.45; ether extract, 2.07; crude fiber, 35.88; nitrogen-free extract, 50.54; protein, 5.06; pentosans, 28.37.

STIPA SETIGERA Presl.

Stipa setigera is decidedly conspicuous in southern California, growing like many of the other species of the genus in large, tall, spreading bunches often 3 feet in height. It appears to make a very fair quality of pasturage, but is never abundant enough to give a distinctive character to the forage outside of very circumscribed areas, and nowhere does it form a complete stand.

No. 7040 (E. O. W.) was collected near San Luis Obispo, Cal., April, 1912. No. 8288 was collected near Banning, Cal., May 14, 1906. This sample was nearly mature and was cut about 2 inches high.

Material analyzed.	Percentage of moisture.	Water-free basis (per cent).					
		Ash.	Ether extract.	Crude fiber.	Nitrogen-free extract.	Protein.	Pentosans.
Our sample No. 7040 (E. O. W.)	5.29	10.35	1.50	34.64	46.32	7.19	28.35
Our sample No. 8288	6.75	6.11	1.64	39.16	47.87	5.22	29.76
Average of both	6.02	8.23	1.57	36.90	47.20	6.20	29.05

STIPA VASEYI Scribn.

Stipa vaseyi (common needle grass) is widely scattered throughout the Rocky Mountain region from southern Montana southward. Although commonly very closely grazed and in many instances nearly, if not quite, exterminated by stock, it has a very bad reputation in some localities. It is known in the Southwest, especially through portions of New Mexico, as sleepy grass, and it is said to have at certain times a very deleterious effect on live stock, especially horses, which graze upon it. The reliable information concerning it, however, is very meager, and requires confirmatory experimentation. It is an interesting fact that the species is very closely related, and, indeed, is considered by some to be doubtfully distinct from what has repeatedly been pronounced a valuable species in the Northwest, namely, *Stipa viridula*. There appear to be no complaints against this latter species from the Dakotas, Montana, or Wyoming, where it is most abundant. In places, the sleepy grass is quite a conspicuous ingredient of native hay. No complaints have come to our attention regarding its effect upon stock when fed to them in a dry condition. In some seasons, comparatively large quantities of it are included in the hay cut upon native meadows in the Cimarron Canyon of New Mexico.

No. 9468 was collected in the Sacramento Mountains of New Mexico, August 5, 1908. The specimen was in early blossom and was cut 3 inches high. Its percentage of moisture was 8.10. Other constituents (on a water-free basis) were as follows: Ash, 7.80; ether extract, 2.77; crude fiber, 34.08; nitrogen-free extract, 41.30; protein, 14.05; pentosans, 20.17.

STIPA VIRIDULA Trin.

As has been stated, *Stipa viridula* is closely related to and sometimes considered indistinguishable from the sleepy grass of the Southwest. It may be looked upon as the northern extension of that species, but it apparently lacks any injurious qualities which the other may have. It grows commonly in large bunches in dry soils and is especially partial to soils which have been somewhat disturbed by scanty cultivation. It has been called feather bunch-grass, but the name is not in very common use. The quality of its hay appears to be very good and it is readily grazed by live stock.

No. 8813 was collected near Fargo, N. Dak., August 11, 1907. The sample represents the plant practically mature, half of the seed having dropped off. It was harvested 2 inches high.

Material analyzed.	Percentage of moisture.	Water-free basis (per cent).					
		Ash.	Ether extract.	Crude fiber.	Nitrogen-free extract.	Protein.	Pentosans.
Our sample No. 8813	6.24	9.79	2.34	33.18	46.36	8.33	25.67
Average of 4 others [1]	....	7.61	2.68	30.30	50.61	8.80	....
Average of all	....	8.04	2.61	30.87	49.77	8.71	....

[1] Colorado Bul. 12, p. 66; Montana Report, 1902, pp. 60, 66, 67; South Dakota Bul. 40, p. 58.

SYNTHERISMA SANGUINALIS (L.) Dulac.

The crab-grass (*Syntherisma sanguinalis*), like many other species, is a vile weed in some sections; in others it is a valuable forage plant. It is remarkable in its persistency and volunteers from seed year after year, often against such tenacious species as Kentucky bluegrass, which may often make a beautiful lawn in the spring only to be disfigured later in the year by brown patches of this weedy crab-grass. It is an introduced species, widely distributed throughout the country at the present time. In portions of the South it is cut for hay, always as a volunteer crop. In many of the orange orchards of Florida, where it volunteers abundantly and makes a tremendous growth after the heavy fertilization given the trees, large crops of a fair quality of hay are taken off in the fall. It also volunteers in different sections in cornfields, with other fall hay crops, and usually forms an important ingredient of the fall crop of forage throughout the South.

No. 8730 was collected at St. Petersburg, Fla., June 13, 1907. The sample was at full maturity and was cut close to the ground. It grew in a favorable situation in a cultivated field.

Material analyzed.	Percentage of moisture.	Water-free basis (per cent).					
		Ash.	Ether extract.	Crude fiber.	Nitrogen-free extract.	Protein.	Pentosans.
Our sample No. 8730	5.67	9.13	2.39	25.55	55.31	7.62	17.11
Average of 20 others [1]	....	10.42	2.98	29.39	46.70	10.51	....
Average of all	....	10.35	2.95	29.21	47.12	10.37	....

[1] Alabama Bul. 127, p. 5. Connecticut Report, 1879, p. 155. Florida Bul. 11, p. 18. Georgia Bul. 6, p. 108. Iowa Bul. 56, p. 486. Kentucky: Bul. 87, p. 116; Report, 1902, p. 302. Louisiana Bul. 34, p. 1175. Mississippi: Bul. 39, p. 159; Report, 1895, pp. 80, 81, 92. Tennessee Bul. 1, vol. 4, p. 7. U. S. Department of Agriculture Report No. 32, 1884, p. 125. Virginia Bul. 180, p. 96.

TRICHLORIS FASCICULATA Fourn.

The distribution of *Trichloris fasciculata* is usually given as dry plains and mesas, but in our experience it commonly inhabits rather favorable situations in the edges of shallow washes, where it receives some benefit from irrigation. It is distributed from Texas to Arizona and southward into Mexico. It sometimes produces a magnificent growth in limited situations in the Salt River Valley of Arizona, where irrigation or seepage water escapes to lands where it has obtained a foothold. In such situations it impresses one as being a favorable grass for cultivation. Its seed habits, however, are rather against it, although these are better than in a good many species of the Chlorideæ. When it gets sufficient moisture, as it often does under artificial conditions in irrigated districts, it will produce two crops a year, one in spring and the other in midsummer. Upon the open ranges of the Southwest at the present time very little of it is seen except an occasional stray stalk 3 feet or more high growing in the protection of thorny shrubs.

No. 8385 was collected near Encinal, Tex., August 12, 1906. The sample was collected when the seed was fully ripe. A great deal of it shattered, but the straw, leaves, and culms were perfectly green. Many of the root leaves, however, were dead and dry and were included in the sample, which was cut 2 inches high. No. 9426 was collected near Devils River, Tex., July 23, 1908. The specimen was overmature, the seed having all fallen, but the remainder of the plant was green and succulent. It was cut about 1 inch high.

Material analyzed.	Percentage of moisture.	Water-free basis (per cent).					
		Ash.	Ether extract.	Crude fiber.	Nitrogen-free extract.	Protein.	Pentosans.
Our sample No. 8385	9.05	11.24	1.92	12.51	66.76	7.57	21.65
Our sample No. 9426	7.59	9.11	2.55	27.06	50.26	11.02	19.35
Average of both	8.32	10.175	2.235	19.785	58.51	9.295	20.50

TRIDENS MUTICUS (Torr.) Nash.

About the same can be said for *Tridens muticus* as for *T. nealleyi*, but the former is more abundant and, on the whole, a more valuable species. It has a wider range, extending from the Pacific coast to Texas and north into Colorado.

No. 7065 (E. O. W.) was collected upon limestone hills in the foothills of the San Andreas Mountains, near Las Cruces, N. Mex., September 8, 1912. Its percentage of moisture was 5.86. Other constituents (on a water-free basis) were as follows: Ash, 6.04; ether extract, 1.72; crude fiber, 35.05; nitrogen-free extract, 49.75; protein, 7.44; pentosans, 25.27.

TRIDENS NEALLEYI (Vasey) Wooton and Stand.

In many situations in the mountains and upon stony ridges and knolls in southwestern Texas and southern New Mexico *Tridens nealleyi* assumes considerable importance on account of its abundance. It furnishes considerable grazing and is a persistent species. Like the other members of the genus it is of second quality in palatability.

No. 7097 (E. O. W.) was collected in the San Andreas Mountains, near Las Cruces, N. Mex., September 23 to October 10, 1912. Its percentage of moisture was 4.55. Other constituents (on a water-free basis) were as follows: Ash, 5.98; ether extract, 1.16; crude fiber, 38.02; nitrogen-free extract, 49.05; protein, 5.79; pentosans, 29.13.

VALOTA SACCHARATA (Buckl.) Chase. (*Panicum lacnanthum*).

Valota saccharata, a conspicuous and attractive cotton-topped species of the southwestern United States and of Mexico, is of decided importance to stock interests. Its seed habits, however, are bad, the seed being covered with long silky hairs, rendering it very difficult to handle. It is therefore of doubtful value for domestication. In many situations, especially in the moister places in the desert foothills of Arizona and the plains of Texas, it grows almost pure over large areas and makes a striking appearance. It grows quite readily from seed, notwithstanding the difficulty of handling. The date of its maturity is very variable in the region indicated above, maturing in central Texas in June if conditions are favorable, or in August if they are not. In southern Arizona its period of development is during the rainy season of summer, in July, August, and September. (Pl. IX, fig. 2.)

No. 8399 was collected near Green, Tex., August 14, 1906. The sample was in early maturity, but no seeds had fallen, and the whole plant was perfectly green. It was cut 1½ inches high. Its percentage of moisture was 7.85. Other constituents (on a water-free basis) were as follows: Ash, 11.96; ether extract, 2.38; crude fiber, 29.97; nitrogen-free extract, 45.72; protein, 9.97; pentosans, 20.46.

ZIZANIOPSIS MILIACEA (Michx.) Doell and Aschers.

The marsh millet (*Zizaniopsis miliacea*) inhabits swamps and banks of streams from Texas eastward and northward to Ohio. It is a tall, rank species, resembling superficially the wild rice of more northern latitudes and from a forage standpoint corresponds very closely to that species. It is always grazed in closely fed pastures, but not until more palatable feeds fail.

No. 9205 was collected at San Antonio, Tex., April 20, 1908. The sample was in blossom and was cut off at the surface of the water about 2 feet high. Its percentage of moisture was 8.77. Other constituents (on a water-free basis) were as follows: Ash, 9.46; ether extract, 1.53; crude fiber, 32.20; nitrogen-free extract, 43.17; protein, 13.64; pentosans, 17.11.

○

BULLETIN OF THE
U.S. DEPARTMENT OF AGRICULTURE

No. 202

Contribution from the Bureau of Animal Industry, A. D. Melvin, Chief.
May 12, 1915.

(PROFESSIONAL PAPER.)

THE ALCOHOL TEST IN RELATION TO MILK.

By S. Henry Ayers, *Bacteriologist*, and William T. Johnson, Jr., *Scientific Assistant, Dairy Division.*

INTRODUCTION.

The alcohol test as generally used consists in the mixing of equal volumes of alcohol and milk. Usually 2 cubic centimeters of 68 per cent alcohol are added to 2 cubic centimeters of milk and shaken gently in a test tube. The test is considered positive when a precipitate is formed, or in other terms, when a coagulum is produced. When a positive test is obtained with fresh milk from a single cow or small herd, it is generally believed that it indicates an abnormal milk, due to physiological or pathological conditions in the cow. A positive test with market milk is supposed to indicate that changes have been produced in the milk as a result of bacterial fermentations.

According to Fleischmann (11)[1] the first account of the alcohol test was published by Martinn in 1890 in the Deutsche (Berliner) Molkerei Zeitung. It is stated that Martinn used 68 per cent alcohol with equal parts of milk. Höft (13) in 1898 used the alcohol test to give an idea of the acidity of milk. He found that the higher the acidity the greater the amount of coagulation by alcohol. In the same year Petri and Maaszen (24) made use of the alcohol test to determine the quality of pasteurized milk, and Weber (31) in 1900 studied the alcohol test in relation to the so-called sterilized milk.

Since 1900 numerous investigators, mostly in Europe, have studied the alcohol test. Of those who have worked with this test Morres is probably its most ardent supporter. He strongly advocates the alcohol test in combination with the alizarin test, which he calls the alizarol test. This test will be described later. Morres and the other advocates of the alcohol test claim that it is of great value, since it affords a simple and quick means of determining the condition and keeping quality of milk.

In this country the alcohol test is used by only one large company which manufactures milk powder. Any milk which shows a precipi-

[1] See list of citations to literature at end of bulletin.

82832°—Bull. 202—15——1

tate when mixed with equal volumes of 75 per cent alcohol is rejected by this company. We are not aware that any practical use of the test is made by any one else in America. In Europe the alcohol test is more generally used, but we are unable to state to what extent the test is employed at present, although Farrington and Woll (9) say that in European creameries and city milk depots the alcohol test is often applied to every can of milk received; milk that is sufficiently sour to be noticed by the taste will coagulate when mixed with an equal volume of 70 per cent alcohol.

The Berlin police regulation of 1902 (32) regarding the sale of milk and cream required that cow's milk coming from a distance must, at the time of delivery to the consumer, stand without coagulation the cooking or alcohol test (mixture of 70 per cent alcohol by volume with equal parts of milk). According to Devarda and Weich (6), only fresh milk, which shows no precipitate or only a very fine coagulation with the alcohol test, is accepted in the Vienna market.

OBJECT OF THIS WORK.

The principal object of this work was to determine the practical value of the alcohol test as a test for the quality of market milk. As incidental to our primary object, it was our purpose to determine some of the causes for the precipitation or coagulation of milk by alcohol.

METHOD OF MAKING THE ALCOHOL TEST.

In our work we have used the single alcohol test; that is to say, a mixture of equal volumes of alcohol and milk. A few investigators have used the double alcohol test, in which two parts by volume of alcohol are mixed with one part of milk. In general equal volumes of 68 per cent alcohol and milk are mixed for the test, but in our work 75 per cent, 68 per cent, and 44 per cent alcohol were used. Three tests were made on each sample of milk, 2 c. c. of alcohol being mixed with 2 c. c. of milk in a test tube. The milk was always at a temperature of from 15° to 20° C. After adding the milk to the alcohol the tube was shaken and examined for the appearance of a precipitate. The precipitate appears as flakes the size of which were recorded as follows: VS for very small, S for small, M for medium-sized, and L for large.

The different percentages of alcohol were obtained by diluting a high grade of absolute alcohol with distilled water. Reiss (27) has shown that alcohol should always be tested for acid before using in the alcohol test, as acetic acid sometimes found in the alcohol may make the milk sufficiently acid to cause a coagulation with alcohol. The acidity was determined by titrating 10 c. c. of milk with N/10 NaOH, and is expressed throughout this paper as per cent of normal acid.

Any special methods employed in this work will be discussed when mentioned in the text.

THE ALCOHOL TEST IN RELATION TO FRESH MILK FROM A SINGLE COW OR HERD.

While reviewing the literature on the alcohol test it became evident that the value of the test must be considered from two standpoints: First, its relation to fresh milk from a single cow or small herd, and, second, its relation to mixed market milk. Although our work on this subject deals principally with the relation of the alcohol test to mixed market milk, we feel justified, after a careful survey of the literature, first in briefly discussing the test in its relation to fresh milk from a single cow or herd.

In the consideration of fresh milk from a single, normal cow we must omit the changes in milk due to bacterial growth and the influences of the changes on the alcohol test. The changes as a result of bacterial activities are of greater importance in the relation of the alcohol test to the mixed market milk and will be discussed later.

It is evident from the results of other investigators and from our own tests on milk from a few cows that fresh, normal milk occasionally coagulates with 68 or 70 per cent alcohol when mixed in equal volumes. Henkel (12) found, after an examination of more than 1,600 samples of milk from a single cow, that 6 showed a coagulation with 68 or 70 per cent alcohol. This is a very low percentage of positive results and he concluded that, generally speaking, the milk of a single animal does not coagulate with 68 or 70 per cent alcohol. After an extensive study of the alcohol test Auzinger (2) concluded that the alcohol coagulation of fresh single milk is not so rare as Henkel had observed. Auzinger (2) also found great fluctuations in the alcohol test (70 per cent) with milk from single cows. Occasionally milk from the same cow gave a positive test in the morning and not in the evening, or vice versa. The test might be positive one day and not the next, but might reappear on the third day. Sometimes he found that the first and last milk from a single cow showed fluctuations in the alcohol test. Auzinger also found that milk from single quarters may coagulate with alcohol independently of the other quarters, although these cases were rare. He concludes that the alcohol test in normal milk from a single cow is independent of the acidity and when the test is positive it is caused by a change in the milk salts, especially the calcium, in their relation to the milk proteids. His opinion as to the reason for the occasional coagulation of fresh, normal milk is strengthened by one of his experiments, in which calcium phosphate was fed to a cow. It was found that the milk from this cow coagulated with a smaller volume of alcohol or with a lower percentage of alcohol than did the normal milk.

When fresh, normal milk from a single cow coagulates with 68 per cent alcohol it is evidently due to some slight change in the composition of the milk. What the exact changes are it is impossible at present to state.

When we speak of fresh, normal milk we mean fresh milk from a healthy cow in the middle of the period of lactation. Milk in the early period of lactation, that is, colostrum milk, or milk taken late in the lactation period—"old" milk, as it is sometimes called—usually coagulates with the alcohol test. Henkel (12), Metzger (17), and also Auzinger (2), found that the milk from a cow in the first of the lactation period, while apparently normal, may show a positive alcohol test at irregular intervals. Auzinger (2) believes that the high albumen and globulin content of colostrum milk and the calcium salts are responsible for the positive alcohol reaction.

EFFECT OF COLOSTRUM AND OF "OLD" MILK ON THE ALCOHOL TEST.

In Table 1 are shown the results of the alcohol tests which we have made on colostrum milk from two cows. Three tests were made, using 75, 68, and 44 per cent alcohol. The results show clearly that colostrum milk gives a positive alcohol test and that the stronger the alcohol the longer the test will be positive. It will be noticed that the milk from cow 16 gave a positive test with 68 per cent alcohol for 24 days, although the acidity was low after the fourth day. It is evident from these results and from those obtained by other investigators that the coagulation of milk in the first of the lactation period by alcohol is largely independent of acidity.

TABLE 1.—*Alcohol tests with colostrum milk.*

Cow No.	Days after calving.	Acidity.	Alcohol test.		
			75 per cent.	68 per cent.	44 per cent.
4	2	2.61	[1] +L	+L	+VS
	3	2.45	+L	+L	+VS
	4	2.25	+L	+M	−
	5	1.87	+L	+S	−
	6	1.80	+M	−	−
	8	1.50	+M	−	−
	9	1.70	+M	−	−
	10	1.55	−	−	−
	11	1.52	+S	−	−
	12	1.50	+M	−	−
	13	1.31	+S	−	−
	19	1.35	−	−	−
	21	2.10	−	−	−
	22	1.12	−	−	−
16	1	2.40	+L	+L	−
	2	2.20	+L	+S	−
	3	2.70	+M	+M	−
	4	2.26	+L	+S	−
	5	1.60	+M	+S	−
	6	1.84	+M	+S	−
	13	1.36	+L	+M	−
	15	1.65	+M	+S	−
	16	1.53	+M	+M	−
	19	1.57	+M	+S	−
	22	1.70	+M	+S	−
	23	1.60	+M	+S	−
	24	1.50	+M	+S	−
	25	1.45	+M	−	−

[1] In this and succeeding tables the initial letters denoting the degree of the positive (+) tests signify: L, large flakes; M, medium flakes; S, small flakes; and VS, very small flakes. Minus sign (−) signifies negative test.

In order to determine whether or not the alcohol test would be positive in a mixed colostrum and normal milk, one experiment was performed. Colostrum milk from two cows 24 hours after calving was mixed in various proportions with fresh, normal milk which gave a negative alcohol test. The results of this experiment, in Table 2, show that from 80 to 90 per cent of colostrum milk had to be mixed with normal milk in order to cause a positive test with 68 per cent alcohol. When 75 per cent alcohol was used the test was positive with as low as 25 per cent of colostrum milk from cow 5, but when colostrum milk from cow 16 was used, a mixture of 80 per cent was required to give a positive reaction with 75 per cent alcohol. It seems evident from these results that the mixing of colostrum and normal milk would not cause a positive alcohol test unless a very large percentage of the milk were colostrum milk.

TABLE 2.—*The alcohol test with a mixture of normal and colostrum milk.*

Colostrum milk from cow No.	Percentage of normal milk.	Percentage of colostrum milk.	Alcohol test.		
			75 per cent.	68 per cent.	44 per cent.
5	10	90	[1] +L	+ L	–
	20	80	+M	+VS	–
	25	75	+M	–	–
	50	50	+S	–	–
	75	25	+S	–	–
	90	10	–	–	–
16	10	90	+M	+ M	–
	20	80	+S	–	–
	25	75	–	–	–

[1] See footnote under Table 1.

Having discussed the relation of the alcohol test to colostrum milk, let us consider its relation to milk drawn at the last of the lactation period, or what is known as "old" milk. Several investigators have shown that "old" milk gives a positive alcohol test. It is well known that milk changes in composition toward the end of the lactation period, and it is undoubtedly these changes which cause the coagulation with alcohol. While no definite changes have been attributed to the positive alcohol reaction, it is believed by some to be due to the high content of solids (not fat). Henkel (12), however, found that this could not explain in all cases the coagulation by alcohol. Auzinger (2) believes that on account of the variation of solids (not fat) the alcohol test has no significance in milk from "old" milk cows.

SUMMARY OF CAUSES FOR POSITIVE TESTS IN MILK OF SINGLE COWS.

It is apparent that fresh milk from a single cow may occasionally give a positive alcohol reaction with 68 or 70 per cent of alcohol. Colostrum milk gives a positive reaction, and the same is true usually of "old" milk—that is, milk from a cow in the last of its lactation period.

The causes for a positive alcohol test may be summarized by the opinion of Ernst (8) who states that a positive alcohol test of fresh milk from a single cow indicates a physiological or severe pathological condition of irritation of the milk glands. There is, however, a difference in the opinions of various investigators as to the reaction of the alcohol test to pathological conditions of the udder. Ruhm (28) noticed the alcohol test in milk from cows with infected udders. In some cases he found the test was positive during the infection and frequently a positive test was observed for three or four weeks later when the milk had a normal appearance and taste. He points out that in udder infection the milk may vary in many ways, and in consequence the alcohol test varies. Auzinger found that there was no relation between streptococci in infected udders and the alcohol test and that a positive test is produced through chemical changes in the secretions. Rullmann and Trommsdorff (29) also observed a positive alcohol reaction in milk from cows with infected udders, but according to these authors the alcohol test shows no definite relation to the leucocyte count. They point out that the variation in ash salts and high albumin content probably influences the alcohol test. Campbell (5) also believes that the alcohol test is of value in determining the diseased condition of the udder. Besides udder infection Auzinger (2) states that the general infections and infections of the vaginal canal may cause a positive alcohol test; also that milk from cows which have aborted may coagulate with alcohol. Metzger (17), however, after a study of the alcohol test with milk from sick cows concludes that the milk from them shows no relation between the acidity and alcohol test. According to this author fever had no influence on the acid and alcohol tests. There was no relation between tuberculosis of the animal and the alcohol test. When animals were very lean from disease the milk inclined toward coagulation with alcohol. Infectious inflammation of the vagina was without influence on the test. Infection of the uterus shows almost regularly with the alcohol test, but not without exception. Metzger also found that there was no relation between the alcohol test and various forms of indigestion. He points out that the chief value of the test lies in its use for the freshness of milk.

We have not had an opportunity to study the alcohol test in its relation to the milk from sick cows, but from a study of the literature on this subject we are inclined to believe that the alcohol test would be of but little value as a routine test of the milk from a single cow or from a small herd. If the alcohol test were used regularly to test fresh milk of single cows a positive reaction would indicate some change in the milk from normal. Subsequent examination of the cow might reveal some pathological condition, or there might be some physiological reason for a slight variation in the composition of the milk. If the test were performed on the milk from a few cows a positive reaction might be caused, as Auzinger (3) believes, by the mixing of milk which is changed by physiological or pathological conditions with milk from normal cows. If there were a large percentage of abnormal milk which gave an alcohol test with a coagulation with large flakes, the mixed milk might show a positive alcohol test in which the coagulation would be in the form of small flakes. When mixed milk from a large number of sources gives a positive alcohol test it must be interpreted in an entirely different manner, and this leads us to another phase of the subject.

THE ALCOHOL TEST IN RELATION TO MARKET MILK.

Since 1900 a considerable number of papers have appeared on the use of the alcohol test in its relation to market milk. According to Kirchner (15), Morres in 1905 showed that the alcohol test was of value for determining the keeping quality of milk and indicating its acidity. Reiss (26) in 1906 pointed out the practical value of the test, and Morres (18) again in 1909 showed the value of the alcohol test as a means of determining the keeping quality of milk. He added 2 c.c. of milk to 2 c.c. of 68 per cent (by volume) alcohol, and states that if the milk coagulates with alcohol then decomposition has already started and the extent is shown by the size of the flakes. If the precipitate is in fine flakes then the acidity corresponds to 4 degrees Soxhlet; however, the coagulation may not be due to an increase in acidity, but may be due to the action of rennet-forming bacteria. In later work Morres has combined the alcohol and alizarin tests. This will be discussed later. Morres considers that the coagulation of mixed market milk is due largely to the formation of acid or the action of rennet-forming bacteria or to a combination of both. Henkel (12) concludes from his work that the alcohol test does not afford a proper means for determining acidity, but that the value of the test lies in the fact that it gives a knowledge of the souring and other changes in the properties of milk or in variations from the normal properties which the acid test does not show. Other investigators believe that the alcohol test is of value only as a preliminary test. Fendler and Borkel (10) after a large number of tests to determine the relation of the acidity of milk to the alcohol test concluded that the double test with 70 per cent alcohol was not a proper criterion for the freshness of market milk, including infants' milk and superior grades of milk. They state that the double test using 50 per cent alcohol is suitable as a preliminary test for food inspectors, but the milk should be submitted to further tests. These authors also found that no consistent relation existed between the alcohol test and the acidity of milk. Rammstedt (25) also agrees with Fendler and Borkel, so far as he found, that no consistent relation existed between the alcohol test and the acidity of milk. He considers that the test gives preliminary knowledge of the hygienic quality of a milk.

It is evident from the literature that in a mixed market milk the acidity plays a part in connection with the alcohol test, so that in considering the factors which influence the test we may first take up the question of acidity.

THE INFLUENCE OF ACIDITY ON THE ALCOHOL TEST.

In our first experiments the acidity of milk was raised by the addition of N/10 lactic acid. The results of two experiments recorded in Table 3 show that a very slight increase in the acidity of milk may cause a positive alcohol test with 75 per cent and 68 per cent alcohol, but a considerably higher acidity is required to cause a positive test with 44 per cent alcohol.

These results show clearly that the alcohol test is sensitive to slight changes in acidity when these changes are produced by the addition of lactic acid. Since an increase in acidity will cause a positive alcohol test it is evident that the growth of acid-forming bacteria in milk will cause a positive test.

TABLE 3.—*Influence of acidity on the alcohol test.*

N/10 lactic acid added to 50 c. c. of milk.	Acidity.	Alcohol test.		
		75 per cent.	68 per cent.	44 per cent.
c. c.				
0	1.81	–	–	–
0.5	1.88	–	–	–
1.0	1.94	[1]+M	+M	–
3.0	2.21	+L	+L	–
3.5	2.38	+L	+L	–
4.0	2.47	+L	+L	+M
0	1.70	–	–	–
.5	1.76	+M	–	–
1.0	1.84	+M	+S	–
2.0	2.00	+L	+L	–
3.0	2.20	+L	+L	–
3.4	2.25	+L	+L	–
3.5	2.26	+L	+L	+few VS
4.0	2.31	+L	+L	+few L

[1] See footnote under Table 1.

In order to determine the relation between the number of acid-forming bacteria, the acidity, and the alcohol test, two experiments were performed, using a pure culture of a lactic-acid-producing organism. The culture was inoculated into sterile skim milk and incubated at 37° C. A bacterial count was made while the acidity and the alcohol test were determined at the same time. From the results shown in Table 4 it may be seen that in Experiment I the alcohol test was negative even after seven hours of incubation. At that time the acidity had increased from 1.98 to 2.14, and the bacteria from from 82,000 to 15,100,000 per cubic centimeter. It is interesting to note that an extensive multiplication of lactic-acid-forming bacteria may occur without causing a positive alcohol test. In the second experiment, also shown in Table 4, a heavier inoculation was used, and it will be seen that the milk at the beginning of the incubation period contained 480,000 bacteria per cubic centimeter. The 68 per cent alcohol test was not positive until the bacteria had increased to 31,400,000 per cubic centimeter.

These figures show that when a pure culture of lactic-acid-forming bacteria is grown in skim milk there must be a very great increase in order to produce acidity enough to cause a positive alcohol test. In these experiments there were no positive alcohol tests until the bacteria had increased from less than 500,000 to over 16,000,000 per cubic centimeter. From these results it is apparent that the growth of acid-forming bacteria in milk may, through the formation of acid, cause a positive alcohol test. However, when there is sufficient acid produced to cause a coagulation with 68 per cent alcohol the number of acid-forming bacteria would be very high.

TABLE 4.—*Influence on the alcohol test of acid produced by the growth of a pure culture of lactic-acid bacteria.*

Experiment No.	Age of culture in hours.	Bacteria per cubic centimeter.	Acidity.	Alcohol test.		
				75 per cent.	68 per cent.	44 per cent.
I	0	82,000	1.98	—	—	—
	2	113,000	....	—	—	—
	4	1,510,000	2.06	—	—	—
	5	4,300,000	2.08	—	—	—
	6	11,700,000	2.09	—	—	—
	7	15,100,000	2.14	—	—	—
II	0	480,000	1.94	—	—	—
	2	1,060,000	....	—	—	—
	4	7,500,000	2.08	—	—	—
	5	16,100,000	2.08	[1]+S	—	—
	6	31,400,000	2.30	+L	+M	—
	7	46,000,000	2.47	+L	+L	—

[1] See footnote under Table 1.

EFFECT OF PHOSPHATES.

We have so far discussed in a general way the effect of increasing the acidity of milk by the addition of lactic acid and by the generation of the acid in milk. Since the acidity of milk when titrated with phenolphthalein is due partly to acid phosphates, it will be of interest to show the effect on the alcohol test of the increase in acidity by acid phosphates. In Table 5 are shown the results of a few tests, using sodium and potassium acid phosphate. Various amounts of a 5 per cent solution of these salts were added to 50 c. c. of milk. It will be seen from the table that when the acidity was increased by sodium acid phosphate from 2.15 to 3.33 the alcohol test with 75 per cent alcohol was positive. At an acidity of 4.27 the milk coagulated with 68 per cent alcohol but the flakes were very small. In order to cause a coagulation with 68 per cent alcohol with medium-sized flakes it was necessary to increase the acidity to 6.16. When potassium acid phosphate was used the results were about the same.

These results show that it is possible by increasing the acidity of milk with acid phosphates to cause a coagulation with the alcohol test, but the acidity has to be increased to a high degree and there would never be enough acid phosphate in a mixed market milk for it to be entirely responsible for a positive alcohol test.

TABLE 5.—*Influence on the alcohol test of the addition of acid phosphates to milk.*

Sodium-acid phosphate.					Potassium-acid phosphate.				
Amount of 5 per cent solution of acid phosphate added to 50 c. c. of milk.	Acidity.	Alcohol test.			Amount of 5 per cent solution of acid phosphate added to 50 c. c. of milk.	Acidity.	Alcohol test.		
		75 per cent.	68 per cent.	44 per cent.			75 per cent.	68 per cent.	44 per cent.
C. c.					*C. c.*				
0	2.15	−	−	−	0	....	−	−	−
1	2.75	−	−	−	1	2.52	−	−	−
2	3.33	[1] +M	−	−	2	3.13	[1] +M	−	−
3	4.27	+M	+VS	−	3	4.00	+M	+VS	−
5	5.50	+M	+VS	−	5	5.20	+M	+VS	−
6	6.16	+M	+M	+VS	6	5.62	+M	+M	+VS

[1] See footnote under Table 1.

In some cases where we increased the acidity of milk by adding lactic acid it was noticed that a very slight increase in acidity caused a positive alcohol test. At other times the acidity had to be increased to a considerable extent before the milk coagulated with alcohol. It occurred to us that the explanation for these differences might be that there were different amounts of dibasic phosphates present in milk and that the acid converted the dibasic phosphate into acid phosphate, which increased the acidity but did not cause a positive alcohol test. In order to test this theory one experiment was performed, the results of which are shown in Table 6. Two flasks of milk were used, each containing 50 c. c. of milk. One flask was left normal and 0.5 per cent dibasic sodium phosphate was added to the other. Various amounts of N/10 lactic acid were then added to each flask. As may be seen from the table, when 3 c. c. of N/10 lactic acid was added to the normal milk, the acidity was 2.37 and the alcohol test was positive with both 75 per cent and 68 per cent alcohol. The flakes were large and medium, respectively. The same amount of acid added to the milk with dibasic phosphate increased the acidity to 2.55 and yet the alcohol test was negative. When 7 c. c. of N/10 lactic acid was added to the normal milk, the acidity was increased to 3.00 and the milk coagulated with large flakes with all the different percentages of alcohol. When 7 c. c. of N/10 lactic acid was added to milk with dibasic phosphate the acidity was increased to 3.05 and only the 75 per cent alcohol test was positive, and the coagulation was in the form of small flakes. When 8 c. c. of acid was added to the milk with dibasic phosphate the acidity was 3.19 and the alcohol test with both 75 per cent and 68 per cent alcohol was positive. It was found by titration that 10 c. c. of a 0.5 solution of dibasic phosphate required 1.56 c. c. of N/10 lactic acid to convert the dibasic into the monobasic phosphate; therefore 50 c. c. of milk containing 0.5 per cent of dibasic sodium phosphate would require 7.8 c. c. of N/10 lactic acid to convert the dibasic into the monobasic phosphate. It will be seen from Table 6 that when from 7 to 8 c. c. of N/10 lactic acid was added to the milk with dibasic phosphate, the alcohol test became positive; that is, when the dibasic phosphate had been converted into monobasic phosphate then further increase in acidity caused a positive alcohol test.

As a very general explanation of this result it may be said that when acid is added to milk it converts the dibasic phosphate into the monobasic phosphate. It follows that the acid and also the monobasic phosphate probably affect the casein and thereby change it into a condition in which it is possible to precipitate the casein by alcohol and cause a positive test. This action on the dibasic phosphate probably explains in part the positive alcohol tests with different low acidities.

TABLE 6.—*Influence on the alcohol test of the addition of dibasic phosphate to milk.*

N/10 lactic acid added to 50 c. c. of milk.	Normal milk.				Normal milk + 0.5 per cent dibasic sodium phosphate.			
	Acidity.	Alcohol test.			Acidity.	Alcohol test.		
		75 per cent.	68 per cent.	44 per cent.		75 per cent.	68 per cent.	44 per cent.
c. c.								
0	1.85	—	—	—	2.03	—	—	—
1	2.01	[1] +S	—	—	2.13	—	—	—
3	2.37	+L	+M	—	2.55	—	—	—
5	2.63	+L	+L	+S	2.81	—	—	—
6	2.80	+L	+L	+M	2.92	—	—	—
7	3.00	+L	+L	+L	3.05	+S	—	—
8	....	....	....	....	3.19	+L	+M	—
9	....	....	....	....	3.43	+L	+L	—
11	....	....	....	....	3.97	+L	+L	+L

[1] See footnote under Table 1.

RESULT OF MIXING SOUR AND NORMAL MILK.

Since a positive alcohol test may be produced by increasing the acidity, several investigators have pointed out that a mixture of sour and normal milks will give a positive test. The amount of sour milk which can be added to fresh milk without causing a positive alcohol test will, of course, depend upon the acidity of the sour milk. In one experiment, the results of which are shown in Table 7, various percentages of sour, raw, and pasteurized milk were added to fresh milk. The addition of 1 per cent of sour milk caused a positive test with 75 per cent alcohol, 2.5 per cent caused a positive test with 68 per cent alcohol, and the addition of 10 per cent of sour milk was necessary to cause a positive test with 44 per cent alcohol.

It must be taken into consideration in this experiment that the sour milk had a high acidity. If the acidity had been low a much higher per cent could undoubtedly have been added to the fresh milk without increasing the acidity sufficiently to cause a positive alcohol test.

TABLE 7.—*The alcohol test with a mixture of normal and sour milk.*

Addition of sour raw milk. Acidity 10.23.					Addition of sour pasteurized milk. Acidity 9.87.				
Per cent of sour milk added.	Acidity.	Alcohol test. 75 per cent.	Alcohol test. 68 per cent.	Alcohol test. 44 per cent.	Per cent of sour milk added.	Acidity.	Alcohol test. 75 per cent.	Alcohol test. 68 per cent.	Alcohol test. 44 per cent.
0.0	1.84	—	—	—	....	....	—	—	—
1.0	1.93	[1]+S	—	—	1.0	1.88	+S	—	—
2.5	2.06	+M	+M	—	2.5	2.00	+M	+M	—
5.0	2.30	+L	+L	—	5.0	2.29	+L	+L	—
10.0	2.70	+L	+L	+M	10.0	2.68	+L	+L	+VS

[1] See footnote under Table 1.

In connection with the relation of acidity to the alcohol test the question arises as to whether or not the acidity of a sour milk can be neutralized so that the alcohol test will be negative. Some investigators have shown that the neutralization of the acidity does not cause a positive test to become negative, although the size of the flakes in the coagulation is somewhat reduced. We have tried one experiment in which various amounts of normal lactic acid were added to fresh milk, after which the acidity was reduced to the original acidity by the addition of sodium hydrate. From the results which are shown in Table 8 it will be seen that when the acidity was increased to 4.3, then neutralized to 1.90, the 68 per cent alcohol test was positive. The positive alcohol tests with 68 per cent alcohol could be made negative at acidities below 4.30 by reducing to about the original acidity of the normal milk.

TABLE 8.—*Effect on the alcohol test produced by neutralizing the acidity of milk.*

Amount of normal lactic acid added to 50 c. c. of milk.	Acidity.	Alcohol test.			Acidity after neutralizing.	Alcohol test.		
		75 per cent.	68 per cent.	44 per cent.		75 per cent.	68 per cent.	44 per cent.
c. c.								
0.0	1.84	—	—	—	....	....	....	....
0.1	2.08	[1] +M	+M	—	1.80	—	—	—
0.3	2.42	+M	+M	—	1.81	—	—	—
0.5	2.99	+L	+M	+VS	1.64	—	—	—
0.8	3.54	+L	+L	+M	1.60	+VS	—	—
1.0	3.94	+L	+L	+L	1.60	+S	—	—
1.5	4.30	+L	+L	+L	1.90	+L	+M	—

[1] See footnote under Table 1.

EFFECT OF HEAT COMBINED WITH ACIDITY.

As a matter of general interest we may mention the effect of heating milk which gave a positive alcohol test. Auzinger (2) found that a milk which gave a positive test at 15° C. sometimes did not give the test when heated for 30 minutes at 60° C. Then again he found that the test might remain positive in milk heated to boiling. In Table 9 is shown the result of an experiment showing the effect of heat on the alcohol test with milk of two different acidities. No effect of heat was found on the sample of milk with an acidity of 2.30, but there was a marked effect when the acidity was lower.

We have no explanation to offer for this negative result of the test when the acidity is low. This action of heat might be of importance when the alcohol test is applied to pasteurized milk.

TABLE 9.—*Effect of heat on the alcohol test which is positive on account of acid action.*

Milk heated to—	Alcohol test.			
	Acidity, 2.		Acidity, 2.30.	
	75 per cent.	68 per cent.	75 per cent.	68 per cent.
°C.				
Not heated...	[1] +M	+S	+L	+L
40...........	+M	+S	+L	+L
60...........	+M	+S	+L	+L
70...........	+M	+VS	+L	+L
80...........	+S	—	+L	+L
90...........	—	—	+L	+L
100..........	—	—	+L	+L

[1] See footnote under Table 1.

INFLUENCE OF THE ACTION OF RENNET.

The relation of the alcohol test to the acidity of milk shows that acidity is one factor which may cause a positive alcohol reaction, but from the work of other investigators it is evident that it is not the sole cause. Morres throughout his papers points out that the alcohol test may be caused by an acid fermentation or by a rennet fermentation or by a mixture of both fermentations.

In order to determine the effect of rennet action in relation to the test, we first tried the effect of prepared rennet. Four flasks of fresh milk were used and to each a different percentage of rennet was added. The milk in each flask was tested by the alcohol test at intervals of one hour. It will be seen from Table 10 that four different percentages of rennet were used, ranging from 0.00005 per cent to 0.0015 per cent. The acidity of the milk increased during the four hours from 1.64 to 1.70; therefore the influence of acidity can be neglected, since it is only a slight change.

The results show that the action of rennet in milk may produce changes which cause a positive alcohol test and that two main factors are of importance, namely, the amount of rennet and the length of time the rennet has to act. Undoubtedly a third factor must be taken into consideration; that is, the temperature at which the milk is held. In our experiments the milk was held at room temperature. These results confirm those obtained by other investigators and indicate that the action of the rennet-forming bacteria might cause a positive alcohol reaction.

TABLE 10.—*Influence of rennet on the alcohol test.*

Hours.	Rennet added.	Alcohol test.		
		75 per cent.	68 per cent.	44 per cent.
	Per cent.			
0	.00005	–	–	–
	.00025	–	–	–
	.0005	–	–	–
	.0015	–	–	–
1	.00005	–	–	–
	.00025	–	–	–
	.0005	–	–	–
	.0015	[1] +M	+M	–
2	.00005	–	–	–
	.00025	–	–	–
	.0005	+M	+M	–
	.0015	+L	+L	+M
3	.00005	–	–	–
	.00025	+M	+M	–
	.0005	+M	+M	–
	.0015	+L	+L	+M
4	.00005	–	–	–
	.00025	+L	+L	L
	.0005	+L	+L	+VS
	.0015	([2])	([2])	([2])

[1] See footnote under Table 1.
[2] Milk curdled by rennet.

In order to show the effect of rennet of bacterial origin, the action of a pure culture of a rennet-forming organism was studied. Two flasks of sterile skim milk were inoculated with different amounts of a pure culture of a rennet-forming organism. These flasks were incubated at 37° C., and the bacterial increase was determined at definite intervals, together with the alcohol test. The results are shown in Table 11. From a study of the table it is evident that rennet-forming bacteria will cause a positive alcohol test, but there must be a large bacterial increase to produce rennet enough to cause a positive test.

The acidity was also increased during the incubation, but we believe this acidity played a minor part in causing the positive alcohol test.

TABLE 11.—*Influence on the alcohol test of rennet produced in milk by the growth of a pure culture of a rennet-forming organism.*

Experiment No.	Age of culture.	Bacteria per cubic centimeter.	Acidity.	Alcohol test.		
				75 per cent.	68 per cent.	44 per cent.
	Hours.					
I	0	34,000	1.98	–	–	–
	2	62,000	....	–	–	–
	4	4,700,000	2.02	–	–	–
	5	9,000,000	2.06	[1] +L	–	–
	6	21,000,000	2.10	+L	+L	–
	7	31,000,000	2.11	+L	+L	+L
II	0	147,000	1.94	–	–	–
	2	200,000	....	–	–	–
	4	15,000,000	2.10	+L	+L	+S

[1] See footnote under Table 1.

DIFFERENTIATION BETWEEN ACIDITY AND RENNET ACTION.

The fact that reducing the acidity did not cause a negative alcohol test, as mentioned above, led us to believe that it might be possible to differentiate between a positive alcohol test caused by acidity and one caused by rennet action. In order to determine whether this was true two flasks of sterile skim milk were prepared. One was inoculated with a pure culture of a lactic-acid-forming organism and the other with equal amounts of a pure culture of lactic-acid bacteria and rennet-forming bacteria. The two flasks were then incubated at 37° C. As may be seen from Table 12, the milk containing the lactic-acid bacteria had an acidity of 2.23 after 3 hours' incubation and the test was positive with both 75 per cent and 68 per cent alcohol. When the acidity was reduced to 1.49 all the alcohol tests were negative. The milk containing a mixed culture of lactic-acid bacteria and rennet-forming bacteria after 3 hours' incubation had an acidity of 2.32 and the alcohol test was positive with 75 per cent and 68 per cent alcohol. In both cases the coagulation was in the form of large flakes. When the acidity was reduced to 1.70 the alcohol test remained positive, although the size of the flakes was reduced. This milk after 5½ hours' incubation had an acidity of 4.38 and the milk coagulated with large flakes with each percentage of alcohol. When the acidity was reduced to 1.49 the alcohol test remained positive, the only change being with the 44 per cent alcohol, in which case the size of the flakes was reduced. This experiment was repeated, as will be seen from Table 12, and the results confirmed those of the first experiment. These results indicate that it may be possible to differentiate between an acid and an acid-and-rennet fermentation in milk, provided the acidity is not high.

TABLE 12.—*Differentiation between an acid and a mixed acid-and-rennet fermentation by neutralizing the acidity and using the alcohol test.*

Experiment No.	Pure culture of—	After incubation at 37° C. for 3 hours.				After incubation at 37° C. for 5½ hours.			
		Acidity.	Alcohol test.			Acidity.	Alcohol test.		
			75 per cent.	68 per cent.	44 per cent.		75 per cent.	68 per cent.	44 per cent.
I.	Lactic-acid bacteria.	2.23	[1]+L	+L	—	3.21	+L	+L	+L
		Neutralized to 1.66.	—	—	—	Neutralized to 1.49.	—	—	—
	Mixture of rennet-forming and lactic-acid bacteria.	2.32	+L	+L	—	4.38	+L	+L	+L
		Neutralized to 1.70.	+S	+VS	—	Neutralized to 1.49.	+L	+L	+S
II.	Lactic-acid bacteria.	....	....	....	....	[2]2.70	+L	+M	—
	Mixture of rennet-forming and lactic-acid bacteria.	[3]2.00	+L	+M	—	[3]3.42	+L	+L	+L
		Neutralized to 1.80.	—	—	—	Neutralized to 1.60.	+L	+M	+VS

NOTE.—Acidity of normal milk in experiment I, 1.75; in experiment II, 1.78.

[1] See footnote under Table 1.
[2] After 4½ hours incubation at 37° C.
[3] Acidity after adding pure cultures to milk and before incubation.

EFFECT OF HEAT COMBINED WITH RENNET ACTION.

Earlier in this paper we have shown the effect of heat on the alcohol test with milk of high and low acidity, and as a matter of general interest the effect of heat on the alcohol test produced by rennet action may now be considered. The results of two experiments shown in Table 13 explain themselves clearly. Sufficient rennet was added to two samples of milk to cause a positive alcohol test with 75 and 68 per cent alcohol. The milk was then heated, and it was found that at 90° C. the milk no longer gave a positive alcohol test. Both experiments showed the same results.

TABLE 13.—*Effect of heat on the alcohol test with milk in which the positive test is due to rennet action.*

Milk heated to—	Alcohol test.			
	75 per cent.		68 per cent.	
	Experiment I.	Experiment II.	Experiment I.	Experiment II.
°*C.*				
Not heated...	[1]+L	+L	+L	+L
40............	+L	+L	+L	+L
60............	+L	+L	+L	+L
70............	+L	+L	+L	+L
80............	+S	+VS	+S	+VS
90............	–	–	–	–

NOTE.—Acidity of milk in experiment I, 1.82; in experiment II, 1.84.

[1] See footnote under Table 1.

The results which we have shown on the effect of rennet action in relation to the alcohol test confirm the work of other investigators, and it is evident that the rennet-forming group of bacteria in milk can play an important part in the production of a positive alcohol test.

INFLUENCE ON THE ALCOHOL TEST OF CARBON DIOXID IN MILK.

There are probably numerous minor factors which influence the alcohol test with market milk. While the two principal factors are probably acidity and the effect of rennet action, it is believed by some investigators that carbon dioxid plays a more or less important part. Auzinger (2) found that milk one hour old which gave a positive alcohol test gave a negative test after it had been held for 18 hours. He believes that carbon dioxid might be partly responsible for such a change.

We have passed carbon-dioxid gas into milk many times and have always been able to cause a positive alcohol test. In one experiment carbon-dioxid gas was passed into milk until the acidity was 2.36 (titration in cold milk with phenolphthalein as an indicator), and a positive alcohol test was obtained with 75 per cent and 68 per cent alcohol. As is shown in Table 14, this milk was heated at different temperatures up to 100° C. With the increase in temperature the acidity was reduced, due probably to the expelling of the CO_2. Barillé (4) has shown that carbon dioxid forms a very unstable compound, which he calls carbono phosphate of calcium and is easily broken up by heat. When the temperature reached 70° C., the alcohol test with 68 per cent alcohol was negative and the acidity had been reduced from 2.36 to 2.05. At 90° C. the acidity was 1.91 and the alcohol test was negative with 75 per cent alcohol.

There can be no doubt as to the fact that carbon dioxid may cause a positive alcohol test, provided there is a large enough amount in the milk. In order to determine how much carbon dioxid was required to cause a positive test with 68 per cent alcohol, the gas was passed into a flask of fresh milk until a positive alcohol test was produced. The amount of CO_2 in this milk and in the original milk was then determined.[1] It was found that the normal milk contained 0.76 per cent of CO_2 by volume at 32° C., and the milk through which the gas had been passed contained 13.05 per cent of CO_2 by volume. In this experiment it was necessary to increase the CO_2 content to 13.05 per cent by volume in order to cause a positive alcohol reaction with 68 per cent alcohol. According to Kastle and Roberts (14) carbon dioxid is present in milk to the extent of 3 to 4 per cent by volume and partly escapes into the air when the milk is drawn. This being the case, it is evident that there is not enough carbon-dioxid gas in normal milk to cause of its own accord a positive alcohol test with 68 per cent alcohol. Of course, the presence of CO_2 may assist other factors to cause a positive alcohol test and in the case of bacterial fermentation where the gas is produced it might play a small part, but we believe that when 68 per cent alcohol is used in the test the influence of CO_2 in mixed market milk would be very small, if it has any effect.

TABLE 14.—*Effect of heat on alcohol test with milk-made acid to phenolphthalein with carbon dioxid.*

Milk heated to—	Acidity.	Alcohol test.	
		75 per cent.	68 per cent.
° C.			
Not heated	2.36	[1] +L	+L
40	2.32	+L	+L
50	2.30	+L	+M
60	2.19	+L	+VS
70	2.05	+M	–
80	2.05	+VS	–
90	1.91	–	–
100	1.92	–	–
Original milk	1.90	–	–

[1] See footnote under Table 1.

THE RELATION OF THE ALCOHOL TEST TO THE BACTERIA IN MIXED MARKET MILK.

Having discussed the effect of acidity and the effect of rennet action on the alcohol test, let us consider the relation of the test to the bacteria in market milk. Since an increased acidity and also rennet action may cause a positive test, it is natural to suppose that there may be some definite relation between the alcohol test and the number of bacteria in milk, as the increase in the acidity and the rennet in milk is the result of bacterial growth.

It is claimed by some authorities that the alcohol test is of great value for determining the freshness of milk, and as this is a question

[1] We are indebted to Dr. Clark, of the Dairy Division laboratory, for this analysis.

of great importance we have examined a number of samples of market milk which had been held for a number of days.

In Table 15 are shown the results of the examination of four samples of market milk. One was raw milk and the others were pasteurized. Each bottle of milk was obtained from a different dairy and was held in a refrigerator at a temperature of about 9° C. The acidity and alcohol test were determined daily and bacterial counts were made on the first day and again when the 68 per cent alcohol gave a positive test.

It is evident from the results obtained that the alcohol test (68 per cent) does not show the freshness of milk. The samples were held from 8 to 13 days at 9° C. before the alcohol test became positive, and during that time the bacteria had increased to more than 100,000,000 per cubic centimeter.

TABLE 15.—*Effect on the alcohol test of holding milk at 9° C.*

Days held.	Raw milk.					Pasteurized milk A.				
	Acidity.	Alcohol test.			Bacteria per cubic centimeter.	Acidity.	Alcohol test.			Bacteria per cubic centimeter.
		75 per cent.	68 per cent.	44 per cent.			75 per cent.	68 per cent.	44 per cent.	
0	1.72	[1]+V.S.	–	–	8,200	......	–	–	–	37,000
1	......	+V.S.	–	–	......	......	–	–	–	......
2	......	+V.S.	–	–	......	......	–	–	–	......
3	......	+V.S.	–	–	......	......	–	–	–	......
4	......	......	......	......	......	......	......	......	......	......
5	......	+V.S.	–	–	......	......	–	–	–	......
6	......	–	–	–	......	......	–	–	–	......
7	......	–	–	–	......	......	–	–	–	......
8	1.88	+V.S.	–	–	......	1.78	–	–	–	......
9	1.95	–	–	–	......	1.88	+S.	–	–	......
10	2.02	–	–	–	......	1.93	+S.	–	–	......
11	......	......	......	......	......	......	......	......	......	......
12	2.08	+ M.	–	–	......	2.30	+L.	+M.	–	242,000,000
13	2.43	+ L.	+M.	–	......	2.48	+L.	+L.	–	......
14	2.72	+ L.	+L.	–	146,000,000	2.75	+L.	+L.	+L.	626,000,000

Days held.	Pasteurized milk B.					Pasteurized milk C.				
	Acidity.	Alcohol test.			Bacteria per cubic centimeter.	Acidity.	Alcohol test.			Bacteria per cubic centimeter.
		75 per cent.	68 per cent.	44 per cent.			75 per cent.	68 per cent.	44 per cent.	
0	1.74	+M.	–	–	182,000	......	–	–	–	133,000
1	......	+L.	–	–	......	......	–	–	–	......
2	......	+M.	–	–	......	1.75	–	–	–	......
3	......	+M.	–	–	......	......	–	–	–	......
4	......	......	......	......	......	......	......	......	......	......
5	......	+M.	–	–	......	......	–	–	–	......
6	1.88	+M.	–	–	......	......	–	–	–	......
7	......	+M.	–	–	......	......	–	–	–	......
8	2.00	+M.	+M.	–	145,000,000	2.12	+M.	+M.	–	221,000,000
9	2.10	+M.	+M.	–	......	2.34	+L.	+L.	–	......
10	2.38	+L.	+L.	–	......	2.77	+L.	+L.	+M.	650,000,000
11	......	......	......	......	......	......	......	......	......	......
12	2.45	+L.	+L.	+M.	700,000,000	......	......	......	......	......
13	......	......	......	......	......	......	......	......	......	......
14	......	......	......	......	......	......	......	......	......	......

[1] See footnote under Table 1.

EFFECT OF HOLDING THE MILK AT DIFFERENT TEMPERATURES.

The temperature at which the milk is held would, of course, affect the length of time before the alcohol test becomes positive. To show the effect of temperature we held samples of raw and pasteurized milk at 9° C. and also at room temperature, and examined them in the same manner as in the preceding experiment. The results are shown in Table 16. In order to have about the same bacterial content in the milk held at the different temperatures, a quart of milk was thoroughly mixed and placed in sterilized pint bottles.

The results show clearly that the temperature at which milk is held has a marked influence on the time when the alcohol test will be positive. Also, as shown by sample of raw milk C, the bacterial content of the milk is an important factor. In all the samples it will be noticed that the bacterial counts show an exceedingly high number when the 68 per cent alcohol test was positive.

TABLE 16.—*Comparison of the alcohol tests with milk held at 9° C. and at 24° C.*

Temperature at which held.	Days held.	Raw milk A.					Pasteurized milk B.				
		Acidity.	Alcohol test.			Bacteria per cubic centimeter.	Acidity.	Alcohol test.			Bacteria per cubic centimeter.
			75 per cent.	68 per cent.	44 per cent.			75 per cent.	68 per cent.	44 per cent.	
9° C.	0	1.85	—	—	—	1,600	1.65	—	—	—	139,000
	1	1.85	—	—	—	....	1.60	—	—	—	....
	2	1.90	—	—	—	....	1.60	—	—	—	....
	3	1.80	—	—	—	....	1.70	—	—	—	....
	4	1.79	—	—	—	....	1.71	—	—	—	....
	5	....	....	....	....	....	....	....	....	....	....
	6	1.85	—	—	—	....	1.60	—	—	—	....
	7	1.90	—	—	—	....	1.80	—	—	—	....
	8	1.80	—	—	—	....	1.65	—	—	—	....
	9	....	—	—	—	....	....	—	—	—	....
	10	1.80	—	—	—	....	1.72	—	—	—	....
	11	....	—	—	—	....	2.00	[1]+S	—	—	197,000,000
	12	....	....	....	....	....	....	....	....	....	....
	13	2.70	+L	+M	—	400,000,000	2.3	+L	+M	—	960,000,000
	14	....	—	—	—	....	....	....	....	....	....
	17	4.1	+L	+L	+L	440,000,000	4.3	+L	+L	+L	....
Room temperature[1, 2]	0	1.85	—	—	—	2,900	1.65	—	—	—	146,000
	1 (9 a.m.)	1.90	—	—	—	....	1.85	+S	—	—	32,600,000
	1 (3 p.m.)	3.1	+L	+L	+L	534,000,000	3.70	+L	+L	+L	694,000,000

[1] See footnote under Table 1.

[2] About 24° C.

TABLE 16.—*Comparison of the alcohol tests with milk held at 9° C. and at 24° C.*—Continued.

Temperature at which held.	Days held.	Raw milk C.				
		Acidity.	Alcohol test.			Bacteria per cubic centimeter.
			75 per cent.	68 per cent.	44 per cent.	
9° C.....	0	1.85	—	—	—	7,870,000
	1	1.80	—	—	—	....
	2	1.95	[1] +S	—	—	93,000,000
	3	2.35	+M	+S	—	130,000,000
	4	2.36	+L	+L	—	188,000,000
	5	....	....	....	....	....
	6	2.88	+L	+L	+M	430,000,000
	7	....	....	....	....	....
	8	....	....	....	....	....
	9	....	....	....	....	....
	10	....	....	....	....	....
	11	....	....	....	....	....
	12	....	....	....	....	....
	13	....	....	....	....	....
	14	....	....	....	....	....
	17	....	....	....	....	....
Room temperature[2].	0	1.85	—	—	—	7,610,000
	1 (9 a.m.)	4.90	....	....	....	Curdled.

[1] See footnote under Table 1. [2] About 24° C.

At various times different investigators have used the alcohol test on market milk. Aurnhammer (1) in an examination of 250 samples of market milk during July and August of 1907 found the 68 per cent alcohol test positive in 82 samples. In a study of market milk in Philadelphia, Campbell (5) found that 37 of 100 samples of milk gave a positive test with 68 per cent alcohol. Of these 37 samples 17 contained less than and 20 more than 1,000,000 bacteria per cubic centimeter. It was found by Nurenberg and Lythgoe (23) during an examination of 2,600 samples of market milk that only 63 gave a positive test with 68 per cent alcohol.

We made alcohol tests on 236 samples of Washington market milk during the period from March 20 to June 4, 1914. These samples and their bacterial counts were supplied by the Health Department, District of Columbia.[1] Of the 236 samples we found that 37 gave an alcohol test with 75 per cent alcohol, 20 with 68 per cent alcohol, and 5 with 44 per cent alcohol. The samples which gave a positive test are tabulated in Table 17 with their acidity and bacterial counts. There were 177 samples of raw milk and 59 samples of pasteurized milk in the 236 samples examined. As may be seen from the table, 35 of the raw-milk samples gave a positive test with 75 per cent alcohol and only 2 of the 59 samples of pasteurized milk.

[1] We take this occasion to express our thanks to Dr. Kinyoun and Dr. Dieter, of the Health Department, for the samples of market milk and their bacterial counts which they so kindly furnished us.

TABLE 17.—*Raw and pasteurized market milk which gave positive alcohol tests.*

Milk.	Sample number.	Acidity.	Bacteria per cubic centimeter.	Alcohol tests.		
				75 per cent.	68 per cent.	44 per cent.
Raw	1	2.01	2,100	[1] +M	+VS	–
	2	2.30	7,000	+L	+M	–
	3	2.00	12,000	+M	–	–
	4	1.60	14,000	+M	+S	–
	5	1.97	18,000	+M	–	–
	6	1.92	24,000	+M	+S	+VS
	7	1.91	24,000	+S	–	–
	8	1.70	29,000	+S	–	–
	9	1.62	51,000	+M	+S	–
	10	2.30	67,000	+L	+M	–
	11	1.79	121,000	+M	+S	+VS
	12	1.75	156,000	+S	–	–
	13	2.00	200,000	+M	–	–
	14	1.94	350,000	+M	–	–
	15	1.90	442,000	+S	–	–
	16	2.06	464,000	+L	+M	–
	17	1.95	1,200,000	+M	+VS	–
	18	1.76	1,300,000	+VS	–	–
	19	1.75	1,500,000	+S	–	–
	20	1.80	1,600,000	+M	+S	–
	21	1.70	2,100,000	+M	–	–
	22	2.03	2,120,000	+S	–	–
	23	1.90	2,200,000	+S	–	–
	24	1.95	2,300,000	+M	+S	–
	25	2.45	2,600,000	+L	+M	+VS
	26	1.95	4,100,000	+M	+M	–
	27	1.93	4,700,000	+VS	–	–
	28	2.15	7,200,000	+M	+S	–
	29	2.19	8,600,000	+M	+S	–
	30	3.65	10,200,000	+L	+L	+L
	31	1.90	10,500,000	+M	–	–
	32	2.05	20,200,000	+M	–	–
	33	1.95	20,400,000	+M	+M	–
	34	2.55	20,600,000	+L	+L	+L
	35	2.10	21,200,000	+L	+M	–
Pasteurized	1	1.68	2,000	+S	–	–
	2	1.90	8,000	+M	+S	–

[1] See footnote under Table 1.

RESULTS OF TESTS WITH SAMPLES OF KNOWN BACTERIAL CONTENT.

When we consider the alcohol test in relation to the number of bacteria in milk, a short survey of the results is sufficient to show that there is no definite relation. Of the 35 samples of raw milk which showed a positive test with 75 per cent alcohol, 16, or 45.7 per cent, contained less than 500,000 bacteria per cubic centimeter. Of the 19 samples positive with 68 per cent alcohol, 8, or 42.1 per cent, contained less, and 11, or 57.9 per cent, more than 500,000 bacteria per cubic centimeter. Of the 5 samples positive with 44 per cent alcohol, 2 samples, or 40 per cent, contained less, and 3, or 60 per cent, more than 500,000 bacteria per cubic centimeter. The number of bacteria in samples which gave a positive alcohol test ranged from 2,100 to 21,200,000 per cubic centimeter.

The samples of pasteurized milk which showed a positive alcohol test had a very low bacterial count.

In order further to show that the alcohol test has no definite relation to the bacterial count, there are tabulated in Tables 18 and 19 the samples of raw and pasteurized milk which gave negative alcohol tests, together with their acidity and bacterial counts. We wish to call particular attention to the bacterial counts of 142 samples of raw milk which ranged from 2,000 to 19,600,000 bacteria per cubic centimeter. Of these 142 samples none gave a positive alcohol test, yet 86, or 60.6 per cent, contained less than and 39.4 per cent more than 500,000 bacteria per cubic centimeter.

The bacterial counts of the samples of pasteurized milk which gave a negative alcohol test ranged from 1,200 to 3,600,000 per cubic centimeter, as may be seen from Table 19.

From our results we believe that there is no definite relation between the alcohol test and the bacterial count, except in special cases where the bacteria have developed to a point where there is sufficient acid produced or where rennet-forming bacteria have acted sufficiently to influence the test.

TABLE 18.—*Acidity and bacterial count of samples of raw market milk which gave negative alcohol tests with 75 per cent, 68 per cent, and 44 per cent alcohol.*

Sample No.	Acidity.	Bacteria per cubic centimeter.	Sample No.	Acidity.	Bacteria per cubic centimeter.	Sample No.	Acidity.	Bacteria per cubic centimeter.
1	1.08	2,000	49	1.82	82,000	97	1.95	812,000
2	2.10	5,000	50	1.75	86,000	98	1.85	840,000
3	1.85	6,000	51	1.08	92,000	99	1.80	860,000
4	1.75	7,000	52	1.90	93,000	100	1.60	880,000
5	1.82	8,000	53	1.85	93,000	101	1.62	906,000
6	2.05	8,000	54	1.60	105,000	102	1.69	910,000
7	2.05	8,500	55	1.70	109,000	103	1.90	910,000
8	1.83	11,000	56	1.93	115,000	104	1.90	910,000
9	1.92	13,000	57	2.00	118,000	105	1.80	920,000
10	1.97	13,000	58	1.87	120,000	106	1.75	1,040,000
11	1.75	14,000	59	2.06	120,000	107	1.75	1,100,000
12	2.00	14,000	60	1.75	130,000	108	1.75	1,170,000
13	2.15	16,000	61	1.75	132,000	109	1.65	1,200,000
14	2.10	18,000	62	2.00	147,000	110	1.70	1,200,000
15	1.75	21,000	63	1.85	149,000	111	1.90	1,210,000
16	1.95	21,000	64	1.90	150,000	112	1.70	1,400,000
17	1.62	22,000	65	1.90	157,000	113	1.85	1,400,000
18	2.15	22,000	66	1.48	160,000	114	1.85	1,460,000
19	1.80	25,000	67	2.00	164,000	115	1.80	1,600,000
20	1.52	26,000	68	1.85	172,000	116	2.08	1,600,000
21	1.80	26,000	69	1.80	206,000	117	1.70	1,630,000
22	1.95	26,000	70	2.00	210,000	118	1.98	1,710,000
23	1.89	27,000	71	2.03	212,000	119	2.20	1,800,000
24	1.65	29,000	72	1.90	214,000	120	2.10	2,120,000
25	2.00	32,000	73	1.85	216,000	121	1.74	2,210,000
26	1.60	33,000	74	2.00	220,000	122	1.75	2,260,000
27	1.84	33,000	75	1.82	238,000	123	1.85	2,340,000
28	1.65	34,000	76	1.83	238,000	124	1.90	2,580,000
29	1.76	34,000	77	2.00	242,000	125	1.85	2,710,000
30	2.10	35,000	78	1.70	266,000	126	1.71	2,840,000
31	1.90	36,000	79	2.02	268,000	127	1.70	2,900,000
32	1.97	36,000	80	1.90	270,000	128	1.80	2,920,000
33	1.74	37,000	81	1.80	278,000	129	1.70	3,300,000
34	1.75	37,000	82	1.80	310,000	130	2.07	3,800,000
35	1.55	38,000	83	1.80	350,000	131	1.85	4,300,000
36	1.80	38,000	84	1.75	360,000	132	1.96	4,800,000
37	2.00	39,000	85	....	422,000	133	2.15	5,100,000
38	1.75	42,000	86	2.10	451,000	134	2.05	5,300,000
39	1.81	42,000	87	1.80	506,000	135	1.80	5,700,000
40	1.70	43,000	88	2.05	510,000	136	1.80	6,400,000
41	1.80	46,000	89	1.90	560,000	137	1.85	6,900,000
42	1.78	51,000	90	1.75	610,000	138	1.90	6,900,000
43	1.90	54,000	91	2.10	620,000	139	1.80	8,800,000
44	1.86	56,000	92	1.88	624,000	140	1.90	12,600,000
45	1.60	63,000	93	1.70	640,000	141	1.85	12,700,000
46	1.75	69,000	94	1.74	740,000	142	2.15	19,600,000
47	1.90	74,000	95	1.75	740,000			
48	1.71	79,000	96	2.00	800,000			

TABLE 19.—*Acidity and bacterial count of samples of pasteurized market milk which gave negative alcohol tests with 75 per cent, 68 per cent, and 44 per cent alcohol.*

Sample No.	Acidity.	Bacteria per cubic centimeter.	Sample No.	Acidity.	Bacteria per cubic centimeter.	Sample No.	Acidity.	Bacteria per cubic centimeter.
1	1.85	1,200	20	1.75	15,000	39	1.85	104,000
2	1.77	1,200	21	1.70	16,000	40	2.05	110,000
3	1.66	1,900	22	1.65	16,000	41	1.65	114,000
4	1.75	3,000	23	2.05	16,000	42	1.76	120,000
5	1.66	4,000	24	1.69	17,500	43	1.80	133,000
6	1.80	5,000	25	1.78	21,000	44	1.75	194,000
7	1.85	7,000	26	1.66	21,000	46	1.73	264,000
8	1.85	7,600	27	1.80	24,000	47	1.70	284,000
9	1.80	8,000	28	1.83	32,000	48	1.90	340,000
10	1.80	9,000	29	1.67	37,000	49	1.76	446,000
11	1.71	9,000	30	1.96	41,000	50	1.85	720,000
12	1.75	11,000	31	1.75	52,000	51	1.65	740,000
13	1.85	11,000	32	1.90	59,000	52	1.75	940,000
14	1.70	11,000	33	1.85	62,000	53	1.74	1,280,000
15	1.65	12,000	34	1.85	64,000	54	1.60	1,660,000
16	1.85	13,000	35	1.70	65,000	55	1.97	2,460,000
17	1.75	14,000	36	1.75	68,000	56	1.60	3,100,000
18	1.75	15,000	37	1.80	71,000	57	2.00	3,600,000
19	1.80	15,000	38	1.70	74,000			

In the early stages of the growth of acid-forming bacteria in milk, when the numbers are low, there is a period in which a rapid increase in numbers takes place without any increase in acidity which can be detected by ordinary chemical methods, or it may occur with only a slight increase in acidity; consequently if the alcohol test were made during that period there would be a high bacterial count and yet not high acidity enough to cause a positive alcohol test. The same is true of the action of the rennet-forming bacteria in their growth and action, as we have shown earlier in this paper when dealing with the relation of acidity, and also the effect of rennet on the alcohol test. Besides these facts there are other groups of bacteria which may develop in milk and yet have no influence on the alcohol test, as, for example, the alkali-forming group of bacteria. We have tried cultures of this group of organisms and found that they did not produce a positive alcohol test. There are other groups of bacteria in the flora of milk, such as the inert group, which also would probably develop without influencing the alcohol test in any way. When we consider all these facts it is not strange that there is no definite relation between the bacterial flora of milk and the bacterial count.

When the 68 per cent alcohol test is positive with a sample of market milk, it is evidence that there is some change in the milk from normal. In some cases it may be due to an increased acidity and in consequence a change in the casein of the milk, due to bacterial action. In other cases it may be due to a pure rennet fermentation or there may be a combination of an acid-and-rennet fermentation. In such cases the bacterial count would undoubtedly be high. However, there still remains to be explained the reason for a positive alcohol test in samples of market milk with a low bacterial count and low acidity.

We can not see that the alcohol test is of any particular value in the control of a market milk supply except as a means of evidence that milk from a particular source is abnormal in some way and should be examined by other tests. It might be of value at a receiving station as a means of detecting sour milk, but the test would be expensive compared with the use of alkaline tablets for the rapid determination of acidity as described by Farrington and Woll (9).

THE TITRATION METHOD OF APPLYING THE ALCOHOL TEST.

From the simple alcohol test in which a definite volume of a definite-percentage alcohol is added to an equal volume of milk there has developed a method in which a definite volume of milk is titrated with certain percentages of alcohol until a coagulation of the milk is produced.

Löhnis (16) has found this titration method to be of value as a test for the quality of market milk. He found that there was quite a definite relation between the titration with 80 per cent alcohol and the bacterial content of market milk. He titrated 2 c. c. of milk in a beaker against a black background with 90, 80, and 70 per cent alcohols, the titration being made at a temperature of from 15° to 20° C. The first appearance of flakes was considered the end point.

We have used this method in the titration of 116 samples of market milk furnished with bacterial counts by Dr. Kinyoun and Dr. Dieter, of the Health Department of the District of Columbia. In our titrations of 92 samples of raw and 24 samples of pasteurized milk we have not found any definite relation between the titration with 90 per cent and 80 per cent alcohols and the bacterial count. In Table 20 is shown the acidity, bacterial counts, and alcohol titration of 92 samples of raw milk, and in Table 21 the results of an examination of 24 samples of pasteurized milk. The bacterial counts of the raw milk ranged from 2,100 to 20,600,000 per cubic centimeter, and the pasteurized milk from 1,200 to 3,100,000 bacteria per cubic centimeter. Consequently we were able to titrate samples having a great variation in their bacterial content. If a study is made of the bacterial counts and the alcohol titrations shown in Tables 20 and 21 it will be seen that there is no definite relation between them. In order to bring this point out more clearly the titrations of samples containing more than 500,000 and less than 500,000 bacteria per cubic centimeter have been averaged, as shown in Table 22. The average titration with 90 per cent alcohol of 46 samples of raw milk containing more than 500,000 bacteria per cubic centimeter was 1.95 c. c., while the average titration of 46 samples containing less than 500,000 per cubic centimeter was 2.39 c. c. The average titration of 46 samples with 80 per cent alcohol was 4.61 c. c. when the bacterial count was more than 500,000 per cubic centimeter and 5.61 c. c. when the counts were less than 500,000 per cubic centimeter. The average titrations of the pasteurized milk samples showed even smaller differences. The small differences in the average titration of samples with a high and a low bacterial count show that there is little, if any, relation between the alcohol titration and the bacterial count. This is shown even more strikingly in Table 23, where the range in titrations among samples grouped according to bacterial counts is recorded. With these extreme ranges among samples of milk with high and low bacterial contents it would be almost impossible to interpret an alcohol titration in terms of bacteria.

TABLE 20.—*Alcohol titrations of raw market milk.*

Sample No.	Acidity.	Bacteria per cubic centimeter.	Alcohol titration.		Sample No.	Acidity.	Bacteria per cubic centimeter.	Alcohol titration.	
			90 per cent.	80 per cent.				90 per cent.	80 per cent.
			c. c.	*c. c.*				*c. c.*	*c. c.*
1	2.01	2,100	1.03	1.86	47	1.80	506,000	1.50	1.80
2	2.30	7,000	.51	.93	48	1.75	610,000	2.93	5.25
3	1.75	7,000	2.17	5.30	49	2.10	620,000	1.80	5.10
4	1.82	8,000	2.76	4.54	50	1.88	624,000	2.91	9.20
5	2.05	8,500	2.00	5.30	51	1.74	740,000	2.96	6.80
6	1.75	14,000	2.21	4.67	52	1.75	812,000	1.91	6.76
7	2.15	16,000	2.80	7.60	53	1.80	860,000	1.62	3.00
8	1.95	21,000	2.70	7.43	54	1.62	906,000	1.68	3.30
9	1.91	24,000	1.59	3.08	55	1.69	910,000	2.08	6.13
10	1.80	25,000	3.29	11.73	56	1.80	920,000	1.85	4.50
11	1.52	26,000	3.12	7.28	57	1.75	1,040,000	1.92	4.37
12	1.65	29,000	2.68	10.07	58	1.75	1,100,000	2.36	4.00
13	2.00	32,000	3.64	9.59	59	1.75	1,170,000	2.20	6.04
14	1.60	33,000	2.56	5.55	60	1.65	1,200,000	1.90	5.76
15	1.65	34,000	2.48	5.51	61	1.76	1,300,000	2.72	6.59
16	2.10	35,000	1.24	2.71	62	1.70	1,400,000	1.63	3.74
17	1.75	37,000	2.26	4.40	63	1.85	1,400,000	2.36	4.42
18	1.80	38,000	2.71	6.50	64	1.85	1,460,000	3.04	9.61
19	1.55	38,000	3.06	6.92	65	1.80	1,600,000	1.23	5.40
20	1.75	42,000	3.00	4.28	66	2.08	1,600,000	2.51	5.94
21	1.80	46,000	2.78	9.68	67	1.70	1,630,000	2.40	6.00
22	2.30	67,000	.50	1.1	68	2.20	1,800,000	1.30	2.37
23	1.75	69,000	2.58	5.98	69	1.70	2,100,000	1.16	1.60
24	1.90	74,000	3.03	6.33	70	2.03	2,120,000	1.16	2.34
25	1.71	79,000	3.50	6.91	71	1.74	2,210,000	2.10	3.96
26	1.85	93,000	1.57	4.36	72	1.75	2,260,000	1.81	4.12
27	1.70	109,000	3.04	5.20	73	1.85	2,340,000	2.42	4.78
28	1.87	120,000	2.46	5.80	74	2.45	2,600,000	.78	.97
29	1.75	130,000	1.60	3.20	75	1.71	2,840,000	2.95	3.97
30	1.75	132,000	2.72	10.45	76	1.70	2,900,000	2.12	6.36
31	2.00	147,000	1.72	3.80	77	1.80	2,920,000	3.00	6.85
32	1.85	149,000	3.54	8.17	78	1.70	3,300,000	2.80	6.30
33	1.80	160,000	1.48	2.49	79	2.00	3,600,000	1.90	5.40
34	1.80	206,000	3.16	5.52	80	1.85	4,300,000	2.05	5.00
35	2.00	210,000	2.68	7.00	81	1.93	4,700,000	1.40	3.90
36	2.03	212,000	2.35	5.70	82	1.96	4,800,000	1.46	2.70
37	1.90	214,000	1.68	4.52	83	2.05	5,300,000	1.60	2.68
38	1.82	238,000	2.75	7.00	84	1.80	5,700,000	2.94	7.25
39	2.00	242,000	1.24	2.90	85	1.85	6,900,000	1.01	2.41
40	1.76	266,000	1.95	3.94	86	2.19	8,600,000	.92	1.86
41	2.02	268,000	2.57	5.20	87	1.80	8,800,000	2.96	10.83
42	1.90	270,000	2.74	4.45	88	1.90	12,600,000	1.83	5.10
43	1.80	278,000	3.22	8.70	89	1.85	12,700,000	1.40	2.43
44	1.80	310,000	2.34	4.58	90	2.15	19,600,000	1.56	3.10
45	1.80	350,000	2.68	4.67	91	1.95	20,400,000	.86	1.40
46	1.75	360,000	2.35	5.29	92	2.55	20,600,000	.52	.60

TABLE 21.—*Alcohol titrations of pasteurized market milk.*

Sample No.	Acidity.	Bacteria per cubic centimeter.	Alcohol titration.		Sample No.	Acidity.	Bacteria per cubic centimeter.	Alcohol titration.	
			90 per cent.	80 per cent.				90 per cent.	80 per cent.
			c. c.	*c. c.*				*c. c.*	*c. c.*
1	1.77	1,200	2.20	5.74	13	1.70	65,000	2.88	5.04
2	1.70	11,000	2.84	6.76	14	1.75	68,000	2.40	5.50
3	1.65	12,000	3.08	8.80	15	1.80	71,000	2.50	4.49
4	1.85	13,000	1.56	4.43	16	1.85	104,000	2.43	3.96
5	1.75	14,000	1.65	3.10	17	1.70	120,000	2.10	5.96
6	1.75	15,000	2.22	3.42	18	1.75	194,000	3.05	6.01
7	1.70	16,000	2.76	4.10	19	1.73	264,000	2.24	3.00
8	1.78	21,000	2.33	5.91	20	1.70	284,000	2.86	5.48
9	1.80	24,000	1.69	6.10	21	1.76	446,000	1.82	5.34
10	1.90	59,000	2.57	3.68	22	1.60	1,600,000	2.10	4.78
11	1.85	62,000	2.23	5.47	23	1.97	2,460,000	2.08	3.66
12	1.60	63,000	2.53	3.24	24	1.60	3,100,000	3.53	7.07

TABLE 22.—*Average alcohol titrations of samples of raw and pasteurized market milk in tables 20 and 21.*

Milk.	Number of samples.	Bacteria per cubic centimeter.	Average alcohol titration.	
			90 per cent.	80 per cent.
			c. c.	*c. c.*
Raw........	46	More than 500,000.	1.95	4.61
	46	Less than 500,000..	2.39	5.61
Pasteurized..	3	More than 500,000..	2.57	5.17
	21	Less than 500,000..	2.28	5.02

TABLE 23.—*Range in alcohol titrations of market milk shown in detail in tables 20 and 21.*

Bacteria per cubic centimeter.	Alcohol titration.			
	90 per cent.		80 per cent.	
	Lowest.	Highest.	Lowest.	Highest.
	c. c.	*c. c.*	*c. c.*	*c. c.*
26 samples with less than 100,000......	0.51	3.64	0.93	11.73
30 samples with from 100,000 to 1,000,000	1.24	3.54	1.80	10.45
36 samples with over 1,000,000........	.52	3.04	.60	10.83

For the sake of clearness we have plotted in figure 1 the bacterial counts and the 90 per cent alcohol titration. In this figure the titrations of 116 samples of milk were plotted as ordinates and the logarithms of the bacterial counts as abscissæ. The numbers 3, 4, 5, 6, 7, and 8 represent the mantissa of the logarithms of the bacterial counts. Consequently from 3 to 4 was plotted the logarithm of samples with a bacterial count of from 1,000 to 9,999; from 4 to 5 counts from 10,000 to 99,999, and so on, as may be seen from the figure. By this method of plotting it is possible to plot bacterial counts ranging from low to high numbers, which would otherwise be impossible in a limited space. A glance at the plot which shows the 90 per cent alcohol titration and the bacterial count of 116 samples indicates clearly that there is no definite relation between them. In figure 2 we have plotted in the same way the 80 per cent alcohol

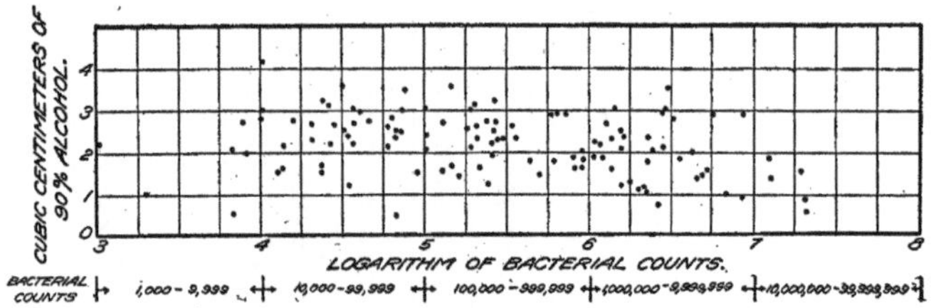

FIG. 1.—Relation o falcohol titration to the bacterial count of milk. Titrations of 116 samples of raw and pasteurized market milk with 90 per cent alcohol.

titration and the bacterial counts. It may be seen that among the 116 samples plotted there is a wide range in titration of samples with low and high bacterial counts. Some samples with a low count show a low titration and others a high titration. Among samples with a high count some show a low and others a high titration.

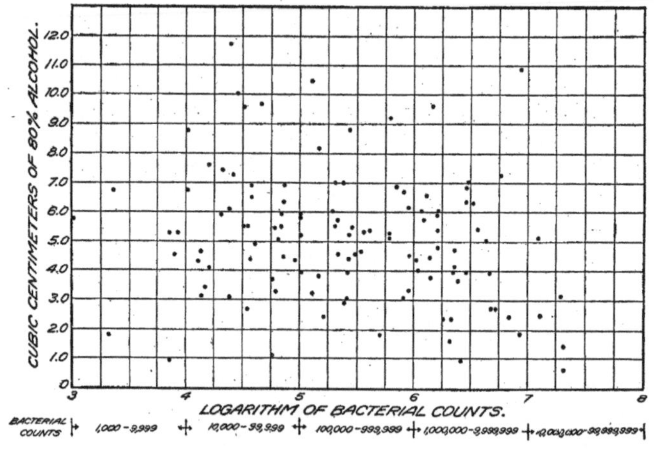

FIG. 2.—Relation of alcohol titration to the bacterial count of milk. Titrations of 116 samples of raw and pasteurized market milk with 80 per cent alcohol.

Our results indicate that there is no definite relation between alcohol titration and acidity unless the acidity is more than about 2.20. This is shown in figure 3, where 116 samples are plotted according to their acidity and titration with 90 per cent alcohol, and also in figure 4, where the 80 per cent titrations and acidities are plotted. The plots show that there is a wide range in the alcohol titration at all acidities until they reach about 2.20, after which the alcohol titration becomes lower in general as the acidities increase. This fact holds true for the small number of samples at these high

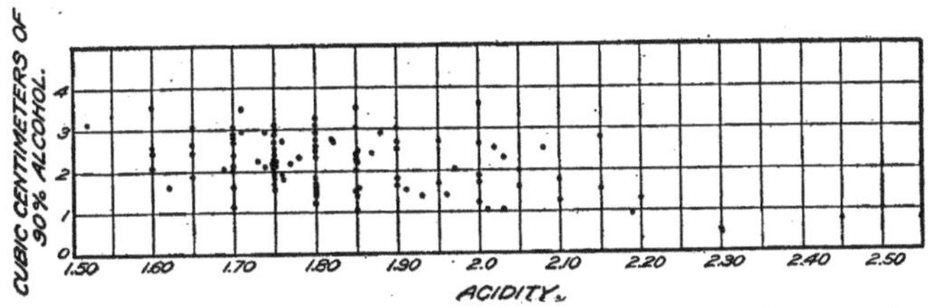

FIG. 3.—Relation of alcohol titration to the acidity of milk. Titrations of 116 samples of raw and pasteurized market milk with 90 per cent alcohol.

acidities and would probably have been brought out more clearly if we had had a larger number of samples with acidity above 2.20.

If we were dealing with pure cultures of organisms which influence the alcohol test the titration with alcohol might be of value in giving an idea of the bacterial numbers, as is shown in Table 24, from the

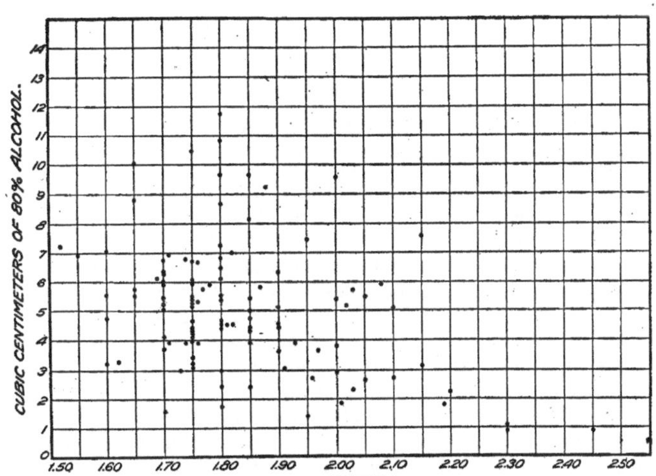

FIG. 4.—Relation of alcohol titration to acidity of milk. Titrations of 116 samples of raw and pasteurized market milk with 80 per cent alcohol.

results of experiments in which we used pure cultures of lactic-acid and rennet-forming bacteria. In milk, however, we have a varied bacterial flora to contend with and we can not see from our results that the alcohol titration method is of much greater value than the simple alcohol test.

TABLE 24.—*Alcohol titrations of milk inoculated with pure cultures of bacteria.*

Experiment.	Culture.	Age of milk culture.	Acidity.	Bacteria per cubic centimeter.	Alcohol titration.	
					90 per cent to 2 c.c. of milk.	80 per cent to 2 c.c. of milk.
		Hours.			*c. c.*	*c. c.*
1.....	Lactic-acid bacteria..........	0	1.95	64,000	3.08	8.88
		2	1.95	....	2.86	9.13
		3	1.90	131,000	3.14	9.42
		4	1.95	120,000	2.60	9.52
		5	1.95	361,000	3.05	9.40
		6	2.05	736,000	3.05	8.85
		6½	2.07	1,660,000	1.85	7.08
	Rennet-forming bacteria.......	0	1.95	....	3.12	9.02
		2	1.90	1,600	3.03	9.52
		3	1.95	70,000	2.50	9.48
		4	2.03	230,000	2.44	9.83
		5	2.04	2,850,000	3.20	9.90
		6	2.04	9,300,000	2.80	8.12
		6½	2.07	11,100,000	1.87	6.18
2.....	Lactic-acid bacteria..........	0	2.00	25,000	3.33	12.55
		2	2.00	184,000	3.58	13.82
		3	2.08	475,000	3.52	11.18
		4	2.04	1,710,000	3.73	9.85
		5	2.18	4,900,000	2.00	7.32
		6	2.26	8,400,000	2.00	5.50
		7	2.33	22,500,000	1.06	1.79
	Rennet-forming bacteria.......	0	2.00	6,100	3.32	13.95
		2	2.00	51,500	3.40	13.36
		3	2.00	234,000	3.98	10.52
		4	2.00	1,325,000	3.57	9.35
		5	2.00	1,300,000	1.56	8.98
		6	2.04	13,000,000	1.25	2.93
		7	2.20	21,800,000	0.83	1.21

THE ALIZAROL TEST.

When the alcohol has alizarin added to it to act as an indicator for the acidity the alcohol test is known as the alizarol test. This name was given to the test by Morres (21). The use of alizarin as an indicator for the acidity of milk has been known for a long time, but Morres (19) was probably the first to combine the alcohol and alizarin test. He pointed out that the alcohol test was of more value than the litmus test and that the combination with alizarin was better than the combination of litmus and alcohol. Morres (20) used a 68 per cent alcohol with 1.2 grams of fresh alizarin paste, or 0.4 gram of dry alizarin to 1,000 c. c. of alcohol. Two cubic centimeters of this alizarin-alcohol solution are mixed with 2 c. c. of milk, the same as in the alcohol test. This author found that from the coagulation by alcohol and the color of the alizarin it was possible to obtain a picture of the condition of the milk. According to Morres (20) the alizarol test shows the following conditions:

1. Lilac-red color. (Milk titrated 7° acid.)
   - (*a*) With no coagulation. The milk should keep sweet more than 6 hours.
   - (*b*) With fine flaky coagulation. The beginning of rennet production is shown here.
   - (*c*) With heavy flocculent coagulation. This indicates advanced rennet formation.

2. Pale-red color. (Milk titrated 8° acid.)
   (a) With no coagulation or only very fine coagulation. This shows the beginning of lactic-acid fermentation.
   (b) With flaky coagulation. Acid and rennet fermentation is indicated.
   (c) With coagulation with very thick flakes. A mixed fermentation is indicated with advanced rennet and the beginning of acid fermentation.
3. Brownish-red color. (Milk titrated 9° acid.)
   (a) With coagulation with fine flakes. Well-advanced pure acid fermentation is indicated.
   (b) With coagulation with thick flakes. A mixed fermentation with advanced rennet and strong acid fermentation is indicated.
   (c) With coagulation with very thick flakes. A very advanced rennet production and little less important acid fermentation is indicated.
4. Reddish-brown color. (Milk titrates 10° acid.)
   (a) With flaky coagulation. Advanced pure acid fermentation is indicated.
   (b) With thick flaky coagulation. Advanced acid fermentation and the beginning of rennet production is indicated.
   (c) With very thick flaky coagulation. A proportional mixed fermentation which is well advanced is indicated.
5. Brown color. (Milk titrates 11° acid.)
   (a) With thick flaky coagulation. Pure acid fermentation is indicated. Milk is sour; to be detected by smell.
   (b) With very thick flaky coagulation. Some rennet production and well advanced acid fermentation is indicated.
6. Yellowish-brown color. (Milk titrates 12° acid.)
   (a) With very thick flaky coagulation. Acid fermentation is indicated. Milk tastes acid.
7. Brownish-yellow color. (Milk titrates 14° acid.)
   (a) With very thick flaky coagulation. Sour taste is distinctly noticeable.
8. Yellow color. (Milk titrates 20° acid.)
   (a) With very thick flaky coagulation. Pure acid fermentation is indicated. Milk smells and tastes strongly acid and is near the normal coagulation point.
9. Violet color. (Milk titrates 7° acid.)
   No fermentation is indicated, but the milk is abnormal.

It can not be disputed that a simple test which will picture conditions in milk, as claimed by Morres, would be of considerable value. But will the alizarol test indicate all that Morres claims? Devarda and Weich (6) in 1913, after working with this test, decided that it had no value over the alcohol test. In a later paper Devarda (7) draws conclusions as follows:

1. For market control the alcohol test is satisfactory for the determination of the quality of milk.

2. The assertion of Morres that the alizarol test can show a pure rennet and mixed fermentation is without scientific or practical significance.

3. In a pure lactic fermentation the alizarol test stands close to the acidity in its color relation, but for the determination of the keeping quality of milk it is of slight significance.

4. The diagnostic value of the alizarol test is limited to an empirical test for milk, principally as to its suitability for cheese making which was already employed by Eugling in 1882.

Thöni (30), in a study of the milk supply of Berne, found that 12 of 85 samples examined were more or less abnormal, according to the alizarol test. Among the other 73 samples of milk, which according to the alizarol test were normal, there were samples which had a high bacterial content and which were abnormal according to the leucocyte and other tests. From his results Thöni believes that the alizarol test is not sufficiently delicate for use in market-milk investigations. However, he believes the test is of value as a quick means for detecting udder infection in animals.

It is evident that there is a diversity of opinion as to the value of the alizarol test, and our experiments have not been extensive enough for us to form a definite opinion in regard to it.

We have tried the test on a number of samples of milk and have not been able to obtain all the color changes which are described by Morres. When the acidity was slightly above normal we found a change from lilac red to pale red and brownish red. In one sample of milk we increased the acidity by the addition of lactic acid and obtained the colors named below.

Amount of N/10 lactic added to 50 c. c. of milk.	Acidity.	Color of alizarol test.
Normal milk	1.85	Lilac red.
2 c. c.	2.10	Pale red.
4 c. c.	2.42	Brownish red.
6 c. c.	2.73	Do.
8 c. c.	3.00	Do.
1.5 c. c. normal acid	5.15	Do.

From our results we believe that alizarin will show slight changes in the acidity when the acidity is low, but that the indicator did not seem to be very sensitive to high acidities in milk. Morres (22), in a paper in 1913, also states that alizarin is of greatest value in indicating the first changes in acidity and that the color change is so gradual at acidities over 16° that the test is of no particular value.

In regard to the value of the alizarol test we believe that wherever the alcohol test can be considered of value, the addition of an indicator, such as alizarin, may increase the value of the alcohol test by possibly giving additional information as to acidity.

On account of the complexity of the bacterial fermentations in market milk we do not believe that the alizarol test gives any very valuable information as to the conditions existing in the milk.

CONCLUSIONS.

In conclusion, we wish to point out again that the alcohol test must be considered from two standpoints: First, in its relation to the milk from a single cow or small herd, and, second, in its relation to mixed market milk.

As to the relation of the alcohol test to milk from a single cow, it seems evident from the work of other investigators, which is confirmed to some extent by our results, that a positive 68 per cent alcohol test indicates some change in the milk from its normal condition. In our opinion the value of the alcohol test with milk from a single cow or small herd lies in the fact that it would show that the milk was abnormal, and in consequence a careful examination should be made of the herd.

When the relation of the alcohol test to mixed market milk is discussed, we must consider it on an entirely different basis. In this case the test with 68 per cent alcohol may be positive as a result of changes produced in milk through bacterial action. The results of our work confirm some of the results of other investigators and show that the alcohol test may be positive as a result of the growth in milk of lactic-acid and rennet-forming bacteria. When the growth of these bacteria has reached a point where the acid or rennet is produced in sufficient quantities to affect the casein, a coagulation is produced when equal volumes of 68 per cent alcohol and milk are mixed. Our results, however, do not show that there is any definite relation between the alcohol test and the number of bacteria in milk. During an examination of 177 samples of raw milk we found that 20 samples gave a positive test with 68 per cent alcohol. Of these 20 samples 8, or 42.1 per cent, contained less than 500,000, and 11, or 57.9 per cent, more than 500,000 bacteria per cubic centimeter. It was also found that 39.4 per cent of 142 samples of milk which gave no positive alcohol tests contained over 500,000 bacteria per cubic centimeter. That there is no definite relation is probably explained by the fact that bacteria may increase in large numbers before there is much acid or rennet produced. Consequently, if an alcohol test were made during that period there would be a high bacterial content and yet not enough change produced in the milk by acid or rennet to cause a positive test. Besides this point it must be remembered that in market milk there is a bacterial flora representing many different species, many of which may increase without influencing the alcohol test.

As stated before, generally speaking, when the bacterial fermentations have advanced to a point where chemical changes are produced, the alcohol test will be positive as a result of lactic or rennet fermentations, or a mixture of both. In such cases the alizarol test may be of more value than the plain alcohol test, so far as it may give additional information as to the kind of fermentation. From our results it seems evident that the acid-and-rennet fermentations may be differentiated by means of neutralization of the acidity by sodium hydrate.

The alcohol titration method according to our tests seems to offer no particular advantages over the alcohol test. In a study of 116 samples we were not able to find any definite relation between the alcohol titration and the bacterial count.

LITERATURE CITED.

1. Aurnhammer, Albert. Milchversorgung der Stadt München. Inaug.-Dissert. Munchen, 1907. *In* Centralblatt für Bakteriologie, Parasitenkunde und Infektionskrankheiten, Abteilung 2, vol. 21, no. 17/19, p. 529, Jena, 1908.
2. Auzinger, August. Studien über die Alkoholprobe der Milch, ihre Verwendbarkeit zum Nachweis abnormer Milchen und ihre Beziehungen zu anderen Prüfungsmethoden pathologischer Milch. *In* Milchwirtschaftliches Zentralblatt, vol. 5, no. 7, p. 293–315; no. 8, p. 352–370; no. 9, p. 393–413; no. 10, p. 430–446, Leipzig, 1909.
3. Auzinger, August. Die Alkoholreaktion der Milch. *In* Molkerei-Zeitung, vol. 28, no. 25, p. 457–459, Hildesheim, March 27, 1914.
4. Barillé, A. De l'existence des carbonophosphates dans le lait. Leur précipitation par la pasteurisation. *In* Comptes Rendus des Séances de l'Académie des Sciences, vol. 149, no. 5, p. 356–358, Paris, Aug. 2, 1909.
5. Campbell, H. C. Biochemic reactions and the bacterial count of milk. *In* U. S. Department of Agriculture, 28th Annual Report of the Bureau of Animal Industry, p. 195–224, Washington, D. C., 1911.
6. Devarda, A., and Weich, A. Die Morressche Alizarolprobe zur Prüfung der Haltbarkeit der Milch. *In* Archiv für Chemie und Mikroskopie, vol. 4, no. 4, p. 207–212, Wien, 1913.
7. Devarda, A. Welchen Wert hat die Alizarolprobe für die Untersuchung der Milch zum Zwecke der Marktkontrolle. *In* Österreichische Molkerei-Zeitung, vol. 21, no. 2, p. 17–19, Wien, Feb. 25, 1914.
8. Ernst, Wilhelm. Grundriss der Milchhygiene für Tierärzte, p. 274, Stuttgart, 1913.
9. Farrington, E. H., and Woll, F. W. Testing milk and its products, Madison, Wis., 1911.
10. Fendler, G., and Borkel, C. Alkoholprobe und Säuregrad der Milch. *In* Zeitschrift für Untersuchung der Nahrungs-und Genussmittel, vol. 21, no. 8, p. 477–480, Berlin, Apr. 15, 1911.
11. Fleischmann, Gustav F. W. Lehrbuch der Milchwirthschaft, Dritte auflage, p. 120. Leipzig, 1901.
12. Henkel, Th. Die Acidität der Milch, deren Beziehungen zur Gerinnung beim Kochen und mit Alkohol, die Säurebestimmungsmethoden, der Verlauf der Säuerung. *In* Milchwirtschaftliches Zentralblatt, vol. 3, no. 8, p. 340–369; no. 9, p. 378–405, Leipzig, 1907.
13. Höft, H. Zur Prüfung und Beurteilung saurer Milch nach der Alkohol und Alizarinprobe. *In* Molkerei-Zeitung, vol. 12, no. 17, p. 277–278, Hildesheim, Apr. 23, 1898.
14. Kastle, Joseph H., and Roberts, Norman. The chemistry of milk. Treasury Department, Public Health and Marine-Hospital Service of the U. S., Hygienic Laboratory bulletin no. 56, p. 313–425, Washington, D. C., 1909.
15. Kirchner, W. Handbuch der Milchwirtschaft, Fünfte auflage, p. 180, Berlin, 1907.
16. Löhnis, F. Die Titration der Milch mit Alkohol von verschiedener Konzentration. *In* Molkerei-Zeitung, vol. 28, no. 9, p. 153–155, Hildesheim, Jan. 30, 1914.
17. Metzger, Karl. Untersuchungen über die Alkoholprobe bei Milch von kranken Kühen. Diss. Stuttgart 1912. *In* Centralblatt für Bakteriologie, Parasitenkunde und Infektionskrankheiten, Abteilung 2, vol. 39, no. 4/7, p. 181, Jena, Oct. 11, 1913.
18. Morres, Wilhelm. Die Haltbarkeitsprüfung der Milch. *In* Molkerei-Zeitung, vol. 19, no. 36, p. 421–422, Berlin, Sept. 4, 1909.
19. Morres, Wilhelm. Zur Alkoholprobe der Milch. *In* Molkerei-Zeitung, vol. 23, no. 47, p. 1319–1321, Hildesheim, Nov. 20, 1909.

20. Morres, Wilhelm. Die Zersetzung der Milch und das einfachste Verfahren, um sowohl ihre Art als auch ihren Grad zuverlässig zu bestimmen. *In* Molkerei-Zeitung, vol. 24, no. 98, p. 1837–1838, Hildesheim, Dec. 16, 1910.

21. Morres, Wilhelm. Die häufigsten Zersetzungsarten der Milch und ihr bestes Erkennungsmittel in der Hand des Molkereipraktikers. *In* Molkerei-Zeitung, vol. 22, no. 38, p. 445–446, Berlin, Sept. 21, 1912.

22. Morres, Wilhelm. Neue Versuche mit der Alizarolprobe. *In* Österreichische Molkerei-Zeitung, vol. 20, no. 21, p. 331–333; no. 22, p. 349–351, Wien, Nov. 1913.

23. Nurenberg, Lewis I., and Lythgoe, Herman C. Detecting pasteurized milk and old milk. *In* The Creamery and Milk Plant Monthly, vol. 11, no. 6, p. 4–6, Chicago, Feb. 1914.

24. Petri, R. J., and Maaszen, Albert. Zur Beurtheilung der Hochdruch-Pasteurisir-Apparate. *In* Arbeiten aus dem Kaiserlichen Gesundheitsamte, vol. 14, p. 53–70, Berlin, 1898.

25. Rammstedt, O. Kochprobe, Alkoholprobe und Säuregrad der Milch. *In* Zeitschrift für Öffentliche Chemie, vol. 17, no. 23, p. 441–455, Plauen, Dec. 1911.

26. Reiss, F. Ueber eine schnellere und billigere Ausführung der Alkoholprobe in den Milchhandlungen. *In* Molkerei-Zeitung, vol. 20, no. 3, p. 50–51, Hildesheim, Jan. 20, 1906.

27. Reiss, F. Wie musz der Alkohol zur Prüfung der Milch auf Kochfähigkeit beschaffen sein? *In* Molkerei-Zeitung, vol. 18, no. 35, p. 831–832, Hildesheim, Aug. 27, 1904.

28. Rühm, G. Untersuchungen über das Vorkommen und die Häufigkeit der Streptokokkenmastitis bei Kühen. *In* Wochenschrift für Tierheilkunde und Viehzucht, vol. 52, no. 7, p. 125–130; no. 8, p. 147, Munich, Feb. 18, 1908.

29. Rullmann, W., and Trommsdorff, R. Milchhygienische Untersuchungen. *In* Archiv für hygiene, vol. 59, no. 3, p. 224–265, Munich und Berlin, 1906.

30. Thöni, J. Untersuchungen über die hygienisch-bakteriologische Beschaffenheit der Berner Marktmilch mit Berücksichtigung des Vorkommens von Tuberkelbacillen. *In* Centralblatt für Bakteriologie, Parasitenkunde und Infektionskrankheiten, Erste Abteilung, Originale, vol. 74, no. 1/2, p. 11–69, Jena, May 27, 1914.

31. Weber, A. Die Bakterien der sogenannten sterilisirten Milch des Handels, ihre biologischen Eigenschaften und ihre Beziehungen zu den Magen-Darmkrankheiten der Säuglinge, mit besonderer Berücksichtigung der giftigen peptonisirenden Bakterien Flügge's. *In* Arbeiten aus dem Kaiserlichen Gesundheitsamte, vol. 17, p. 108–155, Berlin, 1900.

32. Die neue Polizeiverordnung, betreffend den Verkehr mit Kuhmilch und Sahne in Berlin. *In* Molkerei-Zeitung, vol. 16, no. 13, p. 225–226, Hildesheim, Mar. 29, 1902.

ADDITIONAL COPIES
OF THIS PUBLICATION MAY BE PROCURED FROM
THE SUPERINTENDENT OF DOCUMENTS
GOVERNMENT PRINTING OFFICE
WASHINGTON, D. C.
AT
5 CENTS PER COPY
▽

WASHINGTON : GOVERNMENT PRINTING OFFICE : 1915

BULLETIN OF THE
U.S. DEPARTMENT OF AGRICULTURE

No. 203

Contribution from the Bureau of Plant Industry, Wm. A. Taylor, Chief.
April 30, 1915.

(PROFESSIONAL PAPER.)

FIELD STUDIES OF THE CROWN-GALL OF SUGAR BEETS.

By C. O. Townsend,
Pathologist in Charge of Sugar-Beet Investigations.

KINDS OF BEET GALLS.

There are at least two distinct but clearly related kinds of growths occurring upon sugar beets which may be considered under the name of galls. These have been designated as "tumors" and "tuberculosis" in Bulletin No. 213 of the Bureau of Plant Industry.[1] While these two kinds of outgrowths are similar in external appearance, especially in their early stages of development, their internal appearance and their subsequent behavior serve to distinguish the tumor from tuberculosis. Internally, the outgrowths known as tuberculosis of the beet show small, brownish, water-soaked areas, as mentioned on page 194 of the bulletin cited, while the tumor is free from these discolored areas. Externally, both kinds of galls are usually smooth at first, but the tuberculosis galls eventually become decidedly rough, cracked, and very dark, and finally decay. This decay of the galls often causes the beet itself to rot, thereby entailing more or less loss on the grower, according to the prevalence of the disease. On the other hand, the tumor remains comparatively smooth, seldom cracks, does not usually decay, and frequently retains its firmness until the beets are harvested. The quality of the galls and their effect upon the beets from which they arise, as given in this paper, relate for the most part to the tumor variety.

DISTRIBUTION OF BEET GALLS.

The abnormal outgrowths known in this country as crown galls have been observed upon beet plants from time to time for more than 50 years. Indeed, as early as 1839 attention was called to these

[1] Smith, Erwin F., Brown, Nellie A., and Townsend, C. O. Crown-gall of plants: Its cause and remedy. U. S. Dept. Agr., Bur. Plant Indus. Bul. 213, p. 105, 194. 1911.

82778°—Bull. 203—15

peculiar growths upon beet roots, which were spoken of at that time as warts. In 1859 some of these galls were described as larger than the beet roots themselves and were looked upon as curiosities and monstrosities. It appears from a study of the literature upon the subject and from observations in the field from year to year that this disease of the sugar beet has increased rapidly in recent years and that it is still on the increase. Its presence has been recorded in many of the beet-growing countries of Europe, and in our own country it has been found on the sugar beet from Virginia to California. (Fig. 1.) In many localities where only a small number of cases were observed a few years ago, there are now hundreds and sometimes thousands of galled beets each year, especially if beets have been followed by beets for several years in the same field. On the beet itself the galls may appear at any point from the top of the crown to the extreme tip of the root. However, by far the largest number of galls are to be found at or near the surface of the ground, and for this reason these growths have been termed crown galls.

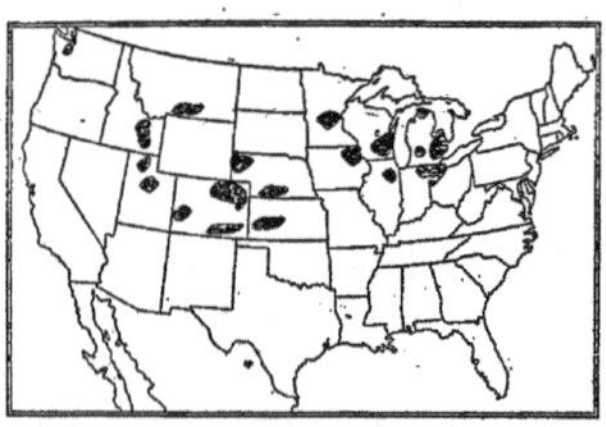

FIG. 1.—Map of the United States, the shaded portions showing the areas where sugar-beet galls have been observed.

APPEARANCE OF BEET GALLS.

The outgrowths, or galls, on the beet do not usually appear until the beets are from one-fourth to one-half grown; that is, until midsummer. From that time on, they may appear at any time until the beets are harvested. Consequently, we may find at harvest time galls in all stages of development, from tiny protuberances that have just begun to grow to what might be called the full-grown gall, several inches in diameter, as shown in Plate I, *A* to *K*. Frequently, these galls push out from the surface of the beet without any distinct line of demarcation between the gall and the beet proper, as seen in Plate II, *B*. In other cases the outgrowths are attached to the beet by very slender necks or threads, and between these extremes may be seen the full range of variation in relative size of the connecting tissue. Whether large or small, the connections are short, so that the gall almost invariably lies close to the beet from which it springs. Sometimes but a single gall is produced on one beet, as shown in Plate I, *F* to *K*, while in other instances several or many galls may develop on the same beet, as illustrated in Plate II, *A*, *B*, *C*, and *F*. In the latter case the galls may be distinct and separate (Pl. II, *A*) or they may occur in groups (Pl. II, *B*). It is not uncommon for the entire crown of the beet to be covered with a mass of galls (Pl. I, *E*).

Usually the galls with slender attachments occur singly, although there may be several on the same beet, while the galls occurring in groups usually have broad bases without any distinct line between the gall and the beet. In the early stages of development—that is, when the galls are young—their surfaces are bright, resembling the surface of the beet proper and indicating active growth; but as the galls grow older they become darker, especially if they are above the surface of the ground. In this way their relative ages may be easily determined. When galls have begun to form they usually increase in size most rapidly on those beets that are making the most rapid growth.

CAUSE OF BEET GALLS.

The primary cause of the formation of crown galls on the sugar beet and many other plants was for a long time in doubt. Few plant diseases have given rise to more extended investigations than has the so-called crown-gall. Different investigators have assigned the origin of these abnormal growths to a great variety of causes, ranging from slime molds to mechanical injuries. However, the investigations set forth in Bulletins Nos. 213 and 255 of the Bureau of Plant Industry[1] prove conclusively that a bacterium or several closely related bacteria are responsible for the origin and development of these outgrowths belonging to the class of so-called crown galls. The organism producing "tumors" is known as *Bacterium tumefaciens* (Smith and Townsend) and the one producing "tuberculosis" is designated as *B. beticolum* (Smith).[2]

The most extensive work on mechanical injuries as the cause of gall formations on sugar beets has been carried on by Spisar.[3] There seems to be no proof, however, that the organism which is capable of producing galls on sugar beets was not present in the fields in which Spisar carried on his experiments. It is apparent that a mechanical injury offers a favorable place for the organism to enter the plant, yet the indications are that gall formations will not result from mechanical injuries unless the gall-producing organism is present. In the field studies on the crown-gall of beets carried on by the writer for several years, it has been frequently noted that when galls begin to appear on the beets in a given field they are at first few in number, increasing from year to year if beets continue to be grown in that field. It has also been noticed that if badly infested fields are followed one or two years with a grain crop and then returned to

[1] Smith, Erwin F., Brown, Nellie A., and Townsend, C. O., op. cit.
Smith, Erwin F., Brown, Nellie A., and McCulloch, Lucia. The structure and development of crown-gall: A plant cancer. U. S. Dept. Agr., Bur. Plant Indus. Bul. 255, 60 p., 2 fig., 109 pl. 1912.

[2] These organisms are described in Bureau of Plant Industry Bulletin 213, which may be obtained from the Superintendent of Documents, Government Printing Office, for 40 cents, 10 cents additional being required for postage to foreign countries.

[3] Spisar, Karl. Über die Bildung des Zuckerrüben-Kropfes. *In* Ztschr. Zuckerindus. Böhmen, Jahrg. 36, Heft 1, p. 1-17, fig. 1-6; Heft 2, p. 57-72, fig. 7-11. 1911.

beets, the galls are greatly reduced in number after one year in grain and practically eliminated after two years. It is true that when galls are present in a field of beets they are frequently more numerous near the ends of the rows, where the greatest amount of mechanical injury is produced by the horses and cultivator in turning. (See Pl. II, *E* and *F*.) However, adjacent fields and even parts of the same field not previously in beets, but in which the beets at the time of the observation were subjected to the same mechanical injuries, were free from galls (Pl. II, *D*), regardless of the fact that the soil, climatic conditions, and cultural methods were the same. While certain plant galls and callus formations may be produced by other agencies, all extensive laboratory, greenhouse, and field studies on the crown-gall of sugar beets lead to the conclusion that in this country the true crown-gall formations of this class are produced by bacteria.

QUALITY OF BEET GALLS.

In topping beets from which sugar is to be obtained, it is customary to cut off the crowns at the line of the lowest leaf scar. The reason for rejecting the crowns, as generally known, depends on the fact that as a rule they contain a high percentage of salts, which tend to prevent the sugar from crystallizing in the mill. In the process of topping the beets it frequently happens that a part or all of the galls that occur on the beets are so located that they are left on the root (Pl. I, *F* to *K*) and are, therefore, put through the mill. In order to find out whether or not the galls might affect injuriously the juices in the mill, a series of tests was made to determine the quality of the galls as compared with the beet crowns and roots. The results of these tests are given in Table I, the analytical work for this and the succeeding table having been performed at the Garden City, Kans., laboratory by Mr. C. A. Hauser.

TABLE I.—*Sugar tests of beets affected with crown-gall.*

Part of beet tested.	Average weight of part tested.	Solids in juice.	Sugar in juice.	Coefficient of purity.	Sugar in part tested.
	Ounces.	*Per cent.*	*Per cent.*	*Per cent.*	*Per cent.*
Experiment 1:					
Galls	3.2	15.32	9.00	58.74	5.00
Crowns	13.6	14.10	10.10	71.63	8.90
Roots	24.0	14.30	11.00	76.92	10.00
Experiment 2:					
Galls	4.0	15.60	8.10	51.92	4.60
Crowns	11.2	12.70	8.20	64.56	7.50
Roots	25.6	14.10	11.00	78.01	10.20
Experiment 3:					
Galls	3.2	16.00	9.20	57.50	7.10
Crowns	13.6	15.40	10.80	70.20	10.20
Roots	29.8	15.00	11.40	76.00	10.70
Experiment 4:					
Galls	5.6	15.30	7.80	50.98	7.00
Crowns	18.4	13.10	9.00	68.70	8.40
Roots	32.8	13.10	10.10	77.09	10.00
Experiment 5:					
Galls	8.0	16.60	9.10	54.81	5.90
Crowns	18.4	14.60	9.90	67.80	8.50
Roots	44.8	14.10	10.50	74.46	9.00

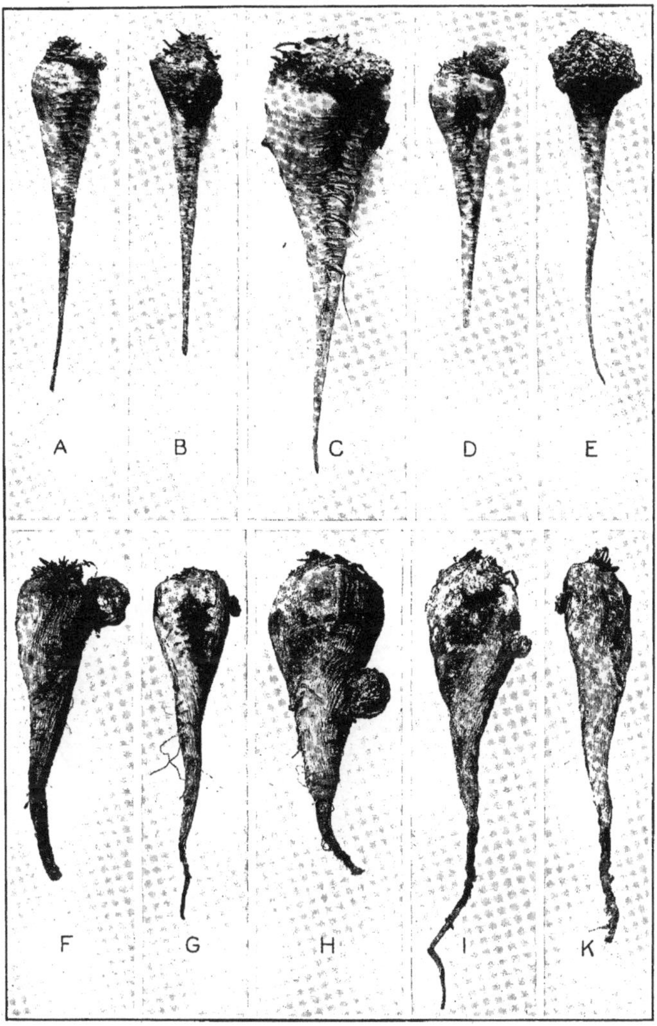

GALLED SUGAR BEETS, SHOWING THE VARIOUS LOCATIONS OF THE GALLS.

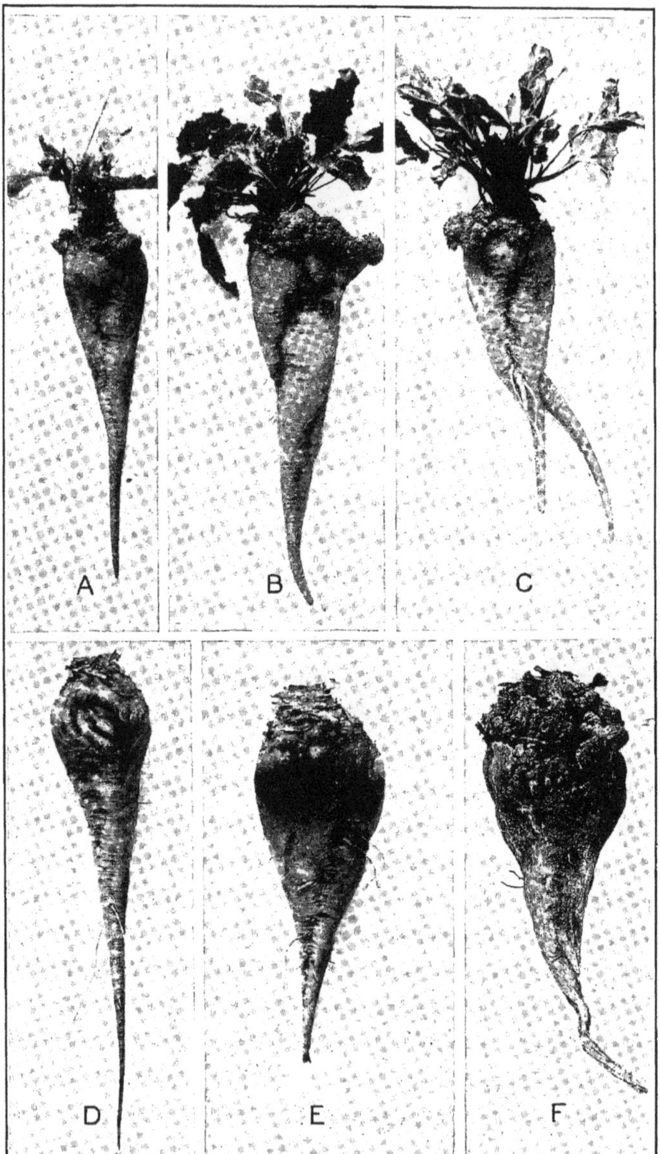

SUGAR BEETS, SHOWING GALLS APPEARING SINGLY AND IN GROUPS (A, B AND C) AND THE RELATION OF INJURY TO GALL FORMATION (D, E, AND F).

TABLE I.—*Sugar tests of beets affected with crown-gall*—Continued.

Part of beet tested.	Average weight of part tested.	Solids in juice.	Sugar in juice.	Coefficient of purity.	Sugar in part tested.
Experiment 6:	*Ounces.*	*Per cent.*	*Per cent.*	*Per cent.*	*Per cent.*
Galls	3.2	17.46	11.10	63.57	10.40
Crowns	8.0	18.40	14.40	78.26	12.50
Roots	30.4	19.56	16.80	85.88	14.00
Experiment 7:					
Galls	2.4	17.20	9.10	52.90	8.30
Crowns	7.2	18.76	15.40	82.08	13.10
Roots	22.4	17.76	14.80	83.33	13.50
Averages:					
Galls	4.23	16.21	9.05	55.60	6.90
Crowns	12.91	15.29	11.11	72.03	9.87
Roots	29.97	15.41	12.23	78.81	11.06

In preparing the material for the analyses which form the basis of this table badly galled beets were taken in groups of five in order to get a sufficient quantity of juice from the galls to make purity as well as sugar determinations of the galls themselves. After removing the leaves only, the beets were thoroughly washed and weighed. The galls were then carefully removed and the beets again weighed. The crowns were then removed and the roots weighed. The three lots of material from each group of five beets were prepared and put through the test for sugar and purity as quickly as possible after the beets were taken from the ground. A study of Table I shows that the galls are decidedly lower in both sugar and purity than even the crowns. It is evident, therefore, that any considerable number of galls on the beet roots would be decidedly injurious to the sugar recovery in the mill, since the large amount of salts in the galls, as indicated by the low purity coefficient, would keep approximately one and a half times as much sugar from crystallizing. Hence, it would be advisable to remove any galls that are attached to the beets below the crowns at the time of topping the beets.

It might not be out of place in this connection to call attention to the high quality of the crowns in some cases, as shown especially in experiment 7. It is possible that the salts were taken up by the galls to the improvement of the crowns to some extent. On the other hand, it is possible that the quality of the crowns might be greatly improved by proper selection, so that the matter of crown tare would not be such an important factor in handling factory beets as it is at present.

EFFECTS OF GALLS UPON QUALITY AND SIZE OF ROOTS.

In an effort to get some definite information regarding the effect of the galls upon the quality of the roots to which they are attached, a series of comparative tests was made between galled beets and beets free from galls. In selecting the beets for these tests a badly galled beet was taken as soon as it was loosened by means of the plow at harvest time, and for comparison another beet was chosen, free from galls, but as nearly the same size and shape as could be found growing in the same row, close to the galled beet. After selecting in the manner described the 26 pairs of beets which form the basis of Table II, each beet was topped, washed, and the galls carefully removed from the galled beet of each pair. The individual roots were then tested for sugar and purity, with the results shown in Table II.

TABLE II.—*Comparison in sugar content and purity of galled beets with beets not so affected.*

Condition of beets.	Solids in juice.	Sugar in juice.	Coefficient of purity.	Sugar in the beet.
	Per cent.	*Per cent.*	*Per cent.*	*Per cent.*
Test No. 1:				
Galled	13.70	10.00	72.99	8.30
No galls	18.10	13.80	76.24	12.20
Test No. 2:				
Galled	13.90	10.50	75.35	9.20
No galls	18.00	13.80	76.66	12.80
Test No. 3:				
Galled	17.60	14.50	82.38	11.70
No galls	21.92	18.60	84.85	16.80
Test No. 4:				
Galled	15.77	13.20	83.70	11.20
No galls	21.50	18.70	86.97	16.80
Test No. 5:				
Galled	15.70	12.80	81.52	10.90
No galls	20.20	17.10	84.65	16.80
Test No. 6:				
Galled	16.30	13.10	80.36	11.40
No galls	20.20	17.10	84.65	16.80
Test No. 7:				
Galled	16.47	13.20	80.14	11.20
No galls	20.17	16.40	81.30	15.10
Test No. 8:				
Galled	10.85	9.30	85.71	8.50
No galls	18.90	15.60	82.53	14.00
Test No. 9:				
Galled	15.27	12.40	81.20	11.70
No galls	16.77	13.90	82.83	13.40
Test No. 10:				
Galled	16.40	13.80	84.14	13.10
No galls	15.77	12.80	81.16	12.00
Test No. 11:				
Galled	16.23	12.10	74.55	11.20
No galls	22.56	19.10	84.66	18.50
Test No. 12:				
Galled	18.77	14.00	74.58	11.50
No galls	22.99	18.20	79.13	17.30
Test No. 13:				
Galled	18.20	14.80	81.31	14.10
No galls	18.77	15.00	79.91	13.80
Test No. 14:				
Galled	17.60	15.40	87.50	14.30
No galls	19.40	16.40	84.53	16.00
Test No. 15:				
Galled	18.07	14.50	80.24	13.10
No galls	19.50	16.10	82.56	16.00
Test No. 16:				
Galled	18.27	15.10	82.64	14.10
No galls	20.50	16.00	78.04	15.70
Test No. 17:				
Galled	18.60	14.80	79.56	13.10
No galls	22.43	19.00	84.70	18.20
Test No. 18:				
Galled	21.00	17.00	81.42	15.40
No galls	21.30	17.90	84.03	16.80
Test No. 19:				
Galled	22.40	18.90	84.37	17.20
No galls	23.00	19.20	83.47	17.20
Test No. 20:				
Galled	16.92	14.00	82.74	14.00
No galls	14.40	12.10	84.02	11.80

TABLE II.—*Comparison in sugar content and purity of galled beets with beets not so affected*—Continued.

Condition of beets.	Solids in juice.	Sugar in juice.	Coefficient of purity.	Sugar in the beet.
	Per cent.	*Per cent.*	*Per cent.*	*Per cent.*
Test No. 21:				
Galled	18.80	16.50	87.76	16.30
No galls	18.32	15.90	86.79	15.20
Test No. 22:				
Galled	16.42	13.30	80.99	12.60
No galls	16.62	13.90	82.39	12.40
Test No. 23:				
Galled	16.50	13.40	81.21	11.70
No galls	17.72	14.60	82.39	13.90
Test No. 24:				
Galled	18.70	15.30	81.81	14.20
No galls	22.12	18.00	81.37	16.70
Test No. 25:				
Galled	14.87	13.00	87.42	12.20
No galls	22.97	19.30	84.02	17.60
Test No. 26:				
Galled	19.07	15.20	79.70	13.90
No galls	16.07	13.60	84.62	12.50
Average:				
Galled	17.01	13.85	81.35	12.54
No galls	19.66	16.21	82.15	15.18

A study of Table II indicates that gall formations on sugar beets have a tendency to reduce both the sugar content and the purity of the roots. The effect upon the sugar content seems to be more marked than upon the purity. Everyone who has studied the individuality of the sugar beet knows that there is a difference in the sugar content and purity of healthy beets growing side by side in the same row. It is not surprising, therefore, that an occasional pair shows qualities favorable to the galled beets, as in tests Nos. 10 and 21 of Table II. It is safe to say, however, that in the great majority of cases the formation of galls upon the roots of sugar beets has a decidedly injurious effect upon either the purity or the sugar content or upon both these factors of quality in the beet root.

It seems to be practically impossible to obtain any accurate data regarding the effect of galls upon the size of the roots affected. We find the largest as well as the smallest beets more or less seriously infested with galls, as shown in Plate I, *A* to *E*, and it is impossible to know whether the galled beets would have been larger or smaller if they had been free from galls. In some infested areas the larger beets are more generally galled, while in other infested areas the smaller beets are the ones most generally affected; and since the individuality of the beet embraces the size and shape, as well as the quality of the roots, a satisfactory comparison of the weights of the galled and not galled beets has not been practicable in any of the areas that have come under the observation of the writer. So far as one can judge from general field observations, however, the galls do not seem to have any marked effect upon the size of the beets. Consequently the tonnage or yield of beets per acre does not seem to be appreciably affected by the disease except in those cases in which the galls cause the beet roots to decay.

CONTROL OF BEET GALLS.

From our present knowledge of the cause of the crown-gall of beets, combined with the field observations already made upon this disease, its elimination or control becomes comparatively simple. As already suggested, a beet field badly infested with the crown-gall organism may be freed from the pest by growing some other crop in that field for two or more years before returning to sugar beets. It is necessary only that the rotation crops other than beets shall be such as are not readily attacked by the crown-gall organism. In Bulletin No. 213 of the Bureau of Plant Industry, already mentioned, it is pointed out that the crown-gall organism will attack a large number of plants in a great variety of families, but there are plants which are attacked with difficulty, if at all, by this organism. In the test mentioned in this bulletin the crop grown was oats, but it is safe to say that any of the small grains, corn, kafir, milo, or sorghum would do well. If only those crops are grown upon which the organism can not feed and thrive, it must eventually die out and the field be left free from the pest. The elimination of crown-gall is, therefore, a simple matter of wise crop rotation, which as a matter of good farming should be practiced by every farmer regardless of the presence of crown-gall.

SUMMARY.

(1) There are at least two distinct types of sugar-beet galls.

(2) The crown-gall of sugar beets is caused by a bacterium or a number of closely related bacteria.

(3) Sugar-beet galls appear to have an injurious effect upon the quality of the roots.

(4) The galls themselves are low in purity and therefore detrimental in the milling processes.

(5) Sugar-beet galls sometimes cause the beet roots to decay, but, so far as general field observations can determine, they do not appear otherwise to affect the tonnage.

(6) This disease may be held in check by a proper system of crop rotation with grain-producing plants.

ADDITIONAL COPIES
OF THIS PUBLICATION MAY BE PROCURED FROM
THE SUPERINTENDENT OF DOCUMENTS
GOVERNMENT PRINTING OFFICE
WASHINGTON, D. C.
AT
5 CENTS PER COPY
▽

WASHINGTON : GOVERNMENT PRINTING OFFICE : 1915

BULLETIN OF THE
U.S. DEPARTMENT OF AGRICULTURE

No. 204

Contribution from the Bureau of Entomology, L. O. Howard, Chief,
May 21, 1915.

REPORT ON THE GIPSY MOTH WORK IN NEW ENGLAND.[1]

By A. F. Burgess,
In Charge of Gipsy Moth and Brown-Tail Moth Work.

INTRODUCTION.

On March 1, 1913, the gipsy-moth work conducted by the Bureau of Entomology, U. S. Department of Agriculture, was reorganized, and the writer was placed in charge under the direction of the chief of the bureau.

The object of this Federal work is to use every measure possible to prevent the spread of the gipsy moth and the brown-tail moth[2] to uninfested parts of the United States.

The main office, which is maintained at 43 Tremont Street, Boston, Mass., furnishes quarters for the men in charge of the main projects and the necessary clerical force. The Gipsy Moth Laboratory, which serves as headquarters for the experimental work, is located at Melrose Highlands, Mass., although one branch of this work is conducted at the Bussey Institution at Forest Hills, Mass. During the past two years a summer laboratory has been maintained for special experiments at Worcester, Mass. A storehouse is located at Melrose Highlands, Mass., where the necessary tools and equipment are stored and repaired.

The work is divided into two distinct lines: (1) Field work, consisting of scouting, and applying hand methods for controlling these insects, as well as a thorough inspection of the plant products shipped from the infested area, and (2) experimental work, which includes the introduction of parasites and natural enemies, together with careful studies of the food plants and other factors, in order to devise more efficient and effective methods of control, as well as an investigation of the relation of silviculture to the gipsy-moth problem. A

[1] This publication is prepared to show the different lines of work which are being taken up and the results that have been secured.

[2] The life history, habits, and methods for controlling these insects have been published in Farmers' Bulletin 564, U. S. Department of Agriculture.

general outline of the problems and investigations and the different activities of the work has already been published[1] in the Journal of Economic Entomology.

During the fiscal year which ended June 30, 1914, an average of 275 men was employed. The greater number were engaged in field operations, but a force of approximately 40 men were employed on different phases of experimental projects.

EXPERIMENTAL WORK.

In carrying on measures for the control of any insect pest it is necessary to conduct many experiments in order to determine the means which are most feasible for reducing the damage. For more than 20 years experiments have been carried on more or less continuously by the State of Massachusetts and other States to which the gipsy moth has spread, as well as by the Bureau of Entomology, for the purpose of perfecting field measures for holding the insect in check, and from time to time improvements have been made which have reduced the cost of handling infested areas. Spraying machinery has been developed so that at the present time it is entirely practical to treat large areas at a moderate cost. The banding of trees with tanglefoot has largely replaced the use of burlap bands and reduced the cost of this method of treatment. In fact, so much work has been done along these lines that the best methods of treatment are well understood and practiced in the areas where the gipsy moth is prevalent. Minor improvements are being made from time to time but in general satisfactory methods of hand suppression have been adopted.

In 1905, when the Federal gipsy-moth work was being organized, it was considered very necessary and desirable to introduce the parasites and natural enemies which occur in foreign countries of both the gipsy moth (*Porthetria dispar* L.) (Pl. I) and the brown-tail moth (*Euproctis chrysorrhoea* L.) (Pl. II). The idea was prevalent that by securing and liberating these natural checks on the increase of these species, it would be possible greatly to reduce the damage, and it was hoped that the parasites would bring the pests as well under control as is the case in Europe. Accordingly arrangements were made by Dr. L. O. Howard, Chief of the Bureau of Entomology, for the collection of a large amount of parasitic material in various European countries, and later similar arrangements were made with entomologists in Japan. This work was carried on for the first five years in cooperation with the State of Massachusetts. Several agents of the Bureau of Entomology have been sent to Europe on different occasions to investigate conditions and forward to this country as large an amount of parasitized material as could be collected. For two seasons this work was conducted by Mr. W. F. Fiske, who was assisted in the summer of 1912 by Mr. L. H. Worthley. Various

[1] Jour. Econ. Ent., v. 7, No. 1, p. 83-87, Feb., 1914.

assistants and collectors were engaged to obtain parasitized material which was forwarded to the Gipsy Moth Laboratory at Melrose Highlands, Mass. After the completion of the foreign work in 1912, it appeared that not only were the parasites, and a contagious disease known as the "wilt," prime factors in controlling the gipsy moth in Europe, but in addition to these a pronounced obstacle to the increase of the pest arose from the fact that forest conditions, particularly in Germany, furnished in the main unfavorable food for the caterpillars. The observations indicated that this factor, in addition to the natural enemies already mentioned, was responsible for rendering the gipsy moth of slight importance to forest growth except at periodic intervals.

In 1912 a number of areas were under observation by Mr. Worthley in the forests of Germany, and at that time the infestation was severe. Deciduous trees in these areas were defoliated and in some cases many trees completely denuded of foliage. Similar studies were made by Mr. Fiske in Italy, where a few infestations were found which were more serious, if possible, than those observed in the German forests. During the summer of 1913 no agent of the bureau was engaged in making foreign observations on the gipsy moth. It seemed best in the spring of 1914 to have the areas in Germany revisited for the purpose of determining the result of the previous infestations and to secure data on the increase or the decrease of the species. Accordingly, early in the spring of that year, Dr. John N. Summers, who for a number of years had been in general charge of the parasite work at the Melrose Highlands Laboratory, was detailed to visit the areas mentioned and to secure all the data possible on the fluctuations of the gipsy moth, as well as to obtain parasitic material for shipment to this country, in case it could be found in collectible quantities. The result of this work has been reported by Dr. Summers, and it appears that in no place in Germany where the insect was reported in 1912 was there a severe or even moderate infestation in 1914. It was impossible, therefore, to obtain parasitized material, and in most cases the insect was so rare that little data beyond the mere fact that it still existed in the areas could be secured.

About the middle of June a report was received that a heavy infestation of the gipsy moth occurred in the Province of Bereg, Hungary. This information was received from Dr. Josef Jablonowski, and Dr. Summers was instructed to take up his investigations in that region. Unfortunately it was impossible for him to arrive in the infested forest until after the feeding of the caterpillars was finished and most of the eggs for the new brood of moths had been laid. Parasites were not present to any marked extent at this time, which was not surprising, owing to the fact that the observations were made too late in the season. Some evidence was secured that the wilt disease was present in the area, but a fairly good increase of the species was noted except at points where the trees had been completely denuded and where the caterpillars had died from starvation or had moved to adjoining tree growth in search of food. Dr. Summers estimates that not less than 5,000 acres were almost completely defoliated in the forests in Hungary where he made his observations. The growth consisted entirely of hardwoods; the oak predominating, and a species of Carpinus, beech, and maple occurring in the order mentioned. A few elm trees were also present.

The results of the European investigations carried on during the past few years, aside from furnishing a good supply of parasitic species, has proved beyond question that as far as the forests are concerned the character of the growth is of prime importance from a gipsy-moth point of view. Coniferous forests predominate in Germany, and these are not injured by the gipsy moth. The deciduous forests in that country are not large, and the injury is periodical and severe. In Hungary large deciduous forests are present and the infestation is more or less common from year to year. Severe defoliation usually continues for about three years before a marked decrease of the moth is observed, and then a few years pass before another outbreak is noticed. This information, with certain data which have been collected in this country for the past few years relative to the increase or decrease of the gipsy moth under New England forest conditions, together with a careful study of the feeding habits of the gipsy-moth caterpillar in all its stages on the various species of tree growth, and the beneficial influence which is being felt to a greater extent each year as a result of the increase of the parasites and natural enemies of the moth and the severity of the wilt disease, all point the way to more effective methods of handling the gipsy-moth problem.

The different phases of the experimental work, as it is being carried on, will be touched upon briefly in order to indicate the changed conditions which are being brought about in the infested area in New England.

PARASITE WORK.

As has already been stated, the first attempts to introduce the parasites and natural enemies of the gipsy moth and brown-tail moth were begun in 1905. In all more than 30 enemies of these insects, which are present to a greater or less extent in their native homes, have been introduced into New England. More than half of the species have been received in sufficient numbers so that colonies could be liberated under field conditions, and they have had an opportunity to demonstrate their ability to withstand climatic conditions and to become established in this country. As should be expected, a large number of the species have failed to survive. A few have been recovered from year to year, showing that while they have the ability to maintain themselves, they have not yet been able to increase to a sufficient extent to become a useful factor in controlling their hosts. A few species have become established and are increasing satisfactorily. In fact, some of them are making sufficient headway so that they have already become a very appreciable

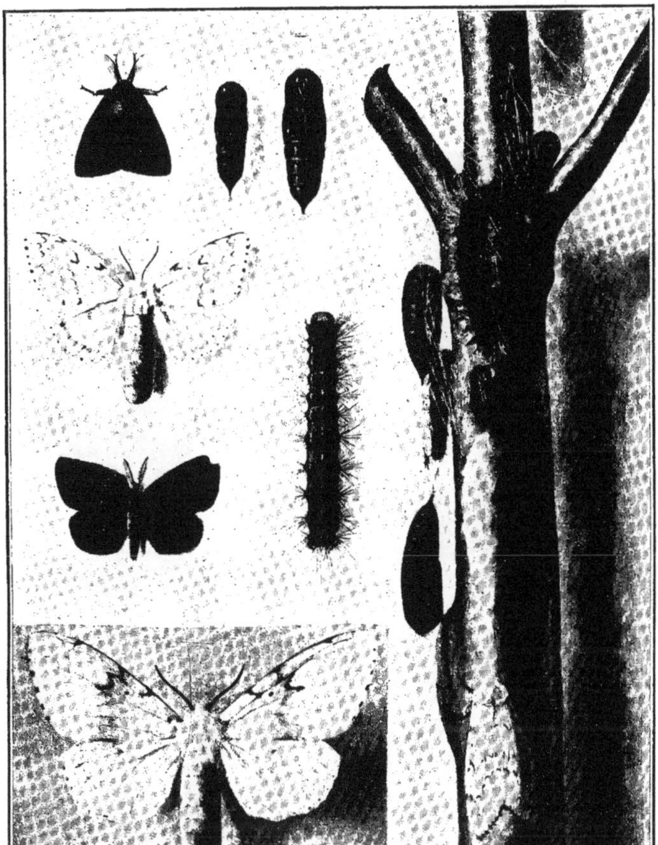

THE GIPSY MOTH (PORTHETRIA DISPAR).

Upper left, male moth with wings folded; just below this, female moth with wings spread; just below this, male moth with wings spread; lower left, female moth, enlarged; top center, male pupa at left, female pupa at right; center, larva; on branch, at top, newly formed pupa; on branch; just below this, larva ready to pupate; on branch, left side, pupæ; on branch, center, egg cluster, on branch, at bottom, female moth depositing egg cluster. All slightly reduced except figure at lower left. (From Howard and Fiske.)

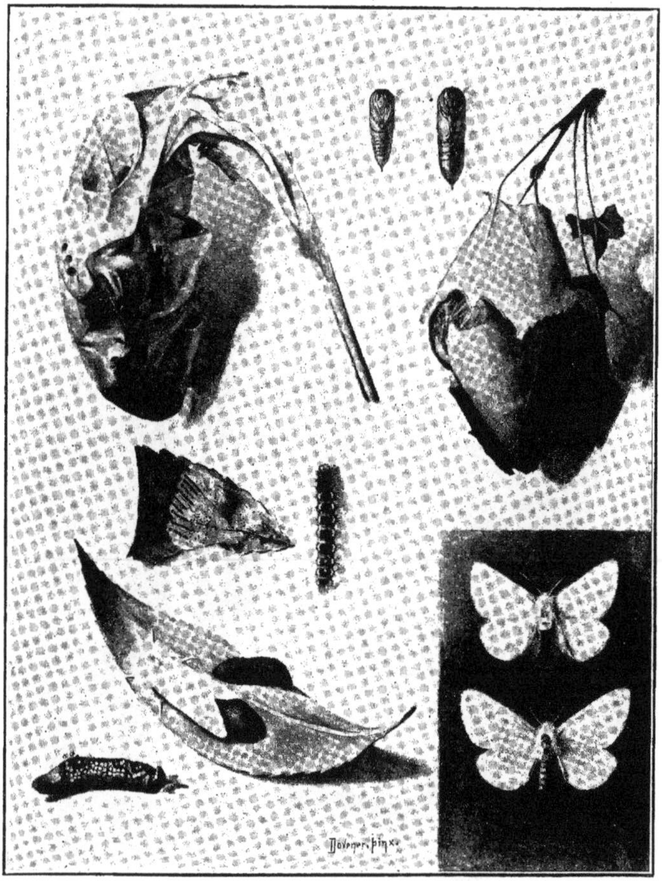

THE BROWN-TAIL MOTH (EUPROCTIS CHRYSORRHOEA).

Upper left, hibernating web; just below this, small larvæ feeding at left, larger larva at right; just below this, female moth depositing eggs at left, egg mass at right; lower left, egg mass with eggs exposed; top center, male pupa at left, female pupa at right; upper right, cocoon incased in leaves; lower right, male moth above, female moth below. All slightly reduced. (From Howard and Fiske.)

factor in reducing the infestation of the gipsy moth even under our adverse food-plant conditions. The most valuable species will be mentioned briefly in order to give an idea of their habits.

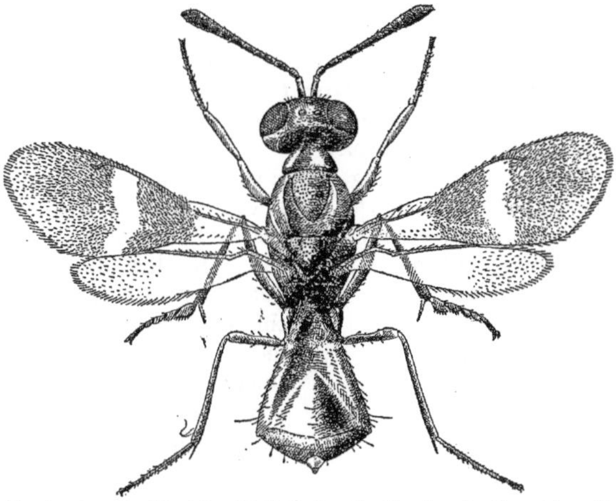

FIG. 1.—*Anastatus bifasciatus:* Adult female. Greatly enlarged. (From Howard.)

Two species of minute hymenopterous parasites which attack the eggs of the gipsy moth have become established in New England. One, *Anastatus bifasciatus* Fonsc. (fig. 1), occurs in Europe and Japan, and although only one brood of this insect is reproduced each

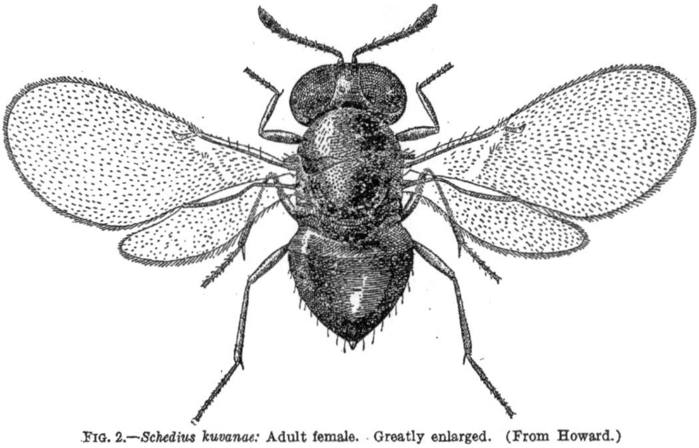

FIG. 2.—*Schedius kuvanae:* Adult female. Greatly enlarged. (From Howard.)

season, it has succeeded in maintaining itself and increasing in practically every locality in which it has been liberated. The other species, *Schedius kuvanae* How. (fig. 2), was imported from Japan.

A brood of this species develops under favorable weather conditions in about four weeks. The first brood appears in August and the insect continues to breed until cold weather sets in. Owing to the fact that several broods develop in a single season, the insect increases very rapidly. It can be reared in the laboratory for the purpose of colonization, and this work is being done each year. Unfortunately the insect does not always survive the winter in good condition, so that its occurrence in the colonies where it is liberated is by no means as uniform as that of Anastatus.

Apanteles lacteicolor Vier. (fig. 3) is a small hymenopterous parasite which deposits its eggs in the small caterpillars of the brown-tail moth in August. The eggs of the parasite hatch in the body of the small caterpillar, but development is very slow during the fall. Caterpillars that are attacked in this way feed and enter the hibernating web with their more fortunate comrades. They pass the winter and emerge with the others early in the spring. As soon as they have become active and begin feeding the Apanteles larva also begins feeding and by the time the caterpillar is about one-fourth of an inch long this internal parasite has become large enough to destroy it. The Apanteles larva then makes its way from the body of the caterpillar, forms a cocoon (Pl. III, fig. 1), and early in June the adult parasite emerges. This is the time of year when small caterpillars of the gipsy moth are feeding, and the parasites attack these caterpillars and pass through one generation with the gipsy moth as a host.

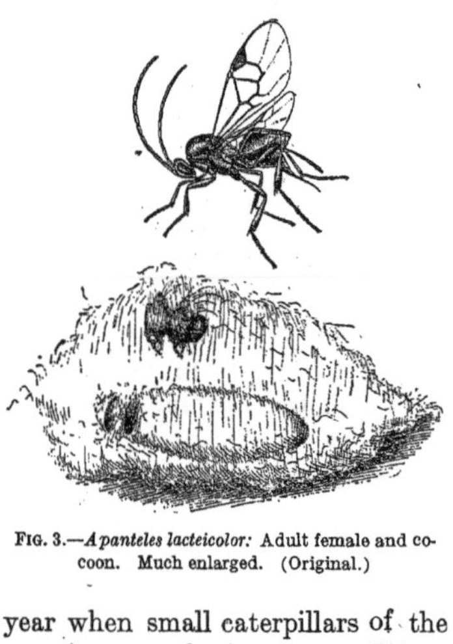

FIG. 3.—*Apanteles lacteicolor:* Adult female and cocoon. Much enlarged. (Original.)

Another species which attacks both the gipsy and brown-tail moth caterpillars is a parasitic fly known as *Compsilura concinnata* Meig. (Pl. III, fig. 2). This insect is about the size of the house fly, although its habits are strictly those of a caterpillar parasite. Early in the spring the female fly deposits a small maggot in the body of the larva of the brown-tail moth which feeds inside the body of the caterpillar and becomes full-grown early in June. At this time the maggot burrows through the epidermis of the host and forms a puparium from which, in about a week, the adult fly emerges. This brood attacks the gipsy-moth caterpillars, the adult flies emerging early in July. One or more broods may follow before cold weather in case native larvæ are at hand to serve as hosts.

A species of Apanteles (*A. melanoscelis* Ratz.), which was received in small numbers from Italy in the summer of 1912, was liberated near the laboratory at Melrose Highlands, Mass. It is double-brooded, both generations being passed on gipsy-moth caterpillars. This species has maintained itself since its introduction and promises to be a most valuable addition to the enemies of the gipsy moth. It has not been imported or recovered in sufficient numbers from the colony liberated in this country so that other colonies could be established, but is considered a very valuable species.

The Calosoma beetle (*C. sycophanta* L.) (Pl. IV), while not strictly a parasite, is at the present time doing more effective work against the gipsy moth than any single introduced species. This large green beetle hibernates in the ground during the winter and emerges about the first of June. It feeds on the caterpillars and pupæ of the gipsy moth and brown-tail moth, as well as on such native species as it may find. These beetles climb trees and are continuously searching for food. They live two or three years and after midsummer burrow into the ground where they remain during the winter. On the average, 100 eggs are deposited in the ground annually by each female. The beetle larvæ hatch in about a week. They are proficient tree climbers and feed constantly on the caterpillars and pupæ of the gipsy moth or other insects until they become full grown about the middle of July. This species has increased and spread in a most satisfactory manner, and has made great inroads on the gipsy moth in many localities. Both the beetles and the larvæ attack the caterpillars of the brown-tail moth, so that double benefit results.

Another parasite, one which attacks the brown-tail moth only, is a hymenopteron known as *Meteorus versicolor* Wesm. It has become well established, but is seldom found in great numbers. It is possible that this species may increase rapidly later on, but at the present time it does not appear to be as beneficial as those that have previously been mentioned. Several species of introduced tachinid flies are recovered occasionally, but in such small numbers as to indicate that they are not at the present time doing effective work.

An enormous amount of careful study and a large number of detailed experiments have been carried on in order to determine the life histories, habits, and utility of the different species which have been introduced. It has been necessary from time to time to develop new methods of handling these species in order to get the data desired, and practically all the equipment and breeding devices used at the laboratory are of original design and have been constructed for the purpose of furthering the gipsy-moth investigations. Much valuable information of a biological nature has been secured which is not only of direct value to the parasite phase of the gipsy-moth work but has been found useful in connection with insect problems in various parts of the country.

RECENT COLONIZATIONS AND RECOVERY OF IMPORTED PARASITES.

During the past two or three years careful investigations have been carried on to determine the increase and spread of the different parasites. In the summer of 1914 this work was in charge of Mr. S. S. Crossman. As large a number as possible of the different species have been liberated in the remote parts of the infested area for the purpose of securing the establishment of these valuable species over the entire territory at the earliest possible date. In the fall of 1913 *Anastatus bifasciatus* was recovered from 41 towns and the parasitism in the collections secured averaged about 30 per cent. From one collection over 43 per cent of the eggs had been destroyed by this insect. As a result of the collection made during the winter, 1,561 colonies of this species, totaling 1,561,000 specimens, were liberated; 1,047 of the colonies were placed in 12 towns in Massachusetts and 514 in three towns in New Hampshire. This insect spreads very slowly, hence it is necessary to liberate many colonies. The plan which is being used is to place a sufficient number of colonies in a town so that no further colonization in that town will be necessary. The work on this insect required the collection in the fall of 1913 of about 7,500 gipsy-moth egg clusters and these were secured from over 100 selected localities.

In the fall of 1913, 33 towns were colonized with *Schedius kuvanae*. The number of colonies placed in a town varied from 1 to 10, depending on the gipsy-moth infestations. Most of the colonies were liberated in the southern part of the infested territory in Massachusetts, as it was believed that this section would be favorable for the survival of the species during the winter. In all 110 colonies were liberated, containing over 375,000 individuals. This species spreads more rapidly than Anastatus, so it is not necessary to place as many colonies in a given area. Over 14,000 gipsy-moth egg clusters were collected from about 100 selected localities within the area bounded by Exeter, N. H., and Berlin, Bolton, and Mashpee, Mass. This material was used at the laboratory to secure records of the percentage of parasitism in colonies that had been liberated in previous years.

The spring of 1913 was very favorable for *Apanteles lacteicolor*, and it was recovered from 69 towns. This was the result of collections of 92,000 brown-tail moth webs, a supply coming from every one of

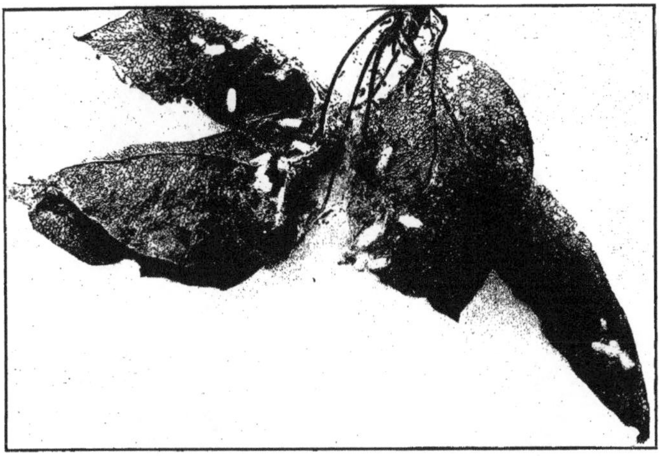

FIG. 1.—COCOONS OF APANTELES LACTEICOLOR IN MOLTING WEB OF THE BROWN-TAIL MOTH. (ORIGINAL.)

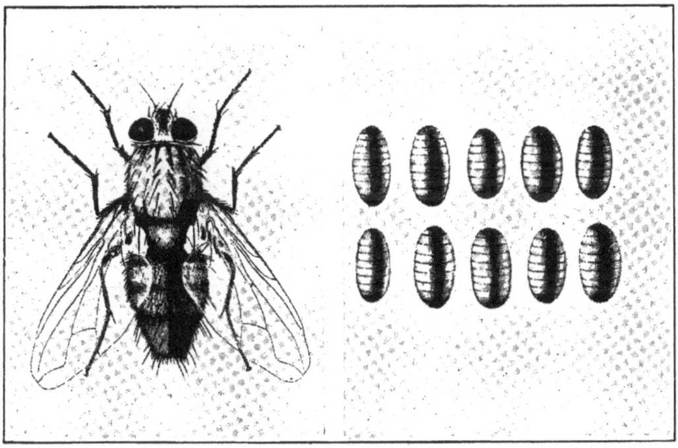

FIG. 2.—THE COMPSILURA FLY (COMPSILURA CONCINNATA): ADULT FLY, MUCH ENLARGED, AT LEFT; PUPARIA, ENLARGED, AT RIGHT. (ORIGINAL.)

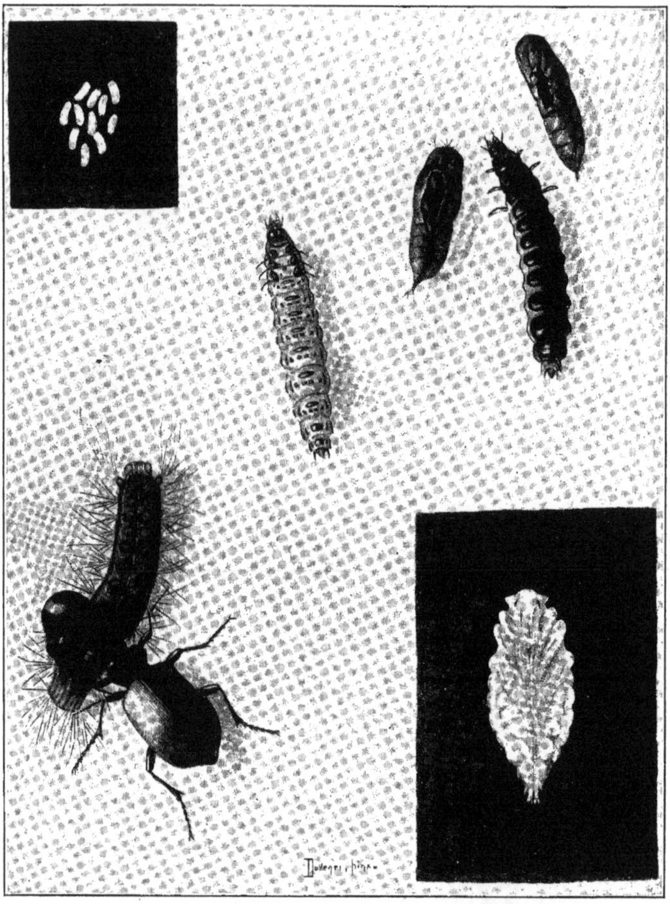

THE CALOSOMA BEETLE (CALOSOMA SYCOPHANTA).

Upper left, eggs; lower left, adult beetle feeding on gipsy moth caterpillar; upper right, gipsy moth pupæ destroyed by Calosoma larvæ; center, Calosoma larva, ventral view; right center, Calosoma larva, dorsal view; lower right, Calosoma pupa in cavity in ground. (From Howard and Fiske.)

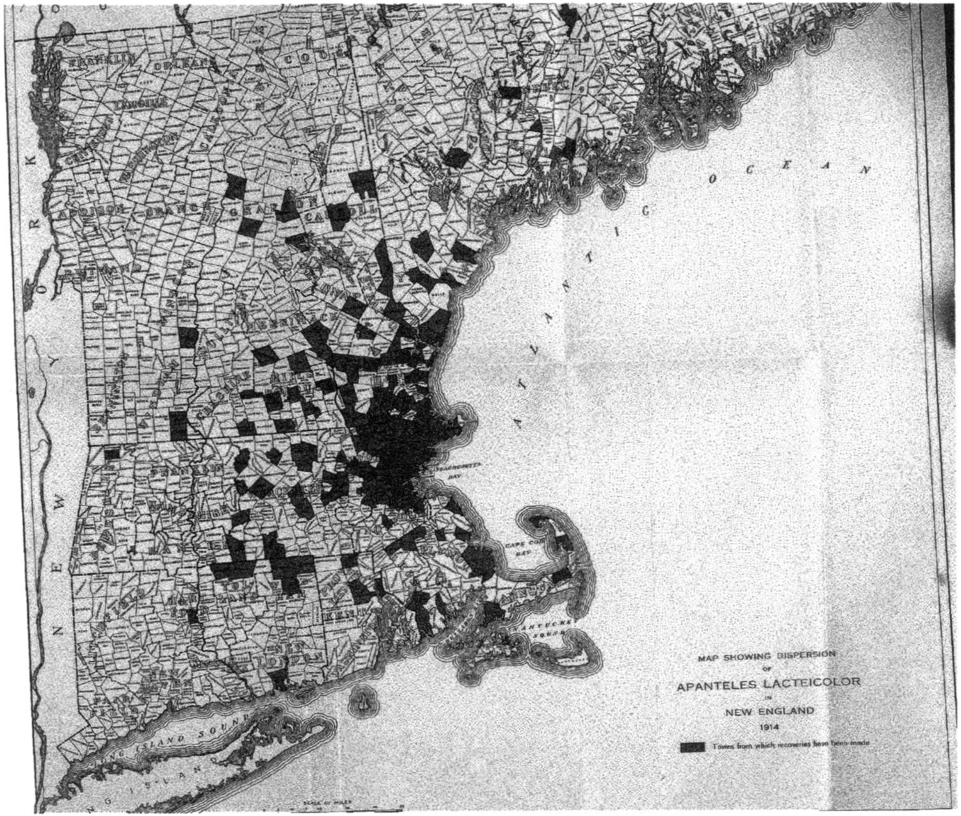
NEW YORK
ATLANTIC OCEAN
LONG ISLAND SOUND
LONG ISLAND
MAP SHOWING DISPERSION
OF
APANTELES LACTEICOLOR
IN
NEW ENGLAND
1914
Towns from which recoveries have been made

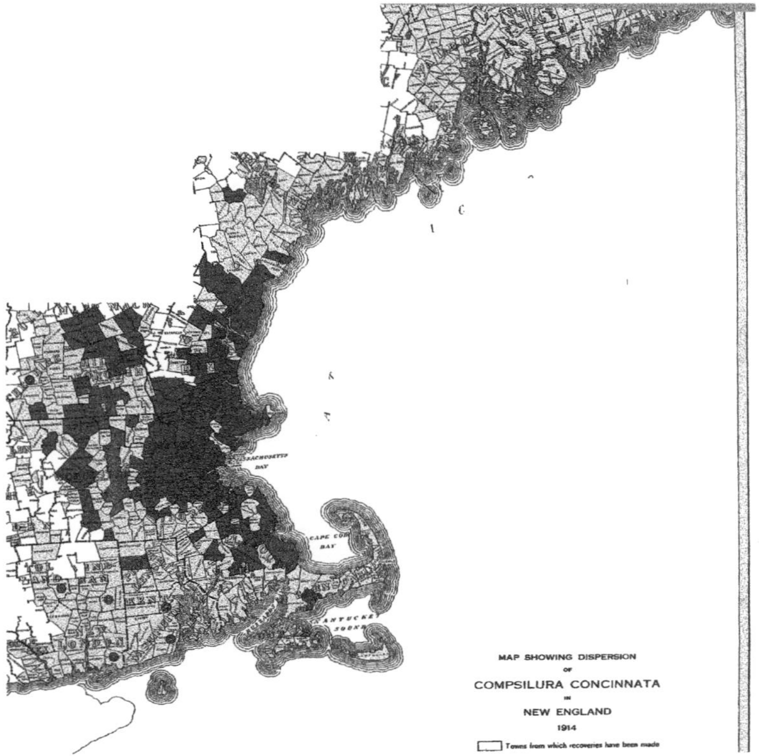
MAP SHOWING DISPERSION
OF
COMPSILURA CONCINNATA
IN
NEW ENGLAND
1914
Towns from which recoveries have been made

the New England States. Fifty-six colonies were liberated in 48 towns, a total of over 76,000 cocoons being placed in the field. During the winter of 1913–14 collections of brown-tail moth webs were made in 72 towns scattered over the infested area in New England. The recovery of the parasite indicates that it has become established as far north as Monson, Me.; west as far as North Adams, Mass.; and south as far as Waterford, Conn. About 2,500 cocoons were liberated in the spring of 1914 in three of the Connecticut Valley towns in Vermont. Our work on this species was supplemented by cooperative work which was carried on by Prof. W. C. O'Kane, State entomologist of New Hampshire. From collections made by his assistants he was able to colonize Apanteles in 11 towns, 1,000 specimens being put in most of these colonies. Similar work is carried on in cooperation with the gipsy-moth laboratory by Maj. E. E. Philbrook, State moth superintendent of Maine, but a definite statement of the number of colonies liberated can not be given at this time. An arrangement was made during the fall of 1913 to continue cooperative parasite work between the laboratory and the entomologist of the Dominion of Canada, Dr. C. Gordon Hewitt. In the spring of 1914 he detailed one of his assistants, Mr. L. S. McLaine, to take up work in Massachusetts, using the gipsy moth laboratory as headquarters. Mr. McLaine secured several assistants, and as a result of his efforts about 1,000 Apanteles cocoons were sent to the brown-tail moth infested area in New Brunswick for the purpose of colonizing the species. Similar efforts were made the previous year and colonies were liberated in New Brunswick and Nova Scotia, and in several of these places the species survived the winter of 1913. (Pl. V.) In general it should be said that the winter of 1913–14 resulted in a marked decrease in the abundance of Apanteles. An unusually high mortality of caterpillars in the brown-tail webs accounts for this decrease. The exact cause of the mortality of the brown-tail moth caterpillars can not be definitely stated, but it seems to be attributable to an unusually severe winter, the presence to a greater or less extent of internal parasites in the caterpillars, and the effects of the brown-tail fungus, a disease which also affects the larvæ of this species.

The parasitism of the gipsy moth by *Apanteles lacteicolor* was not nearly as high in 1914 as during the previous year, and was of course a direct result of the failure of the brown-tail moth caterpillars to bring through the first generation of the parasite.

During the summer of 1913 *Compsilura concinnata* was recovered from 54 new towns. Eleven of these were in Maine, 14 in New Hampshire, and 29 in Massachusetts. In the summer of 1914 this insect was found in 44 new towns—2 in Maine, 21 in New Hampshire, 20 in Massachusetts, and 1 in Rhode Island. It is possible that

Compsilura is present in more localities in Maine, but we have been unable to secure definite records to that effect. The following table is interesting, as it shows the general rate of dispersion of this parasite. The spread recorded is based on distance from Melrose Highlands, Mass., and is mostly due to natural spread, although a few small colonies have been liberated outside of the area where the species was known to occur in 1913.

TABLE I.—*Dispersion of Compsilura concinnata. Distance recovered from Melrose Highlands, Mass.*

	1913	1914
From Melrose Highlands:	*Miles.*	*Miles.*
North	75	100
Northeast	100	130
South	50	50
Southwest	40	55
West	50	65
Northwest	70	80

It is undoubtedly true that this species is now present over an area which would be represented by connecting the points indicated by the directions and distances given in the table for 1914. (Pl. VI.) Four thousand five hundred and sixty-five Compsilura were liberated in 10 new towns in 1913 and 10,000 were placed in 21 new towns in 1914, as follows: Eight in New Hampshire, 5 in Vermont, 2 in Massachusetts, 2 in Rhode Island, 3 in Connecticut, and 1 colony was forwarded to a substation of the Bureau of Entomology at Koehler, N. Mex., in order to test the value of this species as an enemy of the range caterpillar (*Hemileuca oliviae* Ckll.), an insect which is causing enormous damage to the grazing lands in that State. In addition to the number of specimens of this species colonized in 1914, about 5,000 were secured by Mr. McLaine and shipped to New Brunswick; about 3,000 were secured by Mr. R. S. Ferguson, assistant in the moth department of the State of Maine, who, with several assistants, were collecting for the purpose of establishing colonies in that State, and over 2,500 were collected and colonized by Prof. O'Kane's assistants in New Hampshire.

Three hundred and sixty-five sample collections of gipsy-moth larvæ which were secured during the summer of 1914 from scattered localities in Maine, New Hampshire, Massachusetts, and Rhode Island, consisted of over 99,000 caterpillars. This material required the use of over 500 rearing trays at the laboratory and the constant attention of several assistants to feed the larvæ in each tray and record the parasitism, mortality, and other data.

Based on 25 collections of gipsy-moth larvæ taken at widely scattered points in the gipsy-moth-infested area and aggregating 46,000 specimens, an average of 20 per cent of parasitism by Compsilura was found to exist. Several large single colonies showed a degree of parasitism ranging from 40 to 50 per cent. The results secured with this species during the summer of 1914, based on the number of parasites obtained from the collections, indicate that the distribution of this insect is more likely to be local than general, since in areas where it was abundant in the summer of 1913 it was recovered in very small numbers in 1914, in spite of the fact that a moderate infestation was present during the latter year.

Apanteles melanoscelis, a species already referred to, is showing considerable promise. As high as 19 per cent of the second stage gipsy moth larvæ collected at Melrose Highlands during the summer of 1914 were parasitized. This species was recovered from two new towns this year, namely, Stoneham and Saugus.

Considerable additional data have been secured from other imported parasites which have been colonized in this country and have survived in more or less numbers. The details are not given, however, inasmuch as it has not been demonstrated thus far that they are of particular value as parasites of either the gipsy moth or the brown-tail moth.

Pteromalus egregius Först. has been recovered in small numbers from many parts of the territory infested by the brown-tail moth. The larva of this insect works as an external parasite of the small brown-tail moth caterpillars in the webs. *Monodontomerus aereus* Walk., a parasite of gipsy and brown-tail moth pupæ, is known to occur throughout most of the area infested by these insects. It has been reared in small numbers from tachinid puparia and undoubtedly has other unrecorded hosts.

Calosoma sycophanta has been found during the summer of 1914 over a much wider area than that previously recorded (Pl. VII). Owing to the ease with which the beetles and their larvæ could be collected in the field it has been possible to liberate 37 colonies in New Hampshire, Massachusetts, Rhode Island, and Connecticut. These were placed outside the area where the species was previously known to occur. In addition, colonies of Calosoma have been liberated in Maine and New Hampshire by State officials. Colonies have been liberated in New Brunswick, Nova Scotia, and Quebec as a result of collections made by Mr. McLaine and his assistants, and 1,700 specimens were collected by Mr. H. E. Smith and forwarded to Koehler, N. Mex., to test their value as an enemy of the range caterpillar.[1]

[1] This work was carried on by arrangement with Mr. F. M. Webster, who is in charge of the Cereal and Forage Crop Insect Investigations of the Bureau of Entomology.

As a result of the Calosoma scouting work carried on during July and August, 1914, it has been found that this species exists in 18 towns in Maine, 93 in New Hampshire, 170 in Massachusetts, 3 in Rhode Island, and 2 in Connecticut. Data concerning this insect obtained during the present year indicate that the species is able to maintain itself in considerable numbers in areas where the gipsy-moth infestation is slight and that as a rule the species continues to be abundant after it once becomes established in a locality. Owing to the well-known habits of the beetles in migrating considerable distances, it was thought that territory with light infestation would be deserted in favor of areas where caterpillars occurred in abundance. This does not prove to be the case and it is another feature which increases the value of this beneficial insect.

The table below shows the colonization of the principal parasites during 1913 and 1914:

TABLE II.—*Colonization of natural enemies in 1913 and 1914.*

Species.	Number of colonies liberated.		Number of individuals liberated.		Towns where colonies were placed.	
	1913	1914	1913	1914	1913	1914
Anastatus bifasciatus[1]	1,500	1,561	1,500,000	1,561,000	[2] 42	15
Schedius kuvanae	110	502	352,000	2,083,254	33	111
Apanteles lacteicolor[1]	56	14	76,000	13,119	48	14
Compsilura concinnata[1]	10	28	4,565	23,638	10	26
Calosoma sycophanta[1]	45	49	6,175	8,104	42	38

[1] A part of the collections and colonization were made by cooperative arrangements with the State officials of Maine and New Hampshire, with the Dominion Entomologist of Canada, and with Mr. F. M. Webster of this bureau.
[2] In many of these towns only a few colonies were liberated.

The results of the work accomplished by introduced parasites of the gipsy moth during the past year have been excellent. It is true that the increase of *Apanteles lacteicolor* has been seriously retarded but the other species have given a good account of themselves. The fact that Compsilura and Calosoma are becoming established in the remote parts of the area infested with the gipsy moth and are able to maintain themselves under these conditions is very encouraging, as the work of these species will tend to reduce the infestation and be an important factor in preventing the spread along the outside border.

WILT-DISEASE INVESTIGATIONS.

In connection with the parasite work and having a distinct influence on the increase of the gipsy moth in the field, an elaborate series of experiments has been conducted by Mr. R. W. Glaser and several assistants for the purpose of securing information on the identity of the wilt disease (Pl. VIII) and the factors which are favorable to its increase in the field.

MAP SHOWING DISPERSION
OF
CALOSOMA SYCOPHANTA
IN
NEW ENGLAND
1914

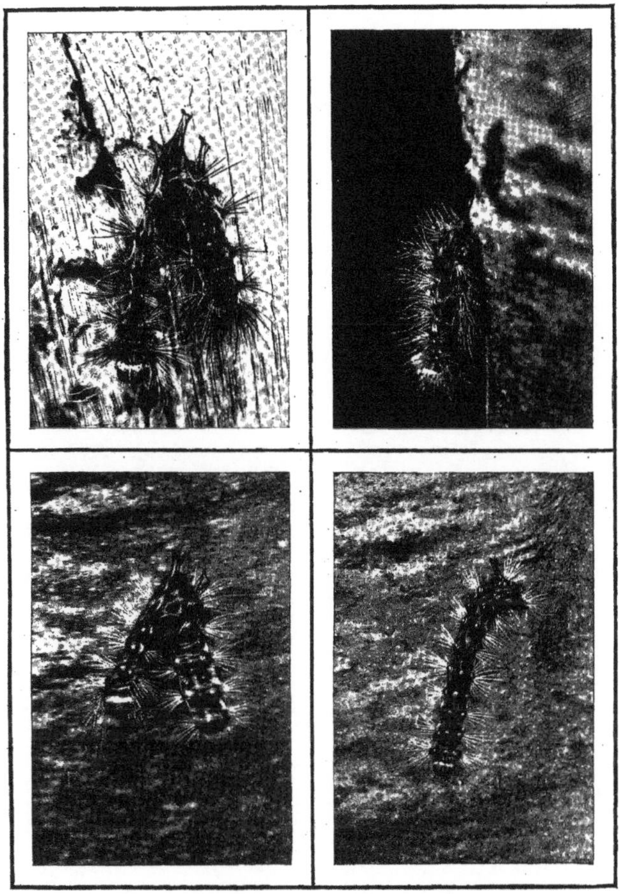

THE WILT DISEASE OF THE GIPSY MOTH. (ORIGINAL.)

Note the typical way in which these caterpillars hang when affected by this disease.

This work has been carried on at the Bussey Institution, Forest Hills, Mass., and a sublaboratory in charge of Mr. J. J. Culver has been maintained during the summer at Worcester, Mass., where special experiments have been conducted to determine the relation of favorable and unfavorable food plants to the development of the disease. A series of field experiments was also conducted in a selected area at Lunenburg, Mass., by Mr. A. W. Young and Mr. R. T. Webber, who made continuous observations in a limited area on the development of the disease under field conditions, with particular reference to the relation of temperature and humidity. Several other points were selected in Massachusetts where continuous temperature and humidity records were secured, as well as at the Lunenburg area, and a careful compilation of this data is expected to give information as to the weather conditions which are most favorable for the development of this disease.

For a number of years the wilt disease has been found in the field in nearly all places where heavy gipsy-moth infestation exists. During the last year or two it has occurred in light infestations and very few localities in the infested area are known where it is not found to a greater or less extent.

The results of the season's work indicate that the disease has been slightly less prevalent during the past summer than the previous year and this was particularly true during June and the first part of July. Cool weather prevailed at this time. Late in July the large caterpillars in many places were seriously affected, so that the increase of the gipsy moth was not as great as was anticipated early in the season.

The technical studies on the wilt disease are very difficult to conduct because it is almost impossible to secure healthy material for experimental purposes. The organism is believed to be a filterable virus and is so minute that it easily passes through the finest bacteriological filters that have yet been devised. It belongs to the same class of organism as yellow fever and a number of other contagious diseases, although all of these were, at one time, supposed to be caused by bacteria. The period when gipsy-moth caterpillars of moderate size are available for experiments covers about six weeks, and this adds to the difficulty of carrying on investigations on account of the limited time when material can be secured. During the past year it has been determined that the wilt disease, or a similar organism, affects eight of our common native caterpillars in addition to the gipsy moth. It is also known to attack the silkworm (*Sericaria mori* L.) and nun moth (*Porthetria monacha* L.), a fairly common European species which is very destructive to pine. Good results have been secured this year, but a large amount of work is necessary in order to establish the essential facts concerning the identity of the organism and the conditions most favorable for its increase and development.

FOOD-PLANT INVESTIGATIONS.

As has already been pointed out, the species of tree growth have an important relation to the ability of the gipsy moth to increase and cause serious damage in the field. Nearly 20 years ago food-plant experiments were conducted in this country to determine the species upon which the gipsy moth would subsist, and a long list of food plants was published by Forbush and Fernald in their excellent book on the gipsy moth. Most of these experiments, however, were carried on by using large caterpillars and feeding them in jars or cages in the laboratory. At that time it did not seem important to determine whether there was variation in the feeding habits of the caterpillars in different stages. As early as 1908 it was observed and proven by an extensive field experiment that the first-stage caterpillars of the gipsy moth could not develop on white pine in the absence of other food. This naturally led to the question of unfavorability of other species to gipsy moth attack. In 1912 a careful series of food-plant experiments was begun. Mr. F. H. Mosher took charge of this work and has been furnished with a number of assistants during the feeding season. The feeding was carried on in individual trays, which were specially constructed for the purpose. One hundred first-stage caterpillars were placed upon a branch of foliage in each tray. In this way the feeding habits could be observed, the foliage renewed daily, and it was possible to determine which food plants were least subject to attack under laboratory conditions. Similar experiments were carried on with caterpillars in the succeeding stages. This work was continued in the summers of 1913 and 1914, so that up to the present time about 250 species of trees and shrubs have been tested.

As a result of these experiments some of the more common species are rated as follows:

I.—Species favored by the gipsy-moth larvæ in all stages:

Alder, speckled.[1]	Oak, black.
Ash, mountain.[1]	Oak, chestnut.
Aspen.[1]	Oak, post.[1]
Balm of Gilead.[1]	Oak, red.
Basswood.	Oak, scarlet.
Beech.	Oak, swamp white.
Birch, gray.[1]	Oak, white.
Birch, paper.	Poplar, big toothed.[1]
Birch, red.[1]	Shadbush.[1]
Boxelder.[1]	Willow.[1]
Larch.	Witch hazel.[1]

[1] Species of low commercial value.

II.—Species favored by the gipsy-moth larvæ after the first stage:

Chestnut.
Hemlock.
Pine, hard.[1]
Pine, red.
Pine, white.
Spruce, black.[1]
Spruce, Norway.
Spruce, red.
Spruce, white.[1]

III.—Species not favored by the gipsy-moth larvæ but capable of supporting it:

Beech, blue.[1]
Birch, black.
Birch, yellow.
Cherry, black.
Elm.
Gum, black.[1]
Hornbeam, hop.[1]
Maple, red.[1]
Maple, silver.[1]
Maple, sugar.
Pignut.
Sassafras.[1]
Shagbark.

IV.—Species unfavored by the gipsy-moth larvæ in all stages:

Arborvitæ.
Ash, black.[1]
Ash, white.
Butternut.
Cedar, red.[1]
Cedar, white.
Fir, balsam.[1]
Hackberry.[1]
Locust, black.
Locust, honey.
Sycamore.[1]
Tulip.

[1] Species of low commercial value.

During 1914 many food plants were tested which do not ordinarily occur in New England except when planted for ornamental purposes. They grow to a greater or less extent in other sections of the United States, and it was desired to make these tests in order to determine whether these plants would be seriously damaged by the gipsy moth in case it should spread from New England. The information is also useful as a guide to the method of treatment which should be applied in case a small colony should become established in some region outside the present infested area. During the first two summers that these experiments were carried on a sublaboratory was maintained at Worcester, Mass., where check experiments were conducted. The food-plant work is now nearly completed and the results will be brought together shortly for publication. In connection with these experiments it should be said that a large number of observations have been made in the field each summer relative to the favorability of different species of trees and undergrowth to gipsy-moth attack. This information serves as a check on the laboratory experiments which are carried on under artificial conditions. The observations in the field have in the main been made in definite areas, which were selected for an entirely different purpose and will be considered under the next experimental project.

EXPERIMENTS IN DETERMINING THE INCREASE OF THE GIPSY MOTH IN THE FIELD.

In view of the importance of parasites, disease, and unfavored food plants in reducing the increase of the gipsy moth, it seemed desirable to secure definite data on the normal increase of this insect in the field and the increase where these deterrent elements were present in varying degrees. The most feasible way to determine the increase is to compare the number of egg clusters in a given locality from year to year. In order to do this arrangements were made in the fall of 1911 to study field conditions in a systematic manner. About 250 areas which have been designated as "observation points" were selected throughout the infested area. This gave an opportunity for ascertaining the effect of latitude, seasonal variation, and altitude on the increase of the species. In selecting these points an attempt was made to secure as many pure stands of forest growth as possible; also, to obtain areas of mixed growth where the proportion of favored food plants varied. Areas were also secured where different species of parasites had been liberated and where the wilt disease had occurred abundantly or in a small amount during the previous year. The degree of infestation was also considered in making a selection and a number of points were obtained where the trees had previously been defoliated to check against some where no defoliation had resulted and the infestation was very light. After an area was selected a tree was marked for a center and a circle 100 feet in diameter was laid out. Each tree within the circle was numbered consecutively and a note made of its species, size, and condition. In the fall, as soon as the foliage had dropped, a careful count was made of the egg clusters on each tree. These results have been secured and tabulated as well as exact information relative to the number of egg clusters found on the ground and undergrowth. Records have also been kept on the condition of the trees from year to year, and the number of trees which died in each area has been carefully noted. The condition of the territory surrounding these points, as regards infestation, has also been noted. This work has been supervised by Mr. C. W. Minott, but it has not been carried on for a sufficient number of years to give all the exact information desired.

The following table gives the gross number of egg clusters found in the points each year, and will be of interest as indicating in a general way the severity of the infestation from 1910 to 1914.

It will be noted that 170 points are given in the table. The balance of the 250 which were originally selected have been discontinued, owing to destruction by fire, promiscuous cutting by the owners, or for other reasons. The area in the points aggregates 30.18 acres, and the surrounding territory which has been watched brings the total under observation up to 863.1 acres. For convenience, the infested territory has been divided into five sections, and the towns in which the points were located are indicated on the accompanying map.

TABLE III.—*Gipsy moth egg clusters recorded in observation points, 1910–1914.*

Locations.	Number of points.	Egg clusters.				
		1910	1911	1912	1913	1914
Eastern New Hampshire and Maine	32	2,074	31,751	29,637	26,147	18,234
Western New Hampshire	33	14,885	23,032	28,618	9,603	13,228
Northern Massachusetts	34	29,399	47,419	30,345	17,603	31,316
Western Massachusetts	30	10,742	26,409	28,301	9,763	17,159
Southern Massachusetts	41	11,486	39,319	42,451	8,222	31,065
Area, 30.18 acres	170	68,586	167,930	159,352	71,338	111,002

The count of the egg clusters recorded under 1910 was made in the fall of 1911 and covered all clusters which were found to have hatched and therefore belong to the 1910 brood of moths. This count was more or less inaccurate, as many of the egg clusters were removed from the trees after a year's exposure to the elements. The count indicates, however, that there was a large increase in infestation between 1910 and 1911, and that in 1912 the gross infestation was slightly reduced. A heavy reduction occurred in 1913, while in 1914 a considerable increase was noted but not nearly as great as was the case from 1910 to 1911.

The conclusion which will inevitably be drawn from these figures will not apply to other localities in the infested area. There are many locations where a marked increase was noted in 1913 or where a marked decrease was noted in 1914, but taking the territory as a whole it gives a general idea of the trend of increase or decrease for the period covered.

Knowing the conditions, one can not fail to be impressed with the results that have already become apparent from the introduction of parasites and the work of the wilt disease. Although the season of 1914 was not as favorable to the natural enemies as was the case in 1910, the proportional increase in the number of egg clusters was considerably smaller. Unfavored food plants have, of course, been instrumental in holding down the increase in some of the points, but the amount of infestation in points where unfavored food predominates has remained rather constant, so that it has not been as great a factor in the reduction noted as the other elements just mentioned.

Much careful work has been required to secure this data. For about six months in each year upward of 20 men have been engaged in this work. During the summer a part of the men made observations on the feeding habits of the gipsy moth caterpillars on different food plants in their sections. Observations on the presence of natural enemies were also made and from time to time collections of egg clusters or caterpillars near the points were obtained and sent to the laboratory in order that the percentage of parasitism might be determined. This work should be continued in order to determine whether after the natural enemies become firmly established the outbreaks of this insect will be periodical over a large territory or whether, as is the case at the present time, the smaller colonies will increase so that stripped areas will be found scattered over the entire region.

DISPERSION WORK.

For the past three or four years considerable attention has been paid to the means by which the gipsy moth spreads. As the female moth does not fly it is apparent that the dispersion of the species must be very slow unless it is carried by other means. Egg clusters may be transported on lumber, forest products, Christmas trees, or other material which is likely to be shipped long distances from the infested area. This matter has been given careful consideration and means have been taken to prevent the spread of the moth in this way. Information concerning methods used are given under the quarantine part of this report.

In the spring of 1910 a number of experiments were conducted which showed that first-stage gipsy-moth caterpillars may be carried by the wind, and the information secured at that time has been published.[1]

Since this work was carried on more elaborate experiments have been conducted by Mr. C. W. Collins and assistants, to obtain long-distance records on the spread in this manner. A study has also been made of the likelihood of the insect being spread by caterpillars drifting in streams, or by wood or other material which is infested with egg clusters floating in rivers and becoming lodged in territory which was not infested. At present wind spread seems to be the chief natural means by which the insect becomes established in new territory. The trend of the spread is toward the north and northeast on account of the fact that the warm prevailing winds before the first of June, when the caterpillars are in the first stage, usually blow in those directions. This has resulted in a large increase in the area infested in Maine, and the territory in that State will probably continue to extend as long as large areas are seriously infested in New Hampshire and Massachusetts. The western spread of the insect has probably been greatly retarded by reason of the fact that low temperature, causing the caterpillars to be inactive, has prevailed when the winds came from the east or northeast. Heretofore serious infestation did not occur in southeastern Massachusetts or Rhode Island; hence winds from the southeast were not an important factor in

[1] Burgess, A. F. The dispersion of the gipsy moth. U. S. Dept. Agr., Bur. Ent., Bul. 119, 62 p., 16 pl., 6 fig., 1 map, Feb. 11, 1913.

causing spread into Connecticut or the area in Massachusetts south of Worcester. Recently, however, the infestation has increased to a great extent in southeastern Massachusetts and Rhode Island, and unless vigorous means are taken to abolish these sources of supply, rapid infestation of eastern Connecticut and territory in Massachusetts lying immediately north of that State will result. In fact, during the past season a large increase has been found in the western tier of towns in Rhode Island and the eastern tier in Connecticut. In eastern Connecticut the white oak, which is one of the most favored food plants of the gipsy moth, is exceedingly common in the woodlands, and the difficulty of controlling the moth under these conditions is very great.

A series of experiments has been conducted to determine how far male moths will be attracted by the females. The purpose is to determine the probability of scattered females being fertilized if they occur at a long distance from a gipsy-moth colony.

SECONDARY INSECT INVESTIGATIONS.

In the fall of 1912 large numbers of oak trees in the areas that had been defoliated by the gipsy moth were found in a dying condition. Examination showed that many of the trees had been attacked by a bark borer, which proved to be *Agrilus bilineatus* Web. The matter was taken up with Dr. A. D. Hopkins, in charge of Forest Insect Investigations of the Bureau of Entomology, and arrangements were made for cooperative study of this insect. Dr. Hopkins was to direct the work, and the salary and expenses of an assistant, Mr. H. A. Preston, who was to give his entire time to the work, were to be paid by this branch. Investigations have been carried on and the life history of the insect worked out. It appears from the information secured that continuous work on this project is not necessary, and the cooperative arrangement was discontinued July 1, 1914. The data relative to the life history and habits, as well as control measures, is in the hands of Dr. Hopkins and will doubtless be published at an early date.

For the information of woodland owners who wish to preserve their oak trees it can be stated that all trees which are in a dying condition in September should be marked so that they can be cut during the winter. The wood should be removed from the lot and if it can be used for fuel the hibernating larvæ will be destroyed. Inasmuch as the oak is very favored as a food plant by the caterpillars of the gipsy moth and as the Agrilus beetles prefer to attack weakened trees, it would seem rather difficult to preserve oak growth unless considerable expense was involved in spraying or treating gipsy-moth egg clusters in order to keep the trees in a vigorous condition. This is impracticable in most woodlands in the infested area. Park or ornamental trees can be handled in this way and the cost is not prohibitive.

RESULTS OF EXPERIMENTAL WORK.

Many of the experimental projects which have been undertaken are nearing completion and detailed reports will be published later.

The information on food plants will now form a definite basis for practical work, and as has been brought out by the observations in Europe on both parasites and food-plant conditions, it will be necessary to bring about in our forests a great reduction of the favored food plants of the gipsy moth before natural enemies can be expected to keep this insect within reasonable bounds.

The parasites and wilt disease, as has already been shown, are doing effective work, but the results would be greatly amplified by eliminating favored food plants.

The study of the increase of the moth in the field furnishes valuable data on all phases of the forest control problem, while the work on dispersion is of special value in connection with the field control work which is being carried on.

Secondary insects are important inasmuch as they may prevent the recovery of many trees which have been defoliated and which would, under normal conditions, gradually recover.

SILVICULTURAL WORK.

During the time the gipsy moth has been known to exist in this country it has done an immense amount of damage to tree growth of the infested region. The injury has caused the death of many of the trees attacked or the retardation of their growth and development, and has produced conditions favorable to the increase of secondary enemies. The tree growth affected may be divided into three classes, (1) fruit trees, (2) shade or ornamental trees, and (3) forest trees. All have suffered severely, but owing to their greater value and relatively smaller numbers it has been possible to prevent a large amount of the injury by applying hand methods of suppression to fruit and shade trees. Gipsy-moth damage to forest trees, however, can not be controlled in the same way owing to the great expense involved, hence the problem of preventing damage in woodlands is a serious one. In some European countries this has been solved to a considerable extent by growing species which are not so susceptible to gipsy-moth attack. The investigations on the food plants and feeding habits of the gipsy moth indicate that the work of eliminating the most susceptible and encouraging the growth of those that are not favored as food by this insect is likely to give good results. As this work involves, to a considerable extent, the practice of silviculture, the Bureau of Entomology requested and received the cooperative assistance of the Forest Service, and these two branches of the Department of Agriculture are now working together on this problem. Mr. George E. Clement, who was formerly an assistant in the Forest

Service, has been appointed to take charge of the investigations along this line. The table given under the "food-plant experiments" indicates in a general way the degree of susceptibility to moth attack of some of our more common forest trees. Certain species, however, are of little commercial value, and it is desired to discourage their growth, as well as those that are particularly susceptible to gipsy-moth attack. In the case of valuable species that are susceptible to attack and for the growth of which a large portion of the infested region is favorable, the only step which can be taken is to determine whether or not they can be sufficiently protected from serious damage by associating with the less susceptible species in small proportions. Of course, the presence of these species may jeopardize the safety of the associated species which would otherwise be immune. However, before abandoning these species careful experiments will be made to determine whether there are associations with which they can join with safety.

The chief fact that reduces the liability of certain species of trees, particularly conifers, to gipsy-moth attack is that the *very young* caterpillars do not feed upon them. Therefore, if there are present no trees or undergrowth upon which the young caterpillars will feed and thereby develop to a size which enables them to attack conifers or similarly susceptible species, they will not be attacked. Thus it appears that certain species can be grown pure or in exclusive association and be free from gipsy-moth attack. Any system of forest management should endeavor to produce in a given area only trees of commercial value, and the foregoing lists (pp. 14–15) indicate the most suitable species for selection.

In converting a given stand of timber into one which shall be immune from gipsy-moth attack, the different classes of trees should be considered for removal in the following order:

(1) Trees of naturally low commercial value and susceptible to gipsy-moth attack.

(2) Trees of low commercial value on account of growing in unfavorable situations and susceptible to gipsy-moth attack.

(3) Trees of commercial value, favorably situated, and subject to gipsy-moth attack.

(4) Trees of naturally low commercial value, but not liable to gipsy-moth attack if properly associated.

(5) Trees of low commercial value on account of growing in unfavorable situations and not liable to gipsy-moth attack.

(6) Trees of commercial value favorably situated and not liable to gipsy-moth attack.

Silvicultural conditions in the woods of the infested region are very poor. Through repeated fires and heavy and inconsiderate cutting, the growth of weed trees has been greatly favored and the growth of some species has been favored in situations quite unsuited to their requirements. This is particularly true in the case of the oaks and gray birch. These species constitute a very large proportion of the deciduous growth of the region and are very susceptible to gipsy-moth attack. On a great deal of the area now covered by these species the white pine would grow to much better advantage, would yield a much more valuable product, and if pure, or nearly so, would prove immune to gipsy-moth attack. The white pine reproduces itself readily under favorable conditions, and is already fairly abundant in numerous localities. For these reasons the white pine recommends itself very strongly as a substitute for the existing moth-susceptible species, and this species has been considered to a very large extent by this department in its experiments to create a safe stand of timber. The deciduous species which are of value and immune to gipsy-moth attack require most favorable situations for their profitable development, and such situations are very few and of small area. An exception in the case of chestnut may be made in this connection. This is a valuable tree and one well suited to grow over a considerable area. Its growth is not recommended on account of its susceptibility to the widespread and fatal chestnut blight. But, like the red oak, it may be found possible to grow it satisfactorily in small numbers with other species.

EXPERIMENTAL WORK.

The experimental work has been conducted by means of small areas known as "sample plats." These vary in size from one-half an acre to 6 acres and occur both scattered and grouped in different parts of the infested region. They are necessarily located on the lands of private owners who are willing to submit their lands to this use.

An effort has been made to distribute this work as widely as possible over the infested region. (Pl. IX.) In this way the greatest variety of conditions is encountered and the results are available to the greatest number of woodland owners. Each sample plat varies from another in one or more of the following points: Composition of stand, age of stand, degree of infestation, and method of treatment. Each sample plot generally consists of two parts. One of these is the portion upon which actual experimental work is done and the other serves as a control or check plat. Upon the latter nothing whatever is done, as its purpose is to provide a means of comparing results under natural and artificial conditions. The corners and boundaries of all plats have been plainly marked, and the areas surveyed and mapped. All trees 1 inch and over in diameter have been calipered on each plat and control, and the measurements recorded. Forest descriptions of each plat have been written.

Where small white pines have occurred in any quantity they have been counted and the numbers have been recorded by foot-height classes. The best available indication of the degree of gipsy-moth infestation seems to be the number of egg clusters, and for this reason the egg clusters have been counted on each plat. Egg clusters will be counted periodically in the future in order to determine the effect of treatment upon the infestations.

After the foregoing steps have been taken, the growth on each of the managed areas has been thinned. Different silvicultural systems have been used, but in general the object has been to remove the greatest number of susceptible trees consistent with the silvicultural requirements of the trees to be left. In some cases the bulk of the stands consisted of susceptible species, and in these the thinning made was preliminary to a later clear cutting.

After cutting, the number of trees of different diameters and species have been counted and recorded, the amounts of products have been measured and recorded, brush has been piled and burned, careful notes of the changed conditions have been made, and an effort has been made to compute the cost of the work and the value of the products on each plat. In some cases numbers of small naturally produced white pine have been supplemented with planted 2-year-old seedlings from the nursery. In cases where plantings were made the cost of the seedlings and the planting was borne by the owner of the woodland. In addition to the sample plats already mentioned, one 10-acre tract has been selected in each of the following towns in New Hampshire: Peterboro, Franklin, Warner, and New Durham. The growth on all these plats is largely inferior hardwoods which are particularly liable to gipsy-moth attack. The infestation in each case is not heavy. As there is more or less white pine growing among the hardwoods the plan is to cut the latter clean and to replace these trees by planting enough white pine to produce a stand which will be free from gipsy-moth damage. The results of these experiments will not be available for several years, and during this period careful notes on conditions will be made.

MIDDLESEX COUNTY FOREST SURVEY.

In order to get some definite information concerning the distribution of the various kinds of timber stands in the region, a rough forest map of the county of Middlesex in Massachusetts has been made. This work has shown that the forest growth is very uneven and complex, and that there is a wide variation in the composition of stands within relatively small areas. The existing growth of trees on any area indicates very infrequently the growth for which the conditions on the area are best suited. From data secured by this survey and observations made througthout the infested region, the crying silvicultural need of the woods is obviously a great reduction of their diversity and the replacement of a large portion of the species by those which have a greater commercial value, and for which the conditions for growth are much better adapted. The steps needed to accomplish this are in many instances precisely those which appear to be necessary in controlling gipsy-moth attack by silvicultural practice.

PROPOSED FOREST EXPERIMENT.

In order to determine the practicability of carrying on an experiment over a large area preliminary surveys have been made of the forest growth in the town of Winchendon, Mass. This work has been attempted in cooperation with the State forester of Massachusetts, Mr. F. W. Rane. The original growth in this town was undoubtedly coniferous, but there has been considerable cutting and as a result hardwood growth of various species has become established. Oak does not predominate, however, in this region and it is hoped that sufficient cooperation can be secured from the woodland owners in the town to handle the forest area so as to bring it into a growth which will not be susceptible to gipsy-moth attack. The preliminary survey has been completed and the data are now being compiled with a view to determining whether a plan of this sort can be worked out on an extensive area.

SCOUTING WORK.

The scouting work consists in examining the territory along the outside border of infestation, and in treating the gipsy-moth colonies adjacent to the border for the purpose of preventing spread of the insects to other parts of the United States. This work is in charge of Mr. L. H. Worthley, who is assisted by Mr. H. L. McIntyre. The territory is divided into six sections with the following men in charge of a section: Mr. D. G. Murphy, Worcester, Mass., H. A. Ames, Athol, Mass., H. N. Bean, Keene, N. H., F. W. Graves, jr., Bradford, N. H., F. W. Foster, Plymouth, N. H., and C. E. Totman, Canaan, N. H. Parties consisting of five trained scouts in charge of a foreman are detailed to make the examinations and treat the infestations, each general foreman having from 5 to 10 crews of scouts under his supervision. In order to check up the thoroughness with which the work is done in the lightly infested territory, a party, usually consisting of two experienced men who are known as special scouts, examines the work after the regular inspection has been made in order to see whether egg clusters of the moth have been missed and that the work was thoroughly done by the scouts. Each scout is required to place a characteristic mark on every tree examined by him so that the responsibility for leaving egg clusters can be readily determined. By following up this plan the force is maintained at a high degree of

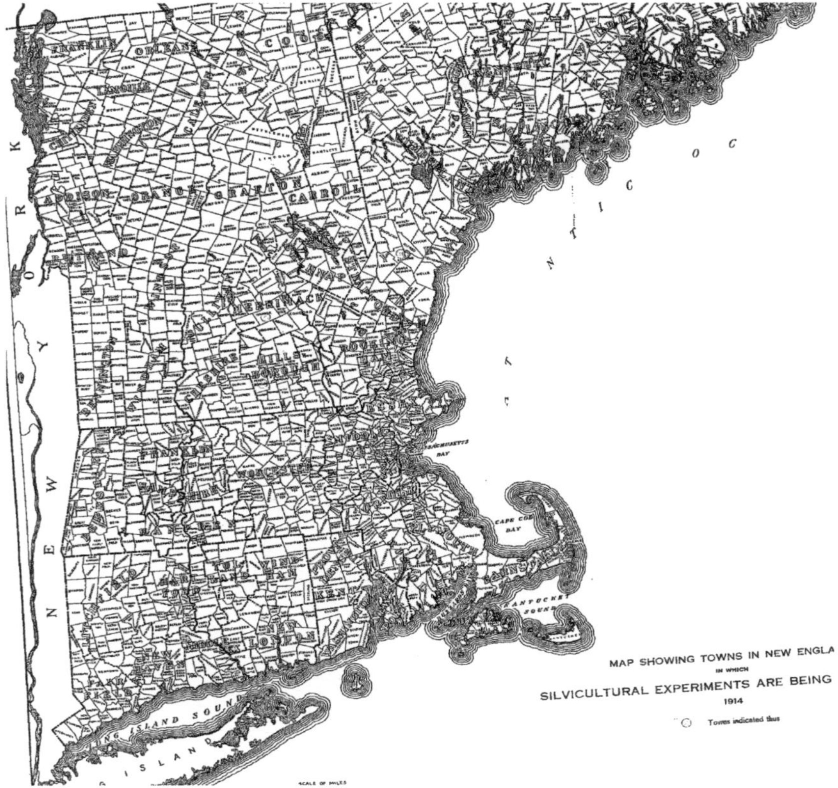
N E W
Y O R K
FRANKLIN
ORLEANS
ADDISON
ORANGE
GRAFTON
CARROLL
MERRIMACK
WORCESTER
CAPE COD BAY
BAY
ISLAND SOUND
SCALE OF MILES
MAP SHOWING TOWNS IN NEW ENGLA
IN WHICH
SILVICULTURAL EXPERIMENTS ARE BEING
1914
Towns indicated thus

CAPE COD BAY
MAP SHOWING AREAS IN NEW ENGLAND
THE GIPSY MOTH AND THE BROWN-TAIL MOTH
1914
Encloses area infested with the gipsy moth
Encloses area infested with the brown-tail moth

efficiency, the careless and negligent men being dropped from the rolls. When large colonies are found crews of woodchoppers are employed temporarily to cut out the worthless trees and clean up the undergrowth in order to render the area in condition for effective operations.

The accompanying map (Pl. X) shows the territory which was known to be infested by the gipsy moth in the fall of 1913. In organizing the work a large party of scouts was sent to Maine for the purpose of determining whether the infestation had spread beyond this line. The results of the examination show that a large number of towns are infested outside the border previously established. The work was continued until late in December, when it was necessary to transfer the men on account of deep snow and extremely cold weather, the temperature for a number of days being as low as 20° to 25° below zero. In all, 155 towns were scouted in Maine, and of these 81 were found infested. The increase in the number of towns over that of previous years is largely explained by the fact that during the winter of 1912–13 the scouting work was not completed on account of snow and also because of the undoubted dissemination of the moth by means of the spread of the small caterpillars by the wind. The manner of this kind of spread has already been explained in this report. Suffice it to say, the general trend of dispersion of this insect has been toward the north and northeast on account of the fact that the prevailing warm winds during the time the caterpillars are hatching blow from the south and southwesterly directions. The work was continued from January until April in New Hampshire, Massachusetts, Rhode Island, and Connecticut.

On February 3, 1914, a report was received that several gipsy-moth egg clusters had been found on an estate at Bratenahl, Ohio, a suburb of Cleveland. The matter was at once investigated and two experienced scouts were detailed to make an examination of the estate and the surroundings. At the time the work was done there was considerable snow on the ground, making inspection work difficult. Seven new egg clusters were found and treated and later in the season the colony was burlapped and the trees sprayed. The work in Ohio was done in close cooperation with the Ohio Agricultural Commission, and work in the colony since the original scouting was done has been carried on by the assistants of Mr. N. E. Shaw, State nursery and orchard inspector.

On May 7, 1914, a report was received from Mr. George G. Atwood, chief of the division of horticulture of the State of New York, that a gipsy-moth colony had been found at North Castle, Westchester County, N. Y. Inspectors from this office were detailed to treat egg clusters, and several experienced scouts were transferred to assist in stamping out this colony. The principal infestation occurred on a large estate, and the caterpillars began hatching soon after the first egg clusters were found. A considerable area was scouted around the infestation, and egg clusters or caterpillars were found over an area of about three-fourths of a square mile. Many of the trees were growing on rough and rocky soil, so that it was very difficult to do thorough work. About 15,000 egg clusters were treated during the month of May.

In addition to the scouting work already mentioned, a special examination was made of the entire town of Geneva, N. Y., but no gipsy-moth egg clusters were found. In 1912 a small colony was found in this city. It has been very thoroughly treated by the assistants of the commissioner of agriculture, and it is now believed that the insect has been exterminated. The scouting party detailed for the Geneva work spent one week in examining trees in Seneca Park, Rochester, N. Y., but no traces of the moth could be found.

Special scouting work was carried on in the towns of Lenox, Stockbridge, and Great Barrington, Mass., during the winter. Infestations have previously been found in these towns, but the examination resulted in finding but one egg cluster in Great Barrington, one in Stockbridge, and two in Lenox, indicating that good results have been secured from the treatment which had been applied during the previous season. A careful inspection was also made in the town of Wallingford, Conn., which was found infested some years ago, but no egg clusters were discovered.

The following table shows the number of towns which have been scouted for the gipsy moth and the number of new towns which were found infested during the winter of 1913–14.

TABLE IV.—*Scouting operations for the gipsy moth during the winter of 1913–14.*

State.	Towns scouted.	Newly infested.
Maine	155	81
New Hampshire	73	6
Massachusetts	36	7
Rhode Island	19	17
Connecticut	13	10
New York	3	1
Ohio	1	1

In nine towns in New Hampshire and two in Massachusetts, infested in 1912–13, no infestations could be found the following winter, and recommendations were made that these towns be excluded from the quarantined area. This was approved by the Federal Horticultural Board, and the border towns of the area quarantined for the gipsy moth include only those that have been found infested during the past winter.

The plan of the work has been to examine the territory in Maine chiefly for the purpose of securing data as to where the quarantine line should extend. It is impossible to prevent the spread of the small caterpillars by the wind, and it has therefore been deemed advisable to confine the clearing-up work along the border to the territory in New Hampshire, Massachusetts, Rhode Island, and Connecticut. Accordingly early in the spring arrangements were made to place tanglefoot bands on trees in all the colonies about three towns wide along the border and from the time this work began the greater part of the scouting force was transferred to the work of applying and patrolling these bands.

In the colony in Westchester County, N. Y., 6,000 tanglefoot and 4,000 burlap bands were applied by the inspectors of the State department of agriculture. The State purchased a high-power spraying machine and very thoroughly sprayed the infested area and surroundings. The colony in Ohio was similarly treated by the State officials, and in both cases excellent results have been secured. This office has kept in constant touch with the work in these States and has also had a representative directing the work in the Berkshire Hills infestations in Great Barrington, Stockbridge, and Lenox.

Inasmuch as many of the new infestations were found on apple trees during the winter, a record has been kept of all such trees inspected and of the number of miles of roads scouted by the men. This information is given in the following table:

Table V.—*Results of scouting operations for the gipsy moth.*

State.	Towns scouted.	Colonies found.	Egg clusters found.	Apple trees inspected.	Miles of road traveled.	Tanglefoot bands applied.
Maine	155	....	....	764,081	4,768	....
New Hampshire	73	1,656	25,427	1,354,908	4,334	68,336
Massachusetts	36	794	11,987	484,731	2,553	58,315
Rhode Island	19	[1] 309	[1] 207	232,190	987	5,324
Connecticut	13	[1] 157	[1] 124	332,036	884	4,767
Total	296	2,916	37,745	3,167,946	13,526	136,742

[1] In a number of these colonies pupa cases only were found.

The following conditions found in 1913 and in 1914 are of interest. In New Hampshire no egg clusters were found in 198 of the colonies that had been treated during the previous years, and in 641 of the 1,656 colonies found in the winter of 1913 no larvæ were found in the spring of 1914. In Massachusetts no egg clusters were found in 68 of the colonies that were treated during the winter of 1912–13, and in 124 of the 794 colonies located in the fall of 1913 no larvæ were found in the spring of 1914. In Rhode Island 276 of the 309 colonies found and treated in the fall of 1913 failed to produce larvæ in the spring of 1914. In Connecticut 136 of the 157 colonies treated in 1913 failed to produce larvæ the following spring.

During the summer of 1914 woodland scouting was carried on in Thompson, Conn., and Rutland, Mass. The former town is heavily wooded and is reported to contain about 30,000 acres of forest, a considerable part of which is oak growth. As a result of the examination of the woodland in this town 73 gipsy-moth colonies were discovered. All of them were small infestations, indicating that the species is established and is well scattered through the woodland.

GENERAL RESULTS SHOWN BY SCOUTING WORK.

The scouting work for the season has shown very encouraging results. In addition to the large number of towns along the outside border where the infestation has been greatly reduced or where it has been cleaned out during the past year, an excellent showing has been made in a number of badly infested towns in Massachusetts and New Hampshire which are just inside the border. In a large number of these towns which were found severely infested in the winter of 1912–13, a large decrease in the number of egg clusters has been found this year. In the town of Bradford, N. H., where over 3,000 egg clusters were treated during the former year, only 200 were found this season. In Hillsboro the records show a reduction of from 8,000 to 500, although the number of small colonies, many containing a single egg cluster, has increased. In Henniker and Warner, N. H., a large decrease has also been noted and the same is generally true in the border towns where work is being carried on.

The work on the tanglefoot bands during the entire season gave very gratifying results, and a very large number of the colonies where caterpillars were present early in the season showed no caterpillars or pupæ at the close of the work on tanglefoot bands on August 1. Only a few caterpillars were found in the western part of the area in New Hampshire, Rhode Island, and Connecticut.

No caterpillars were found in Lenox, Stockbridge, or Great Barrington, Mass. About 400 yards from the old infested area in the latter town 43 egg clusters were found in a rock heap during the caterpillar season which, of course, was under the snow when scouting work was done. Some very thorough work was done at this infestation, and only one pupa was found this season. Of course there is danger of some spread from it, and during the coming season some very thorough scouting will be done in this vicinity.

No caterpillars were found at Wallingford, Conn., this season.

In the badly infested woodland colony in Orange, Mass., where some 1,000 egg clusters were located, there were but 1,182 larvæ found during the summer.

The spraying work during the summer gave very satisfactory results, treatment being applied in border towns from Hubbardston, Mass., as far north as Andover, N. H. Many of the localities where spraying was applied were difficult to reach on account of being inaccessible from roads or water supply, but owing to the careful plans made by the foremen the work was not greatly handicapped on this account. In a number of cases the owners of the areas which were infested offered every cooperation possible in facilitating treatment. A few cases have been found, however, where spraying could not be attempted on account of the unwillingness of the owners to have their pasture trees treated because the grass was needed for grazing stock. In instances of this sort the infestations were cared for by creosoting egg clusters and destroying the caterpillars under tanglefoot bands.

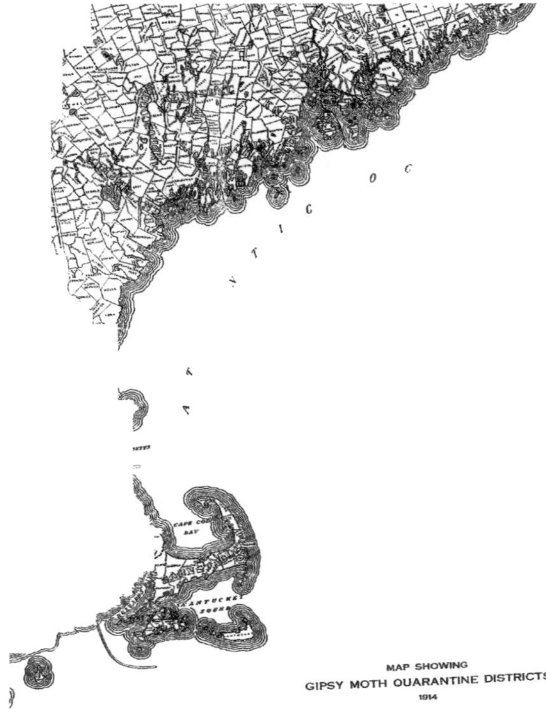

MAP SHOWING
GIPSY MOTH OUARANTINE DISTRICTS
1914

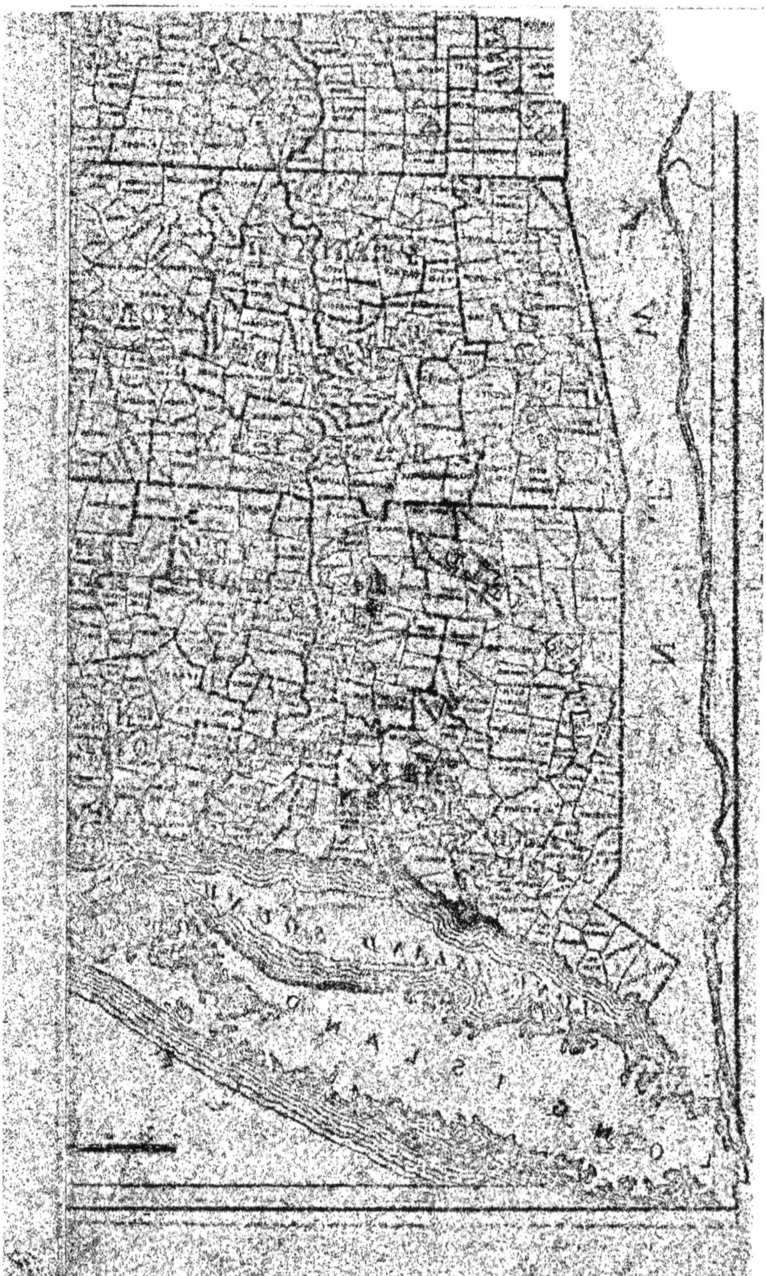

BROWN-TAIL MOTH SCOUTING.

The spread of the brown-tail moth is not easily controlled by artificial means unless the insect can be reduced to minimum numbers. Owing to the large territory over which the insect has spread, it is not possible to carry on extensive scouting or control work by the use of hand-suppressive measures. During the year a considerable area, however, has been examined in Maine, New Hampshire, Vermont, Massachusetts, Connecticut, and New York, and areas have been found infested where the insect was not known previously to exist. The work of the commissioner of agriculture of Vermont and his assistants has been very effective in reducing the infestation in that State. The principal new infestations were found in Connecticut, and a greater part of these were located by the assistants of the State entomologist. Several webs have also been found on Fishers Island and Long Island, N. Y., so that, in all, four towns on these islands are known to be infested. The New York infestations were discovered by the inspectors employed by the State department of agriculture, and several scouts from this office were sent late in the spring to check up the work and cover a part of the area concerned.

QUARANTINE WORK.

The quarantine work is supervised by Mr. D. M. Rogers, who is assisted by Mr. Harry W. Vinton, and the operations are confined to the territory in New England and New York which is infested by the gipsy moth and the brown-tail moth. As a result of the provision of the Federal plant quarantine act, which was passed by Congress August 20, 1912, a domestic quarantine[1] has been declared by the Federal Horticultural Board, covering the territory infested by each of these insects. While the legal authority for declaring quarantine is vested in the board, the cost of administering the work is defrayed by the appropriation for the Bureau of Entomology for "Preventing the spread of moths." The object of this work is to prevent egg clusters or larvæ of the gipsy moth, or winter webs of the brown-tail moth, from being carried out of the infested areas on shipments of trees or forest products. The regulations for enforcing this quarantine provide that all material of this character before being accepted for shipment to points outside the infested district must be inspected and must be accompanied with an official certificate of the Federal Horticultural Board stating that an examination has been made and that the material is free from infestation. Shipment of Christmas trees and similar material to points outside the quarantined area is prohibited. In order to facilitate the work, the infested territory has been divided into 22 sections and a competent inspector has been placed in charge of

[1] For details, see Notice of Quarantine No. 17, of the Federal Horticultural Board, effective Aug. 1, 1914.

each. (Pl. XI.) It is the duty of each inspector carefully to examine all lumber or forest products, cordwood, telephone poles, railroad ties, tan bark, etc., which may be shipped from any points in his district to points outside the infested area after the proper application has been made and to issue certificates of inspection if no infestation is found. In accordance with the provisions of the quarantine regulations, transportation companies are required to reject shipments which are not accompanied with proper certificates. During the season when nursery stock is being moved, examinations are made of all woody plants which are consigned to points outside the quarantined area. A number of special inspectors are employed for this purpose in addition to the men engaged on the regular lumber-inspection work. In order that this work may be of the most thorough character so as to safeguard purchasers in other parts of the United States, a tree-by-tree inspection is made of all trees and plants growing in the nurseries before they are dug for shipment. Another inspection of the plants is made at the time they are being packed for shipment. During the fiscal year 1914, 17,076 shipments have been examined and 4,476 specimens of the gipsy moth and 1,435 specimens of the brown-tail moth in their various stages have been found and the insects destroyed. This has resulted in preventing these pests from spreading to many localities not now infested. The destinations of these shipments ranged as far south as Jacksonville, Fla., as far west as Prineville, Oreg., and as far north as Montreal, Quebec.

The destination of shipments on which infestations were found and destroyed are given below:

State.	Number of shipments.	State.	Number of shipments.	State.	Number of shipments.
Colorado	1	Maine	12	Pennsylvania	10
Connecticut	25	Michigan	4	South Carolina	1
District of Columbia	1	Missouri	5	Vermont	35
Florida	3	New Hampshire	7	Virginia	2
Georgia	1	New Jersey	11	Canada	6
Illinois	14	New York	34	England	1
Iowa	1	North Carolina	1		214
Maryland	2	Ohio	12		
Massachusetts	24	Oregon	1		

BROWN-TAIL MOTH QUARANTINE.

The enforcement of the brown-tail moth quarantine is conducted in connection with the inspections carried on to determine whether shipments are infested with the gipsy moth. It is not necessary, however, to inspect lumber for this purpose. Deciduous nursery stock is examined and all webs of the moth destroyed before shipments are permitted. In order to prevent as far as possible the carriage of the adult female moths on trains, inspectors have been placed at several main railroad junctions along the border of infestations to examine the trains during the time the moths are flying. These insects are strongly attracted to bright light and the results which have been secured from these inspections have been very satisfactory. The inspection work in 1914 began on July 6 and was continued until July 31.

The stations where trains were examined and the number of adults found are given below:

Station.	Brown-tail moths found.	Station.	Brown-tail moths found.
Bellows Falls, Vt	16	North Stratford, N. H	0
Greenfield, Mass	9	Springfield, Mass	1
Gorham, N. H	6	St. Johnsbury, Vt	457
Hartford, Conn	0	Wells River, Vt	247
New London, Conn	7	White River Junction, Vt	1,484

In addition to the foregoing, 296 adults were found and destroyed at arc lights in White River Junction, Vt.

RESULTS OF QUARANTINE WORK.

The results of the quarantine work have been very satisfactory. Only one infested shipment of plant products has been known to pass out of the territory and it was promptly returned.

Several carloads of stone and quarry products have recently been found infested with gipsy-moth egg masses and a quarantine was declared by the Secretary of Agriculture on October 23, 1914. Such products must now be inspected and certified the same as plant products.

Considering the number of infested shipments that have been found and the wide range of country to which they would have been sent if the egg clusters had not been found and treated, it is safe to assert that this work has resulted in enormous saving of money value to the agricultural and forest interests of the United States.

COOPERATIVE WORK.

Since the Federal work was commenced, active cooperation has been secured from the States in which operations were being carried on. While the organization of the State force and that of the Government force are entirely distinct the work is planned in such a way as to avoid duplication and to secure the best results. The general plan is for the Bureau of Entomology to concentrate its efforts in stamping out colonies in the territory along the western border of infestation from Lake Winnipesaukee to Long Island Sound, and to carry on as much work as may be necessary in eliminating the isolated colonies that have been found in New York, Ohio, western Massachusetts, and Connecticut. The State officials concentrate their efforts in the territory inside the border towns. Owing to the hearty spirit of cooperation that has existed between the Bureau of Entomology and the officials in New York, Ohio, and Connecticut, where isolated colonies are present, it has not been necessary for this office to expend much money for control work, as the States concerned have made every effort to stamp out these colonies. A system of following up and checking over the work done by these States has been adopted, so that very satisfactory work has resulted. In the distribution of natural enemies arrangements have been made to cooperate with the State officials, and this has resulted in the establishment of more colonies of parasites than would otherwise have been possible. An arrangement has been made with the Massachusetts State Board of Agriculture so that speakers will be furnished to discuss the gipsy-moth problem at farmers' institutes.

In the spring of 1914 a colored poster was prepared showing the life histories of the gipsy moth and the brown-tail moth and several of the introduced natural enemies. These posters have been distributed to all the post offices in the infested district, to granges, libraries, and educational institutions. Reproductions from this poster have been made in the form of post cards and distributed to schools and parties interested in the work.

During October, 1914, an exhibit covering the gipsy-moth work of the bureau was made at the Boston Pure Food and Domestic Science Exposition, as a part of the Government exhibit. Living parasites were on exhibition as well as mounted specimens and other information.

Efforts are continually being made to advise property owners concerning the methods which should be taken by them to prevent serious damage to their trees, and good results are being accomplished along these lines.

CONCLUSION.

The gipsy-moth work of the Bureau of Entomology is well organized and each section is accomplishing good results.

The scouting work and the quarantine work are doing efficient service and preventing the spread of the gipsy moth, but on account of the enormous area which is infested it is impossible to cover much of the woodland. This has resulted in a gradual spread of the insect. It has been possible to restrict this spread very materially toward the westward.

The work of natural enemies, including the parasites, predacious enemies, and disease, have helped materially in decreasing the amount of infestation, and it seems probable that these influences will become more potent factors in the future.

The importance of bringing forest lands into a growth which is unfavorable to the development of the gipsy moth can not be too strongly urged, as the work of natural enemies is likely to fluctuate from year to year on account of adverse conditions or the decimation of the beneficial species by other parasitic forms. Every movement toward bringing about more unfavorable forest growth is therefore a step in solving the gipsy-moth problem.

WASHINGTON : GOVERNMENT PRINTING OFFICE : 1915

BULLETIN OF THE
U.S. DEPARTMENT OF AGRICULTURE

No. 205

Contribution from the Bureau of Biological Survey, Henry W. Henshaw, Chief.
May 20, 1915.

ELEVEN IMPORTANT WILD-DUCK FOODS.

By W. L. McAtee, *Assistant Biologist.*

INTRODUCTION.

Accounts of the value, nature, range, and methods of propagation of various groups of plants having importance as wild-duck foods are contained in a series of contributions of the Biological Survey to publications of the Department of Agriculture, of which this bulletin is the third. Eleven groups here discussed include 2 assemblages of fresh-water plants of universal distribution in the United States; 2 of more southerly range; 2 trees of southern swamps whose abundant seeds are eagerly eaten by ducks; 1 strictly salt-water duck food, the first thus far recommended by the bureau; 1 brackish-water plant; and 3 others of such luxuriant growth as to be especially adapted for use on duck farms.

MUSK GRASSES.

VALUE AS DUCK FOOD.

Parts of musk grasses (algæ, Characeæ) have been found in the stomachs of the following 14 species of ducks: Mallard, black duck, pintail, wigeon, gadwell, green-winged and blue-winged teals, bufflehead, goldeneye, ruddy duck, little and big bluebills, ringneck, and redhead. The small tubers of these plants are eaten in large numbers; more than 1,100 were contained in the stomach of one goldeneye and more than 1,500 in that of a pintail. However, all parts of musk grasses are eaten. Certain ducks spending the late autumn on Currituck Sound, North Carolina, were feeding extensively on these plants. Three-fifths of the food of 70 little and 35 big bluebills taken in that locality in November, 1909, consisted of musk grasses. The stomachs of 3 pintails collected in the same locality in September contained on the average 52 per cent of musk grasses, and of 2 in October, 90 per cent.

Note.—This bulletin is for general distribution, and shows how 11 groups of plants may be successfully used as food for wild ducks in localities where now unknown, and is the third in a series on this subject, the preceding being Circular 81, Biological Survey, which treated of wild rice, wild celery, and pondweeds; and Bulletin No. 58, Department of Agriculture, which treated of the delta duck potato, wapato, chufa, wild millet, and banana water lily. The groups described in this bulletin are musk grasses, duckweeds, frogbit, thalia, water elm, swamp privet, eel-grass, wigeon-grass, water-cress, water-weed, and coontail.

83175°—Bull. 205—15——1

DESCRIPTION OF PLANTS.

Musk grasses belong to the great group of plants known as algæ, which include forms commonly known as frog spit, green slime, and seaweeds. Most of the musk grasses (Characeæ) live in fresh water and are among the most highly organized algæ that do so. They are attached to the bottom, and over it often form a fluffy blanket a foot or more in thickness. Small round white tubers occur in numbers on the rhizoids (root-like organs) of some species. The slender stems are jointed and bear at the joints whorls of fine tubular leaves, which usually have a beaded appearance (fig. 1), due to the reproductive organs growing there. These are of two sorts: the antheridia, which are spherical and red when mature, and the oögonia, which are ovoid and black, more or less overlaid with white. The oögonia correspond to the seeds of higher plants, and are about half a millimeter in length.

FIG. 1.—A musk grass (*Chara*).

These plants are translucent and fragile, dull green in color, and often (*Chara*) incrusted with lime. This has given them one of their common names, limeweed. Other names are stonewort, fine moss (Michigan), oyster grass and nigger wool (North Carolina), and skunk grass (Massachusetts). The latter name and that here adopted for the plants, namely, musk grass, refer to a strong odor given off by a mass of the plants when freshly taken from the water.

DISTRIBUTION.

Probably no part of the United States entirely lacks representatives of *Chara* or *Nitella*, our two genera of Characeæ. They require lime, however, and hence reach their best development in regions where that mineral is plentiful.

PROPAGATION.

For transplanting, musk grasses should be gathered in quantity in late summer or fall, when some or all of the oögonia are mature. For shipment they should be packed in small units (as in berry crates) open to the air on all sides. This will prevent fermentation; a little drying will not hurt. If they are to be transported long distances, the package should be iced. For planting, bunches of the plant may be weighted and dropped to the bottom. Growth should appear the following summer. Musk grasses will grow on almost any kind of bottom, but it must be remembered that they will not thrive permanently in the absence of lime.

DUCKWEEDS.

VALUE AS DUCK FOOD.

Duckweeds are abundant only under special conditions, but these conditions exist in some of the favorite haunts of our wild ducks. In the still recesses of southern cypress swamps, where duckweeds cover the entire water surface, these plants contribute to the support of all species of wild ducks. A statement of the duckweed content of two lots of stomachs collected at Menesha, Ark., in November and December will serve to show the importance of these plants in that locality. In the first lot were 8 mallards, and duckweeds composed an average of more than 62 per cent of their stomach contents. The proportion in other species was as follows: Spoonbill (1 stomach), 55 per cent; redhead (10), 50.3 per cent; and little bluebill (6), 8.33 per cent. In the second lot were 64 mallards, and they had eaten duckweeds to the average extent of more than 49 per cent. Fifteen ringnecks had consumed on the average 21.7 per cent each, and two wood ducks, 95 per cent. In the woodland ponds also of the Northern States duckweeds abound. Here in the breeding season the wood duck still manifests its preference for these little plants. Some stomachs are filled exclusively with them, thousands being present.

Duckweeds are relished by most of our ducks and have been found in the stomachs of the following species additional to those above mentioned: Pintail, gadwell, black duck, wigeon, blue-winged and green-winged teals, and big bluebill. As duckweeds sink at the approach of cold weather, they are available in the North during only the warmer months. In the South, however, they remain at the surface practically all the year.

DESCRIPTION OF PLANTS.

The duckweeds most commonly seen are the green disks (sometimes more or less tailed on one side, fig. 2, *a*, *b*, *c*, *d*) which cover the surface of quiet and usually shaded waters. These disks are really leaves, the plants being reduced to a leaf, with one or a few roots on the under side. Duckweeds multiply largely by budding, and the parent plant and offsets often cling together in clusters. Individual plants vary in size from one-twelfth to three-fourths of an inch in diameter.

Two genera of duckweeds lack roots. One of these (*Wolffia*, fig. 2, *e, f*) contains the smallest flowering plants. These appear as green granules, one twenty-fourth of an inch or less in diameter, and are often abundant among other duckweeds or about the margins of lakes and ponds. When the hand is dipped into the water large numbers of the plants adhere to it. They look like coarse meal, except for their green color, and feel like it, so that a good name for them would be water meal.

The other genus of rootless duckweeds (*Wolffiella*) consists of strap-shaped plants (fig. 2, *g, h*), narrowed at one or both ends. They are from one-fifth to three-fifths of an inch in length and commonly cohere in radiate bodies or in large masses of less definite structure.

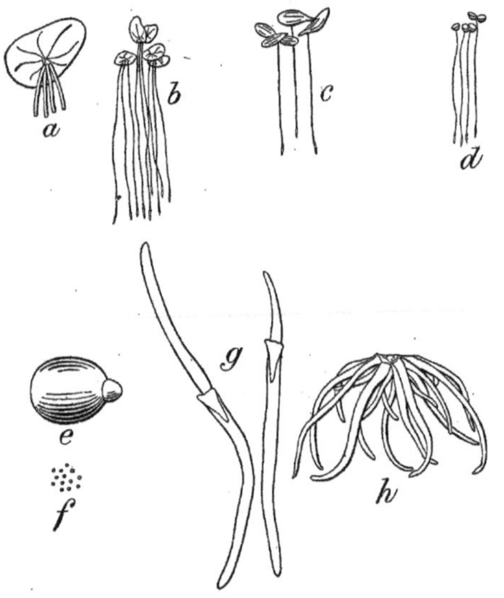

FIG. 2.—Duckweeds: *a, b, Spirodela; c, d, Lemna; e, f, Wolffia; g, h, Wolffiella.*

Duckweeds are known also as duck's meat, water lentils, and seed moss. The latter term, in fact, is used in Arkansas to cover all components of the vegetation of the water surface. Besides duckweeds, this mass includes that green or red, velvety, mosslike plant, *Azolla caroliniana*, and the branching straplike liverworts, *Ricciella*. Both of these are eaten by waterfowl along with the duckweeds, but being less plentiful are of minor importance.

DISTRIBUTION.

Most of the species of duckweeds are wide ranging. Of the single-rooted kind (*Lemna*, fig. 2, *c, d*), 3 species occur throughout the United States, 2 others are confined to the southern part, and 1 to the eastern. The one many-rooted species (*Spirodela*, fig. 2, *a, b*), is of universal distribution. The granulelike rootless forms (*Wolffia*, fig. 2, *e, f*), so far as known, are confined to the eastern half of the country, and the straplike rootless species (*Wolffiella*, fig. 2, *g, h*) to the southeastern quarter.

PROPAGATION.

The seeds of duckweeds are minute and seldom mature. The plants, therefore, must be transplanted bodily. There is no difficulty about this, for if they are not crushed or allowed to ferment or dry, duckweeds are perfectly at home from the moment they are placed in a new body of water. Fermentation may be prevented by shipping in small units freely exposed to the air. Plants which are to be transported a long distance should be iced.

It is useless to put duckweeds in large open bodies of water. They thrive best in small pools and ditches where the water surface is rarely disturbed. In ponds entirely surrounded by forest growth and wooded swamps duckweeds also abound, but they are equally at home in small pools and other openings among the reeds and sedges of marshes. They are strictly fresh-water plants.

FROGBIT.

VALUE AS DUCK FOOD.

Frogbit and the three species next described (thalia, water elm, and swamp privet) are at present known to be of only local importance as wild-duck foods. Frogbit is an abundant inhabitant of some of the shallow cypress-margined lakes in Avoyelles Parish, La. It produces spherical fruits filled with gelatinous matter in which are a multitude of seeds, eagerly sought by ducks. Nearly 18 per cent of the food of 308 mallards collected in that locality from October to March, inclusive, consisted of these seeds. From 8,000 to 10,000 were found in each of several stomachs and one contained 32,000. Other ducks found feeding on frogbit seeds were the pintail and ringneck. Twenty-five stomachs of the latter species collected in December contained on the average over 35 per cent of these eagerly sought seeds.

DESCRIPTION OF PLANT.

Frogbit (*Limnobium spongia*) floats in shallow waters, extending its roots into the muck below, or it may grow on soft mud itself. On stalks from a few inches to a foot in length are several heart-shaped leaves (fig. 3), which have 5 to 7 longitudinal veins springing from the base, and numerous cross-veins. The underside of the leaves is sometimes purplish. Numerous spongy runners help to support the plant in the water, and they also form new plants at the joints. The flowers emerge from conspicuous sheaths, and appear to have 3 sepals which are broader and sometimes reflexed and 3 petals which are narrow and more erect. The stamens, 6 to 12 in number, are given off at different heights from a central column. The stalks supporting the berrylike fruits are thick and recurved. The berry, as previously noted, is filled with a mixture of seeds and gelatinous substance. The seeds are covered by minute tangled processes which cause them to cohere in masses. The fruit ripens in August.

DISTRIBUTION.

Frogbit is a local plant, especially in the northern part of its range. It has been found at Braddock Bay, N. Y., Monmouth County, N. J., and in Delaware, but the normal range probably is from North Carolina and Missouri southward. The range here mapped (fig. 4) is not complete, since the plant has been found in Mexico.

FIG. 3.—Frogbit.

PROPAGATION.

Frogbit is extensively used in aquaria and water gardens, and may be obtained from dealers in plants for such purposes. The plants themselves should be set out in water a few inches deep over a mucky bottom or in soft mud near the water's edge.

THALIA.

VALUE AS DUCK FOOD.

The writer's only experience with thalia (species *divaricata*) as a wild-duck food was on St. Vincent Island, Florida. Here a slough filled with a tall growth of these elegant plants was a favorite resort of ducks, especially mallards, which could always be flushed from

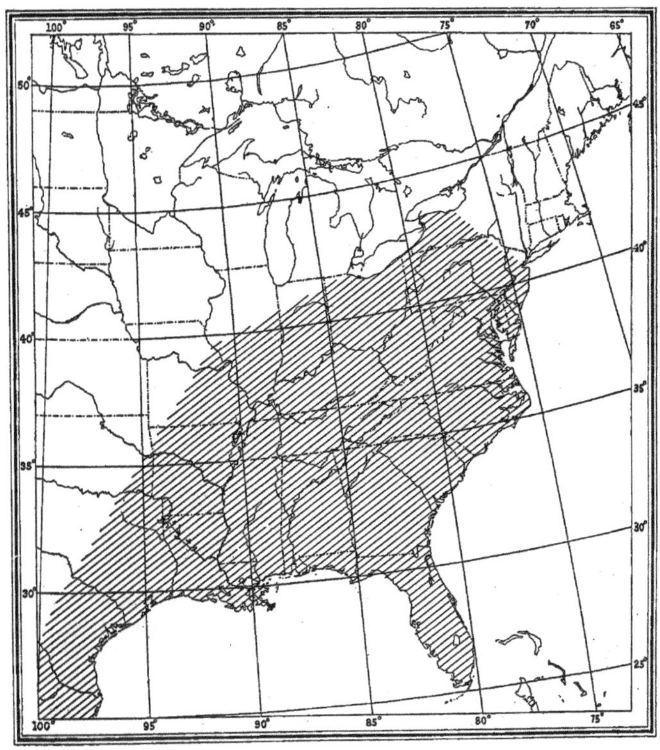

FIG. 4.—Range of frogbit.

this place. However, at the time of the writer's visit only one bird was obtained and its stomach contained a few thalia seeds. Another mallard collected at a later date in the same place, by the late Dr. R. V. Pierce, had fed almost exclusively on these large seeds, and its gullet and gizzard were well filled by 144 entire seeds and fragments of others.

The evidence is sufficient to show that thalia has great possibilities as a wild-duck food. The seeds are large and nutritious and are borne in great abundance. They ripen in July and August and are available to ducks throughout the winter, if the water is not frozen over.

DESCRIPTION OF PLANT.

A single plant of *Thalia divaricata* is a stout, one-leaved stalk from 4 to 15 feet in height, rising from a large tuberlike root, and the stems

FIG. 5.—*Thalia divaricata.*

are usually clustered (fig. 5). The leaf is much like that of canna, is stalked, and may measure 5 inches wide and 15 inches long. The top of the stalk divides and subdivides into a large fruiting head which may bear from 200 to 300 seeds. The ultimate branches of the fruiting head are strongly zigzag. The flowers and seeds are borne in husks, each of which is formed by two purplish bracts, one much larger than the other. The oblong seeds (fig. 6) are plump and vary in length up to three-eighths of an inch. They have thin, closely fitting individual husks, are slightly curved, and bear numerous longitudinal rows of small irregular elevations which are lighter in color than the rest of the surface.

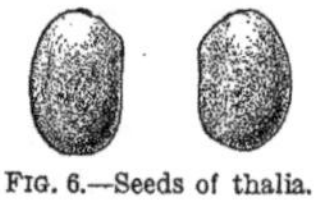

FIG. 6.—Seeds of thalia.

DISTRIBUTION.

Thalia divaricata is native from Florida to southern Arkansas and Texas and southward into Mexico, and doubtless it will thrive as far north as South Carolina and Missouri. Two other species (*T. dealbata* and *T. barbata*) occur in the region from South Carolina and Missouri south to Florida and Texas. Their value as duck food is unknown.

PROPAGATION.

Thalia can be propagated from either seeds or rootstocks. The seeds have a thick shell and the rootstocks are massive, so that neither should be injured if transported with ordinary precautions. Thalia occurs in greatest abundance in muddy sloughs, but it will grow in open water from 2 to 3 feet deep. If planted directly into open water, rootstocks should be used. Seeds should either be placed in shallow water or sprouted in a protected place and the young plants set out after they have attained some size.

WATER ELM.

VALUE AS DUCK FOOD.

That trees should produce food for wild ducks is at first thought surprising, but many do, as oaks, thorns, hollies, ashes, hackberries, and others; none is of more value for this purpose, however, than the water elm.

FIG. 7.—Leaves and fruit of water elm.

The most common wild duck in central Louisiana is the mallard; in fact it outnumbers all other species combined. Foods important to it, therefore, are the important duck-foods of the region. One hundred and seventy-one mallards collected in the vicinity of Mansura and Marksville, during October, November, and December, had fed on the seeds of water elm to the extent of 45.5 per cent of their total subsistence. The largest number of seeds taken by a single duck was upward of 200. These tightly filled the whole gullet and gizzard.

Other species of ducks seem to be fond of the seeds, judging from smaller numbers examined from this region. These include the black duck and the ringneck. Water-elm seeds are eaten by Arkansas mallards also.

DESCRIPTION OF PLANT.

The water elm thrives in swamps and on the margins of sluggish streams. Normally it grows in water which is permanently 2 to 3 feet deep, but it survives prolonged inundation of much greater depth. The tree seldom exceeds 40 feet in height and 20 inches in diameter, and usually is much smaller.

The bark is much like that of the hop hornbeam or ironwood, and the leaves (fig. 7), while obviously similar to those of our other elms, are smaller and have blunter marginal serrations.

FIG. 8.—Seedlings of water elm.

The water elm flowers very early, from February to April, and the fruit usually ripens and falls in a month or six weeks, but occasionally is found on the trees as late as August. The extreme length of a single specimen of the fruit is about a third of an inch. It consists of a plump seed with a shiny blue-black coating, inclosed in a burrlike hull (fig. 7) which is ridged and provided with numerous fleshy projections. The fruits, which are very numerous, drop into the water immediately upon or even before ripening. Seedlings (fig. 8) come up by the thousand in midsummer and young plants in all stages of growth are abundant, proving that, for increase, seed is the main dependence of the tree.

The water elm is also known (in books) as planer tree, and among the French-speaking people of Louisiana as chataignier and charmille.

DISTRIBUTION.

The range (fig. 9) of the water elm (*Planera aquatica*) extends from the lower Wabash Valley in Indiana to the river bottoms of eastern Texas, and from western Tennessee and southeastern North Carolina to Florida.

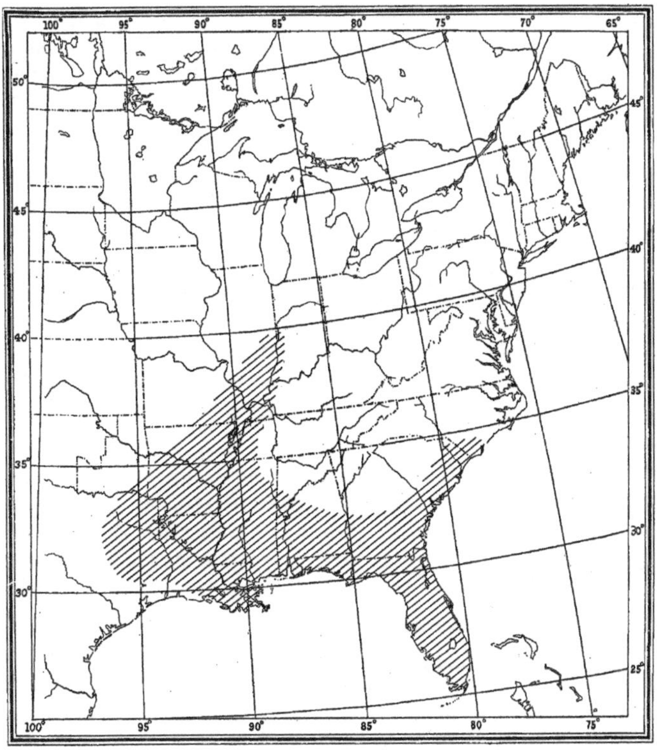

FIG. 9.—Range of water elm.

PROPAGATION.

Seeds of the water elm do not seem to be ripe at the time they usually fall; the real ripening probably occurs as they lie in the water beneath the parent tree. While it is difficult, therefore, to collect seeds in proper condition for planting, young plants of water elm abound and if carefully lifted and packed should stand shipment well. Great care must be taken to prevent the roots from drying. They should be embedded in balls of earth and sewed up in burlap.

Transportation should be as rapid as possible and the young trees should be set out or heeled in immediately upon receipt. Transplanting should be done when the trees are leafless.

SWAMP PRIVET.

VALUE AS DUCK FOOD.

The swamp privet is included principally on account of the testimony of numerous hunters as to its usefulness. Wood ducks in particular are said to feed extensively upon its seeds. Weeks before other species of ducks arrive these birds are abundant in the country where swamp privet grows and are said to consume most of the crop of seeds, leaving little for other ducks. The seeds have been found in numerous mallard stomachs, but in quantity in only one.

FIG. 10.—Leaves of swamp privet.

DESCRIPTION OF PLANT.

Swamp privet (*Forestiera acuminata*) or bois blanc, found in the same kinds of localities as the water elm, is a smooth-barked shrub (sometimes a small tree) usually with drooping stems, which frequently take root at the tip. The smooth, light-green leaves (fig. 10) are opposite, oval, taper-pointed at both ends, and with rounded serrations which are more prominent on the apical half. The fruit of swamp privet is a blue watery berry from one-half to three-fourths of an inch in length. Greatly subject to insect attack, it is usually distorted. The pit is nearly as long as the berry, pointed at both ends, and has numerous lengthwise, fibrous ridges. The seed within is white and smooth. The flowers, borne in clusters, bloom in March and April, and the fruit is ripe in May and June.

As is the case with seeds of the water elm, those of the swamp privet may remain under water for a long period without apparent deterioration. Probably most of the seeds are exposed by the annual lowering of the water level and germinate the summer they are produced. (See fig. 11.) Whether those which fall in deeper water ever germinate is unknown, but it is certain, so far as utility as duck food in concerned, that they keep in perfect condition far into the succeeding spring.

DISTRIBUTION.

Swamp privet is native from central Illinois and Tennessee, near Nashville, south to Texas and Florida (see fig. 12).

PROPAGATION.

Fruits of swamp privet fully ripen upon the tree. The seeds, being protected by a fibrous cover and the pulp of the berry, undoubtedly will stand shipment for ordinary distances. Prompt handling is advisable, however, and the usual precautions against fermentation should be taken. The seeds should be sown in well-watered beds and the young plants grown to some size before setting out. Collected young plants and the offshoots produced by the rooting of the tips of branches of older ones may be handled like those of the water elm.

FIG. 11.—Seedlings of swamp privet.

EEL-GRASS.

VALUE AS DUCK FOOD.

Few who have written of the habits of sea brant have failed to mention its fondness for eel-grass. The relation between this species of bird and plant seems to be as close as, if not closer than, that existing between the noted fresh-water pair, the canvasback duck and wild celery. So far as investigations of the food of the brant are concerned the published record is thoroughly substantiated. All normal stomach contents of the common brant thus far examined consisted exclusively of eel-grass. Other salt-water fowl also feed on eel-grass, as the surf and white-winged scoters. Six birds of the latter species collected at Netarts Bay, Oregon, had made 43 per cent of their last meal of it. The list of other ducks feeding on the plant includes the golden-eye, old squaw, bufflehead, mallard, and black duck, the last-named species sometimes devouring the seeds of

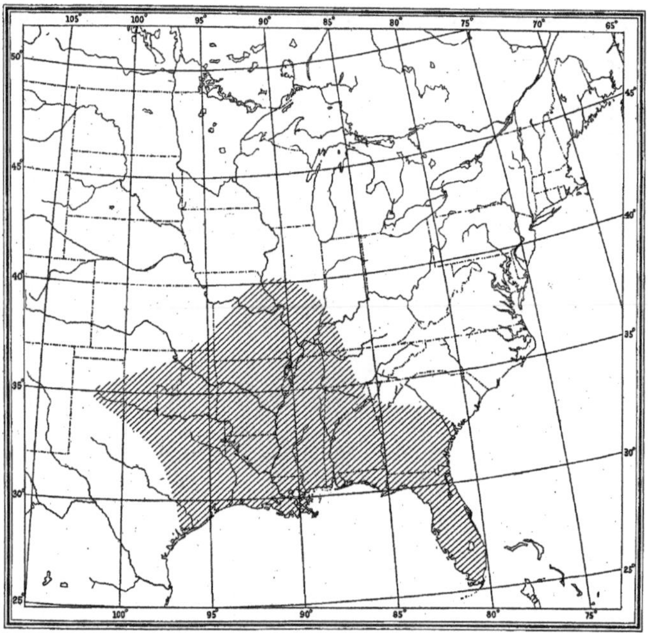

FIG. 12.—Range of swamp privet.

eel-grass in large numbers. The stomachs of 5 black ducks collected at Amityville, Long Island, N. Y., in October and November, contained on the average more than 66 per cent of eel-grass seeds, the number of seeds per stomach varying from 700 to 4,000. Eleven birds taken at Scarboro, Me., during the same months had eaten enough eel-grass seeds to make up 51 per cent of their food. In three cases fully 2,000 seeds had been taken. Thirteen ducks of the same species collected in Massachusetts in January and February had taken eel-grass, including both seeds and leaves, to the extent of more than 11 per cent of their food. The wigeon, a species which prefers foliage to the seeds and roots of aquatic plants, sometimes visits salt water to feed upon this plant. Five of these birds taken at South Island, South Carolina, in February, had made one-fourth of their meal of the leaves of eel-grass.

DESCRIPTION OF PLANT.

Eel-grass (*Zostera marina*) consists of bunches of long tapelike leaves which rise from a jointed fibrous-rooted creeping stem (fig. 13). The leaves bear a strong superficial resemblance to those of wild celery, but they are rarely more than a fourth of an inch wide, while those of wild celery are seldom as narrow. The leaf of eel-grass, furthermore, is tougher and more leathery than that of wild celery. When a mature leaf is torn across, numerous white fibers may be seen at the broken ends. Wild celery lacks these. The color of eel-grass leaves is olive or dark green, that of wild celery clear light green.[1]

The leaves grow in small bundles from the end of the rootstock or its branches, and may reach a length of 6 feet. The rootstocks, which usually are reddish, have joints about every half inch, at which they are easily broken. The numerous fibrous roots spring from these joints. Seeds of eel-grass are formed in sheaths alongside the leaves. They are about one-eighth of an inch in length, are placed end to end, and are barrel-shaped, with the surface conspicuously longi-

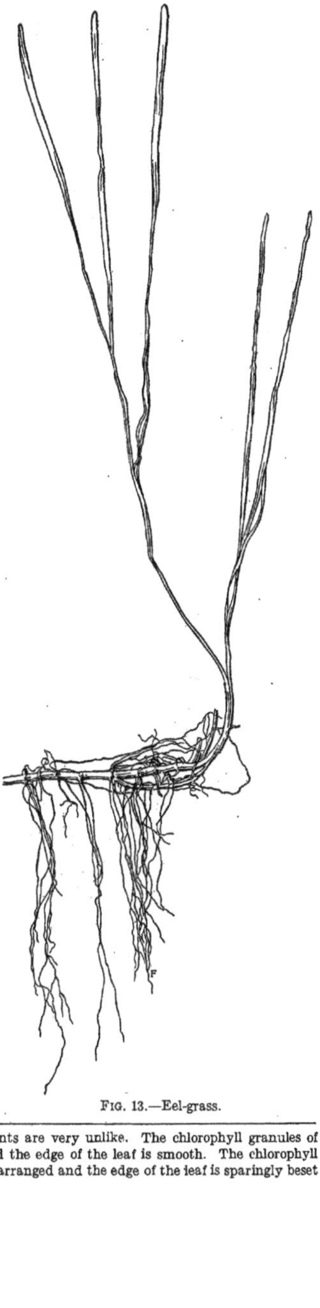

FIG. 13.—Eel-grass.

[1] Under the microscope the leaves of these two plants are very unlike. The chlorophyll granules of *Zostera* are arranged in regular longitudinal rows, and the edge of the leaf is smooth. The chlorophyll granules of *Vallisneria*, on the contrary, are irregularly arranged and the edge of the leaf is sparingly beset with minute teeth.

tudinally ribbed (fig. 14). Eel-grass has numerous common names, among which we may cite sea-wrack or grass-wrack, sea-, sweet-, barnacle-, turtle-, and wigeon-grass.

DISTRIBUTION.

Eel-grass is strictly a maritime species. In its natural habitat it is cosmopolitan. In North America it is found from Greenland to the Gulf of Mexico, and from Alaska to California.

PROPAGATION.

This plant grows only in salt water. It is common along shores facing the open ocean, but also grows in bays and even lagoons where the water must be far less salt than the sea. The seeds are not well protected against drying and for that reason are unsuitable for transplanting.[1] Moreover, unless they can be sown in a very quiet place the chances are against securing a catch. The rootstocks, however, are rather tough and resistant and, furthermore, can be fastened to the bottom. They must not be allowed to dry, but should be shipped wet and handled as rapidly as possible. Bury or fasten to the bottom in water a few feet deep where there is little surf. Once established the plant will spread to more exposed areas.

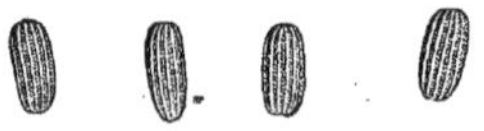

FIG. 14.—Seeds of eel-grass.

WIGEON-GRASS.

VALUE AS DUCK FOOD.

Wigeon-grass is of rather restricted range, but of considerable importance as a duck food almost everywhere it grows. In no locality, so far as known, is it more important than on the coast of Texas. Here the bays that have kept their wigeon-grass have kept their ducks; those in which the plant has been destroyed by influxes of mud and filling up of inlets have lost them. At Rockport, Tex., wigeon-grass still holds its own and is the main dependence of the visiting vegetarian ducks. About 64 per cent of the food of 33 pintails collected at Rockport in December was made up of rootstocks, leaves, and seeds of wigeon-grass. This plant furnished also two-thirds of the food of 3 wigeons, and more than 54 per cent of that of 37 redheads taken at the same time.

Records of the food of ducks on St. Vincent Island, Florida, show two other species of ducks to be very fond of this grass. Nineteen little bluebills collected in January had eaten it, principally the seeds, to the extent of over 63 per cent of their food, the number of seeds per stomach varying from 500 to 4,000. The food of 17 gadwells

[1] They undoubtedly can be preserved by cold storage in salt water, but considering the limited use that can be made of seeds on account of the heavy wash along most shores, this probably would not be profitable.

taken at the same time and place was 84 per cent wigeon-grass; and the stomach of a redhead contained about 5,120 seeds.

Most of the duck stomachs received by the Biological Survey from South Island, South Carolina, have contained wigeon-grass. It composed 41 per cent of the food of 3 blue-winged teals collected there in March, and 27 per cent of that of 8 gadwells obtained in February and March. In Currituck Sound, North Carolina, wigeon-grass grows among too great a profusion of other valuable duck foods to have the importance attained in less favored localities; nevertheless, it is a plant of considerable value. Practically 10 per cent of the food of 35 big bluebills collected there in November was composed of wigeon-grass, as was about the same proportion of the diet of 70 little bluebills.

At Back Bay, Virginia, 17 per cent of the food of 9 pintails collected in February consisted of wigeon-grass, and at Virginia City, Va., 16 per cent of the food of 14 mallards taken in January was of the same composition.

Other ducks found feeding on wigeon-grass are the Florida duck, black duck, green-winged and cinnamon teals, spoonbill, canvasback, ringneck, bufflehead, old squaw, ruddy duck, surf scoter, and hooded merganser.

DESCRIPTION OF PLANT.

Wigeon-grass (*Ruppia maritima*) is similar in habit to sago pondweed or foxtail.[1] Both have long, slender, filamentous leaves on widely spreading, much-branched stems. In wigeon-grass the basal parts of many of the leaves are enlarged (fig. 15), and this, upon close inspection, gives the plant quite a different appearance from sago pondweed. The seeds of sago pondweed are compactly grouped on a central axis, while those of wigeon-grass are borne singly on rather long stalks which radiate from the top of the fruiting peduncle (fig. 16). The latter organ usually is spirally coiled in wigeon-grass; in sago pondweed it never has more than a simple curve. The rootstock of wigeon-grass is tougher than that of sago pondweed, more frequently jointed, and often angled at the joints. There are no tubers. The seeds are black, rounded triangular in outline, with a small pit on each side near the apex, and on one edge an oblong lid which is forced out during germination. Pondweed seeds have a similar lid, but are usually larger than those of wigeon-grass, never black, and lack the apical pits.

Wigeon-grass is usually referred to in books as sea- or ditch-grass; it is also called tassel-grass, tassel-weed, tassel-pondweed, nigger-wool, puldoo-grass, and peter-grass. The last two names are compounded from terms by which the coot is known in southern States, and indicate that wigeon-grass is highly relished by that bird.

---

[1] Described in Biological Survey Circular No. 81, pp. 12-16.

DISTRIBUTION.

Wigeon-grass is a brackish-water plant. It grows in salt water, but probably never in that of full ocean strength. It also grows in water that passes for fresh, as in the upper part of Currituck Sound,

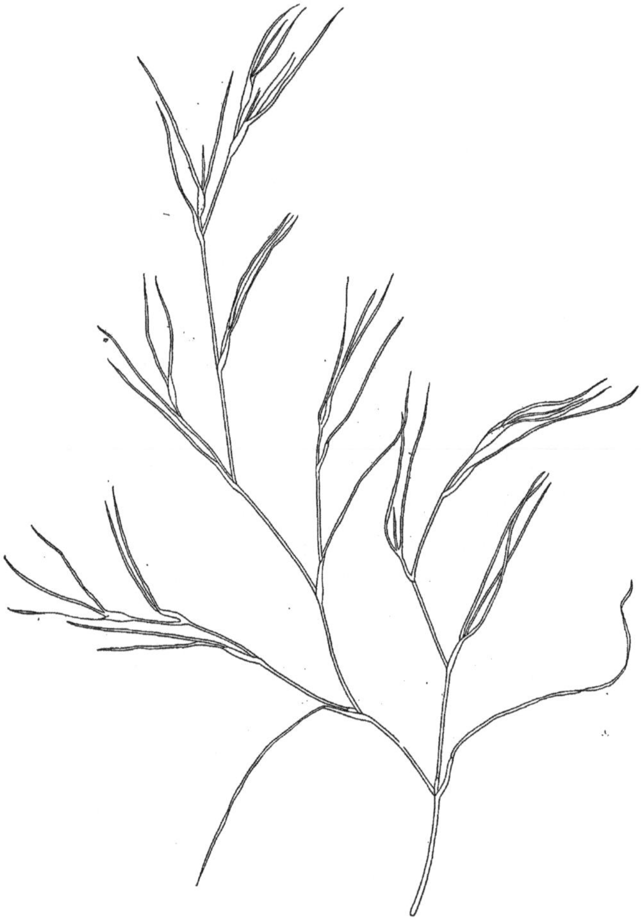

FIG. 15.—Wigeon-grass.

North Carolina, but inlets from the ocean to this part of the sound have existed in recent years and high tides at times cross the narrow beach. Salt in the soil or salt springs, even if covered by fresh water, also give wigeon-grass the conditions necessary for existence; this explains its scattering distribution in the interior of the country (fig. 17). Along the coasts wigeon-grass occurs from the base of the Alaska Peninsula and the Gulf of St. Lawrence south to Central America.[1]

PROPAGATION.

Wigeon-grass may be propagated from the seeds, which ripen in late summer and early autumn. These should be gathered with about 6 inches of the upper part of the plant, as the foliage tends to keep them from drying. This material should not be packed in large masses, but free circulation of air should be provided to prevent fermentation. As little time as possible should intervene between gathering and planting. If it is desired to keep the seeds for some time they may be placed in wet cold storage.

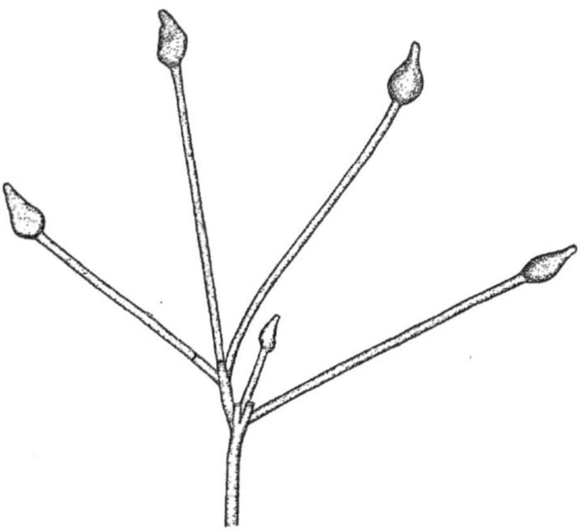

FIG. 16.—Fruits of wigeon-grass.

After soaking the seed until it will sink, sow broadcast, in quiet but not stagnant water over mud bottom. Wigeon-grass grows in water varying in depth from a few inches to 10 feet. It should be sown where the water is permanently 1 to 2 feet deep.

THREE PLANTS FOR DUCK FARMS.

The plants considered under this head are distinguished by rankness of vegetative growth, comparative unimportance of their seeds as duck food, and lack of fleshy rootstocks and tubers. These qualities render the plants generally undesirable for propagation as wild-duck foods, but they are the very things which make them valuable for duck farms. As a rule abundant green food is available to wild ducks, but the birds usually have to search for seeds, fruits, tubers, and like forms of concentrated nutriment. The conditions on a game farm are just the reverse. The birds are supplied grain food constantly, but need roughage, particularly of naturally suitable kinds. Plants of rapid, luxuriant growth are necessary and all requirements are fulfilled by water-cress, water-weed, and coontail.

[1] Authorities hold a variety of views regarding the number of species of *Ruppia* which occur in this area. The purposes of this publication, however, are best served by grouping all the forms under one name.

USE OF THESE PLANTS.

The three plants just mentioned are not recommended for planting in waters where any other growth is desired, since they are such rank growers that they are apt to take complete possession. One of them, namely, coontail, has considerable value as a wild-duck food, however, and may be tried in waters where other plants have failed.

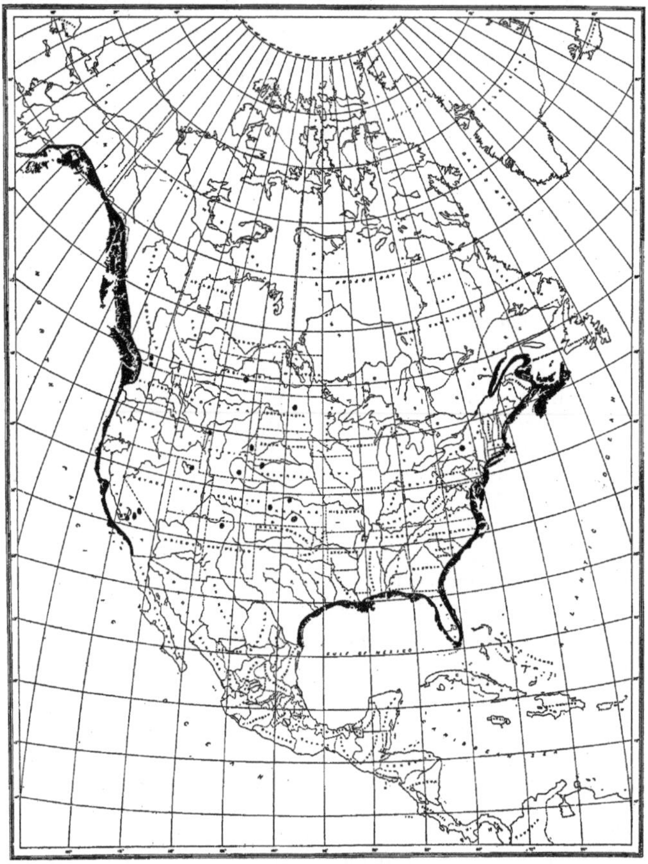

FIG. 17.—Range of wigeon-grass.

On duck farms best results will be obtained if the unit system of ponds be adopted. Ducks can be turned into one pond at a time, and when a pond is eaten out it may be resown, screened off, and allowed to make a new crop. Under favorable conditions waterweed and coontail will grow 6 inches a day.

WATER-CRESS.

VALUE AS DUCK FOOD.

Knowledge of the importance of water-cress as a duck food is derived entirely from breeders of wild ducks, who almost without exception consider it a valuable plant for a duck farm. Not only is it relished, but it is said to grow so fast in some places that the ducks can not eat it out.

DESCRIPTION OF PLANT.

Water-cress (*Sisymbrium nasturtium-aquaticum*) either floats in the water, rooted only at the lower end, or creeps along on mud or in shallow water, throwing out roots at every joint. It is a smooth, fleshy plant, with divided leaves and small white flowers (fig. 18). The leaves consist of 3 to 9 symmetrically arranged oval or roundish segments, of which the apical of each leaf is the largest. The pods vary from one-half to one and one-fourth inches in length, are slightly curved, and contain numerous small seeds. There is a constant succession of flowers and pods throughout the growing season. The plant sometimes is strongly tinged with olive-brown, suggesting one of its common names, brown-cress. Other names are well-cress or -grass, water-kers, -kars, -karse, or -grass, crashes, and brooklime.

FIG. 18.—Water-cress.

DISTRIBUTION.

Water-cress occurs practically throughout the United States.

PROPAGATION.

Water-cress usually is propagated by seed. This may be obtained from most seedsmen. The plant is also easily transplanted by cuttings. It grows in springs, brooks, small streams, and shallow ponds.

Waters in which it is found are usually cool and have some current. It may be sown in similar situations at any time during spring or summer.

WATER-WEED.

VALUE AS DUCK FOOD.

Evidence for the value of water-weed is of the same nature as for water-cress. The density and luxuriance of its growth are such that water-weed maintains its stand even when fed upon daily by a large number of ducks. Small quantities of the plant have been found in stomachs of the mallard, blue-winged teal, and goldeneye.

DESCRIPTION OF PLANT.

Water-weeds (figs. 19 and 20) have long, branching stems with luxuriant foliage and are of a beautiful translucent green color. The leaves, which are set upon the stem in whorls of from 2 to 4 (usually 3), vary from ovate to strap-shaped, and may be pointed or obtuse, and are sometimes finely toothed. They are from one-fourth to one inch or more in length and from one-twelfth to one-eighth of an inch in width. The small flowers are borne on rather long stalks and open at the surface of the water. The fruit, which is rare, is few seeded and ripens under water.

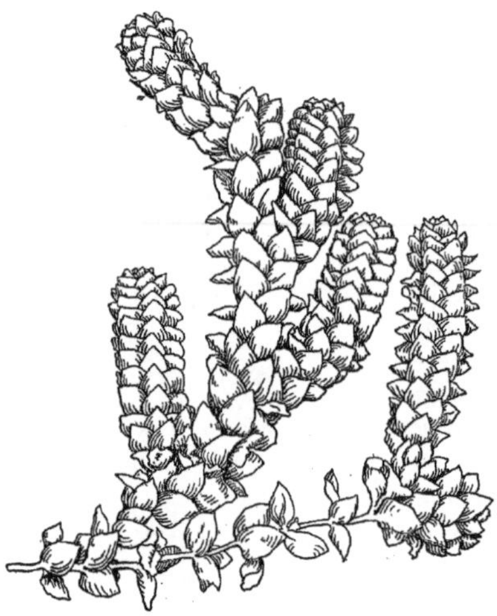

FIG. 19.—Water-weed. A compact form.

This plant was introduced into Great Britain in the middle of the nineteenth century, and spread rapidly, making such rank growth that it soon became a pest, filling ornamental waters, mill races, and canals. It became known there as American water-weed and Babington's curse (because introduced by a botanist of that name). Other names applied to the plant are ditch-moss, water-thyme, thyme-weed, cats-tails, and choke pond-weed.

Some botanists consider that there are several different species of water-weed in the United States. But, having in mind the entirely different aspect wild plants of water-weed assume when transferred to an aquarium, one is inclined to think that differences in the forms, which have been thought to represent distinct species, may be largely due to conditions under which the plants were grown.

Water-weed has had various scientific names applied to it, and the following may be encountered in trade catalogues: *Philotria*, *Elodea*, and *Anacharis*. The specific name that has been most commonly used in this country is *canadensis*. Dealers in aquarium plants usually list a form of water-weed known as *Anacharis canadensis gigantea*.

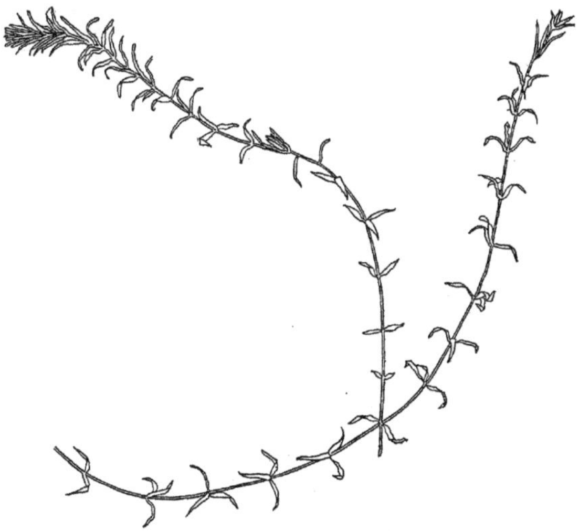

FIG. 20.—Water-weed. A diffuse form.

DISTRIBUTION.

Water-weeds grow naturally throughout most of North America.

PROPAGATION.

Water-weed propagates itself from pieces of leafy stem or root. It is tenacious of life, and if shipment in good condition is achieved, no trouble will be experienced in obtaining a stand of the plant. Bury the roots or bases of stems in the bottom in shallow water for quick results. The plant will grow, however, if only thrown in water shallow enough (3 feet or less) to allow it to send roots to the bottom. It likes a loam or sandy loam and does not grow in clay. Either still or running waters are suitable. When established it will spread to water up to 10 feet in depth.

COONTAIL.

VALUE AS DUCK FOOD.

The seeds of coontail are eaten by practically all wild ducks, but the foliage by a much smaller number and less frequently. Ducks known to feed on this plant are the following: Hooded merganser, mallard, black duck, Florida duck, gadwell, wigeon, green-winged and blue-winged teals, spoonbill, pintail, wood duck, redhead, canvasback, little and big bluebills, ringneck, goldeneye, buffle-head, old squaw, white-winged scoter, ruddy duck, and the whistling swan.

The following instances show the local value of coontail to some of these species of ducks:

About 30 per cent of the food of 171 mallards collected about Mansura and Marksville, La., from October to December consisted of coontail, and as many as 150 seeds were found in a single stomach. Much more than the ordinary proportion of stems and leaves of the plant were taken by these birds.

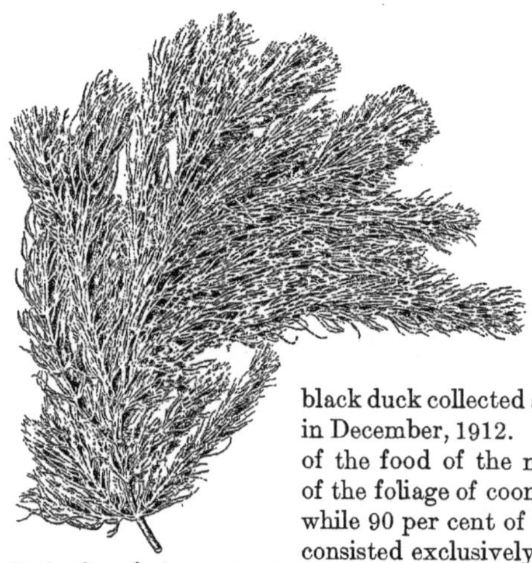

FIG. 21.—Coontail. A compact form.

Another illustration of foliage eating is furnished by 8 mallards and 1 black duck collected at Big Lake, Arkansas, in December, 1912. More than 85 per cent of the food of the mallards was made up of the foliage of coontail, with a few seeds, while 90 per cent of the black duck's food consisted exclusively of coontail foliage.

Sixty-four mallards collected at Menesha, Ark., in November and December, 1909, had fed on coontail seeds to the extent of 7.23 per cent of their diet. Fourteen of the same species of duck, taken at Lake Wapanoca, Arkansas, in November, 1910, had eaten enough seeds, with a little foliage of coontail, to form on the average more than half of their food.

The plant thus has considerable local value as a wild-duck food. However, its tendency to crowd out more desirable species makes transplanting unwise, unless in particularly difficult cases where other plants have failed. The very qualities of coontail that make it a nuisance in natural waters commend it to duck farmers.

DESCRIPTION OF PLANT.

The stems of coontail (*Ceratophyllum demersum*) are thickly clothed with round, dense masses of foliage (figs. 21 and 22), which in shape amply justify the common name so widely used in the South, and which is here adopted for the plant. Coontail is a submerged plant, but only exceptionally is it attached to the bottom, as it has no roots; it usually grows in rather quiet waters from 2 to 10 feet deep. The leaves are composed of slender but rather stiff filaments, twice or thrice forked, and sparingly furnished with small acute projections. They grow in whorls of from 5 to 12, and are usually much crowded on the upper part of the stem.

FIG. 22.—Coontail. A diffuse form.

The fruit of coontail (fig. 23) is composed of a rather large, flattened seed, wedge-shaped at one end and rounded at the other, inclosed in a thin covering which bears various tubercles on the surface and spines on the margin. A common form has one spine at the apex and one at each basal angle of the fruit. One may examine many plants without finding fruit; nevertheless, the frequency with which ducks find it proves that a good crop is produced. Coontail is known also as hornwort, hornweed, morass-weed, coontail moss, fish-blankets, and June grass.

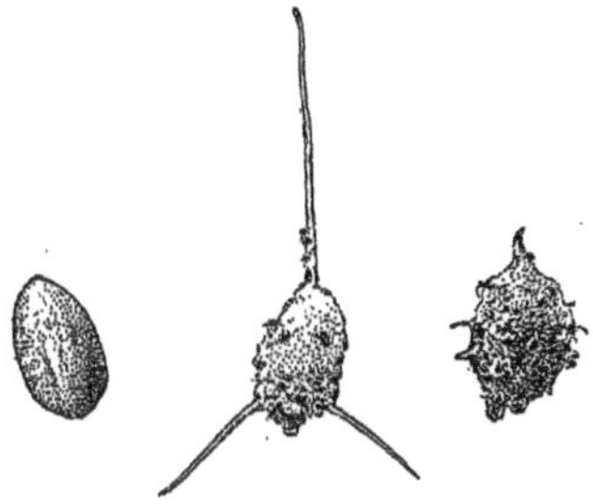

FIG. 23.—Seeds and fruit of coontail.

DISTRIBUTION.

Coontail is practically cosmopolitan and occurs throughout all but the extreme northern parts of North America.

PROPAGATION.

Pieces of coontail broken off from the parent plant promptly make new colonies, a characteristic which makes transplanting easy. Care need be taken only to see that the plants do not lose their vitality either through drying or fermentation during shipment.

Plant in quiet water. As the plant has no roots, it is enabled to thrive over hard or sandy bottoms where many other plants can not establish themselves.

ADDITIONAL COPIES
OF THIS PUBLICATION MAY BE PROCURED FROM
THE SUPERINTENDENT OF DOCUMENTS
GOVERNMENT PRINTING OFFICE
WASHINGTON, D. C.
AT
5 CENTS A COPY

WASHINGTON : GOVERNMENT PRINTING OFFICE : 1915

UNITED STATES DEPARTMENT OF AGRICULTURE
BULLETIN No. 206
Contribution from the Bureau of Animal Industry
A. D. MELVIN, Chief

Washington, D. C. May 25, 1915

THE WOOLGROWER AND THE WOOL TRADE

By

F. R. MARSHALL and L. L. HELLER
Animal Husbandry Division

CONTENTS

WASHINGTON
GOVERNMENT PRINTING OFFICE
1915

BULLETIN OF THE
U.S. DEPARTMENT OF AGRICULTURE

No. 206

Contribution from the Bureau of Animal Industry, A. D. Melvin, Chief.
May 25, 1915.

THE WOOLGROWER AND THE WOOL TRADE.

By F. R. Marshall and L. L. Heller,
Of the Animal Husbandry Division.

CONTENTS.

INTRODUCTION.

The United States ranks as one of the principal wool-producing countries of the world. The amount of wool imported by American manufacturers is equal to more than one-half of the home-grown clip. American and foreign wools are often offered for sale at the same time in the warehouses of Boston and other wool-marketing centers. Some American wools are equally as valuable as the best foreign wools of the same class. On the whole, however, the appearance of American wools compares quite unfavorably with that of most of the foreign wools. The difference is due nearly altogether to the growers' methods of preparing the wool for shipment. Foreign woolgrowers, and Australians in particular, maintain a uniformly high standard in the handling of their wools. This care in preparation and the certainty as to the character of the contents of the bales has given their wools a high reputation that insures their bringing full value at the time of selling to the manufacturer.

Persons familiar with the buying and manufacturing of home-grown and foreign wools assert that on account of poor preparation

Note.—This bulletin discusses the preparation of wools for market and explains the effect upon the value of wool of the factors under the control of the grower. It is of interest to all sheep owners.

American wools net the grower from 1 to 3 cents a pound less than their actual value. This is due to the failure to classify the wool before selling and to defects from the use of improper twine, branding paints, and other minor causes.

The undesirable features which manufacturers have come to look for in American wools constitute a fixed charge which is borne by the producer. There seems to be little doubt that most of the work necessary to place American wools upon a parity with imported wools in our markets can best be done at the time of shearing.

Prevailing methods of selling do little to acquaint the grower with the manufacturers' complaints in regard to his output. In the range States where the clips are large the individual grower may establish for his wool a reputation that will enhance its selling price. To establish fully and realize the benefit of improved methods some form of cooperative effort is necessary. Especially is this true with farm wools where the single clip is small, and ordinarily passes through the hands of a number of uninformed dealers or local buyers and reaches the manufacturers only as part of an offering made up from a large number of clips, varying widely as to quality and care in preparation.

PRESENT METHODS OF DISPOSING OF WOOL BY THE GROWERS.

Western wools.—In the range States sheep are shorn either in sheds located on the premises of the sheep owner or at plants owned by individuals who employ shearers, fleece tiers, and sackers, and shear sheep from various owners at an agreed charge which includes all labor and material necessary to deliver the wool in sacks to its owner. Each individual owner attends to the selling of his own wool. In a few cases manufacturers send their buyers out to purchase wool direct from the growers, but the most of the clips are sold to buyers representing eastern dealers. There is no public market or wool exchange in this country. All transactions in the field or at the points where wool is concentrated by the dealers to be resold to manufacturers are made privately. The newspapers and trade and agricultural papers, upon which the grower must depend for information as to the value of his clip, base their reports of the wool market upon such facts as can be gathered from buyers or sellers at the main wool-selling centers, which are Boston, Philadelphia, Chicago, New York, and St. Louis. In some seasons wool is contracted for before shearing.

If unwilling to sell at the price offered at home the wool grower may consign his wool to a commission house and take chances upon the market falling or rising. Many concerns will either buy wool on speculation or accept it to be sold on commission. In neither case do the wool grower and the maufacturer come in contact with each other, and the former understands the defects of his wool and its handling only as there is chance opportunity to learn of them through the speculator or the distant commission agent.

During the past six seasons a growers' semicooperative selling agency has been in operation in Chicago, with branches in Boston and Philadelphia. The establishment has handled considerable wool, but according to report its growth and service have been less than might have been realized if growers had adhered to the policy of consigning their wool to it instead of using it as a lever to secure higher prices from buyers in the field.

Eastern wools.—The fact that much of the wool produced on farms of the Central and Eastern States is considered as secondary to mutton production does not lessen the need of giving the highest possible value to the grower. Here the producer is even farther removed from the manufacturer than in the case of the range sheepman, who can usually deal with some one acquainted with the values of wools and capable of distinguishing between clips varying in grade and quality. Considerable farm wool is sold to country storekeepers at a uniform price to accumulate into lots of sufficient size to be sold to a traveling buyer. In Minnesota and Wisconsin cooperative selling agencies have been established. The managers of these agencies put the entire amount received into suitable grades for selling to the manufacturers and set a fair price upon each lot of wool received.

Lack of contact between the manufacturer and the wool grower is largely responsible for the latter's failure to place his wool upon the market in such a way as to secure its full value. In order to dispose of wool to the best advantage growers must know the shrinkage and the proper class and grade names for their wools and be able to understand the reports of the market as published.

The pages that follow deal with the factors that determine the value of wool, market reports, grading, sorting, and methods of effecting improvement in the preparation of wool.

FACTORS THAT DETERMINE THE VALUE OF WOOL.

SHRINKAGE.

It is the buyer's first duty in inspecting an offering to make an estimate of the yield of clean or scoured wool. American wools may shrink from 25 to 80 per cent. Since more than 300 pounds of grease wool may be required to produce 100 pounds of scoured, the importance of shrinkage in the eyes of the buyer is readily recognized. Some of the wastes that occur during manufacturing can be used in other types of fabrics, but the loss in scouring is a complete loss.

Shrinkage is due first and chiefly to the oil present in varying quantities in all natural wool. The term "condition" has a special use in the wool trade, referring to the amount of oil or yolk and foreign matter and not to strength or color. Wool from sheep of the breeds that have been bred chiefly for fineness and weight of fleece carries much more oil than that from so-called coarse breeds, or those bred for mutton and having wool of relatively coarser fiber. The weight of a heavy, soggy, greasy fleece may gratify the grower, but the actual commercial value depends solely upon the amount and quality of the clean, scoured wool. American breeders as a rule consider that a large amount of oil is necessary and desirable in the production of a fine quality of wool. It is true that our best wools come from fleeces that shrink rather heavily from oil. At the same time much of the Australian wool shrinks very much less than that of the same fineness produced in this country.

Sand, dust, dirt, burs, and seeds also lower the yield as well as affect the value of the clean wool. The sand present is due to the storms that are experienced in some parts of the West. An instance is related of a sand storm making it necessary to suspend operation at a shearing corral for half an hour. At the end of that time the average weight of fleeces had risen from 6 to 9 pounds, which could hardly be attributed to growth of wool during that time. It is impossible to produce other than heavy-shrinking wools upon some of the sandy ranges, but if there is to be any profit from the operation the wools must be of good character otherwise.

In figuring shrinkages in this country there is no common standard. Some concerns scour cleaner than others, and scour different wools to varying degrees of cleanliness, according to the purpose for which they are to be used. Neither is there any standard as to the amount of moisture present after the wool has been dried. Hot tests are taken immediately after the wool is dried, while in the cold tests the wool has been allowed to "condition," or regain moisture for a time.

The dealers often have sample lots scoured for their own information, and the mills, before buying, may also make a test. Sometimes the shrinkage in the two tests will vary from 1 to 2 per cent, it being to the advantage of the mill to get out every vestige of grease in such a test. A good grader is supposed to estimate within 1 per cent of the actual shrinkage. It has been said that short-fibered wools shrink 2 to 3 per cent more than longer ones of similar character. This statement is in accord with what one would naturally suppose, but there are no available data to show this amount of difference.

Table 1 (prepared by the National Wool Warehouse and Storage Co., of Chicago) indicates the important part that shrinkage plays in fixing prices. At the top are the prices per pound of clean or scoured wool. These are applicable to wools worth from 40 to 70 cents, which limits will cover all ordinary cases. In the column to the left are the percentages of shrinkage. These run from 55 to 75. Take a case of clean wool being worth 40 cents. If it shrinks 60 per cent the wool is worth 16 cents in the grease. On the other hand, if the shrinkage is known and also the grease value, the clean value can be calculated readily.

TABLE 1.—*Relative prices of scoured and raw wool at varying percentages of shrinkage.*

Shrinkage.	Price of clean or scoured wool (cents)—															
	40	41	42	43	44	45	46	47	48	49	50	51	52	53	54	55
Per cent.	*Cts.*	*Cts.*	*Cts.*	*Cts.*	*Cts.*	*Cts.*	*Cts.*	*Cts.*	*Cts.*	*Cts.*	*Cts.*	*Cts.*	*Cts.*	*Cts.*	*Cts.*	*Cts.*
65	18.0	18.4	18.9	19.3	19.8	20.2	20.7	21.1	21.6	22.0	22.5	22.9	23.4	23.8	24.3	24.7
	17.6	18.0	18.5	18.9	19.4	19.8	20.2	20.7	21.1	21.6	22.0	22.4	23.9	23.3	23.8	24.2
57	17.2	17.6	18.1	18.5	18.9	19.3	19.8	20.2	20.6	21.1	21.5	21.9	22.4	22.8	23.2	23.7
58	16.8	17.2	17.6	18.1	18.5	18.9	19.3	19.7	20.2	20.6	21.0	21.4	21.8	22.3	22.7	23.1
59	16.4	16.8	17.2	17.6	18.0	18.4	18.9	19.3	19.7	20.1	20.5	20.9	21.3	21.7	22.1	22.6
60	16.0	16.4	16.8	17.2	17.6	18.0	18.4	18.8	19.2	19.6	20.0	20.4	20.8	21.2	21.6	22.0
61	15.6	16.0	16.4	16.8	17.2	17.5	17.9	18.3	18.7	19.1	19.5	19.9	20.3	20.7	21.1	21.5
62	15.2	15.6	16.0	16.3	16.7	17.1	17.5	17.9	18.2	18.6	19.0	19.4	19.8	20.1	20.5	20.9
63	14.8	15.2	15.5	15.9	16.3	16.6	17.0	17.4	17.8	18.1	18.5	18.9	19.2	19.6	20.0	20.3
64	14.4	14.8	15.1	15.5	15.8	16.2	16.6	16.9	17.3	17.6	18.0	18.4	18.7	19.1	19.4	19.8
65	14.0	14.3	14.7	15.1	15.4	15.7	16.1	16.4	16.8	17.1	17.5	17.9	18.2	18.6	18.9	19.3
66	13.6	13.9	14.3	14.6	15.0	15.3	15.6	16.0	16.3	16.7	17.0	17.3	17.7	18.0	18.3	18.7
67	13.2	13.5	13.9	14.2	14.5	14.8	15.2	15.5	15.8	16.2	16.5	16.8	17.2	17.5	17.8	18.2
68	12.8	13.1	13.4	13.7	14.1	14.4	14.7	15.0	15.4	15.7	16.0	16.3	16.6	17.0	17.3	17.6
69	12.4	12.7	13.0	13.3	13.6	13.9	14.3	14.6	14.9	15.2	15.5	15.8	16.1	16.4	16.7	17.1
70	12.0	12.3	12.6	12.9	13.2	13.5	13.8	14.1	14.4	14.7	15.0	15.3	15.6	15.9	16.2	16.5
71	11.6	11.9	12.2	12.5	12.8	13.0	13.3	13.6	13.9	14.2	14.5	14.8	15.1	15.4	15.7	16.0
72	11.2	11.5	11.8	12.0	12.2	12.6	12.9	13.1	13.4	13.7	14.0	14.3	14.6	14.8	15.1	15.4
73	10.8	11.0	11.3	11.6	11.9	12.1	12.4	12.7	13.0	13.2	13.5	13.8	14.0	14.3	14.6	14.9
74	10.4	10.6	10.9	11.2	11.4	11.7	11.9	12.2	12.5	12.7	13.0	13.3	13.5	13.8	14.0	14.3
75	10.0	10.2	10.5	10.7	11.0	11.2	11.5	11.8	12.0	12.2	12.5	12.8	13.0	13.2	13.5	13.8

Shrinkage.	Price of clean or scoured wool (cents)—														
	56	57	58	59	60	61	62	63	64	65	66	67	68	69	70
Per ct.	*Cts.*	*Cts.*	*Cts.*	*Cts.*	*Cts.*	*Cts.*	*Cts.*	*Cts.*	*Cts.*	*Cts.*	*Cts.*	*Cts.*	*Cts.*	*Cts.*	*Cts.*
55	25.2	25.6	26.1	26.5	27.0	27.4	27.9	28.3	28.8	29.2	29.7	30.1	30.6	31.0	31.5
56	24.6	25.1	25.5	26.0	26.4	26.8	27.3	27.7	28.2	28.6	29.0	29.4	30.0	30.4	30.8
57	24.1	24.5	24.9	25.4	25.8	26.2	26.7	27.1	27.5	28.0	28.4	28.8	29.2	29.7	30.1
58	23.5	23.9	24.4	24.8	25.2	25.6	26.0	26.5	26.9	27.3	27.7	28.1	28.6	29.0	29.4
59	23.0	23.4	23.8	24.2	24.6	25.0	25.4	25.8	26.2	26.7	27.1	27.5	27.9	28.3	28.7
60	22.4	22.8	23.2	23.6	24.0	24.4	24.8	25.2	25.6	26.0	26.4	26.8	27.2	27.6	28.0
61	21.8	22.2	22.6	23.0	23.4	23.8	24.2	24.6	25.0	25.4	25.7	26.1	26.5	26.9	27.3
62	21.3	21.7	22.0	22.4	22.8	23.2	23.6	23.9	24.3	24.7	25.1	25.5	25.8	26.2	26.6
63	20.7	21.1	21.5	21.8	22.2	22.6	22.9	23.3	23.7	24.0	24.4	24.8	25.2	25.5	25.9
64	20.2	20.5	20.9	21.2	21.6	22.0	22.3	22.7	23.0	23.4	23.8	24.1	24.5	24.8	25.2
65	19.6	20.0	20.3	20.7	21.0	21.4	21.7	22.1	22.4	22.8	23.1	23.5	23.8	24.2	24.5
66	19.0	19.4	19.7	20.1	20.4	20.7	21.1	21.4	21.8	22.1	22.4	22.8	23.1	23.5	23.8
67	18.5	18.8	19.1	19.5	19.8	20.1	20.5	20.8	21.1	21.5	21.8	22.1	22.4	22.8	23.1
68	17.9	18.2	18.6	18.9	19.2	19.5	19.8	20.2	20.5	20.8	21.1	21.4	21.8	22.1	22.4
69	17.4	17.7	18.0	18.3	18.6	18.9	19.2	19.5	19.8	20.2	20.5	20.8	21.1	21.4	21.7
70	16.8	17.1	17.4	17.7	18.0	18.3	18.6	18.9	19.2	19.5	19.8	20.1	20.4	20.7	21.0
71	16.2	16.5	16.8	17.1	17.4	17.7	18.0	18.3	18.6	18.9	19.1	19.4	19.7	20.0	20.3
72	15.7	16.0	16.2	16.5	16.8	17.1	17.4	17.6	17.9	18.2	18.5	18.8	19.0	19.3	19.6
73	15.1	15.4	15.7	15.9	16.2	16.5	16.7	17.0	17.3	17.6	17.8	18.1	18.4	18.6	18.9
74	14.6	14.8	15.1	15.3	15.6	15.9	16.1	16.4	16.6	16.9	17.2	17.4	17.7	17.9	18.2
75	14.0	14.3	14.5	14.8	15.0	15.3	15.5	15.8	16.0	16.3	16.5	16.8	17.0	17.3	17.5

CLASSES OF WOOL.

The value of wool is influenced more or less by its length and it is classified accordingly. The longer wools are known as "combing" and the shorter ones as "clothing." These classes are shown in Plate I. This classification is founded upon the English or Bradford system of manufacture, which requires a wool to be about 2½ inches long to be successfully combed. The lower grades of combing wools are usually considerably longer than this, as the coarser wool generally has more length. Clothing wools are shorter. Of late years a class midway between the two has sprung up, known as "baby combing." The French combs handle this length of staple quite satisfactorily.

The combing wools are used in worsted manufacturing. Only the longer straightened fibers are used and these are placed parallel in the yarn. The short, broken, and tangled fibers are removed and make up the "noils." Not only is length required, but also strength. Tender wools will not stand the combing process and are unfitted for this purpose, regardless of length. None but virgin[1] wools are used in the manufacture of worsteds.

Clothing wools are used in the manufacture of woolens, felts, etc. The fibers are laid in every direction, and instead of attempting to arrange them parallel as in worsteds, the opposite extreme is desired. Noils, shoddy, etc., can be used in this process of manufacture.

The difference in value between combing and clothing wools is from 2 to 6 cents per scoured pound in favor of the former.

Coarse, low wools more or less resembling hair are classed as carpet wools. A very small amount of these are produced in America, most of those used being imported from Asia. Some Navajo wool is used in carpet manufacture.

The factors that determine the length of the wool are not all under the control of the flockmaster. The wool does not grow so long on old sheep as it does on a young animal, but short pasture and faulty methods of herding tend to decrease the normal length. Some sheep have been bred for longer staple and naturally produce a greater length of fiber than others

GRADE.

Wool is graded according to fineness, and generally the finer the grade the better the price per scoured pound. Because of their low-shrinking qualities, coarser wools in the grease may sell for as much as or more than the finer ones, but when cleaned there may be as much difference as 20 cents a pound in price. The various grades are discussed on pages 14 to 21.

CHARACTER IN WOOL.

Character in wool will scarcely admit of definition, yet it is very important. Sometimes this may only be acknowledged by preference, or a greater demand at the same price, but at other times there is a difference in price. Color would come under this heading. A white wool is often desired rather than one of a creamy tinge, as the latter tint often shows up after scouring. A wool with lots of "life" or "nature," which means that the fibers are sound and lustrous and that the yolk is of a uniform consistency rather than clotted, is desirable. "Lofty" is another word used to describe a

[1] See glossary of wool terms at end of bulletin for explanation of technical words and phrases.

superior wool of considerable crimp that is uniform in character. Lofty wools possess considerable elasticity and spin higher than those lacking this quality. In well-grown wools the staples or locks are more distinct and the fibers are more nearly parallel than in the frowzy wools. Fleeces from poorly bred sheep show greater variation in diameter of fiber and are more likely to "run out" on the flanks, and this wool is consequently not so valuable. Black fiber shows up occasionally among mutton-bred sheep, and it is objectionable. Kempy wool is worth several cents a pound less than a similar quality free from this defect which denotes poor breeding.

TENDER WOOL.

Wool that has a weak part somewhere in its length must generally go into the clothing class, and in some instances it is inferior even for this. The exact cause of "tender" wool is not always known. It is generally agreed that sickness, a sudden shock from a blizzard, lack of feed, a rapid change from green to dry feed, or vice versa, and overfeeding often cause this condition. Sickness will often cause a distinct "break" in the fiber throughout the fleece. In general, better care and housing conditions decrease the percentage of tender wool, yet this is not always the case. Sheep that have been largely allowed to rough it, but having plenty of feed, have been known to produce better clips than the flock closely housed. "Frowziness" often indicates tender wool. After the wool has been clipped it may become tender through becoming wet. Tender wools are worth several cents per scoured pound less than sound wools. Plates II and III show well-grown, tender, and frowzy wools.

USE OF PAINT FOR BRANDING.

The practice of branding the sheep with paint is very generally established throughout the range country. The brands are usually placed upon the shoulders, side, or back—the most valuable parts of the fleece. Under some conditions it is doubtless necessary to brand, but tar brands should be avoided and the brands used should be as small as possible. At the present time most of the American dealers recognize no brand as soluble in scouring, but regard all paint locks with distrust. The damage done by the paint can scarcely be estimated. It is not only the damage to the locks directly affected, but the fibers carrying the paint are more or less mixed throughout the fleece, and it is almost impossible to get them all out. The amount of damage done varies with the kind of wool and the use to which it is put. One of the prominent felt manufacturing concerns that uses large amounts of the Texas wools for fine felts tries by every means to eliminate the paint. The painted wool is separated in sorting, and yet the scoured wool contains so many specks that it is necessary to "hand pick" it. This process costs from 3 to 5 cents per scoured pound, and with the quantities handled by this firm in one year the expense amounts to between $8,000 and $10,000. This concern will pay one-half to 1 cent extra for wool suitable to its need guaranteed free from paint. Another manufacturer writes: "If the brand marks on a lot of wool were unfailingly and altogether soluble it would enhance its value to us about one-fifth of a cent per pound, the usual cost of clipping." It is good practice to clip off the brands before shearing.

TAGS.

Tags are worth about one-third as much as good wool, depending somewhat upon condition. Ordinary tags shrink much more in scouring than the fleece proper taken from the same sheep. Most clips have the tags on the inside of the fleeces. In buying wool containing tags the buyer usually discounts enough so that he will be safe. It is generally better to remove the tags so that the exact amount can be ascertained, as the grower will generally fare better under this system. It must be admitted, however, that the custom of discounting 1 per cent for tags even after they have been sacked separately does not recognize the value of separate sacking. Another very serious objection to allowing tags to remain in the fleece is that they are likely to stain the surrounding wool, especially when it is wet.

WET WOOL.

Wet wool has been known to "take fire," and there are numerous instances where it has been damaged to the extent of from 1 to 2 cents per pound. The damage is not altogether due to the weakening of the fiber, but also to staining, especially when there are any tags present.

Often wool must be hauled for long distances and piled up along the tracks waiting for shipment. In such case it is sometimes subjected to heavy rain, and while the bags apparently dry out where the air has access, there is no chance for drying inside the pile. When the bags once become wet it often takes months for them to dry out. It is said that as much as 10 per cent of the wools from one of the western States was damaged by moisture in 1913.

WOOL CONTAINING BURS.

Burry fleeces should be separated from the others if there are very many burs present. The hard burs can usually be knocked out during the process of manufacture with a little extra work, but the soft burs entail considerable extra expense. They often open up in a spiral or

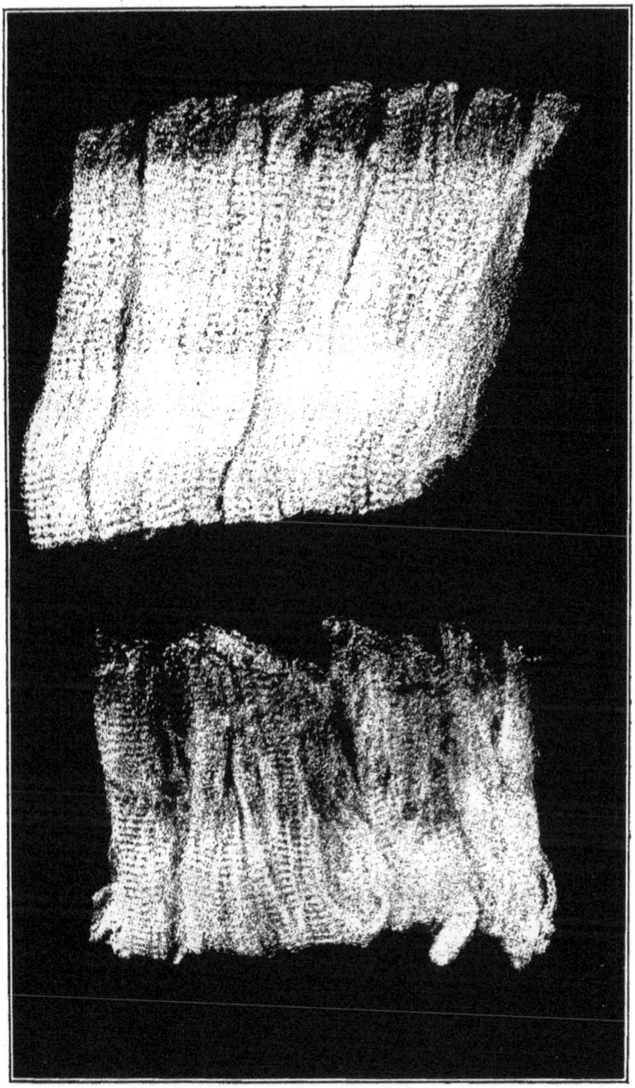

COMBING (UPPER) AND CLOTHING (LOWER) WOOLS.

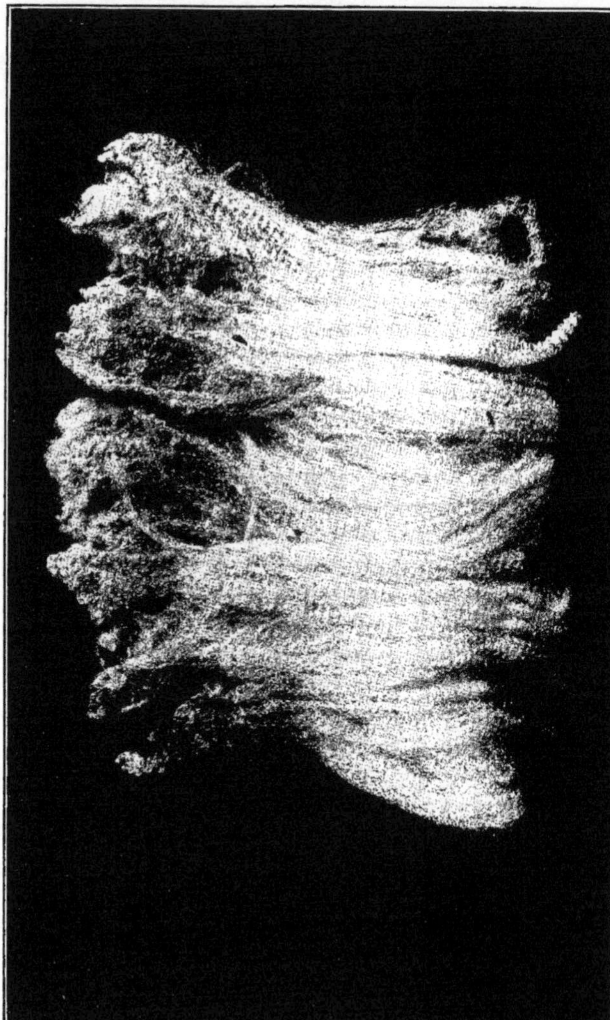

WELL-GROWN WOOL.

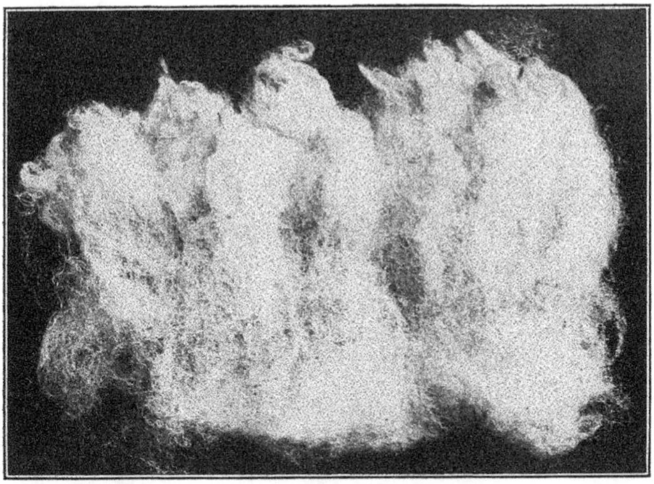

FIG. 1.—FROWZY WOOL.

FIG. 2.—TENDER WOOL, SHOWING BREAK.

WOOL PACKED IN OLD SACKS AND POORLY SEWED.

corkscrew shape and can not be separated in carding. Such wools may be run through a bur picker, which, together with the bur guards on the card, removes them. In the shorter extremely burry wools the process of carbonizing is practiced. This consists of treating with sulphuric acid or aluminum chlorid and heating to about 200° F. The burs and vegetable matter are charred and then removed by crushing and dusting. The process costs from 1½ to 3 cents a pound and results in an average loss of about 10 per cent in weight. Often the shrinkage due to burs is much more than this. Combing wools that are extremely burry are rarely if ever carbonized, as this injures the wool to a certain extent, even under the most favorable circumstances.

IMPROPER TYING OF FLEECES.

The evil of tying the fleeces with sisal twine is constantly recurring. Volumes have been written against this curse of the wool trade, but it is continually coming up again, although of late years it has not been so uniformly common. The "fleece" or farm wools are worse in this respect that the "Territory." A discrimination in price of from 1 to 5 cents a pound and the refusal of some dealers to handle wool thus put up have not eliminated this practice. The pieces of sisal twine adhere to the wool through the processes of manufacture and seriously injure the finished fabric. The large rough jute twine is also undesirable because of the fibers coming off in the fleeces. Growers should insist on having the fleeces in compact bundles that will not open in the ordinary processes of packing.

Locks.—Locks are loose pieces of wool that fall out when the fleeces are handled. They may represent some of the best qualities of the wool, but because of their being in small pieces they are difficult to sort, hence the buyers object to them when they are present in large quantities. Their presence can be avoided by proper tying.

PACKING THE BUCK FLEECES.

Probably the average sheepman can see no reason for keeping the bucks' fleeces separate; nevertheless there is one. These fleeces, especially among the fine and medium wooled sheep, are considerably heavier in grease, and it is undesirable to have too great a variation in shrinkage among fleeces of one grade. The buck fleeces are as a rule easy to detect; they are large, have a strong, musky odor, and the yolk of the fleece has a greenish cast. The statement has been made that the spinning qualities of bucks' fleeces are also lower, but there are no good grounds for this contention. A discount of 50 per cent is often charged against the buck fleeces in western selling contracts. Discrimination to this extent is seldom warranted for buck fleeces sold in the grease.

BLACK WOOL.

No other of the "off sorts" do more damage by being packed with the other wool than the black fleeces. After wool has been packed in bags for a time the fleeces "freeze" together more or less; that is, locks from one fleece adhere to neighboring ones. A lock of black wool in any wool intended for white goods is capable of doing untold damage. To be sure, not all wool goes into white goods, but the dealer, when he is having the wool graded, often does not know to whom it will be sold, nor for what purposes it will be used. The only way to be safe is to pick off all the black locks from the adjacent fleeces. Black wool has been in demand for making a natural gray in the past, but at the present time it is not especially sought after and it sells at from 1 to 2 cents a pound less than the corresponding grade of white wool. When shearing takes place the blacks should be cut out and sheared by themselves, and their wool packed separately and so labeled.

COTTED OR MATTED FLEECES.

The badly cotted or matted fleeces should be placed separately, because it is necessary to run them through an opener, which is not done with ordinary wool. This necessarily causes the breakage of fibers to increase. There are really two kinds of cotts, hard and soft. A soft cott, if it is not in too bad condition, may go through with the other wool.

EFFECTS OF DIPPING.

The effects of dipping upon wools are not always the same. In the Southwest, where there is considerable sand and dirt in the fleeces, it tends to lighten them, while in the Northwest it is said that dipping increases the weight. Most of the dips that have been used do not have any very harmful effect upon the wool, but dealers and manufacturers claim that lime-and-sulphur and caustic-soda dips are harmful. However, no tests have been made in America upon the spinning qualities of dipped and undipped wools.

HAND AND MACHINE SHEARING.

The practice of hand shearing is still quite common in parts of the West. Ridges of wool are left over the sheep's body, and the short wool of the head and belly is largely left on the sheep. Much of the wool is shorter than it would be if machine shorn, and a considerable portion of it is double cut. The large amount of short and cut fibers results in a greater percentage of noil in the combing wools and reduces their value accordingly. Many wools grade as clothing instead of combing solely because of being hand shorn.

In some sections where rapid changes of weather are experienced, the sheepmen object to machine shearing on the ground that the sheep will blister during hot weather if shorn too closely. Losses due to a cold wave following close shearing have also been reported. However, machine shearing does not necessarily mean close shearing, as thicker combs can be used and the fiber cut at a greater distance from the skin; but it does insure more uniformity. A great deal of the prejudice against machine shearing has been aroused by improper handling of the machines.

PACKING WOOL.

Packing lamb, ewe, and wether fleeces together militates against higher prices for wool. Lambs' wool is usually more valuable because of lighter shrinking qualities and because of the fact that it will spin higher than wool from older sheep. Sewing the bags with sisal or other unsuitable twine also creates a bad impression in the mind of the buyer, as there is always the possibility of the sisal fiber getting into the wool and causing damage. Much wool is lost through the bursting of the bags. This is caused by the use of poor twine. A stronger twine used for sewing, such as Andover six-ply, is recommended for this purpose. Examples of poor packing are shown in Plate IV.

Packing dead wool (wool from dead sheep) with good wool is also far too common. The dead wool is usually worth about half as much as the corresponding grade of good wool. Another feature in bad packing that should be discouraged is the tying of the fleeces together. In many cases the two fleeces are not of the same grade and they must be separated by the grader before being assigned to any pile.

Occasionally one hears of frauds being practiced by putting stones, etc., in the center of a fleece or sprinkling sand over the wool after it is shorn, but the actual cases of this kind are very rare. It is true that foreign materials have been found in wool sacks, varying from spectacles to oil stones, but such occurrences are more often due to accident than to intent to defraud.

WOOL GRADING.

Most American-grown wool is sacked just as the fleeces come from the sheep and sold at home to dealers. Before offering wool to the manufacturer the dealer makes up from his various purchases a number of piles, each containing only fleeces of similar character and value. This work constitutes grading and should not be confused with the sorting done at the mill. In the dealer's warehouse the fleeces are not untied, but are graded on the basis of judgment of the fleece as a whole. (Plate V.)

The grading itself is an art with which few American sheepmen are familiar, yet it has many points of interest for them. Passing through the lofts and merely seeing the fleeces go over the grading board is not enough to give one an insight into the complexity of a trade that requires at least three years' apprenticeship. Days and even weeks must be spent there before the importance and significance of numerous points that arise can be appreciated.

The grade has much to do with fixing the price of wool, and every woolgrower should be competent to know how his own wool will grade in the market. The various grades are described later on in connection with the market report following the outline of the work of the grader. Some clips of finer wools, very uniform in character, are resold to the manufacturer in the original bags. This is practicable when the mill produces a variety of fabrics for which different grades of wool are required. (Plate VI.)

AT THE GRADING TABLE.

About the grading table or board are a number of large baskets or box trucks, one for each grade. The wool sacks are rolled up by the table, the ends and one side ripped or cut down, depending upon the kind of sewing, and the fleeces turned out in a roll. The fleeces are separated by helpers, who throw them upon the table. Other helpers bring up the bags and empty the baskets containing the graded fleeces, piling them ceiling high where the wool can be examined by the prospective buyers.

The different grades are merely arbitrary divisions more or less clearly recognized and defined in trade. There is some variation from year to year and among the different houses. The mills often have a higher standard of qualities than the dealers, and the "half-blood" of the dealer may represent the millman's idea of a "three-eighths blood." Fineness is the dominant factor; but many other things are considered in grading.

The grader does not determine fineness, as might be supposed by examination of individual fibers. The handling of innumerable fleeces has given him an intuitive sense of quality, so that he accomplishes in an instant what would take an untrained person a much longer time. For example, say that a half-blood combing fleece has been thrown upon the board. This grade has in general certain characteristics, such as a certain degree of crimp (the finer the crimp the finer the wool, except in very fine wool), and a certain arrangement of the fibers in locks or staples that the grader notes as soon as his eye rests upon it. This gives him something as a guide, but the grade is not yet decided. When his hands come in contact with the fleece he has another source of information. The feel of the different grades is more or less characteristic, and this sense is highly developed in the grader. Illustrating this, a blind buyer formerly operated upon the market with considerable success. He could not only make purchases and distinguish the grade by the touch, but by the odor he could also tell the section of the country from which some wools came. Finer wools usually shrink more than coarser wools, and too wide a range of shrinkage is not desired in any grade, as the scouring liquor is made up of a strength suitable for the average shrink of the grade; thus a higher shrinking fleece would not be suitably scoured.

The grader knows also that a half-blood fleece usually shrinks around 60 per cent, depending upon the season and the location where grown. If the fleece in question is heavier-shrinking, say 65 per cent, the grader will probably take a second look to be sure that he has not "lost his eye." If his first impression as to fineness was correct and the fleece is typically half-blood, or perhaps a trifle high, it will probably be thrown a grade higher, that is, fine medium, on account of its heavy shrinking qualities. The next fleece might offer another problem. Say this one is what is known as a "line" fleece. It is midway between the three-eighths-blood and the quarter-blood. It can go either way. The chances are that if the three-eighths-blood wool has been sold and the dealer is well satisfied with the sale, this fleece will find a resting place on the three-eighths-blood pile. Other conditions might decree it to be a quarter-blood. If the market demands for three-eighths-blood wool were high and the supply a trifle short there would also be some "crowding" of the grades and the three-eighths-blood as a whole would probably average a little lower. There are also "line" fleeces midway between combing and clothing. These are sometimes made into a separate grade known as French combing. It is thus seen that the grades manifest more or less elasticity, depending upon market conditions.

Another fleece might be puzzling because of the wool of the "britch" being much coarser than that of the shoulder. For example, the shoulders might be half-blood quality or higher, while the "britch" was quarter-blood. The grader would simply use his best judgment and trust to chance that the fleece would remain as he throws it. At best the grades can only contain fleeces which contain a large proportion of the quality of wool represented by the grade names. Graded wool ready for sale is shown in Plate V, figure 2.

MARKET GRADES.

The following is a copy of a common form of market report as published in trade and agricultural papers in November, 1914:

BOSTON WOOL MARKET.

DOMESTIC WOOLS.

OHIO AND PENNSYLVANIA FLEECES.

Delaine washed	28 @ 29
XX	27 @ 28
Fine unmerchantable	25 @ ..
½-blood combing	28 @ 29
⅜-blood combing	28 @ 29
¼-blood combing	26½ @ 27½
½, ⅜, ¼ clothing	23 @ ..
Delaine unwashed	23 @ 24
Fine unwashed	23 @ 24
Common and braid	23 @ 24

MICHIGAN AND NEW YORK FLEECES.

Fine unwashed	23 @ ..
Delaine unwashed	21½ @ 22
½-blood unwashed	27 @ 28
⅜-blood unwashed	27 @ 28
¼-blood unwashed	26 @ 27
½, ⅜, ¼ clothing	21 @ 22
Common and braid	23 @ 24

WISCONSIN AND MISSOURI.

⅜-blood	26 @ 27
¼-blood	26 @ 26½
Braid	22 @ 23
Black, burry, seedy cotts	18 @ 19
Georgia	22 @ ..

KENTUCKY AND SIMILAR.

½-blood unwashed	28 @ ..
⅜-blood unwashed	... @ 28
¼-blood unwashed	27 @ ..
Common and Braid	23 @ 24

BOSTON WOOL MARKET—Contd.

SCOURED BASIS.

TEXAS.

Fine 12-months	56 @ 58
Fine 8-months	53 @ 54
Fine Fall	45 @ 47

CALIFORNIA.

Northern	54 @ 55
Middle County	51 @ 52
Southern	48 @ 50
Fall free	46 @ 48
Fall defective	38 @ 40

OREGON.

Eastern No. 1 staple	60 @ ..
Eastern clothing	57 @ 58
Valley No. 1	48 @ 50
Valley No. 2	44 @ 45
Valley No. 3	39 @ 40

TERRITORY.

Fine staple	60 @ 62
Fine medium staple	58 @ 60
Fine clothing	57 @ 58
Fine medium clothing	55 @ 57
½-blood combing	59 @ 60
⅜-blood combing	49 @ 51
¼-blood combing	53 @ 54

DOMESTIC WOOLS.

Ohio and Pennsylvania.—In the foregoing report, which is typical for American wools, the Ohio and Pennsylvania fleeces head the list. These really include the West Virginia clip also. The fine wools from these States are the strongest in the world and they are the most valuable of American wools. More than half of the flocks are of Merino breeding. The sheep pasture upon well-covered sod land and the wools contain little sand or dirt. The entire shrinkage is therefore due to the natural grease. A complete classification of these wools is as follows:

COMBING WOOLS.	CLOTHING WOOLS.
Delaine.	XX and X, washed or fine unwashed.
Half-blood.	Half-blood clothing.
Three-eighths-blood.	Three-eighths-blood clothing.
Quarter-blood.	Quarter-blood clothing.
Low quarter-blood.	
Braid.	

All of the above grades are not always given in the market report. Sometimes not all of them are to be found upon the market and they are eliminated.

Many years ago there were two higher grades, Picklock and XXX, representing, respectively, the wool of the Silesian Merino and the American and Silesian Merino cross. These grades are no longer used upon the market, but they are occasionally seen in some of the mills making very fine woolens. More often these qualities occur only as sorts representing parts of fleeces. The amount of this wool produced, however, is very small and is still diminishing.

The XX grade represents the fineness or quality of an ideal American Merino. Delaine wools are combing wools of this and of X quality. Sometimes they are quoted Fine Delaine, being X quality and above, and Medium Delaine, being about half blood in quality. They are not necessarily from the Delaine type of Merino. The X quality is supposedly the wool from a sheep containing three-quarters Merino blood. It is sometimes referred to as three-quarters blood. Market usage has decreed that XX and X as grade names shall be used only in referring to washed clothing wools, but the terms are sometimes used to indicate the same degrees of quality in other wools. Fine unwashed contains these same qualities, but these wools are heavier shrinking.

Half-blood, three-eighths-blood, and quarter-blood grades, as the terms were coined, referred supposedly to wools from sheep of half, three-eighths, and quarter Merino blood, but they have no such significance now. Wools grading as high as half blood can come from sheep having no trace of Merino blood; the purebred Southdown, for instance, produces wool that sometimes grades that high, and this breed has been kept pure from outside blood for centuries. On the other hand, quarter-blood would rarely come from a sheep containing any Merino blood. Low quarter blood is a grade lower than quarter blood, and braid is the lowest grade of all. It usually refers to luster wool, such as might come from a Lincoln or a Cotswold sheep.

Washed wools.—The practice of washing the sheep has given rise to the terms of washed, unmerchantable, and unwashed. The unmerchantable wool is not unsalable wool, but that which has been poorly washed—sometimes the sheep are merely "driven through the creek." Such fleeces shrink more than those properly washed and could not be fairly placed in an offering of washed wool, as their loss in scouring would be much greater. Fleeces may be unmerchantable for other reasons. These terms do not always mean that the washing operation has actually taken place, the practice of washing being on the decline, but sometimes refer solely to shrinkage. The washed wools are lighter in color and condition, shrinking 3 or 4 per cent less than the unmerchantable, and the latter shrinks about the same amount less than the unwashed.

Michigan and New York.—Michigan and New York have the same classification and the wools are quite similar, some of them being fully as good as Ohio and Pennsylvania wools. As a whole, however, they are not quite up to this standard. The wools from the above States are quite frequently spoken of as the "fleece," "domestic," "native," or "farm" wools.

Kentucky and similar.—Kentucky, Indiana, Missouri, and Wisconsin wools are not so fine in character. They rarely grade higher than half or three-eighths blood, as most of the sheep are of the mutton type. The pasture is much the same as in the "fleece" wool States. The term "bright" is sometimes applied to the wools of these States.

Parts of Tennessee and Virginia are given over to the spring-lamb industry and they produce some wools of a medium quality. Much of it is consumed by local knitting mills. This is some of the lightest shrinking wool in America, some of it not going higher than 35 per cent. Georgia and some of the other Southern States produce some rather coarse, light-shrinking wools.

SCOURED BASIS.

Texas.—Wool from Texas and the "territories" is usually quoted on a scoured basis. The reason for this is that there is such a wide variation in shrinkage in different localities and also from season to season that the clean basis is more satisfactory. In Texas shearing twice a year is often practiced. These short wools are probably the best American felting wools. They are also highly regarded in certain branches of woolen manufacture. The 12-months clip of Texas is probably as near the Ohio type of wool as any western wool. The Merino blood is still strongly dominant here. These wools sometimes shrink as low as 56 to 58 per cent. The average for the entire State, however, has been estimated at 66 per cent. The spring and fall Texas wools come to market untied.

California.—The California wools are quoted as northern, middle, and southern counties. The northern counties wool usually represents a year's growth, and is the most valuable. In the middle and southern counties the wool shrinks more, and shearing is often prac-

FIG. 1.—GRADING WOOL AT WAREHOUSE.

FIG. 2.—GRADED WOOL READY FOR SALE.

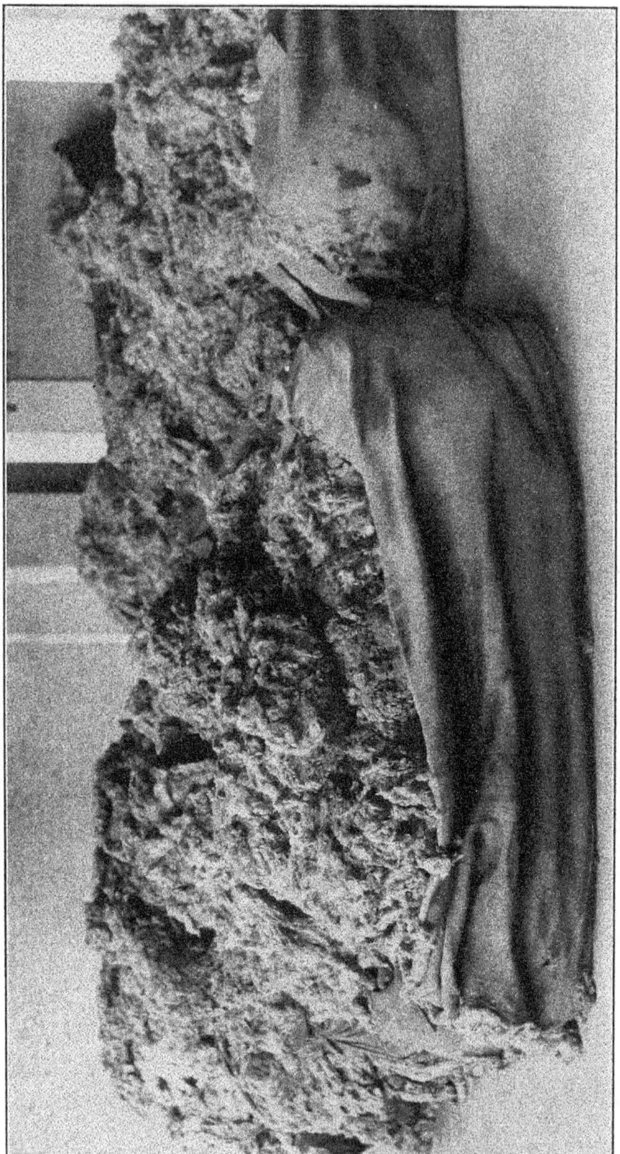

AMERICAN WOOL ON DISPLAY IN THE ORIGINAL BAG.

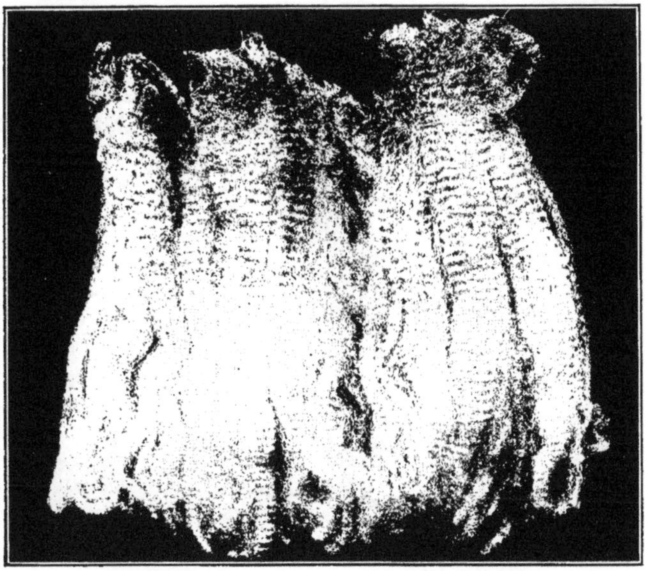

FIG. 1.—COMBING OR STAPLE WOOL OF "FINE" GRADE.

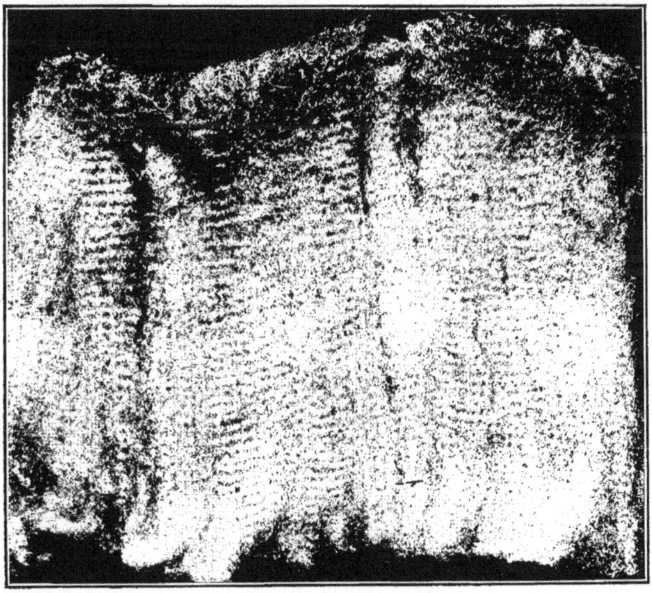

FIG. 2.—HALF-BLOOD COMBING WOOL.

FIG. 1.—THREE-EIGHTHS-BLOOD COMBING WOOL.

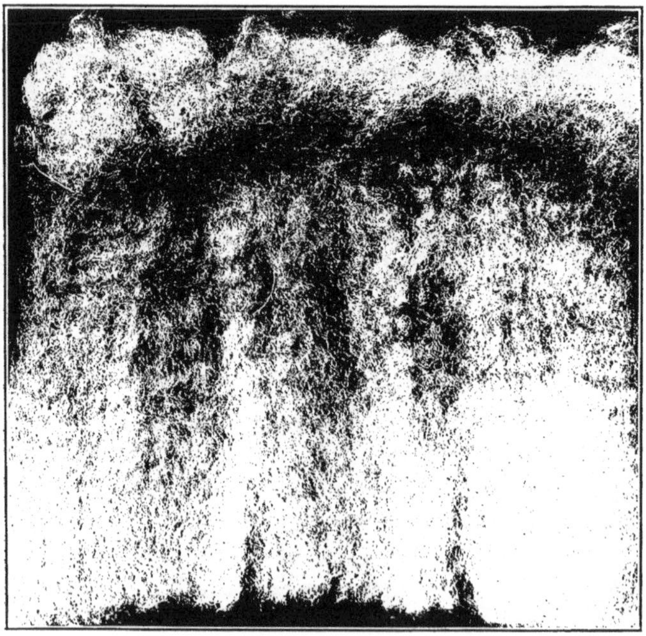

FIG. 2.—QUARTER-BLOOD COMBING WOOL.

ticed twice a year. There are spring, or 8 months, and fall, or 6 months, wools from these sections. The spring wool is usually longer and it shrinks less than the fall. Both spring and fall wools are highly regarded for felting purposes. This is due to the fact that they contain a high percentage of Merino blood and also to the fact that they are short. In the southern part of the State the mestiza bur is very common and many of the wools contain it in varying quantities. These wools are quoted as "defective" in distinguishing them from the "free" wools. This bur can not be removed by mechanical means; hence the wools must be carbonized. The short wools are not tied up in fleeces, but come to market in a loose condition. Some of the California wools are baled to facilitate shipping.

Oregon wools.—Oregon produces some excellent wool, though it is somewhat high in shrinkage. The best of it will grade 80 per cent of staple or combing wool. Excepting the valley wool, it is largely of a fine and fine-medium character. The Lakeview wools of this State are sometimes spoken of separately. The valley wools are quite different from the ordinary clip. They are largely from long-wooled sheep. They are quoted as valley No. 1, No. 2, and No. 3, corresponding roughly to half-blood, three-eighths-blood, and quarter-blood, respectively. These numbers have this same general significance when applied to wools from other sections. The valley wools are somewhat akin to the luster wools of England. Some buyers claim that the heavy rainfall of the valley discolors the wool to a certain extent, but others deny this. These wools are the only western wools that lose weight under normal conditions when being shipped east. They lose from 1 to 2 per cent. Most other wools if dry when shipped gain this amount or even more in transportation.

TERRITORY WOOLS.

Under "territory wools" are grouped all those wools produced west of the Missouri River, and they derived their name from the fact that this section of the country was formerly made up of Territories in distinction to the States of the central and eastern sections. Certain of the wools, however, have more or less distinct characteristics which separate them from the main lot, and they are no longer included in the territory wools. Among these are the clips of California, Oregon, Texas, Arizona, and New Mexico.

The States that produce the territory wools—Montana, Wyoming, Idaho, Utah, Nevada, Colorado, and Washington—are in the main the range States. A great deal of fine-wool blood is present in the flocks, but the use of medium and long wool mutton rams is steadily increasing, and this is having its effect upon the character of wool produced. Considerable sections of the range are more or less sandy and the grass is not as thick as in the central and eastern part of the country. The wind blows with considerable force, creating sand storms in some sections, and much sand and dirt are deposited upon the sheep. These conditions give rise to a heavy-shrinking wool, as would naturally be expected. The wools containing sand usually shrink more than those containing mountain dirt. Occasional fleeces from this district shrink more than 80 per cent, and the average for the different States ranges from 63 to 70 per cent. There is often considerable variation in shrinkage from year to year in the wools from any particular locality. When there has been snow on the ground during the winter, the clips are often 5 per cent lighter than when the range is bare. The selling of territory wools upon the market is consequently upon a clean or scoured basis.

Classification and grades of territory wools.

COMBING.		CLOTHING.	
Fine staple	usually one grade.	Fine clothing.	usually one grade.
Fine medium staple.		Fine medium clothing.	
Half-blood staple.		Half-blood clothing.	
Three-eighths-blood staple.		Three-eighths-blood clothing.	
Quarter-blood staple.		Quarter-blood clothing, or short quarter-blood.	
Lowquarter-blood staple.	often one grade.		
Coarse, common, low, or braid.			

Practically all three-eighths-blood and quarter-blood wools are of combing length.

The term "staple" as applied to a territory wool refers to a combing wool. "Ordinary" is sometimes used to designate clothing wool in this section instead of referring to quality. The terms of fine, fine medium, medium, and low medium have arisen and are used in a general way in referring to territory wools. They are often used in referring to original lots and are largely equivalent to the following:

Fine =XX and X qualities, or fine staple and fine clothing.
Fine medium=X, half-blood and three-eighths-blood.
Medium =Three-eighths-blood and quarter-blood.
Low medium=Low quarter-blood and braid.

It is rather difficult to attempt to characterize the wools from each State, as they grade almost imperceptibly into one another. Often differences appear in the wools that can be recognized, but are difficult to describe.

Montana.—Montana wools as a whole are probably the best of the territory clips. They are light-shrinking compared to the wools of the neighboring States, of good length, and attractive in appearance. They have a slightly creamy tinge which shows up even after scouring. Their felting qualities are good. It is sometimes claimed that wools from this State are more likely to be tender than some of the others, but if this is true the other grade qualities, such as length and quality, overbalance it.

Wyoming.—Wyoming wool has not the soft characteristic feel of the Montana wools. It is somewhat "wild" or harsh in nature. This is said to be due to the influence of the alkali soil over which many of the sheep pass. Wyoming wool scoures out very white. It is quite strong, robust, and of fair length, but is a heavy-shrinking wool. The shrinkage varies widely from year to year. Because of its scouring out so white some manufacturers prefer it to Montana when its heavier shrinkage is discounted.

Idaho.—The Triangle or Soda Springs wools come from a section around the town of the latter name in Idaho. The three points of the triangle are Ogden, Utah; Pocatello, Idaho; and Granger, Wyo. The wools from this section are somewhat lighter-shrinking than the surrounding ones.

The wools from western Idaho are long and fine (often grading 80 per cent staple), but in the eastern part of the State they are generally somewhat shorter.

Utah, Nevada, Colorado, and Washington.—Much of the Utah wool is rather short, there being little staple in it. Overstocking the range is said to be responsible to a certain extent for the poorer qualities of the wools from this State. Nevada is a high-shrinking wool of fairly good quality.

Colorado wool has little character, being a nondescript wool often shrinking from 70 to 72 per cent. There are, however, some lighter-shrinking wools (around 60 per cent) of good quality from certain sections of the northern part of the State. The wool from this State in general is often described as being "breedless." It rarely grades higher than one-half-blood. In southern Colorado the sheep are sometimes sheared twice a year, this short wool coming to market untied.

Washington as a whole probably produces the heaviest-shrinking wools of any western State. It is estimated that the average shrinkage is around 70 per cent. This high shrinkage is due to natural grease, of which there is a great deal in the wool of this section, and to dirt, etc., in the fleeces.

New Mexico and Arizona.—New Mexico and Arizona wools are very uneven in character. The care given the flocks is often very slight, while many of the sheep are poorly bred, and the fleeces run out and kempy. The wools are often very poorly put up. The shrinkage varies from 40 to 75 per cent, though dipping often lightens the wool from these States. It is said that wool from flocks owned by Americans, on account of better handling, is worth an average of 2 cents a pound more than that from flocks of Mexican owners. The

Navajo wool is very uneven. It comes to market untied, the low quarter-blood mixed with the fine grade.

Dakotas, Kansas, and Nebraska.—The wool from the Dakotas, western Kansas, and Nebraska are sometimes included in the territory wools. They are really midway between the "bright" and the territory in condition, having more sand and dirt than the bright but not as much as the territory. The term "semibrights" is sometimes applied to them.

Terms used in other market reports.—The reports of the St. Louis markets often refer to the shrinking qualities of the wool as light-fine, heavy-fine, etc. The amount of vegetable matter present is also indicated by burred, slightly burred, etc. Some other terms are also used that are usually self-explanatory.

FOREIGN GRADES.

Basis of foreign classification.—The quality of English and many other foreign wools is often designated by the counts or number of hanks per pound. The coarser wools are represented by the lower counts, as 18's, 24's, 36's, etc., and the finer ones as 64's, 70's, 80's, etc. These numbers or counts represent the hanks per pound of top to which the wool is supposedly capable of being spun, each hank representing 560 yards. Thus, wool of 50's quality should spin 50×560 yards per pound of top, if spun to the limit. This classification is based on the worsted system of manufacture.

TABLE 2.—*Foreign wool classes and corresponding counts for American grade.*

American grades.	Foreign classes—top-maker's quality.	Counts often spun to in America.
Fine	60's–70's	50's–60's
Half-blood	56's–60's	40's
Three-eighths blood	50's–56's	36's
Quarter-blood	46's–50's	32's
Low quarter-blood	40's–46's	20's
Low, coarse, common, or braid	36's–40's	16's

As a matter of fact the top-maker's quality does not actually represent the counts to which the wool can be spun. The lower grades will not spin up to their number, while the finer ones will spin much higher than their designated numbers. Some fine American wools have been spun to 200 counts for exhibition purposes. Short wools will not spin as high as similar wools of greater length, hence this factor also influences the counts to which the wool will spin.

Another fact worthy of mention is that the wools are rarely spun to their limit, that is, to as fine a yarn as is possible to spin. Wool can be spun several counts higher in England than it can in America. This is due to the fact that the air is moister there and that the labor of the mills is more capable than in the United States. This does not imply that American fabrics are inferior to imported, as a better cloth results if the wool is not so highly spun.

GRADES OF WOOL FROM VARIOUS BREEDS OF SHEEP.

It is impossible to assign wool to a particular grade solely upon the basis of the breeding of the sheep. In the mutton breeds especially there are wide variations within a single breed and within flocks. The following list shows in a general way how wool from the various breeds would be likely to grade:

BREED.	GRADE OF WOOL PRODUCED.
Merino (eastern States)	Delaine, XX, X, or fine unwashed, etc.
Merino (range States)	Fine and fine medium staple or clothing.
Rambouillet	Fine and fine medium staple or clothing and a small amount of half-blood.
Southdown	Half and three-eighths blood (chiefly three-eighths combing or clothing, chiefly clothing).
Shropshire	Mainly three-eighths-blood, combing or clothing. Some quarter-blood.
Hampshire	Three-eighths and quarter blood combing or clothing.
Dorset	Three-eighths and quarter blood combing or clothing.
Suffolk	Three-eighths-blood combing and clothing.
Cheviot	Quarter-blood combing.
Oxford	Quarter and low quarter-blood combing.
Corriedale	Three-eighths-blood combing.
Cotswold, Lincoln, Leicester	Low quarter-blood combing or braid.
Crossbred: Long wool on Merino or Rambouillet	Half-blood, three-eighths-blood, and quarter-blood combing.
Crossbred: Shropshire or Hampshire on Merino or Rambouillet	Half-blood and three-eighths-blood combing or clothing.

SORTING WOOL.

While wool is graded at the warehouses, as a rule sorting is done only at the mills. Its object is to secure lots of wool having greater uniformity as to fineness than could possibly be obtained if the fleeces were not divided. The wool as it grows upon the sheep's body varies in length and quality; consequently the fleeces can not be uniform in quality throughout. There is usually a wider range of quality in the coarse wools, such as Lincolns and Cotswolds and the crossbreds, than among the fine wools. Coarser fleeces might be of a three-eighths-blood grade or even half-blood on the shoulder, while the "britch" would be a quarter-blood. The shoulder wool is considered the best for strength, quality, and length, the sides are next best, and the quality decreases passing backward until the "britch" is reached, which is the coarsest part of all. The wool from the back is likely to contain hayseed or chaff, and it is not of as good quality or strength as that from the shoulder. It is also often shorter. The belly wool is usually finer than any, but it is short, "frowzy," is not so strong, and it lacks character. The wool from over the head is short, coarse, and in the black-faced breeds is likely to contain black fibers. Modern machinery could probably handle these different qualities of wool in the same lot, but more uniform yarn can be made and the wool spun to a finer thread if it is sorted, hence it is an economical advantage to do the sorting. The work is not as exacting as it once was; as a rule not as many sorts are made now as formerly.

The sorting is done over a table that has either a slatted or wire-mesh top, so that the dirt will fall through. The fleeces are untied, shaken out, and piled up beside the table and then passed over the board. A good light is necessary to do the work properly.

The number of sorts made from a fleece or from a bag of wool and the quantity of each will naturally vary with the quality of the wool, the mill where the sorting is done, and the goods for which the wool is intended. Ordinarily four to five major sorts would take care of the bulk of the wool, along with as many more off sorts. There is no uniform system of designating the sorts; each mill uses its own names or numbers.

The regular sorts are made mainly upon quality and length. A little extra length will sometimes cause wool to be thrown higher because of resulting higher spinning qualities. Often the best of a sort, the longer wool, will be separated and used for warp, as a stronger yarn is needed for this purpose than for filling. The off sorts are usually something out of the ordinary. In a worsted mill they are sold for other purposes, as they can not be manufactured on the worsted system.

RESULTS OF SORTING A SAMPLE BAG OF WOOL.

The percentage of the various sorts may vary considerably. The proportion of the main sort varies from 50 to 80 per cent of the weight of a lot of fleeces of a common grade. This is because the quality, condition, and length of the different wools vary, and the dealers' and millmen's ideas concerning grades are not always the same. The market conditions and the quality of the goods into which the wool is to be made may also influence the sorting.

The following is the record of an actual case of sorting a bag of wool, showing the weight, percentage, and value per pound of each sort. This bag contained fleeces that had been graded in the warehouse as "half-blood." The gross weight, was 245 pounds; weight of bag, 4¼ pounds; net weight of wool, 240¾ pounds.

TABLE 3.—*Results of sorting a bag of half-blood Montana wool.*

Sort.	Weight.	Percentage.	Value per pound.
Regular sorts:	*Pounds.*	*Per cent.*	*Cents.*
X or three-quarters-blood	11.21	4.66	21.0
Half-blood combing	88.69	36.84	22.7
Half-blood clothing	12.90	5.36	21.6
Three-eighths-blood combing	64.76	26.90	23.0
Three-eighths-blood clothing	24.33	10.11	20.0
Quarter-blood combing	12.90	5.36	19.0
Short quarter-blood	4.55	1.89	17.0
Low quarter-blood	.55	.23	16.0
Off sorts:			
Stained and gray	.55	.23	14.0
Shorts	3.90	1.62	10.0
Fribs	3.32	1.38	5.0
Clips	2.76	1.15	1.0
String	1.37	.57	....
Loss in sorting	8.90	3.70	....

DESCRIPTION OF SORTS.

Little need be said concerning the regular sorts. They merely represent a more complete division according to quality than was possible in grading. Regarding the off sorts, the "stained and gray" sort is not usually made, except when white goods are to be manufactured and it is necessary to separate them out of the main lot. Their character is implied by their name.

Shorts consist of short wool such as grows about the face and eyes. Part of it may also be due to double cutting in shearing. Fribs are short, sweaty, and dungy locks. Clips are locks so incrusted with foreign material that the wool can not be freed in scouring, but must be clipped off. The string cut from the fleeces is practically valueless, since considerable paper twine is used. The loss of weight in sorting depends upon whether the wools contain much sand or dirt. Other off sorts are often made from wools of various sections. Tags are a very common one. They are sometimes separated at shearing time, but quite often they are separated by the sorters. They are large dung locks and are worth less than half of the value of the other wool.

Paint locks are another quite common sort. The free wool is clipped from the paint, and the short fiber containing paint is sold to hat manufacturers, etc. It is worth about 1½ to 2 cents a pound.

Seedy wool is a sort containing weed seeds, soft burs, etc., that will not be removed by the manufacturing process. It must often be carbonized before using. These carbonized wools are used largely for woolens, felts, etc.

About 25 per cent of the wool bags can be used again; the rest are sold and bring from 5 to 10 cents a pound.

POUNDS OF WOOL PER POUND OF CLOTH.

Some printed statements convey the impression that the entire fleece goes into the production of a garment, so that the amount of finished cloth is equal to the amount of scoured wool. This impression is erroneous, not only because of a certain amount of wool of other sorts than the main ones being present, but also because there is more or less loss all the way along the process of manufacture. True, these other sorts are of value, but they are not generally worth nearly as much as the main lot.

As the weight per yard of goods varies, it is not feasible to give the amount of wool required to manufacture a garment, suit, or so many yards of cloth, but the pounds of wool per pound of cloth can be given. A number of tests reported by different mills and published in the bulletin of the National Association of Wool Manufacturers show that for woolen goods from 3 pounds to 4.64 pounds of grease wool, with an average of 3.73 pounds, were required to make 1 pound of cloth. The average amount of scoured wool required was 1.37 pounds. For worsted cloths from 2.56 pounds to 4.55 pounds of grease wool was required, with an average of 3.66 pounds. The average amount of scoured wool for 1 pound of worsted cloth was 1.55 pounds.

THE NEED OF IMPROVEMENT IN HANDLING AMERICAN WOOLS.

From the discussion in the foregoing pages it can readily be seen that dealers and manufacturers confront many difficulties in handling the average clip of American wool.

PRESENT CONDITIONS.

In October, 1913, the Animal Husbandry Division of the Bureau of Animal Industry, in cooperation with the Bureau of Crop Estimates, made a canvass of a number of sheep owners in Western States to determine the extent to which growers follow the best practices. Because of the way in which the names were secured it is probable that the 383 replies received were from men whose methods are superior to those generally followed in the same localities; consequently the percentages shown at the foot of the table are much higher than would be reported if it had been possible to receive replies from all wool growers in the States shown. The results of this canvass are shown in Table 4.

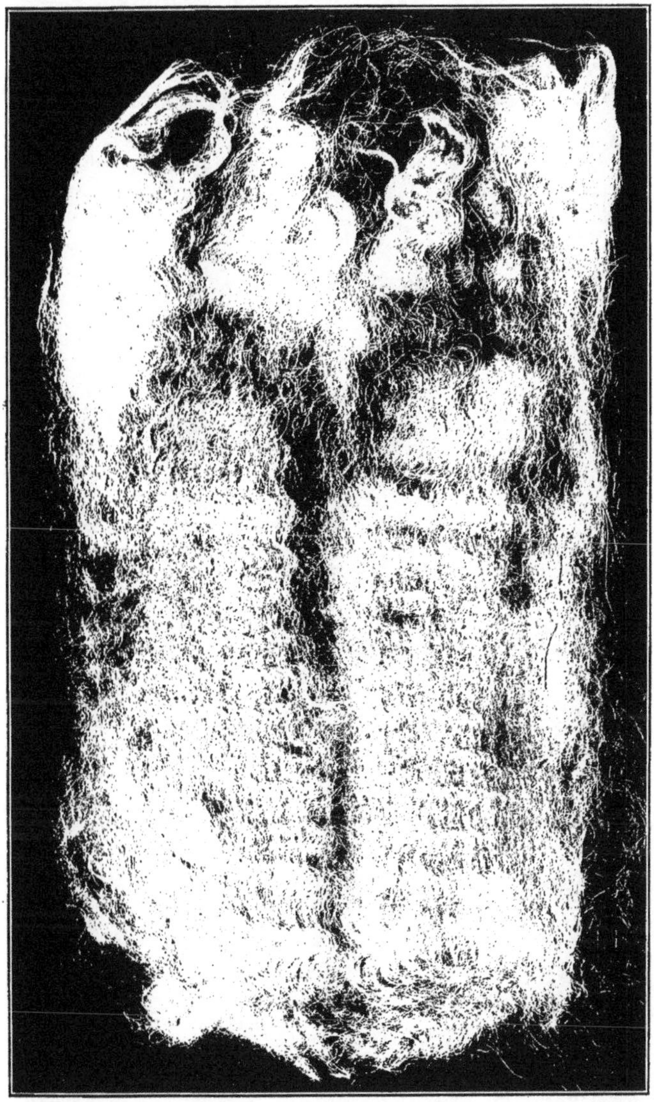

LOW QUARTER-BLOOD COMBING WOOL.

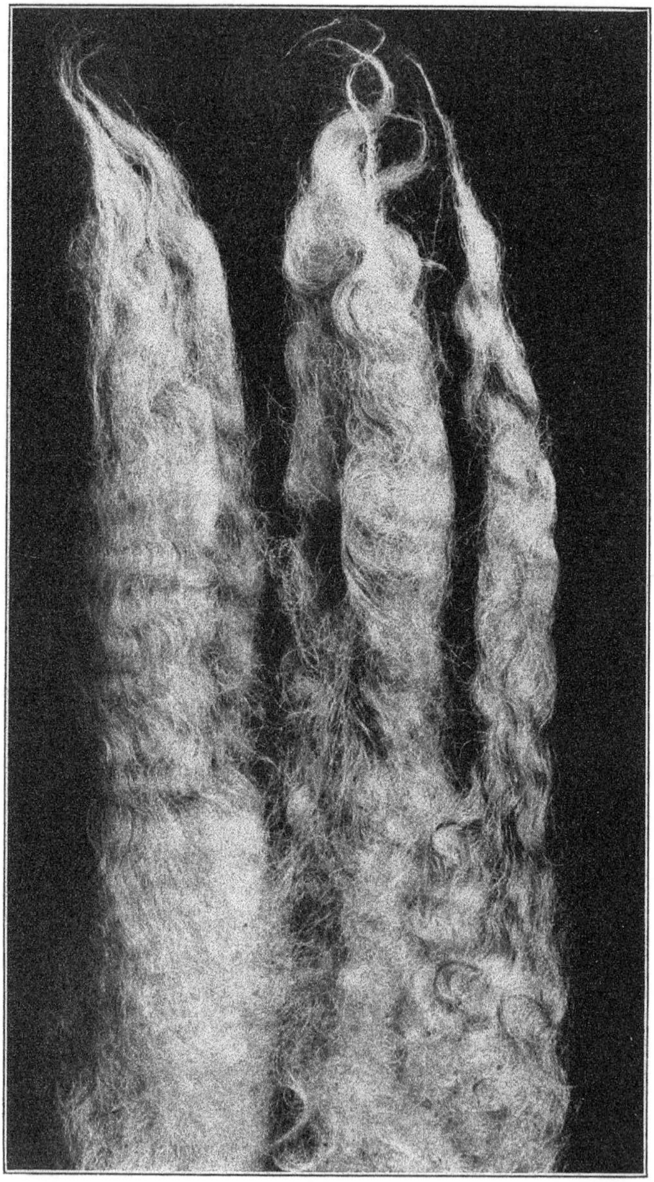

BRAID WOOL.

FOREIGN WOOL SKIRTED, CLASSED, AND BALED, ON DISPLAY AT BOSTON.

TABLE 4.—*Results of investigation of methods of western sheepmen in marketing wool.*

State.	Number of sheep shorn in 1913 by persons reporting.	Number of persons reporting.	Number who sacked ewe, lamb, and buck wool separately.	Number who sacked blacks separately.	Number who used paper twine.	Number who sacked tags separately.	Number of cases where dockage was made for tags.
Arizona	134,422	18	9	6	2	9	3
California	125,302	26	10	5	8	4	7
Colorado	109,695	13	6	8	8	3	4
Idaho	336,249	62	32	48	49	45	26
Montana	518,049	82	46	28	44	51	37
New Mexico	92,011	13	6	10	3	5	....
Oregon	195,246	37	25	23	34	26	11
Utah	309,583	71	17	58	61	24	36
Washington	77,419	13	7	....	11	3	4
Wyoming	371,029	48	32	40	39	33	13
Total	2,269,005	383	190	226	259	203	141
Per cent of total	....	....	49.3	59.0	67.6	53.0	....

Practically one-half the correspondents separated ewes', lambs', and bucks' wool when sacking; 59 per cent put up the black wool separately; and 53 per cent sacked the tags separately. It must be borne in mind, as stated before, that these percentages are undoubtedly much higher than would be the case if it were possible to secure replies from all woolgrowers in any section or State.

The American wool clip is sold by the growers unclassified and in the main very poorly handled. The way in which each of the various defects injures the manufacturing value of the wool has been explained in previous pages. These defects have come to constitute a fixed charge against American wool, which does not apply to wools coming to this country from Australia and some other countries.

Probably the lack of any form of classifying or grading before selling causes the greatest loss to our woolgrowers. The buyer, whether he represents a mill or a firm that buys wool to be sold again after grading, is expected to place a fair valuation upon clips in which there may be many sacks each containing three or four grades of wool. The difference in the scoured values of those grades may not be so serious, but the difference in shrinkage, say, between quarter-blood and half-blood fleeces, is a very great one, and there is no possibility of doing more than making an estimate of the average shrinkage and value of the clip as it is offered. Manifestly the buyer must place the shrinkage estimate sufficiently high to protect himself from loss. In order to get a certain quantity of a particular grade he must buy, even of graded wools, a lot containing other grades that must be sold after sorting.

MANUFACTURER'S TEST OF FOREIGN AND DOMESTIC WOOL.

Even after grading in the eastern warehouses American wools often sell below foreign wools of similar grade and quality because the latter have been skirted and carefully classified before baling, while American fleeces go to the mills in the same shape as they leave the shearing floor, being graded so far as is possible without untying the fleeces.

Comparative results from two lots of wool, one American (Idaho Soda Springs) and one foreign (Australian 50's crossbred), of the same grade and the same value on a scoured basis, as given by a Philadelphia manufacturer, are shown below:

TABLE 5.—*Sorting and scouring test of domestic and foreign wool.*

Item.	Soda Springs.	50's crossbred.
Cost in grease...cents..	18.5	28.0
Loss in weight...per cent..	1.96	.87
Shorts, strings, clips, low, etc...do....	11.25	.17
Main sorts...do....	86.79	98.96
Actual shrinkage main sorts from total weight of wool purchased...do....	57.89	37.36
Shrinkage of net weight of wool scoured...do....	51.46	36.70
Actual cost main sorts in grease...cents..	20.06	28.29
Cost per clean pound...do....	41.32	44.69

As is shown by these figures, the manufacturer bought the American wool for 3.37 cents per clean pound less than exactly similar foreign wool. This was possible mainly because the former lot contained only 86.79 per cent of what was really wanted, against 98.96 per cent in the case of the foreign wool that had been skirted and put up without string. The amount and value of the off sorts in American wools varies, and to the extent of that variation the purchase of these wools involves uncertainty that partakes of gambling and necessitates buying at a figure low enough to cover loss in use or sale of the part not wanted and the greater expense of sorting.

It is the grower who eventually pays all penalties and suffers most of the loss due to inferior preparation of wool. It must not be overlooked that the Australian sheep raiser incurs considerable expense in his method of preparing his wool for the market. He enjoys some advantages favoring the production of extra quality, most marked in the case of fine wools. In the case above cited the wools were of the same grade and the comparison is wholly fair, as the net result shown is on the scoured basis and for wools of equal clean value.

METHODS OF BUYING AND SELLING.

It is the time-honored and oft-repeated statement that buyers pay little attention to the individual clip. Instances are cited in which the dealer buys clips without having seen the wool. However, the dealer may know more concerning the clip than the grower is aware of. He knows the amount of shrinkage for the section for a number of years previous. He knows of the weather conditions, whether or not the winter has been an open one, and he estimates the shrinkage accordingly. He knows whether or not there has been a blizzard and if the wool is likely to be tender. He knows something of the breeding of the sheep and how the owner runs them, for these are all matters of knowledge throughout the country. In fact, he has many sources of information that act as a general guide to values. Yet the grower very often receives little or no benefit for extra pains taken in growing and preparing the wool, and he has just grounds for complaint. In this connection he must appreciate the fact that comparatively few clips are large enough to yield the amount of wool of any one grade that is called for at one time by a manufacturing concern. This being the case, the "fine staple" or the "half blood" of one clip has to be thrown with that of one or more other clips to form a commercial parcel. Unless the buyer of the individual clips is positive that each one has been put up in the same good way he can not insist upon receiving a greater price from the millmen, because they will not relax their safeguards while there is danger of even a very small amount of damage from paint, poor twine, or any one of the vexatious causes that experience has shown are to be looked for.

HOW AMERICAN METHODS OF HANDLING WOOL MAY BE IMPROVED.

If some plan can be worked out whereby American wools can be prepared for market in a manner similar to foreign wools, while they are still the property of the growers, it should be to the advantage of all concerned.

GRADING ON THE RANGE.

It has been claimed that on account of the American growers' comparative nearness to market he should make no attempt to grade his clip. How sound this claim is depends upon how cheaply and how well the work can be done on the range. There is no question that the wool is in better condition for grading immediately after shearing than at any later time. Grading without baling has been practiced in several instances in the west, but the only resulting advantage has been to enable the owner to determine more nearly the value of his clip.

BALING ON THE RANGE.

The statement has been made that baling western wools would militate against higher prices because of resulting poorer appearance. Some southern Wyoming wools have been baled ungraded for a number of years, and a dealer who handles a considerable portion of these says they have not been damaged. Possibly if this wool was baled to the density of foreign wool without being graded and the tags removed, injury would result. The reason these wools have been baled is because they received the benefit of a more favorable freight rate.

Ordinarily the sheep owner can not know as much about the demands of the market and how the wool should be graded as does the wool grader, or, as he is called in Australia, the "classer." This man must always work to the same standard. Attempts of various owners by whom he might be employed to make his work conform to their own ideas would render impossible that uniformity in the classer's work which is necessary to hold the confidence of the buyer as to the put up of the clips.

SKIRTING THE FLEECES.

Skirting fleeces consists in the removal of the belly and the other less valuable parts. When wools are skirted the belly is separated

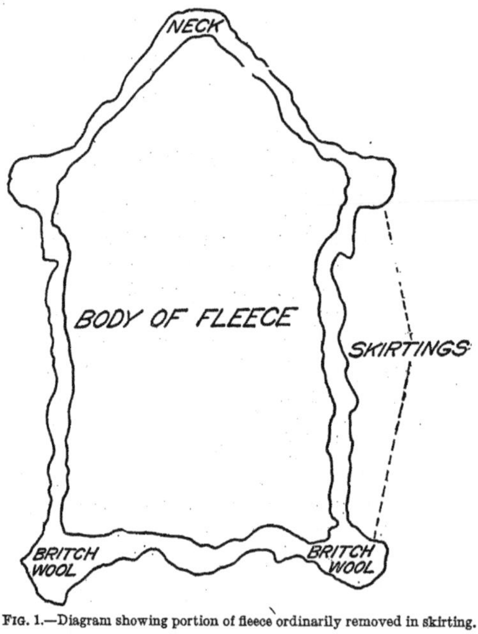

FIG. 1.—Diagram showing portion of fleece ordinarily removed in skirting.

by the shearer and skirting consists of the removal of the parts indicated in figure 1. The belly wool has already been removed from the fleece shown in this figure. The advantage of this lies in the fact that some manufacturers needing higher qualities of wool can buy the bodies of the fleeces alone when they would not care to incur the trouble and expense of separating and reselling the inferior parts, as is necessary when entire fleeces are purchased.

MARKETING GRADED AND SKIRTED WOOL.

The grading and skirting of western American wools is not likely to be economical or satisfactory where less than 10,000 to 20,000 sheep are shorn at one plant. This number need not be the property of one individual, but the wool from such a number should be put up by the same standard and that standard should be the same as applies in other plants in the same territory if our wools are to be as highly esteemed in the markets as foreign wools of the same scoured value.

It is wholly desirable and practicable that small sheep owners, where suitably located, should combine to erect and use a common shearing plant to be conducted upon a high standard. If the practice of grading and skirting is to be adopted some provisions other than those now prevalent will be necessary. The skirtings, locks, and tags from each flock will have varying values, while the main part of the clip will contain not less than two or three grades varying too widely for use by a single mill. An individual wool seller would, therefore, have even greater need than at present of being posted regarding wools and the markets. He would also need to have connection with various branches of the trade in order to dispose of each of the various lots of wool into which his clip was divided. In case of cooperation in ownership and management of the shearing plant the same organization might also be used in effecting the sale of the wool, or each grower might sell at home as opportunity offered or consign to the establishment appearing likely to give the best service.

Marketing farm wools.—For farm wools the greatest advantage is likely to come through such cooperation as will insure the grower's receiving the value of his wool after grading and sale along with other clips sufficient in amount to allow of selling in lots containing not less than 4,000 or 5,000 pounds of each grade.

FUNDAMENTAL RULES FOR THE WOOL GROWER.

Until further improvement can be wrought there are a number of rules that no grower on either farm or range can afford to neglect in order to enhance the reputation of his clip and also—what is equally necessary—the reputation of the wool of his section. These are:

1. Adhere to a settled policy of breeding the type of sheep suitable to the locality.

2. Sack lambs', ewes', wethers', and all buck or very oily fleeces separately. If the bucks or part of the ewes or wethers have wool of widely different kind from the remainder of the flock, shear such separately and put the wool in separate sacks so marked.

3. Shear all black sheep at one time, preferably last, and put the wool in separate sacks.

4. Remove and sack separately all tags, and then allow no tag discount upon the clip as a whole.

5. Have slatted floors in the holding pens.

6. Use a smooth, light, and hard glazed (preferably paper) twine.

7. Securely knot the string on each fleece.

8. Turn sacks wrong side out and shake well before filling.

9. Keep wool dry at all times.

10. Make the brands on the sheep as small as possible and avoid tar brands.

11. Know the grade and value of your wool and price it accordingly.

12. Do not sweat sheep excessively before shearing.

13. Keep the floor sweepings out of the wool.

14. Do not sell the wool before it is grown.

15. When all these rules are followed place your personal brand or your name upon the bags or bales.

GLOSSARY OF TERMS USED IN THE WOOL TRADE.

Black wool.—Includes any wool that is not white.

Braid wool.—Grade name, and synonym for luster wools.

Britch wool.—Wool from the lower thighs of the sheep; usually the coarsest on the body.

Carbonized wool.—That which has been treated with a solution of aluminum chlorid or sulphuric acid to remove the vegetable matter. Carbonizing is rarely practiced with worsted wools.

Carding.—Consists of opening the wool staples, separating to a certain extent the fibers, and condensing and delivering the opened wool in a continuous strand or sliver.

Carpet wool.—Low, coarse wool used in the manufacture of carpets. There is very little produced in the United States.

Combing.—An operation in worsted manufacture which straightens the fibers and separates the short, weak, and tangled fibers known as noils from the continuous strand of long parallel fibers known as top.

Come-back.—In America this refers to a wool fine in quality and having more length than would ordinarily be expected. In Australia it is the result of breeding cross-breds back toward pure Merinos, one of the parents being a pure Merino.

Condition.—Refers to the degree of oil in grease wool. It largely regulates the price. In scoured wool it is used to indicate the degree of moisture.

Cotted fleeces.—A cotted fleece is one in which the fibers are matted or tangled. The cause may be ill health of the sheep or the absence of the proper amounts of yolk or grease in the wool.

Cow tail.—A very coarse fleece, more like hair than wool.

Crimp.—The natural waviness of wool fiber. Uniformity of crimp indicates superior wool.

Crossbred wools.—In the United States the term generally refers to wool from a longwool and finewool cross.

Defective.—Denotes that something will show disadvantageously after the wool is scoured. Fire, water, or moths may cause defective wools. California burry wool is quoted as defective.

Delaine wool.—Delaine originally referred to a fine type of women's dress goods. Delaine wools are fine combing or worsted wools, from Ohio and vicinity, but not necessarily from the Delaine Merino.

Fall wool.—Wool shorn in the fall where shearing is practiced twice a year, as in California and Texas. The fall wool is usually dirtier than the spring clip. It represents from four to six months' growth.

Filling (weft).—Threads that run crosswise and fill in between the warp.

Fribs.—Short and dirty locks of small size. Dungy bits of wool.

Frowzy wool.—A lifeless appearing wool with the fibers lying more or less topsy-turvy. The opposite of lofty wool.

Grease wool.—Wool as it comes from the sheep with the grease still in it.

Hogget wool.—English term for the first wool from a sheep.

Kemp.—Not a dead hair, but an abnormal fiber made up entirely of horny material, such as is on the outside of ordinary wool fiber. It will not dye as well as the ordinary fiber and does not possess spinning qualities.

Line fleeces.—Those midway between two grades as to quality or length.

Lofty wool.—Open wool, full of "life." Springs back into normal position after being crushed in the hand.

Luster wool.—That from Lincoln, Leicester, and Cotswold sheep. It is known as luster wool because the coarse fibers reflect the light.

Modock.—Wool from range sheep that have been fed and sheared in the farm States. The wool has qualities of both regions.

Noil.—A by-product of worsted manufacture consisting of short and tangled fibers. It is used in the manufacture of woolens.

Off sorts.—The by-products of sorting. In fine staple or any other grade there are certain quantities of short, coarse, stained, and colored wools. These are the off sorts.

Picklock wool.—Formerly a grade above XXX. Picklock was the product of Silesian Merino blood. There is no American market grade of that name at present; a little of this quality of wool is produced in West Virginia.

Pulled wool.—Wool taken from the skin of a slaughtered sheep's pelt by slipping, sweating, or the use of depilatory.

Quality.—The diameter of the wool. It largely determines the spinning quality.

Run-out fleece.—One that is not uniform but much coarser on the "britch" than elsewhere. It may be kempy.

Shafty wool.—Wool of good length and spinning qualities.

Shearlings.—Short-wool pulled from skins of sheep shorn before slaughtering. Also English term for yearling sheep.

Shivy wool.—A somewhat broad term. It refers to the presence of vegetable matter in the wool.

Shoddy.—Wool that has been previously used for manufacturing purposes, torn apart and made ready to use again.

Skirting.—Skirting fleeces consists in removing the pieces and the low-quality wool of the britch from the edge of the fleece.

Spring wool.—Six to eight months' growth; shorn in the spring where sheep are shorn twice a year.

Stained wool.—That which is discolored by urine, dung, etc.

Staple.—(*a*) A lock or bunch of wool as it exists in the fleece. (*b*) Western combing wool.

Stubble shearing.—Shearing some distance from the skin, leaving a "stubble."

Suint.—Excretions from sweat glands deposited in the wool.

Sweating sheds.—Sheds in which sheep are "sweated" before shearing. The purpose is to raise the yolk and make shearing easier.

Tags.—Large dungy locks.

Territory wools.—Territory wools are in general those that come from the territory west of the Missouri River.

Tippy wool.—Wool in which the tip or weather end of the fiber is more or less incrusted.

Top.—A continuous untwisted strand of the longer wool fibers straightened by combing. After drawing and spinning it becomes worsted yarn.

Top-maker's qualities or counts.—Top-maker's qualities or counts are the numbers used in designating the quality of certain foreign wools. They range from 12's upward. The numbers are supposed to indicate the number of hanks of yarn a pound of top will spin to. Each hank represents 560 yards.

Tub washed.—Wool that has been washed after having been sheared. Very rare in America; was formerly practiced in Kentucky.

Virgin wool.—Wool that has not previously been used in manufacturing.

Warp.—The threads that run lengthwise in cloth.

Washed wools.—Those from which the suint has been removed by washing the sheep before shearing.

Wether.—In English wools it refers to wool other than the first clip from the sheep. In sheep, a castrated male.

Yolk.—The fatty grease deposited upon the wool fibers from the oil glands.

O

UNITED STATES DEPARTMENT OF AGRICULTURE

BULLETIN No. 207

Contribution from the Forest Service
HENRY S. GRAVES, Forester

Washington, D. C. PROFESSIONAL PAPER July 17, 1915.

THE CYPRESS AND JUNIPER TREES OF THE ROCKY MOUNTAIN REGION

By

GEORGE B. SUDWORTH, Dendrologist

CONTENTS

WASHINGTON
GOVERNMENT PRINTING OFFICE
1915

UNITED STATES DEPARTMENT OF AGRICULTURE

BULLETIN No. 207

Contribution from the Forest Service
HENRY S. GRAVES, Forester

Washington, D. C. PROFESSIONAL PAPER. July 17, 1915.

THE CYPRESS AND JUNIPER TREES OF THE ROCKY MOUNTAIN REGION.

By George B. Sudworth, *Dendrologist.*

CONTENTS.

SCOPE OF THE BULLETIN.

This bulletin describes the distinguishing characters, geographic distribution, and forest habits of all the known species of cypress (Cupressus) and juniper (Juniperus) growing within the Rocky Mountain region. The region embraces western North and South Dakota, Montana, Idaho, Wyoming, western Nebraska, Colorado, Utah, Nevada, Arizona, New Mexico, and western Texas. Such outlying regions as the Dakotas, western Nebraska, and western Texas are included because a few species extend from the main Rocky Mountain region into them. For the same reason Canadian territory lying directly north of the Rockies and Mexican territory adjacent to our Southwest are also included. Canada has no cypress or juniper trees that do not occur at some point within the United States. Mexico, on the other hand, has both cypress and juniper trees that are not found anywhere in this country. Such species, however, are not considered in the present bulletin.

So far as possible the use of technical descriptive terms has been avoided, and only such distinguishing characters (color, texture, etc.) are defined as can not be shown clearly in a black and white drawing. The illustrations represent foliage, fruits, seeds, and other important parts of the trees in their natural size, so that the element of size, so often distinctive, as well as the form in the specimen studied, can be easily compared with the drawing. To insure accuracy in details practically all of the illustrations are line drawings of photographs.

The maps showing the geographical distribution [1] of the different species are photographic reductions of the large folio sheets upon which the distribution data were originally platted, thus affording a more accurate outline of range than is apparent from the small size of the map. These data include all the published and unpublished information now available in the Forest Service.[2] The greater part comprises field notes and unrecorded observations and reports of Forest Service officials who, in the exploration and administration of the National Forests, have special opportunities for gathering such data.

Additional information was obtained from field notes accompanying specimens preserved in the forest herbaria of the Forest Service and the National Museum, Washington, D. C., while through the courtesy of officials in charge similar information was gathered from the Arnold Arboretum, Jamaica Plain, Mass., the Field Museum of Natural History, Chicago, Ill., and the University of Nebraska, Lincoln, Nebr. Field notes, forest photographs, and specimens collected by members of the Bureau of the Biological Survey have also contributed new and valuable range data.[3]

---

[1] Only the botanical range is shown, it being impracticable to combine with this the commercial range of timber-producing species, the supplies of which are constantly reduced by lumbering operations.

[2] The Mexican range of cypresses and junipers is so imperfectly known at present that but few authentic locations are given for them in that region. These locations are shown by small circles of solid color. Further provisional range of these trees in Mexico is indicated by short parallel lines and is based only on reports which have not been verified.

[3] Grateful acknowledgment is made in this connection to Dr. C. Hart Merriam, formerly chief of the Bureau of Biological Survey; to Dr. H. W. Henshaw, present chief of that bureau, and to Dr. A. K. Fisher, Chief of the Division of Economic Ornithology; also to Messrs. Vernon Bailey and H. C. Oberholser, members of the same bureau. To Prof. Charles S. Sargent, director of the Arnold Arboretum, and to Prof. J. G. Jack of the same institution, the author desires especially to acknowledge his hearty appreciation for the loan of herbarium specimens and other helpful courtesies. The writer's cordial thanks are here expressed to Dr. Charles E. Bessey (now deceased), of the University of Nebraska, and to Dr. C. F. Millspaugh, of the Field Museum of Natural History, for the privilege of compiling range data from the herbaria in their departments. For helpful information regarding junipers in Texas acknowledgment is made to Prof. William L. Bray, now of the University of Syracuse, N. Y. Acknowledgment is due also to Mary C. Gannett for the compilation and preliminary mapping of a part of the range data, and to W. H. Lamb and Georgia E. Wharton, of the Section of Forest Distribution, who revised and completed this compilation and prepared final copies of the distribution maps. Finally, the writer wishes to express his grateful appreciation of the assistance received in various ways from Forest officers and other members of the Forest Service.

Naturally the ranges of the better known and more useful trees are more complete than those of the smaller, relatively unimportant ones. Altogether, however, our present knowledge of the geographic distribution of Rocky Mountain cypresses and junipers is still incomplete. It is hoped, therefore, that the publication of range data now available will stimulate the collection of further information.

A key for the identification of junipers is provided on page 36. One for the cypresses is deemed unnecessary, because the two species considered are so strikingly different that they can be quickly identified by consulting the descriptions.

In this connection the writer wishes to say that trees, as is the case with other plants, can be satisfactorily identified only by first becoming familiar with the character and appearance of their foliage, flowers, fruits, bark of the trunk and branches, wood, and habit of growth. Knowledge also of their natural habitat and associates is helpful and an essential part of the life history. Naturally such information can be obtained best by studying trees where they grow. Representative specimens of the different parts of the tree are useful for further study, and should be collected whenever possible. Merely a few sprigs hastily taken in passing a tree will not be a sufficient means of determining and knowing the species.

CLASS AND FAMILY RELATIONSHIP OF CYPRESSES AND JUNIPERS.

The cypresses and junipers belong to a class of plants technically known as Gymnosperms, which are distinguished by their resinous wood and in the fact that their ovules (destined to become seeds) are borne naked or without the usual covering peculiar to the other great class of seed-bearing trees called Angiosperms. Familiar examples of the Gymnosperms are the pines, spruces, firs, etc., while the Angiosperms include the oaks, walnuts, hickories, etc., which do not have resinous wood. Gymnosperms produce wood which is formed in concentric layers or rings of growth, one ring being laid on each year and outside of the preceding one and just beneath the bark. The age of Gymnosperms can, therefore, be accurately told by counting the rings shown on a cross section of the stem cut off at the ground just above where the root is given off.

According to the character of their fruits, Gymnosperms are divided into two families—(1) Coniferæ, trees which bear cone fruits (pines, etc.), and (2) Taxaceæ, trees which bear an olivelike fruit (the seed inclosed in a fleshy sack), as in the yew trees.

Because their fruits are true cones, cypress and juniper trees belong to the family Coniferæ. Other generic groups of this family are the pines (Pinus), spruces (Picea), larches or true tamaracks (Larix), hemlocks (Tsuga), false or bastard hemlocks (Pseudotsuga), firs or "balsam trees" (Abies), "bald," or deciduous-leafed cypress (Taxodium), arborvitæs or "cedars" (Thuja), and redwood and bigtree (Sequoia). All of these trees except the junipers bear a fruit which is a distinctly woody cone, with from two to several naked seeds under each of its overlapping or otherwise closely joined scales. The junipers, however, produce a berrylike fruit, which, though not woody, is, nevertheless, morphologically a cone, the external resemblance to a berry being due to the joining of its fleshy cone scales. The seeds of most conifers have a thin wing, which helps them greatly to be scattered by the wind far from the parent trees, thus providing for their rapid reproduction over a wide area. On the other hand, seeds of some conifers have no wings or merely rudimentary ones, which do not materially aid in distributing the seeds, this being accomplished through the agency of flood waters and animals. Junipers are examples of this class, their wingless seeds and the berry-like fruits containing them being largely dependent for their distribution upon birds, which eat them for the fleshy outside pulp,[1] and upon flood waters, which carry them away from the parent trees.

The leaves of some conifers are scalelike and very small, as in the case of leaves that clothe the twigs of junipers, cedars, and cypresses, while the leaves of all other conifers are needlelike and long, as in the case of the leaves that clothe the twigs and branches of pines, spruces, etc. Of our conifers, all but the bald cypress (Taxodium) and larches (Larix) have leaves that remain green and adhere to the trees for several years, a feature which has given them the popular name of "evergreens." The number of seed-leaves[2] (cotyledons) produced by conifers varies from 2 to about 18.

GENERIC CHARACTERISTICS OF CYPRESSES.

The term "cypress" is popularly applied to three distinct generic groups of North American trees: Taxodium, of the southeastern States; Chamæcyparis, represented in the South Atlantic and Pacific coast forests; and Cupressus, of which native species are found in the southern Rocky Mountain and Pacific coast regions. Strictly speaking, the name cypress should be applied only to the trees of the genera Chamæcyparis and Cupressus, both of which are closely related. Species of Cupressus differ from those of Chamæcyparis in having quadrangular twigs instead of flat ones, and sprays arranged not in one plane but irregularly (Pls. II and V).[3] The overlapping, minute, scalelike leaves of the trees of both groups are arranged in alternately opposite pairs, but those of Cupressus are minutely toothed on their

[1] The hard seeds of the junipers lose none of their germinative vitality by passing through the digestive organs of birds.

[2] Seed-leaves are the first foliar organs appearing above ground when the seeds germinate.

[3] Compare these with figures 65, 66, and 67 in "Forest Trees of the Pacific Slope."

PLATE I.

a

CUPRESSUS ARIZONICA: FOLIAGE AND CLOSED CONES.
a, Newly ripened cones; *b*, detached open cone; *c*, seeds.

CUPRESSUS ARIZONICA.

a, b, Different forms of old cones; *c,* male flower buds (in autumn); *d,* seedling t
(one-half natural size).

margins, while in Chamæcyparis the margins of the leaves are entire or smooth. In Cupressus the leaves of each season's growth remain on the trees from three to four years. The minute flowers, which appear in early spring on the ends of the twigs, are inconspicuous, especially the female flowers. The male flowers, which bear pollen only, and the female flowers, which produce cones and seeds, are borne on different twigs of the same tree. The cones mature at the end of the second season,[1] and bear about 15 or 20 seeds under each fertile cone scale, instead of only 4 or 5 seeds, as in the case of Chamæcyparis. Seeds of native Cupressus differ fundamentally from those of Chamæcyparis in being without thin, membranous wings. The cones of Cupressus are strongly attached to the branches and remain on the trees for a great many years, while those of Chamæcyparis are lightly attached to the twigs and usually fall from the trees within one or two seasons. Seed-leaves of Cupressus are from 3 to 5, and in Chamæcyparis only 2.

The strongly aromatic wood of Cupressus is remarkably durable, but the small size and poor timber form of most native species make it of little commercial value. As forest trees, these cypresses are of considerable importance in assisting to form a protective cover on wind-swept, sandy coasts or dry, arid slopes and in sparsely wooded canyons.

Six species of Cupressus are found in the United States. Four of these are confined to California, while the other two occur in the southern Rocky Mountain region, one extending into Mexico. Trees of this genus are of ancient origin, representatives, now extinct, once growing in Greenland and western Europe.

ARIZONA CYPRESS.

Cupressus arizonica Greene.

COMMON NAME AND EARLY HISTORY.

This little known species has no accepted distinctive common name. Usually it is called "cypress" by the few who know the tree in its mountain habitat, though its occurrence sometimes in moist situations or near streams has earned for it the local name of "water cypress" or "water cedar." The name "Arizona cypress," based on the technical name, is suggested as appropriate because the tree first became known to botanists and foresters through its discovery in southeastern Arizona, where, in 1880, Dr. Edward L. Greene found it "on the mountains back of Clifton, in the extreme eastern part of

[1] Until quite recently this was believed to be another distinction between Cupressus and Chamæcyparis, the latter being thought without exception to mature their fruit in one season. The fruiting habit of Chamæcyparis nootkatensis is now known to be biennial. See Martin W. Gorman, in Nineteenth Annual Report, U. S. Geological Survey, Part V, 339, 1899; Elwes and Henry, Trees of Great Britain and Ireland, V, 1194, 1910; Sudworth, in Review of Forest Service Investigations, II, 7, Pl. I, 1913.

Graham County." Dr. Greene named and described this species in 1882. Later Dr. Rusby discovered an abundant growth of it in canyons on the north slopes of the San Francisco Mountains, central Arizona.[1]

DISTINGUISHING CHARACTERISTICS.

Trees growing in the most favorable situations have narrow, sharply conical crowns with large horizontal branches, straight, rather rapidly tapering trunks, and long slender leaders, characteristics which distinguish the species at a distance from other associated trees. Such trees are from 50 to 80 feet in height, with from 20 to 30 or more feet of clear trunk. Young trees of this type are particularly straight, with very sharp, pointed crowns and horizontal branches. Trees in exposed and otherwise unfavorable situations develop broad, rounded or flat crowns, and seldom reach a height of more than 25 or 30 feet, with very little clear stem. Diameter growth of Arizona cypress varies from 14 inches to nearly 4 feet. (Pl. III, right.)

The trunk bark of large trees is from 1¼ to 1½ inches thick, and of small ones from one-half to three-fourths of an inch. In color the bark is a dull, ashy brown on the outside and pale to dark cinnamon-brown when broken. It is firm, somewhat fibrous, and sharply and deeply furrowed, the main narrow, flat, continuous ridges being connected with small lateral ones. Bark on the branches, twigs, and very young trunks is loosely scaly, the fresh smooth bark beneath the scales being reddish to a dark yellowish-brown. The minute, scale-like, sharp-pointed leaves (Pl. I) have a whitish bloom, which gives the foliage a pale silvery hue, especially pronounced in young trees. The leaves are mainly without pits on the back; very rarely with resinous glands, which when they do occur are exceedingly small. This latter feature and the general absence of pits distinguish the foliage of Arizona cypress from that of smooth cypress (*Cupressus glabra*), which is commonly marked with large glandular pits. Bruised twigs and foliage of Arizona cypress exhale a strong polecat-like odor, while the trees themselves give off an odor which sometimes can be detected at a distance of 100 yards.

Mature cones of Arizona cypress (Pl. I, *b*), which ripen by September of the second season, vary in diameter from seven-eighths of an inch to an inch, and remain on the trees for many years (Pl. II, *a*, *b*), changing with age and exposure from a dark umber-brown to ashy gray. The conspicuous bosses, or protuberances, of the cone scales are usually small and almost pricklelike on cones just matured

[1] Cupressus arizonica was introduced into England, France, and Germany about 32 years ago, where, according to Elwes and Henry (Trees of Great Britain and Ireland, Vol. V, 1184, 1185, 1910), it grows thriftily and has reached a height of from 15 to about 30 feet.

(Pl. I, *a*, *b*), and larger[1] and hornlike on the older fruit (Pl. II, *a*). The deep purplish-brown seeds (Pl. I, *c*) are somewhat triangular in form and irregular in size, but usually about one-eighth of an inch long. The seed-leaves are from 3 to 5 (Pl. II, *d*, lowermost long leaves).

The heartwood of Arizona cypress is a very light brownish-yellow, and the sapwood a pale straw-color. It is moderately soft and of light weight, narrow-ringed and straight-grained, splitting easily. Dry, freshly cut wood has a slight cedarlike odor. When thoroughly seasoned it is fairly durable in contact with the soil, but is used only to a limited extent in supplying local demands for shakes, posts, corral poles, and rough house logs, because the available supply is small and difficult to obtain. The best grades, however, are suitable for sash, doors, blinds, and other building purposes. The lumber seasons well and is readily held in place.

OCCURRENCE AND HABITS.

Arizona cypress grows in moist or rather dry, rocky, shaly, or gravelly soils on mountain slopes, and in the bottoms and on the sides of canyons, at elevations between 4,500 and 8,000 feet. It is especially fond of moist north-slope gulches and benches where the growth is more dense than in drier situations. For the most part it forms pure or nearly pure stands, quite dense on the more favorable sites. The largest and best formed trees occur on north slopes, in coves, and on benches in protected localities, where the soil is moist, deep, and more permeable, while short stunted trees are found in exposed places where the scanty soil is drier and less permeable. Arizona cypress is occasionally associated with Arizona pine, and at higher elevations with huckleberry oak. In some parts of its range repeated forest fires have destroyed the stand over large areas, so that the tree occurs chiefly in patches and in rather small, isolated bodies.

Seedlings and young trees are apparently able to endure dense shade without having their height growth retarded. Later in life trees may still maintain themselves indefinitely under rather heavy top shade, but in such cases growth in diameter and height is very slow. The lateral branches persist for a long time even in very close stands.

Arizona cypress is a prolific seeder and in some localities bears cones every year. Fresh seed shows a moderately high percentage of germination, but the seedlings are likely to come up tardily at irregular intervals. When seeds remain in unopen cones on living

[1] This appears to be due to the growth of tissue about the base of the bosses after the cone matures, and sometimes also throughout the cone and its stem. Cones of Cupressus macnabiana and Cupressus glabra exhibit the same characteristic. (See "Forest Trees of the Pacific Slope," p. 165.) Dried cones, in which the living, spongy, green tissue has become shrunken, do not show this enlargement as conspicuously as cones recently collected.

trees they may retain their vitality for at least several years.[1] Reproduction takes place abundantly where the exposed mineral soil is moist and not subject to washing by mountain floods. Seedlings are scarce, therefore, on steep, rocky slopes, only appearing where the seed has lodged in pockets and crevices. A small amount of the seed is eaten by rodents.

LONGEVITY.

The exact age attained by Arizona cypress is not at present known, but, judging from the few records available, it is evidently long-lived. Trees from 12 to 38 inches in diameter, in full enjoyment of top light, are from 100 to 310 years old, while suppressed, slow-growing trees from 4½ to 5 inches in diameter may be from 50 to 65 years old. The largest trees known would doubtless prove to be from 375 to 400 years old.

SMOOTH CYPRESS.

Cupressus glabra Sudworth.

COMMON NAME AND EARLY HISTORY.

The first reference to this new and handsome cypress was published in 1895 and was based on the discovery of a grove on Pine Creek at "Natural Bridge," central Arizona, by Prof. J. W. Toumey, who believed the tree to be a form of Arizona cypress.[2] It was not distinguished from the latter tree, however, until February, 1910, when it was named and described [3] from a grove of trees discovered by Mr. Arthur H. Zachau on the north slope of a small tributary stream on the west side of the Verde River Canyon, about 16 miles southeast of the town of Camp Verde, Ariz. This grove covers an area about 6 miles long by 1½ miles wide.[4] In size and development the trees there are fairly representative of the species. In 1910 Mr. Willard Drake reported finding the species on the Coconino National Forest, growing with Arizona cypress, while in the same year Mr. R. L. Rogers observed it in the Coronado National Forest. Recently

---

[1] No systematic tests have yet been made to determine exactly how long such seeds will retain their germinative vitality. In many cases, however, the author has found perfectly sound seeds in closed cones that have been attached to living trees for eight or nine years. It is probable that still older seeds could be found.

[2] Garden and Forest, VIII, 32, 1895. While Prof. Toumey referred to the Pine Creek trees as C. arizonica, he nevertheless expressed doubt as to their being the same as the Arizona cypress of the Chiricahua Mountains, for he observed that the bark of the Pine Creek trees "peels off in long shreds."

Prof. Toumey's reference to this characteristic of the bark led the writer to suspect the "Natural Bridge" cypress to be the same as the Verde River Canyon tree. Prof. C. S. Sargent has recently examined specimens of Prof. Toumey's "Natural Bridge" tree and finds it to be C. glabra, so that this grove can now be added to the tree's range.

[3] American Forestry, XVI, 88, 1910.

[4] This grove is partly on a ranch belonging to William A. Tinsley, and approximately in township 11 north, range 5 east, where Mr. Zachau saw it first in 1907, and called the writer's attention to the fact that the trees there had very different bark from that of the Arizona cypress, common in the Chiricahua Mountains. Special credit is due Mr. Zachau for this most important observation, which resulted in an investigation of these trees by the writer and in the discovery then that they are of a distinct species.

CUPRESSUS ARIZONICA (RIGHT) WITH CHARACTERISTIC FURROWED BARK, CUPRESSUS GLABRA (LEFT) WITH SMOOTH SCALY BARK.

CUPRESSUS GLABRA FOLIAGE AND CLUSTER OF NEWLY RIPENED CLOSED CONES.
a, Cluster of very old cones; b, seeds (natural size and enlarged twice natural size).

Mr. Alfred Rehder detected[1] Cupressus glabra in Oak Creek Canyon, about 20 miles south of Flagstaff, Ariz. In the same year Mr. R. D. Forbes found this species at various points in the Tonto National Forest, Arizona. Further search is likely to reveal its existence elsewhere in Arizona and possibly also in New Mexico and Mexico.

The name "smooth cypress" is adopted here as descriptive of the tree's most conspicuous characteristic, its smooth, purple-red bark Settlers in the Verde River Canyon knew this tree long before its technical discovery and called it "yew-wood," doubtless because the bark of the trunk resembles that of the western yew (*Taxus brevifolia*).

DISTINGUISHING CHARACTERISTICS.

In general appearance the foliage of smooth cypress resembles that of the Arizona cypress, though the former species can be distinguished from the latter by the compact, narrowly oval, or somewhat pyramidal crown. The branches of smooth cypress, particularly of younger trees, are strongly upright. Old trees grown in the open develop long, lower branches, which from their great weight are less upright than those of trees of the same age in a close stand. In height the trees range from 25 to 30 feet, and in diameter from 10 to 14 inches, though much larger trees probably exist.[2] The trunk is slightly tapering, while the upper portion is sometimes divided into several branches, in this respect differing from the usual undivided stem of Arizona cypress. Only about one-fourth to one-third of the trunk is clear of branches (Pl. III, left).

The most distinctive characteristic of this tree is its thin, smooth, dark purple-red bark. Each season's growth of bark, from one-sixteenth to one-eighth of an inch thick, breaks irregularly into small, curled, scalelike plates, which fall away during the succeeding autumn and winter, leaving the trunk smooth. Vigorous trees shed their bark more rapidly and completely than less thrifty ones. The foliage is a bright blue-green (glaucous). The minute, scalelike, acutely pointed leaves (Pl. IV), about one-sixteenth of an inch long and closely pressed on old sprays, are thickened and keeled on the back, where in practically every case there is a comparatively large resin gland, a characteristic which distinguishes the leaves from those of Arizona cypress. Young shoots bear closely pressed leaves from one-fourth to one-half of an inch long, with very keen and more or less spreading points (Pl. V, *a*). The leaves die during the second year, turn a bright red-brown, and remain on the twigs for about 4 years, after which they are shed slowly, and later these small branches

[1] Reported to the writer in letter by Prof. C. S. Sargent, Nov. 6, 1914.

[2] According to Prof. J. W. Toumey (loc. cit.) some of the trees in the "Natural Bridge" grove (which must now be considered to be C. glabra) are 3 feet in diameter.

become ashy gray. The spherical cones[1] (Pls. IV, V) are borne on stout stems from one-fourth to one-half of an inch long (Pl. IV, *a*), and mature at the end of the second season. In diameter they range from seven-eighths to one-eighth of an inch, and are composed of from 6 to 8[2] scales, armed with large incurved, somewhat flat-pointed bosses.

The mature cones are smooth, but conspicuously wrinkled, and covered with a deep blue-gray bloom, which when rubbed off reveals a rich dark-brown color beneath. Very old cones (Pl. IV, *a*) are ashy-gray, with bosses much less conspicuous[3] than in newly matured cones (Pl. V). Immature cones of one season's growth are light reddish-brown, with areas of pale-bluish bloom. Mature cones may remain on the trees unopened for from 14 to 18 years, and possibly even longer.[4] The red-brown seeds vary greatly in shape from a rounded to a triangular and somewhat rectangular form, and may be from three-sixteenths to five-sixteenths of an inch long, more often the latter. Each cone contains from about 70 to 112 seeds, the largest number occurring in cones with 8 scales. The large size of the seeds at once distinguishes them from those of Arizona cypress, though in color and form the two are similar. Seed-leaves vary in number from 3 to 4.

The sapwood of smooth cypress is a pale straw-color and the heartwood a very light brownish-yellow. Seasoned wood is hard, rather heavy, strong, and with very narrow rings of growth. As in the case of Arizona cypress, the freshly cut, dry wood has a slightly cedarlike odor, which is less pronounced in green wood. Thoroughly seasoned wood is moderately durable in contact with the soil, fence posts lasting about 20 years, and corral poles 30 to 35 years. Cabins built of the logs 40 years ago are still in a good state of preservation. The small size of the trees and the limited supply have confined the use of the wood mainly to local needs. It has been employed to a limited extent for fence posts, corral poles, and rough house logs, fuel, telephone poles, and mine props.

---

[1] Male flower-buds (Pl. V, *a*) were abundant when the trees were seen in late autumn. The writer has had no opportunity for examining trees in the spring, so that female flowers have not been obtained.

[2] Very young cones may have 10 scales, but at maturity 2 of the basal ones become abortive.

[3] Due to the thickening of the tissue through growth after maturity. In the case of Cupressus glabra the formation of green spongy tissue in old cones appears to enlarge or thicken only the main body of the cone-scales without increasing the size of the bosses, while in the case of C. arizonica this growth enlarges the bosses as well as the body of the scales.

[4] No systematic tests have yet been made of the germination of seeds from cones of different ages. A physical test, however, showed the majority of seeds in the oldest cones to be in a perfectly sound and apparently germinable condition. The almost phenomenal preservation of these seeds can be accounted for only by the green state of the cone, which supplies and maintains an equable amount of moisture, and by the presence of a considerable amount of tannin in the woody parts of the cone-scales which probably prevents decay of the seeds.

OCCURRENCE AND HABITS.

In the Verde River Canyon grove smooth cypress grows abundantly in gravelly and shaly soils on benches, gentle slopes, and low ridges at elevations between 3,700 and 5,500 feet. It is best developed in protected watered gulches and on the gentler slopes and benches where the soil is moist. At low elevations it is associated with Pinus monophylla, Pinus edulis, Quercus chrysolepsis, and Rhus laurina, while higher up it forms nearly pure stands.

Little is known at present regarding the light requirements of smooth cypress during its early stages of growth, but in later life, judging from the greater density of its crown, this species should be as tolerant of shade, if not more so, than Arizona cypress.

Smooth cypress is a prolific seeder, usually producing cones every year. The fresh seed shows a moderately high percentage of germination, while the vitality of older seed probably declines rapidly after the fifth year.

LONGEVITY.

The extreme age attained by this species has not yet been determined, but it is probably as long lived as Arizona cypress. The largest trees found so far are at least 200 or 250 years old.

GENERIC CHARACTERISTICS OF JUNIPERS.

The junipers are evergreen trees that in general appearance somewhat resemble the cypresses, though their berrylike fruits at once distinguish them from the latter. The adult foliage of most junipers covers the branchlets closely and consists of short minute scalelike sharp-pointed leaves arranged in groups (whorls) of three or in opposite pairs, each of the latter alternating in position around the stem. In some species all of the adult leaves occur in threes instead of in pairs and are then much longer, needlelike, standing out loosely at regular intervals (Pls. VI, VII). The margins of the leaves are smooth or minutely toothed. The juvenile or primary foliage produced by seedlings and older young plants of the first group of junipers noted is more or less similar in general appearance to adult foliage of the last group mentioned. This primary foliage gradually gives way, however, as the plants grow older to the adult scalelike form of leaves. The close scalelike type of leaves very often have a pit or resinous gland on the back (Pl. XIII). When bruised, the foliage of junipers emits a pungently aromatic odor.

The needlelike seed-leaves of junipers are 2 to 6 in number (Pl. XIX).

The minute inconspicuous flowers of junipers are of two sexes. Male, or pollen-bearing flowers (Pl. XII, *a*), and female flowers, which develop into fruit, are each borne chiefly on different trees, or in the case of some species on the same tree (XXIV, *a*).

The fruits, popularly called "berries," are morphologically cones, the pulpy berrylike covering being made up of the fleshy flower scales which unite as the fruit develops, so as to inclose the hard seeds (1 to 12 in number; Pl. XI). The points of the flower scales usually project from the surface of the fruit. Most of our native junipers mature their fruit in from one to two seasons (two summers and one winter), while one species requires three seasons (two summers and two winters).[1] When ripe, the berries are dark blue, red-brown, or copper colored, and except in the case of one Texas juniper the surface is covered with a whitish bloom, which is easily rubbed off. The pulpy flesh of the berries is slightly juicy or mealy, sweetish, and often strongly aromatic, due to the presence of resin cells. Both birds and mammals, especially the former, eat the berries and thus play a most important part in the dissemination of the seeds.[2] Otherwise their distribution would be exceedingly slow, for the berries are too heavy to be carried far from the mother trees except on washed slopes.

Junipers are further characterized by their narrow-ringed aromatic durable wood, the "heart" portion of which is dull yellow-brown in some species and a clear rose-purple red in others. The trunk bark is rather soft and distinctly stringy, one species only having brittle checkered hard bark (Pl. XX).

Junipers are small or at most only medium-size trees unfit in most cases for saw timber except for some minor purposes, although the wood itself is suitable for general use. It is used largely for fence posts, fuel, especially in localities where no other trees grow. From the forester's standpoint junipers are important because of their ability to grow on dry barren slopes and exposed situations where few if any other trees will thrive.

Twelve tree junipers inhabit the United States, nine of which occur within the Rock Mountain region. Of the other three species, one is confined to California, while two are found only in the eastern United States.

Junipers are of ancient origin, remains of them in Tertiary rocks showing that they inhabited Europe ages ago.

[1] Prof. John G. Jack was the first to point out that in New England the common dwarf juniper (*Juniperus communis*) requires three seasons for ripening its "berries" (Bot. Gazette, XVIII, 369, Pl. XXXIII. 1893). It is not known whether or not the species has a different habit elsewhere in its wide range.

[2] The hard bony coverings of the seeds are entirely unaffected by digestion except, as is believed, facilitating in some degree their germination.

CUPRESSUS GLABRA: FOLIAGE AND NEWLY RIPENED CLOSED CONES.

a, Male flower buds (in autumn); *b*, new shoot showing large form of leaves.

JUNIPERUS COMMUNIS: STERILE BRANCH.

JUNIPERUS COMMUNIS: FERTILE BRANCH AND RIPE FRUIT.

a, Seeds (natural size and enlarged twice natural size) divested of the pulp.

COMMON JUNIPER.[1]

Juniperus communis Linnæus.

COMMON NAME AND EARLY HISTORY.

The common or dwarf juniper is the most widely distributed tree inhabiting the northern half of the globe.[2] It was technically named and described in 1753, probably from specimens obtained from northern Europe. Apparently, however, it was previously long known in Europe and in Asia. It is difficult to determine when it was first found in North America. The earliest botanical account of it, however, as a native of this country appeared in about 1803. Juniperus communis has a long botanical history in which various forms have been described under about sixteen different specific and varietal names. Thirteen varieties are now distinguished in cultivation, the best marked one being J. communis sibirica. The generally accepted vernacular name of this species, "common juniper," is derived from its technical name. Occasionally it is called "dwarf juniper" and "ground cedar."

DISTINGUISHING CHARACTERISTICS.

Throughout its wide range in North America common juniper attains tree size only in a few counties of southern Illinois, where it grows to a height of from 15 to nearly 25[3] feet and a diameter of from 6 to 8 inches. Elsewhere it is a shrub less than 5 feet high, with numerous slender, half-prostrate stems forming a tangled mass from 5 to 10 feet across. Its very unsymmetrical trunk has conspicuous rounded ridges and intervening grooves at and near the ground. It is clear of branches for only a few feet, and the crown, narrow and very open, has short, slender branches trending upward. The bark, in color a deep chocolate brown tinged with red, is less than one-eighth of an inch thick and composed of loosely attached, extremely thin scales.

The dark, lustrous green, keenly pointed, needlelike, or narrow, lance-shaped leaves (Pls. VI, VII), are chalky white on their upper

[1] The prostrate, high mountain form of this species must be considered a variety, J. communis sibirica (Burgsd.) Rydberg. It differs from J. communis L. in being wholly prostrate, and also in the fact that its foliage is often shorter than that of J. communis.

Another prostrate shrub juniper, more or less common from Maine and New Foundland to Hudson Bay and the eastern slopes of the Rockies in Montana is Juniperus sabina prostrata (Pers.) Loudon. J. sabina, of which this prostrate shrub is held to be a variety, is generally distributed through central and southern Europe and Siberia. It is distinguished from the North American variety by being a strictly upright shrub, or occasionally a small tree. The freshly cut wood and crushed twigs of these plants have a characteristic, rather disagreeable odor. They are further distinguished from J. communis and its variety J. communis sibirica by having the short scalelike, pointed leaves in alternately arranged pairs, the points of the leaves more or less spreading and free. The needlelike leaves of J. communis are arranged in groups of three.

[2] It also grows naturally in northern, central, and eastern Asia, as well as in northern and central Europe.

[3] In Germany and Norway it is said to attain 30 to 40 feet or more in height.

side, a characteristic which clearly distinguishes this juniper from all other native species. The leaves spread widely from the triangular branchlets in groups of three at rather regular intervals, those of each season's growth persisting for five or six years. Young plants of other species, especially of Juniperus virginiana, have sharp-pointed leaves similarly arranged, but much shorter and more slender. Male and female flowers are usually borne on different twigs of the same tree, though sometimes on different trees. The "berries" (Pl. VII) are mature at the end of the third summer, when they are very dark blue, almost black, and coated with whitish bloom. The top of the "berry" is conspicuously marked by three blunt projections, which are points of the ovules (Pl. VII). The soft flesh of the ripe fruit is dry, resinous-aromatic, and sweet, and sometimes contains one, but, commonly, from two to four hard, bony seeds. Birds and mammals eat the berries greedily and thus assist in disseminating the seed; otherwise the fruit may remain on the branches during the following winter or spring, occasionally even until late summer, before falling to the ground.

The heartwood of common juniper is pale, yellowish brown, heavy, rather tough, very narrow-ringed, and exceedingly durable. Even the largest tree form of this juniper known in the United States is too small to be of any commercial value, though the more common shrubby type forms a low, matted ground cover on the highest and most exposed slopes and crests, effectively holding masses of snow until stored water is gradually given up to the soil.

OCCURRENCE AND HABITS.

Common juniper occurs on dry knolls, sandy flats, rocky slopes and ridges, interspersed among spruce and aspen, at elevations between about 2,700 and 10,000 feet.[1] Generally, however, it grows at altitudes between 4,500 and 8,000 feet. It is extremely tolerant of shade, where, however, its growth is very much slower and its foliage less dense than in full light.

Common juniper is a fairly abundant seeder. Seed crops, somewhat larger than the ordinary, occur at irregular intervals of from two to three years. On the whole, reproduction is rather sparse and irregular, due no doubt to the fact that most of the berries are eaten by birds, comparatively few of them reaching the ground in the immediate vicinity of the mother plants, where conditions for germination are most favorable. The fact that berries of this juniper require so long a period to mature may also account in some measure for the lack of natural production.

---

[1] The vertical range of the common juniper varies enormously throughout its world-wide distribution, from sea level on the Pacific coast to 14,000 feet in the Himalayas.

LONGEVITY.

Small trees from 2 to 4 inches in diameter, such as occur in this country, are from 25 to 33 years old. Records of trees grown in Norway show that one 13 inches in diameter was 114 years old, while another 12½ inches through was 300 years old. Sixteen-inch trees ranged from 130 to 150 years in age, and a 14-inch tree had attained 216 years. Dr. Whittmack[1] speaks of a tree of this species, 4 or 5 feet in diameter at the base, cut in the parish of Kokenberg, in Livland, Sweden, which had reached the extreme age of 2,000 years.

WESTERN JUNIPER.

Juniperus occidentalis Hooker.

COMMON NAME AND EARLY HISTORY.

Throughout its natural range this high mountain species is called "juniper," seldom being distinguished from other juniper trees of the same general region. The name "western juniper," adopted here, is coined from the tree's technical name.

Juniperus occidentalis is only sparingly represented in the Rocky Mountain region, its main range lying in the Pacific States. There appears to be no record of the earliest discovery of this tree, which was probably seen by Lewis and Clark on their expedition to our Northwest in 1804 to 1806, for their route took them through a part of its range. The tree received its present technical name, Juniperus occidentalis Hooker, in 1839. Some of the early writers confused the first specimens collected of mountain red cedar with J. occidentalis, but only three other technical names have been applied to it during the nearly 100 years it has been known to science.

DISTINGUISHING CHARACTERISTICS.

Western juniper has a round-topped, open crown, extending to within from 4 to 8 feet of the ground, and a short, thick, conical trunk. In the Rocky Mountain region its height varies from 15 to 20 feet, or occasionally even to 30 feet. Much taller trees, 60 or more feet high and with diameters sometimes as large as 60 inches, occur in protected situations in the Pacific region.

The short chunky stem is ridged and grooved, but is usually straight, or, in the most exposed sites, sometimes bent and twisted. The tree develops enormously long and large roots, which enable it to withstand the fierce winds of high mountains. Huge lower branches often rise like smaller trunks from the base and middle of the stem. Other branches are large and stiff, standing out straight or trending

[1] Gartenflora, xxxvi, 139, 1887.

upward from the trunk, while there are also many short ones. Sometimes the top is divided into two or three thick forks, giving the tree a broader crown than usual. In such cases, if the trees grow on flats with deep soil, the crowns are dense, symmetrical, round-topped, and conical, and extend down to within 6 feet of the ground. Young trees have straight, sharply tapering stems and narrow, open crowns of distant, slender, but stiff-looking, long, upturned branches. In old age the lower and middle-crown branches often droop, but their tips continue to turn upward. The firm stringy bark of the trunk is a clear, light cinnamon-brown, one-half to 1¼ inches thick, distinctly cut longitudinally by wide, shallow furrows, the long flat ridges being connected at remote intervals by narrower diagonal ones. Bark of branchlets that have recently shed their leaves is smooth, very thin, and clear reddish-brown, but later, as the twigs grow larger, is divided into loosely attached, thin scales of lighter red-brown.

The short, pale ashy-green, scalelike leaves (Pl. VIII) clasp the stiff-looking twigs closely, the longer, sharper leaves of young, thrifty shoots spreading slightly at their points (Pl. VIII, *a*). All leaves have a prominent, glandular pit on the back, the abundant whitish resin of which marks the twigs conspicuously and is a distinguishing character. The leaves are arranged on the stems in successive groups of three, thus forming rounded twigs with six longitudinal rows of leaves. The margins of the leaves are minutely toothed. Those produced each season die in about their second year.

Male and female flowers are borne on different trees. The "berries" (Pl. VIII), from one-fourth to one-third of an inch in diameter, mature about the first of September of the second year, when they are bluish black with a whitish bloom. The skin is tough, and only slightly marked at or near the top of the berry by the tips of the female flower scales. The sweetish, pungent aromatic flesh of the ripe berries is scanty, dry, and contains from two to three bony, pitted, and grooved seeds (Pl. VIII, *b*, *c*, *d*). Seed-leaves, two in number, are needlelike, sharp pointed, and about an inch long. Seedling leaves are similar in form, but much shorter, spreading in groups of three at close intervals. The leaves produced in subsequent years are successively shorter and closer in their arrangement, until about the third or fourth year, when a few twigs bear leaves of adult form.

The wood of western juniper is pale brown, tinged with red, with a slight aromatic odor, very narrow-ringed, and, like that of the other brown-wooded junipers, remarkably durable. It is soft and brittle, and splits easily, in this respect resembling the wood of the eastern red-wooded pencil cedars (*J. virginiana* and *J. barbadensis*). The short, often very knotty trunks, are much used locally for posts and fuel, but furnish poor saw timber, though they would give good blocks for pencils.

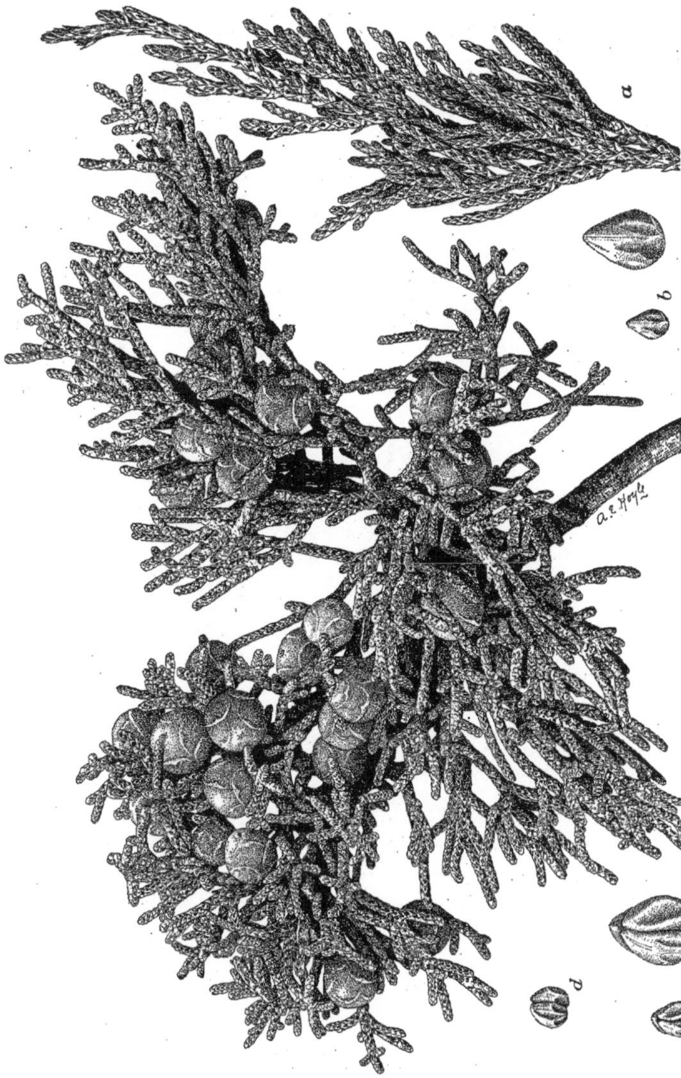

JUNIPERUS OCCIDENTALIS: FOLIAGE AND RIPE FRUIT.

a, New shoot showing large form of leaves; *b*, *c*, *d*, showing variable number of seeds (natural size and enlarged twice natural size) divested of pulp.

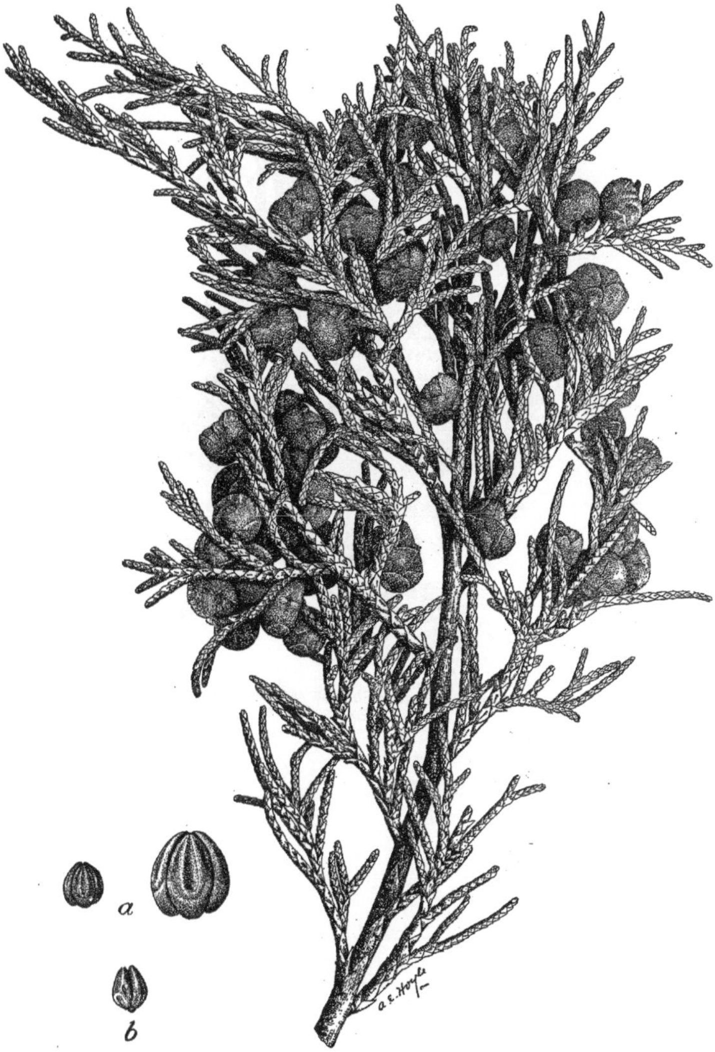

JUNIPERUS SCOPULORUM: FOLIAGE AND RIPE FRUIT FROM TREE IN PROTECTED SITE.

a, b, Variable number of seeds in different berries (natural size and enlarged twice natural size).

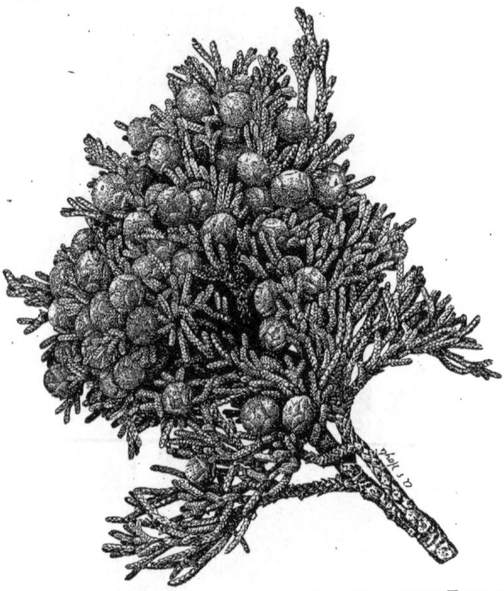

JUNIPERUS SCOPULORUM: FOLIAGE AND RIPE FRUIT FROM TREE IN EXPOSED SITE.

OCCURRENCE AND HABITS.

Western juniper grows on exposed high mountain slopes and sides of canyons, in dry gravelly and rocky soils, and sometimes in crevices of bare rocks. In the Rockies[1] it is found generally at elevations between 2,000 and 9,000 feet, though most often between 6,000 to 8,000 feet, where the best growth occurs. It usually forms very open but practically pure stands, and is sometimes scattered among other trees of its high range. As a rule, pure stands are limited to from a few to 40 or 50 acres. Western juniper is forestrally important because it thrives at high elevations, in dry wind-swept situations, where few other trees can exist. It always grows in the full enjoyment of light, and appears to be decidedly intolerant of shade. Even seedlings in partial shade are much less vigorous than young plants growing in full light.

Western juniper produces its fruit abundantly, yet the seedlings are always much scattered and occur only in pure mineral soil. As in the case of other junipers many of the berries are eaten by birds, which assists in distributing the seed; but very tardy germination of the seed under the particularly unfavorable conditions within the tree's habitat, as well as the fact that seedlings can not grow in better soil under the shade of other trees, probably accounts for the sparse reproduction.

LONGEVITY.

While the extreme age this tree may attain is not yet fully determined, it is known to be exceedingly long-lived. Both height and diameter growth are slow when the tree is rooted in crevices of rock and exposed, as it usually is, to fierce winds. Even in such situations, however, it grows persistently, producing a trunk that is out of all proportion in thickness to its height. The wood of such trees is very narrow-ringed (one-sixth to one-tenth of an inch), indicating great age. In protected mountain coves and on flats with deep washes of loose earth, diameter growth is more rapid and the annual rings wider. Trees of this type, from 20 to 48 inches in diameter, are from 125 to 300 years old, while in general the age of full-grown trees is estimated to be between 500 and 700 years. The largest trees grown in exposed places are probably from 800 to 1,000 or more years old.

[1] Elsewhere in its range this juniper has a widely varying vertical distribution from 600 to about 10,500 feet, the highest elevation attained being in the California Sierras. Its commonest occurrence there is at elevations between 6,000 and 9,000 feet.

MOUNTAIN RED CEDAR.

Juniperus scopulorum Sargent.

COMMON NAME AND EARLY HISTORY.

Mountain red cedar was for a long time supposed to be a western form of the red cedar (*Juniperus virginiana*) of northeastern United States. The two species resemble each other in the general appearance of their foliage and fruit and especially in the dark purple-red color of their heartwood, but the mountain red cedar differs fundamentally from the eastern cedar in that its berries require two seasons to mature, while those of the latter species mature in one.

Mountain red cedar was first discovered in 1804 [1] by Lewis and Clark while on their memorable expedition [2] across this continent. The first technical name applied to the tree is Juniperus excelsa Pursh,[3] which was published in 1814. From 1838 to 1897 other authors referred to this tree mainly as J. virginiana and sometimes as J. occidentalis, while specimens shown at the Centennial Exposition in 1876 were described as J. virginiana var. montana Vasey.[4] Prof. C. S. Sargent [5] distinguished the tree from J. virginiana in 1897 and named it J. scopulorum. A noteworthy fact is, however, that in 1876 Dr. George Vasey, the first botanist of the United States Department of Agriculture, gave to this tree the distinct common name "Rocky Mountain red cedar," [6] and also pointed out the fundamental differences between its crown form and the eastern red cedar. His recognition of these distinctions would seem to show that Dr. Vasey was really the first author to separate this tree from its eastern relative and but for his unfortunate use of a preoccupied name ("var. *montana*") Dr. Vasey's name for the tree probably could now be maintained.

DISTINGUISHING CHARACTERISTICS.

In open, exposed situations mountain red cedar is somewhat bushy and from 10 to 20 feet high, with a short trunk from 6 to 10 inches in diameter, and a rather narrow, rounded crown of large, long limbs trending upward. Often the very short trunk is divided into several stems. In sheltered canyons and other protected places, however, the trunk is straight and sharply tapered, while the tree has an open, slender-branched crown, and attains a height of from 25 to 30 or more feet and a diameter of from 12 to 30 inches. In this form the

[1] Fide Sargent, Silva, XIV, 94, 1902.

[2] History of Expedition under Command of Lewis and Clark, ii, 457 (ed. Coues).

[3] This name is unavailable for the mountain red cedar, because Bieberstein applied it to an Asiatic juniper in 1800.

[4] A name preoccupied by Aiton, who in 1789 applied it to a form of the common juniper (*Juniperus communis*), thus making it unavailable for the Rocky Mountain tree.

[5] Garden and Forest X, 420, fig. 54, 1897.

[6] Report U. S. Dept. Agr. 1875, 185, 1876.

ends of the branches and twigs are often so drooping, or even pendent, that the tree is locally called "weeping juniper." The somewhat stringy bark, shallowly cut into a network of narrow seams and ridges, is grayish on the outside and red-brown within.

The minute, scalelike, pointed, often long-pointed, leaves (Pls. IX, X) cover the slender four-sided twigs in four rows of alternately opposite pairs. The back of each leaf usually has a long, indistinct pit (gland). The margins of the leaves are smooth. The foliage varies in color from a dark to a light green, the latter shade being emphasized by a whitish bloom.

Male and female flowers are borne on different trees. The mature berries (Pls. IX, X) are smooth, and clear blue in color, due to a whitish bloom over the blackish skin. They usually contain 2 seeds, but sometimes 3, and occasionally 1, in a sweetish, resinous pulp. The seeds (Pl. IX, *a*, *b*) are pointed at the top ends, conspicuously grooved, and marked at the base with a short two-parted scar (hilum). The number and character of the seed-leaves are at present unknown.

The wood of mountain red cedar is a dull red, or more often rather bright rose-red, with irregularly disposed yellowish-white streaks. It is narrow-ringed and has a thick layer of white sapwood. Just how durable the heartwood may be is not known, though fence posts made from it are known to have been in a good state of preservation after 20 years of service. It is likely that well-seasoned posts of mountain red cedar would be as durable as those of eastern red cedar, which may remain sound in contact with the soil for 30 or 40 years. The color, "grain," working qualities, and structure of the two woods are very similar. Mountain red cedar is adapted to the same uses to which eastern red cedar is put, but except in a few parts of its range the supply is rather scarce and scattered. The tree is desirable for planting within its natural range, since it thrives on dry soil and produces wood suitable for pencils.

OCCURRENCE AND HABITS.

Mountain red cedar grows on dry, exposed mesas, low, dry mountain slopes, and in rather moist canyon bottoms (where it reaches its best development), in rocky, sandy, or gravelly soils, though seldom in the latter. Within our Rocky Mountain region it occurs at elevations between about 5,000 and 9,000 feet, the lowest elevation being characteristic of the northern distribution, and the highest of its central and southern range. It is most commonly found between 5,000 and 7,000 feet, and is rather rare above 8,000 feet.[1]

Single trees or small groups are usually scattered among piñon pine, one-seed juniper, mountain mahogany, gambel oak, and narrow-leaf cottonwood. Sometimes it is associated with Douglas fir, Engelmann

[1] In its Pacific slope range this species occurs sometimes from sea level to about 3,200 feet.

spruce, and western yellow pine, while small, practically pure stands are occasionally interspersed with pure stands of piñon pine.

The exact light requirements of mountain red cedar are as yet imperfectly known. It endures rather dense shade during the seedling and early sapling stages in moist, cool situations. Later, however, it seems to require top light for height growth, because in close, pure stands and under the dense side shade of other species the trunk branches die. It develops a distinctly thinner and more open crown in protected and shaded situations than in full light. While in early life it has about the same degree of tolerance as eastern red cedar, later on it appears unable to endure as much shade as the latter tree.

Mountain red cedar is usually a very prolific seeder, especially when growing in the open. Some seed is borne practically every year, but particularly heavy crops are produced at intervals of from 2 to 5 years. Reproduction, however, is generally sparse, which may be due primarily to the tardy germination of the seed. The moist soil in pockets, rocky crevices, and on the borders of constantly watered canyons furnish the best seed-beds and are the sites on which seedlings are most often found. Large quantities of the berries are eaten by birds, which assist in distributing the seed.

LONGEVITY.

Little is known regarding the extreme age attained by mountain red cedar. It appears to grow very slowly and to be rather long-lived. Trees from 6 to 8 inches in diameter are from 130 to 175 years old. Under favorable conditions of growth, this cedar probably reaches an age of at least 250 years, possibly 300 years.

ONE-SEED JUNIPER.

Juniperus monosperma (Engelm.) Sargent.

COMMON NAME AND EARLY HISTORY.

This species is commonly called merely "cedar" or "juniper," lay people as a rule not distinguishing it from Utah juniper, with which it often grows. The name one-seed juniper, derived from the technical name of the tree, is appropriate because the small berries usually contain but one seed. This one-seed character, however, can not be depended upon to distinguish Juniperus monosperma from Utah juniper and Juniperus megalocarpa, since both of these have one-seeded fruit.

There is no record of when this tree was first found by early explorers of the southern Rocky Mountain region. The first botanical account of it was published in 1877, when it was named "Juniperus occidentalis var. β monosperma Engelmann," under which varietal name it was known to botanists until 1896. Investigation then showed it to be distinct from J. occidentalis in its smaller twigs, one-seeded fruit, and in its more southern range.

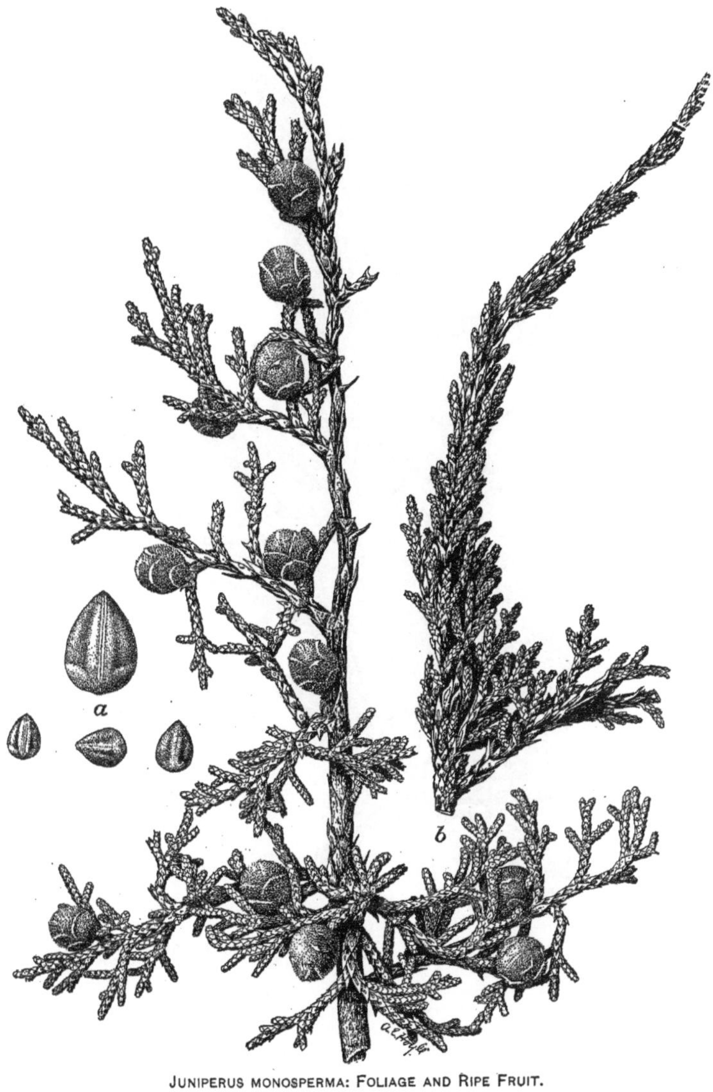

JUNIPERUS MONOSPERMA: FOLIAGE AND RIPE FRUIT.

a, Seeds (enlarged); *b*, young terminal shoot.

: Branch Showing (a) Male Flower Buds (in Autumn).

JUNIPERUS SABINOIDES: FOLIAGE AND RIPE FRUIT.

a, Variable forms and number of seeds in different berries; *b*, young shoot with large form of leaves.

JUNIPERUS SABINOIDES: TYPICAL TRUNK AND CROWN FORM OF TREE GROWN IN OPEN STAND.

DISTINGUISHING CHARACTERISTICS.

One-seed juniper commonly produces several small trunks from a single rootstock, these stems varying in height from 6 to 20 feet and in diameter from 3 to 6 or more inches. The general appearance is often that of a low-crowned, overgrown bush. Single-stem trees are rare, occurring chiefly in protected places. Their height varies from 30 to 50 feet, or occasionally more, with a diameter of from 12 to 24 inches. In all cases the trunk is rather short, often deeply fluted, and widely buttressed. The crowns are open and irregular, owing to the presence of one or several very large branches near the ground. This is a marked characteristic of the species. In the case of trees growing in sheltered situations the large branches leave the trunk above the ground, while in the desert type of tree such branches are given off either at the very base of the stem or at a point below the surface of the ground. Where one-seed juniper and Utah juniper grow together, the latter species may be recognized by its commonly single trunk, which contrasts sharply with the apparently several-stemmed trunk of one-seed juniper.

The bark of the trunk and large branches is light ashy gray on the outside, and a pale reddish or cinnamon brown beneath. On large trees the bark varies in thickness from one-half to three-fourths of an inch, but on smaller trees it rarely exceeds one-fourth of an inch. It is distinctly soft, fibrous, and stringy, narrowly and deeply divided on older trees by slitlike furrows, the narrow, flat ridges being connected with thin, lateral ones. On smaller trees and large limbs the bark is irregularly divided.

The foliage is a pale grayish green and roughish to the touch, due to the slightly spreading points of the scalelike leaves (Pls. XI, XII). The twigs have a notably squarish form, due principally to the projecting points of the leaves, which as a rule are arranged in pairs, though very occasionally in threes. The ordinary leaves of adult twigs (Pl. XI) are about one-eighth of an inch long, sharp-pointed, slightly spreading, and sometimes marked on their keeled backs with a minute, resinlike gland, which may be lacking in other cases. Leaves of thrifty leading shoots (Pl. XI, *b*) and of seedling trees are from one-third to five-eighths of an inch long, with very keen, spreading points, and a resinous gland on the back.[1] The margins of the leaves are minutely toothed.

Male and female flowers are borne on different trees. The thin-fleshed, sweetish berries (Pl. XI), from about one-eighth to one-fourth of an inch in length, are usually copper-colored, though sometimes bluish, and covered with whitish bloom. They are mostly one-seeded,

[1] Resinous glands occur quite regularly on the backs of leaves borne by vigorous leading shoots, while in the case of the smaller or adult foliage of older trees the glands may be present on some leaves and lacking on others.

in exceptional cases being two or three seeded. The fruit of some trees is peculiar in having the top end of the seed partly exposed. The seeds (Pl. XI, *a*) are pale chocolate-brown and marked at the base with a two-lobed, whitish scar (hilum). The seed-leaves are two in number.

The wood of one-seed juniper is very narrow-ringed, hard, and heavy, with a slight cedarlike odor. The sapwood is nearly white and from three-fourths to about 2 inches thick, usually much thinner in old trees than in young ones. The heartwood varies in color from dull yellowish-brown to pale reddish-brown. When thoroughly seasoned it is very durable, and is one of the best and most frequently used woods for fence posts and fuel in arid parts of the Southwest. The fact that the tree is small, crooked, and knotty confines use of the wood to such local but important purposes. Heartwood of old trees grown in protected situations is fairly soft and straight-grained, and blocks would be suitable for certain grades of lead pencils.

OCCURRENCE AND HABITS.

One-seed juniper grows in the dry, rocky, or gravelly soils of high desert plains and mountain slopes, at elevations between 3,500 and 7,000 feet, though it occurs most extensively between 5,000 and 6,500 feet. It forms an open woodland type of forest, and sometimes pure stands of limited extent, but it is more often mixed with Utah juniper, alligator juniper, piñon, and single-leaf pines, and occasionally with western yellow pine and Pinchot juniper (Texas).

Little is known of this juniper's requirement of light. It can probably endure considerable shade in the seedling stages of growth, but the fact that the older trees invariably have open crowns indicates that it requires full sunlight for its later development.

One-seed juniper is a prolific but irregular seeder, and young plants are found only where through washing or in some other way the seed has become buried in mineral soil. Scanty reproduction is due without doubt to the usually dry and generally unfavorable condition of the soil on which the seed falls. A large part of the seed probably never finds sufficient covering or enough moisture to induce germination.

The tree's persistent growth on high desert plains and mountain slopes makes it important in the maintenance of protective woodland cover in the Southwest.

LONGEVITY.

In the more favorable situations the growth of this species is generally uniform and fairly rapid for a juniper. In arid soils and on exposed sites, however, the growth is irregular and often extremely slow. The exact age that one-seed juniper may attain has not yet been determined, but it is probably very long-lived. The oldest trees doubtless reach an age of at least 400 or 500 years. Trees from 5 to 7 inches in diameter are from 170 to 195 years old, and those from 10 to 12 inches are from 315 to 375 years old.

MOUNTAIN CEDAR.

Juniperus sabinoides (H., B. and K.) Nees.

COMMON NAME AND EARLY HISTORY.

Strictly speaking, mountain cedar is not a Rocky Mountain species, since it occurs mainly in central and southeastern Texas and adjacent parts of Mexico. It is included here, however, because its geographic range has climatic and topographic features similar to those in parts of Arizona and New Mexico, and also in order to include all of the junipers occurring west of the one-hundredth meridian, which roughly divides the forest regions of the West from those of the East. The tree has no generally recognized common name, being known in some parts of its range as "mountain cedar" or "rock cedar," and in others as "mountain juniper," or even "juniper cedar." The name "mountain cedar" is the one most commonly applied by those who use the wood of the tree. It is appropriate also because it indicates the general nature of the tree's habitat in Mexico, though in the United States it grows mainly on limestone hills.

Mountain cedar was discovered first in Mexico and subsequently in Texas, but the exact dates of these discoveries are unknown. The earliest technical names applied to the tree is "Cupressus sabinoides H., B. & K.," published in 1817. Subsequently other botanical names given to it were published, from 1826 to 1877. It was not until 1847 that its present name, Juniperus sabinoides (H., B. & K.) Nees (based on Cupressus sabinoides), was permanently established, and for the reason that the name "Cupressus sabinoides H., B. & K." was not generally recognized as applying to our mountain cedar.

DISTINGUISHING CHARACTERISTICS.

The crown of old mountain cedar trees is broadly rounded, while in young ones it is widely conical. Old trees develop very open crowns, while those of younger trees are more compact. The tree is seldom more than 18 feet high, though in sheltered or otherwise favorable situations it may attain a height of 35 or more feet and a diameter of from 12 to 18 inches. Seldom more than one-third of the trunk is free of branches (Pl. XIV), and in very dry, exposed places the tree is often only a many-stemmed, widely spreading shrub, the crooked stems occasionally sprawling upon the ground. In general, the trunks of this juniper are rarely straight and cylindrical for any considerable length, most of them being crooked or variously bent and with irregular ridges and hollows. It is rare for old trees to have single stems. As a rule, the trunks are divided near the ground into large, crooked, sharply ascending branches. The bark is characteristically thin, about one-fourth of an inch thick on small or medium-size trees and from one-third to one-half of an inch on large, old ones. It weathers to a brownish-gray, beneath which the layers of bark are a deep chestnut-brown. It is very stringy and fibrous, and irregularly broken into laterally connected, narrow ridges and deep furrows. Long-persisting loosened shreds of bark often give old trees a more or less shaggy appearance. Bark of the branches is dark brown mottled with white.

The deep bluish-green foliage of mountain cedar is rather roughish and prickly to the touch. The slender twigs are noticeably four-sided, due to the four-ranked arrangement of the scalelike, sharp-pointed, closely overlapping leaves, which occur in pairs and are about one-sixteenth of an inch long (Pl. XIII). The laterally compressed upper ends of the leaves give a keeled appearance to their backs, and emphasize this four-sided feature. The edges of the leaves bear minute, irregular teeth. Vigorous terminal shoots and young plants have very keenly pointed leaves, from one-fourth to one-half of an inch long, the points of which are often slightly spreading. The backs of the leaves are marked with a minuted pit o bear a resinous gland (Pl. XIII).

Male and female flowers are borne on separate trees. The rip berries (Pl. XIII), matured in September at the end of one season' growth, are deep blue and with a whitish bloom. They have tough skin and a thin, pungent, sweetish pulp. As a rule, only th points of the female flower scales are visible on the surface of th berries. The berries contain from 1 to 2 light brown, shiny see (Pl. XIII, *a*), which are pointed, slightly grooved at the top end, an marked at the bottom with a low, narrow, scalelike scar (hilum The seed-leaves are two in number, and narrowly lance-shape Seedlings continue to bear the long awl-shaped form of leaves f 3 or 4 years, when these are gradually succeeded by the shorte adult form.

The wood of mountain cedar is moderately heavy (about 43 poun per cubic foot, seasoned), rather hard, exceedingly narrow-ringe and of a clear cinnamon-brown color, interspersed with irregul paler streaks. The sapwood is very thin, seldom more than o half of an inch thick. Freshly cut, dry, or green wood has a stro cedarlike odor. The heartwood is very durable, and the b sticks are useful for fence posts, telephone and telegraph poles, a light-traffic ties. It is much used locally for fuel. The wood of trees is brittle and can be cut with an easily parted chip, qualit that make clear sections suitable for pencil wood.

JUNIPERUS UTAHENSIS: FOLIAGE AND RIPE FRUIT.

a, Narrow side of seeds; *b*, broad side of seeds (natural size and enlarged twice natural size).

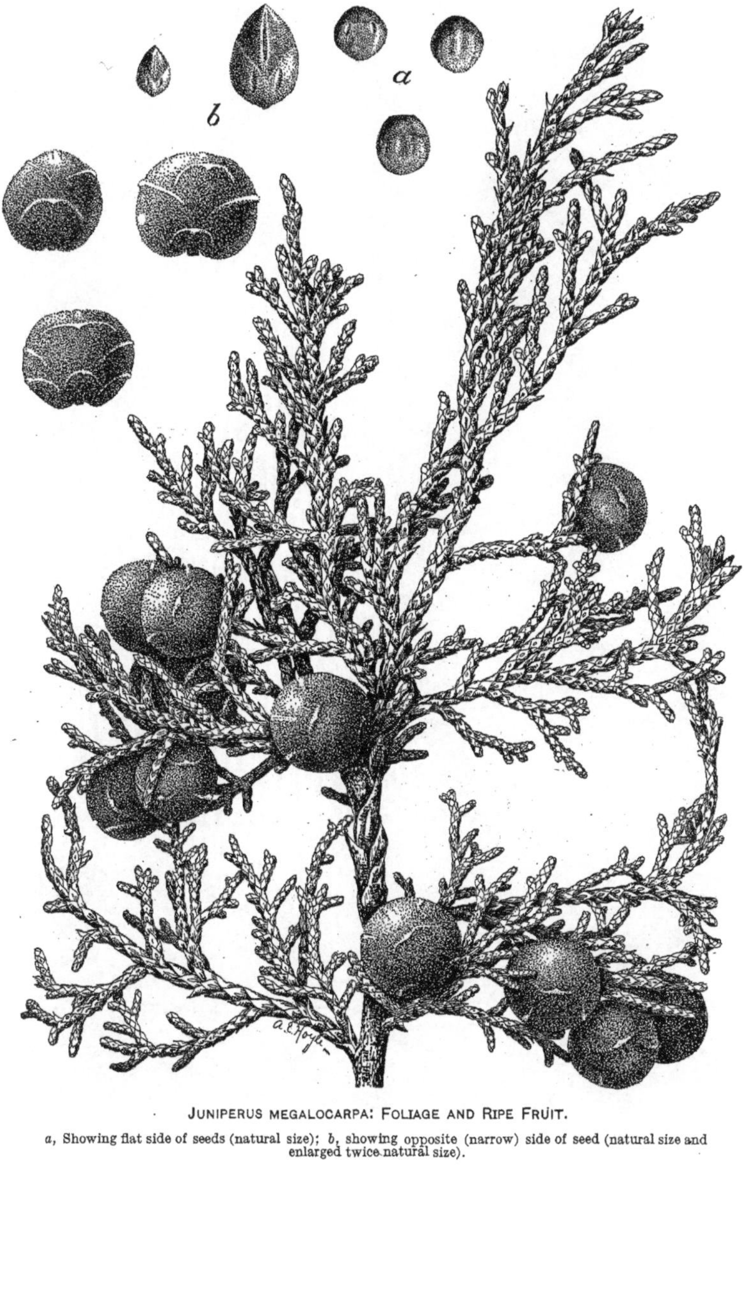

JUNIPERUS MEGALOCARPA: FOLIAGE AND RIPE FRUIT.

a, Showing flat side of seeds (natural size); *b*, showing opposite (narrow) side of seed (natural size and enlarged twice natural size).

JUNIPERUS MEGALOCARPA: SHOWING TYPICAL BARK OF LARGE TREE (26 INCHES IN DIAMETER AND 50 FEET HIGH).

OCCURRENCE AND HABITS.

In the United States mountain cedar forms very dense, pure, or nearly pure, stands, sometimes of vast extent, as on the semiarid limestone hills of the Edwards Plateau in central Texas. It usually grows in dry rocky, gravelly, or sandy soils, often in crevices of bare rock. Mountain cedar also grows both in pure stands and in mixture with other species in lower, sheltered situations in deep-washed soil of good quality. Interspersed with mixed stands are often groups and scattered trees of one-seed juniper, Pinchot juniper, Mexican walnut, live oak, Spanish oak, Durand oak, cedar elm, and hackberry. The dense, sometimes almost impenetrable, stands of this juniper on limestone are locally known as "cedar breaks."[1]

In this country mountain cedar occurs chiefly at elevations between 600 and 2,000 feet. Little is known of its range and habitat in Mexico, where it is said to occur much more extensively and at higher elevations than in the United States.

Mountain cedar is very tolerant of dense shade during the seedling and early sapling stages, as shown by the existence of extremely dense thrifty stands. It appears to be much less tolerant later in life, when its crown becomes thinner and more open (Pl. XIV). In ability to endure shade, however, it compares favorably with red cedar (*Juniperus virginiana*), but probably it would not maintain itself under long suppression as does the latter tree. Local reports of mountain cedar having come up on an area immediately after a full stand of oak had been cut off give further evidence of its tolerance during early life, since on such areas it must have existed for a number of years in a suppressed condition, and recovered when the oak was removed.

Mountain cedar bears seed abundantly, and reproduction is plentiful in loose, permeable soils, and in broken, rocky formations, and also in soil-filled pockets and crevices of bare rock. The sweetish berries are eaten by birds, which assist greatly in a wide distribution of the seed.

LONGEVITY.

Juniperus sabinoides is moderately long-lived, though the extreme age attained is at present unknown. Trees from 5 to 7 inches in diameter, on exposed, rocky sites, are from 150 to 180 years old, while trees from 8 to 10 inches in diameter, in sheltered places on deep, permeable, sandy or gravelly soil, where growth is most rapid, may be only from 95 to 125 years old. Large trees occasionally found in the driest situations are probably at least 250 years old.

[1] Popularly the allusion probably is to the fancied similar lowland "canebrakes," but properly this name appears to refer to the physiographic nature of the plateau region in which dense growths of mountain cedar occur.

UTAH JUNIPER.[1]

Juniperus utahensis (Engelm.) Lemmon.

COMMON NAME AND EARLY HISTORY.

Like most of the other brown-wooded junipers, Juniperus utahensis has no distinctive common name. In the region where it grows, the people usually call it merely "juniper" or sometimes "cedar," seldom if ever distinguishing it from the other species of its kind. The discovery of this tree in Utah led to its being given the technical name "Utahensis," from which the common name employed here is derived. While Utah juniper is the most distinctive name that can be suggested, it is not entirely appropriate, because the tree is not confined to Utah, a large part of its range, in fact, lying outside that State.

Utah juniper was discovered sometime between 1867 and 1869, during the exploration of Nevada and Utah by the United States Geological Survey. The botanical history of the tree shows that its distinguishing characters were imperfectly known until comparatively recent times. The earliest account of it was published in 1871 under "Juniperus occidentalis Watson," the writer supposing it to be a form of the western juniper. In 1877 it was described as "J. californica var. utahensis Engelm.," and finally, in 1890, as "J. utahensis Lemmon." The tree is distinct from the California and western junipers both in its botanical characters and geographic range.

DISTINGUISHING CHARACTERISTICS.

Utah juniper is commonly a low, very short trunked, or many-stemmed, bushy tree, from 6 to 12 feet high,[2] and from 4 to 8 or more

[1] In 1897 Prof. Aven Nelson found a "shrublike tree" juniper in Wyoming (Red Desert region from Seminole Mountains to Green River) which in 1898 he named Juniperus knightii (Bot. Gaz. xxv, 198, fig. 1, 2, 1898).

The writer has not seen authentic specimens of this juniper, and was, therefore, unable personally to decide what final disposition should be made of the tree in the present work. Several authors have, however, reduced Juniperus knightii to a synonym of J. utahensis. Judging from Prof. Nelson's description and illustrations of J. knightii it would seem to be very closely related to J. utahensis and J. megalocarpa. It resembles the former species particularly in the low-branched several-stemmed habit of its crown, and both of these junipers in its large fruit and single large seed. The "copper-colored" fruit ascribed to J. knightii is not, however, strictly speaking, characteristic of J. utahensis and J. megalocarpa.

The author's technical description (loc. cit.) of J. knightii, slightly condensed, follows:

"A scraggy shrub or small tree, usually much branched from the base—i. e., trunkless or breaking up into several subequal trunks also freely branched, branches widely spreading, the lowest close to the ground and almost resting upon it, round-topped, 3-7 meters high or possibly in places exceeding this; leaves 3-ranked, closely appressed * * * entire or rarely minutely denticulate, neither pitted nor glandular * * * berrylike cones blue-green or copper-colored * * * broadly oval, 7-10 millimeters long, dry, the coalesced scales thin, in dried specimens closely and tenaciously adherent to the large single seed; the seed ovate, obtuse, slightly grooved above, rounded or swollen at the base; fruit possibly not maturing till the second year."

[2] The several-stemmed forms of Utah juniper are similar in general appearance to like forms of the one-seed juniper. In the majority of cases, however, if not in all, the trunklike branches of Utah juniper leave the trunk near or above the ground, while in the case of one-seed juniper, the two or more stems usually arise from the main root-stock, or collar, at or slightly below the surface of the ground.

inches thick near the ground, with a wide, rounded, rather open crown of numerous upright, twisted limbs. The short trunk is apt to be one-sided with conspicuous hollows and ridges. Its thin, whitish bark, from one-fourth to three-eighths of an inch thick on large trunks, is cut into long scales.

The minute, sharp-pointed, scalelike, pale yellowish-green leaves (Pl. XV), generally without a pit on the back, are arranged mostly in alternately opposite pairs, and closely overlap each other in four rows on the slender, stiff-looking twigs. Sometimes there are six rows, in which case three leaves occur together at a point. Leaves of vigorous leading shoots are much larger and keenly pointed (Pl. XVI), while those of seed lings are needlelike. The margins of the leaves are minutely toothed. The twigs have a roundish appearance. Leaves of each season's growth persist from 10 to 12 years, or even longer. The bark of larger twigs which have recently shed their leaves is pale reddish-brown and scaly.

Male and female flowers are usually borne on different twigs of the same tree, though sometimes the male flowers are borne on one tree and the female on another. Ripe berries (Pl. XV), matured in the autumn of the second year, have a smooth, tough, red-brown skin, covered with a whitish bloom, which gives the berries a bluish tint. The pulp of the berries is thin, dry, and sweet. They usually contain but one seed (occasionally two), pointed at the top, rather sharply angled (Pl. XV, *a*, *b*), and marked nearly to the top by what appears to be a scalelike, basal covering (hilum). The surface of the berries shows projecting points, which are the ends of minute female flower scales. The pointed seed-leaves are usually 5 in number, but vary from 4 to 6.

The hard, heavy wood of Utah juniper is generally very narrow-ringed, the rings in stunted trees being extremely narrow. The sapwood is very thick and white, while the heartwood, of a light yellowish-brown color, is less pungent in odor than that of other junipers. When thoroughly seasoned the wood is exceedingly durable. Utah juniper is too small and imperfect in form for commercial purposes, though where it is abundant the wood is much used for fuel and fence posts.

OCCURRENCE AND HABITS.

Utah juniper grows on desert foothills and mountain slopes in dry rocky, gravelly, or sandy soils, at elevations between 5,000 and 7,000 feet. It forms extensive, rather open, pure stands, and also grows mixed with single-leaf pine, one-seed juniper, and desert shrubs. Like its associate, one-seed juniper, the tree is important to the forester through its ability to form a woodland type of cover in arid regions.

Little is known regarding the tree's light requirements or its reproduction. In the intolerance of shade, it appears to be very similar to the western and one-seed junipers. It produces an abundance of berries at intervals of about two years, a few being borne nearly every year. Reproduction is usually sparse and widely scattered, due to the failure of most of the seed to germinate in the exceedingly dry soils of the region where the tree grows.

LONGEVITY.

Utah juniper is rather long-lived, the maximum age being about 300 years. Trees from 6 to 10 inches in diameter are from 145 to 250 years old.

BIG-BERRIED JUNIPER.

Juniperus megalocarpa Sudworth.

COMMON NAME AND EARLY HISTORY

This recently discovered juniper is not distinguished by settlers in its range from other southwestern junipers and "cedars." The common name "big-berried juniper," adopted here, is derived from the technical name in reference to the large size of its fruit, a striking and distinctive characteristic.

It was discovered by Mr. W. R. Mattoon of the Forest Service on September 22, 1906, in the southwest corner of the Datil National Forest, Socorro County, southwestern New Mexico, where only about 25 trees were found.[1]

The tree was named and described in June, 1907, from specimens, field notes, and a photograph obtained by Mr. Mattoon.[2]

DISTINGUISHING CHARACTERISTICS.

Big-berried juniper is one of the largest and best formed of our southwestern junipers. It varies in height from 30 to 50 feet, and in diameter from 2 to 4 feet. The crown is compact, broadly pyramidal, with short, stout branches. The trunks are clear of branches for from 15 to 20 feet, or more, and have dark reddish-brown, finely fissured bark, shredded on the surface (Pl. XVIII). The branchlets (Pl. XVII) are short, very dense, and clothed with pale yellowish-green, sometimes bronze-green, foliage, On young trees the foliage

---

[1] This station, approximately in section 11 or 14, township 9 south, an unsurveyed region, is on the west bank of the San Francisco River at a point about halfway between the towns of Alma and Frisco, and 3 miles above the "Widow Kelley's Ranch."

Forest Supervisor William H. Goddard later reported having seen a juniper, which may prove to be J. megalocarpa, on a small tributary of San Francisco River at a point about 6 miles west of Pleasanton, N. Mex., some 20 miles from Mr. Mattoon's type locality and near the east border of Arizona. The writer has not seen specimens of this tree.

Prof. C. S. Sargent also informed the writer (Nov. 6, 1914) that several years ago he collected specimens of this tree on the rim of Oak Creek Canyon, 20 miles south of Flagstaff, Ariz., and that three or four years later Prof. Percival Lowell also collected specimens at Angell, near Flagstaff, Ariz.

Further explorations should extend the tree's range.

[2] Forestry and Irrigation, XIII, figs. 1 and 2 (1907).

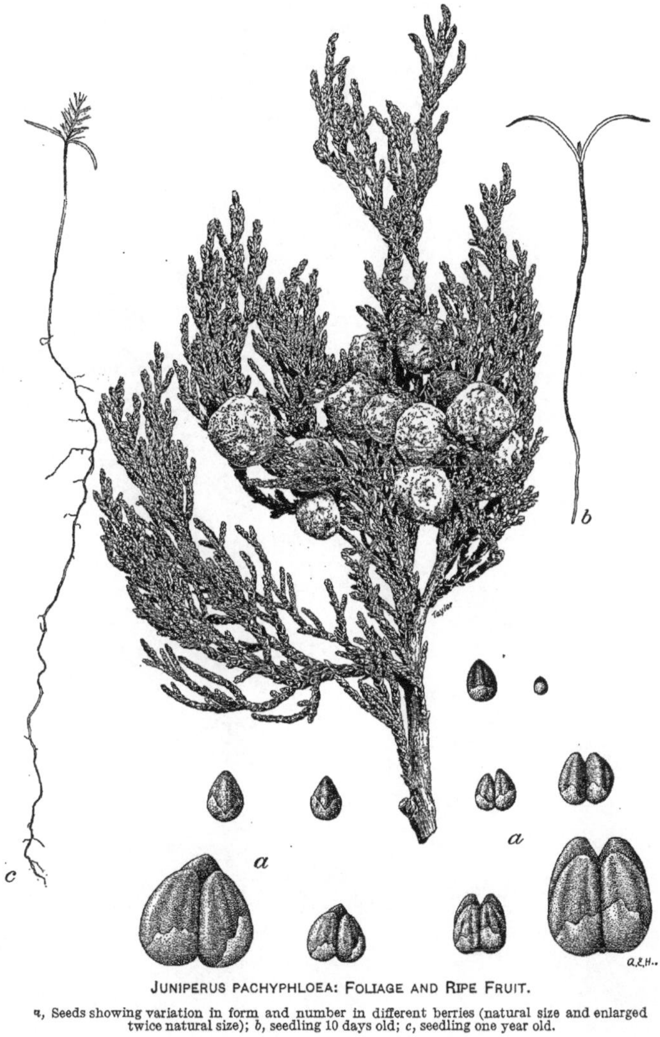

JUNIPERUS PACHYPHLOEA: FOLIAGE AND RIPE FRUIT.

a, Seeds showing variation in form and number in different berries (natural size and enlarged twice natural size); *b*, seedling 10 days old; *c*, seedling one year old.

JUNIPERUS PACHYPHLOEA; SHOWING TYPICAL BARK OF LARGE TREE (37 INCHES IN DIAMETER).

JUNIPERUS PACHYPHLOEA: SHOWING TYPICAL STUNTED FORM OF TREE GROWN IN EXPOSED SITUATIONS.

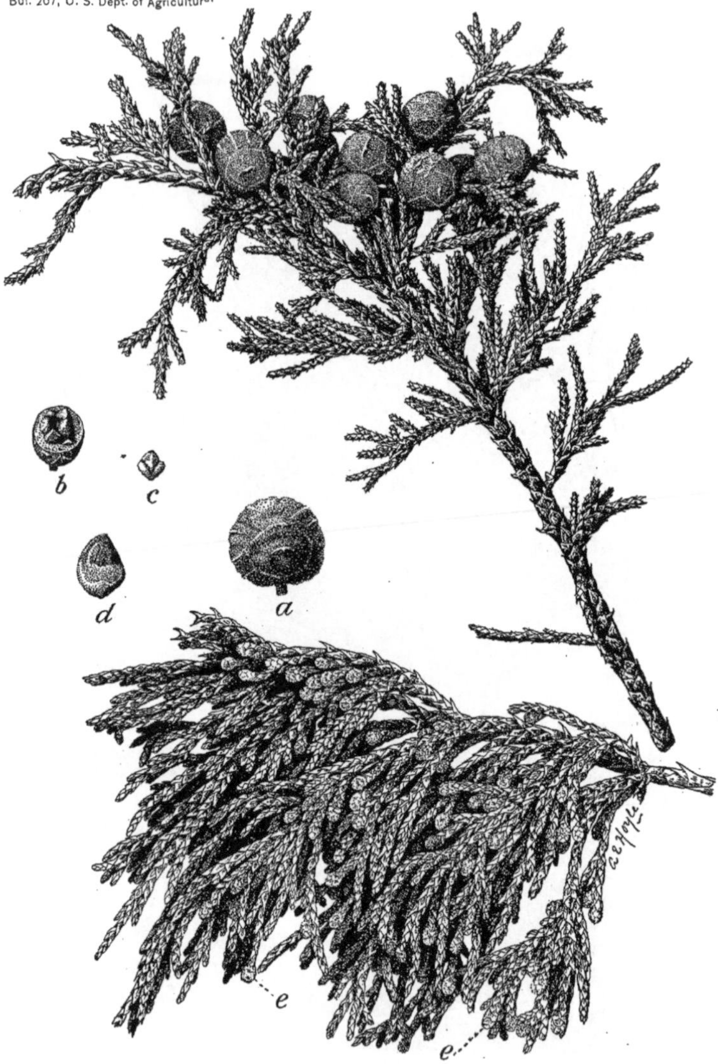

JUNIPERUS FLACCIDA: FOLIAGE AND RIPE FRUIT.

a, Detached large fruit; *b*, berry with top removed showing tiered irregular arrangement of seeds (enlarged one and one-half times natural size); *c*, *d*, detached seeds (natural size and enlarged four times natural size); *e*, male flowers in autumn (natural size).

often has a whitish tinge. The sharp-pointed, scalelike leaves occur in twos and threes, closely overlapping each other, and usually marked on the back with a pit, which often contains a rather conspicuous resin spot. The leaves of vigorous leading shoots have slightly spreading, somewhat slender points and long (decurrent) bases. The margins of the leaves are provided with irregular, minute teeth.

Male and female flowers are borne on separate trees. The fruit of Juniperus megalocarpa matures at the end of the second season. It is spherical or slightly elongated in shape and of exceptionally large size, varying from about nine-sixteenths to eleven-sixteenths of an inch in diameter or length (Pl. XVII). The surface of the berries is roughened only by the united female flower scales and their rather tough skin is reddish-brown and coated with whitish bloom. The sweet flesh of the berries is thick, dry, and firm, and in old and fully matured berries scarcely resinous, though from the presence of old resin cells in the pulp it is evident that immature or newly ripened fruit has a distinct resinous flavor. The berries usually contain but one glossy, chestnut-brown seed—rarely two—marked at the base by a conspicuous 2-lobed scar (hilum), which has distinct short pits or shallow grooves. The top end of the seed is usually abruptly flattened on its two broad sides so as to form a chisellike edge (Pl. XVII *a*, *b*, view of opposite sides). The seeds readily fall out of the dry pulp when the latter is cut or broken open. The number of seed-leaves is unknown.

Juniperus megalocarpa resembles J. utahensis in its large one-seeded fruit and also in the general appearance of its foliage. The much longer vertical creases and furrows and the pointed top of the seeds of J. utahensis distinguish this species from J. megalocarpa.

The wood of big-berried juniper has not been collected, but it is known to have a rather strong, cedarlike odor and to be yellowish-brown in color. Scarcity of post material and fuel in the region where this juniper grows should make it valuable for these purposes.

OCCURRENCE AND HABITS.

The trees found on the Datil National Forest were scattered singly and in small, open groups on deep washed, rather rich, sandy loam or gravelly soils of benches and terraces, from 50 to 150 feet above the bed of the San Francisco River, where the elevation is about 5,400 feet. Interspersed with them were piñon, one-seed juniper, and Emory oak, while mountain red cedar, Arizona oak, and blue oak occur in the same general region.

Big-berried juniper appears to be similar in its requirements of light and reproductive capacity to Utah juniper. No seedlings were found in the vicinity of the fruiting trees, which produce an abundance of berries. The absence of young trees may have been due, however, to the overgrazed state of the ground, which doubtless prevented germination of the seed.

This species is suitable for planting on dry foothills and lower mountain slopes of the Southwest, where it should succeed at elevations between 2,500 and 6,000 feet.

LONGEVITY.

Complete information is not available regarding the longevity of big-berried juniper. Judging from the size of the trees produced in the comparatively dry habitat, however, it probably attains an age of not less than 250 or 300 years.

ALLIGATOR JUNIPER.

Juniperus pachyphlœa Torrey.

COMMON NAME AND EARLY HISTORY.

Alligator juniper is unique in the thick, sharply checkered bark of its trunk (Pl. XX), the resemblance of which to the body scales of an alligator suggested its widely accepted common name, a characteristic which also distinguishes it sharply from all other native junipers. It is sometimes known as "oak-barked juniper" and "thick-barked juniper."

Alligator juniper was discovered in 1851 on the Zuni Mountains of northwestern New Mexico by Dr. S. W. Woodhouse, then a member of Capt. Sitgreaves's exploring party, which descended the Zuni and Colorado Rivers. An account of this discovery was published in 1853,[1] and the tree was technically named and described in 1858.

Three garden varieties of alligator juniper, recently established by Barbier,[2] are distinguished in cultivation, namely, Juniperus pachyphlœa conspicua, J. pachyphlœa elegentissima, and J. pachyphlœa ericoides.

DISTINGUISHING CHARACTERISTICS.

This species is one of the most massive of our junipers. In early life the crown is open and broadly conical, and in old age, dense and round. The trunk is short and clear of branches for 6 or perhaps 10 feet. As a rule, the tree attains a height of from 30 to 40 feet, and a diameter of from 1½ to 3½ feet. Exceptional trees are from 50 to 65 feet or more in height, and from 4 to 6 feet in diameter, with from 15 to 20 feet of clear trunk. In exposed dry situations it is stunted, the trunks often dividing at the ground into several twisted stems (Pl. XXI). The deeply furrowed bark, from one-half

[1] Report of an expedition down the Zuni and Colorado Rivers under the command of Capt. L. Sitgreaves, 35, 1853.

[2] Mitteil. Deutschen Dendr. Gesellschaft 1910, 139, 289.

of an inch thick on trunks 6 to 8 inches through to about 3½ inches on the larger ones, has its flat ridges sharply cut into rectangular plates (Pl. XX). Externally it is usually weathered to a bright ashy-gray, beneath which the color is a dull, dark chocolate-brown. When the slender twigs shed their leaves, they have smooth, reddish purple-brown bark, which becomes scaly as the branchlets grow larger.

The foliage is a pale blue-green; the alternately opposite pairs of minute, scalelike leaves (Pl. XIX), closely pressed and overlapping each other, are arranged in four ranks, giving the twigs a four-sided appearance. Each leaf bears a tiny but conspicuous resin-gland on its back. Leaves of young shoots and seedlings (Pl. XIX, *b*, *c*) are narrowly lance-shaped and keenly pointed. The margins of the leaves are minutely toothed.

Male and female flowers are borne on different trees. The berries, which are matured by October of the second year, vary in shape from spherical to slightly elongated, and may be from about three-eighths to nearly one-half of an inch in diameter or length. Their surface is more or less marked by the points of united female flower-scales, and further roughened by irregular little knobs (Pl. XIX). The firm, deep purplish-brown skin of the berries is covered with a whitish bloom. The flesh of mature berries is dryish and resinous, that of immature ones being very resinous. They contain from 1 to 4 brownish, pointed, distinctly grooved seeds (Pl. XIX, *a*), the bases of which bear a short, two-lobed scar (hilum). The seed-leaves are two in number, pointed, and about one-half an inch long. Ripe berries are shed rather slowly, in some cases continuing to fall during the winter and summer following their maturity.

The wood of alligator juniper is rather light, soft, brittle, and very narrow-ringed. The sapwood is comparatively thin and of a pale straw-color; the heartwood is light brown with a faint reddish tinge, irregularly marked with paler streaks. Seasoned heartwood is durable. Alligator juniper is locally much used for fuel and fence posts, a number of which are often split from large clear logs (Pl. XX). The wood "cuts" freely, with an easily parted chip, a quality which would make it useful for lead pencils, and the probable future use of the best grades for this purpose is likely to give the wood considerable commercial value.

OCCURRENCE AND HABITS.

Alligator juniper is of frequent occurrence throughout its range, sometimes in very scattered, open, pure stands, but oftener mixed with Emory oak, Arizona oak, blue oak, piñon, and Mexican piñon. It grows in the driest rocky and gravelly soils on mountain slopes, plateaus, and canyon sides, where it is likely to be much stunted and distorted. The best developed trees are found in moist, deep washed soils of canyon bottoms and in protected places on the lower mountain benches. The tree's vertical range extends from about 4,500 to nearly 8,400 feet elevation, but it is most abundant between 5,500 and 7,000 feet. Because of its great hardiness this species is one of the most useful of southwestern junipers for maintaining a protective woodland forest on exposed arid hills and lower mountain slopes.

Alligator juniper endures moderate shade during the seedling stage and for a few years afterwards, but requires full overhead light for later development. Continued, dense side shade produces a long clear trunk, and a short, thin-branched, open crown.

This tree bears seed abundantly almost every year, and reproduces itself plentifully whenever the berries find lodgment in washed or broken soil. Reproduction is especially good in light shade where old trees have been cut out. Severely pollarded trees and high-cut stumps often sprout vigorously. Birds eat considerable quantities of the berries and thus assist in disseminating this species, while in seasons when food is scarce squirrels and other rodents eat a good many of the seeds.

LONGEVITY.

Alligator juniper is a very long-lived tree. It grows slowly, however, even in the most favorable situations, and is extremely slow on the least favorable sites. The exact age of very large trees has not been determined. Trees from 12 to 20 inches in diameter are from 165 to 290 years old, while those from 3 to 5 feet in diameter must be from about 500 to 800 years old.

DROOPING JUNIPER.

Juniperus flaccida Schlechtendal.

COMMON NAME AND EARLY HISTORY.

Although very distinct in its general appearance from other southwestern junipers, this species is doubtless unknown to many lay people, and unfamiliar even to a good many foresters and botanists, chiefly because in the United States it grows in an isolated and little frequented section of the country. It is, in fact, essentially a Mexican species, the principal part of its range being in Mexico. The few stockmen and prospectors who have seen the tree know it only as "cedar" or "juniper." The name "drooping juniper," derived from the technical term flaccida, seems both appropriate and distinctive, in that it refers to the nodding or pendent habit of the branchlets, which is a conspicuous and distinctive characteristic of this tree (Pl. XXVI). "Loose-growing Mexican juniper" and "loose-growing juniper" are book names applied about 50 years ago, but neither of these appear to be appropriate, nor has either been adopted in this country.

JUNIPERUS FLACCIDA: SHOWING DROOPING HABIT OF BRANCHLETS OF TREES IN EXPOSED SITES.

a, Detached leaf showing resin gland on back (enlarged five times natural size).

JUNIPERUS FLACCIDA: SHOWING PENDENT BRANCHLETS OF TREES IN SHELTERED SITES.

a, Female flowers (in autumn).

JUNIPERUS FLACCIDA: PRIMARY FOLIAGE OF SEEDLING (ABOUT 6 YEARS OLD).

JUNIPERUS FLACCIDA: SMALL TREE SHOWING CHARACTERISTIC OPEN CROWN AND DROOPING HABIT OF BRANCHLETS IN SHELTERED SITE (ABOUT ONE TWENTY-FIFTH NATURAL SIZE).

Drooping juniper was first discovered in Mexico by the German botanist Schiede, who found it in June, 1830,[1] at "Atotonilco el Chico,"[2] State of Hidalgo. Ehrenberg is also said to have found the drooping juniper at Regla and at other points in Mexico at elevations between 6,000 and 8,000 feet. It first became known to botanists as a Mexican tree in 1838, when it was technically described and named Juniperus flaccida Schlech. The French botanist Carrière informs us that the tree was brought to Europe in that year for purposes of cultivation. The first discovery of drooping juniper within our border was in 1885, when Dr. Valéry Harvard, United States Army surgeon and botanist, found the tree in the Chisos Mountains[3] of southwestern Texas, which is the only location now known for it in the United States.

DISTINGUISHING CHARACTERISTICS.

Drooping juniper varies in size from a bushy tree 8 to 15 feet in height and 3 to 6 inches through to one of medium size, from 20 to 25 feet tall and 12 to 20 inches in diameter. The best developed specimens have straight trunks, clear of branches for from 10 to 15 feet, and rather open, narrowly pyramidal crowns. Trees growing in dry, exposed places are rarely over 10 feet high, densely branched to the ground, and have a dome-shaped crown. The crown is composed of wide-spreading, ascending branches, at the ends of which the slender, drooping twigs (Pls. XXIII, XXIV) give the tree a graceful, weeping appearance. In the case of trees growing in deep shaded canyon bottoms (Pl. XXVI) the drooping habit is especially pronounced, the pendent branchlets often being a foot or more in length. Trees on exposed, drier slopes have very much shorter twigs (Pl. XXII).

The trunk bark is externally grayish brown in color, while within it is a purple or russet brown. On large trunks the bark is fibrous but firm, and distinctly marked with deep furrows and narrow anastomosely arranged ridges. It varies in thickness from one-half an inch on small trees to 1½ inches on larger trees. The bark of twigs that have recently shed their leaves is a russet-brown or purple-brown, composed of easily detached, very thin scales. Bark of the branches is also scaly, but grayish-brown.

The pale yellowish-green foliage is somewhat prickly to the touch, owing to the slightly spreading, keenly pointed leaves. The ordinary adult scalelike leaves are about one-eighth of an inch long (Pl.

---

[1] Schlechtendal in Linnæa, Zwölfter Band, 495. 1838.

[2] "Atotonilco el Chico," also once called "El Chico," a small mining town in Mexico, is now known as Atotonilco and lies due north and near Patchuca, the capital of Hidalgo.

[3] Dr. Harvard's note upon this species (Proceedings of the U. S. Nat. Mus., viii, 504, 1885) is exceedingly brief: "Small tree, only seen in the Chisos Mountains."

XXIII, *a*), while leaves of terminal or rapidly grown shoots are from one-fourth to nearly one-half an inch long. The margins of all leaves have very minute teeth. Adult leaves are arranged alternately in pairs in four ranks, with a prominent resinous gland on the back of each (Pl. XXIII, *a*). The bristlelike, spreading leaves of seedlings, however, are usually arranged in threes (Pl. XXV), but sometimes in twos, these types of leaves persisting for several years.

Male flowers (Pl. XXII, *e*) and female flowers (Pl. XXIV, *a*) are borne on separate trees. The berries mature in the autumn of the second year and are spherical or elongated in shape. The firm, hard, purplish-brown skin is covered with whitish bloom, and distinctly marked by the turned-back points of the united female flower scales (Pl. XXII). Sometimes the surface is also marked with small knobs of irregular shape. The berries vary in diameter or in length from about three-eighths to five-eighths of an inch, the largest fruit being produced by trees in shaded situations, and the smallest in dry exposed places. A striking character of the berries is the several-tiered arrangement of the 6 (rarely 4) to 12 irregularly shaped seeds (Pl. XXII, *a, b, c, d*), of which only a few, or sometimes none, are fully developed. The flesh of the berries is hard, dry, and only slightly resinous. The seed-leaves are pointed, two in number, and about one-half of an inch long.

The wood of drooping juniper is a clear yellowish-brown, with a rather thick layer of nearly white sapwood. It is moderately hard and heavy, straight-grained, and very narrow-ringed. Freshly cut wood has a strong cedar odor. Seasoned heartwood is very durable, and has been extensively used locally for mine timbers and to a limited extent for fence posts. Cattlemen and miners familiar with the Chisos Mountains assert that 40 or 50 years ago this juniper was much more abundant than now, and that large numbers of the best trees were then cut and used in mines near Boquillos, Mexico. The present rather limited occurrence of this species in the United States, however, will prevent further commercial and even local use.

OCCURRENCE AND HABITS.

While in this country the range of drooping juniper is confined to the Chisos Mountains of southwestern Texas, it occurs frequently in all of the canyons there, and stretches up even to the tops of the low divides. It grows alike in the deep, washed, gravelly, and sandy soil of watered canyon bottoms (where it is most abundant and best developed), and on dry, rocky benches, slopes, and ridges, becoming more and more stunted as it ascends to the latter situations. It is usually found at elevations between 6,000 and 7,000 feet, probably not going higher. The limits of vertical range in the Chisos Mountains, however, have not been determined. In its Mexican range drooping juniper is said to grow at elevations between 6,000 and 8,000 feet. In the Chisos Mountains it occurs in small groups or as scattered trees, commonly associated with alligator juniper, Mexican piñon, Texas oak, Mexican mulberry, and Texas madrone. Within its vertical range are found Rocky Mountain scrub oak, Emory oak, western yellow pine, one-seed juniper, stunted Douglas fir, Arizona cypress, and Texas ash.

Drooping juniper bears fruit abundantly, especially when growing on open slopes. Some berries are produced practically every year, and especially large crops are borne at intervals of from two to three years. Reproduction is sparse on dry, rocky slopes, but abundant in moist canyon bottoms and on deep-soiled benches. The seed is probably not disseminated to any extent by birds, as in the case of some of the other junipers, because the berries are dry and unpalatable. The relatively small number of perfect seeds in each berry also account for the slow reproduction of this tree.

Seedlings and young trees grow thriftily in dense shade. Pole-size trees can maintain themselves almost indefinitely under such conditions, though their growth is exceedingly slow. The crowns of shaded trees are much thinner and the foliage less robust than in the case of trees enjoying full light. Dense side shade and moderate top light produce the tallest and clearest trunks, with open crowns. Full sunlight gives short trees, with little or no clear trunk and very dense crowns.

LONGEVITY.

Drooping juniper gives evidence of being a very long-lived tree. So far, however, it has been possible for the writer to determine the age of only one tree, 5 inches in diameter at the collar, which was approximately 200 years old. During the first 150 years of its life, this tree appears to have grown in dense shade. During the last 50 years its crown seems to have received direct light, and in this period its growth nearly equaled that of the previous century and a half. The largest trees (from 14 to 20 inches in diameter) so far found in the Chisos Mountains are growing under somewhat more favorable conditions of light, so that they are probably between 400 and 500 years old.

KEY TO SPECIES OF JUNIPERUS.

Trunk bark divided into squarish plates .... *Juniperus pachyphlœa.*
Trunk bark longitudinally furrowed and ridged:
  Leaves minute, scalelike, closely pressed upon twigs:
    Branchlets drooping[1] .... *Juniperus flaccida.*
    Branchlets not drooping:
      Heartwood purplish or rose-red .... *Juniperus scopulorum.*
      Heartwood yellowish-brown:
        Berries large, mostly over one-fourth of an inch in diameter and bluish:
          One-seeded:
            Seeds round-pointed, furrowed, and creased from top to bottom .... *Juniperus utahensis.*[2]
            Seeds usually chisel-pointed, furrowed only at bottom. *Juniperus megalocarpa.*
          Several-seeded .... *Juniperus occidentalis.*
        Berries small, mostly less than one-fourth of an inch in diameter, and bluish or copper-colored:
          One-seeded .... *Juniperus monosperma.*
          Several-seeded .... *Juniperus sabinoides.*
  Leaves needlelike, spreading or standing out loosely on the twigs. *Juniperus communis.*

[1] The rare "weeping" form of *J. scopulorum* may be easily distinguished from *J. flaccida* by its rose-red heartwood and small bluish berries.
[2] See *J. knightii*, p. 26.

ADDITIONAL COPIES
OF THIS PUBLICATION MAY BE PROCURED FROM
THE SUPERINTENDENT OF DOCUMENTS
GOVERNMENT PRINTING OFFICE
WASHINGTON, D. C.
AT
25 CENTS PER COPY
▽

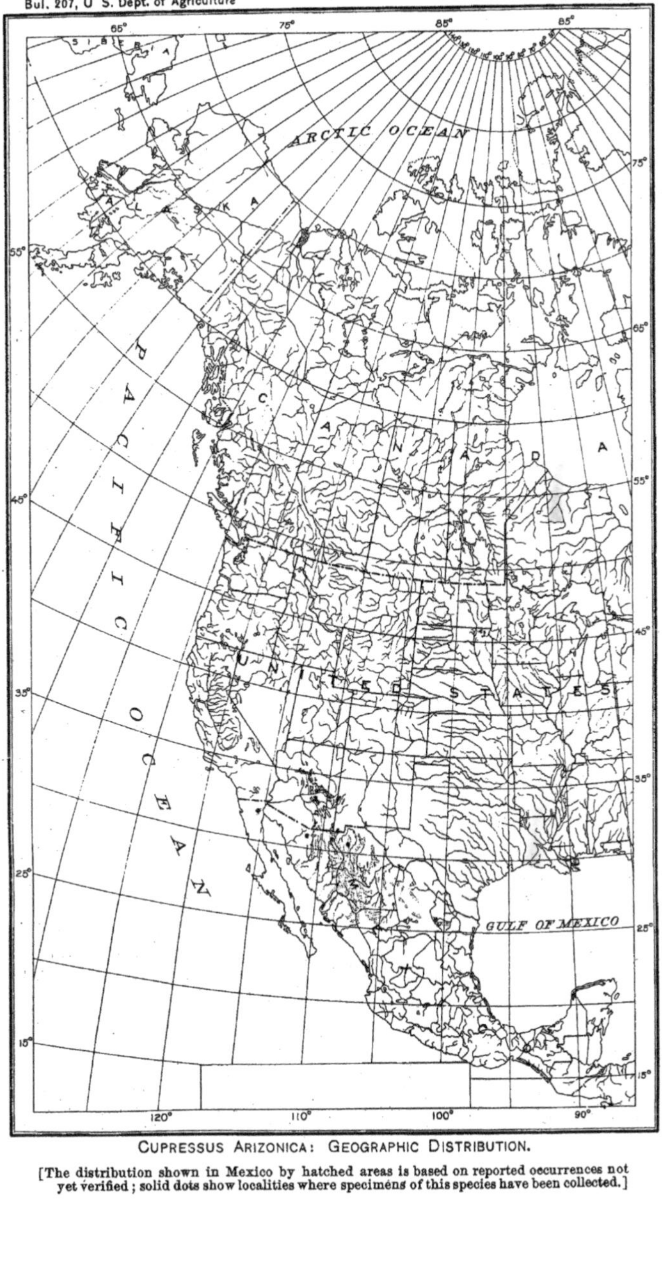

CUPRESSUS ARIZONICA: GEOGRAPHIC DISTRIBUTION.

[The distribution shown in Mexico by hatched areas is based on reported occurrences not yet verified; solid dots show localities where specimens of this species have been collected.]

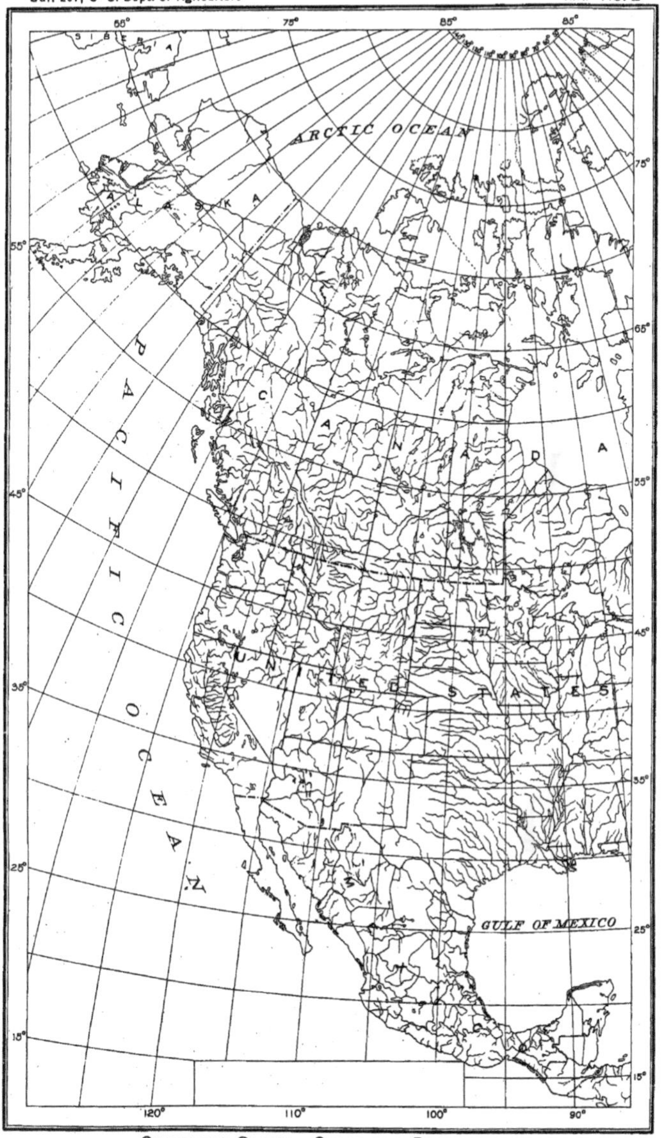

CUPRESSUS GLABRA: GEOGRAPHIC DISTRIBUTION.

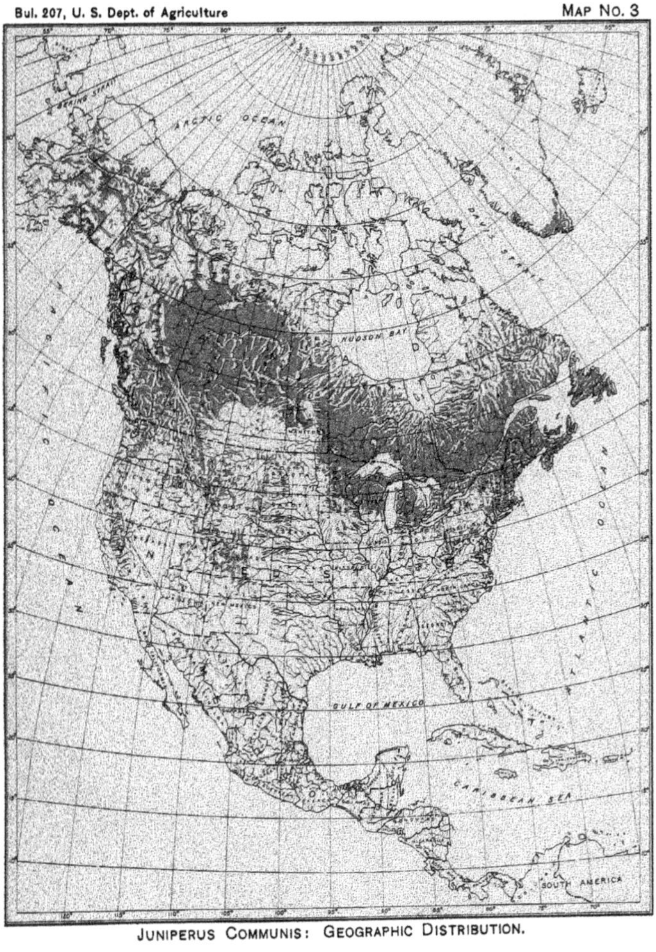

JUNIPERUS COMMUNIS: GEOGRAPHIC DISTRIBUTION.

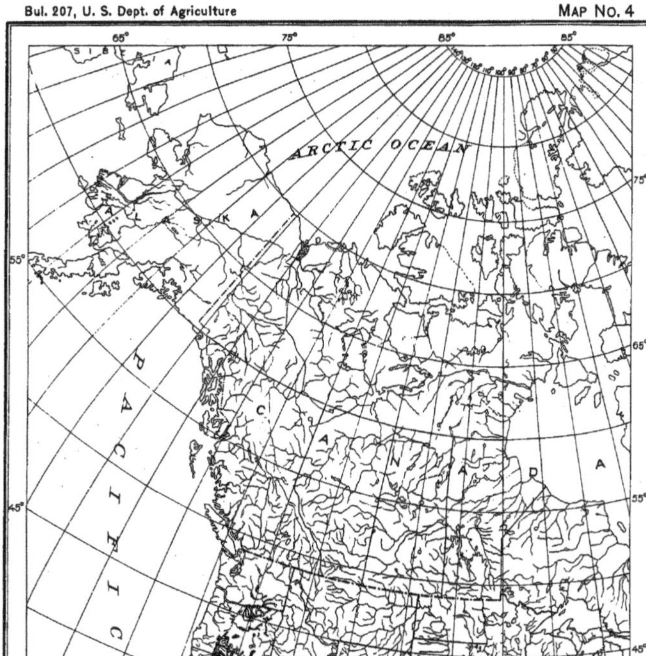

JUNIPERUS OCCIDENTALIS: GEOGRAPHIC DISTRIBUTION.

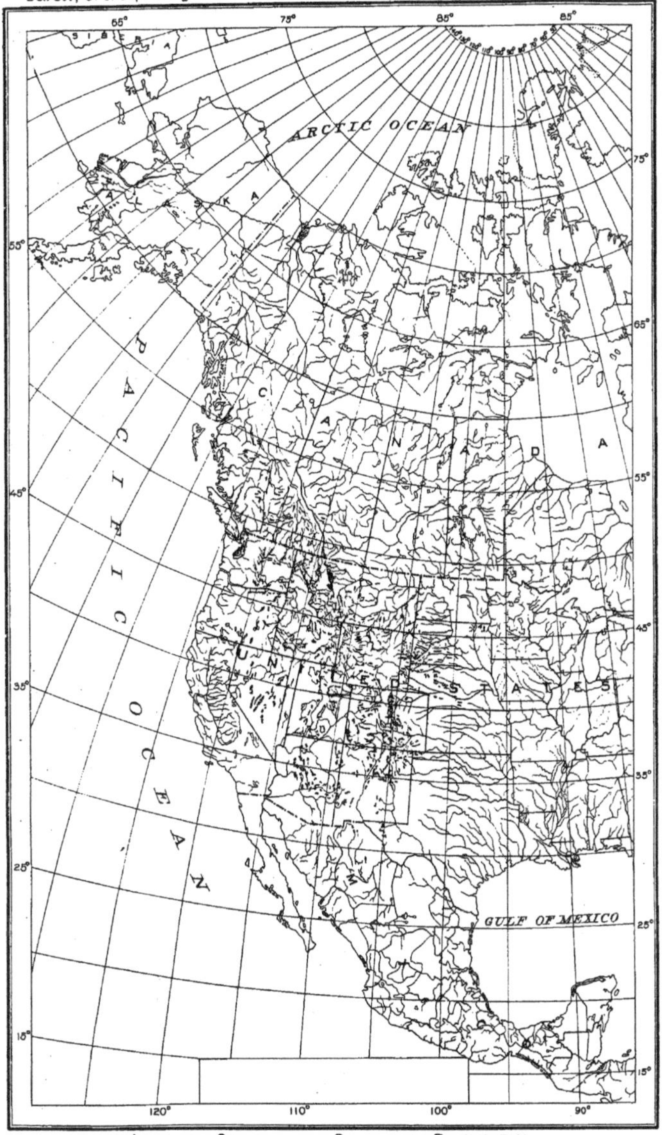

JUNIPERUS SCOPULORUM: GEOGRAPHIC DISTRIBUTION.

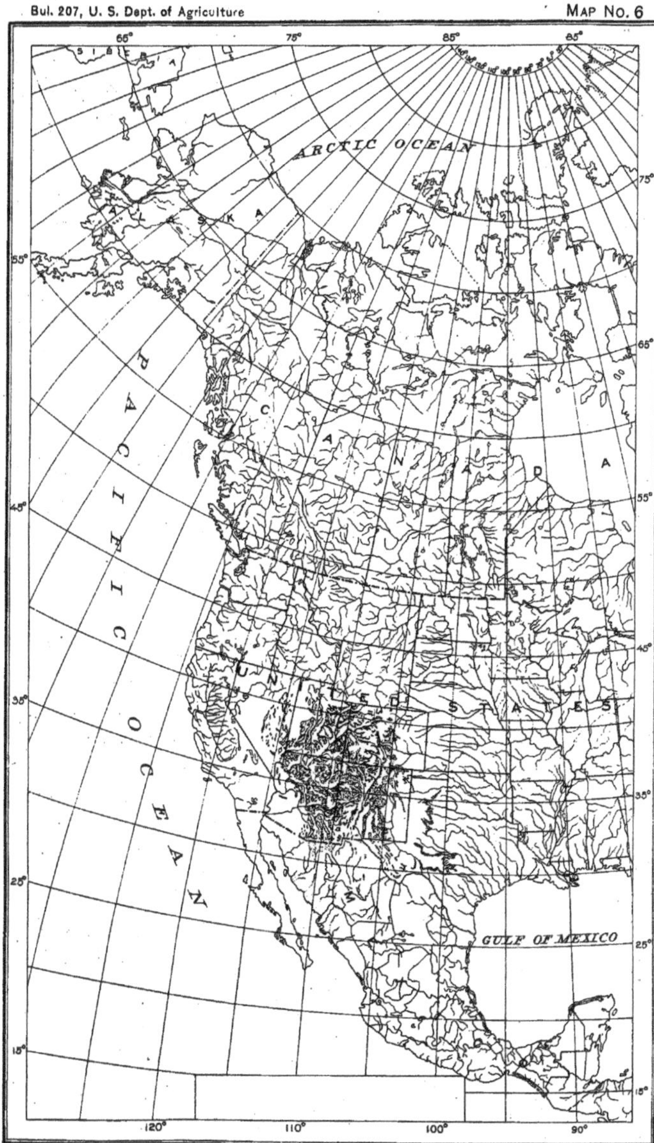

JUNIPERUS MONOSPERMA: GEOGRAPHIC DISTRIBUTION.

[The distribution shown in Mexico by hatched areas is based on reported occurrences not yet verified.]

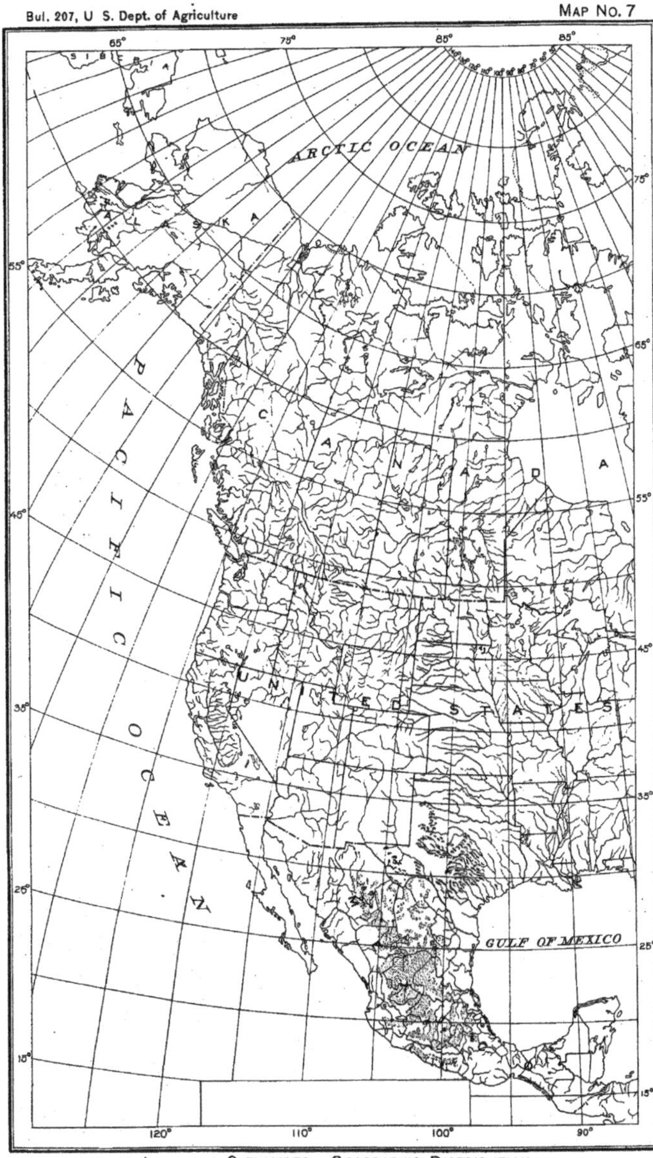

JUNIPERUS SABINOIDES: GEOGRAPHIC DISTRIBUTION.

[The distribution shown in Mexico by hatched areas is based on reported occurrences not yet verified; solid dots show localities where specimens of this species have been collected.]

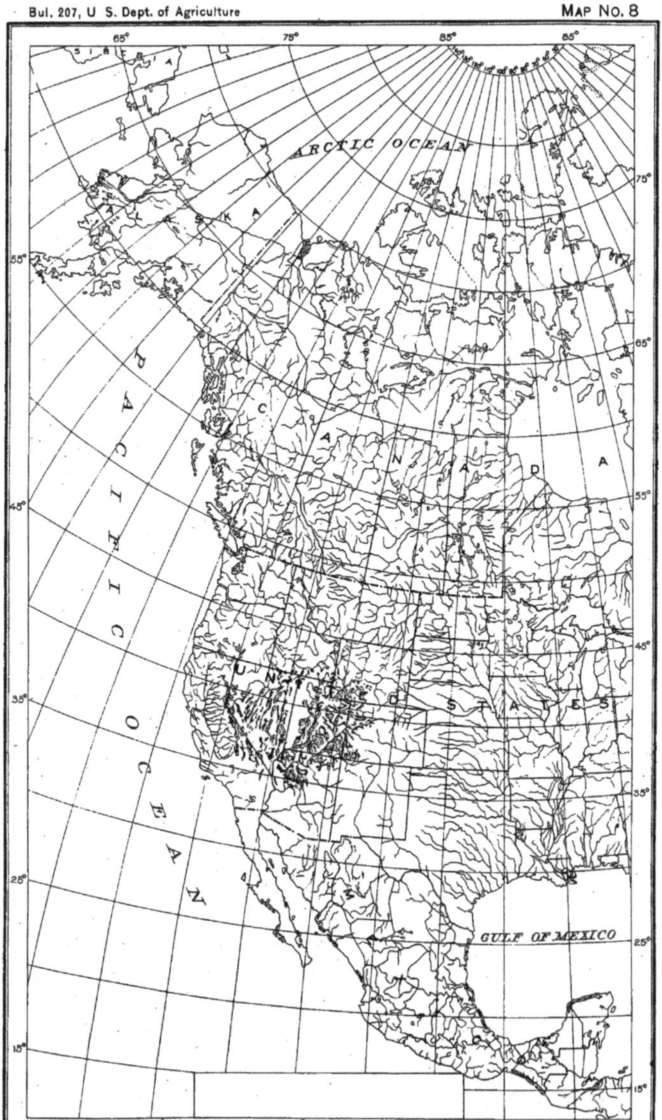

JUNIPERUS UTAHENSIS: GEOGRAPHIC DISTRIBUTION.

JUNIPERUS MEGALOCARPA: GEOGRAPHIC DISTRIBUTION.

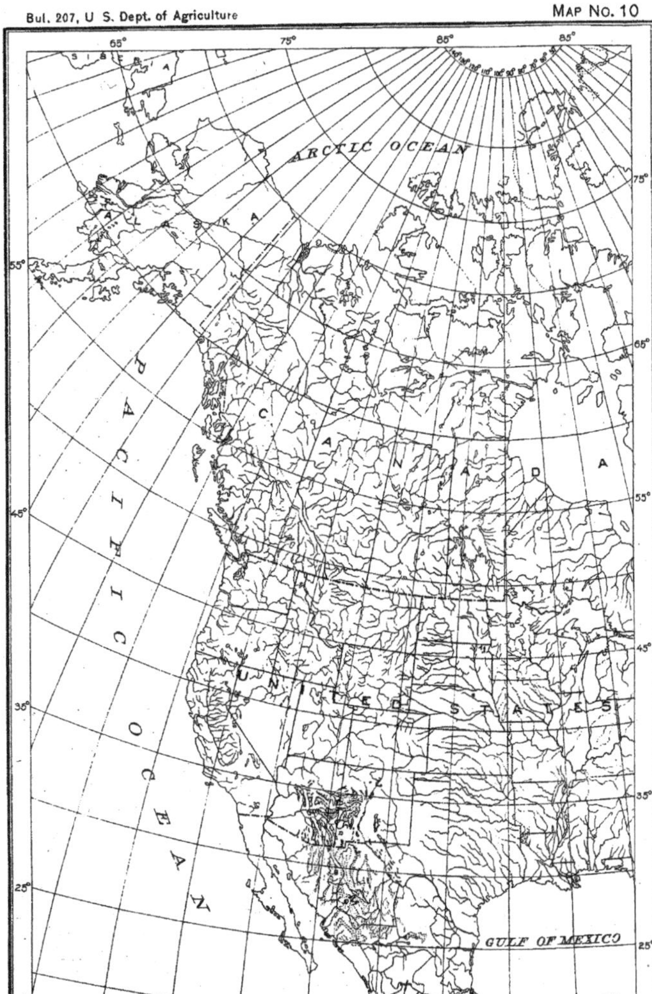

JUNIPERUS PACHYPHLŒA: GEOGRAPHIC DISTRIBUTION.

[The distribution shown in Mexico by hatched areas is based on reported occurrences not yet verified; solid dots show localities where specimens of this species have been collected.]

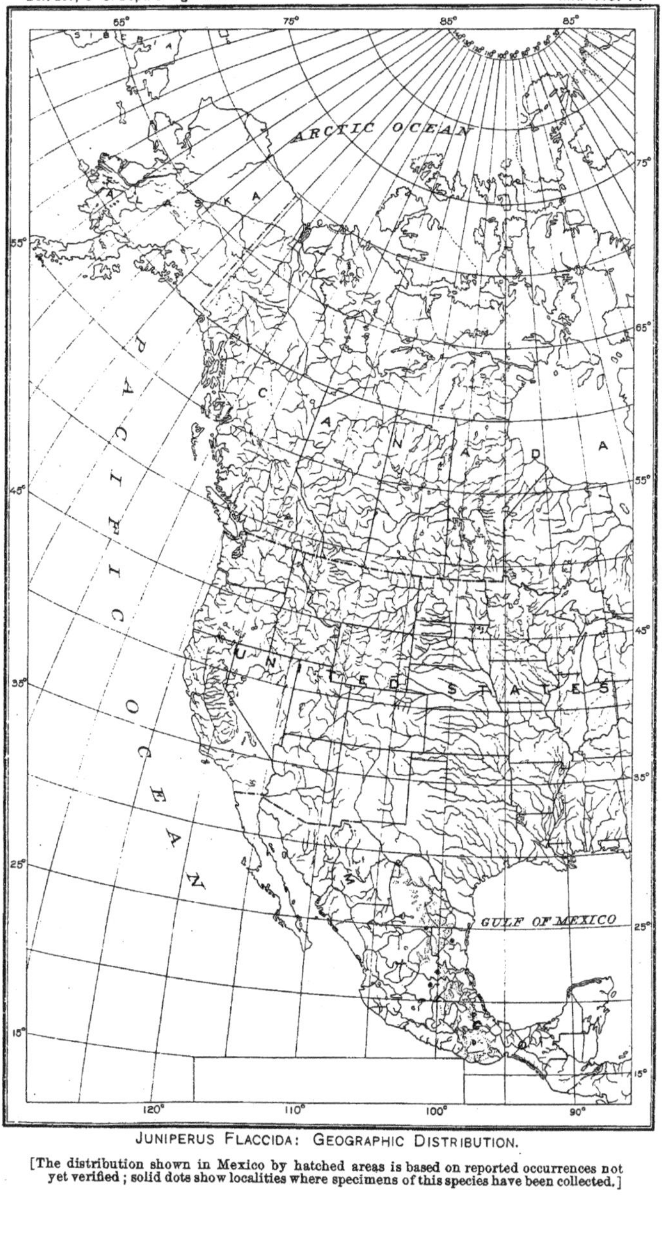

JUNIPERUS FLACCIDA: GEOGRAPHIC DISTRIBUTION.

[The distribution shown in Mexico by hatched areas is based on reported occurrences not yet verified; solid dots show localities where specimens of this species have been collected.]

BULLETIN OF THE
U.S. DEPARTMENT OF AGRICULTURE

No. 208

Contribution from the Bureau of Plant Industry, Wm. A. Taylor, Chief.
May 13, 1915.

YIELDS OF NATIVE PRICKLY PEAR IN SOUTHERN TEXAS.

By DAVID GRIFFITHS, *Agriculturist, Office of Farm Management.*

INTRODUCTION.

When information regarding the value of prickly pear began to be demanded some years ago next to nothing was definitely known about the handling of the crop on an economic basis. Indeed, so far as known, the species of southern Texas had never been systematically planted as a crop. In consequence, some very elementary investigations were necessary in order to furnish the required information. First, it was imperative to determine the yields which could be obtained from the various economic species under cultivation. Data on this phase of the investigations have accumulated to such an extent as to warrant the publication of a summarized statement of yields secured under variable and difficult conditions. The difficulty was due mainly to meager facilities and lack of sufficient constancy and continuation in organization. Although the conditions under which the various yields have been obtained are very variable, they are perfectly interpretable, and some of them at least approach ordinary farm conditions very closely.

Yields for the first plantings made were reported in Bulletin 124 of the Bureau of Plant Industry. In this first 2-year period a yield of about 23 tons per acre was secured for each year. Since that time further observations and tests have been possible with plantings at San Antonio as well as at Brownsville. These two localities are representative of the coastal region of heavy rainfall and of the more inland situation of much more uncertain distribution of moisture.[1] In both places the rainfall is irregular, but at San Antonio it is smaller in quantity. It is neither possible nor necessary here to go into details, but the rainfall at San Antonio is not only on the average smaller in quantity but also of more irregular distribution than at Brownsville.

[1] For a discussion of the relation of the climatic conditions of the San Antonio region to prickly-pear culture, see Bulletin 124 of the Bureau of Plant Industry, entitled "The Prickly Pear as a Farm Crop."

84730°—Bull. 208—15

YIELDS AT BROWNSVILLE.

THE FIRST PLANTING.

In March, 1908, the first planting of native varieties of prickly pear was made on a small scale at Brownsville. At this time two 8-foot rows 458 feet long were established on one side of a varietal collection planted the same summer. Single-joint cuttings were plowed under, as described in previous publications, at a distance of 3 feet apart in the row. This planting was given moderately good cultivation. The middles were kept clean, but often Bermuda grass and other vegetation were allowed to grow in the rows.

In the latter part of October, 1909, or at the end of the second growing season, row 2 was cut and weighed. In harvesting this row, a good stump (Pl. I, figs. 1 and 2) consisting of one to four cuttings, but never over one cutting high, was left attached to the original cutting, set 19 months before. The total material harvested in this manner weighed 17,060 pounds, or 8.53 tons. This showed a yield at the rate of 100.721 tons to the acre for two seasons' growth, or 50.36 tons per acre per annum.

The first row was not harvested at this time, but was reserved until the following February to be cut and used in establishing a 6-acre planting. This row is believed to have yielded considerably more than row 2, harvested in the fall.

In considering these yields, attention should be given to several conditions. It is estimated that not less than 2 tons per acre were left on the ground in the stumps, besides the original cuttings. The increase in weight between October and March, when the 2-year period would be complete, would, in the absorption of water and in growth, amount to several tons per acre. The harvesting was done at a time when the pear contained the least moisture, for it followed a very long dry season. In short, this test is hedged about by such conditions that the results in yield as given appear to be ultra-conservative.

SPECIES PLANTED.

As previously stated, the native species of prickly pear of the Rio Grande delta are unique (Pl. II, fig. 2). They differ from any that have been encountered elsewhere. What is more, they were entirely unstudied when our investigations were begun. A reference to them is found in one of the works of Dr. Engelmann, but this is all; he had never seen any of them.

A general survey of the species of the immediate vicinity was made, and finally two species were selected which appeared to be the most promising. For the sake of comparison a third was selected from a resaca bank near Brownsville. The first two species were secured at Loma Alta, about 6 miles east of Brownsville. They were selected on account of their thrifty, compact growth in nature, the character and number of the spines being left entirely out of consideration. The two species are very similar in stature and general habit, forming a hemispherical shrub about 4 feet high when fully grown. Since their selection and planting, they have been described—one as *Opuntia gommei* and the other as *Opuntia cyanella.*

Opuntia gommei is a bright, more or less glossy, yellowish green species with yellow flowers.

Opuntia cyanella, on the other hand, is glaucous or waxy blue-green, with flowers opening deep red but soon changing to purplish.

Both species have yellow spines and spicules in large numbers; in fact, all the native species of the delta region are among the most spiny of any of the economic species of this genus of plants, their spines and spicules being not only numerous, but large and stout. The spines are so large and stout and die and become inflammable so tardily that these delta species are among the most difficult in the genus to prepare properly as food for stock.

The first two rows previously discussed were planted to a mixture of these two species in about equal quantities.

Besides these two, a third species, which has not been botanically named, having a tall habit of growth and differing in several particulars from the others, was planted in another row, largely for comparison and to verify the writer's judgment of the species most profitable to grow. In other words, it was desirable to determine whether one with a little experience can go into a prickly-pear region which is little known and by ordinary observation unerringly select the species of most economic worth.

At the same time that the plantings of these native species were made a single row of approximately the same length as the others was set in the same way to an introduced species frequently cultivated by the Mexicans about Brownsville. It is the same as one of the Mission varieties so commonly grown in southern California. It is the spiny "tuna blanca" of the region of San Luis Potosi, Mexico, and the "tuna teca," or "tuna blanca teca," of the eastern Jalisco and Aguascalientes regions.

YIELDS.

The third row of the field was planted to this third species (the unnamed one) and it was harvested a week before row 2. The row was 463 feet long and the yield, when harvested precisely as the other, was 13,190 pounds, or at the rate of 77.03 tons to the acre for two seasons' growth. This means an average annual growth of 38.51 tons per acre, as contrasted with 50.36 tons in the case of a mixture of *Opuntia gommei* and *Opuntia cyanella.*

The introduced Mission pear yielded at the rate of 42.75 tons per acre per annum, which was greatly in excess of our expectations.

However, the results here are not quite comparable with those in the other cases, for this species was cut close to the ground. The yields, however, are good enough and close enough to those made by *Opuntia gommei* and *Opuntia cyanella* so that the species becomes one to be considered as an economic possibility, especially as it is much more easily singed than the native species. It also produces a fine quality of fruit, but the fruit often does not set well in this climate, probably owing to the excessive rainfall which is likely to occur when the crop is in blossom.

After this harvesting, all but the first two rows (a mixture of *Opuntia gommei* and *Opuntia cyanella*) were rooted out. Those left were cleaned up with cultivator and hoe and kept well tilled again for the next two years. They were harvested the second time between October 21 and December 27, 1911, or approximately 24 months from the first harvesting. (Pl. I, fig. 2.) The first row yielded at the rate of 191.088 tons per acre and the second at the rate of 236.286 tons, or 95.544 and 118.143 tons per acre per annum, respectively. Averaging these, we have a yield at the rate of 106.843 tons per acre per annum of green, succulent feed.

Late in February and early in March, 1910, a 6-acre planting was established upon an area contiguous to the above. This was planted on poorly prepared land, a part of which was flooded at times and all of which contained more or less Bermuda grass. For the next two years this area was cultivated, but it was, of course, not possible to give it the best tillage, because of the existence of the Bermuda grass and the refractory character of the Cameron clay which extended in a shallow swale diagonally across it. This planting, made to meet the requirements of a feeding experiment conducted by the Bureau of Animal Industry of this department, was harvested according to the demand for the feed between October, 1911, and May, 1913. On account of its being harvested over the entire growing season of 1912 it is not possible to include all of the data, but the weights at the time of harvesting were kept by rows. Consequently, only those rows harvested during the dormant season are available and comparable with other figures obtained elsewhere.

Although this crop can be harvested and fed at any time of the year, estimates of its yield can best be made during the season that the plants are the most dormant, and in order to be exactly comparable they should be made during the same time of the year. Dormancy is only a relative term here, for while no apparent new growth takes place during the winter months, except in heavily pruned plants, there is little doubt that they actually do increase in weight during their dormant period.

As stated above, the harvesting of the 6-acre planting was done as the feed was needed. This planting was contiguous to a varietal

FIG. 1.—A FIELD OF CULTIVATED NATIVE PRICKLY PEAR AT BROWNSVILLE, TEX., SHOWING THE GROWTH FROM SINGLE-JOINT CUTTINGS AT THE CLOSE OF THE SECOND YEAR, ONE ROW HAVING BEEN HARVESTED.

FIG. 2.—ANOTHER VIEW OF THE FIELD ILLUSTRATED IN FIGURE 1, SHOWING THE GROWTH OF TWO YEARS FROM THE STUMPS LEFT AT THE FIRST HARVESTING.

FIG. 1.—A 6-ACRE PLANTING OF NATIVE PRICKLY PEAR AT BROWNSVILLE, TEX., ABOUT THE MIDDLE OF THE SECOND SEASON'S GROWTH.

FIG. 2.—NATIVE UNCULTIVATED PRICKLY PEAR GROWING NEAR BROWNSVILLE, TEX.

collection of prickly pear and agaves, the rows being numbered consecutively, the 6-acre planting beginning at row 20. The yields of rows 20 to 48, inclusive, together with the time of harvesting and the other data necessary to computations and a proper interpretation of them, are given in Table I.

TABLE I.—*Dates of harvesting and yields of native prickly pear at Brownsville, Tex.*

No. of row.	Date of harvesting.	Yield per row.	Length of row.	Total yield per acre.	Annual yield per acre.
	1912.	*Pounds.*	*Feet.*	*Tons.*	*Tons.*
20	Jan. 5 to 13	7,340	501	39.615	19.807
21	Jan. 14 to 20	6,576	501	35.492	17.746
22	Jan. 20 to 30	9,302	501	50.204	25.102
23	Feb. 1 to 12	12,062	499	65.362	32.681
24	Feb. 14 to 28	13,626	500	73.689	36.844
25	Mar. 1 to 15	12,591	501	67.956	33.978
26	Mar. 16 to Apr. 1	13,885	499	75.240	37.620
27	Apr. 1 to 25	17,662	498	95.899	47.949
28	Apr. 9 to May 14	21,662	498	117.619	....
29	May to June	21,662	495	118.331	....
30	May 15 to July 10	23,476	494	128.500	....
31	June 4 to July 14	24,169	490	133.373	....
32	July 15 to Aug. 14	25,957	497	141.221	....
33	Aug. 16 to Sept. 21	22,531	489	124.588	....
34	Sept. 24 to Oct. 21	33,470	487	185.837	....
35	Oct. 22 to Nov. 12	23,525	484	131.428	43.809
36	Nov. 13 to 20	30,224	498	164.108	54.703
37	Nov. 21 to 26	24,239	481	136.262	45.420
38	Nov. 27 to 30	22,708	487	126.083	42.027
39	Dec. 1 to 7	27,306	475	155.443	51.814
40	Dec. 7 to 13	25,268	471	145.063	48.354
41	Dec. 13 to 17	19,488	468	112.597	37.532
42	Dec. 18 to 24	25,476	464	148.463	49.487
43	Dec. 24 to 28	22,005	459	129.633	43.211
	1912–13.				
44	Dec. 29 to Jan. 2	24,249	463	141.618	47.206
45	Jan. 1 to 7	23,718	460	139.421	46.474
46	Jan. 8 to 11	17,160	456	101.756	33.918
47	Jan. 13 to 17	20,216	451	121.206	40.402
48	Jan. 18 to 23	27,078	451	162.347	54.116

It will be seen that the yields are very variable. This is due principally to the varying conditions of the soil. Attention has been called on another page to the low depression running diagonally across the field. This was of stiff Cameron clay, very refractory and difficult to cultivate and flooded at times. Another cause of the differences in yield was the greater prevalence of Bermuda grass in some places than in others.

With reference to rows 20, 21, and 22, it should be stated that the low yields were due to still another factor. The stock for planting these three rows was, contrary to expectations, secured from material cut and dumped into a waste pile several months before. The cuttings were badly withered, and, being planted in very dry soil in a season followed by a long dry summer, they did not start well. Many of the cuttings failed to grow, making the stand poor. During the entire two seasons it was very noticeable that these rows were much lighter than the contiguous rows of the same species but of good stock.

In the last column of Table I the annual yield has been omitted in those rows harvested during the growing season, for reasons already stated. An average of the others gives a yield for the portion harvested during the crop's dormant season of 40.463 tons per acre per annum. Omitting rows 20 to 22, inclusive (which is justifiable on account of the poor stand), the average yield per acre per annum is 43.557 tons. It should be borne in mind that a part of this is averaged for two years' growth and a part for a three-year period. In other words, rows 20 to 27 were harvested after two seasons' growth and rows 35 to 48 after they had attained the growth of three seasons.

The species of prickly pear grown in these experiments were a mixture of the three discussed on page 3, but *Opuntia gommei* and *Opuntia cyanella* greatly predominated. The quantity of the other species grown was negligible.

In addition to what has been said regarding the handling of this plantation, it should be stated that no cultivating at all was done after the second season. Cuttings were set in this planting, as in the other, in 8-foot rows, no attempt being made to space them exactly. Under these conditions, the plants had bridged over the 8-foot rows at the close of the second year's growth to such an extent that animals could not pass through and cultivation had to be abandoned. (Pl. II, fig. 1.)

CONDITION OF THE PLANTATION.

The condition of the plantation was first class during the entire period up to late in the winter of 1913. At this time the common fungous diseases of the region began to be alarmingly prevalent; indeed, so much material had to be discarded in feeding that accurate estimates of yields could not be secured after the first of March. The cause of this condition was not difficult to interpret. The season of 1912–13 had an abnormal rainfall and a winter temperature with a high minimum. Weeds and grass grew thick among the plants and remained green for the most part during the entire winter. The pear itself had grown into an impenetrable thicket, furnishing the best conditions possible for the development of the fungi.

In this region it seems as though the age of the plantation when harvested will have to be considered more than in any other in which we have worked, because of the liability of the development of various diseases when the thicket becomes so dense as to prevent the aeration of the inner delicate vegetative parts. It is possible that when grown under usual conditions it will be necessary, in order to secure the best results, to harvest at from 18 to 36 months rather than let the crop stand for longer periods, as is possible in the San Antonio region or farther inland in general. The common diseased condition of the prickly pear in the brush about Brownsville points to its susceptibility to disease in this region. In all regions, however, much growth is lost after the plants attain a certain size. Even at San Antonio the joints that are heavily shaded in the center of the plant either rot or dry up when the plant is about 3 years old. This means that these plants, like trees and shrubs in general, go through a process of natural pruning which lets light and air into the center of the plant. This natural pruning takes place everywhere, but much more tardily when growth is less rapid.

A summary of the conditions and of the yields obtained at Brownsville is given in Table II.

TABLE II.—*Summary of yields of native prickly pear grown from cuttings or old stumps at Brownsville, Tex.*

Time harvested.	Character of cultivation.	Cuttings or stumps.	Yield per acre per annum.	Species grown.
			Tons.	
October, 1909	Good	Cuttings	50.32	Opuntia gommei and Opuntia cyanella.
Do	do	do	38.42	Unnamed.
Do	do	do	42.75	Mission.
Oct. 21 to Dec. 27, 1911	do	Stumps	106.843	Opuntia gommei and Opuntia cyanella.
Dormant seasons of 1912–13	Good for two seasons; none thereafter.	Cuttings	40.314	Mainly Opuntia gommei and Opuntia cyanella.

YIELDS AT SAN ANTONIO.

Since the publication of the last bulletin [1] detailing the conduct of experiments at San Antonio, Tex., 8 acres of prickly pear, mainly of *Opuntia lindheimeri*, have been grown and harvested from time to time as the condition of the plantings appeared to warrant. An effort has been made on all occasions to make the test practical and comparable with other crops grown in the same vicinity. Although it has not been possible to secure the cultivation deemed necessary, possibly even this brings a closer approximation to usual conditions.

During the entire time that the experiments have been carried on the cultivation has been poor. It has been below the average for farm work in the region; indeed, in nearly every period there was a year with no cultivation at all, and in no case did cultivation to the extent of conserving moisture obtain at any time. The handling has been what could very properly be called poor farming.

YIELD WITHOUT CULTIVATION.

On March 3, 1911, a harvesting was made of an acre of uncultivated planting established five years before. In this instance furrows were opened up with a plow on the native unbroken sod of the region after the mesquite and other shrubs had been grubbed off. The cuttings

[1] Bureau of Plant Industry Bulletin 124, 1908.

were distributed at the side of the furrow and partially covered by pulling the sods back on their bases. No attention was paid to this acre of ground after it was planted. The area was fenced, however, in order to keep stock out of some varieties which were originally planted in an adjoining acre of ground, but the handling in this respect was not at all uniform, for part of the time the cattle were allowed access to the field, when the grass and other vegetation on the plat were grazed closely, like the other native pastures on the place and in the vicinity.

This plat of ground, besides furnishing information on this particular subject, throws important light on the handling of pastures in general. Its irregular, periodical harvesting by dairy cattle, which were herded on the acre of ground on two occasions, showed conclusively that this acre, besides growing the crop of prickly pear, actually furnished more grazing than any other like area of native pasture on the farm. This result was due to periodical as contrasted with continuous grazing. Of course, an exact quantitative comparison between this plat and the remaining native pastures of the farm is obviously impossible, except in so far as one is able to judge from the total results of the farm pastures as compared with the number of animals fed for single days on this acre.

Under the above conditions, which are the same as those of the native cleared pastures of the region except in so far as the periodical grazing and the actual planting of the cuttings may affect the growth of the pear, there was a very low production as compared with even the poorly tilled soil. The growth was of such a character as not to warrant harvesting until after it had attained an age of 5 years instead of 3 years in poorly cultivated and 2 years in well-cultivated ground.

At the end of a 5-year period this acre of ground yielded a crop of 58,920 pounds, which is 29.46 tons, or 5.89 tons per acre per annum. The harvesting was done in a manner comparable with other harvestings discussed elsewhere, leaving small stumps for future growth. The distances apart here were the same as in the cultivated plantings.

Three years later a representative number of rows were again harvested from this area, the growth being, of course, from the old stumps left at the previous harvesting. The yield this time was at the rate of 9.8 tons to the acre each year. Here, as in all other experiments thus far conducted, the growth was considerably greater from old stumps than from freshly set cuttings. This is simply due to the greater productivity of well-established plants.

A few representative rows of this uncultivated acre were harvested at the end of the second growing season and reported upon in Bulletin 124 of the Bureau of Plant Industry. The yield obtained was at the rate of 2.83 tons per annum.

YIELD WITH CULTIVATION.

In April and early May, 1909, there were harvested 3 acres of prickly pear planted in March, 1907. The ground was put in a good state of cultivation when the cuttings were planted and was kept fairly well cultivated the first year. The second year it was given no cultivation.

It was not possible at this time to get weights. The best that could be done was to determine the length of time the area would feed a definite number of dairy cows all the roughage they would consume.

During the feeding there was an extraordinary amount of waste, for here, as in all other cases which have come under our observation, cattle, when their feed is abundant, reject the young growth until the joints are well filled out. The fact that the harvesting was done late in the third growing season does not, therefore, in all probability, introduce any appreciable error into the calculations if the current season is discarded in our reasoning. All the roughage consumed for 1,510 cow-days was furnished by these 3 acres of a 2-year-old crop. This is equivalent to a production of roughage for five cows on 6 acres of ground. When the entire lack of cultivation and the second and only moderate cultivation the first year are taken into account, this yield is comparable with more accurate harvestings made by weighing on another occasion.[1]

In March and April, 1910, another 3 acres of the same field were harvested by being cut and a representative area was weighed. This area was handled the same as the other 3 acres the first two years, and was left and cultivated again the third year. The yield was at the rate of 14.32 tons per acre per annum.

This field was fenced and cattle kept out until the plants were well started; then the gates were left open and cattle allowed to enter the field at will. They did much to keep down certain weeds and native grasses.

In March, 1913, 1 acre of a 3-year-old crop, set from single-joint cuttings in the usual way in the spring of 1910, was cut and weighed. The crop was grown upon land which had been set to a varietal collection for four or five years. It was in a good state of cultivation when planted, so far as weeds were concerned, but it was very dry and cloddy. During the first year the cultivation was satisfactory; the second year it was all but abandoned, and during the third year an ineffectual attempt was made to keep the weeds down. In all, the tract was not over half cultivated during the entire period.

The harvesting was done from March 12 to March 25, 1913, and good stumps were left for future growth. The yield under the circumstances was very satisfactory, a total of 124,114 pounds being secured. This is at the rate of 20.685 tons per acre per annum.

---

[1] See Bureau of Plant Industry Bulletin 124, 1908.

It should be stated that this growth was not all from cuttings. About four rows of the old varietal plantings were preserved, and to this extent the crop was from stumps which had previously had a crop taken from them. The plantings here, as in the other cases at San Antonio, are made approximately 2½ feet apart in 6-foot rows. The varieties grown here are the same as those discussed in previous publications. *Opuntia lindheimeri* has been the principal species, but there has been a small admixture of *O. ferruginispina*, *O. sinclairii*, and other less important species.

In April, 1914, another harvesting of a representative area was made by cutting and weighing two 8-foot rows 416 feet long. The yield for the three-year period from the well-established stumps of the previous harvesting in 1910 was at the rate of 28 tons to the acre each year. During the season of 1910 this area was plowed with a turning plow and cultivated with a spike-tooth harrow three times, which, because of the harvesting and burning over of the previous spring, put the ground in fairly good condition, especially for the penetration of moisture. All the cultivation given consisted in going over the land two or three times with a spike-tooth harrow in 1911. The increase here over the other harvestings, due, it is believed, to the greater vigor of the old established plants, is striking. The beneficial effect of placing the land between the rows in good tilth, even if it be only once in four years, is also shown without doubt. Attention should be called to the fact that no handwork was done in this field after the planting.

A summary of the conditions and of the yields of native prickly pear obtained at San Antonio is given in Table III.

TABLE III.—*Summary of yields of native prickly pear grown from cuttings or old stumps at San Antonio, Tex.*

Time harvested.	Character of cultivation.	Cuttings or stumps.	Yield per acre per annum.	Species grown.
			Tons.	
October, 1907	None	Cuttings	2.83	Opuntia lindheimeri.
April and May, 1909	Very poor	do	(1)	Do.
April, 1910	do	do	14.32	Do.
March, 1911	None	do	5.89	Do.
March, 1913	Poor	do	20.685	Opuntia lindheimeri mostly.
April, 1914	do	Stumps	28.00	Opuntia lindheimeri.
Spring, 1914	None	do	9.8	Do.

1 Roughage for 1 cow on 1¼ acres.

GENERAL CONDITIONS AFFECTING YIELDS.

As shown by the figures cited, other conditions being equal, the yields of prickly pear at a particular place have generally been in direct proportion to the care given the plantation. The most potent factor after the plants are once thoroughly established is cultivation.

The pear does not seem to require anything like a dust mulch or deep cultivation, such as is so commonly practiced with other crops in dry regions. All that experience seems to indicate as necessary is to keep down the weeds, which interfere with the growth of the pear the same as with any other crop. Shallow cultivation appears to be sufficient, but, owing to the fact that our plantations at San Antonio have at times become very weedy, a shallow furrow has been turned toward the rows and subsequently leveled with a spike-tooth cultivator. In our two situations, the maintenance of a dust mulch has not seemed necessary, even in the driest seasons.

In one of our varietal plantings at Brownsville, established upon an old Bermuda-grass sod, a good dust mulch of 2 to 4 inches seemed to be very detrimental. In this case we were dealing with resaca-bank loam in a perfect state of tilth for two years. Under this treatment there was a constant and abundant supply of moisture in the soil. The growth of all species was very rapid for a short time, but they soon rotted off at the surface of the ground, and this condition continued at an alarming rate for two or three seasons after the establishment of the plantation. The spineless and introduced species suffered most, but the native species rotted off also. They simply fell over and took root again on top of the ground, thus becoming reestablished and still making a phenomenal growth. Under these humid conditions a deep dust mulch was decidedly detrimental. Treatment which allowed the soil to dry out more readily was productive of better results. In short, upon the heavier lands of southern Texas, represented by the regions in which this work has been done, a dust mulch does not seem to be essential, but it is necessary to keep down the weeds and give sufficient cultivation to allow a good penetration of moisture at the time of rainfall.

At Chico, Cal., where the summers are long, hot, and dry, all species except those from our driest deserts have withered badly when weeds were not kept out, but when cultivated sufficiently to keep them down no wilting occurs. The desert forms have shown no signs of withering at Chico, even when no cultivation or irrigation was given. Even with poor cultivation, plantings of native prickly pear at Brownsville have never suffered from drought, although the same plants occasionally wither in the brush in the vicinity. At San Antonio our poorly cared for and weedy plantings were often considerably withered. The cultivation there has never been sufficient to do much in the way of conserving moisture, but has usually been enough to cause a good penetration of the rainfall. When no weeds were present the evaporation of this rainfall from a poorly cultivated surface has not caused the plants to wilt.

WASHINGTON : GOVERNMENT PRINTING OFFICE : 1915

ADDITIONAL COPIES
OF THIS PUBLICATION MAY BE PROCURED FROM
THE SUPERINTENDENT OF DOCUMENTS
GOVERNMENT PRINTING OFFICE
WASHINGTON, D. C.
AT
5 CENTS PER COPY

VINIFERA REGIONS OF THE UNITED STATES

By

GEORGE C. HUSMANN, Pomologist in Charge of Viticultural Investigations

CONTENTS

WASHINGTON
GOVERNMENT PRINTING OFFICE
1915

BUREAU OF PLANT INDUSTRY.

Chief of Bureau, William A. Taylor.

Horticultural and Pomological Investigations.

L. C. Corbett, *Horticulturist in Charge*.

PROJECT LEADERS.

G. B. Brackett, *Pomologist.*
C. P. Close, *Pomologist.*
S. J. Dennis, *Refrigeration Technologist.*
H. P. Gould, *Pomologist.*
George C. Husmann, *Pomologist.*
E. R. Lake, *Pomologist.*
F. L. Mulford, *Landscape Gardener.*
H. J. Ramsey, *Pomologist.*
C. A. Reed, *Assistant Pomologist.*
A. D. Shamel, *Physiologist.*
D. N. Shoemaker, *Horticulturist.*
William Stuart, *Horticulturist.*
H. C. Thompson, *Horticulturist.*
W. W. Tracy, sr., *Superintendent of Testing Gardens.*
William F. Wight, *Botanist.*

UNITED STATES DEPARTMENT OF AGRICULTURE

BULLETIN No. 209

Contribution from the Bureau of Plant Industry
WM. A. TAYLOR, Chief

Washington, D. C. PROFESSIONAL PAPER August 6, 1915.

TESTING GRAPE VARIETIES IN THE VINIFERA REGIONS OF THE UNITED STATES.

By George C. Husmann,

Pomologist in Charge of Viticultural Investigations, Office of Horticultural and Pomological Investigations.

CONTENTS.

INTRODUCTION.

A résumé of the viticultural investigations in the Vinifera regions of the United States up to 1910 was reported in Bulletin 172 of the Bureau of Plant Industry. The present publication supplements that bulletin and gives additional data on the investigations then under way, as well as reports upon researches started since the date of that publication. The fundamental problems of the Vinifera region, as determined by the early surveys, were found to require (1) a comprehensive test of the resistant varieties of vines to determine their adaptability to the different soils and climatic conditions; (2) a study of the congeniality of Vinifera varieties to the different resistant-stock varieties; (3) a study of the behavior of fruiting varieties to determine those best adapted to the different localities; and (4) a consideration of all classes of grapes with reference to their resistance to destructive insects and diseases and, if found necessary, the origination of an entirely new class of grapes better adapted to

Pacific coast conditions. These questions still remain the broad cardinal problems, but the facilities for their solution have been much enlarged and a number of subordinate problems that developed in the prosecution of the work have been taken up as far as the means and facilities of the Department of Agriculture permitted.

COOPERATIVE EXPERIMENT VINEYARDS AND THEIR NATURE.

To afford facilities for solving these problems, the Bureau of Plant Industry has established 12 experiment vineyards on the Pacific coast. One of these is at the Plant Introduction Field Station, Chico, Cal., and 11 are located in various other grape-growing centers in cooperation with growers.

A brief description of the purpose, location, soil, and climatic conditions at or near each of these vineyards follows. (Fig. 1.) Those desiring correlation and mechanical analyses of the soils and fuller climatic data are referred to Bulletin 172 of the Bureau of Plant Industry. The soil descriptions are from data furnished by the Bureau of Soils, while the weather data are taken from records furnished by the San Francisco office of the Weather Bureau, through Prof. McAdie, and from observations made in the experiment vineyards.

MAIN VINEYARDS.

Three primary vineyards of 20 acres each are located near Oakville, near Fresno, and at Guasti, Cal.

At the Oakville, Fresno, and Guasti experiment vineyards viticultural material introduced from foreign countries is tested. In these vineyards the adaptability to different localities and the value of grape varieties for different uses is determined; the relative resistance of grape varieties to destructive insects and diseases is inquired into; the congeniality of grape varieties to the different resistant sorts is determined; and grape varieties not now grown in the Vinifera regions of this country are tested, with a view to the possibility of their supplanting some of the varieties now grown. Experiments to determine how the various varieties should be propagated, grafted, pruned, trained, and otherwise cared for are under way. These vineyards offer some opportunity for the broad viticultural research and experimental work that is needed, and furnish practical object lessons in viticulture and facilities for solving some of the many commercial problems of the industry.

OAKVILLE EXPERIMENT VINEYARD.

The Oakville Experiment Vineyard (Pl. I, fig. 1) was established in the spring of 1903, and is located 1 mile west of Oakville, Napa Co., Cal., on the property of the To-Kalon Vineyard Company, at an elevation of 161 feet above sea level. The soil is a dark-brown or black gravelly clay loam or heavy loam, containing a large quantity of organic matter formed in a swamp or lagoon extending in past geological ages up Napa Valley from San Pablo Bay, typical of the greater part of the soils in the valley floor. On weathering, the shales, sandstones, limestones, lime conglomerates, and large quantities of usually lenticular or angular gravel with little erosion of edges are washed down from the steep hills or mountains surrounding Napa Valley on

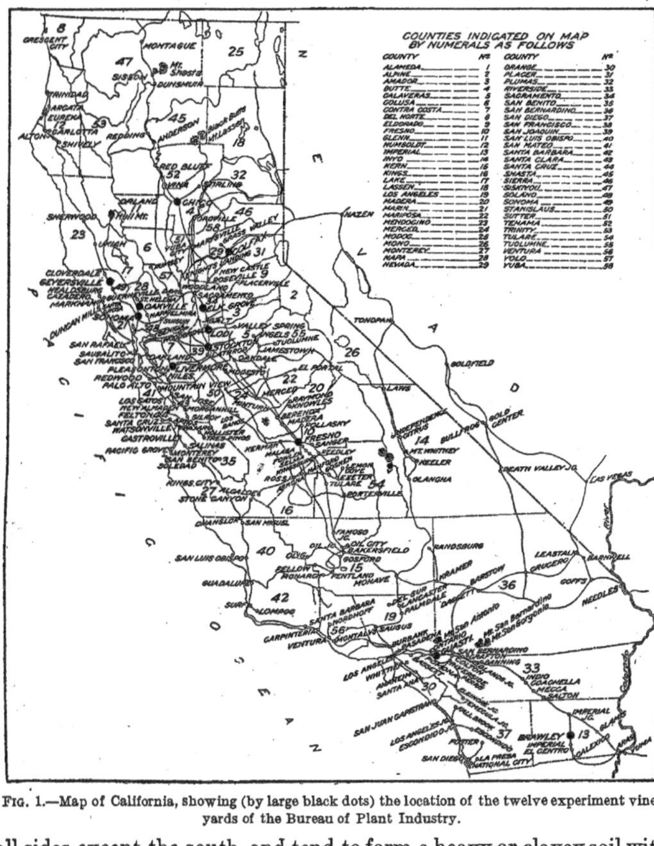

FIG. 1.—Map of California, showing (by large black dots) the location of the twelve experiment vineyards of the Bureau of Plant Industry.

all sides except the south, and tend to form a heavy or clayey soil with only small quantities of sand. No hardpan or alkali appears. The surface is undulating, affording a fairly rapid run-off of surplus rainwater, though in places the subsoil is quite wet during the spring months. No irrigation is necessary. The clay and silt in the subsoils greatly aid in retaining moisture in spite of the large quantity of gravel (20 to 40 per cent) they contain. Cultivation reduces the surface to a good mulch. When grape culture in Napa Valley and the adjoining foothills became important, a reputation for the superior qualities of its dry wines was rapidly made, especially for the excellence of the white wines. This reputation has been sustained, and Napa County has remained one of the leading dry-wine sections of the State.

FRESNO EXPERIMENT VINEYARD.

The Fresno Experiment Vineyard (Pl. I, fig. 2) was established in the spring of 1903. It is located 3 miles east of Fresno on the property of the Fresno Vineyard Company, at an elevation of 290 feet above sea level. The soil is the San Joaquin sandy loam. The fact that it is an outlying isolated portion of soil of this character accounts for the increased depths to hardpan and the sandier subsoil immediately above. The San Joaquin sandy loams are confined to lands adjacent to the lower foothills on the eastern side of the San Joaquin and Sacramento Valleys, where 75,000 acres near Fresno, 6,000 acres near Stockton, and 265,000 acres about Sacramento have already been mapped. The soil is light red in color, granitic in origin, and composed largely of sharp, angular particles. The surface is rolling and generally covered with hog wallows and small mounds.

In the experiment-vineyard plat two varieties of soil were recognized, namely, adhesive sandy loam, closely approaching a true loam, and a friable sandy loam. The former retains moisture longer than the latter, which is a deeper soil of lighter texture. Leveling the plat disturbed the natural soil conditions, decreasing the depth of the sticky, adhesive sandy loam in spots and exposing free sandy loam in others, causing the hardpan underlying the plat to occur at depths varying from scarcely 20 inches to over 6 feet, whereas the average depth at which it occurs is 3½ to 4 feet below the surface. This hardpan, which always accompanies San Joaquin sandy-loam soil, is a red iron-sandstone substance cemented by hydrates of iron and alumina combined with clay. When this occurs at 2 feet or less below the surface, blasting is necessary. Trees and vines thrive when the hardpan is broken or where it lies at a sufficient depth below the surface.

The soils of the plat above the hardpan contain alkali varying from less than 0.05 to more than 20 per cent; but in the lowest grade soil no alkali is visible. Of the salts, over 90 per cent are chlorids, as follows: Calcium, 50; magnesium, 25; sodium, 15; and potassium, about 2 per cent. The remainder consists of calcium sulphate and bicarbonate of soda. The depth of the water table on the tract averages 3 feet.

Fresno is in the center of the raisin industry of the country, and is also one of the most important wine and brandy producing districts of California.

At Oakville there are being assembled and tested on resistant stocks all the grape varieties of the world thought to be of value to the Pacific slope; while at Fresno similar tests are made of raisin, currant, and fleshy varieties.

GUASTI EXPERIMENT VINEYARD.

In view of the entirely different conditions prevailing south of the Tehachapi Pass, especially in the desert region, the Department of Agriculture in the spring of 1904 established another experiment vineyard of like importance and acreage in the San Bernardino desert, at Guasti, Cal., 950 feet above sea level, on the property of the Italian Vineyard Company. (See Pl. I, fig. 3.) The soil mapped as Maricopa gravelly sand is a gray-brown gravelly sand of very uniform texture to an unknown depth. The surface is compact when untilled, because the sharp, angular sand composing the soil becomes somewhat cemented by the organic matter occurring in the topsoil. At a depth of 3 feet the soil is more concentrated and often yellowish from the oxidation of iron in the soil. The soil is almost entirely granitic, and is washed from the Sierra Madres. It contains quantities of undecomposed potash, feldspar particles, which should insure abundant potash for the maturing of grapes. The soil covers most of the San Bernardino Valley floor, and when thoroughly cultivated holds moisture well, the fine sand and silt giving the soil capillary power to bring water up from below. Two of the largest vineyards of the world are in this valley, on similar soil. As the phylloxera is not known to exist here, the plantings in the experiment vineyard are principally Vinifera varieties.

CHICO VARIETAL VINEYARD.

The Chico Varietal Vineyard is located at the plant-introduction field station, 3 miles east of Chico, Butte Co., Cal., and is about 196 feet above sea level (Pl. II, fig. 1). The soil, an alluvium, is composed of material brought down from the mountains and hills on the east and is from 8 to 12 feet deep. It is underlain by a body of sandy water-worn gravel and bowlders, which always carry water. The soil is of light texture, varying from light loam to heavy, fine sandy loam, the heaviest being loam. It is well drained and easily cultivated. The heavy, fine sandy loam consists of from 30 to 36 inches of fine sandy loam, underlain by very fine sandy loam, usually containing some gravel. The light loam has from 10 to 15 inches of fine sandy loam or sandy loam underlain by a heavier structure closely approaching loam. The largest area of this soil is found about Chico, but similar soil occurs in the Feather and the Bear River Valleys.

At the Chico vineyard are being assembled and maintained two plants each of grape varieties that prove of special value for specific purposes, together with grape immigrants from all parts of the world introduced by the Office of Foreign Seed and Plant Introduction. The first plantings were made in the spring of 1906, and the collection here already comprises 308 resistant and direct-producing sorts and 141 Vinifera varieties grafted on resistant stocks.

SMALLER VINEYARDS.

In addition to the main plantations, outlying vineyards of 10 acres each have been established to test varieties at different altitudes, at varying distances from the ocean, bays, and other bodies of water, under different climatic and other conditions, and on the leading types of vineyard soils not found at the Oakville, Fresno, and Guasti vineyards.

BRAWLEY EXPERIMENT VINEYARD.

The Brawley Experiment Vineyard was established in the spring of 1911 on the New River, 1 mile west of Brawley, Imperial Co., Cal., on the property of Mrs. Mabel Oakley, about 110 feet below sea level. (See Pl. II, fig. 2.) The soil, Imperial loam, is sediment brought down by the Colorado River and deposited in strata either while the area was still submerged or from the overflow waters as they spread over the plain. Before irrigation these strata, varying from 1.1 to 2 or 3 inches in thickness, are quite hard and look like shale, but water softens them readily. This soil after irrigation is a sticky reddish loam, a little heavier than a silt loam, having a depth of 4 to 6 feet and resting on a clay or clay-loam subsoil, which in turn is underlain by alternate strata of lighter and heavier material to an indeterminate depth. The surface is usually smooth and level and almost devoid of vegetation. The soil often contains considerable organic matter and when irrigated is productive. Alkali is found in all of it and often greatly in excess of what even the most resistant plants can stand, thus making much reclamation work necessary. This soil is by far the most extensive type in the Imperial Valley. It extends from about the middle of the eastern boundary across in a northwesterly direction into the Salton Sink. A large part of the area west and southwest of Imperial and large tracts between Mesquite Lake and the Mexican line are of this type of soil.

The Imperial Valley is said to be the earliest fruit-ripening district in the United States, and as no phylloxera have been located in it the plantings of 280 grape varieties in this vineyard are all Vinifera.

COLFAX EXPERIMENT VINEYARD.

The Colfax Experiment Vineyard was established in the spring of 1906, on the property of Mr. Louis Cortopassi, in the Sierra Nevada, 2,412 feet above sea level, 1½ miles southwest of Colfax, Placer Co., Cal. (See Pl. II, fig. 3.)

The soil, hilly, usually fairly deep, and well drained, originated in the decomposition of the Mariposa formation, consisting of dark shales or slates, sandstones or quartzite sandstones, and conglomerates. The large amount of iron present from decomposing volcanic-rock material, where exposed to perfect weathering, gives the soil a deep red color. Dark, shallow, conglomerate rocks sometimes outcrop in spots, and rock fragments occur. The first few inches are often dark red from the accumulation of organic matter. The first 8 to 18 inches are usually brownish red clay or clay loam, underlain by 3 to 6 feet of red clay or clay loam, with partially decomposed and weathered rock formations, giving the subsoil a yellow appearance.

Rock outcrops of conglomerates, chert, and slate occur in the higher portions. The native vegetation is manzanita, chaparral, live oak and yellow pine.

The Colfax district is unique in the diversity of the fruit grown on sidehill locations.

GEYSERVILLE EXPERIMENT VINEYARD.

The Geyserville Experiment Vineyard was established in the spring of 1904, on the property of John D. Bosch, just east of Geyserville, Sonoma Co., Cal., against a range of high hills (Pl. III, fig. 1), 236 feet above sea level. To a depth of 2½ to 3 feet the soil consists of a uniform dark gravelly loam with a subsoil of light or yellowish brown color, similar in texture to the topsoil. The soil is very mellow and carries considerable humus, which enables it to retain moisture well. This type of soil extends over considerable areas along the streams and the floor of the Sonoma Valley, having been washed down from the shale, schist, and conglomerate hills.

Soils of this type produce some of the choicest dry wines, both red and white, of the State.

LIVERMORE EXPERIMENT VINEYARD.

The Livermore Experiment Vineyard was established in the spring of 1904, on the property of Mr. C. H. Wente, 3 miles south of Livermore, Alameda Co., Cal., at an elevation of about 450 feet above sea level. (See Pl. III, fig. 2.) The vineyard has a very uniform, level, alluvial soil, derived from decomposed shales and schists, and is full of rounded gravel washed down from the surrounding mountains.

The surface soil is a dark-brown gravelly loam; the second, third, and fourth feet gravelly sandy loam, replaced by gravelly sand in the fifth foot. The humus decreases with the depth, while the gravel increases, varying from 30 to 59 per cent. The proportion of clay is greater than that of silt. This gives the soil a very heavy appearance, the gravel sticking together very tightly when dry or packed. No alkali exists, but ground water is encountered at 5 or 6 feet in some places. These soils are common over the Livermore Valley and produce a superior white wine of the sauterne type. This experiment vineyard was discontinued on July 1, 1914.

LODI EXPERIMENT VINEYARD.

The Lodi Experiment Vineyard was established in the spring of 1904, on the Lawrence & Murray property, about one-fourth of a mile northeast of Lodi, San Joaquin Co., Cal., about 55 feet above sea level. (See Pl. III, fig. 3.) A large body of this soil exists between Lodi and Acampo.

There are two variations on the plat. Phase No. 1 is a brown, free, sandy loam, underlain below 4½ feet by a more adhesive light-brown or yellowish sandy loam. Occasional iron concretions give the subsoil a mottled color. The soil has good capillarity and the water table occurs at 5 to 6 feet. Phase No. 2, an adhesive sand, was formed by an old stream channel. This is light-brown sand to a depth of 3 feet, the subsoil water-washed sand, much looser in texture and lighter in color, and dry to a depth of more than 6 feet, as the soil texture is too loose to exert much capillary force. There is no hardpan or alkali. The soils are, however, deficient in lime; otherwise, they are very productive, comparatively level, unirrigated, and easily tilled. This locality is well known for its table grapes and as a table-grape shipping point.

MOUNTAIN VIEW EXPERIMENT VINEYARD.

The Mountain View Experiment Vineyard was established in the spring of 1904, on the property of Mrs. Caroline Distel, 2 miles west of Mountain View, on the west side of the Santa Clara Valley, 76 feet above sea level. (See Pl. IV, fig. 1.)

The soil is a gravelly Placentia sandy loam. The first 12 inches is a dark-brown, gravelly sandy loam, dark from humus; below this, to 4 feet, the subsoil becomes redder, sandier, and more gravelly until sand is encountered. It is well drained, but inclined to become too dry in summer and fall. The surface soil at times becomes quite compact, and when plowed breaks up into hard clods. When tilled at the right time it works into a very mellow condition. These soils are from washings of granitic sandy shales and schist rocks. Before the destruction of vineyards by phylloxera and other agencies the Santa Clara Valley was the banner dry-wine producing section of California. The following areas of Placentia sandy loam have been surveyed in California: San Jose, 61,500; lower Salinas, 74,000; Los Angeles, 66,000; San Bernardino, 87,000; San Gabriel, 48,800; and Santa Ana, 16,800 acres. Soils of this series occur through the coast range of mountains from San Francisco to the Mexican line, occupying undulating portions of valleys close to the hills. The Mountain View Experiment Vineyard was discontinued on July 1, 1912.

FIG. 1.—OAKVILLE EXPERIMENT VINEYARD.

FIG. 2.—FRESNO EXPERIMENT VINEYARD.

FIG. 3.—GUASTI EXPERIMENT VINEYARD.

FIG. 1.—CHICO VARIETAL VINEYARD.

FIG. 2.—BRAWLEY EXPERIMENT VINEYARD.

FIG. 3.—COLFAX EXPERIMENT VINEYARD.

FIG. 1.—GEYSERVILLE EXPERIMENT VINEYARD.

FIG. 2.—LIVERMORE EXPERIMENT VINEYARD.

FIG. 3.—LODI EXPERIMENT VINEYARD.

FIG. 1.—MOUNTAIN VIEW EXPERIMENT VINEYARD.

FIG. 2.—SONOMA EXPERIMENT VINEYARD.

FIG. 3.—STOCKTON EXPERIMENT VINEYARD.

SONOMA EXPERIMENT VINEYARD.

The Sonoma Experiment Vineyard was established in the spring of 1904, on the property of the Gundlach-Bundschu Wine Company, about 2 miles south of Sonoma, Sonoma Co., Cal., about 110 feet above sea level. (See Pl. IV, fig. 2.) The soil is of rather poor quality, and to a depth of 8 or 10 inches is a gray loam more easily tilled than its texture indicates. The subsoil to 6 feet or more in depth is clay, changing at 4 feet, with an increase of sand, from a light-brown to a yellowish brown color. The soil is found near where weathered shales from the surrounding hills have been partially broken down and transported into the valleys, where they decompose. The soil usually occupies small, undulating ridges, or elevations, and is surrounded by the dark-brown, alluvial clay loam of the valley floor. The surface drainage is good, and no injurious quantity of alkali exists. This soil occupies extensive areas in the Sonoma Valley and in the adjacent bay regions and produces superior white wines of the Riesling, Chasselas, and Traminer types.

STOCKTON EXPERIMENT VINEYARD.

The Stockton Experiment Vineyard was established in the spring of 1907, on the property of the San Joaquin Valley Realty Company, a little over a mile southeast of Stockton, about 15 feet above sea level, on Stockton clay-loam adobe. (See Pl. IV, fig. 3.) This type, locally known as black adobe, was laid down in a swamp or tidal marsh in quiet water, the decomposing vegetation giving it a black color. It is a clay loam in texture, adhesive and sticky when wet and very hard when dry, cracking into large, cubical blocks full of small, cubical fractures. Sufficient rain slacks the clods readily. Cultivated when neither too wet nor too dry, the soil is friable and pulverizes well. The subsoil is a light-yellow silt loam, usually separated from the surface soil at a depth of 2½ feet by a thin stratum, about one-half inch thick, of rather soft marly or calcareous hardpan, which is not always continuous and is often broken or disintegrated. Roots and water readily penetrate the subsoil, often passing through the hardpan. The depth to the water table varies from 3½ to 6 feet for wet seasons and from 6 to 10 feet for dry seasons. This variation is influenced by a thin, marly hardpan which appears to hold the water down under pressure. It is somewhat difficult to establish vineyards on these soils, but when established they are very productive and lasting. Grapes for diverse purposes are grown on them. One of the largest sweet-wine establishments in the world is located near Stockton, and heavy shipments of table grapes grown on these soils are made. Soils of this type have been mapped in California as follows: Stockton, 53,312; Hanford, 5,470; and Fresno, 5,664 acres. It covers many thousand acres between the Marysville Buttes and about North Durham in the Sacramento Valley.

ACREAGE IN THE EXPERIMENT VINEYARDS IN CALIFORNIA.

The plantings and graftings in the California experiment vineyards now comprise the areas shown in Table I.

TABLE I.—*Size of the twelve experiment vineyards in California of the Bureau of Plant Industry and number of varieties planted in each.*

Vineyard.	Area.	Number of varieties.			Vineyard.	Area.	Number of varieties.		
		Resistants and direct producers.	Vinifera. On their own roots.	Vinifera. On resistant stocks.			Resistants and direct producers.	Vinifera. On their own roots.	Vinifera. On resistant stocks.
	Acres.					*Acres.*			
Brawley	2.1	......	209	......	Livermore	1.4	109	......	......
Chico	1.8	308	......	141	Lodi	3.3	112	......	80
Colfax	3.5	122	......	74	Mountain View	2	124	......	......
Fresno	9	187	......	137	Oakville	16.6	306	......	262
Geyserville	1.2	94	......	1	Sonoma	2	117	......	......
Guasti	7	83	317	......	Stockton	1.4	91	......	......

GENERAL PLAN OF PLANTINGS IN THE EXPERIMENT VINEYARDS.

All the plantings for comparative tests and study are made in regular checks of 10 vines of each variety, and all the larger plantings of resistant varieties are grafted in regular checks, usually of 10 vines each, and, where only preliminary readings are desired, the number of grafts of each variety put in have been a divisor of 10 in a check of 10 vines.

PHENOLOGICAL RECORDS.

Each vine or graft receives its block, row, and vine number. A complete history and accurate records are kept of all varieties from the time they are planted or grafted. Their behavior is closely noted, detailed descriptions are made of the vines and their respective fruits, and their value for specific uses and adaptability to different conditions are recorded. Table II summarizes the climatic observations made at the different vineyards.

TABLE II.—*Temperature and rainfall at the twelve experiment vineyards of the Bureau of Plant Industry in California.*

MAXIMUM TEMPERATURES (° F.).

Vineyard.	Jan.	Feb.	Mar.	Apr.	May.	June.	July.	Aug.	Sept.	Oct.	Nov.	Dec.	Annual.
Brawley[1]	80	85	95	106	118	115	115	112	111	105	93	81	118
Chico	74	78	83	94	104	111	114	116	106	96	82	74	116
Colfax	73	88	89	86	98	110	107	108	99	91	82	78	110
Fresno	73	77	84	101	110	107	115	113	108	98	84	74	115
Geyserville	79	83	91	102	108	116	116	110	113	103	98	79	116
Guasti	83	87	88	98	101	105	108	106	105	98	89	80	108
Livermore	77	79	88	95	108	108	113	107	108	99	87	75	108
Lodi	70	72	80	91	104	104	110	104	105	91	78	67	110
Mountain View	76	76	85	94	104	106	111	99	109	95	84	75	111
Oakville	77	75	86	95	106	109	110	105	110	98	84	74	110
Sonoma	77	76	82	91	104	109	106	101	111	97	82	72	111
Stockton	67	70	80	89	102	105	110	103	104	90	84	66	110

[1] Data for four years.

TABLE II.—*Temperature and rainfall at the twelve experiment vineyards of the Bureau of Plant Industry in California*—Continued.

Vineyard.	Jan.	Feb.	Mar.	Apr.	May.	June.	July.	Aug.	Sept.	Oct.	Nov.	Dec.	Annual.
MINIMUM TEMPERATURES (° F.).													
Brawley[1]	24	29	35	38	50	52	57	60	55	40	26	20	20
Chico	18	20	25	30	33	40	46	48	40	34	21	22	18
Colfax	14	19	24	25	30	34	44	38	34	24	18	16	14
Fresno	24	25	30	34	40	42	51	52	42	36	31	24	24
Geyserville	21	21	29	30	33	37	40	39	35	30	26	23	20
Guasti	26	26	30	32	36	39	42	42	44	39	30	26	26
Livermore	23	24	30	30	34	39	41	41	40	34	25	23	23
Lodi	22	24	30	33	38	43	45	44	40	31	25	21	21
Mountain View	25	23	29	29	34	36	40	39	37	30	27	24	23
Oakville	20	24	25	26	30	34	32	34	35	27	25	17	17
Sonoma	23	27	29	27	32	34	41	34	35	32	26	23	23
Stockton	24	24	32	36	40	40	48	42	42	36	25	20	20
MEAN TEMPERATURES (° F.).													
Brawley[1]	54.2	54.3	62.2	69.2	76.3	84.2	89.5	89.3	83.4	71.3	60.9	51.1	70.4
Chico	46.3	49.6	53.0	58.9	65.3	73.0	79.4	77.5	71.4	63.9	52.8	45.8	61.4
Colfax	42.6	44.1	46.3	52.9	59.4	68.6	75.1	73.6	65.7	59.0	51.6	43.5	56.9
Fresno	47.6	50.9	55.4	60.8	66.4	74.5	81.8	80.2	73.1	64.4	54.3	45.7	62.9
Geyserville	47.4	50.3	52.8	57.8	62.4	67.3	69.8	68.2	67.0	62.2	53.9	47.7	58.9
Guasti	49.9	51.7	54.7	58.3	60.7	67.2	75.2	73.2	69.9	64.4	56.5	51.3	60.9
Livermore	48.0	51.0	53.5	57.2	60.5	66.0	70.9	69.8	68.3	62.8	54.5	48.8	59.3
Lodi	46.5	49.4	53.1	57.6	63.0	68.8	72.9	70.6	67.0	60.0	51.5	45.0	58.8
Mountain View	49.1	51.2	53.3	56.1	59.0	62.7	66.0	65.1	64.3	60.2	54.0	48.1	57.4
Oakville	45.4	48.3	50.4	55.1	59.7	64.1	66.8	65.8	65.1	60.8	52.3	45.5	56.6
Sonoma	47.3	50.1	51.7	55.5	59.4	63.8	66.2	64.5	64.2	60.6	52.9	46.3	56.8
Stockton	45.7	48.8	52.5	56.9	62.1	68.3	73.2	71.1	67.8	61.1	51.6	44.2	58.6
PRECIPITATION (INCHES[2]).													
Brawley[3]	......	......	......	......	......	......	......	......	......	......	......	......	......
Chico	6.41	3.77	5.46	1.14	0.96	0.29	T	0.01	1.03	0.79	2.03	3.50	25.39
Colfax	13.12	7.78	11.02	3.00	2.59	.95	T	.002	1.14	2.39	4.98	6.39	53.36
Fresno	2.11	1.30	2.24	.77	.58	.03	.001	T	.30	.56	.72	1.26	9.87
Geyserville	11.08	6.85	9.49	1.40	1.30	.45	T	T	.96	1.59	3.88	5.24	42.25
Guasti	6.05	4.30	6.40	1.29	.93	.12	.02	.01	.44	.56	.87	3.14	24.13
Livermore	4.55	2.00	3.75	.65	.57	.19	T	.03	.31	.43	.90	2.47	15.86
Lodi	5.02	2.68	4.71	.80	1.56	.26	T	.003	.40	.55	1.14	2.94	20.06
Mountain View	4.47	2.46	4.45	.80	.54	.18	T	.04	.52	.51	.96	2.49	17.42
Oakville	8.07	4.42	6.57	1.10	.78	.26	T	.01	.78	.77	2.10	3.95	28.81
Sonoma	6.80	4.91	6.02	.74	.87	.25	.34	T	.82	.83	2.75	4.00	28.33
Stockton	4.24	2.12	3.62	.72	.68	.14	T	.01	.48	.42	.99	2.31	15.73

[1] Data for four years. [2] T=Trace. [3] No data available.

In the care and maintenance of the California experiment vineyards and in prosecuting researches in them, Mr. George C. Husmann, Pomologist in Charge of Viticultural Investigations, is assisted by Mr. Fred L. Husmann, Viticultural Superintendent, and Mr. Richard Schmidt, Assistant in Viticulture.

DESTRUCTION OF VINEYARDS.

In Bulletin 172 of the Bureau of Plant Industry the writer gives an account of the havoc wrought by the phylloxera insect to the vineyards of the Old World as well as to those of the Vinifera regions of this country. Since that bulletin was issued additional heavy losses have occurred.

The destruction in California of once flourishing vineyards covering more than 200,000 acres, through the so-called California vine disease and other agencies, but most largely through phylloxera, has already occurred. All that has been suggested to combat and eradicate the phylloxera has been tried in this and other countries, but it is conceded that, with the exception of vineyards which can be flooded cheaply and sufficiently to kill the insect, the only way successfully to reestablish Vinifera vineyards is by growing the vines on phylloxera-resistant stocks.

FACTORS IN RESISTANCE.

The resistance of vines to phylloxera depends upon two factors: (1) The inherent resistant character of the vine and (2) its adaptation to soil, climatic, and other conditions.

The inherent or natural characteristics of the plant repel or invite the attacks of the phylloxera. The number of swellings, nodosities, and tuberosities from insect punctures and the rotting of the root occasioned by them progress more or less rapidly and deeply in accordance with the texture and character of the root attacked. The weakening and ultimate death of the vine are determined by the extent of the punctures and the progress of the rot upon the roots.

The nodosities rot more or less rapidly in the different grape species. In the Vinifera they are larger and usually rot in a very short time. In the American species the nodosities are smaller and do not rot so quickly, various species differing in this respect. The number of nodosities varies greatly on the different vine varieties, and when the insects have multiplied sufficiently to cover the smaller rootlets with them, eventually the larger roots are attacked, and if cancerous patches of decomposition are found on the more developed roots tuberosities occur.

Some varieties have nodosities on practically all rootlets, while some of the American species are not injured by the phylloxera except that a few nodosities form on their roots. In fact, the resistant ratings of different species are based on a determination of the relative number and size of the nodosities found on their roots.

In order to indicate with some degree of definiteness the resistance to phylloxera (not the value of the stock), scientists have provisionally adopted an arbitrary scale of ratings. In this scale the maximum of resistance or immunity is taken as 20, while absence of resistance (or no resistance) is reckoned as zero.

The necessary degree of resistance for the production of good crops varies with the character of the soil, stocks rating above 16 being considered sufficient for all soils, 14 to 16 for fairly good soils, and 10 to 14 for rich, moist, sandy soils.

ADAPTATION TO SOIL, CLIMATIC, AND OTHER CONDITIONS.

The ability of a vine to withstand or resist the attacks of the phylloxera without serious injury is greatly influenced by the adaptability of the vine to the climatic and soil conditions under which it is grown. These may increase or diminish the vigor of the plant, retard or favor the reparation of the insect injuries, and affect the resistance of the plant by favoring or hindering the dissemination or activity of the insect. For instance, climatic conditions affect the multiplication of the insect and it can travel but little in sandy soils of a certain fineness. Then again, a variety which in one locality has splendid resistant qualities perishes in another locality having a similar soil but a different climate or in another locality having a similar climate but a different soil.

This is due to the fact that some species are adapted to moist soils, while others are variously adapted to dry soils, deep soils, or shallow soils, and also to the fact that the root systems of different species vary in habit of growth, some assuming a horizontal and others a vertical position; some roots are thick and fleshy and others small and wiry; some are soft, while others are firm. (See Pl. V.) Thus, a moisture-loving variety or one having a horizontal root system would not thrive in a dry, hot climate; neither would a variety with a deep root system thrive in a shallow, hard soil, or one adapted to a dry location thrive in a wet soil. For such reasons, a variety grown under congenial soil and climatic conditions will often prove more resistant than one of greater natural resistance grown under adverse soil and climatic conditions.

Resistance to phylloxera is also influenced by the congeniality existing between vine varieties when grafted on other vine varieties. Causes like these, and there are many others, affect the resistant qualities of vines, and it is with the study of the adaptation of varieties to varying conditions and the congeniality existing between vine varieties that the researches reported in this bulletin are particularly concerned.

The European work in the selection and breeding of resistant stocks has been determined largely by the necessity that such stocks be adapted to calcareous-soil conditions rarely encountered in the present Vinifera regions of this country. This renders it necessary for us to undertake our own researches and determinations. The varying soil, climatic, and other conditions in California make the selecting of the right grape species in the reestablishing of vineyards on resistant stocks rather a complex matter.

Of the 23 species of grapes native to North America, the 14 shown in Table III have been found sufficiently resistant to merit the attention of the viticulturist, and they are under test in the experiment vineyards of the United States Department of Agriculture.

Table III shows their natural habitat, the locations, sites, and the character of soil they prefer, the habits of the vines, their relative season of leafing (Pls. VI and VII), their root systems (Pl. V), the flowering and ripening of their fruit, the ease or difficulty of propagating them; their suitability for either bench or field grafting, and their relative resistance to phylloxera, cold, dampness, heat, and drought.

TABLE III.—*Cultural data of fourteen American species of grapes whose varieties or hybrids are under test as resistant stocks in twelve experiment vineyards in California.*[1]

Name and region of nativity.	Preferred location.	Vine.	Roots.	Season of leafing, flowering, and ripening.	Percentage of cuttings taking root.	Grafting adaptation.	Resistance to— Phylloxera (out of a possible 20).	Resistance to— Cold.	Resistance to— Dampness.	Resistance to— Heat.	Resistance to— Drought.
Vitis labrusca (northern fox grape): Allegheny Mountains, from New England to South Carolina.	Wet thickets; granitic soils	Vigorous, medium-sized climber.	Large, fleshy	Very late	85	BF[1]	5	VG		F	F.
V. candicans (mustang grape): Oklahoma, Texas, and New Mexico.	Black waxy lands or adobe	Moderately vigorous, medium climber.	Vigorous, tender	Medium early	30	F	15	F	F	G	G.
V. aestivalis (summer grape): Southern New York to Florida; westward to the Mississippi and Missouri Rivers.	High, warm, gravelly, moist soils.	Vigorous, medium-sized climber.	Rather large, hard, plunging.	Medium late	50	F	14	VG		G	G.
V. linsecomii (post-oak or turkey grape): Texas	High, well drained timber lands, granitic gravelly clay, compact, deep, rich river-bank soils.	Vigorous, good-sized climber.	Medium size, hard, and long.	do	40	F	14	F		G	G.
V. monticola (sweet mountain grape): Texas	Low limestone hills; does moderately well in sandy soils.	Rather small; good grower.	Bushy, plunging	do	65	FB	18	F		G	G.
V. berlandieri (little mountain grape): Texas and Mexico	Tops, sides, and bottoms of limestone hills.	Slender; medium grower.	Strong and plunging	Late	40	F	19	F		G	G.
V. cordifolia (frost or sour winter grape): Great Lakes to Florida, abundant in Illinois, Tennessee, Missouri, and Arkansas.	Deep, rich, loose soils on river banks.	Vigorous, strong climber.	Strong, hard, carneous.	do	25	F	18	VG	F	G	G.
V. cinerea (sweet winter or ashy grape): Illinois to Texas	do	Vigorous, strong grower.	Large, fleshy, plunging	Very late	25	F	15	F	G		
V. champini (adobe-land grape): Texas	Limestone hills; adapts itself to a variety of soils.	Vigorous, spreading grower.	Large, ramified, plunging.	Early to medium	80	FB	12	F	G	G	G.

V. doaniana (Texas Panhandle large grape): Texas	Sandy, limy soils	Slender, fair grower	Numerous, thick, deeply penetrating.	Early	60	F	12	F	G	G	....
V. longii (Solonis, bush or gulch grape): Texas Panhandle, New Mexico, Kansas, and Colorado.	Ravines along streams. Cretaceous, generally rich, sandy, moist, always fresh soils.	Bushy, upright, vigorous grower.	Large, ramified, horizontal, hard.	do	60	F	14	F	G	G	G.
V. rupestris (sand, sugar, or rock grape): From the Rio Grande in Texas mainly into Oklahoma, northwestern Arkansas, southern Missouri, Kentucky, and Tennessee; also in Mountains north to Pennsylvania.	Open places in poor soils and along gravelly banks and ravines.	Vigorous, short, bushy grower.	Long, slender, or strong, plunging.	Very early	80	B	19	G	.....	G	G.
V. vulpina (riparia or riverside grape): From Salt Lake east and from Texas north in all the States as far as 90 miles north of Quebec.	Moist, loose, sandy soils along creeks and river bottoms.	Vigorous; medium size.	Long, thin, slender, hard, wiry, ramified.	do	85	FB	19	VG	G	.....	....
V. bicolor (blue grape): Northern Missouri, Illinois, Wisconsin, Indiana, Michigan, Ohio, Kentucky, Pennsylvania, New York, New Jersey, Maryland, and Ontario.	Black sandy and red siliceous soils.	Fair grower	Rather hard, large, plunging.	Late	40	F	16	VG	.....	G	G.

[1] Abbreviations used in table: Under grafting, B for bench, F for field; under resistance, F for fair, G for good, and V for very.

HYBRIDS.

In the attempts to secure resistants suited to soil, climatic, and other conditions which at the same time would prove congenial, lasting, and productive stocks on which to graft the Vinifera varieties, many difficulties were encountered. For instance, the stock may be adapted to the soil, but it may be so hard to root as to make its commercial use impracticable. Again, the stock may be suited to the soil and it may root easily and be resistant, but not congenial to or make a lasting junction with Vinifera varieties; or the congeniality of the variety may be good, but the fruitfulness of the graft may be impaired.

In many cases also no resistant species are exactly suited to the soil and climatic conditions. To overcome such difficulties and others of like nature, hybrids have been and are being produced, in the breeding of which such of the native American species were selected as possess the various qualities desired. (See Pls. VIII and IX.) In this work some remarkable successes have been achieved, such, for instance, as Riparia × Rupestris, No. 101; Riparia × Rupestris, No. 3306; Riparia × Rupestris, No. 3309; Solonis × Othello, No. 1616; Rupestris × Cordifolia, Nos. 107–11; Riparia × (Cordifolia × Rupestris), Nos. 106–8; Rupestris × Berlandieri, No. 301A; Berlandieri × Riparia, No. 420A; and Monticola × Riparia, No. 18808.

Efforts have also been made to produce hybrids between the Vinifera and American native-grape varieties which would be resistant to phylloxera and at the same time give satisfactory crops of fruit of desirable character and quality. (See Pl. X, fig. 2.) By having such direct producers, the cost of grafting would not only be avoided, but congeniality would not have to be reckoned with. Some remarkable strides are being made along this line. A number of these hybrids are under test in the experiment vineyards, but so far it is not possible to say that any of them are better than or equal to some of our finer varieties of native American grapes or that they have as good phylloxera-resistant qualities.

GROWTH RATINGS OF RESISTANT VINES AND DIRECT PRODUCERS.

In Table IV the upper numbers after each name in the columns headed "Experiment vineyard" show the years when the vines were planted; the lower numbers show the growth ratings, which in all cases were made in the autumn of 1913.

The growth or adaptability of each variety at each vineyard where it is under test is expressed in the form of a percentage rating on a scale in which the growth of the variety under conditions for which it is well adapted is taken as the standard of excellence, 100 per cent.

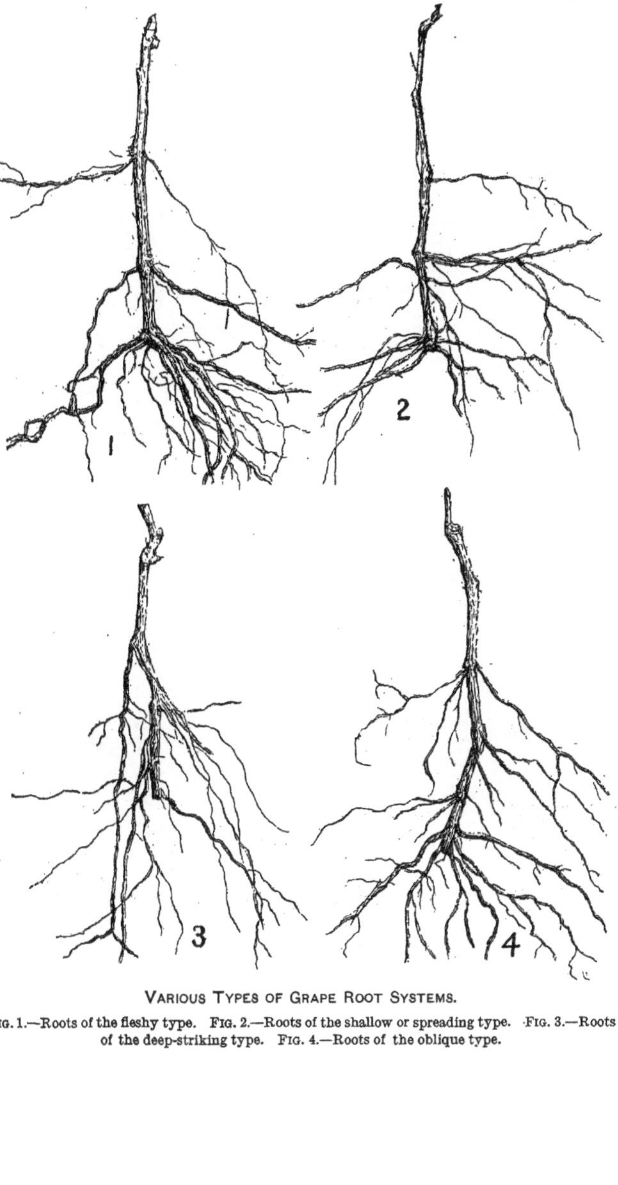

VARIOUS TYPES OF GRAPE ROOT SYSTEMS.

FIG. 1.—Roots of the fleshy type. FIG. 2.—Roots of the shallow or spreading type. FIG. 3.—Roots of the deep-striking type. FIG. 4.—Roots of the oblique type.

LEAVES OF FOUR NATIVE AMERICAN SPECIES OF GRAPES USED AS STOCKS ON WHICH TO GRAFT VINIFERA VARIETIES.

FIG. 1.—*Vitis champini*, upper and lower side of leaf, one-fourth natural size. FIG. 2.—*Vitis doaniania*, upper and lower side of leaf, one-sixth natural size. FIG. 3.—*Vitis candicans*, upper and lower side of leaf, one-fourth natural size. FIG. 4.—*Vitis berlandieri*, upper and lower side of leaf, one-sixth natural size.

LEAVES OF FOUR NATIVE AMERICAN SPECIES OF GRAPES EXTENSIVELY USED AS STOCKS ON WHICH TO GRAFT VINIFERA VARIETIES.

FIG. 1.—*Vitis rupestris*, upper and lower side of leaf, one-fourth natural size. FIG. 2.—*Vitis aestivalis*, upper and lower side of leaf, one-fourth natural size. FIG. 3.—*Vitis labrusca*, upper and lower side of leaf, one-seventh natural size. FIG. 4.—*Vitis riparia*, upper and lower side of leaf, two-fifths natural size.

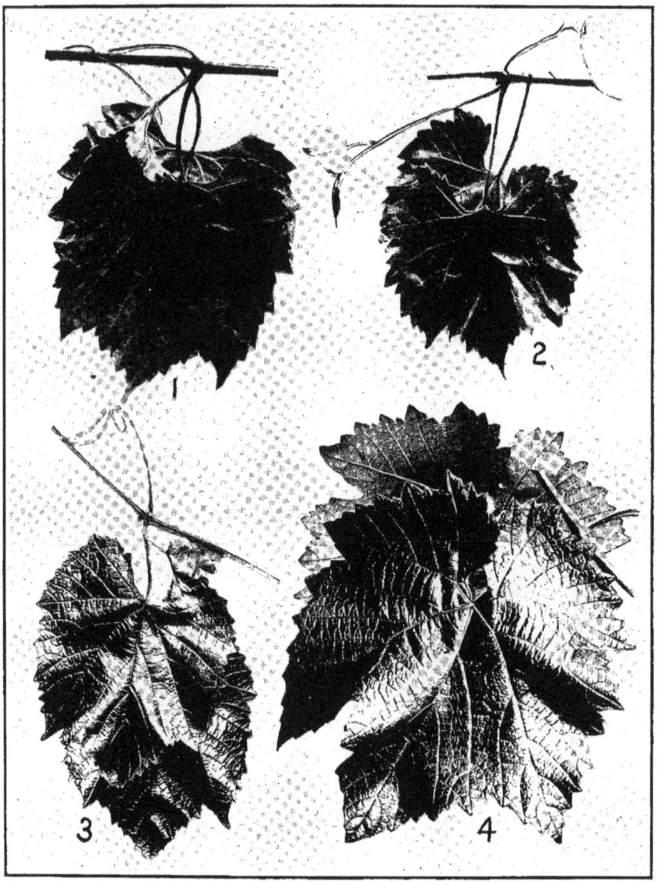

LEAVES OF FOUR GRAPE HYBRIDS USED AS STOCKS ON WHICH TO GRAFT VINIFERA VARIETIES.

FIG. 1.—Monticola × Riparia No. 18808, upper and lower side of leaf, one-sixth natural size. FIG. 2.—Cordifolia × Riparia No. 125-1, upper and lower side of leaf, one-eighth natural size. FIG. 3.—Berlandieri × Riparia No. 420A, upper and lower side of leaf, one-sixth natural size. FIG. 4.—Linsecomii × (Labrusca × Vinifera), upper and lower side of leaf, one-eleventh natural size.

LEAVES OF FOUR GRAPE HYBRIDS ORIGINATED IN FRANCE AND EXTENSIVELY USED AS STOCKS ON WHICH TO GRAFT VINIFERA VARIETIES.

FIG. 1.—Riparia × Rupestris No. 3306, upper and lower side of leaf, one-eighth natural size. FIG. 2.—Mourvedre × Rupestris No. 1202, upper and lower side of leaf, five-sixteenths natural size. FIG. 3.—Riparia × Rupestris No. 101, upper and lower side of leaf, five-fourteenths natural size. FIG. 4.—Riparia × Rupestris No. 3309, upper and lower side of leaf, one-third natural size.

FIG. 1.—A VINIFERA ON RESISTANT STOCK (HUNISA GRAFTED ON DOG RIDGE).

FIG. 2.—A DIRECT PRODUCER ON ITS OWN ROOTS (ALICANTE GANZIN).

These adaptability ratings therefore represent the behavior of each variety under the conditions existing at the several vineyards expressed in terms that permit comparison with its behavior elsewhere. They are not based on a comparison with other varieties in the same vineyard. Each variety is therefore rated on a scale based on its own standard of excellence rather than on any arbitrary scale formulated for application to all varieties. It is believed that this method renders possible a truer expression of the reaction of each variety to different soil and climatic conditions than would be possible by using any arbitrary scale of measurement of growth.

To illustrate, Aramon × Rupestris Ganzin, No. 2, planted at each of three experiment vineyards in 1904, at Fresno was rated 97; at Livermore, 83; and at Lodi, only 46. This shows that at Fresno the growth was very satisfactory, and it was therefore rated at 97. At Livermore the growth was good, but not nearly so good as at Fresno; it was therefore rated at 83. At Lodi it made a very poor growth, which as compared with the growth made at Fresno was as 46 to 97, or when compared to perfect growth as 46 to 100, i. e., 46 per cent.

TABLE IV.—*Resistant and direct-producing varieties of grapes in eleven experiment vineyards in California, showing the year of planting in each vineyard and the relative growth rating.*

Variety.	Experiment vineyard.										
	Chico.	Colfax.	Fresno.	Geyserville.	Guasti.	Livermore.	Lodi.	Mountain View.	Oakville.	Sonoma.	Stockton.
Adobe Giant:											
Year of planting	1906	1906	1903	1904	......	......	......	......	1903	1907	1907
Growth rating	89	93	85	85	......	......	......	......	90	90	87
(Aestivalis × Monticola) × (Riparia × Rupestris, No. 554–5):											
Year of planting	1906	1906	1904	1904	......	......	1904	......	1904	1904	1908
Growth rating	96	87	93	92	......	......	92	......	95	89	89
(Aestivalis × Rupestris) × Riparia, No. 227:											
Year of planting	1906	......	......	......	......	......	......	1905	1905	1905	.....
Growth rating	82	......	......	......	......	......	......	81	95	89	.....
Aramon × Rupestris Ganzin, No. 1:											
Year of planting	1907	1906	1913	1904	......	1904	1904	1904	1904	1904	1908
Growth rating	99	94	......	98	......	96	98	93	98	90	85
Aramon × Rupestris Ganzin, No. 2:											
Year of planting	1907	1906	1904	1904	1907	1904	1904	1904	1904	1904	1908
Growth rating	93	93	97	97	87	83	46	93	98	92	83
Aramon × Rupestris Ganzin, No. 9:											
Year of planting	1906	......	1904	1904	......	1904	1905	1904	1904	1904	1907
Growth rating	98	......	95	71	......	88	94	67	78	94	95
Aramon × Riparia, No. 143A:											
Year of planting	......	......	1904	......	......	......	......	......	1904	......	1907
Growth rating	......	......	96	......	......	......	......	......	87	......	95
Arizonica Phoenix:											
Year of planting	1912	......	......	......	1905	......	......	......	......	......	.....
Growth rating	20	......	......	......	94	......	......	......	......	......	.....
Australis:											
Year of planting	1906	1906	1903	1904	......	1904	1904	1907	1903	1904	1908
Growth rating	91	90	97	92	......	89	90	60	89	92	89
Barnes:											
Year of planting	1906	1906	1903	......	1907	1907	......	1907	1903	......	1907
Growth rating	96	88	94	......	95	87	......	51	99	......	91
Berlandieri, No. 1:											
Year of planting	1906	1906	1904	1904	......	1904	1904	1904	1904	1904	.....
Growth rating	88	81	88	85	......	60	72	78	83	84	.....

TABLE IV.—*Resistant and direct-producing varieties of grapes in eleven experiment vineyards in California, showing the year of planting in each vineyard and the relative growth rating*—Continued.

Variety.	Experiment vineyard.										
	Chico.	Colfax.	Fresno.	Geyserville.	Guasti.	Livermore.	Lodi.	Mountain View.	Oakville.	Sonoma.	Stockton.
Berlandieri, No. 2:											
Year of planting	1906	1906	1904	1906	......	......	......	......	1909	......	......
Growth rating	89	79	65	76	......	......	......	......	85	......	......
Berlandieri Lafont, No. 9:											
Year of planting	1906	......	1904	1904	......	1905	1905	1904	1904	1904	......
Growth rating	88	......	71	93	......	83	66	72	86	77	......
Berlandieri × Riparia, No. 33 E. M.:											
Year of planting	1907	1906	1904	......	......	......	1904	1904	1904	......	1907
Growth rating	92	83	77	......	......	......	68	70	93	......	74
Berlandieri × Riparia, No. 34 E. M.:											
Year of planting	1906	1906	1903	1904	......	1907	......	1904	1903	1907	1907
Growth rating	90	90	87	91	......	85	......	66	93	87	86
Berlandieri × Riparia, No. 157–11:											
Year of planting	1907	1906	1904	1904	......	......	1904	1904	1904	......	1907
Growth rating	99	86	81	89	......	......	76	75	92	......	82
Berlandieri × Riparia, No. 420A:											
Year of planting	1907	1907	1903	1904	1905	1910	1904	1904	1903	1905	1907
Growth rating	97	95	93	75	91	33	93	88	98	92	87
Berlandieri × Riparia, No. 420B:											
Year of planting	1912	1907	1904	......	......	1907	1907	1904	1904	......	......
Growth rating	10	90	85	......	......	85	87	64	88	......	......
(Bourisquou × Rupestris, No. 601) × Calcicola, No. 13205:											
Year of planting	1906	......	1913	1907	......	1905	......	1907	1905	......	......
Growth rating	95	......	91	93	......	91	......	......	94	......	......
Cabernet × Berlandieri, No. 333:											
Year of planting	......	......	1903	1904	......	1904	......	1904	1903	......	1907
Growth rating	......	......	86	91	......	77	......	91	94	......	84
Cabernet × Rupestris Ganzin, No. 33A:											
Year of planting	1909	......	1904	1904	1907	1904	1904	1904	1904	1905	......
Growth rating	85	......	94	93	85	87	82	83	92	72	......
Chasselas × Berlandieri, No. 41B:											
Year of planting	1906	......	1904	1904	......	......	......	1904	1906	1907	1907
Growth rating	90	......	81	94	......	......	......	69	87	84	91
(Cinerea × Rupestris) × Riparia, No. 229:											
Year of planting	1906	......	1905	......	......	......	......	......	1905	......	1908
Growth rating	88	......	87	......	......	......	......	......	90	......	82
Columbaud × Riparia, No. 2502:											
Year of planting	1906	......	1904	......	......	1907	1907	1907	1904	1907	1907
Growth rating	99	......	89	......	......	74	86	80	89	89	92
Columbaud × Rupestris:											
Year of planting	......	......	......	......	......	1907	......	......	1903	1907	......
Growth rating	......	......	......	......	......	94	......	......	96	90	......
Constantia:											
Year of planting	1907	1907	1905	......	1905	......	......	......	1904	......	1907
Growth rating	79	94	96	......	98	......	......	......	99	......	96
Cordifolia × Riparia, No. 125–1:											
Year of planting	1906	......	1904	......	......	1906	1906	......	1904	1907	......
Growth rating	90	......	98	......	......	81	84	......	95	84	......
Cordifolia × Rupestris:											
Year of planting	1906	......	1905	......	......	1905	......	1905	......	......	......
Growth rating	89	......	77	......	......	88	......	60	......	......	......
Dog Ridge:											
Year of planting	1906	1906	1903	1904	1905	1904	1904	1904	1903	1904	1907
Growth rating	97	96	89	97	97	94	94	98	97	97	85
Hotporup:											
Year of planting	1907	......	1903	1904	......	1904	1904	1904	1903	1904	......
Growth rating	97	......	83	89	......	84	93	74	90	92	......
Judge:											
Year of planting	1906	1906	1903	1907	1907	1906	1907	1907	1903	1907	......
Growth rating	85	85	93	77	84	66	83	80	90	86	......
Lenoir:											
Year of planting	1906	1906	1904	1904	1905	1904	1904	1904	1903	1904	1907
Growth rating	100	93	77	95	97	86	96	94	98	95	90
Monticola × Riparia, No. 554:											
Year of planting	1912	......	1904	1904	......	1904	1904	1904	1904	1904	1907
Growth rating	40	......	88	82	......	84	87	80	98	87	88

TABLE IV.—*Resistant and direct-producing varieties of grapes in eleven experiment vineyards in California, showing the year of planting in each vineyard and the relative growth rating*—Continued.

Variety.	Experiment vineyard.										
	Chico.	Colfax.	Fresno.	Geyserville.	Guasti.	Livermore.	Lodi.	Mountain View.	Oakville.	Sonoma.	Stockton.
Monticola × Riparia, No. 18804:											
Year of planting	1906	1906	1904	......	......	1905	1904	1904	1904	1904	1907
Growth rating	95	84	94	......	......	90	91	81	89	91	85
Monticola × Riparia, No. 18808:											
Year of planting	1907	1906	1904	......	......	1905	1904	1904	1904	1904	1907
Growth rating	97	90	94	......	......	90	88	86	91	93	93
Monticola × Riparia, No. 18815:											
Year of planting	1906	1906	1904	......	......	1904	1905	1904	1904	1904	1908
Growth rating	96	92	95	......	......	95	90	86	93	95	92
Motley:											
Year of planting	1906	1906	......	1904	......	1906	1906	1904	1903	1906	......
Growth rating	90	92	......	81	......	76	96	90	86	88	......
Mourvedre × Rupestris, No. 1202:											
Year of planting	1906	1906	1903	1904	1905	1904	1904	1904	1903	1904	1907
Growth rating	93	97	100	99	94	98	97	95	100	92	95
Mourvedre × Rupestris, No. 1203:											
Year of planting	1906	1907	1904	1906	......	1906	1906	......	1906	1906	......
Growth rating	99	91	98	88	......	81	91	......	98	80	......
No name, No. 1:											
Year of planting	......	......	......	......	......	......	......	......	1905	......	......
Growth rating	......	......	......	......	......	......	......	......	95	......	......
No name, No. 2:											
Year of planting	......	......	......	......	......	......	......	......	1905	......	......
Growth rating	......	......	......	......	......	......	......	......	95	......	......
No name, No. 3:											
Year of planting	......	......	......	......	......	......	......	......	1905	......	......
Growth rating	......	......	......	......	......	......	......	......	94	......	......
Pinot Bouschet × Riparia, No. 3001:											
Year of planting	1907	......	1904	......	......	......	......	......	1904	1907	1907
Growth rating	91	......	96	......	......	......	......	......	90	82	83
Pinot × Rupestris, No. 1305:											
Year of planting	1907	1907	1909	1904	1907	1904	1904	1904	1904	1904	1907
Growth rating	99	93	99	93	89	96	93	94	98	95	94
Ramsey:											
Year of planting	1906	1907	1903	......	1907	1910	1907	1906	1903	......	......
Growth rating	90	89	94	......	88	85	92	94	98	......	......
Riparia du Colorado:											
Year of planting	1906	......	1903	1904	1907	1905	1904	1904	1903	1904	......
Growth rating	82	......	72	83	82	51	91	66	66	71	......
Riparia France:											
Year of planting	1906	......	1904	......	1907	1904	1904	......	......	1904	1907
Growth rating	51	......	97	......	84	74	79	......	......	86	87
Riparia Gloire:											
Year of planting	1906	1906	1903	......	1905	1904	1907	......	1903	1904	1907
Growth rating	87	86	85	......	93	82	77	......	88	85	75
Riparia Grand Glabre:											
Year of planting	1909	......	1904	......	1905	1904	1904	1904	1903	1904	1907
Growth rating	56	......	92	......	85	82	82	74	86	89	83
Riparia Martineau:											
Year of planting	1906	......	......	......	......	......	......	......	1904	......	......
Growth rating	92	......	......	......	......	......	......	......	86	......	......
Riparia Ramond:											
Year of planting	1912	......	......	......	1905	......	......	......	1906	......	......
Growth rating	60	......	......	......	92	......	......	......	86	......	......
Riparia Selected:											
Year of planting	......	......	......	......	......	......	......	......	1905	......	......
Growth rating	......	......	......	......	......	......	......	......	89	......	......
Riparia × Berlandieri, No. 161-49:											
Year of planting	1906	1907	......	......	......	......	......	1907	1904	......	......
Growth rating	95	91	......	......	......	......	......	87	90	......	......
Riparia × (Cordifolia × Rupestris), No. 106-8:											
Year of planting	1906	1906	1910	1904	......	1904	1904	1904	1910	1904	1907
Growth rating	88	86	93	86	......	76	85	72	92	90	91
Riparia Grand Glabre × Aramon Rupestris, No. 4110:											
Year of planting	1906	......	1904	......	......	1904	1904	......	1904	1904	......
Growth rating	73	......	89	......	......	92	91	......	91	91	......
Riparia × Rupestris, No. 101:											
Year of planting	1906	1906	1904	1904	......	1904	1904	1904	1904	1904	1907
Growth rating	85	81	95	96	......	91	97	65	93	89	91

TABLE IV.—*Resistant and direct-producing varieties of grapes in eleven experiment vineyards in California, showing the year of planting in each vineyard and the relative growth rating*—Continued.

Variety.	Experiment vineyard.										
	Chico.	Colfax.	Fresno.	Geyserville.	Guasti.	Livermore.	Lodi.	Mountain View.	Oakville.	Sonoma.	Stockton.
Riparia × Rupestris, No. 101-14:											
Year of planting	1906	1906	1904	1904	1905	1904	1904	1904	1904	1904	1907
Growth rating	92	92	93	90	72	90	98	86	94	90	94
Riparia × Rupestris, No. 3306:											
Year of planting	1906	1906	1904	1904	1907	1904	1904	1904	1904	1904	1907
Growth rating	94	92	74	96	89	77	80	91	93	93	90
Riparia × Rupestris, No. 3309:											
Year of planting	1906	1906	1904	1904	1907	1904	1904	1904	1903	1904	1907
Growth rating	89	95	95	97	88	79	94	88	92	91	70
Riparia × Rupestris, No. 108-103:											
Year of planting	......	1906	......	1906	......	......	......	......	1905	1906	1907
Growth rating	......	90	......	91	......	......	......	......	93	91	82
Riparia × Rupestris de Jaeger:											
Year of planting	1909	1906	1904	......	1907	......	1907	......	1904	1904	......
Growth rating	67	91	94	......	86	......	70	......	91	87	......
Riparia × (Rupestris × Aramon) Jaeger, No. 201:											
Year of planting	1906	1906	1904	1904	1907	1904	1904	1904	1904	1904	1907
Growth rating	99	94	85	95	82	95	93	67	96	89	95
Riparia × Rupestris Ramond:											
Year of planting	1906	......	......	......	......	......	......	......	1904	......	......
Growth rating	87	......	......	......	......	......	......	......	77	......	......
Rupestris des Caussettes:											
Year of planting	1906	1906	1903	1904	1905	1904	1904	1904	1903	1904	1907
Growth rating	95	94	91	90	92	85	90	78	91	89	90
Rupestris des Semis, No. 81-2:											
Year of planting	1907	1906	1904	......	......	1907	......	1907	1904	......	1907
Growth rating	100	90	96	......	......	96	......	81	96	......	88
Rupestris Ganzin:											
Year of planting	1906	......	......	......	......	......	......	......	1906	......	......
Growth rating	86	......	......	......	......	......	......	......	93	......	......
Rupestris le Reux:											
Year of planting	1906	......	......	......	1905	......	......	......	1906	......	......
Growth rating	93	......	......	......	89	......	......	......	91	......	......
Rupestris Martin:											
Year of planting	1906	1907	1903	1904	1905	1904	1904	1903	1903	1904	1907
Growth rating	92	83	77	95	79	92	92	75	92	90	89
Rupestris Metallica:											
Year of planting	1906	1906	1903	1904	1905	1904	1904	1904	1903	1906	......
Growth rating	99	92	90	95	95	93	93	82	97	89	......
Rupestris Mission:											
Year of planting	1906	1906	1904	1904	......	1904	1904	1904	1903	1904	1907
Growth rating	91	86	79	85	......	88	87	74	85	81	81
Rupestris Othello:											
Year of planting	1906	......	1904	......	......	1907	......	......	1904	......	1907
Growth rating	98	......	87	......	......	65	......	......	92	......	81
Rupestris Pillans:											
Year of planting	1906	1906	1905	1906	1905	1905	1905	1905	1905	1905	1907
Growth rating	99	92	96	83	95	92	93	80	87	82	87
Rupestris St. George:											
Year of planting	1906	1906	1903	1904	1905	1904	1904	1904	1903	1904	1907
Growth rating	94	99	96	97	95	98	98	87	100	87	97
Rupestris × Berlandieri, No. 219A:											
Year of planting	1907	1906	1902	1904	1905	1904	1904	1904	1903	1904	1907
Growth rating	75	90	82	85	85	88	91	73	83	86	90
Rupestris × Berlandieri, No. 301A:											
Year of planting	1907	1906	1903	1904	......	1904	......	1907	1903	1904	1907
Growth rating	100	83	85	92	......	85	......	88	92	86	84
Rupestris × Berlandieri, No. 301B:											
Year of planting	1906	1907	......	1904	......	......	1905	1905	......	......	......
Growth rating	92	94	......	94	......	......	97	87	......	......	......
Rupestris × Berlandieri, No. 301-37-152:											
Year of planting	1906	1907	1904	......	......	1906	......	1907	1904	......	......
Growth rating	91	89	90	......	......	84	......	82	88	......	......
Rupestris × Chasselas Rose, No. 4401:											
Year of planting	1906	1906	......	......	......	......	......	......	1907	......	......
Growth rating	91	96	......	......	......	......	......	......	98	......	......
Rupestris × Cinerea:											
Year of planting	1909	1907	1904	......	......	......	......	1907	1904	......	1907
Growth rating	60	89	90	......	......	......	......	85	92	......	92

TABLE IV.—*Resistant and direct-producing varieties of grapes in eleven experiment vineyards in California, showing the year of planting in each vineyard and the relative growth rating*—Continued.

Variety.	Experiment vineyard.										
	Chico.	Colfax.	Fresno.	Geyserville.	Guasti.	Livermore.	Lodi.	Mountain View.	Oakville.	Sonoma.	Stockton.
Rupestris × Cordifolia, No. 107–11:											
Year of planting	1906	1907	1904	......	......	1905	1904	1905	1905	1905	.....
Growth rating	71	89	89	......	......	84	94	71	89	85	.....
Rupestris × (Cordifolia × Rupestris), No. 202:											
Year of planting	1907	1907	1904	......	......	......	......	1907	1904	1904	1907
Growth rating	68	91	90	......	......	......	......	82	85	87	77
Rupestris × (Cordifolia × Rupestris), No. 202-5:											
Year of planting	1906	......	1904	1906	......	1906	1907	......	......	1906	.....
Growth rating	90	......	90	89	......	50	78	......	......	90	.....
Rupestris × Hybrid Azemar, No. 215:											
Year of planting	1907	1907	1904	1905	......	1904	1904	1905	1904	1904	.....
Growth rating	93	85	89	70	......	74	83	70	91	92	.....
Rupestris × Petit Bouschet, No. 503:											
Year of planting	1906	......	......	......	......	1904	......	......	......	......	.....
Growth rating	95	......	......	......	......	91	......	......	......	......	.....
Rupestris × Petit Bouschet Jaeger, No. 504:											
Year of planting	1906	......	......	1904	......	1906	......	......	1907	1907	.....
Growth rating	96	......	......	96	......	90	......	......	94	92	.....
Rupestris × Riparia, No. 108–16:											
Year of planting	1912	......	1904	......	......	......	1904	......	1904	1904	.....
Growth rating	75	......	91	......	......	......	78	......	68	81	.....
Salt Creek:											
Year of planting	1906	1906	1903	1904	......	1905	1904	1904	1903	1904	.....
Growth rating	91	87	86	85	......	77	92	68	90	84	.....
Solonis Robusta:											
Year of planting	1906	1906	1903	1904	1905	1904	1904	1904	1903	1905	1907
Growth rating	84	92	92	93	92	83	88	90	92	90	87
Solonis × (Cordifolia × Rupestris), No. 202-4:											
Year of planting	1909	1907	1904	......	......	1906	1906	......	1906	......	.....
Growth rating	60	93	84	......	......	76	84	......	61	......	.....
Solonis × Othello:											
Year of planting	1906	1907	......	1904	......	1904	1904	1904	......	1904	.....
Growth rating	99	93	......	96	......	87	88	88	......	95	.....
Solonis × Othello, No. 1613:											
Year of planting	1906	1906	1903	......	1905	1906	1907	......	1903	......	1907
Growth rating	99	96	100	......	95	90	92	......	100	......	94
Solonis × Riparia, No. 1615:											
Year of planting	1906	1906	1904	......	......	......	1904	1907	1904	1904	1907
Growth rating	93	90	96	......	......	......	91	83	86	89	89
Solonis × Riparia, No. 1616:											
Year of planting	1906	1906	1904	1904	1907	1904	1907	1904	1904	1904	1907
Growth rating	90	91	94	91	86	80	86	80	98	88	94
Taylor Narbonne:											
Year of planting	1906	1907	1904	1904	1907	1904	1904	1904	1904	1904	1907
Growth rating	70	82	89	95	78	70	51	71	91	85	86
Texas:											
Year of planting	......	......	......	......	1905	......	......	......	......	......	.....
Growth rating	......	......	......	......	79	......	......	......	......	......	.....
Tisserand:											
Year of planting	1906	......	1904	......	......	......	1904	......	1904	......	.....
Growth rating	93	......	84	......	......	......	78	......	92	......	.....
Viala:											
Year of planting	1906	1907	1904	......	......	1904	......	......	1903	1907	1907
Growth rating	92	86	89	......	......	71	......	......	97	82	87
Viala × Riparia:											
Year of planting	......	......	1904	......	......	1904	1904	1905	1904	1905	.....
Growth rating	......	......	77	......	......	70	77	78	69	82	.....
Vitis candicans:											
Year of planting	......	......	......	......	......	......	......	1904	1904	......	.....
Growth rating	......	......	......	......	......	......	......	65	89	......	.....

A number of the resistant-stock varieties have been growing a sufficient length of time to show what may be expected of them under similar conditions. In the following list of stocks that are worthy of special mention as having made excellent growth ratings at each of eleven California experiment vineyards, the varieties are given in the order of their ratings, i. e., the best growers first, and so on:

Chico Varietal Vineyard.—Lenoir; Rupestris de Semis, No. 81–2; Rupestris × Berlandieri, No. 301A; Aramon × Rupestris Ganzin, No. 1; Berlandieri × Riparia, No. 157–11; Columbaud × Riparia, No. 2502; Rupestris Metallica; Rupestris Pillans; Solonis × Othello; Solonis × Othello, No. 1613; Aramon × Rupestris Ganzin, No. 9; Rupestris Othello; Berlandieri × Riparia, No. 420A; Dog Ridge; Hotporup; Monticola × Riparia, No. 18808; (Aestivalis × Monticola) × (Riparia × Rupestris, No. 554–5); Barnes.

Colfax Experiment Vineyard.—Rupestris St. George; Mourvedre × Rupestris, No. 1202; Dog Ridge; Solonis × Othello, No. 1613; Berlandieri × Riparia, No. 420A; Riparia × Rupestris, No. 3309; Aramon × Rupestris Ganzin, No. 1; Constantia; Rupestris des Caussettes; Rupestris × Berlandieri, No. 301B; Adobe Giant; Aramon × Rupestris Ganzin, No. 2; Lenoir; Solonis × (Cordifolia × Rupestris), No. 202–4; Solonis × Othello; Monticola × Riparia, No. 18815; Motley; Riparia × Rupestris, No. 101–14.

Fresno Experiment Vineyard.—Mourvedre × Rupestris, No. 1202; Solonis × Othello, No. 1613; Cordifolia × Riparia, No. 125–1; Aramon × Rupestris Ganzin, No. 2; Australis; Riparia France; Constantia; Rupestris des Semis, No. 81–2; Rupestris Pillans; Rupestris St. George; Solonis × Riparia, No. 1615; Aramon × Rupestris Ganzin, No. 9; Monticola × Riparia, No. 18815; Riparia × Rupestris, No. 101; Riparia × Rupestris, No. 3309; Barnes; Monticola × Riparia, No. 18804; Monticola × Riparia No. 18808.

Geyserville Experiment Vineyard.—Mourvedre × Rupestris, No. 1202; Aramon × Rupestris Ganzin, No. 1; Aramon × Rupestris Ganzin, No. 2; Dog Ridge; Riparia × Rupestris, No. 3309; Rupestris St. George; Riparia × Rupestris, No. 101; Riparia × Rupestris, No. 3306; Solonis × Othello; Lenoir; Rupestris Martin; Rupestris Metallica; Taylor Narbonne; Rupestris × Berlandieri, No. 301B; Berlandieri Lafont, No. 9; Solonis Robusta; (Aestivalis × Monticola) × (Riparia × Rupestris, No. 554–5); Australis.

Guasti Experiment Vineyard.—Constantia; Dog Ridge; Lenoir; Barnes; Rupestris Metallica; Rupestris Pillans; Rupestris St. George; Solonis × Othello, No. 1613; Arizonica Phoenix; Mourvedre × Rupestris, No. 1202; Riparia Gloire; Riparia Ramond; Rupestris des Caussettes; Solonis Robusta; Berlandieri × Riparia, No. 420A; Pinot × Rupestris, No. 1305; Riparia × Rupestris, No. 3306; Rupestris le Reux.

Livermore Experiment Vineyard.—Mourvedre × Rupestris, No. 1202; Rupestris St. George; Aramon × Rupestris Ganzin, No. 1; Rupestris des Semis, No. 81–2; Monticola × Riparia, No. 18815; Riparia × (Rupestris × Aramon) Jaeger, No. 201; Dog Ridge; Rupestris Metallica; Rupestris Martin; Rupestris Pillans; Riparia × Rupestris, No. 101; Monticola × Riparia, No. 18804; Monticola × Riparia, No. 18808; Riparia × Rupestris, No. 101–14; Solonis × Othello, No. 1613; Australis; Aramon × Rupestris Ganzin, No. 9; Cordifolia × Rupestris.

Lodi Experiment Vineyard.—Aramon × Rupestris Ganzin, No. 1; Riparia × Rupestris, No. 101–14; Mourvedre × Rupestris, No. 1202; Riparia × Rupestris, No. 101; Lenoir; Motley; Aramon × Rupestris Ganzin, No. 9; Dog Ridge; Riparia × Rupestris,

No. 3309; Rupestris × Cordifolia, No. 107-11; Berlandieri × Riparia, No. 420A; Riparia × (Rupestris × Aramon) Jaeger, No. 201; Rupestris Metallica; Rupestris Pillans; (Aestivalis × Monticola) × (Riparia × Rupestris, No. 554-5); Ramsey; Rupestris Martin; Salt Creek.

Mountain View Experiment Vineyard.—Dog Ridge; Mourvedre × Rupestris, No. 1202; Lenoir; Monticola × Riparia, No. 18804; Aramon × Rupestris Ganzin, No. 1; Aramon × Rupestris Ganzin, No. 2; Riparia × Rupestris, No. 3306; Motley; Solonis Robusta; Berlandieri × Riparia, No. 420A; Riparia × Rupestris, No. 3309; Rupestris × Berlandieri, No. 301A; Solonis × Othello; Riparia × Berlandieri, No. 161-49; Rupestris St. George; Rupestris × Berlandieri, No. 301B; Monticola × Riparia, No. 18808; Monticola × Riparia, No. 18815.

Oakville Experiment Vineyard.—Mourvedre × Rupestris, No. 1202; Rupestris St. George; Solonis × Othello, No. 1613; Barnes; Constantia; Aramon × Rupestris Ganzin, No. 1; Aramon × Rupestris Ganzin, No. 2; Berlandieri × Riparia, No. 420A; Lenoir; Monticola × Riparia, No. 554; Ramsey; Solonis × Riparia, No. 1616; Dog Ridge; Rupestris Metallica; Viala; Rupestris des Semis, No. 81-2; (Aestivalis × Monticola) × (Riparia × Rupestris, No. 554-5); (Aestivalis × Rupestris) × Riparia, No. 227.

Sonoma Experiment Vineyard.—Dog Ridge; Lenoir; Monticola × Riparia, No. 18815; Solonis × Othello; Aramon × Rupestris Ganzin, No. 9; Monticola × Riparia, No. 18808; Riparia × Rupestris, No. 3306; Aramon × Rupestris Ganzin, No. 2; Australis; Berlandieri × Riparia, No. 420A; Mourvedre × Rupestris, No. 1202; Monticola × Riparia, No. 18804; Riparia × Rupestris, No. 3309; Riparia × Rupestris, No. 108-103; Adobe Giant; Aramon × Rupestris Ganzin, No. 1; Riparia × (Cordifolia × Rupestris), No. 106-8; Riparia × Rupestris, No. 101-14.

Stockton Experiment Vineyard.—Rupestris St. George; Constantia; Aramon × Rupestris Ganzin, No. 9; Mourvedre × Rupestris, No. 1202; Riparia × Rupestris, No. 101-14; Solonis × Othello, No. 1613; Solonis × Riparia, No. 1616; Monticola × Riparia, No. 18808; Columbaud × Riparia, No. 2502; Monticola × Riparia, No. 18815; Rupestris × Cinerea; Barnes; Riparia × (Cordifolia × Rupestris), No. 106-8; Riparia × Rupestris, No. 101; Lenoir; Riparia × Rupestris, No. 3306; Rupestris des Caussettes; Rupestris × Berlandieri, No. 219A.

Table V gives the resistant varieties in each vineyard which are estimated to have made the best and most creditable growth records as compared to all the varieties under test. The numbers in line with each name in the vineyard columns show the relative growth rating made by the variety in the respective vineyards where it is under test. The highest rating is expressed by the figure 1, the next by 2, and so on. The ratings therefore represent the behavior of each variety under the conditions existing at the several vineyards, expressed in terms that permit comparison with its behavior elsewhere, and in comparison also with other varieties in the same vineyard. To illustrate: Of all the resistant varieties at Livermore the best record was made by Mourvedre × Rupestris, No. 1202 (rated as 1), whereas at Stockton it was fourth best (expressed by 4), and at Sonoma eleventh best (expressed by 11).

TABLE V.—*Resistant-stock varieties of grapes making the best growth records, showing their relative merits in each of eleven experiment vineyards in California.*

Variety.	Chico.	Colfax.	Fresno.	Geyserville.	Guasti.	Livermore.	Lodi.	Mountain View.	Oakville.	Sonoma.	Stockton.
Adobe Giant		11								15	
Aramon × Rupestris Ganzin:											
No. 1	4	7		2		3	1	5	6	16	
No. 2		12	4	3				6	7	8	
No. 9	11		12			17	7			5	3
Australis			5	18		16				9	
Barnes	18		16		4				4		12
Berlandieri × Riparia:											
No. 420 A	13	5			15		11	1	8	10	
No. 157-11	5										
Columbaud × Riparia, No. 2502	6										9
Constantia		8	7		1				5		2
Cordifolia × Riparia, No. 125-1			3								
Dog Ridge	14	3		4	2	7	8	1	13	1	
Lenoir	1	13		10	3		5	3	9	2	15
Monticola × Riparia:											
No. 18804			17			12		4		12	
No. 18808	16		18			13		17		6	8
No. 18815		16	13			5		18		3	10
Motley		17					6	8			
Mourvedre × Rupestris, No. 1202		2	1	1	10	1	3	2	1	11	4
Ramsey							16		11		
Riparia Gloire					11						
Riparia × Rupestris:											
No. 101			14	7		11	4				14
No. 101-14		18				14	2			18	5
No. 3306				8	17			7		7	16
No. 3309		6	15	5			9	11		13	
Rupestris des Semis, No. 81-2	2		8			4			16		
Rupestris Martin				11		9	17				
Rupestris Metallica	7			12	5	8	13		14		
Rupestris Pillans	8		9		6	10	14				
Rupestris St. George		1	10	6	7	2		15	2		1
Rupestris × Berlandieri:											
No. 301A	3							12			
No. 301B		10		14				16			
Rupestris Cinerea											11
Rupestris × Cordifolia, No. 107-11							10				
Solonis Robusta				16	14			9			
Solonis × Othello	9	15		9				13		4	
Solonis × Othello, No. 1613	10	4	2		8	15			3		6

Table VI gives an alphabetical list of improved American native and Franco-American grape varieties which are being tested on their own roots in the Chico, Colfax, Fresno, Geyserville, Guasti, Livermore, Lodi, Mountain View, Oakville, Sonoma, and Stockton experiment vineyards. The plantings are too young to permit the drawing of conclusions.

TABLE VI.—*Varieties of American native and Franco-American grapes under test on their own roots at eleven experiment vineyards in California.*

[The locations of the tests are indicated by plus (+) marks.]

Varieties.	Chico.	Colfax.	Fresno.	Geyserville.	Guasti.	Livermore.	Lodi.	Mountain View.	Oakville.	Sonoma.	Stockton.
Agawam	+	+									
Albania			+								
Alexander Winter	+								+		
Alicante Ganzin	+	+				+					
Alicante × Rupestris Terrace, No. 20	+			+		+					+
Alice	+								+		
Amber Queen	+										
Ambrosia	+										
Amerbonte								+			

TABLE VI.—*Varieties of American native and Franco-American grapes under test on their own roots at eleven experiment vineyards in California*—Continued.

Varieties.	Chico.	Colfax.	Fresno.	Geyserville.	Guasti.	Livermore.	Lodi.	Mountain View.	Oakville.	Sonoma.	Stockton.
America	+		+	+		+		+	+	+	
Aminia					+						
Antoinette	+										
Arkansas	+								+		
Aroma	+										
Atoka								+			
August Giant	+										
Bacchus	+								+		
Bailey	+										
Barry	+			+		+	+	+		+	
Belle	+								+		
Berckmans	+	+		+			+	+	+		
Bertha	+										
Big Extra	+										+
Big Hope	+										
Bourisquou × Rupestris:											
No. 601	+									+	+
No. 109–4	+			+							+
No. 3907	+					+		+	+		
No. 4306	+			+				+		+	+
No. 4308	+					+					+
Brighton	+	+	+		+						
Brilliant	+					+			+		
Campbell	+								+		
Canada	+	+				+					+
Carignane × Rupestris:											
No. 404	+										+
No. 501	+					+					+
Castel:											
No. 1028	+										
No. 19002	+										
Catawba	+					+					
Cayuga	+										
Centennial	+	+									
Chambrill	+								+		
Champenel	+										+
Champion	+										
Chasselas × Rupestris, No. 901	+							+			+
Clairette Doré Ganzin				+		+		+		+	+
Clevener		+									
Clinton	+										
Cloeta			+					+			
Cochee	+								+		
Colerain	+										
Collier	+										
Columbaud × Rupestris						+				+	
Concord	+			+			+	+			
Continental									+		
Cornucopia	+	+					+		+		
Cottage	+										
Couderc:											
No. 101	+						+				+
No. 201	+										+
No. 503	+						+				+
No. 704											+
No. 1173									+		
No. 3701	+		+		+		+				+
No. 28 × 112	+				+						+
No. 43–06									+		
No. 82 × 32	+						+				
No. 84 × 61	+										+
No. 87 × 115	+						+				+
No. 124 × 30	+										
No. 132–11	+										
Cunningham					+				+		
Cynthiana									+		
Delaware	+			+	+	+		+	+	+	
Diamond	+										
Duchess	+			+		+		+			
Early Victor	+				+				+		
Elvira	+	+									
Fern Munson	+							+			
Governor Ross	+										
Herbemont	+		+								
Herbert	+										
Hexamer	+				+						
Husmann	+										
Isabella	+					+					
Jaeger								+		+	
Lampasas	+										

TABLE VI.—*Varieties of American native and Franco-American grapes under test on their own roots at eleven experiment vineyards in California*—Continued.

Varieties.	Chico.	Colfax.	Fresno.	Geyserville.	Guasti.	Livermore.	Lodi.	Mountain View.	Oakville.	Sonoma.	Stockton.
Lenoir	+										+
Lindley	+							+			
Linn	+										
Lindmar	+								+		
Little Blue	+										
Livingston	+										
Long John	+										
Louisiana	+	+	+								
Lucile	+										
Lukfata	+										
Manito	+		+					+		+	
Marguerite	+	+	+		+			+			
Martha	+										
Mary Favorite	+										
Massasoit	+										
Maxatawney	+										
Mericadel	+		+					+	+		
Merrimac	+										
Missouri Riesling	+										
Montefiore	+										
Moore	+	+	+	+		+	+	+	+	+	
Moyer	+										
Mrs. Munson	+				+						
Muench	+	+									
Niagara	+			+		+	+	+		+	
Noah	+										
Oliatatoo	+	+									
Osage	+										
Olita	+										
Paradox	+										
Paragon	+										
Pardes	+			+			+				+
Peabody	+								+		
Pearl	+								+		
Perkins	+										
Pierce			+	+		+			+		
Plant de Carmes	+		+					+	+	+	
Plant de Gounay									+		
Pocklington	+										
Presley	+								+		
Ragan	+	+			+						
Rebecca	+			+			+				
Red Eagle	+										
Regal	+										
Requa	+										
Rockford	+										
Rogers:											
No. 5	+										
No. 13	+								+		
No. 32	+										
Rommel	+								+		+
Siebel No. 14				+							
Shalah							+				
Wyoming Red	+										

To grow vines on resistant stocks successfully, it should be borne in mind that the resistance of vines depends upon the inherent characters of the vine and its adaptation to soil, climatic, and other conditions, and that the resistant quality of the stock is very materially affected by the congeniality of the varieties grafted on it.

CONGENIALITY AND ADAPTABILITY OF VINES.

Two vine varieties are congenial to each other if both top and root flourish when one is grafted on the other. (See Pl. X, fig. 1.) The congeniality would be called perfect when one variety grafted on another behaves as if the stock were grafted with a scion of itself, the union being perfect and the behavior of the vine the same as that of an entire ungrafted plant.

The term "congeniality" as used in this discussion is limited to the relation of vine varieties to the resistant stocks upon which they are grafted. To discriminate properly between adaptability and congeniality and then to determine the congeniality, it is necessary to know the behavior of the resistant varieties as well as the Vinifera varieties on their own roots. If we have grafted vines of which both the stock and the scion varieties are known to be suited to the soil and climatic conditions and they do not respond, we know that congeniality is lacking.

The adaptability of varieties can be closely forecasted, but their congeniality must be determined by actual tests. Without knowledge of its adaptability to existing conditions, the extent to which differences in the behavior of a variety grafted on different stocks are due to congeniality or to adaptability is impossible of determination.

Saccharine and acid determinations of the fruit from grafted vines have been made for a number of years with a view to ascertain whether the quality of the fruit is influenced by the stock upon which the vine is grafted. (See Pl. X.) Such determinations contrasted with the same season's growth ratings of the same vines indicate a close correspondence between these important chemical constituents of the fruit and the congeniality of grafts and stocks as determined by observations, and they afford a useful check on the congeniality ratings.

Similar growth ratings of a variety grafted on various stocks are found to be accompanied by fairly definite percentages of sugar and acid. Under like conditions of growth the sweetness and the acidity of the fruit, as well as its time of ripening, are materially influenced by the congeniality of the scion and stock. The saccharine and acid contents are two of the leading considerations in the money value of the fruit.

In determining the relative congeniality of vine varieties on diverse resistant stocks, these and the relative quantity of fruit produced, the difference in time of ripening, the relative healthfulness and comparative durability of varieties on different resistant stocks, and the relative amount of wood produced are some of the considerations that appear most important.

BEHAVIOR OF GRAPES GRAFTED AND ON THEIR OWN ROOTS.

In Table VII, column 1 gives (1) the variety name, and indented under it (2) the name of the resistant stock on which it is grafted, or if the variety is on its own roots the fact is so stated. Column 2 shows the experiment vineyard in which the growth was tested, use being made of the following abbreviations: C for Chico, Cx for Colfax, F for Fresno, G for Geyserville, Gi for Guasti, L for Lodi, Li for Livermore, M for Mountain View, O for Oakville, S for Sonoma, St for Stockton. Column 3 shows the year in which the stock was planted, thereby indicating its age, and column 4 gives the year of grafting. Column 5 shows the congeniality, or the growth of each variety on the different stocks, expressed in the form of a percentage rating, on a scale in which the growth of the variety when not grafted but growing as an entire plant on its own root under conditions to which it is well adapted is taken as the standard of excellence, that is, 100 per cent. These ratings therefore represent the behavior of each variety grafted on the several stocks under the conditions existing at the vineyard at which it was found, expressed in terms that permit comparison with its behavior when growing as an entire plant on its own roots under favorable conditions and not based on a comparison with other Vinifera varieties grafted on the same stock in the same vineyard. The rating in each case is the average rating made in different seasons to and including the autumn of 1913. To illustrate: Alicante Bouschet, grafted in the Oakville vineyard in 1906 on different resistant stocks, on Aramon × Rupestris Ganzin, No. 1, was rated at 91; on Riparia × Rupestris, No. 3309, at 88; on Mourvedre × Rupestris, No. 1202, at 72; and on Riparia × Rupestris, No. 101, at 55. This shows that Alicante Bouschet, which is well adapted to the conditions there, when grafted on these different stocks at the same time, under the same conditions, in the same vineyard, and with the same treatment, varied in growth and behavior in comparison with the same variety on its own roots in accordance with the above ratings. Column 6 gives the pruning method, s being used for spurs and c for canes. Column 7 gives the weight of prunings per vine; 8, the nodes bearing fruit; 9 and 10, the growth-starting dates in early and late seasons; 11 and 12, the blossoming dates in early and late seasons; 13 and 14, the fruit-setting dates in early and late seasons; 15 and 16, the fruit-ripening dates in early and late seasons. Columns 17 to 21 give the fruit per vine for the seasons from 1909 to 1913, inclusive; 22, the average percentage of sugar, Balling scale; 23, the average acid, as tartaric, per 100 c. c. Column 24 shows the size of the clusters, m indicating medium; m-l, medium to large; l, large; v, very; s, small. Column 25 shows the shape of the clusters, whether round (r), cylindrical (cy), long (l), or tapering (t). Column 26 designates the density of the clusters, whether compact (c), medium (m), or loose (l). Column 27 shows the size of the berry, whether large (l), medium (m), or small (s). Column 28 gives the shape of the berry, whether round (r), oval (o), or oblong (ob). Column 29 shows the color of the berry, whether black (b), red (r), or white (w). Column 30 indicates the purpose for which the fruit is used, whether for table (t), shipping (s), juice (j), wine (w), or storage (st). In this table the nomenclature of varieties has been brought into conformity with the code of the American Pomological Society in so far as it has appeared practicable.

TABLE VII.—*Relative behavior and value for different purposes of grape varieties tested by grafting on resistant stocks and by growing on their own roots in eleven experiment vineyards in California.*

Variety and stock (on own roots, if so stated).	Experiment vineyard.	Year stock was planted.	Year grafted.	Congeniality.	How pruned.	Weight of pruning per vine.	Nodes bearing fruit.	Growth-starting date.		Blossoming date.		Fruit-setting date.		Fruit-ripening date.	
								Early season.	Late season.	Early season.	Late season.	Early season.	Late season.	Early season.	Late season.
1	2	3	4	5	6	7	8	9	10	11	12	13	14	15	16
				P. ct.		*Lbs.*									
Ach-I-Soum:															
Dog Ridge	O		1910					Mar. 24		May 30		June 3			
Lenoir	O	1904	1910	92	c, s	6.5				May 31	June 1	June 6	June 20		
[illegible]ani Maceron:															
Lenoir	O	1904	1907	89	s	2.9	3 to 4	Mar. 24		May 20	June 5	May 24	June 24	Sept. 26	Oct. 7
Monticola × Rupestris	F	1907	1907	91	s		2 to 5							Oct. 17	
Mourvedre × Rupestris, No. 1202	F	1907	1907	92	c, s	5.5	2 to 5	Mar. 21		May 20	May 25	May 24			
Solonis × Riparia, No. 1616	F	1907	1907	90	c, s	3	2 to 5	Mar. 14	Apr. 1	May 15	May 24	...do		Sept. 15	
Actoniky:															
Lenoir	O	1904	1907	89	s	3.3	2 to 5	Mar. 24		May 23	June 12	May 29	June 29	Sept. 25	Oct. 6
[illegible]la × Rupestris	F	1907	1907	89	c, s	3.7	4 to 5	Mar. 21	Apr. 1	May 19	May 23	May 31	June 1	Sept. 21	
[illegible]y	F	1907	1907	87	c, s	3	3 to 5	Mar. 23	Mar. 28	May 18	...do	May 30			
Admirable:															
Rip aria × Rupestris, No. 3309	O	1904		91	c, s	6.5	2 to 4	Mar. 22		May 15	June 2	May 21	June 19	Sept. 23	Oct. 8
Affenth[illegible]r:															
[illegible]n rots	Gi	1904		83	s			Mar. 14	Mar. 20	May 26	May 27	June 4		Sept. 15	Sept. 24
Agadia:															
Riparia × Rupestris, No. 3309	O		1910	96	c, s	2				May 25	June 1	June 6	June 16		
Ahmeur bon Ahmeur:															
Lenoir	O	1904	1907	88	s	2.8	3 to 6	Mar. 24		May 20	June 7	May 25	June 19	Sept. 30	Oct. 7
Ajaki Odia:															
[illegible]re × Rup[illegible]is, No. 1202	F	1907	1907	97	c, s	4.5	4 to 6	...do	Apr. 3	May 18	May 23	May 29		Sept. 3	Oct. 17
Riparia × Rupestris, No. 101	F	1907	1907	88	c, s		3 to 5	Mar. 20	Mar. 30	May 17	May 21	May 27			
Rupestris [illegible]a	F	1907	1907	85	s	3	3 to 4	...do	Apr. 2	May 15	May 23	May 24		Sept. 6	Sept. 21
Ajmi:															
[illegible]ir	O	1906	1909	88	s	1.5		Mar. 27		June 8	June 13	June 17	June 20		
A[illegible]eo:															
[illegible]n roots	Gi	1904		90	s			Mar. 14	Mar. 25	May 29	May 30	June 2	June 5	Sept. 3	Sept. 23
Dog Ridge	O	1904	1906	91	c, s	3.5	2 to 5	Mar. 20		May 23	June 1	May 28	June 17	Sept. 24	Oct. 6
Lenoir	O	1903	1905	88	s	3.8	2 to 4	Mar. 16		May 21	June 3	May 26	June 19	...do	Oct. 5
Rupestris St. George	O	1903	1905	93	c, s	3	2 to 4	Mar. 18		May 26	...do	June 1	June 17	Sept. 22	Oct. 2
[illegible]or Narbonne	O	1904	1906	81	s	3.2	2 to 5	Mar. 17		May 25	June 8	May 30	June 15	Oct. 4	

TABLE VII.—*Relative behavior and value for different purposes of grape varieties tested by grafting on resistant stocks and by growing on their own roots in eleven experiment vineyards in California*—Continued.

Variety and stock (on own roots, if so stated).	Experiment vineyard.	Year stock was planted.	Year grafted.	Congeniality.	How pruned.	Weight of pruning per vine.	Nodes bearing fruit.	Growth-starting date. Early season.	Growth-starting date. Late season.	Blossoming date. Early season.	Blossoming date. Late season.	Fruit-setting date. Early season.	Fruit-setting date. Late season.	Fruit-ripening date. Early season.	Fruit-ripening date. Late season.
1	2	3	4	5	6	7	8	9	10	11	12	13	14	15	16
Alexandria:				P. ct.		Lbs.									
Own roots	Gi	1904		78	s			Mar. 26	Apr. 1	May 23	do.	June 2	do.	Sept. 16	Sept. 24
Adobe Giant	F	1904	1906	86	s	1.3	2 to 6	Mar. 13	do.	May 14	May 26	May 25	June 2	Sept. 4	Sept. 20
Aramon × Rupestris Ganzin, No. 1	F	1904	1906	83	s	1.5	3 to 5	Mar. 14	do.	May 15	May 24	May 29	June 1	Sept. 12	Sept. 22
Aramon × Rupestris Ganzin, No. 2	F	1907	1909	87	s	2.5		Apr. 1		May 22				Sept. 15	Sept. 27
Australis	F	1907	1909	88	s	3		do.		May 21				Oct. 16	
Berlandieri × Riparia, No. 420A	F	1907	1909	89	s	2		Mar. 24		do.				Sept. 15	Oct. 16
Constantia	F	1907	1909	87	s	2.5		Mar. 23		May 25					
Dog Ridge	F	1904	1906	90	s	2.3	2 to 5	Mar. 14	Apr. 6	May 23	May 29	May 28	June 11	Sept. 8	Sept. 20
Herbemont	F	1903	1905	82	s	1.3	3 to 5	do.	Apr. 1	May 12	May 30	do.	June 8	do.	Do.
Lenoir	F	1903	1905	85	s	1.5	2 to 5	Mar. 18	do.	May 14	May 29	May 24	June 5	Sept. 9	Sept. 15
[illegible]la × Riparia, No. 18808	F	1907	1909	86	s	3		Mar. 29		May 20				Oct. 16	
Monticola × [illegible]	F	1907	1909	88	s	3.6		Mar. 27		May 25				do.	
Mourvèdre × Rupestris, No. 1202	F	1904	1906	86	s	2.5	3 to 5	Mar. 13	Apr. 3	May 14	June 1	May 24	June 10	Sept. 4	Sept. 20
Riparia Gloire	F	1903	1905	83	s	4	3 to 6	Mar. 14	Apr. 1	May 13	May 30	May 25	June 9	Sept. 9	Do.
Riparia × Cordifolia × Rupestris, No. 106-8	F	1907	1909	87	s	5.5		Mar. 24		May 20				Oct. 16	
Riparia × Rupestris, No. 101	F	1904	1906	90	c, s	2	2 to 5	Mar. 12	Apr. 5	do.	May 31	May 28	June 7	Sept. 5	Sept. 20
Riparia × Rupestris, No. 101-14	F	1907	1909	89	s	3.5		Mar. 25		May 26				Oct. 16	
Riparia × Rupestris, No. 3306	F	1907	1909	87	s	2.5		Mar. 31		May 23					
Riparia × Rupestris, No. 3309	F	1904	1906	91	s	4	1 to 5	Mar. 13	Apr. 5	May 18	May 29	May 28	June 5	Sept. 5	Sept. 20
Rupestris Martin	F	1903	1905	85	s	1.6	2 to 5	Mar. 8	Apr. 1	May 13	May 31	May 27	do.	Sept. 8	Do.
Rupestris St. George	F	1903	1905	89	s	2	2 to 5	Mar. 14	do.	May 15	May 28	May 26	do.	do.	Do.
Rupestris × Berlandieri, No. 219A	F	1907	1908	87	s	3		Apr. 1		May 22					
Salt Creek	F	1903	1905	86	s	1.6	3 to 6	Mar. 7	Apr. 1	May 16	May 29	May 21	June 3	Sept. 10	Sept. 20
Solonis Robusta	F	1907	1909	84	s	1		Mar. 29	May 22						
Solonis × Othello, No. 1613	F	1907	1909	86	s	3		Mar 8		May 25				Oct. 16	
Solonis × Riparia, No. 1616	F	1904	1906	88	s	2.4	2 to 5	Mar. 14	Apr. 5	May 22	May 30	May 27	June 8	Sept. 4	Sept. 20
Taylor Narbonne	F	1904	1906	85	s	1.8	3 to 5	Mar. 13	Apr. 1	May 13	May 29	do.	June 4	Sept. 15	Do.
Vialla	F	1907	1911	80	s	1		Mar. 25		May 20					

Alicante:															
Own roots	Gi	1905			s			Mar. 22		do	May 25	May 26	May 29		
[illegible]ir	F	1903	1905	84	s	.8	3 to 5	Mar. 14	Apr. 1	May 15	May 20	May 20	May 26	Aug. 25	Sept. 20
Riparia × Rupestris, No. 3306	O	1904			c, s	2.5		Mar. 4		May 9	May 29	May 15	June 2		
Rupestris St. George	F	1903	1905	87	s	1	3 to 5	Mar. 14	Apr. 3	May 12	May 18	May 22	May 24	Aug. 25	Sept. 19
Al[illegible]e ([illegible] [illegible]ite):															
Own roots	Gi	1905			s			Mar. 12	Mar. 28	May 26	May 27	May 30			
[illegible]ite Bouschet:															
Own roots	Gi	1904			c, s			Mar. 15	do	May 10	May 29	May 31	June 4	Sept. 15	Sept. 23
([illegible]is × Monticola) × (Riparia × Rupestris, No. 554-5)	O	1907	1909	78	s	.8	2 to 3	Mar. 18		May 25	June 1	June 6		Oct. 5	Oct. 30
Aramon × Rupestris Ganzin, No. 1	O	1904	1906	91	s	3.8	2 to 5	do		May 6	do	May 30	June 19	Sept. 25	Oct. 9
Aramon × Rupestris Ganzin, No. 2	O	1907	1909	68	s	.7		do		June 1		June 6			
Berlandieri × Riparia, No. 420A	O	1907	1909	85	s	2	2 to 3	Mar. 20		May 25	June 2	do	June 9	Oct. 5	Oct. 10
Constantia	O	1907	1909	80	s	.5	2 to 3	Mar. 17		May 26	June 1	June 4	June 19	Sept. 25	
Dog Ridge	O	1903	1905	88	s	3.3	2 to 4	Mar. 20		May 21	June 5	May 27	June 22	Sept. 21	Oct. 10
Herbemont	O	1903	1905	79	s	1.9	2 to 6	Mar. 22		May 19	June 1	May 24	June 6	Sept. 29	Oct. 5
Lenoir	O	1903	1905	88	s	3.4	2 to 6	Mar. 24		May 21	June 3	May 26	June 14	Sept. 28	Oct. 15
Mona × [illegible]ia, No. 18808	O	1907	1909	91	s	17		Mar. 16		June 1		June 6	June 17		
Monticola × Riparia, No. 18815	O	1907	1909	83	s	2	2 to 4	Mar. 24		May 29	June 1	June 5	June 20	Oct. 5	Oct. 10
Mourvedre × Rupestris, No. 1202	O	1904	1906	72	s	.5	3 to 5	Mar. 18		May 28		June 6			
Riparia × Rupestris, No. 101	O	1904	1906	55	s	1.6	2 to 6			May 24	June 1	May 30	June 5	Sept. 28	Oct. 11
Riparia × Rupestris, No. 101-14	O	1907	1909	75	s	1.4		Mar. 18		June 1		June 5			
Riparia × Rupestris, No. 3306	O	1907	1909	88	s	1.5	3 to 4	do		do	June 8	June 6	June 20	Oct. 11	Oct. 12
Riparia × Rupestris, No. 3309	O	1904	1906	88	s	2.2	2 to 5	do		May 25	June 1	May 30	June 11	Sept. 26	Oct. 6
Rupestris Martin	O	1903	1905	91	s	3.7	2 to 6	Mar. 31		May 20	do	May 25	June 12	do	Do.
Rupestris Metallica	O	1907	1909	80	s	.5		Mar. 20		May 31		June 4			
Rupestris Mission	O	1907	1909	64	s	1		do		June 2	June 3	June 7	June 15		
Rupestris St. George	O	1903	1905	88	s	3.3	2 to 4	Mar. 19		May 22	June 5	May 25	June 17	Sept. 25	Oct. 10
Salt Creek	O	1903	1905	88	c, s	1.4	3 to 6			May 21		May 26		Sept. 27	Oct. 6
[illegible]is [illegible]ta	O	1907	1909	85	s	1.5		Mar. 18		May 28	June 1	June 4	June 15		
Solonis × Othello, No. 1613	O	1907	1909	85	s	1.5	2 to 3	Mar. 20		June 2	June 5	June 8	do	Sept. 25	
Solonis Riparia, No. 1616	O	1904	1906	78	s	1.8	2 to 5	Mar. 18		May 26	June 3	June 2	June 20	do	Oct. 5
Taylor Narbonne	O	1904	1906	84	s	3	2 to 5	Mar. 17		May 27	June 1	do	June 16	Sept. 26	Oct. 8
Almeria:															
Own roots	Gi	1904			s			Mar. 15	Mar. 28	June 3	June 6	June 13			
[illegible]t	O	1904	1908	89	s	3.2	2 to 5	Mar. 20		do	June 8	June 9	June 30	Oct. 1	Oct. 10
Lenoir	O	1903	1908	86	s	1.3	2 to 7	Mar. 19		June 1	June 10	June 6	June 29	Sept. 25	Oct. 12
Riparia × Rupestris, No. 101	O	1904	1908	91	s	3	2 to 5	Mar. 18		June 3	June 8	June 9	do	Sept. 24	Oct. 10
Riparia × Rupestris, No. 3309	O	1904	1908	94	s	.26	3 to 6	Mar. 24		May 31	June 1	June 5	June 15	do	Oct. 12
Solonis × Riparia, No. 1616	O	1904	1908	91	s	3.2	2 to 6	Mar. 22		do	June 2	June 7	do	Sept. 26	Oct. 1
Aneb el Cadi:															
Adobe Giant	F	1907	1907	96	c, s	9.7	3 to 4	Mar. 23	Apr. 6	May 18	May 22	June 6		Sept. 15	Sept. 21
Lenoir	O	1904	1907	89	c, s	3.2	3 to 4	Mar. 22		May 20	June 7	May 24	June 19	Sept. 29	Oct. 20
Monticola × Rupestris	F	1907	1907	97	c, s	8		Mar. 10	Apr. 5	May 23	May 25	June 11			
Mourvedre × Rupestris, No. 1202	F	1907	1907	93	c, s	5	2 to 6	Mar. 22	Mar. 30	May 16	May 21	May 26		Oct. 17	
Riparia Grand Glabre	F	1907	1907	96	c, s	9.6	2 to 4	Mar. 14	Apr. 5	May 19	May 28	June 5		do	
Angelina:															
Adobe Giant	F	1907	1907	93	c, s	3.25	3 to 6	Mar. 23	Mar. 28	May 14	May 23	May 20			
Lenoir	O	1904	1907	95	s	3.8	2 to 5	Mar. 18		May 22	June 3	May 27	June 16	Sept. 30	Oct. 7
Mourvedre × Rupestris, No. 1202	F	1907	1907	94	c, s	4.6		Mar. 24	Apr. 1	May 15	May 29	May 24		Sept. 5	

TABLE VII.—*Relative behavior and value for different purposes of grape varieties tested by grafting on resistant stocks and by growing on their own roots in eleven experiment vineyards in California*—Continued.

Variety and stock (on own roots, if so stated).	Experiment vineyard.	Year stock was planted.	Year grafted.	Congeniality.	How pruned.	Weight of pruning per vine.	Nodes bearing fruit.	Growth-starting date. Early season.	Growth-starting date. Late season.	Blossoming date. Early season.	Blossoming date. Late season.	Fruit-setting date. Early season.	Fruit-setting date. Late season.	Fruit-ripening date. Early season.	Fruit-ripening date. Late season.
1	2	3	4	5	6	7	8	9	10	11	12	13	14	15	16
Aramon:				*P. ct.*		*Lbs.*									
Aramon × Rupestris [illegible]in, No. 1	O	1904	1906	91	s	3.1	3 to 5	Mar. 19	......	May 22	June 3	May 28	June 17	Sept. 28	Oct. 20
Australis	F	1907	1907	90	c, s	2.5	2 to 5	Mar. 14	Mar. 25	May 5	May 21	May 23	......	Sept. 17	Sept. 21
Barnes	F	1907	1907	87	s	1.9	2 to 5	Mar. 18	Mar. 28	May 14	May 22	May 27	......	Sept. 10	Do.
Cornucopia	F	1907	1907	84	c, s	2	3 to 6	Mar. 12	Mar. 26	May 10	May 21	May 23	......	...do...	Sept. 21
De Grassett	F	1907	1907	91	c, s	3	3 to 7	...do...	......	......	......	...do...	......	Sept. 20	Oct. 17
Dog Ridge	O	1903	1905	92	s	3.1	3 to 6	Mar. 18	......	May 22	June 3	May 28	June 16	Sept. 29	Oct. 25
Herbemont	O	1903	1905	90	s	4.3	2 to 6	...do...	......	...do...	June 10	May 27	June 24	Oct. 5	Oct. 12
Hotporup	F	1907	1907	83	c, s	3	3 to 6	...do...	Apr. 1	May 16	May 21	May 25	......	Oct. 17	
Lenoir	O	1903	1905	93	s	3.7	2 to 5	Mar. 22	......	May 21	May 31	May 27	June 15	Sept. 27	Oct. 15
[illegible]la × Rupestris	F	1907	1907	86	c, s	3.5	3 to 5	Mar. 15	Mar. 28	May 14	May 23	May 24	......	......	
[illegible]e × Rupestris, No. 1202	O	1904	1906	90	s	2.8	3 to 5	Mar. 20	......	May 22	June 3	May 28	June 20	Sept. 27	Oct. 11
Ponroy	F	1907	1907	87	s	3.07	3 to 6	Mar. 19	Mar. 28	May 15	May 23	May 27	......	Sept. 16	Sept. 21
Ramsey	F	1907	1907	92	c, s	3.5	3 to 5	Mar. 12	Mar. 25	May 14	May 20	May 24	......	......	
Riparia × Rupestris, No. 101	F	1907	1907	82	s	2.5	......	Mar. 20	Mar. 28	May 10	May 23	......	......	Sept. 16	Sept. 21
Do	O	1907	1907	87	s	2.3	2 to 5	Mar. 18	......	May 19	June 2	May 24	June 14	Sept. 27	Oct. 15
Riparia × Rupestris, No. 3309	O	1904	1906	87	s	1.5	3 to 5	Mar. 20	......	May 20	June 1	May 26	June 11	...do...	Oct. 8
Riparia × Rup[illegible]tris de [illegible]er	F	1907	1907	83	s	3.2	3 to 5	Mar. 12	Apr. 1	May 16	May 21	...do...	......	Sept. 21	
Rupestris des Caussettes	F	1907	1907	85	c, s	2	......	Mar. 15	Mar. 26	May 15	May 22	May 29	......	......	
[illegible]is des Semis, No. 81-2	F	1907	1907	88	s	3	2 to 5	Mar. 13	Mar. 28	May 12	...do...	May 23	......	Sept. 17	Sept. 21
Rupestris [illegible]n	F	1907	1907	87	s	3.08	3 to 6	Mar. 15	Mar. 26	May 14	...do...	May 25	......	Sept. 10	Do.
Do	O	1903	1905	91	s	3.5	1 to 5	Mar. 20	......	May 24	May 31	May 30	June 11	Sept. 27	Oct. 13
[illegible]is St. [illegible]e	O	1903	1905	92	s	3.7	3 to 6	Mar. 18	......	May 22	June 1	May 27	June 13	Sept. 28	Oct. 10
[illegible]is × Berlandieri, No. 219A	F	1907	1907	87	c, s	2	2 to 5	Mar. 12	Apr. 1	May 12	May 21	May 28	......	Oct. 17	
Salt Creek	F	1907	1907	88	s	3.2	3 to 5	Mar. 11	Mar. 28	May 10	May 23	May 25	......	Sept. 8	Sept. 21
Do	O	1903	1905	91	s	2.1	1 to 5	Mar. 18	......	May 23	June 3	May 29	June 19	Sept. 26	Oct. 11
Solonis × Othello	F	1907	1907	85	s	1.9	3 to 5	...do...	Mar. 25	May 14	May 23	May 25	......	Sept. 16	Sept. 21
Solonis × Riparia, No. 1616	F	1907	1907	86	s	2.8	3 to 7	...do...	Mar. 30	May 17	May 21	May 28	......	...do...	Do.
Do	O	1904	1906	85	s	1.3	3 to 5	Mar. 20	......	May 22	June 2	...do...	June 20	Sept. 27	Oct. 13
[illegible]or Narbonne	O	1904	1906	89	s	3.6	3 to 6	...do...	......	May 21	June 5	May 26	...do...	Sept. 26	Oct. 15
Do	F	1907	1907	84	s	4	......	Mar. 22	......	May 22	......	......	......	Sept. 21	Sept. 26
Valencia	F	1907	1907	91	s	2.6	3 to 6	Mar. 16	Mar. 30	May 12	May 21	May 23	......	...do...	Oct. 5
Vermorel	F	1907	1907	89	c, s	2.6	3 to 5	Mar. 10	Mar. 26	May 15	May 23	May 29	......	Sept. 10	Sept. 21
[illegible]la	F	1907	1907	90	c, s	5	3 to 5	Mar. 20	Mar. 30	May 14	May 25	May 24	......	Sept. 16	Oct. 17

Askari:															
Own roots	Gi	1904			s			Mar. 24	Apr. 1	May 28	May 30	June 6			
[illegible]:															
Own roots	Gi	1904			s			Mar. 12	Mar. 30	May 24	...do...	May 29	June 6	Sept. 20	Sept. 25
[illegible]:															
Adobe Giant	F	1907	1907	80	c,s			Mar. 29		May 23					
Lenoir	O	1904	1907	88	s	3.3	3 to 5	Mar. 17		May 26	June 4	May 30	June 15	Sept. 30	Oct. 10
Baba:															
Own roots	Gi	1904			s			Mar. 18	Mar. 28	May 24	May 30	May 29	June 5	Aug. 29	Sept. 24
Dog Ridge	O	1904	1906	91	s	3.3	2 to 3	Mar. 24		May 25	June 5	June 7	June 21	Sept. 26	Oct. 10
Lenoir	O	1903	1905	90	s	3.3	2 to 4	...do...		May 23	...do...	May 29	June 20	Sept. 25	Oct. 6
Rupestris St. George	O	1903	1905	94	s	3.5	3 to 5	Mar. 21		May 20	...do...	May 26	June 18	Sept. 28	Oct. 8
Taylor Narbonne	O	1906	1906	90	s	3	2 to 5	...do...		May 23	June 8	May 28	June 20	Sept. 26	Oct. 10
Bakator:															
Own roots	Gi	1904		75	s			Mar. 14	Mar. 28	May 25	June 4	May 29	June 10	Sept. 25	
Aramon × Rupestris Ganzin, No. 1	O	1904	1906	90	s	3.5	2 to 4	Mar. 20		May 26	June 5	June 2	June 24	Sept. 22	Oct. 4
Dog Ridge	O	1904	1906	85	s	1.4		...do...		...do...	...do...	May 30	June 18	Sept. 23	Oct. 10
Lenoir	O	1903	1908	83	s	2.5	3 to 4	Mar. 19		May 24	June 10	May 28	June 15	Sept. 21	
Riparia × Rupestris, No. 101	O	1904	1904	90	s	4.4	3 to 4	Mar. 20		May 22	June 3	May 27	June 16	Sept. 23	Oct. 9
Riparia × Rupestris, No. 3309	O	1904	1906	88	c,s	3.5	3 to 4	Mar. 18		May 26	...do...	June 2	June 14	Sept. 20	Oct. 11
Rupestris St. George	F	1903	1905	90	s	3.2	2 to 5	Mar. 13	Mar. 30	May 17	May 22	May 24	May 28	Aug. 24	Sept. 19
Solonis × Riparia, No. 1616	O	1904	1906	89	s	3.4	3 to 5	Mar. 18		May 23	June 10	May 28	June 28	Sept. 22	Oct. 7
Taylor Narbonne	O	1904	1906	93	s	4.3	3 to 4	Mar. 21		May 26	June 5	June 2	June 19	...do...	Oct. 4
Barbarossa:															
Own roots	Gi	1905			c,s			Mar. 14	Apr. 1	May 25	May 27	May 30	June 3	Sept. 24	
Adobe Giant	F	1904	1906	87	c,s	1.9	3 to 5	Mar. 9	...do...	May 13	May 16	May 22	May 27	Aug. 25	Sept. 21
Aramon × Rupestris Ganzin, No. 1	F	1904	1906	93	c,s	4.1	2 to 6	Mar. 14	Mar. 30	...do...	May 20	May 23	May 26	Sept. 10	Sept. 20
Dog Ridge	F	1904	1906	87	s	2.7	3 to 6	Mar. 12	...do...	May 15	...do...	May 25	...do...	Sept. 15	Do.
Do	O	1904	1906	96	c,s	5.5	2 to 4	Mar. 19		May 25	June 1	May 30	June 21	Sept. 27	Oct. 5
Lenoir	F	1903	1905	82	s	1	3 to 6	Mar. 18	Mar. 28	May 15	May 20	May 20	May 29	Aug. 24	Sept. 19
Do	O	1903	1905	89	s	2.8	3 to 5	Mar. 19		May 19	June 1	May 25	June 12	Sept. 25	Oct. 15
Riparia Gloire	F	1903	1905	84	s	2.7	3 to 6	Mar. 11	Apr. 1	May 10	May 16	May 20	May 26	Aug. 24	Sept. 19
Riparia × Rupestris, No. 3309	F	1904	1906	89	s	2.2	3 to 6	Mar. 8	Apr. 5	...do...	May 18	May 22	May 28	Sept. 12	Sept. 20
Rupestris St. George	F	1903	1905	85	s	2.9	3 to 6	Mar. 13	Mar. 30	May 13	May 16	May 21	May 29	Aug. 24	Sept. 19
Do	O	1903	1905	92	c,s	4.9	3 to 6	Mar. 19		May 24	June 2	May 30	June 14	Sept. 25	Oct. 10
Solonis × Riparia, No. 1616	F	1904	1906	87	s	1.9	3 to 6	Mar. 16	Mar. 28	May 13	May 18	May 23	May 25	Aug. 25	Sept. 2
Taylor Narbonne	O	1904	1906	89	s	2	2 to 5	Mar. 20		May 26	June 1	June 2	June 12	Sept. 25	Oct. 5
Barbarossa [illegible]:															
Own roots	Gi	1904			c,s			Mar. 13	Apr. 3	May 27	May 30	May 31	June 5	Aug. 28	Sept. 23
Barbera:															
Own roots	Gi	1904			s			Mar. 15	Mar. 30	May 22	...do...	May 27	...do...	Aug. 29	Sept. 20
Dog Ridge	O	1904	1907	83	s	2.3	2 to 4	Mar. 18		May 19	June 3	May 24	June 15	Sept. 24	
Lenoir	O	1903	1905	87	s	2.6	3 to 4	...do...		May 26	June 5	May 30	June 14	Sept. 20	Oct. 5
Rupestris St. George	O	1903	1905	86	s	1.9	3 to 5	Mar. 19		do.	June 2	June 1	June 13	Sept. 22	Sept. 27
Taylor Narbonne	O	1904	1906	85	s	.9	2 to 3	Mar. 17		do.	May 31	June 2	June 10	...do...	Oct. 10
Barducci:															
Adobe Giant	F	1907	1907	79	s	1.5		Mar. 12	Mar. 25	May 12	May 21	May 23		Sept. 15	Sept. 21
Lenoir	O	1904	1907	88	s	2	2 to 5	Mar. 22		May 21	June 5	May 26	June 17	Sept. 26	

TABLE VII.—*Relative behavior and value for different purposes of grape varieties tested by grafting on resistant stocks and by growing on their own roots in eleven experiment vineyards in California*—Continued.

Variety and stock (on own roots, if so stated).	Experiment vineyard.	Year stock was planted.	Year grafted.	Congeniality.	How pruned.	Weight of pruning per vine.	Nodes bearing fruit.	Growth-starting date. Early season.	Growth-starting date. Late season.	Blossoming date. Early season.	Blossoming date. Late season.	Fruit-setting date. Early season.	Fruit-setting date. Late season.	Fruit-ripening date. Early season.	Fruit-ripening date. Late season.
1	2	3	4	5	6	7	8	9	10	11	12	13	14	15	16
Bastardo:				P. ct.		Lbs.									
On roots	Gi	1904		86	c,s			Mar. 15	Mar. 20	May 26	June 3	May 31	June 10	Aug. 26	Sept. 20
Dog Ridge	O	1904	1906	92	c,s	4.5	3 to 4	Mar. 17		May 27	June 5	June 3	June 20	Sept. 23	Oct. 2
Lenoir	O	1903	1905	90	c,s	5.3	2 to 3	Mar. 15		May 19	May 21	May 24	June 19	Sept. 20	Sept. 24
Rupestris St. George	O	1903	1905	93	s	4.5	2 to 4	Mar. 23		May 22	June 1	May 28	June 15	Sept. 25	Oct. 10
Taylor Narbonne	O	1904	1906	92	s	4.8	2 to 3	Mar. 19		May 28	do.	June 4	do.	do.	Oct. 8
Beclan:															
On roots	Gi	1904			s			Mar. 17	Mar. 30	May 24	May 30	May 29	June 7	Sept. 16	Sept. 25
Dog Ridge	O	1904	1906	90	s	3.6	2 to 4	Mar. 24		May 20	June 8	May 24	June 20	Sept. 28	Oct. 15
Lenoir	O	1903	1905	88	s	2.8	2 to 4	Mar. 19		May 22	do.	May 27	June 22	do.	Do.
Rupestris St. George	O	1903	1905	83	s	2.6	2 to 5	Mar. 16		do.	May 31	do.	June 16	Sept. 26	Oct. 10
Taylor Narbonne	O	1904	1906	83	s	1.3	2 to 5	Mar. 18		May 23	June 1	May 28	June 11	Sept. 29	Do.
Bellino:															
On roots	Gi	1904			s			Mar. 17	Apr. 1	May 27					
Adobe Giant	F	1904	1906	88	s	1.2	3 to 5	Mar. 13	Mar. 28	May 15	May 20	May 20	May 31	Aug. 25	Sept. 21
Aramon × Rupestris Ganzin, No. 1	F	1904	1906	93	c,s	4.5	3 to 6	do.	Mar. 25	May 16	do.	May 24	June 1	do.	Sept. 20
Dog Ridge	F	1904	1906	90	s	5.1	3 to 5	Mar. 14	Apr. 2	May 15	May 29	May 25	June 7	Aug. 24	Do.
Do	O	1904	1906	87	s	3.3	3 to 4	Mar. 24		May 24	June 8	May 29	June 13	Sept. 26	Oct. 8
Lenoir	F	1903	1905	88	s	1.3	3 to 6	Mar. 7	Mar. 30	May 12	May 16	May 21	May 24	Aug. 25	Sept. 13
Do	O	1903	1905	92	s	4.2	3 to 5	Mar. 18		May 26	June 1	June 2	June 20	Sept. 25	
Mourvèdre × Rupestris, No. 1202	F	1904	1906	88	c,s	4.2	3 to 6	Mar. 6	Apr. 1	May 20	May 26	May 24	June 1	Aug. 25	Sept. 20
Ponroy	F	1907	1907	93	c,s	3		Mar. 15	do.	May 15	May 22	May 28		Oct. 17	
Riparia × Rupestris, No. 101	F	1904	1906	90	s	3.1	3 to 5	do.	Mar. 28	May 12	May 20	May 25	May 28	Aug. 25	Sept. 10
Riparia × Rupestris, No. 3309	F	1904	1906	92	c,s	4	3 to 6	Mar. 7	Apr. 1	May 8	do.	May 24	May 27	do.	Sept. 20
Rupestris [illegible]	F	1907	1907	83	c,s	2		Mar. 20		May 22					
Rupestris St. George	F	1903	1905	89	s	3.7	2 to 5	Mar. 12	Mar. 28	May 10	May 20	May 22	May 25	Aug. 25	Sept. 19
Do	O	1903	1905	93	s	3.4	3 to 5	Mar. 14		May 22	June 1	May 28	June 13	Sept. 26	Sept. 30
Solonis × Riparia, No. 1616	F	1904	1906	87	s	1.8	2 to 5	Mar. 7	Mar. 25	May 16	May 20	May 25	May 27	Aug. 25	Sept. 20
Taylor Narbonne	F	1904	1906	87	c,s	3.7	3 to 5	Mar. 18	do.	May 13	May 25	May 22	May 30	do.	Do.
Do	O	1904	1906	90	s	3	2 to 3	Mar. 22		May 21	June 1	May 26	June 14	Sept. 24	Oct. 8
Vermorel	F	1907	1907	86	s	3.5		Mar. 20		May 23				Oct. 16	

Bengi:															
Own roots	O	1904			s			Mar. 25		June 10	[illegible] 13	June 16	June 25		
Bermestia Bianca:															
Rupestris St. George	F	1903	1905	88	s	2.4	3 to 7	Mar. 12	Mar. 20	May 10	May 15	May 20	May 30	Aug. 24	Sept. 19
Besson:															
Own roots	Gi	1904			s			Mar. 15	Mar. 29	May 30	June 3	June 3	June 8	Aug. 27	Sept. 25
Bhokri:															
Own roots	O	1904			s	3.5		Mar. 20		May 12	June 5	May 18	June 18		
B[illegible]:															
Adbe Giant	F	[illegible]04	1906	85		2.1	2 to 5	Mar. 24	Apr. 2	May 17	May 22	May 27	June 6	Aug. 25	Sept. 21
Australis	F	1907	[illegible]07	88	s	2	2 to 5	Mar. 20	Apr. 3	May 16	May 24	May 25		do	Oct. 17
[illegible]s	F	1907	[illegible]07	94	s		3 to 6	do		May 21					
[illegible]eri × Riparia, No. 420B	F	1907	[illegible]07	85	s	4		Mar. 21	Apr. 1	May 15	May 25	May 30			
Constantia	F	1907	[illegible]07	88	c, s	3.6	3 to 5	Mar. 22	Mar. 30	May 18	May 24	June 4		Aug. 25	Sept. 21
De [illegible]tt	F	1907	[illegible]07	85	c, s	5.4	4 to 5	Mar. 23	Apr. 1	May 12	do	May 25			
Dog [illegible]e	O	1904	[illegible]07	86	s	3	3 to 5	Mar. 18		May 23	[illegible] 1	May 29	June 20	Sept. 23	Oct. 4
[illegible]ir	O	1903	[illegible]05	86	s	2.9	2 to 6	Mar. 19	Mar. 21	May 20	June 4	May 25	June 17	do	Oct. 17
[illegible]la × Rupestris	F	1907	[illegible]07	86	c, s	3	4 to 6	Mar. 23	Apr. 3	May 15	May 24	May 28	May 30	Sept. 15	Oct. 7
[illegible]y	F	1907	[illegible]07	93	c, s	7.7	4 to 6	Mar. 17	do	do	May 21	May 23	May 28		
[illegible]ley	F	1907	[illegible]07	90	c, s	5.7	4 to 6	Mar. 21	do	May 14	May 24	May 29		Aug. 25	Sept. 21
Riparia Gloire	O	1904		89	c, s	6	2 to 5	Mar. 19		May 10	June 5	May 16	June 17	Sept. 28	Oct. 4
Riparia × [illegible]s, No. 3306	O	1904		93	c, s	4.5				May 19	June 3	May 24	June 10		
[illegible]a × [illegible], No. 3309	F	1907	1907	96	c, s	10	4 to 5	Mar. 19	Apr. 1	May 17	May 22	May 30		Aug. 25	Sept. 20
[illegible]s [illegible]s [illegible]s	F	1907	1907	85	s	4		Mar. 25	Apr. 3	May 18	May 20	May 29			
[illegible]s St. [illegible]e	O	1903	1905	92	s	4.4	2 to 4	Mar. 22		May 26	June 3	June 2	June 20	Sept. 24	Sept. 30
Do	F	1903	1905	85	s	2.8	2 to 6	Mar. 11	Mar. 30	May 13	May 18	May 20	May 25	Aug. 24	Sept. 19
R[illegible]is × Berlandieri, No. 219A	F	[illegible]07	1907	81	s	2		Apr. 3		May 15		May 26			
Solonis [illegible]a	F	[illegible]07	1907	94	c, s	7.1	3 to 5	Mar. 12	Apr. 1	May 14	May 21	May 24		Sept. 17	Sept. 21
[illegible]r Narbonne	O	1904	1906	70	s	1		Mar. 20		May 21	May 26				
Vala	F	1907	1907	88	c, s	5		Mar. 23		May 22				Aug. 25	Sept. 20
Bl[illegible]k [illegible]ith:															
Own roots	Gi	1904			c, s			Mar. 16	Mar. 27	May 28	June 6	June 1	June 11	Sept. 17	Oct. 10
D[illegible]k [illegible]:															
Own [illegible]s	Gi	1905			s			Mar. 10	Apr. 1	May 25	May 30	May 30		Aug. 28	[illegible]t. 28
B[illegible]k [illegible]:															
Dog Ridge	O	1904	1906	96	s	4.4	3 to 4	Mar. 13		May 30	May 31	June 5	June 12	Sept. 27	
[illegible]ir	O	1904	1906	85	s	2.1	2 to 4	Mar. 20		May 25	June 5	May 28	June 23	Oct. 1	Oct. 15
[illegible]k [illegible]o:															
Own [illegible]s	Gi	1904			s			Mar. 21	Apr. 3	May 26	June 12	June 3	June 19	Sept. 24	[illegible]. 25
[illegible]k [illegible]t:															
Own [illegible]s	Gi	1904			s			Mar. 28	Mar. 30	do	June 7	May 31	June 10	Sept. 15	[illegible]. 24
[illegible]k Prince:															
Own [illegible]s	Gi	1904			s			Mar. 16	Mar. 28	do	[illegible] 5	do	June 11	do	Sept. 25
Dog R[illegible]e	O	1904	1906	93	s	6.5	2 to 4	Mar. 26		[illegible]a	June 11	[illegible] 2	June 24	Sept. 28	Oct. 8
Lenoir	O	1903	1905	95	c, s	4.8	3 to 5	do		May 22	June 7	May 28	June 16	do	[illegible]. 9
[illegible]s St. George	O	1903	1905	93	s	6.8	2 to 4	Mar. 24		do	June 5	[illegible]y 27	June 21	Sept. 26	[illegible]. 10
[illegible]r [illegible]e	O	1904	1906	92	s	3	3 to 6	do		May 27	June 10	June 2	June 19	Sept. 24	Do.
[illegible]k Shahanee:															
Own [illegible]ots	Gi	1904			s			Mar. 12	Apr. 1	do	June 1	June 7		Sept. 20	
Bl[illegible]k Zante:															
Own [illegible]ots	Gi	1904			c, s			Mar. 24	Mar. 26	May 29	June 6	[illegible]e 3	June 13	do	Sept. 24

TABLE VII.—*Relative behavior and value for different purposes of grape varieties tested by grafting on resistant stocks and by growing on their own roots in eleven experiment vineyards in California*—Continued.

Variety and stock (on own roots, if so stated).	Experiment vineyard.	Year stock was planted.	Year grafted.	Congeniality.	How pruned.	Weight of pruning per vine.	Nodes bearing fruit.	Growth-starting date.		Blossoming date.		Fruit-setting date.		Fruit-ripening date.	
								Early season.	Late season.	Early season.	Late season.	Early season.	Late season.	Early season.	Late season.
1	2	3	4	5	6	7	8	9	10	11	12	13	14	15	16
Blanc d'Ambre:				*P. ct.*		*Lbs.*									
Lenoir	O	1904	1907	86	s	2.7	3 to 5	Mar. 17		May 18	May 31	May 23	June 14	Sept. 25	Sept. 25
Monticola × Rupestris	F	1907	1907	80	s	1.8	3 to 5	Mar. 15	Mar. 25	May 14	May 22	May 24			
Mourvedre × Rupestris, No. 1202	F	1907	1907	83	s	3.5		Mar. 14	..do..	May 13		May 25		Sept. 15	
Salt Creek	F	1907	1907	92	s	5	4 to 5	Mar. 24	Apr. 1	May 12	May 22	May 29			
Blauer Portugieser:															
Own roots	Gi	1904			s			Mar. 17	Mar. 29	May 24	May 28	May 30	June 7	Aug. 28	Sept. 20
Dog Ridge	O	1904	1906	92	s	5.2	3 to 4	Mar. 18		May 25	June 1	..do..	June 13	Sept. 23	Oct. 8
Lenoir	O	1903	1905	92	s	4	3 to 5	..do..		May 19	May 31	May 25	June 4	Sept. 10	Oct. 2
Rupestris St. George	O	1903	1905	89	s	2.7	2 to 4	Mar. 19		May 25	June 5	May 30	June 15	Sept. 15	Oct. 4
Boal de Madere:															
Own roots	Gi	1904			s			..do..	Mar. 26	May 24	June 1	May 29	June 7	Aug. 27	Sept. 23
Dog Ridge	O	1904	1907	89	s	3	2 to 4	Mar. 22		..do..	June 2	May 30	June 16	Sept. 28	Oct. 6
Lenoir	O	1903	1905	95	s	4.9	3 to 4	Mar. 19		May 26	June 1	..do..	June 15	Sept. 15	Sept. 24
Rupestris St. George	O	1903	1905	95	c, s	5.1	2 to 4	..do..		May 21	May 30	May 26	June 13	Sept. 24	Oct. 6
Taylor Narbonne	O	1904	1906	92	s	4.1	2 to 4	Mar. 20		May 25	June 1	May 30	..do..	Sept. 25	Oct. 10
Boglich:															
Own roots	Gi				s			Mar. 14	Mar. 28	May 26	May 30	May 31	June 1		
Bolynino:															
Own roots	Gi	1904			s			..do..	Apr. 1	May 20	June 6	May 30	June 13	Sept. 18	Sept. 24
Dog Ridge	O	1904	1906	88	c, s	3.9	2 to 6	Mar. 20		May 25	June 5	..do..	June 20	Sept. 26	
Lenoir	O	1903	1905	91	s	3.4	3 to 5	Mar. 17		May 20	June 3	May 24	June 17	Sept. 28	Oct. 1
Rupestris St. George	O	1903	1905	90	s	4.5	2 to 4	Mar. 19		May 22	June 8	May 27	June 20	Sept. 24	Oct. 8
Taylor Narbonne	O	1904	1906	88	c, s	4.6	2 to 4	Mar. 20		May 23	June 5	May 28	..do..	Sept. 25	Do.
Bonarda:															
Own roots	Gi	1904			s			Mar. 11	Apr. 2	June 3		June 9		Sept. 5	Sept. 23
Boudales:															
Own roots	Gi	1907			s			Mar. 28	Apr. 1	May 27				Sept. 20	
Lenoir	O	1903	1905	93	s	3.8		Mar. 20		May 24	June 6	May 30	June 17	Sept. 27	Oct. 15
Rupestris St. George	O	1903	1905	93	s	4.3	2 to 4	Mar. 22		May 25	June 5	June 2	..do..	..do..	Oct. 8
Bowood Muscat:															
Own roots	Gi	1904			s			Mar. 25	Apr. 5	June 5	June 6	June 14		Sept. 19	Sept. 24

[illegible]o:															
Adobe Giant	F	1907	1907	81	c, s	35		Mar. 20	Mar. 30	May 15	May 23	May 29			
Lenoir	O	1904	1907	87	s	3.2	2 to 5	do.		May 23	May 31	May 28	June 4	Aug. 27	
[illegible]la × Rupestris	F	1907	1907	83	c, s	3.3	3 to 5	Mar. 18	Mar. 28	May 15	May 23	May 24		Sept. 21	
[illegible]e × [illegible]s, No. 1202	F	1907	1907	90	c, s	5	2 to 5	Mar. 11	do.	May 14	May 28	May 28		do.	Oct. 17
[illegible]:															
Lenoir	O	1904	1907	81	s	2.6	3 to 5	Mar. 18		May 25	June 7	May 30	June 22	Sept. 25	Oct. 2
Rupestris St. [illegible]ge	F	1907	1907	91	c, s	2.8	3 to 4	Mar. 19	Mar. 28	May 20	May 26	June 2			
[illegible]d:															
Own roots	Gi	1905			s			Mar. 15	Apr. 3	May 25					
Lenoir	O	1903	1905	83	s	2.2	3 to 4	Mar. 22		May 23	June 5	May 27	June 14	Sept. 22	
[illegible]r:															
Own roots	Gi	1904			s			Mar. 15	Mar. 28	May 21	June 1	May 26	June 6	Aug. 29	Oct. 25
([illegible]lis × [illegible]a) × (Riparia × Rupestris No. 554–5)	O	1907	1909	78	s	2	2 to 4								
[illegible]mon × [illegible]is Ganzin, No. 1	O	1904	1906	89	s	2.7	2 to 6	Mar. 20		May 23	June 10	May 28	June 16	Sept. 30	Oct. 11
Aramon × Rupestris Ganzin, No. 2	O	[illegible]07	[illegible]09	79	s	.8	3 to 5	Mar. 21		June 1	June 5	June 6	June 17	Oct. 1	
[illegible]ri × Riparia, No. [illegible]20A	O	1907	1909	90	s	1.5	2 to 3	Mar. 24		June 2	June 3	do.	June 20	Oct. 10	Oct. 15
Constantia	O	1907	1909	86	s	1.9	2 to 4								
[illegible]d × Rupestris No. 2502	O	1907	1909	90	s	.8	2 to 4	Mar. 19		May 30	June 1	June 6	June 15	Oct. 10	Oct. 15
Dog Ridge	O	1903	1905	89	s	2	2 to 6	Mar. 17		May 22	June 5	May 27	June 21	Sept. 28	Oct. 20
Herbemont	O	1903	1905	80	s	14	3 to 5	Mar. 23		May 23	June 8	May 29	June 23	Sept. 30	Oct. 13
Lenoir	O	1903	1905	78	s	15	2 to 5	Mar. 19		May 24	June 5	do.	June 17	Sept. 27	Oct. 12
Monticola × Riparia, No. 18808	O	1907	[illegible]909	95	s	1.2		Mar. 21		May 28	May 31	June 5	June 15	Oct. 10	
Mourvedre × [illegible]s, No. 1202	O	1904	1906	89	s	2.4	3 to 4	Mar. 20		May 25	June 5	May 30	June 23	Sept. 29	Oct. 11
Riparia × Rupestris, No. 101	O	1904	[illegible]906	82	s	1.2	2 to 5	do.		May 21	June 6	May 26	June 25	Sept. 28	Oct. 20
Riparia × [illegible]o. 101–14	O	1907	1909	80	s	1	3 to 4	Mar. 19		June 1	June 5	June 4	June 19	Oct. 5	
Riparia × Rupestris, No. 3306	O	1907	1909	89	s	14	3 to 4	Mar. 21		June 2	June 8	June 6	June 23	Oct. 10	Oct. 11
Riparia × [illegible]o. 3309	O	1904	1906	60	s	.6	3 to 6	Mar. 20		May 23	do.	May 29	June 27	Sept. 27	Oct. 6
Rupestris [illegible]n	O	1903	1905	85	s	2.1	3 to 6	Mar. 18		May 22	do.	do.	June 20	Sept. 30	Oct. 10
[illegible]ca	O	1907	1909	68	s	.3		do.		May 31	do.	June 4	June 25		
[illegible]is Mission	O	1907	1909	62	s	.4		Mar. 19		June 2		June 6			
[illegible]is St. [illegible]ge	O	[illegible]03	1905	87	s	1.4	2 to 5	Mar. 16		May 22	May 31	May 27	June 10	Sept. 28	Oct. 10
Salt [illegible]eek	O	1903	1905	87	s	2	2 to 5	Mar. 17		May 23	June 3	May 28	June 20	do.	Oct. 11
Solonis Robusta	O	1907	1909	74	s	.7	3 to 5	Mar. 21		June 1	June 10	June 6	June 24	Oct. 10	Do.
Solonis × Othello, No. 1613	O	1907	1909	89	s	1	2 to 5	Mar. 18		June 3	June 5	do.	June 18	do.	Do.
[illegible]nis × Riparia, No. 1616	O	1904	1906	65	s	.7	3 to 5	Mar. 19		May 21	June 8	May 26	June 23	Sept. 27	Oct. 10
[illegible]	O	1904	1906	86	s	2.5	3 to 5	Mar. 17		May 22	June 5	May 29	June 18	Oct. 4	Oct. 15
Cabernet Sauvignon:															
Own [illegible]ts	Gi				s			Mar. 20	Apr. 3	May 27				Sept. 23	
Aramon × Rupestris [illegible]n, No. 1	O	1904	1906	92	c, s	4.3	2 to 5	do.		May 24	June 5	May 29	June 22	Sept. 25	Oct. 5
Dog [illegible]	O	1903	1905	97	c, s	4.7	2 to 4	Mar. 25		May 23	do.	do.	June 20	Sept. 23	Oct. 10
Herbemont	O	1903	1905	93	c, s	4.3	2 to 4	Mar. 24		do.	June 8	May 28	June 21	Sept. 24	Oct. 11
Lenoir	O	1903	1905	92	c, s	4	2 to 4	Mar. 26		May 20	June 7	May 26	June 20	Sept. 15	Oct. 5
Mourvedre × Rupestris, No. 1202	O	1904	1906	91	s	3.2	2 to 4	Mar. 20		May 24	June 10	May 29	June 27	Sept. 25	Oct. 6
Riparia × Rupestris, No. 101	O	1904	1906	88	c, s	3.2	2 to 4	Mar. 21		May 22	June 8	May 27	June 24	do.	Do.
Riparia × Rupestris, No. 3309	O	1904	1906	85	c, s	3.1	2 to 4	Mar. 20		May 26	do.	June 2	June 22	do.	Do.
Rupestris Martin	O	1903	1905	95	c, s	5.3	2 to 5	do.		May 22	June 5	May 25	do.	do.	Oct. 11
Rupestris St. George	O	1903	1905	91	c, s	4.2	2 to 4	Mar. 24		May 20	June 2	May 26	June 20	Sept. 24	Sept. 30
Salt Creek	O	1903	1905	92	c, s	4.1	2 to 4	Mar. 25		May 23	June 4	May 28	June 17	do.	Oct. 11
Solonis × Riparia, No. 1616	O	1904	1906	84	c, s	16	2 to 4	Mar. 20		May 24	June 2	June 2	June 19	Sept. 25	Do.
Taylor Narbonne	O	1904	1906	88	c, s	4.5	2 to 5	Mar. 24		May 26	June 18	do.	June 23	Sept. 22	Oct. 10

TABLE VII.—*Relative behavior and value for different purposes of grape varieties tested by grafting on resistant stocks and by growing on their own roots in eleven experiment vineyards in California*—Continued.

Variety and stock (on own roots, if so stated).	Experiment vineyard.	Year stock was planted.	Year grafted.	Congeniality.	How pruned.	Weight of pruning per vine.	Nodes bearing fruit.	Growth-starting date.		Blossoming date.		Fruit-setting date.		Fruit-ripening date.	
								Early season.	Late season.	Early season.	Late season.	Early season.	Late season.	Early season.	Late season.
1	2	3	4	5	6	7	8	9	10	11	12	13	14	15	16
Calabrian:				P. ct.		Lbs.									
Own roots	GI	1905	....	.....	c, s	....	....	Mar. 26	Mar. 29	May 31	June 4	June 9	....	Aug. 28	Sept. 15
Australis	F	1907	1907	88	c, s	4.5	3 to 5	Mar. 23	Apr. 3	May 16	May 23	May 31	....	Aug. 25	Sept. 5
Lenoir	F	1903	1905	86	s	1.2	4 to 6	Mar. 14	Apr. 1	May 18	May 20	May 22	June 3	Aug. 24	Sept. 19
Do	O	1904	1907	89	s	3.4	3 to 6	Mar. 21	....	May 23	June 5	May 27	June 19	Sept. 28	Oct. 5
Monticola × Rupestris	F	1907	1907	91	c, s	3	3 to 5	Mar. 25	Apr. 1	May 14	May 23	May 28	....	Sept. 25	
Riparia Gloire	F	1903	1905	89	c, s	4.3	2 to 6	Mar. 12	Mar. 30	May 20	May 20	May 24	June 2	Aug. 23	Sept. 16
Rupestris des Caussettes	F	1907	1907	85	c, s	3	3 to 4	Mar. 24	Apr. 3	May 16	May 24	June 1	....	....	
Rupestris St. George	F	1903	1905	94	s	4.2	3 to 6	Mar. 14	Mar. 31	May 12	May 16	May 21	May 27	Aug. 23	Sept. 19
Calmette:															
Adobe Giant	F	1907	1907	82	s	2	2 to 4	Mar. 17	Apr. 5	May 18	May 22	June 2	....	Sept. 6	Sept. 21
Aramon × Rupestris Ganzin, No. 1	F	1907	1907	85	s	2.7	3 to 5	Mar. 18	...do....	May 17	...do....	June 5	....	Sept. 8	Sept. 15
Do	O	1904	1907	92	c, s	4.9	2 to 5	Mar. 20	....	May 23	June 8	May 28	June 20	Sept. 26	Oct. 11
Berlandieri × Riparia, No. 420B	F	1907	1907	81	s	1.5	3 to 5	Mar. 24	Apr. 5	May 15	May 21	May 31	June 2	Sept. 10	Oct. 17
[illegible]a	F	1907	1907	96	c, s	5.8	2 to 5	Mar. 23	Apr. 2	...do....	May 23	May 30	....	....	
Herbemont	O	1904	1909	89	s	2.6	3 to 4	Mar. 20	....	June 1	June 8	June 8	June 20	Oct. 17	
Lenoir	O	1906	1907	82	s	2	2 to 4	Mar. 19	....	May 12	...do....	May 18	June 22	Sept. 28	Oct. 8
[illegible]cola × Riparia, No. 18804	F	1907	1907	85	c, s	2	3 to 5	Mar. 20	Apr. 2	May 10	May 22	May 29	May 30	Oct. 17	
[illegible]ola × Riparia, No. 18815	F	1907	1907	88	c, s	2.3	2 to 4	...do....	Apr. 5	May 15	May 23	May 30	June 3	Sept. 10	Oct. 17
[illegible]ola × Rupestris	F	1907	1907	84	s	1.2	3 to 4	Mar. 24	....	May 25	....	....	....	Sept. 5	Sept. 21
Ponroy	F	1907	1907	85	c, s	1.5	2 to 4	Mar. 21	Apr. 5	May 16	May 22	May 29	....	....	
Ramsey	F	1907	1907	81	s	2.5	3 to 5	...do....	...do....	...do....	May 23	June 4	June 5	Sept. 14	Sept. 21
Riparia × Rupestris, No. 101	F	1907	1907	90	c, s	2.2	3 to 5	Mar. 18	...do....	May 12	May 22	May 31	....	Sept. 21	
Do	O	1904	1907	55	s	2.3	2 to 6	Mar. 20	....	May 21	June 25	May 26	June 30	Sept. 26	Oct. 16
Riparia × Rupestris, No. 3309	F	1907	1907	87	c, s	3.1	2 to 5	...do....	Apr. 5	May 15	May 21	May 29	....	Sept. 19	
Do	O	1904	1907	58	s	2.8	2 to 5	Mar. 25	....	May 27	June 4	June 3	June 19	Sept. 26	Oct. 11
Riparia × Rupestris de Jaeger	F	1907	1907	80	c, s	1.4	3 to 5	Mar. 21	Apr. 6	May 16	May 22	...do....	June 4	Sept. 14	Sept. 20
Rupestris × Berlandieri, No. 219A	F	1907	1907	85	s	.7	2 to 5	Mar. 20	...do....	May 14	May 24	May 30	June 2	...do....	Sept. 21
Rupestris × Berlandieri, No. 301-37-152	F	1907	1907	82	s	2.2	....	Mar. 25	Apr. 1	May 17	May 21	May 29	....	....	
Salt Creek	F	1907	1907	83	s	2.5	....	Mar. 22	Apr. 2	...do....	....	June 2	....	....	
Solonis Robusta	F	1907	1907	76	s	1.5	3 to 5	Mar. 25	Apr. 3	May 23	June 20	June 1	....	Sept. 21	

[illegible] × Othello	F	1907	1907	85	c, s	2.3	2 to 5	Mar. 21	Apr. 5	May 15	May 23	May 29	June 3	Sept. 8	Sept. 21
Solonis × Riparia, No. 1616	F	1907	1907	88	s	4	....	Mar. 27	....	Mar. 23	....	....	....	Sept. 20	Oct. 17
Do.	O	1904	1907	56	s	1.2	2 to 5	Mar. 25	....	May 22	June 4	May 28	June 20	Sept. 28	Oct. 9
Taylor Narbonne	F	1907	1907	86	s	17	2 to 4	...do....	Apr. 6	May 16	May 22	June 2	....	....	
Vermorel	F	1907	1907	85	s	4	2 to 4	...do....	Apr. 1	...do....	...do....	May 29	....	Oct. 17	
Carignane:															
Own roots	Gi	1904	....	....	s	....	....	Mar. 18	Mar. 27	May 27	June 3	May 30	June 10	Sept. 20	Sept. 26
Aramon × Rupestris Ganzin, No. 1	O	1904	1906	92	s	3	[illegible]	Mar. 19	....	May 26	June 5	June 1	June 21	Sept. 28	Oct. 20
Dog Ridge	O	1903	1905	95	s	3.3	[illegible]	Mar. 23	....	May 25	June 7	...do....	June 23	...do....	Oct. 10
Herbemont	O	1903	1905	92	s	3.9	[illegible]	...do....	....	May 24	June 5	May 30	June 19	Sept. 24	Oct. 11
Lenoir	O	1903	1905	93	s	4.5	3 to 6	Mar. 26	....	May 25	June 7	...do....	June 21	Sept. 28	Oct. 12
Mourvedre × Rupestris, No. 1202	O	1904	1906	92	s	2.9	3 to 6	....	....	May 24	June 13	...do....	June 29	...do....	Oct. 11
Riparia × Rupestris, No. 101	O	1904	1906	92	s	2.2	[illegible]	Feb. 19	....	...do....	June 3	May 29	June 24	Sept. 25	Oct. 10
Riparia × Rupestris, No. 3309	O	1904	1906	9[illegible]	s	2.8	[illegible]	Mar. 17	....	May 24	June 3	May 29	June 24	Sept. 27	Oct. 6
[illegible]	O	[illegible]3	1905	90	c, s	4	[illegible]	Mar. 22	....	...do....	June 5	...do....	June 20	...do....	Oct. 7
Rupestris St. George	O	1903	1905	85	s	4.2	[illegible]	...do....	....	May 23	June 8	May 28	June 21	...do....	Oct. 8
[illegible]	O	1903	1905	95	c, s	2	[illegible]	Mar. 23	....	May 24	June 12	May 30	June 26	...do....	Oct. 10
Solonis × [illegible] No. 1616	O	1904	1906	90	s	2.1	[illegible]	Mar. 17	....	May 23	June 10	May 28	June 24	...do....	Oct. 11
Taylor Narbonne	O	1904	1906	90	c, s	3	[illegible]	Mar. 20	....	May 26	June 5	June 1	June 20	Sept. 29	Oct. 10
Cast[illegible]:															
[illegible]a × [illegible]stris, No. 3309	O	....	[illegible]0	90	s	2.1	....	....	....	June 3	June 15	June 7	June 29	....	
[illegible]to a la Porta:															
Own roots	Gi	1904	....	....	s	....	....	Mar. 25	Mar. 30	May 28	June 10	June 2	June 15	Sept. 15	Sept. 20
Ch[illegible]ach:															
Own roots	Gi	1904	....	....	s	....	....	Mar. 13	Mar. 25	May 29	June 3	June 10	....	Aug. 25	Do.
Lenoir	O	....	1910	91	s	4.5	2 to 3	Mar. 15	....	May 18	June 9	May 23	June 13	Sept. 24	
Chaouch Rose:															
Lenoir	O	1904	1907	97	c, s	4.3	3 to 5	Mar. 18	....	...do....	June 1	May 22	June 20	Sept. 29	
Ch[illegible]do:															
Own roots	Gi	1907	....	....	s	....	....	...do....	Apr. 5	May 27	....	....	....	Sept. 25	
Dog Ridge	O	1904	1906	92	c, s	5.5	2 to 4	....	....	May 24	....	May 29	....	Oct. 3	
Lenoir	O	1903	1905	93	c, s	3.9	2 to 5	....	....	May 21	....	May 26	....	Sept. 28	
Rupestris St. George	O	1903	1905	91	c, s	4	2 to 5	....	....	May 25	....	May 30	....	Sept. 27	Sept. 30
Riparia × Rupestris, No. 101	O	1904	1906	90	s	2.5	3 to 5	Mar. 18	....	May 24	June 8	...do....	June 20	Sept. 28	Oct. 6
Riparia × Rupestris, No. 3309	O	1904	1906	90	s	2.7	2 to 5	Mar. 20	....	May 26	...do....	June 2	June 21	Sept. 27	Do.
Solonis × Riparia, No. 1616	O	1904	1906	84	s	2	2 to 5	...do....	....	May 23	June 5	May 27	June 20	Sept. 24	Oct. 11
Taylor Narbonne	O	1904	1906	87	s	2.3	2 to 5	Mar. 17	....	May 24	...do....	May 29	...do....	Sept. 26	Oct. 10
Chasselas Bouches du Rhone:															
Own roots	Gi	1905	....	....	c, s	....	....	Mar. 18	Apr. 1	May 28	....	....	....	Sept. 5	Sept. 25
Dog Ridge	O	1904	1906	91	s	3.5	3 to 5	Mar. 15	....	May 24	June 1	May 29	June 16	Sept. 9	Oct. 10
Lenoir	O	1903	1905	90	c, s	3.3	2 to 5	Mar. 13	....	May 20	...do....	May 24	June 15	...do....	Oct. 9
Rupestris St. George	O	1903	1905	93	s	5.2	3 to 4	Mar. 17	....	May 21	June 5	May 26	June 21	...do....	Oct. 10
Taylor Narbonne	O	1904	1906	70	s	.5	3 to 5	Mar. 18	....	May 20	June 2	May 25	June 10	...do....	Sept. 21
Chasselas [illegible]:															
Dog Ridge	O	1904	1906	92	s	4	3 to 5	Mar. 15	....	May 23	June 1	May 29	June 13	Sept. 21	Oct. 10
Lenoir	O	1903	1905	87	s	4.2	2 to 5	...do....	....	May 20	June 8	May 23	June 21	Sept. 23	Sept. 25
Rupestris St. George	O	1903	1905	94	s	4.4	2 to 5	Mar. 14	....	May 24	June 1	May 30	June 13	Sept. 9	Sept. 20
Taylor Narbonne	O	1904	1906	75	s	1.6	3 to 5	Mar. 18	....	...do....	...do....	May 29	June 9	Sept. 23	Oct. 1

TABLE VII.—*Relative behavior and value for different purposes of grape varieties tested by grafting on resistant stocks and by growing on their own roots in eleven experiment vineyards in California*—Continued.

Variety and stock (on own roots, if so stated).	Experiment vineyard.	Year stock was planted.	Year grafted.	Congeniality.	How pruned.	Weight of pruning per vine.	Nodes bearing fruit.	Growth-starting date. Early season.	Growth-starting date. Late season.	Blossoming date. Early season.	Blossoming date. Late season.	Fruit-setting date. Early season.	Fruit-setting date. Late season.	Fruit-ripening date. Early season.	Fruit-ripening date. Late season.
1	2	3	4	5	6	7	8	9	10	11	12	13	14	15	16
Chasselas [illegible]t:				P. ct.		Lbs.									
Own roots	Gi	1907			s			Mar. 17	Apr. 10	May 28					
Dog Ridge	O	1904	1906	91	s	3.3	2 to 5	..do..		May 21	June 2	May 26	June 15	Sept. 9	Oct. 10
Lenoir	O	1903	1905	87	s	2.9	2 to 5	..do..		..do..	June 3	May 24	June 14	..do..	Oct. 1
Rupestris St. George	O	1903	1905	88	s	3.9	2 to 5	..do..		..do..	June 1	May 25	June 20	..do..	Oct. 2
Chasselas Doré:															
Own rots	Gi	1905			c, s			Mar. 20	Mar. 26	May 29	June 2	June 7		Aug. 24	Sept. 21
Dog Ridge	O	1904	1906	91	s	2.8	3 to 5	Mar. 14		May 25	May 31	May 30	June 12	Sept. 9	Oct. 10
Lenoir	O	1903	1905	94	c, s	3.5	3 to 5	..do..		May 21	June 1	May 24	June 20	..do..	Oct. 9
Rupestris St. George	O	1903	1905	94	s	6.1	2 to 5	Mar. 15		May 23	June 3	May 29	..do..	..do..	Oct. 2
Chas[illegible]s Duhamel:															
Aramon × Rupestris Ganzin, No. 1	O	1904		92	c, s	5	2 to 4	Mar. 21		May 31	June 1	June 2	June 13	Sept. 29	Oct. 8
Dog Ridge	O	1904	1906	91	s	4	3 to 4	Mar. 15		May 21	June 3	May 26	June 19	Sept. 9	Oct. 10
Lenoir	O	1903	1905	90	s	3.1	3 to 5	..do..		May 20	..do..	May 28	June 14	..do..	Sept. 30
Rupestris St. George	O	1903	1905	94	s	4.1	2 to 5	Mar. 21		May 21	June 8	May 26	June 24	..do..	Oct. 2
Taylor Narbonne	O	1904	1906		s	2.5								..do..	
Chasselas de Fontainebleau:															
[illegible]is St. George	F	1903	1905	85	s	1.5	2 to 6	Mar. 14	Mar. 30	May 15	May 17	May 20	May 24	Aug. 19	Sept. 19
Chasselas [illegible]:															
Own rots	Gi	1905			s			Mar. 8	Apr. 21	May 27	June 1	June 7		Sept. 23	
Dog [illegible]ge	O	1904	1906	91	s	4.7	2 to 5	Mar. 15		May 24	..do..	May 30	June 12	Sept. 9	Oct. 10
Lenoir	O	1903	1905	91	s	3.1	3 to 5	Mar. 16		May 22	May 31	May 27	June 15	..do..	Oct. 9
[illegible]is St. [illegible]ge	O	1903	1905	91	s	3.9	2 to 4	Mar. 17		May 25	June 1	June 1	June 18	..do..	Do.
Taylor Narbonne	O	1904	1906	82	s	1	2 to 3	Mar. 16		May 22	..do..	May 27	June 12	Sept. 21	
Chasselas Montauban:															
Own roots	Gi	1905			c, s			Mar. 18	Apr. 1	..do..	May 27	May 26			
Lenoir	O	1903	1905	95	s	2.5	2 to 6	Mar. 16		May 23	June 3	May 28	June 17	Sept. 9	Sept. 25
Rupestris St. [illegible]ge	O	1903	1907	91	s	4.7	2 to 5	Mar. 24		May 21	June 5	May 26	June 20	..do..	Oct. 12
Chasselas [illegible]e Vrai:															
Own rots	Gi	1907			s			Mar. 15	Mar. 20	May 25				Sept. 25	
Dog Ridge	O	1904	1906	91	s	3.2	2 to 5	Mar. 16		May 22	June 1	May 27	June 20	Sept. 9	Oct. 10
Lenoir	O	1903	1905	88	s	3.9	2 to 5	Mar. 20		May 20	..do..	May 24	June 18	..do..	Oct. 9
Rupestris St. George	O	1903	1905	94	s	6.2	1 to 4	Mar. 17		May 23	..do..	May 28	June 15	..do..	Oct. 10

Chasselas [illegible]:														
Own roots	Gi	1905	......	......	s	......	......	Mar. 6	Apr. 8	May 22	...do...	May 27	June 6	Sept. 21	
Dog Ridge	O	1904	1906	85	s	3.6	2 to 5	Mar. 17	......	May 24	June 3	May 29	June 19	Sept. 9	Oct. 1
[illegible]ir	O	1903	1905	90	s	3.6	2 to 5	Mar. 20	......	May 19	June 1	May 24	June 16	...do...	Oct. 9
[illegible]	O	1904	......	63	s	4	......	Mar. 16	......	...do...	...do...	May 14	June 12	......	
[illegible]s St. George	F	1903	1905	85	s	1.5	2 to 6	Mar. 13	Mar. 30	May 15	May 19	May 23	June 1	Aug. 5	Sept. 4
Do	O	1903	1905	88	s	4.6	2 to 5	Mar. 16	......	May 22	June 1	May 27	June 18	Sept. 9	Oct. 10
Taylor [illegible]	O	1904	1906	87	s	23	2 to 4	...do...	......	May 21	June 2	May 26	June 11	...do...	Do.
Chasselas [illegible]:															
Own roots	Gi	1904	......	......	s	......	......	Mar. 18	Apr. 3	May 28	May 30	June 7	......	Sept. 5	Sept. 24
Chasselas Rose de Falloux:															
Own roots	Gi	1905	......	......	s	......	......	Mar. 6	Apr. 1	...do...	...do...	June 6	......	...do...	Sept. 28
Aramon × Rupestris Ganzin, No. 1	O	1904	1906	90	s	3.1	2 to 6	Mar. 18	......	May 21	June 5	May 27	June 17	Sept. 9	Oct. 11
Do	F	1907	1907	79	s	1.5	2 to 7	Mar. 20	Apr. 1	May 15	May 22	May 30	......	Aug. 25	Sept. 12
Australis	F	1907	1907	79	s	2.2	3 to 6	Mar. 18	......	May 22	......	......	......	...do...	Sept. 26
Dog Ridge	O	1904	1906	88	s	2.7	3 to 5	...do...	......	May 26	June 2	June 1	June 18	Sept. 9	Oct. 11
Lenoir	O	1903	1905	89	s	3.2	2 to 6	Mar. 17	......	...do...	...do...	...do...	June 16	...do...	Sept. 26
Mourvedre × Rupestris, No. 1202	O	1904	1906	90	s	48	2 to 6	Mar. 20	......	...do...	June 5	do...	June 24	Sept. 23	Oct. 13
Riparia × Rupestris, No. 101	F	1907	1907	80	s	2.5	2 to 5	Mar. 28	......	May 21	......	......	......	Sept. 21	
Do	O	1904	1906	88	s	2.7	3 to 6	Mar. 22	......	May 23	June 9	May 28	June 24	Sept. 9	Sept. 25
Riparia × Rupestris, No. 3309	F	1907	1907	75	s	......	......	Mar. 20	Apr. 1	May 13	......	May 26	......	......	
Do	O	1904	1906	88	s	18	3 to 6	Mar. 19	......	May 24	June 1	May 29	June 20	Sept. 9	Oct. 12
Rupestris St. George	F	1903	1905	86	s	2.2	3 to 6	Mar. 12	Apr. 1	May 16	May 22	May 24	June 5	Aug. 10	Sept. 4
Do	O	1903	1905	92	s	5.4	2 to 6	Mar. 18	......	May 23	June 8	May 28	June 14	Sept. 9	Oct. 12
Salt Creek	F	1907	1907	86	c, s	5	3 to 7	Mar. 23	Mar. 30	May 14	May 23	May 27	......	......	
Solonis × Riparia, No. 1616	O	1904	1906	82	s	1.5	3 to 4	......	......	May 20	June 8	May 25	June 20	Sept. 9	Oct. 12
Taylor Narbonne	F	1907	1907	75	s	.7	4 to 7	Mar. 22	......	...do...	......	......	......	Sept. 21	
Do	O	1904	1906	80	s	2.9	2 to 5	Mar. 17	......	May 21	June 1	May 26	June 20	Sept. 9	Oct. 10
Chasselas Rose Royal:															
Aramon × Rupestris Ganzin, No. 1	O	1904	......	92	c, s	4.5	2 to 4	Mar. 18	......	May 31	...do...	June 5	June 13	Sept. 25	Sept. 26
Dog Ridge	O	1904	1906	81	s	2	3 to 5	Mar. 16	......	May 26	June 2	June 2	...do...	Sept. 9	Sept. 21
Lenoir	O	1903	1905	89	c, s	4	3 to 5	Mar. 14	......	May 22	June 7	May 26	June 16	...do...	Oct. 2
Rupestris St. George	O	1903	1905	92	s	4.7	2 to 4	Mar. 15	......	...do...	June 8	May 27	June 23	...do...	Sept. 20
Taylor Narbonne	O	1904	1906	50	s	.7	3 to 4	Mar. 20	......	May 20	June 9	May 26	June 14	...do...	Sept. 23
Chasselas Rouge:															
Own roots	Gi	1905	......	......	s	......	......	Mar. 8	Apr. 1	...do...	......	May 30	......	Sept. 5	Sept. 25
Lenoir	O	1903	1905	90	s	4.1	2 to 6	Mar. 19	......	do...	June 5	May 24	June 19	Sept. 9	Oct. 1
Rupestris St. George	O	1903	1905	88	s	4	2 to 4	Mar. 24	......	May 22	June 4	May 27	June 21	...do...	Oct. 10
Chasselas St. Bernard:															
Canada	F	1909	1909	76	s	1.5	......	Mar. 13	Apr. 1	May 12	May 20	May 25	......	......	
Lenoir	O	1904	1907	79	s	2.1	2 to 5	Mar. 20	......	May 16	June 3	May 24	June 18	Sept. 30	
Riparia × Rupestris, No. 101	F	1907	1907	73	s	1	......	Mar. 18	Mar. 28	May 12	......	May 26	......	......	
Rupestris des Caussettes	F	1907	1907	80	s	1.5	......	Mar. 13	Apr. 1	May 1	May 18	May 24	......	......	
Rupestris St. George	F	1907	1907	78	s	1.7	......	Mar. 12	Mar. 30	May 15	......	......	......	......	
Valencia	F	1907	1907	82	s	1.5	......	Mar. 21	Apr. 1	May 11	......	May 24	......	......	
Chauche Noir:															
Own roots	Gi	1904	......	......	c, s	......	......	Mar. 11	Mar. 26	May 29	May 30	June 5	......	Aug. 25	Sept. 20
Dog Ridge	O	1904	1906	95	c, s	5.2	2 to 4	Mar. 18	......	May 23	June 5	May 29	June 17	Sept. 20	Oct. 1
Lenoir	O	1903	1905	94	c, s	3.6	2 to 4	Mar. 15	......	May 21	June 1	May 26	June 14	Sept. 16	Sept. 25
Rupestris St. George	O	1903	1905	93	c, s	7.2	2 to 4	Mar. 20	......	May 23	June 5	May 29	June 17	Sept. 15	Do.
[illegible]sh:															
Lenoir	O	1906	1909	88	s	.5	......	Mar. 17	......	June 5	June 13	June 21	......	......	

TABLE VII.—*Relative behavior and value for different purposes of grape varieties tested by grafting on resistant stocks and by growing on their own roots in eleven experiment vineyards in California*—Continued.

Variety and stock (on own roots, if so stated).	Experiment vineyard.	Year stock was planted.	Year grafted.	Congeniality.	How pruned.	Weight of pruning per vine.	Nodes bearing fruit.	Growth-starting date.		Blossoming date.		Fruit-setting date.		Fruit-ripening date.	
								Early season.	Late season.	Early season.	Late season.	Early season.	Late season.	Early season.	Late season.
1	2	3	4	5	6	7	8	9	10	11	12	13	14	15	16
Chenin Blanc:				*P. ct.*		*Lbs.*									
Own roots	Gi	1905	.....	.....	c, s	.....	.....	Mar. 15	Mar. 28	May 26	May 30	May 30	June 5	Aug. 28	Sept. 25
Dog Ridge	O	1904	1906	91	c, s	3.6	2 to 4	Mar. 20	.....	May 24	June 1	May 29	June 15	Sept. 23	Oct. 17
Lenoir	O	1903	1905	93	s	5.8	2 to 5	Mar. 18	.....	May 21	...do...	May 24	June 20	Sept. 15	Sept. 28
Rupestris St. George	O	1903	1906	90	s	5.6	2 to 4	Mar. 19	.....	May 24	...do...	May 29	June 17	Sept. 20	Oct. 1
Child of Hall:															
Lenoir	O	1904	1907	89	s	3.2	3 to 5	Mar. 18	.....	May 23	...do...	May 28	June 16	Sept. 28	Oct. 6
Cinsaut:															
Own roots	Gi	1904	.....	.....	s	.....	.....	Mar. 21	Mar. 29	May 26	June 4	May 30	June 9	Aug. 28	Sept. 20
Lenoir	O	1903	1905	84	s	2.2	2 to 5	Mar. 17	.....	May 24	June 1	June 2	June 10	Sept. 28	Oct. 4
Rupestris St. George	O	1903	1905	93	s	3.9	2 to 4	Mar. 20	.....	...do...	June 5	May 29	June 17	Sept. 26	Sept. 30
Cipro Nero:															
Own roots	Gi	1904	.....	.....	s	.....	.....	Mar. 27	Apr. 1	June 4	...do...	June 9	.....	Sept. 24	
Clairette à Gros Grain:															
Lenoir	O	1904	1907	88	s	3	2 to 5	Mar. 16	.....	May 25	...do...	May 29	June 20	Sept. 30	Oct. 8
[illegible]la × Rupestris	F	1907	1907	82	c, s	2.3	3 to 6	Mar. 14	Mar. 30	May 14	May 22	May 30	.....	Sept. 21	
Clairette Blanche:															
Own roots	Gi	1904	.....	.....	c, s	.....	.....	Mar. 20	Apr. 1	May 27	June 4	May 31	June 9	Sept. 20	Sept. 28
Clairette Mazel:															
Own roots	Gi	1905	.....	.....	c, s	.....	.....	...do...	.....	May 29	June 2	June 2	June 7	Aug. 28	Sept. 20
Lenoir	O	1906	1912	85	c, s	4	3 to 4	Mar. 22	.....	May 30	May 31	June 4	...do...	Sept. 5	Oct. 7
Riparia Gloire	O	1904	.....	89	s	4	.....	Mar. 19	.....	June 1	June 8	June 6	June 23	Sept. 22	Do.
Coarna Negra:															
Australis	F	1907	1907	88	s	4.8	.....	Mar. 20	.....	May 25	.....	.....	.....	.....	
Lenoir	O	1904	1907	84	s	2.8	2 to 4	Mar. 19	.....	May 24	May 31	May 30	June 13	Sept. 30	Oct. 3
Rupestris Martin	F	1907	1907	90	c, s	5.7	2 to 5	Mar. 23	.....	May 27				.....	
[illegible]m [illegible]do B[illegible]undo:															
Own roots	Gi	1904	.....	.....	s	.....	.....	Mar. 21	Mar. 30	May 24	June 6	May 29	June 12	Aug. 29	Sept. 26
[illegible]ur:															
Riparia × Rupestris, No. 3306	O	1904	.....	85	s	6.5	2 to 3	Mar. 20	.....	May 12	June 1	May 17	June 15	Sept. 25	Oct. 1

Corbeau Noir Shar:															
Own roots	Gi	1904	....	......	s	....	....	Mar. 18	Mar. 30	May 26	June 3	June 9	....	Sept. 17	Sept. 25
Corinthe Blanc:															
Lenoir	O	1906	1909	91	c, s	.5	....	Mar. 17	....	May 30	[illegible] 8	June 8	June 25	....	
Corinthe à Gros Grain:															
Canada	F	1907	1907	96	c, s	5	3 to 5	Mar. 25	Apr. 3	May 18	May 23	May 30	....	Sept. 25	
Lenoir	O	1904	1907	90	s	2.2	3 to 6	Mar. 19	....	May 23	June 9	May 29	June 24	Sept. 23	Oct. 26
Mourvedre × Rupestris, No. 1202	F	1907	1909	92	c, s	3.3	....	Mar. 24	Apr. 3	May 22	May 25	[illegible] 2	....	Aug. 25	Sept. 25
Ramsey	F	1907	1907	89	c, s	4	3 to 4	Mar. 20	Apr. 2	May 21	May 29	June 1	....	Sept. 21	
Riparia × Rupestris, No. 3309	F	1907	1907	92	s	4	3 to 4	Mar. 24	Apr. 1	[illegible] 18	May 25	June 4	....	Aug. 25	Sept. 21
Rupestris St. George	F	1907	1907	93	c, s	4.8	3 to 5	Mar. 25	Apr. 3	May 20	..do....	May 30	....	Sept. 7	Sept. 25
Solonis × Riparia, No. 1616	F	1907	1907	95	c, s	6.1	3 to 5	Mar. 17	....	May 23	....	....	....	Sept. 17	
Corinthe Rose:															
Adobe Giant	F	1907	1907	98	c, s	9.6	3 to 5	Mar. 20	Apr. 1	May 12	May 22	May 23	....	....	
Canada	F	1907	1908	100	c, s	5	....	..do....	....	May 19	May 24	May 31	....	Sept. 21	
Constantia	F	1907	1907	96	c, s	7.7	1 to 6	Mar. 14	Apr. 28	May 16	May 22	May 25	....	....	
Lenoir	O	1904	1908	90	c, s	3.1	3 to 5	Mar. 22	....	May 25	June 6	May 29	June 25	Sept. 10	Sept. 15
Monticola × Rupestris	F	1907	1907	85	c, s	3.3	....	Mar. 23	Apr. 3	May 18	May 27	...do....	....	Aug. 10	
Mourvedre × Rupestris, No. 1202	F	1907	1907	95	c, s	4.1	....	Mar. 21	...do....	...do....	May 25	...do....	....	Aug. 15	
Riparia Grand Glabre	F	1907	1907	96	s	9.7	3 to 7	Mar. 15	Apr. 1	May 13	May 22	May 25	....	....	
Riparia × Rupestris, No. 101	F	1907	1907	97	c, s	9	3 to 7	Mar. 23	...do....	May 14	...do....	May 26	....	....	
Vermorel	F	1907	1907	93	c, s	7.1	....	Mar. 19	Mar. 28	May 18	...do....	May 25	....	....	
Coristano:															
Australis	F	1907	1907	97	c, s	7.5	3 to 5	Mar. 23	Apr. 1	...do....	May 24	June 1	....	Sept. 17	Oct. 17
Barnes	F	1907	1907	96	c, s	4.3	2 to 5	Mar. 25	...do....	May 16	May 21	May 29	....	....	
[illegible]	O	1904	1907	83	s	2	2 to 6	Mar. 20	....	May 26	[illegible] 7	May 30	June 23	Sept. 30	Oct. 26
[illegible]la × Rupestris	F	1907	1907	96	c, s	6.3	2 to 6	Mar. 28	Apr. 1	May 19	May 25	June 4	....	[illegible] 17	[illegible] 17
Rupestris [illegible]in	F	1907	1907	90	c, s	5.5	2 to 6	Mar. 24	Apr. 1	May 17	May 22	May 30	....	Sept. 17	Sept. 21
Rupestris St. [illegible]ge	F	1907	1907	96	c, s	7	2 to 5	Mar. 25	...do....	May 20	May 23	[illegible] 3	....	Sept. 10	Do.
[illegible]:															
Own roots	Gi	1904	....	......	c, s	....	....	Mar. 17	Mar. 27	May 30	June 6	June 4	June 13	Sept. 19	Oct. [illegible]
[illegible]n × [illegible]pis [illegible], No. 1	O	1904	1907	93	s	3.5	3 to 4	Mar. 24	....	May 22	June 10	May 28	June 27	Sept 27	
Lenoir	O	1906	1907	89	s	4.1	3 to 4	Mar. 22	....	May 23	June 6	...do....	June 20	Oct. 13	
Riparia [illegible]re	O	1904	....	90	s	6	....	...do....	....	May 17	[illegible] 8	May 23	June 25	....	
Rupestris × Berlandieri, No. 301A	F	1907	1907	90	c, s	4.5	3 to 4	Apr. 5	....	May 23	....	....	....	Sept. 26	
Solonis Robusta	F	1907	1907	92	c, s	4.7	3 to 5	Mar. 12	Apr. 6	May 18	May 24	May 29	....	Sept. 15	
Crabbs Burgundy:															
[illegible]n rots	......	1907	....	......	s	....	....	Mar. 18	Apr. 10	May 25	....	....	....	Sept. 23	....
Aramon × Rupestis [illegible]n, No. 1	O	1904	1906	87	s	3.8	2 to 4	....	Mar. 20	May 19	June 6	May 24	June 18	Sept. 28	Oct. 12
Dog Ridge	O	1904	1906	95	c, s	4	3 to 4	Mar. 17	....	May 26	June 2	June 1	June 21	...do....	Oct. 8
Lenoir	O	1903	1905	91	s	3.9	2 to 5	Mar. 15	....	May 20	June 5	May 25	June 20	...do....	Oct. 12
Riparia × Rupestris, No. 101	O	1904	1906	88	s	1.2	2 to 4	Mar. 22	....	May 21	June 4	May 27	June 17	Sept. 27	Oct. 11
Riparia × [illegible]is, No. 3309	O	1904	1906	92	s	2.7	3 to 4	Mar. 20	....	May 20	June 1	May 25	...do....	Sept. 28	Do.
Rupestris St. [illegible]e	O	1903	1905	88	s	2.8	2 to 4	Mar. 16	....	May 23	...do....	May 29	...do....	Sept. 29	Oct. 8
Solonis × Riparia, No. 1616	O	1904	1906	79	s	1.1	3 to 5	Mar. 20	....	May 19	June 10	May 24	June 27	...do....	Oct. 11
[illegible]or [illegible]e	O	1904	1906	85	s	2.1	2 to 5	...do....	....	May 21	May 31	May 26	June 12	Sept. 28	Oct. 10
[illegible]to:															
Own rots	Gi	1904	....	......	s	....	....	Mar. 19	Apr. 1	May 24	June 3	May 29	June 9	Aug. 29	Sept. 27
Crujidero:															
[illegible]n roots	Gi	1904	....	......	s	....	....	Mar. 17	Mar. 26	May 28	June 6	June 2	June 13	Sept. 22	Oct. 15

TABLE VII.—*Relative behavior and value for different purposes of grape varieties tested by grafting on resistant stocks and by growing on their own roots in eleven experiment vineyards in California*—Continued.

Variety and stock (on own roots, if so stated).	Experiment vineyard.	Year stock was planted.	Year grafted.	Congeniality.	How pruned.	Weight of pruning per vine.	Nodes bearing fruit.	Growth-starting date. Early season.	Growth-starting date. Late season.	Blossoming date. Early season.	Blossoming date. Late season.	Fruit-setting date. Early season.	Fruit-setting date. Late season.	Fruit-ripening date. Early season.	Fruit-ripening date. Late season.
1	2	3	4	5	6	7	8	9	10	11	12	13	14	15	16
Danugue:				P. ct.		Lbs.									
Own roots	Gi	1904			s			Mar. 24	Mar. 28	June 2	June 4	June 7		Sept. 24	
Dog Ridge	O	1904	1907	86	s	2	2 to 5	Mar. 17		May 25	May 31	May 30	June 12	Sept. 9	Sept. 25
Lenoir	O	1903	1905	89	s	3.1	3 to 5	Mar. 15		May 20	June 1	May 26	June 14	do	Do.
Rupestris St. George	O	1903	1905	92	c, s	3.9	3 to 4	Mar. 20		May 23	June 2	May 29	June 7	do	Do.
Taylor Narbonne	O	1904	1906	84	s	1.8	2 to 4	do		May 19	June 9	May 24	June 15	do	
Dattier de Beyrouth:															
Lenoir	O	1903	1912	58	s	2.5		Mar. 16		June 4		June 9			
Deacon Superb:															
Own roots	Gi	1907			c, s			Mar. 10	Apr. 1	May 26				Sept. 19	
Diamant:															
Own roots	Gi	1905			s			Mar. 23	do					Sept. 25	
Dodrelabi:															
Own roots	Gi	1904			s			Mar. 18	Mar. 28	May 2	June 1	May 31	June 7	Sept. 20	Sept. 26
Aramon × Rupestris Ganzin, No. 1	O	1904	1909				3 to 4	Mar. 16		June 3	June 8	June 8	June 22		
Dog Ridge	O	1904	1907	94	s	3.5	3 to 4	Mar. 20		May 25	June 5	May 29	June 20	Oct. 10	Oct. 20
Herbemont	O	1904	1909	89	s	3.1	3 to 4	Mar. 18		June 3	June 8	June 9	June 25	Oct. 2	Oct. 15
Lenoir	O	1903	1905	90	s	2.7	2 to 4	Mar. 17		May 24	June 5	May 30	June 17	Sept. 10	Oct. 10
Mourvèdre × Rupestris, No. 1202	O	1904	1909	95	s	3	3 to 4	Mar. 21		June 3	June 6	June 8	June 20	Oct. 5	Oct. 12
Rupestris St. George	O	1903	1905	89	s	3.3	2 to 4	Mar. 19		May 22	June 2	May 28	June 21	Sept. 28	Oct. 10
Solonis × Riparia, No. 1616	O	1904	1909	93	s	4.2	2 to 4	Mar. 23		May 25	June 4	June 8	June 15	Oct. 5	Oct. 12
Taylor Narbonne	O	1904	1906	87	s	2.2	3 to 4	Mar. 18		May 27	June 1	June 2	June 13	Sept. 30	Oct. 4
Drnekusa:															
Own roots	Gi	1904			s			Mar. 14	Mar. 24	May 28	June 5	do	June 10	Aug. 29	Sept. 25
Dronkane:															
Lenoir	O	1904	1907	88	s	3	3 to 5	Mar. 26		May 26	June 15	June 1	June 30	Sept. 25	Oct. 25
Rupestris des Caussettes	F	1907	1907	88	s	2	4 to 5	Mar. 21	Apr. 1	May 16	May 22	May 27		Oct. 17	
Duc de Magenta:															
Rupestris St. George	F	1903	1905	86	s	2.3	5 to 7	Mar. 9	Mar. 15	May 10	May 16	May 20	May 26	Aug. 5	Sept. 13
Duc de Malakoff:															
Own roots	Gi	1905			c, s			Mar. 18	Mar. 27	May 29	May 31	June 6		Aug. 28	Sept. 25

Em[illegible]a:															
Dog Ridge	O	1904	1908	.....	.....	.....	.....	Mar. 15	.....	[illegible] 4	June 5	June 8	June 20	.....	
[illegible]ir	O	1904	1908	90	s	1.5	.....	...do....	.....	[illegible] 3	.....	June 7	June 18	Sept. 20	Oct. 7
Emperor:															
[illegible]ir	O	1903	1909	96	s	2.5	.....	Mar. 21	.....	[illegible] 5	[illegible] 6	June 10	June 21	.....	
[illegible]is St. George	O	1903	1909	93	s	4.2	.....	...do....	.....	May 31	[illegible] 1	June 6	June 14	.....	
[illegible]:															
Lenoir	O	1906	1909	85	s	.8	.....	Mar. 19	.....	[illegible] 6	[illegible] 14	June 12	.....	.....	
[illegible]re de [illegible]:															
[illegible] roots	Gi	1904	.....	.....	s	.....	.....	Mar. 18	Mar. 22	May 29	May 30	June 7	.....	.....	
[illegible]:															
[illegible]ir	O	1904	1907	90	s	3.1	3 to 6	[illegible] 17	.....	May 25	June 8	May 29	June 24	Sept. 30	Oct. 13
[illegible]is St. George	F	1907	1907	92	c, s	6.5	2 to 4	Mar. 14	Mar. 30	May 14	May 21	May 25	.....	Aug. 5	Sept. 21
[illegible]y:															
[illegible]ir	O	1904	1907	85	c, s	2.4	3 to 6	Mar. 18	.....	May 24	June 8	May 29	June 20	[illegible] 29	Oct. 15
[illegible] × [illegible]is, No. 3309	F	1909	1909	94	c, s	5.5	.....	[illegible] 13	.....	May 22	.....	.....	.....	[illegible] 25	Oct. 17
[illegible]p [illegible]is St. [illegible]	F	1907	1907	93	c, s	5.5	.....	[illegible] 12	Apr. 5	May 18	May 22	June 4	.....	Sept. 16	[illegible]
Feher G[illegible]r [illegible]:															
[illegible] roots	Gi	1904	.....	.....	s	.....	.....	Mar. 15	Mar. 24	May 22	May 30	May 27	June 5	[illegible] 15	Sept. 25
[illegible]r Som:															
[illegible]ir	O	1904	1907	89	s	2.6	2 to 4	[illegible] 21	.....	May 25	[illegible] 8	June 1	June 6	[illegible] 26	Oct. 7
[illegible]is St. George	F	1907	1907	85	s	3	2 to 4	Mar. 20	Mar. 28	May 16	May 23	May 30	.....	Oct. 17	
[illegible]r Szagos:															
[illegible]	F	1904	1906	87	s	1.7	2 to 4	Mar. 15	Mar. 30	...do....	[illegible]	May 27	May 31	Sept. 14	Sept. 20
[illegible] × [illegible]is [illegible], No. 1	F	1904	1906	96	c, s	6	2 to 5	Mar. 13	Mar. 25	...do....	May 29	May 21	[illegible] 6	Sept. 15	Do.
Dog Ridge	F	1903	1905	91	c, s	2	2 to 4	Mar. 12	...do....	May 20	May 20	May 25	[illegible] 1	Sept. 5	[illegible]
[illegible]	F	1903	1905	84	c, s	1.7	2 to 5	[illegible] 8	[illegible] 20	May [illegible]	...do....	...do....	May 26	...do....	[illegible]
[illegible]ir	F	1903	1905	85	s	1.4	2 to 5	[illegible] 11	[illegible] 30	May 14	May 16	May 21	May 27	Sept. 12	Sept. 15
[illegible]re × [illegible], No. 1202	F	1904	1905	93	c, s	3.7	2 to 6	Mar. 6	[illegible] 25	May 15	May 20	May 24	...do....	Sept. 8	Sept. 20
[illegible]a Gloire	F	1903	1905	90	s	2.6	2 to 5	[illegible] 14	[illegible] 27	May 13	...do....	May 22	May [illegible]	Sept. 13	Sept. 19
[illegible]a × [illegible]is, No. 101	F	1904	1906	88	s	3.3	3 to 6	...do....	[illegible] 28	May 16	May 21	May 24	May [illegible]	Sept. 15	Sept. 20
[illegible]a × [illegible], No. 3309	F	1904	1906	95	c, s	3.4	2 to 6	Mar. 8	[illegible] 30	May 14	May 23	May 26	May 28	...do....	[illegible]
[illegible]is [illegible]	F	1903	1905	82	s	1.8	3 to 6	[illegible] 2	Mar. 25	May 20	May 22	...do....	May [illegible]	Sept. 10	[illegible]
[illegible]is St. George	F	1903	1905	93	s	3	2 to 5	[illegible] 12	...do....	May 15	May 20	May 22	June 1	...do....	Sept. 19
Salt [illegible]	F	1903	1905	85	s	1.5	2 to 5	[illegible] 6	Apr. 1	May 17	...do....	May 25	[illegible] 5	Sept. 30	[illegible] 20
Solonis × [illegible], No. 1616	F	1904	1906	92	c, s	4.6	2 to 5	Mar. 8	Mar. 30	May 15	May 22	May [illegible]	May 30	Sept. 13	Do.
[illegible]r [illegible]	F	1904	1906	86	c, s	2.5	2 to 5	Mar. 13	Mar. 25	May 12	May 20	May 25	May 29	Sept. 10	[illegible]
Ferrara:															
[illegible]int	O	1904	1908	92	s	3.2	2 to 5	Mar. 22	.....	[illegible] 6	[illegible] 11	June 10	June 25	Sept. 27	Oct. 4
[illegible]ir	O	1904	1908	86	s	2.1	3 to 5	[illegible] 18	.....	[illegible] 4	[illegible] 13	[illegible] 9	June 30	Oct. 12	
Fin[illegible]:															
[illegible]	Gi	1907	.....	.....	s	.....	.....	[illegible] 24	Apr. 1	May 24	May 28	May 30	.....	[illegible] 25	
Dog [illegible]	O	1904	1906	87	s	3.3	2 to 5	...do....	.....	[illegible] 28	June 6	[illegible]	June 21	Sept. 27	[illegible] 15
Lenoir	O	1903	1905	88	s	2	3 to 5	...[illegible]...	.....	May 24	[illegible] 8	May [illegible]	June 23	...do....	Do.
[illegible]is St. George	O	1903	1905	89	s	3.2	2 to 5	[illegible] 22	.....	May 23	[illegible] 5	May 27	June 19	[illegible] 15	Oct. 10
[illegible]r Narbonne	O	1904	1906	88	s	2.3	2 to 4	Mar. 24	.....	[illegible] 21	[illegible] 8	May [illegible]	June 21	Sept. 25	[illegible] 4
Flame Tokay:															
O[illegible]	Gi	1904	.....	.....	s	.....	.....	Mar. 18	Mar. 29	May 28	[illegible] 7	May 31	June 11	[illegible] 20	Sept. 26
Canada	F	1907	1907	91	s	5	3 to 4	[illegible] 20	Apr. 2	May 13	May 23	May 26	.....	Sept. 26	
[illegible]	O	1904	1907	94	s	3.5	2 to 4	[illegible] 24	.....	May 24	June 8	[illegible] 1	June 24	[illegible] 30	Oct. 20
[illegible]ir	O	1904	1907	93	s	3.5	3 to 4	[illegible] 21	.....	...do....	[illegible] 5	May 29	June 10	[illegible] 27	Oct. 14

TABLE VII.—*Relative behavior and value for different purposes of grape varieties tested by grafting on resistant stocks and by growing on their own roots in eleven experiment vineyards in California*—Continued.

Variety and stock (on own roots, if so stated).	Experiment vineyard.	Year stock was planted.	Year grafted.	Congeniality.	How pruned.	Weight of pruning per vine.	Nodes bearing fruit.	Growth-starting date. Early season.	Growth-starting date. Late season.	Blossoming date. Early season.	Blossoming date. Late season.	Fruit-setting date. Early season.	Fruit-setting date. Late season.	Fruit-ripening date. Early season.	Fruit-ripening date. Late season.
1	2	3	4	5	6	7	8	9	10	11	12	13	14	15	16
Flame Tokay—Continued.				*P. ct.*		*Lbs.*									
Monticola × Riparia, No. 554	F	1907	1907	96	c, s	6	3 to 5	Mar. 22	Apr. 1	May 17	May 22	May 30		Sept. 29	
[illegible]la × Riparia, No. 18804	F	1907	1907	95	c, s	7	3 to 5	Mar. 23	...do...	May 18	May 26	May 28		...do...	
Monticola × Riparia, No. 18808	F	1907	1907	97	s	7	3 to 6	Mar. 24	Apr. 6	May 20	May 25	May 30			
[illegible]la × [illegible]ria, No. 18815	F	1907	1907	97	s	6.9	3 to 6	...do...	...do...	...do...	May 22	...do...		Sept. 29	
Riparia à [illegible]es [illegible]es	F	1907	1907	90	s	4.9	3 to 5	Mar. 23	Apr. 2	May 14	May 23	May 24		Sept. 25	
Riparia × Rupestris, No. 101	O	1904	1907	94	s	3.1	2 to 4	Mar. 21		May 24	June 1	May 30	June 21	Sept. 30	Oct. 12
Riparia × Rupestris, No. 3309	O	1904	1907	94	s	4.2	3 to 5	Mar. 22		May 25	June 3	...do...	June 14	Sept. 29	Oct. 8
Do	F	1907	1907	93	c, s	7.1	3 to 5	Mar. 25	Apr. 2	May 21	May 23	June 1			
Rupestris Martin	F	1907	1907	89	c, s	2.7		Mar. 23	...do...	May 19	May 24	May 30		Sept. 26	
Salt Creek	F	1907	1907	91	c, s	4.2	3 to 5	Apr. 1		May 23				Sept. 12	
Taylor Narbonne	F	1907	1907	95	c, s	4.4	3 to 4	Mar. 23	Apr. 2	May 14	May 24	May 24		Sept. 25	
Folle B[illegible]nche:															
[illegible]tris St. George	F	1903	1905	79	s	.9	3 to 6	Mar. 8	Mar. 30	May 15	May 20	May 20	June 5	Sept. 13	Sept. 19
F[illegible]der:															
Own [illegible]o[illegible]ts	GI	1905			s			Mar. 15	Mar. 28	May 24	May 27	May 30	June 5	Sept. 5	Sept. 20
Lenoir	F	1903	1905	88	s	1.4	3 to 6	Mar. 11	Mar. 25	May 13	May 18	May 22	May 28	Aug. 24	Sept. 22
Riparia Gloire	F	1903	1905	84	s	1.8	3 to 5	Mar. 14	Mar. 30	May 12	May 19	May 23	May 25	Aug. 23	Sept. 19
Rupestris St. [illegible]ge	F	1903	1905	90	s	3	2 to 6	Mar. 15	...do...	May 15	May 20	May 21	June 4	Aug. 24	Sept. 10
Frankenthal Precoce:															
Herbemont	O	1904	1909	72	s	1.1		Mar. 24		June 2	June 7	June 7	June 20		
Lenoir	O	1903	1905	90	c, s	2.2	3 to 5	Mar. 18		May 20	June 1	May 29	June 14	Sept. 23	Oct. 5
[illegible]la × [illegible]ria, No. 18808	F	1907	1907	90	c, s	3.3		Mar. 20	Mar. 30	May 14	May 24	May 28		Aug. 25	Oct. 17
Monticola × Riparia, No. 18815	F	1907	1907	87	c, s	2.7	4 to 6	...do...	...do...	May 16	May 23	...do...		Aug. 30	Do.
Rupestris St. George	O	1903	1905	92	c, s	2.2	3 to 4							Sept. 23	Sept. 30
Solonis × Othello	F	1907	1907	90	c, s	3	3 to 4	Mar. 29		May 22				Oct. 17	
Sonis × Riparia, No. 1616	F	1907	1907	89	s	3.7	3 to 5	Mar. 25	Apr. 2	May 15	May 22	May 28		Sept. 1	Sept. 21
Fredericton:															
Dog [illegible]ge	F	1907	1907	92	c, s	5		...do...	Apr. 1	May 18	May 23	May 19			
Lenoir	O	1904	1907	91	s	2.8	3 to 4	Mar. 17		May 25	June 5	May 30	June 17	Sept. 25	Sept. 28
Rupestris St. George	F	1907	1907	92	s	5		Mar. 31	Apr. 1	May 21	May 23	June 4			

Fresa de Monferat:															
Own roots	Gi	1904			s			Mar. 16	Mar. 29	May 26	May 30	June 6		Sept. 23	
[illegible]ay de Bourgogne:															
Own roots	Gi	1907			s			Mar. 8	Apr. 8	May 20		May 28		Sept. 15	
Dog Ridge	O	1904	1906	92	s	3.6	2 to 4	Mar. 20		May 19	May 31	May 24	June 11	Sept. 9	Oct. 6
Lenoir	O	1903	1905	91	s	2.4	3 to 5	Mar. 16		do	May 30	May 23	June 15	Sept. 8	Sept. 26
Rupestris St. George	O	1903	1905	92	s	4.3	2 to 4	Mar. 18		do	June 1	May 24	June 8	Sept. 24	Sept. 25
Gamay [illegible]:															
[illegible]s	Gi	1904			s			do	Apr. 3	May 27	June 3	June 6		Aug. 25	Sept. 20
Dog Ridge	O	1904	1906	90	c, s	3.6	3 to 6	Mar. 16		May 19	May 31	May 24	June 9	[illegible] 22	Sept. 28
Lenoir	O	1903	1905	88	s	2.2	2 to 5	Mar. 15		May 24	do	June 1	June 11	Sept. 24	Oct. 5
Rupestris St. George	O	1903	1905	91	s	3.3	2 to 5	Mar. 19		May 25	June 3	May 30	June 10	Sept. 25	[illegible] 4
Taylor Narbonne	O	1904	1906	73	s	.8	2 to 5			May 19	May 31	May 25	June 8	Sept. 22	Oct. 1
[illegible]rz Traminer:															
Own roots	Gi	1904			c, s			Mar. 12	Apr. 1	May 29	May 30	June 6		Aug. 28	Sept. 22
Golden [illegible]pion:															
Own roots	Gi	1905			c, s			Mar. 27	Mar. 30	May 28	June 3	June 2	June 8	Sept. 19	Sept. 20
Do	F	1904			s			Mar. 12	Apr. 13	May 10	May 24	May 24	May 29	Sept. 6	Sept. 8
Dog Ridge	O	1904	1906	89	s	4	3 to 5	Mar. 23		May 24	June 5	May 29	June 20	[illegible] 29	Oct. 25
[illegible]	O	1903	1905	93	s	3.5	2 to 5	Mar. 20		do	do	May 27	do	Sept. 28	Oct. 9
Rupestris St. George	O	1903	1906	89	s	3.7	3 to 5	Mar. 17		May 21	do	May 26	June 19	Sept. 30	Oct. 15
Golden [illegible]burg:															
Lenoir	O	1906	1909	90	s	.5		Mar. 16		June 5	June 8	June 9	June 20		
Golden Queen:															
Lenoir	O	1906	1909	91	c, s	.7		Mar. 19		May 21	do	June 6	June 18		
[illegible]e:															
Own roots	O	1904		90	c, s	4.5	3 to 4	Mar. 18		May 12	May 31	May 18	do	Sept. 23	Oct. 8
Gradiska:															
[illegible]s	Gi	1907			s			Mar. 12	Apr. 10	May 26				Sept. 25	
Dog Ridge	O	1904	1907	92	s	2.7	2 to 4	Mar. 22		May 23	June 1	May 29	June 17	Sept. 23	Oct. 10
[illegible]	O	1903	1905	90	s	2.4	2 to 5	Mar. 20		May 19	June 8	May 23	June 20	do	Oct. 8
St. George	O	1903	1905	86	s	2.9	2 to 4	Mar. 24		May 24	June 3	June 1	June 16	Sept. 22	Oct. 10
Taylor Narbonne	O	1904	1906	83	s	1.4	3 to 4	Mar. 20		May 21	June 8	May 26	June 7	do	Oct. 4
[illegible]en Hungarian:															
[illegible]ts	Gi	1904			s			Mar. 12	Apr. 1	May 27	May 30	May 31	June 5	Sept. 19	Sept. 25
[illegible]is × [illegible]a) × (Riparia × Rupestris, No. 554-5)	O	1907	1909	82	s	2				June 7		June 12			
Aramon × [illegible]	O	1904	1906	86	s	3	3 to 5	Mar. 22		May 22	June 8	May 28	June 20	Sept. 30	Oct. 20
[illegible]on × Rupestris Ganzin, No. 2	O	1907	1909	76	s	.5	2 to 4	Mar. 21		June 1	do	June 5	June 24	Oct. 5	Oct. 14
Berlandieri × [illegible]0A	O	1907	1909	75	s	.7		Mar. 19		do	June 5	June 6	June 20		
[illegible]ia	O	1909	1909	74	s	.9		Mar. 20		May 28	May 31	June 5	June 4		
Dog Ridge	O	1903	1905	89	s	3.8	[illegible]5	Mar. 19		May 25	June 5	June 1	June 21	Sept. 30	Oct. 15
Herbemont	O	1903	1905	78	s	1.3	2 to 5	Mar. 18		May 24	June 14	May 30	June 24	Sept. 30	Oct. 17
[illegible]oir	O	1903	1905	87	c, s	2.1	2 to 5	do		May 25	June 7	do	June 21	Sept. 28	Oct. 8
Monticola × [illegible]o. 18808	O	1907	1909	92	s	3	2 to 3	Mar. 19		June 2	June 5	June 7	June 20	Oct. 1	Oct. 10
Mourvedre × [illegible], No. 1202	O	1904	1906	86	s	16	3 to 5			May 24		May 29		Sept. 30	Oct. 6
Riparia × [illegible]o. 101	O	1904	1906	73	s	1.5	3 to 5	Mar. 22		May 20	June 5	May 26	June 20	do	Oct. 15
Riparia × [illegible]o. 3306	O	1907	1909	80	s	.9	2 to 4	Mar. 21		June 1	do	June 5	June 18	Oct. 10	
[illegible]ia × [illegible]o. 3309	O	1904	1906	92	s	3	3 to 4			May 21		May 26		Oct. 6	
[illegible]i	O	1907	1909	65	s	.2		Mar. 21		June 1		June 5			

TABLE VII.—*Relative behavior and value for different purposes of grape varieties tested by grafting on resistant stocks and by growing on their own roots in eleven experiment vineyards in California*—Continued.

Variety and stock (on own roots, if so stated).	Experiment vineyard.	Year stock was planted.	Year grafted.	Congeniality.	How pruned.	Weight of pruning per vine.	Nodes bearing fruit.	Growth-starting date.		Blossoming date.		Fruit-setting date.		Fruit-ripening date.	
								Early season.	Late season.	Early season.	Late season.	Early season.	Late season.	Early season.	Late season.
1	2	3	4	5	6	7	8	9	10	11	12	13	14	15	16
Green Hungarian—Continued.				P. ct.		Lbs.									
Rupestris Mission	O	1907	1909	67	s	1		Mar. 18		June 2	June 5	..do..			
Rupestris St. George	O	1903	1905	79	s	1.4	2 to 5	..do..		May 26	June 1	June 2	June 12	Sept. 29	Oct. 10
Salt Creek	O	1903	1905	90	s	2	2 to 5			May 24		May 29		Oct. 6	
Solonis Robusta	O	1907	1909	82	s	1.5	3 to 5	Mar. 21		May 25	June 1	June 6	June 20	Oct. 1	Oct. 11
Solonis × Othello, No. 1613	O	1907	1909	83	s	.9	2 to 3	Mar. 20		June 1		..do..		Oct. 5	
Solonis × Riparia, No. 1616	O	1904	1906	68	s	1.9	2 to 5	Mar. 19		May 24	June 10	May 30	June 22	Sept. 30	Oct. 15
Taylor Narbonne	O	1904	1904	84	s	1.7	3 to 5	Mar. 22		May 25	June 1	..do..	June 12	Sept. 29	Do.
Grenache:															
Own roots	Gi	1904			s			..do..	Mar. 28	May 28	May 31	June 1	June 7	Sept. 20	Oct. 24
Dog Ridge	O	1904	1906	91	c, s	4.2	2 to 4	Mar. 24		May 20	June 2	May 26	June 19	Sept. 29	Oct. 15
Lenoir	O	1903	1905	91	c, s	4	2 to 4	Mar. 20		May 21	June 3	May 27	June 18	Sept. 25	Oct. 6
Rupestris St. George	O	1903	1905	90	s	4.7	2 to 4	Mar. 19		..do..	June 8	..do..	June 26	..do..	Oct. 9
Taylor Narbonne	O	1904	1906	88	s	2.8	2 to 4	Mar. 22		May 24	June 1	May 30	June 19	Sept. 29	Oct. 10
Gros Blanc de Lausanne:															
Lenoir	O	1904	1907	86	s	2	3 to 6	Mar. 20		May 20	June 10	May 25	June 20	Sept. 28	Oct. 7
Solonis × Othello	F	1907	1907	85	c, s	2.5	3 to 4	Mar. 16	Mar. 30	May 10	May 21	May 29		Aug 25	
Gros Guillaume:															
Lenoir	O	1904	1911	90	s	2.5									
Gros Manzenc:															
Own roots	Gi	1904			s			Mar. 16	Apr. 1	May 26	May 30	June 5		Sept. 15	Sept. 25
Gros Maroc:															
Own roots	Gi	1905			s			Mar. 13	..do..	May 18	May 29	May 21	June 4	Sept. 25	
Gros Verdot:															
Own roots	Gi	1907			s			Mar. 20	..do..	May 26				..do..	
Dog Ridge	F	1903	1905	92	s	4	3 to 6	Mar. 13	..do..	May 16	May 20	May 26	June 4	Aug. 24	Sept. 20
Do	O	1904	1906	90	s	4.5	3 to 5	Mar. 17		May 25	May 31	May 30	June 15	Sept. 28	Oct. 5
Lenoir	O	1903	1905	90	s	2.8	2 to 4	Mar. 18		May 23	June 3	May 27	June 14	Sept. 27	Do.
Do	F	1903	1905	80	s	1	2 to 4	Mar. 14	Mar. 30	May 15	May 18	May 23	May 29	Aug. 24	Sept. 19
Rupestris St. George	F	1903	1905	88	s	1.7	2 to 5	Mar. 12	Apr. 1	May 14	May 20	May 24	May 30	..do..	Do.
Do	O	1903	1905	89	s	3.7	2 to 5	Mar. 20		May 20	May 31	May 26	June 20	Sept. 30	Oct. 10
Taylor Narbonne	O	1904	1906	86	s	2.1	2 to 4	..do..		May 23	June 4	June 3	..do..	Sept. 27	Oct. 6

Hebron:															
Lenoir	O	1904	1907	85	s	3.4	2 to 4	Mar. 21		May 25	June 3	May 30	June 16	Sept. 29	Oct. 12
Rupestris St. George	F	1907	1907	94	c, s	5.7		Mar. 22	Apr. 8	May 15		June 2		Sept. 21	
Solonis × Othello, No. 1613	F	1907	1907	95	c, s	7.5		Mar. 23	...do...	May 20		June 4		...do...	
Huasco:															
Own roots	H	1904	1904		s			Mar. 24	Apr. 3	May 24	June 10	May 28	June 16	Sept. 14	Sept. 22
[illegible] × [illegible] No. 1	F	1904	1906	88	s	3	2 to 5	Mar. 13	...do...	May 15	May 28	...do...	June 3	Sept. 8	Sept. 20
Do	O	1904	1907	91	s	2	3 to 5	Mar. 26		June 8	June 9	June 16	June 22	Oct. 5	
[illegible] × [illegible] No. 2	F	1909	1909	85	s	3		Mar. 8		May 27				Oct. 16	
Australis	F	1907	1909	90	s	2		Apr. 5		May 23				Sept. 5	
[illegible] × [illegible] No. 420A	F	1907	1909	84	s	1		Apr. 1		May 24				Sept. 10	Oct. 16
[illegible]	F	1903	1905	86	s	1.4	2 to 5	Mar. 6	Apr. 1	May 12	May 20	May 23	May 30	...do...	Sept. 15
[illegible] × [illegible], No. 3308	F	1907	1909	90	s	4.5		Apr. 2		May 27				Oct. 16	
[illegible] × [illegible] 1202	F	1904	1906	89	s	2.8	2 to 5	Mar. 22	Apr. 5	May 14	June 2	May 30	June 12	Sept. 5	Sept. 20
[illegible]	F	1903	1905	84	c, s	4.4	2 to 5	Mar. 12	Apr. 1	May 24	May 29	May 29	June 11	Sept. 10	Sept. 19
Riparia × ([illegible] × Rupestris, No. 106-8)	F	1907	1909	88	s	25		Apr. 1		May 27				Sept. 5	
[illegible] × R[illegible], No. 101	F	1904	1906	88	s	2.1	2 to 5	Mar. 17	Mar. 26	May 14	May 29	May 26	June 7	Sept. 4	Sept. 20
Do	O	1904	1907	90	s	1.1	3 to 4	Mar. 24		June 6	June 10	June 10	June 26	Sept. 28	
[illegible] × Rupestris, No. 3309	F	1904	1906	88	s	3.4	2 to 5	Mar. 23	Apr. 5	May 13	May 27	May 28	June 3	Sept. 10	Do.
[illegible] St. George	F	1903	1905	90	s	2.3	2 to 5	Mar. 12	...do...	May 20	May 30	June 1	June 4	Sept. 9	Sept. 19
Solonis [illegible]	F	1907	1909	88	s	3		Apr. 1		May 24				Oct. 16	
Solonis × [illegible], No. 1616	F	1904	1906	84	s	2		Mar. 22	Apr. 3	May 20	May 23	May 28	June 4	Sept. 10	
[illegible]	F	1904	1906	92	s	3.1	2 to 6	Mar. 7	Mar. 29	May 17	May 30	May 30	June 6	Sept. 17	Sept. 20
[illegible]	F	1907	1909	89	s	2		Apr. 1		May 29				Sept. 25	
Huni[illegible]:															
[illegible] Giant	F	1904	1906	86	s	1.5	3 to 5	Mar. 8	Mar. 26	May 16	May 28	May 27	June 4	Sept. 5	
Australis	F	1907	1909	91	c, s	4		Mar. 27		May 21				Sept. 30	Oct. 18
[illegible] × Riparia, No. 420A	F	1907	1909	90	c, s	4		Mar. 24		May 23				Oct. 18	
[illegible]	F	1907	1909	92	c, s	5		Mar. 23		May 24				Oct. 5	
Dog Ridge	F	1903	1906	95	c, s	29	4 to 5	Mar. 5	Mar. 28	May 20	May 25	May 28	June 5		
Riparia × [illegible], No. 3309	F	1907	1907	97	s			Mar. 30	Apr. 5	May 19	...do...	June 1			
Solonis [illegible]	F	1907	1909	98	s	3		Mar. 21		May 23				Sept. 25	
Solonis × Riparia, No. 1616	F	1907	1907	96	c, s	8.3	3 to 5	Mar. 23	Apr. 1	May 16	May 26	May 30			
[illegible]sa (S. P. I. No. 6124):															
Own roots	O	1904			s	8				June 5	June 8	June 11			
Hunisa (S. P. I. No. 8583):															
Own roots	O	1904			c, s	6.7	2 to 4	Mar. 16		May 15	June 12	May 21	June 27	Oct. 10	
[illegible]b:															
Own roots	Gi	1904			c, s			Mar. 29	...do...	June 1	June 6	June 13			
Hycales:															
Lenoir	O	1904	1907	88	s	2.2	2 to 5	Mar. 18		May 19	June 5	May 24	June 17	Sept. 28	Oct. 7
Rupestris [illegible]	F	1907	1907	97	c, s	10	1 to 4	Mar. 22	Apr. 5	May 16	May 23	May 31			
[illegible] St. [illegible]	F	1907	1907	97	c, s	4.4	2 to 4	Mar. 20	Mar. 28	May 5	May 22	May 25		Aug. 25	Oct. 9
Solonis × [illegible], No. 1613	F	1907	1907	90	c, s	3	1 to 4	Mar. 17	Apr. 8	May 15	May 22	May 29		Sept. 20	Oct. 17
Imperial:															
Own roots	Gi	1905			c, s			Mar. 26	Apr. 1	May 26	June 6	May 30	June 12	Sept. 25	
[illegible]ia Bianca:															
Lenoir	O	1904	1907	84	s	1.8	2 to 4	Mar. 24		May 22	June 7	May 27	June 20	Sept. 23	Oct. 7
Rupestris St. George	F	1907	1907	90	[illegible]	4.1	3 to 5	Mar. 23	Apr. 1	...do...	May 24	June 3		Aug. 25	Sept. 21

TABLE VII.—*Relative behavior and value for different purposes of grape varieties tested by grafting on resistant stocks and by growing on their own roots in eleven experiment vineyards in California*—Continued.

Variety and stock (on own roots, if so stated).	Experiment vineyard.	Year stock was planted.	Year grafted.	Congeniality.	How pruned.	Weight of pruning per vine.	Nodes bearing fruit.	Growth-starting date.		Blossoming date.		Fruit-setting date.		Fruit-ripening date.	
								Early season.	Late season.	Early season.	Late season.	Early season.	Late season.	Early season.	Late season.
1	2	3	4	5	6	7	8	9	10	11	12	13	14	15	16
Johannisberg:				*P. ct.*		*Lbs.*									
Own roots	GI	1904	....	......	c, s	....	....	Mar. 15	Mar. 26	May 29	....	June 3	....	Sept. 5	Sept. 20
Jura Muscat:															
Lenoir	F	1903	1905	81	s	.8	2 to 5	Mar. 7	Mar. 25	May 4	May 18	May 20	May 25	Aug. 10	Sept. 19
Riparia Gloire	F	1903	1905	89	s	3.3	3 to 5	Mar. 8	Mar. 20	May 12	May 21	May 25	May 31	Aug. 20	Do.
Rupestris St. George	F	1903	1905	91	s	2.5	3 to 5	Mar. 9	...do...	May 15	May 18	May 21	....	Aug. 5	Do.
[illegible]k:															
Own roots	O	1904	....	......	s	8	2 to 3	Mar. 22	....	May 16	June 1	...do...	June 20	Sept. 29	Oct. 15
Kadarka:															
Own roots	Gi	1904	....	......	c, s	....	....	Mar. 25	Mar. 27	May 30	June 6	June 11	....	Sept. 15	Sept. 25
Dog Ridge	F	1903	1905	93	s	4.8	2 to 6	Mar. 14	Apr. 3	May 23	May 30	May 30	June 10	Sept. 10	Sept. 20
Lenoir	F	1903	1905	92	c, s	3.3	2 to 6	Mar. 7	Apr. 1	May 20	May 22	May 27	June 4	...do...	Sept. 19
Riparia Gloire	F	1903	1905	90	c, s	3.9	3 to 7	Mar. 8	Apr. 5	...do...	May 27	May 28	June 7	Sept. 5	Do.
Rupestris St. George	F	1903	1905	95	c, s	4	1 to 6	Mar. 13	Apr. 1	May 11	May 20	May 24	May 30	Sept. 12	Do.
Kechmisn-Aly-Blanc:															
Lenoir	O	1904	1907	84	s	2.6	3 to 5	Mar. 21	....	May 25	June 12	May 30	June 28	Sept. 23	Oct. 5
Solonis × Othello, No. 1613	F	1907	1907	92	s	3.5	....	Mar. 23	Mar. 30	May 20	May 22	June 4	....	....	
Keropodia:															
Lenoir	O	1904	1907	90	c, s	4	2 to 5	Mar. 22	....	...do...	June 5	May 29	June 23	Sept. 23	Oct. 20
Riparia × Rupestris, No. 3309	F	1907	1907	90	c, s	5.5	....	Mar. 20	Apr. 5	May 16	May 23	June 2	....	....	
C[illegible]y:															
[illegible]t	O	1904	1909	47	s	.9	....	Mar. 22	....	June 5	June 7	June 12	June 17	....	
Lenoir	O	1904	1906	83	s	2	1 to 5	Mar. 24	....	May 27	June 13	June 1	June 22	Sept. 30	Do.
Kleinburger:															
Own roots	Gi	1904	....	......	s	....	....	Mar. 10	Apr. 5	May 22	May 30	May 27	June 5	Aug. 29	Sept. 23
K[illegible]ler:															
Own roots	Gi	1904	....	......	s	....	....	...do...	Mar. 30	May 27	...do...	May 31	...do...	Sept. 10	Sept. 26
Dog Ridge	O	1904	1906	88	c, s	2.6	2 to 4	Mar. 17	....	...do...	June 3	June 1	June 15	Sept. 26	Oct. 3
Lenoir	O	1903	1905	89	s	2.4	2 to 6	Mar. 15	....	May 23	June 8	May 27	June 21	...do...	Oct. 15
Rupestris St. George	O	1903	1905	88	s	2.8	3 to 5	Mar. 16	....	...do...	June 1	May 28	June 17	...do...	Oct. 10
Taylor [illegible]e	O	1904	1906	73	s	.8	2 to 4	Mar. 18	....	May 22	...do...	...do...	June 13	...do...	Oct. 4

Kuristi Mici:															
Lenoir	O	1904	1907	81	s	2.1	3 to 5	Mar. 25		May 25	June 9	May 29	June 25	Oct. 7	Oct. 10
[illegible]:															
Own roots	Gi	1904			s			Mar. 20	Mar. 29	May 30	June 1	June 6		Sept. 24	Sept. 25
Do.	O	1904			s	3	3 to 4	Mar. 25		May 19	June 8	May 24	June 18	Sept. 28	
[illegible]ntraube:															
Own roots	F	1903	1905	76	s	.7	2 to 7	Mar. 12	Mar. 25	May 15	May 22	May 20	June 4	Aug. 24	Sept. 25
Riparia Gloire	F	1903	1905	83	s	1.8	2 to 5	Mar. 13	do.	May 12	May 17	May 21	May 23	Aug. 20	Sept. 19
Rupestris St. George	F	1903	1905	85	s	2.4	3 to 6	Mar. 12	do.	do.	May 18	do.	May 25	Aug. 25	Do.
[illegible]ani Zolo:															
Rupestris St. George	F	1903	1905	89	s	2.3	3 to 5	Mar. 11	Mar. 27	May 13	May 17	May 22	May 26	Aug. 26	Do.
Lignan Blanc:															
Own roots	Gi	1905			c, s			Mar. 12	Mar. 29	May 27				Sept. 19	
Aramon × Rupestris Ganzin, No. 1	F	1904	1906	89	s	2.4	2 to 6	do.	Apr. 1	May 15	May 23	May 27	May 31	Sept. 10	Do.
Dog Ridge	O	1904	1906	83	s	1.2	4 to 6	Mar. 19		May 24	June 3	May 29	June 10	Sept. 25	[illegible] 3
Do.	F	1904	1906	89	c, s	3.4	2 to 5	Mar. 13	Apr. 1	May 20	May 28	May 26	June 2	Sept. 12	Sept. 20
Hotporup	F	1907	1907	89	s	2		Mar. 25	Apr. 3	May 12	May 24	do.			
Lenoir	O	1903	1905	89	c, s	2.7	3 to 5	Mar. 15		May 26	June 3	June 2	June 13	Sept. 26	Oct. 9
Do.	F	1903	1905	80	s	.4	2 to 6	Mar. 12	Mar. 30	May 15	May 19	May 23	May 26	Sept. 12	Sept. 25
[illegible]re × Rupestris, No. 1202	O	1904	1909	95	s			Mar. 20	June 1	June 10	June 5	June 25			
Do.	F	1904	1906	87	c, s	1.6	2 to 6	Mar. 23	Apr. 1	May 20	May 24	May 26	May 30	Sept. 14	Sept. 20
[illegible]Gloire	F	1903	1905	86	c, s	2.6	3 to 7	Mar. 8	do.	May 15	May 21	May 23	June 2	Sept. 13	Sept. 19
Riparia × Rupestris, No. 101	O	1904	1906	82	s	1.6	2 to 5	Mar. 14	do.	do.	May 23	May 25	May 28	Sept. 15	Sept. 20
Riparia × Rupestris, No. 3309	F	1904	1906	88	c, s	2	2 to 6	Mar. 13	do.	May 13	May 26	do.	June 3	Sept. 13	Do.
[illegible]is St. George	O	1903	1905	91	s	2.9	3 to 5	Mar. 17		May 24	May 31	May 30	June 13	Sept. 26	Oct. 1
Do.	F	1903	1905	87	c, s	2.8	2 to 6	Mar. 13	Mar. 30	May 15	May 20	May 22	May 28	Sept. 10	Sept. 19
[illegible]is × [illegible]llo	F	1907	1907	88	c, s	2.3		Mar. 18	do.	May 10	May 22	May 27		Sept. 17	[illegible] 21
[illegible]is × [illegible], No. 1616	F	1904	1906	83	s	1.4	2 to 5	Mar. 20	Apr. 1	May 17	May 23	May 23	May 30	Sept. 12	Sept. 20
[illegible]or [illegible]	F	1904	1906	85	s	1	2 to 5	do.	do.	May 20	do.	May 28	do.	do.	Do.
Do.	O	1904	1906	84	s	1.6	2 to 5	Mar. 18		May 21	June 11	May 26	June 15	Sept. 25	Oct. 4
[illegible]:															
Own roots	Gi	1904			s			Mar. 16	Mar. 31	May 22	June 1	May 27	June 6	Sept. 20	Sept. 23
[illegible]is × [illegible]) × (Riparia × [illegible], No. 554-5)	O	1907	1909	89	s	2.1	2 to 3	Mar. 22		May 30	June 5	June 9	June 14	Sept. 25	Oct. 10
[illegible] × [illegible], No. 1	O	1904	1906	97	s	3.5	2 to 4	Mar. 18		May 19	June 3	May 25	June 20	Sept. 21	[illegible] 4
Aramon × Rupestris [illegible], No. 2	O	1907	1909	86	s	.9	2 to 4	Mar. 19		May 26	June 2	June 8	June 14	Sept. 20	
Berlandieri × [illegible], No. 420B	F	1907	1907	96	c, s	7	2 to 5	Mar. 26	Apr. 1	May 10	May 22	May 26		Aug. 26	
[illegible] × [illegible], No. 2502	O	1907	1909	89	s	2.1		Mar. 18		May 30	June 3	June 7	June 15	Oct. 10	
[illegible]	O	1907	1909	92	s	3.8	2 to 3	do.		May 25	May 31	June 4	June 12	Sept. 23	Oct. 10
[illegible]ia	F	1907	1907	90	s	4.3	2 to 4	Mar. 21	Apr. 1	May 18	May 22	June 1		Aug. 25	Sept. 21
De [illegible]	F	1907	1907	94	c, s	5	2 to 5	Mar. 26	Apr. 3	May 15	May 24	June 2		do.	Oct. 17
Dog Ridge	O	1903	1905	93	s	3.5	2 to 5	Mar. 18		May 26	June 4	May 30	June 20	Sept. 23	Oct. 10
[illegible]nt	O	1903	1905	88	s	2.2	1 to 4	Mar. 21		May 22	June 5	May 28	June 19	Sept. 22	[illegible] 5
Lenoir	O	1903	1905	87	s	2.7	2 to 5	Mar. 20		May 20	do.	May 25	June 20	Sept. 16	[illegible] 10
Monticola × Riparia, No. [illegible]	F	1907	1907	95	c, s	5.5	1 to 5	Mar. 21	Apr. 3	May 18	May 23	June 4		Aug. 25	Sept. 21
[illegible]a × Riparia, No. [illegible]	O	1907	1909	92	s	2.8	3 to 4	Mar. 20		June 3	June 5	June 8	June 20	Sept. 25	
Mourvedre × Rupestris, No. [illegible]	O	1904	1906	95	s	5	2 to 5	Mar. 18		May 25	June 8	May 30	June 24	Sept. 21	Oct. 11
Riparia × [illegible], No. 101	O	1904	1906	93	s	3.2	3 to 4	do.		May 20	do.	May 25	June 30	Sept. 22	Do.
Do.	F	1907	1907	87	s	2.5	2 to 4	Mar. 24	Apr. 5	May 18	May 24	May 30		Sept. 21	
Riparia × R[illegible]tris, No. 101-14	O	1907	1909	86	s	1.1	3 to 4	Mar. 17		May 28	May 31	June 4	June 15	Sept. 20	Oct. 11

TABLE VII.—*Relative behavior and value for different purposes of grape varieties tested by grafting on resistant stocks and by growing on their own roots in eleven experiment vineyards in California*—Continued.

Variety and stock (on own roots, if so stated).	Experiment vineyard.	Year stock was planted.	Year grafted.	Congeniality.	How pruned.	Weight of pruning per vine.	Nodes bearing fruit.	Growth-starting date.		Blossoming date.		Fruit-setting date.		Fruit-ripening date.	
								Early season.	Late season.	Early season.	Late season.	Early season.	Late season.	Early season.	Late season.
1	2	3	4	5	6	7	8	9	10	11	12	13	14	15	16
Listan—Continued.				P. ct.		Lbs.									
Riparia × [illegible]estris, No. 3306	O	1907	1909	94	s	1.3	3 to 4	Mar. 18	...	May 31	June 8	June 4	June 21	Sept. 25	
Riparia × Rupestris, No. 3309	F	1907	1907	92	c, s	3.2	4 to 5	Mar. 21	Apr. 2	May 12	May 21	May 26	...	Sept. 21	
Do	O	1904	1906	92	s	2.3	3 to 4	Mar. 18	...	May 23	June 8	May 28	June 14	Sept. 26	Oct. 9
Rupestris [illegible]tin	O	1903	1905	93	s	3.8	2 to 5	Mar. 20	...	May 22	June 5	...do...	June 10	Sept. 22	Oct. 6
Rupestris [illegible]a.	O	1907	1909	88	s	1.2	3 to 4	Mar. 17	...	June 8	...	June 13	June 20	Sept. 25	
Rupestris Mission	O	1907	1909	87	s	.9		...do...	...	June 3	...	June 6	...	...	
Rupestris St. George	F	1903	1905	86	s	1.5	4 to 6	Mar. 13	Apr. 1	May 16	May 20	May 22	June 1	...	
Do	O	1903	1905	87	s	2.1	2 to 5	Mar. 18	...	May 20	June 1	May 26	June 13	Sept. 18	Oct. 8
Rupestris × Berlandieri, No. 219A	F	1907	1907	90	c, s	5.2	1 to 4	Mar. 22	...	May 22	...	...	...	Sept. 21	
Salt Creek	O	1903	1905	94	s	3.4	2 to 5	Mar. 19	...	...do...	June 5	May 27	June 10	...do...	Oct. 5
Solonis Robusta	F	1907	1907	97	c, s	6.4	1 to 4	...do...	Apr. 2	May 15	May 22	May 30	...	Aug. 25	Sept. 21
Do	O	1907	1909	90	s	4	2 to 4	Mar. 18	...	June 2	June 10	June 7	June 18	Sept. 20	Oct. 11
Solonis × [illegible]o.	F	1907	1907	97	c, s	6.8	2 to 5	Mar. 25	Apr. 1	May 16	May 22	May 30	...	Sept. 5	Sept. 21
Solonis × Othello, No. 1613	O	1907	1909	88	s	1.2	3 to 4	Mar. 20	...	June 2	June 5	June 8	June 10	Sept. 25	Oct. 11
Solonis × Riparia, No. 1616	O	1904	1906	91	c, s	3.2	2 to 4	Mar. 18	...	May 25	June 3	May 30	June 11	Sept. 21	Oct. 9
Taylor N[illegible]e	O	1904	1906	93	c, s	3.3	2 to 4	Mar. 16	...	May 22	June 7	May 28	...do...	Sept. 22	Oct. 8
Valencia	F	1907	1907	96	c, s	8.5	2 to 5	Mar. 19	Apr. 1	May 15	May 23	May 31	...	Aug. 25	Sept. 21
Luglienga [illegible]a:															
Adobe Giant	F	1904	1906	82	s	1.5	3 to 5	Mar. 13	...do...	May 18	May 20	May 25	May 30	Sept. 14	Do.
Dog Ridge	F	1903	1905	86	s	1.7	3 to 6	Mar. 7	Apr. 3	May 14	...do...	May 21	May 29	Aug. 25	Sept. 20
Riparia × Rupestris, No. 3309	F	1907	1907	88	c, s	1.5	...	Mar. 15	...	May 23	...	...	...	Sept. 21	
Rup[illegible]is St. George	F	1903	1905	87	c, s	2.1	4 to 6	Mar. 14	Mar. 25	May 10	May 19	May 21	May 23	Aug. 25	Sept. 19
[illegible]unier:															
Own rots	Gi	1907	...	...	s	...	...	Mar. 10	Apr. 5	May 20	May 25	May 25	June 5	Sept. 4	Sept. 20
[illegible]e [illegible]ne:															
Own roots	Gi	1905	...	...	s	...	...	...do...	Mar. 30	May 25	June 2	June 1	June 7	Aug. 29	
Dog Ridge	O	1904	1907	90	s	1.8	2 to 5	...	...	May 19	May 30	May 24	June 11	Sept. 20	Oct. 2
Lenoir	O	1903	1905	90	s	2.6	2 to 4	Mar. 15	...	May 24	May 26	May 28	June 6	...do...	Oct. 8
Rupestris St. George	O	1903	1905	89	s	5.1	2 to 4	Mar. 16	...	May 25	May 31	June 1	June 15	Sept. 22	Sept. 25
[illegible]e Blanche:															
Own roots	Gi	1905	...	...	c, s	...	...	Mar. 25	Mar. 29	May 30	June 6	June 3	June 11	Aug. 28	Sept. 19

Mad ine d'Ambre:															
Dog Ridge	O	1904	1906	9[illegible]	c, s	5.3	3 to 4	Mar. 19		May 23	June 5	May 28	June 16	Oct. 4	Oct. 15
Lenoir	O	1903	1905	94	s	4	3 to 4	Mar. 22		May 24	June 4	May 27	June 7	Sept. 23	Oct. 2
Rupestris St. George	O	1903	1905	95	s	6	2 to 5	Mar. 20		do.	June 5	May 29	June 17	Sept. 24	Sept. 30
Me Re:															
Own roots	Gi	1905			c, s			do.	Mar. 30	June 1				Sept. 25	
Riparia Gloire	O	1904		88	c, s	4	2 to 4	Mar. 22		do.		June 5	June 20	Sept. 23	Oct. 2
Madeleine Royale:															
Own rts	Gi	1905			c, s			Mar. 12	Mar. 28	May 25				Sept. 15	
Dog Ridge	O	1904	1906	93	s	4.9	2 to 5	Mar. 27		May 19	May 31	May 25	June 8	Sept. 20	Oct. 1
nhir	O	1903	1905	90	s	3.7	2 to 5	Mar. 16		May 13	May 24	do.	June 11	do.	Do.
a:															
Own roots	Gi	1904			c, s			do.	Mar. 25	May 24	May 29	May 29	June 4	Aug. 29	Sept. 20
dabe Giant	F	1904	1906	93	c, s	4	2 to 4	Mar. 10	Mar. 26	May 15	May 21	May 22	May 30	Sept. 15	Do.
mon × is Ganzin, No. 1	F	1904	1906	90	c, s	4.7	2 to 5	Mar. 9	Mar. 25	May 16	May 29	May 23	June 6	do.	Do.
da	F	1907	1907	97	s	3	1 to 4	Mar. 15	Mar. 29	May 19	May 23	May 30			
Constantia	F	1907	1907	84	s	2.7	1 to 4	Mar. 18	Mar. 25	May 17	May 22	May 27		Sept. 16	
Dog Ridge	F	1903	1905	95	c, s	6	1 to 4	Mar. 7	do.	May 14	May 21	May 24	May 29	Sept. 8	Sept. 20
Herbemont	F	1903	1905	84	s	1.6	2 to 4	do.	do.	May 12	May 20	do.	May 26	Sept. 12	Do.
Lenoir	F	1903	1905	85	c, s	1.6	2 to 5	Mar. 10	Mar. 20	May 14	May 22	May 27	May 29	Sept. 10	Do.
Mourvedre × Rupestris, No. 1202	F	1904	1906	95	c, s	6.7	2 to 5	Mar. 7	do.	do.	May 20	May 21	May 26	do.	Do.
Riparia Gdre	F	1903	1905	96	c, s	5.8	2 to 5	Mar. 8	Mar. 25	May 13	May 18	do.	May 23	Sept. 5	Sept. 19
Riparia × Rupestris, No. 101	F	1904	1906	93	c, s	5.1	2 to 5	Mar. 13	do.	May 12	May 24	May 23	May 30	Sept. 12	Sept. 20
Riparia × is, No. 3309	F	1904	1906	95	c, s	5.1	2 to 4	Mar. 12	do.	May 16	May 22	May 27	do.	Sept. 14	Do.
is tin	F	1903	1905	88	s	2.7	2 to 4	Mar. 17	do.	May 14	May 21	May 25	May 29	Sept. 12	Do.
R is St. George	F	1903	1905	94	c, s	4.9	2 to 5	Mar. 12	Mar. 20	May 15	May 26	May 23	May 30	Sept. 10	Sept. 19
Salt Creek	F	1903	1905	89	c, s	2.7	2 to 5	Mar. 6	Mar. 30	do.	May 27	May 24	do.	Sept. 5	Sept. 20
Solonis × Riparia, No. 1616	F	1904	1906	93	c, s	3.5	2 to 4	Mar. 9	Mar. 27	May 18	May 27	do.	June 3	Sept. 13	Sept. 16
Taylor Narbonne	F	1904	1906	90	c, s	3.8	2 to 5	Mar. 6	Mar. 23	May 8	May 17	May 22	May 27	Sept. 1	Sept. 20
Malaga Blanc:															
Lenoir	F	1903	1905	85	s	1.7	2 to 6	Mar. 23	Apr. 3	May 15	May 20	May 24	June 4	Sept. 7	Sept. 15
Riparia Gloire	F	1903	1905	89	c, s	3.3	1 to 5	Mar. 24	do.	May 22	May 30	May 28	June 8	Sept. 3	Sept. 19
Rupestris St. George	F	1903	1905	89	c, s	2.5	2 to 6	Mar. 15	Mar. 31	May 12	May 18	May 21	May 30	Sept. 9	Do.
k:															
On roots	Gi	1907			c, s			Mar. 16	Mar. 28	May 30		June 5		Aug. 27	Sept. 23
ia:															
Own roots	Gi	1904			s			Mar. 20	Apr. 2	May 22	May 30	May 27	June 6	Aug. 28	Sept. 24
Lenoir	O	1904	1909	88	s	2		Mar. 19		May 30	June 2	June 7	June 10		
Rupestris St. George	O	1902	1909	85	s	2.7		Mar. 22		June 3	June 5	June 9	June 17		
Malvasia de Broglio:															
Own ros	Gi	1904			s			Mar. 21	Mar. 31	May 30	June 3	June 4	June 8	Sept. 20	Sept. 23
ia ia:															
Own ts	Gi	1904			s			Mar. 18	Apr. 1	May 28	do.	June 2	June 9	Sept. 18	Se. 25
Dog Ridge	F	1903	1905	93	c, s	5.4	3 to 5	Mar. 8	Apr. 6	May 22	June 1	May 30	do.	Sept. 5	Sept. 20
t	O	1904	1909	93	s	3.6									
Lenoir	F	1903	1905	80	s	.8	3 to 6	Mar. 20	Apr. 3	May 18	May 21	May 23	June 4	Sept. 14	Sept. 17
Riparia Gloire	F	1903	1905	91	c, s	2.6	2 to 6	Mar. 13	Apr. 1	May 15	May 26	May 29	June 3	Sept. 10	Sept. 19
Rupestris St. George	F	1903	1905	90	s	2.3	2 to 6	do.	do.	May 18	May 30	May 23	June 5	Sept. 8	Do.
a Rovasenda:															
Own oots	Gi	1904			s			Mar. 18	do.	May 22	June 2	May 27	June 9	Sept. 5	Sept. 22

TABLE VII.—*Relative behavior and value for different purposes of grape varieties tested by grafting on resistant stocks and by growing on their own roots in eleven experiment vineyards in California*—Continued.

Variety and stock (on own roots, if so stated).	Experiment vineyard.	Year stock was planted.	Year grafted.	Congeniality.	How pruned.	Weight of pruning per vine.	Nodes bearing fruit.	Growth-starting date.		Blossoming date.		Fruit-setting date.		Fruit-ripening date.	
								Early season.	Late season.	Early season.	Late season.	Early season.	Late season.	Early season.	Late season.
1	2	3	4	5	6	7	8	9	10	11	12	13	14	15	16
Mamelon:				*P. ct.*		*Lbs.*									
Own roots	Gi	1907			s			Mar. 15	Apr. 8	May 20	May 30	May 30	June 2		
Dog Ridge	O	1904	1907	91	c, s	3.1	3 to 5	Mar. 17		May 25	June 5	...do...	June 15	Sept. 22	Oct. 8
Lenoir	O	1903	1905	94	c, s	4.2	2 to 5	Mar. 16		May 23	June 5	May 27	June 13	Sept. 19	Oct. 6
Rupestris St. George	O	1903	1905	90	s	4.7	2 to 4	Mar. 17		May 24	June 8	May 30	June 15	Sept. 21	Sept. 30
Taylor Narbonne	O	1904	1906	87	s	2.3	3 to 5	Mar. 21		...do...	...do...	May 29	June 16	Sept. 20	Oct. 4
Valencia	F	1907	1907	89	c, s	.9		Mar. 12		...do...				Oct. 17	
Mantuo de Pilas:															
Own roots	Gi	1904			c, s			Mar. 10	Mar. 24	May 26	June 3	May 30	June 9	Sept. 20	Sept. 25
Adobe Giant	F	1904	1906	88	s	2.4	3 to 4	Mar. 11	Mar. 26	May 13	May 19	May 19	May 27	Sept. 15	Sept. 20
Aramon × Rupestris Ganzin, No. 1	F	1904	1906	95	c, s	2.6	3 to 6	Mar. 10	Mar. 25	May 12	...do...	May 23	May 26	Sept. 5	...do...
Dog Ridge	F	1903	1905	86	c, s	2.5	3 to 5	Mar. 13	Mar. 27	May 14	May 20	May 24	May 30	Sept. 15	...do...
Herbemont	F	1903	1905	83	s	2	3 to 5	Mar. 7	Mar. 24	May 15	May 23	May 27		Sept. 5	...do...
Lenoir	F	1903	1905	87	s	1.8	3 to 5	...do...	Mar. 27	May 14	May 18	May 20	May 26	Sept. 10	Sept. 23
Do	O	1903	1905	89	s	2.9	3 to 4	Mar. 24		May 20	June 1	May 23	June 14	Sept. 23	Oct. 9
Mourvedre × Rupestris, No. 1202	F	1904	1906	93	c, s	3.7	3 to 6	Mar. 12	Mar. 26	May 15	May 20	May 24	May 30	Sept. 10	Sept. 20
Riparia Gloire	F	1903	1905	93	c, s	3.1	3 to 5	...do...	Mar. 20	...do...	May 21	May 25	...do...	Sept. 14	Sept. 19
Riparia × Rupestris, No. 101	F	1904	1906	89	c, s	2.8	2 to 6	...do...	...do...	May 12	May 23	...do...	May 29		
Riparia × Rupestris, No. 3309	F	1904	1906	93	c, s	2.9	3 to 6	Mar. 1	Mar. 30	May 13	May 22	...do...	May 28	Sept. 14	Sept. 20
Rupestris Martin	F	1903	1905	86	s	1.3	3 to 5	Mar. 13	Mar. 26	May 17	May 20	May 24	June 4	Sept. 8	Do.
Rupestris St. George	F	1903	1905	92	c, s	3.4	2 to 6	Mar. 12	Mar. 25	May 14	May 18	May 23	June 2	Sept. 10	Sept. 19
Do	O	1903	1908	87	s	3.1	2 to 4	Mar. 20		May 21	June 2	May 27	June 15	Sept. 22	Sept. 30
Salt Creek	F	1903	1905	86	s	1.7	2 to 6	Mar. 6	Mar. 30	May 13	May 21	May 24	June 3	Sept. 5	Sept. 20
Solonis × Riparia, No. 1616	F	1903	1905	92	c, s	4	4 to 6	Mar. 12	...do...	May 14	May 23	May 25	May 28	Sept. 13	Sept. 16
Taylor Narbonne	F	1904	1906	91	c, s	3.2	2 to 5	Mar. 6	Mar. 25	May 15	...do...	May 23	May 29	...do...	Do.
Marascina:															
Own roots	Gi	1905			c, s			Mar. 25	Mar. 30	May 30	June 6	June 5	June 12	Sept. 23	Sept. 24
Lenoir	O	1904		84	s	3.5		Mar. 23	May 10	June 1	May 16	June 18			
Maraville de Malaga:															
Lenoir	O	1904	1907	85	s	2.1	3 to 5	...do...		May 22	June 8	May 27	June 24	Sept. 24	Oct. 20
Riparia × Rupestris, No. 3309	F	1907	1907	92	c, s	6.3		Mar. 13	Apr. 8	May 20	May 23	...do...		Sept. 25	
Solonis × Othello, No. 1613	F	1907	1907	87	s	2.1	3 to 5	Mar. 11	...do...	May 21	May 26	June 2		Sept. 20	Sept. 21

Marmola Blad:														
Own roots	Gi	1904			s			Mar. 23	Apr. 10	May 29				Sept. 24
Marmora:														
Lenoir	F	1903	1905	85	s	1.5	2 to 6	Mar. 15	Apr. 3	May 18	May 20	May 24	May 30	Aug. 24	Sept. 27
Riparia Gloire	F	1903	1905	85	s	2.2	3 to 6	Mar. 8	Apr. 1	May 15	...do	May 25	June 4	...do	Sept. 19
Rupestris St. George	F	1903	1905	86	c, s	2	3 to 7	Mar. 15	Mar. 28	May 18	May 25	May 23	June 7	...do	Do.
Marsanne:															
Own roots	Gi	1904			s			...do	Mar. 27	May 26	June 4	May 31	June 9	Aug. 28	Sept. 22
Marzemino:															
Own roots	Gi	1904			s			Mar. 12	Apr. 3	...do		June 2		Sept. 20	Sept. 23
Do	O	1904			s		3 to 4	Mar. 23		May 9	June 5	May 15	June 17	Sept. 23	
Mataro:															
Own roots	Gi	1907			s			Mar. 20	Apr. 1	May 28				...do	
Aramon × Rupestris Ganzin, No. 1	O	1904	1906	90	s	3.4	2 to 5	Mar. 18		May 23	June 7	May 29	June 20	Sept. 27	Oct. 15
Dog Ridge	O	1903	1905	92	s	2.4	2 to 5			May 24	June 9	June 1	June 14	Sept. 22	Oct. 10
Herbemont	O	1903	1905	86	s	1.2	3 to 5			May 23	June 4	May 28	June 10	Sept. 28	Oct. 11
Lenoir	O	1903	1905	96	s	3.2	2 to 6	Mar. 22		May 24	June 6	May 29	June 12	Sept. 22	Oct. 8
Mourvèdre × Rupestris, No. 1202	O	1904	1906	89	s	3.1	2 to 4	Mar. 17		...do	June 5	...do	June 20	Sept. 28	Oct. 6
Rupestris Martin	O	1903	1905	91	s	3.3	3 to 5			May 22	June 6	May 27	June 11	Sept. 27	Oct. 11
Rupestris St. George	O	1903	1905	94	s	3.7	2 to 4			May 24	June 5	May 29	June 9	Sept. 24	Oct. 10
Salt Creek	O	1903	1905	89	s	1.7	2 to 4	Mar. 20		May 23	June 12	...do	June 16	Sept. 7	Oct. 11
Taylor Narbonne	O	1904	1906	88	s	2.8	2 to 4	Mar. 24		...do	June 8	...do	June 22	Sept. 27	Oct. 10
Melon:															
Dog Ridge	F	1903	1905	90	s	3.6	4 to 6	Mar. 12	Mar. 30	May 15	May 25	May 27	June 10	Aug. 25	Sept. 20
Rupestris St. George	F	1903	1905	88	s	2.1	4 to 5	Mar. 11	Mar. 28	May 12	May 17	May 20	May 27	...do	Sept. 19
Merlot:															
Own roots	Gi	1904			s			Mar. 15	Apr. 1	May 26	May 30	June 5		Sept. 15	
Meslier:															
Own roots	Gi	1905			s			Mar. 8	Apr. 3	May 20	...do	May 31	June 5	...do	Sept. 22
Aramon × Rupestris Ganzin, No. 1	O	1904		92	s	5	2 to 3	Mar. 19		May 29	May 31	June 5	June 16	Sept. 25	Oct. 10
Lenoir	O	1903	1905	89	s	4	2 to 5	Mar. 16		May 26	...do	May 29	June 12	Sept. 20	Oct. 8
Rupestris St. George	O	1903	1905	92	s	4.3	2 to 4	Mar. 21		May 21	May 30	May 26	...do	...do	Oct. 10
Meunier:															
Own roots	Gi	1905			s			Mar. 15	Apr. 1	May 22	May 26	...do	June 4	Aug. 23	Aug. 23
Dog Ridge	O	1904	1906	88	s	3.7	2 to 4	Mar. 20		May 10	June 5	May 24	June 17	Sept. 20	Oct. 3
Lenoir	O	1903	1905	85	s	3.4	3 to 5	Mar. 16		May 20	May 31	May 26	June 13	Sept. 25	Oct. 18
Rupestris St. George	O	1903	1905	90	c, s	4.3	2 to 5	Mar. 17		May 22	...do	May 27	June 7	Sept. 15	Oct. 8
Meyer, No. 59:															
Dog Ridge	O	1904	1906	90	s	2.5	2 to 5	Mar. 18		May 26	June 8	June 1	June 16	Sept. 24	Oct. 4
Lenoir	O	1904	1906	89	s	3.2	3 to 4	Mar. 20		May 23	June 12	May 27	June 17	Sept. 25	
Meyer, No. 60:															
Dog Ridge	O	1904	1906	93	s	3.1	3 to 5	Mar. 23		May 26	June 7	June 2	June 14	Sept. 23	Oct. 1
Lenoir	O	1904	1906	88	c, s	3.9	3 to 4	Mar. 20		May 25	June 5	May 29	June 19	Sept. 25	
Meyer, No. 65:															
Lenoir	O	1904	1906	93	s	4.3	3 to 5	Mar. 18		May 21	June 8	May 25	June 20	Sept. 28	Oct. 20
Meyer, No. 94:															
Dog Ridge	O	1904	1906	95	s	4.3	3 to 5	Mar. 17		May 22	May 31	May 27	June 12	Sept. 27	
Lenoir	O	1904	1906	91	s	5.3	3 to 4	Mar. 20		May 20	June 4	May 23	June 17	Sept. 26	Oct. 11
Meyer, No. 95:															
Dog Ridge	O	1904	1906	93	s	5.9	3 to 5	...do		May 26	June 5	June 2	June 14	Sept. 29	Oct. 4
Lenoir	O	1904	1906	93	s	5.3	3 to 5	Mar. 17		May 22	...do	May 25	June 17	Sept. 30	Oct. 7

TABLE VII.—*Relative behavior and value for different purposes of grape varieties tested by grafting an resistant stocks and by growing on their own roots in eleven experiment vineyards in California*—Continued.

Variety and stock (on own roots, if so stated).	Experiment vineyard.	Year stock was planted.	Year grafted.	Congeniality.	How pruned.	Weight of pruning per vine.	Nodes bearing fruit.	Growth-starting date.		Blossoming date.		Fruit-setting date.		Fruit-ripening date.	
								Early season.	Late season.	Early season.	Late season.	Early season.	Late season.	Early season.	Late season.
1	2	3	4	5	6	7	8	9	10	11	12	13	14	15	16
Mr, No. 103:				*P. ct.*		*Lbs.*									
Lenoir	O	1904	1906	88	s	2.4	....	Mar. 18	....	May 22	June 9	May 26	June 17	....	
Mr, No. 107:															
Lenoir	O	1904	1906	94	c, s	4.4	2 to 4	Mar. 16	....	May 19	June 4	May 23	June 8	Oct. 7	Oct. 10
Mr, No. 116:															
Dog Ridge	O	1904	1906	94	s	3.2	3 to 5	Mar. 19	....	May 26	June 9	June 1	June 24	Sept. 26	
Lenoir	O	1904	1906	90	s	4.8	3 to 5	Mar. 21	....	May 19	June 5	May 25	June 9	...do...	
Meyer, No. 515:															
Dog Ridge	O	1904	1906	85	s	2.1	3 to 4	...do...	....	May 23	...do...	May 29	June 11	Sept. 29	Oct. 15
Lenoir	O	1904	1906	89	s	3.3	....	....	....	...do...	....	May 24	....	Sept. 26	Oct. 10
Millenium:															
mon × Rupestris Ganzin, No. 1	O	1904	1907	90	s	3.7	2 to 4	Mar. 16	....	May 21	June 2	May 26	June 12	Sept. 26	Oct. 9
Lenoir	O	1904	1906	74	s	1.2	3 to 5	Mar. 22	....	May 24	June 1	May 28	June 10	Sept. 28	Oct. 2
Riparia × Rupestris, No. 101	O	1904	1907	70	s	.9	2 to 5	Mar. 18	....	May 21	June 2	May 26	June 15	Sept. 27	Oct. 6
Riparia × Rupestris, No. 3309	O	1904	1907	61	s	1.3	3 to 5	Mar. 20	....	May 20	June 1	May 25	June 13	Sept. 28	
Solonis × Riparia, No. 1616	O	1904	1907	68	s	.5	3 to 4	...do...	....	May 19	May 28	May 24	June 12	Sept. 25	Oct. 5
Mission:															
Own roots	Gi	1904	....	....	c, s	....	....	Mar. 22	Mar. 27	May 26	June 4	May 30	June 9	Sept. 15	Sept. 28
Adobe Giant	F	1904	1906	90	s	4.3	3 to 4	Mar. 11	Apr. 1	May 1	May 25	May 8	May 30	Sept. 8	Sept. 21
Dog Ridge	F	1903	1905	92	c, s	4	4 to 6	Mar. 14	Mar. 30	May 15	May 28	May 28	June 7	Sept. 5	Sept. 20
Do	O	1903	1907	94	s	3.8	2 to 4	Mar. 22	....	May 25	June 8	May 30	June 14	Sept. 28	Oct. 5
Herbemont	F	1903	1905	82	c, s	4.8	2 to 4	Mar. 13	Apr. 1	May 20	May 30	May 29	June 6	Sept. 5	Sept. 20
Do	O	1903	1905	91	s	4.1	2 to 5	Mar. 20	....	May 22	June 10	May 28	June 24	Sept. 28	Oct. 11
Lenoir	F	1903	1905	84	s	1.3	3 to 6	Mar. 9	Mar. 30	May 15	May 20	May 23	May 30	Sept. 10	Sept. 18
Do	O	1903	1905	93	s	4	2 to 4	Mar. 20	....	May 23	June 1	May 28	June 11	Sept. 27	Oct. 10
Riparia Gloire	F	1903	1905	90	c, s	3.3	2 to 5	Mar. 12	Mar. 25	May 20	May 27	May 24	June 10	Sept. 8	Sept. 19
Rupestris Mission	F	1903	1905	87	c, s	2.4	2 to 4	Mar. 14	Mar. 26	May 13	May 23	May 21	June 28	Sept. 11	Sept. 20
Do	O	1903	1905	96	s	3.8	2 to 4	Mar. 21	....	May 23	June 8	May 29	June 22	Oct. 1	Oct. 1
Rupestris St. George	F	1903	1905	95	c, s	5	3 to 7	Mar. 10	Mar. 31	May 18	May 26	May 23	June 2	Sept. 10	Sept. 19
Do	O	1903	1905	95	s	5.1	2 to 5	Mar. 21	....	May 20	June 1	May 26	June 11	Sept. 25	Oct. 10
Salt Creek	F	1903	1905	88	c, s	2.3	2 to 4	Mar. 13	Apr. 1	May 23	May 28	May 29	June 10	Sept. 8	Sept. 20
Do	O	1903	1905	91	s	2.8	2 to 5	Mar. 22	....	May 21	June 10	May 26	June 20	Sept. 26	Oct. 10

Molinera Gordo:															
Lenoir	O	1904	1907	82	s	3.2	3 to 5	Mar. 23	....	May 19	...do....	May 25	June 16	...do....	Do.
Mondeuse:															
Own roots	Gi	1904			s			Mar. 20	Mar. 30	May 26	May 28	May 30	June 5	Sept. 10	Sept. 24
Aramon × Rupestris Ganzin, No. 1	O	1904	1906	93	s	4.4	3 to 6	Mar. 21		May 24	June 3	May 29	June 10	Sept. 27	Oct. 5
Dog Ridge	O	1903	1905	91	s	3.8	2 to 4	Mar. 22		May 22	June 10	May 28	June 17	Sept. 5	Oct. 10
Herbemont	O	1903	1905	83	s	3.7	3 to 6	Mar. 18		May 25	June 5	May 30	June 18	Sept. 27	Oct. 11
Lenoir	O	1903	1905	93	s	4.6	2 to 4	Mar. 19		..do....	..do....	..do....	June 15	Sept. 22	Oct. 8
Mourvedre × Rupestris, No. 1202	O	1904	1906	91	c, s	3	3 to 5	Mar. 20		May 24	June 4	May 29	..do....	Sept. 23	Oct. 9
Riparia × Rupestris, No. 101	O	1904	1906	89	s	26	3 to 6			May 23		May 28		Sept. 26	Oct. 16
Riparia × Rupestris, No. 3309	O	1904	06	91	s	25	2 to 5	Mar. 17		May 20	June 4	May 26	June 16	Sept. 25	Oct. 11
Rupestris Martin	O	1903	1905	91	s	3.3	3 to 5	Mar. 20		May 21	June 5	..do....	June 19	Sept. 28	Oct. 6
Rupestris St. George	O	1903	1905	92	s	4.1	3 to 5	..do....		..do....	..do....	..do....	June 20	Sept. 29	Oct. 1
Salt Creek	O	1903	1905	90	c, s	2.2	3 to 6			May 22		May 28		Sept. 27	Oct. 6
Solonis × Riparia, No. 1616	O	1904	1906	86	s	2.3	2 to 5	Mar. 17		May 21	June 10	May 26	June 19	Sept. 25	Oct. 5
Taylor Narbonne	O	1904	1906	87	s	4.5	2 to 6	Mar. 21		May 24	June 5	May 29	June 17	..do....	Oct. 10
[illegible] Nero:															
Own roots	Gi	1904			s			Mar. 20	Mar. 30	May 28	June 6	June 2	June 11	Aug. 29	Sept. 25
[illegible]:															
Own roots	Gi	1904			s			Mar. 14	Apr. 1	..do....	June 3	June 1	June 10	Sept. 15	Do.
Aramon × Rupestris Ganzin, No. 1	O	1904	1906	90	s	3.3	2 to 4	Mar. 19		May 25	..do....	May 30	June 18	Sept. 29	Oct. 12
Dog Ridge	O	1904	1906	89	s	2.4	2 to 4	Mar. 20		..do....	June 1	..do....	June 15	Oct. 4	Oct. 10
Herbemont	O	1904	1909	91	s	3	2 to 5	Mar. 21		June 5	June 10	June 9	June 26	Oct. 5	Oct. 13
Lenoir	O	1903	1909	94	s	1		Mar. 24		June 2	June 8	June 5	June 20		
Riparia × Rupestris, No. 101	O	1904	1906	90	s	26	2 to 6	Mar. 20		May 24	June 5	May 29	June 18	Sept. 24	Oct. 15
Riparia × Rupestris, No. 3309	O	1904	1906	92	s	28	3 to 6	Mar. 18		..do....	..do....	..do....	June 20	Sept. 25	Oct. 11
Solonis × Riparia, No. 1616	O	1904	1906	88	s	2.1	2 to 5	..do....		May 26	..do....	June 2	June 19	Sept. 29	Oct. 10
Taylor Narbonne	O	1904	1906	90	s	3.4	3 to 5	..do....		..do....	June 3	..do....	..do....	Sept. 26	Oct. 5
Mourisco Bianca:															
Own roots	Gi	1904			s			Mar. 15	Mar. 26	..do....	June 1	May 31	June 6	Sept. 18	Sept. 25
Dog Ridge	O	1904	1906	93	s	3.7	2 to 5	Mar. 18		May 19	..do....	May 24	June 12	Sept. 30	Oct. 5
Lenoir	O	1903	1905	93	s	3.2	3 to 5	Mar. 20		May 20	June 3	May 25	June 13	Sept. 28	Sept. 30
Rupestris St. George	O	1903	1905	93	s	4.6	2 to 5	Mar. 17		May 21	June 1	May 26	..do....	Sept. 25	Do.
Taylor Narbonne	O	1904	1906	93	s	2.8	2 to 4	Mar. 20		May 25	June 7	May 30	June 11	Sept. 20	Oct. 4
Mourisco Preto:															
Own roots	Gi	1904			s			Mar. 18	Mar. 25	May 26	May 30	May 31	June 3	Aug. 29	Sept. 20
Dog Ridge	O	1904	1906	95	c, s	6.1	2 to 4	Mar. 20		May 27	June 3	June 2	June 15	Sept. 25	Oct. 5
Lenoir	O	1903	1905	95	c, s	4.7	2 to 4	Mar. 16		May 20	May 31	May 25	June 10	..do....	Oct. 6
Rupestris St. George	O	1903	1905	93	s	5.5	2 to 4	..do....		May 26	..do....	May 30	June 15	Sept. 30	Oct. 8
Muscadelle du Bordelais:															
Adobe Giant	F	1904	1906	82	s	1	3 to 5	Mar. 13	Mar. 27	May 11	May 16	May 21	May 25	Aug. 20	Sept. 20
Aramon × Rupestris Ganzin, No. 1	F	1904	1906	90	s	3.4	3 to 6	Mar. 6	Mar. 25	May 12	..do....	May 20	May 26	Aug. 3	Do.
Lenoir	F	1903	1905	87	s	1.4	3 to 6	Mar. 7	Mar. 30	May 10	May 15	May 19	May 25	Aug. 5	Sept. 10
Mourvedre × Rupestris, No. 1202	F	1904	1906	90	c, s	3	3 to 6	Mar. 18	Mar. 27	May 14	May 19	May 20	May 27	Aug. 1	Sept. 20
Riparia Gloire	F	1903	1904	88	c, s	3.2	2 to 5	Mar. 11	Mar. 25	May 17	..do....	May 23	..do....	Aug. 15	Sept. 4
Riparia × Rupestris, No. 101	F	1904	1906	88	c, s	2.4	3 to 5	Mar. 8	Mar. 28	May 10	May 17	May 20	May 25	Aug. 10	Sept. 20
Riparia × Rupestris, No. 3309	F	1904	1906	89	s	33	2 to 6	Mar. 12	Apr. 1	..do....	May 16	..do....	..do....	Aug. 5	Do.
Rupestris St. George	F	1903	1905	86	c, s	2.4	2 to 5	..do....	Mar. 30	..do....	May 15	May 15	..do....	Aug. 3	Sept. 19
Solonis × Riparia, No. 1616	F	1904	1906	86	s	1.7	3 to 6	Mar. 7	Mar. 28	May 14	May 16	May 20	May 24	Aug. 1	Sept. 3
Taylor Narbonne	F	1904	1905	88	s	23	3 to 5	Mar. 6	Mar. 25	May 12	..do....	..do....	May 31	Aug. 5	Sept. 20

TABLE VII.—*Relative behavior and value for different purposes of grape varieties tested by grafting on resistant stocks and by growing on their own roots in eleven experiment vineyards in California*—Continued.

Variety and stock (on own roots, if so stated).	Experiment vineyard.	Year stock was planted.	Year grafted.	Congeniality.	How pruned.	Weight of pruning per vine.	Nodes bearing fruit.	Growth-starting date.		Blossoming date.		Fruit-setting date.		Fruit-ripening date.	
								Early season.	Late season.	Early season.	Late season.	Early season.	Late season.	Early season.	Late season.
1	2	3	4	5	6	7	8	9	10	11	12	13	14	15	16
Mat (S. P. I. No. 3063):				P. ct.		Lbs.									
roots	O	1904	....	.....	s	.2	3 to 4	Mar. 20	....	May 12	June 12	May 17	June 16	Oct. 10	
Mat ns:															
Own roots	Gi	1905	....	.....	s	....	....	...do.....	Mar. 28	...do.....	May 29	May 18	June 4	Aug. 27	Sept. 25
on × is in, No. 1	F	1904	1906	87	s	2.1	2 to 6	Mar. 22	Apr. 1	May 20	May 23	May 27	May 31	Aug. 20	Sept. 2
ir	F	1903	1905	87	c, s	1.7	2 to 6	Mar. 13	Mar. 30	May 12	May 19	May 23	May 27	Aug. 23	Sept. 15
re × Rupestris, No. 1202	F	1904	1906	92	c, s	4.8	2 to 6	Mar. 14	...do.....	May 15	May 20	May 21	June 1	Aug. 18	Sept. 20
Riparia Gloire	F	1903	1905	84	s	2.6	2 to 5	Mar. 20	Apr. 1	May 13	May 18	May 22	May 26	Aug. 20	Sept. 19
Riparia × s, No. 101	F	1904	1906	87	s	2.7	2 to 5	Mar. 13	Mar. 30	May 16	May 20	May 24	...do.....	...do....	Sept. 20
ia × s, No. 3309	F	1904	1906	91	c, s	5.7	2 to 5	Mar. 23	Apr. 1	May 12	May 23	May 21	May 28	Aug. 8	Do.
is St. G ege	F	1903	1905	92	s	4.3	2 to 5	Mar. 24	...do.....	May 14	May 16	...do.....	May 29	Aug. 20	Sept. 19
Solonis × Riparia, No. 1616	F	1904	1906	85	s	1.4	3 to 5	Mar. 21	Mar. 30	May 12	May 20	May 25	May 27	Aug. 18	Sept. 2
Taylor ne	F	1904	1906	88	s	3	3 to 6	Mar. 12	...do.....	May 13	...do.....	May 24	May 26	Aug. 15	Sept. 20
Mat Bonod:															
ri × Riparia, No. 420A	F	1909	1909	.....	s	1	....	Mar. 22	Apr. 8	May 18	May 22	May 29	....	Sept. 15	
De Grasset	F	1909	1909	80	s	2	....	Mar. 26	....	May 24	....	....	....	Oct. 17	
Lenoir	O	1904	1907	79	s	1.7	2 to 5	...do.....	....	May 23	June 10	May 28	June 25	Sept. 28	Oct. 25
Riparia × s, No. 101	F	1907	1907	82	s	1.7	3 to 5	Mar. 24	Apr. 8	May 18	May 24	May 29	....	Oct. 17	
Riparia × Rupestris, No. 3309	F	1907	1907	89	s	3.5	3 to 5	Mar. 25	Apr. 5	May 20	...do.....	June 3	....	...do.....	
Rupestris St. e	F	1907	1907	87	s	2	2 to 5	Mar. 24	Apr. 8	May 26	May 26	June 2	....	Sept. 15	
nis ta	F	1907	1907	90	s	3.3	2 to 5	Mar. 21	Apr. 5	May 16	...do.....	May 30	....	Sept. 21	
ia	F	1907	1907	92	s	4	2 to 5	Mar. 23	....	May 28	....	....	....	Oct. 17	
Mat es:															
n rots	Gi	1905	....	.....	c, s	....	....	Mar. 18	Mar. 27	May 26	May 27	May 30	....	Sept. 10	
Dog ge	O	1904	1906	79	s	2.8	2 to 5	Mar. 26	....	...do.....	June 11	...do.....	June 15	Sept. 20	
ir	O	1903	1905	85	s	2.1	2 to 4	Mar. 18	....	May 21	May 31	May 26	June 14	Sept. 9	Sept. 21
Rupestris St. George	O	1903	1905	85	s	3.4	2 to 5	...do.....	....	May 26	June 3	June 1	...do.....	...do.....	Sept. 23
r:															
n roots	Gi	1905	....	.....	c, s	....	....	Mar. 17	Mar. 28	...do.....	...do.....	June 8	....	Aug. 27	Sept. 20
Dog ge	F	1903	1906	89	c, s	2.4	3 to 5	Mar. 8	Mar. 26	May 14	May 20	May 25	May 29	Aug. 5	Do.
ir	F	1903	1905	87	s	1.2	3 to 6	Mar. 12	Mar. 25	May 10	May 14	May 16	May 24	Aug. 24	Sept. 10
loire	F	1903	1905	76	s	1.2	3 to 5	Mar. 10	...do.....	May 16	May 20	May 24	May 29	Aug. 21	Sept. 19
Rupestris St. George	F	1903	1905	89	c, s	2.3	3 to 5	Mar. 13	...do.....	May 8	May 18	May 14	May 24	Aug. 20	Do.

Muscat Gros Noir Hatif:														
Own roots	Gi	1905	....	......	s	....	....	Mar. 18	Mar. 27	My 14	My 27	My 20	June 1	Aug. 27	Sept. 23
Dog Ridge	O	1904	1906	90	s	2.9	3 to 4	Mar. 20	....	May 25	May 31	May 30	June 10	Sept. 15	Oct. 10
Lenoir	O	1903	1905	84	s	2.2	2 to 5	Mr. 17	....	May 22	une 1	My 28	June 12	...do.....	Ot. 6
Rupestris St. George	O	1903	1905	86	s	2.9	3 to 6	Mar. 18	....	...do.....	do.....	...do.....	June 14	Spt. 10	Spt. 26
T ar Narbonne	O	1904	1906	84	s	2.6	1 to 4	do.....	....	My 24	...do.....	My 29	...do....	Sept. 15	O.. 4
t g:															
Own roots	Gi	1905	....	......	c, s	....	....	...do.....	Mar. 28	May 26	May 27	May 30	June 3	Aug. 27	Spt. 23
Aramon × pestris Ganzin, No. 1	F	1907	1907	86	s	3	2 to 4	Mar. 24	Apr. 1	May 16	May 23	May 27	....	Aug. 20	
Dog Ridge	O	1904	1906	87	s	3.9	2 to 5	Mar. 22	....	May 25	June 5	May 30	June 17	Spt. 25	Oct. 4
Lenoir	O	1903	1905	83	s	2	3 to 5	Mar. 24	....	May 30	June 1	June 6	June 15	...do.....	Oct. 6
Monticola × Rupestris	F	1907	1907	88	s	2.2	3 to 4	Mar. 26	Apr. 1	May 15	May 22	May 28	....	Aug. 24	
Riparia × Rupestris, No. 3309	F	1907	1907	83	s	1.6	....	Mar. 23	Apr. 2	May 18	do.....	May 27	....	Aug. 15	Aug. 25
Rupestris St. George	O	1903	1905	90	s	3.9	2 to 6	Mat. 17	....	May 19	June 3	May 24	June 16	Sept. 15	Sept. 30
Rupestris × Berlandieri, No. 219A	F	1907	1907	84	s	18	3 to 5	Mar. 20	Apr. 2	May 17	May 22	May 29	....	Aug. 15	Aug. 25
Taylor Narbonne	O	1904	1906	80	s	2.2	3 to 6	Mar. 19	....	May 21	June 2	May 27	June 17	Spt. 25	Oct. 4
Muscat Hamburg Noir d'Hongrie:															
Own roots	Gi	1905	....	......	s	....	....	Mr. 26	Apr. 1	My 26	June 1	My 30	Jne 6	Aug. 27	Sept. 20
Muscat Noir d'Hongrie:															
Lenoir	F	1903	1905	83	s	1.7	t05	Mar. 14	Mar. 30	May 14	May 18	May 18	May 26	Aug. 24	Spt. 18
Do	O	1903	1905	90	s	2.8	t05	Mar. 22	....	May 24	June 4	May 29	June 18	Spt. 25	Oct. 6
Riparia Gloire	F	1903	1905	90	c, s	3.6	t05	Mar. 10	Apr. 1	May 12	May 18	May 22	May 29	Aug. 20	Sept. 19
Rupestris St. George	F	1903	1905	89	s	3.7	2 to 5	Mar. 14	Mar. 25	May 10	May 16	May 19	May 25	Aug. 22	D.
Do	O	1903	1905	90	s	5.4	t05	Mar. 16	....	May 22	June 1	May 27	June 14	Sept. 15	Oct. 8
Muscat Nir e:															
n × Rupestris Ganzin, No. 2	F	1907	1907	91	s	3.5	t06	Mar. 21	Apr. 1	May 16	May 23	May 26	....	Aug. 25	Aug. 29
Dog Ridge	O	904	1906	81	s	.9	2to 4	Mar. 22	....	May 23	May 31	May 29	June 13	Sept. 28	Oct. 8
ebir	O	1903	1905	88	s	2.9	t04	Mar. 18	....	May 26	June 3	June 1	June 10	...do.....	Do.
Lukfata	F	1907	1907	93	s	5	3 to 5	Mar. 25	Apr. 1	May 16	May. 22	May 29	....	Aug. 20	Aug. 25
la × Riparia, No. 18804	F	1907	1907	92	c, s	6.3	3 to 5	Mar. 21	...do.....	...do.....	...do.....	...do.....	....	d.....	
Rupestris St. George	O	1903	1905	91	s	4	t04	Mar. 20	....	May 24	May 30	...do.....	June 10	Sept. 20	Sept. 30
Rupestris × Berlandieri, No. 219A	F	1907	1907	88	s	2.8	t06	...do.....	Apr. 1	May 15	May 22	May 27	....	Aug. 20	Aug. 24
Solonis × Othello	F	1907	1907	89	s	3.5	3 to 6	Mar. 25	....	May 22	....	....	....	Aug. 29	
Taylor Narbonne	O	904	1906	85	s	2	t05	Mar. 22	....	May 23	June 4	May 28	June 16	Spt. 25	Oct. 8
Muscat e:															
Dog ge	F	1903	1906	88	c, s	2.8	3 to 7	Mar. 7	Mar. 30	May 13	May 18	May 24	May 28	Aug. 26	Sept. 20
Lenoir	F	1903	1905	82	s	1	2 to 6	Mar. 6	Mar. 25	May 12	do.....	May 21	May 25	Aug. 5	Spt. 10
Riparia e	F	1903	1905	88	c, s	3.9	2 to 6	Mar. 12	...do.....	May 15	May 16	May 20	May 31	Aug. 1	Sept. 19
Rupestris St. George	F	1903	1905	86	c, s	3.3	3 to 6	do.....	Mar. 28	May 12	May 15	May 18	May 27	Aug. 10	Do.
Muscat e de Madre:															
bir	F	1903	1905	76	s	1	3 to 5	Mar. 16	Mar. 30	My 11	d.....	My 19	My 24	....	
Riparia Gloire	F	1903	1905	86	c, s	3.3	2 to 6	Mar. 10	pr. 1	My 10	My 21	May 24	My 26	Aug. 5	Sept. 19
is St. George	F	1903	1905	88	c, s	4.3	2 to 5	Mar. 12	Mar. 28	My 12	My 15	My 18	My 25	Aug. 24	Do.
Mat t:															
Own te	Gi	1905	....	......	s	....	....	Mar. 15	Apr. 3	My 26	My 28	Jne 1	....	Sept. 18	
bir	O	1903	1905	86	s	3.3	3 to 6	do.....	....	My 23	ne 5	My 27	June 18	Sept. 9	Sept. 25
Rupestris St. George	O	1903	1907	86	s	4.5	....	Mar. 23	....	My 25	...do.....	May 30	June 14	...do.....	Do.
M:															
Own ots	Gi	1904	....	......	s	....	....	do.....	Apr. 1	My 24	Jne 6	My 29	June 13	Sept. 10	Sept. 22

TABLE VII.—*Relative behavior and value for different purposes of grape varieties tested by grafting on resistant stocks and by growing on their own roots in eleven experiment vineyards in California*—Continued.

Variety and stock (on own roots, if so stated).	Experiment vineyard.	Year stock was planted.	Year grafted.	Congeniality.	How pruned.	Weight of pruning per vine.	Nodes bearing fruit.	Growth-starting date.		Blossoming date.		Fruit-setting date.		Fruit-ripening date.	
								Early season.	Late season.	Early season.	Late season.	Early season.	Late season.	Early season.	Late season.
1	2	3	4	5	6	7	8	9	10	11	12	13	14	15	16
				P. ct.		*Lbs.*									
Nasa Valentiana:															
Own roots	Gi	1905			c, s			Mar. 8	Mar. 30	May 25	May 30	June 1	June 3	Sept. 21	
Rupestris St. George	F	1903	1905	83	s	1.8	2 to 5	Mar. 3	Mar. 15	May 10	May 15	May 20	May 28	Aug. 25	Sept. 19
Nebbiolo:															
Own roots	Gi	1905			s			Mar. 15	Apr. 3	May 22	June 1	May 27	June 5	Sept. 5	Sept. 24
Dog Ridge	O	1904	1906	93	s	4.4	2 to 4	Mar. 20		May 25	June 2	May 29	June 12	Sept. 25	Oct. 4
Lenoir	O	1904	1906	90	s	3.4	2 to 4	Mar. 19		May 24	June 5	May 28	June 17	...do...	Oct. 8
Rupestris St. George	O	1903	1905	84	s	2	2 to 4	Mar. 24		May 20	June 3	May 26	June 15	Sept. 27	Sept. 30
Nebbiolo Bourgu:															
Dog Ridge	O	1904	1906	93	s	4.1	3 to 5	Mar. 17		May 22	June 5	May 28	June 19	Sept. 23	Oct. 8
Lenoir	O	1903	1905	88	s	3.8	2 to 5	Mar. 14		May 19	May 30	May 23	June 14	Sept. 25	
Rupestris St. George	O	1903	1905	88	s	4.1	2 to 4	Mar. 18		May 24	May 31	May 30	June 10	Sept. 24	Sept. 30
Taylor [illegible]	O	1904	1907	81	s	1.6	4 to 5	Mar. 30		May 19	May 28	May 24	June 9	Sept. 23	Oct. 2
[illegible]lo Fino:															
Dog Ridge	O	1904	1906	89	s	4	3 to 5	Mar. 18		...do...	June 1	May 25	June 15	...do...	Oct. 4
Lenoir	O	1903	1905	86	s	2.8	3 to 5	Mar. 16		...do...	...do...	May 23	June 13	...do...	Sept. 28
[illegible]is St. George	O	1903	1905	84	s	2.8	2 to 4	Mar. 20		May 24	May 25	May 29	June 2	...do...	Sept. 30
[illegible]or Narbonne	O	1904	1906	78	s	1.2	3 to 4	Mar. 24		May 19	May 30	May 24	June 10		
[illegible]ra di Gattinara:															
Own roots	Gi	1904			s			Mar. 14	Apr. 1	May 22	...do...	May 27	June 5	Sept. 16	Sept. 22
Negro [illegible]aro:															
Own roots	Gi	1904			s			Mar. 20	Mar. 29	May 24	June 3	May 30	June 10	Aug. 27	Sept. 23
Neiretta di [illegible]lla:															
Own roots	Gi	1904			c, s			Mar. 10	Mar. 30	May 22	May 28	May 27	June 3	Sept. 23	Sept. 25
Ocru di Boe:															
Own roots	Gi	1904			c, s			Mar. 17	Mar. 28	May 28				Sept. 15	Sept. 21
[illegible]z:															
Lenoir	O	1906	1909	93	s	1.2		Mar. 18		June 5	June 14	June 9	June 20		
Olivette [illegible]he:															
[illegible]be Giant	F	1907	1907	98	c, s	7.7	2 to 5	Mar. 21	Apr. 2	May 19	May 23	May 29		Sept. 21	
Lenoir	O	1907	1907	88	s	2.8	2 to 5	Mar. 20		May 20	June 8	May 26	June 20	Sept. 30	Oct. 10
Riparia à Grandes Feuilles	F	1907	1907	96	c, s	6.6	3 to 5	Mar. 12	Apr. 1	May 21	May 23	June 1		Aug. 25	Sept. 21
Riparia × Rupestris, No. 101	F	1907	1907	97	c, s	6.2	3 to 5	Mar. 22	...do...	May 19	May 24	May 30		Aug. 26	

Olivette Chaptal:															
Lenoir	O	1904	1907	83	s	2.1	2 to 5	Mar. 24	....	May 21	June 10	May 26	June 17	Sept. 26	Oct. 26
Solonis Robusta	F	1907	1907	92	s	8.1	3 to 5	...do...	Apr. 1	...do...	May 22	May 29	....	Sept. 21	
Olivette Noir:															
Lenoir	O	1904	1907	81	s	2	3 to 6	Mar. 26	....	May 23	June 10	May 27	June 25	Sept. 27	Oct. 20
[illegible]de × [illegible]is, No. 1202	F	1907	1907	91	c, s	6.3	3 to 5	Mar. 24	Apr. 5	May 20	May 25	May 29	....	Sept. 15	
Riparia × Rupestris, No. 3309	F	1907	1907	94	c, s	7.3	....	Mar. 23	...do...	May 21	...do...	May 30	....	Sept. 17	
Solonis × Othello, No. 1613	F	1907	1907	95	c, s	8.6	2 to 5	Mar. 25	...do...	May 20	...do...	May 31	....	Sept. 15	
[illegible]te Rose:															
Lenoir	O	1904	1907	89	s	3.1	2 to 4	Mar. 19	....	May 24	June 5	May 29	June 20	Sept. 27	Oct. 16
[illegible]:															
[illegible]eir	O	1904	1907	87	s	2.2	3 to 5	Mar. 20	....	May 19	...do...	May 24	June 17	....	
[illegible]:															
Own roots	Gi	1904	....	....	c, s	....	....	...do...	Mar. 26	May 26	June 3	May 31	June 8	Aug. 29	Sept. 25
[illegible]to:															
Own roots	Gi	1904	....	....	s	....	....	Mar. 10	Mar. 27	...do...	June 8	...do...	June 14	Sept. 20	Do.
Dog Ridge	O	1904	1906	94	s	5.6	1 to 4	Mar. 20	....	May 25	...do...	May 30	June 20	Sept. 28	Oct. 10
Lenoir	O	1903	1905	90	c, s	4.1	3 to 5	Mar. 16	....	May 26	June 5	June 1	June 19	Sept. 27	Oct. 8
Rupestris St. George	O	1905	1905	94	s	5.8	3 to 5	Mar. 17	....	...do...	June 1	...do...	June 13	...do...	Oct. 10
Taylor Narbonne	O	1904	1906	83	s	2	2 to 4	Mar. 18	....	May 19	...do...	May 25	June 11	Sept. 28	Do.
Palarusa:															
Own roots	Gi	1904	....	....	s	....	....	Mar. 26	Mar. 28	May 26	June 10	May 31	June 15	Sept. 20	Sept. 30
Panariti:															
Adobe Giant	F	1904	1906	94	c, s	10.1	2 to 4	Mar. 7	...do...	May 14	May 19	May 24	June 1	Aug. 3	
Aramon × Rupestris Ganzin, No. 1	F	1904	1906	95	c, s	6.5	2 to 4	Mar. 10	Apr. 1	May 13	May 22	...do...	June 27	July 28	Aug. 1
Dog Ridge	F	1903	1905	91	s	3.2	2 to 4	Mar. 7	Mar. 27	...do...	...do...	May 26	May 28	July 25	Do.
[illegible]nt	F	1903	1905	76	s	1.7	2 to 5	...do...	Mar. 30	May 12	May 18	May 29	...do...	....	
Lenoir	F	1903	1905	90	c, s	1.7	2 to 4	Mar. 8	Mar. 25	May 11	...do...	May 22	May 24	July 25	
[illegible]dre × Rupestris, No. 1202	F	1904	1906	94	s	5.5	3 to 5	Mar. 5	Apr. 1	May 15	May 20	May 25	June 4	...do...	Aug. 8
[illegible]re	F	1903	1905	94	c, s	5.5	2 to 5	...do...	Mar. 25	May 10	May 18	May 23	May 25	...do...	Aug. 3
Riparia × Rupestris, No. 101	F	1904	1906	73	s	1.2	....	...do...	...do...	May 14	May 20	May 25	May 29	....	
Riparia × Rupestris, No. 3309	F	1904	1906	94	c, s	5.6	2 to 4	Mar. 8	Mar. 27	May 12	...do...	May 21	May 25	July 25	Aug. 1
Rupestris Martin	F	1903	1905	86	s	1.9	....	Mar. 12	Mar. 25	May 13	May 16	May 25	May 27	....	
Rupestris St. George	F	1903	1905	96	c, s	6.1	3 to 6	Mar. 11	...do...	...do...	May 18	May 23	May 30	July 25	Do.
Salt Creek	F	1903	1905	90	c, s	5.1	2 to 5	Mar. 9	...do...	May 12	...do...	...do...	May 26	...do...	
Solonis × Riparia, No. 1616	F	1904	1906	90	c, s	4.8	3 to 5	Mar. 7	...do...	...do...	May 20	May 25	May 27	...do...	Do.
Taylor Narbonne	F	1904	1906	92	c, s	3.4	2 to 4	...do...	Mar. 28	May 13	...do...	...do...	May 28	July 28	
Parc de Versailles:															
Adobe Giant	F	1904	1906	93	c, s	5.5	2 to 5	Mar. 14	Mar. 25	May 12	May 23	May 22	...do...	Aug. 20	Sept. 21
[illegible]mon × [illegible]is Ganzin, No. 1	F	1904	1906	91	c, s	6.1	2 to 5	Mar. 6	...do...	May 14	May 16	May 21	May 27	Aug. 5	Sept. 20
Dog Ridge	F	1904	1906	95	s	7.3	2 to 5	Mar. 7	Mar. 30	May 12	May 25	May 24	May 30	...do...	Do.
Lenoir	F	1903	1905	90	c, s	3.2	2 to 5	Mar. 5	Mar. 15	May 18	May 20	May 22	May 25	Aug. 25	Sept. 19
[illegible]e × Rupestris, No. 1202	F	1904	1906	81	s	1.8	3 to 5	Mar. 4	...do...	May 15	May 22	June 1	June 5	...do...	Sept. 20
Ponroy	F	1907	1907	93	c, s	10.5	3 to 5	Mar. 21	....	May 21	....	....	....	Sept. 21	
Riparia Gloire	F	1903	1905	91	c, s	6.7	2 to 4	Mar. 8	Mar. 20	May 10	May 20	May 20	May 26	Aug. 5	Sept. 19
Riparia × Rupestris, No. 101	F	1904	1906	80	s	1.4	3 to 5	Mar. 20	Mar. 29	...do...	May 15	May 24	May 25	....	
Riparia × Rupestris, No. 3309	F	1904	1906	94	c, s	5.4	2 to 5	Mar. 8	Mar. 28	May 12	May 25	May 27	May 30	Aug. 10	Sept. 20
Rupestris [illegible]	F	1907	1907	92	s	5	3 to 6	Mar. 20	....	May 21	....	....	....	Oct. 17	
Rupestris St. George	F	1903	1905	96	c, s	7.6	2 to 5	Mar. 10	Mar. 15	May 8	May 17	May 20	May 23	Aug. 20	Sept. 19
Solonis × Riparia, No. 1616	F	1904	1906	84	s	2.8	4 to 5	Mar. 6	Mar. 25	May 11	May 20	May 25	May 28	Aug. 25	Sept. 20
[illegible]lor [illegible]e	F	1904	1906	96	c, s	6	3 to 6	Mar. 5	...do...	...do...	May 23	May 24	...do...	Aug. 5	Do.

TABLE VII.—*Relative behavior and value for different purposes of grape varieties tested by grafting on resistant stocks and by growing on their own roots in eleven experiment vineyards in California*—Continued.

Variety and stock (on own roots, if so stated).	Experiment vineyard.	Year stock was planted.	Year grafted.	Congeniality.	How pruned.	Weight of pruning per vine.	Nodes bearing fruit.	Growth-starting date.		Blossoming date.		Fruit-setting date.		Fruit-ripening date.	
								Early season.	Late season.	Early season.	Late season.	Early season.	Late season.	Early season.	Late season.
1	2	3	4	5	6	7	8	9	10	11	12	13	14	15	16
Pedro Ximines:				P.ct.			Lbs.								
Own roots	Gi	1904	......	......	c, s	......	......	Mar. 12	Mar. 28	May 22	May 30	May 29	June 6	Aug. 29	Sept. 25
Adobe Giant	F	1904	1906	84	s	.8	2 to 4	Mar. 7	Mar. 26	May 13	May 20	May 24	May 26	Sept. 15	Sept. 21
Aramon × Rupestris Ganzin, No. 1	F	1904	1906	88	c, s	2.7	3 to 5	Mar. 5	Mar. 30	May 20	May 28	May 25	June 4	Sept. 8	Sept. 15
Dog Ridge	F	1903	1905	90	s	2.4	3 to 5	Mar. 13	Mar. 26	May 14	May 22	May 27	May 30	Sept. 10	Sept. 20
Herbemont	F	1903	1905	72	s	1.1	3 to 5	...do.....	Mar. 25	May 15	May 20	May 24	June 1	Sept. 13	Do.
Lenoir	F	1903	1905	88	s	.9	2 to 5	...do.....	Mar. 27	...do.....	...do.....	May 22	May 29	Sept. 15	Sept. 19
Mourvèdre × Rupestris, No. 1202	F	1904	1906	94	c, s	3.7	3 to 6	...do.....	Mar. 26	May 14	...do.....	May 24	May 26	Sept. 10	Sept. 20
Riparia Gloire	F	1903	1905	89	c, s	3	2 to 5	Mar. 8	Mar. 20	May 15	May 28	May 21	June 5	...do.....	Sept. 19
Riparia × Rupestris, No. 101	F	1904	1906	94	c, s	3.8	4 to 7	Mar. 12	Mar. 26	May 14	May 20	May 22	May 26	Sept. 5	Sept. 20
Riparia × Rupestris, No. 3309	F	1904	1906	95	c, s	3.6	3 to 5	Mar. 11	Mar. 25	May 11	...do.....	May 25	...do.....	Sept. 8	Do.
Rupestris Martin	F	1903	1905	84	s	1.5	2 to 5	Mar. 13	Mar. 28	May 15	May 18	May 23	May 25	Sept. 10	Sept. 16
Rupestris St. George	F	1903	1905	93	c, s	3.2	4 to 6	...do.....	Mar. 20	May 12	May 16	May 21	May 30	Sept. 8	Sept. 19
Salt Creek	F	1903	1905	81	s	1.3	3 to 5	Mar. 10	Mar. 30	May 15	May 23	May 23	May 28	Sept. 10	Sept. 20
Solonis × Riparia, No. 1616	F	1904	1906	92	c, s	2.9	3 to 5	Mar. 6	Apr. 1	...do.....	...do.....	May 25	...do.....	...do.....	Do.
Taylor Narbonne	F	1904	1906	90	c, s	2.2	3 to 5	Mar. 11	Mar. 25	May 14	May 20	May 23	May 27	Sept. 15	Do.
Perle Blanche:															
Lenoir	O	1903	1905	89	s	3.4	3 to 6	....	....	May 20	June 5	May 26	June 20	Sept. 23	Sept. 28
Rupestris St. George	O	1903	1905	91	s	4.4	2 to 4	Mar. 19	....	May 23	June 4	May 27	June 18	...do.....	Oct. 15
Lenoir	O	1904	1907	80	s	1.2	2 to 6	Mar. 21	....	May 18	June 3	May 24	June 15	Sept. 25	
Perruno:															
Own roots	Gi	1904	......	......	s	......	......	Mar. 14	Mar. 29	May 24	June 4	May 29	June 10	Sept. 10	Sept. 23
Persian, No. 21:															
Own roots	Gi	1904	......	......	c, s	......	......	Mar. 18	Mar. 30	May 30	....	....	....	Sept. 20	
Persian, No. 25:															
Own roots	Gi	1904	......	......	c, s	......	......	Mar. 16	Mar. 25	...do.....	June 3	June 10	....	Sept. 24	
Persian, No. 26:															
Own roots	Gi	1904	......	......	c, s	......	......	Mar. 20	Mar. 28	June 3	June 5	June 11	....	...do.....	
Peru:															
Lenoir	O	1903	1909	92	s	3.2	3 to 4	Mar. 26	....	June 9	June 10	June 13	June 27	Sept. 25	Oct. 8

[illegible]lt Syr[illegible]:															
[illegible] [illegible]ts	G	1907			s			Mar. 27	Apr. 1	May 30					
[illegible] Giant	G	1904	1909	83	s	1.2		Mar. 7	Mar. 29	May 29		June 1		Sept. 20	
([illegible]s × [illegible]a) × [illegible]a × Rupestris, No. 554–5)	G	1904	1909	90	s	4.2		Mar. 9	Apr. 1	May 25	May 27	June 10		Sept. 28	Do.
Aramon × [illegible]l	G	1904	1909	95	s	4.1		Mar. 6	Apr. 2	May 28				Sept. 23	Do.
Do.	O	1904	1906	85	s	3.7	2 to 5	Mar. 18		May 20	June 1	May 26	June 12	Sept. 24	Oct. 6
[illegible] [illegible]o. 2	G	1904	1909	95	s	3.5		Mar. 8	Mar. 30	May 27	June 3	June 12		Sept. 20	Oct. 4
Aramon × Rupestris Ganzin, No. 9	G	1904	1909	60	s	.5		Mar. 2		June 15				Oct. 7	
Australis	G	1904	1909	91	s	1.1		Mar. 10	Apr. 1	May 27				Sept. 22	Oct. 8
[illegible]i, [illegible]l	G	1904	1909	78	s	1.5		Mar. 6	do.	June 3	June 18	July 2		Sept. 26	Oct. 7
Berlandieri, No. 2	G	1904	1909	86	s	1		Mar. 10	Mar. 27	June 1				Sept. 28	Oct. 1
Berlandieri Lafont, No. 9	G	1904	1909	91	s	.5		Mar. 5	Mar. 30	do.				do.	Do.
[illegible]i × Riparia, No. 34EM	G	1904	1909	90	s	35		Mar. 2	Apr. 1	May 28				Sept. 30	Oct. 8
Berlandieri × Riparia, No. 157–11	G	1904	1909	82	s	1.8		Mar. 4	Mar. 27	do.				do.	Do.
Berlandier[illegible] [illegible]o. 420A	G	1904	1909	72	s	.5		Mar. 6	Mar. 28					Sept. 20	
Do.	O	1907	1909	76	s	1.1	2 to 4	Mar. 21		June 1	June 4	June 8	June 13	do.	Do.
Bourisquou × Rupestris, No. 109–4	G	1904	1909	88	s	3		Mar. 5	Apr. 1	May 27		June 3		do.	Oct. 12
(Bourisquou × Rupestris, No. 601) × [illegible]a, No. 13205	G	1907	1909	86	s	1.7		do.	Apr. 3	May 30				Sept. 26	Oct. 7
Bourisquou × [illegible], No. 3907	G	1904	1909	97	s	3.5		Mar. 7	Apr. 1	June 2				Sept. 20	Do.
Cabernet × Berlandieri, No. 333	G	1904	1909	90	s	.7		Mar. 8	Mar. 28	June 1	June 20	June 4		Sept. 26	Oct. 8
[illegible]et × [illegible]is [illegible], No. 33A	G	1904	1909	90	s	2.2		Mar. 6	Apr. 3					do.	Do.
Captain	G	1908	1909	86	s	2		Mar. 3	Apr. 1	May 23	June 1	June 9		Oct. 10	
Chasselas × Berlandieri, No. 41B	G	1904	1909	91	s	2		Mar. 2	Apr. 2	June 1	June 15	June 25		Sept. 26	Oct. 7
Constantia	O	1907	1909	87	s	2.3	2 to 4	Mar. 20		June 2	do.	June 7	June 20	Oct. 10	
Dog Ridge	G	1904	1909	95	s	3		Mar. 6	Mar. 30	June 1				Sept. 26	Oct. 8
Do.	O	1903	1905	88	s	2.9	3 to 5	Mar. 19		May 19	June 5	May 25	June 12	Sept. 27	Oct. 15
Herbemont	O	1903	1905	86	s	2.8	2 to 5	Mar. 17		May 25	do.	May 30	June 17	Sept. 25	Oct. 6
Hotporup	G	1904	1909	93	s	2.2		Mar. 3	Mar. 10	May 20	June 4	June 12		Sept. 20	Oct. 8
Joly	G	1907	1909	80	s	1.1		Mar. 1	Apr. 3	June 1				do.	Do.
Judge	G	1907	1909	70	s	.4		Mar. 4	Apr. 1	do.				do.	Do.
Lenoir	O	1903	1905	89	s	2.9	3 to 5	Mar. 20		May 23	June 5	May 29	June 11	Sept. 25	Oct. 6
[illegible]a × [illegible]ia, No. 554	G	1904	1909	85	s	15		Mar. 6	Apr. 1	May 25	June 3	June 10		do.	Do.
[illegible]a × [illegible]a, No. 18808	O	1907	1909	87	s	2.2		Mar. 22		June 2	do.	June 6	June 17	Oct. 10	
[illegible]a × [illegible]s	G	1906	1909	85	s	1.2		Mar. 10	Apr. 1	May 30				Sept. 20	Do.
[illegible]ey	G	1904	1909	86	s	.4		Mar. 8	do.	May 28	June 1	June 12		do.	Oct. 10
[illegible]re × Rupestris, No. 1202	G	1904	1909	95	s	3.2		Mar. 6	do.	do.	do.	June 17		do.	Oct. 7
Do.	O	1904	1909	92	s	2	3 to 4	Mar. 21		June 12		June 25		Oct. 5	
[illegible]e × [illegible]is, No. 1203	G	1905	1909	78	s	.6		Mar. 4		June 1		June 18		Sept. 25	
Pardes	G	1907	1909	90	s	2.2		Mar. 6	Mar. 20	May 25	May 30	June 9		Sept. 20	Oct. 4
[illegible]a [illegible] [illegible]o	G	1904	1909	86	s	1		Mar. 10	do.	May 28				Sept. 26	Oct. 8
R[illegible]a × ([illegible]ia × Rupestris) No. 106–8	G	1904	1909	89	s	35		do.	Mar. 30	do.				do.	Do.
[illegible]a × [illegible]estris, No. 101	G	1904	1909	94	s	2.5		Mar. 6	Apr. 2	May 30				Sept. 25	Do.
Do.	O	1904	1906	85	s	2	3 to 5	Mar. 21		May 20	June 7	May 26	June 20	Sept. 27	Oct. 6
[illegible]a × [illegible], No. 101–14	G	1904	1909	90	s	17		Mar. 10	Mar. 30	June 1		June 16		Sept. 26	Oct. 8
Do.	O	1907	1909	72	s	.5		Mar. 19		June 2	June 10	June 7	June 25		

TABLE VII.—*Relative behavior and value for different purposes of grape varieties tested by grafting on resistant stocks and by growing on their own roots in eleven experiment vineyards in California*—Continued.

Variety and stock (on own roots, if so stated).	Experiment vineyard.	Year stock was planted.	Year grafted.	Congeniality.	How pruned.	Weight of pruning per vine.	Nodes bearing fruit.	Growth-starting date. Early season.	Growth-starting date. Late season.	Blossoming date. Early season.	Blossoming date. Late season.	Fruit-setting date. Early season.	Fruit-setting date. Late season.	Fruit-ripening date. Early season.	Fruit-ripening date. Late season.
1	2	3	4	5	6	7	8	9	10	11	12	13	14	15	16
Petit Syrah—Continued.				P. ct.		Lbs.									
Riparia × Rupestris, No. 108–103	G	1905	1909	75	s	1.2		Mar. 2	Apr. 3	June 5				Sept. 26	
Riparia × Rupestris, No. 3306	G	1904	1909	98	s	3.2		Mar. 9	Mar. 27	May 27				do	Oct. 8
Do	O	1907	1909	88	s	1.5	2 to 4	Mar. 19		May 30	June 2	June 6	June 15	Sept. 25	Oct. 1
Riparia × Rupestris, No. 3309	G	1904	1909	93	s	3.7		Mar. 10	Apr. 3	June 1				Sept. 26	Oct. 7
Do	O	1904	1906	91	s	2	2 to 5	Mar. 17		May 24	June 7	May 30	June 22	Sept. 25	Oct. 11
Rupestris des Caussettes	G	1904	1909	89	s	2.7		Mar. 8	Mar. 30	May 28	June 1	June 9		Sept. 26	Oct. 8
Rupestris Martin	G	1904	1909	94	s	2.6		Mar. 11	Mar. 27	June 1				Sept. 28	Do.
Do	O	1903	1905	89	s	3.1	2 to 5	Mar. 18		May 24	June 3	May 29	June 20	Sept. 24	Oct. 13
Rupestris Metallica	G	1904	1909	91	s	1.2		Mar. 6	Apr. 3	May 29				Sept. 25	Oct. 8
Do	O	1904	1909	84	s	1.2	2 to 3	Mar. 20		June 3	June 5	June 9	June 2	Oct. 1	
Rupestris Mission	G	1904	1909	86	s	1.2		Mar. 9	Mar. 27	May 27				Sept 28	Oct. 8
Do	O	1907	1909	88	s	.8		Mar. 5	Apr. 1	May 29				Sept. 26	Do.
Rupestris St. George	G	1904	1909	88	s	3.2		Mar. 4	Mar. 30	June 4		June 10		Sept. 22	Oct. 4
Do	O	1903	1905	90	s	3.2	2 to 5	Mar. 20		May 24	May 31	May 29	June 17	Sept. 27	Oct. 8
Rupestris × Berlandieri, No. 219A	G	1904	1909	92	s	1.6		Mar. 7	Apr. 3	June 1		June 14		Sept. 25	Oct. 10
Rupestris × Berlandieri, No. 301A	G	1904	1909	87	s	2.8		Mar. 8	Mar. 21	May 30	June 1	June 12		do	Do.
Rupestris × Berlandieri, No. 301B	G	1904	1909	93	s	2		Mar. 6	Apr. 3	do				Sept. 26	
Rupestris × (Cordifolia × Rupestris) No. 202–5.	G	1905	1909	85	s	1.3		Mar. 4	do	June 1				do	Oct. 8
Rupestris × Hybrid Azemar, No. 215.	G	1904	1909	83	s	.6		Mar. 10	Mar. 18	May 26				Sept. 20	Do.
Salt [illegible]k	G	1904	1909	83	s	1.4		Mar. 9	Apr. 1	May 27	June 1	June 12		Sept. 25	Do.
Do	O	1903	1905	88	s	1.5	2 to 5			May 22	do	May 27	June 6	do	Oct. 11
Solonis Ordinaire	G	1904	1909	70	s	.4		Mar. 7	Apr. 5	May 6	June 10	June 11	June 20	Sept. 26	Oct. 8
Solonis Robusta	G	1904	1909	91	s	1.7		Mar. 8	Apr. 1	May 28	do	June 15		do	Oct. 7
Do	O	1907	1909	88	s	.6	3 to 4	Mar. 19		June 5	do	June 9	June 20	Sept. 25	
Solonis × Othello	G	1904	1909	91	s	1.2		Mar. 2	Apr. 1	May 28		June 13		Sept 26	Oct. 8
Solonis × Othello, No. 1613	O	1907	1909	77	s	.9	2 to 4	Mar. 21		May 30	June 3	June 7	June 15	Sept. 25	
Solonis × Riparia, No. 1616	G	1904	1909	82	s	1.2		Mar. 6	Mar. 30	May 27				Sept. 28	Oct. 7
Do	O	1904	1906	83	s	1.4	2 to 5	Mar. 17		May 25	June 10	June 1	June 17	Sept. 23	Oct. 5
Taylor [illegible]e	G	1904	1909	83	s	2.5		Mar. 1	Apr. 2	May 28	do			Sept. 20	Oct. 9
Do	O	1904	1906	88	s	1.9	2 to 4	Mar. 23		May 25	June 8	May 30	June 19	Sept. 26	Oct. 8

Petit Verdot:															
Own roots	Gi	1904	......	......	s	......	......	Mar. 17	Apr. 1	May 26	June 1	...do...	June 7	Sept. 18	Sept. 20
Dog Ridge	O	1904	1906	95	s	4.5	3 to 5	Mar. 18	......	May 27	May 31	June 3	June 14	Sept. 24	Oct. 10
Lenoir	O	1903	1905	94	s	5.4	2 to 4	Mar. 15	......	...do...	...do...	June 2	June 15	Sept. 25	Oct. 6
Rupestris St. George	O	1903	1905	94	s	6.1	3 to 5	Mar. 18	......	May 20	June 1	May 26	June 20	...do...	Oct. 10
Taylor Narbonne	O	1904	1906	84	s	2.3	3 to 4	Mar. 17	......	May 21	June 3	...do...	June 16	...do...	Oct. 4
Peverella:															
Own roots	Gi	1904	......	......	s	......	......	Mar. 20	Mar. 28	May 26	May 29	May 30	......	Sept. 10	Sept. 20
Dog Ridge	O	1904	1906	90	s	2.7	3 to 5	...do...	......	May 24	June 8	May 29	June 19	Sept. 26	Oct. 7
Lenoir	O	1903	1905	85	s	2.3	3 to 5	...do...	......	May 23	...do...	May 28	June 20	Sept. 25	Oct. 15
Rupestris St. George	O	1903	1905	88	s	3.4	2 to 5	Mar. 22	......	...do...	June 5	...do...	...do...	Sept. 28	Oct. 20
Taylor Narbonne	O	1904	1906	88	s	2.4	2 to 5	Mar. 19	......	May 27	...do...	June 3	...do...	...do...	Oct. 6
[illegible]ul:															
Own roots	Gi	1904	......	......	c, s	......	......	Mar. 18	Mar. 28	May 30	......	June 7	......	Sept. 20	Sept. 24
[illegible]it:															
Lenoir	O	1904	1907	90	s	4	3 to 5	Mar. 26	......	May 27	June 10	June 2	June 25	Sept. 28	Oct. 20
[illegible]ice [illegible]at:															
Own roots	Gi	1905	......	......	c, s	......	......	Mar. 20	Mar. 27	May 25	June 4	May 30	......	Aug. 28	Sept. 25
[illegible]u de [illegible]:															
Own roots	Gi	1904	......	......	c, s	......	......	Mar. 15	Mar. 28	May 26	May 30	May 31	June 6	Sept. 18	Sept. 26
Aramon × Rupestris Ganzin, No. 1	O	1904	1906	90	c, s	4.3	2 to 4	Mar. 21	......	May 19	June 5	May 25	June 19	Oct. 5	
Dog Ridge	O	1903	1905	94	s	3.6	3 to 4	Mar. 20	......	...do...	May 31	...do...	June 14	Sept. 18	Oct. 3
Herbemont	O	1903	1905	84	s	2.3	2 to 5	Mar. 19	......	...do...	June 1	May 24	June 12	Sept 20	Oct. 5
Lenoir	O	1903	1905	93	s	4.1	2 to 4	Mar. 16	......	May 22	May 31	May 26	June 4	Sept. 3	Sept. 25
Mourvèdre × Rupestris, No. 1202	O	1904	1906	92	c, s	3.2	2 to 5	Mar. 18	......	May 19	June 3	May 24	June 24	Oct. 4	
Riparia × Rupestris, No. 101	O	1904	1906	84	s	1.8	2 to 5	Mar. 20	......	...do...	...do...	...do...	June 26	Sept. 20	
Riparia × Rupestris, No. 3309	O	1904	1906	88	s	3.4	2 to 5	Mar. 19	......	...do...	May 31	May 25	June 8	...do...	Oct. 4
Rupestris Martin	O	1903	1905	86	s	3.1	2 to 5	Mar. 20	......	...do...	June 2	May 24	June 10	Sept. 22	Oct. 6
Rupestris St. George	O	1903	1905	91	s	4	3 to 4	Mar. 16	......	...do...	May 30	May 26	...do...	Sept. 15	Sept. 17
Salt Creek	O	1903	1905	89	s	3.1	2 to 5	......	......	May 20	May 31	...do...	June 4	Sept. 20	Sept. 23
Solonis × Riparia, No. 1616	O	1904	[illegible]07	85	s	2.5	3 to 5	Mar. 18	......	May 19	June 1	May 24	June 14	Sept. 25	Sept. 27
Taylor Narbonne	O	1904	1906	91	s	2.8	2 to 4	Mar. 20	......	...do...	May 30	...do...	June 11	Sept. 18	Oct. 2
Pineau de [illegible]rs:															
Own roots	Gi	1905	......	......	s	......	......	Mar. 12	Mar. 29	May 27	May 28	June 2	June 3	Aug. 29	Sept. 25
Dog Ridge	O	1904	1906	92	s	3.6	2 to 4	Mar. 20	......	May 19	......	May 24	......	Sept. 27	Oct. 3
Lenoir	O	1903	1905	84	c, s	3.1	2 to 5	Mar. 21	......	May 20	May 27	May 25	June 13	Sept. 23	Sept. 28
Rupestris St. George	O	903	1905	84	c, s	2	2 to 5	......	......	May 23	......	May 28	......	Sept. 24	Sept. 30
Pineau Noir Epernay:															
Own roots	Gi	1905	......	......	c, s	......	......	Mar. 16	Mar. 29	May 26	May 28	June 1	......	Aug. 27	Sept. 21
Lenoir	O	1903	1905	83	s	2.4	2 to 4	Mar. 19	......	May 19	May 31	May 24	June 10	Sept. 22	
Rupestris St. George	O	1903	1905	82	s	3.4	2 to 4	...do...	......	May 20	...do...	May 16	June 8	Sept. 12	Sept. 21
Pinot Blanc:															
Own roots	Gi	1904	......	......	c, s	......	......	Mar. 10	Mar. 28	May 26	May 27	June 2	......	Sept. 15	Sept. 20
Pinot St. George:															
Own roots	Gi	1904	......	......	s	......	......	Mar. 20	Mar. 31	May 27	May 30	May 31	June 5	Aug. 28	Do.
Dog Ridge	O	1904	1906	93	s	3.6	2 to 4	...do...	......	May 24	June 5	May 30	June 20	Sept. 25	Oct. 4
Lenoir	O	1903	1905	88	s	3.1	2 to 4	...do...	......	May 20	May 31	May 25	June 14	Sept. 20	Oct. 6
Rupestris St. George	O	1903	1905	85	s	1.9	2 to 4	...do...	......	...do...	June 5	May 26	June 17	Sept. 15	Oct. 8
Pinot Vert Doré:															
Own roots	Gi	1904	......	......	c, s	......	......	Mar. 15	Mar. 31	May 27	May 30	June 5	......	Sept 5	Sept. 20

TABLE VII.—*Relative behavior and value for different purposes of grape varieties tested by grafting on resistant stocks and by growing on their own roots in eleven experiment vineyards in California*—Continued.

Variety and stock (on own roots, if so stated).	Experiment vineyard.	Year stock was planted.	Year grafted.	Congeniality.	How pruned.	Weight of pruning per vine.	Nodes bearing fruit.	Growth-starting date. Early season.	Growth-starting date. Late season.	Blossoming date. Early season.	Blossoming date. Late season.	Fruit-setting date. Early season.	Fruit-setting date. Late season.	Fruit-ripening date. Early season.	Fruit-ripening date. Late season.
1	2	3	4	5	6	7	8	9	10	11	12	13	14	15	16
Pis de Chèvre des Alps:				P. ct.		Lbs.									
Own roots	Gi	1904	.....	.....	s	.....	.....	Mar. 15	Mar. 29	May 26	June 2	May 31	June 9	Sept. 24	
Dog Ridge	O	1904	1906	86	s	3.1	2 to 4	Mar. 23	.....	May 19	May 31	May 24	June 12	Sept. 23	Oct. 10
Lenoir	O	1903	1905	90	s	2.9	3 to 5	Mar. 21	.....	..do..	June 8	May 23	June 24	..do..	Oct. 9
Rupestris St. George	O	1903	1905	92	s	4.9	2 to 3	Mar. 22	.....	May 24	May 31	May 3	June 12	Sept. 22	Oct. 12
Pis de Chevre Rouge:															
Noir	O	1904	1907	86	s	3.2	3 to 5	Mar. 20	.....	May 23	June 6	May 28	June 20	Sept. 20	Sept. 21
Pizzutella:															
Own roots	Gi	1904	.....	.....	c, s	.....	.....	Mar. 20	Mar. 28	May 30	June 1	June 5	.....	Sept. 10	Sept. 23
Adobe Giant	F	1904	1906	89	c, s	4	3 to 5	Mar. 25	Apr. 3	May 20	May 30	May 27	June 7	..do..	Sept. 20
Aramon × Rupestris Ganzin, No. 1	F	1904	1906	95	c, s	6.6	2 to 4	Mar. 12	Apr. 1	..do..	May 29	May 26	June 3	Sept. 12	Do.
Dog Ridge	F	1903	1905	80	s	1.1	2 to 5	Mar. 8	Mar. 30	May 15	May 22	May 27	May 28	Sept. 16	Do.
Herbemont	F	1903	1905	73	s	1.1	3 to 5	Mar. 6	Mar. 25	..do..	May 25	May 30	June 1	Sept. 9	
Lenoir	F	1903	1905	91	s	2	2 to 5	..do..	Mar. 30	May 12	May 20	May 26	May 27	Sept. 10	Sept. 15
Mourvedre × Rupestris, No. 1202	F	1904	1906	87	c, s	4.9	3 to 5	Mar. 20	Apr. 1	May 14	May 29	..do..	June 4	Sept. 5	Sept. 20
Riparia Gloire	F	1903	1905	96	c, s	7.3	2 to 6	Mar. 14	..do..	May 18	May 28	May 23	June 3	Sept. 8	Sept. 19
Riparia × Rupestris, No. 101	F	1904	1906	98	c, s	13.3	2 to 5	Mar. 20	Apr. 6	May 20	May 29	May 27	June 5	Sept. 10	Sept. 20
Riparia × Rupestris, No. 3309	F	1904	1906	95	c, s	5.1	3 to 5	Mar. 13	Apr. 2	May 14	May 25	..do..	May 30	..do..	Do.
Rupestris Martin	F	1903	1905	82	s	2	.....	Mar. 12	Mar. 30	May 16	May 21	May 25	May 27	Sept. 8	Sept. 9
Rupestris St. George	F	1903	1905	95	c, s	6.5	2 to 5	Mar. 15	Apr. 1	..do..	May 28	May 22	June 8	Sept. 10	Sept. 19
Salt Creek	F	1903	1905	86	s	2.5	3 to 6	Mar. 14	Mar. 30	May 21	May 23	May 25	June 5	Sept. 5	Sept. 20
Solonis × Riparia, No. 1616	F	1904	1906	96	c, s	5.6	2 to 5	Mar. 24	Apr. 1	May 20	May 29	May 28	June 6	Sept. 10	Do.
Taylor Narbonne	F	1904	1906	87	c, s	3.7	3 to 5	Mar. 14	Mar. 31	May 15	May 24	May 26	May 28	Sept. 8	Do.
Poulsard:															
Own roots	Gi	1904	.....	.....	s	.....	.....	Mar. 17	Mar. 28	May 27	.....	June 5	.....	Sept. 15	Sept. 21
Precoce de Courtiller:															
Lenoir	O	1903	1905	79	s	2.4	2 to 4	Mar. 18	.....	May 22	May 30	May 26	June 14	Sept. 9	Sept. 25
Rupestris St. George	O	1903	1907	82	s	3.4	2 to 4	Mar. 22	.....	..do..	May 31	May 29	June 10	Sept. 22	Do.
Prune de Cazouls:															
Aramon × Rupestris Ganzin, No. 2	F	1907	1909	88	s	.....	.....	Mar. 26	.....	May 21	.....	.....	.....	Sept. 25	
Australis	F	1907	1909	90	s	.....	.....	Mar. 31	.....	May 25	.....	.....	.....	Oct. 5	
Berlandieri × Riparia, No. 420A	F	1907	1909	87	s	.....	.....	Mar. 23	.....	May 21	.....	.....	.....	Sept. 15	

Lenoir	O	1904	1907	91	s	2.8	2 to 5	Mar. 22		May 25	June 8	May 30	June 20	Sept. 28	Oct. 10
[illegible]ia × Riparia, No. 18804	F	1907	1909		s			Apr. 3		May 23				Sept. 15	
[illegible]ia × Riparia, No. 18808	F	1907	1909	90	s			Mar. 21		May 18				Sept. 30	
Monticola × Rupestris	F	1907	1909	90	s			Mar. 20		May 22				Sept. 20	
Riparia × [illegible]ia × R[illegible]is, No. 0[illegible]-8)	F	1907	1909	87	s			Mar. 26		May 23				do.	
Riparia × Rupestris, No. 101-14	F	1907	1909		s			Apr. 5		do.				Sept. 30	
[illegible]aria × R[illegible]is, No. 3306	F	1907	1909		s			Mar. 24		do.				Sept. 25	
Rupestris Martin	F	1907	1909	89	s			Mar. 22		do.				Oct. 10	
Purple Damascus:															
Own roots	Gi	1905			c, s			Mar. 26	Mar. 28	May 30	June 6	June 13		Sept. 10	Sept. 24
Adobe Giant	F	1904	1906	86	s	1.6	3 to 5	Mar. 12	do.	May 16	May 23	May 23	May 30	Sept. 8	Sept. 21
[illegible]n × Rupestris Ganzin, No. 1	F	1904	1906	95	c, s	5.9	2 to 5	do.	Mar. 27	May 11	May 20	May 25	May 28	Sept. 11	Sept. 20
Dog Ridge	F	1904	1906	92	c, s	7.3	2 to 5	Mar. 13	Apr. 5	May 17	May 23	May 26	June 2	Sept. 8	Do.
Lenoir	F	1903	1905	92	c, s	2.5	2 to 5	Mar. 7	Apr. 1	May 16	May 20	May 23	May 30	Sept. 12	Sept. 22
[illegible]re × Rupestris, No. 1202	F	1904	1906	95	c, s	5.8	3 to 5	Mar. 13	do.	May 20	May 25	May 28	June 4	Sept. 8	Sept. 20
Riparia [illegible]e.	F	1903	1905	89	c, s	4.1	2 to 5	Mar. 7	do.	May 15	May 20	May 24	June 1	Sept. 10	Sept. 19
Riparia × Rupestris, No. 101	F	1904	1906	88	s	3.7	3 to 5	Mar. 8	Mar. 30	May 8	May 24	do.	May 29	Sept. 5	Sept. 20
Riparia × Rupestris, No. 3309	F	1904	1906	93	s	4.8	2 to 5	Mar. 12	Apr. 3	May 20	May 28	May 26	June 4	[illegible] 12	Do.
Rupestris St. George	F	1903	1905	95	c, s	6.8	3 to 5	Mar. 14	Mar. 25	May 16	May 20	May 24	do.	Sept. 10	Sept. 19
Solonis × Riparia, No. 1616	F	1904	1906	87	s	2.7	3 to 5	Mar. 15	Mar. 28	May 10	May 24	May 21	May 29	Sept. 12	Sept. 20
Taylor Narbonne	F	1904	1906	92	c, s	4.5	3 to 5	Mar. 14	Mar. 26	May 14	May 21	May 26	May 27	do.	Do.
Quagliano:															
Own roots	Gi	1904			s			Mar. 19	Apr. 1	May 26	June 6	May 30	June 11	Sept. 19	Sept. 25
Dog Ridge	O	1904	1906	82	s	1.3	3 to 4	do.		do.	June 8	June 2	June 14	Sept. 29	Oct. 6
Lenoir	O	1903	1905	90	s	3.1	3 to 5	do.		May 23	do.	May 29	June 13	Sept. 28	Oct. 8
Rupestris St. George	O	1903	1905	91	s	2.6	3 to 5	Mar. 20		May 21	June 5	May 27	June 10	do.	Oct. 10
Taylor [illegible]ne	O	1904	1906	89	s	2.2	2 to 4	Mar. 19		May 23	do.	May 29	June 11	Sept. 29	Do.
Razaki Zolo:															
Own roots	Gi	1905			c, s			Mar. 26	Mar. 31	May 26	June 6	May 26	June 6	Sept. 15	Sept. 23
Rupestris St. George	F	1903	1905	89	c, s	4.5				May 10		May 10		Sept. 23	
Riparia × Rupestris, No. 3306	O	1904		90	c, s	4.2	2 to 4	Mar. 21		do.	June 8	May 15	June 13	do.	Oct. 1
Refosco:															
Own roots	Gi	1904			s			Mar. 20	Apr. 10	May 29	May 30	June 6		do.	
Dog Ridge	O	1904	1906	91	c, s	4	2 to 4	Mar. 24		May 23	June 8	May 28	June 15	Sept. 25	Oct. 8
Lenoir	O	1903	1905	90	c, s	3.2	2 to 4	Mar. 16		do.	June 5	May 29	June 17	Sept. 24	Oct. 15
Rupestris St. George	O	1903	1905	92	s	3.8	3 to 4	Mar. 19		May 25	May 31	June 2	June 13	Sept. 23	Oct. 8
T[illegible]lor Narbonne	O	1904	1906	88	s	2.8	2 to 4	Mar. 22		May 27	June 3	do.	June 20	do.	Do.
Ribier:															
Lenoir	O	1903	1905	92	s	3.5	3 to 5	Mar. 15		May 23	June 1	May 26	June 14	Sept. 28	
Rupestris St. George	O	1903	1905	93	s	6	2 to 5	Mar. 23		May 22	June 3	May 28	June 17	Sept. 29	
Robin Noir:															
Own roots	Gi	1904			s			Mar. 16	Mar. 27	May 26	May 30	May 31	[illegible]ne 2	Aug. 20	Sept. 23
Rodites:															
Lenoir	O	1904	1907	91	s	3.6	3 to 6	Mar. 21		May 25	June 8	May 30	June 25	Sept. 29	Oct. 20
Rose d'Italie:															
Lenoir	O	1903	1905	84	s	1.8	2 to 4	Mar. 17		May 22	June 5	May 28	June 29	Sept. 20	Oct. 11
Riparia × Rupestris, No. 3309	O	1904	1908	89	s	2.5	2 to 5	Mar. 24		[illegible]ne 1	June 3	June 7	June 17	do.	Oct. 1
Rupestris St. George	O	1903	1905	90	c, s	3.8	3 to 5	Mar. 16		May 23	May 31	May 28	June 12	Sept. 26	Sept. 30
Solonis × Riparia, No. 1616	O	1904	1908	92	s	3.1	2 to 5	Mar. 24		June 1		June 6	June 17	Sept. 20	Oct. 8
Taylor Narbonne	O	1904	1908	84	s	1.2	2 to 5	Mar. 16		June 2	June 3	June 7	June 14	Sept. 15	Oct. 10

TABLE VII.—*Relative behavior and value for different purposes of grape varieties tested by grafting on resistant stocks and by growing on their own roots in eleven experiment vineyards in California*—Continued.

Variety and stock (on own roots, if so stated).	Experiment vineyard.	Year stock was planted.	Year grafted.	Congeniality.	How pruned.	Weight of pruning per vine.	Nodes bearing fruit.	Growth-starting date.		Blossoming date.		Fruit-setting date.		Fruit-ripening date.	
								Early season.	Late season.	Early season.	Late season.	Early season.	Late season.	Early season.	Late season.
1	2	3	4	5	6	7	8	9	10	11	12	13	14	15	16
Rothgipfler:				*P. ct.*		*Lbs.*									
Own roots	Gi	1904			c, s			Mar. 15	Mar. 28	May 24	June 1	May 29	June 7	Aug. 24	Oct. 20
Roussaou:															
Own roots	Gi	1905			c, s			Mar. 18	Mar. 30	May 25	June 6	...do	June 12	Aug. 26	Sept. 23
Dog Ridge	O	1904	1906	91	c, s	4.2	3 to 5	Mar. 16		...do	Mar. 30	...do	June 15	Sept. 25	Oct. 10
Lenoir	O	1903	1905	87	s	5.2	2 to 4	...do		May 27	May 31	June 2	June 16	Sept. 20	Oct. 9
Riparia × Rupestris, No. 3306	O	1904		91	c, s	4.7	1 to 3	Mar. 20		May 15	June 5	June 5	June 18	Sept. 23	Oct. 5
Riparia × Rupestris de Jaeger	F	1907	1907	91	c, s	3.8		Mar. 19		May 22				Aug. 25	Oct. 17
Rupestris St. George	O	1903	1905	90	s	2.4	2 to 4	Mar. 16		May 16	June 5	May 27	June 17	Sept. 15	Sept. 26
Solonis × Riparia, No. 1616	F	1907	1907	84	s	2.2		Mar. 19		May 21				Oct. 17	
Taylor Narbonne	O	1904	1906	80	s	1.5	2 to 4	Mar. 21		May 19	June 1	May 24	June 10	Sept. 25	
Royal Ascot:															
Own roots	Gi	1905			s			Mar. 15	Mar. 26	May 20	...do	May 26	June 6	Aug. 27	Do.
Saint Laurent:															
Own roots	Gi	1905			s			Mar. 18	Apr. 1	May 26	May 30	May 30	June 5	Aug. 29	Sept. 23
Adobe Giant	F	1904	1906	83	s	2.4	3 to 5	Mar. 24	...do	May 15	May 18	May 23	May 28	Aug. 10	Sept. 6
Aramon × Rupestris Ganzin No. 1	F	1904	1906	90	c, s	3.7	2 to 6	Mar. 14	Apr. 2	May 16	May 19	May 22	May 30	Aug. 5	Sept. 10
Dog Ridge	F	1903	1905	81	s	2.6	2 to 5	Mar. 15	Apr. 1	May 14	May 22	May 24	May 31	Aug. 1	Sept. 6
Herbemont	F	1903	1905	74	s	3.7	2 to 5	Mar. 14	...do	May 20		May 25	June 1	...do	Sept. 10
Lenoir	F	1903	1905	67	s	.8	2 to 6	Mar. 12	Mar. 30	May 12	May 20	May 24	May 27	Aug. 24	Sept. 11
Mourvedre × Rupestris, No. 1202	F	1904	1906	89	c, s	3.3	2 to 6	Mar. 15	...do	May 15	...do	May 25	May 31	Aug. 1	Sept. 8
Riparia Gloire	F	1903	1905	82	s	1	2 to 5	Mar. 18	Apr. 1	May 14	...do	May 22	May 26	Aug. 3	Do.
Riparia × Rupestris, No. 101	F	1904	1906	86	s	2.1	2 to 5	Mar. 14	Mar. 30	May 7	...do	May 23	May 27	Aug. 1	Sept. 10
Riparia × Rupestris, No. 3309	F	1904	1906	83	s	1.5	2 to 5	Mar. 13	Apr. 1	May 14	May 17	...do	May 29	...do	Sept. 4
Rupestris Martin	F	1903	1905	69	s	1.5	2 to 5	Mar. 24	Apr. 5	...do	May 18	May 22	May 31	Aug. 5	Sept. 8
Rupestris St. George	F	1903	1905	91	c, s	2.4	2 to 6	Mar. 15	Mar. 31	May 13	May 17	May 21	May 30	Aug. 1	Do.
Salt Creek	F	1903	1905	75	s	1.3	2 to 6	...do	Mar. 27	May 15	May 20	...do	May 25	Aug. 5	Do.
Solonis × Riparia, No. 1616	F	1904	1906	72	s	1.1	2 to 6	Mar. 6	Mar. 30	May 14	May 17	May 22	May 29	Sept. 9	
Taylor Narbonne	F	1904	1906	50	s	1.3		Mar. 14	Mar. 19	May 16	...do	May 21	May 26	Aug. 24	Do.
Saint Macaire:															
Own roots	Gi	1904			s			Mar. 12	Mar. 31	May 24	June 2	May 28	June 7	Sept. 18	Sept. 25
Aramon × Rupestris Ganzin, No. 1	O	1904	1909	94	s	3.7	3 to 5							Oct. 1	
Dog Ridge	O	1904	1906	91	s	3.2	2 to 4	Mar. 19		May 25	June 5	May 30	June 20	Sept. 28	Oct. 8

Lenoir	O	1903	1905	94	s	4.9	2 to 5	Mar. 20	....	May 22	June 10	May 28	June 26	Sept. 28	Oct. 12
Mourvedre × Rupestris, No. 1202	O	1904	1909	95	s	....	....	do	....	June 2	June 12	June 6	June 25	....	
Rupestris St. George	O	1903	1905	92	s	3.5	2 to 4	Mar. 17	....	May 25	June 8	June 1	June 26	Sept. 28	Oct. 8
Solonis × Riparia, No. 1616	O	1904	1909	91	s	2	....	....	....	....	....	....	....	....	
[illegible] Narbonne	O	1904	1906	92	s	2.7	2 to 4	Mar. 20	....	May 27	June 1	June 2	June 15	Sept. 25	Oct. 10
San Gioveto:															
Dog Ridge	O	1904	1906	90	s	6	2 to 4	Mar. 24	....	May 23	June 8	May 29	June 19	Sept. 26	
Lenoir	O	1903	1905	91	s	2.3	2 to 4	Mar. 16	....	May 16	June 3	May 21	June 18	...do....	
Rupestris St. George	O	1903	1905	87	c,s	4.2	3 to 4	Mar. 21	....	May 26	...do....	May 30	June 16	Sept. 20	Sept. 26
[illegible]	O	1904	1907	94	s	5.8	....	Mar. 18	....	...do....	...do....	June 1	June 14	....	
S[illegible]in Blanc:															
Dog Ridge	O	1904	1906	82	s	1.2	....	Mar. 22	....	May 19	....	May 24	....	Sept. 21	
Lenoir	O	1903	1905	87	s	3.4	3 to 5	Mar. 17	....	...do....	May 31	May 23	June 11	Sept. 8	Sept. 20
Rupestris St. George	O	1903	1905	86	s	3.6	3 to 4	Mar. 20	....	May 20	June 4	May 30	June 13	Sept. 9	Do.
Sauvignon Blanc:															
Own roots	Gi	1907	....	......	s	....	....	Mar. 28	Apr. 5	May 27	....	....	....	Sept. 23	
Dog Ridge	O	1904	1906	90	s	3.9	3 to 5	Mar. 22	....	May 23	June 1	May 28	June 14	Sept. 22	Oct. 10
Lenoir	O	1903	1905	92	s	3.1	3 to 5	Mar. 17	....	May 26	June 8	May 30	June 22	Sept. 23	Oct. 9
Rupestris St. George	O	1903	1906	91	s	3.7	2 to 4	Mar. 19	....	May 25	June 5	June 1	June 20	Sept. 21	Oct. 1
Sauvignon [illegible]:															
Own roots	Gi	1904	....	......	c,s	....	....	Mar. 20	Mar. 29	May 24	June 2	May 28	June 8	Sept. 19	Sept. 20
Aramon × Rupestris Ganzin, No. 1	O	1904	1906	95	c,s	4.5	3 to 6	Mar. 30	....	May 23	June 8	May 29	June 20	Sept. 25	Oct. 11
Aramon × Rupestris Ganzin, No. 2	O	1907	1909	85	s	.8	2 to 3	Mar. 18	....	May 30	June 2	June 7	June 12	Sept. 20	
Berlandieri × Riparia, No. 420A	O	1907	1909	84	s	1.6	2 to 4	...do....	....	June 3	June 5	do....	June 20	...do....	Oct. 8
[illegible]ia	O	1907	1909	92	s	2.4	2 to 4	Mar. 20	....	May 30	June 3	June 8	June 16	...do....	
Dog Ridge	O	1903	1905	93	c,s	3.2	2 to 6	Mar. 16	....	May 23	June 6	May 29	June 17	Sept. 25	Oct. 10
Herbémont	O	1903	1905	85	c,s	2.6	[illegible] to 6	Mar. 21	....	May 25	June 10	May 30	June 24	...do....	Oct. 9
Lenoir	O	1903	1905	91	s	2.9	2 to 6	Mar. 16	....	May 22	June 8	May 28	June 21	...do....	Oct. 6
Monticola × Riparia, No. 18808	O	1907	1909	89	s	1.7	2 to 4	...do....	....	June 3	June 5	June 7	June 20	...do....	
Mourvedre × Rupestris, No. 1202	O	1904	1906	95	c,s	5.4	2 to 6	Mar. 19	....	May 26	...do....	June 2	June 19	...do....	Oct. 11
Riparia × Rupestris, No. 101	O	1904	1906	93	c,s	3	2 to 6	Mar. 20	....	May 23	June 10	May 28	June 30	Sept. 26	Do.
Riparia × Rupestris, No. 101–14	O	1907	1909	87	s	1.2	3 to 4	...do....	....	June 2	June 8	June 8	June 24	Sept. 20	
Riparia × Rupestris, No. 3306	O	1907	1909	91	s	19	2 to 3	Mar. 18	....	June 3	June 5	June 10	June 20	...do....	
Riparia × Rupestris, No. 3309	O	1904	1906	91	c,s	4.1	3 to 6	Mar. 19	....	May 23	...do....	May 28	...do....	Sept. 23	Oct. 4
Rupestris Martin	O	1903	1905	91	c,s	3.5	3 to 6	...do....	....	May 24	June 3	May 29	June 17	Sept. 27	Oct. 5
Rupestris St. George	O	1903	1905	86	s	3.2	3 to 6	Mar. 17	....	May 23	June 6	May 27	June 21	Sept. 25	Oct. 10
Salt Creek	O	1903	1905	90	c,s	2.5	3 to 6	Mar. 16	....	May 22	June 5	May 28	June 19	Sept. 20	Oct. 9
[illegible]ta	O	1907	1909	90	s	1.7	2 to 4	Mar. 18	....	June 1	...do....	June 10	June 20	...do....	
Solonis × Othello, No. 1613	O	1907	1909	87	c,s	2.1	2 to 3	Mar. 17	....	...do....	June 3	June 8	June 21	...do....	Oct. 11
Solonis × Riparia, No. 1616	O	1904	1906	92	c,s	3.6	3 to 6	...do....	....	May 26	June 10	June 2	June 23	Sept. 25	Oct. 9
[illegible]ne	O	1904	1906	93	c,s	4.8	2 to 5	Mar. 20	....	May 27	June 3	June 3	June 15	Sept. 24	Oct. 8
Schiradzouli [illegible]:															
Lenoir	O	1904	1907	86	s	2.5	2 to 4	Mar. 18	....	May 24	June 8	May 28	June 20	Sept. 28	Oct. 13
Schiradzouli [illegible]let:															
Lenoir	O	1904	1907	88	s	2.8	2 to 5	...do....	....	May 26	...do....	May 30	June 23	Sept. 25	Oct. 7
Semillon:															
Own roots	Gi	1904	....	......	c,s	....	....	...do....	Mar. 27	May 20	May 29	May 31	June 5	Aug. 28	Sept. 24
Aramon × Rupestris Ganzin, No. 1	O	1904	1906	88	s	2.5	2 to 5	Mar. 20	....	May 23	June 10	May 29	June 21	Sept. 23	Oct. 11
Berlandieri × Riparia, No. 420A	O	1907	1909	83	s	.9	....	...do....	....	May 30	June 3	June 8	June 18	Oct. 6	
Dog Ridge	O	1903	1905	94	c,s	3.6	2 to 4	Mar. 19	....	May 24	...do....	May 30	June 17	Sept. 21	Oct. 8
Herbemont	O	1903	1905	85	c,s	2.5	2 to 5	Mar. 20	....	...do....	June 7	May 29	June 20	Sept. 23	Oct. 11

TABLE VII.—*Relative behavior and value for different purposes of grape varieties tested by grafting on resistant stocks and by growing on their own roots in eleven experiment vineyards in California*—Continued.

Variety and stock (on own roots, if so stated).	Experiment vineyard.	Year stock was planted.	Year grafted.	Congeniality.	How pruned.	Weight of pruning per vine.	Nodes bearing fruit.	Growth-starting date. Early season.	Growth-starting date. Late season.	Blossoming date. Early season.	Blossoming date. Late season.	Fruit-setting date. Early season.	Fruit-setting date. Late season.	Fruit-ripening date. Early season.	Fruit-ripening date. Late season.
1	2	3	4	5	6	7	8	9	10	11	12	13	14	15	16
Semillon—Continued.				*P. ct.*		*Lbs.*									
Lenoir	O	1903	1905	88	c, s	2.2	2 to 6	Mar. 22		May 20	June 5	May 26	June 18	Sept. 23	Oct. 8
[illegible]la × Riparia, No. 18808	O	1907	1909	85	s	3.8		Mar. 16		May 30	June 3	June 7	June 17		
[illegible]e × Rupestris, No. 1202	O	1904	1906	89	s	2.8	2 to 4			May 26		June 2		Sept. 23	Oct. 6
Riparia × Rupestris, No. 101	O	1904	1906	89	c, s	2.4	3 to 4	Mar. 21		May 23	June 2	May 29	June 18	Sept. 24	Oct. 11
Riparia × Rupestris, No. 3306	O	1907	1909	91	c, s	1.7	3 to 4	Mar. 20		June 2	June 8	June 6	...do...	Sept. 20	Do.
Riparia × Rupestris, No. 3309	O	1904	1906	89	c, s	2	2 to 4			May 23		May 29		Oct. 5	
Rupestris Martin	O	1903	1905	88	c, s	4.7	2 to 4	Mar. 20		...do...	June 4	May 28	June 20	Sept. 24	Oct. 5
Rupestris St. [illegible]	O	1903	1905	86	s	1.9	3 to 4	Mar. 16		May 26	May 31	June 1	June 11	Sept. 22	Oct. 8
Salt Creek	O	1903	1905	89	s	2.7	2 to 4	Mar. 19		May 23	June 10	May 29	June 24	Sept. 20	Oct. 11
[illegible]lis × [illegible]1613	O	1907	1909	88	s	1.1		Mar. 20		May 25	June 3	June 8	June 11		
Solonis × Riparia, No. 1616	O	1904	1906	88	c, s	2.7	2 to 4	Mar. 17		...do...	June 5	May 30	June 21	Sept. 24	Oct. 4
Taylor Narbonne	O	1904	1906	90	c, s	2.9	2 to 4	Mar. 20		May 26	...do...	June 2	June 18	...do...	Oct. 8
[illegible]on [illegible]c:															
Own roots	Gi	1905			c, s			Mar. 19	Mar. 31	May 28	May 29	June 1	June 4	Aug. 29	Sept. 25
Serine:															
Own roots	Gi	1904			s			Mar. 10	Mar. 29	May 27	May 30	June 6		Sept. 20	Sept. 22
Dog Ridge	O	1904	1907	91	c, s	4.3	3 to 6	Mar. 18		May 25	June 1	May 30	June 21	Sept. 23	Oct. 10
Lenoir	O	1903	1905	89	s	3.7	3 to 4	Mar. 17		May 22	June 5	May 26	June 18	Sept. 20	Oct. 6
Rupestris St. George	O	1903	1905	91	s	5	3 to 5	Mar. 20		May 19	June 3	...do...	June 14	Sept. 15	Do.
[illegible]lor N[illegible]bonne	O	1904	1906	86	s	3.6	2 to 4	Mar. 19		May 22	June 2	May 27	...do...	Oct. 2	Oct. 10
Servan Rose:															
Lenoir	O	1904	1907	86	s	2.5	2 to 5	Mar. 18		...do...	June 7	May 28	June 20	Sept. 28	Oct. 13
[illegible]ilien:															
Own roots	Gi	1905			s			Mar. 26	Apr. 1	May 28	May 29	June 4		Aug. 28	Sept. 27
Aramon × Rupestris Ganzin, No. 1	O	1904		88	s	6	2 to 3	Mar. 18		June 1	June 5	June 3	June 10	Sept. 29	Oct. 15
Lenoir	O	1904	1907	87	s	2.9	3 to 6	Mar. 16		May 21	June 4	May 27	June 20	Sept. 9	Oct. 6
Slankamenka:															
Own roots	Gi	1904			s			Mar. 14	Apr. 3	May 29	May 30	June 5		Aug. 23	Sept. 22
Souvenir du Congrès:															
Dog Ridge	O	1904	1906	85	s	2	3 to 5			May 12	June 1	June 3	June 17	Sept. 21	Oct. 1
Lenoir	O	1903	1905	93	s	6.2	3 to 4	Mar. 20		May 28	June 3	May 30	...do...	Sept. 23	
Rupestris St. George	O	1903	1906	89	s	3.7	2 to 4	Mar. 19		...do...	...do...	June 1	June 16	Sept. 20	Sept. 22

Sparbonna:															
Own roots	Gi	1904			s			Mar. 17	Apr. 1	May 27				Aug. 29	Sept. 24
Sucré de Marseille:															
Dog Ridge	O	1904	1907	87	c, s	3.5	2 to 4	Mar. 21		May 19	June 2	May 25	June 15	Sept. 20	Oct. 8
Lenoir	O	1903	1905	80	s	1.6	3 to 5	Mar. 16		May 22	June 3	May 26	June 16	Sept. 15	Sept. 28
Rupestris St. George	O	1903	1905	92	s	4.4	2 to 5	Mar. 24		May 25	June 5	May 30	June 19	Sept. 21	Oct. 12
[illegible] Narbonne	O	1904	1906	70	s	1.3		Mar. 18		May 19	June 2	May 25	June 7	do.	
Sufetha:															
Own roots	O	1904		86	s	8	2 to 5	do.		May 6	June 8	May 12	June 19	Oct. 12	
Sultana:															
Own roots	Gi	1904			c, s			Mar. 14	Apr. 1	May 29	June 6	June 2	June 13	Sept. 5	
Sultanina:															
Own roots	Gi	1904			c, s			Mar. 12	Mar. 29	May 28	June 3	do.	June 10	Sept. 16	
Do.	O	1904			s	3.2	2 to 4	Mar. 24		May 11	May 31	May 16	June 16	Sept. 24	Oct. 8
Aramon × Rupestris Ganzin, No. 1	O	1904	1907	94	s	5	3 to 5	Mar. 26		May 24	June 14	May 29	June 28	do.	Oct. 3
Do.	F	1907	1907	93	c, s	5.3	3 to 6	Mar. 10	Mar 25	May 17	May 25	June 4		Aug. 30	Sept. 21
Aramon × Rupestris Ganzin, No. 2	F	1909	1909	90	s	4.5		Mar. 22		May 28				Oct. 16	
Australis	F	1909	1909	95	s	6		Mar. 20		May 24				Sept. 10	Oct. 16
Dog Ridge	O	1904	1907	93	c, s	4	2 to 6	do.		do.	June 10	May 30	June 22	Sept. 26	
[illegible]	F	1909	1909	90	s	2.5		Mar. 14		May 25				Oct. 16	
Lenoir	O	1904	1907	92	c, s	82	3 to 5	Mar. 8		May 23	June 15	May 29	June 30	Sept. 24	Sept. 30
[illegible] × [illegible], No. 554	F	1907	1907	86	c, s	2.8	3 to 6	Mar. 12	Mar. 30	May 18	May 23	June 7		Aug. 25	Oct. 17
Monticola × Riparia, No. 18804	F	1907	1907	96	c, s	5	3 to 6	Mar. 16	Mar. 27	May 15	May 22	June 5		Sept. 21	
Monticola × Riparia, No. 18808	F	1909	1909	98	s	11		Mar. 17		May 25				Sept. 5	
[illegible] × [illegible], No. 18815	F	1907	1907	88	s	3		Mar. 20		May 26				Aug. 26	
[illegible] × Rupestris	F	1909	1909	93	s	3.5	3 to 6	Mar. 12		May 21				Sept. 21	
[illegible]	F	1907	1907	94	c, s	3.8		Mar. 19	Mar. 27	May 18	May 23	June 6		Aug. 27	
Ramsey	F	1907	1907	96	c, s	39	3 to 6	Mar. 18	do.	do.	do.	do.		Aug. 25	
Riparia × (Cordifolia × Rupestris, No. 106–8)	F	1909	1909	92	s	3.5		Mar. 7		May 22				Oct. 16	
Riparia × Rupestris, No. 101	O	1907	1907	92	s	4.8		Mar. 22		May 23	June 13	May 28	June 25	Sept. 24	Oct. 1
Riparia × Rupestris, No. 101–14	F	1909	1909	95	s	3.6	3 to 5	Mar. 8		May 20				Oct. 16	
Riparia × Rupestris, No. 3306	F	1909	1909	88	s	2.6		Mar. 20		May 21				do.	
Riparia × Rupestris, No. 3309	O	1904	1907	96	c, s	4.7	3 to 5	Mar. 24		May 27	June 12	June 2	June 14	Sept. 23	Oct. 5
Riparia × [illegible]is de [illegible]ger, No. 201	F	1907	1907	83	c, s	2.1	3 to 6	Mar. 18		May 22				Sept. 21	
[illegible]	F	1907	1907	88	c, s	2	3 to 5	Mar. 19	Mar. 31	May 16	May 24	June 4		do.	
[illegible]	F	1909	1909	87	s	2.5		Mar. 20		May 21				Oct. 16	
Rupestris Mission	F	1907	1909	93	s	4.6		Mar. 12		May 24				do.	
Rupestris × Berlandieri, No. 219A	F	1907	1909	85	c, s	2.3	3 to 5	Mar. 20	Mar. 30	May 18	May 23	June 5		Sept. 5	Oct. 16
Salt Creek	F	1907	1907	96	c, s	4.3	3 to 6	Mar. 16	Mar. 27	May 19	do.	June 4		Aug. 25	
Solonis Robusta	F	1907	1909	95	s	5.5		Mar. 22		May 23					Oct. 16
Solonis × Othello, No. 1613	F	1907	1909	88	s	4.5		Mar. 23		May 25					Do.
Solonis × Riparia, No. 1616	O	1904	1907	91	c, s	4.8	2 to 6	Mar. 16		May 24	June 10	May 29	June 25	Sept. 23	Sept. 28
Vermorel	F	1907	1907	93	c, s	4.3	3 to 6	Mar. 18	Mar. 27	May 17	May 22	June 6		Aug. 27	Sept. 21
Viala	F	1907	1909	92	c, s	4		Mar. 19		May 23				Sept. 5	Oct. 16
Sultanina Rosea:															
Lenoir	O	1904	1908	82	s	2.1		Mar. 20		May 24	June 8	May 28	June 20	Sept. 26	Oct. 6

TABLE VII.—*Relative behavior and value for different purposes of grape varieties tested by grafting on resistant stocks and by growing on their own roots in eleven experiment vineyards in California*—Continued.

Variety and stock (on own roots, if so stated).	Experiment vineyard.	Year stock was planted.	Year grafted.	Congeniality.	How pruned.	Weight of pruning per vine.	Nodes bearing fruit.	Growth-starting date.		Blossoming date.		Fruit-setting date.		Fruit-ripening date.	
								Early season.	Late season.	Early season.	Late season.	Early season.	Late season.	Early season.	Late season.
1	2	3	4	5	6	7	8	9	10	11	12	13	14	15	16
Sylvaner:				P. ct.		Lbs.									
Own roots	Gi	1904			c,s			Mar. 17	Mar. 26	May 26	May 28	May 31	June 1	Aug. 28	Sept. 23
Aramon × Rupestris Ganzin, No. 1	O	1904	1906	95	c,s	6.4	2 to 4	Mar. 19		May 19	June 8	May 24	June 20	Sept. 20	Oct. 11
Dog Ridge	O	1903	1905	91	c,s	3.8	2 to 5	Mar. 15		May 20	June 3	..do..	June 15	Sept. 22	Oct. 8
Herbemont	O	1903	1905	92	s	4.5	2 to 5	Mar. 22		..do..	June 2	May 25	June 13	Sept. 20	Oct. 9
Lenoir	O	1903	1905	93	c,s	5.9	2 to 4	Mar. 18		May 19	..do..	May 24	June 16	Sept. 21	Oct. 6
Riparia × Rupestris, No. 101	O	1904	1906	90	c,s	2.2	1 to 4	Mar. 21		..do..	..do..	..do..	June 15	Sept. 22	Oct. 9
Riparia × Rupestris, No. 3309	O	1904	1906	89	c,s	3.6	2 to 4	Mar. 17		..do..	June 3	..do..	June 24	Sept. 20	Oct. 8
Rupestris Martin	O	1903	1905	86	c,s	3.1	2 to 5	Mar. 20		May 23	June 2	May 28	June 19	..do..	Oct. 5
Rupestris St. George	O	1903	1905	86	s	3.5	2 to 4	Mar. 21		May 18	June 1	May 23	June 14	..do..	Oct. 6
Syrian:															
Own roots	Gi	1904			s			Mar. 20	Apr. 1	May 28	June 3	June 9		Sept. 18	Oct. 25
Tadone:															
Dog Ridge	O	1904	1906	88	c,s	1.9	3 to 5	Mar. 18		May 24	June 1	May 29	June 17	Sept. 30	Oct. 4
Lenoir	O	1903	1905	90	s	2.2	2 to 6	Mar. 15		May 26	June 2	May 30	June 19	Sept. 28	Oct. 8
Rupestris St. George	O	1903	1905	88	s	2.8	2 to 4	Mar. 16		May 24	June 3	May 29	June 18	..do..	Oct. 10
Taylor Narbonne	O	1904	1906	84	s	1.6	2 to 6	Mar. 19		May 26	June 2	June 2	June 16	Sept. 27	Oct. 4
Tannat:															
Own roots	Gi	1904			c,s			Mar. 15	Mar. 29	May 27	June 4	May 30	June 9	Aug. 29	Sept. 23
Dog Ridge	O	1904	1906	93	s	3.5	3 to 5	Mar. 26		May 25	June 7	May 29	June 25	Sept. 28	Oct. 2
Lenoir	O	1903	1905	89	s	2.1	2 to 5	Mar. 20		May 23	June 5	May 28	June 16	Sept. 20	Oct. 4
Rupestris St. George	O	1903	1905	89	s	4.1	3 to 6	..do..		..do..	June 10	..do..	June 25	Sept. 27	Oct. 6
Taylor Narbonne	O	1904	1907	74	s	1.5	2 to 4	Mar. 24		May 24	June 6	May 29	June 20	Sept. 24	Oct. 8
Teneron:															
Own roots	Gi	1904			s			Mar. 14	Mar. 28	May 22	June 4	May 27	June 9	Sept. 15	Sept. 24
Lenoir	O	1904	1907	89	s	2.6	2 to 6	Mar. 24		May 25	June 8	June 1	June 20	Sept. 26	Oct. 7
Riparia × Rupestris, No. 3306	O	1904		94	c,s	7	2 to 4	Mar. 20		May 12		May 16	May 18	Oct. 1	Oct. 8
Terret Monstre:															
[illegible] Giant	F	1907	1907	95	c,s	3.3	2 to 4	..do..	Mar. 30	May 18	May 23	May 30		Sept. 16	Sept. 21
[illegible]	F	1907	1907	97	s	5.1	3 to 4	Mar. 14	..do..	May 15	..do..	May 29		..do..	Do.
Lenoir	O	1904	1907	89	s	2.4	2 to 5	Mar. 25		May 24	June 8	..do..	June 23	June 28	Oct. 7
Riparia × Rupestris, No. 101	F	1907	1907	95	c,s	5.5	3 to 5	Mar. 23	Apr. 1	May 20	May 21	May 31		Sept. 15	Sept. 21

[illegible]	F	1907	1907	97	c,s	4.7	3 to 5	Mar. 20	...do...	May 16	May 23	May 30		Sept. 16	Do.
[illegible] × [illegible], No. 1616	F	1907	1907	94	c,s	5.1	3 to 5	...do...	...do...	do	...do...	May 28		...do...	Oct. 17
[illegible]	F	1907	1907	98	s	78	3 to 4	Mar. 17	Mar. 20	May 17	May 22	May 30		...do...	
Tinta [illegible]:															
[illegible]	Gi	1904			s			Mar. 18	Mar. 30	May 28	June 3	June 2	June 6	Sept. 18	Sept. 20
Dog Ridge	O	1904	1906	95	c,s	6.6	2 to 4	Mar. 19		May 27	...do...	June 3	June 16	Sept. 25	Oct. 6
Lenoir	O	1903	1905	90	c,s	4	2 to 4	...do...		May 20	...do...	May 26	June 15	...do...	Do.
[illegible]is St. [illegible]	O	1903	1905	94	s	4.7	2 to 4	Mar. 17		May 24	June 5	May 29	June 17	Sept. 26	Do.
Taylor Narbonne	O	1904	1906	88	s	2.3	2 to 4	Mar. 21		May 25	...do...	May 30	June 18	June 25	Oct. 4
Tinta [illegible]:															
Own roots	Gi	1904			s			Mar. 15	Apr. 5	May 24	May 30	May 29	June 7	Aug. 29	Sept. 22
Dog Ridge	O	1904	1906	94	c,s	7.7	2 to 4	Mar. 21		...do...	June 5	...do...	June 17	...do...	Oct. 8
[illegible]	O	1903	1905	95	s	49	2 to 4	Mar. 17		May 19	June 8	May 24	June 24	Sept. 25	Do.
[illegible]s St. George	O	1903	1905	94	s	5.1	2 to 5	Mar. 20		...do...	June 1	May 25	June 15	Sept. 26	Oct. 6
Taylor [illegible]ne	O	1904	1906	90	s	36	1 to 4	Mar. 19		May 23	May 11	May 29	June 12	Sept. 30	Oct. 4
Tinta d[illegible] [illegible]re:															
Own roots	Gi	1904			s			Mar. 15	Mar. 29	May 24	May 30	...do...	June 7	Aug. 28	Sept. 20
[illegible]	O	1904	1907	92	c,s	5.8	2 to 4	Mar. 19		May 25	June 1	June 1	June 15	Sept. 29	Oct. 2
[illegible]r	O	1903	1905	94	s	6.3	2 to 4	Mar. 18		May 26	June 6	June 2	June 17	Sept. 24	Oct. 4
[illegible]is St. George	O	1903	1905	96	c,s	6	2 to 4	Mar. 20		May 21	May [illegible]	May 27	June 16	Sept. 10	Sept. 23
Taylor [illegible]rbonne	O	1904	1907	87	s	2	2 to 4	Mar. 18		May 26	June 3	June 2	June 7	Sept. 24	
[illegible]k [illegible] [illegible]r:															
Own roots	Gi	1904			s			Mar. 12	Mar. 28	...do...	May 31	May 31	June 5	Sept. 18	Sept. 25
[illegible]r:															
Own roots	Gi	1907			s			Mar. 16	Apr. 1	...do...				Sept. 23	
[illegible]on × [illegible]s Ganzin, No. 1	O	1904	1906	88	s	2.7	[illegible] to 5	Mar. 20		...do...	June 3	June 2	June 15	Sept. 25	Oct. 5
Dog Ridge	O	1903	1905	89	c,s	26	2 to 4	Mar. 18		May 22	June 23	May 28	June 17	...do...	Oct. 10
Herbemont	O	1903	1905	82	s	1.7	[illegible] to 5	Mar. 20		May 20	June 6	May 26	June 12	Sept. 20	Oct. 5
[illegible]ir	O	1903	1905	90	s	3.1	[illegible] to 5	Mar. 18		May 25	June 2	June 20	June 20	Sept. 23	Oct. 6
[illegible] [illegible]s, No. 1202	O	1904	1906	84	s	1.5	[illegible] to 5	Mar. 20		May 26	June 3	...do...	...do...	Sept. 26	Do.
[illegible]ia [illegible]ris, No. 101	O	1904	1906	85	s	13	2 to 4	Mar. 18		May 22	June 2	May 28	...do...	Sept. 24	Do.
[illegible], No. 3309	O	1904	1906	89	c,s	2.7	[illegible] to 5	Mar. 17		May 20	June 1	May 26	...do...	Sept. 25	Oct. 4
[illegible]is [illegible]n	O	1903	1905	85	s	2.2	[illegible] to 5	Mar. 20		May 23	June 4	May 28	June 18	Sept. 24	Oct. 6
[illegible]	O	1903	1905	92	c,s	35	[illegible] to 4	Mar. 18		May 24	June 1	May 29	June 10	Sept. 12	Sept. 30
[illegible]ek	O	[illegible]903	1905	88	s	19	2 to 5	...do...		May 22	June 5	May 27	June 17	Sept. 26	Oct. 6
[illegible]is × [illegible]ia, No. 1616	O	1904	1906	88	s	23	2 to 4	May 17		May 26	June 10	June 2	June 25	Sept. 24	Oct. 5
Taylor Narbonne	O	1904	1906	92	s	3.4	2 to 5	Mar. 18		May 27	June 1	June 3	June 12	Sept. 23	
[illegible]h:															
[illegible]	Gi	1904			s			Mar. 15	Apr. 1	May 26	May 28	June 2		Sept. 20	
[illegible]r	O	1903	1905	91	c,s	3.3	3 to 5	...do...		...do...	June 5	June 1	June 16	Sept. 9	Oct. 1
[illegible]is St. George	O	1903	1905	90	c,s	2.1	2 to 4	Mar. 22		May 22	June 2	May 28	June 10	Sept. 24	Oct. 8
Trifere du [illegible]n:															
Lenoir	O	1904	1907	84	s	2.6	2 to 6	Mar. 20		May 23	June 10	May 29	June 6	Sept. 29	Oct. 10
[illegible]he:															
[illegible]r	O	1907	1907	92	s	2.9	3 to 5	Mar. 16		...do...	June 5	...do...	June 18	Sept. 27	Oct. 15
Trivoti:															
Own roots	Gi	1904			s			Mar. 20	Apr. 10	May 31	June 12	June 6	June 19	Sept. 24	Oct. 25
Trojka:															
Own roots	Gi	1904			s			Mar. 26	Mar. 29	May 24	June 3	May 29	June 10	Aug. 29	Sept. 24

TABLE VII.—*Relative behavior and value for different purposes of grape varieties tested by grafting on resistant stocks and by growing on their own roots in eleven experiment vineyards in California*—Continued.

Variety and stock (on own roots, if so stated).	Experiment vineyard.	Year stock was planted.	Year grafted.	Congeniality.	How pruned.	Weight of pruning per vine.	Nodes bearing fruit.	Growth-starting date.		Blossoming date.		Fruit-setting date.		Fruit-ripening date.	
								Early season.	Late season.	Early season.	Late season.	Early season.	Late season.	Early season.	Late season.
1	2	3	4	5	6	7	8	9	10	11	12	13	14	15	16
Trousseau:				*P. ct.*		*Lbs.*									
Own roots	Gi	1904	......	......	c, s	......	......	Mar. 20	Mar. 26	May 26	May 30	May 31	June 7	Aug. 24	Sept. 20
Dog Ridge	O	1904	1906	93	s	4.6	1 to 5	Mar. 22	....	...do....	June 3	June 2	June 15	Sept. 25	Oct. 8
Lenoir	O	1903	1905	95	c, s	5.1	2 to 4	Mar. 20	....	May 26	June 1	June 1	June 13	Sept. 24	Sept. 28
Rupestris St. George	O	1903	1905	95	c, s	4.8	1 to 4	Mar. 16	....	May 24	...do...	May 30	June 14	...do....	Sept. 25
Taylor Narbonne	O	1904	1906	94	s	6.5	2 to 4	Mar. 21	....	May 27	June 3	June 3	...do....	Sept. 23	
Ulliade Blanche d'Ambre:															
Own roots	Gi	1905	......	......	c, s	......	......	Mar. 20	Mar. 31	May 28	May 30	...do....	....	Sept. 15	Sept. 25
Valandova:															
Dog Ridge	O	1904	1906	92	s	4	2 to 4	Mar. 16	....	May 26	June 3	June 2	June 15	Sept. 27	
Lenoir	O	1904	1906	90	s	3	3 to 4	Mar. 18	....	May 27	...do....	June 1	June 14	Sept. 28	Oct. 7
Valdepenas:															
Own roots	Gi	1904	......	......	s	......	......	Mar. 10	Apr. 1	May 26	May 30	May 30	June 5	Aug. 29	Sept. 23
Aramon × Rupestris Ganzin, No. 1	O	1904	1906	95	c, s	4.7	2 to 5	Mar. 20	....	May 21	June 4	May 27	June 15	Sept. 24	Oct. 11
Dog Ridge	O	1903	1905	94	c, s	3.9	1 to 4	...do....	....	May 24	June 5	May 29	June 20	Sept. 20	Oct. 8
Herbemont	O	1903	1905	95	c, s	5.7	1 to 4	Mar. 25	....	...do....	...do....	...do....	June 17	...do....	Oct. 11
Lenoir	O	1903	1905	95	s	4.4	2 to 4	Mar. 15	....	...do....	June 3	...do....	...do....	Sept. 25	Oct. 8
Mourvedre × Rupestris, No. 1202	O	1904	1906	95	c, s	3	2 to 5	Mar. 18	....	...do....	June 1	May 30	June 13	...do....	Oct. 5
Riparia × Rupestris, No. 101	O	1904	1906	94	s	3.9	2 to 5	Mar. 20	....	...do....	June 2	May 29	June 15	Sept. 24	Oct. 9
Riparia × Rupestris, No. 3309	O	1904	1906	94	s	4.2	2 to 3	Mar. 18	....	May 25	May 31	May 30	...do....	Sept. 23	Oct. 5
Rupestris Martin	O	1903	1905	96	s	6.3	1 to 4	...do....	....	May 21	June 3	May 26	June 18	Sept. 24	Oct. 6
Rupestris St. George	O	1903	1905	97	s	5.6	2 to 4	Mar. 20	....	May 20	May 31	May 25	June 17	Sept. 25	Oct. 8
Salt Creek	O	1903	1905	92	c, s	2.8	2 to 5	...do....	....	May 22	June 3	May 27	June 16	Sept. 22	Oct. 11
Solonis × Riparia, No. 1616	O	1904	1906	91	s	3.4	2 to 5	Mar. 18	....	May 23	June 10	May 29	June 25	Sept. 24	Oct. 4
Taylor Narbonne	O	1904	1906	92	c, s	5	2 to 5	Mar. 23	....	May 25	June 8	May 28	June 23	Sept. 23	Oct. 10
Veltliner:															
Own roots	Gi	1904	......	......	c, s	......	......	Mar. 13	Mar. 28	May 22	May 28	May 27	June 3	Aug. 28	Sept. 20
Dog Ridge	O	1903	1905	92	s	3	3 to 5	Mar. 20	....	May 24	June 1	May 29	June 16	Sept. 24	Oct. 8
Herbemont	O	1903	1905	88	c, s	2.7	3 to 5	Mar. 24	....	May 20	June 5	May 26	June 17	Sept. 23	Oct. 9
Lenoir	O	1903	1905	90	s	3.1	2 to 4	Mar. 20	....	...do....	June 3	May 25	June 16	Sept. 24	Oct. 8
Riparia × Rupestris, No. 3306	O	1907	1909	79	s	.9	......	...do....	....	June 1	...do....	June 5	June 14	....	
Rupestris Martin	O	1903	1905	84	s	1.8	2 to 4	...do....	....	May 19	June 5	May 25	June 20	Sept. 26	Oct. 6
Rupestris St. George	O	1903	1905	85	s	2.1	2 to 5	Mar. 24	....	May 20	May 31	May 27	June 10	Sept. 25	Do.
Salt Creek	O	1903	1905	88	s	2.4	2 to 5	Mar. 20	....	May 19	June 1	May 25	June 16	Sept. 20	Oct. 11

[illegible]:														
Own roots	Gi	1905	......	......	c, s	......	......	Mar. 15	Mar. 27	May 24	June 8	May 29	June 13	Sept. 19	Sept. 26
Dog Ridge	O	1904	1907	89	s	3.5	2 to 5	Mar. 22	......	May 26	June 5	June 1	June 20	Sept. 30	Oct. 15
Do	F	1903	1905	96	c, s	4.6	3 to 7	Mar. 14	Mar. 26	May 20	May 24	May 29	June 4	Sept. 6	Sept. 20
[illegible]	O	1903	1905	98	c, s	3.8	3 to 5	Mar. 18	......	May 26	June 8	May 30	June 22	Sept. 28	Oct. 9
Rupestris St. George	O	1903	1905	93	s	5.7	3 to 6	...do...	......	...do...	...do...	June 2	...do...	Sept. 29	Oct. 3
Do	F	1903	1905	92	s	3.3	3 to 6	Mar. 12	Apr. 3	May 15	May 20	May 25	May 29	Sept. 10	Sept. 19
Verdel:															
Own roots	Gi	1904	......	......	s	......	......	Mar. 20	Apr. 10	May 26	June 4	May 31	June 10	Sept. 20	Sept. 28
Adobe Giant	F	1904	1906	93	c, s	3.8	2 to 6	Mar. 14	Mar. 25	May 15	May 20	May 25	May 27	Sept. 5	Sept. 21
Aramon × Rupestris Ganzin, No. 1	F	1904	1906	93	c, s	6.1	2 to 6	Mar. 12	...do...	May 13	May 19	May 22	May 30	...do...	Sept. 20
Dog Ridge	F	1904	1906	97	c, s	15.3	3 to 6	Mar. 25	Apr. 1	May 15	May 21	May 26	May 31	...do...	Do.
Mourvedre × Rupestris, No. 1202	F	1904	1906	95	c, s	7	3 to 6	Mar. 7	Mar. 25	May 13	May 22	May 28	......	Sept. 10	Do.
Riparia × Rupestris, No. 101	F	1904	1906	87	c, s	3.1	3 to 6	Mar. 18	...do...	May 10	May 20	May 25	May 27	Sept. 5	Do.
Riparia × Rupestris, No. 3309	F	1904	1906	97	c, s	8.7	2 to 6	Mar. 12	Mar. 20	May 16	May 18	May 24	...do...	...do...	Do.
Rupestris St. George	F	1903	1905	95	c, s	6.4	2 to 6	Mar. 6	Mar. 31	May 15	May 17	May 20	June 3	Sept. 10	Sept. 19
Solonis × Riparia, No. 1616	F	1904	1906	87	s	2.4	2 to 5	Mar. 8	Mar. 25	May 14	May 20	May 25	May 28	Sept. 8	Sept. 20
Taylor Narbonne	F	1904	1906	92	c, s	5.1	3 to 5	Mar. 6	Mar. 30	May 15	May 26	May 24	May 30	Sept. 12	Do.
[illegible]o:															
Own roots	F	1904	......	......	c, s	......	......	Mar. 14	Mar. 28	May 27	May 29	June 4	......	Aug. 29	Sept. 28
Verdelho de Madere:															
[illegible]	F	1907	......	......	s	......	......	Mar. 10	Apr. 5	......	......	......	......	Sept. 23	
Aramon × Rupestris Ganzin, No. 1	F	1904	1906	85	s	2	1 to 4	Mar. 7	Mar. 30	May 11	May 17	May 22	May 26	Aug. 16	Sept. 20
Dog Ridge	F	1904	1906	80	s	1.6	1 to 4	Mar. 6	Apr. 1	May 15	May 18	...do...	May 30	Aug. 19	Do.
Riparia × Rupestris, No. 3309	F	1904	1906	82	c, s	1.4	2 to 4	Mar. 13	...do...	May 11	May 16	May 21	May 25	Aug. 20	Do.
Rupestris St. George	F	1903	1905	86	s	2.8	1 to 5	Mar. 5	Mar. 27	May 13	May 15	May 20	May 30	Aug. 15	Sept. 19
Solonis × Riparia, No. 1616	F	1904	1906	83	s	1.4	2 to 5	Mar. 7	Mar. 25	...do...	May 17	May 23	...do...	...do...	Sept. 20
Ver[illegible]o:															
Own roots	F	1904	......	......	c, s	......	......	Mar. [illegible]	Mar. 29	May 26	June 6	May 30	June 12	Aug. 29	Sept. 25
Adobe Giant	F	1904	1906	89	s	2.8	2 to 5	Mar. 14	Apr. 1	May 20	May 23	May 26	June 6	Sept. 8	Sept. 20
Aramon × Rupestris Ganzin, No. 1	F	1904	1906	90	s	4.8	2 to 5	Mar. 12	...do...	...do...	June 1	May 30	June 10	Sept. 5	Do.
Dog Ridge	F	1903	1905	89	c, s	2.4	2 to 5	Mar. 14	...do...	May 14	May 30	May 28	June 7	Sept. 14	Do.
Herbemont	F	1903	1905	81	s	1.4	2 to 4	Mar. 7	Mar. 25	May 13	May 20	May 24	May 31	Sept. 5	Do.
Lenoir	F	1903	1905	85	s	.9	2 to 5	Mar. 12	Apr. 1	May 3	May 23	May 25	May 28	Sept. 10	Sept. 19
Mourvedre × Rupestris, No. 1202	F	1904	1906	88	s	3.5	2 to 4	Mar. 8	Mar. 25	May 15	May 25	May 26	June 3	Sept. 8	Sept. 20
Riparia Gloire	F	1903	1905	80	c, s	2.1	2 to 4	...do...	Mar. 20	May 16	May 23	May 23	June 7	Sept. 10	Sept. 19
Riparia × Rupestris, No. 101	F	1904	1906	86	s	1.6	2 to 5	Mar. 14	Apr. 5	May 18	May 28	May 21	June 2	Sept. 8	Sept. 20
Riparia × Rupestris, No. 3309	F	104	1906	95	c, s	4.7	[illegible]	Mar. 12	Apr. 1	May 12	...do...	May 27	June 5	Sept. 10	Do.
[illegible]n	F	1903	1905	84	s	1.7	2 to 4	...do...	Mar. 30	May 16	May 21	May 26	May 30	...do...	Do.
Rupestris St. George	F	1903	1905	92	c, s	3	2 to 5	Mar. 14	Apr. 2	...do...	May 29	May 21	June 3	Sept. 8	Sept. 19
Salt Creek	F	1903	1905	72	c, s	1.8	2 to 5	Mar. 10	Mar. 25	...do...	May 22	May 25	May 31	Sept. 5	Sept. 16
Solonis × Riparia, No. 1616	F	1904	1906	91	c, s	3.7	2 to 5	Mar. 12	Apr. 1	May 14	May 23	May 27	May 28	Sept. 10	Sept. 20
Taylor Narbonne	F	1904	1906	90	c, s	3.2	2 to 4	Mar. 8	...do...	May 12	May 25	May 26	May 30	Sept. 16	Do.
Vernaccia Sarda:															
Own roots	Gi	1904	......	......	s	......	......	Mar. 16	Mar. 31	May 26	June 1	May 31	June 8	Aug. 29	Sept. 24
Vigne de Zericho:															
[illegible]	O	1904	1907	93	s	3.2	2 to 5	Mar. 21	......	May 20	June 8	May 26	June 21	Sept. 30	Oct. 7
Mourvedre × Rupestris, No. 1202	F	1907	1907	98	c, s	7.6	3 to 4	Mar. 18	......	May 18	May 24	May 31	......	Sept. 15	Sept. 21
Wälschriesling:															
Own roots	Gi	1904	......	......	c, s	......	......	Mar. 17	Apr. 1	May 26	May 30	...do...	June 5	Aug. 27	Sept. 23
Werme:															
Own roots	Gi	1904	......	......	s	......	......	Mar. 13	Apr. 3	...do...	May 29	June 3	......	Aug. 29	Sept. 20

TABLE VII.—*Relative behavior and value for different purposes of grape varieties tested by grafting on resistant stocks and by growing on their own roots in eleven experiment vineyards in California*—Continued.

Variety and stock (on own roots, if so stated).	Experiment vineyard.	Year stock was planted.	Year grafted.	Congeniality.	How pruned.	Weight of pruning per vine.	Nodes bearing fruit.	Growth-starting date.		Blossoming date.		Fruit-setting date.		Fruit-ripening date.	
								Early season.	Late season.	Early season.	Late season.	Early season.	Late season.	Early season.	Late season.
1	2	3	4	5	6	7	8	9	10	11	12	13	14	15	16
White Hanepoot:				P. ct.		Lbs.									
Adobe [illegible]t	F	1904	1906	88	s	1.5	3 to 5	Mar. 24	Apr. 2	May 20	May 28	May 29	June 4	Sept. 5	Sept. 12
[illegible] × Rupestris Ganzin, No. 2	F	1907	1909	88	s	1.5		Mar. 20		May 25					
Australis	F	1907	1909	90	s	3		Mar. 30		May 21				Oct. 16	
[illegible] × Riparia, No. 420A	F	1907	1909	88	s	3		Apr. 1		May 22				do	
Dog Ridge	F	1904	1906	91	s	3.8	2 to 5	Mar. 13	Apr. 6	May 18	May 30	May 29	June 8	Sept. 5	Sept. 20
Hotporup	F	1907	1909	87	s	2.2		Mar. 20		May 21				Oct. 16	
Monticola × Rupestris	F	1907	1909	89	s	4		Mar. 27		May 27				do	
[illegible]re × [illegible]s, No. 1202	F	1903	1905	89	s	3.5	3 to 5	Mar. 14	Apr. 5	May 20	May 25	May 30	June 7	Sept. 8	Sept. 20
Riparia × [illegible]ia × Rupestris, No. 106-8)	F	1907	1909	90	s	3.5		Mar. 24		do				Oct. 16	
Riparia × Rupestris, No. 101	F	1904	1906	86	s	1.3	2 to 5	Mar. 12	Apr. 2	May 15	May 31	May 25	June 7	Spt. 16	Sept. 20
Riparia × Rupestris, No. 3306	F	1907	1909	88	s	3		Mar. 30		May 22				Oct. 16	
Riparia × Rupestris, No. 3309	F	1904	1906	92	s	4.1	2 to 5	Mar. 14	Apr. 1	May 20	May 30	May 26	June 8	Sept. 5	Sept. 20
[illegible]is [illegible]	F	1907	1909	80	s			Mar. 23		May 24				Sept. 10	
[illegible]is St. [illegible]	F	1903	1905	84	s	2.9	3 to 6	Mar. 15	Apr. 5	May 21	May 27	May 29	June 6	Sept. 12	Sept. 19
[illegible]is × Berlandieri, No. 219A	F	1907	1909	82	s	2		Mar. 31		do				Oct. 16	
[illegible]	F	1904	1906	89	s	2.6	3 to 6	Mar. 8	Apr. 3	May 15	May 25	May 26	May 30	Sept. 4	Sept. 20
Viala	F	1907	1909	87	s	2		Mar. 24		May 24				Oct. 16	
W[illegible]te Tokay:															
Own roots	Gi	1904			s			Mar. 12	Mar. 28	May 22	May 30	May 27	June 5	Aug. 18	Sept. 24
[illegible] Hamburg:															
[illegible]n roots	O	1904			s	2.7	3 to 4	Mar. 18		May 16	May 31	May 21	do	Sept. 29	
Do	Gi	1905			c, s			Mar. 14	Mar. 28	May 27	May 28	June 2		Aug. 28	Sept. 25
Wilmot, No. 16:															
[illegible]n roots	Gi	1905			c, s			Mar. 20	Mar. 31	May 15	May 26	May 29		Sept. 25	
Dog Ridge	O	1904	1906	89	s	2.4	3 to 6	do		May 20	June 2	May 26	June 12	Sept. 28	Oct. 10
Lenoir	O	1903	1905	91	s	2.8	2 to 5	Mar. 21		May 25	May 31	May 29	June 16	do	Oct. 15
[illegible]is St. George	O	1903	1905	89	s	2.2	3 to 6	Mar. 20		May 22	do	May 28	June 14	Sept. 25	Sept. 30
Zante:															
Own roots	Gi	1904			s			Mar. 22	Mar. 27	do	May 22	do	June 7	Sept. 5	Sept. 24

Zinzillosa:														
Own roots	Gi	1904			s			Mar. 20	Apr. 1	May 24	June 3	May 30	June 9	Aug. 29	Sept. 25
Zinfandel:															
Own roots	Gi	1907			s			do	Mar. 30	June 27				Sept. 15	Sept. 23
[illegible] × Rupestris Ganzin, No. 1	O	1904	1906	92	s	4.1	2 to 5	do		May 26	June 1	June 2	June 14	Sept. 20	Oct. 11
Berlandieri × Riparia, No. 420A	O	1907	1909	83	s	1	2 to 3	Mar. 19		May 30	June 4	June 9	June 15	Sept. 25	
Dog Ridge	O	1903	1905	93	s	3	2 to 5	Mar. 22		May 23	June 5	May 29	June 17	do	Oct. 8
Herbemont	O	1903	1905	86	s	2.5	2 to 5	Mar. 24		May 22	do	May 28	do	do	Oct. 11
Lenoir	O	1903	1905	91	s	2.9	2 to 4	Mar. 17		do	do	May 27	June 20	Sept. 20	Oct. 8
[illegible] × Riparia, No. 18815	O	1907	1909	85	s	1.9	2 to 3	Mar. 18		June 1		June 6	June 21	do	Oct. 10
[illegible] × Rupestris, No. 1202	O	1904	1906	89	s	2.9	3 to 5	Mar. 20		May 23	June 3	May 28	June 23	Sept. 25	Oct. 11
Riparia × [illegible], No. 101	O	1904	1906	82	s	2.5	2 to 5	do		May 22	June 1	May 27	June 20	Sept. 20	Oct. 5
Riparia × [illegible] No. 101-14	O	1907	1909	82	s	1.3		do		May 30	May 31	June 4	June 16		
[illegible] × Rupestris, No. 3306	O	1907	1909	86	s	1.3	2 to 3	Mar. 18		May 31	June 1	do	June 24	Sept. 20	Oct. 11
[illegible] × Rupestris, No. 3309	O	1904	1906	89	s	1.8	2 to 5	Mar. 20		May 24	June 2	May 29	do	do	Oct. 8
Rupestris Martin	O	1903	1905	87	s	3.5	2 to 5	do		do	June 6	May 30	June 19	Sept. 25	Oct. 13
Rupestris Metallica	O	1907	1909	70	s	.4		do		May 31	do	June 5	June 21		
Rupestris [illegible]	O	1907	1909	87	s	1	2 to 4	do		do		June 4		Sept. 20	
[illegible] St. [illegible]	O	1903	1905	92	s	3.1	3 to 5	Mar. 18		May 22	June 1	May 27	June 13	Sept. 28	Oct. 10
Salt Creek	O	1903	1905	86	s	1.5	2 to 6	Mar. 22		May 23	June 10	May 29	June 24	Sept. 20	Oct. 11
Solonis Robusta	O	1907	1909	79	s	1.6	2 to 5	Mar. 18		May 30	June 1	June 6	June 15	do	do
Solonis × [illegible], No. 1613	O	1907	1909	68	s	1	3 to 4	Mar. 20		June 1	June 5	June 5	June 20	Sept. 25	
Solonis × [illegible], No. 1616	O	1904	1906	72	s	1.1	2 to 5	do		May 23	June 10	May 29	June 26	Sept. 29	Oct. 10
[illegible] Narbonne	O	1904	1906	82	s	2.1	2 to 5	do		May 20	June 8	May 25	June 22	Sept. 25	Oct. 8

TABLE VII.—*Relative behavior and value for different purposes of grape varieties tested by grafting on resistant stocks and by growing on their own roots in eleven experiment vineyards in California*—Continued.

Variety and stock (on own roots, if so stated).	Weight of fruit per vine (pounds). 1909	1910	1911	1912	1913	Sugar, Balling scale.	Acid, as tartaric (grams per 100 c. c.).	Cluster. Size.	Cluster. Shape.	Cluster. Compact or loose.	Berry. Size.	Berry. Shape.	Berry. Color.	Use.
1	17	18	19	20	21	22	23	24	25	26	27	28	29	30
Ach-I-Soum:						*P. cent.*								
Dog Ridge								m	t	l	l	r	w	s, st
Lenoir								m	t	l	l	r	w	s, st
Actoni Maceron:														
Lenoir	2	10			3	21.8	0.5780	m-l	t	l	v, l	o	w	s, t
[illegible]la × Rupestris				3	3	28	.4200	m-l	t	l	v, l	o	w	s, t
[illegible]re × Rupestris, No. 1202								m-l	t	l	v, l	o	w	s, t
Solonis × Riparia, No. 1616			6		3	24.5	.4200	m-l	t	l	v, l	o	w	s, t
[illegible]y:														
Lenoir	6	3	7			24.8	.1750	l	t	l	v, l	o	w	s, t
Monticola × Rupestris				2		20	.0050	l	t	l	v, l	o	w	s, t
[illegible]ey								l	t	l	v, l	o	w	s, t
Admirable:														
Riparia × Rupestris, No. 3309	25		21	7		22.5	.7150	m	cy	m	m	r	w	t, w
Affenthaler:														
Own roots	10	1½	8	19		25.4	.7125	m	t	c	l	ob	b	s, t
A[illegible]ga:														
Riparia × Rupestris, No. 3309					5			m	cy	c	l	r	w	s, st, t
Ahmeur bou Ahmeur:														
Lenoir	8	8	3			21.8	.5600	l	t	c	l	o	r	s, t
Ajaki Odia:														
[illegible]re × Rupestris, No. 1202			6			28.5	.6562	l	cy	m	l	o	w	t
Riparia × Rupestris, No. 101								l	cy	m	l	o	w	t
[illegible]aris Metallica			3	6		24.5	.5475	l	cy	m	l	o	w	t
Ajmi:														
Lenoir								m	t	s	l	o	w	t
A[illegible]eo:														
Own roots	5	3	3	25		29	.7294	l	t	c	m	r	b	t, w
Dog Ridge	25	10	5	2	5	27	.8325	l	t	c	m	r	b	t, w
[illegible]ir	25	10	14		29	23.5	.8900	l	t	c	m	r	b	t, w
Rupestris St. George	40	12	15	1	27½	26.5	.8456	l	t	c	m	r	b	t, w
Taylor Narbonne		3				23.2	.8500	l	t	c	m	r	b	t, w

[illegible]ria:														
Own roots		6	2	8		25.2	.6600	n	t	l	l	o	w	r, s, st, t, w, j
Adobe Giant	8	26	2	12	11	26	.5900	m	t	l	l	o	w	r, s, st, t, w, j
[illegible] × [illegible]estris Ganzin, No. 1	5		2			26.5	. [illegible]060	n	t	l	l	o	w	r, s, st, t, w, j
Aramon × [illegible]stris [illegible], No. 2			8	4		27.5	.5300	n	t	l	l	o	w	r, s, st, t, w, j
[illegible]s				5½		28.5	.5250	m	t	l	l	o	w	r, s, st, t, w, j
Berlandieri × [illegible]A			11½	9		[illegible]9	.5250	m	t	l	l	o	w	r, s, s[illegible]t, w, j
Constantia								n	t	l	l	o	w	r, s, st, t, w, j
[illegible]	16	15	3	8	5½	26.5	.6281	m	t	l	l	o	w	r, s, st, t, w, j
[illegible]	2		½	⅛	0	25.5	.5281	m	t	l	l	o	w	r, s, st, t, w, j
Lenoir	8	1	8	2½		27	. [illegible]66	m	t	l	l	o	w	r, s, st, t, w, j
[illegible] × [illegible]ia, No. 18808				4		28	.6150	m	t	l	l	o	w	r, s, st, t, w, j
[illegible] × Rupestris				12		28	.5325	n	t	l	l	o	w	r, s, st, t, w, j
[illegible] × [illegible], No. 1202	10	1	3	5	0	26.5	.6550	n	t	l	l	o	w	[illegible], st, t, w, j
[illegible] Gloire	15	1	3	12	2	27	.6018	m	t	l	l	o	w	r, s, st, t, w, j
Riparia × C[illegible]ia × Rupestris, No. 106–8)				8½		27	.5350	m	t	l	l	o	w	r, s, st, t, w, j
Riparia × Rupestris, No. 101	10		3	7	18	28.5	. [illegible]60	n	t	l	l	o	w	r, s, st, t, w, j
[illegible]a × [illegible]str s, No. 101–14				3		27	.4575	m	t	l	l	o	w	r, s, st, t, w, j
Riparia × Rupestris, No, 3306								m	t	l	l	o	w	r, s, st, t, w, j
Riparia × [illegible]stris, No. 3309	12	1½	5	5	18	27.5	.6490	m	t	l	l	o	w	r, s, st, t, w, j
[illegible]s [illegible]in			¼	½	0	25.5	.4987	m	t	l	l	o	w	r, s, st, t, w, j
[illegible]t. George	2	1½	[illegible]	5	½	27	.5250	m	t	l	l	o	w	r, s, st, t, w, j
[illegible]s × Berlandieri, No. 219A								n	t	l	l	o	w	r, s, st, t, w, j
Salt Creek	10	1	1	2	1	26.7	.5788	n	t	l	l	o	w	r, s, st, t, w, j
Solonis [illegible]a								m	t	l	l	o	w	r, s, st, t, w, j
Solonis × [illegible]o. 1613				3		19	.8700	m	t	l	l	o	w	r, s, st, t, w, j
[illegible]s × a[illegible]a, No. 1616	4	5	2	10	½	28	.5181	n	t	l	l	o	w	r, s, st, t, w, j
Taylor [illegible]e		10	½	2	0	28	.6425	n	t	l	l	o	w	r, s, st, t, w; j
Viala								m	t	l	l	o	w	r, s, st, t, w, j
[illegible]:														
Own roots								l	t	m	n	o	b	t, w
Lenoir	25	10	2	10		24.4	.7068	l	t	m	n	o	b	t, w
Riparia × R[illegible]stris, No. 3306								l	t	n	m	o	b	t, w
[illegible]s St. [illegible]e	30	12	3	25		24	.7020	l	t	n	n	o	b	t, w
Ali [illegible] [illegible]e):														
Own roots								l	t	n	n	o	b	t, w
Alicante Bouschet:														
Own roots	25	15	8	17	5	24.8	.6680	m	cy	c	m	r	b	w
(A[illegible]s × Monticola) × (Riparia × Rupestris, [illegible]. 45)			7	4	5	21.5	1.3200	m	cy	c	m	r	b	w
[illegible]n × [illegible]s Ganzin, No. 1	40	30	8	5	1	24.9	.9767	n	cy	c	m	r	b	w
An × [illegible]up[illegible]is Ganzin, No. 2					3			m	cy	c	n	r	b	w
Berlandieri × R[illegible]a[illegible]ia, No. 420A			1½	4	4	22	1.0612	m	cy	c	m	r	b	w
[illegible]a			2½		6	24.5	.9075	m	cy	c	n	r	b	w
Dog [illegible]e	40	8	9½	6	10	21	1.1672	n	cy	c	n	r	b	w
[illegible]t	20	6				20	.8300	n	cy	c	n	r	b	w
Lenoir	50		13	8	7	20.6	1.0008	m	cy	c	m	r	b	w
Monticola × Riparia, No. 18808								n	cy	c	m	r	b	w
Monticola × Riparia, No. 18815			3	4	5	21.5	1.0270	m	cy	c	m.	r	b	w
Mourvedre × Rupestris, No. 1202								n	cy	c	m	r	b	w

TABLE VII.—*Relative behavior and value for different purposes of grape varieties tested by grafting on resistant stocks and by growing on their own roots in eleven experiment vineyards in California*—Continued.

Variety and stock (on own roots, if so stated).	Weight of fruit per vine (pounds).					Sugar, Balling scale.	Acid, as tartaric (grams per 100 c. c.).	Cluster.			Berry.			Use.
	1909	1910	1911	1912	1913			Size.	Shape.	Compact or loose.	Size.	Shape.	Color.	
1	17	18	19	20	21	22	23	24	25	26	27	28	29	30
Alicante Bouschet—Continued.						*P. cent.*								
Riparia × Rupestris, No. 101	60	10	......	25	2	21.5	1.0000	m	cy	c	m	r	b	w
Riparia × Rupestris, No. 101-14	......	......	......	......	4	......	......	m	cy	c	m	r	b	w
Riparia × Rupestris, No. 3306	......	......	11	3	5	21	1.3237	m	cy	c	m	r	b	w
Riparia × Rupestris, No. 3309	60	10	6	......	3	23.8	.9650	m	cy	c	m	r	b	w
Rupestris [illegible]	60	10	8	......	15	23	.8750	m	cy	c	m	r	b	w
Rupestris Metallica	......	......	......	......	3	......	......	m	cy	c	m	r	b	w
Rupestris Mission	......	......	......	......	......	......	......	m	cy	c	m	r	b	w
Rupestris St. George	60	15	8	8	6	22.4	.9073	m	cy	c	m	r	b	w
Salt Creek	60	6	......	......	4	22.5	.7612	m	cy	c	m	r	b	w
Solonis Robusta	......	......	......	......	5	......	......	m	cy	c	m	r	b	w
Solonis × Othello, No. 1613	......	......	4	......	4	23	1.0350	m	cy	c	m	r	b	w
Solonis Riparia, No. 1616	40	20	7	......	5	23	.8810	m	cy	c	m	r	b	w
Taylor Narbonne	50	8	9	3	7	22	1.8950	m	cy	c	m	r	b	w
Almeria:														
Own roots	......	......	......	......	......	......	......	l	t	c	l	o	w	s, st, t
Herbemont	......	25	12	......	......	23	.7537	l	t	c	l	o	w	s, st, t
Lenoir	20	15	......	......	......	20.8	.6100	l	t	c	l	o	w	s, st, t
Riparia × Rupestris, No. 101	8	10	6	......	3	23.5	.6500	l	t	c	l	o	w	s, st, t
Riparia × Rupestris, No. 3309	10	15	11	15	8	22.6	.7650	l	t	c	l	o	w	s, st, t
Solonis × Riparia, No. 1616	30	30	20	......	......	23.5	.6700	l	t	c	l	o	w	s, st, t
Aneb el Cadi:														
Adobe Giant	......	......	6	......	10	25.5	.7837	l	cy	m	m-l	ob	b	s, st, t
Lenoir	10	10	9	......	......	20	.7533	l	cy	m	m-l	ob	b	s, st, t
Monticola × Rupestris	......	......	......	......	......	......	......	l	cy	m	m-l	ob	b	s, st, t
Mourvedre × Rupestris, No. 1202	......	......	......	8	......	23	.5700	l	cy	m	m-l	ob	b	s, st, t
Riparia Grand Glabre	......	......	......	12	......	25	.6150	l	cy	m	m-l	ob	b	s, st, t
Angelina:														
Adobe Giant	......	......	......	......	......	......	......	v l	t	c	l	ob	r	s, st, t
Lenoir	4	2	8	......	3	21.2	.5825	v l	t	c	l	ob	r	s, st, t
Mourvedre × Rupestris, No. 1202	......	......	2	......	......	26	.3105	v l	t	c	l	ob	r	s, st, t

Aramon:														
Aramon × Rupestris Ganzin, No. 1	60	20	19	4	8	20.7	.9300	l	t	c	l	ob	b	w, s, t
Australis		3	15	43		20.5	1.0008	l	t	c	l	ob	b	w, s, t
Barnes		5	2			22.6	.7158	l	t	c	l	ob	b	w, s, t
Cornucopia			1			23	.6000	l	t	c	l	ob	b	w, s, t
De [illegible]tt			8			23.5	.8925	l	t	c	l	ob	b	w, s, t
Dog Ridge	40	12	20	7	6	19.8	.9399	l	t	c	l	ob	b	w, s, t
Herbemont	50	20	12	3	12	20	.9319	l	t	c	l	ob	b	w, s, t
Hotporup				20		24	.5625	l	t	c	l	ob	b	w, s, t
Lenoir	60		22	12		18	1.0200	l	t	c	l	ob	b	w, s, t
[illegible]la × Rupestris								l	t	c	l	ob	b	w, s, t
Mourvedre × Rupestris, No. 1202	40	8	15	2	3	19.5	.9469	l	t	c	l	ob	b	w, s, t
[illegible]y			3	36		22	.9187	l	t	c	l	ob	b	w, s, t
Ramsey								l	t	c	l	ob	b	w, s, t
Riparia × Rupestris, No. 101			8	24		21.7	.7912	l	t	c	l	ob	b	w, s, t
Do	60	12	16		2	20.7	.9051	l	t	c	l	ob	b	w, s, t
Riparia × Rupestris, No. 3309	50	10			2	19	.8287	l	t	c	l	ob	b	w, s, t
Riparia × Rupestris de Jaeger				15		22	.8100	l	t	c	l	ob	b	w, s, t
Rupestris des C[illegible]es								l	t	c	l	ob	b	w, s, t
Rupestris des Semis, No. 81-2		4				23.4	.8812	l	t	c	l	ob	b	w, s, t
[illegible]is Martin		3	1		16	24.5	.8225	l	t	c	l	ob	b	w, s, t
Do	50	10	11	4		21.5	.9537	l	t	c	l	ob	b	w, s, t
Rupestris St. [illegible]ge	55	20	20	½	12	20	.9150	l	t	c	l	ob	b	w, s, t
Rupestris × Berlandieri, No. 219A						24	.9750	l	t	c	l	ob	b	w, s, t
Salt [illegible]k		5	1			21.8	.9333	l	t	c	l	ob	b	w, s, t
Do	60	10	17	2	5	20.8	.8169	l	t	c	l	ob	b	w, s, t
Solonis × Othello		3	6	26		22.9	.9100	l	t	c	l	ob	b	w, s, t
Solonis × Riparia, No. 1616			4			21	.7575	l	t	c	l	ob	b	w, s, t
Do	40	25	9	1		19.4	.8812	l	t	c	l	ob	b	w, s, t
[illegible]or Nar[illegible]onne	55	20	15			20.8	.8700	l	t	c	l	ob	b	w, s, t
Do			4	13		20.5	.8200	l	t	c	l	ob	b	w, s, t
Valencia			15	25		23	.5812	l	t	c	l	ob	b	w, s, t
Vermorel		3	3			22.2	.7175	l	t	c	l	ob	b	w, s, t
Vi[illegible]		4	8			23.6	.9200	l	t	c	l	ob	b	w, s, t
[illegible]:														
Own rots								m	cy	l	m-l	o	b	s, t
Aspiran Noir:														
Own rots	20	25	30	25		20.5	.8206	m	t	c	m	o	b	s, t, w
[illegible]:														
[illegible]e Giant								l	t	l	l	r	b	s, t
Lenoir	3	1½	5		4	20.8	.6050	l	t	l-	l	r	b	s, t
Baba:														
Own roots	25	12		25	18	23.6	.3213	m	t	l	m	r	w	w
Dog Ridge	20	8	8	2		22.4	.5250	m	t	l	m	r	w	w
Lenoir	40	15	10	1		25	.5250	m	t	l	m	r	w	w
Rupestris St. George	30	10	30	½	11	21	.5586	m	t	l	m	r	w	w
Taylor Narbonne	50	8	8	4		25	.5475	m	t	l	m	r	w	w

TABLE VII.—*Relative behavior and value for different purposes of grape varieties tested by grafting on resistant stocks and by growing on their own roots in eleven experiment vineyards in California*—Continued.

Variety and stock (on own roots, if so stated).	Weight of fruit per vine (pounds).					Sugar, Balling scale.	Acid, as tartaric (grams per 100 c. c.).	Cluster.			Berry.			Use.
	1909	1910	1911	1912	1913			Size.	Shape.	Compact or loose.	Size.	Shape.	Color.	
1	17	18	19	20	21	22	23	24	25	26	27	28	29	30
Bakàtor:						*P. cent.*								
Own roots				3	3	23	0.6825	l	t	c	m	r	r	t, w
Aramon × Rupestris Ganzin, No. 1	15	20				22.1	.6970	l	t	c	m	r	r	t, w
Dog Ridge	15	3	1½		2	21.8	.8618	l	t	c	m	r	r	t, w
Lenoir	15					22.2	.7875	l	t	c	m	r	r	t, w
Riparia × Rupestris, No. 101	25	8		1		21.4	.7585	l	t	c	m	r	r	t, w
Riparia × Rupestris, No. 3309	10	6	6	3		23.4	.8525	l	t	c	m	r	r	t, w
Rupestris St. George	20	5	1	8	5	23.2	.4950	l	t	c	m	r	r	t, w
Solonis × Riparia, No. 1616	10	25				21.2	.7912	l	t	c	m	r	r	t, w
Taylor Narbonne	20	1½	2			22.8	.8200	l	t	c	m	r	r	t, w
Barbarossa:														
Own roots				¼	1	22	1.1925	m	t	c	m	r	r	t, w
Adobe Giant	35	25	5	25		23	.5430	m	t	c	m	r	r	t, w
Aramon × Rupestris Ganzin, No. 1	40		5	7	20	23	.5375	m	t	c	m	r	r	t, w
Dog Ridge			8	12		22.5	.6187	m	t	c	m	r	r	t, w
Do	5	3	2			22.6	.6575	m	t	c	m	r	r	t, w
Lenoir	20	20	3	4	14	22.5	.5418	m	t	c	m	r	r	t, w
Do	40	15	15	3	32	24.3	.6318	m	t	c	m	r	r	t, w
Riparia Gloire	10	21	5	43	23	22.6	.5381	m	t	c	m	r	r	t, w
Riparia × Rupestris, No. 3309	30		25	26	8	25	.3950	m	t	c	m	r	r	t, w
Rupestris St. George	35	24	15	43	24	22.3	.5256	m	t	c	m	r	r	t, w
Do	20	5	19	2	35	23.5	.6868	m	t	c	m	r	r	t, w
Solonis × Riparia, No. 1616	30	10	25		3	24.3	.4025	m	t	c	m	r	r	t, w
Taylor Narbonne	40	2	3			23.8	.6400	m	t	c	m	r	r	t, w
Barbarossa Finnebourgo:														
Own roots	1½	1		3		26	.6300	m	t, cy	l	m-l	o	r	t, s, w
Barbera:														
Own roots	3	2	8			26	.6933	m	cy	c	s	ob	b	w
Dog Ridge	½					24.2	.8775	m	cy	c	s	ob	b	w
Lenoir	12	1	3½		½	25.7	1.0440	m	cy	c	s	ob	b	w
Rupestris St. George	12	2	5		1½	22.8	.7006	m	cy	c	s	ob	b	w
Taylor Narbonne	10		3			25.6	1.2440	m	cy	c	s	ob	b	w

Barducci:														
Adobe Giant	....	....	8	1½	....	22.5	.62	l	cy	s	s	r	w	w
Lenoir	10	....	....	....	17	19.6	.[illegible]	l	cy	s	s	r	w	w
Bastardo:														
Own roots	6	3	....	15	2	28	.7375	l	cy	c	l	r	b	w
Dog Ridge	8	2	6	....	....	26	.7000	l	cy	c	l	r	b	w
Lenoir	50	5	11	....	2	25.9	.6750	l	cy	c	l	r	b	w
Rupestris St. George	60	4	....	¾	4½	24.3	.5208	l	cy	c	l	r	b	w
Taylor Narbonne	8	....	....	½	....	23.8	.9412	l	cy	c	l	r	b	w
Beclan:														
Own roots	20	10	10	8	....	23.6	.5418	m	cy	l	m	r	b	w
Dog Ridge	45	6	4	15	....	22.9	.6581	m	cy	l	m	r	b	w
Lenoir	50	....	7½	5	20	19.7	.8225	m	cy	l	m	r	b	w
Rupestris St. George	50	8	9	6	19½	23.3	.6693	m	cy	l	m	r	b	w
Taylor Narbonne	40	6	....	2	4	21	.6250	m	cy	l	m	r	b	w
Bellino:														
Own roots	....	....	....	....	....	....	....	m	t	c	m-l	r	b	t,s,w
Adobe Giant	½	8	3	25	....	21.4	.5235	m	t	c	m-l	r	b	t,s,w
Aramon × Rupestris Ganzin, No. 1	6	10	2	8	12	21.3	.5775	m	t	c	m-l	r	b	t,s,w
Dog Ridge	12	11	10	10	....	21.4	.5603	m	t	c	m-l	r	b	t,s,w
Do	6	....	....	1	1	23	.6937	m	t	c	m-l	r	b	t,s,w
Lenoir	12	1	1	7	3	21.9	.4931	m	t	c	m-l	r	b	t,s,w
Do.	5	....	....	....	1½	25	.5025	m	t	c	m-l	r	b	t,s,w
[illegible]e × R[illegible]tris, No. 1202	10	8	14	11	20	23.4	.5700	m	t	c	m-l	r	b	t,s,w
Ponroy	....	....	....	....	....	24	.6675	m	t	c	m-l	r	b	t,s,w
Riparia × Rupestris, No. 101	8	12	2	....	12	21.2	.4637	m	t	c	m-l	r	b	t,s,w
Riparia × Rup[illegible]tris, No. 3309	12	15	4	23	5	22.6	.5600	m	t	c	m-l	r	b	t,s,w
Rupestris des C[illegible]s	....	....	....	....	....	....	....	m	t	c	m-l	r	b	t,s,w
Rupestris St. George	8	1½	....	3	8	22.4	.6408	m	t	c	m-l	r	b	t,s,w
Do.	12	1	....	....	....	21.9	.7237	m	t	c	m-l	r	b	t,s,w
[illegible]nis × Riparia, No. 1616	6	4	....	½	½	24.2	.5475	m	t	c	m-l	r	b	t,s,w
[illegible]r N[illegible]e	12	2	1	3	14	23	.6970	m	t	c	m-l	r	b	t,s,w
Do	8	2	2	....	....	24.4	.6600	m	t	c	m-l	r	b	t,s,w
Vermorel	....	....	....	....	....	21	.6675	m	t	c	m-l	r	b	t,s,w
Bengi:														
Own [illegible]	....	....	....	....	....	....	....	m	t	c	l	r	b	t,s
Bermestia [illegible]a:														
[illegible]is St. George	20	18	3	½	3	22.3	.4275	m	t	c	m-l	ob	w	t,s
Besson:														
Own roots	2	....	¼	2	2	26	.5575	m	cy	c	m	r	w	t,s,w
[illegible]:														
Own roots	....	....	....	....	....	....	....	l	t	c	m	....	w	t,s
[illegible]e:														
[illegible]e [illegible]nt	20	12	3	26	....	23	.5831	m	r	l	l	ob	w	t,s
[illegible]lis	....	1½	9	....	....	23.9	.5875	m	r	l	l	ob	w	t,s
Barnes	....	....	....	....	....	....	....	m	r	l	l	ob	w	t,s
Berlandieri × Riparia, No. 420B	....	....	....	....	....	....	....	m	r	l	l	ob	w	t,s
[illegible]a	....	2	2	13	....	23.6	.6425	m	r	l	l	ob	w	t,s
De Grassett	....	....	....	....	....	....	....	m	r	l	l	ob	w	t,s
Dog Ridge	20	5	9	....	....	22.6	.7875	m	r	l	l	ob	w	t,s

TABLE VII.—*Relative behavior and value for different purposes of grape varieties tested by grafting on resistant stocks and by growing on their own roots in eleven experiment vineyards in California*—Continued.

Variety and stock (on own roots, if so stated).	Weight of fruit per vine (pounds). 1909	1910	1911	1912	1913	Sugar, Balling scale.	Acid, as tartaric (grams per 100 c. c.).	Cluster. Size.	Cluster. Shape.	Cluster. Compact or loose.	Berry. Size.	Berry. Shape.	Berry. Color.	Use.
1	17	18	19	20	21	22	23	24	25	26	27	28	29	30
Bicane—Continued.						*P. cent.*								
Lenoir	11	2	3½		7	20	0.8735	m	r	l	l	ob	w	t, s
[illegible]la × Rupestris			4	7	4	24	.6691	m	r	l	l	ob	w	t, s
Ponroy					10			m	r	l	l	ob	w	t, s
[illegible]y		3	4		4	21.7	.8850	m	r	l	l	ob	w	t, s
[illegible]a Gloire	40	2				20.7	.5700	m	r	l	l	ob	w	t, s
Riparia × Rupestris, No. 3306								m	r	l	l	ob	w	t, s
Riparia × Rup[illegible]s, No. 3309		3	9			23	.6375	m	r	l	l	ob	w	t, s
Rupestris [illegible]s C[illegible]s								m	r	l	l	ob	w	t, s
Rupestris St. [illegible]ge	3	2	1			21.6	.8725	m	r	l	l	ob	w	t, s
Do.	12	10		2½	2	24.3	.5298	m	r	l	l	ob	w	t, s
[illegible]is × [illegible]eri, No. 219A								m	r	l	l	ob	w	t, s
[illegible]is Robusta		3				22	.9562	m	r	l	l	ob	w	t, s
[illegible]r Narb[illegible]nne								m	r	l	l	ob	w	t, s
Viala		2	3½			23.5	.6262	m	r	l	l	ob	w	t, s
Black Corinth:														
Own roots		4	25	12		25	.2771	m	cy	c	v, s	r	b	t, r
Black Hamburg:														
Own roots	15	½		8		24.7	.5713	m	r	c	l	ob	b	t, s, w
Black [illegible]ari:														
Dog Ridge	30					22.2	.4875	m	cy	c	m-l	o	b	t, s, w
Lenoir	30		2			19.7	.6700	m	cy	c	m-l	o	b	t, s, w
Black Morocco:														
Own roots	5	20				21.6	.7275	m-l	t	c	l	r	b	t, s
Black Muscat:														
Own roots			½	7		24	.7537	m-l	t	l	m	o	b	t, s, r
Black Prince:														
Own roots	2	1		38		25.1	.5375	l	t	l	m	o	b	t, s, r
Dog Ridge	60	8	20	¾	8	22.3	.6262	l	t	l	m	o	b	t, s, r
Lenoir	30	12	20	3	34	20.7	.7218	l	t	l	m	o	b	t, s, r.
Rupestris St. George	40	10	19	1	30	23	.6180	l	t	l	m	o	b	t, s, r
Taylor Narbonne	40	2		1½		23.7	.5725	l	t	l	m	o	b	t, s, r

Black [illegible]:														
Own roots				3		28	.8625	l						
Black Zante:														
Own roots		1½		9		23	.6525	m	t	c	s	r	b	t, r
Blanc d'Ambre:														
Lenoir	2		2		2	23.5	.5025	m-l	cy	l	s	r	w	t, w
[illegible]a × Rupestris								m-l	c	l	s	r	w	t, w
Mourvedre × Rupestris, No. 1202			3			27	.3750	m-l	cy	l	s	r	w	t, w
Salt [illegible]k								m-l	cy	l	s	r	w	t, w
[illegible]r Portugieser:														
Own roots	4	4	1	⅓	12	25	.6138	m	cy	c	s	r	b	t, w
Dog Ridge	30	3	4	½		25.8	.5512	m	cy	c	s	r	b	t, w
Lenoir	30	8	10	2	30	27.8	.4875	m	cy	c	s	r	b	t, w
Rupestris St. George	35	2	8	½	2	26.3	.5531	m	cy	c	s	r	b	t, w
Boal de [illegible]:														
Own roots	3	8	6	30	2	26.5	.6231	m	cy	l	s	r	w	t, w
Dog Ridge	40	8	15	2		25.5	.7612	m	cy	l	s	r	w	t, w
Lenoir	40	8	9		12	26.6	.6950	m	cy	l	s	r	w	t, w
Rupestris St. George	40	5	14½		43	26.7	.6600	m	cy	l	s	r	w	t, w
[illegible]r [illegible]ne	40	5	4			24.7	.7931	m	cy	l	s	r	w	t, w
Boglich:														
Own roots								m-l	t	l	l	r	b	t, s
Bolynino:														
Own roots	12	20		18	7	23.5	.6635	m	cy	c	m	o	b	w
Dog Ridge	40				2	22.2	.8250	m	cy	c	m	o	b	w
Lenoir	40	18	1⅜		9	21.3	1.0325	m	cy	c	m	o	b	w
Rupestris St. George	35	10	15	1½	23	23.2	.4437	m	cy	c	m	o	b	w
Taylor [illegible]e	40	10	12	2½	1	23	.9448	m	cy	c	m	o	b	w
Bonarda:														
Own roots						25	.7237	m-l	cy	c	m-l	r	b	t, s
[illegible]s:														
Own roots				3		29	.8475	m-l	t	l	l	ob	b	t, s, w
[illegible]r	45	4	14	4	25	22.2	.6431	m-l	t	l	l	ob	b	t, s, w
Rupestris St. George	35	8	15	¼	28	23.4	.8043	m-l	t	l	l	ob	b	t, s, w
Bowood [illegible]at:														
Own roots		6	4	7		24.7	.6125	m	t	l	m	ob	w	t, s, r
Brustiano:														
[illegible]e [illegible]it								l	t	l	l	ob	w	t, s
Lenoir	6				3	22.8	.4200	l	t	l	l	ob	w	t, s
[illegible]a × [illegible]s				4		23	.5250	l	t	l	l	ob	w	t, s
[illegible]e × Rupestris, No. 1202						22	.5770	l	t	l	i	ob	w	t, s
[illegible]:														
Lenoir	8	3	5½		6	24.3	.6248	l	t	l	m	r	w	t, w
Rupestris St. George								m-l	t	l	m	r	w	t, w
[illegible]:														
Own roots								l	t	l	m	r	w	t, s, w
Lenoir	6					22.2	.4950	l	t	l	m	r	w	t, s, w
Burger:														
Own roots	20	30	22	40	12	26.1	.7350	l	t	c	l	r	w	w
(Aestivalis × Monticola) × (Riparia × Rupestris No. 554-5)			8			16	1.1025	l	t	c	l	r	w	w
Aramon × Rupestris Ganzin, No. 1	60	10	20	6	15	18.5	.9581	l	t	c	l	r	w	w

TABLE VII.—*Relative behavior and value for different purposes of grape varieties tested by grafting on resistant stocks and by growing on their own roots in eleven experiment vineyards in California*—Continued.

Variety and stock (on own roots, if so stated).	Weight of fruit per vine (pounds).					Sugar, Balling scale.	Acid, as tartaric (grams per 100 c. c.).	Cluster.			Berry.			Use.
	1909	1910	1911	1912	1913			Size.	Shape.	Compact or loose.	Size.	Shape.	Color.	
1	17	18	19	20	21	22	23	24	25	26	27	28	29	30
Burger—Continued.						*P. cent.*								
Aramon × Rupestris Ganzin, No. 2	......	......	4	......	3	17	0.9525	l	t	c	l	r	w	w
Berlandieri × Riparia, No. 420A	......	......	2	4	3	21.5	.7350	l	t	c	l	r	w	w
Constantia	......	......	3	......	12	21	.8625	l	t	c	l	r	w	w
Columbaud × Rupestris No. 2502	......	......	14	6	4	20.5	.9650	l	t	c	l	r	w	w
Dog Ridge	60	5	18	3	20	17.9	1.0475	l	t	c	l	r	w	w
Herbemont	30	15	4	4	4	19	.7300	l	t	c	l	r	w	w
Lenoir	20	......	10	3	......	19	1.0200	l	t	c	l	r	w	w
[illegible]la × Riparia, No. 18808	......	......	......	5	......	24	1.9250	l	t	c	l	r	w	w
[illegible]e × Rupestris, No. 1202	60	10	10	5	5	22.2	.7744	l	t	c	l	r	w	w
Riparia × Rupestris, No. 101	40	10	12	1	......	19	1.0050	l	t	c	l	r	w	w
Riparia × Rupestris, No. 101–14	......	......	4	......	......	23	.8925	l	t	c	l	r	w	w
Riparia × [illegible]s, No. 3306	......	......	15	1	15	20	1.1742	l	t	c	l	r	w	w
Riparia × Rupestris, No. 3309	60	15	......	......	......	18.7	.7662	l	t	c	l	r	w	w
Rupestris [illegible]n	50	10	12	......	10½	17.9	1.0294	l	t	c	l	r	w	w
u[illegible]s [illegible]a	......	......	......	......	4	......	......	l	t	c	l	r	w	w
Rupestris [illegible]n	......	......	......	......	......	......	......	l	t	c	l	r	w	w
Rupestris St. George	30	5	10	4	......	21.1	.7462	l	t	c	l	r	w	w
Salt Creek	30	10	8	1	6	19.5	1.0168	l	t	c	l	r	w	w
Solonis Robusta	......	......	2½	2	4	21.5	.9667	l	t	c	l	r	w	w
[illegible]s × Othelló, No. 1613	......	......	13	10	2	22	1.1670	l	t	c	l	r	w	w
Solonis × Riparia, No. 1616	15	15	4	......	5	20.5	.5756	l	t	c	l	r	w	w
[illegible]r Narbonne	50	15	19	6	8	16.7	.9337	l	t	c	l	r	w	w
[illegible]t [illegible]n:														
Own roots	......	......	......	½	1	24.5	.7950	m	t	m	m	r	b	w
A[illegible]n × [illegible]s [illegible]n, No. 1	15	6	5	......	......	24.3	.7825	m	t	m	m	r	b	w
[illegible]g [illegible]e	30	2	......	17	5	23.6	.8525	m	t	m	m	r	b	w
Herbemont	20	3	11	2	4	23	.7706	m	t	m	m	r	b	w
Lenoir	25	8	4	......	......	21.4	.7925	m	t	m	m	r	b	w
Mourvedre × Rupestris, No. 1202	10	4	......	......	......	23.2	.6562	m	t	m	m	r	b	w
Riparia × Rupestris, No. 101	20	3	5	......	......	24.3	.7458	m	t	m	m	r	b	w
Riparia × [illegible]s, No. 3309	20	2	6	......	2	25.4	.7100	m	t	m	m	r	b	w

Rupestris Martin	25	2	6	½	3	22.2	.9475	m	t	m	m	r	b	w
Rupestris St. George	25	3	6			23.5	.7258	m	t	m	m	r	b	w
Salt Creek	20	5	9	1	5	25.1	.8775	m	t	m	m	r	b	w
Solonis × Riparia, No. 1616	20	12	6	2		23.6	.7862	m	t	m	m	r	b	w
Taylor Narbonne	25	4	9	3		20.6	.9225	m	t	m	m	r	b	w
Calabrian:														
Own roots		3	2			23.6	. 82	l	cy	l	l	r	w	t, s
Australis		5	3			24.6	. 165	l	cy	l	l	r	w	t, s
Lenoir	2	8	1	½	9	23.8	.5556	l	cy	l	l	r	w	t, s
Do	8	1	4		3	25.4	. 660	l	cy	l	l	r	w	t, s
[illegible]a × [illegible]stris			6½		10	25.5	.5175	l	cy	l	l	r	w	t, s
[illegible]a [illegible]e	12	7	3	4	17	26	. 83	l	cy	l	l	r	w	t, s
Rupestris [illegible]s [illegible]s								l	cy	l	l	r	w	t, s
Rupestris St. George	10	9	15	24	8	23.6	.5531	l	cy	l	l	r	w	t, s
[illegible]tte:														
A[illegible]e [illegible]nt		5	3			24.2	.7225	m	t	l	l	r	b	w
Aramon × [illegible]s [illegible]in, No. 1		2	4			24	.7425	m	t	l	l	r	b	w
Do	40	40	9	2	15	21.6	.7775	m	t	l	l	r	b	w
Berlandieri × Riparia, No. 420B		5	6			25.2	.6625	m	t	l	l	r	b	w
Constantia								m	t	l	l	r	b	w
[illegible]t		10				21.3	.9900		t	l	l	r	b	w
Lenoir	20	8	6	2½		22.5	.8131	m	t	l	l	r	b	w
[illegible]a × Riparia, No. 18804				7		28	.6367	m	t	l	l	r	b	w
[illegible]la × Riparia, No. 18815	4	4	13			26	.6700	m	t	l	l	r	b	w
[illegible]a × Rupestris		2	4			22.6	.6725	m	t	l	l	r	b	w
Ponroy								m	t	l	l	r	b	w
[illegible]y			6	16		25	. 060	m	t	l	l	r	b	w
Riparia × [illegible]s, No. 101						23	. 650	m	t	l	l	r	b	w
Do	40	30	13			20.1	.8430	m	t	l	l	r	b	w
[illegible]a × [illegible], No. 3309				28		26	. 360	m	t	l	l	r	b	w
Do	50	20	14	1	8	18.8	.8183	m	t	l	l	r	b	w
Riparia × [illegible]stris de Jaeger			4	6		26.5	. 850	m	t	l	l	r	b	w
Rupestris × Berlandieri, No. 219A		6	6	13		24.7	. 708	m	t	l	l	r	b	w
[illegible]s × Berlandieri, No. 301-37-152								m	t	l	l	r	b	w
Salt C[illegible]k								m	t	l	l	r	b	w
Solonis [illegible]a						23	.7800	m	t	l	l	r	b	w
[illegible]s × [illegible]o		10	4	22		23.5	.7450	m	t	l	l	r	b	w
Sol[illegible]s × Riparia, No. 1616			3½			25.5	.6520	m	t	l	l	r	b	w
Do	30	15	3		3	21.1	.6350	m	t	l	l	r	b	w
[illegible]r Narbonne								m	t	l	l	r	b	w
[illegible]l				5		28	.6450	m	t	l	l	r	b	w
Carign[illegible]ne:														
Own [illegible]s	20	20	5	35	12	22.7	.8475	m	t	l	m	r	b	w
[illegible]n × [illegible]s [illegible], No. 1	60	40	15	9	15	22.7	. 095	m	t	l	m	r	b	w
Dog Ridge	60	12	20	16	28	21.7	1. 505	m	t	l	m	r	b	w
Herbemont	50	10	14	5	18	22	.9015	m	t	l	m	r	b	w
Lenoir	55	20	16	12	10	20.5	.9619	m	t	l	m	r	b	w
[illegible]e × Rupestris, No. 1202	60	15	15	8	12	21	1.2924	m	t	l	m	r	b	w
Riparia × Rupestris, No. 101	60	10	11	5	7	22.4	.8006	m	t	l	m	r	b	w

TABLE VII.—*Relative behavior and value for different purposes of grape varieties tested by grafting on resistant stocks and by growing on their own roots in eleven experiment vineyards in California*—Continued.

Variety and stock (on own roots, if so stated).	Weight of fruit per vine (pounds).					Sugar, Balling scale.	Acid, as tartaric (grams per 100 c. c.).	Cluster.			Berry.			Use.
	1909	1910	1911	1912	1913			Size.	Shape.	Compact or loose.	Size.	Shape.	Color.	
1	17	18	19	20	21	22	23	24	25	26	27	28	29	30
Carignane—Continued.						*P. cent.*								
Riparia × Rupestris, No. 3309	50	10	13	......	10	21.8	1.0160	m	t	c	l	ob	b	s, w
Rupestris Martin	50	12	10	......	32	20.6	1.0082	m	t	c	l	ob	b	s, w
Rupestris St. George	60	20	16	3	18	22.3	.8620	m	t	c	l	ob	b	s, w
Salt Creek	60	12	12	4	12	23.7	1.1437	m	t	c	l	ob	b	s, w
Solonis × Riparia, No. 1616	50	57	9	5	5	22.2	.9000	m	t	c	l	ob	b	s, w
Taylor Narbonne	50	20	15	8	12	21	.9884	m	t	c	l	ob	b	s, w
Castiza:														
Riparia × Rupestris, No. 3309	......	......	......	......	......	......	......	m	t	c	m	ob	r	s, t
Catarratto a la Porta:														
Own roots	......	¼	¼	1½	4	26.2	.7111	m	t	c	l	ob	b	w
Chaouch:														
Own roots	......	......	......	......	......	29.2	.4912	m	cy	c	l	ob	w	s, t
Lenoir	......	......	......	......	......	23.4	.6375	m	cy	c	l	ob	w	s, t
Chaouch Rose:														
Lenoir	10	......	......	......	1	20.8	.3750	m	cy	c	l	ob	r	s, t
Charbono:														
Own roots	......	......	......	2	2	21	.8250	m	t	l	m	r	b	w
Dog Ridge	5	......	......	......	......	20.8	.5745	m	t	l	m	r	b	w
Lenoir	35	20	......	......	......	20.9	.7612	m	t	l	m	r	b	w
Rupestris St. George	50	15	......	......	......	22.6	.5325	m	t	l	m	r	b	w
Riparia × Rupestris, No. 101	40	10	9	......	4	21.7	.6881	m	t	l	m	r	b	w
Riparia × Rupestris, No. 3309	50	8	13	......	8	22.3	.7237	m	t	l	m	r	b	w
Solonis × Riparia, No. 1616	50	20	12	4	6	22.5	.7108	m	t	l	m	r	b	w
Taylor Narbonne	35	15	11	4	5	21.2	.6712	m	t	l	m	r	b	w
Chasselas Bouches du Rhone:														
Own roots	......	......	1	1½	......	23.2	.3562	m	cy	c	m	r	w	w, t
Dog Ridge	15	......	6½	2	6	21.2	.5493	m	cy	c	m	r	w	w, t
Lenoir	30	......	1	......	10	21.2	.5400	m	cy	c	m	r	w	w, t
Rupestris St. George	15	......	14	½	3	21.7	.4968	m	cy	c	m	r	w	w, t
Taylor Narbonne	15	......	......	......	......	21.8	.4645	m	cy	c	m	r	w	w, t

Chas[illegible]s [illegible]y:														
[illegible]ge	30	......	3	3	8	21	.5518	m	cy	c	m	r	w	w, t
Lenoir	18	......	15	......	......	21	.5587	m	cy	c	m	r	w	w, t
Rupestris [illegible] George	8	......	7	......	......	20.6	.4981	m	cy	c	m	r	w	w, t
Tay[illegible]r [illegible]e	2	......	1	......	1	20	.4612	m	cy	c	m	r	w	w, t
[illegible]elas [illegible]t:														
[illegible]n [illegible]s	......	......	......	......	1	......	......	s	cy	c	m	r	w	w, t
[illegible]	18	......	......	10	8	21.3	.5075	s	cy	c	m	r	w	w, t
Lenoir	6	......	2	......	3	21.7	.5300	s	cy	c	m	r	w	w, t
[illegible]s St. George	4	......	½	......	6	22	.5925	s	cy	c	m	r	w	w, t
[illegible]s [illegible]é:														
[illegible]n roots	10	3	......	......	......	26	.3862	m	cy	m	m	r	w	w, t
D[illegible]g R[illegible]e	20	8	......	......	1	21.2	.5350	m	cy	m	m	r	w	w, t
[illegible]ir	12	......	5	2	8	21.7	.5681	m	cy	m	m	r	w	w, t
Rupestris St. George	8	......	4	......	......	19.9	.5125	m	cy	m	m	r	w	w, t
Chas[illegible]s [illegible]l:														
Aramon × Rupestris [illegible]in, No. 1	8	......	......	......	......	20	.5325	m	cy	m	m	r	w	w, t
[illegible]ge	8	......	7	3	4	20.8	.[illegible]694	m	cy	m	m	r	w	w, t
[illegible]ir	15	......	10	......	......	20.2	.5555	m	cy	m	m	r	w	w, t
[illegible]s St. George	20	......	9	......	......	21.5	.5200	m	cy	m	m	r	w	w, t
Taylor [illegible]e	......	......	......	......	......	20.4	.5700	m	cy	m	m	r	w	w, t
[illegible]elas de [illegible]u:														
Rupestris St. [illegible]e	2½	4	1	7	15	26.4	.4627	m	t	l	m	r	r	w, t
[illegible]s [illegible]e:														
[illegible]n [illegible]s	4	......	......	......	12	23	.3450	m	cy	m	m	r	w	w, t
Dog Ridge	12	......	2½	......	5	23.1	.5475	m	cy	m	m	r	w	w, t
[illegible]ir	20	......	⅛	......	4	21.6	.5075	m	cy	m	m	r	w	w, t
Rupestris St. George	5	......	5	1	7	22.7	.5906	m	cy	m	m	r	w	w, t
Tay[illegible]r [illegible]e	2	......	......	......	3	25	.3975	m	cy	m	m	r	w	w, t
[illegible]elas [illegible]:														
[illegible]n [illegible]s	......	......	......	......	20	......	......	m	cy	m	m	r	w	w, t
Lenoir	......	......	2	......	3	21.3	.5775	m	cy	m	m	r	w	w, t
Rupestris St. [illegible]e	10	......	14	......	......	21.7	.5525	m	cy	m	m	r	w	w, t
[illegible]s [illegible]e [illegible]i:														
Own [illegible]s	......	......	......	3	......	23	.7850	s	cy	l	m	r	w	w, t
D[illegible]g R[illegible]e	20	......	4	10	10	21.2	.6306	s	cy	l	m	r	w	w, t
Lenoir	30	......	......	1	4	21.4	.5644	s	cy	l	m	r	w	w, t
[illegible]s St. [illegible]e	6	......	17	⅓	2	21.8	.7690	s	cy	l	m	r	w	w, t
Chas[illegible]s [illegible]nt:														
[illegible]n [illegible]s	3	......	......	......	......	23	.3375	m	cy	c	m	r	w	w, t
Dog Ridge	10	......	5	......	2	20.8	.4150	m	cy	c	m	r	w	w, t
[illegible]r	20	......	7	2	4	21	.4950	m	cy	c	m	r	w	w, t
[illegible]a Gloire	......	......	......	......	......	......	......	m	cy	c	m	r	w	w, t
Rupestris [illegible] [illegible]e	8	3	10	5	2	23.6	.4200	m	cy	c	m	r	w	w, t
[illegible]o	15	......	2	⅓	8	20.4	.5531	m	cy	c	m	r	w	w, t
Tay[illegible]r [illegible]e	15	......	5	3	3	22.1	.5175	m	cy	c	m	r	w	w, t
[illegible]elas Rose:														
[illegible]n [illegible]s	2	......	4	3	......	24.4	.3925	m	cy	c	m	r	r	w, t

TABLE VII.—*Relative behavior and value for different purposes of grape varieties tested by grafting on resistant stocks and by growing on their own roots in eleven experiment vineyards in California*—Continued.

Variety and stock (on own roots, if so stated).	Weight of fruit per vine (pounds). 1909	1910	1911	1912	1913	Sugar, Balling scale.	Acid, as tartaric (grams per 100 c. c.).	Cluster. Size.	Shape.	Compact or loose.	Berry. Size.	Shape.	Color.	Use.
1	17	18	19	20	21	22	23	24	25	26	27	28	29	30
Chasselas Rose de Falloux:						P. cent.								
Own roots	2	......	6	......	......	21.6	0.3375	m	cy	c	m	r	r	w, t
Aramon × Rupestris Ganzin, No. 1	25	......	4	1½	7	21.2	.6115	m	cy	c	m	r	r	w, t
Do	......	4	4½	......	4	20.5	.3667	m	cy	c	m	r	r	w, t
Australis	......	3	3½	16	......	21.9	.4850	m	cy	c	m	r	r	w, t
Dg [illegible]e	20	......	2	½	......	20.8	.5643	m	cy	c	m	r	r	w, t
[illegible]:	16	......	9	......	5	20.2	.5458	m	cy	c	m	r	r	w, t
[illegible]e × R[illegible], No. 1202	20	......	1	½	½	19.8	.5550	m	cy	c	m	r	r	w, t
Riparia × Rupestris, No. 101	......	......	......	6	5	20	.4200	m	cy	c	m	r	r	w, t
Do	20	......	4	......	6	20.8	.1510	s	cy	c	m	r	r	t, s, w
[illegible]a × [illegible], No. 3309	......	......	......	......	10	......	......	s	cy	c	m	r	r	t, s, w
Do	30	......	12	......	4	20.6	.6243	s	cy	c	m	r	r	t, s, w
[illegible]s St. George	12	4	8	3	10	24.8	.4131	s	cy	c	m	r	r	t, s, w
Do	20	......	11	......	4	21.2	.5700	s	cy	c	m	r	r	t, s, w
St [illegible]k	......	......	......	......	......	......	......	s	cy	c	m	r	r	t, s, w
Solonis × Riparia, No. 1616	20	......	5	2	2½	20.8	.5412	s	cy	c	m	r	r	t, s, w
[illegible]r [illegible]e	......	......	......	4	8	17	.5400	s	cy	c	m	r	r	t, s, w
Do	15	......	......	1	6	21.8	.5225	s	cy	c	m	r	r	t, s, w
[illegible]s [illegible]e [illegible]:														
[illegible]n × [illegible]s [illegible], No. 1	10	......	3	......	......	20.3	.4870	s	cy	c	m	r	r	t, s, w
Dg [illegible]e	25	......	......	......	......	20.6	.4125	s	cy	c	m	r	r	t, s, w
Lanoir	25	......	4	......	3	22.3	.4350	s	cy	c	m	r	r	t, s, w
Rupestris St. [illegible]e	11	......	6½	......	2	23	.5275	s	cy	c	m	r	r	t, s, w
Ta[illegible]r [illegible]e	3	......	......	......	......	21.2	.4725	s	cy	c	m	r	r	t, s, w
Chas[illegible]s Rouge:														
[illegible]n [illegible]s	4	......	5	5	18	21.9	.4346	s	cy	c	m	r	r	t, s, w
[illegible]r	20	......	5	......	8	20.8	.4675	s	cy	c	m	r	r	t, s, w
Rup[illegible]s St. George	15	......	8	½	3	22	.5146	s	cy	c	m	r	r	t, s, w
Cha selas St. Bernard:														
[illegible]a	......	......	......	......	......	......	......	m	cy	l	m	r	w	t, s
[illegible]r	6	......	......	......	......	17.8	.3600	m	cy	l	m	r	w	t, s
R[illegible]a × Rupestris, No. 101	......	......	......	......	......	......	......	m	cy	l	m	r	w	t, s

[illegible]s des Caussettes								m	cy	l	m	r	w	t, s
Rup[illegible] [illegible]s St. George								m	cy	l	m	r	w	t, s
[illegible]a								m	cy	l	m	r	w	t, s
[illegible]e [illegible]r:														
[illegible] [illegible]s		1	3½		6	32.2	.5625	s	cy	c	s	r	b	w
Dog Ridge	10	2	2			28.2	.5065	s	cy	c	s	r	b	w
L[illegible]r	20	2			6	28.5	.4537	s	cy	c	s	r	b	w
[illegible]s St. George	15	1½	4½		½	27.9	.6200	s	cy	c	s	r	b	w
[illegible]:														
Lenoir								s						
[illegible]in [illegible]:														
[illegible] [illegible]s	2	3½	1	8		22.8	.7701	m	cy	c	s	r	w	w
[illegible]g R[illegible]e	6	5	4	2		24.9	.7835	m	cy	c	s	r	w	w
L[illegible]r		2	15		27	23.2	.8500	m	cy	c	s	r	w	w
Rup[illegible] [illegible]s St. George	20	10	13			24.9	.8300	m	cy	c	s	r	w	w
Child of Hall:														
L[illegible]r	1		4		1	24.4	.7750	m	t	l	m-l	ob	w	t
Cin [illegible]:														
[illegible] [illegible]s	1	4	6	12	12	24.5	.7125	m-l	t	m	m	r	b	w
L[illegible]r	25	5	1	12	12	23.9	. 306	m-l	t	m	m	r	b	w
Rup[illegible] [illegible]s St. George	25	3	20		30	23.7	. 669	m-l	t	m	m	r	b	w
[illegible]o N[illegible]o:														
[illegible] [illegible]s				7		22	. [illegible]60	m	t	l	l	o	b	t, s
Clairette à [illegible]s [illegible]in:														
L[illegible]r	40	15	13		18	22.3	.8406	m	t	l	s	o	w	t, w
[illegible]a × Rupestris				22		25	.7875	l	t	l	s	o	w	t, w
[illegible]e [illegible]:														
[illegible] [illegible]s	6	15	8	5	8	22.1	.6523	m	t	l	s	ob	w	t, w
[illegible]e [illegible]:														
[illegible] [illegible]		½		11		25.6	.6067	s	cy	l	s	ob	w	t, w
[illegible]oir	15	5	1			24	.4100	s	cy	l	s	ob	w	t, w
[illegible]loire	15	5				24	.3750	s	cy	l	s	ob	w	t, w
[illegible]a Neagra:														
[illegible]lls								m	cy	l	l	o	b	t, s
L[illegible]r	5		4		3	19.1	.7250	m	cy	l	l	o	b	t, s
Rupestris [illegible]								m	cy	l	l	o	b	t, s
[illegible]m [illegible]o [illegible]o:														
[illegible] roots	4	4	2	12	18	23	.6830	m	t	l	m	r	w	t
[illegible]r:														
Riparia × Rupestris, No. 3306	50	10				27.4	.6125	m	cy	c	l	ob	w	t, w
[illegible]u [illegible]r Shar:														
[illegible] [illegible]s	6	8		4	8	23.9	.6881	m	cy	c	s	r	b	t, w
[illegible]e B[illegible]c:														
[illegible]ir								m	cy	c	s	r	w	t, r, w
[illegible]e à [illegible]s Grain:														
Canada			13			24.5	. [illegible]25	l	t	c	l	ob	r	t, s, w
Lenoir	15	4	14		6	20.5	. 744	l	t	c	l	ob	r	t, s, w
[illegible]e × Rupestris, No. 1202		2	16			24.5	.6037	l	t	c	l	ob	r	t, s, w
[illegible]y				16		23.5	.8850	l	t	c	l	ob	r	t, s, w
[illegible]a × Rupestris, No. 3309		1		10		24.5	. [illegible]37	l	t	c	l	ob	r	t, s, w
[illegible]s St. [illegible]e		4	9			24.8	.7387	l	t	c	l	ob	r	t, s, w
Solonis × [illegible]a, No. 1616		4				22.1	. 0[illegible]5	l	t	c	l	ob	r	t, s, w

TABLE VII.—*Relative behavior and value for different purposes of grape varieties tested by grafting on resistant stocks and by growing on their own roots in eleven experiment vineyards in California*—Continued.

Variety and stock (on own roots, if so stated).	Weight of fruit per vine (pounds).					Sugar, Balling scale.	Acid, as tartaric (grams per 100 c. c.).	Cluster.			Berry.			Use.
	1909	1910	1911	1912	1913			Size.	Shape.	Compact or loose	Size.	Shape.	Color.	
1	17	18	19	20	21	22	23	24	25	26	27	28	29	30
Corinthe Rose:						*P. cent.*								
Adobe Giant								l	cy	c	s	r	r	t, r, w
Canada				1½		23	0.8400	l	cy	c	s	r	r	t, r, w
Constantia								l	cy	c	s	r	r	t, r, w
Lenoir			2		3	26.5	.9400	l	cy	c	s	r	r	t, r, w
[illegible]la × Rupestris			2			28	.6525	l	cy	c	s	r	r	t, r, w
Mourvedre × Rupestris, No. 1202			2			26	.5475	l	cy	c	s	r	r	t, r, w
Riparia Grand Glabre								l	cy	c	s	r	r	t, r, w
Riparia × Rupestris, No. 101								l	cy	c	s	r	r	t, t, w
Vermorel								l	cy					
Coristano:														
Australis		15	41			20.6	1.1058	vl	t	c	s	r	r	t, w
Barnes								vl	t	c	s	r	r	t, w
Lenoir	20	4	10	8	28	18.4	.8890	vl	t	c	s	r	r	t, w
[illegible]la × Rupestris		6	37	25		21.1	.6750	vl	t	c	s	r	r	t, w
Rupestris Martin		4				19.8	1.0870	v, l	t	c	s	r	r	t, w
Rupestris St. George		8	10			19.6	1.2050	v, l	t	c	s	r	r	t, w
Cornichon:														
Own roots		8	6	12		20	.5750	l	t	l	l	o	b	t, s
Aramon × Rupestris Ganzin, No. 1	40					20.2	.6525	l	t	l	l	o	b	t, s
Lenoir			8			21	.9375	l	t	l	l	o	b	t, s
Riparia Gloire								l	t	l	l	o	b	t, s
Rupestris × Berlandieri, No. 301A			8			20	.9575	l	t	l	l	o	b	t, s
Solonis Robusta			8			21	.7725	l	t	l	l	o	b	t, s
[illegible]bs Burgundy:														
Own roots				4	3	22	.9186	m	cy	c	m	r	b	w
Aramon × Rupestis Ganzin, No. 1	45		10		3	21.4	.8017	m	cy	c	m	r	b	w
Dog Ridge	30	12	4	2		21.3	.8419	m	cy	c	m	r	b	w
Lenoir	40	10	24½	12	16	21.2	.8880	m	cy	c	m	r	b	w
Riparia × Rupestris, No. 101	50	8	10	1		21.2	.8275	m	cy	c	m	r	b	w
Riparia × Rupestris, No. 3309	60	5	13	5	5	22.4	.7665	m	cy	c	m	r	b	w
Rupestris St. George	30	8	17	4	31	22.6	.8055	m	cy	c	m	r	b	w
Solonis × Riparia, No. 1616	30	20		3		19.5	.8150	m	cy	c	m	r	b	w
Taylor [illegible]ne	30	8		3	3	21.8	.6844	m	cy	c	m	r	b	w

Croetto:													
Own roots	5	4	10	8	12	20	.8355	m	t	l	s	o	b	w
Crujidero:													
Own roots	20		25	5	7	23.9	.5868	m	t	l	l	o	w	t
Danugue:													
Own roots				21		22	.8025	m	t	l	l	r	b	t, s
Dog Ridge	5		1½		1	24.1	.5100	m	t	l	l	r	b	t, s
Lenoir	35			6		25.4	.5220	m	t	l	l	r	b	t, s
Rupestris St. George	40		4½		4	23.9	.5494	m	t	l	l	r	b	t, s
[illegible]						22.6	.6150	m	t	l	l	r	b	t, s
Dattier de Beyrouth:													
Lenoir								l	cy	l	l	ob	w	t, s, r
Deacon Superb:													
Own roots				½		27	.9300	l	cy	c	l	ob	w	t
Diamant:													
Own roots				6		22	.6225	m	t	c	l	r	w	t, s
Dodrelabi:													
Own roots	2	2		3		21.8	.4200	m	r	l	l	r	b	t, s
Aramon × Rupestris Ganzin, No. 1								m	r	l	l	r	b	t, s
Dog Ridge	60	10	11	6	2	16.7	.6990	m	r	l	l	r	b	t, s
Herbemont		8	12		4	18.8	.7375	m	r	l	l	r	b	t, s
Lenoir	40	10	12	1½	9	18.9	.6540	m	r	l	l	r	b	t, s
[illegible]e × Rupestris, No. 1202			3			18	.8437	m	r	l	l	r	b	t, s
Rupestris St. George	30	10	28		12	19.6	.5700	m	r	l	l	r	b	t, s
Solonis × Riparia, No. 1616			8	3	5	20	.7600	m	r	l	l	r	b	t, s
Taylor Narbonne	50	3	9			20.2	.6545	m	r	l	l	r	b	t, s
Drnekusa:													
Own roots		3	25	25	6	22.3	.5661	m	t	l	l	ob	b	t, s
Dronkane:													
Lenoir	10	2	13			22.8	.8348	v, l	l	l	l	ob	w	t, s
Rupestris des Caussettes				8		27	.7500	v, l	l	l	l	ob	w	t, s
Duc de Magenta:													
Rupestris St. George	15	20	3		3	23.5	.5231	l	l	l	l	ob	w	t, s
Duc de Malakoff:													
Own roots		1	4	7	8	24.8	.7106	l	t	m	l	r	w	t, s
Emathia:													
Dog Ridge								m	t	l	l	o	w	t, s, st
Lenoir		4	5			23	.5737	m	t	l	l	o	w	t, s, st
Emperor:													
Lenoir								l	t	l	l	r	b	t, s
Rupestris St. George								l	t	l	l	r	b	t, s
Erz ([illegible]):													
Lenoir													
Etraire de l'Adhui:													
Own roots					7	27	1.0125	m	m	c	m	ob	b	w
Fajoumi Jaune:													
Lenoir	6		5			21.2	.8095	l	cy	l	l	ob	w	t, s
Rupestris St. George			2	1½		20	.6445	l	cy	l	l	ob	w	t, s
Faphly:													
Lenoir	25	10	13		15	19.7	.7369	v, l	cy	l	l	ob	r	t, s, st
Riparia × Rupestris, No. 3309			8			27	.6367	v, l	cy	l	l	ob	r	t, s, st
Rupestris St. George		2	2½			26.6	.7500	v, l	cy	l	l	ob	r	t, s, st

TABLE VII.—*Relative behavior and value for different purposes of grape varieties tested by grafting on resistant stocks and by growing on their own roots in eleven experiment vineyards in California*—Continued.

Variety and stock (on own roots, if so stated).	Weight of fruit per vine (pounds).					Sugar, Balling scale.	Acid, as tartaric (grams per 100 c. c.).	Cluster.			Berry.			Use.
	1909	1910	1911	1912	1913			Size.	Shape.	Compact or loose.	Size.	Shape.	Color.	
1	17	18	19	20	21	22	23	24	25	26	27	28	29	30
Feher Goher Noir:						*P. cent.*								
Own roots	15	12	10	35	......	23	0.7406	l	cy	c	l	o	b	t, s, w
Feher Som:														
Lenoir	10	5	6	......	12	24.5	.8775	l	cy	c	l	o	b	t, s, w
Rupestris St. George	......	......	......	4	......	29	.6150	l	cy	c	l	o	b	t, s, w
Feher Szagos:														
Adobe Giant	3	35	10	29	19	27	.5205	l	t	l	l	o	w	t, s, r
Aramon × Rupestris Ganzin, No. 1	40	30	8	1	20	22.1	.5745	l	t	l	l	o	w	t, s, r
Dog Ridge	30	25	3	20	9	24.5	.6230	l	t	l	l	o	w	t, s, r
Herbemont	10	4	¼	3	......	25.2	.6076	l	t	l	l	o	w	t, s, r
Lenoir	20	10	2	3	......	23.1	.5300	l	t	l	l	o	w	t, s, r
Mourvedre × Rupestris, No. 1202	40	20	4	9	4	23.8	.5320	l	t	l	l	o	w	t, s, r
Riparia Gloire	20	30	8	20	5	23.6	.5260	l	t	l	l	o	w	t, s, r
Riparia × Rupestris, No. 101	40	40	5	15	......	23.5	.5043	l	t	l	l	o	w	t, s, r
Riparia × Rupestris, No. 3309	50	20	30	31	......	20.5	.5700	l	t	l	l	o	w	t, s, r
Rupestris Martin	6	......	½	......	......	26	.4575	l	t	l	l	o	w	t, s, r
Rupestris St. George	6	40	10	25	6	21.6	.5535	l	t	l	l	o	w	t, s, r
Salt Creek	15	12	½	6	0	24.1	.5081	l	t	l	l	o	w	t, s, r
Solonis × Riparia, No. 1616	40	3	20	28	9	21.2	.4990	l	t	l	l	o	w	t, s, r
Taylor Narbonne	10	15	6	28	3	27.4	.4890	l	t	l	l	o	w	t, s, r
Ferrara:														
Herbemont	25	15	......	......	......	23.6	.5812	v l	l	l	l	ob	b	t, s, st
Lenoir	......	12	......	......	......	19	.7575	v l	l	l	l	ob	b	t, s, st
Fintendo:														
Own roots	......	......	......	......	......	23.5	.7950	m	cy	c	m	ob	b	t, s, w
Dog Ridge	30	5	12	6	2	21.9	.7695	m	cy	c	m	ob	b	t, s, w
Lenoir	25	18	8	4	27	22.1	.7860	m	cy	c	m	ob	b	t, s, w
Rupestris St. George	30	5	14	1½	23	22	.8175	m	cy	c	m	ob	b	t, s, w
Taylor Narbonne	35	8	9	......	10	22.4	.7175	m	cy	c	m	ob	b	t, s, w

Flame [illegible]:															
[illegible]	1	2	3	25		21.4	.5212	l	t	c	l	ob	r	t, s
[illegible]			24			25	.4800	l	t	c	l	ob	r	t, s
Dog Ridge	30	12	18			20.8	.6600	l	t	c	l	ob	r	t, s
[illegible]ir	8		14			21.6	.5250	l	t	c	l	ob	r	t, s
[illegible]a × R[illegible]a, No. 554			22			22	.5230	l	t	c	l	ob	r	t, s
[illegible]a × R[illegible], No. 18804			18			27	.7575	l	t	c	l	ob	r	t, s
Monticola × R[illegible], No. 18808								l	t	c	l	ob	r	t, s
[illegible]a × [illegible], No. 18185			18			26	.5850	l	t	c	l	ob	r	t, s
[illegible]a à [illegible]es [illegible]les			11			24	.4875	l	t	c	l	ob	r	t, s
[illegible] × [illegible]is, No. 101	30	25	6			22.1	.5950	l	t	c	l	ob	r	t, s
[illegible] × [illegible]is, No. 3309	30	15	15			21.9	.6225	l	t	c	l	ob	r	t, s
Do.								l	t	c	l	ob	r	t, s
Rupestris [illegible]n			8			21	.4800	l	t	c	l	ob	r	t, s
Salt [illegible]k			4			24	.5325	l	t	c	l	ob	r	t, s
Taylor Narbonne			13			26	.5175	l	t	c	l	ob	r	t, s
Folle Blanche:														
[illegible]is [illegible]. George	20	15		4	3	21.7	.8175	m	t	l	m	r	w	w
Foster:														
[illegible]n [illegible]ots	25		4			26	.4612	m	t	c	l	r	w	t, s, w
[illegible]ir		10	4	7	2	23.5	.5119	m	t	c	l	r	w	t, s, w
[illegible]ia [illegible]e	6	7	3	8	15	25.4	.5535	m	t	c	l	r	w	t, s, w
Rupestris St. [illegible]e	20	12	8	15	15	25.6	.5920	m	t	c	l	r	w	t, s, w
[illegible]l [illegible]ce:														
Herbemont								l	l	m	l	r	b	s, t, w
Lenoir	15	2	4			24.1	.7350	l	l	m	l	r	b	s, t, w
[illegible]a × Riparia, No. 18808		3	3	15		23	.6425	l	l	m	l	r	b	s, t, w
[illegible]a × [illegible]a, No. 18815			4	12		24.5	.6600	l	l	m	l	r	b	s, t, w
[illegible]is St. George	20	1				25.4	.6487	l	l	m	l	r	b	s, t, w
Solonis × Othello				8		28	.7125	l	l	m	l	r	b	s, t, w
S[illegible]is × [illegible]ria, No. 1616			4	2		20.5	.6900	l	l	m	l	r	b	s, t, w
[illegible]:														
Dog Ridge								m	t	l	l	ob	b	s, t
Lenoir	8		7			21.8	.8025	m	t	l	l	ob	b	s, t
[illegible]is St. [illegible]rge								m	t	l	l	ob	b	s, t
Fresa [illegible]e [illegible]t:														
[illegible]n roots				½		26	.8925	m	cy	l	m	ob	b	w
Gamay [illegible]e Bourgogne:														
[illegible]n [illegible]ts				½		23	.8025	m	cy	c	m	r	b	w
Dog Ridge	25		9½	4		25.9	.9525	m	cy	c	m	r	b	w
Lenoir	20		6		2	24.8	1.0762	m	cy	c	m	r	b	w
Rupestris St. George	15	3				25.7	.9712	m	cy					
Gamay Teinturier:														
Own roots		2	1	5	½	28	.6581	s	cy	c	s	r	b	w
Dog Ridge	50	3				26.6	.7912	s	cy	c	s	r	b	w
Lenoir	30	3	9		15	24.7	.8500	s	cy	c	s	r	b	w
Rupestris St. George	50	8	12	1	14	26.9	.9225	s	cy	c	s	r	b	w
Taylor Narbonne	40	2				28.1	.7420	s	cy	c	s	r	b	w
Gerwürz Traminer:														
Own roots		4	1	3	9	24.9	.5625	s	cy	c	l	r	w	w

TABLE VII.—*Relative behavior and value for different purposes of grape varieties tested by grafting on resistant stocks and by growing on their own roots in eleven experiment vineyards in California*—Continued.

Variety and stock (on own roots, if so stated).	Weight of fruit per vine (pounds).					Sugar, Balling scale.	Acid, as tartaric (grams per 100 c. c.).	Cluster.			Berry.			Use.
	1909	1910	1911	1912	1913			Size.	Shape.	Compact or loose.	Size.	Shape.	Color.	
1	17	18	19	20	21	22	23	24	25	26	27	28	29	30
Golden Champion:						*P. cent.*								
Own roots		2		20		25.9	0.8512	m	t	c	l	r	w	s, t
Do	8		2			25.6	.5212	m	t	c	l	r	w	s, t
Dog Ridge	30	3	18	4	1	20	.8385	m	t	c	l	r	w	s, t
Lenoir	60	15	4	2	18	20.5	.7240	m	t	c	l	r	w	s, t
Rupestris St. George	25	8	6	1	6	20.2	.8300	m	t	c				
Golden Hamburg:														
Lenoir								m	cy	c	l	r	w	s, t
Golden Queen:														
Lenoir								m	t	c	l	r	w	s, t
Goolabie:														
Own roots	40	15	6	7		23.8	.5831	m l	l	l	l	ob	b	s, t, w
Gradiska:														
Own roots				2½	3	20.5	.8037	m l	l	l	l	ob	w	s, t
Dog Ridge	40	15	12	3		21.1	.6056	m l	l	l	l	ob	w	s, t
Lenoir	30		13	4	8	18.6	.6450	m l	l	l	l	ob	w	s, t
St. George	20	10	19	⅓		22.7	.6349	m l	l	l	l	ob	w	s, t
[illegible]r N [illegible]onne	20	6	7			21	.6250	m l	l	l	l	ob	w	s, t
Green Hungarian:														
Own roots	12	10	2	18		22.1	.5605	m l	t	l	l	r	w	w
([illegible]is × M[illegible]la) × (Riparia × Rupestris, No. 5[illegible]-5)								m l	t	l	l	r	w	w
[illegible]n × [illegible]is [illegible], No. 1	15	5	9		4	18.1	.5835	m l	t	l	l	r	w	w
Aramon × Rup[illegible]is [illegible], No. 2			3	2	2	18.8	.7375	m l	t	l	l	r	w	w
[illegible]i × R[illegible]a, No. [illegible]A								m l	t	l	l	r	w	w
[illegible]la					3	21	.7125	m l	t	l	l	r	w	w
Dog Ridge	40	12	14	5	19	19.8	.7170	m l	t	l	l	r	w	w
Herbemont	30	10	2			17.1	.6717	m-l	t	l	l	r	w	w
Lenoir	40	8	6	4	8	20.8	.7460	m-l	t	l	l	r	w	w
[illegible]la × [illegible]e No. 18808			4	2	3	22	.7945	m-l	t	l	l	r	w	w
[illegible] × [illegible]is, No. 1202	30	3			4	20.6	.5626	m-l	t	l	l	r	w	w

Riparia × Rupestris, No. 101	40	5	8	1	18	20.6	.7185	m-l	t	l	l	r	w	w
[illegible] × [illegible]s, No. 3306	......	......	3	......	5	19.5	.7725	m-l	t	l	l	r	w	w
Riparia × [illegible] [illegible], No. 3309	......	10	......	......	5	21.3	.7325	m-l	t	l	l	r	w	w
[illegible] [illegible]artin	......	......	......	......	......	......	......	m-l	t	l	l	r	w	w
[illegible] [illegible]on	......	......	......	......	4	22	.8100	m-l	t	l	l	r	w	w
Rup[illegible] St. George	30	4	4	4	2	19	.7435	m-l	t	l	l	r	w	w
Salt [illegible]	......	12	......	......	4	20.4	.6470	m-l	t	l	l	r	w	w
Solonis [illegible]	......	......	4	......	......	21.5	.8212	m-l	t	l	l	r	w	w
Solonis × Othello, No. 1613	......	......	8	......	5	21	.8137	m-l	t	l	l	r	w	w
[illegible]is × Riparia, No. 1616	25	10	3	......	......	17.8	.7575	m-l	t	l	l	r	w	w
Tay[illegible] [illegible]	50	10	11	4	4	19.6	.7290	m-l	t	l	l	r	w	w
Grenache:														
Own roots	10	30	20	32	30	24	.7245	m-l	t	c	m	ob	b	t, w
[illegible]	40	12	15	2	......	22.5	.8794	m-l	t	c	m	ob	b	t, w
Lenoir	50	15	18	11	36	22.8	.7800	m-l	t	c	m	ob	b	t, w
[illegible]is St. [illegible]ge	40	3	4	¾	23	24	.9075	m-l	t	c	m	ob	b	t, w
[illegible] N[illegible]	50	5	11	......	2	24.8	.7170	m-l	t	c	m	ob	b	t, w
Gros [illegible]:														
[illegible]ir	20	8	11	......	17	22.2	.5250	m	t	c	m	ob	w	w
Solonis × Othello	......	2	......	......	......	23.3	.4950	m	t	c	m	ob	w	w
Gros [illegible]:														
[illegible]ir	......	......	......	......	1½	28	.5250	m	r	c	l	r	b	t, s
[illegible] [illegible]:														
Own [illegible]	½	......	⅛	8	......	25.6	.5091	m	cy	l	m	r	b	w
Gros [illegible]oc:														
Own roots	......	......	......	......	......	21.5	.8250	m	t	c	l	ob	b	s, t, st
Gros Verdot:														
Own [illegible]	......	......	......	½	......	21	.9000	m	cy	c	l	r	b	w
[illegible]	35	20	......	35	12	23.5	.8118	m	cy	c	l	r	b	w
Do	20	3	5	......	......	23.1	1.0075	m	cy	c	l	r	b	w
Lenoir	40	15	12	......	31	20.7	.7181	m	cy	c	l	r	b	w
Do	12	12	......	4	2	24.1	.5962	m	cy	c	l	r	b	w
Rupestris St. George	25	15	......	20	15	23.8	.8081	m	cy	c	l	r	b	w
Do	30	10	14	6	38	22.5	.8445	m	cy	c	l	r	b	w
Taylor Narbonne	20	5	9	......	......	22	.7108	m	cy	c	l	r	b	w
Hebron:														
Lenoir	3	5	8	......	......	22.3	.5825	m-l	t	l	m	r	w	w
Rupestris St. George	......	......	......	2	......	21	.7875	m-l	t	l	m	r	w	w
Solonis × Othello, No. 1613	......	......	......	1½	......	20	.7500	m-l	t	l	m	r	w	w
Huasco:														
Own roots	......	6	2	4	......	26	[illegible]	m	t	l	l	o	w	s, t, r
Aramon × Rupestris Ganzin, No. 1	15	10	5	3	2	26	[illegible]	m	t	l	l	o	w	s, t, r
Do	......	......	10	......	......	22	[illegible]	m	t	l	l	o	w	s, t, r
Aramon × Rupestris Ganzin, No. 2	......	......	......	12	......	28	[illegible]	m	t	l	l	o	w	s, t, r
Australis	......	......	4	......	......	25	.5850	m	t	l	l	o	w	s, t, r
Berlandieri × Riparia, No. 420A	......	......	3	5	......	29.5	[illegible]	m	t	l	l	o	w	s, t, r
Lenoir	10	8	3	½	......	26.5	[illegible]	m	t	l	l	o	w	s, t, r
Monticola × Riparia, No. 18808	......	......	......	4	......	30	[illegible]	m	t	l	l	o	w	s, t, r
Mourvedre × Rupestris, No. 1202	15	6	3	19	3	26	[illegible]	m	t	l	l	o	w	s, t, r
Riparia Gloire	......	......	½	12	1	26	[illegible]	m	t	l	l	o	w	s, t, r
Riparia × (Cordifolia × Rupestris, No. 106-8)	......	......	6	......	......	25.5	[illegible]	m	t	l	l	o	w	s, t, r

TABLE VII.—*Relative behavior and value for different purposes of grape varieties tested by grafting on resistant stocks and by growing on their own roots in eleven experiment vineyards in California*—Continued.

Variety and stock (on own roots, if so stated).	Weight of fruit per vine (pounds).					Sugar, Balling scale.	Acid, as tartaric (grams per 100 c. c.).	Cluster.			Berry.			Use.
	1909	1910	1911	1912	1913			Size.	Shape.	Compact or loose.	Size.	Shape.	Color.	
1	17	18	19	20	21	22	23	24	25	26	27	28	29	30
H[illegible] [illegible]d.						P. cent.								
[illegible]ia × [illegible], No. 101	4		1	2		29.9	0.5717	m	t	l	l	o	w	s, t, r
Do		2				26.3	.6225	m	t	l	l	o	w	s, t, r
[illegible]ia × [illegible], No. 3309			3	2		24.5	.5262	m	t	l	l	o	w	s, t, r
[illegible]is St. George	15	11	5	8	4	27	.6000	m	t	l	l	o	w	s, t, r
[illegible]s Robusta				5		29	.5500	m	t	l	l	o	w	s, t, r
[illegible]s × [illegible]ia, No. 1616			½			28	.4950	m	t	l	l	o	w	s, t, r
Taylor N[illegible]b[illegible]me		5		½	½	27.2	.6750	m	t	l	l	o	w	s, t, r
[illegible]la				8		27	.5100	m	t	l	l	o	w	s, t, r
[illegible]a:														
[illegible]be[illegible]a			2			28	.5175	l	cy	l	l	o	b	s, t, st
[illegible]			12	35		20	.7725	l	cy	l	l	o	b	s, t, st
[illegible]i × Riparia, No. 420A				15				l	cy	l	l	o	b	s, t, st
ar[illegible]ia			12	22		21	.5325	l	cy	l	l	o	b	s, t, st
[illegible]g [illegible]e								l	cy	l	l	o	b	s, t, st
i[illegible]ia × u[illegible]stris, No. 3309								l	cy	l	l	o	b	s, t, st
Sonis [illegible]ta			14	12		21	.5775	l	cy	l	l	o	b	s, t, st
Solonis × Riparia, No. 1616								l	cy	l	l	o	b	s, t, st
Hunisa (S. P. I. No. 6124):														
Own o[illegible]s								l	cy	l	l	o	b	s, t, st
[illegible]a (S. [illegible]. I. No. 8583):														
[illegible]n o[illegible]s	10					18.2	1.0125	l	cy	l	l	o	b	s, t, st
Hutab:														
Own roots					2	22	.5850	m	l	l	m	o	w	t
[illegible]s:														
Lenoir	15	10	13		9	22	.6850	l	t	l	m	r	w	s, t, w
[illegible]stris Mission								l	t	l	m	r	w	s, t, w
[illegible]estris St. George		2	19			23	.4815	l	t	l	m	r	w	s, t, w
Sonis × Othello, No. 1613			9	12		25.2	.4762	l	t	l	m	r	w	s, t, w
Imperial:														
Own roots				8	5	20.5	.6442	m	t	c	m-l	r	b	t, s, w

Inzolia Bianca:														
[illegible]ir	8	5	5	......	2	23.1	.6267	m-l	t	c	m	ob	w	t, w
R[illegible]s St. George	......	1½	10	......	......	23	.6950	m-l	t	c	m	ob	w	t, w
[illegible]:														
Own o[illegible]ts	2	......	4	15	3	25.2	.6562	s	cy	c	s	r	w	w
Jura Muscat:														
[illegible]ir	1½	5	1	2	2	26.5	.6555	m	cy	c	s	r	r	t, w
[illegible]Gloire	12	3	......	28	6	27.7	.6400	m	cy	c	s	r	r	t, w
Rupestris St. George	16	6	3	20	4	28.8	.7095	m	cy	c	s	r	r	t, w
K[illegible]k:														
Own o[illegible]s	30	......	......	......	......	17.6	.6712	m	t	c	m-l	ob	w	t, s
Kadarka:														
Own roots	2	35	8	35	20	22.7	.5850	l	cy	c	s	r	b	w
[illegible]g [illegible]e	40	30	10	30	25	23.4	.6644	l	cy	c	s	r	b	w
n[illegible]r	15	30	4	2	22	23.7	.4950	l	cy	c	s	r	b	w
Riparia Gloire	8	15	5	18	7	23.9	.5365	l	cy	c	s	r	b	w
[illegible]s S. George	20	40	10	36	26	24.8	.4305	l	cy	c	s	r	b	w
[illegible]-Blanc:														
Lenoir	2	......	2½	......	......	24.1	.7425	l	t	l	m	o	w	t, r, w
S[illegible]s × Othello, No. 1613	......	......	......	......	......	......	......	l	t	l	m	o	w	t, r, w
Keropodia:														
n[illegible]ir	20	5	11	......	4	24	.7652	l	t	l	m	o	w	w
[illegible]ia × [illegible], No. 3309	......	......	......	......	......	......	......	l	t	l	m	o	w	w
Key:														
[illegible]nt	......	......	......	......	......	......	......	l	t	c	l	r	b	s, t, w
[illegible]ir	20	3	5	......	35	21.4	.5796	l	t	c	l	r	b	s, t, w
[illegible]r:														
Own roots	4	2	1	½	......	24.9	.6262	s	cy	c	s	r	w	w
Kölner:														
Own roots	3	½	1	10	4	25.3	.6510	m	cy	l	l	r	b	w
Dog [illegible]e	15	1½	10	......	......	23	.8717	m	cy	l	l	r	b	w
[illegible]ir	15	8	9½	4	20	22.4	.7765	m	cy	l	l	r	b	w
[illegible]s St. George	45	7	12	1	21	21.2	.9210	m	cy	l	l	r	b	w
[illegible]r n[illegible]e	15	2	......	......	......	24.3	.4395	m	cy	l	l	r	b	w
[illegible]i M[illegible]:														
n[illegible]ir	......	3	6	......	......	22.1	.5550	m	t	l	l	ob	r	s, t
[illegible]ka:														
Own o[illegible]s	......	......	⅛	4	......	21.2	.5250	l	cy	l	m	ob	w	w
Do	50	......	......	......	......	20.3	.7050	l	cy	l	m	ob	w	w
[illegible]e:														
Own [illegible]s	15	7	½	......	......	23.3	.7037	m-l	l	l	l	ob	w	w, s, t
Riparia Gloire	15	8	1	12	......	26	.6944	m-l	l	l	l	ob	w	w, s, t
Rupestris St. [illegible]e	30	10	8	6	3	24.3	.7350	m-l	l	l	l	ob	w	w, s, t
[illegible]i Zolo:														
p[illegible]s St. [illegible]e	30	40	8	30	18	22.3	.5130	m	cy	c	s	r	w	w
[illegible]n Blanc:														
Own roots	......	......	......	3	......	27.5	.8475	s	cy	c	s	r	w	w
[illegible]on × [illegible]s [illegible]in, No. 1	40	30	5	43	0	22.3	.6094	s	cy	c	s	r	w	w
Dog [illegible]	10	6	......	......	......	22.6	.6187	s	cy	c	s	r	w	w
Do	42	35	14	47	7	22.6	.6388	s	cy	c	s	r	w	w

TABLE VII.—*Relative behavior and value for different purposes of grape varieties tested by grafting on resistant stocks and by growing on their own roots in eleven experiment vineyards in California*—Continued.

Variety and stock (on own roots, if so stated).	Weight of fruit per vine (pounds).					Sugar, Balling scale.	Acid, as tartaric (grams per 100 c. c.).	Cluster.			Berry.			Use.
	1909	1910	1911	1912	1913			Size.	Shape.	Compact or loose.	Size.	Shape.	Color.	
1	17	18	19	20	21	22	23	24	25	26	27	28	29	30
Lignan Blanc—Continued.						*P. cent.*								
Hotporup	......	6	4	......	......	24.1	.6175	s	cy	c	s	r	w	w
Lenoir	25	5	3	1½	5	23.2	.6660	s	cy	c	s	r	w	w
Do	28	10	2	2	4	21.3	.6990	s	cy	c	s	r	w	w
Mourvedre × Rupestris, No. 1202	......	......	......	......	......	......	......	s	cy	c	s	r	w	w
Do	25	30	3	41	8	22.3	.6315	s	cy	c	s	r	w	w
R[illegible]ia Gloire	8	35	8	40	11	24.8	.6615	s	cy	c	s	r	w	w
Riparia × Rupestris, No. 101	30	30	20	6	0	22.9	.6276	s	cy	c	s	r	w	w
Riparia × Rupestris, No. 3309	20	50	25	13	4	23	.6135	s	cy	c	s	r	w	w
Rupestris St. G[illegible]ge	40	10	10	......	10½	22.8	.6950	s	cy	c	s	r	w	w
Do	40	30	5	18	26	22.4	.6185	s	cy	c	s	r	w	w
Solonis × Othello	......	4	......	......	......	23	1.0462	s	cy	c	s	r	w	w
Solonis × Riparia, No. 1616	10	20	15	12	0	24	.5174	s	cy	c	s	r	w	w
[illegible]r Narbonne	6	40	10	23	0	22.4	.5681	s	cy	c	s	r	w	w
Do	50	5	3	......	......	24.2	.6150	s	cy	c	s	r	w	w
Listan:														
Own roots	10	10	15	21	8	23.6	.5090	l	l	l	m	r	w	w, s, t
([illegible]is × Monticola) × (Riparia × [illegible]upestris, No. 554–5)	......	......	6	1	6	23	.6300	l	l	c	m	r	w	w, s, t
[illegible]n × Rupestris Ganzin, No. 1	40	40	26	......	8	23.3	.5806	l	l	c	m	r	w	w, s, t
Aramon × Rup[illegible]is [illegible], No. 2	......	......	3	......	2	24.5	.6187	l	l	c	m	r	w	w, s, t
Berlandieri × Riparia, No. 420B	......	5	......	......	......	23.7	.4800	l	l	c	m	r	w	w, s, t
[illegible]d × Riparia, No. 250 2	......	......	......	3	......	22	.5025	l	l	c	m	r	w	w, s, t
Constantia	......	......	4	2	8	23.8	.6375	l	l	c	m	r	w	w, s, t
Cornucopia	......	4	4	......	......	23.3	.3475	l	l	c	m	r	w	w, s, t
De [illegible]tt	......	6	......	6	......	25.6	.4950	l	l	c	m	r	w	w, s, t
Dog Ridge	30	10	17	8	12	23.3	.6375	l	l	c	m	r	w	w, s, t
Herbemont	15	12	2	......	4	22.3	.5344	l	l	c	m	r	w	w, s, t
Lenoir	6	5	9	......	5	23.1	.5450	l	l	c	m	r	w	w, s, t
[illegible]la × Riparia, No. 18804	......	5	1	26	......	23.7	.4495	l	l	c	m	r	w	w, s, t
[illegible]la × Riparia, No. 18808	......	......	1½	......	4	24.5	.6070	l	l	c	m	r	w	w, s, t
[illegible]re × Rupestris, No. 1202	30	10	13	2	15	22.9	.6630	l	l	c	m	r	w	w, s, t

Riparia × Rupestris, No. 101	25	10	16	2	2	22.3	.6300	l	l	c	m	r	w	w, s, t
Do.						21	.6300	l	l	c	m	r	w	w, s, t
Riparia × [illegible]tris, No. 101–14			2			24	.6487	l	l	l	m	r	w	w, s, t
Riparia × [illegible]is, No. 3306			3		5	24	.6750	l	l	l	m	r	w	w, s, t
Riparia × Rupestris, No. 3309				19		23	.6255	l	l	l	m	r	w	w, s, t
Do.	60	15	9		5	23.3	.6660	l	l	l	m	r	w	w, s, t
Rupestris M[illegible]in	30	10	1½		8	24	.6287	l	l	l	m	r	w	w, s, t
Rupestris M[illegible]a			5		3	25	.6412	l	l	l	m	r	w	w, s, t
Rupestris M[illegible]n					2	25	.5475	l	l	l	m	r	w	w, s, t
Rupestris St. [illegible]ge								l	l	l	m	r	w	w, s, t
Do.	6	3	2	½		22.7	.5469	l	l	l	m	r	w	w, s, t
[illegible]tis × Berlandieri, No. 219A				1½		23	.5250	l	l	l	m	r	w	w, s, t
Salt C[illegible]	15	8	5		10	25	.6075	l	l	l	m	r	w	w, s, t
[illegible]is Robusta		6	4			24.5	.4575	l	l	l	m	r	w	w, s, t
Do.			5	2	4	23.3	.6800	l	l	l	m	r	w	w, s, t
[illegible]is × Othello			1			23	.4537	l	l	l	m	r	w	w, s, t
[illegible]is × Othello, No. 1613			1½	2	4	24	.6450	l	l	l	m	r	w	w, s, t
[illegible]is × [illegible]ia, No. 1616	15	50	19	3		24.1	.6469	l	l	l	m	r	w	w, s, t
Taylor Narbonne	30	10	25	3	8	24.6	.5845	l	l	l	m	r	w	w, s, t
Valencia		3	3			24.2	.4825	l	l	l	m	r	w	w, s, t
L[illegible]a:														
[illegible]be Giant	30	10	4	26		22.4	.5931	m-l	r	c	l	ob	b	w, s, t
Dog R[illegible]e	45	25		6	8	24	.5594	m-l	r	c	l	ob	b	w, s, t
Riparia × [illegible]is, No. 3309				2		24	.6825	m-l	r	c	l	ob	b	w, s, t
[illegible]is St. [illegible]e	20	25	5	43	6	27	.4740	m-l	r	c	l	ob	b	w, s, t
M[illegible]ar:														
[illegible]n r[illegible]s	1½			4	1	25	.6917	s	cy	c	s	ob	b	w
M[illegible] [illegible]gevine:														
[illegible]n roots		3			2	22.6	.4950	m-l	t	l	m	ob	w	w, t
Dog R[illegible]e	15	2	12		1	24.5	.5392	m-l	t	l	m	ob	w	w, t
Lenoir	15	2	1		2½	22.3	.5420	m-l	t	l	m	ob	w	w, t
Rupestris St. George	6	2	2		3	24.7	.5756	m-l	t	l	m	ob	w	w, t
M[illegible]e [illegible]he:														
[illegible]n r[illegible]e						25.9	.6975	m-l	t	l	m	ob	w	w, t
Mad[illegible]ine d'Ambre:														
Dog Ridge		½	16	½		23.5	.7800	m-l	t	l	m	ob	w	w, t
Lenoir	6	2	½		5	20.9	.7294	m-l	t	l	m	ob	w	w, t
Rup[illegible]tris St. [illegible]ge	3	2			3	21.3	.8057	m-l	t	l	m	ob	w	w, t
[illegible]leine Rose:														
[illegible]n roots				2		22	.7500	m-l	t	l	m	ob	w	w, t
[illegible]ria Gloire			2			25.5	.5587	m-l	t	l	m	ob	w	w, t
[illegible]e ([illegible]le):														
[illegible]n roots				4		31	.7500	m-l	t	l	m	ob	w	w, t
Dog R[illegible]e	25	4			4	27.4	.5725	m-l	t	l	m	ob	w	w, t
Lenoir	10	2	½		3	25.7	.6600	m-l	t	l	m	ob	w	w, t
[illegible]:														
[illegible]n r[illegible]s	20	25	2	7	9	23.9	.5205	l	t	m	l	ob	w	s, t, r
([illegible]e G[illegible]t	60	70	15	42	30	22.6	.5550	l	t	m	l	ob	w	s, t, r
[illegible]n × [illegible]tis [illegible]in, No. 1	50	40	3	43	8	22.7	.6045	l	t	m	l	ob	w	s, t, r
[illegible]a								l	t	m	l	ob	w	s, t, r
[illegible]ntia			10			23	.5775	l	t	m	l	ob	w	s, t, r

TABLE VII.—*Relative behavior and value for different purposes of grape varieties tested by grafting on resistant stocks and by growing on their own roots in eleven experiment vineyards in California*—Continued.

Variety and stock (on own roots, if so stated).	Weight of fruit per vine (pounds). 1909	1910	1911	1912	1913	Sugar, Balling scale.	Acid, as tartaric (grams per 100 c. c.).	Cluster. Size.	Cluster. Shape.	Cluster. Compact or loose.	Berry. Size.	Berry. Shape.	Berry. Color.	Use.
1	17	18	19	20	21	22	23	24	25	26	27	28	29	30
[illegible]d.						*P. cent.*								
Dog R[illegible]e	60	40	10	20	32	23.1	0.6150	l	t	m	l	ob	w	s, t, r
[illegible]t	2	20	2	...	...	24.8	.6093	l	t	m	l	ob	w	s, t, r
I [illegible]eir	30	20	20	4	2	22.8	.4392	l	t	m	l	ob	w	s, t, r
[illegible]e × Ru[illegible]s, No. 1202	45	30	15	45	12	22.9	.5950	l	t	m	l	ob	w	s, t, r
[illegible]a [illegible]e	50	25	15	44	18	22.7	.6489	l	t	m	l	ob	w	s, t, r
[illegible]a × [illegible]s, No. 101	40	70	20	43	10	23.6	.6120	l	t	m	l	ob	w	s, t, r
[illegible]a × [illegible]s, No. 3309	40	30	30	22	18	23.7	.5995	l	t	m	l	ob	w	s, t, r
[illegible]s Martin	11	7	½	1½	1	22.5	.4790	l	t	m	l	ob	w	s, t, r
[illegible]s St. [illegible]e	40	30	15	30	20	22.9	.5715	l	t	m	l	ob	w	s, t, r
Salt Creek	30	15	5	31	8	22.8	.6165	l	t	m	l	ob	w	s, t, r
[illegible]s × Riparia, No. 1616	50	70	35	...	12	22.7	.6006	l	t	m	l	ob	w	s, t, r
[illegible]r Narbonne	60	60	15	33	4	23.9	.5600	l	t	m	l	ob	w	s, t, r
[illegible]a Blanc:														
Lenoir	15	18	3	...	...	26.9	.5425	m-l	l	l	m	ob	w	w
[illegible]a Gloire	4	15	1	7	4	25.3	.5790	m-l	l	l	m	ob	w	w
Rup[illegible]s St. George	15	25	4	30	26	26.5	.5720	m-l	cy	c	s	r	b	w
M[illegible]ck:														
[illegible]n [illegible]s	...	2	2	22	3	24	.8025	s	t	c	l	ob	b	s, t, w
Malvasia:														
[illegible]n [illegible]s	2	6	2	27	...	26	.5556	s	t	c	l	ob	b	s, t, w
[illegible]ir	...	...	...	...	...	...	...	s	t	c	l	ob	b	s, t, w
Rup[illegible]s St. [illegible]e	...	...	...	...	3	24	.9375	s	t	c	l	ob	b	s, t, w
[illegible]sia de Broglio:														
[illegible]n roots	4	...	...	15	...	23.1	.6375	l	t	l	m	r	w	w
[illegible]a [illegible]a:														
[illegible]n [illegible]s	15	8	2	12	...	24.5	.7162	l	t	c	l	ob	b	w
Dog R[illegible]e	40	50	5	40	0	23.4	.7125	l	t	c	l	ob	b	w
Herbemont	...	...	4½	...	...	21	.8625	l	t	c	l	ob	b	w
Lenoir	25	15	½	...	6	24.3	.6354	l	t	c	l	ob	b	w
Riparia Gloire	30	40	5	20	26	22.4	.6495	l	t	c	l	ob	b	w
[illegible]s St. George	25	25	10	10	0	24.1	.6469	l	t	c	l	ob	b	w

[illegible]ia Rovasenda:														
[illegible]n [illegible]	10	20	10	3	3	25	.6862	l	t	c	l	ob	b	w
[illegible]n:														
Own roots					6	21	.7200	l	t	c	l	ob	w	s, t
[illegible]g [illegible]e	4	8	24	6		25.2	.6787	l	t	c	l	ob	w	s, t
[illegible]ir	20	12		4	37	24.1	.6360	l	t	c	l	ob	w	s, t
Rupestris St. [illegible]e	15	10			4	24.3	.6200	l	t	c	l	ob	w	s, t
Tay dr [illegible]e	15	8	10		7	26.6	.6300	l	t	c	l	ob	w	s, t
Val [illegible]a				5		23	.7500	l	t	c	l	ob	w	s, t
Man [illegible]o de [illegible]as:														
Own roots	20	20	20	21	10	22.2	.5715	l	t	l	m	ob	w	s, t, w
[illegible]e [illegible]it	30	40	15	39	16	23.1	.4980	l	t	l	m	ob	w	s, t, w
[illegible]n × [illegible]s [illegible]n, No. 1	45	50	8	28	20	22.7	.3903	l	t	l	m	ob	w	s, t, w
[illegible]g R[illegible]e	25	30	15	26	3	21.5	.3660	l	t	l	m	ob	w	s, t, w
[illegible]t	5	2	¼		1	24.1	.5040	l	t	l	m	ob	w	s, t, w
[illegible]ir	40	30	3	2½	3	21.3	.3255	l	t	l	m	ob	w	s, t, w
Do	12	15	6	1	23	21.6	.5565	l	t	l	m	ob	w	s, t, w
[illegible]e × R[illegible], No. 1202	45	45	5	13	18	22.2	.40	l	t	l	m	ob	w	s, t, w
[illegible]a Gloire	20	40	5	28	18	2.6	.3200	l	t	l	m	ob	w	s, t, w
Riparia × Rupestris, No. 101	30	50	15	12	6	25.6	.3870	l	t	l	m	ob	w	s, t, w
[illegible]a × Rupestris, No. 3309	45	50	20	13	15	23.1	.4525	l	t	l	m	ob	w	s, t, w
Rupestris [illegible]n	10	6	1½	1	2	22.5	.5100	l	t	l	m	ob	w	s, t, w
[illegible]s St. [illegible]e	45	50	5	30		22.9	.3494	l	t	l	m	ob	w	s, t, w
Do	15	2	7		15	22.8	.4800	l	t	l	m	ob	w	s, t, w
Salt [illegible]k	15	40	¼	5	4	22.5	.4216	l	t	l	m	ob	w	s, t, w
[illegible]s × Riparia, No. 1616	40	50	30		17	23	.3787	l	t	l	m	ob	w	s, t, w
[illegible]r [illegible]e	40	15	10		5	24.1	.4087	l	t	l	m	ob	w	s, t, w
Mar [illegible]:														
Own roots	1			15		23.3	.6675	m	cy	m	m	r	w	w
[illegible]ir								m	cy	m	m	r	w	w
Maraville de [illegible]a:														
[illegible]ir	8	3	14		8	22.5	.5681	v, l	t	m	m	r	b	s, t, w
Rip[illegible]a × [illegible]s, No. 3309			6			22	.5020	v, l	t	m	m	r	b	s, t, w
Sol[illegible]s × [illegible]o, No. 1613			7	15		23.5	.4162	v, l	t	m	m	r	b	s, t, w
[illegible]a [illegible]d:														
Own [illegible]ts						22	1.0500	m	t	l	m	ob	b	s, t, w
[illegible]:														
[illegible]r	30	5	2	3	2	22.9	.4630	m-l	t	m	l	r	w	st, t
[illegible]a Gloire	2	4	3	32	12	24.5	.4395	m-l	t	m	l	r	w	st, t
Rupestris St. George	12	7	3	25	6	24.8	.4680	m-l	t	m	l	r	w	st, t
[illegible]:														
Own [illegible]s	15	18	8	10	25	26.2	.5595	m	t	l	s	r	w	w
[illegible]o:														
Own [illegible]ts	3		¼	5		24	.5050	m	l	m	m	r	b	w
Do	1					26	.6025	m	l	m	m	r	b	w
[illegible]:														
Own [illegible]s						24	.6075	m	cy	c	m	r	b	w
[illegible]n × [illegible]s [illegible]n, No. 1	55	38	9	2	4	21.7	.6810	m	cy	c	m	r	b	w
Dog Ridge	50	12		16	2½	22.7	.7481	m	cy	c	m	r	b	w
[illegible]nt	45			3	8	19.6	.8325	m	cy	c	m	r	b	w
[illegible]ir	60	5		4		21.9	.7675	m	cy	c	m	r	b	w

TABLE VII.—*Relative behavior and value for different purposes of grape varieties tested by grafting on resistant stocks and by growing on their own roots in eleven experiment vineyards in California*—Continued.

Variety and stock (on own roots, if so stated).	Weight of fruit per vine (pounds). 1909	1910	1911	1912	1913	Sugar, Balling scale.	Acid, as tartaric (grams per 100 c. c.).	Cluster. Size.	Cluster. Shape.	Cluster. Compact or loose.	Berry. Size.	Berry. Shape.	Berry. Color.	Use.
1	17	18	19	20	21	22	23	24	25	26	27	28	29	30
Mataro—Continued.						*P. cent.*								
[illegible]e × [illegible], No. 1202	50	5	6	....	4	21.1	0.8587	m	cy	c	m	r	b	w
[illegible]s Martin	40	8	2	16	....	21.4	.8212	m	cy	c	m	r	b	w
Rupestris St. [illegible]e	50	12	....	15	10	21.7	.7200	m	cy	c	m	r	b	w
Salt C[illegible]k	45	12	....	4	4	22	.8719	m	cy	c	m	r	b	w
[illegible]r [illegible]e	30	10	8	10	4	22.6	.7350	m	cy	c	m	r	b	w
M[illegible]n:														
Dog R[illegible]e	20	20	....	10	15	23.1	.5131	m	r	c	l	ob	w	s, t
[illegible]s St. George	15	15	....	15	8	23.5	.5096	m	r	c	l	ob	w	s, t
M[illegible]t:														
Own roots	2	....	2	....	½	24.7	.5950	m	cy	m	s	r	b	w
M[illegible]r:														
Own [illegible]ts	3	1½	1	....	....	24.7	.9300	s	cy	c	s	r	w	w
[illegible]n × [illegible]s [illegible]n, No. 1	6	....	5	....	....	22.4	1.0650	s	cy	c	s	r	w	w
L[illegible]ir	8	3	....	4	20	21.7	1.0918	s	cy	c	s	r	w	w
[illegible]s St. [illegible]e	15	1	5½	1	6	22.8	.9224	s	cy	c	s	r	w	w
M[illegible]r:														
Own roots	4	2	....	2	....	28.4	.6975	s	cy	c	s	r	b	w
Dog R[illegible]e	25	1	16	....	....	25.1	.7050	s	cy	c	s	r	b	w
Lenoir	20	3	5	....	9	21.5	.8344	s	cy	c	s	r	b	w
Rupestris St. George	40	3	29	3	7	28.4	.8160	s	cy	c	s	r	b	w
[illegible]r, No. 59:														
Dog Ridge	12	5	....	....	....	25.8	.5250	l	t, cy	c	m	ob	w	s, t, w
Lenoir	....	....	6	....	....	22	.5325	l	t, cy	c	m	ob	w	s, t, w
[illegible]r, No. 60:														
Dog R[illegible]e	30	....	3½	....	....	25.1	.6112	l	t, cy	c	m	ob	w	s, t, w
[illegible]ir	1	....	4	....	....	22	.7349	l	t, cy	c	m	ob	w	s, t, w
[illegible]r, No. 65:														
[illegible]ir	20	8	13	....	19	20.6	.6885	l	t	m	m	r	r	w
[illegible]r, No. 94:														
Dog R[illegible]e	20	....	....	....	....	21.2	.2400	m-l	cy	m	l	ob	w	s, t
[illegible]ir	2	½	11	....	....	20.2	.3316	m-l	cy	m	l	ob	w	s, t

[illegible]r, No. 95:														
Dog Ridge	10	2				21.1	.6150	l	t	l	l	ob	w	s, t
[illegible]r	20	3	13			19	.5875	l	t	l	l	ob	w	s, t
[illegible]r, No. 103:														
Lenoir					5	23	.6000	s	r	c	s	r	b	w
[illegible]r, No. 107:														
[illegible]r		2	9			19	.8637	l	r	c	l	ob	w	s, t
[illegible]r, No. 116:														
Dog Ridge	5					23.2	.6300	l	l	l	m	r	b	w
Lenoir	3		4			24.1	.5925	l	l	l	m	r	b	w
[illegible]r, No. 515:														
Dog Ridge	10	2	5½			20.1	.7425	l	t	c	l	ob	b	w
[illegible]r	8	15			6½	20.6	.7275	l	t	c	l	ob	b	w
[illegible]m:														
[illegible]n × [illegible]stris Ganzin, No. 1	25	20	11	5	4	23.7	.6885	m-l	t	c	l	r	w	s, t, w
Lenoir	40	3	11		6	23.4	.7237	m-l	t	c	l	r	w	s, t, w
Riparia × [illegible]tris, No. 101	25	5	2			22.5	.5950	m-l	t	c	l	r	w	s, t, w
Rip[illegible]ia × Rupestris, No. 3309	30					21.9	.7125	m-l	t	c	l	r	w	s, t, w
Solonis × Riparia, No. 1616	30	5	1			22.3	.6825	m-l	t	c	l	r	w	s, t, w
[illegible]in:														
Own roots	30	30	10	45	15	20.2	.5885	l	t	m-c	m	r	b	w, s, t
[illegible]	30	20	4	26	12	26.6	.5010	l	t	m-c	m	r	b	w, s, t
Dog Ridge	20	25	5	15	16	26.4	.4889	l	t	mc	m	r	b	w, s, t
Do	60	15	20		20	21.2	.7500	l	t	m-c	m	r	b	w, s, t
Herbemont	4	10	2			29.4	.4837	l	t	m-c	m	r	b	w, s, t
Do	65	20	12	10	9	21.5	.7295	l	t	m-c	m	r	b	w, s, t
Lenoir	20	30	3	3	1	24.6	.5070	l	t	m-c	m	r	b	w, s, t
Do	50		15	10	15	19.1	.6125	l	t	m-c	m	r	b	w, s, t
[illegible]a Gloire	15	10	2	20	15	27.2	.4871	l	t	m-c	m	r	b	w, s, t
[illegible]s Mission	3	15	2	11	4	25.1	.4605	l	t	m-c	m	r	b	w, s, t
Do		5	10	1	23	22	.7395	l	t	m-c	m	r	b	w, s, t
Rupestris St. George	40	30	10	13	12	26.5	.5450	l	t	m-c	m	r	b	w, s, t
Do	60		19	8	15	23	.5910	l	t	mc	m	r	b	w, s, t
S[illegible]lt [illegible]k	20	15	5	3	12	27.1	.5685	l	t	m-c	m	r	b	w, s, t
Do	30	10	16		5	23.5	.6412	l	t	m-c	m	r	b	w, s, t
Molinera Gordo:														
Lenoir	3		5½			23	.5175	t	l	m	l	r	r	s, t
Mondeuse:														
Own roots	15	4	15	3	6	25.4	.6170	m	cy	m	m	r	b	w
Aramon × Rupestris Ganzin, No. 1	45	15	14		4	25.2	.7781	m	cy	m	m	r	b	w
Dog Ridge	50	8	8½	5	3	24.4	.9930	m	cy	m	m	r	b	w
Herbemont	30	20	7	2	3	22.4	.6895	m	cy	m	m	r	b	w
Lenoir	25	20		10	8	21.7	.6991	m	cy	m	m	r	b	w
Mourvedre × Rupestris, No. 1202	40	10	5	2	4	25.4	.8930	m	cy	m	m	r	b	w
Riparia × Rupestris, No. 101	40	12			5	24	.8125	m	cy	m	m	r	b	w
Riparia × Rupestris, No. 3309	40	10	6	3	5	25.4	.9162	m	cy	m	m	r	b	w
Rupestris Martin	50	5	6			20.3	.8750	m	cy	m	m	r	b	w
Rupestris St. George	5	5	15	6	8	21.8	.8220	m	cy	m	m	r	b	w
Salt Creek	60	10			12	23.7	.7700	m	cy	m	m	r	b	w
Solonis × Riparia, No. 1616	25	25	5			23.5	.7600	m	cy	m	m	r	b	w
Taylor Narbonne	35	10	13	9		24.3	.8231	m	cy	m	m	r	b	w

TABLE VII.—*Relative behavior and value for different purposes of grape varieties tested by grafting on resistant stocks and by growing on their own roots in eleven experiment vineyards in California*—Continued.

Variety and stock (on own roots, if so stated).	Weight of fruit per vine (pounds).					Sugar, Balling scale.	Acid, as tartaric (grams per 100 c. c.).	Cluster.			Berry.			Use.
	1909	1910	1911	1912	1913			Size.	Shape.	Compact or loose.	Size.	Shape.	Color.	
1	17	18	19	20	21	22	23	24	25	26	27	28	29	30
Moneca Nero:						*P. cent.*								
Own roots	5	10	4	18		23.8	0.5700	l	t	c	m	r	b	w, t
Mourastel:														
Own roots	3	3	2	8	6	20.2	.8235	m-l	t	m	m	r	b	w
Aramon × Rupestris Ganzin, No. 1	40		19	10	12	19.9	1.0500	m-l	t	m	m	r	b	w
Dog Ridge		10		12		23.1	1.0125	m-l	t	m	m	r	b	w
Herbemont			11	2		20	.8850	m-l	t	m	m	r	b	w
Lenoir					31	24	.8250	m-l	t	m	m	r	b	w
Riparia × Rupestris, No. 101	60	8	15	4	6	22.5	.9330	m-l	t	m	m	r	b	w
Riparia × Rupestris, No 3309	60	5	12	3	15	22.2	.9825	m-l	t	m	m	r	b	w
Solonis × Riparia, No. [illegible]61	40	25	11	3	2	21.7	.9855	m-l	t	m	m	r	b	w
[illegible]r [illegible]e	60	10	11		12	22.2	.9622	m-l	t	m	m	r	b	w
Mo[illegible] Bianca:														
Own roots	10	6	6	18	2	23	.5490	l	t	l	m	ob	w	t, s, w
Dog Ridge	50	10			8	21	.4450	l	t	l	m	ob	w	t, s, w
Lenoir	60	10			40	19.4	.6725	l	t	l	m	ob	w	t, s, w
Rupestris St. George	25	12	18		30	24.4	.5750	l	t	l	m	ob	w	t, s, w
[illegible]r [illegible]ne	40	2	6			23.4	.5300	l	t	l	m	ob	w	t, s, w
Mourisco Preto:														
Own roots	12	10	2	3		25.7	.5662	m	t	c	s	o	b	w
Dog Ridge	50	6	10		2	24.8	.7687	m	t	c	s	o	b	w
Lenoir	40	8	8	2	21	23.3	.8401	m	t	c	s	o	b	w
Rupestris St. George		7	6½	½	6	24.7	.7516	m	t	c	s	o	b	w
[illegible]adelle du Bordelais:														
Adobe Giant	10	4	2	9	4	25.4	.6615	m-l	l	m	m	r	w	w
Aramon × Rupestris Ganzin, No. 1	12	8	8	2	2	27.3	.5420	m-l	l	m	m	r	w	w
Lenoir	3	5	2	3	3	26.5	.6445	m-l	l	m	m	r	w	w
[illegible]e × Rupestris, No. 1202	15	9	5	8	12	28.9	.5885	m-l	l	m	m	r	w	w
Riparia Gloire	1	4	5	8	4	28.8	.6355	m-l	l	m	m	r	w	w
Riparia × Rupestris, No. 101	20	7	8	19	16	28.2	.5730	m-l	l	m	m	r	w	w
Riparia × Rupestris, No. 3309	20	8	10	15	3	27.7	.5750	m-l	l	m	m	r	w	w
Rupestris St. George	25	6	8	28	4	28.2	.6245	m-l	l	m	m	r	w	w
Solonis × Riparia, No. 1616	10	0	3			30.5	.5772	m-l	l	m	m	r	w	w
[illegible]r [illegible]ne	10	½	5	8		32.1	.6450	m-l	l	m	m	r	w	w

[1] [illegible] (S. P. I. No. 3063):													
Own [illegible]s	15					16.2	.6600	m-l	t, cy	m	m	ob	b	s, t
[illegible] [illegible]ns:													
Own [illegible]s	4	1		5	2	23.2	.7569	m-l	l	m	m	ob	b	s, t
Aramon × Rupestris Ganzin, No. 1	8	8	1			27	.5225	m-l	l	m	m	ob	b	s, t
Lenoir	12	3	3	1½	2	24.9	.5125	m-l	l	m	m	ob	b	s, t
[illegible]e × [illegible]s, No. 1202	25	10	3	18	20	26.6	.4940	m-l	l	m	m	ob	b	s, t
[illegible]a Gl[illegible]e	10	6	2	32	1	26.2	.5580	m-l	l	m	m	ob	b	s, t
[illegible]a × Rupestris, No. 101	8	12	1	21	6	27.6	.5060	m-l	l	m	m	ob	b	s, t
Riparia × Rupestris, No. 3309	30	0	10	13	8	26.4	.4462	m-l	l	m	m	ob	b	s, t
Rupestris St. George	15	5	8	8	6	28	.5635	m-l	l	m	m	ob	b	s, t
[illegible]is × [illegible]a, No. 1616	5	0	1	2		27.1	.4375	m-l	l	m	m	ob	b	s, t
[illegible]r Narbonne	6	4	5	18		24.7	.4312	m-l	l	m	m	ob	b	s, t
[illegible]t [illegible]:													
[illegible]ri × Riparia, No. 420A			13			23	.7500	m	t	l	m-l	o	w	s, t
De [illegible]t				3		30	.4650	m	t	l	m-l	o	w	s, t
[illegible]ir	10	2	9½		2	22.3	.6094	m	t	l	m-l	o	w	s, t
Riparia × Rupestris, No. 101						28	.5250	m	t	l	m-l	o	w	s, t
[illegible]a × Rupestris, No. 3309				14		31	.5475	m	t	l	m-l	o	w	s, t
Rupestris [illegible]. George						25	.6750	m	t	l	m-l	o	w	s, t
[illegible]s Robusta						27	.8325	m	t	l	m-l	o	w	s, t
[illegible]a				8		28	.5175	m	t	l	m-l	o	w	s, t
[illegible]t [illegible]s:													
Own [illegible]s				3		29	.8250	l	t	l	m-l	o	b	s, t
Dog Ridge	15					27.2	.6500	l	t	l	m-l	o	b	s, t
Lenoir	40		6			25.3	.7173	l	t	l	m-l	o	b	s, t
[illegible]s St. George	40		11		4	24.3	.7575	l	t	l	m-l	o	b	s, t
[illegible]r:													
Own roots		5	1	12	6	25.4	.6525	m	cy	c	s	r	w	s, w
[illegible]g Ridge	8	4	15	9	2	28.3	.6555	m	cy	c	s	r	w	s, w
Lenoir	4	4	½	1	2	25.2	.7080	m	cy	c	s	r	w	s, w
Riparia [illegible]e	1		1	1		25.5	.6200	m	cy	c	s	r	w	s, w
Rupestris St. George	20	3	1	6	10	30.1	.5790	m	cy	c	s	r	w	s, w
[illegible]t [illegible]s [illegible]ir Hatif:													
Own [illegible]s	3	½		4		23.7	.6350	m-l	l	l	m-l	o	b	s, t, w
Dog R[illegible]e	25	2	3	9		25	.7540	m-l	l	l	m-l	o	b	s, t, w
[illegible]ir	20	5	5	1	4	24.4	.7500	m-l	l		m-l	o	b	s, t, w
[illegible]s St. George	12	5	7			23.3	.8075	m-l	l	l	m-l	o	b	s, t, w
[illegible]r n[illegible]e	30	5	2			24.4	.8525	m-l	l	l	m-l	o	b	s, t, w
[illegible]t [illegible]g:													
Own [illegible]s						26.7	.5550	m	l	l	m	o	b	s, t, w
Aramon × Rupestris [illegible], No. 1			3			27	.5775	m	l	l	m	o	b	s, t, w
Dog R[illegible]e	30	1½	4		2	24.5	.7080	m	l	l	m	o	b	s, t, w
L[illegible]ir	40	2	10	½	2	23	.6285	m	l	l	m	o	b	s, t, w
[illegible]a × Rupestris		4				28.2	.6075	m	l	l	m	o	b	s, t, w
[illegible]a × Rupestris, No. 3309		4	2			24.5	.6050	m	l	l	m	o	b	s, t, w
[illegible]s [illegible]. [illegible]e	25	12	13			22.7	.6150	m	l	l	m	o	b	s, t, w
Rupestris × Berlandieri, No. 219A		3	2½			26.5	.5625	m	l	l	m	o	b	s, t, w
[illegible]r Narbonne	15	5				23.8	.6025	m	l	l	m	o	b	s, t, w
[illegible]t [illegible]g [illegible]ir d'Hongrie:													
Own roots	3	2	½	15		23.8	.6918	m	l	l	m	o	b	s, t, w

TABLE VII.—*Relative behavior and value for different purposes of grape varieties tested by grafting on resistant stocks and by growing on their own roots in eleven experiment vineyards in California*—Continued.

Variety and stock (on own roots, if so stated).	Weight of fruit per vine (pounds).					Sugar, Balling scale.	Acid, as tartaric (grams per 100 c. c.).	Cluster.			Berry.			Use.
	1909	1910	1911	1912	1913			Size.	Shape.	Compact or loose.	Size.	Shape.	Color.	
1	17	18	19	20	21	22	23	24	25	26	27	28	29	30
Muscat Noir d'Hongrie:						*P. cent.*								
Lenoir	8	6	½	1½	3	27	0.4650	m	l	l	m	o	b	s, t, w
Do	50	10	10	1		22.6	.6731	m	l	l	m	o	b	s, t, w
Riparia Gloire	15	15	3			27.8	.6285	m	l	l	m	o	b	s, t, w
Rupestris St. George	12	8	1	16	2	28.1	.5520	m	l	l	m	o	b	s, t, w
Do	30	8	9	½	2	23.6	.6675	m	l	l	m	o	b	s, t, w
Muscat Noir Precoce:														
Aramon × Rupestris Ganzin, No. 2		4	10			23.9	.6187	m	l	l	m	o	b	s, t, w
Dog Ridge	25	2		4		22.8	.5625	m	l	l	m	o	b	s, t, w
Lenoir	60	8	13	1	4	21.5	.6010	m	l	l	m	o	b	s, t, w
Lukfata		2	5			24.1	.6337	m	l	l	m	o	b	s, t, w
Monticola × Riparia, No. 18804			4			25	.5625	m	l	l	m	o	b	s, t, w
Rupestris St. George	25	8	12		½	23.3	.5587	m	l	l	m	o	b	s, t, w
Rupestris × Berlandieri, No. 219A		3	3			26.3	.5437	m	l	l	m	o	b	s, t, w
Solonis × Othello			6			26	.5100	m	l	l	m	o	b	s, t, w
Taylor Narbonne	40	8	12			23.5	.5850	m	l	l	m	o	b	s, t, w
Muscat Rose:														
Dog Ridge	10	3	6	5	2	27.3	.6837	m	cy	c	s	r	r	s, t, w
Lenoir	7	0	3	½		27.9	.6400	m	cy	c	s	r	r	s, t, w
Riparia Gloire	2	2	2	5		29.7	.5156	m	cy	c	s	r	r	s, t, w
Rupestris St. George	15	1	4	8	2	28.7	.5025	m	cy	c	s	r	r	s, t, w
Muscat Rouge de Madère:														
Lenoir								m	cy	c	s	r	r	s, t, w
Riparia Gloire			½	2	2	29	.9325	m	cy	c	s	r	r	s, t, w
Rupestris St. George		2		6	6	28.6	.7500	m	cy	c	s	r	r	s, t, w
Muscat Talabot:														
Own roots	5					26	.3525	s	cy	l	s	r	r	s, t, w
Lenoir	10		¼		19	22.9	.5494	s	cy	l	s	r	r	s, t, w
Rupestris St. George			2		9	22.5	.6600	s	cy	l	s	r	r	s, t, w
Napoleon:														
Own roots			2	2		23.5	.6637	m	r	l	l	ob	w	s, t, w

Nasa Valentiana:														
Own roots	1					22	.4575	m	t	m	l	r	w	s, t, w
Rupestris St. George	5	10		3	2	24.6	.4706	m	t	m	l	r	w	s, t, w
Nebbiolo:														
Own roots	5	½	3½	3½	4	22.7	.7202	m	cy	c	m	r	b	w
Dog Ridge	40	15	8			24.4	.6133	m	cy	c	m	r	b	w
Lenoir	35	8	12	2	34	22.8	.7050	m	cy	c	m	r	b	w
Rupestris St. George	5	4			6½	25.3	.5400	m	cy	c	m	r	b	w
Nebbiolo Bourgu:														
Dog Ridge	10	1½	8	½		24.3	1.0012	m	t	c	m-l	r	b	w
Lenoir	20				1½	23.5	.9632	m	t	c	m-l	r	b	w
Rupestris St. George	5	5			9	23.8	.8666	m	t	c	m-l	r	b	w
Taylor Narbonne	5	2				25	.8587	m	t	c	m-l	r	b	w
Bilo Fino:														
Dog Ridge	12	½	2½			23.7	1.0125	m	t	c	m-l	r	b	w
Lenoir	15	2				23.9	.7987	m	t	c	m-l	r	b	w
Rupestris St. George	10	1	6		4	24.3	.9262	m	t	c	m-l	r	b	w
Taylor [illegible]ne								m	t	c	m-l	r	b	w
Negrara di Gattinara:														
Own roots	2	⅓	2			26.3	.5550	m	lt	c	m-l	r	b	w
Negro [illegible]o:														
Own roots	8	8	½	19	1	27.5	.9950	m	t	c	s	r	b	w
[illegible]ta di Costilla:														
Own [illegible]ts	3		2	3		23.8	.5450	m	t	m	m	r	b	w
[illegible]ru di Boe:														
Own roots	1		2	15	7	25.5	.7313	s	cy	c	m	ob	b	w
Ohanez:														
[illegible]ir								l	t	m	l	ob	w	s, t, st
Oli[illegible]te Blanche:														
Adobe Giant				32		17	.8475	l	t	m	l	ob	w	s, t
Lenoir	12	4	8		4	19.7	.9000	l	t	m	l	ob	w	s, t
Riparia à [illegible]es Feuilles		3		21		20.1	.7125	l	t	m	l	ob	w	s, t
Riparia × Rupestris, No. 101	3					23.6	.5325	l	t	m	l	ob	w	s, t
[illegible]te [illegible]:														
Lenoir	8		4			22.1	.6825	l	t	m	l	ob	w	s, t
Solonis Robusta						19	.9825	l	t	m	l	ob	w	s, t
[illegible]te Noir:														
Lenoir	8	2	6½			21	.5775	l	t	m	l	ob	b	s, t
[illegible]re × Rupestris, No. 1202			15			24	.4050	l	t	m	l	ob	b	s, t
Riparia × Rupestris, No. 3309		3				26.2	.8100	l	t	m	l	ob	b	s, t
Solonis × Othello, No. 1613			14			24	.5250	l	t	m	l	ob	b	s, t
Oli[illegible]tte Rose:														
Lenoir	20		5½		3	20	.7925	l	t	m	l	ob	r	s, t
Opiman:														
Lenoir								l	t	l	l	ob	w	s, t
Orleans:														
Own rots	3	3		4		21.5	.7925	s	cy	c	s	r	w	w
Pagadebito:														
Own rots	3	10	6	10		22	.6112	m	cy	m	m	r	b	w, s, t
Dog Ridge	40	2	10	1	4	23	8957	m	cy	m	m	r	b	w, s, t

TABLE VII.—*Relative behavior and value for different purposes of grape varieties tested by grafting on resistant stocks and by growing on their own roots in eleven experiment vineyards in California*—Continued.

Variety and stock (on own roots, if so stated).	Weight of fruit per vine (pounds).					Sugar, Balling scale.	Acid, as tartaric (grams per 100 c. c.).	Cluster.			Berry.			Use.
	1909	1910	1911	1912	1913			Size.	Shape.	Compact or loose.	Size.	Shape.	Color.	
1	17	18	19	20	21	22	23	24	25	26	27	28	29	30
Pagadebito—Continued.						*P. cent*								
Lenoir	$40\frac{4}{5}$	3	7	10	38	23.6	0.7530	m	cy	m	m	r	b	w, s, t
Rupestris St. George	35		11		28	22.6	.8035	m	cy	m	m	r	b	w, s, t
Taylor Narbonne	15	4	5	2	1	23.4	.6945	m	cy	m	m	r	b	w, s, t
Palarusa:														
Own roots		8	20	30		18.6	.8325	l	cy-t	c	m	ob	w	s, t
Panariti:														
Adobe Giant	3					32	.7735	m-l	cy	c	vs	r	b	r, w, s
Aramon × Rupestris Ganzin, No. 1	10		10			32.8	.7050	m-l	cy	c	vs	r	b	r, w, s
Dog Ridge	3		4			33	.6562	m-l	cy	c	vs	r	b	r, w, s
Herbemont								m-l	cy	c	vs	r	b	r, w, s
Lenoir			4			29	.5700	m-l	cy	c	vs	r	b	r, w, s
Mourvèdre × Rupestris, No. 1202	2		3			29.8	.6562	m-l	cy	c	vs	r	b	r, w, s
Riparia Gloire	2		3			28.1	.7387	m-l	cy	c	vs	r	b	r, w, s
Riparia × Rupestris, No. 101								m-l	cy	c	vs	r	b	r, w, s
Riparia × Rupestris, No. 3309	3		5			34.8	.6375	m-l	cy	c	vs	r	b	r, w, s
Rupestris Martin								m-l	cy	c	vs	r	b	r, w, s
Rupestris St. George	2		5			34.5	.6337	m-l	cy	c	vs	r	b	r, w, s
Salt Creek			3			29	.6000	m-l	cy	c	vs	r	b	r, w, s
Solonis × Riparia, No. 1616	3		5			33.5	.6070	m-l	cy	c	vs	r	b	r, w, s
Taylor Narbonne			2			31	.6900	m-l	cy	c	vs	r	b	r, w, s
Parc de Versailles:														
[illegible]	10	2	3	27	6	21.5	.5225	m	t	m	l	ob	w	s, t
Aramon × Rupestris Ganzin, No. 1	2	3	2	3	18	21.5	.5353	m	t	m	l	ob	w	s, t
Dog Ridge	5	4	$2\frac{1}{2}$	$18\frac{1}{2}$	13	19.3	.7450	m	t	m	l	ob	w	s, t
[illegible]	$\frac{1}{2}$	3		5	3	21.8	.5362	m	t	m	l	ob	w	s, t
Mourvèdre × Rupestris, No. 1202	1	2		5	2	21.9	.5431	m	t	m	l	ob	w	s, t
Ponroy						20	.6150	m	t	m	l	ob	w	s, t
Riparia Gloire	6	1	4	41	20	22.2	.4875	m	t	m	l	ob	w	s, t
Riparia × Rupestris, No. 101								m	t	m	l	ob	w	s, t
Riparia × Rupestris, No. 3309	1	4	2	12	9	22.1	.5460	m	t	m	l	ob	w	s, t

Rupestris Metallica	......	......	......	6	......	23	.5400	m	t	m	l	ob	w	s, t
[illegible]s St. George	10	1½	1½	15	8	20.3	.5055	m	t	m	l	ob	w	s, t
Solonis × Riparia, No. 1616	10	2	......	7	4	22.9	.5306	m	t	m	l	ob	w	s, t
Tay[illegible] N[illegible]be	5	1½	3	21	8	22.6	.5220	m	t	m	l	ob	w	s, t
Pedro X[illegible]s:														
Own roots	20	22	10	21	11	23.3	.5153	m	t	l	m	ob	w	w
[illegible]be Giant	15	20	15	3	2	22.1	.5845	m	t	l	m	ob	w	w
Aramon × [illegible]s Ganzin, No. 1	30	40	3	......	12	23.7	.4950	m	t	l	m	ob	w	w
Dog R[illegible]e	35	50	12	2	15	22.2	.5290	m	t	l	m	ob	w	w
Herbemont	10	4	......	......	......	23.3	.5350	m	t	l	m	b	w	w
Lenoir	40	30	2	2	1	21.9	.5130	m	t	l	m	ob	w	w
[illegible]e × Rupestris, No. 1202	40	50	8	20	28	22.5	.5355	m	t	l	m	ob	w	w
[illegible]ria Gloire	20	50	2	28	20	21	.5430	m	t	l	m	ob	w	w
[illegible]ia × Rupestris, No. 101	30	75	5	39	29	22	.4645	m	t	l	m	ob	w	w
Riparia × [illegible]s, No. 3309	50	60	10	43	17	22.3	.604	m	t	l	m	ob	w	w
[illegible]s Martin	10	4	6	......	1	22.4	.5137	m	t	l	m	ob	w	w
[illegible]is St. [illegible]e	45	40	5	18	10	22.1	.4[illegible]0	m	t	l	m	ob	w	w
Salt Creek	25	10	¼	3	2	21.4	.4890	m	t	l	m	ob	w	w
Solonis × [illegible]a, No. 1616	25	60	2	15	23	23	.5695	m	t	l	m	ob	w	w
[illegible]r [illegible]e	30	40	20	25	18	21.4	.4665	m	t	l	m	ob	w	w
Perle [illegible]e:														
[illegible]ir	20	3	5	......	3	23.2	.7806	m	t, cy	m	m	ob	w	w
[illegible]ris St. George	20	3	1½	......	8	19.7	.835	m	t, cy	m	m	ob	w	w
Lenoir	4	......	......	......	......	22	.3975	m	t, cy	m	m	ob	w	w
Perruno:														
Own roots	2	......	1	½	4	24	.4275	m	t, cy	l	l	ob	w	s, t
Persian, No. 21:														
Own roots	......	......	......	2	......	28	.555	m	t	l	m	ob	w	s, t
[illegible]n, No. 25:														
Own roots	......	......	......	3	......	24	.6075	m	t	l	m	ob	w	s, t
[illegible]n, No. 26:														
Own [illegible]s	......	......	......	1	......	24	.7125	m	t	l	m	ob	w	s, t
Peru:														
Lenoir	......	......	6½	3	5	23.3	.6275	m	t	m	l	ob	b	s, t, w
[illegible]tit r[illegible]h:														
Own roots	......	......	......	......	12	20	1.0500	m	t, cy	c	m	r	b	w
[illegible]e G[illegible]t	......	......	6	......	5	21	.7312	m	t, cy	c	m	r	b	w
[illegible]s × Monti[illegible]ola) × (Riparia × Rupestris, No. 554-5)	......	......	19	25	21	20	.8125	m	t, cy	c	m	r	b	w
[illegible]n × Rupestris [illegible]in, No. 1	......	......	11	7½	29½	20.6	.9025	m	t, cy	c	m	r	b	w
Do	25	20	9	......	......	23.1	.8325	m	t, cy	c	m	r	b	w
Aramon × [illegible]s [illegible]in, No. 2	......	......	4	4½	3	22	.8733	m	t, cy	c	m	r	b	w
[illegible]n × Rupestris [illegible]in, No. 9	......	......	......	1	3	23.5	.8250	m	t, cy	c	m	r	b	w
[illegible]is	......	......	6	1½	9½	20.3	.7345	m	t, cy	c	m	r	b	w
Berlandieri, No. 1	......	......	3	3	21	21	.7550	m	t, cy	c	m	r	b	w
Berlandieri, No. 2	......	......	9	4	8	21.6	.7683	m	t, cy	c	m	r	b	w
[illegible]ri [illegible]fant, No. 9	......	......	8	4	30	23	.7900	m	t, cy	c	m	r	b	w
[illegible]ri × Riparia, No. 34EM	......	......	......	......	......	......	......	m	t, cy	c	m	r	b	w
Berlandieri × Riparia, No. 157-11	......	......	4	3	10	22	.8825	m	t, cy	c	m	r	b	w
[illegible]dieri × Riparia, No. 420A	......	......	2	......	3	25	.8600	m	t, cy	c	m	r	b	w
Do	......	......	3	2	......	25.5	.9562	m	t, cy	c	m	r	b	w

TABLE VII.—*Relative behavior and value for different purposes of grape varieties tested by grafting on resistant stocks and by growing on their own roots in eleven experiment vineyards in California*—Continued.

Variety and stock (on own roots, if so stated).	Weight of fruit per vine (pounds). 1909	1910	1911	1912	1913	Sugar, Balling scale.	Acid, as tartaric (grams per 100 c. c.).	Cluster. Size.	Cluster. Shape.	Cluster. Compact or loose.	Berry. Size.	Berry. Shape.	Berry. Color.	Use.
1	17	18	19	20	21	22	23	24	25	26	27	28	29	30
Petit Syrah—Continued.						*P. cent.*								
[redacted]u × [redacted], No. 109-4	......	......	17	1/3	12	21	1.1850	m	t, cy	c	m	r	b	w
[redacted]u × [redacted]is, No. 601) × Calcicola, No. 1[redacted]5	......	......	9	3⅓	18½	21.8	.7800	m	t, cy	c	m	r	b	w
[redacted]u × [redacted]s, No. 3907	......	......	8	7	9	21.6	.8041	m	t, cy	c	m	r	b	w
r[redacted]t × Berlandieri, No. 333	......	......	8	6 7/10	10½	20.3	.8600	m	t, cy	c	m	r	b	w
r[redacted]t × [redacted]s Ganzin, No. 33A	......	......	6	2	16	22	1.2833	m	t, cy	c	m	r	b	w
Captain	......	......	......	2	......	18	.6750	m	t, cy	c	m	r	b	w
[redacted]s × [redacted]ri, No. 41B	......	......	5	1 7/10	19	21.6	.8275	m	t, cy	c	m	r	b	w
[redacted]a	......	......	4	1	8	23	.7725	m	t, cy	c	m	r	b	w
Dog R[redacted]e	......	......	24	5	35	20.6	.8150	m	t, cy	c	m	r	b	w
Do	50	10	11	8	6	20.2	.8670	m	t, cy	c	m	r	b	w
[redacted]nt	25	25	4	......	12	20.5	.8700	m	t, cy	c	m	r	b	w
Hotporup	......	......	14	2	11	21.3	.7975	m	t, cy	c	m	r	b	w
Joly	......	......	6	3	13	18.3	.7517	m	t, cy	c	m	r	b	w
Judge	......	......	1	1	5½	21.3	.7700	m	t, cy	c	m	r	b	w
[redacted]ir	30	18	40	8	6	23.1	.7365	m	t, cy	c	m	r	b	w
[redacted]la × [redacted]a, No. 554	......	......	3	2	20	21.6	.7917	m	t, cy	c	m	r	b	w
[redacted]la × [redacted]a, No. 18808	......	......	......	3	4	23.5	1.0087	m	t, cy	c	m	r	b	w
[redacted]la × Rupestris	......	......	8	3	12½	23.3	.7550	m	t, cy	c	m	r	b	w
Motley	......	......	5	3	5	21	.8225	m	t, cy	c	m	r	b	w
[redacted]e × [redacted]s, No. 1202	......	......	8	6½	30	23.6	.8775	m	t, cy	c	m	r	b	w
Do	......	......	20	......	19	22.5	.8175	m	t, cy	c	m	r	b	w
Mourvedre × Rupestris, No. 1203	......	......	......	......	1½	23	.9750	m	t, cy	c	m	r	b	w
Pardes	......	......	1	2	22½	21.6	.7600	m	t, cy	c	m	r	b	w
Riparia du Colorado	......	......	4	2 3/16	15½	19.6	.7850	m	t, cy	c	m	r	b	w
Riparia × (Cordifolia × Rupestris), No. 106-8	......	......	7	5	28½	19.6	.6508	m	t, cy	c	m	r	b	w
Riparia × Rupestris, No. 101	......	......	20	5⅛	34	22.3	.8600	m	t, cy	c	m	r	b	w
Do	50	5	11	......	2	22	.8725	m	t, cy	c	m	r	b	w
Riparia × Rupestris, No. 101-14	......	......	11	4½	28½	19.3	.7617	m	t, cy	c	m	r	b	w
Do	......	......	......	......	......	......	......	m	t, cy	c	m	r	b	w
Riparia × Rupestris, No. 108-103	......	......	8	......	12½	21	.8512	m	t, cy	c	m	r	b	w
Riparia × Rupestris, No. 3306	......	......	34	2½	37½	20.7	.8325	m	t, cy	c	m	r	b	w

Do.			7	1	3	23.3	.9450	m	t, cy	c	m	r	b	w
[illegible]a × [illegible]s, No. 3309			26	8	32	23	.6900	m	t, cy	c	m	r	b	w
Do.	60	6	9	3	4	22.2	.7853	m	t, cy	c	m	r	b	w
[illegible]s des [illegible]ettes			7	1	21½	21.3	.8617	m	t, cy	c	m	r	b	w
[illegible]s [illegible]			16	5		19	.9332	m	t, cy	c	m	r	b	w
Do.	45	8	9	1	6	22.4	.9885	m	t, cy	c	m	r	b	w
[illegible]s [illegible]a			5	3½	12½	21	.8020	m	t, cy	c	m	r	b	w
Do.			9			22	1.1025	m	t, cy	c	m	r	b	w
[illegible]s [illegible]n			8	4½	13½	20	.8825	m	t	l	m	ob	w	w
Do.			9	4	12½	20.5	.9000	m	t	l	m	ob	w	w
[illegible]s St. [illegible]ge			16	4	28	22.3	.7 60	m	t	l	m	ob	w	w
Do.	50	12	13	6	8	21.5	.8060	m	t	l	m	ob	w	w
[illegible]s × Berlandieri, No. [illegible]9A			12	6	29	19	.9250	m	t	l	m	ob	w	w
[illegible]is × [illegible]e[illegible], No. 301A			8	3½	28	17.8	1.0300	m	t	l	m	ob	w	w
[illegible]is × [illegible]ri, No. [illegible]1B			13		32½	20	.8125	m	t	l	m	ob	w	w
[illegible]s × (Cordifolia × Rup[illegible]tris), No. 202-5			10	3½	17	20.3	.7696	m	t	l	m	ob	w	w
Rupestris × Hybrid [illegible]r, No. 215			2	1 7/10	1½	22.6	.8275	m	t	l	m	ob	w	w
Salt C[illegible]k			7	3½	13	21.6	.7425	m	t	l	m	ob	w	w
Do.	40	3	5	4	3	20.7	.826	m	t	l	m	ob	w	w
[illegible]s [illegible]e			2	2	2	20	.7900	m	t	l	m	ob	w	w
[illegible]s Robusta			7	5	23½	22	.7300	m	t	l	m	ob	w	w
Do.			8			27	.8475	m	t	l	m	ob	w	w
[illegible]s × Othello			15	4	31½	19.9	.7200	m	t	l	m	ob	w	w
[illegible]is × [illegible]llo, No. 1613			4			23	.8625	m	t	l	m	ob	w	w
[illegible]s × Riparia, No. 1616			24	3	28	21.6	.7450	m	t	l	m	ob	w	w
Do.	60	15	9			24.1	.8325	m	t	l	m	ob	w	w
[illegible]r [illegible]e			4	2	7	19.6	.8000	m	t	l	m	ob	w	w
Do.	50	8	18	5	8	23.4	.8301	m	t	l	m	ob	w	w
[illegible]t Verdot:														
[illegible]n [illegible]s	3	4		1	2	24.7	.7700	m	cy	c	m	r	b	w
Dog R[illegible]ge	35	7	12	½		22.8	.8231	m	cy	c	m	r	b	w
Lenoir	40	10	10⅓	3	16	24.2	.7115	m	cy	c	m	r	b	w
[illegible]s St. [illegible]ge	45	5	8	¼	18	23.7	.7325	m	cy	c	m	r	b	w
Tay[illegible]r [illegible]e	30	5	3		1	23.3	.6844	m	cy	c	m	r	b	w
[illegible]ella:														
[illegible]n [illegible]ts	2		8	17	18	26	.7819	m-l	cy	c	m	r	w	w
Dog Ridge	40		8	½		22.3	.9175	m-l	cy	c	m	r	w	w
Lenoir	50	10	12	3	3	22.1	.8715	m-l	cy	c	m	r	w	w
[illegible]s St. [illegible]ge	50	10	14	¾	24	22.8	.8520	m-l	cy	c	m	r	w	w
Taylor N[illegible]e	40	8	3	½	2	25	.5130	m-l	cy	c	m	r	w	w
Picpoul:														
[illegible]n [illegible]ts			8	11		22.5	.6862	s	cy	l	s	ob	w	w
[illegible]:														
[illegible]ir	15	8	12			18.1	.6200	v-l	l	l	l	ob	r	s, t, st
[illegible]e [illegible]t:														
[illegible]n [illegible]s		2		2		21.5	.6937	m	l	c	m	ob	b	s, t
[illegible]u de Chardo[illegible]nay:														
[illegible]n [illegible]	4	8		10		25	.6137	s	cy	c	s	r	w	w
[illegible]n × [illegible]s Ganzin, No. 1		4				24.3	.6150	s	cy	c	s	r	w	w
Dog R[illegible]e	8	2	2		2	25.2	.7281	s	cy	c	s	r	w	w
[illegible]t.	2	4				24.9	.7912	s	cy	c	s	r	w	w
[illegible]ir	12	1	1		2	23.3	.7581	s	cy	c	s	r	w	w

TABLE VII.—*Relative behavior and value for different purposes of grape varieties tested by grafting on resistant stocks and by growing on their own roots in eleven experiment vineyards in California*—Continued.

Variety and stock (on own roots, if so stated).	Weight of fruit per vine (pounds).					Sugar, Balling scale.	Acid, as tartaric (grams per 100 c. c.).	Cluster.			Berry.			Use.
	1909	1910	1911	1912	1913			Size.	Shape.	Compact or loose.	Size.	Shape.	Color.	
1	17	18	19	20	21	22	23	24	25	26	27	28	29	30
[illegible] de Chardonnay—Continued.						*P. cent.*								
[illegible] × [illegible], No. 1202		5				28.3	0.7125	s	cy	c	s	r	w	w
[illegible] × [illegible], No. 101	4					27	.6600	s	cy	c	s	r	w	w
[illegible] × Rupestris, No. 3309	4	1½	4			27.9	.8475	s	cy	c	s	r	w	w
[illegible] Martin	3	1	2		2½	25.6	.7744	s	cy	c	s	r	w	w
[illegible] St. [illegible]	7		2			27.5	.7527	s	cy	c	s	r	w	w
Salt [illegible]	8		1		3	25.3	.8128	s	cy	c	s	r	w	w
Solonis × [illegible], No. 1616	25		9½			21.5	.5512	s	cy	c	s	r	w	w
Taylor [illegible]	2	1	1			28.3	.6791	s	cy	c	s	r	w	w
[illegible] de [illegible]:														
[illegible]	4	1½	2	18		23.1	.7031	s	cy	c	s	r	w	w
[illegible]	15	2	3			23.3	.6858	s	cy	c	s	r	w	w
[illegible]	15	5	7			21.7	.8375	s	cy	c	s	r	w	w
[illegible] St. George	20	10				23.5	.7200	s	cy	c	s	r	w	w
[illegible]:														
[illegible]	3	1½				27.5	.5187	s	cy	c	s	r	b	w
[illegible]	10				4	25.1	.4837	s	cy	c	s	r	b	w
[illegible] St. George	15	3	4			26.1	.7175	s	cy	c	s	r	b	w
[illegible]:														
[illegible] roots			½	3	3	25.6	.7683	s	cy	c	s	r	w	w
[illegible] St. George:														
[illegible] roots	12	4	8	26	9	24.7	.6560	m	cy	m	m	ob	b	w
[illegible]	35	5	12		2	23.5	.6806	m	cy	m	m	ob	b	w
[illegible]	15	1		3	20	24.5	.6356	m	cy	m	m	ob	b	w
[illegible] St. George	10	2	3	½	8	24.7	.6210	m	cy	m	m	ob	b	w
[illegible]:														
[illegible]	2		1	3		27.7	.6450	s	t	c	s	ob	w	w
Pis de [illegible] Alps:														
[illegible]						24	.5375	m-l	t	l	m	ob	r	w
[illegible]	25	8	⅓	3		21.3	.6618	m-l	t	l	m	ob	r	w
[illegible]	10	15		2	12	19.2	.7412	m-l	t	l	m	ob	r	w
[illegible] St. George	20	15	12	½	7	22.6	.7605	m-l	t	l	m	ob	r	w
Pis de [illegible]:														
Lenoir	2		1½			25.1	.8062	m-l	t	l	m	ob	r	w

[illegible]la:														
Own roots			½	2		23	.3787	l	t	n	l	o	w	s, t, r
Adobe Giant	12	20	2	4	16	22.4	.4020	l	t	m	l	o	w	s, t, r
Aramon × Rupestris Ganzin, No. 1	8	12	4	4½	12	24.5	.4660	l	t	m	l	o	w	s, t, r
Dog Ridge	3	3	2			232	.3[illegible]1	l	t	m	l	o	w	s, t, r
Herbemont						24.8	.3075	l	t	n	l	o	w	s, t, r
Lenoir	10	6	4	1	2	23	.3485	l	t	m	l	o	w	s, t, r
Mourvedre × Rupestris, No. 1202	6	10	5	12	3	23.6	.4005	l	t	m	l	o	w	s, t, r
Riparia Gloire	6	3	3	12	7	235	.2[illegible]0	l	t	n	l	o	w	s, t, r
Riparia × Rupestris, No. 101	12	25	2	12	2	24.6	.4726	l	t	m	l	o	w	s, t, r
Riparia × Rupestris, No. 3309	10	10	3	8	1	22.3	.3[illegible]0	l	t	m	l	o	w	s, t, r
Rupestris Martin	3	0	½			27.8	.3300	l	t	m	l	o	w	s, t, r
Rupestris St. George	15	10	4	5	8	24.9	.3336	l	t	m	l	o	w	s, t, r
Salt Creek	4	2	1	2	1	23.6	.4635	l	t	m	l	o	w	s, t, r
Solonis × Riparia, No. 1616	10			12	1	25.1	.5110	l	t	m	l	o	w	s, t, r
Taylor Narbonne	1	20	1	8	2	23.7	.2950	l	t	m	l	o	w	s, t, r
Poulsard:														
Own roots	5		½	1½		27	.6466	l	cy	c	l	o	b	s, t, w
Precoce de Courtiller:														
Lenoir	4		½		2	22.1	.8006	s	cy	l	m	r	w	s, t, w
Rupestris St. George	4		5			22.1	.8058	s	cy	l	m	r	w	s, t, w
Prune de Cazouls:														
Aramon × Rupestris Ganzin, No. 2			25			22	.8162	l	t	c	l	o	b	s, t, st
Australis			12			18	.8475	l	t	c	l	o	b	s, t, st
Berlandieri × Riparia, No. 420A			8			25.5	.6262	l	t	c	l	o	b	s, t, st
Lenoir	18	5	12		6	20.2	.7550	l	t	c	l	o	b	s, t, st
Cordifolia × Riparia, No. 18804			12			25	.4275	l	t	c	l	o	b	s, t, st
Cordifolia × Riparia, No. 18808			32			21	.8925	l	t	c	l	o	b	s, t, st
Cordifolia × Rupestris			30			22	.7650	l	t	c	l	o	b	s, t, st
Riparia × (Cordifolia × Rupestris, No. 106–8)			20			25	.6625	l	t	c	l	o	b	s, t, st
Riparia × Rupestris, No. 101–14			12			22	.7800	l	t	c	l	o	b	s, t, st
Riparia × Rupestris, No. 3306			24			22	.7875	l	t	c	l	o	b	s, t, st
Rupestris Martin			15			20	.7950	l	t	c	l	o	b	s, t, st
Purple Damascus:														
Own roots			½	2½		23	.6075	m-l	t, cy	n	l	ob	b	s, t
Adobe Giant	40	40	2	12	3	232	.5630	m-l	t, cy	m	l	ob	b	s, t
Aramon × Rupestris Ganzin, No. 1	30	30	3	35	23	23.1	.7515	m-l	t, cy	m	l	ob	b	s, t
Dog Ridge	13	45	4½	10	6	23	.7[illegible]80	m-l	t, cy	m	l	ob	b	s, t
Lenoir	25	30	3	8	4	21.7	.[illegible]05	m-l	t, cy	m	l	ob	b	s, t
Mourvedre × Rupestris, No. 1202	20	50	10	20	2	22.1	.7065	m-l	t, cy	n	l	ob	b	s, t
Riparia Gloire	12	29	5	15	14	23.1	.6420	m-l	t, cy	m	l	ob	b	s, t
Riparia × Rupestris, No. 101	15	25	2	7	6	23.3	.5050	m-l	t, cy	m	l	ob	b	s, t
Riparia × Rupestris, No. 3309	15	40	3	36	22	23.1	.6795	m-l	t, cy	m	l	ob	b	s, t
Rupestris St. George	30	35	5	18	12	22.1	.5970	m-l	t, cy	n	l	ob	b	s, t
Solonis × Riparia, No. 1616	12	30	2	20	8	22.2	.5521	m-l	t, cy	m	l	ob	b	s, t
Taylor Narbonne	20	50	30	15	2	22.1	.5170	m-l	t, cy	n	l	ob	b	s, t
Quagliano:														
Own roots	10	10		30	7	23.5	.5606	m-l	cy	c	m	r	b	s, t, w
Dog Ridge	15	3	9		½	20.5	.6400	m-l	cy	c	m	r	b	s, t, w
Lenoir	60	17	13	6	33	20	.8085	m-l	cy	c	m	r	b	st, w
Rupestris St. George	40	5	13	1	17	22.7	.6285	m-l	cy	c	m	r	b	st, w
Taylor Narbonne	6	9	12	6		21.9	.6744	m-l	cy	c	m	r	b	s, t, w

TABLE VII.—*Relative behavior and value for different purposes of grape varieties tested by grafting on resistant stocks and by growing on their own roots in eleven experiment vineyards in California*—Continued.

Variety and stock (on own roots, if so stated).	Weight of fruit per vine (pounds).					Sugar, Balling scale.	Acid, as tartaric (grams per 100 c. c.).	Berry.			Cluster.			Use.
	1909	1910	1911	1912	1913			Size.	Shape.	Compact or loose.	Size.	Shape.	Color.	
1	17	18	19	20	21	22	23	24	25	26	27	28	29	30
Razaki Zolo:						*P. cent.*								
Own roots	2	4	1	2	.....	22.9	0.5400	m	cy	l	m	ob	r	s, t
Rupestris St. George	12	.....	.....	.....	.....	20.8	.5250	m	cy	l	m	ob	r	s, t
Riparia × Rupestris, No. 3306	12	.....	13	.....	.....	20.9	.6262	m	cy	l	m	ob	r	s, t
Refosco:														
Own roots	.....	.....	.....	2¼	.....	25	.8475	s	cy	c	m	r	b	w
Dog Ridge	30	10	6	6	4	28.7	.6840	s	cy	c	m	r	b	w
Lenoir	50	15	13½	8	28	23.2	.6995	s	cy	c	m	r	b	w
Rupestris St. George	40	15	10	3	32	24.1	.6690	s	cy	c	m	r	b	w
Taylor Narbonne	30	6	1½	1	3	24.5	.7005	s	cy	c	m	r	b	w
Ribier:														
Lenoir	10	.....	.....	.....	.....	22	.6750	s	cy	c	m	r	b	w
Rupestris St. George	10	.....	.....	.....	.....	21.5	.4800	s	cy	c	m	r	b	w
Robin Noir:														
Own roots	15	10	3	10	.....	25.5	.7337	l	cy	m	m	ob	b	w
Rodites:														
Lenoir	25	3	12	.....	.....	21.1	.6641	v, l	t	l	l	ob	r	s, st, l
Rose d'Italie:														
Lenoir	5	8	½	3	.....	23.2	.7250	m	t	l	m-l	ob	r	s, t, w
Riparia × Rupestris, No. 3309	15	7	4	.....	.....	26	.6100	m	t	l	m-l	ob	r	s, t, w
Rupestris St. George	10	1	.....	.....	.....	26.2	.6750	m	t	l	m-l	ob	r	s, t, w
Solonis × Riparia, No. 1616	15	12	15	2	.....	26.8	.6656	m	t	l	m-l	ob	r	s, t, w
Taylor Narbonne	5	.....	1	½	.....	23.6	.6850	m	t	l	m-l	ob	r	s, t, w
Rothgipfler:														
Own roots	20	3	20	8	.....	25.1	.6687	m	t	c	m	o	w	w
Roussaou:														
Own roots	10	1	.....	25	4	24.5	.7294	m	t	c	m	ob	w	w
Dog Ridge	15	10	9	2	.....	21.8	.6712	m	t	c	m	ob	w	w
Lenoir	20	15	5	2½	36	22.1	.5900	m	t	c	m	ob	w	w
Riparia × Rupestris, No. 3306	40	.....	12	.....	.....	24.3	.5625	m	t	c	m	ob	w	w
Riparia × Rupestris de Jaeger	.....	2	.....	2	.....	23.6	.5437	m	t	c	m	ob	w	w
Rupestris St. George	25	8	11	.....	23	24.4	.5212	m	t	c	m	ob	w	w

Solonis × Riparia, No. 1616	...	...	3	...	...	27	.5175	m	t	c	m	ob	w	w
Taylor Narbonne	20	...	...	...	...	23.2	.3750	m	t	c	m	ob	w	w
Royal [illegible]:														
Own roots	20	6	...	23	...	20.7	.6150	s	r	c	l	ro	b	s, t, st
Saint Laurent:														
Own roots	1½	3	1½	3	...	26.3	.4625	m	cy	c	m-l	o	w	s, t
Adobe Giant	8	14	8	3	...	25.4	.4218	m	cy	c	m-l	o	w	s, t
Aramon × Rupestris Ganzin, No. 1	8	10	10	12	2	24	.4130	m	cy	c	m-l	o	w	s, t
Dog Ridge	10	16	2	5	2	25.6	.4170	m	cy	c	m-l	o	w	s, t
Herbemont	12	1	3	...	1	25	.4512	m	cy	c	m-l	o	w	s, t
[illegible]	2	6	...	...	...	25.3	.4462	m	cy	c	m-l	o	w	s, t
Mourvedre × Rupestris, No. 1202	12	12	6	12	8	24.1	.4555	m	cy	c	m-l	o	w	s, t
Riparia Gloire	5	4	¾	2½	11	26.2	.4939	m	cy	c	m-l	o	w	s, t
Riparia × Rupestris, No. 101	8	12	2	3	2	26.5	.4710	m	cy	c	m-l	o	w	s, t
Riparia × Rupestris, No. 3309	...	15	3	1	2	24.1	.4287	m	cy	c	m-l	o	w	s, t
Rupestris Martin	10	½	4	...	...	26.2	.4125	m	cy	c	m-l	o	w	s, t
Rupestris St. George	5	10	12	10	8	25.8	.4545	m	cy	c	m-l	o	w	s, t
Salt Creek	10	5	2	1	...	27.2	.1594	m	cy	c	m-l	o	w	s, t
Solonis × Riparia, No. 1616	8	...	...	...	...	28	.3975	m	cy	c	m-l	o	w	s, t
Taylor Narbonne	12	½	...	...	...	29.1	.1360	m	cy	c	m-l	o	w	s, t
Saint Macaire:														
Own roots	12	4	4	11	...	22.2	.9056	m-l	r	c	m	ob	b	w
Aramon × Rupestris Ganzin, No. 1	...	...	2½	...	...	26	.8175	m-l	r	c	m	ob	b	w
Dog Ridge	20	5	11	2	2	23.6	.8630	m-l	r	c	m	ob	b	w
Lenoir	40	15	13	9	20	22	1.0275	m-l	r	c	m	ob	b	w
Mourvedre × Rupestris, No. 1202	...	...	...	...	6	24	.8250	m-l	r	c	m	ob	b	w
Rupestris St. George	40	10	11	3	20	24.8	.9400	m-l	r	c	m	ob	b	w
Solonis × Riparia, No. 1616	...	...	...	...	4	25	.7950	m-l	r	c	m	ob	b	w
Taylor Narbonne	50	10	9	½	3	22.4	1.1085	m-l	r	c	m	ob	b	w
San Gioveto:														
Dog Ridge	½	...	...	...	...	24	1.0500	s	t, cy	l	s	r	b	w
Lenoir	½	...	...	...	...	24	.8775	s	t, cy	l	s	r	b	w
Rupestris St. George	½	...	3	...	...	26.2	.9112	s	t, cy	l	s	r	b	w
Taylor Narbonne	...	...	...	...	...	...	...	s	t, cy	l	s	r	b	w
Satin Blanc:														
Dog Ridge	6	...	...	...	...	24	.3975	m	cy	c	m	r	w	s, t
Lenoir	3	...	...	...	2	24.7	.4700	m	cy	c	m	r	w	s, t
Rupestris St. George	8	...	...	...	6	23.3	.4950	m	cy	c	m	r	w	s, t
Sauvignon Blanc:														
Own roots	...	...	...	⅓	...	25	.5475	m	cy	c	m	r	w	s, t
[illegible]	12	10	12	6	3	21	.8190	m	cy	c	m	r	w	s, t
Lenoir	25	12	5½	3	36	20.6	.8635	m	cy	c	m	r	w	s, t
Rupestris St. George	5	...	14	...	7	22.3	.9100	m	cy	c	m	r	w	s, t
Sauvignon Vert:														
Own roots	10	10	15	24	23	25.1	.4785	s	t, cy	l	m	r	w	w
Aramon × Rupestris Ganzin, No. 1	60	40	19	10	15	23.4	.6495	s	t, cy	l	m	r	w	w
Aramon × Rupestris Ganzin, No. 2	...	...	2	...	...	27	.5775	s	t, cy	l	m	r	w	w
Berlandieri × Riparia, No. 420A	...	...	10	6	7	25.3	.6300	s	t, cy	l	m	r	w	w
[illegible]	...	...	1½	...	8	27.5	.6225	s	t, cy	l	m	r	w	w
Dog Ridge	55	12	16	20	21	22.7	.5975	s	t, cy	l	m	r	w	w
Herbemont	60	15	12	4	12	22.9	.5970	s	t, cy	l	m	r	w	w

TABLE VII.—*Relative behavior and value for different purposes of grape varieties tested by grafting on resistant stocks and by growing on their own roots in eleven experiment vineyards in California*—Continued.

Variety and stock (on own roots, if so stated).	Weight of fruit per vine (pounds). 1909	1910	1911	1912	1913	Sugar, Balling scale.	Acid, as tartaric (grams per 100 c. c.).	Cluster. Size.	Cluster. Shape.	Cluster. Compact or loose.	Berry. Size.	Berry. Shape.	Berry. Color.	Use.
1	17	18	19	20	21	22	23	24	25	26	27	28	29	30
S[illegible]in t[illegible]d.						*P. cent.*								
L[illegible]ir	45	15	9	5	5	24.4	0.5970	s	t, cy		m	r	w	w
[illegible]la × Riparia, No. 18808	½	1	3	......	......	24.3	.6530	s	t, cy	l	m	r	w	w
[illegible]re × Rupestris, No. 1202	50	12	13	2	18	22.8	.6825	s	t, cy	l	m	r	w	w
Riparia × Rupestris, No. 101	50	12	13	6	18	22.4	.6915	s	t, cy	l	m	r	w	w
Riparia × [illegible]s, No. 101–14	......	......	2	......	2	24.5	.5137	s	t, cy	l	m	r	w	w
Riparia × Rupestris, No. 3306	......	......	10	......	7	24.5	.6937	s	t, cy	l	m	r	w	w
Riparia × Rupestris, No. 3309	60	10	10	8	10	25.6	.6013	s	t, cy	l	m	r	w	w
Rupestris Martin	60	12	8	......	23	23.1	.5130	s	t, cy	l	m	r	w	w
Rupestris S[illegible]. [illegible]ge	55	8	5	2	4	25.1	.6325	s	t, cy	l	m	r	w	w
Salt [illegible]k	50	12	9	3	7	24.1	.5805	s	t, cy	l	m	r	w	w
Solonis Robusta	......	......	2	......	2	27	.6262	s	t, cy	l	m	r	w	w
Solonis × [illegible]lo, No. 1613	......	......	5½	2	4	25	.6466	s	t, cy	l	m	r	w	w
Solonis × Riparia, No. 1616	55	45	13	15	4	24.9	.5390	s	t, cy	l	m	r	w	w
Taylor [illegible]e	60	10	20	2	12	24.4	.6185	s	t, cy	l	m	r	w	w
S[illegible]li B[illegible]c:														
[illegible]r	2	2	9	......	......	23	.4625	m	t	c	m	o	w	s, t, st
S[illegible]li [illegible]t:														
Lenoir	2	......	5	......	......	21	.6150	m	t	c	m	o	r	s, t, st
Semillon:														
Own roots	8	3	2	15	4	24.6	.5670	m	cy	l	m	r	w	w
Aramon × Rupestris Ganzin, No. 1	30	10	12	½	......	24.2	.7556	m	cy	l	m	r	w	w
Berlandieri × Riparia, No. 420A	......	......	......	½	4	25.5	.7680	m	cy	l	m	r	w	w
Dog Ridge	30	3	13	8	10	24.5	.7635	m	cy	l	m	r	w	w
Herbemont	40	15	15	5	12	22.3	.7200	m	cy	l	m	r	w	w
Lenoir	20	5	5	3	......	21.2	.7275	m	cy	l	m	r	w	w
Monticola × Riparia, No. 18808	......	......	......	......	4	27	.5400	m	cy	l	m	r	w	w
Mourvedre × Rupestris, No. 1202	20	2	......	......	......	24	.5850	m	cy	l	m	r	w	w
Riparia × Rupestris, No. 101	20	8	9	2	5	22.9	.6360	m	cy	l	m	r	w	w
Riparia × Rupestris, No. 3306	......	......	3	3	4	25.6	.8075	m	cy	l	m	r	w	w
Riparia × Rupestris, No. 3309	35	5	......	......	3	21.8	.6921	m	cy	l	m	r	w	w
Rupestris Martin	20	2	2	......	4½	25	.5819	m	cy	l	m	r	w	w
Rupestris St. George	20	8	7	½	3	22.6	.6015	m	cy	l	m	r	w	w

Salt Creek	25	5	6	1	4	25.2	.7620	m	cy	l	m	r	w	w
Solonis × Othello, No. 1613					3	25	.9675	m	cy	l	m	r	w	w
Solonis × Riparia, No. 1616	25	5			2	27.2	.5275	m	cy	l	m	r	w	w
Taylor Narbonne	25	4	4	½	2	25.4	.6900	m	cy	l	m	r	w	w
Semillon Blanc:														
Own roots	3	4		4	8	23.8	.6206	m	cy	l	m	r	w	w
Serine:														
Own roots	2		1	3	2	25.5	.7312	s	cy	c	s	r	b	w
Dog Ridge	15	5	9		3	26.9	.8460	s	cy	c	s	r	b	w
Lenoir	25	8	7	6	14	25	.6662	s	cy	c	s	r	b	w
Rupestris St. George	35	15	19	2	10	25.9	.8145	s	cy	c	s	r	b	w
Taylor Narbonne		10		3		26	.7387	s	cy	c	s	r	b	w
Servan Rose:														
Lenoir	8		6		6	20	.150	m	r	l	l	ob	r	s, t, st
Sicilien:														
Own roots		1		3		20.5	.7162	l	l	l	l	ob	w	s, t, st
Aramon × Rupestris Ganzin, No. 1	16					17.4	.6937	l	l	l	l	ob	w	s, t, st
Lenoir	4		5½		½	24.3	.4875	l	l	l	l	ob	w	s, t, st
Slankamenka:														
Own roots	2	1	2	10		25	.7181	l	l	l	l	ob	w	s, t, st
[illegible] du [illegible]ès:														
Dog Ridge	11		1			22.6	.5550	s	cy	l	s	r	w	w, t
Lenoir	2					23	.5325	s	cy	l	s	r	w	w, t
Rupestris St. George	3		½			22	.6825	s	cy	l	s	r	w	w, t
Sparbonna:														
Own roots	6	3	1	15		21.1	.7237	m	r	l	m	r	b	w
Sucre de [illegible]ille:														
Dog Ridge	20	2	2	10	3	24.7	.5830	s	r	l	m	r	w	w
Lenoir	20	5	9		5	24	.6137	s	r	l	m	r	w	w
Rupestris St. George	10	3	1½		8	24.8	.6075	s	r	l	m	r	w	w
Taylor Narbonne	5					26.8	.4875	s	r	l	m	r	w	w
Sufetha:														
Own roots	25					15.9	1.1475	s	cy	c	m	ob	w	st, s, t
Sultana:														
Own roots			½		4	23.5	.8887	l	l	l	m	r	w	s, t, r, w
Sultanina:														
Own roots		⅓			4	25.5	.6187	vl	l	l	m	ob	w	s, t, r, w
Do	20	10				24	.5425	vl	l	l	m	ob	w	s, t, r, w
Aramon × Rupestris Ganzin, No. 1	12	12				25.5	.6112	vl	l	l	m	ob	w	s, t, r, w
Do			4	46		25.5	.5850	vl	l	l	m	ob	w	s, t, r, w
Aramon × Rupestris Ganzin, No. 2				4		24	.4500	vl	l	l	m	ob	w	s, t, r, w
[illegible]lis			9	13		25	.5100	vl	l	l	m	ob	w	s, t, r, w
Dog Ridge	25					23	.4950	vl	l	l	m	ob	w	s, t, r, w
Hotporup				6		22	.5025	vl	l	l	m	ob	w	s, t, r, w
Lenoir	8		4			23.5	.6070	vl	l	l	m	ob	w	s, t, r, w
Monticola × Riparia, No. 554		3	2	9		24.1	.5500	vl	l	l	m	ob	w	s, t, r, w
Monticola × Riparia, No. 18804						23	.5775	vl	l	l	m	ob	w	s, t, r, w
Monticola × Riparia, No. 18808			8			23	.5325	vl	l	l	m	ob	w	s, t, r, w
Monticola × Riparia, No. 18815		5				25.1	.5100	vl	l	l	m	ob	w	s, t, r, w
Monticola × Rupestris				4		23	.6850	vl	l	l	m	ob	w	s, t, r, w
Ponroy						23	.6150	vl	l	l	m	ob	w	s, t, r, w

TABLE VII.—*Relative behavior and value for different purposes of grape varieties tested by grafting on resistant stocks and by growing on their own roots in eleven experiment vineyards in California*—Continued.

Variety and stock (on own roots, if so stated).	Weight of fruit per vine (pounds). 1909	1910	1911	1912	1913	Sugar, Balling scale.	Acid, as tartaric (grams per 00 c.c.).	Cluster. Size.	Cluster. Shape.	Cluster. Compact or loose.	Berry. Size.	Berry. Shape.	Berry. Color.	Use.
1	17	18	19	20	21	22	23	24	25	26	27	28	29	30
Sultanina—Continued.						*P. cent.*								
Ramsey		2	8			24.7	0.5470	vl	l	l	m	ob	w	s, t, r, w
Riparia × (Cordifolia × Rupestris, No. 106-8)				15		25	.5475	vl	l	l	m	ob	w	s, t, r, w
Riparia × Rupestris, No. 101	15	2				26.6	.5850	vl	l	l	m	ob	w	s, t, r, w
Riparia × Rupestris, No. 101-14				5		25.5	.5062	vl	l	l	m	ob	w	s, t, r, w
Riparia × Rupestris, No. 3306				4		23	.4950	vl	l	l	m	ob	w	s, t, r, w
Riparia × Rupestris, No. 3309	20	3	5			25.2	.6025	vl	l	l	m	ob	w	s, t, r, w
Riparia × Rupestris de Jaeger, No. 201				16		22	.9250	vl	l	l	m	ob	w	s, t, r, w
Rupestris des Caussettes				7		20	.5625	vl	l	l	m	ob	w	s, t, r, w
Rupestris Martin				3		25	1.2175	vl	l	l	m	ob	w	s, t, r, w
Rupestris Mission				10		26	.5025	vl	l	l	m	ob	w	s, t, r, w
Rupestris × Berlandieri, No. 219A			6	14		24.8	.5645	vl	l	l	m	ob	w	s, t, r, w
Salt Creek			10			25	.5400	vl	l	l	m	ob	w	s, t, r, w
Solonis Robusta				5		29	.5775	vl	l	l	m	ob	w	s, t, r, w
Solonis × Othello, No. 1613				11		24	.5625	vl	l	l	m	ob	w	s, t, r, w
Solonis × Riparia, No. 1616	25	20				27.8	.5925	vl	l	l	m	ob	w	s, t, r, w
Vermorel			3			23	.6000	vl	l	l	m	ob	w	s, t, r, w
Viala			5	20		25	.5041	vl	l	l	m	ob	w	s, t, r, w
Sultanina Rosea:														
Lenoir	½	2				25.2	.6675	l	l	l to c	m	ob	r	s, st, t, l
Sylvaner:														
Own roots	3	2	4	18		25.5	.5868	s	cy	c	s	r	w	w
Aramon × Rupestris Ganzin, No. 1	20	10	11	3		24.4	.6450	s	cy	c	s	r	w	w
Dog Ridge	20	6	9	4	6	25	.7365	s	cy	c	s	r	w	w
Herbemont	20	12	6	2		25.6	.7312	s	cy	c	s	r	w	w
Lenoir	10	3	10	1		24.7	.6994	s	cy	c	s	r	w	w
Riparia × Rupestris, No. 101	25	9	4	2	7	25.2	.7475	s	cy	c	s	r	w	w
Riparia × Rupestris, No. 3309	20	10	6	1		26.5	.7069	s	cy	c	s	r	w	w
Rupestris Martin	15	2	8		6	26.5	.7106	s	cy	c	s	r	w	w
Rupestris St. George	24	2	7	1	2	27.7	.7500	s	cy	c	s	r	w	w
Syrian:														
Own roots		1½	10	5		23	.6650	l	l	l	l	ob	w	s, st, t

Tadone:														
Dog Ridge	30	5				21.1	.7725	l	t	c	m	r	b	w
Lenoir	55	7	4	1½	13	21.9	.9660	l	t	c	m	r	b	w
Rupestris St. George	15	4	6½	1	12	23.9	.9090	l	t	c	m	r	b	w
Taylor Narbonne	6	5	8½			22.9	.8550	l	t	c	m	r	b	w
Tannat:														
Own roots	8	1	5	30	4	24.6	.5651	m	cy	c	m	r	b	w
Dog Ridge	50	8	18		.5	22.8	.9187	m	cy	c	m	r	b	w
Lenoir	40	12	7½	7	23	25	1.0413	m	cy	c	m	r	b	w
Rupestris St. George	40	15		4	24	25.5	.7400	m	cy	c	m	r	b	w
Taylor Narbonne	10	3		2½		27.6	1.0325	m	cy	c	m	r	b	w
Teneron:														
Own roots	8	½	4	½	4	24.6	.6165	l	t	c	l	r	w	s, st, t
Lenoir	6	3	6		4	22.5	.7530	l	t	c	l	r	w	s, st, t
Riparia × Rupestris, No. 3306			23	12	36	22.3	.9500	l	t	c	l	r	w	s, st, t
Terret Monstre:														
Adobe Giant	4	5				23.7	.7550	l	t	m	l	o b	w	s, st, t
Canada	7	6				22.6	.7575	l	t	m	l	o b	w	s, st, t
Lenoir	8	8	15		6	21.5	.6862	l	t	m	l	o b	w	s, st, t
Riparia × Rupestris, No. 101		8	5	27		22.3	.7300	l	t	m	l	o b	w	s, st, t
Rupestris [illegible]		3	10			22.7	.7700	l	t	m	l	o b	w	s, st, t
Solonis × Riparia, No. 1616		7	8			23.7	.6725	l	t	m	l	o b	w	s, st, t
[illegible]a			4			25	.6525	l	t	m	l	o b	w	s, st, t
Tinta Amarella:														
Own roots		12	8		12	23.4	.7257	m-l	t	c	m	r	b	w
Dog Ridge	30	15	15	1		23.2	.8169	m-l	t	c	m	r	b	w
Lenoir	40	5	15	5	32	22.6	.7560	m-l	t	c	m	r	b	w
Rupestris St. George	50	10	15	3	11	23.4	.7160	m-l	t	c	m	r	b	w
Taylor Narbonne	60	10	9		4	22.1	.7125	m-l	t	c	m	r	b	w
Tinta Cao:														
Own roots	10	8	5	10		24.5	.5619	m	cy	m	s	r	b	w
Dog Ridge	25	3	8½	1		22.4	.7712	m	cy	m	s	r	b	w
Lenoir	30	15	13	3	18	23.1	.7250	m	cy	m	s	r	b	w
Rupestris St. George	40	3	10	1½	5	23.9	.7680	m	cy	m	s	r	b	w
Taylor Narbonne	20	5			4	25	.5580	m	cy	m	s	r	b	w
Tinta de [illegible]:														
Own roots		3	¼	2	1	25.3	.6281	m	cy	c	s	ob	b	w
Dog Ridge	5	1	11			24.6	.7700	m	cy	c	s	ob	b	w
Lenoir	15	3	6	2	3	27.4	.6390	m	cy	c	s	ob	b	w
Rupestris St. George	30	1½	5		20	26.9	.6750	m	cy	c	s	ob	b	w
Taylor Narbonne	10					28.2	.4350	m	cy	c	s	ob	b	w
Torok Goher Noir:														
Own roots	6	½		18		22.5	.4675	m-l	cy	m	m-l	ob	b	w
[illegible]r:														
Own roots				2½	1	23	.8175	m	t	m	m-l	r	w	w, t
Aramon × Rupestris Ganzin, No. 1	40	12	10		4	25.5	.6412	m	t	m	m-l	r	w	w, t
Dog Ridge	40	15	6½	10	18	22	.7665	m	t	m	m-l	r	w	w, t
Herbemont	25	10	4		2	24.2	.4806	m	t	m	m-l	r	w	w, t
Lenoir	40	20	9½	5	4	22.7	.7365	m	t	m	m-l	r	w	w, t
Mourvedre × Rupestris, No. 1202	50	4				22.6	.6862	m	t	m	m-l	r	w	w, t
Riparia × Rupestris, No. 101	40	6	2		2	24.8	.6862	m	t	m	m-l	r	w	w, t

TABLE VII.—*Relative behavior and value for different purposes of grape varieties tested by grafting on resistant stocks and by growing on their own roots in eleven experiment vineyards in California*—Continued.

Variety and stock (on own roots, if so stated).	Weight of fruit per vine (pounds). 1909	1910	1911	1912	1913	Sugar, Balling scale.	Acid, as tartaric (grams per 100 c. c.).	Cluster. Size.	Cluster. Shape.	Cluster. Compact or loose.	Berry. Size.	Berry. Shape.	Berry. Color.	Use.
1	17	18	19	20	21	22	23	24	25	26	27	28	29	30
Traminer—Continued.						*P. cent.*								
Riparia × Rupestris, No. 3309	50	4	13		7	26	0.7631	m	t	m	m-l	r	w	w, t
Rupestris [illegible]	30	3	3		13	22.4	.6712	m	t	m	m-l	r	w	w, t
[illegible]s St. [illegible]ge	50	15	19		15	23.2	.7612	m	t	m	m-l	r	w	w, t
Salt Creek	50	8	5			23.1	.6750	m	t	m	m-l	r	w	w, t
[illegible]is × [illegible]a, No. 1616	50	15	3			24.5	.7400	m	t	m	m-l	r	w	w, t
Taylor N[illegible]e	55				5	25	.8312	m	t	m	m-l	r	w	w, t
Trentham:														
Own roots	3			4		27	.5025	m	t	m	l	ob	b	s, st, w
Lenoir	15		6		4	24.6	.5212	m	t	m	l	ob	b	s, st, w
Rupestris St. George	20	2			15	24.8	.5655	m	t	m	l	ob	b	s, st, w
Trifere du Japon:														
Lenoir	10	1	8			17.6	.5958	l	r	c	l	ob	b	s, st, t
[illegible]e:														
Lenoir	10	8	15		3½	19.1	.9637	l	r	c	l	ob	b	s, st, t
[illegible]:														
Own roots	4	5	6		5	21.1	.8175	l	cy	c	l	ob	b	w
Trojka:														
Own roots	1	2	20	18	18	21.1	.7905	l	t	m	l	ob	w	t, st, s
[illegible]au:														
Own roots		2	2	4	12	28.1	.6532	s	cy	c	s	r	b	w
Dog Ridge	10	1	2	1		26.7	.6375	s	cy	c	s	r	b	w
Lenoir	20	5	5		3	25	.7425	s	cy	c	s	r	b	w
[illegible]ris St. George	20	4	5		1	25.3	.7376	s	cy	c	s	r	b	w
[illegible]r N[illegible]bonne	15					26	.5550	s	cy	c	s	r	b	w
Ulliade [illegible]he d'Ambre:														
Own roots			6			21.5	.6112	s	cy	c	s	r	w	w
[illegible]a:														
Dog Ridge	10					22.2	.3825	m	r	m	l	ob	r	s, st, t
Lenoir	5	2				21.8	.5250	m	r	m	l	ob	r	s, st, t

Valdepenas:														
Own roots	2	5	2	10	....	23.8	.7294	m	cy	m	m	ob	b	w
Aramon × Rupestris Ganzin, No. 1	30	6	22	10	10	24.5	.[illegible]45	m	cy	m	m	ob	b	w
Dog Ridge	30	5	9	10	18	24.5	.6705	m	cy	m	m	ob	b	w
[illegible]t	45	15	5	1½	10	23.2	.6705	m	cy	m	m	ob	b	w
Lenoir	40	8	5½	4	18	23.8	.7530	m	cy	m	m	ob	b	w
Mourvedre × Rupestris, No. 1202	....	3	10	....	3	26.1	.6763	m	cy	m	m	ob	b	w
Riparia × Rupestris, No. 101	30	5	7	2	....	24.6	.[illegible]37	m	cy	m	m	ob	b	w
Riparia × Rupestris, No. 3309	30	8	....	....	15	24	.5975	m	cy	m	m	ob	b	w
Rupestris Martin	45	5	7	....	29	25.7	.6144	m	cy	m	m	ob	b	w
Rupestris St. George	50	3	20	½	12	24.9	.6074	m	cy	m	m	ob	b	w
Salt Creek	30	7	18	3	5	24.1	.7065	m	cy	m	m	ob	b	w
Solonis × Riparia, No. 1616	25	15	11	....	4	25.7	.6131	m	cy	m	m	ob	b	w
Taylor Narbonne	30	2	13	2	3	24.7	.6420	m	cy	m	m	ob	b	w
[illegible]r:														
Own roots	3	4	4	12	7	26.7	.6345	m	t	l	m	r	r	w
Dog Ridge	50	5	6½	2	18	27.2	.6415	m	t	l	m	r	r	w
[illegible]t	35	15	3	2	3	25.6	.7305	m	t	l	m	r	r	w
Lenoir	40	3	1	1	....	23.9	.6356	m	t	l	m	r	r	w
Riparia × Rupestris, No. 3306	....	....	....	....	2	25	.7425	m	t	l	m	r	r	w
Rupestris M[illegible]	30	1½	....	....	3	23.6	.6925	m	t	l	m	r	r	w
Rupestris St. George	40	3	8	½	....	25	.7069	m	t	l	m	r	r	w
Salt Creek	40	....	6	1	....	24	.6850	m	t	l	m	r	r	w
Verdal:														
Own roots	20	5	20	12	....	21.3	.6606	m	t	l	l	ob	w	s, st, t
Dog Ridge	40	3	18	4	3	19.4	.8598	m	t	l	l	ob	w	s, st, t
Do	60	70	8	60	20	21.3	.7479	m	t	l	l	ob	w	s, st, t
Lenoir	60	17	22	10	7	20	.8310	m	t	l	l	ob	w	s, st, t
Rupestris St. George	25	5	14	....	....	20.1	.8300	m	t	l	l	ob	w	s, st, t
Do	50	50	8	40	20	21.9	.6860	m	t	l	l	ob	w	s, st, t
Verdel:														
Own roots	1	8	10	8	5	21.9	.7815	s	cy	c	s	r	b	w
[illegible]e [illegible]t	30	30	4	12	7	24.3	.5820	s	cy	c	s	r	b	w
Aramon × Rupestris Ganzin, No. 1	15	30	3	15	23	24.2	.6035	s	cy	c	s	r	b	w
Dog Ridge	20	30	6	10	10	22.9	.6975	s	cy	c	s	r	b	w
Mourvedre × Rupestris, No. 1202	30	35	12	25	....	24.8	.6537	s	cy	c	s	r	b	w
Riparia × Rupestris, No. 101	16	10	½	⅓	14	25.7	.4640	s	cy	c	s	r	b	w
Riparia × Rupestris, No. 3309	40	50	5	38	22	24	.6180	s	cy	c	s	r	b	w
Rupestris St. George	30	40	5	12	12	24.8	.6723	s	cy	c	s	r	b	w
Solonis × Riparia, No. 1616	15	5	2	8	5	25.7	.4530	s	cy	c	s	r	b	w
Taylor Narbonne	15	20	6	15	4	24.5	.4935	s	cy	c	s	r	b	w
[illegible]o:														
Own roots	8	1½	....	3	3	25.6	.8006	m	t	l	m	ob	w	w
[illegible]o de M[illegible]:														
Own roots	....	....	....	2	....	26	.6750	m	t	l	m	ob	w	w
Aramon × Rupestris Ganzin, No. 1	3	3	6	2	....	26.6	.7681	m	t	l	m	ob	w	w
Dog Ridge	2	5	....	9	....	28.9	.7275	m	t	l	m	ob	w	w
Riparia × Rupestris, No. 3309	8	9	5	5	1	26.7	.7165	m	t	l	m	ob	w	w
Rupestris St. George	10	8	5	12	4	27.6	.7245	m	t	l	m	ob	w	w
Solonis × Riparia, No. 1616	8	4	1	3	....	27.6	.7144	m	t	l	m	ob	w	w

TABLE VII.—*Relative behavior and value for different purposes of grape varieties tested by grafting on resistant stocks and by growing on their own roots in eleven experiment vineyards in California*—Continued.

Variety and stock (on own roots, if so stated).	Weight of fruit per vine (pounds).					Sugar, Balling scale.	Acid, as tartaric (grams per 100 c. c.).	Cluster.			Berry.			Use.
	1909	1910	1911	1912	1913			Size.	Shape.	Compact or loose.	Size.	Shape.	Color.	
1	17	18	19	20	21	22	23	24	25	26	27	28	29	30
						P. cent.								
Ver mio:														
On roots	10	20	20	8		22.1	0.5720	m-l	t	m	l	ob	w	w
e t	50	35	3	25	18	22.3	.5730	m-l	t	m	l	ob	w	w
n × s Ganzin, No. 1	25	30	5	5	16	22.7	.4755	m-l	t	m	l	ob	w	w
Dog Ridge	10	40	10	8	8	22.7	.4225	m-l	t	m	l	ob	w	w
t						23.5	.5647	m-l	t	m	l	ob	w	w
r	25	15	3	3	6	22.3	.4950	m-l	t	m	l	ob	w	w
e × Rupestris, No. 1202	20	40	5	15	12	23.9	.4865	m-l	t	m	l	ob	w	w
Gloire	20	30	5	10	2	22.6	.4890	m-l	t	m	l	ob	w	w
a × s, No. 101	15	50	3	38	10	22.2	.5670	m-l	t	m	l	ob	w	w
Riparia × s, No. 3309	30	50	10	25	30	21.9	.5370	m-l	t	m	l	ob	w	w
s Martin	5	4	½	1½	0	24.4	.5550	m-l	t	m	l	ob	w	w
s St. e	50	30	15	20	12	22.8	.5057	m-l	t	m	l	ob	w	w
Salt Creek	25	30	1		5	22.9	.4694	m-l	t	m	l	ob	w	w
Solonis × , No. 1616	30	30	6	35	12	21.9	.4890	m-l	t	m	l	ob	w	w
r e	12	50	12	35	24	23.2	.4455	m-l	t	m	l	ob	w	w
a Sarda:														
On roots	12	6	3	32	16	25.6	.8265	m	t	l	m	ob	w	s, st, t, w
e de Zericho:														
Lenoir	4	1½	13			19.2	.7363	l	t	c	l	ob	w	s, st, t
e × Rupestris, No. 1202			24	13		22	.6188	l	t	c	l	ob	w	s, st, t
Wälschriesling:														
On s	6	3	3	8	6	25.8	.6165	s	cy	c	s	r	w	w
Werme:														
On roots	4	2	2	3	1	26.1	.6120	m	t	t	m	r	w	w
e t:														
e t	10	10	6		7	27.4	.5812	m	t	l	l	ob	w	s, st, t, r
n × stris Ganzin, No. 2			15			24	.6900	m	t	l	l	ob	w	s, st, t, r
s				6		29	.4425	m	t	l	l	ob	w	s, st, t, r
ri × , No. 420A				5		31	.5625	m	t	l	l	ob	w	s, st, t, r
Dg e	15	15	3	20	3	25.5	.5565	m	t	l	l	ob	w	t, st, t, r

[illegible]p	....	....	....	9½	....	29.5	. [illegible]5	m	t	l	l	ob	w	s, st, t, r
[illegible]a × [illegible]s	....	....	....	7	....	27	. [illegible]5	m	t	l	l	ob	w	s, st, t, r
Mourvedre × [illegible]s, No. 1202	15	10	5	8	3	26	.5650	m	t	l	l	ob	w	s, st, t, r
Riparia × [illegible]lia × Rupestris, No. 106–8)	....	....	....	6	....	28.5	.5250	m	t	l	l	ob	w	s, st, t, r
[illegible]a × Rupestris, No. 101	....	....	½	5	....	27.5	.5072	m	t	l	l	ob	w	s, st, t, r
[illegible]a × Rupestris, No. 3306	....	....	....	1½	....	29	.5100	m	t	l	l	ob	w	s, st, t, r
[illegible]a × Rupestris, No. 3309	10	5	11	12	....	28	.5625	m	t	l	l	ob	w	s, st, t, r
[illegible]s [illegible]Min	....	....	6	....	....	26	.5700	m	t	l	l	ob	w	s, st, t, r
[illegible]s [illegible]. George	20	7	5	2	6	25.3	.5790	m	t	l	l	ob	w	s, st, t, r
[illegible]s × Berlandieri, No. 219A	....	....	....	5	....	28	.4800	m	t	l	l	ob	w	s, st, t, r
[illegible]r [illegible]e	6	....	....	6	....	27.9	.5572	m	t	l	l	ob	w	s, st, t, r
[illegible]la	....	....	....	4	....	28	.5025	m	t	l	l	ob	w	s, st, t, r
[illegible]e [illegible]y:														
[illegible]n roots	15	3	2	12	....	25.5	.7294	m	t	l	m	ob	w	s, st, t
[illegible]t Hamburg:														
[illegible]n [illegible]s	50	....	....	....	....	20	.6675	m	t	c	l	r	b	s, t, w
Do	10	1	....	15	....	23.9	.5125	m	t	c	l	r	b	s, t, w
Wilmot, No. 16:														
Own roots	....	....	....	5	....	23	.6900	m	t	c	l	r	b	s, t, w
Dog Ridge	20	13	....	2½	2	21.6	.6844	m	t	c	l	r	b	s, t, w
Lenoir	45	10	9	....	10	20.3	.6206	m	t	c	l	r	b	s, t, w
Rupestris St. George	40	10	8	3	....	23.4	.6487	m	t	c	l	r	b	s, t, w
Zante:														
Own roots	....	15	3	29	....	25	.4850	m	cy	c	v, s	r	b	s, t, r
Zinzillosa:														
Own roots	1	1	1	4	1½	22.5	.7560	m	t	m	m	r	b	w
Zinfandel:														
Own roots	....	....	4	12	3	22.6	.7691	m-l	cy	c	m	r	b	w
Aramon × Rupestris Ganzin, No. 1	30	20	13	12	18	24.2	1.0080	m-l	cy	c	m	r	b	w
Berlandieri × Riparia, No. 420A	....	....	6	....	5	25.5	.9788	m-l	cy	c	m	r	b	w
Dog Ridge	50	8	11½	5	12	23.2	1.1130	m-l	cy	c	m	r	b	w
Herbemont	30	20	7	2	15	22.2	.8640	m-l	cy	c	m	r	b	w
Lenoir	40	15	60	5	15	23.9	1.0260	m-l	cy	c	m	r	b	w
[illegible]a × [illegible], No. 18815	....	....	3	4	....	23	1.2412	m-l	cy	c	m	r	b	w
[illegible]e × Rupestris, No. 1202	40	4	10	2	8	23.8	.9815	m-l	cy	c	m	r	b	w
[illegible]a × Rupestris, No. 101	50	8	12	....	6	21.9	1.0025	m-l	cy	c	m	r	b	w
[illegible]a × Rupestris, No. 101–14	....	....	....	....	5	25	.9000	m-l	cy	c	m	r	b	w
[illegible]a × [illegible]s, No. 3306	....	....	9	4	8	24.6	1.0150	m-l	cy	c	m	r	b	w
[illegible]a × [illegible]s, No. 3309	40	10	8	2	7	22.8	.9870	m-l	cy	c	m	r	b	w
[illegible]s [illegible]Min	40	8	10	2	8	20.2	.8995	m-l	cy	c	m	r	b	w
[illegible]s [illegible]a	....	....	....	....	3	23	.8625	m-l	cy	c	m	r	b	w
[illegible]s [illegible]n	....	....	2	....	5	23	1.0312	m-l	cy	c	m	r	b	w
[illegible]s St. [illegible]e	45	8	13	1	10	22	1.0577	m-l	cy	c	m	r	b	w
Salt [illegible]k	50	5	7	4	4	23.7	.9125	m-l	cy	c	m	r	b	w
[illegible]is [illegible]a	....	....	7	1	3	24.3	1.[illegible]1	m-l	cy	c	m	r	b	w
[illegible]s × Othello, No. 1613	....	....	2	....	4	25	.9150	m-l	cy	c	m	r	b	w
Solonis × [illegible], No. 1616	30	10	....	....	3	19.5	.7525	m-l	cy	c	m	r	b	w
[illegible]r [illegible]e	40	8	5½	8	....	23	.9480	m-l	cy	c	m	r	b	w

Table VIII gives an alphabetical list of additional Vinifera varieties grafted on resistant stocks which are under test at the Chico, Colfax, Fresno, Geyserville, Lodi, and Oakville experiment vineyards. Arabic figures are used to indicate the number of different stocks upon which each is grafted and the location of the same. The tests are too young to permit the drawing of conclusions.

TABLE VIII.—*Additional Vinifera varieties of grapes under test on resistant stocks at six experiment vineyards in California.*

[Arabic figures are used to indicate the number of different stocks upon which each variety is grafted and the location of the same.]

Varieties.	Chico.	Colfax.	Fresno.	Geyserville.	Lodi.	Oakville.
Ach-I-Soum						1
Actoni Maceron	1					
Actoniky	1	2	3		4	4
Agadia						1
Agra-Ash						2
Ahmeur bon Ahmeur	2	4			4	5
Ah Saibe						1
Ajaki-Odia	1					
Ajmi	1					5
Ak-Uzum						2
Albardiens	1					
Aldara						1
Alexandria			4			
Alicante	2					
Almeria	1				7	
Amlachu						1
Aneb el Cadi	1	4			4	5
Angelina	2	5			5	7
Aramon	1					
Arecussia						1
Ash Khuta						2
Askaree	1					4
Asmi						6
Atch Gau						2
Aswad Kari						2
Atch Kiek						2
Aturk-Ash						2
Angulata	1	7	1		5	3
Awasarghua						2
Bokator						1
Barducci	2	4	2		5	4
Bermestia Bianca	1					
Bicane	1	5	1		6	5
Black Hamburg	2	2			2	2
Black Monukka	1		18		1	8
Black Morocco	1	7			2	
Black Prince	1					
Black Seedless						3
Black Shahanee	1					5
Blanc d'Ambre	1	4			5	5
Blaney White	1	3			6	9
Blauer Portugieser	1					
Bowood Muscat	1					
Brustiana	2	5			7	8
Buccleugh	1	5			5	8
Buckland	1					8
Calabrian	1	7			7	6
Calmette	1		3			2
Carignane	1					6
Castiza		4			4	5
Chadeh Arabieh	2					6
Chaouch Blanche	1	6			6	5
Chaouch Rose	1	9			8	8
Chasselas Rose de Falloux			1			
Chasselas Rouge	1	2				3
Chasselas St. Bernard	1	2	5		5	4
Chavooschee	1					
Chauche Gris						3
Chaweesh	1					5

Varieties.	Chico.	Colfax.	Fresno.	Geyserville.	Lodi.	Oakville.
Child of Hall	2	5			5	4
Cinsaut	1					
Clairette à Gros Grain	1	6			6	9
Coarna Neagra	2	5			5	6
Corinthe Blanc			9		1	
Corinthe à Gros Grain	1	5	2		6	7
Corinthe Rose	2	6	12		4	7
Coristano	1	8			6	8
Cornichon	2	4	3		6	4
Damas Rose			17			
Danugue	1					
Dattier de Beyrouth						3
Deis-al-A'anze	1				1	6
Dizmar	1					
Dodrelabi	1					
Drnekusa	2					5
Dronkane	1	6	2		10	6
Emathia						1
Emperor	1	3	6		3	9
Erz Roumli	1					5
Fajoumi Jaune	1	5			6	2
Faphly		8	1		9	16
Feher Som	1	7			7	5
Feher Zagos	1					
Ferrara	1	3	25			6
Fintendo	2					
Flame Tokay	1	9	4		4	3
Frankenthal Précoce	2		2			
Fredericton	1	5	1		6	5
Ghulabi						2
Golden Champion						6
Golden Hamburg						5
Golden Queen	1				3	11
Goolabie	1	5	24		2	2
Green Hungarian	1					5
Grenache	1					
Gros Blanc de Lausanne	1	5	1		7	5
Gros Guillaume			24			5
Hebron	1	8			6	10
Huasco			10			
Hunisa	1	6	14			1
Hycales	1	12	1		8	16
Insolia Bianca	2	6	2		6	5
Jauzani						2
Jbâ'i						1
Jeresiana						2
Joannenc						2
Jubeili						6
Kabbajuk						2
Kadarka	1					
Kandihar						2
Kara-sarma						1
Kara-uzum						1
Kharashani						1
Kâsûfi-dakar						2
Kâsûfi-inti						5
Katchitch						1
Kechmish-Aly-Blanc	2	5	2		7	3
Keropodia	1	7	2		7	8
Key	1	2			2	6

TABLE VIII.—*Additional Vinifera varieties of grapes under test on resistant stocks at six experiment vineyards in California*—Continued.

Varieties.	Chico.	Colfax.	Fresno.	Geyserville.	Lodi.	Oakville.	Varieties.	Chico.	Colfax.	Fresno.	Geyserville.	Lodi.	Oakville.
Khudud-ul-Banat						3	Prune de Cazouls	2	5	23		8	5
Kishmish					5	2	Purple Damascus	2	6				2
Kishmish Daba						1	Quagliano	1					
Kishmish Red						1	Red Hanepoot			17			1
Kishmishi	1					1	Ribier	1					
Kordash						2	Rodites	1	11	25		7	14
Korsa Kishmish						1	Ronde Weisse						1
Ksil-isjum						1	Rose d'Italie	1	6			3	4
Kurdi	1					1	Roussaou			2			
Kuristi Mici	1	5	2		7	4	Saibe						2
Kurtelaska	1						St. Macaire	1					
Leani Zolo	2					5	Satin Blanc	1	8			6	8
Lignan	1	2	2			3	Schiradzouli Violet	1	7	22		7	8
Listan	1		6			1	Semillon						9
Madeleine Royale						1	Servan Rose	1	6	2		7	7
Malvasia	1	6			4	5	Sev-ursa						1
Malvasia Rosaria						1	Sgotoruk						1
Mantua de Pilas	1						Shahmani						5
Maraville de Malaga	1	6	23		6	5	Shakaifi						2
Marmora	1						Shakaribira						1
Melon	1	7				1	Shanzi						1
Meyer No. 64						1	Shatawi						5
Meyer No. 114						2	Shirshira						1
Meyer No. 115						1	Sicilien	1	9	1		6	11
Meyer No. 801						3	Slankamenka	2					
Meyer No. 803						1	S. P. I. No. 601						1
Meyer No. 832						2	S. P. I. No. 611						1
Meyer No. 866						1	S. P. I. No. 614						1
Miksâsi						5	S. P. I. No. 6914						1
Millenium	1	3	5			8	S. P. I. No. 30042						1
Molinera Gordo	2	8	2		5	10	Sultana			1			2
Monake						1	Sultanina			14			4
Mondeuse	1						Sultanina Rosea		3	38		6	22
Mourestel	1					4	Suri						6
Mukhkh-ul-Baghl						2	Sylvaner						5
Muscat Albardiens		6					Syrian					3	
Muscat Bonod	1	6	2		9	10	Tavris						1
Muscat Capusines	1					4	Tavrish						1
Muscat Gros Noir Hatif	2		1				Teneron	1	9	3			12
Muscat Hamburg			5				Terret Monstre	1	8	2		8	6
Muscat Noir Precoce	1		2		1		Tififihi Ahmer	1					3
Nasa Valentiana	1						Tinta Amerella	1					
Nebbiolo						1	Trifere du Japon	1	13	2		5	15
Ohanez	1	13	48	79	10	6	Triomphe	2	8			5	8
Olivette Blanche	1	15	5		9	17	Trojka	1					
Olivette Chaptal	1	9	1		6	10	Ubeide						6
Olivette Noir	2	10			6	10	Uva de Casta						6
Olivette Rose			1				Uva de Embarque						6
Opiman	2	3			4	3	Valandova			25			
Pagadebito	1						Valdepenas	1					
Palarusa	2						Veltliner						11
Panariti	1		25				Velusa						1
Panse de Roquevaire						5	Verdal		2			1	1
Paykanee Razuki	1						Verdelho de Madere			1			
Pearl de Casaba	1				3	3	Vigne de Zericho	1	6	22		7	6
Pedro Ximines	2						West Prolific						4
Perle Imperial Blanche	2	7			3	11	White Hanepoot			10			
Peru	1	1			1	2	White Kapadjulari						2
Petit Syrah	1			1		3	White Luglienga	1	12	2		10	14
Philipi						1	White Tokay	1	1				2
Piment	1	5	29		10	6	Zabalkanski	1					3
Pis des Chevre Rouge	1	6	3		6	5	Zeine						6
Pizzutella	2						Zinfandel	1					4

The following is an alphabetically arranged list of Vinifera varieties in the Brawley Experiment Vineyard (Pl. II, fig. 2), the plantings of which are as yet too young to permit the drawing of conclusions relative to their adaptability:

Ach-I-Soum, Actoni, Actoniky, Agadia, Ahmeur bon Ahmeur, Ajmi, Aleatico, Alexandria, Almeria, Aneb-el-Cadi, Angelina, Augulata, Askari, Aspiran-Noir, Atch Kiek, Awasarghua.

Barducci, Beclan, Bermestia Bianca, Boal de Madera, Bowood Muscat, Black Morocco, Black St. Peter, Black Shahanee, Black Zante, Blanc d'Ambre, Blaney White, Blauer Portugieser, Buccleuch, Brustiana.

Carignane, Calabrian, Catarratto a la Porta, Castiza, Chadieh Arabieh, Chavooschee, Chaouch, Chaouch Rose, Chasselas Bouches du Rhone, Chasselas Dore, Chasselas Fontainebleau, Chasselas Florence, Chasselas Montauban, Chasselas Musque Vrai, Chasselas Negrepont, Chasselas Rose, Chasselas Rose de Falloux, Chasselas Rouge, Chasselas St. Bernard, Child of Hall, Cinsaut, Clairette à Gros Grain, Clairette Blanche, Coarna Neagra, Commandeur, Corinthe Rose, Corinthe à Gros Grain, Cornichon, Coristana, Crujidero.

Damascus, Danugue, Dattier de Beyrouth, Dizmar, Dodrelabi, Downing, Drnekusa, Dronkane, Duc de Magenta.

Emperor.

Fajaumi Jaune, Faphly, Feher Goher Noir, Feher Som, Feher Zagos, Ferrara, Fintendo, Flame Tokay, Foster, Frankenthal Precoce, Fredericton.

Golden Champion, Golden Hamburg, Golden Queen, Goolabie, Gradiska, Green Hungarian, Grenache, Gros Blanc de Lausanne, Gros Maroc.

Hebron Hycales, Hunisa, Huasco, Hutab.

Insolia Bianca.

Jura Muscat.

Kadarka, Kahallillee, Kakour, Keropodia, Kishmish, Kuristi Mici, Kurtelaska.

Lahntraube, Lampasas, Leani Zolo, Luglienga.

Madeleine Angevine, Madeleine Blanche, Madeleine Rose, Madeleine Royale, Mamelon, Malaga, Malvasia, Malvasia Rosario, Maraville de Malaga, Marascina, Marzamina, Meslier, Millenium, Mission, Molinera Gordo, Mondeuse, Mourisco Bianca, Muscateller, Muscatelle Fino, Muscat Albardiens, Muscat Bonod, Muscat Capusines, Muscat Gros Noir Hatif, Muscat Hamburg, Muscat Madera Rose, Muscat Noir de Hongrie, Muscat Noir Precoce, Muscat Talabot.

Napoleon, Nasa Valentiana, Negrara di Gattinara, Neiretta di Costillo.

Ocru di Boe, Ohanez, Olivette Blanche, Olivette de Cadenet, Oliver de Serres, Olivette Noir.

Pagadebito, Parc de Versailles, Palarusa, Panariti, Paykanee Razuki, Pearl de Casaba, Perruno, Persian, No. 20; Persian, No. 21; Persian, No. 23; Persian, No. 25; Persian, No. 26; Persian, No Number; Persian, No Tag; Philipi, Piment, Pince Muscat, Prune de Cazouls.

Rose de Italie, Royal Ascot, Rozaki Zolo.

Schach-I-Soum, Schiradzouli Blanc, Schiradzouli Violet, Servan Blanc, Servan Rose, Sgotoruk, Shiraz, Sicilian, Slankamenka, St. Laurient, Sultana, Sultanina, Sultanina Rosea, Syrian.

Terret Monstre, Tinta Amerilla, Torok Goher Noir, Trentham Black, Trifere du Japon, Triomphe, Trivoti, Trojka, Trousseau, Tsien Tsien.

Valdepenas, Veltliner, Verdal, Vernaccia Sarda, Vigne de Zericho.

Wilmot Hamburg, Wilmot No. 16, White Corinth, White Tokay.

Zante.

Table IX shows additional tests of improved American native and Franco-American grape varieties grafted on resistant stocks which are being made at the Fresno and Oakville experiment vineyards. (See Pl. I, figs. 1 and 2.) Arabic figures are used to indicate the number of different stocks upon which each is grafted and the location of the same. The tests are too young to permit the drawing of conclusions.

TABLE IX.—*Varieties of American native and Franco-American grapes under test on resistant stocks at the Fresno and Oakville experiment vineyards, showing the number of different stocks included in the test.*

Varieties.	Fresno.	Oakville.	Varieties.	Fresno.	Oakville.
Agawam............stocks..	1	4	Concord............stocks..	5	10
America × Malaga No. 2:			Concord Improved.....do....	....	1
No. 1............stocks..	....	1	Continental...........do....	....	1
No. 2..............do....	....	2	Lindley..............do....	4	11
No. 16.............do....	....	1	Lucile...............do....	....	6
Armistead Seedling....do....	....	1	Massasoit............do....	....	1
Barry...............do....	1	4	Moore...............do....	1	7
Brighton.............do....	4	6	Niagara..............do....	5	6
Brilliant.............do....	....	4	Perkins..............do....	....	1
Campbell.............do....	....	5	Rebecca..............do....	1	4
Catawba..............do....	1	9	Riggs No. 16..........do....	....	1
Champion.............do....	....	2			

The explanation of columns already given for Table VII will apply for the most part to Table X, showing the relative behavior and value for different purposes of improved American native and Franco-American grape varieties, except that the parentage of the varieties displaces the designation of the stock, the column for the "Year grafted" is omitted, and the congeniality column is changed to a growth-rating column, because all the varieties are on their own roots. The column for weight of pruning is also omitted. The abbreviations used to designate the parent species are as follows: Aest. for Aestivalis, Bourq. for Bourquiniana, Champ. for Champini, Lab. for Labrusca, Lins. for Linsecomii, Rip. for Riparia, Rup. for Rupestris, Vin. for Vinifera.

TABLE X.—*Relative behavior and value for different purposes of improved native American and Franco-American varieties of grapes growing on their own roots in eleven experiment vineyards in California.*

Variety and parentage.	Experiment vineyard.	Year planted.	Growth rating.	How pruned.	Nodes bearing fruit.	Growth-starting date.		Blossoming date.		Fruit-setting date.		Fruit-ripening date.	
						Early season.	Late season.	Early season.	Late season.	Early season.	Late season.	Early season.	Late season.
1	2	3	4	5	6	7	8	9	10	11	12	13	14
Agawam:			*Per ct.*										
Lab. × Vin	O	1905	88	s	1 to 3	Mar. 25	Mar. 26	May 15	May 27	May 21	May 31	Sept. 18	Oct. 6
Do.	F	1905	88	s		Mar. 5	Mar. 20	May 3	May 20	May 12	May 24	Aug. 29	Sept. 17
Albania:													
× [illegible]t. × Lab. × Bourq.)	O	1903	88	s	2 to 4	Mar. 19	Apr. 4	May 22	June 6	May 27	June 20	Sept. 23	
Alicante [illegible]:													
Vin. × Rup	O	1907	80	s	2 to 3	do	Apr. 3	May 20	May 30	May 29	June 12	Sept. 24	Oct. 8
Alicante × Rupestris Terrace, No. 20:													
Vin × Rup	O	1903	94	s	1 to 4	Mar. 14	Apr. 1	May 15	May 27	May 27	May 31	Sept. 26	Oct. 7
Do.	Gi	1905	94	s		Mar. 8	Mar. 25	May 9	May 24	May 13	May 29	Sept. 18	Sept. 28
Do.	Cx	1906	96	c, s		Mar. 17	Apr. 1	June 1	June 8	June 5	June 13	Sept. 15	Oct. 2
Amerbonte:													
Burq. × (Lins. × Rup.)	F	1903	44	s		Mar. 12	do	May 20	May 30	May 26	June 3		
Do	C	1907	94	c, s		Mar. 28	do	May 1	May 20	May 5	June 4		
Do	O	1903	94	s		Mar. 20	Apr. 5	June 2	June 8	June 7	June 19		
A[illegible]a:													
L(ins. × Rup.) × (Bourq. × Lab.)	F	1903	88	s		Mar. 12	Mar. 30	May 12	May 20	May 20	May 25	Aug. 29	Sept. 17
Do	O	1903	97	s	3 to 5	Mar. 15	Apr. 7	May 22	June 1	May 27	June 20	Sept. 24	
[illegible]y:													
Lab. × Vin	F	1905	77	s		Mar. 7	Mar. 25	Apr. 25	May 12	May 9	May 14	Aug. 15	Sept. 4
Do	O	1905	77	s	1 to 4	Mar. 30		May 15	May 30	May 24	June 1	Sept. 8	
[illegible]s:													
[illegible]. × (Lab. × Bourq.)	F	1904	57	s		Mar. 5	Mar. 13	Apr. 25	May 15	May 10	May 21	Aug. 15	Sept. 20
Do	S	1904	80	s		Mar. 16	Apr. 1	May 27	June 25	May 31	June 29	[illegible] 30	Oct. 4
Big [illegible]tra:													
[illegible]ns. × (Lab. × Vin.)	Cx	1907	90	s		Mar. 19	Apr. 9	May 1	June 14	May 8	June 20	Sept. 24	Do.
Do.	F	1904	87	s		Mar. 8	Apr. 2	May 18	May 27	May 20	June 7	Aug. 30	Sept. 21
Do.	G	1904	85	s		Mar. 1	Mar. 28	May 23	June 18	May 27	June 23	Sept. 20	Sept. 28
Do	Li	1904	67	s		Mar. 11	Apr. 3	May 24	June 20	May 28	June 24	Oct. 1	Oct. 10
Do	L	1904	90	c, s		Mar. 10	do	May 20	June 8	May 25	June 13	Sept. 24	Oct. 26

Do.	M	04	93	s		[illegible] 30	[illegible] 8	[illegible] 9	[illegible] 18		[illegible] 23	Sept. 26	
Do.	O	1903	87	s	3 to 5	[illegible] 20	do.	My 21	[illegible] 8	May 26	June 25	Sept. 10	[illegible] 28
Do.	S	04	89	s		[illegible] 16	Apr. 10	My 26	[illegible] 25	May 30	June 29	Sept. 24	[illegible] 15
[illegible]:													
[illegible] × Aest.) × L(ns. × Lab.)	F	03	53	s		[illegible] 14	[illegible] 1	[illegible] 18	My 25	May 22	May 30	Sept. 5	[illegible] 17
Do.	O	03	86	s	1 to 4	[illegible] 20	[illegible] 8	My 19	[illegible] 5	May 23	June 20	Sept. 25	[illegible] 12
[illegible] × [illegible], No. 601:													
Vin. × [illegible]	Cx	1906	90	s		[illegible] 18	[illegible] 10	May 3	J ne 7	May 9	June 11	Sept. 5	[illegible] 6
Do.	Gi	1905	87	s		[illegible] 14	Apr. 1	May 8	My 23	May 12	May 28	do.	[illegible] 25
Do.	F	1903	93	c, s		[illegible] 8	Mar. 30	My 10	My 18	do.	May 23	Sept. 6	[illegible] 17
Do.	Li	1907	90	s		[illegible] 14	Apr. 1	[illegible] 19	[illegible] 5	May 25	June 9	Sept. 25	[illegible] 10
Do.	M	1906	65	s		[illegible] 26	Mar. 29	My 27	do.	June 1	June 11	Oct. 8	
Do.	O	1903	95	s	1 to 3	[illegible] 21	[illegible] 3	My 18	[illegible] 29	May 23	June 8	Sept. 24	[illegible] 8
[illegible] × Rupestris, No. 603:													
Vin. × Rup.	Cx	06	90	s		[illegible] 19	[illegible] 6	[illegible] 2	[illegible] 15		June 20	Oct. 5	Oct. 6
Do.	F	04	84	s		[illegible] 12	[illegible] 1	[illegible] 15	My 23	May 20	May 27	Sept. 10	[illegible] 24
Do.	Li	05	91	s		[illegible] 14	Apr. 3	[illegible] 10	[illegible] 5	May 13	June 10	Sept. 25	[illegible] 5
Do.	L	05	93	s		[illegible] 11	Mar. 31	do.	June 3	May 14	June 6	Oct. 8	
Do.	M	05	79	s		[illegible] 21	[illegible] 4	[illegible] 25	[illegible] 5		June 10	Sept. 23	Oct. 8
Do.	O	04	92	s	1 to 4	[illegible] 22	[illegible] 1	[illegible] 16	My 28	May 21	do.	Sept. 29	[illegible] 15
Do.	S	05	87	s		[illegible] 17	[illegible] 5	My 23	[illegible] 10	May 26	June 14	Sept. 25	
[illegible] × [illegible], No. 109-4:													
Vin. × Rup.	Cx	07	93	s		[illegible] 16	Apr. 6	[illegible] 29	J ne 1	June 5	June 13	do.	Oct. 5
Do.	Gi	07	89	s		[illegible] 25	M[illegible] 28	My 7	My 21			Sept. 5	Sept. 25
Do.	F	04	93	s		[illegible] 5	Mr. 24	[illegible] 1	My 15	May 18	My 23	Sept. 11	Sept. 22
Do.	Li	04	94	s		[illegible] 10	Apr. 5	My 23	[illegible] 10	May 28	[illegible] 15	Sept. 20	Oct. 1
Do.	L	04	97	s		do.	Apr. 1	[illegible] 9	My 28	May 13	June 1	Oct. 2	
Do.	M	04	84	s		[illegible] 28	Mar. 30	My 23	[illegible] 8	May 27	[illegible] 14	Sept. 26	
Do.	O	04	98	s	2 to 3	[illegible] 17	Mar. 26	[illegible] 12	[illegible] 24	May 17	[illegible] 28	Sept. 23	
Do.	S	05	98	s		[illegible] 12	[illegible] 3	My 20	[illegible] 10	May 25	[illegible] 15	Sept. 24	Oct. 15
Bourisquou × [illegible], No. 3907:													
Vin. × Rup.	Cx	06	91	s		[illegible] 19	Apr. 9	My 1	J ne 8	May 7	June 14	Sept. 5	Oct. 4
Do.	Gi	07	90	s		[illegible] 12	Mar. 22	My 8	My 23			do.	Sept. 22
Do.	F	04	94	s		[illegible] 6	[illegible] 13	[illegible] 5	My 15	May 18	My 26	Sept. 9	Sept. 20
Do.	G	04	93	s		[illegible] 2	Mar. 18	My 8	[illegible] 7	May 22	[illegible] 11	Sept. 25	
Do.	L	04	97	s		[illegible] 13	Apr. 2	My 19	[illegible] 8	May 24	[illegible] 12		
Do.	S	04	87	s		[illegible] 16	Apr. 10	My 21	[illegible] 1	May 25	[illegible] 20	Sept. 24	Oct. 14
[illegible] × [illegible], No. 4306:													
Vin. × Rup.	Cx	1907	94	s		[illegible] 19	Apr. 8	[illegible] 4	[illegible] 7	June 8	[illegible] 12	Oct. 2	
Do.	F	1904	99	s		[illegible] 18	[illegible] 1	My 8	My 20	May 15	My 25	Sept. 9	Sept. 20
Do.	Li	1907	94	s		[illegible] 13	Apr. 3	My 19	[illegible] 10	May 25	[illegible] 15	Sept. 30	Oct. 1
Do.	O	1904	98	s	2 to 4	[illegible] 20	Apr. 1	My 20	My 23	May 27	[illegible] 5	Sept. 28	
[illegible] × [illegible], No. 4308:													
Vin. × [illegible]	Cx	1906	92	s		[illegible] 30	Apr. 3	June 4	[illegible] 8		June 14	Sept. 5	Oct. 2
Do.	Gi	1907	89	s		[illegible] 10	Mr. 25	My 10	My 23	May 14		Sept. 23	
Do.	F	1904	96	s		[illegible] 14	Apr. 3	[illegible] 8	[illegible] 18	May 15	May 23	Sept. 8	Sept. 20
Do.	M	1904	85	s		[illegible] 20	Mar. 26	My 27	[illegible] 8	June 2	June 14	Sept. 26	
Do.	O	1904	95	s	2 to 3	[illegible] 18	Mr. 29	My 19	My 25	May 30	June 5	Sept. 22	
[illegible]:													
[illegible] × Vin.	O	1905	87	s	2 to 3	[illegible] 15	Apr. 7	May 18	My 28	May 24	May 31	Sept. 9	

TABLE X.—*Relative behavior and value for different purposes of improved native American and Franco-American varieties of grapes growing on their own roots in eleven experiment vineyards in California*—Continued.

Variety and parentage.	Experiment vineyard.	Year planted.	Growth rating.	How pruned.	Nodes bearing fruit.	Growth-starting date. Early season.	Growth-starting date. Late season.	Blossoming date. Early season.	Blossoming date. Late season.	Fruit-setting date. Early season.	Fruit-setting date. Late season.	Fruit-ripening date. Early season.	Fruit-ripening date. Late season.
1	2	3	4	5	6	7	8	9	10	11	12	13	14
Brilliant:			Per ct.										
Lab. × (Vin. × Bourq.)	Gl	1905	77	s		Mar. 6	Apr. 1	May 26	May 30	June 3		Sept. 5	Sept. 25
Do.	F	1904	80	s		Mar. 12	...do....	May 10	May 20	May 15	May 24	Aug. 20	Sept. 4
Do.	G	1905	73	s		[illegible] 2	Mar. 20	May 22	June 18	May 26	June 23	Sept. 20	
Do.	M	1904	84	s		[illegible] 26	Mar. 31	May 30	June 7	June 10	June 11	Oct. 4	
Canada:													
(Rip. × Lab.) × Vin.	F	1903	87	s		[illegible] 10	Mar. 25	May 10	May 25	May 15	May 30	Sept. 5	Sept. 19
Do.	L	1906	88	s		[illegible] 17	Apr. 15	May 8	May 30	May 12	June 4	Sept. 20	Sept. 22
Do.	O	1903	96	s	1 to 3	ar. 20	Apr. 4	May 19	May 25	May 22	June 10	Sept. 10	Sept. 23
Do.	S	1906	93	s		ar. 10	Apr. 12	May 25	June 15	June 19		Sept. 24	Sept. 26
Carignane × Rupestris, No. 404:													
Vin. × Rup.	F	1904	97	s		ar. 7	Mar. 30	May 10	May 20	ay 15	My 26	Sept. 9	Sept. 17
Do.	G	1904	95	s		ar. 16	Mar. 20	May 19	June 7	ay 24	ne 12	Sept. 26	
Do.	Li	1905	94	s		ar. 13	Apr. 1	May 23	June 10	J ne 8	ne 14	Sept. 23	Oct. 1
Do.	M	1904	87	s		Mr. 29	...do....	May 28	June 8	J ne 2	ne 13	Sept. 26	Oct. 8
Do.	O	1904	96	s	1 to 3	Mr. 18	Apr. 3	May 22	May 27	ay 26	ne 1	...do....	Oct. 7
Do.	S	1907	89	s		ar. 12	...do....	May 29	June 5	J ne 4	ne 20	Sept. 24	
Carignane × Rupestris, No. 501:													
Vin. × Rup.	L	1904	92	s		[illegible] 7	Mar. 30	May 10	June 3	ay 14	ne 5	Oct. 26	
Do.	M	1904	90	s		ar. 26	Mar. 29	June 3	June 12	J ne 5	ne 17	Oct. 10	
Do.	O	1904	95	s	1 to 3	ar. 16	Apr. 1	May 14	May 18	J ne 1	ne 10	Sept. 27	Oct. 1
Do.	S	1907	90	s		ar. 14	Mar. 30	May 27	June 10	...do....	ne 14	Oct. 17	
Carman:													
Lins. × (Vin. × Lab. × Bourq.)	F	1904	52	s		...do....	Mar. 20	May 21	May 26	My 25	J ne 3	Aug. 23	Sept. 19
Do.	O	1903	74	s	1 to 3	[illegible] 16	Apr. 3	May 22	May 31	May 27	J ne 23	Sept. 10	Sept. 25
Castel, No. 1028:													
Rip. × Vin.	O	1907	84	s	2 to 4	Mar. 20	Apr. 6	May 28	May 29	June 2	J ne 13	Sept. 9	Oct. 6
Castel, No. 19002:													
(Lab. × Rup.) × Vin.	O	1907	87	s	2 to 4	[illegible] 19	Apr. 1	May 7	May 25	ay 21	[illegible] 27	Sept. 22	Oct. 9

Catawba:													
Lab. × Vin.	Cx	1906	68	s		Mar. 20	Apr. 8	May 26	June 3	May 30	June 8	Sept. 24	
Do.	F	[illegible]	68	s		Mar. 7	Apr. 1	May 5	May 15	May 17	May 20	Sept. 11	Sept. 15
Do.	G	1905	91	s		Mar. 10	Mar. 31	May 24	June 5	May 28	June 9	Sept. 26	
Do.	L	1905	88	s		Mar. 11	Apr. 3	May 12	May 18	May 16	May 27	Sept. 23	Oct. 3
Do.	M	1905	87	s		Mar. 26	Apr. 10	May 30	June 3	June 3	June 16	Oct. 10	
Do.	O	1905	77	s	1 to 4	Mar. 22	Apr. 1	May 17	May 25	May 22	June 11	Sept. 9	Oct. 10
Do.	S	1905	90	c, s		Mar. 12	Apr. 2	May 20	June 10	May 30	June 14	Sept. 24	Oct. 14
Centennial:													
Lab. × Æst.	Gi	1905	87	s		Mar. 15	Apr. 1	May 9	May 27			Sept. 25	
Do.	F	1904	86	s		Mar. 13	Mar. 25	May 10	May 18	May 24	May 25	Sept. 5	Sept. 21
Do.	O	1905	79	s	2 to 3	Mar. 14	Apr. 1	May 16	May 28	May 21	June 1	Sept. 9	Oct. 6
Champenel:													
Champ. × Lab.	O	1903	94	s	2 to 3	Mar. 22	Apr. 3	May 19	May 24	May 24	June 11	Sept. 27	
Chasselas × Rupestris, No. 901:													
Vin. × Rup.	F	1904	91	s		Mar. 6	Mar. 15	May 6	May 16	May 15	May 21	Sept. 8	Sept. 12
Do.	O	1904	95	s	1 to 2	Mar. 17	Mar. 25	May 19	May 25	May 24	June 1	Sept. 27	
Clairette Doré Ganzin:													
Vin. × Rup.	F	1903	88	c, s		Mar. 9	Apr. 5	May 12	May 20	May 20	May 26		
Do.	Gi	1905	90	s		do.	Mar. 27	May 26	June 3	May 30	June 9	Sept. 25	Sept. 30
Do.	L	1907	78	s		Mar. 6	Mar. 20	May 13	May 22	May 18	May 26	Sept. 24	Sept. 27
Do.	O	1903	94	s	2 to 4	Mar. 16	Mar. 22	May 20	May 30	May 24	June 4	Sept. 30	Oct. 15
Clevener:													
Lab. × (Rip. × Aest.)	O	1907	83	s		Mar. 22	Mar. 30	May 8	May 22	May 12	May 29	Oct. 9	
Cloeta:													
(Lins. × Rup.) × (Lab. × Vin.)	O	1903	90	s	2 to 4	Mar. 21	Apr. 9	May 19	May 29	May 24	June 3	Sept. 24	
Columbaud × Rupestris:													
Vin. × Rup.	O	1903	96	s	2 to 4	Mar. 17	Mar. 25	May 22	May 28	June 1	June 5	Sept. 26	
Concord:													
Lab.	Cx	1906	88	s		Mar. 23	Apr. 6	June 1	June 7	June 5	June 12	Oct. 4	
Do.	Gi	1905	68	s		Mar. 18	Apr. 1	May 26				Sept. 25	
Do.	O	1904	76	s	2 to 4	Mar. 17	Mar. 30	May 12	May 28	May 17	June 2	Oct. 7	
Do.	S	1904	83	s		Mar. 12	Apr. 10	May 20	June 1	June 5	June 7	Sept. 20	
[illegible]ia:													
Vin. × Rup.	F	1903	56	s		Mar. 1	Apr. 1	May 1	May 10	May 15		Sept. 6	
Do.	S	1907	88	s		Mar. 12	Mar. 27	May 22	June 8	May 27	June 13	Oct. 15	
Couderc, No. 101:													
Vin. × Rip.	Cx	1907	94	s		Mar. 15	Apr. 4	May 28	June 4	June 8	June 12	Sept. 15	Oct. 3
Do.	F	1904	93	c, s		Mar. 8	Mar. 15	May 6	May 24	May 25	May 29	Sept. 10	Sept. 17
Do.	G	1904	93	s		Mar. 4	Mar. 14	do.	May 16	May 12	May 21	Sept. 25	Oct. 10
Do.	Li	1904	94	s		Mar. 9	Mar. 30	May 12	June 8	May 16	June 13	Sept. 24	Oct. 1
Do.	M	1904	86	s		Mar. 26	Apr. 4	May 29	June 6	June 3	June 10	Sept. 26	Oct. 8
Do.	O	1904	93	s	1 to 5	Mar. 18	Mar. 25	May 17	May 25	May 23	May 29	Sept. 25	Oct. 9
Do.	S	1904	91	s		Mar. 10	Apr. 8	May 20	June 15	May 24	June 19	Sept. 22	Sept. 28
No. 201:													
Rip. × (Rup. × Vin.)	Gi	1907	90	s		Mar. 17	Mar. 28	May 10	May 25	May 25		Sept. 20	Sept. 25
Do.	F	1904	98	c, s		Mar. 10	Mar. 25	do.	May 20	May 17	May 25	Sept. 4	Sept. 20
Do.	G	1904	95	s		Mar. 2	Mar. 22	May 17	June 17	May 21	June 16	Sept. 25	Oct. 10
Do.	Li	1905	96	s		Mar. 12	Apr. 6	May 23	June 8	May 29	June 12	Sept. 23	Oct. 1
Do.	M	1904	87	s		Mar. 26	do.	May 26	June 10	May 31	June 14	Sept. 26	Oct. 8
Do.	O	1904	94	s	2 to 5	Mar. 20	Apr. 7	May 18	May 24	May 18	May 31	Sept. 27	Oct. 9
Do.	S	1904	90	s		Mar. 10	Apr. 5	May 27	June 8	May 31	June 13	Sept. 20	Oct. 7

TABLE X.—*Relative behavior and value for different purposes of improved native American and Franco-American varieties of grapes growing on their own roots in eleven experiment vineyards in California*—Continued.

Variety and parentage.	Experiment vineyard.	Year planted.	Growth rating.	How pruned.	Nodes bearing fruit.	Growth-starting date. Early season.	Growth-starting date. Late season.	Blossoming date. Early season.	Blossoming date. Late season.	Fruit-setting date. Early season.	Fruit-setting date. Late season.	Fruit-ripening date. Early season.	Fruit-ripening date. Late season.
1	2	3	4	5	6	7	8	9	10	11	12	13	14
Couderc, No. 503:			*Per ct.*										
Rup. × Vin.	Cx	1907	88	s		Mar. 18	Apr. 9	June 1	...do...	June 5	June 15	Sept. 26	Oct. 4
Do.	Gi	1907	89	s		Mar. 20	Apr. 1	May 18	May 24	May 22		Sept. 25	
Do.	F	1904	96	c, s		Mar. 13	Mar. 30	May 12	May 23	May 18	May 31	Sept. 6	Sept. 19
Do.	G	1904	85	s		Mar. 6	Mar. 20	May 17	June 1	May 21	June 17	Sept. 20	Sept. 25
Do.	Li	1904	93	s		Mar. 12	Apr. 5	May 20	June 8	May 24	June 13	Sept. 23	Oct. 1
Do.	M	1904	84	s		Mar. 28	Apr. 6	May 28	...do...	June 2	June 12	Sept. 28	Oct. 10
Do.	O	1904	97	s	1 to 5	Mar. 18	Apr. 2	May 17	May 27	May 23	June 9	Sept. 27	Do.
Couderc, No. 704.	S	1904	90	s		Mar. 2	Apr. 10	May 22	June 15	May 27	June 20	Sept. 20	Oct. 17
Do.	G	1904	79	s		Mar. 6	Mar. 25	May 12	...do...	May 16	...do...	Sept. 25	Do.
Do.	M	1904	73	s		Mar. 25	Apr. 1	June 5	June 12	June 13	June 17	Sept. 26	Oct. 8
Do.	O	1904	89	s	1 to 3	Mar. 20	Mar. 27	May 17	June 7	May 23	June 12	...do...	Oct. 9
Do.	S	1904	90	s		Mar. 12	Apr. 15	May 26	June 15	May 31	June 20	Sept. 24	Oct. 15
Couderc, No. 3701:													
Vin. × Rup.	Cx	1907	94	c, s		Mar. 16	Apr. 5	June 1	June 10	June 5	June 16	Sept. 26	Oct. 4
Do.	G	1904	95	s		Mar. 3	Mar. 17	May 15	...do...	May 19	...do...	Sept. 25	Oct. 7
Do.	Li	1904	97	s		Mar. 12	Apr. 5	May 25	June 4	May 29	June 9	Sept. 15	Sept. 30
Do.	M	1904	88	s		Mar. 28	...do...	May 28	June 5	June 2	...do...	Sept. 27	Oct. 8
Do.	O	1904	96	s	1 to 4	Mar. 20	Mar. 30	May 16	June 3	May 21	...do...	Sept. 25	Oct. 9
Do.	S	1904	92	s		Mar. 11	Apr. 5	May 30	...do...	June 8	June 13	Sept. 24	Oct. 7
Couderc, No. 4401:													
Rup. × Vin.	O	1907	89	s	2 to 4	Mar. 20	Apr. 2	May 20	May 23	May 28	June 9	Sept. 22	Oct. 8
Couderc, No. 28 × No. 112:													
Vin. ? × Rup.	Cx	1907	94	c, s		Mar. 16	Apr. 5	June 4	June 8	June 8	June 13	Sept. 26	Oct. 3
Do.	F	1904	89	c, s		Mar. 10	Mar. 20	May 6	May 16	May 20	May 22	Sept. 5	Sept. 20
Do.	G	1904	96	s		Mar. 11	Mar. 23	May 16	June 15	...do...	June 21	Sept. 20	
Do.	Li	1904	91	s		Mar. 14	Apr. 5	May 24	June 8	May 29	June 14	Sept. 15	Sept. 30
Do.	L	1904	96	s		Mar. 12	Mar. 30	May 8	May 25	May 12	May 30	Sept. 24	
Do.	M	1904	93	s		Mar. 26	Apr. 4	Apr. 26	May 30	Apr. 30	June 10	Oct. 8	

Do.	O	1904	99	s	2 to 4	Mar. 21	Apr. 1	May 17	May 26	May 23	May 29	Sept. 25	Oct. 5
Do.	S	1904	89	s	....	Mar. 10	..do....	May 31	June 15	June 5	June 20	Sept. 24	Oct. 14
Couderc, No. 71-06: Rup. × (Lins. × Vin.)	O	1907	82	s	2 to 3	Mar. 23	Mar. 27	May 17	June 8	May 21	June 14	Sept. 25	Oct. 10
Couderc, No. 71-20: Rup. × (Lins. × Vin.)	O	1907	85	s	2 to 5	..do....	Mar. 25	..do....	June 6	..do....	June 11	Sept. 21	Oct. 8
Couderc, No. 74-17: Complex Hybrid	O	1907	86	s	1 to 3	Mar. 24	Apr. 1	May 23	May 28	June 1	June 5	Oct. 6	Oct. 10
Couderc, No. 82 × 32: Complex Hybrid	Cx	1907	91	c, s	....	Mar. 25	Apr. 10	May 2	June 12	May 9	June 17	Sept. 25	Do.
Do.	F	1904	90	s	....	Mar. 15	Mar. 22	May 15	May 25	May 21	June 1	Sept. 1	Sept. 19
Do.	G	1904	95	s	....	Mar. 2	Mar. 25	May 23	June 1	May 27	....	Sept. 20	
Do.	Li	1904	88	s	....	Mar. 15	Apr. 5	May 24	June 10	May 29	....	Sept. 15	Sept. 23
Do.	M	1904	91	s	....	Mar. 26	..do....	June 9	June 18	June 22	....	Sept. 28	Oct. 4
Do.	O	1904	94	s	....	Mar. 16	..do....	May 20	June 10	May 26	June 16	Sept. 22	Oct. 10
Do.	S	1904	90	s	....	Mar. 12	Apr. 7	May 28	June 30	June 2	July 3	Sept. 30	Oct. 14
Couderc, No. 84 × 61: (Vin. × Rup.) × Vin.	Cx	1907	82	s	....	Mar. 17	Apr. 2	May 26	June 4	June 8	June 11	Sept. 20	Oct. 4
Do.	Gi	1907	87	s	....	Mar. 10	Apr. 8	May 20	....	May 30	....	Sept. 15	Sept. 23
Do.	F	1904	59	s	....	Mar. 11	Mar. 20	May 12	May 26	May 20	May 31	Sept. 8	Sept. 20
Do.	G	1904	72	s	....	Mar. 5	Mar. 16	May 16	June 8	..do....	June 12	Sept. 20	Oct. 8
Do.	Li	1904	66	s	....	Mar. 10	Mar. 25	May 26	June 10	May 30	June 14	..do....	Oct. 1
Do.	L	1907	69	s	....	Mar. 3	Mar. 26	May 12	May 29	May 17	June 4	Sept. 24	Oct. 4
Do.	M	1904	72	s	....	Mar. 29	Apr. 1	Apr. 26	June 9	Apr. 30	June 19	Sept. 26	Oct. 9
Do.	O	1904	37	s	2 to 4	Mar. 20	Mar. 30	May 18	June 10	May 23	June 16	Sept. 27	Oct. 2
Do.	S	1904	72	s	....	Mar. 13	May 26	June 1	June 18	June 23	....	Sept. 24	Oct. 17
Couderc, No. 85 × 113: (Vin. × Rup.) × Vin.	O	1907	86	s	2 to 4	Mar. 24	Apr. 1	May 31	June 1	June 3	June 20	Sept. 23	Oct. 10
Couderc, No. 87 × 115: Vin. × (Rup. × Vin.)	Cx	1907	89	s	....	Mar. 16	Apr. 5	June 1	June 18	June 5	June 23	Sept. 15	
Do.	Gi	1907	83	s	....	Mar. 8	Apr. 1	May 6	May 14	May 10	....	Sept. 5	Sept. 23
Do.	F	1904	91	s	....	Mar. 12	Mar. 20	May 15	May 25	May 25	May 29	Aug. 24	Sept. 19
Do.	G	1907	92	s	....	Mar. 2	Mar. 25	May 16	June 5	May 20	June 12	Sept. 23	Oct. 10
Do.	Li	1907	88	s	....	Mar. 9	Mar. 30	May 26	June 18	May 29	June 22	..do....	Oct. 1
Do.	M	1904	93	s	....	Mar. 27	Apr. 3	Apr. 25	June 9	Apr. 29	June 23	Sept. 24	Oct. 7
Do.	O	1904	88	s	1 to 2	Mar. 18	Apr. 1	May 17	June 7	May 22	June 12	Sept. 26	Oct. 9
Do.	S	1907	88	s	....	Mar. 12	..do....	May 29	June 22	June 2	June 27	Sept. 24	Oct. 17
Couderc, No. 124 × 30: Vin. × (Rup. × Vin.)	G	1907	87	s	....	Mar. 7	Mar. 28	May 10	May 25	....	....	Sept. 25	
Do.	F	1904	87	s	....	Mar. 10	Mar. 25	May 14	May 24	May 20	May 29	Sept. 9	Sept. 17
Do.	G	1904	90	s	....	Mar. 2	Mar. 30	May 21	June 15	May 25	June 20	Sept. 25	
Do.	Li	1904	91	s	....	Mar. 13	Apr. 3	May 12	June 14	May 18	..do....	Sept. 22	Oct. 5
Do.	L	1904	91	s	....	Mar. 14	Apr. 1	..do....	May 29	May 16	June 3	Sept. 24	Do.
Do.	M	1904	82	s	....	Mar. 28	Apr. 2	Apr. 25	June 1	Apr. 29	June 20	Sept. 26	Oct. 8
Do.	O	1904	89	s	1 to 3	Mar. 18	Mar. 27	May 17	June 5	May 24	June 10	Sept. 27	Oct. 10
Do.	S	1904	86	s	....	Mar. 12	Apr. 1	May 22	June 12	May 27	June 17	Sept. 20	Sept. 25
Couderc, No. 132-11: Complex Hybrid	O	1907	85	s	1 to 3	Mar. 24	Mar. 25	May 26	June 3	May 30	June 9	Sept. 27	Oct. 30
Couderc, No. 199-88: Vin. × (Rup. × Vin.)	O	1907	78	s	1 to 2	Mar. 25	....	..do....	May 31	May 24	June 4	Sept. 25	Oct. 5
Couderc, No. 241-125: Vin. × (Rup. × Vin.)	O	1907	87	s	2 to 4	Mar. 27	Mar. 28	..do....	June 6	May 30	June 13	Sept. 24	Oct. 8

TABLE X.—*Relative behavior and value for different purposes of improved native American and Franco-American varieties of grapes growing on their own roots in eleven experiment vineyards in California*—Continued.

Variety and parentage.	Experiment vineyard.	Year planted.	Growth rating.	How pruned.	Nodes bearing fruit.	Growth-starting date.		Blossoming date.		Fruit-setting date.		Fruit-ripening date.	
						Early season.	Late season.	Early season.	Late season.	Early season.	Late season.	Early season.	Late season.
1	2	3	4	5	6	7	8	9	10	11	12	13	14
No. 2677:			*Per ct.*										
Complex Hybrid	O	1907	88	s	2 to 3	Mar. 21	Mar. 24	May 24	May 30	May 27	June 5	Sept. 30	Oct. 15
Couderc, No. 272-60:													
Complex Hybrid	O	1907	90	s	1 to 4	...do...	Apr. 3	May 26	May 29	May 31	June 4	Sept. 22	Oct. 8
Delaware:													
Lab. × Bourq. × Vin.	F	1904	52	s		Mar. 6	Mar. 30	May 10	May 20	May 15	May 28	Aug. 5	Sept. 20
Do.	L	1904	65	s		Mar. 11	Apr. 10	May 16	June 8	May 20	June 13	Sept. 25	
Diamond:													
Lab. × Vin.	Gi	1905	80	s		Mar. 10	Apr. 8	May 9	May 21	May 14	May 25	Aug. 29	Sept. 10
Do.	F	1905	69	s		Mar. 7	Apr. 1	...do...	May 17	May 15	May 22	Sept. 19	
Do.	O	1905	66	s	2 to 3	Mar. 20	Apr. 6	May 19	May 31	May 23	June 4	Sept. 8	
Diana:													
Lab. × Vin. × Aest.	Gi	1905	84	s		Mar. 11	Apr. 3	May 9	May 21	May 13	May 25	Sept. 11	Sept. 19
Do.	O	1905	86	s	2 to 4	Mar. 14	Apr. 1	May 24	May 31	May 28	June 2	Sept. 8	Oct. 9
Dutchess:													
Lab. × Vin. × Aest.	Cx	1906	80	s		Mar. 17	Apr. 6	Apr. 26	June 8	May 3	June 14	Sept. 10	Sept. 26
Do.	F	1905	69	s		Mar. 6	Mar. 13	May 10	May 16	May 20	May 25	Aug. 29	Sept. 5
Do.	L	1905	88	s		Mar. 9	Mar. 30	May 20	June 1	May 25	June 6	Sept. 24	
Do.	O	1905	91	s	1 to 4	Mar. 12	Apr. 1	May 19	June 7	May 24	June 12	Sept. 9	Oct. 3
Do.	S	1905	88	s		Mar. 15	Apr. 7	May 25	June 18	May 30	June 23	Sept. 20	Oct. 16
Elvira:													
Rip. × Lab.	Gi	1905	79	s		Mar. 10	Apr. 3	May 20	May 21	May 25	May 26	Sept. 1	Sept. 22
Do.	F	1904	83	s		Mar. 7	Mar. 30	May 8	May 14	May 12	May 19	Aug. 24	Sept. 21
Do.	L	1904	90	c, s		Mar. 10	Apr. 2	May 10	May 22	May 14	May 26	Sept. 24	Sept. 27
Do.	O	1904	64	s	2 to 3	Mar. 15	Mar. 29	May 2	May 27	May 5	May 30	Oct. 7	Oct. 7
Fern Munson:													
Lin. × (Vin. × Lab.)	Cx	1910	91	c, s		Mar. 20	Apr. 2	Apr. 25	June 12	Apr. 30	June 17	Sept. 20	Oct. 4
Do.	O	1903	86	s	3 to 6	Mar. 16	Apr. 3	May 21	June 2	May 26	June 7	...do...	Oct. 1
Do.	S	1904	88	s		...do...	...do...	May 29	June 18	June 1	June 23	Sept. 24	Oct. 16

Gold [illegible]:													
[illegible]t. × Lab.	F	1904	60	s	....	Mar. 23	Apr. 8	May 12	May 30	May 20	June 6	[illegible] 5	Sept. 19
Do.	G	1904	79	s	....	Mar. 7	Apr. 5	May 18	June 14	June 18	....	Sept. 20	Oct. 7
Do.	O	194	67	s	3 to 4	Mar. 16	Apr. 8	May 30	June 1	June 3	June 15	[illegible] 25	
Do.	S	904	85	s	....	Mar. 10	Apr. 12	May 28	June 18	June 1	June 23	[illegible] 24	Oct. 16
[illegible]r [illegible]s:													
Lab. × Vin.	Gi	1904	88	s	....	Mar. 20	Apr. 8	May 20	June 3	May 25	June 10	[illegible] 18	
[illegible]t:													
Bourq.	Cx	1906	92	c, s	....	Mar. 18	Apr. 3	Apr. 21	June 18	Apr. 28	June 24	Sept. 25	Oct. 4
Do.	Gi	1905	84	s	....	Mar. 10	Apr. 5	May 26	May 31	May 29	May 31	Sept. 19	Sept. 30
Do.	M	1904	87	s	....	Mar. 9	Apr. 1	Apr. 30	May 13	May 4	....	Sept. 26	Oct. 8
Do.	O	1903	84	s	2 to 3	Mar. 22	...do...	May 22	June 5	May 27	June 9	...do...	Oct. 10
Do.	S	1904	78	s	....	Mar. 12	Mar. 25	May 25	...do...	June 8	June 11	....	
[illegible]t:													
Lab. × Vin.	F	1905	70	s	....	Mar. 5	Mar. 10	May 1	....	May 20	....	Aug. 25	Sept. 10
Do.	O	1905	87	s	....	[illegible] 14	Apr. 1	May 18	May 28	May 22	June 1	[illegible] 9	
[illegible]r:													
Lins. × ([illegible]b. × Vin.)	F	1905	85	....	....	Mar. 9	Apr. 5	May 15	May 20	May 19	May 26	[illegible] 9	Sept. 17
Do.	O	1905	89	s	2 to 4	Mar. 15	Apr. 6	May 17	June 12	May 22	June 18	Sept. 8	Oct. 15
[illegible]n:													
Lins. × (Vin. × Lab.)	O	1906	73	s	2 to 3	...do...	Apr. 2	May 19	June 8	May 24	June 14	[illegible] 7	Oct. 6
[illegible]l:													
Vin. × Lab.	Gi	1905	91	c, s	....	...do...	Apr. 1	May 26	June 6	May 30	June 12	[illegible] 25	
[illegible]a:													
Lab. × Vin.	Cx	1906	91	s	....	Mar. 19	Mar. 31	Apr. 30	June 5	May 6	June 10	[illegible] 15	Oct. 2
Do.	Gi	1905	73	s	....	Mar. 10	Apr. 15	May 10	May 23	May 14	[illegible]y 26	....	
Do.	F	1905	90	s	....	Mar. 5	Mar. 25	May 5	May 14	May 15	[illegible]y 19	[illegible] 12	Sept. 20
Do.	G	1905	91	s	....	Mar. 6	Mar. 18	May 15	June 3	May 21	[illegible]e 9	....	
Do.	L	1905	88	s	....	Mar. 9	Apr. 1	May 8	May 25	May 11	[illegible]y 28	Sept. 25	
Do.	M	1905	81	s	....	Mar. 25	Apr. 3	May 28	[illegible]e 5	June 1	[illegible]e 10	....	
Do.	O	1905	91	s	1 to 5	Mar. 16	Apr. 1	May 15	May 26	May 21	[illegible]y 30	....	
Do.	S	1905	97	c, s	....	Mar. 10	[illegible] 30	May 20	[illegible]e 10	May 24	[illegible]e 15	Sept. 24	Oct. 17
Jaeger:													
Lins. × Bourq.	F	1904	68	s	....	Mar. 15	Apr. 3	May 14	May 22	May 20	May 27	Sept. 5	Sept. 19
Do.	G	1904	87	s	....	Mar. 4	Apr. 5	May 20	June 5	May 28	June 12	Sept. 20	Sept. 25
Do.	L	1904	70	s	....	Mar. 20	Apr. 6	May 12	May 20	May 10	May 24	....	
Do.	O	1903	79	s	1 to 3	Mar. 25	Apr. 2	May 28	[illegible]e 5	June 3	[illegible]e 17	Sept. 25	
[illegible]h:													
Lab. × Vin.	C	1906	80	s	....	Mar. 31	Apr. 16	May 30	[illegible]e 3	...do...	June 8	....	
Do.	O	1905	69	s	1 to 3	Mar. 24	Apr. 1	May 16	May 28	May 22	May 31	Sept. 23	Oct. 4
[illegible]a:													
Lins. × [illegible]q.	F	1903	55	s	....	Mar. 10	Mar. 12	Apr. 18	May 3	May 5	May 12	....	
Do.	O	1903	86	s	2 to 3	Mar. 24	Apr. 5	May 28	June 7	June 3	June 12	Sept. 27	
Lamp[illegible]s:													
L[illegible]b. × Aest.	F	1908	91	c, s	....	Mar. 10	Mar. 18	May 8	May 15	May 15	....	....	
[illegible]l:													
Lins. × (Lab. × Aest.)	F	1904	27	s	....	Mar. 12	Mar. 25	May 5	May 17	May 23	....	Sept. 19	
[illegible]:													
Bourq.	Cx	1906	93	c, s	....	Mar. 23	Apr. 2	[illegible]e 9	June 12	[illegible]e 14	June 17	Sept. 10	Sept. 23
Do.	Gi	1905	98	s	....	Mar. 18	Mar. 28	May 25	May 30	May 30	June 5	Sept. 20	Sept. 29
Do.	F	1904	79	s	....	Mar. 14	Mar. 20	May 15	....	May 20	....	Sept. 8	Sept. 12

TABLE X.—*Relative behavior and value for different purposes of improved native American and Franco-American varieties of grapes growing on their own roots in eleven experiment vineyards in California*—Continued.

Variety and parentage.	Experiment vineyard.	Year planted.	Growth rating.	How pruned.	Nodes bearing fruit.	Growth-starting date. Early season.	Growth-starting date. Late season.	Blossoming date. Early season.	Blossoming date. Late season.	Fruit-setting date. Early season.	Fruit-setting date. Late season.	Fruit-ripening date. Early season.	Fruit-ripening date. Late season.
1	2	3	4	5	6	7	8	9	10	11	12	13	14
[illegible]d.			Per ct.										
Bourq.	G	1904	95	s		Mar. 2	Mar. 27	May 24	June 5	May 29	June 29	Sept. 22	Oct. 7
Do.	Li	1904	94	s		Mar. 8	Mar. 28	May 23	do.	May 28		Sept. 25	Sept. 28
Do.	L	1904	96	c, s		Mar. 12	Mar. 31	May 18	May 20	May 25	May 31	Sept. 24	Oct. 3
Do.	M	1904	82	s		Mar. 27	Apr. 5	May 26	June 15	May 30	June 20	Sept. 26	Oct. 8
Do.	O	1903	98	s	3 to 5	Mar. 16	Apr. 3	May 19	June 1	May 23	June 5	Sept. 29	Oct. 3
Do.	S	1904	93	s		Mar. 4	Apr. 2	May 27	June 15	June 1	June 29	Sept. 24	Oct. 16
Lindley:													
Lab. × Vin.	Cx	1906	89	s		Mar. 22	Apr. 1	Apr. 30	June 5	May 7	June 20	Sept. 10	Oct. 4
Do.	Gi	1905	83	s		Mar. 10	Mar. 28	May 15	May 24	May 20	May 28	Sept. 20	
Do.	F	1904	88	s		Mar. 12	Apr. 1	May 9	May 15	May 12	May 21	Aug. 24	Sept. 21
Do.	O	1905	93	s	2 to 4	Mar. 16	Mar. 26	May 10	May 27	May 14	June 1	Sept. 9	Oct. 7
[illegible]a:													
Bourq.	O	1903	57	s	2 to 4	Mar. 20	Apr. 15	May 22	June 10	May 27	June 23	do.	Do.
Do.	S	1907	86	s		Mar. 14	Apr. 5	May 30	June 12	June 4		Oct. 10	
Lukfata:													
[illegible]. × Lab.	F	1903	83	s		Mar. 10	Apr. 1	Apr. 3	May 10	May 6	May 14	Sept. 23	
Do.	L	1904	88	s		Mar. 5	Apr. 5	May 12	May 25	May 26	May 30		
Do.	O	1903	95	s		Mar. 19	Apr. 4	do.	May 23	May 16	May 28		
[illegible]:													
(Lab. × Vin. × Bourq.) × (Lins. × Rup.)	O	1903	93	s	2 to 3	Mar. 16	do.	May 18	June 1	May 23	June 6	Sept. 10	Sept. 26
[illegible]:													
Lins. × Bourq.	G	1904	86	s		Mar. 6	Apr. 3	June 5				Sept. 19	
Do.	L	1904	76	s		Mar. 18	do.	May 25	June 5	May 29			
Do.	O	1903	91	s		Mar. 19	Apr. 9	June 4	June 10	June 7	June 23		
Do.	S	1904	92	s		Mar. 12	Apr. 7	May 29	June 15	June 2	June 30	Oct. 14	
Martha:													
Lab. × Vin.	Gi	1905	60	s		Mar. 20	Apr. 15	May 25		June 3		Sept. 25	

[illegible] Riesling:													
Rip. × Lab.	F	1904	83	s	....	Mar. 13	Apr. 1	May 8	May 17	May 18	May 22	Sept. 5	Sept. 19
Do.	L	1904	82	s	....	..do.....	Apr. 6	..do.....	May 28	May 12	June 1	Sept. 24	Sept. 25
Do.	O	1904	70	s	1 to 3	Mar. 14	Apr. 3	May 12	May 27	May 17	May 31	Sept. 20	Oct. 5
Mrs. Munson:													
Lins. × Bourq.	O	1905	80	s	3 to 5	Mar. 12	Apr. 6	May 19	June 15	May 23	June 22	Sept. 22	Oct. 1
[illegible]:													
Lins. × Bourq.	F	1904	87	s	....	Mar. 22	Apr. 1	May 18	May 30	May 22	June 6	Sept. 6	Sept. 19
Do.	O	1903	92	s	3 to 4	Mar. 20	..do.....	May 20	June 1	May 25	..do.....	Sept. 25	Sept. 27
Niagara:													
Lab. × Vin.	Cx	1906	88	s	....	Mar. 19	Apr. 5	May 3	..do.....	May 12	June 7	Sept. 5	Oct. 4
Do.	F	1905	71	s	3 to 7	Mar. 7	Apr. 1	May 6	May 14	..do.....	May 19	Aug. 24	Aug. 26
Do.	O	1905	89	s	1 to 3	Mar. 13	Mar. 25	May 16	May 27	May 20	June 21	Sept. 10	Sept. 21
Oli atoo:													
(Vin. × Lab.) × (Lins. × (Vin. × Lab.))	O	1907	81	s	2 to 4	Mar. 20	Mar. 30	June 8	June 10	June 12	June 16	Sept. 8	
Pardes:													
Vin. × Rup.	Cx	1907	94	s	....	Mar. 19	Apr. 3	Apr. 27	June 5	May 2	[illegible]	Sept. 25	Oct. 4
Do.	Gi	1905	98	s	....	Mar. 8	Mar. 25	May 20	May 21	May 24	May 25	Sept. 19	Sept. 26
Do.	F	1904	89	c, s	....	Mar. 5	Mar. 28	May 5	May 15	May 15	May 21	Sept. 8	Sept. 20
Do.	Li	1904	73	s	....	Mar. 7	Mar. 25	May 10	May 28	May 16	June 16	Sept. 15	Sept. 28
Do.	M	1904	53	s	....	Mar. 20	Mar. 29	June 6	June 12	June 11	....	Sept. 25	Oct. 10
Do.	O	1904	93	s	2 to 4	Mar. 18	Mar. 25	May 15	May 28	May 20	June 3	Sept. 26	Oct. 9
Do.	S	1904	95	s	....	Mar. 14	Mar. 27	May 26	June 10	May 31	June 14	Sept. 24	Oct. 14
Pierce:													
Lab. × Vin.	L	1905	88	s	....	Mar. 11	Apr. 3	May 4	May 18	May 7	May 23	..do.....	Oct. 2
Do.	M	1905	85	s	....	Mar. 27	Apr. 1	May 21	June 8	May 26	June 13	Oct. 6	
Do.	S	1905	92	s	....	Mar. 14	Apr. 5	May 23	June 3	May 27	June 9	Sept. 30	
Rebecca:													
Lab. × Vin.	F	1905	63	s	....	Mar. 9	Apr. 1	May 6	May 18	May 18	May 23	Aug. 25	Aug. 30
Do.	M	1905	81	s	....	Mar. 28	Apr. 6	June 3	June 8	June 11	June 16	Oct. 4	
Do.	O	1905	69	s	1 to 3	Mar. 19	Apr. 3	May 12	May 24	May 16	May 29	Sept. 9	Oct. 10
Do.	S	1905	84	s	....	Mar. 13	Apr. 5	May 28	June 15	June 1	June 18	Sept. 24	Oct. 16
Rommel:													
Lab. × (Rip. × Vin.)	F	1904	84	s	....	Mar. 9	Mar. 25	May 7	May 18	May 15	May 23	Aug. 10	Sept. 20
Do.	L	1904	86	c, s	....	Mar. 18	Apr. 3	May 10	May 27	May 14	June 1	Sept. 24	Oct. 5
Do.	S	1907	89	s	....	Mar. 12	Apr. 1	May 24	June 28	May 28	July 1	Oct. 17	
R. W. Munson:													
Lins. × (Lab. × Vin.)	C	1906	90	c, s	....	Mar. 27	Apr. 8	May 8	May 20	May 7	June 4	....	
Do.	Cx	1906	80	s	....	Mar. 23	Apr. 5	May 1	June 10	May 9	June 15	....	
Do.	Gi	1907	80	s	....	Mar. 9	..do.....	May 18	May 26	....	....	....	
Do.	F	1904	83	s	....	Mar. 6	Apr. 1	May 12	..do.....	May 18	May 31	Aug. 24	Sept. 15
Do.	G	1904	91	s	....	Mar. 4	Apr. 3	May 22	....	May 29	....	....	
Do.	Li	1904	71	s	....	Mar. 10	Apr. 1	June 2	June 15	June 8	June 20	....	
Do.	L	1904	78	s	....	Mar. 11	Apr. 3	May 13	May 18	May 17	May 23	....	
Do.	M	1904	92	s	....	Mar. 29	..do.....	June 8	June 14	....	June 19	....	
Do.	O	1903	91	s	2 to 5	Mar. 22	..do.....	May 18	May 30	May 24	June 4	Sept. 26	
Do.	S	1904	85	s	....	Mar. 13	Apr. 12	May 26	June 20	May 31	June 25	....	

TABLE X.—*Relative behavior and value for different purposes of improved native American and Franco-American varieties of grapes growing on their own roots in eleven experiment vineyards in California*—Continued.

Variety and parentage.	Experiment vineyard.	Year planted.	Growth rating.	How pruned.	Nodes bearing fruit.	Growth-starting date.		Blossoming date.		Fruit-setting date.		Fruit-ripening date.	
						Early season.	Late season.	Early season.	Late season.	Early season.	Late season.	Early season.	Late season.
1	2	3	4	5	6	7	8	9	10	11	12	13	14
Seibel, No. 1:			*Per ct.*										
Rup. × (Lins. × Vin.)	C	1907	93	s		Mar. 29	Apr. 13	May 2	May 20	May 27			
Do.	Cx	1907	91	s		Mar. 19	Apr. 2	May 30	June 3	June 5	June 8	Sept. 26	Oct. 15
Do.	Gi	1905	94	s		Mar. 15	Apr. 1	May 20	May 26	May 25	June 2	Sept 16	Sept. 28
Do.	F	1904	74	s		Mar. 11	...do...	May 5	May 25	May 15	May 31	Aug. 20	Sept. 15
Do.	G	1904	90	s		Mar. 4	...do...	May 21	June 18	May 25	June 24	Sept. 24	Sept. 30
Do.	Li	1904	48	s		Mar. 14	Apr. 5	May 15	June 15	May 20	June 20		
Do.	L	1904	89	s		Mar. 13	Apr. 1	May 13	June 4	May 17		Sept. 20	Oct. 3
Do.	M	1904	63	s		Mar. 27	Apr. 4	June 9	June 15		June 20	Sept. 26	Oct. 8
Do.	O	1904	86	s		Mar. 21	Mar. 30	May 15	June 5	May 20	June 10	Sept. 28	Oct. 9
Do.	S	1904	91	s		Mar. 16	Apr. 10	May 21	June 18	May 25	June 23	Sept. 24	Oct. 12
Do.	St	1907	86	s		Mar. 20	Apr. 1	May 15	June 1	May 20	June 5		
Seibel, No. 2:													
Rup. × (Lins. × Vin.)	C	1910	93	s		Mar. 28	Apr. 6	May 16	May 27	May 21	June 1		
Do.	Cx	1907	90	s		Mar. 24	...do...	June 5	June 9	June 10	June 14	Sept. 24	Oct. 5
Do.	Gi	1905	92	s		Mar. 20	Mar. 30	May 20	May 27	May 24	June 4	Sept. 18	Sept. 25
Do.	F	1904	78	s		Mar. 10	Mar. 20	May 13	May 25	May 20	May 30	Aug. 23	Do.
Do.	G	1904	82	s		Mar. 6	Apr. 1	May 28	June 10		June 14		
Do.	Li	1904	41	s		Mar. 14	...do...	May 16	June 20	May 20	June 25	Sept. 25	Oct. 5
Do.	L	1904	88	s		Mar. 12	Mar. 30	May 19	June 3	May 22	June 10	Sept. 23	
Do.	M	1904	82	s		Mar. 28	Apr. 6	May 26	...do...	June 1	June 9	Sept. 25	Oct. 8
Do.	O	1904	82	s	2 to 4	Mar. 21	Mar. 25	...do...	May 31	May 30	June 2	Sept. 28	Oct. 9
Do.	S	1904	82	s		Mar. 17	Apr. 8	...do...	June 18	...do...	June 22	Sept. 25	Oct. 12
Do.	St	1907	87	s		Mar. 15	Mar. 25	May 15	June 2	May 20	June 7		
Seibel, No. 14:													
Rup. × (Lins. × Vin.)	C	1906	92	s		Mar. 31	Apr. 10	May 26	June 1	May 30	June 6		
D.	Cx	1906	95	s		Mar. 20	Apr. 5	May 4	June 12	May 11	May 17	Sept. 5	Sept. 23
Do.	Gi	1905	93	s		Mar. 9	Mar. 25	May 9	May 27	May 13	May 30	Sept. 19	Sept. 25
Do.	O	1904	84	s		Mar. 17	Apr. 1	May 19	May 29	May 24	June 3	Sept. 20	Oct. 9

Seibel, No. 29: Rup. × (Lins. × Vin.)	O	1907	88	s	2 to 4	Mar. 25	Apr. 12	June 1	June 15	June 5	June 20	Sept. 26	Oct. 15
Seibel, No. 38: Rup. × (Lins. × Vin.)	C	1906	93	s	....	Mar. 27	Apr. 21	May 20	June 1	....	June 7	....	
Seibel, No. 60: Rup. × (Lins. × Vin. × Rup.)	O	1907	70	s	....	Apr. 5	....	May 29	June 8	June 2	June 12	....	
Seibel, No. 70: Rup. × (Lins. × Vin. × Rup.)	O	1907	81	s	2 to 5	Mar. 19	Apr. 1	May 26	June 5	June 1	June 10	Sept. 25	Oct. 10
Seibel, No. 78: Rup. × (Lins. × Vin.)	O	1907	80	s	2 to 5	Mar. 26	Mar. 28	...do....	June 8	...do....	June 14	Sept. 23	Oct. 2
Seibel, No. 80: Rup. × (Lins. × Vin.)	O	1907	89	s	2 to 5	Mar. 24	...do....	May 21	May 30	May 25	June 5	Sept. 24	Oct. 7
Seibel, No. 128: Rup. × (Lins. × Vin.)	O	1907	83	s	2 to 4	...do....	Apr. 1	May 26	June 11	June 1	June 16	Sept. 21	Oct. 8
Seibel, No. 156: Rup. × (Lins. × Vin.)	O	1907	84	s	2 to 3	Mar. 21	Apr. 3	May 27	June 7	...do....	June 13	Sept. 23	Oct. 15
Seibel, No. 209: Rup. × (Lins. × Vin.)	O	1907	82	s	2 to 4	Mar. 25	Mar. 28	May 31	June 12	June 4	June 18	Sept. 24	Oct. 8
Seibel, No. 215: Rup. × (Lins. × Vin.)	C	1906	93	s	....	Mar. 30	Apr. 10	May 16	June 3	May 21	June 9	....	
Do.	Gi	1905	76	s	....	Mar. 20	Mar. 30	May 25				Sept. 15	Sept. 20
Do.	O	1907	86	s	2 to 4	Mar. 21	Apr. 3	May 26	June 9	June 1	June 14	Sept. 22	Oct. 27
Seibel, No. 334: Rup. × (Lins. × Vin. × Rup.)	O	1907	78	s	2 to 5	Mar. 24	Mar. 28	May 5	June 8	May 30	...do....	Sept. 23	Do.
Seibel, No. [illegible]: Rup. × (Lins. × Vin.)	O	1907	82	s	2 to 5	Mar. 16	Apr. 10	May 28	June 10	June 2	...do....	Sept. 22	Oct. 6
Seibel, No. [illegible]: Rup. × (Lins. × Vin.)	O	1907	86	s	2 to 5	Mar. 22	Apr. 2	May 27	...do....	June 1	...do....	Sept. 20	Oct. 9
Seibel, No. 1077: Rup. × (Lins. × Vin.)	O	1907	81	s	3 to 5	Mar. 26	Apr. 10	May 29	June 15	June 2	June 21	Sept. 29	Oct. 7
Seibel, No. [illegible]: Rup. × (Lins. × Vin.)	O	1907	82	s	2 to 5	Mar. 24	Mar. 30	May 24	June 3	May 28	June 8	Sept. 30	Oct. 15
Seibel, No. [illegible]: Rup. × (Lins. × Vin.)	O	1907	86	s	2 to 5	Apr. 8	....	May 28	June 18	June 1	June 23	Sept. 24	
Seibel, No. [illegible]: Rup. × (Lins. × Vin.)	O	1907	85	s	2 to 3	Mar. 22	Mar. 24	May 24	June 5	May 28	June 10	Sept. 28	Oct. 10
Seibel, No. 2043: Rup. × (Lins. × Vin. × Rup.)	St	1910	69	s	....	Mar. 5	Mar. 29	May 17	May 27	May 20	May 31	....	
Seibel, No. 2044: Rup. × (Lins. × Vin. × Rup.)	O	1907	88	s	1 to 5	Mar. 24	Apr. 1	May 22	May 30	May 26	June 6	Sept. 23	Oct. 15
Seibel, No. 2056: Rup. × (Lins. × Vin. × Rup.)	O	1907	89	s	3 to 5	Mar. 26	...do....	May 26	...do....	May 30	June 3	Sept. 30	Oct. 9
Shala: Lins. × (Rup. × Lab.)	C	1903	90	s	....	Mar. 31	Apr. 17	May 5	May 20	May 9	May 25	....	
Do.	O	1903	90	s	....	Mar. 19	Apr. 5	May 19	June 2	May 23	June 7	....	
[illegible]: Lab. × (Aest. × Vin.)	O	1905	80	s	....	Mar. 21	Apr. 2	June 3	June 7	June 5	June 12	....	
Wine King: (Aest. × Lab.) × (Lins. × Rup.)	C	1907	97	s	....	Mar. 31	Apr. 8	May 4	May 30	May 9	June 4	....	
Do.	O	1903	93	s	2 to 4	Mar. 16	Apr. 3	May 19	May 31	May 25	June 3	....	

TABLE X.—*Relative behavior and value for different purposes of improved native American and Franco-American varieties of grapes growing on their own roots in eleven experiment vineyards in California*—Continued.

Variety and parentage.	Experiment vineyard.	Year planted.	Growth rating.	How pruned.	Nodes bearing fruit.	Growth-starting date. Early season.	Growth-starting date. Late season.	Blossoming date. Early season.	Blossoming date. Late season.	Fruit-setting date. Early season.	Fruit-setting date. Late season.	Fruit-ripening date. Early season.	Fruit-ripening date. Late season.
1	2	3	4	5	6	7	8	9	10	11	12	13	14
Worden:			*Per ct.*										
Lab.	C	1906	72	c, s		Mar. 30	Apr. 20	May 8	May 20		May 26		
Do.	Cx	1906	81	s		Mar. 25	Apr. 5	June 1	June 5	June 5		Sept. 20	Sept. 30
Do.	F	1905	67	s		Mar. 15	do.	May 5	May 30		June 4	Aug. 29	Sept. 15
Do.	G	1905	56	s		Mar. 5	Apr. 3	May 15	June 1		June 6		
Do.	L	1905	72	s		Mar. 11	Apr. 5	May 10	May 23	May 14	May 28		
Do.	M	1905	74	s		Mar. 26	Apr. 6	May 25	June 8	May 30	June 13	Sept. 9	
Do.	O	1905	47	s	1 to 2	Mar. 18	Apr. 5	May 17	May 30	May 23	June 5	do.	
Do.	S	1905	80	s		Mar. 11	Apr. 8	May 25	June 9	June 8	June 12		
Wyoming Red:													
Lab.	F	1905	71	s		Mar. 7	Mar. 25	May 8	May 20	May 12	May 24	Aug. 25	Sept. 5
Do.	G	1905	82	s		Mar. 2	do.	May 24	June 5	May 28	June 10		
Do.	Li	1905	45	s		Mar. 11	Apr. 5	May 25	June 1	June 4	June 5		
Do.	L	1905	66	s		do.	Apr. 1	May 10	May 27	May 14	May 29		
Do.	M	1905	70	s		Mar. 30	Apr. 5	June 5	June 7	June 10			
Do.	O	1905	85	s	1 to 3	Mar. 18	Mar. 30	May 16	May 25	May 23	June 2		
Do.	S	1905	82	s		Mar. 16	Apr. 5	May 24	June 18	May 27	June 22		
Xinta:													
(Lins. × Rup.) × (Vin. × Lab.)	C	1907	80	s		Mar. 29	Apr. 17	May 2	May 10	May 7	May 20		
Do.	F	1903	61	s		Mar. 5	Mar. 25	May 10	May 15	May 15	do.		
Do.	O	1903	76	s	2 to 3	Mar. 16	Apr. 1	May 18	June 5	May 24	June 18	Sept. 20	Oct. 1

Variety and parentage.	Weight of fruit per vine (pounds).					Sugar, Balling scale.	Acid, as tartaric, grams per 100 c. c.	Cluster.			Berry.			Use.
	1909	1910	1911	1912	1913			Size.	Shape.	Compact or loose.	Size.	Shape.	Color.	
1	15	16	17	18	19	20	21	22	23	24	25	26	27	28
Agawam:						*Per ct.*								
Lab. × Vin.	2				1½	24.6	0.655	m	cy	c	m, l	r	r	s, st, t
Do.	3	4	¼			22.5	.6175	m	cy	c	m, l	r	r	s, st, t
Albania:														
Lins. × ([illegible]t. × Lab. × Bourq.)	4					24.6	.4425	l	t	m	m	r	w	w, s, st, t
a[illegible]te Ganzin:														
Vin. × Rup.	6	3			16	24.2	.8920	l	t	c	m	r	b	w
[illegible]te × Rupestris Terrace, No. 20:														
[illegible]n. × [illegible]	50	8				25.2	.6913	s	cy	c	s	r	b	w
Do.	20	5	15			24.7	.5425	s	cy	c	s	r	b	w
Do.		1½	8	10		25.6	.86	s	cy	c	s	r	b	w
Amerbonte:														
Bourq. × (Lins. × Rup.)								l	t	m	s	r	r	w, s, t
Do.								l	t	m	s	r	r	w, s, t
Do.								l	t	m	s	r	r	w, s, t
[illegible]a:														
([illegible]s. × Rup.) × (Bourq. × Lab.)	10	6		2	2	28.8	.8022	l	t	m	s	r	r	w, s, t
Do.	8					24.9	.9155	l	t	m	s	r	r	w, s, t
Barry:														
[illegible]. × Vin.			1	1		25.5	.6525	m	cy	m	l	r	b	s, st, t
Do.						25.2	.7875	m	cy	m	l	r	b	s, st, t
[illegible]s:														
Rip. × (Lab. × Bourq.)			⅓	½		25.5	.8588	m	cy	c	m	r	r	w, st, t
Do.			1			23	.825	l	cy	c	m	r	b	w, st, t
Big Extra:														
[illegible]s. × (Lab. × Vin.)		¼		2		25.8	.8362	l	cy	c	m	r	b	w, st, t
Do.	8		2	16	1	22.4	.6631	l	cy	c	m	r	b	w, st, t
Do.			1		2½	22	.9825	l	cy	c	m	r	b	w, st, t
Do.			1			21	.8025	l	cy	c	m	r	b	w, st, t
Do.		½		1		20.6	.9358	l	cy	c	m	r	b	w, st, t
Do.		2				23.2	1.2006	l	cy	c	m	r	b	w, st, t
[illegible].	10	5				22.9	.8075	l	cy	c	m	r	b	w, st, t
Do.		4			1	23.8	.8581	l	cy	c	m	r	b	w, st, t
[illegible]:														
[illegible]rq. × Aest.) × (Lins. × Lab.)	4	3	½			22.6	.6617	l	cy	c	m	r	w	w, t
Do.	6		5			24.3	.5737	l	cy	c	m	r	w	w, t

TABLE X.—*Relative behavior and value for different purposes of improved native American and Franco-American varieties of grapes growing on their own roots in eleven experiment vineyards in California*—Continued.

Variety and parentage.	Weight of fruit per vine (pounds).					Sugar, Balling scale.	Acid, as tartaric, grams per 100 c. c.	Cluster.			Berry.			Use.
	1909	1910	1911	1912	1913			Size.	Shape.	Compact or loose.	Size.	Shape.	Color.	
1	15	16	17	18	19	20	21	22	23	24	25	26	27	28
[illegible] × Rupestris, No. 601:						*Per ct.*								
Vin. × Rup.			2	7½		25.5	1.0537	l	t	m	s	r	b	w
Do.	15		8	13		23.9	.7571	l	t	m	s	r	b	w
Do.	15	25	10		16	25.5	.8631	l	t	m	s	r	b	w
Do.			7	2		22.5	1.117	l	t	m	s	r	b	w
Do.				3		22	.9825	l	t	m	s	r	b	w
Do.	30	15	10	5		23.2	1.1381	l	t	m	s	r	b	w
[illegible] × Rupestris, No. 603:														
Vin. × Rup.			2	4		21.5	.737	l	t	m	s	r	b	w
Do.	15	18	10	4	23	21.3	.8155	l	t	m	s	r	b	w
Do.			4			21	1.2225	l	t	m	s	r	b	w
Do.				6		22	.9112	l	t	m	s	r	b	w
Do.		3		6		20.1	.94	l	t	m	s	r	b	w
Do.	20		6		24	21	.9187	l	t	m	s	r	b	w
Do.		4	3		16	23.6	.7631	l	t	m	s	r	b	w
[illegible] × Rupestris, No. 109-4:														
Vin. × Rup.			1			27	.93	l	t	m	s	r	b	w
Do.			4	6		20	.8437	l	t	m	s	r	b	w
Do.	15	20	10	13		27.1	.9693	l	t	m	s	r	b	w
Do.		1½	5	1		25	1.0858	l	t	m	s	r	b	w
Do.						26	.9525	l	t	m	s	r	b	w
Do.		3				23.2	1.1570	l	t	m	s	r	b	w
Do.	15					23.2	.6975	l	t	m	s	r	b	w
Do.		3	2		8	24.9	.9350	l	t	m	s	r	b	w
[illegible] × [illegible], No. 3907:														
Vin. × Rup.			1½	4½		25	1.012	l	t	m	s	r	b	w
Do.			½	8		24	.8962	l	t	m	s	r	b	w
Do.	20	20	10	8	8	25.2	.8846	l	t	m	s	r	b	w
Do.					9½	32	1.1250	l	t	m	s	r	b	w
Do.								l	t	m	s	r	b	w
Do.		5	2		5	24.4	.7631	l	t	m	s	r	b	w
Bourisquou × Rupestris, No. 4306:														
Vin. × Rup.				2		25	1.02	m	cy	m	s	r	b	w
Do.	6			20		23.6	.9295	m	cy	m	s	r	b	w
Do.			1	½		22	1.005	m	cy	m	s	r	b	w
Do.	12					23.8	.75	m	cy	m	s	r	b	w

Bourisquou × Rupestris, No. 4308:															
Vin. × Rup.			2	4½		24.5	1.113	m	cy	m	s	r	b	w
Do.				5		27	.8625	m	cy	m	s	r	b	w
Do.	10			12		25.6	.8625	m	cy	m	s	r	b	w
Do.	4					21.4	1.4275	m	cy	m	s	r	b	w
Do.	12					25.2	.78	m	cy	m	s	r	b	w
Brighton:															
Lab. × Vin.						22.7	.705	l	t	m	m	r	r	s, st, t
Brilliant:															
Lab. × (Vin. × Bourq.)	4	⅓	1	7		26.1	.6355	m	cy	c	m	r	r	s, st, t
Do.	6		2	2½		26.1	.5825	m	cy	c	m	r	r	s, st, t
Do.			2			21	.6	m	cy	c	m	r	r	s, st, t
Do.			½			26	.975	m	cy	c	m	r	r	s, st, t
Canada:															
(Rip. × Lab.) × Vin.	15	15	½	2		23.1	.7031	m	cy	c	m	r	b	s, st, t
Do.		1		2		28.4	.7791	m	cy	c	m	r	b	s, st, t
Do.	15		9		10	25	.7800	m	cy	c	m	r	b	s, st, t
Do.		6	6		22	23.4	.8337	m	cy	c	m	r	b	s, st, t
Carignane × Rupestris, No. 404:															
Vin. × Rup.	7	25	12			22.9	.8033	m	t	m	m	r	b	w
Do.			12		20½	20.8	.7775	m	t	m	m	r	b	w
Do.		2	10	2½		24.1	.8572	m	t	m	m	r	b	w
Do.		6	2	8		22.2	.887	m	t	m	m	r	b	w
Do.	25	5				23.2	.6337	m	t	m	m	r	b	w
Do.			6			23	.712	m	t	m	m	r	b	w
Carignane × Rupestris, No. 501:															
Vin. × Rup.						26	.645	m	t	m	m	r	b	w
Do.				3½		22	.9012	m	t	m	m	r	b	w
Do.	15	3				24.3	.7462	m	t	m	m	r	b	w
Do.					7	23	.6	m	t	m	m	r	b	w
Carman:															
Lins. × (Vin. × Lab. × Bourq.)	3	¼	¼	1		26.6	.5669	m	t	m	m	r	b	w, t
Do.	4		4			24.8	.6275	m	t	m	m	t	b	w, t
Castel, No. 1028:															
Rip. × Vin.	3				3½	25.2	.6100	m	cy	m	m	r	b	w
Castel, No. 19002:															
(Lab. × Rup.) × Vin.	5	7	2		12	25.9	.5970	m	cy	m	m	r	b	w
Catawba:															
Lab. × Vin.		1				28	.57	m	cy	c	m	r	r	w, st, t
Do.	3		½			21.7	.397	m	cy	c	m	r	r	w, st, t
Do.			½			20	.6	m	cy	c	m	r	r	w, st, t
Do.		1		4		25.2	.8925	m	cy	c	m	r	r	w, st, t
Do.				½		21	1.005	m	cy	c	m	r	r	w, st, t
Do.	8		2		2	24.3	.8255	m	cy	c	m	r	r	w, st, t
Do.		5	4		16	23.5	.697	m	cy	c	m	r	r	w, st, t
Centennial:															
Lab. × Aest.				½		23	.9825	s	t	c	m	r	r	w, t
Do.	2	3	3	5		24.3	.6602	s	t	c	m	r	r	w, t
Do.					3½	23.4	.7912	s	t	c	m	r	r	w, t
Champenel:															
Champ. × Lab.	5					22.8	.78	m	cy	c	m	r	b	w, t

TABLE X.—*Relative behavior and value for different purposes of improved native American and Franco-American varieties of grapes growing on their own roots in eleven experiment vineyards in California*—Continued.

Variety and parentage.	Weight of fruit per vine (pounds).					Sugar, Balling scale.	Acid, as tartaric, grams per 100 c. c.	Cluster.			Berry.			Use.
	1909	1910	1911	1912	1913			Size.	Shape.	Compact or loose.	Size.	Shape.	Color.	
1	15	16	17	18	19	20	21	22	23	24	25	26	27	28
Chasselas × Rupestris, No. 901:						*Per ct.*								
Vin. × Rup.	5		10			26.5	.6337	m	cy	c	m	r	b	w
Do.	8					25	.7275	m	cy	c	m	r	b	w
Clairette Doré Ganzin:														
Vin. × Rup.								l	t	l	m	r	w	w
Do.	4			29		20.4	1.1437	l	t	l	m	r	w	w
Do.		2		2		25.1	.9825	l	t	l	m	r	w	w
Do.	60	20	13	8	42	18.3	1.2255	l	t	l	m	r	w	w
Clevener:														
Lab. × (Rip. × Aest.)					2	25	.7875	s	cy	c	s	r	b	w
Cloeta:														
(Lins. × Rup.) × (Lab. × Vin.)		4				22.9	.66	l	cy	l	m	r	b	w, t
Columbaud × Rupestris:														
Vin. × Rup.	10					21.9	.78	m	t	m	m	r	b	w
Concord:														
Lab.						24	.3975	m	cy	m	m, l	r	b	w, st, t
Do.				4		23	.3525	m	cy	m	m, l	r	b	w, st, t
Do.						22.4	.57	m	cy	m	m, l	r	b	w, st, t
Do.			⅛			26	1.132	m	cy	m	m, l	r	b	w, st, t
Cornucopia:														
Vin. × Rip.	4					25	.825	l	cy	c	m	r	b	st, t
Do.					5	25	.8625	l	cy	c	m	r	b	st, t
Couderc, No. 101:														
Vin. × Rip.		1	3	½		28.3	1.1275	s	cy	c	s	r	b	w
Do.	15	20	5		24	24.4	.8344	s	cy	c	s	r	b	w
Do.			4	⅔	12½	21	.8675	s	cy	c	s	r	b	w
Do.		2	8			25.1	1.0225	s	cy	c	s	s	b	w
Do.		5	4	4		22.3	1.0916	s	cy	c	s	r	b	w
Do.	40	8	10	5	4½	22	1.0355	s	cy	c	s	r	b	w
Do.		4	3		9	26.1	.9693	s	cy	c	s	r	b	w
Couderc, No. 201:														
Rip. × (Rup. × Vin.)			2	15	6	21	.8818	s	cy	c	s	r	b	w
Do.	15	20	8	15	23	24.2	.7935	s	cy	c	s	r	b	w
Do.			1	3	3	19	1.1300	s	cy	c	s	r	b	w
Do.		½	7	½		24	1.1193	s	cy	c	s	r	b	w

Do	...	6	4	4½	...	21.6	1.0716	s	cy	c	s	r	b	w
Do	30	6	11	5	15	26	.9570	s	cy	c	s	r	b	w
Do	...	8	8	...	21	23	1.0423	s	cy	c	s	r	b	w
Couderc, No. 503:														
Rup. × Vin.	...	⅓	3	2	...	23.1	.8	l	t	l	s	r	b	w
Do	...	...	...	8	1	21	.8437	l	t	l	s	r	b	w
Do	20	25	10	37	18	21.8	.8190	l	t	l	s	r	b	w
Do	...	...	2	...	16	19.5	1.042	l	t	l	s	r	b	w
Do	...	3½	10	3	...	23.3	.795	l	t	l	s	r	b	w
Do	...	8	6	18	...	20.4	.8731	l	t	l	s	r	b	w
Do	60	10	14	13	28½	20.8	.736	l	t	l	s	r	b	w
Couderc, No. 704	...	10	6	...	24	23.1	.8137	s	cy	s	s	r	b	w
Do	...	...	8	4	10½	21	.8100	s	cy	s	s	r	b	w
Do	...	8	4	20	...	22.3	.9383	s	cy	s	s	r	b	w
Do	40	8	11	3	20	22.8	.7065	s	cy	s	s	r	b	w
Do	...	8	6	...	16	22.8	.8493	s	cy	s	s	r	b	w
Couderc, No. 3701:														
Vin. × Rup.	...	½	2	4	...	24.6	1.055	m	t	c	m	r	b	w
Do	...	...	5	¾	19½	21	.9000	m	t	c	m	r	b	w
Do	...	3	12	2	...	24.4	.9575	m	t	c	m	r	b	w
Do	...	4	...	9	...	22.1	1.0162	m	t	c	m	r	b	w
Do	25	8	6½	5	8	23.6	.8879	m	t	c	m	r	b	w
Do	...	5	6	...	8	23.6	.9031	m	t	c	m	r	b	w
Couderc, No. 1401:														
Rup. × Vin.	5	2	...	...	2	26	.7075	m	cy	m	s	r	b	w
Couderc, No. 28 × No. 112:														
M? × Rup.	...	3	4	3	...	23.8	1.1125	m	cy	m	m	r	b	w
Do	10	30	10	33	25	24	.9513	m	cy	m	m	r	b	w
Do	...	...	6	...	18½	21.2	.9712	m	cy	m	m	r	b	w
Do	...	2½	8	1½	...	21.5	1.0856	m	cy	m	m	r	b	w
Do	...	...	...	...	...	25.2	.975	m	cy	m	m	r	b	w
Do	...	...	...	5½	...	22	.9825	m	cy	m	m	r	b	w
Do	10	5	12	...	...	24.5	1.0341	m	cy	m	m	r	b	w
Do	...	3	4	...	13	25	.9631	m	cy	m	m	r	b	w
Couderc, No. 71–06:														
Rup. × (Lins. × Vin.)	4	2	½	...	3½	25	.6543	m	cy	m	m	r	b	w
Couderc, No. 71–20:														
Rup. × (Lins. × Vin.)	3	4	2	4	5	26.6	.8580	m	cy	m	m	r	b	w
Couderc, No. 74–17:														
[illegible] Hybrid	...	...	...	1½	6	24.5	.6575	m	cy	m	m	r	b	w
Couderc, No. 82 × 32:														
Complex Hybrid	...	½	½	6	...	22.1	.65	m	cy	l	l	o	w	w, t, st
Do	6	8	1½	9	...	22.6	.8819	m	cy	l	l	o	w	w, t, st
Do	...	...	3	...	1½	19	.9458	m	cy	l	l	o	w	w, t, st
Do	...	⅓	2	...	...	24.5	.997	m	cy	l	l	o	w	w, t, st
Do	...	...	2	¾	...	23	.727	m	cy	l	l	o	w	w, t, st
Do	15	3	6	3	2	21.1	.7800	m	cy	l	l	o	w	w, t, st
Do	...	...	½	...	...	24	.907	m	cy	l	l	o	w	w, t, st
Couderc, No. 84 × 61:														
(Vin. × Rup.) × Vin.	...	1	4	1½	...	25.3	.9425	m	t	m	m	r	b	w
Do	...	...	1½	8	...	24.5	.499	m	t	m	m	r	b	w
Do	20	20	1	5	3	23.3	.6032	m	t	m	m	r	b	w

TABLE X.—*Relative behavior and value for different purposes of improved native American and Franco-American varieties of grapes growing on their own roots in eleven experiment vineyards in California*—Continued.

Variety and parentage.	Weight of fruit per vine (pounds). 1909	1910	1911	1912	1913	Sugar, Balling scale.	Acid, as tartaric, grams per 100 c. c.	Cluster. Size.	Cluster. Shape.	Cluster. Compact or loose.	Berry. Size.	Berry. Shape.	Berry. Color.	Use.
1	15	16	17	18	19	20	21	22	23	24	25	26	27	28
Couderc, No. 84 × 61—Continued.						*Per ct.*								
(Vin. × Rup.) × Vin.	......	......	2	1	3	20.6	.9275	m	t	m	m	r	b	w
Do.	......	½	3	10	......	24	.7969	m	t	m	m	r	b	w
Do.	......	½	......	2	......	23.8	.645	m	t	m	m	r	b	w
Do.	......	6	4	16	......	21.5	1.077	m	t	m	m	r	b	w
Do.	......	15	......	1½	......	22.5	.715	m	t	m	m	r	b	w
Do.	......	6	4	......	6	26.5	.8468	m	t	m	m	r	b	w
Couderc, No. 85 × 113:														
(Vin. × Rup.) × Vin.	6	4	2½	2½	......	23.7	.8156	m	cy	m	m	r	b	w
Couderc, [illegible] × 115:														
Vin. × (Rup. × Vin.)	......	......	1	3	......	24	.57	l	cy t	l	s	r	b	w
Do.	......	......	2	4	......	26	.6562	l	cy t	l	s	r	b	w
Do.	20	4	......	34	21	23.9	.572	l	cy t	l	s	r	b	w
Do.	......	......	2	1	9	20	.7975	l	cy t	l	s	r	b	w
Do.	......	½	4	2½	......	23.8	.8925	l	cy t	l	s	r	b	w
Do.	......	6	6	19	......	24.7	1.0125	l	cy t	l	s	r	b	w
Do.	35	10	13	6	......	21.8	.6224	l	cy t	l	s	r	b	w
Do.	......	6	......	......	22	21.7	.7612	l	cy t	l	s	r	b	w
Couderc, No. 124 × 30:														
Vin. × (Rup. × Vin.)	......	......	......	2	12	21.7	.877	m	cy	m	l	r	b	w
Do.	25	15	8	7	8	22.3	.9105	m	cy	m	l	r	b	w
Do.	......	......	......	......	11½	19.5	.8937	m	cy	m	l	r	b	w
Do.	......	3	7	4	......	23	1.0744	m	cy	m	l	r	b	w
Do.	......	1½	......	6	......	23.3	.995	m	cy	m	l	r	b	w
Do.	......	6	4	17	......	21.8	1.1655	m	cy	m	l	r	b	w
Do.	40	5	14	......	28	21.8	.8868	m	cy	m	l	r	b	w
Do.	......	8	4	......	12	22.3	.9702	m	cy	m	l	r	b	w
Couderc, No. 132–11:														
[illegible]x Hybrid	6	2	2	2	18	22.7	.5106	l	t	m	m	r	b	w
Couderc, No. 199–88:														
Vin. × (Rup. × Vin.)	......	2	½	......	......	26	.6632	m	t	m	m	r	w	w, t
Couderc, No. 241–125:														
Vin. × (Rup. × Vin.)	......	1	......	......	3	26	.7162	m	cy	m	s	r	b	w
Couderc, No. 267–27:														
Complex Hybrid	......	3	2	½	10	29	.6262	m	cy	m	m	r	b	w

[illegible]rc, No. 272-60:														
[illegible]x Hybrid			3	6	20	28	.6300	m	t	m	m	r	r	w, t
Delaware:														
Ab. × Bourq. × [illegible]			2	1		29	.7237	s	cy	c	s	r	r	w, st; t
Do				½		28	.5025	s	cy	c	s	r	r	w, st, t
[illegible]:														
Ab. × Vin	1	½			2	25.8	.4350	m	cy	m	l	r	w	st, t
Do				½		22	.57	m	cy	m	l	r	w	st, t
Do						24	.6225	m	cy	m	l	r	w	st, t
Diana:														
Lab. × Vin. × Aest	½	1½				23.4	.585	m	cy	l	m	r	r	w, st, t
Do	10				3	22.9	.468	m	cy	l	m	r	r	w, st, t
Dutchess:														
Lab. × Vin. × Aest		1		½		24	.5025	l	t	m	s	r	w	w, t
Do			½			23.3	.4925	l	t	m	s	r	w	w, t
Do		1				23.4	.5425	l	t	m	s	r	w	w, t
Do	6		½		3½	26.1	.6037	l	t	m	s	r	w	w, t
Do		3	½		4	29	.3635	l	t	m	s	r	w	w, t
Elvira:														
Rip. × Lab	5		1	8	2	29.	.5906	m	cy	c	m	r	w	w, t
Do	10	3	3	9	3	24	.5959	m	cy	c	m	r	w	w, t
Do		4		5		26.2	.6175	m	cy	c	m	r	w	w, t
Do		½				23.5	.48	m	cy	c	m	r	w	w, t
Fern [illegible]son:														
[illegible]s. × (Vin. × Lab.)			½	½		24	1.32	l	cy	m	m	r	b	w, t
Do	2		3			24.2	1,3383	l	cy	m	m	r	b	w, t
Do		3			1	25	1.0108	l	cy	m	m	r	b	w, t
Gold Coin:														
Est. × Lab		2	¼	⅓		23	.5746	m	cy	m	m	r	w	t, st
Do			½	¾	3	22	.7650	m	cy	m	m	r	w	t, st
Do	1					26.6	.445	m	cy	m	m	r	w	t, st
Do		1½			1	23	.607	m	cy	m	m	r	w	t, st
[illegible]or [illegible]ss:														
Ab. × Vin				7		30	.7125	l	cy	m	l	o	w	t
Herbemont:														
Bourq			4	1½		23	1.030	m	cy	c	s	r	b	w, st, t
Do		8	4	12		21	.7350	m	cy	c	s	r	b	w, st, t
Do		3		5		22	1,132	m	cy	c	s	r	b	w, st, t
Do	15	2	5	3		23	.8081	m	cy	c	s	r	b	w, st, t
Do						26		m	cy	c	s	r	b	w, st, t
Herbert:														
Ab. × Vin	3	⅓				25	.5587	m	cy	m	l	r	b	st, t
Do					3	22	.6375	m	cy	m	l	r	b	st, t
Hexamer:														
Lins. × (Lab. × Vin.)	4	2				23	1.0532	m	cy	m	m	o	b	w, t
Do	2		5½	1	2	22.4	1.0589	m	cy	m	m	o	b	w, t
[illegible]n:														
Lins. × (Vin. × Lab.)	2				3	25	.7658	m l	cy	l	l	r	b	w, t
Imperial:														
Vin. × Lab				15	8	20	.6487	l	cy	m	l	r	w	t

TABLE X.—*Relative behavior and value for different purposes of improved native American and Franco-American varieties of grapes growing on their own roots in eleven experiment vineyards in California*—Continued.

Variety and parentage.	Weight of fruit per vine (pounds). 1909	1910	1911	1912	1913	Sugar, Balling scale.	Acid, as tartaric, grams per 100 c. c.	Cluster. Size.	Cluster. Shape.	Cluster. Compact or loose.	Berry. Size.	Berry. Shape.	Berry. Color.	Use.
1	15	16	17	18	19	20	21	22	23	24	25	26	27	28
Isabella:						*Per ct.*								
Lab. × Vin		2	2	1		26	1.658	m	cy	c	m	r	b	st, t
Do								m	cy	c	m	r	b	st, t
Do			½			18	.587	m	cy	c	m	r	b	st, t
Do								m	cy	c	m	r	b	st, t
Do				1½		28	.72	m	cy	c	m	r	b	st, t
Do								m	cy	c	m	r	b	st, t
Do	3		1½			23	.3037	m	cy	c	m	r	b	st, t
Do			6		22	22	.7837	m	cy	c	m	r	b	st, t
Jaeger:														
Lins. × oBrq	6		¼		1½	25	.6931	m	cy	c	s	r	b	w
Do			½		3	23	1.027	m	cy	c	s	r	b	w
Do								m	cy	c	s	r	b	w
Do	3					24.9	.81	m	cy	c	s	r	b	w
Jefferson:														
Lab. × Vin								m	cy	c	l	r	r	st, t
Do	3	1			1	29	.3777	m	cy	m	l	r	b	w, t
Ki wa:														
Lins. × Bourq								m	cy	m	l	r	b	w, t
Do	3					20.8	.66	s	cy	m	m	r	r	t
Lampasas:														
L b. × Aest								m	cy	c	m	r	b	t
[illegible]l:														
Lins. × (Lab. × Aest.)				¼		23	.5625	l	t	l	s	r	b	w
Lenoir:														
Bourq		2	2			29.2	.977	l	t	l	s	r	b	w
Do	5	5	5	30	10	23.6	1.3334	l	t	l	s	r	b	w
Do	15	6	1			29.2	.7375	l	t	l	s	r	b	w
Do			2	2	9	22	.995	l	t	l	s	r	b	w
Do			1½	5		24	1.1212	l	t	l	s	r	b	w
Do		1½		18		24.9	1.1141	l	t	l	s	r	b	w
Do		5		5½		22	1.235	l	t	l	s	r	b	w
Do	15	2				24	1.0575	l	t	l	s	r	b	w
Do		6	2		4	23.8	.8493	l	t	l	s	r	b	w

						[sugar?]	[acid?]							
Lindley:														
Lab. × Vin	......	½	2	1½	......	26.4	.5000	m	cy	l	m	r	r	w, t
Do	......	......	......	½	1	22.5	.5512	m	cy	l	m	r	r	w, t
Do	8	1	......	5	8	23.1	.4500	m	cy	l	m	r	r	w, t
Do	4	......	......	......	1	23.3	.5300	m	cy	l	m	r	r	w, t
[illegible]ina:														
[illegible]	12	......	5	......	6	25.5	.7350	s	cy	c	s	r	b	w, t
Do	......	......	......	......	2	30	.6325	s	cy	c	s	r	b	w, t
[illegible]ta:														
Champ. × Lab	......	......	......	1½	......	20	.7275	m	cy	c	l	r	b	t
Do	......	......	......	......	......	......	......	m	cy	c	l	r	b	t
Do	......	......	......	......	......	......	......	m	cy	c	l	r	b	t
Manito:														
(Lab. × Vin. × Bourq.) × (Lins. × Rup.)	3	......	......	......	......	23.6	.7012	m	cy	c	m	r	b	t
[illegible]arguerite:														
Lins. × Bourq	......	......	......	......	......	22	.6075	m	cy	c	m	r	b	w, t
Do	......	......	......	......	......	26.5	.90	m	cy	c	m	r	b	w, t
Do	......	......	......	......	......	......	......	m	cy	c	m	r	b	w, t
Do	......	......	......	......	2	26	.9	m	cy	c	m	r	b	w, t
Martha:														
[illegible]. × Vin	......	......	......	......	......	23	.51	m	t	l	m	r	w	t
[illegible] Riesling:														
Rip. × Lab	2	4	1	4	6	23.9	.5791	s	cy	c	s	r	w	w
Do	......	1½	......	½	......	25.6	.6300	s	cy	c	s	r	w	w
Do	3	1	1½	......	......	25.5	.4900	s	cy	c	s	r	w	w
[illegible]rs. [illegible]n:														
[illegible]s. × Bourq	4	½	1	......	......	23.6	.6775	m	cy	l	m	r	b	t
e[illegible]:														
Lins. × Bo[illegible]q	4	6	2	8	4	25.7	.6790	m	cy	c	s	r	b	w
Do	2	......	4	......	......	23.9	.8662	m	cy	c	s	r	b	w
[illegible]iagara:														
Lab. × Vin	......	......	1	1½	......	26	.51	m l	cy	m	l	r	w	w, st, t
Do	1½	½	½	......	......	25.8	.485	m l	cy	m	l	r	w	w, st, t
Do	4	......	......	......	3	25.6	.7275	m l	cy	m	l	r	w	w, st, t
Oli[illegible]tao:														
(Vin. × Lab.) × (Lins. × (Vin. × Lab.))	......	......	......	......	......	25.6	.8625	m	t	l	m	r	w	w, t
Pardes:														
Vin. × Rup	......	......	3	3½	......	23.5	.8925	m	cy	m	s	r	b	w
Do	20	5	5	15	......	2.9	.825	m	cy	m	s	r	b	w
Do	15	......	5	23	20	2.4	.65	m	cy	m	s	r	b	w
Do	......	1½	4	2	......	25.3	.9[illegible]2	m	cy	m	s	r	b	w
Do	......	......	½	2½	......	2.5	.8612	m	cy	m	s	r	b	w
Do	25	3	11	4	10	23.8	.9725	m	cy	m	s	r	b	w
Do	......	4	4	......	15	25.1	.8775	m	cy	m	s	r	b	w
Pierce:														
Lab. × Vin	......	2	......	1½	......	24.1	.6208	m	cy	c	l	o	b	st, t
Do	......	......	......	2	......	21	.9825	m	cy	c	l	o	b	st, t
Do	......	6	1	......	......	19.7	.9187	m	cy	c	l	o	b	st, t
Rebecca:														
Lab. × Vin	1½	......	......	......	......	24.6	.5137	m	cy	m	s	o	w	t
Do	......	......	......	7	......	26	.75	m	cy	m	s	o	w	t
Do	6	......	......	......	3	22.2	.4012	m	cy	m	s	o	w	t
Do	......	4	2	......	11	23	.6244	m	cy	m	s	o	w	t

TABLE X.—*Relative behavior and value for different purposes of improved native American and Franco-American varieties of grapes growing on their own roots in eleven experiment vineyards in California*—Continued.

Variety and parentage.	Weight of fruit per vine (pounds).					Sugar, Balling scale.	Acid, as tartaric, grams per 100 c. c.	Cluster.			Berry.			Use.
	1909	1910	1911	1912	1913			Size.	Shape.	Compact or loose.	Size.	Shape.	Color.	
1	15	16	17	18	19	20	21	22	23	24	25	26	27	28
Rommel:						*Per ct.*								
Lab. × (Rip. × Vin.)	6	3	5	6	6	25	.4925	m	cy	l	l	r	w	w, t
Do		2½		2		23.1	.5362	m	cy	l	l	r	w	w, t
Do					8	23	.975	m	cy	l	l	r	w	w, t
R. W. Munson:														
Lins. × (Lab. × Vin.)								m-l	cy	l	l	r	b	w, t
Do								m-l	cy	l	l	r	b	w, t
Do								m-l	cy	l	l	r	b	w, t
Do	3	¼	½			26.2	.5975	m-l	cy	l	l	r	b	w, t
Do								m-l	cy	l	l	r	b	w, t
Do								m-l	cy	l	l	r	b	w, t
Do								m-l	cy	l	l	r	b	w, t
Do								m-l	cy	l	l	r	b	w, t
Do	2					26.6	.7513	m-l	cy	l	l	r	b	w, t
Do								m-l	cy	l	l	r	b	w, t
Seibel, No. 1:														
Rup. × (Lins. × Vin.)								m	cy	l	l	r	b	w
Do		2	1	6½		37	.7918	m	cy	l	l	r	b	w
Do	18	15	15			22.8	.9081	m	cy	l	l	r	b	w
Do	30	7	2	5	1	26	.5580	m	cy	l	l	r	b	w
Do			4		14	22	.9037	m	cy	l	l	r	b	w
Do						24.7	.705	m	cy	l	l	r	b	w
Do		3		4		28.1	.765	m	cy	l	l	r	b	w
Do		2	3	7		22.2	.9986	m	cy	l	l	r	b	w
Do	50	5		9		25.1	.7437	m	cy	l	l	r	b	w
Do		10	3		6	25.4	.8418	m	cy	l	l	r	b	w
Do								m	cy	l	l	r	b	w
Seibel, No. 2:														
Rup. × (Lins. × Vin.)								m	cy	l	l	r	b	w
Do		2	3	5½		26	1.1766	m	cy	l	l	r	b	w
Do	25	18	18			24	1.2825	m	cy	l	l	r	b	w
Do	30	6	2	18	3	26	.7290	m	cy	l	l	r	b	w
Do			2	4½	23½	20	.7225	m	cy	l	l	r	b	w
Do			⅛			25	.9487	m	cy	l	l	r	b	w

Do.		3		7		25.5	1.1737	m	cy	l	l	r	b	w
Do.		3	4	6		23.1	1.0991	m	cy	l	l	r	b	w
Do.	50	2	6	3	4	23.5	1.115	m	cy	l	l	r	b	w
Do.		8	½		3	24	1.0177	m	cy	l	l	r	b	w
Do.								m	cy	l	l	r	b	w
Seibel, No. 14:														
Rup. × (Lins. × Vin.)								m	cy	l	l	r	b	w
Do.		1	1			29	.960	m	cy	l	l	r	b	w
Do.	20	6		8		23	.7750	m	cy	l	l	r	b	w
Do.	15		10		10	24	1.3325	m	cy	l	l	r	b	w
Seibel, No. 29:														
Rup. × (Lins. × Vin.)	2	3	½	3	13	24	.8895	s	cy	c	s	r	b	w
Seibel, No. 38:														
Rup. × (Lins. × Vin.)								s	cy	c	s	r	b	w
Seibel, No. 60:														
Rup. × (Lins. × Vin. × Rup.)								s	cy	c	s	r	b	w
Seibel, No. 70:														
Rup. × (Lins. × Vin. × Rup.)	5	3	2	4	13	25	.9144	s	cy	c	s	r	b	w
Seibel, No. 78:														
Rup. × (Lins. × Vin.)	4				6	28	.6212	m	cy	c	m	r	b	w
Seibel, No. 80:														
Rup. × (Lins. × Vin.)	4	4			18	26.2	.6725	m	cy	c	m	r	b	w
Seibel, No. 128:														
Rup. × (Lins. × Vin.)	1½	2			8	26	.9335	m	t	m	m	r	b	w
Seibel, No. 156:														
Rup. × (Lins. × Vin.)	2	1	1½	¼		31	.9518	m	t	m	m	r	b	w
Seibel, No. 209:														
Rup. × (Lins. × Vin.)		1			9	26	.7912	m	t	m	m	r	b	w
Seibel, No. 215:														
Rup. × (Lins. × Vin.)								m	cy	m	m	r	b	w
Do.	6	10				22.3	.8375	m	cy	m	m	r	b	w
Do.	½	4	25	3	6½	24	.8250	m	cy	m	m	r	b	w
Seibel, No. 334:														
Rup. × (Lins. × Vin. × Rup.)	2		1		6	25	1.150	l	cy	c	m	r	b	w
Seibel, No. 1004:														
Rup. × (Lins. × Vin.)	4	4	1½	3	11	23	.9555	l	cy	m	m	r	b	w
Seibel, No. 1070:														
Rup. × (Lins. × Vin.)	5	5	3		9	23	.9593	l	cy	m	m	o	b	w
Seibel, No. 1077:														
Rup. × (Lins. × Vin.)	1				6	21	.7275	m	cy	c	m	r	b	w
Seibel, No. 2010:														
Rup. × (Lins. × Vin.)		½	1	2	3	23	.8487	s	cy	c	m	r	b	w
Seibel, No. 2029:														
Rup. × (Lins. × Vin.)		1				27.4	1.155	s	cy	c	m	r	b	w
Seibel, No. 2033:														
Rup. × (Lins. × Vin.)	3	2	3		12	23.5	.8812	l	cy	c	m	r	b	w
Seibel, No. 2043:														
Rup. × (Lins. × Vin. × Rup.)								s	cy	c	m	r	b	w
Seibel, No. 2044:														
Rup. × (Lins. × Vin. × Rup.)	3	1½	2	5	6	26.⅗	1.1535	s	cy	c	m	r	b	w
Seibel, No. 2056:														
Rup. × (Lins. × Vin. × Rup.)		1			6	23.5	.9750	s	cy	c	m	r	b	w

TABLE X.—*Relative behavior and value for different purposes of improved native American and Franco-American varieties of grapes growing on their own roots in eleven experiment vineyards in California*—Continued.

Variety and parentage.	Weight of fruit per vine (pounds).					Sugar, Balling scale.	Acid, as tartaric, grams per 100 c. c.	Cluster.			Berry.			Use.
	1909	1910	1911	1912	1913			Size.	Shape.	Compact or loose.	Size.	Shape.	Color.	
1	15	16	17	18	19	20	21	22	23	24	25	26	27	28
Shala:						Per ct.								
Lins. × (Rup. × Lab.)								l	cy	c	l	r	b	w, t
Do								l	cy	m	l	r	b	w, t
Winchell:														
Lab. × (Aest. × Vin.)								l	t	l	s	r	w	w, t
Wine King:														
(Aest. × Lab.) × (Lins. × Rup.)								l	cy	c	m	r	b	w
Do						22.8	0.9000	l	cy	c	m	r	b	w
Worden:														
Lab.								m	cy	l	m	r	b	t
Do			½	½		27	.4850	m	cy	l	m	r	b	t
Do	3		¼			23.3	.5325	m	cy	l	m	r	b	t
Do								m	cy	l	m	r	b	t
Do								m	cy	l	m	r	b	t
Do								m	cy	l	m	r	b	t
Do						20.9	.5775	m	cy	l	m	r	b	t
Do								m	cy	l	m	r	r	t
Wyoming Red:														
Lab.	1½	¼	1			24.9	.5300	m	cy	l	m	r	r	t
Do								m	cy	l	m	r	r	t
Do								m	cy	l	m	r	r	t
Do								m	cy	l	m	r	r	t
Do								m	cy	l	m	r	r	t
Do						24.8	.6150	m	cy	l	m	r	r	t
Do								m	cy	l	m	r	r	t
Xlnta:														
(Lins. × Rup.) × (Vin. × Lab.)								l	cy	m	m	r	b	w
Do								l	cy	m	m	r	b	w
Do			4			23	.9375	l	cy	m	m	r	b	w

CONCLUSIONS AND SUGGESTIONS.

Varying soil, climatic, and other conditions complicate the successful establishment of vineyards on resistant stocks.

The adaptability of varieties to soil, climatic, and other conditions can be closely forecasted, but congeniality has to be determined by actual test.

The best results are obtained where the scion and stock are congenial and both are suited to all the conditions of the environment.

When both scion and stock varieties are suited to the conditions but do not thrive, congeniality is probably lacking.

The ideal vine is one having a most resistant root which is congenial to a top that produces the best fruit abundantly.

Different species used as stocks with the same variety grafted on them (Table VII) may increase or diminish its vigor and productiveness; increase or diminish the quality, size, and appearance of the fruit; cause it to ripen earlier or later; and bring about results varying from perfect success to almost complete failure.

Extensive saccharine and acid determinations made (Table VII) of varieties grafted on resistant stocks and contrasted with the congeniality and growth ratings made of the same vines the same season show a close correspondence between these important chemical constituents of the fruit and the congeniality of graft and stock. Similar growth ratings of a variety grafted on various stocks are found to be accompanied by fairly definite percentages of sugar and acid. The congeniality of the variety to the stock materially affects the resistant qualities of the stock.

The quantity and quality of the fruit are usually in opposition on the soils and vines producing most abundantly; the fruit is usually not of as much value per given unit as it is on vines that are relatively less productive.

Most vine varieties making perfect growth on resistant stocks are found to yield heavier crops than the same variety when grown on its own roots.

The best results can be obtained only when the varieties are placed under soil, climatic, and other conditions to which they are adapted and by using the methods of pruning, training, and culture best suited to each one.

A number of the new grape introductions of the Department of Agriculture are proving to be superior to the varieties that are now commercially grown for certain purposes.

The relative rooting qualities of resistant varieties are an important consideration in the cost of establishing resistant vineyards.

Some stocks are suited for bench grafting, while others are especially valuable for vineyard grafting.

Cuttings of many hybrids root easily, although the cuttings from one of the parents may be hard to root.

Where conditions are not suited to a given species, they are often well adapted to hybrids of that species with some other species.

As cuttings of Monticola, Berlandieri, Aestivalis, Linsecomii, Bicolor, and Candicans (Pls. VI, VII, and VIII) are hard to root, they should be rooted in the nursery and grafted there, or planted in the vineyard and grafted afterwards.

Riparia cuttings root easily and are excellent stocks well suited for vineyard and bench grafting, but they are adapted to but few California soils. Soils in which Riparia varieties thrive usually produce large crops of only fair quality.

Rupestris cuttings root and graft easily and are best adapted to bench grafting. When so used the dormant eyes should be cut out of the stock. Many varieties are not congenial to Rupestris, and their fruit is usually somewhat later in ripening than when grown on some other stock.

In most instances Riparia, Berlandieri, Champini, and Aestivalis stocks (Pl. VI, VII, and VIII) are congenial to Vinifera varieties. Their fruitfulness is increased and the time of ripening hastened in comparison with the same varieties grown on other stocks.

Some of the hybrid resistant-stock varieties are making enviable records as stocks under California conditions.

Where all the qualities desired can not be found in a hybrid, a complex hybrid—that is, a hybrid of hybrids—may yield the desired results.

A grower of Vinifera grapes should decide before locating his vineyard what varieties he desires to grow, and then choose soil and other conditions suited to such varieties. He should know whether stocks are to be established in the vineyard and grafted afterwards or whether the plantings are to be of bench or nursery grafts. He should then select the resistant varieties best suited to the purpose and conditions and which at the same time are congenial to the varieties he intends to grow. He should familiarize himself with all the operations necessary in establishing a resistant vineyard.

The amount of money practically thrown away in the reestablishment of Vinifera vineyards in this country since the first appearance of phylloxera in them can not be even approximately estimated.

The direct causes of this waste of money have been due to lack of information and the fact that there was no source from which data could be obtained. This has resulted in the taking of chances by the growers in planting nonresistants, or in using the wrong resistants, or in using resistants which were not congenial to the varieties they were growing. Other causes for this waste have been the purchase of bench grafts on resistant stocks not true to name and the lack of proper care and management of resistant vineyards, such as allowing roots to grow from Vinifera tops grown on resistant stocks. These mistakes have delayed the general use of resistants. There should be no further delay of this kind. The Department of Agriculture is now prepared and will be glad to give information of value along all these lines.

O

BULLETIN OF THE U.S. DEPARTMENT OF AGRICULTURE

No. 210

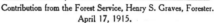

Contribution from the Forest Service, Henry S. Graves, Forester.
April 17, 1915.

(PROFESSIONAL PAPER.)

SEED PRODUCTION OF WESTERN WHITE PINE.[1]

By RAPHAEL ZON, *Chief of Forest Investigations.*

PROBLEMS INVOLVED IN DETERMINING SEED PRODUCTION.

When, several years ago, an attempt was made by the Forest Service to collect seed on a large scale for forestation purposes, it was keenly realized for the first time how little knowledge exists in this country regarding the seed production of our trees and the factors which influence it. One should be able to foretell with a reasonable degree of certainty the amount of seed which different species will produce at definite intervals. Aside from the practical value of such knowledge, it is of the greatest scientific interest. Our knowledge of the life history of forest trees will be incomplete until the mysterious occurrence of seed years and the factors that influence them are fully understood. Of all the forest problems, seed production is the most difficult one to solve. This may be readily inferred from the fact that although seed production excited great interest on the part of European foresters even in the early days, and several attempts were made to penetrate into the mystery of it, little as yet is known regarding the factors which influence the seed production of even the few European species.

The investigation of seed production of forest trees consists of four distinct problems: (1) The determination of the amount of the seed crop, (2) the determination of the periodicity of seed production, (3) the determination of the various external and internal factors which affect the amount and the periodicity of seed production, and (4) the solution of the biological problem of seed production. Each of these problems must be solved in the order indicated, since the solution of one furnishes the basis for the solution of those which follow.

The first and immediate problem is to determine the amount of seed produced by each species. This may not be as simple an under-

[1] *Pinus monticola* Dougl.

NOTE.—This bulletin contains a report upon an investigation of the seed production of western white pine and a discussion of the method of measuring the seed crop.

85754°—Bull. 210—15

taking as it seems. Should the seed crop be estimated ocularly or actually measured on representative trees or sample plots? If it is to be measured, what is to be taken as the unit of measure—the number of cones produced by a few individual trees, the number of cones produced per unit of area, or the quantity of germinable seed produced by individual trees on a given area?

When a method is agreed upon, the problem of the periodicity of seed crops can be attacked. To solve this problem, repeated comparable investigations of the first problem carried on for years is necessary.

In the solution of the third problem there enters the determination, first, of the external factors such as climate, soil, exposure, light, injury, and destruction of seed by animals and fungi, and, second, of internal factors, such as composition, age, density, and health of the stand. The solution of this complicated question, or rather of this series of complicated questions, requires systematic, parallel, and uninterrupted series of investigations, which can not be undertaken by one individual, but must be carried on by permanently organized forest experiment stations.

The fourth problem, the solution of which is the final aim of the whole investigation, is the most difficult of all, and requires, in addition to the other lines of work, a series of chemical, physiological, and anatomical investigations.

In this paper an attempt will be made to discuss merely the method of measuring seed crops.

METHOD EMPLOYED IN MEASURING THE SEED CROP.

The production of seed in forest trees is not a function of an individual tree, but really of the whole stand, since the development of the life processes of each tree is determined by the density, composition, and age of the stand, and by the position of the tree in the stand. Therefore, in determining the amount of the seed crop, the quantity of seed produced per unit of area, and not the amount produced by individual trees, should be made the basis of measurement. Further, the cone production can not alone serve as a basis for measuring the seed crop. The seed production must be measured not by the quantity of cones but by the amount of seed produced, because the final aim in the study of seed crops is not the cones but the seed. The quality of seed, therefore, viz, its viability, must be taken into account. Two stands may produce different quantities of cones per tree, yet the stand with the smaller average number of cones per tree may furnish more germinable seed than the stand with the larger number of cones. Barren seed are biologically nothing but impurities, and it would therefore be a mistake not to leave them out of consideration in determining the amount of seed production. Thus, in measuring the seed crop, three things must be determined: (1) The seed production for the stand per unit of area (not for individual trees), (2) the quantity of seed, and (3) viability of the seed. The weight of germinable seed per unit of area must be accepted as the standard for measuring seed crops. If a is the weight of clean air-dried seed obtained from 1 acre, and p is their germination per cent, then the seed crop, or x, may be expressed by the formula $x=ap$.

Since the aim is to determine the amount of seed produced per unit of area, the best method of studying seed production is by means of sample areas. These areas may be from one-quarter of an acre to one-half of an acre in extent, in accordance with the density of the stand. Each sample area, however, should include at least 100 trees of the principal species composing the stand.

It would, of course, be more accurate to gather cones and obtain the seed from all of the trees on the sample area. This, however, would necessitate the cutting down of the trees, which is not always practicable or possible. Moreover, this operation would require a great deal of time, which would make such an investigation difficult. For this reason it is preferable to collect the cones and extract the seed only from sample trees.

It is a well-established fact that light is a necessary condition for seed production, and observations show that the greater the amount of light received by the tree the greater is its crown development and the amount of seed produced. It may be already accepted a priori that individual trees in a stand do not produce equal amounts of seed, but vary in accordance with their crown development. In the selection of the sample trees, therefore, one must be guided by the form and development of the crown of the individual tree. In the different species the different parts of the crown have varying importance; thus in Douglas fir the upper part of the crown is of the most importance, since it is there that the largest number of cones are developed; in other species it may be the extremities of the largest lower branches.

In order that the amount of seed obtained from the sample trees should, when multiplied by the total number of trees on the sample plot, actually represent the amount of seed produced on the plot, the sample trees must include representatives of all groups of trees which differ in any way in their crown development. With this end in view, all the trees on the sample plot are divided into groups in accordance with their crown development, and their diameters tallied. From these groups the sample trees are selected. As a basis for dividing the trees into groups in accordance with their crown development, the ordinary classification into dominant (I), codominant

(II), intermediate (III), oppressed (IV), and suppressed (V) may be followed. Since, however, the crown development of trees in the codominant and intermediate classes may not be uniform, these two classes may be subdivided and designated by the letters *a*, *b*, *c*, and *d*. In this way there may be from seven to ten classes or groups of trees.

At the time the trees are measured and divided into groups a note is made for each tree as to whether or not it is bearing cones. These data, which are very interesting in themselves, become absolutely essential in case of partial seed production, when not all of the trees bear cones.

In the work of dividing the trees into groups, the investigator must carefully examine each crown from all sides, observing its habitus. Experience has taught that in order to avoid errors of crown classification the total number of trees on a sample plot must not exceed 100. The size of the sample plot will depend, therefore, upon the age, density, and composition of the stand.

The enumeration of the trees may be made by marking each tree with white paper tags, and the record kept on a form similar to the one given below:

Number.	Diameter.	Class.	Cones present (+) or absent (−).
	Inches.		
1	25	IIIa	+
1	13	V	−
Aspen	27		

When in a mixed stand a tree of secondary species occurs, its name should be given in the first column, but columns 3 and 4 left blank. After the number of trees in each class is computed, a certain number of sample trees are selected from the various classes. For ordinary investigations, 10 per cent of the total number of trees on the sample plot may be sufficient. For more intensive investigations, however, a larger percentage should be taken.

The more carefully the division into classes is done and the more uniform the crowns of each class, the easier it is to select the sample trees. It is advisable to select sample trees separately for each class—that is, first select the trees of Class I, then take up the next class, and so on.

When not all trees in the stand are bearing cones, the sample trees should be selected from the cone-bearing ones, and, in determining the amount of seed production, the percentage of seed-bearing trees for each group must be taken into account.

The sample trees are felled, care being taken in falling that they do not touch the crowns of other trees and thus knock off their own cones or those of their neighbors. From the felled sample trees all the cones are gathered very carefully, those which still hang on the branches as well as those which were knocked off in felling the tree. It is necessary to avoid collecting cones which were knocked off from other trees. This can often be very readily accomplished, since the cones of each tree differ from those of others in size and form, especially in the case of western white pine. The cones gathered from each sample tree are put in separate sacks, properly labeled, and after being slightly dried at ordinary room temperature are subjected to further investigation.

The total height and age and health of each of the sample trees are determined, the number of cones from each counted, their lengths measured, and their volumes and green weights determined. The cones are then dried and the seed extracted. Coniferous tree seeds are separated from their wings, cleaned, and weighed. If there is any foreign matter present its percentage is determined by weighing several grams of the sample, then cleaning it of all foreign matter and reweighing. After the seeds are cleaned, 200 are taken, their weights determined to one one-hundredth of a gram, and these are then germinated. After the germination percentage is determined, the amount of seed per unit of area—for instance, an acre—can be ascertained by means of the formula, $x=ap$.

SEED PRODUCTION OF WESTERN WHITE PINE.

The method of investigation described was applied in 1911 to the study of seed-bearing characteristics of the western white pine in Idaho on the Kaniksu and Coeur d'Alene National Forests, where this pine reaches its optimum development. In all there were located four sample plots, three on the Kaniksu and one on the Coeur d'Alene Forest. About 10 per cent of the white-pine trees of the different crown classes which bore cones were felled, the cones carefully gathered, and kept separately for each tree. The seed from each tree was extracted by hand and its purity and germinability determined. The results for each sample plot follow.

TABLE 1.—*Classification of trees according to character of crown and presence or absence of cones; number of cones and amount of seed produced by sample trees, and total seed production on plot No. 1, Kaniksu National Forest (area, one-half acre).*

CROWN CLASSIFICATION OF TREES AND NUMBER BEARING CONES.

Diameter breast high (inches).	Number of trees, by crown class.					Trees with cones.		Trees without cones.	
	Class I.	Class II.	Class III.	Class IV.	Class V.	Number.	Per cent.	Number.	Per cent.
1 to 5					4			4	100
6 to 8				2	3			5	100
9 to 10			2	5	1			8	100
11 to 12			2	3				5	100
13 to 14		1	2	2		2	40	3	60
15 to 16									
17 to 18		1	1			1	50	1	50
19 to 20	1	5	2			6	75	2	25
21 to 22	3	5				7	87	1	13
23 to 24	1	6				6	86	1	14
25 to 26	7	2				8	89	1	11
27 to 28	4					4	100		
29 to 30	1	1				1	50	1	50
31 to 32	3					3	100		
33 to 34									
35 to 36	1					1	100		
Total	21	21	9	12	8	38	[1] 54	33	[1] 46
Per cent	30	30	12	17	11	54		46	
Per cent of each class with cones	100	83	18	0	0				

NUMBER OF CONES AND AMOUNT OF SEED PRODUCED BY SAMPLE TREES.

Tree No.	Crown class.	Diameter.	Age.	Height.	Cones open or closed.	Number of cones by inch lengths.			
						3 to 4 inches.	5 to 6 inches.	7 to 8 inches.	Total.
		Inches.	*Years.*	*Feet.*					
1	I	28	230	166	Closed	9	139	77	225
2	I	28	230	152	...do	2	26	24	52
3	I	21	223	147	...do		4	17	21
					Open		4	37	41
1	II	24	215	154	Closed		14	6	20
2	II	21	200+	146	...do	4	5		9
					Open	1	4		5
3	II	21	200+	152	Closed	5	55	9	69
1	III	14	[2] 200	104	...do			7	7
Total (7 trees)						21	251	177	449

Tree No.	Average length of cone.	Total weight of cones.	Total volume of cones.	Weight of clean seed.	Number of clean seed per pound.	Per cent of germination.	Per cent germinating in first 144 days of test.
	Inches.	*Pounds.*	*Bushels.*	*Grams.*			
1	5.8	23.3	1.215	330.27	38,069	22	19.0
2	6.2	4.5	.325	58.58	30,362	45	31.0
3	7.0	1.5	.204	8.79	31,690	18	13.5
	7.3	3.5	.478	17.10	29,813		
1	6.1	2.1	.137	40.21	26,880	52.5	33.5
2	4.4	.2	.027	.82	35,200	26	25.0
	5.0	.15	.045	4.02	56,960		
3	5.3	4.1	.341	94.32	33,876	67.5	34.0
1	7.2	.7	.090	13.06	24,320	56	33.0
Total (7 trees).	[1] 5.8	40.1	2.862	567.19			

[1] Per cent of total. [2] Rotten.

TABLE 1.—*Classification of trees according to character of crown and presence or absence of cones; number of cones and amount of seed produced by sample trees, and total seed production on plot No. 1, Kaniksu National Forest (area, one-half acre)*—Continued.

TOTAL SEED PRODUCTION.

Crown class.	Total trees.		Total sample trees.		Yield from sample trees.			Yield of germinable seed.		
					Cones.	Cleaned seed.	Germinable seed.[1]	Per plot.	Per acre.	
	No.	*Per ct.*	*No.*	*Per ct.*	*Bush.*	*Grams.*	*Grams.*	*Grams.*	*Grams.*	*No.*
I	21	30	3	14	2.22	414.75	103.68	725.78	1,451.56	114,408
II	21	30	3	14	.55	139.38	86.04	487.54	975.086	68,680
III	9	12	1	11	.09	13.06	7.31	14.63	29.26	1,704
IV	12	17	......	......	......	......	......	......	......	......
V	8	11	......	......	......	......	......	......	......	......
Total	71	100	7	10	2.86	567.19	......	1,227.95	[2] 2,455.906	184,792

[1] Weight of pure seed multiplied by their percentage of germination. [2] Equivalent to 5.4 pounds.

TABLE 2.—*Classification of trees according to character of crown and presence or absence of cones; number of cones and amount of seed produced by sample trees, and total seed production on plot No. 2, Kaniksu National Forest (area, one-half acre).*

CROWN CLASSIFICATION OF TREES AND NUMBER BEARING CONES.

Diameter breast high (inches).	Number of trees, by crown class.					Trees with cones.		Trees without cones.	
	Class I.	Class II.	Class III.	Class IV.	Class V.	Number.	Per cent.	Number.	Per cent.
1 to 5	......	......	......	......	3	......	......	3	100
6 to 8	......	......	......	2	18	......	......	20	100
9 to 10	......	......	......	8	2	......	......	10	100
11 to 12	......	......	3	6	......	......	......	9	100
13 to 14	......	......	5	5	......	2	20	8	80
15 to 16	......	3	3	......	......	4	66	2	34
17 to 18	......	7	1	......	......	7	87	1	13
19 to 20	2	6	1	......	......	8	89	1	11
21 to 22	5	1	......	......	......	6	100	......	......
23 to 24	5	......	......	......	......	5	100	......	......
25 to 27	1	......	......	......	......	1	100	......	......
Total	13	17	13	21	23	33	38	54	62
Per cent	15	20	15	24	26	38	......	62	......
Per cent of each class with cones	100	94	30	0	0	......	......	......	......

NUMBER OF CONES AND AMOUNT OF SEED PRODUCED BY SAMPLE TREES.

Tree No.	Crown class.	Diameter.	Age.	Height.	Cones open or closed.	Number of cones, by inch lengths.				
						3 to 4 inches.	5 to 6 inches.	7 to 8 inches.	9 to 10 inches.	Total.
		Inches.	*Years.*	*Feet.*						
1	I	20	144	150	Closed	......	4	6	1	11
2	I	22	145	164	Open	1	17	5	......	23
					Closed	2	39	19	......	60
1	II	20	145	160	Open	......	6	8	1	15
					Closed	......	......	12	5	17
2	II	16	147	141	Open	......	5	3	......	8
3	II	18	146	144	..do	......	......	14	3	17
					Closed	1	2	20	3	26
1	III	14	134	133	Open	......	2	1	1	4
2	III	16	145	134	..do	......	2	......	......	2
3	III	17	144	138	Closed	......	11	1	1	13
Total (8 trees)		......	......	......	......	4	88	89	15	196

TABLE 2.—*Classification of trees according to character of crown and presence or absence of cones; number of cones and amount of seed produced by sample trees, and total seed production on plot No. 2, Kaniksu National Forest (area, one-half acre)*—Continued.

NUMBER OF CONES AND AMOUNT OF SEED PRODUCED BY SAMPLE TREES—Contd.

Tree No.	Average length of cone.	Total weight of cones.	Total volume of cones.	Weight of clean seed.	Number of clean seed per pound.	Per cent of germination.	Per cent germinating in first 144 days of test.
	Inches.	*Pounds.*	*Bushels.*	*Grams.*			
1	6.6	1.0	0.077	14.910	31,200	63.5	25.0
2	5.7	1.5	.171	12.861	24,352	56.5	37.5
	5.8	4.8	.410	63.659	26,458		
1	6.0	1.2	.171	8.670	27,520	37	6.0
	7.8	1.9	.189	53.421	26,619		
2	5.9	.5	.080	.555	37,600	(1)	....
3	7.7	1.6	.273	18.283	31,467	40	10.0
	7.2	2.6	.273	25.035	26,187		
1	7.1	.2	.060	2.364	31,520	15.5	13.0
2	5.5	.1	.015	1.196	38,800	(1)	....
3	6.0	1.0	.070	33.522	26,920	34.5	24.5
Total (8 trees)	6.4	16.4	1.789	234.476	....	....	....

TOTAL SEED PRODUCTION.

Crown class.	Total trees.		Total sample trees.		Yield from sample trees.			Yield of germinable seed.		
					Cones.	Cleaned seed.	Germinable seed.[2]	Per plot.	Per acre.	
	No.	*Per ct.*	*No.*	*Per ct.*	*Bush.*	*Grams.*	*Grams.*	*Grams.*	*Grams.*	*No.*
I	13	15	2	15	0.66	91.43	52.702	342.563	685.126	40,352
II	17	20	3	18	.99	105.96	40.523	216.128	432.256	26,016
III	13	15	3	23	.14	37.08	12.344	16.460	32.920	2,032
IV	21	24	....	....	....	....	....	....	....	....
V	[illegible]	26	....	....	....	....	....	....	....	....
Total	87	100	8	11	1.79	234.47	....	575.151	[3]1,150.302	68,400

[1] Not tested.
[2] Weight of pure seed multiplied by their percentage of germination.
[3] Equivalent to 2.5 pounds.

TABLE 3.—*Classification of trees according to character of crown and presence or absence of cones; number of cones and amount of seed produced by sample trees, and total seed production on plot No. 3, Kaniksu National Forest (area, one-half acre).*

CROWN CLASSIFICATION OF TREES AND NUMBER BEARING CONES.

Diameter breast high (inches).	Number of trees, by crown class.					Trees with cones.		Trees without cones.	
	Class I.	Class II.	Class III.	Class IV.	Class V.	Number.	Per cent.	Number.	Per cent.
1 to 5	....	....	....	....	2	....	....	2	100
6 to 8	....	....	....	8	10	....	....	18	100
9 to 10	....	....	2	20	2	....	....	24	100
11 to 12	....	2	6	6	....	2	15	12	85
13 to 14	1	9	8	....	....	9	50	9	50
15 to 16	1	8	2	....	....	7	64	4	36
17 to 18	7	3	....	....	....	9	90	1	10
19 to 20	1	....	....	....	....	1	100	....	....
21 to 22	....	....	....	....	....	....	....	....	....
24	....	....	....	....	....	....	....	....	....
29	....	....	....	....	....	....	....	....	....
Total	10	22	18	34	14	28	28.5	70	71.5
Per cent	10	23	18	35	14	28.5	....	71.5	....
Per cent of each class with cones	100	66	17	0	0	....	....	....	....

TABLE 3.—*Classification of trees according to character of crown and presence or absence of cones; number of cones and amount of seed produced by sample trees, and total seed production on plot No. 3, Kaniksu National Forest (area, one-half acre)*—Continued.

NUMBER OF CONES AND AMOUNT OF SEED PRODUCED BY SAMPLE TREES.

Tree No.	Crown class.	Diameter.	Age.	Height.	Cones, open or closed.	Number of cones, by inch lengths.				
						3 to 4 inches.	5 to 6 inches.	7 to 8 inches.	9 to 10 inches.	Total.
		Inches.	*Years.*	*Feet.*						
1	I	18	150	151	Closed		3	3	1	7
					Open		3	8	2	13
2	I	18	130	139	Closed		8	9		17
1	II	17	145	136	..do		2	11	3	16
					Open			12	5	17
2	II	13	153	129	Closed		4	2		6
3	II	15	145	134	..do		5	5		10
(1)	III									
Total (5 trees)							25	50	11	86

Tree No.	Average length of cone.	Total weight of cones.	Total volume of cones.	Weight of clean seed.	Number of clean seed per pound.	Per cent of germination.	Per cent germinating in first 144 days of test.
	Inches.	*Pounds.*	*Bushels.*	*Grams.*			
1	6.9	0.8	0.056	14.180	31,744	19.5	13.5
	6.9	1.1	.183	8.106	32,000		
2	6.3	1.4	.255	10.183	26,960	36.5	22.5
1	7.4	1.6	.255	9.280	28,267	46.5	42.0
	7.7	1.7	.292	13.855	25,472		
2	5.5	.5	.045	6.130	34,560	22	18.5
3	6.5	1.0	.073	14.385	29,312	35.5	23.0
(1)				6.130	34,560		
Total (5 trees)	6.9	8.1	1.159	82.249			

TOTAL SEED PRODUCTION.

Crown class.	Total trees.		Total sample trees.		Yield from sample trees.			Yield of germinable seed.		
					Cones.	Cleaned seed.	Germinable seed.[2]	Per plot.	Per acre.	
	No.	*Per ct.*	*No.*	*Per ct.*	*Bush.*	*Grams.*	*Grams.*	*Grams.*	*Grams.*	*No.*
I	10	10	2	20	0.49	32.47	8.064	40.320	80.640	5,560
II	22	23	3	14	.66	43.65	17.214	86.070	172.140	10,380
III	18	18				6.13	1.349	4.047	8.094	570
IV	34	35								
V	14	14								
Total	98	100	5	5	1.15	82.25		130.437	[3] 260.874	16,510

[1] Results of tree No. 2, Crown Class II, used for this tree.
[2] Weight of pure seed multiplied by their percentage of germination.
[3] Equivalent to 0.6 pound.

TABLE 4.—*Classification of trees according to character of crown and presence or absence of cones; number of cones and amount of seed produced by sample trees, and total seed production on plot No. 4, Coeur d'Alene National Forest (area, 0.9 acre).*

CROWN CLASSIFICATION OF TREES AND NUMBER BEARING CONES.

Diameter breast high (inches).	Number of trees, by crown class.							Trees with cones.		Trees without cones.	
	Class I.	Class II.	Class IIa.	Class III.	Class IIIa.	Class IV.	Class V.	Number.	Per cent.	Number.	Per cent.
4 to 6						4	7			11	100
7 to 8					6	7	2			15	100
9 to 10				4	10	1				15	100
11 to 12		1	2	10				4	30	9	70
13 to 14		4	3	3				5	50	5	50
15 to 16		9	6		1			12	75	4	25
17 to 18	1	5	3					8	89	1	11
19 to 20	1	3						4	100		
21 to 22	2	1						3	100		
23 to 24	2		1					3	100		
25 to 26	2							2	100		
Total	8	23	15	17	17	12	9	41	41	60	59
Per cent	8	22	15	17	17	12	9	41		59	
Per cent of each class with cones	100	91	73	6	0	0	0				

NUMBER OF CONES AND AMOUNT OF SEED PRODUCED BY SAMPLE TREES.

Tree No.	Crown class.	Diameter.	Age.	Height.	Cones open or closed.	Number of cones, by inch lengths.				
						5 to 6 inches.	7 to 8 inches.	9 to 10 inches.	11 to 12 inches.	Total.
		Inches.	*Years.*	*Feet.*						
1	I	19.8	107	127		2	19	17	1	39
1	II	16.0	84	108		7	25	1		33
1	IIa	14.5	92	100		1	3	6	1	11
1	III	12.2	72	78			1			1
1	IIIa	8.5	80	77						
1	IV	7.2	72	67						
1	V	6.0	83	47						
Total (7 trees)						10	48	24	2	84

Tree No.	Average length of cone.	Total weight of cones.	Total volume of cones.	Weight of clean seed.	Number of clean seed per pound.	Per cent of germination.	Per cent germinating in first 144 days of test.
	Inches.	*Pounds.*	*Bushels.*	*Grams.*			
1	7.97	6.0	0.295	118.901	23,840	61	39
1	6.93	3.8	.215	62.773	29,840	33	24
1	8.45	1.9	.102	38.667	21,771	37.5	19
1	8	.1	.008	2.805	21,920	90	50
1							
1							
1							
Total (7 trees).	7.6	11.8	.620	223.146			

TABLE 4.—*Classification of trees according to character of crown and presence or absence of cones; number of cones and amount of seed produced by sample trees, and total seed production on plot No. 4, Cœur d'Alene National Forest (area, 0.9 acre)*—Continued.

TOTAL SEED PRODUCTION.

Crown class.	Total trees.		Total sample trees.		Yield from sample trees.			Yield of germinable seed.		
					Cones.	Cleaned seed.	Germinable seed.[1]	Per plot.	Per acre.	
	No.	*Per ct.*	*No.*	*Per ct.*	*Bush.*	*Grams.*	*Grams.*	*Grams.*	*Grams.*	*No.*
I	8	8	1	12	0.295	113.90	72.530	580.240	644.711	33,929
II	23	22	1	4	.215	62.77	20.715	435.015	483.350	31,593
IIa	15	15	1	6	.102	38.67	14.500	159.500	177.222	8,727
III	17	17	1	5	.008	2.80	2.525	2.525	2.806	137
IIIa	17	17	1	5	....	....	....	....	....	....
IV	12	12	1	8	....	....	....	....	....	....
V	9	9	1	11	....	....	....	....	....	....
Total	101	100	7	7	.620	223.14	110,270	1,177.280	[2] 1,308.089	74,386

[1] Weight of pure seed multiplied by their percentage of germination.
[2] Equivalent to 2.9 pounds.

CONCLUSIONS.

The material collected so far is not sufficient to allow of final conclusions. Those here presented are offered chiefly to point out the still unknown factors into which the problem of seed production resolves itself and of demonstrating the suitability of the proposed method for solving them.

1. Perhaps the most striking fact brought out by this investigation is that the different crown classes do not participate equally in the production of seed. Thus 98.8 per cent of all the seed in 1911 was produced by the first two crown classes, while the third contributed only 1.2 per cent. It is interesting to note that though 1911 was a year of a moderately good seed crop, the crown classes IV and V did not bear any seed at all.

If we divide the average percentage of seed production of each crown class by the average percentage of trees in each class, we secure, roughly, the ratios in which the different crown classes of western white pine bear seed.

TABLE 5.—*Distribution of the seed crop of western white pine, by crown classes.*

	Ratios of seed production of crown classes.[1]					
	Class I.	Class II.	Class III.	Class IV.	Class V.	Total.
Plot No. 1.						
Total yield.......per cent..	59.1	39.7	1.2	0	0	100
Number of trees.......do....	30	30	12	17	11	100
Plot No. 2.						
Total yield.......do....	59.5	37.6	2.9	0	0	100
Number of trees.......do....	15	20	15	24	26	100
Plot No. 3.						
Total yield.......do....	30.9	66.0	3.1	0	0	100
Number of trees.......do....	10	23	18	35	14	100
Plot No. 4.						
Total yield.......do....	49.3	50.5	0.2	0	0	100
Number of trees.......do....	8	37	34	12	9	100
Average.......	54.3	44.5	1.2	0	0	100
	15	27	21	22	15	100

[1] Expressed in percentage of seed produced in each crown class of the plot divided by percentage of trees in the crown class.

The ratios of productivity of trees of different crown classes in round figures are 3.5, 1.5, 0.05, 0.0. Thus a tree of crown Class I bears 70 times and a tree of crown Class II 30 times more seed than a tree of Class III.

The participation of the different crown classes in the production of seed may serve as an index of the seed crop. In exceptionally good seed years not only the dominant classes bear seed, but even the oppressed trees have occasional cones, while in poor seed years cones are to be found only in the dominant class (I), and even then not on all trees or parts of their crowns. Between these two extremes range seed crops of various abundance. The abundance of the seed crop can, therefore, be prognosticated very early in the summer by observing in the forest the kind of trees that bear cones. In order to establish a regular yield for the seed production of western white pine, it would be necessary accurately to measure the crop by the method described over several seed years of various intensity. After the seed production for the poorest, moderate, and exceptionally good seed years is ascertained, the determination of whether the crop of a given year is good, fair, or poor can then be forecasted easily and early by merely observing the different crown classes of trees that are bearing cones.

An attempt to penetrate deeper into the causes that determine the average amount of seed produced by an individual tree of each crown class meets with difficulties because of the many counteracting factors, some of which still remain unexplained. Aside from the length and width of the crown, which has been accepted as a most decisive influence in seed production, there are other factors that affect the amount of viable seed produced by a tree, such as the size of the cones, average number of seed in a cone, size of the seed, its germinability, the age of the tree, and the still little understood individual energy of each tree in producing seed.

2. The largest amount of germinable seed was invariably produced by trees chiefly of the first and also of the second crown class. The largest amount of germinable seed recorded (2½ ounces) belonged to two trees of crown Class I, and in only one case has this amount been closely reached by a tree of crown Class II. Crown development thus seems to be the most important factor in the seed production of trees.

3. The age of the trees evidently has an effect upon the amount and quality of seed produced. Thus the younger trees (in plot No. 4), ranging from 72 to a little over 100 years in age, have produced practically in all three crown classes a larger quantity of germinable seed than the older trees. Apparently the age has also something to do with the average length of the cones, since the younger trees possessed, on an average, longer cones which yielded a larger number of pure seeds per cone than the older trees. The germination percentage was also greater in the younger trees than in the old ones; the highest germination percentage reached (90) was found in a tree 72 years old, while the highest found in the older trees was 67.5.

4. The relation between the length of the cone and the size of the seed (the number of seed per pound) is clearly shown. Thus the longest cones, 8 inches and over, yielded about 22,000 seed to the pound, while cones 5 inches long occasionally yielded as many as 57,000 seed to the pound.

5. The vigor of growth apparently influences favorably the amount and quality of seed produced. Thus trees which grew at the rate of 0.19 of an inch in diameter and about 1.25 feet in height annually produced a larger amount of germinable seed than trees which grew at a slower rate. This, however, may be indirectly the effect of the age of the tree, since the younger trees have not yet passed the period of most rapid growth.

6. While a relation between the size of the seed and its germinative vigor [1] is not clearly brought out, yet there seems to be a tendency for the larger seeds to have the highest germinative vigor. This tendency is shown in Table 6.

[1] The germinative vigor is gauged by the percentage of seed which germinated within 144 days after being sown.

TABLE 6.—*Size of seed and period of rest.*

Number of seeds per pound.	Seed that germinated within 144 days.	Number of seeds per pound.	Seed that germinated within 144 days.
	Per cent.		*Per cent.*
22,000	34.5	31,000	17.5
24,000	36.5	32,000	13.4
25,000	42.0	34,000	26.3
26,000	23.8	35,000	25.0
27,000	21.6	36,000	
28,000	24.0	37,000	
29,000	23.0	38,000	19.0
30,000	22.8		

The failure of such relationship to be clearly apparent is probably due more to deficient field data than to the actual absence of any such relationship.

The size of the seed and the germination percentage are closely connected, as shown by Table 7.

TABLE 7.—*Relation of size of seed to germination.*

Number of seeds per pound.	Average germination.
	Per cent.
25,000	60
30,000	39
35,000	31
40,000	22
55,000	26

The percentage of germination decreases with the increase in the number of seed per pound—with the decrease in size of the seed.

8. Similarly, the length of cone has a perceptible effect upon the quality of the seed, as shown in Table 8.

TABLE 8.—*Relation between length of cones and germination.*

Length of cones.	Average germination.
	Per cent.
4 to 5 inches	26
5 to 6 inches	41
6 to 7 inches	40
7 to 8 inches	43

Thus it is fairly evident that seed from shorter cones possess a lower germination percentage than seed from longer cones.

9. Since the size of the cones goes hand in hand with the weight, the following generalization may be made: *The larger or heavier the cones the larger is the seed, and the larger the seed the greater is the*

germination percentage; therefore, the larger the cones the better is the quality of the seed. This is of importance in seed collection.

10. An idea of the reproductive capacity of a single tree may be gained from the record of the largest yield by an individual white-pine tree, which was 2½ ounces, or 6,000 germinable seed.

11. If from individual trees we turn to stands, we find that normally stocked stands bear from 2½ to 5 pounds of germinable seed per acre, or, assuming an average of 30,000 seed to the pound, from 75,000 to 150,000 germinable seed. The apparently small yield of plot No. 3 (a little over one-half pound) is explained by the overcrowded condition of the stand. The average of 3 pounds, or 90,000 germinable seed, per acre for a moderately good seed year may therefore be accepted as the average seed crop for the white pine on the Kaniksu and Coeur d'Alene National Forests. Applying this average figure to the different forest types found on the Kaniksu and Coeur d'Alene Forests, and assuming that there are 45,000 acres of white-pine land of which plot No. 1 is representative, 20,000 acres of which plot No. 2 is a sample, and 15,000 acres which may be represented by plot No. 3, the total amount of germinable seed produced in 1911 on the Kaniksu Forest would be in the neighborhood of 300,000 pounds.

This amount is for a moderately good seed year. In exceptionally abundant seed years it would be much larger. These estimates, of course, do not take into consideration any possible destruction of seed by insects or disease, either in the cone or flower.

12. It is interesting to compare the total yield of germinable seed with the amount of seed actually collected by the Forest Service. In 1911 the collection of seed was conducted on an extremely large scale, 6,700 pounds being gathered on 20,676 acres. The total amount of clean seed produced during this same year on that area, as ascertained by the study, was 225,368 pounds. The amount collected by the Forest Service constituted, therefore, about 3 per cent of the total amount of seed produced that year. This conveys some idea of the portion of seed which man is able to collect out of the total amount produced by the forest. The remainder is either left on the ground for future natural reproduction or is destroyed by squirrels and other animals.

WASHINGTON : GOVERNMENT PRINTING OFFICE : 1915

UNITED STATES DEPARTMENT OF AGRICULTURE

BULLETIN No. 211

Contribution from the Bureau of Plant Industry
WM. A. TAYLOR, Chief

Washington, D. C. ▼ May 26, 1915

FACTORS AFFECTING RANGE MANAGEMENT IN NEW MEXICO

By

E. O. WOOTON, Agriculturist, Office of Farm Management

CONTENTS

WASHINGTON
GOVERNMENT PRINTING OFFICE
1915

BULLETIN OF THE U.S. DEPARTMENT OF AGRICULTURE

No. 211

Contribution from the Bureau of Plant Industry, Wm. A. Taylor, Chief.
May 26, 1915.

FACTORS AFFECTING RANGE MANAGEMENT IN NEW MEXICO.

By E. O. Wooton,
Agriculturist, Office of Farm Management.

CONTENTS.

INTRODUCTION.

Stock raising is more patently influenced by and dependent upon its physical environment than most other industries appear to be. The topographic and climatic conditions are fundamental, because they determine the kind and quantity of feed the animals must eat, the temperature and other extremes they must endure, and the various dangers which they must avoid.

The laws and customs of the region determine the character of the tenure and control of the land which produces the feed upon which the animals subsist. They are but the expression of the public opinion that warrants the existence of that industry in that place. And not less important, but probably less often considered, is the relation which the business bears to other industries in operation in the same region. From this standpoint, the industry is to be considered as in a certain stage of development toward a better and more complex adjustment among all industries, and a statement of its present condition must be taken as in the nature of a report of progress. It is not what it once was, nor yet what it will be. Thus, while we are

NOTE.—The various factors influencing the live-stock industry in New Mexico, especially as affecting range management, are presented and discussed in this bulletin.

here mainly concerned with the details of the purely physical basis of the industry, the factors of control and relation to other industries are so closely connected with any proper kind of management that they must be considered somewhat at length; and a study of range conditions is but preliminary to an understanding of methods of management and the requirements necessary for the further improvement of the industry.

THE TOPOGRAPHY OF NEW MEXICO.

New Mexico is almost square in outline, being about 350 miles long from north to south, nearly as wide at the southern end, and somewhat narrower along the northern boundary. Only the southern boundary is a broken line. The State consists essentially of a high, arched plateau, the axis of the arch being near the middle and running north and south, the northern end being higher than the southern. This plateau is about 7,000 feet above sea level at its highest point on the northern boundary line and drops to about 3,500 feet at its southern end.

Apparently resting upon this plateau, which is but a part of the great Rocky Mountain uplift, are numerous mountain ranges that seem to rise out of the sweeping plains as islands from the sea. These mountains are of two fairly well-defined types—narrow, rocky ridges, with but a scanty covering of low bushes and scattering trees, and great mountain masses, consisting of numerous associated ridges more or less densely covered with forests and woodland. Nearly all the main ranges have a northerly and southerly trend. Some of the mountains are composed of granites, rhyolites, gneisses, and other igneous and metamorphic rocks, while many of them are great monoclinal piles of tilted, stratified rocks with sharp escarpment faces upon one side. In actual altitude they range from less than 5,000 feet to more than 14,000 feet, there being numerous peaks and ranges over 10,000 feet high.

Large lava flows have occurred in several places, resulting in sheets of black, vesicular basalt, covering extensive areas. Associated with these flows are several large, extinct volcanoes and numerous small cones. The lava sheets have done much to modify the relief features, since the lava (or mal pais, as it is locally known) is harder than the underlying rocks and protects them from erosion. This has resulted in a number of high mesas and buttes that almost take on the dimensions of mountains. (Pl. I, fig. 1.)

The wide stretches of seemingly level plains that lie between the mountain ranges are nowhere really level. Many of them are typical bolsons, or basins, into which drains all the water that falls in the region. These bolsons are independent of each other and may occur at any altitude (Pl. I, fig. 2). The San Augustine Plains in central

Socorro County and the Estancia Valley in Torrance County are typical examples. These plains are everywhere dissected by dry watercourses, or arroyos, which serve to collect the flood waters that are sometimes temporarily very abundant, and sheet erosion of unprotected soil surfaces is everywhere very rapid, largely because of the steep gradient of even that part of the surface, which, by comparison with the bolder relief features, seems to be level. Many of the striking topographic features, both of sculpture and deposition, are due to wind action. On the eastern side of the State the mountains and mesas gradually subside into the wide expanse of the Staked Plains, while to the west Arizona is but a repetition of the alternation of plains and mountains so characteristic of New Mexico but at a slightly lower general level.

The river valleys are narrow and not infrequently constricted to the river channels alone or "boxed in" where they cut through mountains or mesas. The two largest rivers, the Rio Grande and Rio Pecos, run entirely or almost across the State from north to south. The San Juan and the Gila flow out of the State westwardly in San Juan and Grant Counties, respectively, while the northeastern part of the State contains some of the tributaries of the Arkansas River and the headwaters of the Canadian, all of which flow eastwardly. The most conspicuous feature of all these streams is the small number of permanent tributaries possessed by each when the size of its drainage area is considered. The valley bottoms throughout the State, wherever there is a permanent flow of water, are always turned into cultivated fields, and many acres of such lands produce alfalfa. (Pl. II; fig. 2.)

CLIMATE.

Precipitation.—Precipitation is everywhere relatively small in amount in New Mexico. On the plains of the southern part of the State and in all of the river valleys outside of the mountains it is always scanty. In the mountains at altitudes of 5,500 feet or more it is more abundant, but even in the more moist regions the amount of water that falls during the year is rarely equal to that which is common in the humid regions farther east.

To say that there is a summer rainy season does not mean what the same expression tells in regard to a tropical country. It merely says that most of the rain of the year comes during July, August, and September, and that this is the growing season on the plains and almost everywhere in the mountains. In some of the higher mountains, where there is considerable snow during the winter, the ground is left wet enough by the melting of these snows to cause a certain spring and early-summer growth; and some of the perennials of even the drier plains put out their blossoms and grow some new leaves in May and June each year if there has been a normal rainfall the previous summer. But it is true of practically all of the State that May and June are the driest months of the year, and summer arrives without any heralding by spring. It has been said that there are but two seasons in the southern valleys, summer and late fall, and the longer of these is summer. The summer rains usually occur as rather violent local showers of short duration. The water falls from clouds that are high above the earth, and the air next the ground may be relatively dry; in fact, it is not infrequent to see small, high clouds that are evidently producing some rain, but the water evaporates at a lower level and never reaches the ground. Drizzling rains from low-hung, drifting clouds that roll along only a few hundred feet above the earth are only occasional anywhere except upon the cloud-capped peaks of the high mountains; and heavy general storms moving steadily over large areas are very rare.

A study of the United States Weather Bureau reports indicates that there are two factors fundamental in nature which determine in a general way what the average precipitation of any point in the State shall be. The first of these is the well-known relation between precipitation and altitude, depending upon the effect of forcing currents of moisture-laden warm air to higher atmospheric levels through the upward deflection of such currents by the mountains. It thus happens that, other things being equal, the precipitation increases with altitudinal increase, though not always in a direct ratio.

The average precipitation of any station in the State also seems to be in some way dependent upon its distance from the southeast corner. If localities having the same altitude be considered, it appears that those in the southeastern corner have the greatest average rainfall, and that this rainfall gradually diminishes as one goes west and north. This fact would seem to suggest that the source of the moisture lies to the southeast, possibly the Gulf of Mexico. Local factors enter into the case, sometimes decreasing, sometimes augmenting the amount of precipitation for a particular location. Some of the extreme records for the State follow and will give an idea of the limits of variation. A normal rainfall chart for New Mexico has been published by the State immigration bureau.

The maximum precipitation in the State recorded for any single calendar year is for Elk, 39.1 inches, in 1905. There is possibly some inaccuracy in this record, or the station is subjected to local conditions which tend to increase the normal expectancy for this altitude, 7,400 feet. Cloudcroft (8,650 feet) received 32.32 inches in 1905; Chama (7,851 feet) received 32.83 inches in 1891; and the highest record for Windsor (8,200 feet) is 27.92 inches in 1907. The lowest records occur in the lower valleys. San Marcial (4,439 feet)

FIG. 1.—VIEW IN THE NORTHEASTERN PART OF NEW MEXICO, SHOWING THE TOPOGRAPHY AS AFFECTED BY LAVA SHEETS.

FIG. 2.—A TYPICAL BOLSON, OR BASINLIKE MESA, IN THE SOUTHERN PART OF NEW MEXICO, SHOWING THE SHRUBBY ASSOCIATION ON THE GRAVELLY PORTIONS OF SUCH AN AREA.

FIG. 1.—AN AREA IN NEW MEXICO HAVING A TYPICAL COMPACT GROWTH OF BLUE GRAMA, COMMON ON THE NORTHERN PLAINS.

FIG. 2.—A SMALL VALLEY IN THE NORTHERN PART OF NEW MEXICO, SHOWING IRRIGATED LANDS PRODUCING ALFALFA.

The growth shown in the foreground is typical of the unirrigated land of the region when the range is protected.

received 3.44 inches in 1894; Mesilla Park (3,863 feet) received 3.49 inches in 1873; Deming (4,333 feet) received 3.42 inches in 1910, while the same year Carlsbad (3,120 feet) received only 3.95 inches.

The variation in the amount of precipitation from year to year is also great. An extreme case is shown at Mesilla Park. In a record for this region extending over 47 years, the average rainfall is 8.62 inches. For five of those years the total amount was just about half of the normal supply. Five other years show from one and one-half to nearly two times the average. It will thus be seen that there is a range from the lowest amount recorded, 3.49 inches, to almost five times that amount, 17.09 inches, the highest record. For one period of ten consecutive years the total annual precipitation was each year below the average quoted above, and periods of three to five years in which the annual rainfall is two-thirds of the normal or less have occurred three times within the time for which the observations have been made.

Snow occurs at some time every winter at all points in the State. At the lower levels the occurrence is rare and the quantity that falls is small, nor does it lie long. In the higher mountains of the northern part of the State considerable of the precipitation comes as snow, and in favorable locations it drifts and lies for most of the winter. From such regions stock are excluded for at least part of the year.

Cloudy weather is the exception, and one bright sunshiny day after another is the rule throughout the State.

Temperature.—The most characteristic peculiarity of the temperature and one which applies at all points in the State is the great range which occurs, yearly, monthly, and daily. A daily range of 45° F. is not uncommon, and one of 30° or more may be said to be almost the rule. This condition is, of course, due to the altitude and the lack of moisture in the air.

The mean temperatures of different localities are exceedingly misleading when one is considering climate in New Mexico, because they are made up of high maximum and low minimum temperatures. This statement applies to all the means, daily, monthly, and annual. The highest recorded temperature for the State is 113° F. at San Marcial. A summer maximum of over 100° F. is common for many of the stations at the lower altitudes. The higher elevations, of course, have lower temperatures. The absolute minimum temperatures recorded for the different stations range from 4° to −29° F., and there is always a winter season of three months or more anywhere in the State during which one may expect it to freeze any night. This condition would hardly be expected when one considers the latitude alone and is another consequence of high altitude and aridity.

When it is remembered that the months of spring and early summer are usually quite dry, as well as cold at night, the late starting of the native plants is explained. At high elevations the growing season is short, and above 8,500 feet frosts are recorded for almost every month in the year.

Wind motion.—Wind motion is an important climatic factor throughout the State. The air is nearly always dry and frequently very dry, and the wind blows much of the time. The spring is apt to be particularly windy, and the most violent sand storms are usually accompanied by low humidity and consequent rapid evaporation. Many young seedlings are dried out or cut off by the sand during these windstorms, and much damage is done to cultivated crops even in the irrigated fields.

Exposure.—Differences in exposure to the sun's rays, arising from the direction of slope of all hills and mountain sides, cause striking differences in the climate of stations at the same level and near together, with the consequent differences in vegetation. This effect is readily seen when traversing a mountain canyon that runs east or west. The north-facing slope is always occupied by a plant association entirely different from that of the south-facing slope at similar altitudes above the bottom of the canyon.

Vegetation.—Notwithstanding the various unfavorable climatic conditions that plants must be able to endure, there is a covering of vegetation of some kind practically all over the State except locally in spots where the soil is of drifting sand or so alkaline as to kill plants, or on the flat playas that are subject to occasional inundation, or on exposed rocky surfaces where there is little or no soil. This vegetation is frequently very scanty and scattered, often scrubby and spiny, showing in many ways its adaptation to a scanty supply of water. Many of the plants are valueless as forage, but many times more are good for this purpose, and when examined in detail the wonder grows that so many and not so few are usable by stock at one time or another.

"Finally, it is clear that man, whether by reforestation or deforestation, by flooding a desert or by draining a swamp, can produce no important or extended modifications of natural climate. This is governed by factors beyond human control." [1]

There seems to be no doubt of the correctness of this generalization. But it is possible to materially improve or impair the living conditions for humanity in a given region by the management of those industries that man carries on which are dependent upon the adaptation of these industries to the existing climate of that region. The truth of this statement is recognized without question in a humid

[1] Ward, R. de C. Climate . . . p. 363, New York, 1908.

region and accepted as the natural order of things; but it is of vastly more importance in regions of scanty rainfall. Here any kind of management that permits or assists in the waste of water in any way tends in the long run to the desiccation of the region. Hence, any practice that increases the rapidity or amount of superficial run-off or increases the evaporation of water (other than that which passes through the bodies of growing plants) makes for the gradual drying out and increased sterility of the region. These processes are cumulative, and regions that are easily habitable under one kind of treatment may be gradually changed to desert wastes by another procedure which, to the careless observer, does not seem materially different from the first.

SOILS.

Speaking very generally, the soils of most localities in the State have been formed almost in situ by the disintegration of the underlying or near-by rocks and necessarily have the chemical composition arising from the breaking up of these rocks, mechanical or chemical, or both. The soils of the river valleys have been transported considerable distances and the particles assorted to size by the action of the water. They consist mostly of sand or adobe and are uniform in character and depth only for very short distances, because of the great variations in the volume and velocity of the waters of the streams that have deposited them.

The soils of the larger and higher mountains, wherever they occur, are mostly a rather rich loam, due to the nearly complete chemical decomposition of the rocks, and contain considerable humus derived from the vegetation of such regions. The foothills of the mountains are mostly flanked by talus slopes and outwash plains composed of partially disintegrated rock particles of various sizes, forming gravelly ridges and slopes in which proper soil particles constitute only a small part of the volume.

The soils of the plains and bolsons are largely wind-blown sand or loess. In the bottoms of the basins such soils are sometimes deep, but mostly they form only a thin layer.

Wherever the water collects, evaporation goes on rapidly, with a consequent accumulation of the soluble salts of sodium and calcium known as alkali. Alkali often occurs in the river valleys in the soil of terraces whose surfaces are but 2 or 3 feet above the water table, as a result of the concentration of these salts at the surface by evaporation.

The lava-covered areas are in places but bare black rock, with scattered patches of loess or sand in depressions and behind projecting angles. In other places, where the lava is older, the basalt has decomposed to a rich reddish loam, a soil that is recognizedly one of the best.

Outside of the timber-covered mountains, the soils have little or no humus, because the conditions are unfavorable for the production or decomposition of any large amount of vegetable matter.

A characteristic feature of many of the plains is a layer of white, calcareous material, a few to several inches in thickness, lying a foot or so below the surface. This is known as caliche, or hardpan, and is probably a concentration of this material leached from the lower soil layers by an upward movement of the soil water due to prolonged surface evaporation.

SUBDIVISIONS OF THE LAND.

New Mexico contains a little less than 78,500,000 acres of land. According to the Thirteenth Census (1909 data), 11,270,021 acres, or 14.4 per cent of the total area, were included in farms. This designation is quite misleading, as will be seen farther on; it certainly does not mean that that much land is under cultivation.

Of the above-named area, 1,467,191 acres—only 1.9 per cent of the total area of the State and 13 per cent of the area reported as included in farms—were improved land. The same authority states that 35.9 per cent of the farms were irrigated and that these irrigated farms contained 31.5 per cent of the improved land. Irrigation plants then in existence were able to water 644,970 acres, and irrigation projects were then completed or under way that would irrigate 1,102,291 acres.

Newell[1] estimates the total water supply of the State as sufficient to irrigate 4,000,000 acres. The governor's report for 1909–10[2] states that "thorough investigations which have been carried on during the past four years by the engineering department show conclusively that we have no less than 3,000,000 acres which may be reclaimed by practicable diversion, storage, and pumping projects."

The area of farming land has been markedly increased within the past six or seven years by the introduction of the so-called dry-farming methods in the eastern part of the State. Some of the best land of northeastern Eddy and eastern Chaves Counties and considerable of that in Roosevelt, Curry, Quay, Torrance, Guadalupe, San Miguel, Mora, Union, and Colfax Counties has been patented, and some small part of it has been improved. Estimates made by men well acquainted with the development going on in that region place the area of this land under cultivation in 1911 at 417,000 acres, and these estimates are believed to be conservative. The year 1912 saw more of it in cultivation than ever before, but in 1914 the greater part of it was not cultivated and many of the farms were deserted.

It is probable that this change in the method of using this land will ultimately increase the total number of stock grown in the State,

[1] Newell, F. H. Irrigation in the United States, p. 55. New York, 1902.

[2] Curry, George. Report of the Governor of New Mexico to the Secretary of the Interior. [1909]-10, p. 24. Washington, 1910.

after the people have become adjusted to the conditions of the region. No exact data are available as to the total area that may be cultivated in this way, but an estimate by good authorities places it at approximately 15,000,000 acres, which is doubtless large enough to cover all possibilities.

The national forests of the State now contain 9,881,660 [1] acres of more or less densely timber-covered lands, practically all of which is used as grazing land for at least a part of the year.

Large areas are included in the old Spanish land grants, but much of this land is unfenced and is treated as open range. That portion of it which is arable is included in the farming lands previously referred to; the remainder is grazing land of greater or less value.

As an endowment for the public educational, penal, and charitable institutions, several million acres of land have been given to the State by the Federal Government, and these lands are managed by a State commissioner of public lands. Much of this land is leased, and doubtless most of it will be in the not distant future.

Large areas of land (about 4,000,000 acres) were given to some of the transcontinental railroads when they were first built, but considerable of it has been surrendered for lieu-land scrip or sold outright. About one-half of their present holdings of 2,500,000 acres is rented for grazing purposes, but none of it is fenced.

About 5,000,000 acres of land are held in Indian, military, and other Government reservations, not including the national forests. Stock is run on most of this land, sometimes by the Indians themselves, or the land is leased for grazing purposes by the agents in charge.

On July 1, 1913, there were 31,298,621 acres of Government land open for entry in the State of New Mexico, almost all of which is classified as broken or grazing land. It is probably safe to say that 40 per cent of the total area of the State is still Government land, and therefore used without legal right and controlled only by custom. It is also true that many of the State lands and the Mexican grant lands that might be placed under legal control for one reason or another are not so controlled to-day, though this is a continually decreasing area.

A careful analysis of these data shows that but a relatively small part of the State is fitted for the growing of field crops, and it emphasizes the fact that by far the greater part of the total area, under whatever form of tenure it may be held, is grazing land and is likely to remain so, at least until some method of farming with a smaller supply of water is developed.

[1] Apr. 1, 1914. The gross area includes over 1,000,000 acres of alienated lands.

RELATIVE IMPORTANCE OF STOCK RAISING.

Manufacturing in the Territory is still in its infancy. The mining of coal, copper, gold, and silver are of considerable importance, but the principal pursuits are stock raising and agriculture.[1]

It is somewhat difficult to get reliable statistics concerning the relative economic importance of stock raising in New Mexico, because the summaries made in most reports do not have their component factors combined in the same manner and are therefore not comparable. The Territorial and State auditors' annual reports have been compiled from the county assessors' reports and show only the property returned for taxation. This showing is confessedly inaccurate, being always less than the actual facts, especially as to the number of range animals, which are almost never counted, the returns being based upon an estimate. And taxation values are always based upon some percentage less than 100 of the current selling price at the time of making up the returns.

The figures collected by the United States Census Bureau for the Thirteenth Census are, in the opinion of the present State auditor, probably slightly in excess of the actual facts. These figures, however, are perhaps the most accurate of any available, and in so far as they are usable for our present purpose they will constitute our most reliable data. Unfortunately, the system adopted in the grouping of some of the items is not designed to bring out the comparisons we wish to make. This report does not differentiate between the range lands and the agricultural or cultivated lands. All patented lands are referred to as "Land in farms," and the subdivisions "Improved land in farms," "Woodland in farms," and "Other unimproved land in farms" do not assist in separating the areas of land used as actual farming land from the proper range lands.

There is evidently some difference in the classification of the lands given in the census report and the Territorial auditor's report for the same year, 1909, since the latter shows a larger acreage under the heads of grazing and agricultural lands together than all the "Land in farms" as given in the former, and there can be no doubt that the auditor's report is not in excess of the actual taxable acreage, since taxes were assessed on all the lands so listed. There can hardly be any doubt, either, that the group "Land in farms" of the census report is intended to include agricultural and grazing lands, though some of the lands used for grazing may have been reported to the census taker as mineral or timber lands, or part of the proper timber or mineral lands may have been returned as grazing land in the auditor's report in order to benefit by a lower rate of taxation.

Since practically all timber and mineral lands are used as grazing lands and since there is very little opportunity to falsify the returns of land acreage, the figures given in the auditors' reports are probably very close to the truth regarding the division of the patented lands between the grazing and agricultural industries.

[1] United States 13th Census, 1910, v. 9, Manufactures, Reports by States, p. 787. 1912.

In Table I is shown a summary of the number of acres of land, both grazing and agricultural, and the number of domestic animals (omitting swine and fowls) that were returned for taxation in the years 1909, 1910, 1911, 1912, and 1913. In column 3 of this table is shown the report of the Thirteenth Census upon the same subjects, while in column 2 appears the factor by which the auditor's number for 1909 must be multiplied in order to produce the census number for the same item the same year. This column of figures is interesting as showing the correctness of the auditor's generalization that the valuations returned for assessment have been for a number of years scarcely 50 per cent of the actual value of the property.

From this table may be seen the area of patented land used in stock raising[1] and that which is under cultivation in some kind of farm crops. It should be kept in mind that about 5 per cent of the cattle are dairy cows and are on the agricultural lands or in the towns, that probably two-fifths to one-half of the horses are also on the farms or in the towns, as are practically all of the mules, and that nearly all the sheep, goats, and burros are range animals, the number of these animals that are kept on the farms or in the towns being so small a percentage of the whole as to be negligible.

TABLE I.—*Comparison of the reports of the Territorial and State auditors of New Mexico for the last five years with the Thirteenth Census report.*

Land and animals.	Factor.	Thirteenth Census (1909).	1909	1910	1911	1912	1913
Land (acres):							
Grazing			11,180,159	11,218,856	11,572,790	12,654,535	13,686,833
Agricultural			[1] 2,164,952	1,735,776	1,774,049	2,443,875	2,696,426
Farms		11,270,021	[2] 13,345,111	[2] 12,954,111	[2] 13,346,839	[2] 15,098,410	[2] 16,383,259
Live stock (number):							
Cattle (all kinds)	2.48	1,081,663	480,558	390,155	359,308	386,565	570,939
Horses	2.02	171,525	84,847	79,711	74,963	83,936	104,253
Mules	1.69	14,937	8,804	9,239	9,145	9,248	9,638
Burros	2.81	11,853	4,207	4,722	5,146	5,555	5,794
Sheep	2.27	3,346,984	1,472,866	1,368,460	1,280,467	1,463,691	1,693,970
Goats	2.24	412,050	183,872	151,639	133,734	145,165	190,658

[1] To understand why more agricultural land was returned in 1909 than in 1910 and 1911, it is necessary to remember that 1909 was a year of large influx of settlers into the dry-farming area. The next year was dry and many claims were deserted, and much of the land was returned as grazing land after title had been obtained by commuting.

[2] This is the sum of the area of grazing and agricultural lands and is comparable with the Census report figures.

Figures 1, 2, and 3 show the approximate density of distribution of range animals by counties. These charts were prepared from the Thirteenth Census reports and are from enumerations made in 1909.

[1] This takes no account of the large area of State lands leased for grazing, the national forests grazed under a permit system, or the immense area of Government lands used without charge of any kind.

As will be seen by consulting Table I, these figures are greatly in excess of the latest available tax returns (1913), but if the tax returns for 1913 are compared with those for 1909 it will be observed at once that the numbers of different kinds of stock returned for the two years are not very dissimilar. There are some fluctuations in the returns for the different counties, but the general variations are small.

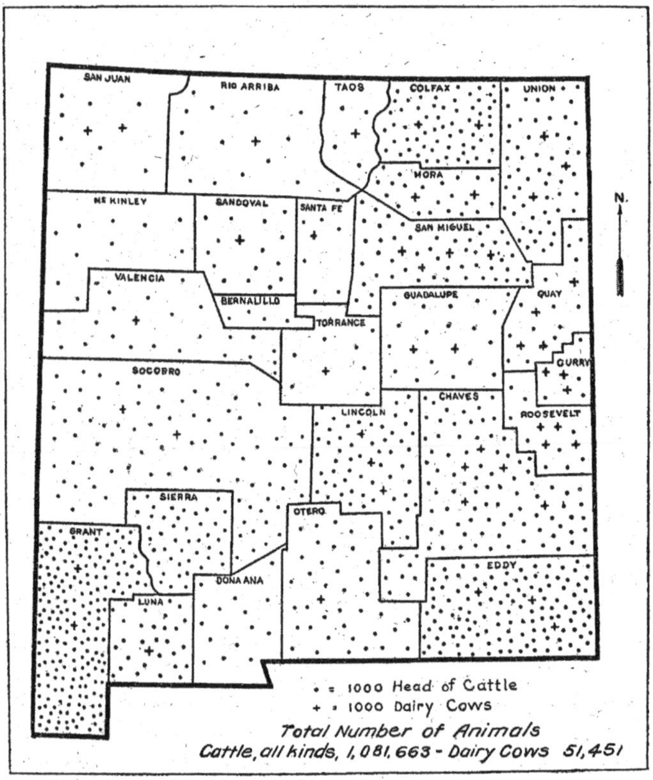

FIG. 1.—Outline map of New Mexico, showing the distribution (by counties) of cattle of all kinds and dairy cows, according to the Thirteenth Census.

The charts show the ordinary geographic distribution and relative importance of each kind of stock as well as it could be presented without assuming much smaller units of area requiring more detailed data. From these diagrams we learn that the central, northern, and northeastern parts of the State are most heavily stocked with sheep, while the southwestern, southeastern, and northeastern corners are more heavily stocked with cattle. Horses, mules, and burros are about uniformly distributed over the State, and goats occur mainly in the southwest corner and in the north-central part.

Table II shows the percentage of the total valuation which each large group of property represents in the assessment returns. It is

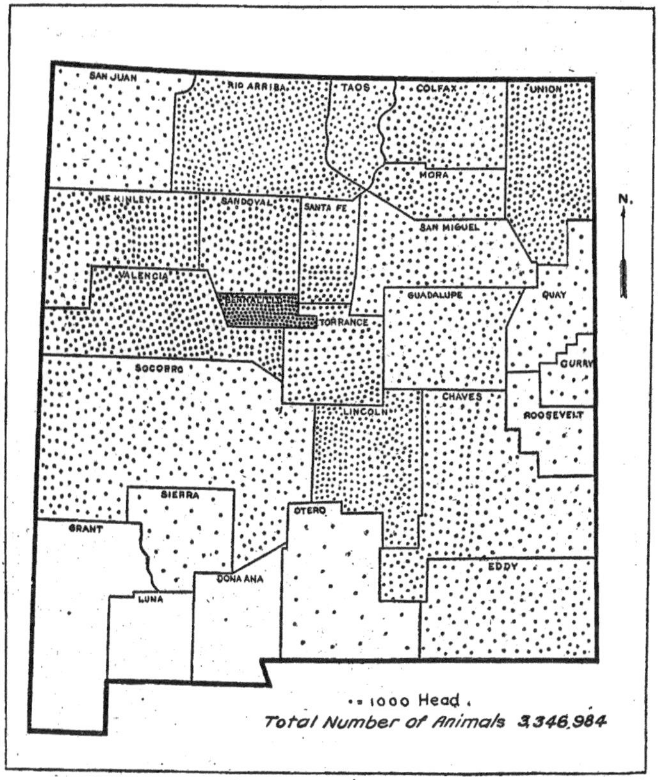

FIG. 2.—Outline map of New Mexico, showing the distribution (by counties) of sheep, according to the Thirteenth Census.

recognized that the valuations ascribed are not correct, but the general reduction in values is so nearly uniform as to make the percentages of valuation represented by each class of property quite accurate. The relative importance of the different classes of property is also indicated.

TABLE II.—*Percentage of the total assessed valuation in New Mexico contributed by each different kind of property.*

[Data taken from Territorial and State auditors' reports.]

Classes of property.	1909	1910	1911	1912	1913
	Per cent.	*Per cent.*	*Per cent.*	*Per cent.*	*Per cent.*
Railroads	24.218	25.056	24.307	26.460	32.826
City property and improvements	17.621	18.512	18.142	15.929	13.942
Agricultural lands and improvements	12.220	13.444	13.976	14.929	14.275
Grazing lands and improvements	13.383	13.082	14.595	14.238	11.009
Cattle (all kinds)	7.042	5.917	5.392	5.809	7.139
Merchandise	4.683	4,637	4.438	3.733	3.212
Sheep and goats (all kinds)	4.427	4.127	3.847	3.079	2.821
Stocks, bonds, money, public utilities, mills, etc	4.043	3.645	3.729	3.448	3.722
Household goods, musical instruments, watches, clocks, sewing machines, vehicles of all kinds, saddles, harness, farming implements, etc	3.532	3.460	3.370	3.123	2.115
Mineral and timber lands, with all improvements and products	3.434	3.404	3.844	5.090	4.808
Horses, mules, and burros	3.022	2.849	2.622	2.632	2.377
All other property	2.375	1.867	1.738	1.919	1.614

Table III is a grouping of the percentages taken from Table II, which shows approximately what part of the total tax valuation of the property of the State is invested as capital in the business of stock raising. The data available do not permit of an accurate distribution of land area and improvements, stock, and other property so as to show the exact relation of stock raising to agriculture and other forms of industry, but the estimates offered in Table III do show the percentage values of grazing land, improvements, and stock upon the ranges. If the proper percentage of the valuation of vehicles, saddles, harness, farm implements, and household property belonging to and being used in the stock-raising industry be added to the totals given in this table, it will be seen that the business utilizes about one-fourth of the taxable property in the State, to say nothing of the value obtained from the use of public lands.

TABLE III.—*Approximation of the percentage of the assessed valuation of the property of New Mexico that is invested as capital in the stock-raising industry.*

Property.	1909	1910	1911	1912	1913
	Per cent.	*Per cent.*	*Per cent.*	*Per cent.*	*Per cent.*
Grazing land and improvements	13.383	13.082	14.595	14.238	11.009
Total cattle (less dairy cows = 5 per cent)	6.690	5.621	5.122	5.519	6.782
Total sheep and goats (all kinds)	4.427	4.127	3.847	3.079	2.821
One-half total horses, mules, and burros	1.511	1.424	1.311	1.316	1.188
Total	26.011	24.054	24.875	24.152	21.800

Judged as an industry by the capital invested in the business, stock raising stands second in importance to the railroads only, and it has reached this status but recently, partly by a marked increase in the valuation of the railroad property for taxation by the assessor. It is directly comparable on the same basis to farming as an industry, which it surpasses slightly. It very noticeably exceeds in taxable valuation all the city and town property of the State; and when we take into consideration that it is a productive business, continually bringing into existence new wealth and not merely shifting value from one holder to another, the importance of the industry is still more apparent and it becomes at once one of the most important industries, if not the most important industry, of the State.

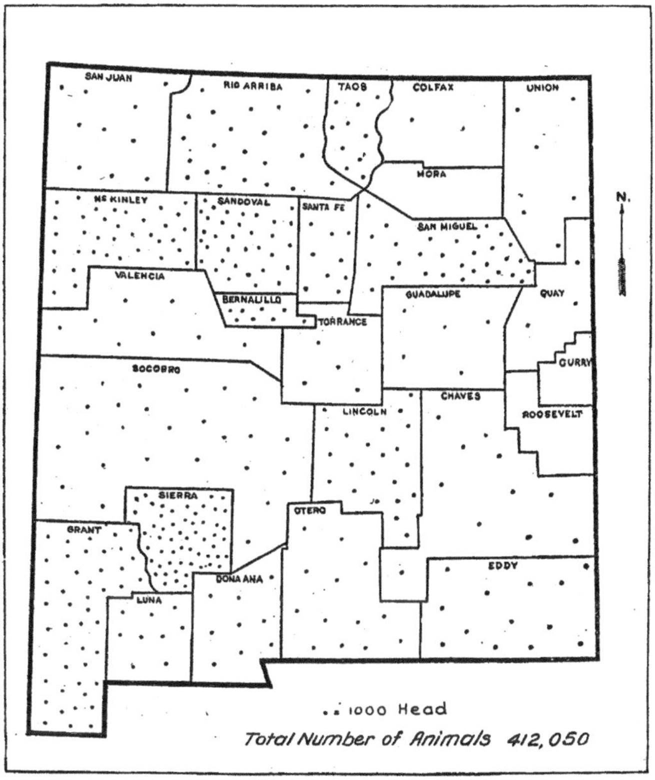

FIG. 3.—Outline map of New Mexico, showing the distribution (by counties) of goats, according to the Thirteenth Census.

LEGAL STATUS OF THE BUSINESS.

Every business must have a proper standing before the law.

There is a steadily increasing demand for beef and mutton, hides and wool, and the supplying of this demand is recognized as a legitimate business.

The cheap production of these commodities calls for the use of large bodies of low-priced lands.

New Mexico has large areas of cheap land upon which these products may be grown and which are not well suited to any other business.

Naturally they have been occupied by stockmen, but the difficulty of obtaining and maintaining control of the land has materially retarded the natural growth of the industry, and to-day this lack of legalized control of the land is not only reducing the output and rendering the business precarious, but is causing marked deterioration of the range itself, besides causing great and frequent losses of valuable property, to say nothing of the suffering of thousands of animals that die of starvation.

A careful examination into the conditions, laws, and customs now controlling the business is here attempted.

Under another heading attention has been called to the relative areas of land held under legal tenure of one kind or another. It is of importance to know how possession of the Government lands is maintained and to understand how this form of tenure affects the stock-raising industry.

It must be kept in mind that only such land to which the claimant has title or right or is in process of obtaining such title by the method prescribed by the land laws may be inclosed with a fence.[1] To this group belong (1) the patented homesteads, desert claims, timber claims, lieu-land selections, or all Government lands that have been filed upon according to some existing land law; (2) all railroad land grants which have not been exchanged for lieu-land scrip; (3) all the lands included in the old Mexican land grants that have been confirmed by the courts; (4) the State lands which have been given to the State by the National Government as an endowment for its educational, penal, and charitable institutions,[2] and (5) land held in small areas under mineral claims, such areas being held from one year to the next by performing the assessment work each year. It goes without saying that all such lands may be fenced and controlled according to the will of the claimants.

All other lands, not including various reservations like national forests, Indian reservations, etc., are Government lands and according to the rulings of the General Land Office may not be inclosed with a fence. They are public property and in the sight of the law may be used by everybody in general and nobody in particular. This situation arises as the result of lack of legislation concerning the

[1] Under certain conditions special permission to fence limited areas of Government land within the national forests may be obtained. Recently the policy of building drift fences has been to some extent adopted and is strongly recommended by the United States Forest Service. (See Graves, H. S., Report of the Forester, United States Department of Agriculture, 1912, p. 69. Washington, 1912.)

[2] This area consists of four sections in each township for the grade schools and several hundred thousand acres scattered over the State for the other institutions named.

disposal of such land. It was assumed when the existing land laws were made that all land was about equally good and that 160 acres of it was amply sufficient for the support of one man's family; that if he wanted any of it he might have that much and welcome; and that all of it would ultimately be given by the Government to its individual citizens.

It has since been learned that much of the land will not support a family upon 160 acres, but that in certain places from 20 to 50 times that area is necessary. Of course, the original lawmakers assumed such land to be desert and therefore valueless. It has a certain value as pasture land, however, and in order that its best use may be secured it is necessary that it should be used to some degree in severalty instead of in common. It being impossible to obtain legal control of it in bodies of sufficient size to carry on stock raising with profit, men were forced to control it some other way or not use it.

The need of stock water is as great as that of stock feed, and the pioneers in the stock business at once perceived that the water could be controlled. So to-day throughout the region the permanent watering places are all held under some kind of legal right, and it is through the control of the water that the range is controlled.

This set of conditions gave rise to the custom that men should use and claim as their own the pasture lands surrounding their watering places. Whenever a conflict of interests arose, the men concerned had to settle it among themselves. Community of interests and the desire for an amicable agreement have led to a set of customs that have the force of unwritten laws. These differ to some extent in different localities, mainly because of local conditions, but the basal principles, being dependent upon the requirements of the business itself, are quite uniform. The worst differences arose between the cattlemen and sheepmen, because the methods of caring for their stock are of necessity different, and hence their interests are strongly competitive instead of parallel. As long as there was plenty of unoccupied land to which the more venturesome spirits might move, severe competition was only local and sporadic, but as soon as the available range was all occupied, competition became more and more strenuous. Competition is generally not vigorous between those subdivisions of the industry of the same kind and approximately equal grade. Thus a group of small cattlemen in a region get along fairly well together, having only petty personal jealousies. Large cattlemen recognize the rights of their equals in the business.

On an open range it is, of course, necessary to have all water open, and cattle and horses go where they will to drink, though they are generally "located" in some particular region. It is the common custom to allow all stock of whatever ownership to water at any watering place, and the man who would exclude any of his neighbors' stock from his water troughs would be ostracized. But this necessity of the business makes it possible for the stingy or thievish man to "edge in" on every other owner in his district. He "develops" water at a certain place, but not in sufficient quantity to supply the number of animals he puts upon the range. It follows that his animals get some of their water from his neighbors, and water costs money in the range country at any place. Thus, the small man is a thorn in the side, especially of the large owner who has a first-class equipment. The latter may retaliate by throwing large numbers of his stock into the small man's range long enough to eat it out in a short time, or by instituting legal proceedings on trumped-up charges, thereby causing the small man loss of time and unnecessary expenditure of money. These are but a few of the more patent of the competitive methods in use among cattlemen, and another similar set is to be found among the large and small sheepmen.

The battles between the sheep and cattle industries have been told time and again. The sheepman has the advantage in most respects. His stock are herded all the time; they can be held on any spot as long as he desires; if held long enough they will practically obliterate the vegetation on such an area; they require much less water than cattle, and with green succulent feed may go for long periods without any water at all; they may be driven in almost any place where other stock can go. He is thus able to drive over a cattleman's range and leave desolation in his wake if he wants to; and he may do this, too, without overstepping his legal rights.

For convenience in handling the sheep at night, the herders build brush corrals. These corrals burn readily after the brush is dry. When not in a corral, sheep may easily be stampeded and scattered at night. A herder's camp fire at night is a conspicuous target, but the immediate vicinity is very unsafe when rifle practice at such target is going on, and a band of sheep without a herder is soon lost. Such gentle hints as any of these may be taken to indicate to the sheepman that it is time for him to move on.

The industry is now developed to such a state that if a man wishes to enter it he must either buy a range and its rights or develop some of the few remaining unoccupied areas, where water is hard to obtain and where the supply of feed is scanty and uncertain. In either case, he must be able to invest considerable capital in the business. This means that the industry is upon a much more permanent basis and is consequently more highly organized.

Perhaps no other demand of the business is so well recognized by all those interested in it as the desirability of control of the range, and nothing but the selfish interest of the few who are getting the lion's share under the present régime and the fear of the many that the last state might be worse than the first have for years prevented legislation.

Advantage has been taken of various methods to obtain control and to divide up the range. Natural barriers, like mountains or impassable lava flows, have always been used. Until recently, areas without water have been natural barriers, but such areas are now very rare. The railroad rights of way have been fenced and now act as drift fences. Miles of drift fence have been constructed since a ruling of the Commissioner of the General Land Office was made, deciding that such fences might be allowed to stand, since they do not inclose Government lands. The law allowing a county road to be fenced has resulted in the establishment of some very queer-looking county roads. All such fences and natural barriers have resulted in cutting up the country into large, more or less independent areas, and have given some individuals in favored localities practically complete—though not legal—control of their ranges. Such individuals have little to obtain from any legalized system of control except the necessity of paying for what they now get for nothing.

Individuals or corporations who have had the money necessary have bought lieu-land scrip and placed it on compact bodies of land or have bought such of the Mexican land grants as they could obtain title to. For years most of these grants have been treated as the United States public lands; at first, because the grants had not been confirmed in the land courts. Later, since the titles were confirmed, it has been difficult to get the authority for the management of such lands delegated to any representative of the owners, because too many claimants had to be considered. Recently, some of these grants have been sold and fenced, and others are leased in severalty without fencing, much as the national forests are treated.

Similarly, the lands given to the State and its institutions by Congress may be leased in large bodies. The practice of leasing the school section and fencing it for a pasture is a common one, and it is a not uncommon habit in places to rent a given school section and fence one or more sections that happen to be conveniently located, with scant regard for the terms of the rental contract. Land inspectors come around at very rare intervals, and even then they do not know where the township and section corners are and can not demonstrate without an expensive survey that the area fenced is not the same as that leased. Hence, the fences stand and the fenced areas increase in number and in size. Sometimes State lands have been so located as to cover natural waters, like springs and streams in the mountains or places where wells might easily be dug. These lands have then been leased, and by this means the water and range have been controlled and possible settlers have been kept out.

A large part of the railroad lands was surrendered for lieu-land scrip. The remainder now in the possession of the railroads is rented for grazing purposes so far as possible. Practically none of these lands are fenced, because they are the alternate sections.

The grazing privilege on the national forests is controlled by a permit system that guarantees the proper use of such ranges, rendering the business less hazardous and at the same time increasing the carrying capacity.

It will thus be seen that the desire of all parties engaged in the business is some sort of legalized control of the range lands; and wherever this has been obtained and is at the same time associated with the proper kind of management, the result has been beneficial to the industry and to the range also, and consequently to the State

NATURE OF THE FORAGE CROP AND ITS DISTRIBUTION.[1]

Plains.—Much of the area of New Mexico consists of open, nearly flat stretches that pass under such names as prairies, plains, or mesas. They range in elevation from about 3,500 to nearly 7,000 feet above sea level, a few, like Johnsons Mesa, reaching 8,000 feet. Such plains are usually covered with a more or less dense covering of grasses, which in the northern part of the State forms a tolerably thick sod. (Pl. II, fig. 1.) In the southern part of the State the grass covering is always less dense and rarely, if ever, forms a true sod (Pl. III, fig. 1), while in many places the ground is absolutely bare over areas many acres in extent (Pl. III, fig. 2). Over large sections, often of many thousands of acres of these plains, the soil consists of loose sand and is covered with a more or less scattered growth of sand, bunch, and sage grasses (Pl. IV, fig. 1) or a scrub oak known as shinry (Pl. IV, fig. 2). Often the tight soils of the southern part of the State carry a growth of shrubs which are valuable browse plants, of which mesquite and shadscale (locally called sagebrush or coarse sage) are the most important. (Pl. V, fig. 1.)

Besides the grasses and shrubs already referred to, there is a long list of herbaceous annuals and perennials that appear in the growing season. The spring growth is fairly constant where some winter rain or snow may be depended upon, but in the southern part of the State these spring weeds only appear abundantly when three favorable conditions occur in sequence. There must be enough rain in the fall to germinate the seeds; the winter must be wet enough and warm enough to produce good root growth; and the spring must not be so

[1] A detailed treatment of the forage plants of New Mexico will be found in New Mexico Experiment Station Bulletins 66, 78, 81, and 87.

FIG. 1.—VIEW IN THE SOUTH-CENTRAL PART OF NEW MEXICO, SHOWING A TYPICAL AREA OF OPEN OR SCATTERED GRASSES.

FIG. 2.—VIEW IN THE SOUTHERN PART OF NEW MEXICO, SHOWING AN AREA OF PERFECTLY BARE SOIL.

FIG. 1.—VIEW IN THE SOUTHEASTERN PART OF NEW MEXICO, SHOWING GROWTH OF SAGE OR SAND GRASSES ON SANDY LAND.

FIG. 2.—VIEW IN THE SOUTHEASTERN PART OF NEW MEXICO, SHOWING THE GROWTH OF SHINRY ON SAND HILLS.

FIG. 1.—VIEW IN THE SOUTH-CENTRAL PART OF NEW MEXICO, SHOWING THE SHADSCALE AND MESQUITE ASSOCIATION OF PLANTS.

FIG. 2.—A BRUSH-COVERED AREA IN NEW MEXICO, SHOWING A SMALL SPOT HAVING AN ALMOST PURE STAND OF GRASS.

FIG. 1.—VIEW IN NEW MEXICO, SHOWING AN AREA ALMOST COMPLETELY COVERED BY SNAKEWEED AS THE RESULT OF OVERSTOCKING.

FIG. 2.—VIEW IN NEW MEXICO, SHOWING A CHARACTERISTIC GROWTH OF THE ROCKY MOUNTAIN BEE PLANT DUE TO OVERSTOCKING.

dry and windy as to dry up or cut off the young seedlings. In an experience extending over about twenty years but three such springs occurred at one point in the region mentioned. In the summer after the rains there is commonly an abundant crop of such plants.

Many of these plains are really bolsons, or basins, without a drainage outlet, and in all such low places where the water collects and evaporates, as well as in many places in the river valleys where the water table is near the surface, alkali occurs in greater or less abundance. In such places may be found an association of alkali-loving plants, many of which are usable as forage in default of something better.

Porous gravelly mesas.—In the southern part of the State are large bodies of dry, porous, gravelly soil that usually lie as bands of greater or less width paralleling the mountain chains. The dominant plants of these areas are shrubs of no forage value, and there are few forage plants of any kind in the association. The factor which in the last analysis determines the distribution of this association is probably one of soil aeration, though it may be dependent upon the amount of available water.[1]

Where wind-transported sand or loess collects under the protection of bushes, bluffs, or other obstructions, a spot of soil of an entirely different texture is formed and other plants occur. It is not uncommon to find in these bush-covered areas spots of this kind, from a few square feet to several acres in extent, upon which occurs an almost pure stand of grass. (Pl. V, fig. 2.)

Sometimes there is a good crop of annuals upon these gravelly mesas, but this crop is rarely used, since at such times there is an abundance of better feed elsewhere. These areas also are poorly supplied with watering places, because the feed will not warrant the expense. If some drought-resistant shrub having a value as forage could be found that might replace the valueless shrubs of these areas, much land now useless could be rendered productive, at least to some degree. The amount of vegetation now produced upon these areas is about the same as that upon the tight soils of the region, but it is not usable because of its kind. Hence, there is hope that a valuable plant may be found that will grow here.

Arroyos.—In most general terms, the plants that grow in the arroyos or dry watercourses are the same that grow in the foothills of the near-by mountains and have followed the drainage channel downward, or those that have followed back up these channels from the

[1] An investigation carried on at the New Mexico Agricultural College by a student assistant of the writer, Mr. O. B. Metcalfe, demonstrated pretty completely that a pronounced tension line between almost pure creosote-bush and shadscale associations was not due (as we had long believed) to a difference in alkalinity of the soils. Careful examination, chemically and physically, of the soils to a depth of 6 feet at several places across the tension line showed no differences in soil except those arising from the size of the particles. The soil upon which the creosote-bush association grew was very gravelly, and some of the bowlders contained in it were so large that it was necessary several times to dig a pit instead of using the soil auger to get the soil samples. The soil supporting the shadscale association was much more finely grained, being mostly a sandy loam at the surface and not gravelly below.

lower levels into which the arroyos debouch, with a few that have come in from the adjacent mesas or ridges.

The physical factors that determine this distribution relate in some way to local water and air drainage. While the upper courses of such arroyos are likely to be deep and full of plants, the lower reaches are usually dry, broad, flat, gravelly channels, at most but a few feet lower than the surrounding land and practically bare of vegetation or occasionally having a crop of range weeds.

Woodlands.—As used here, the term woodlands refers to those areas that are covered with a more or less scattering growth of low trees, a plant formation occupying a zone between the grass-covered plains and the forest-covered areas of the higher mountains. Typical woodlands occur on the lower parts of the mountains, ranging upward from 1,000 to 2,000 feet above the level of the surrounding plains. Where these plains are relatively low, as they are in the southern part of the State, the wooded areas begin at about 5,000 feet elevation, while farther north, where the plains are much higher, the lower limit of woodland is sometimes as high as 7,000 feet. Throughout the State the area is characterized by the presence in greater or less abundance of low scrubby trees and numerous shrubs. Among these occur various bunch grasses and numerous herbs during the growing season. This plant formation often covers the lower drier ridges and mountains to the summits, especially on the southern exposures where the zone is nearly always broad, while on the higher mountains and especially on steep northern slopes the zone is apt to be narrow or sometimes almost absent.

Forests.—Above the woodland zone in the mountains come the forests. First, as one goes upward, are the open forests of western yellow pine with interspersed parks (the transition zone), then the denser forests of pine and Douglas spruce (mainly the Canadian zone), and last the dense spruce forests (Hudsonian zone), reaching the timber line. These forests exist only because of the rainfall that occurs at these levels, and the growing conditions thus produced result in an abundant and varied flora, most of which is readily eaten by stock. As the elevation increases, the forests become denser, darker, and wetter. The growing season also is shortened, as is the grazing season, the area above the transition zone being mostly summer pasture.

Above the timber line there are some ridges and peaks which have a short-lived crop of grass, sedges, herbs, and a few low shrubs, but this area is very rarely reached by stock even in the warmest of the summer weather.

Practically all of the lands held by the Federal Government lying in the woodland zone and those above it are now administered as national forest.

UNDESIRABLE RANGE PLANTS.

Besides the useless shrubs occurring on the gravelly mesas, two other types of undesirable plants occur. These may be called for convenience range weeds and poisonous plants. Range weeds are of two kinds—native and introduced—and their presence upon the range is due to two facts: First, and of much the greater importance, because the animals will not eat these plants at all or only when forced to do so by extreme hunger; and, second, because their natural plant dominants (both biologic and economic) have been removed by overstocking.

In the main, those native plants which have become the commonest and apparently most important range weeds are not very aggressive and would not occupy the large areas they do but for the effective assistance in their struggle for existence which they receive from the animals. Yet so important has this factor of animal interference with the adjustment of plants in different associations become that large areas are often occupied by almost pure stands of plants that would normally form but an insignificant part of the vegetable covering.

The best example of this kind of a range weed is found in the snakeweed (*Gutierrezia* spp.), which also is called by its Mexican name yerba del vibora (Pl. VI, fig. 1). In many places it is called sheep weed because of its abundance on overstocked sheep ranges. So infrequent is this plant on a normal range which has not been overstocked that the average observer rarely sees it, and it has often been sent to the writer as an example of a recently introduced and very harmful weed.

In response to the oft-repeated question of how to get rid of the snakeweed, there is but one method economically possible, and that is to give the grama grass a chance and it will crowd out the snakeweed. In the eastern counties of the State, where the influx of settlers several years ago drove range stock out and gave much of what had been range land a long and much-needed rest, this very thing happened. It usually happens inside the fences of the railroad rights of way. There is little doubt also that the burning of the dead grass, a custom of the Indian days, was very destructive to the snakeweed, which is quite resinous, burns readily, and is easily killed by fire, but it did little damage to the grass except to destroy the standing dry crop. Advantage might be taken of this fact locally to hasten the eradication of this weed. Rabbit brush (*Chrysothamnus* spp.) occasionally assumes this rôle in certain localities.

Another common, though less important, weed of the open parks in the forests is the Rocky Mountain bee plant, which in places occupies large areas to the more or less complete exclusion of some of the best of the forage plants. (Pl. VI, fig. 2.)

Of more importance is a group of introduced weeds, about the probable effects of which we know less and whose spread within recent years has been rather ominous. These are mostly tumble-weeds, of which the Russian thistle (*Salsola pestifer*) is far and away the worst. (Pl. VII, fig. 1.) Their seed-distribution habits are admirably adapted to an open country with strong winds, and they scatter their abundant crops of seed over wide areas. Most of the species are able to endure extreme drought and great heat; their seeds germinate readily and the seedlings endure very unfavorable conditions and grow into plants that mature seed whether they be but a few inches high or reach maximum size. They practically all belong in the goosefoot or amaranth families and have to their credit the fact that they are all to some extent valuable as forage when young, and they are eaten when nothing better is available.

In regions having a rainfall of over 15 inches the Russian thistle is very much at home, and wherever the native grasses have been killed out either by stock or by the plow it is a pestiferous weed. For a short time, while it is young and tender, it is a fairly good feed, and it has been used as hay and silage when other crops have failed in the dry-farming regions; but these uses are always make-shift attempts to utilize a product that is not desired. Ordinarily, it does not seem to be able to crowd out the native grasses, but in the dry-farming areas, where the sod has been broken and the land deserted for any reason, it usually takes the ground completely. It also takes badly overstocked places on the ranges, especially where sheep have been held too long. Whether the native grasses will be able to crowd their way back into such areas or not still remains to be seen. If they are not, then the importance of this pest is increased many times.

Certain poisonous plants are also of some considerable menace to the ranges, especially where any overstocking is going on. Speaking very generally, these plants form a very small and numerically unimportant part of the natural flora until the factor of overstocking enters. Of course, the different species differ in importance merely on the basis of the readiness with which they reproduce themselves and their ability to compete with their plant associates. Under normal conditions, unless pressed by hunger, grazing animals of all kinds let them alone and hence do not in any way interfere with their natural rate of reproduction and spread. Like other weeds that are not eaten, they thus tend to spread much more rapidly when relieved of their plant competitors by the animals. In fact, under these circumstances there is nothing left but their animal and plant parasites to hold them in check, unless man should interfere.[1]

[1] A few species of loco weed have become so abundant on some of the sheep ranges of California that it is now the custom in certain localities for the herder to carry a spud or a spade, dig these plants up, collect them, and burn them. The practice evidently pays or it would not be followed.

FIG. 1.—VIEW IN THE NORTHWESTERN PART OF NEW MEXICO, SHOWING A TYPICAL GROWTH OF RUSSIAN THISTLE ON AN OVERGRAZED SHEEP RANGE.

FIG. 2.—A PUMPING PLANT AND RESERVOIR IN NEW MEXICO, THE WELL IN CONNECTION THEREWITH BEING 330 FEET DEEP.

FIG. 1.—VIEW IN THE NORTHERN PART OF NEW MEXICO, SHOWING THE BEGINNING OF AN ARROYO ON AN OVERSTOCKED RANGE.

FIG. 2.—VIEW IN NEW MEXICO, SHOWING THE RESULT OF A SUMMER SHOWER WHICH LASTED BUT A SHORT TIME AND ILLUSTRATING MOST CHARACTERISTICALLY THE IMPORTANCE OF THE RUN-OFF.

Whatever may be said of the undesirability of weeds on a range, there is one thing to be said in their favor. Any vegetable covering in an arid region is better than none, since such a covering prevents to some degree the removal of the soil, and any plant association occupying an area is to be looked upon as merely one stage in the production of that ultimate assemblage of plants which is best adapted to that place and its conditions.

EROSION.

To the observer from a humid climate, perhaps no one characteristic of the arid regions of the Southwest is so startling as the evidence on all sides of the forceful action of water as an erosive agent. And this in a land where water is the one thing that is everywhere lacking.

But the reason is patent after a summer in the region, and the conditions are common to all arid countries of high relief. The erosive effects that one sees so plainly are the resultant of several factors. During the warm weather, the only season of the year in which large volumes of moist air are brought into the region, the air next the ground is always warm and therefore relatively dry. Hence, rain occurs only when masses of humid air are forced into the cold upper strata. Such conditions arise only locally and produce showers of restricted size, but such showers are mostly torrential in character, a large amount of water falling on a restricted area in a very short time.

Let such a downpour occur on what seems to be a flat plain, and in a few minutes the lower levels are flooded and the roadbed of any obstructing railroad is apt to suffer severely. Thus, we are forever hearing of railroad washouts in a region that is called a desert and is wanting governmental irrigation systems established. (Pl. VIII, fig. 2.)

The land is but sparsely covered with any kind of vegetation and there is little to obstruct the run-off. The gradient is high at almost any place. Add to this the fact that the soil has been loosened by daily expansion and nightly contraction, due to large diurnal variations of temperature, and the conditions for maximum efficiency of the erosive agent are supplied; and the consequences are not only not singular but were to be expected instead of wondered at.

The factor which more than anything else tends to prevent the same kind of results in a humid region on an even larger scale is the protective cover of vegetation everywhere abundant, and no one factor is so efficacious in producing rapid erosion on the arid grazing lands as the more or less complete removal of their already scanty cover of plants by overstocking.

A common sight on an overstocked range is the arroyo made by the run-off which has not been held back by the grass and bushes until the water could soak into the ground. (Pl. VIII, fig. 1.) So the removal of even the grass and low shrubbery results in the partial loss of the soil and much of the ground water.

These effects, like many others of the range country, are cumulative. Once a cut is started it soon becomes a trench into which the water drains, the soil is gradually all carried away and in the end nothing is left but the gravel and bowlder-strewn channel where little or nothing can grow. Many of the ranges in New Mexico that years ago were gently rolling grass-covered plains are to-day cut and scarred by arroyos that are almost impassable to a horseman, and all because the region has been overstocked.

RANGE MANAGEMENT.[1]

As stated in another place, in New Mexico to-day the stockman usually owns the land upon which he has "developed" water, and he is warranted by the custom of the country in the use of the range half way from his last watering place to the nearest water of his nearest neighbor, on all sides. He must maintain at his watering place a supply sufficient for the number of stock he may have watering at that place. Such watering places must be open to all stock that come to them of their own volition. Only animals which are driven through the country are expected to have their water paid for, and this recognizedly legitimate charge is often not exacted.

The stockmen's wars, so common a number of years ago, are mostly of the past, for everybody concerned has learned that such methods do not pay. There is still more or less friction among individuals in a small way, as they overreach or are overreached. But in general there is a desire to play fair, or at least within what are recognized as the "rules of the game." What is needed for the improvement of the business is a pronounced change in the rules.

The routine work of the ordinary cattle ranch of to-day consists in maintaining the watering places, moving stock from one place to another as the feed varies, looking after old cows or dogy calves, riding bog, and going after strays, with the heavy work of the spring and fall round-ups, and the incidental branding of calves that have been missed. Owing to the fact that the cattle are in no way restricted in their movements and that all distances which must be traversed are large, such work requires much riding by a number of men, depending upon the size of the ranch.

[1] The word management as used in this bulletin in every case means the financially profitable regulation of the individual enterprise considered as a productive business unit. The principles apply as well to the man with a hundred or so cattle or horses or a single band of sheep as they do to the owner of thousands of animals and large equipment.

With sheep there is the continual round of driving to the feeding grounds in the day and back to the bed grounds at night, with a trip to water every few days, depending upon the kind of feed and amount of water available. The camping place must be changed at frequent intervals, and there is the eternal hunt for good feed. There must be persistent care to prevent the splitting of the herd or losing a bunch of stragglers, and to keep predatory animals out of the flock; and in the spring comes lambing, shearing, and dipping, though in some places shearing is done twice and dipping may also have to be repeated. Most of such work must be done on foot and always in the open, whatever the weather.

When the dry seasons come there is work for all and a hard time for the animals. Though all the stockmen know that the dry seasons will surely come, there is at present little chance of making any preparation for them.

The ideal toward which the individual stockman must always strive is to manage the factors under his control so as to produce upon his range the largest and most valuable crop of forage that it is able to maintain season after season under use, and the adjustment of the proper number of animals to the ranch needs excellent judgment in order to get the best returns. In the opinion of the writer, considerable of the overstocking now done on controlled ranges is due to a lack of accurate knowledge of their carrying capacity, which results in poor judgment in making the adjustment mentioned.

Everybody knows in a general way that there are already too many animals on the range under the present form of management. Many of the more thoughtful stockmen know that it would pay them to reduce the number of stock on their ranches and give the grass a chance to grow, but there are always new men coming into any range country who do not know the rate of feed production of the region. Such men recognize the possibility of developing water in favorable positions, and if they find grass in any quantity which is apparently not being used, they think they have found the place they are looking for. If Mr. A, who has been in possession of that region for maybe twenty years and who does know what the region will carry, complains to the newcomer that the latter is crowding in where there is no place for his stock, Mr. A has absolutely no means of convincing the new arrival of either his knowledge or his sincerity.

The land is all open to entry. The new man can take up a claim and develop the necessary water and turn his stock on the open range, and no one can prevent him. Nor can anyone either protect Mr. A in his claims or insist that only so much stock shall run on a given area. If the seasons are good for a year or so, the range may carry the additional stock, and the newcomer is sure he was right, but when the dry years come both men are bound to lose heavily.

It does no good then for Mr. A to say "I told you so," and his only hope is that he can endure the losses longer than the new man and that the latter will be forced to leave.

There are only two other things that Mr. A can do. He may either buy the newcomer out and so get rid of him—a practice that sometimes induces men to dig wells to sell to established stockmen who have made money—or he may develop another watering place near the newcomer, thus restricting the latter's range to a minimum, and wait for the dry years. Any way that the matter may now be adjusted ultimately results in a direct loss for both men (accompanied by great suffering by the stock), an indirect loss to the general business interests of the region, and a serious depreciation in the value of the range.

An experienced and successful cattleman in the southern part of New Mexico, commenting to the writer on this state of affairs not long ago, said:

> I can better afford to take the $2,500 loss of stock which I know I will have when the dry years come than to take my stock off my range and try to save the grass which I know I will need in those dry years. I hold my range now only by having my stock on it. If I take my stock off, someone else will take my range, and I can afford to lose the stock better than lose the range.

Every stockman using Government range lands is forced into this kind of action whether he be astute enough to have reasoned it out or not. Yet these same lands under a better type of management (possible only under legalized control) would carry safely all the time more and better stock than they now carry with such uncertainty.

Now the crux of the situation is expressed in the phrase "possible only under legalized control." The mere fact that the stockman is not able to protect his range against willful misuse by himself is the best of evidence that the industry has reached the limit of its possible development under the system of management now in operation. The earlier growth of the industry occurred under a condition of what was practically unlimited free range and was satisfactory in most ways as long as this condition continued; but as soon as all the range land was occupied a new system became necessary; and this necessity has been seen by investigators and far-sighted stockmen for a long time. Before the industry can develop further it must become possible to determine how many animals may be put on a given area. But control of such animals as cattle, horses, mules, and burros can be maintained only by fences. Under the present system sheep and goats *can* be managed so as to prevent overstocking, but they rarely are. With a properly fenced range even they are better off, and the range is also. Let us assume that the right to fence the range lands in severalty has been obtained and consider the changes in management rendered possible thereby.

The necessity of allowing feed to mature.—It is a well-known botanical fact that in order for ordinary green plants to grow they must have leaves, since the food from which new growth is made is elaborated mostly in the leaves. This point has been emphasized by various writers, but no definite data as to the exact effect of pasturage upon the quantity of feed produced have been obtained till recently. Studies carried on by Drs. Briggs and Shantz have given some very definite data for alfalfa. From their work it appears probable that whenever range land is closely pastured during the growing season its total productivity is automatically reduced approximately two-thirds, or possibly more. Or, stated generally, close grazing during the growing season reduces the carrying capacity about two-thirds.

One way to diminish this effect is to divide the range into a number of relatively small pastures and give each pasture a rest in turn. Each pasture must be given as long a time to grow its crop as is possible, keeping in mind all the time the fact that the stock must grow as rapidly as possible. It is probably better to put a large number of animals on a relatively small acreage for a short time, thus giving the plants a long period of growth. This procedure makes a larger number of watering places necessary.

The utilization of summer feed.—Subdividing the range is beneficial in another way. In many places there are areas that produce forage which is good feed only while it is green. On other near-by areas forage which cures standing occurs. The latter is the natural winter feed of the region, but these plants are usually preferred by animals while they are green. Thus, if the animals are allowed to range freely and select their feed they eat the winter feed in the summer time. From the standpoint of sustenance the summer feed is all right in the summer, but poor in the winter. Hence, good management requires that it be eaten while at its best. Similarly, the winter feed should be saved till the winter time. Without fences such management is impossible, and the selective action of the stock is always operating to destroy the best feed on the range, for they always graze it more closely, even when the range is properly stocked.

In the higher mountain country some of the range is available only in the summer, because it is covered with snow in the winter. There is some tendency for free-ranging stock to go to the higher levels in the summer, which is advantageous to the stockman. While cattle will climb the hills if they have to, they will congregate in the open valleys and parks as long as the feed lasts, unless they are fenced out. But the valleys and parks may be pastured earlier and later than the mountain sides and should be fenced. Many such treeless areas are capable of cultivation or may be turned into meadows where a good crop of hay may be grown.

Thus in a number of ways the ability to subdivide the range into pastures makes a much more effective utilization of the forage crops possible and so increases the carrying capacity.

The importance of reserve feed.—Attention has been called to the variability of the climate of the region. It is as safe to prophesy lean years in New Mexico as it was in Egypt in Joseph's time, and they usually come in cycles of two or more seasons in which the precipitation is below the average. Only two ways of adjusting the stock business to these years of scanty growth are possible. One must either reduce the number of stock or be able to fall back on a reserve supply of feed. The forced sale of the stock nearly always means financial loss, largely because of the condition of the stock. They have been held in expectation that the rain will occur at what is generally referred to as the usual time. The stock at this time have just passed the season of poor feed and are not in first-class condition for sale, and the longer the rain is delayed the poorer and less valuable they become. If the owner sells at this time, he is bound to lose heavily. Yet, if the rain does come even late in the summer, growth is so rapid that there will be feed enough to carry over to what may be a better year. So he hopes and holds on. But if rain does not come at all, the weak stock and many of the young will die. Thus a large percentage of the breeding stock is lost and the next year's crop much reduced. On much of the New Mexico range country two or three such seasons in succession will put many of the stockmen out of business and kill thousands of animals. Yet these cycles of dry seasons come, and everyone knows they will come again, but no one can get ready for them, because he can not fence his range.

Developing water.—Attention has already been called to the fact that the control of the range is now maintained by the control of the stock water. Of course, it must be understood that wherever there is sufficient water for irrigation purposes it is always so used. In New Mexico there is almost everywhere sufficient stock water to supply all the animals which the range will carry, and in many places quite a little more could be developed. This is one of the factors which have made overstocking not only possible but unavoidable under the present system of tenure.

Wherever there is underground water within 500 feet of the surface, the earth tank and cased well, with its big windmill and gasoline engine, furnish a supply that can be depended upon. (Pl. VII, fig. 2.) Such equipment is, however, the sign of the investment of considerable money; the deeper the well, the larger the expense, and likewise the greater the cost of use and maintenance.

Springs and small streams are always used, unless the supply is large enough for irrigation purposes. Just in the edge of the foothills, where the flood-water channels open out upon the flats, sites may be found where a small earth dam and a proper spillway will make a tank that will catch and hold a large quantity of water. (Pl. IX, fig. 1.) These tanks are usually not very expensive, and, notwithstanding the high rate of evaporation, water is often maintained in such tanks throughout the year. The deeper the tank in proportion to its area the smaller the relative amount of loss by evaporation. Even in the plains country there is always sufficient run-off to collect large quantities of water in tanks properly located. (Pl. IX, fig. 2.) A little judgment in the selection of a site and the use of some plows and scrapers are all that is necessary to develop a valuable supply.

In the mountainous country it is frequently very easy to make lakes of considerable size by deflecting the flow of the smaller streams into natural basins, where a small dam will make a lake several acres in extent. The construction of such lakes is one of the best things that can be done upon a ranch, since all such bodies of water help to regulate the run-off. They always afford a supply of water for stock, and they frequently change intermittent streams into permanent ones, thus distributing the water so that the stock do not need to congregate. They thus reduce the run-off and tend to remove the main cause of trail making, both of which factors are very potent in reducing erosion.

No other one factor is so important as the abundance of good, clean water, well distributed over the ranch, and there are relatively few ranches that now have the water so well distributed that the range may be uniformly grazed. Stock mostly have to go too far for water, with the result that much grass is trampled out around the watering places, and the range is apt to be cut up by trails that ultimately become arroyos. And it is equally true that much more water could be developed upon most ranges, a procedure that would materially help the business. But under the present uncertainty of tenure of the range lands such expenditures are not warranted.

Reducing the effects of erosion.—There are two ways by which the effects of erosion may be reduced. Attention has already been called to the regulation of the run-off and the making of trails. What is necessary on many ranches to-day is the repair of arroyos already made. The aggregate area of land that now produces no forage as the result of the erosive action of water is large. More or less intricate systems of drainage channels have been established where formerly there was but gently rolling country with no definite channels. The original condition existed because the plant cover of the soil prevented the water from collecting into streams. The run-off occurred mostly as a thin sheet of water gently moving over all slopes, the motion being so slow as to allow most of it to soak into the soil. This is the best possible condition for the conservation of both the moisture and the soil, as well as for the maximum production of forage, and it should be brought about wherever possible.

All arroyos should be gradually filled. This can not be done economically except very slowly and by letting the water do it. The cutting occurs because of the velocity of the water, which depends upon the quantity of water and the slope of the land. It is necessary to begin work at the heads of such channels, deflect the water from the main channels, and cause it to run over the more gently sloping land as a sheet. Large obstructions across deep ditches or gullies are of little value unless they are so strong as to hold all the water which can collect behind them, as in a tank or lake.

The same is, of course, true of the broader channels, where more extensive dams would be necessary. If such dams were built and should burst, much greater damage would be done, because of the large volume of water stored before the obstruction gave way. Small obstructions which allow a small quantity of soil to collect behind them upon which the grass may grow are of great advantage in channels, provided most of the flood waters can be kept out of the channel by deflection at the head.

All permanent lakes or tanks become local levels below which cutting can not occur in the drainage basin above them and are, of course, desirable.

The general principle to be kept in mind is that the transporting power of water varies as the sixth power of its velocity. In other words, if the velocity of a stream be doubled, the weight of the largest particles it will push along is 64 times as great as that of the stream at the original velocity. But the velocity increases with the depth and with the gradient. The importance of inducing the water to flow slowly over the surface as a thin sheet is thus apparent. And a relatively small amount of work properly applied will produce important results in restoring to productivity land which is now only used to carry away water that should go into the ground. But none of this improvement work will be done until the worker knows he will be allowed to reap the benefit of his labor.

Reseeding operations.—So far, experiments attempting to reseed artificially the ranges of most of New Mexico have resulted negatively. There are good reasons for this, to which we wish to call attention. There are, however, large areas where artificial reseeding will prove successful. Many high mountain valleys that receive considerable water, but have a short, cool season, can be set in timothy or redtop. Orchard grass, tall fescue, or brome-grass will grow in many localities if properly treated. Oats, barley, and wheat are already grown in many of the open parks of the higher mountain timbered lands, and much of the plains country of the eastern side of the State will grow kafir, milo, or some of the other sorghums. Such lands are range lands

FIG. 1.—VIEW IN THE SOUTH-CENTRAL PART OF NEW MEXICO, SHOWING A SMALL TANK IN THE FOOTHILLS.

FIG. 2.—VIEW IN THE SOUTHEASTERN PART OF NEW MEXICO, SHOWING A LARGE TANK ON THE PLAINS.

only temporarily, until their owners learn that they can produce much more feed per acre by cultivating them, when they become agricultural lands, and it is no longer an experiment to try to cultivate such lands.

The commonly cultivated pasture grasses will not grow on much the larger part of the lands of the State, because of insufficient moisture, and these are the only pasture grasses whose seeds can be had in quantity from dealers. There is little doubt that it would pay to sow grama-grass seed over large areas of the range lands if good seed could be had in quantity at a reasonable price, and this same statement is true of several other valuable native grasses. But such seed can not be bought in quantity at any price. Hence, the main reseeding method is that of allowing the plants to reseed themselves. This necessitates the protection of the seeding plants till the mature seeds are distributed. The process is very slow at the start if the range is badly eaten out, for relatively few viable seeds are then produced, and germination conditions are rarely ever good even for the native plants. But this method of improvement is, like all the others so far mentioned, dependent upon the control of the land and the ability to keep the stock off during the growing season.

The control of stock.—Much of what has already been said in favor of legalized range control has assumed the regulation of the number of head of animals that may be allowed to graze on a given area. The point of view, however, in each case has been that of advantage in the production, preservation, or utilization of feed.

Of equal importance in the management of any range is the control of stock, i. e., the possibility of knowing where any given animal may be found at any time. It is much easier to maintain a watch over cattle and horses by "riding fence" than by "riding range." It takes fewer men and fewer horses, and the information obtained as to the condition of the stock is much more accurate. If a hundred cows are put into a given pasture [1] it is only necessary to ride around the fence to know whether any animals have broken in or out. One merely needs to ride to the watering place at the proper time of day to find a particular animal. Very rarely, indeed, must strays be hunted, and bog holes may generally be fenced in, the danger being thus removed.

Even though the pasture be many square miles in extent, it will take only a few men to gather all the animals that are in it if the country is open as is the case with most of New Mexico; and if the number of head in the pasture is known, the number of head gathered shows the efficiency of the men and makes it possible to ascertain the amount and causes of all losses.

1 It must be remembered that this word is stretched from its ordinary usage so as to include areas that may be many sections in extent instead of a few acres.

With a fenced range, the spring and fall round-ups become merely the gathering of the stock in the separate pastures and can be done by a few men. The operations on each ranch thus become independent of each other and are not subject to a time schedule that may be inconvenient. The need of extra help is not so pressing. The branding can be done at the corral, where a "squeezer" obviates the necessity of running, roping, and throwing the animals, with the consequent losses that attend this method, losses that range all the way from the effects of overheating the horses and cattle to the killing of an occasional animal. Working at the corral often obviates the necessity of the round-up wagon, with its attendant expenses. To summarize: The fencing of a range and its division into separate pastures reduces the operative force necessary to handle a given area and makes the work itself easier for the men and not so hard on the stock.

The control of breeding operations.—Probably the most important function of a fence on a cattle or horse ranch is the control that it gives to the breeding operations. All stockmen recognize the importance of producing only well-bred animals, but this can be done on an open range only by the enforcement of laws controlling the character of males that are allowed at large. Considerable has been done in this respect in New Mexico as regards bulls, and the manner of handling sheep gives control of the bucks. There is at present but poor control of stallions and burros. Even with good laws there is great difficulty in their enforcement, since opinions differ very much as to what is a desirable animal for breeding purposes. Many of the men, for pecuniary reasons, especially if their means are limited, do not see how they can afford to buy well-bred animals for their small ranches, so they allow grade bulls to run and all their neighbors must put up with the consequences. One of the commonest complaints of the progressive owner is that his neighbors do not buy good bulls or enough of them. This is one of the exasperating losses which the larger single owners and practically all of the big companies have to endure under the present system. Yet all stockmen know that the practice is economically a bad one.

It is probably desirable upon some of the ranches in the higher mountains to restrict the breeding to certain months in the year, in order to avoid the losses resulting from the birth of calves during the cold weather. This plan has been tried in a few places; and while the percentage of calves dropped is smaller, the losses are noticeably less, and the total calf crop is about the same, with some advantage in favor of the practice because of the strength of the calves. With the proper precautions taken as to the number and distribution of bulls, it is likely that the percentage of dry cows could be reduced to the normal for the open range, even under this system.

Fenced inclosures also make possible the classification of the stock. The steers may be taken out of the cow herd, thereby increasing to some degree the fecundity. Young animals may be kept in pastures containing only their own kind. Uniformity in the grading of the animals makes them more attractive and more easily salable when the buyer is inspecting them. It makes possible the weaning of the calves at the proper age, which allows their mothers to recover flesh while carrying their young.

Quarantine and disease eradication.—The importance of a fence for use in the control and eradication of various diseases that attack range animals is excellently set forth in a petition [1] recently presented to the President of the United States by those residents of southeastern New Mexico who are either directly or indirectly interested in stock raising. It reads as follows:

In addition to what has been said herein as to the manifest advantages of the individual control of the range, it should be remembered that the splendid work which has for the past twelve years been carried on by the Bureau of Animal Industry would be *very greatly* facilitated. The officials of this department have done excellent and efficient work in clearing this part of New Mexico of various infectious diseases to which cattle and sheep are subject; but they have been greatly hampered and their work delayed and made infinitely more expensive and difficult by the fact that there has been no method whatever of isolating such infected herds as graze on the public domain. It is practically impossible to thoroughly eradicate even the least virulent of these diseases, such as scabies, pleuro-pneumonia, and anthrax, as long as the diseased animals can not be permanently isolated from the healthy ones, which, with herds running at large, is impossible. If under the present conditions of the range such an infection as foot-and-mouth disease, which has appeared twice in the United States in the past twelve years, should become distributed, the cattle industry would be practically annihilated. It has been fully demonstrated in this and other districts that where animals were under control in privately owned pastures, the eradication of disease has been entirely practicable, while at the same time in contiguous open ranges vast herds have perished as a result of these diseases, and their owners have been practically ruined.

Feeding range stock.—Very little feeding of range stock has been done in New Mexico for any purpose whatever, and it is still a common practice to let animals die of starvation if there is not sufficient feed on the range to maintain them. Aside from the humanitarian argument, this is really very poor business, with meat at its present price.

Within the past decade a considerable area of the State has come into cultivation by the development of various irrigation enterprises or by dry-farming methods. In consequence, a much greater area of land, previously some of the best grazing land of the State, has ceased temporarily to be used for this purpose; but in all the dry-farming area (where at present less than half the land is occupied,

[1] Written by ex-Governor Hagerman, of New Mexico.

and a still smaller acreage is cultivated) the important cultivated crops are forage crops, much of which will not admit of shipment, on account of their bulk as compared with their value. They must, therefore, be used near the place of production. Any concentrated feeds produced may seek an outside market, and the production of such feed within the State, where a large quantity of such feed should be used to carry animals over the periods of scarcity, is advantageous in many ways. The producers need a market; the stockmen need cheap feed; the railroads need the haul; the State needs the industries; and the country needs the meat.

There is little doubt that the areas into which the homesteaders have been coming for some time, and which thereby have produced much less meat for a number of years, will in the end produce much more than they originally did, unless some marked improvement is made in agricultural operations with a limited supply of water. Kafir, milo, or some other sorghum and the silo, with stock raising or dairying, seem to be one solution of the problem of living in these regions. The experience of the stockmen in other States indicates that cattlemen and sheepmen alike can very well afford to feed grain to their stock during periods of shortage of range feed.

Sheepmen are accustomed to assume that all of these generalizations that apply so patently to cattle do not affect their business. But this is not correct. It has been shown by experiment[1] that even in the heart of the forest in the high mountains, where predatory animals are most numerous and active, half of a band of sheep protected by a fence and a hunter with dogs produced more mutton and more wool and left the pasture in better shape than the other half of the band under the ordinary care given by herding. Nor is this all.

Many of the flockmasters of southwestern Texas are building fences that, with the aid of proper dogs, will protect their sheep from coyotes and wolves. This is being done because the herders of the region are becoming less reliable and at the same time more expensive. When that region is once cut up by fences into pastures of a few sections each, the coyotes and wolves can be exterminated. The cost of construction and maintenance of the fence and of keeping down the jack rabbits is the main expense which must be met in lieu of the wages and subsistence of the herders and camp tenders necessary when the sheep are handled on an open range; and the increased carrying capacity of the range, the increased amount and quality of the wool, and the increased quantity of mutton produced must be taken into account when comparisons are made.

[1] Jardine, J. T., and Coville, F. V. Preliminary report on grazing experiments in a coyote-proof pasture. U. S. Dept. Agr., Forest Serv. Circ. 156, 32 p., 2 fig. 1908.

CHARACTER OF THE PRESENT OPPOSITION TO CONTROL.

What are the interests opposed to legalized control of the range country? There are at least two that are more or less actively opposed to the idea. They are those owners who, by the nature of their stock and the region they are in, are able to get a lion's share of the benefits to be derived from the business, or they are those who, by the particularly favorable location of the ranges they now occupy, already have practical control and would only increase their expenses by gaining a legalized control. There are only a few such owners in New Mexico. But there are many who are afraid that any change which might be made would result in loss to themselves. They want control, but are passively obstructing any move tending toward that end, because they fear that in any new adjustment they would lose part or all of what they now claim.

There is nothing to criticize in any of these attitudes, since they are those of all competitive business. Each stockman is merely getting all he can out of his business under the conditions in which he finds himself, and he is warranted in so doing so long as he breaks no existing laws. But would it not be much better business to get some sort of legalized control system established which would do away with the present uncertainties and losses and make a better type of management possible?

The industry would be placed upon a much better footing. Its returns would be much more certain and could be calculated in advance with much greater accuracy. By virtue of this certainty a more complex and more remunerative type of business could be developed, which would result in an output both larger in quantity and better in quality. Hence the business would be more remunerative to those engaged in it and would improve the general business status of the State. From the standpoint of the great majority of the stockmen of New Mexico there is everything to gain and almost nothing to lose by the establishment of a system which will allow them to fence their lands and hold them in severalty, while from the standpoint of the business the promise of improvement is slight, if any (due mainly to the increased prices of the meat produced), with all the factors tending toward a diminution of productivity so long as the present form of tenure is the only one possible.

SUMMARY.

(1) The present status of the stock-raising industry in New Mexico is but one phase of the adjustment of the various industries of the State among themselves and to the physical environment.

(2) The topographic, climatic, and soil characters of the State restrict by far the greater part of its total area to the business of stock raising so long as the present agricultural methods continue.

(3) While much of the land is held under one form of tenure or another, over 31,000,000 acres, although in continuous use, now lack legal control.

(4) From the best statistics available it is shown that the stock-raising industry in New Mexico pays taxes on almost one-fourth of the total assessed valuation of the property of the State and is probably the most productive industry in the State.

(5) The present method of controlling the Government lands depends upon the legal control of the stock water and a custom which has the force of an unwritten law. This condition has arisen from lack of legislation which takes all the conditions into consideration. No type of legislation is here recommended, because it would be out of place; but that some type of legal control is not only desirable but very necessary for the further development of the industry is forcibly urged.

(6) The nature of the forage crops and their distribution are indicated in this bulletin in general terms, as are some of the undesirable plants, and methods of eradicating the latter are suggested.

(7) The management of the controlled range is contrasted with that now possible. It is shown that the present form of control can result in nothing but overstocking. Closely cropped range plants produce probably not more than one-third as much forage as when they are allowed to mature before being grazed. Feed which is good only in the summer, either by virtue of its kind or its position, can be properly utilized only on a controlled range. The more or less regular recurrence of cycles of dry years makes the reservation of feed necessary. This is rarely, if ever, possible on an open range. The distribution of stock water is to-day poor when considered from the standpoint of the demands of the business. Much could be done to improve this condition, but the necessary expenditure is not warranted while the right of control is so uncertain. Much damage has been done to the ranges by erosion. Efforts to correct this condition and to stop the consequent losses to the range and industry are not warranted so long as a man may not know that he is to profit by his effort. Reseeding operations will pay in some places, but the effort and expense are not warranted without the guaranty of returns. Fencing gives more complete control of stock and reduces the expense of operation in many ways. It allows a better organization of the business and makes the reduction of losses and increase of output possible. It also makes the improvement of the quality of the stock possible by giving control of the breeding operations. It renders the classification and grading of the animals feasible, thereby tending to increase salability. Protection from and eradication of diseases and all types of quarantine operations are much more easily applied to inclosed areas, and some of the more desirable operations are impossible on an

open range. Feeding stock in times of scarcity of range feed is indicated even under the present system of management, but this very desirable improvement can hardly be expected to occur till a better form of land tenure is guaranteed.

(8) The opposition to some legalized system of control is to-day more a passive than an active one and is due mostly to a fear of quite uncertain and indefinite possible, but not probable, consequences. There is every reason to expect that, whatever the system, those in possession of the range would be given legal control of the land they occupied at the time the system went into effect, assuming that they complied with the requirements.

ADDITIONAL COPIES
OF THIS PUBLICATION MAY BE PROCURED FROM
THE SUPERINTENDENT OF DOCUMENTS
GOVERNMENT PRINTING OFFICE
WASHINGTON, D. C.
AT
15 CENTS PER COPY
▽

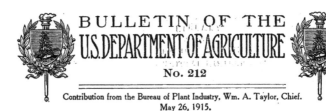

BULLETIN OF THE U.S. DEPARTMENT OF AGRICULTURE

No. 212

Contribution from the Bureau of Plant Industry, Wm. A. Taylor, Chief.
May 26, 1915.

(PROFESSIONAL PAPER.)

OBSERVATIONS ON THE PATHOLOGY OF THE JACK PINE.

By James R. Weir,
Forest Pathologist, Office of Investigations in Forest Pathology.

INTRODUCTION.

A discussion of the fungous diseases of a particular forest tree is incomplete unless the general habitat in which the tree grows and which influences the occurrence and virulence of its diseases is considered. In general, a description of the characteristic home of the jack pine (*Pinus divaricata* (Ait.) Du Mont. de Cours.) is essentially that of the sandy plains in the region of the Great Lakes, where it attains its greatest size. Here the sand deposits are usually of great thickness and heavily mixed with glacial drift. The soil is composed chiefly of the same materials. With the exception of some of the lower plains and old lake levels the humus soil is very thin. In most regions within the range of the jack pine there is practically no humus. Where humus does exist in any appreciable thickness it is so much a part of the underlying sand and gravel that it dries out very rapidly, affording no opportunity for a luxuriant and uniform forest cover. Exceptions to this occur in parts of Minnesota and Canada. The improvement in the quality of the soil is at once reflected by the larger size of the jack pine and incidentally in the nature and virulence of the diseases attacking it. Observations show that a continuous and sustained growth in the case of the jack pine is not conducive to much injury from wood-destroying fungi.

Owing to the rapidity with which the soil of the jack-pine "plains" dries out and to the inflammable nature of the slight ground cover, favorable conditions are furnished for forest fires. This, in turn, likewise greatly influences the presence of fungous diseases as a result of injuries caused by the fires. Severe and rapid changes in temperature and a fluctuation of the mean annual precipitation are other factors characteristic of the jack-pine habitat. The susceptibility of forest trees, and likewise of the fungi attacking them, to the influence of soil and climate directly or indirectly produces conditions favor-

35752°—Bull. 212—15

able or unfavorable to the best development and spread of disease. The fungi inhabiting the bark and leaves are probably influenced by these factors in a far greater degree than are those attacking the heartwood.

Pathologically, the jack pine may be divided, in most regions of its range, into two forest types, which are determined largely by the amount of moisture in the soil. The fungi at work in the moist or swamp type may occur in the drier and more arid type, but may show considerable variation in the abundance of any one species. Another factor of considerable importance is the absence or presence of any associate tree of the type which may prove equally or even more susceptible to cosmopolitan fungi and thus increase the chances of infection for all members of the stand. In many parts of its range the jack pine occurs in pure stands. In mixture with other species it is usually attacked by a greater number of diseases than in pure stands.

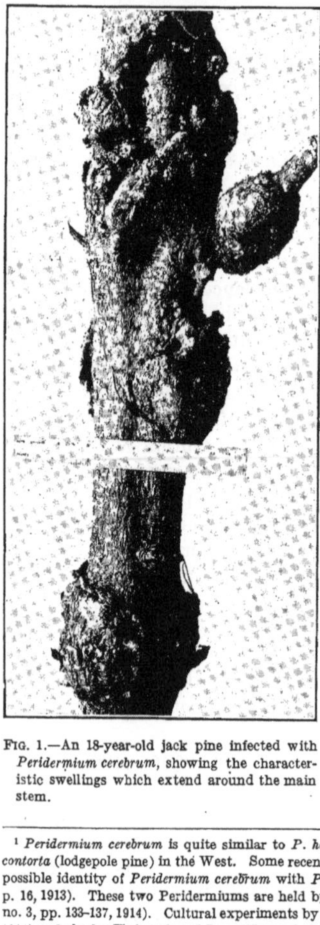

FIG. 1.—An 18-year-old jack pine infected with *Peridermium cerebrum*, showing the characteristic swellings which extend around the main stem.

DISEASES.

The fungus causing the greatest immediate injury to the jack pine of all age classes, as determined by pathological surveys in Michigan and Minnesota, is *Peridermium cerebrum* Peck (*Cronartium quercus* (Brondeau) Schrot.).[1] The galls (fig. 1) produced through the stimulative effect of the fungus are in May and June covered with globoid swellings somewhat after the manner of the convolutions of the

[1] *Peridermium cerebrum* is quite similar to *P. harknessii* Moore, which causes much damage to *Pinus contorta* (lodgepole pine) in the West. Some recent observations by Hedgcock and Meinecke indicate the possible identity of *Peridermium cerebrum* with *P. harknessii* on *Pinus radiata* (Phytopathology, vol. 3, p. 16, 1913). These two Peridermiums are held by Arthur and Kern to be identical (Mycologia, vol. 6, no. 3, pp. 133–137, 1914). Cultural experiments by Arthur and Kern (Mycologia, vol. 6, no. 3, pp. 133–137, 1914) and also by Hedgcock and Long (Journal of Agricultural Research, vol. 2, pp. 247–249, 1914) demonstrate the identity of *Peridermium fusiforme* with *P. cerebrum*. *Peridermium globosum* Arthur and Kern founded on a single specimen and supposed to occur on *Pinus strobus* has been acknowledged by the authors to be *P. cerebrum* on *Pinus divaricata*. The error arose from a misidentification of the host (Mycologia, vol. 6, no. 3, pp. 133–137, 1914).

brain—cerebroid. These blisterlike swellings are orange-yellow at first; after the rupture of the peridium and the dispersal of the golden yellow æciospores they become whitish. The gall formation causes great injury to the trunk and branches (fig. 1). The infection usually begins by means of some injury to the bark or cambial layer.[1] The gall swellings gradually increase from year to year from the growth of a perennial mycelium, so that they finally encompass the entire branch, resulting eventually, if the galls are near the trunk, in its death below and above the hypertrophy. Whether or not the entire branch dies depends upon the presence of lateral, leafed branches below the gall.

In dry sandy areas *Peridermium cerebrum* confines itself more generally to the branches, occurring rarely on the trunk but frequently in the axils of the branches. This latter condition usually results in a combination trunk and branch gall, which in numerous instances produces greater damage than either of the other two types of galls. The branch and trunk are girdled by abnormal wood tissue and are thus weakened (fig. 2). This results usually in either the branch or the tree being blown down by the wind. Personal observations show that borers and wood-rotting fungi entering at the burl often hasten the decline of the tree.

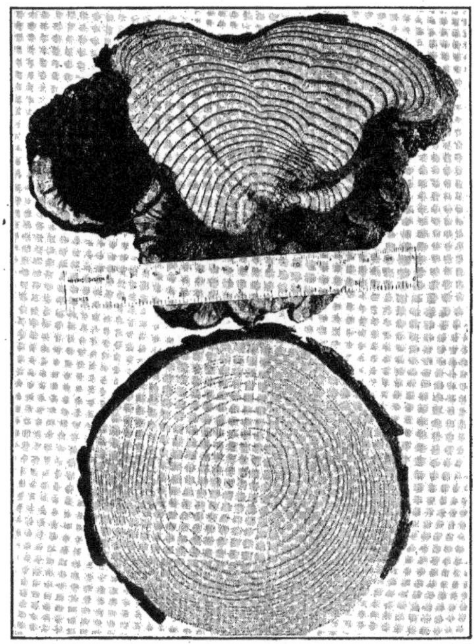

FIG. 2.—Cross sections of the main trunk of a jack pine heavily infected with *Peridermium cerebrum*. Note the progressive girdling by the resinous burl tissues in the upper figure and its effects on the increment of the trunk below, as shown in the lower figure.

From a careful examination of young twigs showing very recent infections at leaf scales, leaf traces, and at the bases of young pistillate

[1] Wounds made by sapsuckers, ovipositors of bark-stinging insects, rodents, and ice and snow breaks are common means of entrance for *Peridermium cerebrum*.

flowers, it is believed that *Peridermium cerebrum* can enter young seedlings or the tender portions of more mature growth without first having the bark broken. Entrance in this manner must, out of necessity, be aided by sufficient moisture for germination and to permit a rapid penetration by the young mycelium. On the sandy plains of the Great Lakes region rain water disappears almost immediately and the sand becomes heated about the isolated tree groups, causing a rapid evaporation from the surface of the trunk and branches and leaving the moisture content of the outer bark at a minimum. In whatever manner the fungus may enter its host, directly or through wounds, the number of galls and imperfect branches is usually much less on trees of the sandy barrens than in more moist regions.

In swampy areas the jack pine grows in close stands. Here the percentage of infected trees is much greater. The trunks of the 6 to 12 year old jack pines are often covered with swellings stunting the growth of the trees very rapidly (Pl. I, fig. 1). Trees so infected never reach maturity and may continue living for an indefinite period in a stunted condition, to be finally blown over by the wind or broken down by the snow. The 1 to 4 year old seedlings are quite often attacked. With these, as is often the case with larger trees which through mechanical injury may become infected at the ground, the gall is formed directly at the base of the main stem. When a seedling is infected there or higher up on the stem, it develops into a deformed growth after the manner of a witches'-broom (Pl. I, fig. 2) and never attains a height of more than 2 or 3 feet. The perennial mycelium of the fungus thrives in the cambial layer and in the living parts of the sapwood. Trees with a single infection on the trunk occurring at the age of 4 to 6 years are known to support the living mycelium of the fungus to the advanced age of 70 to 80 years. Usually, however, the excessive production of resin in the infected tissues infiltrates the woody portion of the trunk, and the sap supply is cut off so that death results in a comparatively short time (fig. 2). This is especially true in young seedlings. Peridermium galls are frequently observed a foot or more in diameter. Trees supporting galls of this size had succumbed in every instance to the disease.

Some knowledge of the damage done by *Peridermium cerebrum* to the jack pine may be obtained from notes of a pathological survey by the writer in the national forests of Michigan. Out of 100 trees of an average plat on dry sandy soil, not selected because of any pronounced diseased condition, 50 per cent were heavily infected, while only an occasional tree out of a second hundred on similar but moister soil was absolutely free from the disease. Out of 100 trees taken from the swamp type, practically all were infected. Not all the trees were infected seriously. A tree bearing a single branch gall

FIG. 1.—A 6-YEAR-OLD JACK PINE INFECTED WITH PERIDERMIUM CEREBRUM.

The complete girdling of the main stem by two oppositely arranged galls is shown. Note the wedge-shaped gall tissues.

FIG. 2.—FOUR-YEAR-OLD SEEDLINGS OF JACK PINE, SHOWING THE CHARACTERISTIC SWELLINGS OF PERIDERMIUM CEREBRUM.

The entire crown of the seedlings develops into spherical brooms.

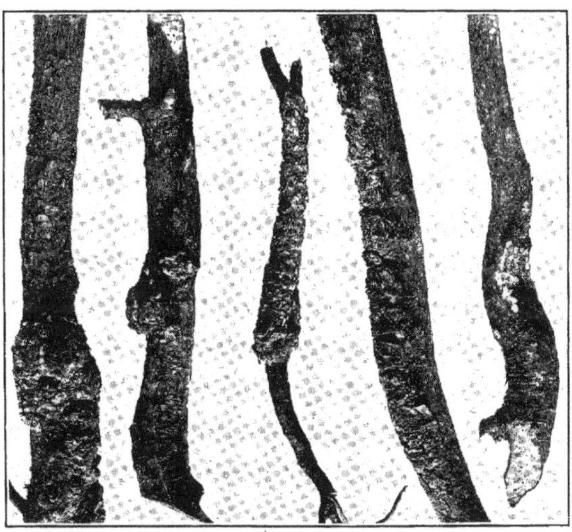

FIG. 3.—VARIOUS TYPES OF INFECTION OF YOUNG JACK PINE BY PERIDERMIUM COMPTONIAE.

Note that in the central figure the fungus has invaded the underground tissues of the stem.

was marked "infected." Four trees specifically studied yielded by actual count an average of 220 burls on the branches and 13 on the trunks. The cones produced by these trees, although of average number, were small, with a higher percentage of abortive sporophylls than is commonly the case with this species (fig. 3). Comparative germination tests of seeds from heavily infected and vigorous non-infected jack pine of the same age and type conditions showed for the former a germination of 19 per cent below that of the latter. For this experiment 10 samples, consisting of a dozen or more cones, were taken from each of five heavily infected and five uninfected pines. Fifty seeds from each of these samples were planted in sand, kept moist with distilled water, and allowed to stand at laboratory temperature (about 70° F.) for 90 days.

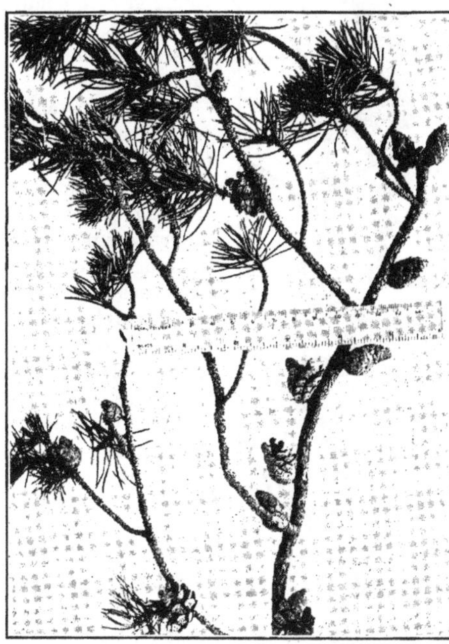

FIG. 3.—Branch of jack pine with aborted cones, the result of a severe attack of *Peridermium cerebrum*. Note that some of the cones did not open and that most of them are less than an inch in length. Average normal cones measure from 1½ to 2 inches.

The prolific development of *Peridermium cerebrum* in many parts of the jack-pine forests of the Great Lakes region is a factor in reforestation which should be carefully considered. The fact that the fungus occurs so commonly on young seedlings in the natural forest and occasionally in the nursery shows that it is a menace to the best development of the species. The largest and best formed jack pine in all the regions studied where the Peridermium was abundant was almost entirely devoid of this injurious disease. However this may be interpreted as to the original differences in vigor, the fact that heavily infected trees were invariably scrubby and ill formed is, in the mind of the writer, directly referable to the effects of the parasite. The fact that *P. cerebrum* has its telial stage on the leaves of several species of Quercus [1] should be of much significence in control work. *Quercus velutina* and *Q. coccinea* are two scrub oaks frequently forming a conspicuous part of the jack-pine type, particularly in Michigan. Methods could be devised for the eradication of these worthless species, thus removing the alternate host of the fungus. However impracticable this may be on a large scale, in wood lots and small holdings this would not be a very difficult matter. The removal of infected branches of young growth could be done in the orchard-like stands of jack pine on the more sandy soils, thus saving many young trees from early suppression.

FIG. 4.—Young jack pine infected with *Peridermium comptoniae*. Note the ruptured peridia with their serrate margins.

In a few instances, in the region studied, young jack pine was found to be diseased by *Peridermium comptoniae* (Arthur) Orton and Adams (*Cronartium comptoniae* Arthur). (Fig. 4.) In the experience of the writer this fungus was not common. The æcial stage of the fungus is chiefly characterized by a slight fusiform swelling, seldom forming the spherical galls so characteristic for *P. cerebrum*. The peridia rupture with a sharply serrate or spiny margin. The fungus is further distinguished from *P. cerebrum* by attacking principally young seedlings (Pl. I, fig. 3) and causing excessive brooming of the branches. It was not found on more mature growth. *P. cerebrum* attacks both young and old trees. *P. comptoniae* has its alternate stage on sweet fern [2] (*Comptonia peregrina* and *Myrica gale*). Without the production of the teliospores on these plants the fungus can not reproduce itself on the jack pine.

As a precaution against these Peridermiums entering the forest nursery and the possibility of their transportation to other regions, all alternate hosts, such as species of oaks and sweet ferns, should be removed from the vicinity of the nursery. This immunity zone should be extended as far back from the nursery as time and means will allow. Before new nurseries are established a pathological survey of the immediate region should be made as to the presence of these heterœcious pine rusts. Much attention should also be given

[1] Demonstrated by Dr. C. L. Shear, Jour. Myc., vol. 12, p. 89, 1906.

[2] Demonstrated by G. P. Clinton, Conn. Agr. Exp. Sta. Rept., 1907, pp. 380-383, 1908.

the selection of nursery sites, with regard to the topography and prevailing winds of the region.

With the exception of *Peridermium cerebrum* and *P. comptoniae*, few fungi of economic importance attack the living jack pine in the drier parts of its range. On the dry pine barrens of the Lake States the jack pine reaches its normal age without much defect in the wood arising from fungous diseases, although exceptionally old trees of 90 years and more frequently show considerable decay. In mixture with other species in the more moist regions of its range, particularly in parts of northern Minnesota and of Canada, *Trametes pini* (Brot.) Fr. causes considerable heart-rot in trees of 60 years and older. In general, however, this fungus is in negligible quantities. In close stands jack pine prunes readily during its most rapid growing period, forming straight clear stems. The rapid occlusion of the branch knots shortens the danger period for infection by wound fungi. It is principally due to this fact that some of the most serious wood-destroying fungi do not effect an entrance until the tree has reached its period of decline.

Polyporus schweinitzii Fr., causing a butt rot, is usually in greater abundance than *Trametes pini*, but the percentage of infected trees, even on the more protected soils, is seldom more than 2 to 4 per cent of the stand. The jack pine is a deep-rooted species and unless the root system comes in contact with a hard stratum of clay and gravel, root-destroying fungi are largely a negligible quantity. In this class are *Fomes annosus* Fr. and *Armillaria mellea* (Vahl.) Quél., which very rarely occur on the jack pine. Only a few isolated and unimportant infections have ever been recorded by the writer.

The jack pine does not suffer any material injury from needle fungi. Those that do occur are mostly of a saprophytic nature. *Lophodermium pinastri* Schrad. is found only occasionally.

On dry soils in open stands the jack pine frequently shows a tendency to form witches'-brooms. The terminal shoot, which is the part usually affected, develops into a thick-matted broom, precluding any further growth in that direction. Trees thus infected usually show a rapid falling off in increment, probably dating from the time when the influence of the parasite was first felt. Another type of broom formation is confined to the lower and older branches and has a similar effect on the growth of the host. These brooms are probably caused by some perennial fungus. In the absence of any fruiting structures the causal organism can not be determined.

The jack pine in its eastern range is not subject to mistletoe injury. Macoun [1] reports the occurrence of *Razoumofskya americana* (Nutt.) Kuntze, the lodgepole-pine mistletoe, on the jack pine in Canada.

[1] Macoun, John. Catalogue of Canadian Plants, pt. 3, p. 422. Montreal, 1886.

The writer finds this mistletoe to be the cause of serious damage to the jack pine at its most western extension or where it approaches the zone of the lodgepole pine in the north.

SAPROPHYTIC FUNGI.

Aside from the previously mentioned wood-destroying species, which in many cases continue alive after the death of the host,[1] the usual strictly saprophytic fungi of coniferous woods are found on cut or fire-killed jack pine. *Ceratostomella pilifera* Fr., the blue-stain fungus, appears very rapidly after the death of the tree. In moist situations, species of Auricularia and Dacryomyces are surprisingly abundant, but can be of little importance, as the mycelium does not penetrate the wood to any appreciable distance. The first fungus of importance is *Polystictus abietinus* Dicks. This is a sap-rotting species and is seldom absent from fire-killed trees after the second or third year. Second in importance is *Lenzites sepiaria* Fr., which works both in the sap and in the heartwood and usually appears on the fallen trunks after they have lain for three or four years, following up the first-mentioned fungus. The Lenzites appearing on jack pine is invariably the true, small, thin-fruited form, with radiating gills. *Lenzites sepiaria* is as easily recognized by the orange-yellow color of its growing margin as the young, growing *Polystictus abietinus* is by its beautiful purple tinge. *Fomes pinicola* Fr. has very little to do with the decay of fallen jack pine. This fungus has not been found to be very common. *Polyporus palustris* Berk. and Curt. occasionally appears, but is more common on dead Norway pine. *Fomes carneus* "Nees" very rarely occurs on jack pine. *Lentinus lepideus* Fr., *Polyporus sulphureus* Fr., and *Trametes sepium* have been collected by the writer on dead jack pine, but they are very rare. Resupinate Thelephoraceæ occur only in the moist stands of mixed species. Those which may be considered of importance in the decay of fire-killed timber in the forest are *Corticium byssinum* (Karst.) Burt., *C. sulphureum* Pers., *C. galactinum* (Fr.) Burt., *Coniophora olivaceae* (Fr.) Bres., and *Peniophora globifera* E. and E. A yellowish white Poria which goes under the name of *P. subacida* Peck is occasionally found on fallen jack pine in Minnesota. This fungus has been observed by the writer in a fruiting condition on old boxes and barrel staves made from newly felled living trees. This indicates its probable parasitism on jack pine in the living forest.

[1] This is a fact that is not generally appreciated, and on it depends the solution of some very important pathological problems in the forest. Vigorously growing sporophores of *Trametes pini* springing from original infections in the living tree have been collected from a fallen western larch which had lain on the ground for more than 100 years. This was determined by the age of a western red cedar growing astride the fallen trunk. Practically all the more serious wound and root fungi of the genera Trametes, Fomes, Polyporus, and Agaricus in moist situations continue alive indefinitely after the death of their hosts.

INJURIES DUE TO OTHER CAUSES.

In the absence of an adequate snow protection on the flat wind-swept pine barrens of the Lake States, winter injury sometimes results to young growth from long exposure to freezing temperatures. Winter-injured seedlings of jack pine, however, recover more rapidly than those of the more sensitive associate species and when in this condition are not so apt to be attacked by secondary deteriorating agents. It has already been stated that the deep root system of the jack pine is unfavorable to some root-destroying fungi. In like measure this is a safeguard against injury by wind. It is very unusual to find jack pine blown down by the wind when the trees are in a healthy condition. Very old trees sometimes succumb to strong winds, but it is found that such trees are usually mechanically weakened by wood-destroying fungi. The jack pine may be considered very windfirm. Porcupines and squirrels are known to do considerable injury to jack pine during the winter months when food is scarce. The latter animal is much addicted to gnawing the galls of *Peridermium cerebrum* in the spring during the period of the exudation from the diseased bark of a sweet yellow liquid which bears the conidiospores of the fungus. Since squirrels also gnaw the galls when the æciospores are mature, they may be considered a factor in the distribution of this fungus. The bark of the galls is frequently completely gnawed away, killing the infection.

In general, the jack pine is very sensitive to fire, which usually causes the greatest injury in the typical dry sandy jack-pine plains. In many cases fire injury in jack pine results from repeated burnings, the tree having successfully withstood the first slight ground fires. Fires in the more typical jack-pine forests pass through very quickly, so that the thickened bark immediately at the base of the tree affords sufficient protection until it is burned off by succeeding fires, which frequently occur notwithstanding the meager ground cover. The fact that the species frequently grows in orchardlike stands or in isolated groups, more or less separated from one another by free areas, greatly lessens the damage of the fire spreading from one group to another. However, the low-spreading branches, which often extend to the ground, increase the danger from crown fires.

CONCLUSIONS.

With reference to the prevalence and severity of its fungous enemies, two distinct forest types for the jack pine may be recognized: The pure dry sandy-plain type and the mixed type of moist protected soils.

The most important fungous disease of the jack pine is *Peridermium cerebrum* Peck, the control of which in many localities is quite a serious forest problem. The fungus attacks all age classes, causing the death or early suppression of trees of tender years and seriously interfering with the propagation and development of more mature growth.

From the standpoint of merchantability, wood-destroying fungi in the living tree are in almost all regions a negligible quantity. The two most important are *Trametes pini* (Brot.) Fr. and *Polyporus schweinitzii* Fr. These, however, do not produce any appreciable decay till after the tree reaches its period of decline, which is attained after a comparatively rapid early growth. This period may be placed approximately at from 60 to 80 years.

The wood of dead jack pine rapidly deteriorates under the influence of a number of saprophytic fungi and may not be expected to remain sound in the forest for more than two or three years.

Jack pine is sensitive to heat, but suffers only occasionally from winter injury.

Because jack pine in general is comparatively free from a number of the diseases which are common on other conifers and is resistant to drought, winter injury, and frost, it is admirably suited for reforesting many of the dry sandy regions of the North-Central States.

ADDITIONAL COPIES
OF THIS PUBLICATION MAY BE PROCURED FROM
THE SUPERINTENDENT OF DOCUMENTS
GOVERNMENT PRINTING OFFICE
WASHINGTON, D. C.
AT
5 CENTS PER COPY
▽

WASHINGTON : GOVERNMENT PRINTING OFFICE : 1915

BULLETIN OF THE U.S. DEPARTMENT OF AGRICULTURE

No. 213

Contribution from the Office of Experiment Stations, A. C. True, Director.
April 15, 1915.

THE USE OF LAND IN TEACHING AGRICULTURE IN SECONDARY SCHOOLS.

By EUGENE MERRITT, *Assistant in Agricultural Education, Office of Experiment Stations.*

CONTENTS.

INTRODUCTION.

This bulletin is the result of an attempt to determine how land is being used in the teaching of agriculture in secondary schools in the United States. In gathering the material upon which the bulletin is based two questionnaires were sent out, one in April, 1914, to all high schools receiving State aid for agriculture, to special agricultural schools, and to normal schools known to have courses in agriculture. To this 400 replies were received. In September another questionnaire was sent to the same high schools and special agricultural schools, but not to the normal schools, which were omitted because a great part of their instruction relates to school gardens and not to work tending toward farm practice. Out of the 385 schools replying to the first questionnaire, 257 reported that some land was used in connection with their agricultural instruction. The schools so reporting were distributed as follows: Ten in the New England States,

NOTE.—This bulletin describes how land is being used in the teaching of agriculture in secondary schools and discusses some of the problems involved. It is written to aid all persons who are engaged or interested in the teaching of agriculture.

16 in the Middle Atlantic, 31 in the East North Central, 86 in the West North Central, 15 in the South Atlantic, 36 in the East South Central, 50 in the West South Central, 6 in the Mountain, and 7 in the Pacific.

SCHOOLS REPORTING SCHOOL FARMS AND FARM ANIMALS.

Of the 27 special agricultural schools, 25 reported that they had land and 2 that they had none. Of the 259 high schools, 166 reported land, and of the 101 normal schools, 66. Of schools with land, 20 of the 25 special schools, 43 of the 166 high schools, and 19 of the 66 normal schools reported that they had farm animals. In other words, of the 257 schools with land only 82 reported farm animals. In many instances the farm animals consisted of a horse or team which was used on the farm and for driving by the instructor in agriculture.

SIZE AND TENURE OF THE FARMS.

The reports indicated that 40 of the 257 school farms had 1 acre or less; 23, 2 acres; 23, 3 acres; 10, 4 acres; 21, 5 acres; 16, 6 acres, and the remainder had 6 acres or more. In other words, over one-half of the 257 school farms had 6 acres or less. There were 58 farms with over 20 acres. The records of the College of Agriculture of the University of Minnesota showed that one-half of the school farms in that State were rented. There is no information to indicate whether this is true in other States or not, but in several States the law requires that the farms shall not be leased for less than five years, which would indicate that the schools could use rented land.

USE MADE OF THE FARMS.

The reports show that of the 257 school farms, 150 were growing corn; 129, garden crops; 84, potatoes; 75, oats; 61, alfalfa; 42, cotton; 35, wheat; 29, clover; and 20, sweet potatoes.

Out of the 3,900 acres reported by 84 schools, only 12 acres belonging to 22 schools were reported as being used for the raising of laboratory material. Twelve of the 84 schools reported a total of 10 acres used for projects for individual pupils Fifty-two acres were reported as used for school gardens. Some of the larger uses to which the land was put were 827 acres for crop rotation, 593 acres for general demonstrations, 382 acres for raising pure-bred seed for distribution among the farmers and the pupils, 206 for dormitory supplies, 166 for fertilizer demonstration, and 166 for general experiments.

IS A SCHOOL FARM NECESSARY?

A question was asked as to whether the school could conduct its agricultural instruction without a school farm. Of the 104 schools which reported having land 39 replied "yes" and 65 "no." If the replies were used as they stand they would indicate a majority opposed to the school farm. However, of the 29 having no land, 26 reported that they could get along without the school farm and 3 considered it essential. By taking both those with land and those without land, 65 replied that they could get along without land, and 68 that they could not get along without it. In other words, there is a majority of 3 in favor of school farms. But an analysis of these replies indicated that the schools with the small farm seem to feel that they could get along without the farm in their agricultural instruction, and the schools with the large farms seemed to feel that it was an advantage and that they could not carry on their work without it. The small farms are mostly in the Northern and Eastern States, and the large farms in the Southern States. Most of the schools in the South are more or less of a boarding type, whereas those in the North and East have a large proportion of the pupils who are at home morning and night. Detailed data as to the replies are given in the table below:

Analysis of replies to question "Could you conduct your agricultural instruction successfully without school farm or plat?"

Geographic divisions.	Having land and answering yes.	Having land and answering no.	Having no land and answering yes.	Having no land and answering no.
New England	4	3	6	
Middle Atlantic	2	2	8	
East North Central	3	1	1	
West North Central	27	21	10	2
South Atlantic	1	9	1	
East South Central	1	12		1
West South Central	1	17		
Total	39	65	26	3

ADVANTAGES AND DISADVANTAGES.

In the first questionnaire the agricultural instructor was asked to state the advantages and disadvantages of the school farm in his work. All the advantages seemed to be educational, and all the disadvantages seemed to be in connection with the management of the school farm. The principal advantages were that the school farm made the instruction real, it gave the student some practical agricultural work, it supplied laboratory material, and it gave the agricultural instructor an opportunity to carry on demonstrations for the benefit of the farmer and his pupils. The principal disadvantages were that help was hard to get, the land poor, and the instructor's time was poorly spent.

From a farm-management point of view a more difficult problem could not be presented to an agricultural instructor than is found in the school farm as it exists in the Northern and Eastern States. Most of the farms have a small acreage. Sixty-one of the 84 schools in Minnesota depend entirely upon day help, all the team work is hired, and the land is expensive. In Minnesota the average value per acre is $150. It generally takes two or three years to put this land in shape to be used for agricultural purposes. Many farms are without farm buildings. If they have buildings, the investment is high in proportion to the acreage cultivated and to the crops obtained. The majority of them have little or no machinery, so when they want to cultivate or gather their crops they must borrow. The majority have no live stock, so that they have to purchase their manure. It is only in exceptional instances that the agricultural instructor lives on or near the school farm.

MANAGEMENT OF THE SCHOOL FARM.

Considering these factors from a farm-management point of view, it can be readily seen that the agricultural instructor has a peculiar problem on his hands. The majority of them have not been able to solve it satisfactorily. The agricultural instructor who can not make his farm pay has very little standing among the farmers, since as long as the farm does not pay he has to admit that he can not produce crops with a profit. What farmer would have any confidence in such a man? Those schools which succeed must practice an intensive system of agriculture. The school farms which seem to have met with the best success are those which are growing pure-bred corn, pure-bred small grains, potatoes, alfalfa, cabbage, and the like. This gives them a high-priced crop and enables the school to get good seed to be distributed in the neighborhood. Thirty-three of the eighty-four schools reporting on this point were using a part of their land for raising pure-bred seed for distribution. Some had extended this idea to the growing of fruit trees and berry vines to be distributed in a similar manner.

The school adds to its effectiveness if it becomes the distributing center of high-class seed and trees. Indeed, where they have live stock they should develop the same idea by extending the service of the sires in the neighborhood and distributing their young among the farmers. Several instances were found in the South where the boys in the pig-club work were being furnished with pigs from the school farm in the same way that boys in the corn clubs in the North were being furnished with corn from school farms.

KINDS OF WORK PUPILS ENGAGE IN.

The kinds of crops grown and the types of farming carried on have already been ascertained. The next point of interest is the kinds of work that the student is engaged in on the school farm. The three types that stand out most prominently are the preparation of the land, the planting of the crops, and the harvesting of the same. In most of the agricultural schools the pupil has little or no part in the cultivating of the crops. The different kinds of labor in which the pupils engage are shown in the following table:

Kinds of labor in which students are engaged on the school farm or plat.

Improvement of school ground	2	Mulching trees	2
Gardening	12	Spraying trees	6
Harvesting	1	Dairying	3
Digging potatoes	3	Caring for stock	2
Corn raising	4	Poultry	3
Selecting seed corn	8	Bees	1
Planting grains	2	Greenhouses	2
Planting potatoes	4	Grading land	1
Harvesting alfalfa	1	Drainage	2
Harvesting grains	4	Running survey lines	2
Haying	1	Ditching	1
Picking cotton	1	Terracing	1
Picking peas	1	Applying fertilizers	2
Renovating orchards	1	Preparation of land	10
Orchards	5	Plowing	2
Pruning	3	Harvesting	1
Berry patch	2	Fencing	4
Planting trees	2		

USE OF LAND TO TEACH GENERAL PRINCIPLES.

A question was asked as to whether the agricultural instructor used the land to teach technique or general principles. The invariable answer was general principles. When it is considered that most schools have an average of 30 to 40 pupils to an agricultural instructor and from 5 to 10 acres on which to give them instruction, it can be realized that the student can get but little actual experience in the ordinary farm operations and that the instructor can simply show what has happened under certain conditions.

HOME PROJECTS.

In the second questionnaire several questions were asked in regard to home projects. Seventy-four of the 156 schools reported that their students were doing home-project work, 61 reporting corn, 37 garden, 26 poultry, 25 potatoes, 14 dairying, 12 orchards, 12 alfalfa, and 10 keeping herd records. There was but one report for cotton. That there were few home projects in the South can be readily explained when it is considered that the agricultural schools are of the boarding type and that the districts served are generally congressional districts or some larger area. There seems to be but little supervision by the agricultural instructor except in the New England and Middle

Atlantic States. Instructors in the West North Central States did not visit their pupils on an average of more than three times during the year. The replies indicate that a large number of the instructors had more than 200 miles on their project circuit. Data for home projects reported are given in the following table:

Home projects reported.

Corn	61	Berries	3
Garden	37	Crops	3
Poultry	26	Rotation	3
Potatoes	25	Oats	2
Dairying	14	Cabbage	2
Orchard	12	Barley	2
Alfalfa	12	Pop corn	2
Herd record	10	Bees	2
Fertilizer	9	Cotton	1
Accounts	6	Sweet clover	1
Wheat	5	Tobacco	1
Hotbed	5	Reforesting	1
Beans	4	Cover crop	1
Spraying	4	Cement construction	1
Tomato canning	4	Surveying	1
Pruning	3	Cold frames	1

The returns of the agricultural instructor indicated that the number of farms on the home-project list were higher in the West than in the East, the average for the West North Central States being 33 per agricultural instructor, 8 more than the maximum allowed under the Massachusetts system. These returns indicated that not all of the pupils in the agricultural instructor's class in the North Central States were on his home-project list. In some instances the agricultural instructor had as many as 130 pupils in his classes. In the following table are shown the number of schools reporting and not reporting home projects and the average number of home projects per school:

Number reporting home projects and average number of home-project pupils per school.

Geographic divisions.	Number reporting home projects.	Number not reporting home projects.	Average number of home projects per school.
New England	9	3	12
Middle Atlantic	13	3	16
East North Central	3	2	15
West North Central	35	51	33
South Atlantic	2	5	18
East South Central	....	13	....
West South Central	12	1	9

EXTENSION WORK OF AGRICULTURAL INSTRUCTOR.

Over one-half of the agricultural instructors reported that they were engaged in some kind of boys' and girls' club work, and in the majority of instances they were acting as local leaders, although in some cases they were merely cooperating. Eighty-one of the 157 agricultural instructors indicated that they were doing other types of extension work. The principal types were organizing farmers' clubs, cow-testing and live-stock work, seed selection, speaking at meetings—generally in connection with their farmers' clubs, and giving advice to individual farmers. Details as to the kind of extension work carried on by the agricultural instructor are shown in the following table:

Principal kinds of extension work reported.

Spraying	8	Alfalfa plats	15
Pruning	2	Weed identification	2
Associations	6	Corn club	8
Grange work	3	Seed corn	6
Organizing clubs	7	Wheat breeding	5
Farmers' club	16	Demonstration	12
Speaking at meetings	15	Experiments	5
Cow testing	8	Consultations	4
Testing milk	10	Farm visits	3
Dairy improvement	4	Fertilizing	3
Purchase of live stock	2	Answering questions	4
Hog cholera	8	Soil drainage	6
Assist in vaccinating hogs	2	School contests	7
Stock improvement	2	Advice	9
Care of cattle	2	Lecture work	9
Introducing pure-bred seeds	3	Poultry club	2
Seed testing	4	Plowing	3

Records of the College of Agriculture, University of Minnesota, show that of the 117 agricultural instructors in Minnesota reporting in regard to extension work, 92 stated that they had organized 273 farmers' clubs; 35, shipping associations; and 31, cow-testing associations, testing 42 herds containing 960 cows. In five instances the boys in the agricultural classes were doing the testing. The instructors were also carrying on farm-demonstration work in corn, barley, alfalfa, and small grains. Twenty-three of the schools had taken part in the vaccination of hogs for cholera, 73 had helped in planning and building silos, and 29 had helped to plan farmsteads.

A question was asked as to whether the agricultural instructors were employed for nine months or for the entire year, to learn whether they could carry on home-project work. Ninety-nine out of the 157 were so employed. One hundred and thirty-one were graduates of agricultural colleges, and their average salaries were between

$1,200 and $1,300. Thus far the land and the agricultural instructor have been considered. The next and most important feature is the pupil.

SOURCE AND DISTANCE FROM SCHOOL OF PUPILS STUDYING AGRICULTURE.

The returns indicated that 40 per cent of the pupils studying agriculture were living at home on farms, 40 per cent were living at home but not on farms, and 20 per cent were boarding during the school year. In other words, 60 per cent of the pupils studying agriculture were from farm homes, and one-third of them were not at home during the school year. In the East North Central and West North Central States 43 and 47 per cent, respectively, of the pupils were not from farms. In the New England and Middle Atlantic States about 60 per cent were living at home on farms. The following table shows the distribution by geographic divisions and by residence of the pupils studying agriculture, as reported in the questionnaire:

Sources of pupils studying agriculture.

Geographic divisions.	Total number studying agriculture.	Number living at home on farms.	Number living at home not on farms.	Number not living at home during school year.	Average maximum distance from which pupils are drawn.
					Miles.
New England	272	162	29	81	8.41
Middle Atlantic	391	224	132	35	7.36
East North Central	245	78	106	61	9.40
West North Central	3,233	1,233	1,546	454	11.30
South Atlantic	447	219	106	122	18.12
East South Central	801	259	187	355	21.69
West South Central	481	181	266	34	8.92

Since such a large percentage of the pupils are not living at home the average area from which they are drawn was ascertained. The returns, as the above table shows, indicated that in the New England and Middle Atlantic States the maximum distance is on the average 8 miles; in the East North Central and West North Central States between 10 and 12 miles, and in the South, where the schools have a boarding department, the areas are even larger. If the student lives more than 4 miles from the school and goes and comes each day, it would be practically impossible for him to take any part in the farm operations unless he did it on Saturday.

RELATIVE PROPORTION OF BOYS AND GIRLS STUDYING AGRICULTURE IN HIGH SCHOOLS.

The returns to the Bureau of Education for 1913[1] indicated that one-third of the high-school students studying agriculture in the United States were girls. In many of the agricultural classes visited the number of girls exceeded the number of boys. When the instructor was asked why so many girls were in his classes, he replied that if the girls were to teach in the rural districts they would be required to pass an examination in agriculture, and so were attending his classes for this purpose. It would seem that this fact would call for a modification in the methods of teaching agriculture and in the use of the school land and the home project. In the following table are included all schools which have courses in agriculture, whether they receive State aid or not. Of course, they comprise a much larger number than were used in obtaining information in regard to the use of land. This table shows the relative number of boys and girls studying agriculture.

Number of public high schools reporting agricultural courses, and number of pupils in attendance.[1]

Geographic divisions.	Schools reporting.	In agricultural courses.		
		Boys.	Girls.	Total.
United States	1,414	19,749	10,076	29,825
North Atlantic Division	132	1,524	507	2,031
North Central Division	742	8,730	5,356	14,086
South Atlantic Division	136	1,922	958	2,880
South Central Division	267	5,024	2,729	7,753
Western Division	137	2,549	526	3,075

THE PERIOD BETWEEN GRADUATION AND STARTING FARMING ON OWN ACCOUNT.

It can safely be assumed that the average boy leaves school at 18 years of age. From the best information available the average farmer does not start farming on his own account until he is somewhere between 25 and 30 years of age. In other words, there is a period of the farmer's life, when he is between 18 and 30 years of age, when he is not working on his own farm nor is he his own master. It would seem that wherever the home-project method has been introduced an effort should be made to follow up the boy and, if possible, arrange in some way for him to continue his home-project work and gradually becomes a partner with his father in the farm business. This feature should be a part of the extension work of the agricultural instructor.

[1] Rpt. Comr. Education [U. S.], 1913, II, p. 489.

AGRICULTURAL SCHOOL AND THE SHIFTING-TENANT PROBLEM.

Farmers are recruited from two sources, from the sons of farmers and the sons of agricultural laborers. In going over the original census schedules of 1910 for farmers of Iowa County, Wis., this rather interesting fact developed, that where the tenant and landlord had the same name the tenant had been on the farm that he was on the day the census was taken for a much longer period than where their names were different. It was found that 31 per cent of the cash tenants who were related to the owner had been tenants on the farms which they were on, at the census date, for two years or less, while the per cent for those where no relationship existed was 65. For share tenants the figures were 50 and 80 per cent respectively. In other words, where there is relationship there is less of the shifting-tenant problem than where relationship does not exist. From other records it was learned that of the total years a man had been a tenant, he had been a tenant on the farm where he was at the time the records were taken 76 per cent of the total time when kinship existed and 50 per cent when there was no relationship. The returns also indicated that where relationship existed 33 per cent had attended high school, but where there was no relationship only 18 per cent had attended high school. In other words, if through the school the farmer could be made to take an interest in the agricultural training of the boy and they could be established in a partnership relation, the shifting-tenant problem would be partially solved.

EFFICIENCY IN AGRICULTURAL PRODUCTION.

It should be remembered in all vocational training that the boy or girl is always of greater importance than the subject taught. Much is said in these days in regard to the superiority of European agriculture compared with that of the United States. If Germany is taken as an example and the yields per acre compared with those of the United States, it would appear that Germany is 50 per cent more efficient than the United States. But the average German agricultural laborer cultivates but $7\frac{1}{10}$ acres, whereas the average agricultural laborer in the United States cultivates over 27 acres and produces two and one-half times as much as the German laborer, measured by the crops obtained.

According to G. F. Warren the four principal factors in efficient farming are the size of the business, diversity of crops, crop yields, and production per animal. A large production per acre may not indicate that the farm is being used to the greatest advantage. It was important to determine whether the agricultural instructors were considering this in marking their pupils. Consequently they were asked what standard they had adopted in giving the boy a passing mark in his farm work. The replies indicated that if the boy passed his examination on work in the classroom and laboratory his efficiency in performing the farm operations was of little importance.

THE PLACE OF PERSONAL EFFICIENCY IN AGRICULTURAL INSTRUCTION.

Two other questions were asked to determine whether the agricultural instructor had anything definite in mind in the practical work that he gave the boy. Either the questions were not understood, or the instructor had not considered this phase of the work. The two questions were whether he had standardized any of the principal farm operations in the community, and also to give standard movements or processes in the principal farm operations of his community. None of the answers seemed to indicate that the agricultural instructor had analyzed the farm operations in which the pupils were engaged. Apparently most of the agricultural instructors are requiring of the boy that he get a certain piece of farm work done, and no effort is made to show the boy the most efficient method of performing that operation. It would seem that in this respect the agricultural instructor laid more emphasis on growing a crop than on developing the boy. It would seem especially important that the agricultural instructor should increase the efficiency of his pupils in those phases of farm operations which limit the area cultivated or the number of animals kept.

SUMMARY.

The principal facts developed by this investigation were that in the New England States the majority of the pupils are living at home and have easy access to the school, that the school farms are small, and that the home project is more or less closely supervised, also that the majority of the agricultural instructors are of the opinion that they could easily get along without the school farm.

In the North Central States the school farms are small, the pupils are drawn from greater distances than those in the New England States, and they have not as good means of transportation. It is also evident that there are a large number of boys from towns and cities, and of girls desiring to become teachers, in the classes studying agriculture.

In Minnesota the agricultural instructor has not only to teach but to do extension work, with the result that he has more than he can properly care for. The part that he would like most to neglect is the school farm. Wherever the home project has become a part of his method of teaching agriculture he has not had the time properly to supervise or to work out the details. For these two parts of the country the reasons given for the desire to do away with the school farm are not educational but pertain to the management of a farm of uneconomical size. Since the primary purpose of the school farm is educational, this should not count in making a decision. The considerations that should decide are whether the school farm could be used to make the agricultural workers of that community more efficient, or whether some other method could be devised to take the place of the school farm, as, for example, the home project.

In the South, the majority of the agricultural schools have a boarding department and a large farm, so that the agricultural pupils have a better opportunity to participate in the farm operations, and home projects have not been developed; but even in these schools, where the pupils carry on the farm operations under the direct supervision of the agricultural instructor, it would seem that not enough attention has been paid to making the pupils efficient in the ordinary farm operations and too much attention has been given to getting the farm work done. Thus, the use of land in agricultural teaching presents three different and distinct problems which have no common ground for working out their solution.

The returns indicated that some of the things that could be done most extensively by all the schools having farms are the distribution of pure-bred seed, the introduction of new varieties of plants, fruits, and shrubs, and the extending of the services of pure-bred animals in the community.

ADDITIONAL COPIES
OF THIS PUBLICATION MAY BE PROCURED FROM
THE SUPERINTENDENT OF DOCUMENTS
GOVERNMENT PRINTING OFFICE
WASHINGTON, D. C.
AT
5 CENTS PER COPY
▽

WASHINGTON : GOVERNMENT PRINTING OFFICE : 1915

NITED STATES DEPARTMENT OF AGRICULTURE

BULLETIN No. 214

Contribution from the Bureau of Plant Industry
WM. A. TAYLOR, Chief

SPRING WHEAT IN THE GREAT PLAINS AREA

RELATION OF CULTURAL METHODS TO PRODUCTION

By

E. C. CHILCOTT, Agriculturist in Charge, and J. S. COLE
and W. W. BURR, Assistants, Office of
Dry-Land Agriculture

CONTENTS

WASHINGTON
GOVERNMENT PRINTING OFFICE
1915

BULLETIN OF THE U.S. DEPARTMENT OF AGRICULTURE

No. 214

Contribution from the Bureau of Plant Industry, Wm. A. Taylor, Chief.
May 1, 1915.

SPRING WHEAT IN THE GREAT PLAINS AREA:

RELATION OF CULTURAL METHODS TO PRODUCTION.

By E. C. Chilcott, *Agriculturist in Charge*, and J. S. Cole and W. W. Burr, *Assistants, Office of Dry-Land Agriculture.*[1]

CONTENTS.

INTRODUCTION.

This bulletin contains a study of the yields of spring wheat obtained under various methods of seed-bed preparation at 14 stations in the Great Plains region. The area considered in these

[1] All of the members of the scientific staff of the Office of Dry-land Agriculture have contributed more or less to this paper by having charge of field investigations and by assisting in the preparation of data for records or for publication. The scientific staff as at present constituted consists of the following members, named in the order of length of service: W. W. Burr, Denver, Colo.; E. F. Chilcott, Woodward, Okla.; O. J. Grace, Akron, Colo.; J. S. Cole, Denver, Colo.; J. M. Stephens, Moccasin, Mont.; A. L. Hallsted, Hays, Kans.; O. R. Mathews, Belle Fourche, S. Dak.; J. C. Thysell, Dickinson, N. Dak.; M. Pfaender, Mandan, N. Dak.; H. C. McKinstry, Hettinger, N. Dak.; W. M. Osborn, North Platte, Nebr.; W. D. Griggs, Dalhart, Tex.; C. A. Burmeister, Amarillo, Tex.; J. E. Mundell, Big Spring, Tex.; F. L. Kelso, Ardmore, S. Dak.; W. A. Peterson, Mandan, N. Dak.; J. T. Sarvis, Ardmore, S. Dak.; G. W. Morgan, Huntley, Mont.; J. H. Jacobson, Mitchell, Nebr.; H. G. Smith, Tucumcari, N. Mex.; L. N. Jensen, Woodward, Okla.; J. G. Lill, Garden City, Kans.; R. S. Towle, Edgeley, N. Dak.; A. J. Ogaard, Williston, N. Dak.; C. B. Brown, Dalhart, Tex.; L. D. Willey, Archer, Wyo.; J. B. Kuska, Colby, Kans.; and A. E. Seamans, Akron, Colo.

The following-named men have held positions on the scientific staff of the Office of Dry-land Agriculture during the past nine years, but have resigned or have been transferred to other offices of the Department of Agriculture: Sylvester Balz, F. L. Kennard, J. E. Payne, L. E. Hazen, C. A. Jensen, H. R. Reed, W. O. Whitcomb, C. H. Plath, F. Knorr, and R. W. Edwards.

The data here reported from the stations in Kansas, Nebraska, North Dakota, and Montana have been obtained in cooperation with the agricultural experiment stations of the respective States. In South Dakota, Colorado, Texas, Oklahoma, and New Mexico the stations are operated by the United States Department of Agriculture.

Field, office, and laboratory facilities, teams, and implements have been provided by the Office of Western Irrigation Agriculture, at Huntley, Mont., Belle Fourche, S. Dak., and Mitchell, Nebr., and by the Office of Cereal Investigations at Amarillo, Tex., and Archer, Wyo. The Biophysical Laboratory has cooperated in obtaining the meteorological data reported.

Note.—This bulletin is intended for all who are interested in the agricultural possibilities of the Great Plains area.

investigations consists of about 400,000 square miles of territory (fig. 1). It is bounded on the east by the ninety-eighth meridian of longitude, on the west by the foothills of the Rocky Mountains (indicated by the 5,000-foot contour), on the north by the Canadian boundary, and on the south by the thirty-second parallel. The area covers parts of 10 States, and includes all of the stations herein considered except the one at Archer, Wyo.

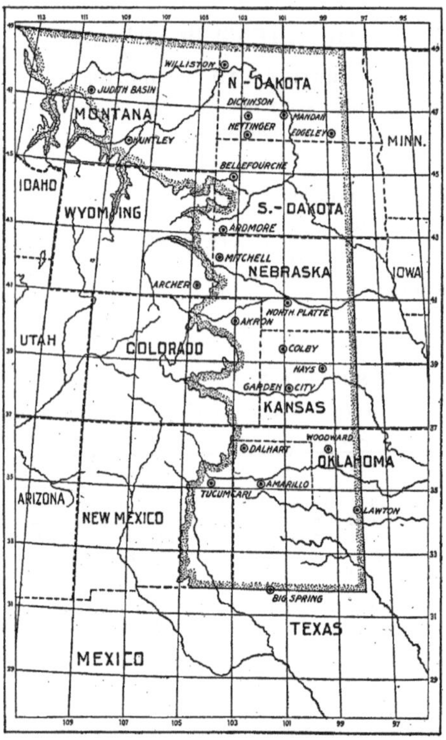

FIG. 1.—Sketch map of the Great Plains area, which includes parts of ten States and consists of about 400,000 square miles of territory. Its western boundary is indicated by the 5,000-foot contour. The location of each field station within the area is shown by a dot within a circle (⊙).

The study as here presented deals only with spring wheat and is made in such a way as to show the effect of cropping and cultivation in only the year preceding its growth. Reference hereafter is made to the crop only as wheat, but it should be borne in mind that spring wheat is meant. The yields of winter wheat and its response to cultural methods are in many cases very different from spring wheat. There is also given a study of the comparative cost of production of wheat under each of the methods studied and the resulting profit or loss.

The work here reported from 14 stations covers an aggregate of 73 station years and embodies the data from a total of 1,683 plat years. By station year is meant one year at one station; by plat year is meant one plat at one station for one year. It is manifestly impossible in dealing with such a mass of data to go into much detail; only some of the broader phases of the evidence are here considered.

Dealing as it does with only one crop, to which certain sections of the Plains are obviously not adapted, this report does not afford a measure of judging the agricultural value or possibilities for other crops of any section of the country.

In 1906 the Office of Dry-land Agriculture of the United States Department of Agriculture began field investigations of the problems in methods of crop production in the Great Plains. The work begun at that time has been constantly and steadily added to, until in 1914 work was conducted at 20 stations. The results here presented are from 14 stations, records covering only one or two years having been excluded.

The method of work adopted was that of raising the standard crops of each section both in rotation and by different methods of preparation under systems of continuous cropping. In no case have rotations requiring more than 6 years been used. Those of even this length have been tried only when sod of tame grass crops are included. More of the work has been done with 3-year and 4-year rotations.

Figure 2 shows a diagram of the plats in the experimental field laid out in 1908 at the Judith Basin Field Station. This station, being a representative one, will serve to illustrate the general scheme and plan of work. The plats here, as in all the work, are one-tenth acre in size. Their dimensions are 2 by 8 rods. Along their larger dimension the plats are separated by bare alleys 4 feet in width. Along the ends of the plats they are separated by roads 20 feet wide. At this station six crops are represented in a series of continuously cropped plats lettered from A to F or G. In this group, plats C and D are alternately cropped and summer tilled, so that each year a crop is grown on land that was summer tilled the previous year and a plat is summer tilled for cropping the next year.

The remainder of the field is in rotations in which each plat is known by a rotation number and letter. On the field diagram the separation of rotations is indicated by heavy lines.

The movement of the crops in the rotation is in the direction from Z to A and from A back to the letter that marks the other end of the rotation.

In figure 2 the diagram is filled out to show the cropping in 1914. The letters following the crop indicate the treatment given the ground in preparation for it, S. P. standing for spring plowed, F. P. for fall plowed, Fal., or S. F., for summer tilled, G. M. for green manured, and D. C. for disked corn land. The addition of the letter M indicates the use of manure. To illustrate: In 1914 plat A of the 4-year rotation No. 14 was in corn on spring-plowed land, plat B was in wheat on disked corn ground, and plat C was in winter rye on fall-plowed land. This would be plowed under for green manure. Plat D was in oats where winter rye had been turned under the year before. In 1915 A will be in wheat, B in winter rye, C in oats, and D in corn.

In the present stage of development of the work, the effect of the immediately preceding crop and of the method of handling its stubble in preparing the seed bed greatly overshadows the effects of the rotations considered as units. Some of the rotations are calculated to conserve or to accumulate fertility and organic matter in the soil, while others may perhaps deplete it, but on the naturally fertile soils of the Plains such results are not strongly evidenced in the first years of treatment. The controllable factors that exert the greatest influence on production are water supply, physical condition of the seed bed, and a recognized if not understood effect of the immediately preceding crop. The crop of a single year brings the land back so near to uniformity in these factors that their probable residual effect is not great enough in the work in hand to introduce serious error into a study as here made.

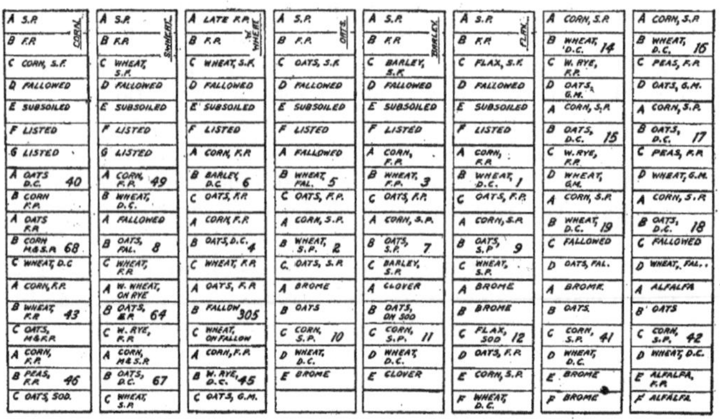

FIG. 2.—Diagram of the dry-land rotation field at the Judith Basin Field Station. The lettering shows the cropping practiced in 1914. The explanation of abbreviations used is as follows: D. C. = disked (corn land), Fal., or S. F.=summer tilled, F. P.=fall plowed, G. M.=green manured, M.=manured, S. P.= spring plowed.

It seems advisable at the present time to prepare a series of bulletins discussing in each the results secured with one crop, as determined by the treatment of the land in only the one year preceding its growth.

CLIMATIC CONDITIONS.

The annual precipitation at the various stations varies from about 15 to 21 inches. The average increases from north to south and from west to east. An increase in the average daily evaporation from north to south prevails. The rainfall is fluctuating in character. Years of heavy rainfall may follow years when it is deficient, and vice versa.

Or a succession of years may be either comparatively wet or comparatively dry.

The seasons of light rainfall are usually accompanied by other unfavorable conditions, such as higher wind velocity, higher temperature, and lower humidity. The distribution of the rainfall is also very important in its influence on crop production. A crop may be produced on a relatively small seasonal rainfall if it is well distributed. On the other hand, a season of higher rainfall, because of unfavorable distribution, may result in crop failure.

Space in this bulletin will not permit the presentation of a complete record of the climatic conditions at the various stations during the time the work here reported was being done. It is, however, available in publications of the United States Weather Bureau. Table I gives the lowest, highest, and average annual and seasonal precipitation for the time covered by the work. The seasonal evaporation is also shown. By seasonal is meant the precipitation or evaporation for the period between the average time of seeding and the average time of harvesting. No attempt is made to show other climatic factors, all of which are important.

Table I.—*Annual and seasonal precipitation and seasonal evaporation at fourteen stations in the Great Plains area.*[1]

Station.	Altitude[2] (feet).	Precipitation[3] (inches).						Seasonal evaporation[3] (inches).		
		Annual.			Seasonal.					
		Minimum.	Maximum.	Average.	Minimum.	Maximum.	Average.	Minimum.	Maximum.	Average.
Judith Basin	4,228	14.96	23.78	18.06	6.50	10.90	8.62	19.117	26.273	21.330
Huntley	3,000	11.92	11.92	11.92	5.00	7.35	6.18	19.820	20.594	20.207
Williston	1,875	10.28	18.99	14.84	5.62	12.00	8.31	21.104	28.269	24.705
Dickinson	2,543	11.93	21.22	16.69	5.31	16.27	10.06	18.379	27.366	22.377
Edgeley	1,468	11.94	21.95	16.71	5.08	15.73	9.60	17.664	25.362	20.657
Hettinger	2,253	12.72	15.68	14.20	8.82	12.89	10.69	20.111	24.248	22.430
Belle Fourche	2,950	6.64	17.73	13.11	1.92	12.75	6.82	23.627	33.906	27.220
Scottsbluff	3,950	13.77	18.51	16.14	5.56	8.26	7.11	24.698	26.647	25.718
North Platte	3,000	11.18	23.01	18.05	4.38	11.25	7.77	25.954	35.255	30.253
Akron	4,600	14.51	22.46	18.28	5.32	9.52	7.82	25.917	32.691	28.781
Hays	2,050	15.59	27.80	21.30	3.87	12.87	9.55	29.390	41.317	32.628
Garden City	2,900	11.82	23.58	18.54	5.01	8.16	6.85	33.315	38.926	35.332
Dalhart	4,000	13.69	16.35	15.11	4.54	14.86	8.17	33.381	41.002	38.596
Amarillo	3,676	10.69	27.80	18.28	5.03	11.49	7.05	32.305	40.704	36.709

[1] The years covered are the same as for the data shown in the other tables for each station.

[2] The altitude given is for the field where the work was done and is based in most cases on that of the nearest town.

[3] The record of annual precipitation for 1914 is not included. The records of seasonal precipitation and evaporation for 1914 are included for all stations, the evaporation being figured from Apr. 1 to July 31. The seasonal rainfall is the amount from Apr. 1 to July 31 for stations north of and including that at Belle Fourche. For stations south of Belle Fourche it is the amount between Mar. 1 and June 30. Evaporation measurements are made from a free water surface in a tank sunk into the soil to almost its full depth. The water surface is kept about level with the surface of the ground.

GENERAL PLAN OF THE INVESTIGATIONS.

Durum wheat has been used in these trials. The aim has been to use at each station the best standard variety available for general use. Changes are made only when necessitated by loss of seed or when varietal tests, breeding, or seed selection makes available for general use a better variety. The same seed is used on all plats at any one station in any particular year.

All seeding is done with a drill. Drill rows are spaced from 6 to 8 inches. As compared with more humid sections, light seeding is practiced. The rate varies from 2 to 4 pecks, depending upon the location and the consequent average climatic conditions. At Edgeley, N. Dak., where summer rains are more frequent and weeds more troublesome, the seeding rate is 6 pecks per acre. Generally speaking, the drier the condition the lighter the seeding. The seeding rate, date, and manner of seeding are the same for all plats at the same station in any one year.

For comparative study of the effect of environment and for securing data on production certain of the work is made uniform at all stations. This results in the attempted growth of spring wheat and other crops in sections to which they are not adapted and in their growth at certain stations by methods not adapted to the conditions obtaining there. Such work, however, is limited, the most intensive studies at each station being undertaken on the crops which are of greatest promise in that locality.

In the present study a table is presented for each station. The first part of such table shows the yields that have been obtained in each year by each of the different methods under which wheat has been grown, considering only the treatment during the one year immediately preceding the crop. The reasons for not differentiating the study further have already been stated.

Where more than one plat has been grown under the same treatment for the previous year, only the average yield of the whole number of plats so grown is given. Column 2 of the table shows the number of plats so averaged. In the presentation of yields, the column headed "Treatment and previous crop" indicates the method of preparation, whether fall plowed, spring plowed, listed, subsoiled, disked, green manured, or summer tilled. Some of these are again subdivided to show the previous crop. To illustrate: The table for Judith Basin (Table V) shows that there were five plats of wheat each year grown on fall-plowed land. On two of these the wheat followed corn, on two it followed oats, and on one it followed wheat. The average yield on fall plowing as given is the average of the five plats, not the average of the given averages. To obtain these averages it is necessary to use the figures as many times as there were plats averaged in obtaining them. The succeeding columns need no explanation, as they are the yields for each year as indicated and the average of each method for the whole period of years. In the last column, where the average appears under the heading "Average," the calculation is from the left. For a rough comparison of seasons, the bottom line of the first half of the table gives an average of all plats for each year, the average of the yearly average yields appearing in the last column to the right.

Throughout the tables, where wheat is shown as following corn on either fall or spring plowing, it is in a 3-year rotation in which the other crop is oats. Where wheat is shown as following oats on fall or spring plowing, it is in a 3-year rotation where in the third year the land is either cropped to corn or is summer tilled. Where wheat follows wheat under any treatment it is in a system of continuous cropping to wheat by the method indicated.

The methods of operation have been similar at all stations. Fall plowing is done early, except after crops like corn that are not removed from the ground early. It is done to a good depth, the standard being set at 8 inches. Ground may be either worked down or left rough over winter. Spring-plowed land may be disked in the fall or may be undisturbed until spring, when plowing is done just before seeding. Plowing is done to a good depth, usually at about 8 inches. This applies to all wheat plats except one plat at each station on which wheat follows wheat. The stubble of this plat is undisturbed until spring, when it is plowed shallow (at about 4 inches) and is then given a minimum of cultivation, which usually consists of one or two harrowings. In those cases where an additional plat appears under spring plowing after wheat, it is plowed deep instead of shallow.

Under the subhead "Listed" there is shown at some stations the yield from one plat continuously cropped to wheat. Instead of plowing this plat, it is furrowed out with a lister at the time of fall plowing. It is cultivated down level by seeding time.

Under the subhead "Subsoiled" there is shown at the stations where it has been tried the results from a plat continuously cropped to wheat. At the time of plowing, a subsoil plow is run in the bottom of the furrow, usually loosening the soil to a total depth of about 14 inches. The variation from this depth is hardly more than 2 inches either way. In general, subsoiling has been done two years in succession and then omitted for two years.

Under the subhead "Disked" is given the average of a considerable number of plats of wheat following corn. These occur in alternate cropping to wheat and corn, in 3-year rotations in which the other crop is oats, and in 4-year rotations in which the other crops are summer tillage and oats or barley. In sod rotations, wheat on disked corn ground is the third crop after breaking the sod. At some stations are shown additional plats on disked ground following potatoes and following sorghum. These are in 4-year rotations.

Under the subhead "Green manured" are given the yields of wheat following the plowing under of rye, peas, or sweet clover, as specified. This treatment is in 4-year rotations in which one of the other crops is corn and the other is one of small grain.

At each station several plats of spring wheat are grown on summer-tilled land. One of these is from land alternately summer tilled and cropped to wheat; one is from a 3-year rotation of summer tillage, wheat, and oats; and others are from 4-year rotations in which the other crops are corn or potatoes and oats or barley.

The method of summer tillage practiced has been of the intensive type. The ground is fall plowed and clean cultivation is continued through the next year and until the wheat is seeded in the second spring. In some cases it is necessary in order to destroy weeds to replow during the summer when the land is fallow. At other stations summer-tilled plats are plowed but once. Experiments not here reported are under way to ascertain the best method of fallowing. Indications are that equally good results can be obtained with a less intensive method than has been practiced in the investigations here reported.

The yields given in these tables begin with the second year of crop production at each station. All crops are produced the first year on land uniform in its treatment. In some cases an entire crop has been lost by hail. These years are not considered in computing averages, as the crops resulting from all methods alike were destroyed.

By the use of the basic data which follows in Tables II, III, and IV there has been compiled a second part embodying a summarized statement of the table of yields for each station. In this summary are brought together in different form the yields in the first part of such table. The value of the average yields thus obtained is shown together with the cost of production (as computed from the available data). In the last line of the table is given the average profit or loss resulting from the production of wheat by the method shown at the head of the column. Loss is indicated by the minus sign.

COMPARISON OF CULTURAL METHODS ON THE BASIS OF COST.

In order to make a comparison of the relative profits or losses of the several cultural methods, as shown in the second part of the table for each station, it was necessary to establish the average cost of production under each of these methods. The methods under study vary a great deal in the labor involved and in the consequent cost of preparation. Table IV has therefore been compiled in order to show the average cost of the methods under study as determined from the data of eight of the stations having the most trustworthy records. An average of the records for 5½ years at each station has been used in compiling this table. This is equivalent to a record of 44 years at one station. An accurate record has been kept of all the farm operations performed under the various methods under trial. These have been averaged for the eight stations. The amount of work required for some methods of treatment varies with the season and with the soil, and the expense of some operations varies with the soil. The amount of labor performed under each of the methods was neither more nor less than that which the man in charge believed to be necessary to bring about the results sought.

In computing the cost of the various operations a fixed wage of $2 per day for a man and $1 a day for a horse was adopted. This may be above or below the actual labor cost in any particular locality, but it is believed to be a fair average and one that will afford a profitable market to the farmer for his labor. The time required for men and teams to cover a given acreage in each of the several farm operations obviously varies with soils and other conditions. The average shown in Table II has been determined from the actual experience of a large number of men connected with these investigations, which experience has extended over a wide range of conditions and many years of time.

The factors included in the cost of production are calculated on an acre basis for each of the separate operations performed, beginning with the preparation of the land and ending with the harvesting and shocking of the grain. To these items are added the cost of seed at 85 cents per acre, interest and taxes on the land investment, calculated at 8 per cent on a valuation of $20 per acre, and the deterioration and repairs of the binder at 15 cents per acre. No allowance is made for deterioration of other farm equipment, as it is believed that the wages allowed for men and teams are sufficient to cover this item for the remainder of the equipment. The above-mentioned items are fixed charges per acre; that is, they do not vary greatly with the yield per acre, except the item of twine, but this variation is not sufficient to materially affect the relative total cost of production under the several methods.

Table II shows the cost per acre based upon what is considered an average day's work for each of the farm operations involved at the above-mentioned wage. As before stated, the type of soil and seasonal conditions will determine to a certain extent the labor required and the consequent cost per acre. The cost of production as computed in Tables II and IV is not offered as being absolute for any locality, either in the amount of labor required or its cost, but is given as a working basis for the comparison of the results by different methods of preparation.

TABLE II.—*Average cost per acre*[1] *of the farm operations involved in growing spring wheat in the Great Plains area.*

[The wage scale assumed is $2 per day for each man and $1 per day for each horse.]

Operation.	Force employed.		Day's work.	Item cost.	Cost per acre.
	Men.	Horses.			
			Acres.		
Plowing	1	4	3½		$1.71
Disking	1	4	8		.75
Harrowing	1	4	35		.17
Subsoiling	1	3	3½		1.43
Drilling	1	4	15		.40
Cultivating	1	4	16		.38
Listing	1	4	10		.60
Harvesting:					
Cutting and binding	1	4	15	$0.40	.93
Shocking	1			.13	
Twine				.25	
Binder wear and repair				.15	

[1] The cost of thrashing is not included in the cost per acre, but it is estimated at 10 cents per bushel and deducted from the price of 80 cents in the granary, thus giving a value of 70 cents per bushel in the shock.

The costs of hauling, stacking, and thrashing are not included in the per-acre cost of production because they can be calculated more accurately on the basis of cost per bushel, as hereafter explained.

The average farm price of wheat used in these computations is based on the data given in Table III, furnished by the Bureau of Crop Estimates. The four States of Kansas, Nebraska, North Dakota, and South Dakota were selected because their extensive wheat production has given them established market prices, which are not greatly influenced by local conditions.

TABLE III.—*Average price of spring wheat at the farm granary for 10 years in four States of the Great Plains area.*

[The quotations are given in cents per bushel. Those for the year 1914 are for the date of Nov. 1; in other years Dec. 1 is taken as the date.]

Year.	North Dakota.	South Dakota.	Nebraska.	Kansas.	Average.	Year.	North Dakota.	South Dakota.	Nebraska.	Kansas.	Average.
1905	69	67	66	71	68¼	1911	89	91	87	91	89½
1906	63	61	57	58	59¾	1912	69	69	69	74	70¼
1907	87	89	79	82	84¼	1913	73	71	71	79	73½
1908	92	92	84	88	89	1914	97	90	92	94	94¼
1909	92	90	89	96	91¾						
1910	90	89	80	84	85¾	Average.	82	81	77	82	80½

Table III shows that the average farm price of wheat on December 1 for the past 10 years has been, in round numbers, 80 cents per bushel. It costs about 10 cents per bushel to take the grain from the shock, thrash it, and put it in the granary on the farm. This cost per bushel does not vary greatly with the yield and is therefore a fixed price per bushel instead of a fixed price per acre, as is the case with the other costs of production. It is therefore obvious that the relative profits of producing wheat under the different methods can best be determined by finding the difference between the fixed cost per acre and the value per acre of the grain at the point where the fixed cost per acre ends, which, as before stated, is when the grain is in the shock. Knowing that the average farm value of wheat in the granary is 80 cents per bushel, and that it costs 10 cents per bushel to take it from the shock, thrash it, and put it in the granary, it is obvious that it would be worth 70 cents per bushel in the shock. This valuation of 70 cents per bushel has therefore been used as a basis for calculating the relative crop values, costs, and profits per acre of these various methods.

In conformity with the foregoing explanation, Table IV gives in detail the cost of producing wheat in the shock, expressed in dollars and cents, and in bushels per acre at 70 cents per bushel in the shock.

TABLE IV.—*Cost per acre of producing wheat in the shock in the Great Plains area, showing averages of data from eight stations.*

Method of preparation.	Number of operations.						Cost of preparation.	Cost per acre.			Interest and taxes.	Total cost of production.	
	Plowing.	Harrowing.	Disking.	Subsoiling.	Listing.	Drilling.		Seed.	Drilling.	Harvesting.		Per acre.	In bushels at 70 cents per bushel.
Disked corn land	......	1.3	1	......	......	......	$0.97	$0.85	$0.40	$0.93	$1.60	$4.75	6.8
Listed	......	1.6	1.2	......	1	......	1.77	.85	.40	.93	1.60	5.55	7.9
Spring plowed	1	1.3	.5	......	......	......	2.31	.85	.40	.93	1.60	6.09	8.7
Fall plowed	1	2.3	.9	......	......	......	2.78	.85	.40	.93	1.60	6.56	9.4
Subsoiled	1	1.7	.9	0.5	......	......	3.39	.85	.40	.93	1.60	7.17	10.2
Summer tilled	1.5	9.2	2.6	......	......	......	6.12	.85	.40	.93	3.20	11.50	16.4
Green manured:													
With rye [1]	2	6.5	2.4	......	......	1	7.73	.85	.40	.93	3.20	13.11	18.7
With peas [2]	2	5.8	2.7	......	......	1	10.73	.85	.40	.93	3.20	16.11	23.0
Average cost of green manuring	......	......	......	......	......	......	......	......	......	......	......	14.61	20.8

[1] The cost of rye for seeding one acre is estimated at $1.
[2] The cost of peas for seeding one acre is estimated at $4.

RESULTS AT THE SEVERAL STATIONS.

Accompanying the presentation of the results for each station is a brief soil description, with particular reference to the depth of the soil and its water-holding capacity. Only such information is given as is necessary to understand fully the interpretation of the results.

JUDITH BASIN FIELD STATION.

The field station at Moccasin, Mont., in the Judith Basin, is located on a heavy clay soil of limestone origin. The soil is apparently very rich in available fertility. It is underlain, at a depth of approximately 3 feet, by a limestone gravel that is closely cemented with lime materials. The gravel subsoil, which extends to a depth of about 30 feet, is practically free from soil. While it is so closely cemented that it does not unduly drain the soil, it is not of a character that allows the storage of available water or the development of roots within it. The presence of gravel in the surface soil does not permit the taking of satisfactory samples for the study of soil moisture. Enough has been done, however, to make certain that only a limited supply of water available to the crop can be stored in the soil. This shallowness of the soil and the consequent limitation of the supply of water that can be stored in it and recovered by a crop make the crop dependent in large part upon the rains that fall while the crop is growing.

TABLE V.—*Yields and cost of production of spring wheat by different methods at the Judith Basin Field Station, 1909 to 1914, inclusive.*

Treatment and previous crop.	Number of plats averaged.	Yield per acre (bushels).						
		1909	1910	1911	1912	1913	1914	Average.
Fall plowed:								
Corn	2	31.3	13.2	21.4	[a] H	24.9	18.1	21.8
Oats	2	36.8	11.5	24.7	H	23.5	19.1	23.2
Wheat	1	33.4	14.0	22.0	H	18.5	15.8	20.7
Total or average	5	33.9	12.7	22.8	....	23.1	18.0	22.1
Spring plowed:								
Corn	1	33.1	11.6	21.3	H	23.8	18.5	21.7
Oats	2	[b] 31.6	10.0	20.8	H	24.1	18.1	20.9
Wheat	2	35.6	9.2	24.1	H	25.4	16.7	22.2
Total or average	5	[c] 34.0	10.0	22.6	....	24.5	17.6	21.7
Listed: Wheat	1	33.3	8.3	26.5	H	23.3	17.1	21.7
Subsoiled: Wheat	1	36.3	15.0	23.5	H	22.8	16.5	22.8
Disked: Corn	8	35.0	10.8	23.9	H	23.6	19.4	22.5
Green manured:								
Rye	1	34.0	9.0	19.0	H	28.0	15.1	21.0
Peas	1	28.3	11.0	20.5	H	20.5	18.3	19.7
Total or average	2	31.2	10.0	19.8	....	24.3	16.7	20.4
Summer tilled	4	[d] 34.1	7.2	20.1	H	22.9	19.5	20.8
Average of all 26 plats	....	34.1	10.6	22.6	....	23.6	18.4	21.9

SUMMARY OF YIELDS AND DIGEST OF COST.

Yields, values, etc. (average per acre).	Tillage treatment.							Previous crop.	
	Fall plowed (5 plats).	Spring plowed (5 plats).	Disked (8 plats.)	Listed (1 plat).	Sub-soiled (1 plat).	Green manured (2 plats).	Summer tilled (4 plats).	Corn (11 plats).	Small grain (9 plats).
Yields of grain:									
1909 bushels	33.9	[c] 34.0	35.0	33.3	36.3	31.2	[d] 34.1	[e] 34.1	[f] 34.9
1910 do	12.7	[c] 10.0	10.8	8.3	15.0	10.0	[d] 7.2	[e] 11.3	[f] 11.1
1911 do	22.8	[c] 22.6	23.9	26.5	23.5	19.8	20.1	23.2	[f] 23.8
1912 do	H	H	H	H	H	H	H	H	H
1913 do	23.1	24.5	23.6	23.3	22.8	24.3	22.9	23.8	23.4
1914 do	18.0	17.6	19.4	17.1	16.5	16.7	19.5	19.1	17.5
Average	22.1	21.7	22.5	21.7	22.8	20.4	20.8	21.9	22.1
Crop value, cost of production, etc.:									
Value	$15.47	$15.19	$15.75	$15.19	$15.96	$14.28	$14.56	....	....
Cost	6.56	6.09	4.75	5.55	7.17	14.61	11.50	....	....
Profit or loss	8.91	9.10	11.00	9.64	8.79	− .33	3.06	....	....

[a] H=Destroyed by hail.
[b] Yield of 1 plat only.
[c] Average of 4 plats.
[d] Average of 3 plats.
[e] Average of 10 plats.
[f] Average of 8 plats.

The most significant fact shown by Table V is the lack of material differences in yield resulting either from different methods of handling the soil in preparation for spring wheat or from the effect of the crop immediately preceding. This indicates that the place given to spring wheat in a rotation is comparatively unimportant. This is rather to be expected when the factors that determine production are understood in the light of recent information. There is not space here to discuss the subject, but suffice it to say: (1) On this rich, virgin, limestone soil, production is not immediately dependent upon increased fertility or greatly influenced by additions to or removal of its elements; (2) the shallowness of the soil where it is underlain by nonfunctioning gravel, together with the usually heavy spring rains, makes it impossible to realize the benefits that might be expected to accrue from methods of cultivation calculated to add to the total moisture supply by storage of moisture in the soil.

The problems appear to be those of good seed, good stand, freedom from weeds, and getting work done in proper season rather than those of certain methods of tillage. How soon results may become apparent from rotations that either add to or take from the fertility of the soil, it is impossible to predict.

The variations in yields have been so small up to the present time that it is possible all may be within the limits of experimental error or due to variations existing in the soil. It would therefore be unprofitable to discuss in detail the small variations that appear. The results are, however, of great importance in the evidence they offer that no one of the methods tried is essential to success in the growth of spring wheat and in the consequent freedom allowed in arranging a cropping system which need not necessarily include any unduly expensive or laborious method as a requisite of production.

Since there are no essential differences in yields from different methods at this station, it follows that the relative profit or loss has been largely determined by the cost of production. The spring wheat crop has been raised at a profit by all methods except that of green manuring. The largest profit has been obtained from disked corn ground. The value of it as a farm practice would depend upon the profitable growth or utilization of the corn crop in a farming system.

The next highest profits have been obtained from listing instead of plowing. This again is due to the low cost of preparation. While the yield from summer tillage has been about the same as from other methods, the increased cost of this method has been sufficient to reduce the profit from $11 per acre on disked corn ground to $3.06 per acre on summer-tilled land.

The heavy cost of green manuring has caused it to be done at the nominal loss of 33 cents per acre, when its whole cost is charged to the first crop that follows it. From the standpoint of actual yields in bushels per acre it appears that no particular method of preparation for spring wheat is essential at this station. From the standpoint of profits per acre it would appear that the greatest profits are derived from the least expensive methods.

HUNTLEY FIELD STATION.

The field station at Huntley, Mont., is located in the valley of the Yellowstone River at the foot of the first bench. The soil is a heavy gumbo to a depth of about 8 feet. Underlying the soil is a considerable depth of free-drained gravel. This soil carries a large proportion of available water and allows deep feeding of the crop. It is consequently possible to store in it a maximum quantity of water that can be recovered by the crop.

TABLE VI.—*Yields and cost of production of spring wheat by different methods at the Huntley Field Station, 1913 and 1914.*

Treatment and previous crop.	Number of plats averaged.	Yield per acre (bushels). 1913	1914	Average.
Fall plowed:				
Corn	1	19.3	21.5	20.4
Oats	2	15.8	27.8	21.8
Wheat	1	11.8	20.2	16.0
Total or average	4	15.7	24.3	20.0
Spring plowed:				
Corn	1	18.6	24.6	21.6
Oats	1	14.3	24.8	19.6
Wheat	1	16.0	18.3	17.2
Total or average	3	16.3	22.6	19.5

Treatment and previous crop.	Number of plats averaged.	Yield per acre (bushels). 1913	1914	Average.
Listed: Wheat	1	16.5	19.5	18.0
Subsoiled: Wheat	1	14.5	17.5	16.0
Disked: Corn	8	18.2	26.5	22.4
Green manured:				
Rye[1]	1	15.0	26.0	20.5
Peas	1	21.3	26.8	24.1
Total or average	2	18.2	26.4	22.3
Summer tilled	3	25.5	26.3	25.9
Average of all 22 plats		18.2	24.8	21.5

SUMMARY OF YIELDS AND DIGEST OF COST.

Yields, values, etc. (average per acre).	Tillage treatment. Fall plowed (4 plats).	Spring plowed (3 plats).	Disked (8 plats).	Listed (1 plat).	Subsoiled (1 plat).	Green manured (2 plats).	Summer tilled (3 plats).	Previous crop. Corn (10 plats).	Small grain (7 plats).
Yields of grain:									
1913 ... bushels	15.7	16.3	18.2	16.5	14.5	18.2	25.5	18.4	15.0
1914 ... do	24.3	22.6	26.5	19.5	17.5	26.4	26.3	25.8	22.3
Average	20.0	19.5	22.4	18.0	16.0	22.3	25.9	22.1	18.7
Crop value, cost of production, etc.:									
Value	$14.00	$13.65	$15.68	$12.60	$11.20	$15.61	$18.13	....	....
Cost	6.56	6.09	4.75	5.55	7.17	14.61	11.50	....	....
Profit	7.44	7.56	10.93	7.05	4.03	1.00	6.63	....	....

[1] Barley was used in place of rye in 1913.

The results of only two years are available for study from the Huntley station. Both were years of good to heavy production, but years when production was determined to a considerable degree by the amount of water stored in the soil at seeding time. There was consequently rather sharp response to those methods that start a crop with more available soil water than others.

The highest average yield, 25.9 bushels per acre, has been obtained from summer tillage. The next highest yield, 24.1 bushels, has been from the use of peas as green manure. Disked corn ground with a yield of 22.4 bushels has been better than corn ground plowed either in fall or spring. The data on the effects of fall and spring plowing of either corn ground, wheat, or oat stubble being rather contradictory and inconsistent among themselves, are hardly sufficient to admit the drawing of conclusions. Indications are that marked differences are not to be expected. The same lack of significant difference exists between the yields from listing and plowing. The yields from subsoiled land have just equalled those from land similarly treated in every way except subsoiling. Green manure, on the average, was productive of yields intermediate between those on summer-tilled ground and those on cropped ground. The crop raised in 1913 where peas were plowed under was much superior to that raised where barley was plowed under. In 1914 there was little difference between the crop after peas and that after winter rye.

Wheat has been produced at a profit by all methods. The greatest profit, $10.93 per acre, has come from disked corn land. This is due both to high yield and low cost of preparation. Between fall plowing, spring plowing, and listing there is little difference, the profits from them exceeding $3 per acre less than from disked corn ground. Subsoiling, on account of its low yield and higher cost, has reduced the profits to $4.03 per acre. The high cost of production on summer fallow has overcome the high yield to the extent that the profit from it has been somewhat less than that realized from land cropped every year. The least profit, $1 per acre, has been from the use of green manure.

WILLISTON FIELD STATION.

The experimental work at the Williston Field Station, in North Dakota, is conducted on a silt soil that carries a considerable proportion of available water and on which the depth of feeding is limited only by the depth to which the character of the crop limits its development of roots.

The results of five years are available for study from Williston station. The production for two of these years was very heavy, the average yield from all plats in 1912 being the highest yet recorded in this work. The year 1913 was one of good but not excessive yields, while in 1910 and 1911 nearly all yields were so low as to be practical failures. With this wide diversity in seasons and yields, the results from year to year have been fairly consistent, the most serious departure being the low yield on disked corn ground in 1914. Minor differences, it is true, have been manifested, particularly as to the relative merits of fall and spring plowing, but on the whole there is a remarkable uniformity.

TABLE VII.—*Yields and cost of production of spring wheat by different methods at the Williston Field Station, 1910 to 1914, inclusive.*

Treatment and previous crop.	Number of plats averaged.	Yield per acre (bushels).					
		1910	1911	1912	1913	1914	Average.
Fall plowed:							
Corn	1	0.7	1.8	36.5	16.1	23.3	15.7
Oats	2	.9	1.7	35.1	9.5	31.0	15.6
Wheat	1	1.3	2.3	33.8	11.7	22.5	14.3
Total or average	4	.9	1.9	35.1	11.7	26.9	15.3
Spring plowed:							
Corn	1	.7	5.5	38.2	14.4	26.8	17.1
Oats	1	1.8	4.0	32.2	13.0	31.5	16.5
Wheat	1	1.7	2.7	25.2	16.8	23.8	14.0
Total or average	3	1.4	4.1	31.9	14.7	27.4	15.9
Disked: Corn	7	.9	5.8	39.7	15.3	19.5	16.2
Green manured:							
Rye	1	2.8	.8	36.0	18.8	37.3	19.1
Peas	1	2.0	2.5	33.0	19.7	32.7	18.0
Total or average	2	2.4	1.7	34.5	19.3	35.0	18.6
Summer tilled	3	4.9	8.2	39.9	17.8	30.3	20.2
Average of all 19 plats	....	1.8	4.6	37.0	15.2	25.7	16.9

SUMMARY OF YIELDS AND DIGEST OF COST.

Yields, values, etc. (average per acre).	Tillage treatment.					Previous crop.	
	Fall plowed (4 plats).	Spring plowed (3 plats).	Disked (7 plats).	Green manured (2 plats).	Summer tilled (3 plats).	Corn (9 plats).	Small grain (5 plats).
Yields of grain:							
1910 ... bushels	0.9	1.4	0.9	2.4	4.9	0.9	1.3
1911 ... do	1.9	4.1	5.8	1.7	8.2	5.3	2.5
1912 ... do	35.1	31.9	39.7	34.5	39.9	39.2	32.3
1913 ... do	11.7	14.7	15.3	19.3	17.8	15.3	12.1
1914 ... do	26.9	27.4	19.5	35.0	30.3	20.8	27.9
Average	15.3	15.9	16.2	18.6	20.2	16.3	15.2
Crop value, cost of production, etc.:							
Value	$10.71	$11.13	$11.34	$13.02	$14.14	....	....
Cost	6.56	6.09	4.75	14.61	11.50	....	....
Profit or loss	4.15	5.04	6.59	− 1.59	2.64	....	....

The highest average yield, 20.2 bushels per acre, has been obtained from summer tillage. The plowing under of rye or peas for green manure has resulted in the next highest average yield. Spring rye is used at this station and is plowed under at the same time as peas. This is done in early summer, and the land is then handled as an intensively cultivated bare fallow until seeding time. While results have fluctuated between the two crops used for green manure from year to year, the variations have probably been within the limits of experimental error.

As to the relative merits of fall and spring plowing and disking as a means of preparation for wheat, the yields show such lack of consistency from year to year that it would be unwise to attempt to draw general conclusions from the data at hand, unless it were that the results attending these practices will vary with the season and that no particular one is essential to success.

Wheat, on both spring and fall plowing after oats, appears on the average to yield better than wheat after wheat.

When the cost of production is figured, it is found that the average yields of the five years under study have been sufficient to allow a profit from all methods except that of green manure. While the yield from this method was next to the highest, it was not enough to offset the heavy cost of production.

The greatest profit, $6.59 per acre, was obtained from disked corn ground, and the least, $2.64 per acre, from summer tillage.

DICKINSON FIELD STATION.

The soil at the Dickinson Field Station, in North Dakota, is somewhat lacking in uniformity. In general, however, it is characterized as a sandy loam to a depth of approximately 5 feet. Below this depth is a lighter soil, which in some cases becomes very sandy or pure sand. The soil has the capacity to retain a large proportion of water and to give up to the crop a large share of what is retained. This feature, in connection with the depth to which a crop may feed, makes it possible to store in this soil an exceptionally large quantity of water that can be recovered by the crop.

While records for the Dickinson station are available for study since and including 1908, the yields and averages are made up from the results of six years, as the crop of 1912 was destroyed by hail shortly after heading. As the fall plowing that year was done exceptionally early, on account of the opportunity offered by the early removal of the crop, it shows up relatively much better than usual in 1913. On this account it approached summer tillage and green manure both in opportunity and in results.

Four of the years studied have been years of heavy wheat production from all methods. The year 1911 was one of low general average, but of exceptional differences between methods. It was a year of drought during the late stages of growth, which made it possible to realize a maximum benefit from the water previously stored in the soil by some methods. The crop of 1914 was damaged at least 25 per cent by hail shortly before harvest.

TABLE VIII.—*Yields and cost of production of spring wheat by different methods at the Dickinson Field Station, 1908 to 1914, inclusive.*

Treatment and previous crop.	Number of plats averaged.	Yield per acre (bushels).							
		1908	1909	1910	1911	1912	1913	1914	Average.
Fall plowed:									
Corn	1	35.0	37.3	24.0	4.7	[1] H	27.5	15.9	24.1
Manured corn	1	33.8	40.7	22.5	3.2	H	27.5	13.2	23.5
Oats	2	19.7	34.7	19.2	.7	H	26.8	11.3	18.7
Wheat	1	17.7	25.2	18.2	1.4	H	20.5	8.9	15.3
Total or average	5	25.2	34.5	20.6	2.1	....	25.8	12.1	20.1
Spring plowed:									
Corn	1	35.0	39.7	27.8	14.0	H	28.0	12.0	26.1
Oats	1	18.7	30.7	18.1	1.3	H	17.0	15.2	16.8
Wheat	1	24.3	26.8	17.4	5.7	H	13.5	10.5	16.4
Total or average	3	26.0	32.4	21.1	7.0	....	19.5	12.6	19.8
Disked: Corn	9	32.3	37.9	22.7	3.8	H	27.8	15.3	23.3
Green manured:									
Rye	2	32.1	38.3	19.7	5.6	H	28.0	20.0	24.0
Peas	2	30.0	36.0	17.4	1.2	H	24.8	18.6	21.3
Sweet clover	1	31.0	32.3	19.0	1.3	H	24.5	13.7	20.3
Total or average	5	31.0	36.1	18.6	3.0	....	26.0	18.2	22.2
Summer tilled	3	33.6	36.9	26.0	22.1	H	27.2	19.2	27.5
Average of all 25 plats	....	30.0	36.1	21.7	5.9	....	25.9	15.4	22.5

SUMMARY OF YIELDS AND DIGEST OF COST.

Yields, values, etc. (average per acre).	Tillage treatment.					Previous crop.	
	Fall plowed (5 plats).	Spring plowed (3 plats).	Disked (9 plats).	Green manured (5 plats).	Summer tilled (3 plats).	Corn (12 plats).	Small grain (5 plats).
Yields of grain:							
1908........bushels	25.2	26.0	32.3	31.0	33.6	33.0	20.0
1909........do	34.5	32.4	37.9	36.1	36.9	38.3	30.4
1910........do	20.6	21.1	22.7	18.6	26.0	23.2	18.4
1911........do	2.1	7.0	3.8	3.0	22.1	4.9	2.0
1912........do	H	H	H	H	H	H	H
1913........do	25.8	19.5	27.8	26.0	27.2	27.8	20.9
1914........do	12.1	12.6	15.3	18.2	19.2	14.9	11.4
Average	20.1	19.8	23.3	22.2	27.5	23.7	17.2
Crop value, cost of production, etc.:							
Value	$14.07	$13.86	$16.31	$15.54	$19.25	....	....
Cost	6.56	6.09	4.75	14.61	11.50	....	....
Profit	7.51	7.77	11.56	.93	7.75	....	....

[1] H=Destroyed by hail.

Some indications shown in Table VIII are rather striking. The effect of the preceding crop and the preparation for spring wheat divide rather sharply into two groups, as indicated by the results obtained. When wheat followed summer tillage, corn, or green manure it has given comparatively high yields. When it followed small grains, the yields have been comparatively low, regardless of preparation.

As between oats and wheat, whether spring or fall plowed, or between spring or fall plowing of either wheat or oat stubble, no decision is apparently to be made from the data at hand. The advantage, if any, seems to be in favor of fall-plowed oat stubble.

The highest average yield, and it is a very high average, 27.5 bushels per acre, has been obtained by summer tillage. But spring-plowed corn ground has averaged 26.1 bushels; fall-plowed corn ground, 24.1 bushels; and nine plats of disked corn ground, well distributed over the field, have averaged 23.3 bushels per acre. Considering the importance of corn in a general farming system and the small advantage shown by summer tillage over corn land in producing wheat, it would seem that even here where summer tillage has been productive of such high yields, it can have no regular place in a permanent farming system.

The use of manure on corn does not appear to have had as yet any appreciable effect upon the wheat that followed the corn.

The use of winter rye plowed under as green manure has thus far been productive of considerably better results than the similar use of either peas or sweet clover. This difference in yield is probably due to the fact that winter rye may be plowed under considerably earlier than either the peas or sweet clover.

Both high yield and low cost of production have combined to give the greatest profit per acre, $11.56, from wheat on disked corn ground. The high yield of wheat on summer tillage has been scarcely sufficient to overcome the increased cost of this method. It shows a profit of $7.75 per acre, while spring-plowed land that had been cropped shows a profit of $7.77 per acre, and fall-plowed land shows $7.51. While green manuring shows about the same production as land from which a crop was removed, the high cost of the method has reduced the profit from it to 93 cents per acre.

EDGELEY FIELD STATION.

The field station at Edgeley, N. Dak., is located on a soil that is derived from the decomposition of shale. Shale in undecomposed particles is found very near the surface. In the third foot the shale, while broken and offering fairly free passage to water, is not as yet broken down into soil. The depth of feeding of crops is practically limited to the first 2 feet. The first foot carries an exceptionally large proportion of water available to the crop. The limited depth of soil that functions in the storage of water and in the development of the crop, however, limits the supply of water that can be carried in the soil to about half of that carried by soils of greater depths. This makes the crop peculiarly dependent upon rains that fall while it is growing.

TABLE IX.—*Yields and cost of production of spring wheat by different methods at the Edgeley Field Station, 1907 to 1914, inclusive.*

Treatment and previous crop.	Number of plats averaged.	Yield per acre (bushels).								
		1907	1908	1909	1910	1911	1912	1913	1914	Average.
Fall plowed:										
Corn	1	12.6	20.8	32.5	6.3	1.5	36.7	23.0	16.8	18.8
Oats	2	9.5	13.0	27.6	4.7	1.0	30.3	15.9	17.1	14.9
Wheat	1	7.0	15.3	23.3	5.2	.5	27.0	12.1	9.2	12.5
Total or average	4	9.7	15.5	27.7	5.2	1.0	31.1	16.7	15.1	15.3
Spring plowed:										
Corn	2	[a] 13.2	[a] 15.8	28.0	4.7	.8	35.5	22.7	16.7	17.2
Oats	1	4.2	13.5	25.8	3.8	.2	31.3	20.6	17.5	14.6
Wheat	1	4.1	13.3	28.3	4.0	.7	35.0	16.3	11.3	14.1
Total or average	4	7.2	14.2	27.5	4.3	.6	34.3	20.6	15.5	15.5
Disked: Corn	12	[b] 13.4	[c] 18.1	27.8	5.7	2.6	33.6	23.6	17.0	17.7
Green manured:										
Rye	1	10.5	19.8	30.5	2.6	.3	36.7	21.8	12.8	16.9
Peas	1	10.2	18.2	28.6	6.3	.2	37.5	22.1	20.3	17.9
Sweet clover	1	......	11.7	23.1	3.6	.2	34.2	24.5	14.3	15.9
Total or average	3	[d] 10.4	16.6	27.4	4.2	.2	36.1	22.8	15.8	16.7
Summer tilled	5	[d] 10.9	15.8	27.5	8.0	3.2	35.4	26.1	16.0	17.9
Average of all 28 plats	....	[e] 10.6	[f] 16.6	27.6	5.7	1.9	33.9	22.5	16.2	16.9

SUMMARY OF YIELDS AND DIGEST OF COST.

Yields, values, etc. (average per acre).	Tillage treatment.					Previous crop.	
	Fall plowed (4 plats).	Spring plowed (4 plats).	Disked (12 plats).	Green manured (3 plats).	Summer tilled (5 plats).	Corn (15 plats).	Small grain (5 plats).
Yields of grain:							
1907 .... bushels	9.7	[g] 7.2	[b] 13.4	10.4	10.9	[h] 13.2	6.9
1908 .... do	15.5	[g] 14.2	[c] 18.1	16.6	15.8	18.2	13.6
1909 .... do	27.7	27.5	27.8	27.4	27.5	28.1	26.5
1910 .... do	5.2	4.3	5.7	4.2	8.0	5.6	4.5
1911 .... do	1.0	.6	2.6	.2	3.2	2.3	.7
1912 .... do	31.1	34.3	33.6	36.1	35.4	[i] 34.0	30.8
1913 .... do	16.7	20.6	23.6	22.8	26.1	23.4	16.1
1914 .... do	15.1	15.5	17.0	15.8	16.0	17.0	14.4
Average	15.3	15.5	17.7	16.7	17.9	17.7	14.2
Crop value, cost of production, etc.:							
Value	$10.71	$10.85	$12.39	$11.69	$12.53	....	....
Cost	6.56	6.09	4.75	14.61	11.50	....	....
Profit or loss	4.15	4.76	7.64	− 2.92	1.03	....	....

[a] Yield of 1 plat.
[b] Average of 5 plats.
[c] Average of 9 plats.
[d] Average of 2 plats.
[e] Average of 18 plats.
[f] Average of 22 plats.
[g] Average of 3 plats.
[h] Average of 7 plats.
[i] Average of 11 plats.

This station presents for study the results of eight years. Five of these have been years of good to heavy production. In one year the production was light, in another it was very poor, while the remaining year was one of practical failure of all methods under study.

The wide differences in yield resulting from different methods of preparation that were obtained at some stations during some years are not exhibited at this station in either the good or the poor years. The reason for this is to be found in the shallowness of the soil that functions for the growth of the crop and for the storage of water that can be recovered by the crop. This shallowness makes the crop dependent for its growth upon seasonal rains that fall while the crop is growing. It may be that this shallowness makes it possible to realize quicker results from the cumulative effect of the use of manure than would be realized on deeper soils.

The relative merits of fall or spring plowing of either wheat or oat stubble seem to be a matter of season. In no case does it make a great difference, and on the average the difference has been negligible. It should be noted that the result from the one plat of wheat on spring-plowed wheat land deserves but little consideration. On account of its location and of continual spring plowing, it has accumulated blowing soil until it is now built up several inches above its original level, or the present level of other plats.

Fall-plowed corn ground has apparently had an advantage over corn ground, either spring plowed or disked, in preparation for wheat. The results are determined from 1 plat of fall-plowed corn as against 12 plats of disked corn ground, which are distributed over the whole field; the advantage, therefore, may be due to a particularly favorable location of the one plat.

With the exception of the high yield of wheat in 1914 on peas used as green manure, there is little choice between them and rye similarly used. Both have been better than sweet clover plowed under. The average yield of wheat following peas as green manure is exactly the same as the average on summer tillage.

Summer tillage has given an average yield of 17.9 bushels per acre for the eight years. This is exceeded only by the yield on fall-plowed corn ground. When this is compared with a similar average yield of 17.7 bushels per acre from disked corn ground and 14.2 bushels from wheat under all methods following small-grain crops, it is seen that summer tillage is an unnecessary practice and one not to be recommended for this section. This is brought out strongly by Table IX, which shows the cost of production and the resultant profit or loss from each method. Disked corn ground shows an average 8-year profit of $7.64 per acre, spring plowing $4.76, and fall plowing $4.15, while the cost of summer tillage has reduced the profit to $1.03. The average loss for the green manures has been $2.92 per acre.

HETTINGER FIELD STATION.

The soil at the Hettinger (N. Dak.) station is a heavy clay loam. The seasons during which the work has been carried on have been such that the results of soil-moisture study are not yet conclusive in determining the proportion of water that can be stored in the soil and recovered by a crop. It is probable, however, that the depth of feeding is not limited by any physical peculiarity of the soil and that the quantity of water that can be stored is large. It is reasonable therefore to expect that on this soil the maximum effect will be realized from methods of tillage calculated to store water.

TABLE X.—*Yields and cost of production of spring wheat by different methods at the Hettinger Field Station, 1912, 1913, and 1914.*

Treatment and previous crop.	Number of plats averaged.	Yield per acre (bushels).			
		1912	1913	1914	Average.
Fall plowed:					
Manured corn	1	9.0	18.0	11.7	12.9
Corn	1	13.8	17.8	12.0	14.5
Oats	2	17.8	12.7	14.1	14.9
Wheat	1	12.0	10.7	6.2	9.6
Total or average.	5	14.1	14.4	11.6	13.4
Spring plowed:					
Corn	1	13.0	26.3	10.3	16.5
Oats	1	8.3	16.5	10.8	11.9
Wheat	1	14.3	13.8	10.0	12.7
Total or average.	3	11.9	18.9	10.4	13.7

Treatment and previous crop.	Number of plats averaged.	Yield per acre (bushels).			
		1912	1913	1914	Average.
Disked:					
Corn	11	17.5	18.4	11.7	15.9
Potatoes	1	11.7	16.7	11.7	13.4
Total or average.	12	17.0	18.3	11.7	15.7
Green manured:					
Rye	2	16.0	21.3	11.4	16.2
Peas	1	18.3	23.5	9.0	16.9
Sweet clover	1	11.2	8.2	7.8	9.1
Total or average.	4	15.4	18.6	9.9	14.6
Summer tilled	8	19.9	29.6	11.8	20.4
Average of all 32 plats	......	16.6	20.6	11.4	16.2

SUMMARY OF YIELDS AND DIGEST OF COST.

Yields, values, etc. (average per acre).	Tillage treatment.					Previous crop.		
	Fall plowed (5 plats).	Spring plowed (3 plats).	Disked (12 plats).	Green manured (4 plats).	Summer tilled (8 plats).	Corn (14 plats).	Small grain (5 plats).	Potatoes (1 plat).
Yields of grain:								
1912 bushels	14.1	11.9	17.0	15.4	19.9	16.3	14.0	11.7
1913 do	14.4	18.9	18.3	18.6	29.6	18.6	13.3	16.7
1914 do	11.6	10.4	11.7	9.9	11.8	11.6	11.0	11.7
Average	13.4	13.7	15.7	14.6	20.4	15.5	12.8	13.4
Crop value, cost of production, etc.:								
Value	$9.38	$9.59	$10.99	$10.22	$14.28	....	....	....
Cost	6.56	6.09	4.75	14.61	11.50	....	....	....
Profit or loss	2.82	3.50	6.24	−4.39	2.78	....	....	....

The results of three years at this station are available for study. The most striking things shown by the arrangement of yields for the present study are the increased production of wheat on summer tillage, on rye and peas as green manure, and on corn ground either disked or plowed in the spring. When yields are studied in connection with cost of production, it is seen that, owing to good yield and cheap cost of preparation, the greatest profit, $6.24 per acre, has been obtained from wheat on disked ground. Of the disked plats,

11 were corn ground and 1 was potato ground. Spring plowing has been productive of an average profit of $3.50 and fall plowing of $2.82. Despite the increased yield on summer tillage, the high cost of the method has reduced the profits from it to $2.78 per acre. The still higher cost of preparation and the lower yields from green manuring have contributed to make it show a loss of $4.39 per acre.

BELLE FOURCHE FIELD STATION.

The field-station farm near Newell, S. Dak., on the Belle Fourche Reclamation Project, is located on a heavy gumbo clay soil, which is derived from the decomposition of Pierre shale. From the soil at the surface there is a rapid change to broken but undecomposed shale. Near the bottom of the second foot is a comparatively impervious layer of soil. The first foot and at least a part of the second foot carry a large proportion of available water. It is probable that little use is made of either water or soil below the first 2 feet. In spite of the heavy soil and the large quantity of water that can be obtained by the plant from that portion of it near the surface, the shallowness of feeding reduces the quantity of water that can be carried in the soil to about one-half of that available on deeper soils. The result of this is shown in the yields.

While the results of six years are available from this station, two of them have been years of total failure of the wheat crop. These failures were due to drought so extreme that no methods of culture were able to overcome it. A third year produced some light yields, but the crop was practically a failure for all methods. These three dry years in succession afforded no opportunity to profit from methods calculated to store moisture. The rainfall was so light and its distribution so unfavorable as to make the accumulation of water in the soil impossible. In two other years there was production from all methods, but the yields were light. In only the first year of the series under consideration was the general production heavy.

Neither in the average of the series nor in any of the years within the series has there been evidenced sufficient difference in production to warrant an extended discussion of the relative merits of the methods under trial. The only partial exception to this statement is to be found in the advantage of summer tillage over other methods in resisting the dry seasons of 1913 and 1914. However, in 1913 it was able to produce only 15.6 bushels per acre, as against an average of 8.7 bushels on fall-plowed land that had been in crop the year before. In 1914 it produced an average of 16.1 bushels per acre, while the production on disked corn land was 10 bushels and on fall-plowed ground only 5.8 bushels per acre. In 1912 all the available water in the soil was used, but in no case was it sufficient to make a crop.

TABLE XI.—*Yields and cost of production of spring wheat by different methods at the Belle Fourche Field Station, 1909 to 1914, inclusive.*

Treatment and previous crop.	Number of plats averaged.	Yield per acre (bushels).						
		1909	1910	1911	1912	1913	1914	Average.
Fall plowed:								
Corn	1	23.6	0	0	0	7.3	6.3	6.2
Oats	2	31.5	0	0	0	9.8	6.1	7.9
Wheat	1	23.3	0	0	0	7.9	4.8	6.0
Total or average	4	27.5	......	......	......	8.7	5.8	7.0
Spring plowed:								
Corn	1	23.9	3.0	0	0	5.6	4.5	6.2
Oats	1	26.1	2.4	0	0	7.9	6.0	7.1
Wheat	1	23.8	2.8	0	0	6.2	4.0	6.1
Total or average	3	24.6	2.7	......	......	6.6	4.8	6.5
Listed: Wheat	1	28.7	0	0	0	9.5	6.8	7.5
Subsoiled: Wheat	1	28.5	0	0	0	6.8	4.7	6.7
Disked:								
Corn	10	29.8	3.8	0	0	10.3	10.0	9.0
Potatoes	1	27.5	1.7	0	0	12.3	11.3	8.8
Sorghum	1	20.8	.3	0	0	9.4	9.0	6.6
Total or average	12	28.9	3.3	......	......	10.4	10.0	8.8
Green manured:								
Rye	1	30.6	5.7	0	0	13.4	13.8	10.6
Peas	1	29.9	1.3	0	0	13.5	11.3	9.3
Sweet clover	2	24.5	0	0	0	12.0	13.9	8.4
Total or average	4	27.4	1.8	......	......	12.7	13.2	9.2
Summer tilled	5	32.7	4.3	0	0	15.6	16.1	11.5
Average of all 30 plats	......	28.7	2.5	......	......	10.8	10.1	8.7

SUMMARY OF YIELDS AND DIGEST OF COST.

Yields, values, etc. (average per acre).	Tillage treatment.							Previous crop.			
	Fall plowed (4 plats).	Spring plowed (3 plats).	Disked (12 plats).	Listed (1 plat).	Subsoiled (1 plat).	Green manured (4 plats).	Summer tilled (5 plats).	Corn (12 plats).	Small grain (7 plats).	Potatoes (1 plat).	Sorghum (1 plat).
Yields of grain:											
1909...bushels	27.5	24.6	28.9	28.7	28.5	27.4	32.7	a 29.3	27.6	27.5	20.8
1910.....do....	0	2.7	3.3	0	0	1.8	4.3	3.4	.7	1.7	.3
1911.....do....	0	0	0	0	0	0	0	0	0	0	0
1912.....do....	0	0	0	0	0	0	0	0	0	0	0
1913.....do....	8.7	6.6	10.4	9.5	6.8	12.7	15.6	9.7	8.3	12.3	9.4
1914.....do....	5.8	4.8	10.0	6.8	4.7	13.2	16.1	9.3	5.5	11.3	9.0
Average	7.0	6.5	8.8	7.5	6.7	9.2	11.5	8.6	7.0	8.8	6.6
Crop value, cost of production, etc.:											
Value	$4.90	$4.55	$6.16	$5.25	$4.69	$6.44	$8.05	......	......	......	......
Cost	6.56	6.09	4.75	5.55	7.17	14.61	11.50	......	......	......	......
Profit or loss	−1.66	−1.54	1.41	−.30	−2.48	−7.17	−3.45	......	......	......	......

a Average of 11 plats.

The only method that shows a profit here is disked corn ground. This, on account of the low cost of preparation, shows an average annual profit of $1.41 per acre. All other methods indicate the production of wheat at a loss ranging from 30 cents on listed land to $7.17 an acre on green manure. Generally speaking, the more expensive the method of preparation the greater the yield. But the yields did not increase in the same ratio as the expense; it accordingly follows that the less the expense of preparation the less the loss that attended the use of any method.

SCOTTSBLUFF FIELD STATION.

The work at Scottsbluff, Nebr., is conducted at a field station located on the North Platte Reclamation Project. The soil is a comparatively light, sandy loam. At a depth varying from 5 to 8 feet there is a sharp break from this soil to either sand or Brule clay. Above this point the soil offers no unusual resistance to the downward passage of water or the development of roots. Owing to its light character, however, it is possible to store in it only a moderate proportion of available water. While the evidence on this point is not yet complete, the amount of water that can be stored in this soil is known to be somewhat intermediate between the corresponding amounts that can be stored in the Belle Fourche and North Platte soils.

The results of three years are available for study at this station. All have been years of comparatively light yields, but one of them shows heavy production from one method.

Spring plowing has been generally better than fall, irrespective of whether it were wheat, oat, or corn stubble that was plowed. Marked benefit was apparently derived one year from the use of manure in growing the corn that preceded one plat of wheat.

Furrowing with a lister and leaving the ground rough through the winter instead of plowing was apparently beneficial one year, but of neutral value in the others.

Disked corn ground was the second best method in one year, but it seemed to be of little benefit in increasing production in the other two years. Disked corn ground has each year given larger returns of wheat than were obtained by plowing it either in spring or fall.

The results from green manure are not consistent either among themselves or in comparison with other methods. In average production it stands third on the list, being exceeded by summer tillage and disked corn ground.

The highest yields each year have been obtained from summer tillage. This method has an average yield of 19.9 bushels per acre as against 14 bushels, the next highest average, from disked corn ground.

TABLE XII.—*Yields and cost of production of spring wheat by different methods at the Scottsbluff Field Station, 1912, 1913, and 1914.*

Treatment and previous crop.	Number of plats averaged.	Yield per acre (bushels). 1912	1913	1914	Average.
Fall plowed:					
Corn	1	11.6	8.0	9.5	9.7
Manured corn	1	20.8	9.8	9.5	13.4
Oats	2	7.7	9.0	10.3	9.0
Wheat	1	6.3	7.8	6.7	6.9
Total or average	5	10.8	8.7	9.3	9.6
Spring plowed:					
Corn	1	17.3	11.3	11.0	13.2
Oats	1	11.7	9.5	12.0	11.1
Sorghum	1	18.7	11.2	9.0	13.0
Wheat	1	8.7	12.0	5.7	8.8
Total or average	4	14.1	11.0	9.4	11.5
Listed:					
Wheat	1	15.0	7.2	6.0	9.4
Subsoiled:					
Wheat	1	12.3	6.3	9.5	9.4
Disked:					
Corn	11	19.1	11.8	11.1	14.0
Green manured:					
Rye	1	15.0	13.0	13.6	13.9
Peas	1	11.7	14.2	12.0	12.6
Total or average	2	13.4	13.6	12.8	13.3
Summer tilled	3	27.8	18.1	13.8	19.9
Average of all 27 plats	27	17.0	11.6	10.7	13.1

SUMMARY OF YIELDS AND DIGEST OF COST.

Yields, values, etc. (average per acre).	Tillage treatment. Fall plowed (5 plats).	Spring plowed (4 plats).	Disked (11 plats).	Listed (1 plat).	Subsoiled (1 plat).	Green manured (2 plats).	Summer tilled (3 plats).	Previous crop. Corn (14 plats).	Small grain (7 plats).	Sorghum (1 plat).
Yields of grain:										
1912..bush	10.8	14.1	19.1	15.0	12.3	13.4	27.8	18.6	9.9	18.7
1913...do	8.7	11.0	11.8	7.2	6.3	13.6	18.1	11.4	8.3	11.2
1914...do	9.3	9.4	11.1	6.0	9.5	12.8	13.8	10.9	8.6	9.0
Average	9.6	11.5	14.0	9.4	9.4	13.3	19.9	13.6	8.9	13.0
Crop value, cost of production, etc.:										
Value	$6.72	$8.05	$9.80	$6.58	$6.58	$9.31	$13.93	......	......	......
Cost	6.56	6.09	4.75	5.55	7.17	14.61	11.50	......	......	......
Profit or loss	.16	1.96	5.05	1.03	−.59	−5.30	2.43	......	......	......

Having next to the highest yield and the lowest cost of preparation, disked corn ground shows the greatest profit, $5.05 per acre. Other methods that show profits are spring plowing, summer tillage, listing, and fall plowing. Subsoiling and green manure show losses.

NORTH PLATTE FIELD STATION.

The work here presented was conducted on the table-land of the North Platte, Nebr., station. The soil is of the type generally known as loess. With the exception of the humus accumulated near the surface it is practically uniform to great depths. The storage and use of water is not limited by the depth of soil or any peculiarities in it. The development of roots is limited only by the physiological character of the crops grown and the available moisture. It is a soil on which maximum results from tillage methods would be expected.

TABLE XIII.—*Yields and cost of production of spring wheat by different methods at the North Platte Field Station, 1907 to 1914, inclusive.*

Treatment and previous crop.	Number of plats averaged.	Yield per acre (bushels).								
		1907	1908	1909	1910	1911	1912	1913	1914	Average.
Fall plowed:										
Corn	2	22.5	28.7	21.3	7.6	0	6.4	4.1	5.5	12.0
Oats	2	26.3	27.3	16.0	6.8	0	4.7	1.3	6.1	11.1
Wheat	1	26.0	27.3	15.3	6.7	0	11.2	1.8	5.2	11.7
Total or average	5	24.7	27.8	18.0	7.1	......	6.7	2.5	5.7	11.6
Spring plowed:										
Corn	1	23.7	24.0	17.2	5.2	0	5.3	1.5	5.0	10.2
Oats	1	20.8	17.5	16.7	8.7	0	8.8	1.8	2.2	9.6
Wheat	1	24.5	22.7	23.0	6.8	0	12.8	2.0	6.0	12.2
Sorghum	1	23.5	20.3	16.3	8.7	0	3.8	3.3	5.2	10.1
Total or average	4	23.1	21.1	18.3	7.4	......	7.7	2.2	4.6	10.6
Disked:										
Corn	8	24.5	24.2	14.5	7.3	0	4.6	3.0	5.1	10.4
Potatoes	1	......	......	......	......	......	5.2	4.2	6.9	5.4
Total or average	9	[a] 24.5	[a] 24.2	[a] 14.5	[a] 7.3	......	[a] 4.6	3.1	5.3	10.5
Summer tilled	3	28.9	41.4	22.6	15.3	0	7.1	6.8	12.5	16.8
Average of all 19 plats	....	24.7	26.3	17.1	8.7	......	[b] 6.4	[c] 3.2	6.3	11.6

SUMMARY OF YIELDS AND DIGEST OF COST.

Yields, values, etc. (average per acre).	Tillage treatment.				Previous crop.		
	Fall plowed (5 plats).	Spring plowed (4 plats).	Disked (8 plats).	Summer tilled (3 plats).	Corn (11 plats).	Small grain (5 plats).	Sorghum (1 plat).
Yields of grain:							
1907 ... bushels	24.7	23.1	24.5	28.9	24.1	24.8	23.5
1908 ... do	27.8	21.1	24.2	41.4	25.0	24.4	20.3
1909 ... do	18.0	18.3	14.5	22.6	16.0	17.4	16.3
1910 ... do	7.1	7.4	7.3	15.3	7.1	7.2	8.7
1911 ... do	0	0	0	0	0	0	0
1912 ... do	6.7	7.7	4.6	7.1	5.0	8.4	5.8
1913 ... do	2.5	2.2	3.0	6.8	3.0	1.6	3.3
1914 ... do	5.7	4.6	5.1	12.5	5.2	5.1	5.2
Average ... do	11.6	10.6	10.4	16.8	10.7	11.1	10.1
Crop value, cost of production, etc.:							
Value	$8.12	$7.42	$7.28	$11.76	....	....	....
Cost	6.56	6.09	4.75	11.50	....	....	....
Profit	1.56	1.33	2.53	.26	....	....	....

[a] Average of 8 plats. [b] Average of 22 plats. [c] Average of 23 plats.

Some of the results of the work of eight years are exhibited in Table XIII. Three of these years have been productive of good to heavy crops of wheat; in four years the average yields were light; and in the remaining year under study the crop was a total failure on account of drought, together with some damage from grasshoppers. The general averages of spring-wheat yields for the eight years range from 9.6 to 16.8 bushels per acre, according to the preparation and previous cropping of the land. A comparison of the wheat crops raised on corn ground, oat stubble, and wheat stubble with those on spring-plowed or fall-plowed ground after any crop, or on disked-corn ground as a preparation for wheat, shows no wide differences in yields. A small average difference in favor of fall over spring plowing is shown. Fall plowing of corn ground in preparation for wheat appears from the returns of two plats so treated to have been considerably better than either disking or spring plowing it.

The one plat of wheat on spring plowing following wheat has given an average yield of 12.2 bushels per acre. This plat is plowed shallow while the others are plowed deep, as heretofore explained. The departure of this method from the others in yield appears to have been dependent upon the seasons and is not consistent from year to year.

Summer tillage for wheat at this station seems to stand by itself as a means of increasing the yield. The largest increases in bushels from this method have been obtained in the best years. After the first year of a period of dry years, which began in 1910, summer tillage has not been able, except in 1914, to increase yields or even, in some cases, to maintain them at the standard set by less expensive methods. While it is not shown in the present study, a much greater response to summer tillage is obtained with winter wheat.[1] Consequently, in spite of the fact that this method has been productive on the average of more bushels per acre of spring wheat than any other, it will not find favor in farm management as a general practice for the growth of spring wheat.

When the cost of production is considered, it is seen that the yield obtained by summer tillage has been enough to pay for the cost of the method. For the eight years under study it shows an average profit of 26 cents per acre. Fall plowing and spring plowing show profits of only $1.56 and $1.33 per acre for the same period. The low cost of preparation is responsible for making disked corn ground show an average annual profit of $2.53.

While the spring wheat crop has been raised without much net profit, it seems that it might afford a market for the labor of men and teams and pay for the use of the land.

AKRON FIELD STATION.

The soil at the field station at Akron, Colo., is of a clay-loam type, locally known as "tight land." It is characterized in the native vegetation by a growth of short grass. As it carries in each unit section a considerable proportion of water available to the crop and as it offers no physical resistance to the development of roots, it is possible to store in it a large quantity of water available to a crop. It

[1] See Nebraska Experiment Station Bulletin 135.

is a soil on which maximum results from methods of tillage calculated to store water would be expected.

TABLE XIV.—*Yields and cost of production of spring wheat by different methods at the Akron Field Station, 1909 to 1914, inclusive.*

Treatment and previous crop.	Number of plats averaged.	Yield per acre (bushels).						
		1909	1910	1911	1912	1913	1914	Average.
Fall plowing:								
Corn	1	19.2	11.2	3.4	30.3	1.4	14.3	13.3
Oats	3	10.3	5.8	3.7	18.8	.6	13.6	8.8
Wheat	a 2	10.3	6.2	2.1	17.5	.7	11.0	8.0
Total or average	5	12.1	6.9	3.1	20.6	.8	12.8	9.4
Spring plowing:								
Corn	1	20.8	15.3	1.3	26.5	6.8	18.5	14.9
Oats	1	14.3	6.3	.2	20.3	1.0	21.2	10.6
Wheat	b 2	12.2	8.9	2.9	21.3	4.8	22.2	12.1
Total or average	4	14.9	10.0	1.5	22.7	4.2	20.6	12.3
Listed: Wheat	1	9.6	7.1	1.2	17.2	2.1	14.2	8.6
Subsoiled: Wheat	1	11.2	5.5	1.5	16.0	.5	9.8	7.4
Disked: Corn	4	15.5	11.4	1.7	19.0	2.8	16.7	11.2
Green manured:								
Rye	1	14.7	11.7	3.7	19.2	1.5	15.3	11.0
Peas	1	12.0	12.4	1.7	20.3	1.5	13.3	10.2
Sweet clover	1	10.1	3.8	1.7	20.5	3.9	11.2	8.5
Total or average	3	12.3	9.3	2.4	20.0	2.3	13.3	9.9
Summer tilled	2	18.4	12.2	4.8	20.5	9.0	22.5	14.6
Average of all 20 plats	....	13.8	9.2	2.5	20.0	2.9	16.5	10.8

SUMMARY OF YIELDS AND DIGEST OF COST.

Yields, values, etc. (average per acre).	Tillage treatment.						Previous crop.		
	Fall plowed (5 plats).	Spring plowed (4 plats).	Disked (4 plats).	Listed (1 plat).	Subsoiled (1 plat).	Green manured (3 plats).	Summer tilled (2 plats).	Corn (6 plats).	Small grain (9 plats).
Yields of grain:									
1909....bushels	12.1	14.9	15.5	9.6	11.2	12.3	18.4	17.0	11.2
1910....do	6.9	10.0	11.4	7.1	5.5	9.3	12.2	12.0	6.7
1911....do	3.1	1.5	1.7	1.2	1.5	2.4	4.8	1.9	2.3
1912....do	20.6	22.7	19.0	17.2	16.0	20.0	20.5	22.1	18.5
1913....do	.8	4.2	2.8	2.1	.5	2.3	9.0	3.2	1.3
1914....do	12.8	20.6	16.7	14.2	9.8	13.3	22.5	16.6	14.5
Average	9.4	12.3	11.2	8.6	7.4	9.9	14.6	12.1	9.1
Crop value, cost of production, etc.:									
Value	$6.58	$8.61	$7.84	$6.02	$5.18	$6.93	$10.22	....	....
Cost	6.56	6.09	4.75	5.55	7.17	14.61	11.50	....	....
Profit or loss	.02	2.52	3.09	.47	−1.99	− 7.68	− 1.28	....	....

a Only 1 plat up to 1911. b Only 1 plat after 1910.

The results of six years are available for study at this station. Three years have been years of good yields, one of light yield, and the other two of poor yields.

The best average yield for the six years from any one method of treatment is 14.9 bushels per acre from corn ground plowed in the spring before seeding to wheat. This is closely approached by summer tillage, with an average yield of 14.6 bushels per acre. The next highest yield, 13.3 bushels per acre, has been from corn ground plowed in the fall before seeding to wheat.

Disked corn ground has yielded an average of 11.2 bushels per acre. This yield is exceeded by nine-tenths of a bushel per acre by wheat following wheat on spring plowing.

Spring plowing has been productive of markedly heavier crops than fall plowing, irrespective of whether it was corn, wheat, or oat stubble that was plowed.

Furrowing with a lister and leaving the ground rough through the winter has given results practically the same as fall plowing similar stubble.

Subsoiling has been done at the expense of a decrease in the yields every year except the first, when its increase over similar stubble plowed at the same time was only 0.9 bushel per acre.

Green manuring has given about the same yields as land from which a crop was harvested. Of the different crops used for green manure rye has been the best and sweet clover the poorest, as judged by the yields obtained immediately following them.

When the cost of production is considered in connection with the yields obtained from different methods, the arrangement as presented shows a profit of $3.09 per acre from disked corn ground and $2.52 from spring plowing. Fall plowing and listed land both show merely nominal profits of a few cents per acre. Subsoiling and summer tillage show losses of $1.99 and $1.28, respectively. The high cost of green manure has increased the loss from it to $7.68 per acre. A more detailed presentation would show that the greater part of the profit from both spring and fall plowing was from corn ground.

HAYS FIELD STATION.

The soil on which the experimental work has been conducted at Hays, Kans., is a heavy silt loam. Penetration of water to the lower depths is slow. The very compact zone in the third foot offers marked resistance both to the downward passage of water and to the development of roots. While the evidence is not as complete as might be desired, it appears that the proportion of water that can be stored in the soil is comparatively high.

The results of five years are available from the Hays station, the crop of 1909 having been lost through a hail storm that destroyed it before maturity. Only two years have been productive of fair crops. The year 1914 has not been considered in computing averages. Indications are that under ordinary farm conditions yields might have been fair, but soil blowing on the experimental plats delayed seeding until it was so late that the crop did not produce grain.

TABLE XV.—*Yields and cost of production of spring wheat by different methods at the Hays Field Station, 1908 to 1914, inclusive.*

Treatment and previous crops.	Number of plats averaged.	Yield per acre[1] (bushels).							
		1908	1909	1910	1911	1912	1913	1914	Average.
Fall plowed:									
Corn	1	3.9	[2] H	11.8	0	14.6	2.1	......	6.5
Oats	3	4.7	H	12.7	0	15.4	1.8	......	6.9
Wheat	1	4.5	H	9.6	0	15.2	.5	......	6.0
Total or average	5	4.5	......	11.9	......	15.2	1.6	......	6.6
Spring plowed:									
Corn	1	1.5	H	10.3	0	8.4	1.8	......	4.4
Oats	1	2.2	H	11.6	0	12.8	1.8	......	5.7
Wheat	1	1.2	H	7.6	0	11.6	1.0	......	4.3
Total or average	3	1.6	......	9.8	......	10.9	1.5	......	4.8
Listed: Wheat	1	5.2	H	15.0	0	11.8	1.5	......	6.7
Subsoiled: Wheat	1	5.2	H	12.6	0	12.7	1.3	......	6.4
Disked: Corn	1	3.7	H	10.6	0	16.2	4.3	......	7.0
Summer tilled	2	4.2	H	11.3	2.2	15.2	7.3	......	8.0
Average of all 13 plats	....	3.8	......	11.5	.3	13.8	2.6	......	6.4

SUMMARY OF YIELDS AND DIGEST OF COST.

Yields, values, etc. (average per acre).	Tillage treatment.						Previous crop.	
	Fall plowed (5 plats).	Spring plowed (3 plats).	Disked (1 plat).	Listed (1 plat).	Sub-soiled (1 plat).	Summer tilled (2 plats).	Corn (3 plats).	Small grain (8 plats).
Yields of grain:								
1908 ... bushels	4.5	1.6	3.7	5.2	5.2	4.2	3.0	4.0
1909 ... do	H	H	H	H	H	H	H	H
1910 ... do	11.9	9.8	10.6	15.0	12.6	11.3	10.9	11.8
1911 ... do	0	0	0	0	0	2.2	0	0
1912 ... do	15.2	10.9	16.2	11.8	12.7	15.2	13.1	13.8
1913 ... do	1.6	1.5	4.3	1.5	1.3	7.3	2.7	1.5
1914 ... do	....	....	....	....	....	....	....	....
Average	6.6	4.8	7.0	6.7	6.4	8.0	5.9	6.2
Crop value, cost of production, etc.:								
Value	$4.62	$3.36	$4.90	$4.69	$4.48	$5.60	....	....
Cost	6.56	6.09	4.75	5.55	7.17	11.50	....	....
Profit or loss	−1.94	−2.73	.15	− .86	−2.69	− 5.90	....	....

[1] Danger of soil blowing on experimental plats in 1914 delayed seeding until it was too late to mature grain
[2] H=Destroyed by hail.

The yields show very consistently an advantage of fall plowing over spring plowing, irrespective of the kind of stubble that is plowed. They also show wheat doing better after oats than after wheat, whether the stubble is plowed in the fall or in the spring.

Very small gains have attended both subsoiling and opening over winter with a lister instead of plowing.

Disking corn ground has been better than plowing it.

The best average results have been obtained from summer tillage. The gain of this method over disked corn ground, the next highest yielding method, has been, however, only 1 bushel per acre. In one year of fair production, summer tillage for wheat was done at the expense of a distinct loss in yield as compared with nearly all other methods.

While the differences noted are of value as indicators, the yields are all so light and the average difference between the best and the poorest method so small as to make them perhaps of little practical moment. Considering the apparent impossibility of materially increasing yields by any method of tillage or management of the soil and considering a thing not shown in this study—the greater adaptation of winter wheat as shown by its higher and more certain yields and its greater response to tillage operations—it would appear that spring wheat has little or no place in the farm economy of this section.

The only method under trial that shows any profit is disked corn ground. In spite of its low average yield the cheapness of this preparation leaves it with the nominal profit of 15 cents per acre. The losses by other methods range from 86 cents for listing to $5.90 for summer tillage. There being less differences in yield than in cost of production, it follows that the least loss has been from the least expensive method.

GARDEN CITY FIELD STATION.

The work at the field station at Garden City, Kans., is on a high upland. The soil is a light silt loam. With the exception of the accumulated humus near the surface it is practically uniform to a depth of at least 15 feet. The development of roots is limited only by the depth to which water is available and the physiological character of the crop. The lighter character of the soil, however, makes it possible to store in each unit of it but a comparatively small proportion of water. This limited storage is not entirely overcome by the unlimited depth of soil. The results in storing water have been determined largely by the limited quantity of water available for storage. In no year, under any method practiced, has the soil been filled with water to as great a depth as it is possible for the crop to develop roots and to use available water.

The results of five years with spring wheat are available from this station, exclusive of 1913 when the crop was destroyed by hail on July 4. In 1911, which is included in the averages, the crop was a total failure from drought so extreme that it was not overcome by any method under trial.

The yields so far from any of the methods under trial have not been sufficient to indicate any possibility of the crop being a profitable one. Neither do the results attending any of the methods, which cover a wide range, indicate the possibility of sufficiently overcoming conditions by cultural methods to make it such. The work, however, has been of great value in the information it has supplied that may find application in the growth of other crops better adapted to conditions. The benefit of the stored moisture accumulated in the soil by summer tillage or other methods is usually seen in the increased growth of straw, but never has it together with the rainfall been sufficient to mature the crop of grain it has promised. This indicates the advisability of growing feed crops which can be saved and utilized even though they do not mature grain.

TABLE XVI.—*Yields and cost of production of spring wheat by different methods at the Garden City Field Station, 1909 to 1914, inclusive.*

Treatment and previous crop.	Number of plats averaged.	Yield per acre (bushels).						
		1909	1910	1911	1912	1913	1914	Averaged.
Fall plowed:								
Corn	1	2.2	9.2	0	7.3	[a] H	5.7	4.9
Oats	3	1.6	5.1	0	7.5	H	8.0	4.4
Wheat	2	3.4	5.0	0	3.9	H	3.9	3.2
Total or average	6	2.3	5.8	....	6.3	....	5.9	4.1
Spring plowed:								
Corn	1	4.0	3.5	0	8.2	H	([b])	3.9
Oats	1	2.5	2.7	0	10.0	H	3.1	3.7
Wheat	1	2.1	2.5	0	3.5	H	1.5	1.9
Total or average	3	2.9	2.9	....	7.2	....	2.3	3.1
Listed	1	3.2	5.7	0	11.0	H	5.8	5.1
Subsoiled	1	2.9	5.2	0	7.7	H	5.3	4.2
Disked: Corn	2	1.2	5.2	0	10.0	H	6.7	4.6
Green manured:								
Rye	1	1.4	5.8	0	8.8	H	([b])	[c] 4.0
Peas	1	0.9	4.8	0	7.5	H	([b])	[c] 3.3
Total or average	2	1.2	5.3	....	8.2	....	([b])	[c] 3.7
Summer tilled	3	5.6	7.6	0	8.8	H	7.9	6.0
Average of all 18 plats	....	2.8	5.4	....	7.8	....	5.6	4.3

SUMMARY OF YIELDS AND DIGEST OF COST.

Yields, values, etc. (average per acre).	Tillage treatment.							Previous crop.	
	Fall plowed (6 plats).	Spring plowed (3 plats).	Disked (2 plats).	Listed (1 plat).	Subsoiled (1 plat).	Green manured (2 plats).	Summer tilled (3 plats).	Corn (4 plats).	Small grain (9 plats).
Yields of grain:									
1909.....bushs..	2.3	2.9	1.2	3.2	2.9	1.2	5.6	2.1	2.5
1910......do....	5.8	2.9	5.2	5.7	5.2	5.3	7.6	5.8	4.6
1911......do....	0	0	0	0	0	0	0	0	0
1912......do....	6.3	7.2	10.0	11.0	7.7	8.2	8.8	8.9	6.9
1913......do....	H	H	H	H	H	H	H	H	H
1914......do....	5.9	2.3	6.7	5.8	5.3	....	7.9	6.2	4.9
Average	4.1	3.1	4.6	5.1	4.2	3.7	6.0	4.6	3.8
Crop value, cost of production, etc.:									
Value	$2.87	$2.17	$3.22	$3.57	$2.94	$2.59	$4.20	....	....
Cost	6.56	6.09	4.75	5.55	7.17	14.61	11.50	....	....
Loss	−3.69	−3.92	−1.53	−1.98	−4.23	−12.02	−7.30	....	....

[a] H=Destroyed by hail. [b] Crop blown out. [c] Average of 4 years only.

DALHART FIELD STATION.

The soil at the field station at Dalhart, Tex., is a sandy loam. In some respects it behaves like sand. In other respects it exhibits the characteristics of heavy clay soil. Its water-holding capacity is comparatively limited. The crops appear, however, to be able to utilize its water to the depth of a normal development.

TABLE XVII.—*Yields and cost of production of spring wheat by different methods at the Dalhart Field Station, 1909 to 1914, inclusive.*

Treatment and previous crop.	Number of plats averaged.	Yield per acre (bushels).						
		1909	1910	1911	1912	1913	1914	Average.
Fall plowed:								
Corn	1	0	[1] H	0	[1] H	0	6.3	1.6
Oats	3	0	H	0	H	0	9.0	2.3
Wheat	1	4.0	H	0	H	0	9.0	3.3
Total or average	5	.8	....	....	....	....	8.1	2.2
Spring plowed:								
Corn	2	0	H	0	H	0	7.0	1.8
Oats	1	0	H	0	H	0	....	0
Wheat	1	0	H	0	H	0	7.8	2.0
Total or average	4	....	....	....	....	....	7.4	1.9
Listed: Wheat	1	8.8	H	0	H	0	12.9	5.4
Disked: Corn	3	0	H	0	H	0	7.0	1.8
Green manured:								
Rye	1	0	H	0	H	1.1	....	.3
Peas	1	0	H	0	H	1.0	....	.3
Total or average	2	....	....	....	....	1.1	....	.3
Summer tilled	2	9.1	H	0	H	.7	13.5	5.8
Average of all 16 plats	....	1.9	....	....	....	.2	9.5	2.9

SUMMARY OF YIELDS AND DIGEST OF COST.

Yields, values, etc. (average per acre).	Tillage treatment.						Previous crop.	
	Fall plowed (5 plats).	Spring plowed (3 plats).	Disked (3 plats).	Listed (1 plat).	Green manured (2 plats).	Summer tilled (2 plats).	Corn (6 plats).	Small grain (6 plats).
Yields of grain:								
1909......bushels	0.8	0	0	8.8	0	9.1	0	2.1
1910......do	H	H	H	H	H	H	H	H
1911......do	0	0	0	0	0	0	0	0
1912......do	H	H	H	H	H	H	H	H
1913......do	0	0	0	0	1.1	.7	0	0
1914......do	8.1	7.4	7.0	12.9	(2)	13.5	6.8	9.7
Average	2.2	1.9	1.8	5.4	.3	5.8	1.7	3.0
Crop value, cost of production, etc.:								
Value	$1.54	$1.33	$1.26	$3.78	$0.21	$4.06	....	....
Cost	6.56	6.09	4.75	5.55	14.61	11.50	....	....
Loss	−5.02	−4.76	−3.49	−1.77	−14.40	− 7.44	....	....

[1] H=Destroyed by hail. [2] Discontinued.

Methods covering a wide range have been under trial in attempts to grow spring wheat each year since the station was started in 1908. Practically no success has attended these efforts. The crops have been lost by hail, drought, and soil blowing. In only three years of the six have any yields at all been obtained. In 1909, 9.1 bushels per acre were obtained from summer tillage and 8.8 bushels per acre from ground furrowed with a lister in the fall. In 1913 green manures and summer tillage produced yields not exceeding 1.1 bushels per acre. In 1914 yields were obtained from all methods except on those plats which were exposed to blowing from adjoining fields. The highest yield of spring wheat yet obtained on the station was 13.5 bushels on fallow in 1914.

While feed crops and late-planted crops have been grown here with success, the type of soil represented on the station farm is not adapted to the growth of small grains under the climatic conditions that exist.

AMARILLO FIELD STATION.

The soil at the field station at Amarillo, Tex., is a heavy clay silt. It is of the type locally known as "tight land" or "short-grass land." While the evidence is not as complete as could be desired, it appears that the storage of water and the development of the feeding roots of the crop are interfered with by a comparatively impervious layer of soil in the third foot. The soil above this, however, is competent to care for all the water that it has been possible to store, even under a system of alternate cropping and summer tillage.

The results of six years are available from this station. The year 1910 is not included; owing to a forced necessity for changing the location of the farm, the crops of that year were all grown on land uniform in its preparation.

Following corn, where the fall plowing is necessarily late, spring plowing has averaged better than fall and exactly the same as disked corn ground. Following both wheat and oats, fall plowing is done early, and has averaged better than spring plowing. Furrowing with a lister has averaged better than plowing. Subsoiling has resulted in exactly the same yields as plowing the same stubble at the same time without subsoiling.

Green manuring has been productive of practically the same yields as upon land from which a grain crop was harvested. Summer tillage has succeeded in raising the yields in a marked degree, but not enough to furnish compensation for the use of the method necessary to obtain them.

TABLE XVIII.—*Yields and cost of production of spring wheat by different methods at the Amarillo Field Station, 1908 to 1914, inclusive.*

Treatment and previous crop.	Number of plats averaged.	Yield per acre (bushels).							
		1908	1909	a 1910	1911	1912	1913	1914	Average.
Fall plowed:									
Corn	1	8.5	0	......	5.7	1.3	0	11.7	4.5
Oats	2	13.5	0	......	6.3	4.3	1.2	9.4	5.8
Wheat	b 2	14.0	2.8	......	10.0	8.5	1.5	11.9	8.1
Total or average	5	12.5	.7	......	7.1	4.6	1.1	10.8	6.2
Spring plowed:									
Corn	1	8.0	0	......	11.6	9.3	.5	10.2	6.6
Oats	1	5.3	0	......	6.8	6.2	.2	3.3	3.6
Wheat	c 1	16.2	0	......	9.4	6.3	0	11.0	7.2
Total or average	3	11.4	0	......	9.3	7.3	.2	8.2	6.1
Listed: Wheat	1	14.3	0	......	12.9	4.7	1.5	11.0	7.4
Subsoiled: Wheat	1	16.2	4.0	......	11.3	4.2	.8	12.3	8.1
Disked: Corn	1	8.3	0	......	12.1	6.3	1.0	11.8	6.6
Green manured:									
Rye	1	14.2	4.3	......	7.5	9.2	2.3	11.7	8.2
Peas	1	19.7	0	......	11.4	8.7	2.5	10.7	8.8
Total or average	2	17.0	2.2	......	9.5	9.0	2.4	11.2	8.6
Summer tilled	d 6	16.3	10.0	......	18.7	9.8	8.1	12.7	12.6
Average of all 19 plats	....	13.3	2.1	......	10.5	7.2	3.3	11.2	7.9

SUMMARY OF YIELDS AND DIGEST OF COST.

Yields, values, etc. (average per acre).	Tillage treatment.							Previous crop.	
	Fall plowed (5 plats).	Spring plowed (3 plats).	Disked (1 plat).	Listed (1 plat).	Sub-soiled (1 plat).	Green manured (2 plats).	Summer tilled (6 plats).	Corn (3 plats).	Small grain (8 plats).
Yields of grain:									
1908...bushels..	12.5	11.4	8.3	14.3	16.2	17.0	16.3	8.3	13.7
1909......do....	.7	0	0	0	4.0	2.2	10.0	0	.9
1910 a.....do....	....	....	....	....	....	....	....	....	....
1911......do....	7.1	9.3	12.1	12.9	11.3	9.5	18.7	9.8	9.0
1912......do....	4.6	7.3	6.3	4.7	4.2	9.0	9.8	5.6	5.5
1913......do....	1.1	.2	1.0	1.5	.8	2.4	8.1	.5	1.0
1914......do....	10.8	8.2	11.8	11.0	12.3	11.2	12.7	11.2	10.0
Average	6.2	6.1	6.6	7.4	8.1	8.6	12.6	5.9	6.7
Crop value, cost of production, etc.:									
Value	$4.34	$4.27	$4.62	$5.18	$5.67	$6.02	$8.82	....	....
Cost	6.56	6.09	4.75	5.55	7.17	14.61	11.50	....	....
Loss	−2.22	−1.82	−.13	−.37	−1.50	−8.59	−2.68	....	....

a Location of station changed in 1910; records not used.
b One plat only to 1912.
c Two plats averaged to 1911.
d Only two plats were averaged up to 1912.

None of the methods under trial show the production of spring wheat at a profit. More profitable crops are produced from a group of crops not treated in this publication—the grain sorghums. It appears from the evidence at hand that the spring-sown small grains are not destined to occupy a place of major importance in the agriculture of this section.

GENERAL DISCUSSION OF RESULTS.

In the preceding pages data have been presented and briefly discussed separately for each station without reference to results at other stations. In the following pages some of the more important bearings and indications are considered from a more general standpoint.

To facilitate this study, Table XIX has been compiled, in which are brought together for each station the average yields as grouped for this study under different methods of preparation. The figures here given are taken from the last column of the tables as given for each station. The yield and cost of production data are also assembled in such a way as to show the profit or loss in dollars and cents per acre for the average crop for each method for which it has been computed at each station.

TABLE XIX.—*Comparison of the average yields and profit or loss on the production of spring wheat, by different methods of tillage at 14 stations in the Great Plains area.*

Statement of data.	Number of years averaged.	Methods of tillage.						
		Fall plowed.	Spring plowed.	Listed.	Subsoiled.	Disked.	Green manured.	Summer tilled.
1	2	3	4	5	6	7	8	9
Yields per acre (bushels):[1]								
Judith Basin	5	22.1	21.7	21.7	22.8	22.5	20.4	20.8
Huntley	2	20.0	19.5	18.0	16.0	22.4	22.3	25.9
Williston	5	15.3	15.9	....	....	16.2	18.6	20.2
Dickinson	6	20.1	19.8	....	....	23.3	22.2	27.5
Edgeley	8	15.3	15.5	....	....	17.7	16.7	17.9
Hettinger	3	13.4	13.7	....	....	15.7	14.6	20.4
Belle Fourche	6	7.0	6.5	7.5	6.7	8.8	9.2	11.5
Scottsbluff	3	9.6	11.5	9.4	9.4	14.0	13.3	19.9
North Platte	8	11.6	10.6	....	....	10.4	....	16.8
Akron	6	9.4	12.3	8.6	7.4	11.2	9.9	14.6
Hays	6	6.6	4.8	6.7	6.4	7.0	....	8.0
Garden City	5	4.1	3.1	5.1	4.2	4.6	3.7	6.0
Dalhart	4	2.2	1.9	5.4	....	1.8	.3	5.8
Amarillo	6	6.2	6.1	7.4	8.1	6.6	8.6	12.6
Average[1]	....	11.6	11.6	10.0	10.1	13.0	13.3	16.2
Profit or loss (—) per acre:								
Judith Basin	5	$8.91	$9.10	$9.64	$8.79	$11.00	—$0.33	$3.06
Huntley	2	7.44	7.56	7.05	4.03	10.93	1.00	6.63
Williston	5	4.15	5.04	....	....	6.59	— 1.59	2.64
Dickinson	6	7.51	7.77	....	....	11.56	.93	7.75
Edgeley	8	4.15	4.76	....	....	7.64	— 2.92	1.03
Hettinger	3	2.82	3.50	....	....	6.24	— 4.39	2.78
Belle Fourche	6	—1.66	—1.54	— .30	—2.48	1.41	— 7.17	—3.45
Scottsbluff	3	.16	1.96	1.03	— .59	5.05	— 5.30	2.43
North Platte	8	1.56	1.33	....	....	2.53	....	.26
Akron	6	.02	2.52	.47	—1.99	3.09	— 7.68	—1.28
Hays	5	—1.94	—2.73	— .86	—2.69	.15	....	—5.90
Garden City	4	—3.69	—3.90	—1.98	—4.23	—1.53	—12.02	—7.30
Dalhart	6	—5.02	—4.76	—1.77	....	—3.49	—14.40	—7.44
Amarillo	6	—2.22	—1.82	— .37	—1.50	— .13	— 8.59	—2.68

[1] The averages of columns 3, 4, 7, and 9 are strictly comparable with each other; columns 5 and 6 approximately so; column 8 is not comparable with any other.

Table XIX shows a rather natural division of the stations into two groups. At the 10 more northern stations spring wheat has been grown at a profit by at least one method. At Belle Fourche the only profit was $1.41, from disked corn ground. At the 4 more southern stations the only profit realized from any method has been 15 cents an acre from disked corn ground at Hays.

When tests on fall-plowed ground following corn, oats, and wheat are averaged together and compared with spring plowing following the same crops, the averages of the two methods at the 14 stations are the same for the years averaged. At only 3 stations—Scottsbluff, Akron, and Hays—are the average differences greater than 1 bushel per acre. At Hays the advantage is with fall plowing and at the other 2 stations with spring plowing. At most stations the average difference is too low to receive much consideration. The advantage of one over the other depends chiefly upon the season, as is shown in the detailed tables. The data indicate the importance of understanding the general principles that govern the observed seasonal variations and the importance of adjusting this work to the general economy of the farm organization. This subject is too broad to be considered here, and a separate publication dealing with it in detail is in preparation. The small difference in cost of the two methods makes relative profits and losses from them follow closely the differences in yields.

Disked corn ground has given consistently high yields. This, together with the low cost of this preparation for wheat, has resulted in its uniform showing of the greatest profit per acre at those stations where it has been possible to raise wheat at a profit and the least loss at those stations where wheat has been raised only at a loss. The only exception to this is at Dalhart, Tex., where yields have been so low as to be of little practical moment. The realization of these profits depends, of course, upon the successful growth of corn as a general farm crop in competition with other crops.

It should be borne in mind that at all stations disking corn ground as a preparation for all small grain crops has been done upon corn land kept free from weeds. If weeds were allowed to develop in the corn similar results should not be expected. To the extent that the weeds developed or were unhindered in their growth, the corn ground would approach a grain stubble in the condition of the seed bed. If the weeds matured seed, further damage might be done by their growth in the succeeding crop. Where moisture is the limiting factor, weed growth is decidedly detrimental.

Subsoiling, as compared with similar wheat stubble fall plowed without subsoiling, has been of doubtful utility as a means of increasing yields. As a means of overcoming drought it is without value. Only at Judith Basin and Scottsbluff has it been able to account for an increase of more than 1 bushel per acre. At Judith Basin the increase has been 1.9 bushels and at Scottsbluff 2.5 bushels. This evidence from eight stations, some of which have records for study covering eight years, together with the evidence at hand but not here reported of other work on depth of plowing, which includes deep tilling and dynamiting, would seem to be conclusive that the nature of the Plains and the trend of their agriculture are not to be changed by the simple expedient of working them to a greater depth than is reached by the ordinary plow and equipment.

Listing wheat stubble instead of plowing it in the fall has resulted in a small increase of yield at seven of the eight stations where it has been tried. At Amarillo it has increased the yields in the years of heaviest wheat production, but it shows on the average a loss of 0.6 bushel per acre at this station. As it is a somewhat cheaper method of preparation than fall plowing, it has consequently been a more profitable one.

Except at the Judith Basin and Akron stations, summer tillage has given the highest average yields of any method under trial. At Akron the yield on summer tillage has been exceeded by that on spring-plowed corn ground by 0.3 bushel per acre. The reason for the departure at the Judith Basin station from the general rule is discussed under that station. For the whole 14 stations under study the average increase in yield over disked corn ground has been 3.1 bushels per acre. Summer tillage requires the use of the land two years to produce a crop and requires an extra amount of cultivation to keep it free from weeds in the fallow year. It consequently has the highest acre cost of any method under trial except that of green manuring. A study of the relative profits and losses from different methods, as given in Table XIX, shows that the increase in cost of production by summer tillage has been relatively greater than the increase in yields resulting from it. With one or two exceptions the highest yields have been obtained by this method. It has not at any station been the most profitable when a profit was realized nor has it been the source of the least loss where wheat has been raised at a loss. At eight stations it shows a profit, but a smaller one than was realized from some other method or methods. At three other stations it has resulted in a loss while some other methods have resulted in profit. At the remaining three stations its practice has increased the loss attending the use of less expensive methods.

Green manuring is the most expensive method under trial. It resembles a fallow in that it requires the use of the land for two years for the production of one harvested crop, with the added expense of seed and seeding. There is a saving in cultivation during the spring while the crop is growing, but this is offset by the necessity of plowing to turn the crop under and is not sufficient to make up for the cost of seed and seeding. Yields have not been commensurate with the increased cost of producing them. At no station have the average yields following any green manure exceeded those from summer tillage. At Huntley and Dickinson, the two stations having the highest average yields, small profits have been realized from this method in spite of its high cost. At the 10 other stations at which it has been under trial the result has been a monetary loss, both actually and in comparison with other methods.

It is hardly fair to charge the whole expense of green manuring to the one crop that immediately follows it, as is here done. It should have a cumulative effect in building up the soil or remedying its deficiency in organic matter. The available evidence is that on normal soils in the Great Plains, at least in the first years of the work, little effect is shown on other than the first crop. This effect is that of a fallow to the extent that the green manure approaches a fallow in the storage of water during the period after the crop is plowed under.

At different times and in different sections certain methods have been exploited as the solution of the problems of dry farming. Each of these systems may have merit, but any and all fall far short of a panacea under all conditions. The observations and investigations that have developed these systems, or upon which the advocacy of special methods have been founded, have been altogether too limited both in geographic extent and in range of time. There is always, too, the temptation to magnify the importance of those single years which may be exceptional, but whose results point strongly in the desired direction, losing sight of the fact that it is the average of a long series of years upon which the agricultural organization and practices of a section are and must be based.

The scope of the work in hand is broad enough, both in length of time and in geographic distribution, to overcome these objections. One fact conclusively shown is that cultivation is not an unfailing solution of the problem of drought. It will doubtless alleviate it to some extent, but can never fully overcome it. Some methods have shown consistent merit under some soil conditions. The same system when transplanted to some other environment may show little or no merit. With the exception of one year at one station the greatest difference in yield between the supposedly good and the supposedly poor method has been in the good years rather than the bad years. This shows that good systems have more efficacy in augmenting the results obtained in a good year than in overcoming the conditions of a very unfavorable year.

A study of the data given in the tables will show that at some stations no material difference has resulted from the various methods of tillage used in preparing the soil for spring wheat.

On shallow soil, where the development of roots and the recovery of water is limited by underlying shale, or on shallow soils underlain by gravel impervious to plant roots, one can not expect to get any material benefit from systems of tillage calculated to increase the storage of water in the soil. The shallowness of the soil will of itself limit the amount of water that can be stored in it. It may be that one heavy rain or rainy period will be sufficient to fill such a soil completely. After it has been filled to its carrying capacity it is obvious that no amount of cultivation will increase its water content. Crops grown on such soils are dependent upon seasonal rainfall.

The soils upon which these investigations have been made are in the main fertile. In most cases they have been but recently broken from the native sod and in no case has the fertility been dissipated by long-continued cropping. Unless some abnormal factor enters in, such as hail or injurious insects, the yield obtained is largely determined by the available water. Since the water available to the crop on shallow soils can not be materially increased by cultivation, and since on these soils water is the chief limiting factor, it is unreasonable to expect much increase in yield from one method of tillage over another.

On uniform soils of sufficient depth to allow the accumulation of a surplus of water, wider variations in yields are to be expected from the various methods, under climatic conditions favorable to the storage of water. Such results have been obtained at several of the stations. The differences in yields, however, from different methods of tillage, have not been the same from year to year, even on the most responsive soils, but have varied with the climatic conditions. In some years comparatively wide differences are obtained. In another year the climatic conditions may be unfavorable and little or no differences in yield are shown. The rainfall might be so distributed that it could not be accumulated in the soil by one method more than by another. If only light showers came, or dry weather prevailed during the practice of some system calculated to accumulate water in the soil, it is obvious that little or no water would be stored. If the rains came later in sufficient amount and falling slowly enough to avoid run-off, the soils under all methods would be filled with water, which would tend to equalize the resulting yields. If, on the other hand, little or no rain came and none had been stored, the results would be equalized in failure. It must be borne in mind that cultivation of itself does not accumulate the water in the soil. There must first be rain. The cultivation can assist only in getting the water into the soil and in preventing its loss through weeds, by run-off, or by vaporization and loss through shrinkage cracks.

At some stations the yields have been so nearly practical failures that it is evident that the growing of spring wheat is not a profitable practice. At other stations one or two crops show a profit, while the remaining ones are practical failures. They indicate that the farmer may not find spring wheat profitable on the average even though some years show a profit. That a certain locality is not favorable to the growing of spring wheat does not mean that it is not a farming section. It simply indicates that soil and climatic conditions are not favorable to the production of this crop. Other crops may find their most favorable environment at such a place. Only one crop is herein discussed. At every station some crops have been grown that have given good returns. At the southern stations, for example, the grain sorghums have done well and should be considered the main crops.

Where work has been carried on for several years with no material difference in yield obtained from the various methods, it indicates that more freedom may be used by the farmer in planning his operations. If spring plowing, fall plowing, or disking after some intertilled crop gives practically the same yields, the rational thing to do is to take advantage of this fact. It is desirable to plow when it can be done most economically for men and teams. If the cropping system includes intertilled crops and disking is as effective and can be done at less labor cost, it is advisable to disk the land to prepare for wheat. Unless there is a gain from some certain method of tillage or crop sequence, one should adjust the work from the standpoint of economical operation. The farmer can then give his thought to procuring better seed, keeping ahead with his work, and preventing the growth of weeds.

CONCLUSIONS.

These conclusions apply only to the yields of spring wheat as affected by the cropping and cultivation of the one year immediately preceding their growth.

(1) Some seasons are so unfavorable as to result in failure of the spring-wheat crop without regard to the cultural methods under investigation. Extremely unfavorable climatic conditions can not be overcome by cultural methods.

(2) It is only in those seasons when the rainfall deficit is so small that it can be overcome by moisture stored in the soil that the cultural methods under investigation have shown important effects upon yields.

(3) When the differences in value of the yields are less than the differences in cost of production, then cost becomes the determining factor.

(4) Some soils, even in the regions of profitable spring-wheat production, show little response to cultural methods.

(5) Reducing the cost of production has in most cases in these investigations proved a more important factor in determining profits than increasing yields by cultural methods.

(6) Northern Colorado and Kansas seem from these investigations to be the southern limit of profitable spring-wheat production on the Great Plains. This limitation does not apply to winter wheat and other crops under investigation.

(7) Disked corn ground has given consistently high yields. This, together with the low cost of preparation, has resulted in its showing the highest average profit or lowest average loss of any of the methods tried at all of the fourteen stations except one. These profits are based on the assumption that the corn crop was so utilized as to pay for the cost of its production. (If the corn crop was grown at a loss, this loss should be deducted from the profits on the wheat crop following it.)

(8) Furrowing with a lister and leaving the surface ridged through the winter has resulted in a small increase in yield over plowing at seven of the eight stations where it has been tried. As it is a somewhat cheaper method of preparation than plowing, it has consequently been more profitable.

(9) The average difference in the yields of spring wheat following fall plowing and spring plowing are very small. At most stations the advantage of one over the other depends upon the season.

(10) Subsoiling has been of doubtful utility as a means of increasing yields. As a means of overcoming drought it is without value.

(11) Summer tillage without crop has given the highest average yields of any method under trial at 12 of the 14 stations. However, on account of its high cost, due to extra labor and alternate-year cropping, it has not been the most profitable practice.

(12) The most expensive method under trial is green manuring. It has produced less profit or greater loss than any other method under investigation.

ADDITIONAL COPIES
OF THIS PUBLICATION MAY BE PROCURED FROM
THE SUPERINTENDENT OF DOCUMENTS
GOVERNMENT PRINTING OFFICE
WASHINGTON, D. C.
AT
10 CENTS PER COPY
▽

UNITED STATES DEPARTMENT OF AGRICULTURE

BULLETIN No. 215

Contribution from the Bureau of Chemistry
CARL L. ALSBERG, Chief

Washington, D. C. PROFESSIONAL PAPER May 21, 1915

COMPOSITION OF CORN (MAIZE) MEAL MANUFACTURED BY DIFFERENT PROCESSES AND THE INFLUENCE OF COMPOSITION ON THE KEEPING QUALITIES

By

A. L. WINTON, W. C. BURNET, and J. H. BORNMANN

CONTENTS

WASHINGTON
GOVERNMENT PRINTING OFFICE
1915

BULLETIN OF THE
U.S. DEPARTMENT OF AGRICULTURE

No. 215

Contribution from the Bureau of Chemistry, Carl L. Alsberg, Chief.
May 21, 1915.

(PROFESSIONAL PAPER.)

COMPOSITION OF CORN (MAIZE) MEAL MANUFACTURED BY DIFFERENT PROCESSES AND THE INFLUENCE OF COMPOSITION ON THE KEEPING QUALITIES.

By A. L. Winton,[1] W. C. Burnet, *Chemist in Charge, Savannah Food and Drug Inspection Laboratory*, and J. H. Bornmann, *Assistant Chemist*.

CONTENTS.

INTRODUCTION.

The cause, detention, and prevention of the spoilage of Indian corn have been given special attention by the investigators in the Bureau of Plant Industry who have studied the subject from the chemical, biological, and toxicological standpoints. In view of the fact that an excess of moisture is conducive to spoilage as well as shrinkage, Brown and Duvel[2] have introduced a rapid method for the determination of this constituent which has come into extensive use in grain standardization laboratories as well as in elevators and mills. The percentages of moisture obtained by this process are important factors in determining the grade of market corn.

While moisture is doubtless the most important of the controllable factors causing deterioration, the determination of acidity has come to be recognized as the best chemical means of detecting actual

[1] Dr. Winton was formerly chemist in charge, Food Investigation Laboratory.

[2] Brown, Edgar, and Duvel, J. W. T. A Quick Method for the Determination of Moisture in Grain. U. S. Dept. Agr., Bureau of Plant Industry Bul. 99.

NOTE.—This bulletin is of interest to corn millers and dealers in corn and corn products and is suitable for distribution in all parts of the country.

spoilage, or at least a tendency in that direction. Italian and Austrian authorities have for some time placed dependence upon this determination in conjunction with certain qualitative tests which appear to have local significance. The Austrian chemist, Schindler,[1] described a method for acidity, and Black and Alsberg[2] in the United States have elaborated the details of the process in order to make it applicable for the use of those unskilled in laboratory manipulation. The process described by these authors has been further popularized by Besley and Baston,[3] and applied in their investigations on the soundness of corn. A certain amount of acid-reacting material, residing chiefly in the germ, is present in sound corn although no sour taste or smell is evident. During spoilage this acidity rapidly increases through the agency of molds or bacteria, or both, until the limit of tolerance is exceeded.

Although the spoilage of corn, as such, has been the chief subject of investigation by the authors named, Black and Alsberg have also shown that the corn meal on the American market often contains an amount of acidity in excess of 30, the arbitrary limit adopted by the Austrian chemist Schindler. This figure, in chemical language, represents the number of cubic centimeters of normal alkali required to neutralize the acidity in the extract from 1,000 grams of the meal.

The main purpose of this paper is to show the general composition of American table meal milled by different processes, and especially the keeping qualities of the extreme types, dried to different degrees and stored in different localities. Incidentally, the composition of grits and the by-products are considered.

The writers desire to express their appreciation for the assistance furnished by corn millers in various parts of the country who have permitted the inspection of their plants and furnished samples of corn and meal for analysis. Special thanks are due Mr. H. Bates, jr., president of the American Hominy Co., also Mr. F. C. Atkinson, chemist, and Mr. Charles Highstreet, general superintendent of that company, who threw open their mill at Terre Haute, Ind., for the experiments. Acknowledgment should also be made for the cooperation of Mr. W. J. McGee, former chief of the New Orleans Food and Drug Inspection Laboratory, and for the analytical work carried out by Mr. L. Patton, assistant chemist at the Savannah Food and Drug Inspection Laboratory.

CONSUMPTION OF CORN MEAL.

The consumption of corn meal is greatest in the Southern States of the Union, where in certain sections meal and grits are the principal

[1] Schindler, Josef. Anleitung zur Beurteilung des Maises und seiner Mahlprodukte mit Rücksicht auf ihre Eignung als Nahrungsmittel. Innsbruck, 1909.

[2] Black, O. F., and Alsberg, C. L. The Determination of the Deterioration of Maize, with Incidental Reference to Pellagra, U. S. Dept. Agr., Bureau of Plant Industry Bul. 199.

[3] Besley, H. J., and Baston, G. H. Acidity as a Factor in Determining the Degree of Soundness of Corn, U. S. Dept. Agr. Bul. 102.

cereal foods. Hon. E. J. Watson, commissioner of agriculture, commerce, and industries of the State of South Carolina, who has been particularly active in repressing the sale of spoiled meal in his State, is responsible for the statement that in South Carolina corn meal is not only the principal cereal product, but the most important of all articles of diet.[1] The same statement applies to many other regions in the South, particularly the rural districts, where wheat flour is of secondary importance and in some cases even a rarity. In many southern families, even in the cities, corn meal in some form or other is eaten three times a day, and in most families at least once a day.

Among the common corn-meal dishes eaten in the South are hoecake, a mixture of corn meal and water with or without salt, cooked in a frying pan or griddle; corn bread or pone, made with the addition of baking powder or its equivalent and baked in the oven; griddle cakes, prepared from a thin batter with the addition of a leavening agent; egg or spoon bread, differing from ordinary corn bread in that eggs are used; and corn dumplings, usually cooked with either meat or vegetables. Corn meal is used in puddings, waffles, poultry dressing, meat and fish dishes. There is also a large consumption of mush made from hominy or grits and of lye hominy prepared from the whole grain after removal of the hull with caustic soda.

The corn and grits used in the South are prepared almost exclusively from white dent corn in both northern and southern mills. In the North, where corn products are consumed to a less degree, the preference is usually given to meal made from yellow corn, although the so-called hominy (grits) made from white corn is a common breakfast cereal. Hasty pudding (corn mush) and Johnny cake (corresponding to the hoecake of the South) have been made in New England households since colonial days. Indian pudding, a popular dessert prepared from corn meal, milk, and eggs, has long been regarded as one of the necessary adjuncts to the New England Thanksgiving dinner.

The dent varieties, both white and yellow, are generally used in the manufacture of meal and grits. A white variety known as "hominy corn," extensively grown in eastern Illinois and western Indiana, is preferred by many millers. In Rhode Island white flint corn has been milled for generations to produce a kind of meal much esteemed by the residents of that State, and in some other regions flint corn is milled to a limited extent.

MANUFACTURE OF CORN MEAL.

Although the consumption of meal is greatest in the South, the production of corn is greatest in the States of the Middle West forming the "corn belt." In the South the acreage is given up largely to the production of cotton, and the corn crop is not sufficient to

[1] Personal communication.

supply the local demand. While the southern corn is used as far as it goes, and is usually preferred, the larger part of the meal is either ground by southern mills from western corn or is milled in the North, usually in or near the region where the corn is grown.

THE STONE PROCESS.

With few exceptions the southern mills grind the corn by stones. The chief difference between the process of the small country mill with a single "run of stone," which grinds the grist that the farmer brings in on his back, and that of the large mill, with several to 40 or 50 "run of stone," is in the perfection of the grain-cleaning and the bolting systems. In many of the mills native stones, notably the so-called Esopus stones from New York quarries, are preferred to French buhrs for the reason that they produce a soft, smooth meal, which is highly esteemed by southern cooks.

The term "water meal" has been applied indiscriminately to old-fashioned, stone-ground meal regardless of the fact that at the present time steam or even electricity is often the motive power. Naturally the nature of the milling machinery and not the power determines the character of the meal. Stone-ground meal is either milled from corn without bolting, and consequently does not differ in composition from the whole grain, except for the removal of a small amount of chaff by a simple fan device, or is bolted to remove the coarse bran and germ. It is stated that when unbolted meal is used the cook is accustomed to put it through a sifter, thus removing the greater part of the coarse, branny tissues, so that the final result attained is the same as if bolted meal had been used. Stone-ground meal, owing to the incomplete removal of the fatty matter of the germ, is characterized by its rich oily flavor, the taste for which when once acquired is not satisfied by degerminated meal in which the fat content is reduced to the minimum.

In the small stone mills no attempt is made to dry either the corn or the meal, although it is well known that the corn must be moderately dry in order to prevent gumming in the mill and to insure keeping for a reasonable length of time. The friction of grinding, especially when the stones are set for producing a very fine, soft meal, develops considerable heat, which serves to drive off much of the moisture. In certain of the large mills drying apparatus is used to some extent for removing the excess of moisture from either the corn or the meal. In many of the mills, however, dependence is placed on the heat developed during grinding as well as on the exposure of the hot meal to the air in open conveyors.

THE ROLLER PROCESS.

In northern mills rolls have largely replaced stones, the process being one of gradual reduction similar to that employed in wheat milling. Preliminary to grinding, the corn is put through the "degerminator," which loosens the germ, permitting its separation for the manufacture of corn oil. In some mills corrugated rolls take the place of the degerminator, but the product thus obtained may be contaminated with a considerable amount of oil. Reels and sifters similar to those employed in wheat milling are used in making the separation. In addition to the "degerminator" special forms of aspirators and driers, quite unknown in wheat milling, are peculiar to this process.

Corn, like wheat, is tempered by steam or water preliminary to the milling process, but it is considered necessary to dry the products, except in the summer months after the corn has become dry through long standing. This drying is usually effected in revolving horizontal cylinders containing steam pipes. The products and by-products are subjected to this drying process either before or after separation. The drying of the corn itself preliminary to milling is unusual.

PRODUCTS OF CORN MILLING.

Not only corn meal, but usually also grits and corn flour, as well as germ and feed, are obtained as the products and by-products of the roller process. In some mills two or more grades of meal are separated. These are designated either for table or brewers' use, or, according to the size of the particles, as coarse or fine. Grits and meal for brewers' use are the main products of some of the largest mills.

The grits are either used as such by the brewer or are rolled or "flaked" in order to facilitate malting. Special machines turn out continuous ribbons of rolled grits which are later broken up into thin flakes a fraction of an inch in size. A similar product serves for the manufacture of toasted corn flakes, a well-known, ready-for-use breakfast cereal.

Brewers' meal differs from table meal in that it contains more of the floury part of the kernel. The difference, however, is not marked and either can be used for both purposes. The brewing industry demands that both grits and meal contain not only the highest possible amount of starch, but also a low percentage of fat. A low percentage of moisture is also desired, not merely to increase thereby the percentage of starch but also to insure better keeping qualities.

Corn flour, the finely divided material separated by bolting, may be regarded as a by-product of the gradual reduction process. It serves as an ingredient of pancake flour and also as a filler or binder for sausage.

The germ, detached from the grain in the early stage of the process by the degerminator, is pressed for the manufacture of corn oil. Corn cake, the residue from the presses, is utilized for cattle food.

Corn bran corresponds to the bran obtained in the milling of wheat in the modern flour mill, and corn feed is the cattle food consisting usually of a mixture of bran and the finely divided offal analogous to red dog flour of the wheat mill. The ground corn cake is often an ingredient of corn feed.

COMPOSITION OF THE PRODUCTS OF CORN MILLING.

The analyses reported under this head are of samples obtained from corn mills in different sections of the country. With few exceptions the samples of meal were taken at the mills by the authors, so far as possible from the streams of corn going to the milling apparatus and of finished products going to the packers. They represent the products of forty-one mills located in thirty-two towns and seventeen States. The samples were shipped without delay to the Chicago Food and Drug Inspection Laboratory for analysis, the determinations being made as soon as the samples were received.

METHODS OF ANALYSIS.

The analyses were made by the methods of the Association of Official Agricultural Chemists, with the exception of the acidity, which was determined by the method employed by Schindler [1] and described in detail by Black and Alsberg.[2]

The determination of moisture by drying for five hours at the temperature of boiling water in a current of dry hydrogen was carried out in the apparatus devised by Winton.[3] The results obtained by means of this apparatus were about 1 per cent higher than those obtained by drying for the same length of time and at the same temperature in an open dish. The reason for this difference is not clear, but is probably, in part at least, physical. The fact that the difference was well marked in the case of degerminated meal containing less than 1 per cent of fat precludes the assumption that the cause lies in the prevention of oxidation by the hydrogen method.

Great annoyance and sometimes heated disputes have resulted from discrepancies in the results of a moisture determination by different methods and in different laboratories, particularly those of the buyer and seller. As the process used in these experiments has given concordant results in mill laboratories as well as in those of the department, it is believed that the extra labor and expense involved as compared with drying in an open dish will recommend it, at least for use in standardizing such shorter processes as the official or trade chemist may find convenient. In this connection attention is directed to the modification of the Brown and Duvel apparatus adapted for the determination of moisture in meal which has recently been devised by Cox.[4] It is hoped that this method will be of great value

[1] Loc. cit. p. 37.

[2] Loc. cit. p. 10.

[3] Winton, A. L. Conn. Agr. Expt. Sta. Rept., 1889, p. 187; Leach, Albert E. Food Inspection and Analysis, p. 62.

[4] Cox, John H. A Special Flask for the Rapid Determination of Water in Flour and Meal. U. S. Dept. Agr. Bul. 56.

to the trade. So far there has not been opportunity to compare the results obtained by this apparatus with those by the gravimetric method employed in these investigations.

FULL SET OF PRODUCTS OF TWO ROLLER MILLS.

In Table 1 are given analyses of samples representing all the products and by-products obtained in two corn mills, one, grinding white corn, located in the Middle West, the other, grinding yellow corn, on the Pacific slope.

PROCESS OF MANUFACTURE.

A description of the process used in the white-corn mill, as furnished by the chemist, follows:

Number three[1] white corn is carried from the elevator or bin through a magnetic separator to remove nails, etc., then through a screen to remove large pieces of cobs or other foreign matter and over a fine screen to remove sand and grit. It is then aspirated with a strong air current to remove impurities of a light, fluffy nature.

The cleaned corn now goes through the tempering device and to the degerminator. In the latter machine the kernels are broken open, the germs are partly broken loose from the starchy portion of the grain, and the bran is partially removed. This broken corn is dried and allowed to flow through the hominy separator. In this machine the stock is led through a revolving sheet-iron cylinder, through the metal of which are numerous narrow slots. Within this cylinder are beaters revolving in the opposite direction from the cylinder. This removes some bran and most of the rotten grains, which latter are shattered into very fine particles as they pass through the degerminators.

From this cylinder the stock passes through a sizing reel which removes all the material fine enough to pass a number seven screen (seven meshes to the linear inch). At the same time it is aspirated to remove dust and bran. The coarse portion from this machine, which is now quite well cleaned, is passed through the first, second, and third break rolls, being screened after each break, separating flour, meal, fine grits, coarse grits, and hominy.

As the products attain the desired degree of fineness they are aspirated thoroughly before bagging.

In the yellow-corn mill both dent and flint corn, either separately or mixed, are milled, the process, as described by the head miller, being as follows:

The corn first passes through a degerminator which removes the bran and germ. It is then thoroughly dried and allowed to remain in the bin long enough to cool to about its normal temperature. From thence it passes through a series of rolls, being gradually reduced to the proper fineness. The chaffy material is removed by suction, after which the meal is sterilized at a temperature of 218° F., the process requiring a little over three minutes. When the meal has cooled off slightly it is packed in sacks or other suitable containers.

ANALYSES OF THE PRODUCTS.

A study of the analyses in Table 1 shows that the percentages of fat and ash in the white corn grits and in the coarse yellow corn meal correspond very closely to the percentages of these constituents

[1] This is the old No. 3 grade used by the trade prior to the adoption of the Government corn grades in July, 1914. Corn graded No. 4 on account of moisture is often used. No. 2 corn is found comparatively rarely and then only in summer and early fall.

in patent wheat flour, showing that the gradual reduction process eliminates quite completely the bran and impurities. The percentages of fat and ash in both kinds of white corn meal and in the fine yellow corn meal are about the same as those present in clear wheat flour. The analogy ceases in the case of protein, as the corn products with low fat and ash contents contain relatively high amounts of protein, whereas the reverse is true of the different grades of wheat flour.

TABLE 1.—*Composition of the products and by-products of corn milling.*

Product.	Analysis as received.							Analysis calculated to moisture-free basis.					
	Moisture.	Acidity.	Protein (N×6.25).	Fat.	Nitrogen-free extract.	Crude fiber.	Ash.	Acidity.	Protein (N×6.25).	Fat.	Nitrogen-free extract.	Crude fiber.	Ash.
White corn, products, and by-products:	*P. ct.*		*P. ct.*	*P. ct.*	*P. ct.*	*P. ct.*	*P. ct.*		*P. ct.*	*P. ct.*	*P. ct.*	*P. ct.*	*P. ct.*
Corn	13.52	27.5	9.12	3.62	70.50	2.02	1.22	31.8	10.55	4.19	81.51	2.34	1.41
Grits, coarse	13.07	16.4	8.78	.48	76.78	.53	.36	18.9	10.10	.55	88.33	.61	.41
Grits, fine	12.12	16.6	8.66	.64	77.68	.48	.42	18.9	9.85	.73	88.39	.55	.48
Meal, cream	11.97	19.1	7.85	1.41	77.65	.56	.56	21.7	8.92	1.60	88.20	.64	.64
Meal, brewers'	11.95	18.1	8.00	1.23	77.59	.64	.59	20.6	9.08	1.40	88.12	.73	.67
Flour	11.19	22.1	6.78	2.87	77.61	.80	.75	24.9	7.63	3.23	87.40	.90	.84
Germ	6.64	59.3	16.62	23.79	40.30	6.04	6.61	63.5	17.80	25.48	43.17	6.47	7.08
Germ cake	2.14	68.6	20.22	7.26	54.39	7.90	8.09	70.1	20.66	7.42	55.58	8.07	8.27
Feed (including bran)	11.00	52.4	11.69	8.44	60.99	5.03	2.85	58.9	13.13	9.48	68.54	5.65	3.20
Bran	10.13	49.2	8.43	6.71	62.85	9.72	2.16	54.7	9.38	7.47	69.93	10.82	2.40
Yellow corn, products, and by-products:													
Corn	13.45	35.4	9.16	5.10	68.89	2.06	1.34	40.9	10.58	5.89	79.60	2.38	1.55
Meal, bolted, coarse	12.88	18.0	9.78	.90	75.60	.45	.39	20.7	11.23	1.03	86.77	.52	.45
Meal, bolted, fine	13.10	21.1	9.09	2.19	74.48	.53	.61	24.3	10.46	2.52	85.71	.61	.70
Germ	11.29	62.5	13.34	18.07	49.25	3.98	4.07	70.5	15.04	20.37	55.51	4.49	4.59
Bran	10.37	66.5	9.06	11.00	57.19	9.68	2.70	74.2	10.11	12.27	63.81	10.80	3.01

It should be especially noted that the acidity of both the grits and the meal is much less than that of the corn, the figures being well within the limit 30, notwithstanding the high amount in the corn which was characteristic of the crop of 1913.

Corn flour is not comparable with any of the commercial grades of wheat flour, although in respect to both process and composition it has some resemblance to break flour. The acidity, fat, and ash contents are higher in the flour than in the meal and grits, whereas the protein content is lower.

The germ is characterized by its high content of acidity, protein, fat, fiber, and ash, all of which constituents, except the fat, are obviously further increased in percentage amount by pressing. The high acidity at once shows the chief seat of the acid-reacting materials and the advantage of degermination.

The samples of bran, while containing about the same amount of protein as the corn, are characterized by their higher fat, fiber, and ash content. The feed is still richer in fat and ash as well as in protein. These results show the value of this offal for feeding, but the high acidity is significant proof of its unsuitability for human food.

WHOLE-KERNEL STONE-GROUND MEAL.

The samples without exception were from southern mills. Analyses of both the meal and the corn from which it was milled appear in Table 2. As the corn was ground without the removal of any constituent other than some of the thin, papery chaff or "bee wing," the meal when ground should not differ materially from the corn in composition, except for a possible change in moisture content. Whether or not the moisture is less or greater than in the corn depends on the dryness of the latter and on the climate. Ordinarily there is a loss in grinding.

TABLE 2.—*Composition of whole-kernel, stone-ground meal and of corn from which meal was milled.*

Product.	Analysis as received.							Analysis calculated to moisture-free basis.					
	Moisture.	Acidity.	Protein (N×6.25).	Fat.	Nitrogen-free extract.	Crude fiber.	Ash.	Acidity.	Protein. (N×6.25).	Fat.	Nitrogen-free extract.	Crude fiber.	Ash.
White corn and meal:													
Mill No. 1, Alabama—	*P. ct.*		*P. ct.*	*P. ct.*	*P. ct.*	*P. ct.*	*P. ct.*		*P. ct.*	*P. ct.*	*P. ct.*	*P. ct.*	*P. ct.*
Corn, Middle West	13.05	32.0	8.47	3.70	71.49	2.00	1.29	36.8	9.74	4.26	82.22	2.30	1.48
Meal, unbolted	13.28	32.2	8.38	3.59	71.34	2.12	1.29	37.2	9.66	4.14	82.26	2.45	1.49
Mill No. 2, Alabama—													
Corn, Tennessee	12.41	20.0	8.25	4.16	71.90	2.00	1.28	22.8	9.42	4.75	82.09	2.28	1.46
Meal, unbolted	12.30	34.1	8.00	4.27	72.00	2.05	1.38	38.9	9.12	4.87	82.10	2.33	1.58
Mill No. 3, Georgia—													
Corn, Indiana	13.28	25.2	8.19	3.75	71.52	2.07	1.19	29.0	9.44	4.32	82.49	2.38	1.37
Meal, unbolted	11.97	26.0	8.47	3.65	72.52	2.15	1.24	29.5	9.62	4.15	82.38	2.44	1.41
Mill No. 4, Georgia—													
Corn	13.99	25.4	8.81	3.78	70.19	1.95	1.28	29.5	10.24	4.40	81.61	2.26	1.49
Meal, unbolted	12.38	27.4	8.66	3.81	71.83	1.98	1.34	31.3	9.88	4.35	81.98	2.26	1.53
Mill No. 5, Georgia—													
Corn, Middle West	14.04	23.0	8.59	3.55	70.54	2.04	1.24	26.8	10.00	4.13	82.06	2.37	1.44
Meal, unbolted	12.51	28.0	8.31	3.75	71.97	2.19	1.27	32.0	9.50	4.29	82.25	2.51	1.45
Mill No. 6, South Carolina—													
Corn, South Carolina	11.73	18.0	7.90	4.45	72.69	2.05	1.18	20.4	8.95	5.04	82.35	2.32	1.34
Meal, unbolted	11.16	20.7	7.94	4.39	73.21	2.10	1.20	23.3	8.94	4.94	82.41	2.36	1.35
Mill No. 7, Tennessee—													
Corn, Tennessee	11.82	18.0	7.00	4.29	73.56	2.07	1.26	20.4	7.94	4.87	83.42	2.34	1.43
Meal, entire kernel	13.09	24.5	7.25	4.18	72.25	2.01	1.22	28.2	8.34	4.81	83.13	2.32	1.40
Mill No. 8, Mississippi—													
Corn, Mississippi	12.13	31.0	9.09	4.42	71.06	2.07	1.23	35.3	10.35	5.03	80.87	2.35	1.40
Meal, unbolted	13.18	37.2	8.47	4.25	70.60	2.17	1.33	42.9	9.75	4.90	81.32	2.50	1.53
Mill No. 9, Mississippi—													
Corn, Kentucky	12.54	30.0	9.22	4.24	70.73	1.91	1.36	34.3	10.54	4.85	80.87	2.19	1.55
Meal, unbolted	12.31	42.7	9.41	4.18	70.74	1.99	1.37	48.7	10.73	4.77	80.67	2.27	1.56
Mill No. 10, Mississippi—													
Corn, Mississippi	11.86	24.7	8.19	4.63	71.88	2.09	1.35	28.1	9.29	5.26	81.55	2.37	1.53
Meal, unbolted	11.58	25.1	7.97	4.49	73.09	1.55	1.32	28.4	9.01	5.08	82.66	1.76	1.49
Mill No. 11, Missouri—													
Corn, Middle West	15.83	21.3	8.78	3.67	68.65	1.84	1.23	25.3	10.44	4.36	81.56	2.18	1.46
Meal, straight	10.17	21.3	9.03	3.56	74.52	1.36	1.36	23.7	10.05	3.96	82.96	1.51	1.52
Meal: Maximum	13.28	42.7	9.41	4.49	74.52	2.19	1.38	48.7	10.73	5.08	83.13	2.51	1.58
Meal: Minimum	10.17	20.7	7.25	3.56	70.60	1.36	1.20	23.3	8.34	3.96	80.67	1.51	1.35
Meal: Average	**12.18**	**29.0**	**8.35**	**4.01**	**72.19**	**1.97**	**1.30**	**33.1**	**9.51**	**4.57**	**82.19**	**2.25**	**1.48**

The remarkable agreement in the percentages other than moisture and acidity is as would be expected, but the greater amount of acidity in the meal requires explanation. That the acidity of both corn and freshly ground meal would be the same is obvious, but the increase in the meal is much more rapid than in the corn. In cases where the acidity of the meal is in excess the cause is directly traceable to delay in delivery of the samples, which in some instances was a week or more. Experience shows that corn will not materially increase in acidity during that time.

The acidity given in Table 2 for the corn should in all cases be taken as that of the corresponding meal at the time of grinding.

The excessive amount of acidity in some of the samples of meal when analyzed merely illustrates the difficulty in keeping meal of this type, which fact is further brought out by the results of the later experiments. (See Tables 12 and 14.)

BOLTED UNDEGERMINATED MEAL.

Results obtained in the analysis of bolted, undegerminated meal, as well as of the corn from which it was milled, appear in Table 3. The mills in which the corn was ground are all located in the South except No. 18, which is in Iowa, and No. 35, which is in Rhode Island. In most of the mills grinding was done by stones; in Nos. 18, 36, 37, and 38, however, rolls were used. The corn ground in all the southern mills was white dent, in the Iowa mill it was yellow dent, and in the Rhode Island mill it was white flint.

TABLE 3.—*Composition of bolted, undegerminated corn meal and of corn from which meal was milled.*

Product.	Analysis as received.							Analysis calculated to moisture-free basis.					
	Moisture.	Acidity.	Protein (N×6.25).	Fat.	Nitrogen-free extract.	Crude fiber.	Ash.	Acidity.	Protein (N×6.25).	Fat.	Nitrogen-free extract.	Crude fiber.	Ash.
White corn and meal:													
Mill No. 1, Alabama—	*P. ct.*		*P. ct.*	*P. ct.*	*P. ct.*	*P. ct.*	*P. ct.*		*P. ct.*	*P. ct.*	*P. ct.*	*P. ct.*	*P. ct.*
Corn, Middle West..	13.05	32.0	8.47	3.70	71.49	2.00	1.29	36.8	9.74	4.26	82.22	2.30	1.48
Meal, bolted.........	14.94	33.8	7.75	2.92	72.53	.83	1.03	29.8	9.11	3.43	85.27	.98	1.21
Mill No. 4, Georgia—													
Corn.................	13.99	25.4	8.81	3.78	70.19	1.95	1.28	29.5	10.24	4.40	81.61	2.26	1.49
Meal, bolted.........	12.60	27.7	9.09	3.72	71.94	1.48	1.17	31.7	10.40	4.26	82.30	1.70	1.34
Mill No. 34, Georgia—													
Corn.................	12.79	23.5	8.93	4.30	70.62	2.06	1.30	26.9	10.24	4.93	80.98	2.36	1.49
Meal, bolted.........	11.32	26.2	9.22	4.35	72.12	1.64	1.35	29.6	10.39	4.90	81.34	1.85	1.52
Mill, No. 5, Georgia—													
Corn, Middle West..	14.04	23.0	8.59	3.55	70.54	2.04	1.24	26.8	10.00	4.13	82.06	2.37	1.44
Meal, bolted.........	11.60	25.5	8.87	3.78	72.77	1.68	1.30	28.8	10.04	4.27	82.32	1.90	1.47
Mill No. 21, Missouri—													
Corn, Middle West..	14.87	25.8	8.75	3.58	69.47	1.99	1.34	30.3	10.28	4.20	81.62	2.34	1.56
Meal, bolted.........	12.78	24.1	8.97	3.04	72.92	1.17	1.12	27.6	10.28	3.49	83.61	1.34	1.28
Mill No. 9, Mississippi—													
Corn, Kentucky.....	12.54	30.0	9.22	4.24	70.73	1.91	1.36	34.3	10.54	4.85	80.87	2.19	1.55
Meal, bolted.........	12.45	44.5	9.06	4.72	70.88	1.38	1.51	50.8	10.35	5.39	80.96	1.58	1.72
Mill No. 35, Rhode Island—													
Corn, R. I. flint.....	12.93	22.5	9.50	4.47	69.94	1.83	1.33	25.8	10.91	5.13	80.33	2.10	1.53
Meal, bolted.........	10.12	21.7	8.97	4.83	73.39	1.31	1.38	24.2	9.98	5.38	81.64	1.46	1.54

TABLE 3.—*Composition of bolted, undegerminated corn meal and of corn from which meal was milled*—Continued.

Product.	Analysis as received.							Analysis calculated to moisture-free basis.					
	Moisture.	Acidity.	Protein (N×6.25).	Fat.	Nitrogen-free extract.	Crude fiber.	Ash.	Acidity.	Protein (N×6.25).	Fat.	Nitrogen-free extract.	Crude fiber.	Ash.
White corn and meal—Continued.													
Mill No. 36, Tennessee—	*P. ct.*		*P. ct.*	*P. ct.*	*P. ct.*	*P. ct.*	*P. ct.*		*P. ct.*	*P. ct.*	*P. ct.*	*P. ct.*	*P. ct.*
Corn, Middle West	13.14	26.2	8.28	3.85	71.45	2.04	1.24	30.2	9.54	4.43	82.25	2.35	1.43
Meal, plain	13.72	46.0	8.78	4.83	69.33	1.73	1.61	53.3	10.17	5.59	80.37	2.01	1.86
Meal, bolted	14.25	45.5	9.03	5.14	68.31	1.62	1.65	53.1	10.53	6.00	79.66	1.89	1.92
Mill No. 37, Tennessee—													
Corn, uncleaned	12.60	24.7	8.34	3.73	72.06	2.00	1.27	28.3	9.55	4.27	82.44	2.29	1.45
Meal, cream	14.39	31.0	7.47	2.75	73.76	1.77	.86	36.2	8.72	3.22	86.15	.90	1.01
Mill No. 38, Tennessee—													
Corn, Tennessee	13.81	19.2	9.40	4.63	68.83	1.94	1.39	22.3	10.91	5.38	79.85	2.25	1.61
Meal, bolted	15.09	27.5	8.47	3.58	70.54	1.15	1.17	32.3	9.97	4.22	83.07	1.36	1.38
Mill No. 39, Tennessee—													
Corn, Tennessee	14.19	21.7	9.09	4.18	69.46	1.75	1.33	25.3	10.59	4.87	80.96	2.03	1.55
Meal, bolted	13.31	24.0	9.18	4.11	71.19	.86	1.35	27.7	10.59	4.74	82.13	.99	1.55
Meal, pearl	12.87	20.7	8.78	2.98	73.54	.83	1.00	23.8	10.07	3.42	84.41	.96	1.14
Mill No. 40, Virginia—													
Corn, Middle West	14.69	27.7	8.72	3.55	69.67	2.14	1.23	32.5	10.23	4.16	81.66	2.51	1.44
Meal, bolted	12.51	28.5	8.84	3.90	71.66	1.77	1.32	32.6	10.11	4.45	81.90	2.03	1.51
Meal: Maximum	15.09	46.0	9.22	5.14	73.76	1.77	1.65	53.3	10.59	6.00	86.15	2.03	1.92
Meal: Minimum	10.12	20.7	7.47	2.75	68.31	.77	.86	23.8	8.72	3.22	79.66	.90	1.01
Meal: **Average**	**12.99**	**30.5**	**8.75**	**3.90**	**71.79**	**1.30**	**1.27**	**35.1**	**10.05**	**4.48**	**82.51**	**1.50**	**1.46**
Yellow corn and meal:													
Mill No. 18, Iowa—													
Corn, Middle West	16.95	19.6	8.59	3.55	67.58	2.06	1.27	23.6	10.35	4.28	81.37	2.48	1.52
Meal, Porto Rico trade	16.82	24.3	7.16	1.95	72.79	.66	.62	29.2	8.61	2.35	87.52	.79	.73

The effect of bolting in all cases was a decrease in fiber, but further than this no general rule can be deduced, as conditions such as fineness of grinding and the size of the meshes of the bolts exert more influence than the mere fact of bolting. The markedly high acidity in the meal from mills 9 and 36 was doubtless due to the length of time elapsing between grinding and analysis, which for reasons already stated was from 9 to 12 days.

DEGERMINATED BOLTED ROLLER-GROUND MEAL.

The general name "cream meal" is applied to degerminated, bolted, roller-ground meal when made from white corn, but various terms are used for the corresponding product from yellow corn. Analyses of both white and yellow meal and of the corn from which the meal was milled will be found in Table 4. The samples were from mills located in the Northern States and in Tennessee. All the mills were equipped with rolls and modern machinery for cleaning the grain as well as for separating and drying the products. Most of the mills employed degerminators, while others depended on corrugated rolls for loosening the germ and bran from the endosperm.

TABLE 4.—*Composition of degerminated, bolted, roller-ground meal and of corn from which meal was milled.*

Product.	Analysis as received.							Analysis calculated to moisture-free basis.					
	Moisture.	Acidity.	Protein (N×6.25).	Fat.	Nitrogen-free extract.	Crude fiber.	Ash.	Acidity.	Protein (N×6.25).	Fat.	Nitrogen-free extract.	Crude fiber.	Ash.
White corn and meal:													
Mill No. 12, Illinois—	P. ct.		P. ct.	P. ct.	P. ct.	P. ct.	P. ct.		P. ct.	P. ct.	P. ct.	P. ct.	P. ct.
Corn, Middle West	16.28	19.0	8.41	3.39	68.72	2.00	1.20	22.7	10.03	4.04	82.11	2.39	1.43
Meal, pearl	13.08	10.6	6.56	.99	78.40	.62	.35	12.2	7.54	1.14	90.21	.71	.40
Mill No. 13, Illinois—													
Corn, Middle West	13.92	18.5	8.63	3.55	70.49	2.19	1.22	21.5	10.02	4.12	81.91	2.54	1.41
Meal, cream	16.17	13.2	6.63	.80	75.36	.67	.37	15.7	7.90	.94	89.93	.80	.43
Mill No. 14, Illinois—													
Corn, Middle West	17.11	23.8	8.16	3.37	68.12	2.06	1.18	28.7	9.84	4.07	82.19	2.48	1.42
Meal, brewers'	14.58	15.6	5.81	1.15	77.35	.73	.38	18.2	6.80	1.35	90.55	.85	.45
Mill No. 15, Indiana—													
Corn, Middle West	17.38	19.8	8.25	3.34	67.86	2.00	1.17	23.9	9.96	4.03	82.18	2.42	1.41
Meal, cream	14.44	11.9	6.16	1.28	77.06	.67	.39	13.9	7.18	1.49	90.09	.78	.46
Mill No. 16, Indiana—													
Corn, Middle West	17.32	19.0	8.50	3.26	67.75	2.02	1.15	22.9	10.25	3.93	82.00	2.44	1.38
Meal, cream	13.85	13.5	7.50	.87	76.85	.58	.35	15.6	8.69	1.00	89.24	.67	.40
Mill No. 17, Iowa—													
Corn, Middle West	16.24	22.5	8.81	3.17	68.54	2.02	1.22	26.9	10.52	3.79	81.82	2.41	1.46
Meal, cream	13.97	15.7	7.19	.75	77.07	.61	.41	18.2	8.36	.87	89.59	.71	.47
Mill No. 18, Iowa—													
Corn, Middle West	16.09	27.8	8.50	3.77	68.45	1.98	1.21	33.1	10.13	4.49	81.58	2.36	1.44
Meal, pearl	18.28	20.8	7.00	1.22	72.41	.60	.49	25.5	8.57	1.50	88.60	.74	.59
Mill No. 19, Maryland—													
Corn, Chicago	14.71	21.2	8.31	3.68	70.04	2.09	1.17	24.9	9.74	4.31	82.13	2.45	1.37
Meal, fancy cream	13.78	23.0	6.28	1.43	77.35	.68	.48	26.7	7.29	1.66	89.70	.79	.56
Mill No. 20, Michigan—													
Corn, Middle West	12.92	23.1	8.59	3.70	71.47	2.07	1.25	26.5	9.87	4.25	82.06	2.38	1.44
Meal	12.83	18.9	7.97	1.54	76.39	.64	.63	21.7	9.14	1.76	87.64	.74	.72
Mill No. 21, Missouri—													
Corn, Middle West	14.87	25.8	8.75	3.58	69.47	1.99	1.34	30.3	10.28	4.20	81.62	2.34	1.56
Meal, cream	12.81	21.6	8.84	2.08	74.59	.87	.81	24.7	10.14	2.39	85.56	.99	.92
Mill No. 22, Missouri—													
Corn	15.19	24.2	8.81	3.54	69.20	1.92	1.34	28.4	10.39	4.17	81.59	2.27	1.58
Meal, cream	13.77	14.5	7.47	1.80	75.64	.69	.63	16.8	8.66	2.08	87.73	.80	.73
Mill No. 23, Missouri—													
Corn	16.19	23.3	8.00	3.52	69.10	1.96	1.23	27.8	9.54	4.20	82.45	2.34	1.47
Meal, cream	14.78	19.1	6.81	1.60	75.58	.70	.53	22.3	7.99	1.88	88.69	.82	.62
Mill No. 24, New York—													
Corn, Middle West	13.25	21.1	8.81	3.77	70.88	2.06	1.23	24.4	10.16	4.35	81.70	2.37	1.42
Meal, cream	13.56	14.7	5.91	1.45	77.86	.72	.50	17.1	6.83	1.68	90.07	.84	.58
Mill No. 25, Pennsylvania—													
Corn, Middle West	14.10	27.0	8.56	3.56	70.48	2.11	1.19	31.4	9.97	4.14	82.05	2.45	1.39
Meal, cream	14.08	20.2	6.65	1.75	76.12	.77	.63	23.6	7.75	2.04	88.58	.90	.73
Meal, Southern trade	13.59	22.3	6.66	2.04	76.25	.80	.66	25.8	7.70	2.36	88.24	.93	.77
Mill No. 26, Tennessee—													
Corn, Illinois	13.87	26.0	7.97	3.60	71.26	2.08	1.22	30.2	9.25	4.19	82.73	2.42	1.41
Meal, cream	12.41	17.5	6.84	2.00	77.48	.60	.67	20.0	7.81	2.28	88.45	.69	.77
Mill No. 27, Tennessee—													
Corn, Middle West	12.63	24.2	8.31	3.67	72.16	2.06	1.17	27.7	9.51	4.20	82.59	2.36	1.34
Meal, cream	12.54	18.7	7.72	2.31	75.74	.96	.73	21.4	8.82	2.64	86.60	1.10	.84
Mill No. 28, Tennessee—													
Corn, Middle West	12.74	21.0	9.22	4.72	70.43	1.72	1.17	24.1	10.56	5.41	80.72	1.97	1.34
Meal, cream	11.97	15.4	7.47	1.44	77.87	.72	.53	17.5	8.48	1.63	88.47	.82	.60
Mill No. 29, Wisconsin—													
Corn	17.83	26.1	8.50	3.28	67.24	2.03	1.12	31.7	10.34	3.99	81.84	2.47	1.36
Meal, cream	15.18	15.6	6.56	.70	76.46	.73	.37	18.4	7.73	.83	90.14	.86	.44
Meal Maximum	18.28	23.0	8.84	2.31	78.40	.96	.81	26.7	10.14	2.64	90.55	1.10	.92
Meal Minimum	11.97	10.6	5.81	.70	72.41	.58	.35	12.2	6.80	.83	85.56	.67	.40
Meal Average	**13.98**	**17.0**	**6.95**	**1.43**	**76.42**	**.70**	**.52**	**19.7**	**8.07**	**1.66**	**88.85**	**.82**	**.60**
Yellow corn and meal:													
Mill No. 30, Iowa—													
Corn	17.92	20.8	8.31	3.77	66.72	2.09	1.19	25.2	10.12	4.58	81.32	2.54	1.44
Meal, fine	16.18	14.5	6.63	.75	75.63	.55	.26	17.3	7.91	.89	90.24	.65	.31
Meal, granular	15.54	14.0	7.94	.33	75.49	.46	.24	16.6	9.40	.39	89.39	.55	.27

TABLE 4.—*Composition of degerminated, bolted, roller-ground meal and of corn from which meal was milled*—Continued.

Product.	Analysis as received.							Analysis calculated to moisture-free basis.					
	Moisture.	Acidity.	Protein (N×6.25).	Fat.	Nitrogen-free extract.	Crude fiber.	Ash.	Acidity.	Protein (N×6.25).	Fat.	Nitrogen-free extract.	Crude fiber.	Ash.
Yellow corn and meal—Continued.													
Mill No. 18, Iowa—	*P. ct.*		*P. ct.*	*P. ct.*	*P. ct.*	*P. ct.*	*P. ct.*		*P. ct.*	*P. ct.*	*P. ct.*	*P. ct.*	*P. ct.*
Corn, Middle West..	16.75	19.7	8.53	3.68	67.63	2.14	.27 1	23.6	10.25	4.42	81.24	2.57	1.52
Meal, cream..........	17.85	19.0	7.37	1.47	71.98	.72	.61	23.1	8.98	1.79	87.62	.88	.73
Mill No. 31, Michigan—													
Corn, Middle West..	12.73	21.9	8.97	3.77	71.16	2.12	1.25	25.1	10.27	4.34	81.53	2.43	1.43
Meal, cream..........	13.33	19.2	7.50	1.81	76.02	.69	.65	22.2	8.65	2.09	87.72	.79	.75
Mill No. 32, Michigan—													
Corn, Middle West..	14.87	23.0	8.34	3.72	69.53	2.24	1.30	27.1	9.80	4.37	81.67	2.63	1.53
Meal, granular......	14.71	17.9	7.47	.78	75.97	.59	.48	21.0	8.75	.92	89.08	.69	.56
Mill No. 24, New York—													
Corn, Middle West..	12.91	25.5	8.72	3.88	70.86	2.29	1.34	29.3	10.01	4.45	81.37	2.63	1.54
Meal, table..........	13.01	19.7	8.63	1.40	75.64	.76	.56	22.7	9.92	1.61	86.96	.87	.64
Mill No. 33, Wisconsin—													
Corn, Dakota........	16.87	31.0	8.56	3.69	67.65	2.10	1.13	37.3	10.29	4.44	81.39	2.52	1.36
Meal, granular.......	14.12	16.2	8.00	.59	76.40	.59	.30	18.8	9.32	.69	88.95	.69	.35
Meal, bolted.........	14.88	15.7	6.63	.82	76.64	.69	.34	18.4	7.79	.96	90.04	.81	.40
Meal Maximum...	17.85	19.7	8.63	1.81	76.64	.76	.65	23.1	9.92	2.09	90.24	.88	.75
Meal Minimum....	13.01	14.0	6.63	.33	71.98	.46	.24	16.6	7.79	.39	86.96	.55	.27
Meal **Average**....	**14.95**	**17.0**	**7.52**	**.99**	**75.48**	**.63**	**.43**	**20.0**	**8.84**	**1.17**	**88.75**	**.74**	**.50**

The analyses calculated to the moisture-free basis show that the process invariably yielded a meal containing less acidity, protein, fat, fiber, and ash, as well as more nitrogen-free extract than the corn. The range in acidity of the white meal is from 10.6 to 23, and of the yellow meal from 14 to 19.7, in all cases calculated to the material as received.

The fact that the acidity and fat are much lower than in the corn shows superior keeping qualities. The tendency to spoilage is further diminished by drying, at least during the winter and spring when the corn carries an excessive amount of moisture. Without drying the meal may contain even more moisture than the corn, due to the tempering with steam or water to facilitate separation of the germ and bran. The keeping qualities of meal of this type are further brought out in the experiments described on subsequent pages (see Tables 8, 10, 12, and 14).

LOW GRADE OR "STANDARD" TABLE MEAL.

Analyses of low grade or "standard" table meal and of the corn from which the meal was milled appear in Table 5. This type of meal is a by-product of mills producing a higher grade of meal or grits or both and is intermediate between such products and the feed. While it differs greatly in composition, the average amounts of acidity, protein, fat, fiber and ash are more and of nitrogen-free extract less than in cream meal. As compared with the corn, it is sometimes richer and sometimes poorer in fat. This "standard" meal is consumed largely by the poorer classes in the South.

TABLE 5.—*Composition of low grade ("standard") table meal and of corn from which the meal was milled with removal of grits or high grade meal and feed.*

Product.	Analysis as received.							Analysis calculated to moisture-free basis.					
	Moisture.	Acidity.	Protein (N×6.25).	Fat.	Nitrogen-free extract.	Crude fiber.	Ash.	Acidity.	Protein. (N×6.25).	Fat.	Nitrogen-free extract.	Crude fiber.	Ash.
White corn and meal:													
Mill No. 19, Maryland—	*P. ct.*		*P. ct.*	*P. ct.*	*P. ct.*	*P. ct.*	*P. ct.*		*P. ct.*	*P. ct.*	*P. ct.*	*P. ct.*	*P. ct.*
Corn, Middle West..	14.71	21.2	8.31	3.68	70.04	2.09	1.17	24.9	9.74	4.31	82.13	2.45	1.37
Meal, standard......	14.65	26.2	7.06	2.83	73.81	.80	.85	30.7	8.27	3.31	86.48	.94	1.00
Mill No. 11, Missouri—													
Corn................	15.83	21.3	8.78	3.67	68.65	1.84	1.23	25.3	10.44	4.36	81.56	2.18	1.46
Meal, standard......	10.01	24.1	9.97	4.34	72.31	1.80	1.57	26.7	11.07	4.82	80.37	2.00	1.74
Mill No. 22, Missouri—													
Corn, Middle West..	15.19	24.2	8.81	3.54	69.20	1.92	1.34	28.4	10.39	4.17	81.59	2.27	1.58
Meal, standard......	11.51	21.8	8.59	3.36	74.39	.99	1.16	24.6	9.72	3.80	84.05	1.12	1.31
Mill No. 23, Missouri—													
Corn................	16.19	23.3	8.00	3.52	69.10	1.96	1.23	27.8	9.54	4.20	82.45	2.34	1.47
Meal, standard......	13.42	20.8	8.15	3.96	72.05	1.12	1.30	24.0	9.42	4.58	83.20	1.30	1.50
Mill No. 37, Tennessee—													
Corn, Illinois.......	12.60	24.7	8.34	3.73	72.06	2.00	1.27	28.3	9.55	4.27	82.44	2.29	1.45
Meal, standard......	14.03	44.5	9.15	5.26	68.26	1.74	1.56	51.8	10.65	6.12	79.40	2.02	1.81
Mill No. 26, Tennessee—													
Corn, Illinois.......	13.87	26.0	7.97	3.60	71.26	2.08	1.22	30.2	9.25	4.19	82.73	2.42	1.41
Meal, standard......	12.10	19.7	7.94	3.48	74.33	.98	1.17	22.5	9.03	3.96	84.56	1.12	1.33
Mill No. 27, Tennessee—													
Corn................	12.63	24.2	8.31	3.67	72.16	2.06	1.17	27.7	9.51	4.20	82.59	2.36	1.34
Meal, standard......	12.03	23.2	8.62	3.61	73.15	1.44	1.15	26.4	9.79	4.10	83.16	1.64	1.31
Mill No. 28, Tennessee—													
Corn................	12.74	21.0	9.22	4.72	70.43	1.72	1.17	24.1	10.56	5.41	80.72	1.97	1.34
Meal, standard......	11.56	21.5	9.90	4.32	71.40	1.29	1.53	24.3	11.20	4.88	80.73	1.46	1.73
Meal {Maximum...	14.65	44.5	9.97	5.26	74.39	1.80	1.57	58.1	11.20	6.12	86.48	2.02	1.81
Meal {Minimum....	10.01	19.7	7.05	2.83	68.26	.80	.85	22.5	8.27	3.31	79.40	.94	1.00
Meal {**Average.....**	**12.41**	**25.2**	**8.67**	**3.89**	**72.48**	**1.27**	**1.28**	**28.9**	**9.89**	**4.15**	**82.74**	**1.45**	**1.47**

GRITS.

Table 6 shows the composition of five samples of table grits and six samples of brewers' grits taken from mills in the Middle West. The difference in composition between the two classes lies chiefly in the lower percentage of fat in the brewers' grits.

TABLE 6.—*Composition of table and brewers' corn grits.*

Product.	Analysis of original material.							Analysis calculated to moisture-free basis.					
	Moisture.	Acidity.	Protein (N×6.25).	Fat.	Nitrogen-free extract.	Crude fiber.	Ash.	Acidity.	Protein. (N×6.25).	Fat.	Nitrogen-free extract.	Crude fiber.	Ash.
Table grits:	*P. ct.*		*P. ct.*	*P. ct.*	*P. ct.*	*P. ct.*	*P. ct.*		*P. ct.*	*P. ct.*	*P. ct.*	*P. ct.*	*P. ct.*
Mill No. 15, Indiana	14.12	15.0	7.41	0.86	76.64	0.61	0.36	17.5	8.63	1.00	89.24	0.71	0.42
Mill No. 16, Indiana	14.12	16.2	7.47	.73	76.70	.62	.36	18.9	8.69	.85	89.32	.72	.42
Mill No. 17, Iowa	14.20	15.6	8.50	.85	75.40	.58	.47	18.2	9.91	.99	87.87	.68	.55
Mill No. 11, Missouri	10.92	18.3	9.28	2.32	75.68	.88	.92	20.5	10.40	2.61	84.97	.99	1.03
Mill No. 23, Missouri	12.53	14.3	8.13	1.68	76.28	.79	.59	16.3	9.29	1.92	87.22	.90	.67
Maximum	14.20	18.3	9.28	2.32	76.70	.88	.92	20.5	10.40	2.61	89.32	.99	1.03
Minimum	10.92	14.3	7.41	.73	75.40	.58	.36	16.3	8.63	.85	84.97	.68	.42
Average	**13.18**	**15.9**	**8.16**	**1.29**	**76.13**	**.70**	**.54**	**18.3**	**9.38**	**1.47**	**87.73**	**.80**	**.62**
Brewers' grits:													
Mill No. 12, Illinois	13.42	13.1	7.78	.43	77.60	.54	.23	15.1	8.98	.50	89.62	.63	.27
Mill No. 13, Illinois	15.87	23.9	7.75	.72	74.63	.67	.36	28.3	9.21	.86	88.70	.80	.43
Mill No. 14, Illinois	14.11	14.8	7.12	.75	77.03	.65	.34	17.2	8.29	.87	89.69	.75	.40
Mill No. 41, Indiana	15.63	15.7	7.56	.69	75.28	.52	.32	18.6	8.95	.82	89.25	.61	.37
Mill No. 22, Missouri	13.80	14.1	8.22	.72	76.34	.59	.33	16.3	9.54	.83	88.56	.68	.39
Mill No. 29, Wisconsin	15.12	16.8	7.84	.72	75.22	.73	.37	19.8	9.23	.85	88.62	.86	.44
Maximum	15.87	23.9	8.22	.75	77.60	.73	.37	28.3	9.54	.87	89.69	.86	.44
Minimum	13.42	13.1	7.12	.43	74.63	.52	.23	15.1	8.29	.50	88.56	.61	.27
Average	**14.66**	**16.4**	**7.71**	**.67**	**76.01**	**.62**	**.33**	**19.2**	**9.03**	**.79**	**89.08**	**.72**	**.38**

As shown by the analyses in Table 1, grits contain less fat, fiber and ash, but more protein than meal of the same mill run, although the difference is not always well marked, especially as much of the cream meal may be classed as a kind of fine grits.

SPOILAGE OF MEAL.

It is well recognized that spoiled corn should not be used for table meal and that when good corn is used the corn or the product should be dried to insure keeping. Spoilage is most common during the spring which is designated by the trade as the "germinating season." At this season when the whole kernel is ready to germinate it is reasoned that the germ tissues in the meal also show a tendency toward activity. The relation of season to spoilage is more probably that of temperature. Meal should keep through the germinating season if held in cold storage. On the other hand, it will spoil in the winter months if it contains an excess of moisture and is kept in warm storage. That the presence of the germ in the meal increases the tendency to spoilage has been known in a general way to the trade and has been emphasized by Schindler, Black, and Alsberg and other investigators.

Other things equal, grits keep better than meal, and meal made from the horny part of the kernel better than that containing the floury part. Evidently the mechanical condition as well as the composition is an important factor in determining the keeping qualities.

RELATION OF MOISTURE CONTENT TO KEEPING QUALITY OF DEGERMINATED BOLTED ROLLER-GROUND MEAL.

These experiments were carried on in two series, the first with ton lots and the second with carload lots. The meal used in both series was ground during the month of May, 1913, at the mill of the American Hominy Company, Terre Haute, Indiana. Each lot of meal was divided into two parts, one of which was shipped to Savannah, Georgia; the other to Chicago, Illinois. At both places the meal was stored in public warehouses designed for products of this nature, sample bags being withdrawn from month to month for chemical analysis and tests as to quality. The analyses of the meal as ground were made at the Chicago Food and Drug Inspection Laboratory, as were also the analyses at the end of each period of the meal stored at that center. Analyses of the meal stored at Savannah were made at the Government food laboratory located in that city. In addition to the usual chemical determinations, the general appearance of the meal and the taste and flavor of the mush prepared from the meal were noted.

STORAGE EXPERIMENTS WITH TON LOTS OF MEAL MILLED MAY 7, 1913.

DESCRIPTION AND ANALYSES OF THE MEAL AS MILLED.

Five lots of 1 ton each were milled to contain percentages of moisture ranging from 11.41 to 16.86. Since the corn used, owing to the good quality of the crop of 1912 and the lateness of the season, was quite dry, the meal ground without any drying whatever (lot B) contained only 15.04 per cent of moisture. In order to secure one lot with a higher moisture content, such as would have been present in undried meal milled earlier in the season, water in addition to the amount usually employed for tempering was added to the corn. In this manner the percentage of moisture in lot A was raised to 16.86. It was recognized that meal thus prepared was not strictly comparable with that made without the addition of water from corn with a higher moisture content, and due allowance was made in interpreting the results.

TABLE 7.—*Composition of ton lots of degerminated, bolted, roller-ground corn meal, containing different amounts of moisture, as milled May 7, 1913, for use in storage experiments.*

Product.	Moisture.	Acidity.	Protein (N×6.25).	Fat.	Nitrogen-free extract.	Crude fiber.	Ash.
	Per cent.		*Per cent.*	*Per cent.*	*Per cent.*	*Per cent.*	*Per cent.*
Meal as milled:							
Lot A, undried, water added	16.86	14.7	6.53	0.71	75.13	0.49	0.28
Lot B, undried	15.04	14.0	6.50	.94	76.65	.52	.35
Lot C, medium dried	13.41	14.1	6.69	1.05	77.87	.59	.39
Lot D, medium dried	13.27	13.4	6.66	.80	78.32	.59	.36
Lot E, high dried	11.41	11.9	6.72	1.32	79.47	.62	.46
Moisture-free meal:							
Lot A, undried, water added	......	17.7	7.85	.86	90.36	.59	.34
Lot B, undried	......	16.5	7.65	1.11	90.22	.61	.41
Lot C, medium dried	......	16.3	7.73	1.21	89.92	.69	.45
Lot D, medium dried	......	15.5	7.68	.92	90.30	.68	.42
Lot E, high dried	......	13.4	7.58	1.49	89.71	.70	.52

Lots C, D, and E were dried to different degrees, the meal containing 13.41, 13.27, and 11.41 per cent of moisture, respectively. It should be noted that lots C and D contained practically the same amount of moisture and might be regarded as duplicates were it not that lot C was somewhat richer in fat and therefore more susceptible to spoilage.

Part of each lot was packed in 100-pound and part in 25-pound cotton bags, the weight in each case being accurately determined by standard scales. It was believed that the gain or loss in moisture during storage would furnish useful data in connection with the net weight amendment of the Food and Drugs Act, as well as for the special purposes of this investigation.

SHIPMENT AND STORAGE.

Shipment was made to Chicago and Savannah in ordinary freight cars with the larger lots of meal of the next series of experiments. The warehouse in Chicago was several stories high and of fireproof construction. The windows admitted some air but little sunlight, and the temperature responded slowly to outside changes. The Savannah warehouse was three stories high with board floors, and was exceptionally light and airy, the temperature of the air within and without being practically the same. Each lot of bags was separately piled, care being taken not to allow those with an extreme moisture content to come in contact with one another.

ANALYSES AND TESTS OF THE STORED MEAL.

The results of determinations of moisture, acidity, fat, and protein contents made at the end of each four weeks' period are given in Table 8. This table also gives notes as to the physical condition and permits comparison of the loss in weight and loss in moisture. The same general results were obtained at both Savannah and Chicago, and with both 100 and 25-pound bags.

Moisture.—Lots A and B show a steady loss of moisture and lot E a steady gain, while lots C and D remain practically constant. The changes in weight in most cases follow closely the changes in moisture.

Acidity.—Lots D and E in no case reached the limit 30, and lot C just barely reached that limit after several months' storage. Lot B slightly exceeded the limit after 16 weeks' storage, and lot A exceeded the limit in 12 weeks.

Fat.—There was no marked change except in the case of lot A where the percentage of fat diminished as the acidity increased.

Protein.—No significant change took place.

Taste and appearance.—Lot A was found to be musty after 20 weeks' storage. No deterioration was detected in any of the other samples.

TABLE 8.—*Analyses of degerminated, bolted, roller-ground corn meal containing different amounts of moisture, showing changes during storage; ton lots, milled May 7, 1913.*

Product.	Stored in 100-pound bags.						
	Moisture.	Acidity.	Protein (N×6.25).	Fat.	Change in weight.	Change in moisture.	Taste and appearance.
Meal stored at Chicago:	*Per cent.*		*Per cent.*	*Per cent.*	*Per cent.*	*Per cent.*	
Lot A, undried, water added—							
When milled	16.86	14.7	6.53	0.71	....	....	Good.
Stored 4 weeks	15.72	20.5	....	.74	−0.50	−1.14	Do.
Stored 8 weeks	15.50	25.5	....	.67	−1.47	−1.36	Do.
Stored 12 weeks	15.52	35.6	....	.65	−1.83	−1.34	Do.
Stored 16 weeks	14.92	43.2	....	.42	−2.79	−1.94	Do.
Stored 20 weeks	14.75	44.3	6.37	.39	−2.51	−2.11	Musty
Stored 24 weeks	14.24	39.3	6.81	.44	−2.96	−2.62	Do.
Lot B, undried—							
When milled	15.04	14.0	6.50	.94	....	....	Good.
Stored 4 weeks	14.57	18.5	....	.95	− .12	− .47	Do.
Stored 8 weeks	14.61	23.7	....	.93	+ .28	− .43	Do.
Stored 12 weeks	14.78	28.0	....	.97	− .33	− .26	Do.
Stored 16 weeks	14.42	29.7	....	.91	− .06	− .62	Do.
Stored 20 weeks	14.32	31.3	6.38	.85	....	− .72	Do.
Stored 24 weeks	13.97	31.0	6.50	.87	....	−1.07	Do.
Lot C, medium dried—							
When milled	13.41	14.1	6.69	1.05	....	....	Do.
Stored 4 weeks	13.39	18.0	....	1.03	+ .15	− .02	Do.
Stored 8 weeks	13.57	23.5	....	1.08	+ .10	+ .16	Do.
Stored 12 weeks	13.98	28.0	....	1.11	+ .18	+ .57	Do.
Stored 16 weeks	13.65	29.2	....	1.02	+ .26	+ .24	Do.
Stored 20 weeks	13.76	29.8	6.78	1.02	....	+ .35	Do.
Stored 24 weeks	13.50	29.7	6.81	1.03	....	+ .09	Do.
Lot D, medium dried—							
When milled	13.27	13.4	6.66	.80	....	....	Do.
Stored 4 weeks	13.37	16.5	....	.76	+ .12	+ .10	Do.
Stored 8 weeks	13.69	20.0	....	.82	....	+ .40	Do.
Stored 12 weeks	13.86	22.5	....	.80	+ .63	+ .59	Do.
Stored 16 weeks	13.56	23.4	....	.79	....	+ .29	Do.
Stored 20 weeks	13.58	23.6	6.65	.73	+ .22	+ .31	Do.
Stored 24 weeks	13.36	21.7	6.72	.74	+ .31	+ .09	Do.
Lot E, high dried—							
When milled	11.41	11.9	6.72	1.32	....	....	Do.
Stored 4 weeks	12.15	14.5	....	1.30	+1.12	+ .74	Do.
Stored 8 weeks	12.58	19.0	....	1.32	+1.45	+1.17	Do.
Stored 12 weeks	12.87	23.0	....	1.30	+1.74	+1.46	Do.
Stored 16 weeks	12.55	23.7	....	1.24	+1.94	+1.14	Do.
Stored 20 weeks	12.80	24.3	6.66	1.29	....	+1.39	Do.
Stored 24 weeks	12.63	23.2	6.69	1.25	....	+1.22	Do.
Meal stored at Savannah:							
Lot A, undried, water added—							
When milled	16.86	14.7	6.53	.71	....	....	
Stored 4 weeks	14.92	27.0	7.06	.66	−2.50	−1.94	
Stored 8 weeks	13.48	30.0	6.92	.70	−3.00	−3.38	
Stored 12 weeks	13.18	31.0	6.83	.56	−3.45	−3.68	
Stored 16 weeks	13.21	33.1	7.00	.53	−3.81	−3.65	
Stored 20 weeks	13.76	26.5	6.94	.59	−3.38	−3.10	
Stored 24 weeks	13.85	26.0	6.74	.49	−3.77	−3.01	
Lot B, undried—							
When milled	15.04	14.0	6.50	.94	....	....	
Stored 4 weeks	14.25	24.2	6.75	.96	− .37	− .79	
Stored 8 weeks	13.04	25.0	6.66	.98	− .94	−2.00	
Stored 12 weeks	12.77	26.0	6.66	1.01	....	−2.27	
Stored 16 weeks	12.86	32.8	6.57	.94	−1.37	−2.18	
Stored 20 weeks	13.54	24.5	6.75	.96	−1.28	−1.50	
Stored 24 weeks	13.73	25.5	6.64	.94	−1.56	−1.31	
Lot C, medium dried—							
When milled	13.41	14.1	6.69	1.05	....	....	
Stored 4 weeks	13.10	24.0	6.75	1.03	−3.75	− .31	
Stored 8 weeks	12.25	24.0	6.66	1.05	− .62	−1.16	
Stored 12 weeks	12.04	23.5	6.92	1.13	− .96	−1.37	
Stored 16 weeks	12.59	31.9	6.97	1.05	− .79	− .82	
Stored 20 weeks	13.46	23.5	6.83	1.07	+ .38	+ .05	
Stored 24 weeks	13.22	24.0	6.91	1.13	−1.11	− .19	
Lot D, medium dried—							
When milled	13.27	13.4	6.66	.80	....	....	
Stored 4 weeks	13.15	20.0	6.87	.89	+ .19	− .12	
Stored 8 weeks	12.56	20.0	6.66	.79	− .25	− .71	
Stored 12 weeks	12.43	21.0	6.83	.87	− .19	− .84	
Stored 16 weeks	12.83	25.8	6.62	.77	− .19	− .44	
Stored 20 weeks	13.08	19.5	6.66	.75	+ .34	− .19	
Stored 24 weeks	13.15	18.2	6.74	.85	−1.61	− .12	

TABLE 8.—*Analyses of degerminated, bolted, roller-ground corn meal containing different amounts of moisture, etc.*—Continued.

Product.	Stored in 100-pound bags.						
	Moisture.	Acidity.	Protein (N×6.25).	Fat.	Change in weight.	Change in moisture.	Taste and appearance.
Meal stored at Savannah—Continued.	*Per cent.*		*Per cent.*	*Per cent.*	*Per cent.*	*Per cent.*	
Lot E, high dried—							
When milled	11.41	11.9	6.72	1.32	....	....	
Stored 4 weeks	11.89	19.0	6.55	1.25	+1.13	+ .48	
Stored 8 weeks	11.51	19.5	6.39	1.30	....	+ .10	
Stored 12 weeks	11.55	20.5	6.75	1.37	+1.38	+ .14	
Stored 16 weeks	12.66	25.9	6.79	1.29	+1.34	+1.25	
Stored 20 weeks	12.78	19.5	6.79	1.25	+ .34	+1.37	
Stored 24 weeks	12.56	20.0	6.64	1.35	+1.78	+1.15	

Product.	Stored in 25-pound bags.					
	Moisture.	Acidity.	Protein (N×6.25).	Fat.	Change in weight.	Change in moisture.
Meal stored at Chicago:	*Per cent.*		*Per cent.*	*Per cent.*	*Per cent.*	*Per cent.*
Lot A, undried, water added—						
When milled	16.86	14.7	6.53	0.71	....	....
Stored 4 weeks	16.00	20.5	....	.70	−1.04	−0.86
Stored 8 weeks	15.39	25.7	....	.72	−1.83	−1.47
Stored 12 weeks	15.16	31.3	....	.73	−2.61	−1.70
Stored 16 weeks	14.37	32.5	....	.59	−3.26	−2.49
Stored 20 weeks	14.30	31.7	6.88	.60	−3.59	−2.56
Stored 24 weeks	13.84	32.0	6.91	.63	−3.39	−3.02
Lot B, undried—						
When milled	15.04	14.0	6.50	.94	....	....
Stored 4 weeks	14.52	18.5	....	.97	− .26	− .52
Stored 8 weeks	14.52	24.3	....	.90	− .39	− .52
Stored 12 weeks	14.55	28.3	....	.91	− .65	− .49
Stored 16 weeks	13.78	30.2	....	.89	−1.31	−1.26
Stored 20 weeks	13.80	29.6	6.47	.94	−1.50	−1.15
Stored 24 weeks	13.64	30.2	6.69	.93	−1.57	−1.40
Lot C, medium dried—						
When milled	13.41	14.1	6.69	1.05	....	....
Stored 4 weeks	13.44	18.5	....	1.03	+ .73	+ .03
Stored 8 weeks	13.67	23.5	....	1.06	+ .59	+ .26
Stored 12 weeks	13.88	28.0	....	1.10	+ .65	+ .47
Stored 16 weeks	13.51	28.7	....	1.02	+ .13	+ .10
Stored 20 weeks	13.47	29.8	6.72	1.02	− .06	+ .06
Stored 24 weeks	13.22	30.0	6.75	1.01	+ .59	− .19
Lot D, medium dried—						
When milled	13.27	13.4	6.66	.80	....	....
Stored 4 weeks	13.38	16.0	....	.80	+ .78	+ .11
Stored 8 weeks	13.57	20.0	....	.75	+ .26	+ .30
Stored 12 weeks	13.71	23.0	....	.81	− .07	+ .44
Stored 16 weeks	13.23	23.2	....	.75	.00	− .04
Stored 20 weeks	13.42	23.3	6.66	.81	− .20	+ .15
Stored 24 weeks	13.22	22.0	6.97	.74	+ .20	− .05
Lot E, high dried—						
When milled	11.41	11.9	6.72	1.32	....	....
Stored 4 weeks	12.22	15.0	....	1.29	+1.30	+ .81
Stored 8 weeks	12.68	19.0	....	1.22	+1.50	+1.27
Stored 12 weeks	13.08	23.0	....	1.36	+1.37	+1.67
Stored 16 weeks	12.66	23.7	....	1.24	+1.31	+1.25
Stored 20 weeks	12.73	24.3	6.59	1.30	− .46	+1.32
Stored 24 weeks	12.56	25.0	6.59	1.28	+1.95	+1.15
Meal stored at Savannah:						
Lot A, undried, water added—						
When milled	16.86	14.7	6.53	.71	....	....
Stored 4 weeks	14.96	29.5	7.06	.62	−2.47	−1.90
Stored 8 weeks	13.33	28.5	6.92	.65	−3.78	−3.53
Stored 12 weeks	13.06	31.0	6.92	.60	−4.29	−3.78
Stored 16 weeks	13.46	34.7	6.73	.48	−4.17	−3.40
Stored 20 weeks	14.06	28.5	6.66	.48	−3.90	−2.80
Stored 24 weeks	....	....	....	....	....	....

TABLE 8.—*Analyses of degerminated, bolted, roller-ground corn meal containing different amounts of moisture, etc.*—Continued.

Product.	Stored in 25-pound bags.					
	Moisture.	Acidity.	Protein (N×6.25).	Fat.	Change in weight.	Change in moisture.
Meal stored at Savannah—Continued.	*Per cent.*		*Per cent.*	*Per cent.*	*Per cent.*	*Per cent.*
Lot B, undried—						
When milled	15.04	14.0	6.50	0.94	......	......
Stored 4 weeks	14.09	24.0	6.69	.93	−1.17	−0.95
Stored 8 weeks	12.83	25.0	6.66	1.03	−1.76	−2.21
Stored 12 weeks	12.39	26.0	6.75	1.00	−2.08	−2.65
Stored 16 weeks	13.69	31.7	6.69	.97	−5.47	−1.35
Stored 20 weeks	13.88	23.5	6.54	.95	−1.89	−1.16
Stored 24 weeks	......	......	......	......	......	......
Lot C, medium dried—						
When milled	13.41	14.1	6.69	1.05	......	......
Stored 4 weeks	13.27	23.5	6.73	1.05	− .52	− .14
Stored 8 weeks	12.23	23.2	6.70	1.00	−1.79	−1.18
Stored 12 weeks	12.02	25.2	6.75	1.10	− .37	−1.39
Stored 16 weeks	12.89	30.0	6.71	1.10	− .00	− .52
Stored 20 weeks	13.73	26.5	6.83	1.05	+ .07	+ .32
Stored 24 weeks	......	......	......	......	......	......
Lot D, medium dried—						
When milled	13.27	13.4	6.66	.80	......	......
Stored 4 weeks	13.13	20.0	6.81	.82	− .65	− .14
Stored 8 weeks	12.21	20.0	6.83	.85	− .65	−1.06
Stored 12 weeks	12.26	20.2	6.92	.85	− .78	−1.01
Stored 16 weeks	13.60	23.5	6.53	.81	− .58	+ .33
Stored 20 weeks	13.69	18.5	6.66	.81	− .26	+ .42
Stored 24 weeks	......	......	......	......	......	......
Lot E, high dried—						
When milled	11.41	11.9	6.72	1.32	......	......
Stored 4 weeks	12.18	18.5	6.50	1.31	+ .39	+ .77
Stored 8 weeks	11.32	20.2	6.44	1.33	+ .91	− .09
Stored 12 weeks	11.62	20.0	6.56	1.33	+ .80	+ .21
Stored 16 weeks	12.81	24.8	6.71	1.34	+1.04	+1.40
Stored 20 weeks	13.10	21.0	6.54	1.34	+1.50	+1.69
Stored 24 weeks	......	......	......	......	......	......

STORAGE EXPERIMENTS WITH CARLOAD LOTS OF MEAL MILLED MAY 23, 1913.

DESCRIPTION AND ANALYSES OF THE MEAL AS MILLED.

This experiment was carried out with carload lots (40 tons) of undried and highly dried meal. The meal was packed in 100-pound cotton sacks. As it was impracticable to mix thoroughly all of the meal of each lot, one ton (20 bags) was taken out for subsequent sampling, turned over on a floor with a shovel until uniform, and rebagged. One of these bags furnished the sample at the end of each period at each of the cities where the meal was stored. In both the cars and storage warehouse these sample bags were kept in the middle of the pile with bags of the same lot on all sides. Analyses of the meal when milled appear in Table 9.

TABLE 9.—*Composition of carload lots of degerminated, bolted, roller-ground corn meal, as milled with and without drying, May 23, 1913, for use in storage experiments.*

Product.	Moisture.	Acidity.	Protein (N×6.25).	Fat.	Nitrogen-free extract.	Crude fiber.	Ash.
Meal as milled:	*P. ct.*		*Per cent.*	*P. ct.*	*Per cent.*	*P. ct.*	*P. ct.*
Lot A, undried	15.73	16.2	7.12	1.02	75.19	0.51	0.43
Lot B, high dried	9.86	13.0	7.46	1.16	80.37	.67	.48
Moisture-free meal:							
Lot A, undried	......	19.2	8.45	1.21	89.22	.61	.51
Lot B, high dried	......	14.4	8.28	1.29	89.16	.74	.53

SHIPMENT AND STORAGE.

Each lot was divided into two parts and the two half lots shipped in the same car with the meal of the preceding experiment to Savannah and Chicago, where it was stored as already described.

ANALYSES AND TESTS OF THE STORED MEAL.

Determinations of moisture, acidity, fat, and protein were made at intervals of four weeks. The changes in weight, taste, and appearance were also recorded (Table 10).

Moisture.—Lot A showed a loss in moisture which was somewhat greater in Savannah than in Chicago, due either to the hotter climate or to the nature of the warehouse, or both. Lot B gained about the same amount at both places. The gain or loss of moisture was practically the same as the gain or loss in weight.

Acidity.—Lot A reached the limit 30 in 12 weeks at Chicago, and in 8 weeks at Savannah. The acidity of lot B after 24 weeks was only 21.8 and 19.0, respectively, at the two cities.

Fat.—The percentage of fat in lot A slowly diminished in both cities, but that of lot B did not change perceptibly. In all of the experiments, whenever there was a great increase in acidity or spoilage, there was a diminution of fat, due doubtless to the formation of ether-insoluble oxidation products.

Protein.—The changes were insignificant.

Taste and appearance.—In no case was there evidence of spoilage, even at the end of the experiment.

TABLE 10.—*Analyses of degerminated, bolted, roller-ground corn meal, milled with and without drying, showing changes during storage; carload lots, milled May 23, 1913, stored in 100-pound bags.*

Product.	Moisture.	Acidity.	Fat.	Protein (N×6.25).	Change in weight.	Change in moisture.	Taste and appearance.
Meal stored at Chicago:							
Lot A, undried—	*P. ct.*		*P. ct.*	*Per cent.*	*P. ct.*	*P. ct.*	
When milled	15.73	16.2	1.02	7.12	....	....	Good.
Stored 4 weeks	15.22	22.7	.98	....	−0.33	−0.51	Do.
Stored 8 weeks	15.68	28.1	.97	....	− .36	− .05	Do.
Stored 12 weeks	15.44	33.2	1.00	....	− .48	− .29	Do.
Stored 16 weeks	14.70	40.7	.78	....	− .93	−1.03	Do.
Stored 20 weeks	14.53	40.5	.81	7.19	−1.39	−1.20	Do.
Stored 24 weeks	14.20	42.4	.74	7.22	−1.64	−1.53	Do.
Lot B, high dried—							
When milled	9.86	13.0	1.16	7.46	....	....	Do.
Stored 4 weeks	9.90	15.6	1.18	....	+ .36	+ .04	Do.
Stored 8 weeks	10.88	17.3	1.17	....	+ .95	+1.02	Do.
Stored 12 weeks	10.94	18.7	1.25	....	+1.12	+1.08	Do.
Stored 16 weeks	11.07	20.5	1.17	....	+1.48	+1.21	Do.
Stored 20 weeks	11.20	20.8	1.16	7.43	+1.39	+1.34	Do.
Stored 24 weeks	10.96	21.8	1.18	7.53	+1.37	+1.10	Do.
Meal stored at Savannah:							
Lot A, undried—							
When milled	15.73	16.2	1.02	7.12	....	....	Do.
Stored 4 weeks	15.35	24.0	1.06	6.87	− .51	− .38	Do.
Stored 8 weeks	14.16	32.5	.99	7.10	−1.08	−1.57	Do.
Stored 12 weeks	13.53	32.7	.92	7.01	−1.80	−2.20	Do.
Stored 16 weeks	13.70	32.8	.91	7.31	−2.30	−2.03	Do.
Stored 20 weeks	13.50	29.0	.84	6.91	−2.83	−2.23	Do.
Stored 24 weeks	13.23	32.0	.90	7.00	−3.55	−2.50	Do.
Lot B, high dried—							
When milled	9.86	13.0	1.16	7.46	....	....	Do.
Stored 4 weeks	10.25	15.0	1.33	7.51	+ .48	+ .39	Do.
Stored 8 weeks	9.75	18.0	1.30	7.53	+1.23	− .11	Do.
Stored 12 weeks	10.30	19.0	1.29	7.58	+1.36	+ .44	Do.
Stored 16 weeks	10.74	19.3	1.21	7.56	+ .98	+ .88	Do.
Stored 20 weeks	11.22	16.5	1.27	7.26	+1.86	+1.36	Do.
Stored 24 weeks	11.10	19.0	1.23	7.18	+1.65	+1.24	Do.

COMPARATIVE KEEPING QUALITY OF WHOLE-KERNEL STONE-GROUND MEAL AND DEGERMINATED BOLTED ROLLER-GROUND MEAL.

In this investigation a comparison in regard to fat content was made of the keeping quality of meal of the extreme types, ground from the same corn and containing practically the same amounts of moisture. The experiments were carried out in two series, the first with meal milled in December, in parallel lots, dried to different degrees so as to contain from less than 11 to over 19 per cent of moisture, the second with meal ground in April without drying.

The whole-kernel meal was ground in an under-runner bevel mortise-geared buhr mill which was set up for the purpose at the Terre Haute plant of the American Hominy Company. The mill was adjusted to yield a fine, soft meal, such as is preferred by the southern trade, nothing being added to the corn and nothing taken away. The degerminated meal was the usual somewhat granular product of the mill known in the trade as "cream meal." The corn used was No. 3 white dent of the crop of 1913. The quality was quite poor, much inferior to that of the preceding year, which was exceptionally good. It thus appears that in the experiments of the two years the extremes in quality were encountered.

In all the experiments the stream of cleaned corn was divided, part going to the roller system and part to the buhr stones. The bags that received each kind of meal were numbered consecutively and the process so regulated that the meal of the two kinds in bags bearing the same number was from the same corn. As the capacity of the buhr mill was much less than that of the roller system it was necessary to draw the corn for the whole-kernel meal from the divided stream into bags arranged in the proper order and continue the grinding, after the cream meal was milled and sacked.

As in the experiments of the preceding year, it was impracticable to mix all of the meal in each lot. Accordingly ton portions were taken out, mixed, analyzed, and bagged in specially marked sacks, one of which was used for the tests at the end of each storage period. Care was taken that these sublots for sampling, representing the two kinds of meal of the same moisture content, were from the bags bearing the same numbers and therefore were comparable not only as to moisture, but also as to corn.

STORAGE EXPERIMENTS WITH PARALLEL LOTS OF WHOLE-KERNEL AND DEGERMINATED MEAL, OF DIFFERENT DEGREES OF DRYNESS, MILLED DECEMBER, 1913.

DESCRIPTION AND ANALYSES OF THE MEAL AS MILLED.

This experiment involved the serious difficulty of drying both kinds of meal of each pair of the series so that they should be alike as to corn and moisture. As the drying apparatus of the stone system differed from that of the roller system in kind and capacity, it was only after repeated trials that suitable lots were secured. A laboratory was set up at the mill. Here tests for moisture and acidity were made on the meal immediately after milling, the remainder of the analyses being finished at the Chicago Food and Drug Inspection Laboratory.

The analyses in Table 11 represent the six parallel lots finally secured. It will be noted that the percentage of moisture in the two kinds of meal of each pair are reasonably close together, thus permitting satisfactory comparison of the results obtained after storage; furthermore, that the range in moisture (less than 11 to over 19 per cent) is sufficiently great to cover the trade conditions. As the corn varied from day to day, it was found impossible to keep the composition of the meal of the different lots uniform. This, however, seemed unnecessary so long as the two kinds of meal of each pair were from the same corn and of practically the same moisture content.

TABLE 11.—*Composition of carload lots of corn meal containing different amounts of moisture, as milled December, 1913, and used in storage experiments.*

Product.	Whole-kernel, stone-ground meal.						
	Moisture.	Acidity.	Protein (N×6.25).	Fat.	Nitrogen-free extract.	Crude fiber.	Ash.
Meal as milled:	*P. ct.*		*P. ct.*	*P. ct.*	*P. ct.*	*P. ct.*	*P. ct.*
Lot A, undried	19.27	23.1	8.56	3.26	66.06	1.75	1.10
Lot B, extra low dried	17.25	28.5	8.76	3.45	67.71	1.73	1.10
Lot C, low dried	15.71	19.9	9.00	3.47	68.95	1.79	1.08
Lot D, medium dried	13.44	21.3	9.16	3.71	70.42	2.06	1.21
Lot E, high dried	12.25	24.6	9.44	3.55	71.65	1.95	1.16
Lot F, extra high dried	10.79	21.8	9.82	3.71	72.42	2.03	1.23
Moisture-free meal:							
Lot A, undried		27.6	10.60	4.04	81.83	2.17	1.36
Lot B, extra low dried		34.4	10.59	4.17	81.82	2.09	1.33
Lot C, low dried		23.6	10.68	4.12	81.80	2.12	1.28
Lot D, medium dried		24.6	10.58	4.29	81.34	2.39	1.40
Lot E, high dried		28.0	10.76	4.05	81.65	2.22	1.32
Lot F, extra high dried		24.4	11.01	4.16	81.17	2.28	1.38

Product.	Degerminated, bolted, roller-ground meal.						
	Moisture.	Acidity.	Protein (N×6.25).	Fat.	Nitrogen-free extract.	Crude fiber.	Ash.
Meal as milled:	*P. ct.*		*P. ct.*	*P. ct.*	*P. ct.*	*P. ct.*	*P. ct.*
Lot A, undried	19.20	16.0	7.38	0.67	71.94	0.46	0.32
Lot B, extra low dried	17.73	17.6	7.50	.83	73.01	.57	.36
Lot C, low dried	15.72	13.8	7.38	.75	75.25	.56	.34
Lot D, medium dried	13.78	13.3	7.28	1.05	76.81	.64	.44
Lot E, high dried	12.91	13.0	7.41	.92	77.73	.60	.43
Lot F, extra high dried	11.26	13.9	7.25	1.06	79.31	.70	.42
Moisture-free meal:							
Lot A, undried		19.8	9.14	.83	89.06	.57	.40
Lot B, extra low dried		21.4	9.12	1.01	88.74	.69	.44
Lot C, low dried		16.4	8.76	.89	89.29	.66	.40
Lot D, medium dried		15.4	8.45	1.22	89.08	.74	.51
Lot E, high dried		14.9	8.51	1.06	89.25	.69	.49
Lot F, extra high dried		15.7	8.17	1.19	89.38	.79	.47

SHIPMENT AND STORAGE.

Half of each lot was shipped to Savannah and half to New Orleans, the analyses being made from month to month in the Government laboratories located in these cities. Each of the three cars destined for each city contained two parallel lots—that is to say, two half lots of whole-kernel meal and two of cream meal, representing two degrees of dryness. Care was taken not to allow the two kinds of meal, or meal of the same kind with extreme moisture content, to come in contact either in the car or the storage warehouse, also to so bury the bags for analysis in the piles that they should be surrounded by bags of the same lot on all sides. The storage warehouse at Savannah was similar to that used in the preceding experiment, while that at New Orleans was a large, modern structure of several stories, dimly lighted but quite well ventilated.

ANALYSES AND TESTS OF THE STORED MEAL.

The analyses shown in Table 12 are the most instructive of all those given in this bulletin and show conclusively the superior keeping qualities of degerminated meal.

Moisture.—The lots with high moisture, i. e., A, B, and C, regardless of the kind of meal, lost weight during storage, while the drier lots, D, E, and F, in most instances gained. In cases where the meal heated the loss in weight was not only considerable but noticeably greater than the loss in moisture, indicating that carbon dioxid was given off in appreciable amount.

Acidity.—The whole-kernel meal, even when dried to less than 11 per cent of moisture, became sufficiently acid to exceed the limit of 30 in from four to eight weeks and finally reached from two to over three times that limit. On the other hand, the degerminated meal gained slowly in acidity, the limit being exceeded in sixteen weeks only in lot B stored at New Orleans. The highest acidity that was reached in the degerminated meal of lots C, D, E, and F, which contained 15.72 to 11.26 per cent of moisture at the outset, was 30.1 and that only after 28 weeks' storage.

TABLE 12.—*Comparative analyses of whole-kernel, stone-ground corn meal and degerminated, bolted, roller-ground corn meal, containing different amounts of moisture, showing changes during storage; carload lots, milled December, 1913, and stored in 100-pound bags.*

Product.	Whole-kernel, stone-ground meal.						
	Moisture.	Acidity.	Protein (N×6.25).	Fat.	Change in weight.	Change in moisture.	Taste and appearance.
Meal stored at New Orleans:							
Lot A, undried—	*Per ct.*		*Per ct.*	*Per ct.*	*Per ct.*	*Per ct.*	
When milled	19.27	23.1	8.56	3.26	....	....	Good.
Stored 4 weeks	14.73	83.6	9.28	2.61	−6.81	−4.54	Hot, musty, caked.
Stored 8 weeks	14.56	81.2	9.06	2.39	−7.50	−4.71	Rancid, caked, dark.
Stored 12 weeks	13.75	81.0	9.22	2.39	−8.00	−5.52	Do.
Stored 16 weeks	14.02	89.6	8.97	2.47	−7.70	−5.25	Do.
Stored 20 weeks	13.80	92.7	9.16	2.16	−8.22	−5.47	Do.
Stored 24 weeks	13.50	93.0	8.94	2.41	−7.94	−5.77	Do.
Stored 28 weeks	13.27	88.2	9.25	2.39	−8.67	−6.00	Do.
Lot B, extra low dried—							
When milled	17.25	28.5	8.76	3.45	....	....	Good.
Stored 4 weeks	17.17	42.0	8.72	3.49	− .34	− .08	Musty.
Stored 8 weeks	13.70	95.8	9.09	2.85	−5.22	−3.55	Hot, rancid, caked.
Stored 12 weeks	13.60	97.7	9.16	2.85	−5.27	−3.65	Rancid, caked.
Stored 16 weeks	13.80	103.0	8.97	2.92	−4.90	−3.45	Do.
Stored 20 weeks	13.68	107.2	9.09	2.62	−5.06	−3.57	Do.
Stored 24 weeks	13.45	107.6	9.12	2.96	−5.31	−3.80	Do.
Stored 28 weeks	13.19	107.6	9.13	2.86	−5.39	−4.06	Do.
Lot C, low dried—							
When milled	15.71	19.9	9.00	3.47	....	....	Good.
Stored 4 weeks	15.18	28.9	8.76	3.40	− .27	− .53	Do.
Stored 8 weeks	15.25	42.0	9.15	3.47	− .59	− .46	Do.
Stored 12 weeks	14.75	49.7	9.06	3.43	−1.09	− .96	Do.
Stored 16 weeks	14.94	59.7	8.94	3.43	− .73	− .77	Rancid.
Stored 20 weeks	13.86	86.7	9.09	3.26	−2.31	−1.85	Rancid, warm, lumpy.
Stored 24 weeks	12.87	93.0	9.15	2.75	−3.51	−2.84	Do.
Stored 28 weeks	12.34	104.1	9.19	2.50	−4.01	−3.37	Do.
Lot D, medium dried—							
When milled	13.44	21.3	9.16	3.71	....	....	Good.
Stored 4 weeks	13.61	31.5	9.12	3.55	+ .37	+ .17	Do.
Stored 8 weeks	13.78	39.2	9.06	3.62	+ .33	+ .34	Do.
Stored 12 weeks	13.68	47.9	9.19	3.53	+ .22	+ .24	Do.
Stored 16 weeks	13.64	53.0	8.97	3.56	+ .47	+ .20	Rancid.
Stored 20 weeks	13.56	69.5	9.00	3.60	+ .52	+ .12	Do.
Stored 24 weeks	13.26	76.9	9.15	3.58	+ .02	− .18	Do.
Stored 28 weeks	12.60	87.2	9.19	3.61	− .20	− .84	Do.
Lot E, high dried—							
When milled	12.25	24.6	9.44	3.55	....	....	Good.
Stored 4 weeks	12.43	39.0	9.25	3.55	+ .11	+ .18	Do.
Stored 8 weeks	12.55	50.0	9.44	3.54	+ .14	+ .30	Do.
Stored 12 weeks	12.47	61.6	9.12	3.56	+ .06	+ .22	Do.
Stored 16 weeks	12.48	71.0	9.22	3.66	+ .34	+ .23	Rancid.
Stored 20 weeks	12.64	93.4	9.44	3.54	+ .45	+ .39	Do.
Stored 24 weeks	12.38	90.2	9.34	3.50	+ .25	+ .13	Do.
Stored 28 weeks	12.21	105.5	9.50	3.55	+ .36	− .04	Do.
Lot F, extra high dried—							
When milled	10.79	21.8	9.82	3.71	....	....	Good.
Stored 4 weeks	10.95	26.8	9.62	3.72	+ .14	+ .16	Do.
Stored 8 weeks	11.34	37.4	9.59	3.68	+ .86	+ .55	Do.
Stored 12 weeks	11.13	44.8	9.75	3.62	+ .86	+ .34	Do.
Stored 16 weeks	11.57	55.6	9.72	3.59	+1.14	+ .78	Do.
Stored 20 weeks	11.55	72.5	9.81	3.51	+1.44	+ .76	Rancid.
Stored 24 weeks	11.47	86.5	9.69	3.69	+1.28	+ .68	Do.
Stored 28 weeks	11.43	86.7	9.63	3.55	+1.20	+ .64	Do.
Meal stored at Savannah:							
Lot A, undried—							
When milled	19.23	23.1	8.56	3.26	....	....	Good.
Stored 4 weeks	14.10	61.0	8.25	2.10	−7.52	−5.13	Warm, musty, caked.
Stored 8 weeks	14.27	69.3	8.79	2.40	−7.27	−4.96	Musty, caked.
Stored 12 weeks	13.77	64.0	8.55	2.31	−7.46	−5.46	Do.
Stored 16 weeks	14.16	64.0	9.06	2.17	−7.77	−5.07	Do.
Stored 20 weeks	13.60	77.0	8.66	2.33	−8.27	−5.63	Do.
Stored 24 weeks	13.90	77.0	8.66	1.95	−8.58	−5.33	Do.
Stored 28 weeks	12.78	84.0	8.84	2.11	−9.29	−6.45	Do.

TABLE 12.—*Comparative analyses of whole-kernel, stone-ground corn meal and degerminated, bolted, roller-ground corn meal, etc.*—Continued.

Product.	Whole-kernel, stone-ground meal.						
	Moisture.	Acidity.	Protein (N×6.25).	Fat.	Change in weight.	Change in moisture.	Taste and appearance.
Meal stored at Savannah—Contd.							
Lot B, extra low dried—	*Per ct.*		*Per ct.*	*Per ct.*	*Per ct.*	*Per ct.*	
When milled	17.25	28.5	8.76	3.45	....	....	Good.
Stored 4 weeks	16.51	35.0	8.25	3.00	−.71	−.74	No record.
Stored 8 weeks	14.44	74.0	8.51	2.38	−4.08	−2.81	Warm.
Stored 12 weeks	13.87	77.0	8.43	2.60	−4.96	−3.38	Caked.
Stored 16 weeks	14.24	78.5	8.71	2.41	−4.58	−3.01	Do.
Stored 20 weeks	13.63	90.5	9.11	2.22	−5.48	−3.62	Do.
Stored 24 weeks	13.43	91.0	8.75	2.13	−6.02	−3.82	Do.
Stored 28 weeks	12.78	94.5	8.75	2.15	−6.27	−4.47	Do.
Lot C, low dried—							
When milled	15.71	19.9	9.00	3.47	....	....	Good.
Stored 4 weeks	15.08	22.4	8.65	3.45	−.46	−.63	Do.
Stored 8 weeks	14.88	34.0	8.60	3.40	−.77	−.83	Do.
Stored 12 weeks	14.88	43.5	8.60	3.47	−.90	−.83	Do.
Stored 16 weeks	14.48	46.0	8.78	3.32	−1.15	−1.23	Do.
Stored 20 weeks	13.47	74.0	9.11	3.38	−2.27	−2.24	Warm, caked.
Stored 24 weeks	12.48	81.2	8.75	3.23	−3.40	−3.23	Caked.
Stored 28 weeks	12.41	88.3	8.39	2.55	−4.08	−3.30	Do.
Lot D, medium dried—							
When milled	13.44	21.3	9.16	3.71	....	....	Good.
Stored 4 weeks	13.30	17.5	8.86	3.70	+.11	−.14	No record.
Stored 8 weeks	13.48	36.3	8.87	3.57	+.11	+.04	Do.
Stored 12 weeks	13.56	39.0	8.79	3.50	+.21	+.12	Do.
Stored 16 weeks	13.45	44.0	8.97	3.69	+.34	+.01	Do.
Stored 20 weeks	13.28	65.5	9.11	3.80	−.21	−.16	Do.
Stored 24 weeks	12.99	70.5	9.02	3.50	−.40	−.45	Do.
Stored 28 weeks	12.54	76.7	8.17	3.80	−.71	−.90	Do.
Lot E, high dried—							
When milled	12.25	24.6	9.44	3.55	....	....	Good.
Stored 4 weeks	11.82	24.3	9.04	3.60	+.05	−.43	No record.
Stored 8 weeks	12.67	45.5	8.87	3.58	+.27	+.42	Do.
Stored 12 weeks	12.60	53.0	8.87	3.72	+.11	+.35	Do.
Stored 16 weeks	12.46	56.0	8.87	3.76	+.58	+.21	Do.
Stored 20 weeks	12.58	77.0	9.11	3.68	+.17	+.33	Do.
Stored 24 weeks	12.35	88.5	9.11	3.79	−.02	+.10	Do.
Stored 28 weeks	12.15	99.5	8.53	3.54	+.02	−.10	Do.
Lot F, extra high dried—							
When milled	10.79	21.8	9.82	3.71	....	....	Good.
Stored 4 weeks	10.39	17.5	9.63	3.63	+.64	−.40	No record.
Stored 8 weeks	11.08	30.5	9.02	3.59	+.98	+.29	Do.
Stored 12 weeks	11.27	39.0	9.50	3.78	+.92	+.48	Do.
Stored 16 weeks	11.32	46.5	9.68	3.62	+1.16	+.53	Do.
Stored 20 weeks	11.51	70.5	9.64	3.76	+1.23	+.72	Do.
Stored 24 weeks	11.45	73.5	9.56	3.55	+1.05	+.66	Do.
Stored 28 weeks	11.54	83.0	9.56	3.58	+1.20	+.75	Do.

Product.	Degerminated, bolted, roller-ground meal.						
	Moisture.	Acidity.	Protein (N×6.25).	Fat.	Change in weight.	Change in moisture.	Taste and appearance.
Meal stored at New Orleans:							
Lot A, undried—	*Per ct.*		*Per ct.*	*Per ct.*	*Per ct.*	*Per ct.*	
When milled	19.20	16.0	7.38	0.69	....	....	Good.
Stored 4 weeks	19.21	22.0	7.60	.60	−0.33	+0.01	Warm, musty.
Stored 8 weeks	16.72	16.2	7.72	.26	−3.59	−2.48	Musty, lumpy, pink.
Stored 12 weeks	16.58	16.1	7.75	.25	−3.78	−2.62	Do.
Stored 16 weeks	16.68	17.3	7.22	.21	−3.61	−2.52	Do.
Stored 20 weeks	16.20	17.7	7.62	.22	−4.11	−3.00	Do.
Stored 24 weeks	15.99	18.4	7.13	.16	−3.87	−3.21	Do.
Stored 28 weeks	15.77	18.8	7.81	.20	−4.23	−3.43	Do.
Lot B, extra low dried—							
When milled	17.73	17.6	7.50	.83	....	....	Good.
Stored 4 weeks	17.37	19.2	7.60	.85	−.42	−.36	Do.
Stored 8 weeks	16.89	25.1	7.56	.77	−1.00	−.84	Slighty musty.
Stored 12 weeks	16.23	28.0	7.56	.76	−1.50	−1.50	Good.
Stored 16 weeks	16.09	34.5	7.31	.63	−1.40	−1.64	Do.
Stored 20 weeks	15.58	41.7	7.66	.36	−2.42	−2.15	Stale, lumpy.
Stored 24 weeks	15.22	37.6	7.78	.31	−2.75	−2.51	Musty, lumpy.
Stored 28 weeks	14.98	41.2	7.81	.28	−3.44	−2.75	Do.

TABLE 12.—*Comparative analyses of whole-kernel, stone-ground corn meal and degerminated, bolted, roller-ground corn meal, etc.*—Continued.

Product.	Degerminated, bolted, roller-ground meal.						
	Moisture.	Acidity.	Protein (N×6.25).	Fat.	Change in weight.	Change in moisture.	Taste and appearance.
Meal stored at New Orleans—Con.							
Lot C, low dried—	*Per ct.*		*Per ct.*	*Per ct.*	*Per ct.*	*Per ct.*	
When milled	15.72	13.8	7.38	0.75	....	....	Good.
Stored 4 weeks	15.57	16.1	7.35	.70	−0.14	−0.15	Do.
Stored 8 weeks	15.51	18.0	7.40	.74	− .45	− .21	Do.
Stored 12 weeks	15.29	18.7	7.44	.77	− .80	− .43	Do.
Stored 16 weeks	15.45	19.6	7.28	.74	− .30	− .27	Do.
Stored 20 weeks	15.40	24.8	7.38	.72	− .53	− .32	Stale.
Stored 24 weeks	15.23	25.9	7.44	.76	− .44	− .49	Do.
Stored 28 weeks	14.82	28.9	7.63	.69	−1.51	− .90	Do.
Lot D, medium dried—							
When milled	13.78	13.3	7.28	1.05	....	....	Good.
Stored 4 weeks	14.61	16.4	7.25	1.04	− .14	+ .83	Do.
Stored 8 weeks	14.39	15.7	7.31	1.04	+ .56	+ .61	Do.
Stored 12 weeks	14.46	18.1	7.31	1.01	+ .66	+ .68	Do.
Stored 16 weeks	14.39	19.2	7.09	1.04	+ .80	+ .61	Do.
Stored 20 weeks	14.43	25.7	7.28	1.03	+ .37	+ .65	Do.
Stored 24 weeks	14.54	24.7	7.19	1.02	+ .36	+ .76	Do.
Stored 28 weeks	14.23	30.1	7.25	1.00	+ .65	+ .45	Do.
Lot E, high dried—							
When milled	12.91	13.0	7.41	.92	....	....	Do.
Stored 4 weeks	13.20	14.5	7.32	.95	+ .23	+ .29	Do.
Stored 8 weeks	13.42	14.5	7.31	.93	+ .70	+ .51	Do.
Stored 12 weeks	13.39	14.9	7.38	.96	+ .61	+ .48	Do.
Stored 16 weeks	13.62	16.3	7.37	.96	+ .95	+ .71	Do.
Stored 20 weeks	13.83	22.1	7.25	.96	+1.16	+ .92	Do.
Stored 24 weeks	13.58	19.6	7.19	.99	+1.08	+ .67	Do.
Stored 28 weeks	13.54	26.6	7.38	.92	+1.08	+ .63	Do.
Lot F, extra high dried—							
When milled	11.26	13.9	7.25	1.06	....	....	Do.
Stored 4 weeks	11.79	12.8	6.94	1.13	+ .45	+ .53	Do.
Stored 8 weeks	12.31	13.0	7.22	1.08	+1.25	+1.05	Do.
Stored 12 weeks	12.08	12.6	7.31	1.10	+1.48	+ .82	Do.
Stored 16 weeks	12.68	14.7	7.41	1.10	+1.50	+1.42	Do.
Stored 20 weeks	12.69	18.0	7.38	1.07	+2.09	+1.43	Do.
Stored 24 weeks	12.72	21.3	7.00	1.10	+2.12	+1.46	Do.
Stored 28 weeks	12.81	22.7	7.25	1.03	+2.30	+1.55	Do.
Meal stored at Savannah:							
Lot A, undried—							
When milled	19.20	16.0	7.38	.69	....	....	Do.
Stored 4 weeks	18.38	17.5	7.30	.73	− .65	− .82	No record.
Stored 8 weeks	17.67	20.0	7.60	.70	−1.83	−1.53	Do.
Stored 12 weeks	16.87	17.5	7.26	.60	−3.02	−2.33	Do.
Stored 16 weeks	16.40	18.5	7.61	.48	−3.52	−2.80	Do.
Stored 20 weeks	16.19	24.0	7.31	.36	−4.08	−3.01	Do.
Stored 24 weeks	15.70	25.0	7.50	.36	−4.52	−3.50	Musty.
Stored 28 weeks	14.95	22.0	6.79	.38	−5.29	−4.25	Do.
Lot B, extra low dried—							
When milled	17.73	17.6	7.50	.83	....	....	Good.
Stored 4 weeks	17.05	15.8	6.90	.88	− .46	− .68	No record.
Stored 8 weeks	16.70	22.0	6.90	.89	− .83	−1.03	Do.
Stored 12 weeks	16.66	24.0	7.18	.95	−1.46	−1.07	Do.
Stored 16 weeks	16.09	27.5	7.31	.84	−1.65	−1.64	Do.
Stored 20 weeks	15.75	33.7	7.59	.49	−2.40	−1.98	Do.
Stored 24 weeks	14.97	36.5	7.34	.53	−3.21	−2.76	Do.
Stored 28 weeks	14.50	33.2	7.41	.51	....	−3.23	Do.
Lot C, low dried—							
When milled	15.72	13.8	7.38	.75	....	....	Good.
Stored 4 weeks	15.31	12.0	7.31	.65	− .21	− .41	Do.
Stored 8 weeks	15.44	15.8	7.09	.83	− .46	− .28	Do.
Stored 12 weeks	15.49	16.5	6.82	.77	− .46	− .23	Do.
Stored 16 weeks	15.25	17.5	7.26	.79	− .46	− .47	Do.
Stored 20 weeks	15.02	22.5	7.59	.72	− .77	− .70	Do.
Stored 24 weeks	15.00	25.5	7.24	.72	−1.15	− .72	Do.
Stored 28 weeks	14.22	24.5	6.97	.87	−1.65	−1.50	Do.
Lot D, medium dried—							
When milled	13.78	13.3	7.28	1.05	....	....	Do.
Stored 4 weeks	13.98	10.3	7.35	1.13	+ .36	+ .20	Do.
Stored 8 weeks	14.16	15.8	7.09	1.07	+ .73	+ .38	Do.
Stored 12 weeks	14.13	15.5	6.82	1.12	+ .54	+ .35	Do.
Stored 16 weeks	14.09	17.0	7.26	1.09	+ .36	+ .31	Do.
Stored 20 weeks	14.30	23.0	7.15	1.12	+ .36	+ .52	Do.
Stored 24 weeks	14.07	25.5	7.23	1.05	− .08	+ .29	Do.
Stored 28 weeks	13.68	25.7	7.15	1.14	....	− .10	Do.

TABLE 12.—*Comparative analyses of whole-kernel, stone-ground corn meal and degerminated, bolted, roller-ground corn meal, etc.*—Continued.

Product.	Degerminated, bolted, roller-ground meal.						
	Moisture.	Acidity.	Protein (N×6.25).	Fat.	Change in weight.	Change in moisture.	Taste and appearance.
Meal stored at New Orleans—Con.							
Lot E, high dried—	*Per ct.*		*Per ct.*	*Per ct.*	*Per ct.*	*Per ct.*	
When milled	12.91	13.0	7.41	0.92	....	....	Good.
Stored 4 weeks	12.16	9.5	7.00	.95	+0.23	−0.75	Do.
Stored 8 weeks	13.39	13.5	7.00	.98	+ .61	+ .48	Do.
Stored 12 weeks	13.35	14.5	7.09	1.00	+ .48	+ .44	Do.
Stored 16 weeks	13.45	15.0	7.00	1.03	+ .67	+ .54	Do.
Stored 20 weeks	13.58	19.0	7.15	1.09	+ .61	+ .67	Do.
Stored 24 weeks	13.32	20.5	7.24	1.00	+ .39	+ .41	Do.
Stored 28 weeks	13.27	22.5	7.10	1.04	+ .52	+ .36	Do.
Lot F, extra high dried—							
When milled	11.26	13.9	7.25	1.06	....	....	Do.
Stored 4 weeks	11.17	9.3	7.09	1.14	+ .73	− .09	Do.
Stored 8 weeks	11.49	12.0	7.45	1.15	+1.11	+ .23	Do.
Stored 12 weeks	12.30	13.0	7.09	1.13	....	+1.04	Do.
Stored 16 weeks	12.13	12.7	7.18	1.13	+1.11	+ .87	Do.
Stored 20 weeks	12.30	17.5	7.16	1.10	+1.48	+1.04	Do.
Stored 24 weeks	12.40	16.5	7.05	1.13	+1.42	+1.14	Do.
Stored 28 weeks	12.64	18.8	7.01	1.16	+1.67	+1.38	Do.

Special attention should be directed to the degerminated meal of lot A, which heated during the first four weeks and also became musty and lumpy. Notwithstanding the spoilage evident to the senses, this meal did not increase appreciably in acidity—in fact, at the end of 28 weeks it had less acidity than most of the dried meal. The pink color, as well as the mycological examination by Dr. C. Thom, showed that the flora of the sample was peculiar and evidently such as to produce spoilage without development of acidity.

Fat.—A marked diminution in the percentage of fat accompanied heating. This was evident in lots A, B, and C of the whole-kernel meal and lots A and B of the degerminated meal. This diminution was also noted in the experiments of the preceding year.

Protein.—The results show no significant change in total crude protein.

Taste and appearance.—Both the whole-kernel and the degerminated meal of lot A were hot, musty, and unfit for food four weeks after milling, and the whole-kernel meal of lot B was musty at the same period. The remainder of the whole-kernel meal became rancid in from 20 to 24 weeks. The degerminated meal of lots B and C was stale at the end of 20 weeks, but none of the lots with lower moisture content suffered appreciably in quality, even up to the end of the experiment.

CONCLUSIONS.

Whole-kernel meal prepared from corn of the quality of the crop of 1913, even when thoroughly dried, develops excessive acidity in so short a time as to demand immediate consumption. If meal of this type is preferred because of its greater nutritive value or more oily flavor, it should, as recommended by Commissioner Watson, be milled locally in small quantities and consumed within a short period.

In regard to keeping qualities, whole-kernel meal may be compared to cream in that it must be delivered and consumed without delay, while degerminated meal may be compared to butter, which within reasonable limits keeps until used.

STORAGE EXPERIMENTS WITH WHOLE-KERNEL AND DEGERMINATED MEAL, MILLED WITHOUT DRYING, APRIL 3, 1914.

The analyses of the meal as milled April 3, 1914, appear in Table 13, and of the meal after storage at New Orleans in Table 14. The percentages of moisture at the time of milling were 18·45 and 18.46, and of fat 3.34 and 0.79, respectively, in the whole-kernel and the degerminated meal.

TABLE 13.—*Composition of carload lots of whole-kernel, stone-ground corn meal and degerminated, bolted, roller-ground corn meal, as milled, without drying, Apr. 3, 1914, for use in storage experiments.*

Product.	Moisture.	Acidity.	Protein (N×6.25).	Fat.	Nitrogen-free extract.	Crude fiber.	Ash.
Meal as milled:	*Per ct.*		*Per cent.*	*P. ct.*	*Per cent.*	*Per ct.*	*P. ct.*
Whole-kernel stone-ground	18.45	30.0	8.94	3.34	66.23	1.78	1.26
Degerminated bolted roller-ground	18.46	17.9	6.97	.79	72.91	.46	.41
Moisture-free meal:							
Whole-kernel stone-ground		36.8	10.96	4.10	81.22	2.18	1.54
Degerminated bolted roller-ground		22.0	8.55	.97	89.42	.56	.50

TABLE 14.—*Comparative analyses of whole-kernel, stone-ground corn meal and degerminated, bolted, roller-ground corn meal, milled without drying, showing changes during storage.*

[Carload lots milled Apr. 17, 1914, and stored in 100-pound bags at New Orleans.]

Product.	Moisture.	Acidity.	Protein (N×6.25).	Fat.	Change in weight.	Change in moisture.	Taste and appearance.
Whole-kernel, stone-ground meal:	*Per ct.*		*Per cent.*	*Per ct.*	*Per ct.*	*Per cent.*	
When milled	18.46	30.0	8.94	3.34			Good.
Stored 2 weeks	15.41	82.7	8.85	2.79	−4.36	−3.04	Hot, musty, caked.
Stored 4 weeks	14.47	90.0	9.25	2.76	−5.72	−3.98	Musty, caked.
Stored 6 weeks	14.48	98.1	9.44	2.52	−5.73	−3.97	Rancid, caked.
Stored 8 weeks	14.55	98.7	9.38	2.78	−5.66	−3.90	Do.
Stored 12 weeks	13.85	94.8	9.38	2.71	−6.00	−4.60	Do.
Degerminated, bolted, roller-ground meal:							
When milled	18.46	17.9	6.97	.79			Good.
Stored 2 weeks	18.50	21.9	7.18	.73	− .30	+ .04	Not good.
Stored 4 weeks	16.06	20.3	7.31	.31	−3.81	−2.40	Musty, lumpy, pink.
Stored 6 weeks	15.53	21.0	7.53	.27	−4.67	−2.93	Do.
Stored 8 weeks	15.67	22.2	7.25	.34	−4.51	−2.79	Do.
Stored 12 weeks	15.19	22.1	6.75	.29	−4.56	−3.27	Do.

Neither kind of meal was fit for food at the end of two weeks' storage, the deterioration being evident from the taste and appearance, as well as in the case of the whole-kernel meal, from the acidity. As in lot A of the preceding experiment, the degerminated meal spoiled without developing excessive acidity.

SUMMARY.

1. The products of a white-corn mill may be arranged in the following order in regard to acidity, fat, fiber, and ash, beginning with the lowest percentage: Grits, meal, flour, feed, and germ. They may be arranged in the following order in regard to protein: Flour, meal, grits, feed, and germ. The percentage of nitrogen-free extract is not strikingly different in the grits and meal, but is lower in the feed and lowest in the germ.

2. Samples of meal taken from 41 mills located in 32 towns and 17 States are classified under four heads: (1) Whole-kernel, stone-ground meal; (2) bolted, undegerminated meal; (3) degerminated, bolted, roller-ground meal ("cream meal"); and (4) low-grade or "standard" meal.

3. Whole-kernel meal at the time of grinding is the same in composition as the corn except in regard to moisture, but soon develops a greater acidity.

4. Bolted, undegerminated meal contains less fiber than the corn, but no other general rule can be formulated owing to the variable conditions of manufacture.

5. Degerminated, bolted meal contains less protein, fat, fiber, and ash, but more nitrogen-free extract than the corn.

6. Low-grade ("standard") meal contains sometimes more and sometimes less of each constituent than the corn.

7. Ton lots of degerminated, bolted meal, with a range in moisture content, were stored at Savannah and Chicago. The lot containing 16.86 per cent of moisture showed an excess of acidity in 12 weeks, a loss of fat in 16 weeks, and a musty taste in 20 weeks. The lot containing 15.04 per cent of moisture only slightly exceeded the limit for acidity (30) in 24 weeks, and did not suffer in taste or appearance, while those with 13.41 per cent or less kept well in all respects up to the end of the experiment (24 weeks).

8. Carload lots of degerminated, bolted meal, with 15.73 per cent of moisture, showed an excess of acidity at Savannah in 8 weeks and at Chicago in 12 weeks, but did not suffer appreciably in quality. Highly dried meal with 9.86 per cent of moisture after 24 weeks showed a maximum acidity of only 21.8.

9. Comparative tests with whole-kernel and degerminated, bolted meal, undried and dried to different degrees and stored at Savannah and New Orleans, showed the superior qualities of the latter. Even when dried to 10.79 per cent of moisture, the whole-kernel meal developed excessive acidity in 8 weeks and became rancid in 20

weeks, while with 15.71 per cent of moisture or higher, in addition to becoming acid, it sooner or later heated and caked. The loss in weight accompanying heating exceeded the loss of moisture.

Degerminated, bolted meal containing 13.78 per cent or less of moisture kept in all respects for 28 weeks, and that containing 15.72 per cent, although it became stale in 20 weeks, did not develop excessive acidity. The undried meal containing 19.20 per cent of moisture, although it heated within 4 weeks, unlike the whole-kernel meal, did not increase markedly in acidity.

10. Meal of the two kinds milled April, 1914, without drying and containing about 18.50 per cent of moisture, spoiled within 2 weeks at New Orleans. Only the whole-kernel meal developed an excess of acidity.

11. A study of all the results leads to the conclusion that degerminated, bolted meal containing not over 14 per cent of moisture and 1 per cent of fat, as determined by the method of the Association of Official Agricultural Chemists, properly stored, should keep for 6 months; with a moisture content of 15 per cent it should keep 3 months. Schindler's limit for moisture, namely 13½ per cent, obtained by drying in an open dish, corresponds to about 14½ per cent by the method of the Association of Official Agricultural Chemists.

12. Whole-kernel meal, like cream, should be produced locally and consumed soon after grinding; properly dried, degerminated meal, like butter, keeps well during transportation and long storage.

ADDITIONAL COPIES
OF THIS PUBLICATION MAY BE PROCURED FROM
THE SUPERINTENDENT OF DOCUMENTS
GOVERNMENT PRINTING OFFICE
WASHINGTON, D. C.
AT
5 CENTS PER COPY
▽

BULLETIN OF THE
U.S. DEPARTMENT OF AGRICULTURE

No. 216

Contribution from the Office of Markets and Rural Organization,
Charles J. Brand, Chief.
April 26, 1915.

COTTON WAREHOUSES:

STORAGE FACILITIES NOW AVAILABLE IN THE SOUTH.[1]

By Robert L. Nixon, *Assistant in Cotton Marketing.*

INTRODUCTION.

This bulletin is the result of a survey made for the purpose of determining the extent of storage facilities now available in the cotton-producing States. An attempt has been made to determine not only the storage capacity of the cotton warehouses now in use, but to learn something of the conditions under which cotton is stored, the charges for storage, the insurance rates paid, and other factors affecting cotton in storage. Particular attention was given to the different types of buildings with reference to cost of construction, insurance rates, and general economy in handling cotton, and also to the distribution of these storage houses with reference to the production of cotton, and the availability of such warehouses to farmers who may wish to store their cotton. Efforts also were made to determine something of the importance of the warehouses in protecting cotton from fire and damage by weather, in handling and marketing, and in financing the cotton crop. The relation of the cotton warehouse to other business and its importance to the farmer and to business men generally has been kept in mind.

The warehouse survey of Georgia and North Carolina was made during the early part of 1914, so the resulting figures, which are given in tabular form in this bulletin, relate to the amount of storage space that was available during the 1913–14 season, except in Table VI, which is an estimate of the storage space now available. Letters

[1] The figures in this bulletin relating to the storage facilities now available in the cotton belt were secured from a comprehensive survey of Georgia and North Carolina, and also by means of a letter of inquiry which was sent to all the county agents of the Farmers' Cooperative Demonstration Work of the Southern States. The work in North Carolina was done in cooperation with the Marketing Division of the Agricultural Experiment Station. In Georgia the survey was conducted entirely by the Office of Markets and Rural Organization. However, the State College of Agriculture furnished office space and extended other courtesies to the writer while making the survey which greatly facilitated the work.

Note.—This bulletin deals with the cotton warehouse situation of the South, with special reference to conditions in Georgia and North Carolina. An attempt has been made to determine what storage facilities are now available, the importance of the warehouse in financing the cotton crop, and the general relation of a system of warehouses to other lines of business. It should be of special interest to farmers, warehousemen, and cotton factors, merchants, and bankers of the South.

86344°—Bull. 216—15——1

were sent to all ginners and cotton dealers in Georgia and North Carolina asking for the names and addresses of all cotton-storage companies, both public and private. A tentative warehouse list was made up from the replies to this inquiry, and a letter and blank asking for details as to cost of construction, storage capacity, insurance rates, and charges for storage were sent to each individual or company on the list. These were followed, in many cases, by other inquiries and special correspondence. In addition to this, the writer visited many of the warehouses and conferred with a large number of warehousemen, cotton dealers, and others interested in the cotton industry.

In August, 1914, when it became apparent that the price of cotton would be seriously depressed on account of a limited demand, it was obvious that there would be an unusual demand for storage space. In order to get data concerning storage facilities in the cotton-producing States, a letter of inquiry was sent to all the county agents of the Farmers' Cooperative Demonstration Work in the Southern States. This letter asked for the names of all warehouse companies in the sections where the various agents were located and the storage capacity of the buildings operated by these companies. The agents responded readily to this inquiry, and the results obtained enabled us to form a good idea of the available storage facilities throughout the South. In this connection it should be remembered that an immediate report was requested from the county agents. This made it impossible for them to make a very thorough investigation which would enable them to report all storage houses. Many of the cotton-producing counties have no agents, so the number of warehouses reported from this source is further limited. In addition, many of the nonproducing counties in the cotton belt where no agents are stationed have warehouses with a large aggregate storage capacity. Taking all of these facts into consideration it is quite evident that the reports from the county agents necessarily are far short of the actual number of warehouses in the various States. But these reports are especially valuable as a basis for comparison of conditions between the States where surveys have been made and the States where no such investigations have been conducted.

IMPORTANCE OF THE WAREHOUSE IN FINANCING THE COTTON CROP.

Financing the cotton crop is one of the most difficult, and at the same time one of the most important problems confronting the southern farmer and the southern business man. In the light of all the facts, it seems reasonable to state that but little cotton would be stored or insured if it were not necessary to do so in order to negotiate loans with cotton as collateral. The banks are entirely willing to advance money on cotton on liberal terms when it is properly stored and insured, but they are not always able to advance these necessary funds. Even in years when prices are satisfactory, and but little cotton is held, it takes enormous sums of money to finance the marketing of the crop, and when the market is unsatisfactory and many persons wish to hold their cotton for better prices, it is almost impossible for the present banking institutions to supply the necessary funds. The farmer frequently has no operating capital and that of the bank is limited. Consequently, when a market for cotton practically disappears, it is impossible for the banks of the cotton-producing section to meet their obligations. Success in developing an adequate and efficient system of storage houses depends largely upon obtaining sufficient capital to finance the cotton crop. Many letters from bankers, warehousemen, and business men generally, indicate an entire willingness and even eagerness on their part to erect storage houses of sufficient capacity, if only money could be obtained in order to enable farmers and others to hold cotton.

It would seem that the banks would increase their capital stock to such an extent that they would be in position to advance all the funds needed. But it must be remembered here, as stated in connection with storing cotton, that it is only when the market is unsatisfactory that the farmer needs to hold his cotton and therefore needs an unusual amount of capital. The banks, of course, can not keep on hand unlimited funds to meet this occasional demand. It also must be remembered that the farmer is not always reasonable in his demand for funds at such a time. When cotton is bringing 13 or 14 cents per pound he often sells his crop as fast as it is ginned without reference to the disastrous effect it may have on the market, spends the proceeds, and devotes all his energies to raising a large crop the following year. While the cotton is growing he spends for his supplies on the basis of a full crop for which he expects to receive the maximum price. When, because of overproduction or unusual pressure on the market, the price falls appreciably, he finds that the merchant's equity in the cotton is greater than its cash value. He then expects the banks to advance him money on the basis of the prices that prevailed when conditions were favorable, or perhaps on the cost of production. While cotton is recognized as the best collateral it will not be accepted by business men on such conditions.

Bankers and other southern business men believe that cotton when properly stored and insured is the very best collateral. The most substantial bankers state definitely that they prefer it to real estate, and will advance funds on it as readily as on Government bonds. When making the survey of Georgia and North Carolina special efforts were made to determine whether the bankers in general regarded cotton as desirable collateral. They were practically unanimous in their opinion that it is the very best that can be offered.

From careful observation it appears that in North Carolina most of the loans on cotton are made by banks at a rate of from 6 to 8 per cent. The average would doubtless be 7 per cent or less. These same banks charge 8 per cent or more for ordinary loans on personal security or real estate. In Georgia the rate on loans on cotton ranges from 7 to 10 per cent. The average is probably about 8 per cent. This refers to comparatively small loans made by banks to individuals and small companies. Doubtless many of the Georgia cotton companies obtain money at the rate of 6 per cent. The rate on personal notes in Georgia ranges from 8 to 12 per cent, with an average of not less than 9 per cent. In both States the interest charged on store accounts (which is usually included in the selling price) ranges from 10 to 35 or 40 per cent. The average is not less than 20 per cent. All these facts show that in both States loans can be obtained when cotton is offered as collateral at a much lower rate than when personal security is given.

It can readily be seen that one of the greatest needs of the cotton farmer is to get away from the present credit system. Many, especially those of the tenant class, pay the supply merchant an advance of from 25 to 35 cents on a dollar's worth of supplies, and these supplies are actual necessities. These accounts ordinarily run from six to eight months. Such exorbitant rates of interest would be disastrous to any class of people. When the crop is harvested the farmer disposes of his cotton and settles his accounts with the proceeds, provided, of course, that he receives sufficient funds for this purpose. Then it is usually necessary for him to mortgage his next year's crop to the supply merchant in order to obtain credit, which is necessary to enable him to live while the crop is being made. While it is difficult to see how this situation can be remedied, owing to the fact that these tenants have no means of living while the crop is being made without trading with supply merchants, it does seem that the situation would be improved greatly by establishing a system of warehouses and encouraging the tenants to store such cotton as is not absolutely necessary to settle their accounts. If this plan should be pursued for two or three years, while economy in living was exercised, many could eventually free themselves from the present system.

The merchant is almost as helpless as the farmer. He advances supplies while expecting cotton to bring a fairly good price. In most cases he has bought his stock on time and can not meet his own obligations until the farmers' accounts are paid. Whenever the price is so low that the farmer fails to meet his obligations, the merchant is likely to be seriously embarrassed. Late in 1914 for instance, many farmers refused positively to sell their cotton, and many of them failed to meet their obligations, thus making it especially hard on the merchant. When the price is unusually low, as in the present emergency, the merchant can not afford to "close out" the tenant. The cotton, if thrown on the market, would not bring enough to settle the account. If the merchant insisted on selling the cotton he necessarily would lose much of the money due him.

It is equally true that the local banker is helpless in such a situation. His bank advances some money to local merchants and some to the farmers. He has borrowed most of this money from some larger institution which is usually located outside of the cotton-producing section. He is supposed to pay this money back at the time that cotton is picked. When the farmer fails to meet his obligation the merchant naturally finds it difficult to pay his banker. Then the local banker is dependent upon the mercy of the larger institution.

A well-organized system of cotton warehouses would be of the greatest assistance to the farmer, the supply merchant, and the local banker in financing the cotton crop, especially in tiding over an emergency. There is a serious need for warehouses whose receipts would be accepted as an absolute guarantee that a certain amount of cotton of a definite grade and in marketable condition had been stored with the warehouse company. Under such conditions it would be very easy for the farmer to store his cotton and offer the receipts to his supply merchant as collateral for extending the time in which his account must be paid. The merchant in turn could surrender these receipts to the local banker and extend the time of his loan. The local banker would then use these receipts in a similar way to extend the time of his loan with the larger institution. In practically every instance the large banker would be glad to extend the time of payment when these receipts were offered as collateral. In many instances the rate of interest would be greatly reduced. This is one of the very important functions of an efficient system of warehouses, and the need of such a system is extremely urgent.

GENERAL DISCUSSION OF STORAGE FACILITIES.

It will be shown (Table VII, p. 17) that the warehouses now in use are entirely ample in total storage capacity when we consider the South as a whole. The investigations indicate that if all storage houses, including those belonging to cotton mills in the cotton-growing States, were used, every bale of an average crop could be stored. There is never a year when there is a demand for this amount of storage space. Some cotton is always shipped direct from the gins through the compresses to New England and to Europe. Some is kept on the farm for several months. When this is taken into consideration, it appears that the storage capacity of the buildings now in use is entirely adequate.

DISTRIBUTION OF WAREHOUSES.

This, however, does not mean that every person who has cotton is able to get it stored on favorable terms. While the facilities in a general way are ample in most of the States, in others they are entirely inadequate. By referring to Table VII it will be seen that the warehouses of Virginia, Florida, Tennessee, and Louisiana have a storage capacity much greater than the production of cotton in those States, but most of the warehouses are located in the shipping centers, namely, Norfolk, Newport News, Jacksonville, Pensacola, Memphis, and New Orleans. While from a glance at the table it would seem that the facilities in these States are adequate, probably it is true that the cotton-producing sections are very poorly supplied with storage houses. A farmer who wishes to hold cotton in these sections would have to keep it on the farm uninsured or ship it to a cotton factor in one of the large towns.

GEORGIA.

In Table I (p. 7) an attempt is made to illustrate the distribution of warehouses in Georgia. The first half of the table shows the 10 counties having public and private cotton warehouses with the greatest aggregate storage capacity, and the second section shows the 10 counties producing the most cotton in 1913. The same table shows the total production of cotton in 1913 in running bales for all the counties listed. The first section shows 103 public and private warehouses reported in the 10 counties, with a total storage capacity of 419,280 bales. The 47 cotton mills reporting can store 192,475. This makes a total capacity for the 10 counties of 611,755 bales. These figures are for uncompressed cotton. Many of these warehouses usually receive compressed cotton. There are also 37 warehouses located in these counties which have not reported. Taking this into consideration it would be safe to say that, in all, the warehouses in these 10 counties could store almost 1,000,000 bales of cotton. The table shows further that the production of these counties for 1913 was only 170,375 bales, as reported by the United States Census Bureau.

The second section of this table shows the conditions in the 10 counties producing the most cotton in 1913. It will be seen that 112 warehouses in these counties have a storage capacity of only 118,255 bales. The 10 cotton mills reporting can store 15,400 bales, making a total storage capacity for the 10 counties of only 133,655 bales, while the 1913 production for these counties was 437,605 bales.

TABLE I.—*Showing the production of cotton in certain counties in Georgia, in running bales, and the distribution of warehouses, their number, character, and storage capacity, in flat bales.*

County.	Production in running bales, 1913.	Mill warehouses.		Other warehouses.		Total warehouse capacity in flat bales.
		Number reporting.	Capacity in flat bales.	Number reporting.	Capacity in flat bales.	
Bibb	10,690	3	19,800	7	40,500	60,300
Chatham				8	53,000	53,000
Clarke	13,291	7	7,300	5	35,500	42,800
Dooly	39,365			18	22,780	22,780
Fulton	2,544	8	32,900	3	44,100	77,000
Jackson	44,550	3	3,800	16	19,850	23,650
Muscogee	7,940	8	47,875	4	37,500	85,375
Richmond	10,765	6	25,000	20	121,950	146,950
Stewart	16,178			15	22,850	22,850
Troup	25,052	12	55,800	7	21,250	77,050
Total	170,375	47	192,475	103	419,280	611,755
Bulloch	41,667			2	4,000	4,000
Burke	53,687			6	6,800	6,800
Carroll	39,878	3	5,500	17	10,575	16,075
Dooly	39,365			18	22,780	22,780
Emanuel	41,298			10	9,850	9,850
Jackson	44,550	3	3,800	16	19,850	23,650
Laurens	53,740	1	1,200	16	11,550	12,750
Sumter	39,005			11	13,000	13,000
Terrell	38,614			10	10,350	10,350
Walton	45,801	3	4,900	6	9,500	14,400
Total	437,605	10	15,400	112	118,255	133,655

It will be seen that the number of warehouses in the first group of counties is less than the number in the second group. The average storage capacity in the first group is approximately 4,000 bales, while in the other it is approximately 1,000. It will be seen further that only two counties appear in both of these groups. This table is presented to illustrate the fact that the warehouses are not distributed with reference to production. It also shows that the larger and better storage houses are located in the nonproducing counties. It is well to note the fact that Georgia has a greater number of warehouses than any other State, and that their distribution is probably better, but even in this State the distribution is not such as to best serve the farmer.

NORTH CAROLINA.

Table II (p. 8) gives the same information for certain counties in North Carolina that Table I gives for Georgia. It is interesting to note that some of the counties of this State which have warehouses with large combined storage capacity have a very small production. It will be noticed further that some of the counties which produce large amounts of cotton have very few warehouses or frequently none at all. When the survey of this State was being made, it was very noticeable that the facilities available were entirely inadequate, and that those storage houses which were in use were not so distributed as to be of the greatest benefit to the cotton producer. It will be seen that 10 counties have 39 warehouses, with a total capacity of 133,770 bales. These are the 10 counties having the largest amount of storage space, yet the production for the same counties in 1913 was 183,483 bales, or approximately 50,000 bales more than could be stored in all the public and private warehouses. These counties also have 90 cotton mills, whose warehouses have a total capacity of 107,525 bales, making a combined storage capacity for these counties of 241,295 bales.

TABLE II.—*Showing the production of cotton in certain counties in North Carolina, in running bales, and the distribution of warehouses, their number, character, and storage capacity in flat bales.*

County.	Production in running bales, 1913.	Mill warehouses.		Other warehouses.		Total warehouse capacity in flat bales.
		Number reporting.	Capacity in flat bales.	Number reporting.	Capacity in flat bales.	
Cleveland	23,482	17	13,625	7	5,570	19,195
Cumberland	19,155	7	7,600	3	11,300	18,900
Franklin	15,536	1	3,500	5	6,800	10,300
Gaston	13,706	35	34,150	6	9,600	43,750
Guilford	435	7	22,500	1	15,000	37,500
Mecklenburg	31,164	13	14,750	5	32,000	46,750
New Hanover	....	2	750	2	30,000	30,750
Sampson	21,510	....	....	4	9,300	9,300
Wake	28,530	6	8,050	3	5,100	13,150
Wayne	29,965	2	2,600	3	9,100	11,700
Total	183,483	90	107,525	39	133,770	241,295
Edgecombe	29,676	4	8,100	4	1,800	9,900
Halifax	32,110	5	11,400	2	1,700	13,100
Johnston	38,751	6	9,900	2	1,200	11,100
Mecklenburg	31,164	13	14,750	5	32,000	46,750
Nash	29,860	....	....	....	....	....
Robeson	54,039	6	12,400	3	3,700	16,100
Scotland	27,649	6	10,300	....	....	10,300
Union	31,409	4	5,600	3	4,200	9,800
Wake	28,530	6	8,050	3	5,100	13,150
Wayne	29,965	2	2,600	3	9,100	11,700
Total	333,153	52	83,100	25	58,800	141,900

In the second part of this table it will be seen that the 10 counties listed have only 25 warehouses and that these can store only 58,800 bales. On the other hand, the total production of cotton is 333,153 bales, or almost six times the amount of the total storage capacity of all the public and private warehouses. More than one-half of this space is located in one county, and this is used almost entirely by cotton dealers. These counties have 52 cotton mills which can store 83,100 bales. Adding this to the capacity of public and private warehouses, we have a maximum possible storage space for these counties of only 141,900 bales, which is less than one-half the annual production for the same counties. When we take into consideration the fact that very few of the cotton mills allow the farmer to use any of their storage houses and that many of the other warehouses are intended primarily for the private use of merchants and cotton factors, it will be seen that the farmers at best could store only a very small proportion of their annual production.

In many primary markets there are no storage houses at all. Cotton frequently remains on the ground, in public yards, and about supply stores for weeks, where it is damaged by weather and endangered by fire. In North Carolina cotton is stored by the dealer in order to aid in financing his transactions, but seldom by anyone for protection from "country damage."

GEORGIA AND ALABAMA.

On further examination Table VII seems to indicate that Georgia and Alabama are best served at present, especially when we take into consideration the distribution of warehouses with reference to production. These States have by far a greater number of warehouses than any others. In Georgia 1,089 public and private warehouses and the storage houses belonging to 151 cotton mills have a combined capacity of 2,105,780 bales, which is not far short of the 1913 production. Something of the distribution of these warehouses has been shown in Table I. As previously noted, it appears that, with reference to distribution, Georgia is better supplied with cotton warehouses than any other State. The available storage space in Alabama is greater than the annual production, and the fact that there are 581 warehouses seems to denote that those now in use in that State are fairly well distributed.

SOUTH CAROLINA, MISSISSIPPI, AND OKLAHOMA.

Reports indicate that the situation in South Carolina, Mississippi, and Oklahoma is about the same. We see from Table VII that each of these States has a storage capacity slightly in excess of the production, but the number of warehouses in each of these States is much less than in Georgia and Alabama. Owing to the fact that the investigations in these States have been very limited, it is not possible to state the situation definitely. But the comparatively small number of warehouses would seem to indicate that they are located in the principal towns. This means that many of the small and even medium-sized towns are not well supplied with storage houses. The trouble in these States is not necessarily with the total storage capacity of the cotton warehouses, but with the poor distribution of those now in use.

ARKANSAS AND NORTH CAROLINA.

It will be seen (Table VII) that the warehouse space in Arkansas is insufficient to shelter the annual production and that the number of warehouses is small. It must be considered further that a number of large warehouses are located in Pine Bluff and Fort Smith. This would seem to show that many of the small towns are not properly supplied. The situation is very much the same in North Carolina. It will be seen that the number of warehouses, not including those belonging to the cotton mills, is very small. The combined storage capacity of public and private warehouses and storage houses belonging to cotton mills falls far short of the annual production. It is known that comparatively few of the mills permit farmers to use their warehouses. Many of the mills buy the cotton which they use from other States. From a rather thorough investigation of conditions in this State it has been found that very few of the small towns have any warehouses. Most of the warehouses in the State are located in a few of the central markets and are controlled and used primarily by the dealers. North Carolina is probably in more serious need of storage houses than any of the other cotton-producing States. It would seem that many new warehouses could be constructed and operated at a profit in this State. The warehouses at Norfolk, Va., are used largely, however, by North Carolina merchants, and this tends to relieve the situation, especially in the northeastern part of the State.

TEXAS.

It will be seen (Table VII) that the storage capacity (as offered) of all the warehouses in Texas is more than a million bales short of the annual production. Reports from this investigation show that more than half of this space is located in Galveston and Houston. This shows clearly that the warehouses in the producing sections are entirely inadequate. As there are only 497 warehouses in the State, it can be assumed that most of them are large and located in the more important towns. This seems to be conclusive proof that only a comparatively small percentage of the farmers could store their cotton if they wished to do so.

SUMMARY OF DISTRIBUTION.

In summarizing the storage situation it may be repeated that the cotton warehouses now in use have an ample storage capacity, but they are so located and the conditions under which they operate are such that in many cases they do not serve their purposes. In North Carolina, Arkansas, and Texas the total capacity of all of the warehouses is not equal to the annual production, and those that are in use are not properly distributed. In Georgia and Alabama storage facilities seem to be ample in volume and fairly well distributed, but the service is not of the best. In the other States facilities are ample in storage capacity, but the warehouses are not properly distributed nor are they so operated as best to serve the producers. In all States a majority of the cotton warehouses do not appear to be rendering efficient service to the industry as a whole.

SERVICE OF WAREHOUSES NOT SATISFACTORY.

SPACE NOT AVAILABLE.

While an attempt has been made to show that in storage capacity the warehouses now in use are fully adequate, it is not meant to convey the impression that those who produce cotton can get proper and efficient warehouse service. This is far from the case. Most of the best storage houses belong to the cotton mills and to cotton factors or commission merchants. The mills have built their warehouses for storing the cotton which they buy for spinning. They were never intended as public storage houses, and they are available for such use in very few instances. The factors have not built warehouses for the purpose of doing a storage business, but in order to aid in their regular transactions. But few of these persons would build warehouses for the storage fees they collect, but they are forced to operate the warehouses in order to handle the cotton which is consigned to them for sale. It will be seen, therefore, that but few of the best storage houses now in use are available to the farmer unless he is willing to ship his cotton to the factor and pay him a fee for selling it, in addition to regular storage charges. Many farmers are averse to shipping their cotton to another town and consigning it to a factor or commission merchant. They usually expect to receive the money at the time the cotton is delivered. Many farmers are reluctant to pay any charges whatever. This attitude is unfortunate, for it eliminates them from participation in the use of the best storage facilities.

THE SMALL WAREHOUSE RENDERS POOR SERVICE.

The service rendered by the small warehouses in the primary markets is almost universally unsatisfactory. The warehouse owners are not to blame for this poor service. The cost of handling is much greater than in the case of larger establishments, and the insurance rate is usually four or five times as great as in the standard warehouses in larger towns. One might at first be inclined to think that they should erect costly buildings, but in most cases this would not pay, for there is not a sufficient volume of business. Very few farmers will store their cotton when the market price is fairly satisfactory. A good storage building might be erected in a small town and a fair profit be made for one year, but it might be four years or even longer before it would again be well patronized. The chances are that during this period the fees collected would not pay the cost of operation. The investor would lose all of the money made in one year in addition to the interest on the funds invested in the building. The result is that most of the warehouses erected in such towns are owned primarily by merchants or cotton buyers for use in connection with their business. They are not intended for the use of farmers, and when a year of very low prices comes they are not in position to render the service that the farmer expects.

COOPERATION ON THE PART OF FARMERS.

From the foregoing it would seem that the most satisfactory solution of the situation would be for the farmers to form cooperative associations and build their own storage houses. They can not expect others to invest thousands of dollars in storage houses that will lie idle for several years and make a profit for only one year. No business men will invest their money in such a way. Farmers must build their own storage houses or remain dependent upon the merchants and cotton factors. It would seem also that the mills and trade in general should encourage the preservation of cotton by storage by discriminating individually against "country damaged" cotton. This would put a premium on cotton in good condition and would thus tend to encourage storage.

WAREHOUSES NOT WELL DISTRIBUTED.

It has been stated that in aggregate storage capacity present facilities are ample but the warehouses are not properly distributed. The investigation showed that in many places in every State, including those with the greatest number of warehouses, thousands of bales of cotton are "stored" on the streets and platforms, or left about gins and farms, while all the warehouses in use are filled to their greatest capacity. In other sections of the same State, frequently in the same county, warehouses were found that are used very little. This indicates that very poor judgment has been exercised in the location of storage houses and that those who have cotton to be protected can not get the service which might be expected from the figures shown in Table VII. Doubtless many new warehouses should be erected in sections that are not now served. Many of the houses which have been improperly planned should be reconstructed in order to obtain better insurance rates and render better service. Some of the inferior houses should be destroyed or used for hay barns or for other purposes. Wherever possible, the farmer should be allowed the use of cotton mill and other private warehouses, and he should be encouraged in every possible way to store and protect his cotton. On the other hand, he should be willing to change his present practice and his ideas in regard to the storage business.

STORAGE FACILITIES NOW AVAILABLE.

GEORGIA AND NORTH CAROLINA.

Table III (p. 13) gives the results of the survey in Georgia and North Carolina. It will be seen that the storage capacity of warehouses is given in flat or uncompressed bales, in cotton as offered, and also in the compressed form. All the figures relating to the storage capacity of warehouses belonging to cotton mills refer to uncompressed or flat cotton. In the investigation in these States information as to the storage capacity of all warehouses in flat bales was requested. From this list a careful estimate has been made of the quantity in compressed cotton which these same warehouses could store. A detailed study of the entire situation has been made in order to ascertain which warehouses ordinarily receive flat cotton and which receive compressed cotton. "Capacity as offered" in the table represents the total number of bales which these warehouses would hold, in the form in which it is usually offered, as thus estimated. This table also shows the total number of warehouses in the State, the number reporting, and the number not reporting. The capacities entered in the table are for those warehouses which made reports.

Table III also shows the storage capacity of the warehouses owned by cotton mills in Georgia and North Carolina. The data upon which this table is based were secured directly from the mills. A letter of inquiry was sent to all cotton mills in these States asking for information regarding storage facilities, including the capacity of their warehouses, and insurance rates. The table shows the number of mills reporting, together with the total storage capacity of the warehouses belonging to those of each State.

TABLE III.—*Number and storage capacity of warehouses in Georgia and North Carolina (beginning of 1913–14 season).*

Kind of warehouses.	State.	Total number	Number reporting.	Number not reporting.	Capacity in bales.[2]		
					Flat.	As offered.	Compressed.
Public and private.	Georgia	990	668	322	1,038,445	1,281,745	1,746,060
	North Carolina	128	114	14	182,705	229,205	318,855
Cotton mill	Georgia	151	123	28	397,875		
Do	North Carolina	326	274	52	368,495		

[1] Data secured from warehouses.
[2] The totals given here include only the warehouses reporting.

THE COTTON BELT IN GENERAL.

Table IV (p. 14) gives the result of a letter of inquiry sent to the county agents in the cotton-growing States. Written reports were received from these agents which gave the names and storage capacities of the number of warehouses in each State entered in this table. Some of these reports referred to cotton in the uncompressed form, some to compressed bales, and still others did not indicate to which form they referred. As a result of a careful estimate, there is shown in one column the number of flat bales these warehouses could store, and in another the number of compressed bales. The form in which cotton is ordinarily offered for storage has also been determined as nearly as possible, and the capacity as thus estimated is given under the column headed "As offered."

TABLE IV.—*Number and storage capacity of warehouses in the cotton belt (August, 1914) as reported by the county agents.*

State.	Number reporting.	Storage capacity in bales.		
		Flat.	As offered.	Compressed.
Alabama	264	740,425	856,525	1,246,150
Arkansas	106	365,100	508,400	631,900
Florida	46	204,600	325,300	345,700
Georgia	214	605,350	690,500	1,009,800
Louisiana	91	519,000	689,900	774,700
Mississippi	76	405,700	693,550	757,200
North Carolina	55	60,550	60,550	101,700
Oklahoma	47	244,365	379,665	419,475
South Carolina	153	597,800	746,800	1,006,400
Tennessee	28	529,350	835,850	850,010
Texas	226	1,223,820	1,904,670	2,221,950
Virginia	27	199,900	287,800	299,150
Total	1,333	5,695,960	7,979,510	9,664,135

Table V (p. 14), which is an estimate of the storage capacity of the warehouses available at the end of the 1913–14 season, is made up from a detailed comparison of Tables III and IV. By referring to Table III it will be seen that the complete list of Georgia contains 990 warehouses. Of these, 668 have reported, and as shown in Table III they have a storage capacity of 1,038,445 flat bales, 1,281,745 bales as offered, or 1,746,060 compressed bales. This is an average capacity for the warehouses reporting of 1,555 flat bales, 1,770 as offered, or 2,600 compressed. From a careful survey of the State it has been ascertained that many warehouses not reporting have a large storage capacity, and it is believed that the average capacity of those not reporting is as great, if not greater, than the average for the 668 which reported. But in making these estimates, in order to be very conservative, it is assumed that the average capacity of those not reporting in flat bales is only 600, as offered 800, and compressed 1,000. If these amounts are added to the amounts actually reported, the total storage capacity for Georgia is: Flat, 1,231,645 bales; as offered, 1,539,345 bales; and compressed, 2,068,060 bales.

TABLE V.—*Estimated number and storage capacity of warehouses in the cotton belt (beginning of the 1913–14 season).*

State.	Total number.	Storage capacity in bales.		
		Flat.	As offered.	Compressed.
Alabama	528	1,480,850	1,713,050	2,492,300
Arkansas	212	649,800	878,000	925,000
Florida	46	204,600	325,300	345,700
Georgia	990	1,231,645	1,539,345	2,068,060
Louisiana	182	736,000	996,300	1,145,900
Mississippi	152	811,400	1,387,100	1,514,400
North Carolina	128	191,105	240,405	332,855
Oklahoma	94	488,730	759,330	838,950
South Carolina	306	1,051,600	1,239,600	1,715,800
Tennessee	28	529,350	835,850	850,010
Texas	452	1,769,540	2,284,840	3,210,700
Virginia	27	199,900	287,800	299,150
Total	3,145	9,344,520	12,486,920	15,738,825

The same plan was followed in arriving at the storage capacity of North Carolina warehouses. By referring again to Table III, it will be seen that the average storage capacity for the 114 warehouses reporting from this State is 1,602 flat bales, 2,015 bales as offered, and 2,709 compressed bales. This is very close to the average in Georgia, and the same figures have been used in determining the probable storage capacity of the 14 warehouses not reporting; namely, 600 flat, 800 as offered, and 1,000 compressed. This gives the following total capacity for North Carolina: Flat bales, 191,105, as offered 240,405, and compressed 332,855.

By referring further to Table III, it will be seen that the complete list for Georgia comprises 990 warehouses. Table IV shows that the county agents reported only 214 warehouses with the storage capacity indicated. This is less than one-fourth of the number on the complete list. In North Carolina the agents reported only 55 warehouses, which is less than one-half the number that are in use in that State. In arriving at the number of warehouses for the different States it would seem justifiable to estimate that the agents reported about one-third or one-fourth of the actual number, inasmuch as they reported less than one-fourth of the number actually existing in the States of Georgia and North Carolina combined, where detailed surveys had been made. But in order to be on the safe side, it has been assumed that they reported approximately one-half of the number in each cotton State, except Georgia and North Carolina, in which States the number indicated by the survey has been used. Doubling the number of warehouses reported by the county agents as shown in Table IV, there results the number given in Table V. The exact number reported in Virginia, Florida, and Tennessee is shown, as the warehouses in these three States are located chiefly in large cities, and it is believed that fairly complete figures have been obtained.

The next problem is to arrive at the storage capacity in the different States. It has been explained how this estimate was made for Georgia and North Carolina, and, it will be remembered, this was based on a comprehensive survey of these States. Comparing again Tables IV and V, it will be seen that the reports of the county agents for Georgia show a total storage capacity of less than one-half of that actually developed by the comprehensive survey. In North Carolina the same reports cover less than one-third of the storage space which actually exists. This seems to be sufficient justification for multiplying the capacities shown in Table IV by two and one-half or even by three. But instead of doing this, after eliminating the large shipping centers, the capacities reported by the county agents have been doubled, except in Georgia and North Carolina, where the figures of the complete survey are used. The reported capacity of warehouses for Virginia, Florida, and Tennessee has not been increased. In addition, the storage space as reported for Charleston,

New Orleans, Houston, Galveston, Memphis, and Pine Bluff (Ark.), is given as reported. In these towns there are many large storage houses, and the reports seem to indicate that they cover the complete storage capacity.

Table VI (p. 16) is derived directly from Table V. The figures given in Table V are believed to be a very safe estimate of the available storage facilities in the South in the early part of 1914 or during the cotton season of 1913-14. It is impossible to state, of course, just how many new warehouses have been erected and how much the total storage capacity has been increased in this way. Many storage houses have been constructed to help meet the present emergency. This increase has been estimated at 10 per cent, which is a very conservative estimate. Table VI is the same as Table V with a 10 per cent increase in the number of warehouses and a like increase in the total storage capacity. In another column is shown the 1913 production by States in running bales [1] as reported by the Census. In this way a comparison between the storage facilities now available and the production can be made very readily.

TABLE VI.—*Estimated number and storage capacity of all warehouses in the cotton belt, making allowance for a 10 per cent increase since August, 1914, compared with the production in running bales, by States.*

State.	Number.	Storage capacity in bales.			1913 production in running bales.
		Flat.	As offered.	Compressed.	
Alabama	581	1,628,935	1,884,355	2,741,530	1,483,669
Arkansas	233	714,780	965,800	1,017,500	1,038,293
Florida	51	225,060	357,830	380,270	66,700
Georgia	1,089	1,354,810	1,693,280	2,274,866	2,346,237
Louisiana	200	809,600	1,095,930	1,260,490	436,865
Mississippi	167	892,540	1,525,810	1,665,840	1,251,841
North Carolina	149	210,216	264,446	366,141	842,499
Oklahoma	[1] 120	540,600	842,330	927,845	837,995
South Carolina	337	1,156,760	1,363,560	1,887,380	1,418,704
Tennessee	31	582,285	919,435	935,011	366,786
Texas	497	1,946,494	2,513,324	3,531,770	3,773,024
Virginia	30	219,890	316,580	329,065	24,569
All others	......	....	....	....	95,629
Total	3,485	10,281,970	13,742,680	17,317,708	13,982,811

[1] The names of 26 companies reporting to us have been added. This is more than the 10 per cent added for other States from which no reports were received of the number of new warehouses.

In connection with the estimate of the probable increase in storage facilities, it may be well to state that the Marketing Division of the North Carolina Experiment Station has published the results of an investigation which indicate that the storage space provided since the 1913-14 season in that State would be sufficient to store 134,915 bales. By referring to Table V it will be seen that this is an increase of almost 100 per cent over the space available in 1913-14.

In Oklahoma 41 warehouse companies were chartered from the first of September, 1914, to about the middle of October of the same

[1] By the term "running bales" is meant the actual number of bales produced, which is not exactly the same as the number of 500-pound bales ordinarily used for statistical purposes.

year. Letters were sent to these companies to determine whether they had actually constructed buildings, and if so, the storage capacities of these new warehouses. Replies were received which show that 26 of the 41 companies have actually constructed buildings and are doing a storage business. The reported capacity of these 26 warehouses is 53,250 bales. This is an increase of over 10 per cent in the cotton storage space in the State, and 20 per cent in the number of warehouses. It is certain that many other warehouses have been constructed since that time, and, in all probability, a number of persons who have not applied for charters are doing a storage business. In view of the fact that these two investigations show such a large increase in the apparent storage facilities in the autumn of 1914, the estimate of 10 per cent as the average increase for the cotton belt must appeal to everyone as being very conservative.

ESTIMATED STORAGE CAPACITY OF COTTON-MILL WAREHOUSES.

GEORGIA.

In Georgia there are 151 cotton mills (Table VII). Reports received from 123 of these show that the total capacity of their warehouses is 398,875 bales of uncompressed cotton (see Table III). This is an average of 3,317 bales per mill. Making the supposition that the 28 mills not reporting have warehouses of equal average capacity, their total storage capacity is almost 100,000 bales. This, added to the figures actually reported, would give a combined storage capacity of almost 500,000 bales. In order to avoid any overestimation, it has been assumed that only 15 of the 28 cotton mills have storage houses and that the average capacity of these warehouses is 1,000 bales, or less than one-third the average capacity of those reporting. This would give a total storage capacity of 15,000 bales. Adding this to the 397,875 bales actually reported gives an estimated total capacity for the mill warehouses of the State of 412,500 bales. Any error that may exist in this estimate is on the conservative side.

TABLE VII.—*Estimated number and storage capacity of warehouses and cotton-mill warehouses now in use compared with the production of each State, in running bales, for 1913.*

State.	Warehouses.		Cotton mills.		Combined storage capacity.	1913 production in running bales.
	Number.	Capacity in bales as offered.	Number.	Capacity in flat bales.		
Alabama	581	1,884,355	62	62,000	1,946,355	1,483,669
Arkansas	233	965,800	6	6,000	971,800	1,038,293
Florida	51	357,830	1	1,000	358,830	66,700
Georgia	1,089	1,693,280	151	412,500	2,105,780	2,346,237
Louisiana	200	1,095,930	6	6,000	1,101,930	436,865
Mississippi	167	1,525,810	18	18,000	1,543,810	1,251,841
North Carolina	149	264,446	326	400,995	665,441	842,499
Oklahoma	120	842,330	7	7,000	849,330	837,995
South Carolina	337	1,363,560	164	300,000	1,663,560	1,418,704
Tennessee	31	919,435	27	27,000	946,435	366,786
Texas	497	2,513,324	36	36,000	2,549,324	3,773,024
Virginia	30	316,580	19	19,000	335,580	24,569
All others						95,629
Total	3,485	13,742,680	823	1,295,495	15,038,175	13,982,811

NORTH CAROLINA.

In North Carolina there are 326 cotton mills (Table VII). Reports were received from 274 of these, showing the total storage capacity of these mill warehouses to be 368,495 flat bales, or an average of 1,346 bales each. If it is assumed that the mills not reporting have an average capacity equal to those reporting, their combined storage capacity would amount to about 70,000 bales. Adding this to the amount actually reported, we have a total of about 440,000 bales, but, as in the case of Georgia, in order to avoid the possibility of any overestimation it has been assumed that only 26 of the 52 mills have warehouses and that the average storage capacity of these is only 1,250 bales. Their combined capacity at this rate would be 32,500 bales, which, added to the amount actually reported, gives the aggregate storage capacity of the cotton mills of the State as 400,995 bales. There is every reason to believe that this is a very low estimate. Some of the largest mills of the State are among those which failed to make reports. The average storage capacity of the warehouses belonging to the cotton mills thus failing to report is doubtless greater than that of those which have reported.

SOUTH CAROLINA.

In South Carolina there are 164 cotton mills. Reports from county agents show that 62 of these mills have warehouse space for 234,900 bales, or an average of 3,600 bales each. If the average for all the cotton mills of the State should equal the 62 included in these reports, a total of 590,000 bales could be stored. From general observations and conferences with many of the cotton-mill men in South Carolina it is believed that the storage space of the mills is on the average very large. An estimate of 600,000 bales apparently would be justified by the reports at hand. However, an estimate of only 300,000 bales for the State, or approximately one-half of the apparent storage capacity, has been used.

OTHER STATES.

For all the remaining States it is assumed that each cotton mill has a storage capacity of 1,000 bales. In no State which has been investigated in detail is the average storage space of the mills so small as this. Estimates of the capacity of mill warehouses in each of the cotton-producing States, determined in the manner just explained, will be found in Table VII, which shows the storage capacity of warehouses for cotton as offered, as given in Table VI, with the figures for the cotton mills added. This table shows the estimated number of warehouses and their storage capacity in bales as offered, and the number of cotton-mill warehouses with their estimated capacity in flat bales. But many of the mills use compressed cotton, so the estimate for the warehouses belonging to cotton mills might be increased greatly without danger of making it too great. In the column headed "Combined storage capacity for State" is shown the total of both the public and private warehouses and cotton-mill warehouses.

STORAGE CAPACITY COMPARED WITH PRODUCTION.

The next column (Table VII) shows the 1913 production of each of the States. It will be seen that the storage capacity of all the warehouses is greater than the production. In addition to making conservative estimates in every case, the list does not include warehouses in St. Louis, Evansville, and the storage houses belonging to the cotton mills in Missouri. Cotton is moving to eastern ports constantly and being exported, and extensive warehouses belonging to the cotton mills in New England are used, all of which tends to increase the available storage space. Further, efforts have been made to exclude compress sheds and terminal sheds belonging to railroads and other transportation companies, so in presenting this estimate it is believed that it is too low throughout rather than too high in any instance.

INSURANCE RATES AND COST OF BUILDINGS.

DISCUSSION OF TYPES.

Table VIII (p. 20) gives important data relating to the different types of warehouses now in use. It is particularly interesting to notice the difference in the cost of constructing the same type of warehouse in different States. A comparison of cost and insurance rates of different types in the same State is also interesting. For example, the ordinary brick warehouse costs more than a standard warehouse with board ends and fire walls, and at the same time pays a much higher insurance rate. Further, it is shown that those warehouses that are equipped with automatic sprinklers (Table IX) have cost very little more than the others; yet they have a very much lower insurance rate. The automatic sprinkler is costly, but the reduction of insurance rates helps to offset the additional cost of installation. The data in the tables show clearly that it is best to construct standard warehouses and equip them with automatic sprinklers. This unquestionably will effect a great saving. In Georgia and North Carolina the insurance rate is reduced about 80 per cent by the use of sprinklers. It is decidedly interesting to notice the lower cost of construction and the lower insurance rate on the warehouses belonging to the cotton mills in each of the States (Table X). From this it may be concluded that a great saving could be effected by the erection and proper equipment of modern warehouses conforming to the standards promulgated and recommended by the underwriters associations.

TABLE VIII.—*Comparative cost, storage capacity, insurance rates, and other data concerning public and private warehouses classified according to construction.*

State.	Type of warehouse (construction).	Number.	Total capacity in flat bales.	Average capacity in flat bales.	Total cost.	Cost per bale capacity.	Average insurance rate.
Georgia	Wood	26	14,250	548	$48,350	$3.40	$3.30
	Corrugated iron	69	53,935	782	125,820	2.35	2.70
	Brick	215	280,170	1,303	1,089,500	3.89	1.95
	Standard	5	10,700	2,140	31,750	2.97	1.52
	Concrete or stone	22	20,750	944	76,500	3.64	2.29
North Carolina	Brick	11	14,000	1,273	40,950	2.925	1.96
	Standard	5	13,250	2,650	30,450	1.54	1.25
Oklahoma	Corrugated iron	22	27,850	1,266	27,820	1.00	2.20

TABLE IX.—*Comparative cost, storage capacity, insurance rates, and other data concerning public and private warehouses classified according to sprinkler equipment.*

State.	Equipment of warehouses.	Number.	Total capacity in flat bales.	Average capacity in flat bales.	Total cost.	Cost per bale capacity.	Average insurance rate.
Georgia	With sprinklers	30	129,200	4,307	$527,900	$4.09	$0.246
	Without sprinklers	30	63,200	2,107	248,600	3.77	1.67
North Carolina	With sprinklers	8	47,900	5,988	173,500	3.62	.238
	Without sprinklers	8	8,600	1,075	22,950	2.67	1.52

PLAN, EQUIPMENT, AND COST.

It is impossible to overestimate the importance of proper planning, construction, and equipment of cotton warehouses. These have an important bearing not only upon the cost of the structure itself and the cost of handling cotton but also upon insurance rates. The public warehouses now in use which are equipped with automatic sprinklers have cost about $4 per bale storage capacity, and cotton stored in these buildings is insured at an average of about 25 cents on the $100 per annum. These investigations show clearly that the average cost of warehouses not so equipped is not very much less than $4 per bale storage capacity, while the insurance rate is very much higher, comparatively speaking. It is admitted that the automatic sprinkler equipment is expensive, but the warehouses now in use which are equipped with sprinklers are comparatively large, most of them have been built according to the underwriters' standards, and in a general way they have been planned and built on a business basis, which accounts for the saving in cost of construction.

If the present crop of cotton is assumed to be 16,000,000 bales, new warehouses to store all of it could be constructed and equipped with automatic sprinklers for $64,000,000 or less. If all of this crop should be stored for a period of six months the cost of insurance at $2 per $100, which is lower than the average paid at present, would amount to $8,000,000 if the cotton is valued at $50 per bale. In the new warehouses costing $64,000,000 this cotton could be stored for the same length of time at $1,000,000, or 25 cents on the $100 per annum. It seems a radical statement, but it will be seen that if every warehouse now in existence were destroyed and new ones constructed to protect the entire crop, the expenditure of the $64,000,000 would effect an annual saving of $7,000,000, assuming that all the cotton would be stored for a period of six months. This saving of $7,000,000 would represent a fair income on twice the cost of the warehouses.

This is a rather remarkable showing, but if we would profit by the experience of the cotton mills and adopt their methods this saving could be greatly increased. At the cost of constructing the present cotton-mill warehouses (Table X), it would be possible to erect buildings to store the 16,000,000 bales of cotton at a cost of $44,800,000. This would represent a saving in cost of construction of $19,200,000 over the assumed cost. It will be seen further from Table X that the mills in many instances pay an insurance rate of less than 12½ cents on $100. On this basis the 16,000,000 bales of cotton valued at $50 per bale could be stored for six months for $500,000. The figures show that it would be possible to make a saving of $7,500,000 per annum by the investment of approximately $45,000,000 for standard and properly equipped warehouses.

INSURANCE RATES.

A careful examination of the insurance records in the cotton-producing States shows that the average insurance rate is about 3 per cent per annum, including all cotton risks. These investigations show clearly that the average rate on cotton in the present warehouses is not less than 2 per cent per annum, and if cotton in compress sheds, terminal yards, and various other hazardous places is included, it would seem that an estimate of 3 per cent is not too high. It is therefore safe to use 2 per cent as the basis of the estimates in the preceding paragraphs. Table VIII shows that a large number of brick warehouses in Georgia and North Carolina pay approximately 2 per cent and that the buildings constructed of wood, corrugated iron, concrete, and stone pay a much higher rate, and the cost of construction is also very high for most of these types.

TABLE X.—*Comparative cost, storage capacity, insurance rates, and other data concerning cotton-mill warehouses with automatic sprinklers.*

State.	Number.	Total capacity in flat bales.	Average capacity in flat bales.	Total cost.	Cost per bale capacity.	Average insurance rate.
Georgia	64	164,700	2,573	$461,698	$2.80	$0.122
North Carolina	73	109,950	1,506	301,900	2.76	.13

In comparing the cost of the corrugated iron warehouses in Georgia and Oklahoma, it is well to remember that most of the buildings in Georgia have wooden floors with costly brick foundations, while most of those in Oklahoma have dirt floors, which are very much cheaper and carry a lower insurance rate. It is also true that many of the houses in Oklahoma have been erected expressly for the storage of cotton, while some of the houses in Georgia are used both for cotton and other products, which general use is responsible for a higher rate of insurance.

GENERAL CONCLUSIONS.

BENEFITS TO BE DERIVED FROM A SYSTEM OF WAREHOUSES.

It would be impossible to enumerate all of the benefits, direct and indirect, that might be derived from the inauguration of an ample and efficient system of storage houses, but it is evident that such a system would be of great assistance in handling and financing the cotton crop. It would benefit not only the farmer but the merchant, the local banker, and other business men. A storage system properly operated and used would eventually free the cotton farmer from the present destructive credit system. It would improve conditions in the cotton market. Much "country damage" and loss from unnecessary sampling would be prevented, and much of the duplication in handling and marketing cotton under the present complex system would be eliminated. Such a system would enable the farmer to distribute the sales of cotton throughout the year, and in this way avoid depressed prices. Under present conditions the farmer rushes his cotton to market as fast as it can be picked and ginned, and thus "bears" his own market.

DIFFICULTIES UNDER PRESENT CONDITIONS.

There are many disadvantages connected with the storage business as conducted at present, and there are serious difficulties that must be overcome before an adequate system can be inaugurated. The present facilities are poorly distributed and frequently not available to the farmer. The service rendered by many of the companies is poor, and their charges, including insurance, are unusually high owing to the small amount of cotton ordinarily stored by the farmer. His business is undesirable, for it is much more trouble to handle cotton in small lots. The cotton mills do not encourage the farmer to store his cotton, as their usual practice is to make a general allowance for tare and damage. This average is charged against all cotton, whether it reaches the mill in good or bad condition, so there is little incentive for the farmer and trade in general to go to any trouble or extra expense in protecting the staple. The farmer, therefore, receives practically no benefit from the system now in operation, and it is not at all certain that he would take kindly to any system which might be devised. As a general proposition, he is averse to storing his cotton, especially when he has to pay any direct charge for the service. The majority of farmers have been accustomed to selling their own cotton and receiving the money for it when it is delivered. It is not believed that they would generally patronize any storage house, if to do so it were necessary to ship their cotton to another town. It is equally true that they will not cooperate readily with each other in building storage houses near the place of production.

SELLING COTTON THROUGH FACTORS.

To anyone spending much time in the cotton markets it becomes evident that our cotton crop is supporting entirely too many men. This is particularly true of buyers and merchants in the primary markets. It is not uncommon, in those cities where from 10,000 to 15,000 bales are marketed in one season, to see four or five and frequently a larger number of buyers on the street. Naturally these men must be paid for their services, and it is quite evident that the cotton itself is taxed to cover this expense. If such a town had one good warehouse and one competent cotton man to represent the farmers, these buyers could be eliminated, and the farmer would receive the benefit in the form of better prices for his cotton. It is true that most farmers prefer making their own sales, but in very few cases do they know the grade of their cotton or the price it should bring. Consequently they are not in a position to make an intelligent sale. It would be much better for farmers to pay a nominal fee for the services of an experienced man. This would save time and trouble and eventually place the cotton trade on a business basis. It would not only eliminate unnecessary persons connected with the markets, but it would save the farmer much time now lost in going to town to make his sale and would prevent the waste resulting from unnecessary sampling.

VALUE OF PLANS.

The importance of taking the necessary precautions in planning warehouses and adhering to the standards of the underwriters' associations is forcibly illustrated by a comparison of five standard warehouses with sprinkler equipment with five warehouses without such equipment, all of which are located in the same Georgia city. The five warehouses without sprinklers have a total storage capacity of 21,000 flat bales, or an average of 4,200 bales for each warehouse. These buildings cost a total of $82,500, or an average of $3.92 per bale storage capacity. The other five buildings have a total storage capacity of 46,000 bales, or an average capacity of 9,200 bales for each warehouse. These buildings cost $161,000, or $3.50 per bale capacity. The first group of buildings have no automatic sprinkler equipment, and the average insurance rate on cotton stored in these buildings is $2.57 per $100 per annum. The second group of buildings are fully standard, and have approved automatic sprinkler equipment, and the insurance rate on cotton stored in these buildings is only 35 cents per $100 per annum. Those without the sprinklers are small buildings and are not properly planned, and such poor business methods were used in their construction that they cost more than was necessary. On the other hand the five buildings with automatic sprinkler equipment were properly planned. They were erected at a minimum cost, with the greatest efficiency, and have a low insurance rate.

SIZE OF WAREHOUSE.

It is impossible to state definitely the best size for a public warehouse. These investigations show conclusively that the large, properly organized, advantageously located storage houses pay well, while the small warehouses in most cases do not pay. Other things being equal, it might be said that the larger the storage house the better. Building a large house saves much in cost of construction and reduces the cost of handling the cotton. On the other hand, it is impossible to build only large houses and have them properly distributed. These two points must be taken into consideration, and the proper size for the house will be a compromise between the two. Where towns are very small and shipping facilities to large centers are ample it might be best to have no storage house. On the other hand, many towns where a considerable amount of cotton is marketed annually will do well to have a warehouse. It is frequently the case that in very small towns two or three men each build storage houses. None of them can give efficient service, and they are forced to charge too much for storage, while at the same time they lose money. It would certainly seem that there is a most urgent need of cooperation in the small towns.

IDEAL WAREHOUSE SYSTEM.

It would probably be unwise to attempt to outline in detail a theoretically ideal warehouse system, but it does seem proper to indicate some essential features of such a system. It should be organized intelligently on a sound business basis, with the best financial standing and connections. Both the company and custodian should be bonded. Some provision should be made for State or Federal inspection. This would give the receipts of the company the greatest possible value, and the holder of such a receipt would be able to borrow money on the very best terms. Each warehouse should be intelligently managed. The man in charge should be well posted on grades and market conditions. This would enable him to render the most efficient service in marketing the farmers' cotton, and thereby avoid the unnecessary profits of the buyer and eliminate various other losses. It is needless to say that the storage houses operated by such a system should be standard in every respect. Cotton should be fully protected by insurance, and convenient forms should be provided for making and recording all transactions. This system should aim eventually to store cotton in the compressed form in order to increase the storage capacity of the building. All warehouses should use uniform receipts, and so far as it is practicable the business should be fully standardized.

SUMMARY.

1. Financing is one of the greatest problems in marketing cotton. A sufficient number of warehouses would be erected if it were possible in the present emergency to borrow on cotton when stored.

2. Cotton is considered the very best collateral, but it is not available unless safely stored and insured. The banks are always willing to accept cotton as security, but during emergencies their capital is insufficient to meet demands.

3. A system of warehouses would simplify our financial system and eventually free the southern cotton farmer from the present disastrous credit system. It would stabilize the price of cotton by distributing sales throughout the year. The farmer would stop depressing the price of his own products by selling his cotton as soon as it is ginned.

4. In storage capacity the present cotton warehouses are ample, but these warehouses are poorly distributed. The best warehouses are not available to the farmer. The charges of the others are too high because they must pay a high insurance rate and the cost of handling is necessarily great. Some new standard buildings should be erected, but many of those now in use should be remodeled.

5. Cotton keeps in storage better than any other farm product. Protected from the weather it never deteriorates. It resists decay even when exposed. Consequently, it is neglected more than any other valuable product. The cotton mills should encourage storing by paying a premium for cotton in good condition.

6. The dealers, or middlemen as they are frequently called, are in much better position to hold cotton than the farmers. They not only control the best storage houses, but have better financial connections which enable them to get money more readily and on better terms. The farmer sells his cotton when prices are depressed and the dealer gets the full benefit of any advance after the rush is over.

7. A large standard storage house pays ample dividends, while most of the owners of small warehouses actually lose money on the

investment. The fact that the best warehouses belong to the factors and the cotton mills and are not available to the farmer makes it desirable for the farmers to cooperate in building their own houses. If they do not, they must remain dependent upon the factors.

8. All warehouses should conform fully to the standards recognized by the underwriters' associations. This will save cost in construction, in handling cotton, and in insurance.

ADDITIONAL COPIES
OF THIS PUBLICATION MAY BE PROCURED FROM
THE SUPERINTENDENT OF DOCUMENTS
GOVERNMENT PRINTING OFFICE
WASHINGTON, D. C.
AT
5 CENTS PER COPY
▽

WASHINGTON : GOVERNMENT PRINTING OFFICE : 1915

BULLETIN OF THE U.S. DEPARTMENT OF AGRICULTURE

No. 217

Contribution from the Bureau of Biological Survey, Henry W. Henshaw, Chief.
May 26, 1915.

MORTALITY AMONG WATERFOWL AROUND GREAT SALT LAKE, UTAH.

(PRELIMINARY REPORT.)

By Alex Wetmore, *Assistant Biologist.*

INTRODUCTION.

It is widely known that in recent years vast numbers of waterfowl frequenting the marshes along the eastern shore of Great Salt Lake, Utah, have died, apparently from disease. Untold thousands of wild ducks, snipe, sandpipers, and other birds of less economic value have perished. Nor is the effect of this mortality confined to the region in question. While countless numbers of waterfowl have perished in comparatively small areas, the effect upon the abundance of these birds in other regions is widespread. In the marshes around Great Salt Lake are bred annually great numbers of waterfowl, and hordes from more northern regions migrate through in spring and fall. These breeding and migrant birds form an important percentage of those migrating or wintering farther south, and serious diminution of their numbers in the affected localities will be felt heavily in other regions. The question of the causes of this mortality and possible measures for its prevention are therefore of widespread interest and importance.

It is to be noted that a similar mortality occurs in other localities, as Tulare and Owens Lakes, Cal., where for several years thousands of birds have perished annually. Reports not yet fully investigated have been received from other districts, and apparently the trouble may occur anywhere in the West under similar conditions.

Early in the investigations a number of dead ducks sent to the Biological Survey were turned over to the Bureau of Animal Industry for examination, the results of which are discussed on another page. Later, agents of that bureau made brief field inquiries into the mortality in Utah. A preliminary examination of the conditions around

Note.—This bulletin is a report of progress in investigating the causes of mortality among ducks and other waterfowl in marshes about Great Salt Lake, Utah. It is for the information of sportsmen and others interested in game birds.

87711°—Bull. 217—15

Great Salt Lake was made in the latter part of August, 1913, by S. E. Piper, of the Biological Survey. Following this, the writer began investigations in July, 1914' continuing the work throughout the summer and fall. The present paper discusses the results obtained and may be considered a report of progress. It is planned to continue the investigations during the present year (1915).

HISTORY.

The fact that many ducks were dying around Great Salt Lake was noted in the newspapers in Salt Lake City and Ogden in 1908 or 1909, but the prevalence of a malady among waterfowl was known many years earlier. Fred Hansen, who lives near the mouth of Bear River, says that in October, 1896, two guides brought 400 mallards from Klondike (at the mouth of Bear River), part of which were found dead and the rest alive but helpless. Dr. M. R. Stewart, of Salt Lake City, says that in 1902 or 1903 a few birds died on the New State Gun Club grounds at the mouth of the Jordan River. At the mouth of the Weber River birds were occasionally found helpless in the growths of "bayonet grass" during the fall of 1904, and were the subject of much speculation among the hunters. Early in the season of 1909 a few sick birds were noticed at the mouth of the Jordan River; and in the fall others, thought by some to be crippled birds from the fall shooting, were reported.

About July 15, 1910, sick birds appeared at the mouth of the Jordan River, and shortly after others were found on the Weber. Later, birds were found dying on the great expanse of mud flats and marshes built up in the delta of Bear River. Attention was now fully aroused, and as the mortality among ducks and other waterfowl increased, many theories as to its cause were advanced. The season was exceedingly dry, the water in the marshes was low, and the birds died in enormous numbers, the trouble continuing on Bear River until November. How many wild ducks and other waterfowl perished during that year will never be known. Thousands died both on the Jordan and the Weber, while on the Bear River marshes the mortality was almost incredible. V. T. Davis, in charge of the Bear River Club grounds, estimated that 85 per cent of all ducks on the lake died, and this statement was fully corroborated by others. The stench in South Bay arising from the dead bodies is said to have been unbearable.

Mortality among the birds began again in 1911, but was not so disastrous as during the preceding year. In 1912 few birds died on the New State Gun Club grounds, on the Jordan River, as the marshes were drained and water was not admitted until September 20. Elsewhere, however, conditions were more serious. At this time the trouble was considered contagious, and it was decided to clear the marshes of dead birds. On Bear River 44,462 wild ducks (from the present the two lakes first named are dry and the third contains an abundance of fresh water. On Tulare Lake, however, conditions are unchanged. In November, 1914, it was estimated by Tipton Matthews, deputy game warden of Kern County, and the writer that at least 15,000 birds had perished there during the preceding summer. Mr. Matthews stated that he has known of sick birds around Goose Lake and at Browns Knolls (Widgeon Gun Club grounds) for at least 20 years when the water was low in summer. Goose Lake is now dry, and as the water at Browns Knolls is kept fresh by artesian wells there is little trouble.

In June, 1891, Dr. A. K. Fisher, of the Biological Survey, noted large numbers of eared grebes and spoonbills dead around the shore of Owens Lake, Cal., and estimated the number of dead grebes at 35,000.[1] From the 12th to the 14th of November, 1914, the writer found many dead birds of these same species in this locality, and he was informed that this was an annual occurrence.

TERRITORY COVERED IN INVESTIGATIONS.

On July 12, 1914, work was begun in the Salt Lake Basin and continued until October 30. Investigations were made at the mouths of the Jordan, Weber, and Bear Rivers, the main areas affected (see Pls. I and III). Because of the large area involved, diversified conditions, and convenience of access to the marshes, most of the experimental work was carried on at the mouth of Bear River. In addition to the localities mentioned, conditions were studied at Willard Spur, Promontory Point on Great Salt Lake, and Locomotive Springs near Kelton.

From November 3 to 11 Tulare Lake, in California, was visited, in order to investigate the mortality in that region, and conditions at Owens Lake in the same State were studied from November 12 to 14.

At the mouth of Bear River, in Utah, quarters were furnished at the Duckville Gun Club, and thanks are due the officers and members of the club for assistance and facilities extended. Much assistance was rendered by A. P. Bigelow, of Ogden, and L. B. McCornick, of

[1] North American Fauna No. 7, 1893, p. 12-13.

Salt Lake City, who were deeply interested in the work. Valuable information was obtained also from V. T. Davis, in charge of the grounds of the Bear River Club. At the mouth of the Weber River, W. O. Belnap gave all possible assistance, as did other members of the North Shore Gun Club. At the mouth of the Jordan River work was done at the New State Gun Club. Permits for shooting such birds as were necessary for purposes of investigation were granted by the State fish and game commissioner, Fred W. Chambers. In California the State fish and game commission furnished an assistant, Tipton Matthews, deputy warden of Kern County, whose aid rendered the work around Tulare Lake effective.

NATURE OF THE TROUBLE.

During the season's work in Utah 27 species of birds of 11 families were found to be affected. Among these were 9 species of ducks, 10 of shorebirds, and 8 miscellaneous forms ranging from grebes and snowy herons (see Pl. III, fig. 1) to the pipit. Among ducks the pintail and green-winged teal seemed to be most susceptible, while the mallard, spoonbill, and cinnamon teal followed them closely. Avocets and stilts suffered more heavily than any other shorebirds.

The birds affected first lose the power of flight and are unable to rise in the air, though in some cases they can flutter across the water, and in others can fly for a few rods before dropping back. The legs next become affected and the power of diving is lost. As the birds grow weaker, they crawl out on the mud bars, if able to do so, or hide in growths of grass or rushes. In a later stage of the affection they are unable to rise. Finally the neck relaxes and the head lies prostrate (see Pl. II, figs. 1 and 2). If in the water, death comes by drowning, but on land, birds may live for two days or more in this condition.

A large series of postmortem examinations revealed no pathological lesions other than that the intestine was reddened and firm and hard to the touch. When the gut was slit, washed, and examined under a low magnification, the capillaries in the intestinal villi were found to be distended, showing intense irritation. The reddening of the canal appeared sometimes in spots, most severe at the bends of the intestine, but at others it extended continuously from the duodenal loop to the cæca. Clots of extravasated blood, partially digested, were found in most cases, and not uncommonly the cæca were distended with this matter. A severe dysentery occasioned by the irritation of the intestine was the obvious external symptom. The feces were greenish and stained the feathers about the anus and sometimes well up on the abdomen. Large quantities of renal matter were present, white and almost solid, and with an offensive odor. As the food residue in the intestine worked off, this renal matter constituted an increasing proportion of the feces, frequently solidifying

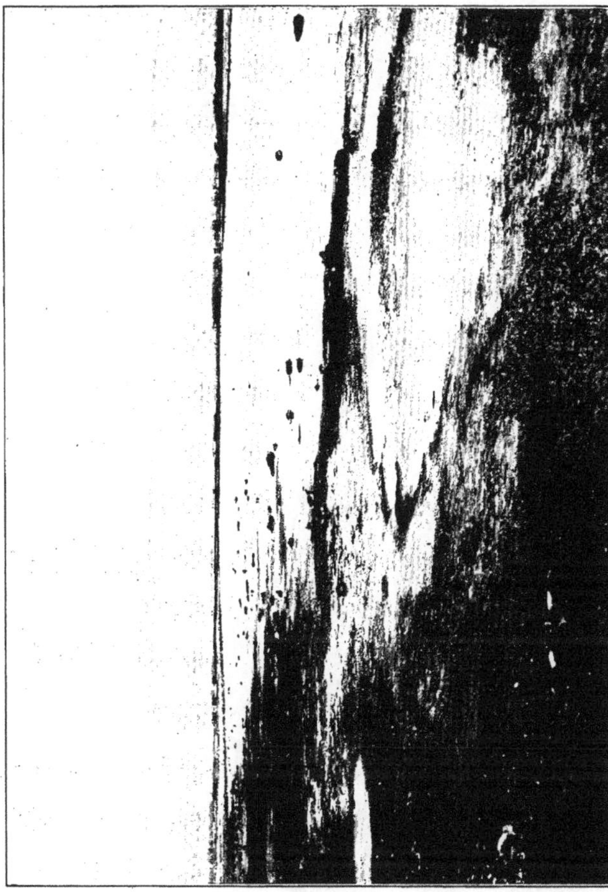

DUCKS DEAD FROM THE SO-CALLED "DUCK MALADY."

Helpless birds may be seen in the foreground. Photograph taken at mouth of Weber River, Utah, September 14, 1914.

FIG. 1.—TWO MALLARDS, ONE HELPLESS, THE OTHER DEAD.
Photograph taken at mouth of Bear River, Utah.

FIG. 2.—A SICK MALLARD.
The head has fallen on the back; otherwise the bird would have drowned. This bird recovered when given fresh water.

FIG. 1.—SNOWY HERONS DEAD FROM THE SO-CALLED "DUCK MALADY."
Photograph taken September 22, 1914, at mouth of Bear River, Utah.

FIG. 2.—ROW OF EXPERIMENT PENS AT MOUTH OF BEAR RIVER, UTAH.
In these inclosures ducks were kept under experimental conditions. Similar pens were stationed at other localities on the mud flats.

into a chalky mass which closed the anal opening. In about one-third of the birds kept under observation a secondary trouble developed in the course of two days or more after they lost the power of flight. A watery exudate came from the eyes and nasal chamber, and through the internal nares ran into the throat. This occasioned trouble in breathing. At times the discharge thickened into a whitish, cheesy mass and cemented the eyelids together.

THEORIES AS TO CAUSE.

Many theories have been advanced to account for the mortality. It has been variously ascribed to bacterial infection, typhoid infection from the presence of sewage, parasitic nematodes, poisoning from the deposition of sulphur or arsenic from smelters, and waste water from sugar factories. Other minor hypotheses need not be noted.

BACTERIAL INFECTION.

The fact that so many species of birds are affected militates against the theory of bacterial infection, and no bacillus apparently capable of transmitting the trouble has been isolated. Dr. J. R. Mohler, of the Bureau of Animal Industry, writes as follows concerning the ducks examined in that bureau:

> Relative to our investigations concerning the cause of death of large numbers of ducks in Utah, the information at hand points to the probability that death is due to an acute poisoning, and not to a disease of bacterial origin. The suggestion has frequently been made in the past that the water which the ducks drink is poisoned by the discharge of sulphuric acid, arsenic, copper, and other materials from smelters. A duck in captivity can be easily poisoned by administering any of these substances; but it is very doubtful whether a large body of running water in which large numbers of ducks in flight could obtain water could be poisoned even if a large chemical works discharged its entire output into the stream. Dilute sulphuric acid in small amounts is harmless, and it is doubtful whether ducks would drink a solution of sulphuric acid of any appreciable strength because of the sour taste. Estimations were made of the amounts of sulphates, sulphuric acid, arsenic, and copper in the stomach contents and tissues of ducks from Utah. In no case did the results obtained point to any of these substances as the probable cause of death. Small amounts of sulphates, arsenic, and copper can be found in the tissues of any animal, and are no indication of abnormal conditions.
>
> Practically all the live ducks forwarded to Washington for study promptly recovered, while the dead ducks received were autopsied, but failed to show lesions of diagnostic value. Numerous inoculations were made from the different organs of the ducks, both on culture media and into experimental animals, but up to the present no special organism has been found which might be regarded as the causative agent of the disease. The earlier incrimination of the coccidia found in the intestinal canal of a number of ducks, as the exciting factors of the disease, has not been substantiated by later investigations.

PARASITIC NEMATODES.

Microscopic examinations in the field of a large number of blood smears failed to reveal the presence of nematodes, and a collection of material from the feeding grounds of the ducks near the mouth of the

Weber River was forwarded to the department for study. This was critically examined by Dr. N. A. Cobb, of the Bureau of Plant Industry, a leading authority on nematodes, who reports as follows:

A preliminary examination of the nematodes collected from material from the Weber River, Utah, does not disclose any reason for supposing any of the nematodes found could be connected with the great mortality noticed among wild ducks feeding in the locality whence I understand this material comes. A single specimen has been seen which is of a doubtful character and may perhaps be connected with some parasitic nematode form. This specimen, however, is of small importance, considering the large number of specimens that have been so far looked over. I think it is quite safe to assume that nothing in the way of an explanation of the mortality of the ducks will come as a result of these examinations.

SMELTER AND FACTORY WASTE.

Sulphur poisoning has been held by many to be at the root of the trouble, but the presence of ducks and other birds in California apparently suffering from the same disorder, in localities where there is no appreciable trade waste of sulphur, is sufficient to disprove this theory. Birds kept under experimental conditions were given various solutions of sulphuric acid, but they failed to show symptoms similar to those exhibited in nature. None of the changes incident to death from arsenical poison were found in the internal organs of the large number of birds examined.

In regard to waste water from sugar factories on the Weber River, high water in the fall of 1914 came down in mid-September, carrying with it drainage from the settling ponds of the sugar factory, and though the toxic matter present was sufficient to kill large numbers of carp and chubs, conditions among the ducks improved immediately with the rush of water to the flats.

AN ALKALINE POISON AS THE CAUSE.

While it is not yet possible to set aside all these theories as groundless, it is believed that further investigations will disclose a poison as the real cause of the trouble. The work of the past summer leads to the conclusion that the mortality results from an alkaline poison, the exact nature of which is still to be determined. That this is the case appears from several facts.

As formerly stated, no lesions were present in any of the organs of the many birds examined, other than a severe irritation in the lumen of the intestine. Practically all the birds affected are fat, even though found helpless or dead; not until they begin to recover do they get thin. In birds relatively strong the kidneys make a vigorous effort to throw off the matter absorbed through the intestines, and thus the excretion of renal matter is greatly increased and is given off in almost solid form.

It is well known that a large percentage of the afflicted birds recover if they are given fresh water. During the investigations at the mouth of Bear River, 586 sick ducks of 6 species were taken from the flats and placed in pens at the Duckville Gun Club, where there was running water from Bear River. Of this number, 426 birds, or 73 per cent (see p. 9), entirely recovered. Had the cause of the trouble been bacterial infection, such a recovery would not have been possible. The large assortment of species of birds affected, ranging from grebes, ducks, gulls, shorebirds, and snowy herons to an occasional land bird, is in itself an argument against the disease theory and points unmistakably to the conclusion that a poison is the real cause. Diseases which are fatal to even closely allied species are not common, and one involving many species among birds belonging to several different orders is unknown.

The fact that a similar mortality occurs in California also goes to prove that the trouble is due to a salt or an alkali. In a careful study of local conditions there, it was possible to establish this similarity and to check doubtful points encountered in the Utah work.

Around Great Salt Lake the birds undoubtedly sicken in the shallow water bordering the mud flats. As these flats dry after high water, salts and alkalis crystallize on the surface of the ground. When light rains form pools on the flats, or when a steady wind blows the water across the dry barrens, pintails, green-winged teal, and other waterfowl follow, eager to feed on the newly flooded lands. As the highly soluble salts are taken up by the water from the previously dry surface, the birds feeding here sicken and die in large numbers. Every unusual outbreak on Bear River during the past summer was found to correspond with some such phenomenon. In other localities, as the mouth of the Weber, the poorly drained pools contain a solution concentrated by evaporation. As soon as irrigation ceases and there is a great increase in the amount of water coming down the river the constant flow steadily drains the flats, removing the stagnant water, and the mortality ceases almost at once.

At Tulare Lake, Cal., it may be found that the mortality will increase when the water is blown out by the wind to cover new ground. During the summer of 1914 large areas along the south shore of the lake were flooded before wheat planted there was ready to harvest, and on these flats were found great numbers of ducks and other birds dead.

Birds resident on Bear River undoubtedly establish a certain degree of immunity from the mortality. In spring when migrants first return from the south it is said that a few sick birds may be found along the overflows. Later these disappear and few of the breeding individuals are markedly affected until mid-July. It is certain, however, that water harmless to these individuals is highly toxic to migrants gathering from near-by breeding grounds to feed, molt, and pass the early fall in the accustomed security of the great marshes. Large numbers of the birds found dead in July and August undoubtedly have come to these marshes from other localities. In the brief account given of the history of the trouble it was shown that sick birds have occurred for a longer time than is commonly believed. In fact there can be little doubt that for many years under certain conditions a few sick birds have been present annually in alkaline pools and on mud flats bordering the mouths of the rivers. The sudden increase in the mortality may be explained by the increased amount of water used for irrigating purposes. Undoubtedly the quantity of water reaching the lake through the rivers has been greatly reduced within the past 15 years. Alkalis and salts are leached from the soil by irrigation and carried off in the drainage to be deposited in the deltas of the rivers and elsewhere. An instance of this leaching is shown in the freshening of the ground water north of Bear River near Corinne. Under these changing conditions disaster came with the dry summer of 1910.

SUGGESTED REMEDIES.

Fresh water is the only remedial agency yet discovered for dealing with this mortality among waterfowl. In the marshes at the mouth of the Jordan River the problem may be considered as settled. Water from the Jordan is carried through the marsh in a series of canals, and as long as it is abundant these are kept full. When the supply fails, as it may in dry years, the marsh can readily be drained and dried. Under normal conditions there are only two points in these channels where stagnation and consequent mortality may occur to any extent; namely, near the Mallard Holes and about the Duck Puddles on the west side. On the flats below the dams on the lake front a small number of birds will undoubtedly die, even though the marshes are drained, but under present conditions this can not be remedied.

At the mouth of the Weber River the situation is more difficult. Here the north channel at present marks the true course of the stream, though in late summer there is little water, as the whole supply is diverted near Ogden for irrigation purposes. Toward the lake are level flats with shallow pools of water connected by a very slight current, or cut off in places from the main body. The south channel has higher banks and runs as a narrow stream supplied by waste water from irrigation ditches. Few, if any, sick birds occur in this channel, as it is deeper and well drained. However, the ducks elect to use the shallow flats along the north channel, and probably less than 10 per cent of the birds that gather there during the summer are alive by the opening of the shooting season on October 1. If the lower course of this north channel from the North Shore Gun Club eastward can be ditched and the water prevented from spreading on the shallows, as it does now, conditions will undoubtedly improve. This should cause the ducks to use the better drained south channel and alleviate the trouble. When the irrigation dams are opened in September and there is an abundance of water, the flats could again be covered, attracting the birds for the fall shooting. Here it might be possible also to establish ponds fed by artesian water which would save many birds could they be induced to visit them to feed and drink.

The extensive flats at the mouth of the Bear River present a still more serious problem. So large an area is involved that drainage under present conditions is impracticable, but even if it were possible this course would deprive enormous numbers of water birds of a summer home. Apparently the only solution here is to increase by some means the water supply during July, August, and the early part of September. If an agreement could be made with the canal companies controlling the irrigation project dams across Bear River whereby more water could be allowed to pass their dams, reservoirs might be established higher up, and a supply might be reserved for the summer months. It might even be practicable to utilize for this purpose some of the water from Bear Lake. The construction of a low dam across South Bay and East Pass in order to raise the water level has been considered. As such a dam would be cut out each year by the ice, an endeavor to increase the water supply would be more practicable. In damming up the bay there is danger of too much stagnant water, and this might add to the trouble.

A measure which might be adopted in all three localities, and one strongly recommended, is to station men on the marshes to gather up the helpless birds and pen them on fresh water. Considering the great number of birds that might be saved in this way the expense will be slight, and in dry seasons this may prove the only feasible means of relief. From August 11 to September 26 there were brought in to the Duckville Gun Club 586 ducks, of 6 species. The following table gives the percentage of recoveries and deaths:

Species.	Number.	Recovered.	Died.
		Per cent.	*Per cent.*
Mallard	59	80	20
Gadwall	5	80	20
Pintail	233	77	23
Green-winged teal	258	69	31
Cinnamon teal	16	63	37
Spoonbill	15	60	40
Total	586	73	27

When large and small ducks were inclosed together the stronger pintails and mallards crowded the teal and spoonbills, and many were drowned. It also developed that very weak birds should be separated from the others. Under more favorable conditions the percentage of recoveries could be markedly increased. California sportsmen will be interested to know that at present this appears to be the only measure that will prove successful on Tulare Lake. It is even possible that birds once cured may become to a greater or less extent immune, and will not readily be affected again.

In order to obtain data on this possible immunity and on the subsequent longevity of birds which have recovered from the poisoning, aluminum bands were placed upon the legs of 270 of the birds released during the past summer. Each band bears a number on one side and on the reverse the inscription "Notify U. S. Dept. Agr., Wash., D. C." By this means the birds may be identified should any of them be found or captured.[1] Already reports have been received concerning more than 20 of these birds. Should more of these bands be secured it is hoped they will be forwarded to the Department of Agriculture with full information as to date taken and attending circumstances.

[1] Valuable information in another line of investigation will be forthcoming from these bands. At present knowledge of the routes of migration followed by waterfowl is based upon observation as to the dates of arrival or departure of the birds in various localities. These, properly tabulated, show the movement of the species in question as a whole. The actual lines of flight pursued by individual birds are almost entirely unknown. The importance of information on this point can not be overestimated.

ADDITIONAL COPIES
OF THIS PUBLICATION MAY BE PROCURED FROM
THE SUPERINTENDENT OF DOCUMENTS
GOVERNMENT PRINTING OFFICE
WASHINGTON, D. C.
AT
5 CENTS PER COPY
▽

WASHINGTON : GOVERNMENT PRINTING OFFICE : 1915

UNITED STATES DEPARTMENT OF AGRICULTURE

BULLETIN No. 218

Contribution from the Bureau of Plant Industry
WM. A. TAYLOR, Chief

Washington, D. C. ▼ May 28, 1915

OATS IN THE GREAT PLAINS AREA

RELATION OF CULTURAL METHODS TO PRODUCTION

By

E. C. CHILCOTT, Agriculturist in Charge, and J. S. COLE and W. W. BURR, Assistants, Office of Dry-Land Agriculture

CONTENTS

WASHINGTON
GOVERNMENT PRINTING OFFICE
1915

BULLETIN OF THE U.S. DEPARTMENT OF AGRICULTURE

No. 218

Contribution from the Bureau of Plant Industry, Wm. A. Taylor, Chief.
May 28, 1915.

OATS IN THE GREAT PLAINS AREA: RELATION OF CULTURAL METHODS TO PRODUCTION.

By E. C. CHILCOTT, *Agriculturist in Charge*, and J. S. COLE and W. W. BURR, *Assistants, Office of Dry-Land Agriculture.*[1]

CONTENTS.

INTRODUCTION.

This bulletin contains a study of the yields of oats from different methods of cultivation and seed-bed preparation at fourteen field stations on the Great Plains.

[1] All of the members of the scientific staff of the Office of Dry-Land Agriculture have contributed more or less to this paper by having charge of field investigations and by assisting in the preparation of data for records or for publication. The scientific staff as at present constituted consists of the following members, named in the order of length of service: W. W. Burr, Denver, Colo.; E. F. Chilcott, Woodward, Okla.; O. J. Grace, Akron, Colo.; J. S. Cole, Denver, Colo.; J. M. Stephens, Moccasin, Mont.; A. L. Hallsted, Hays, Kans.; O. R. Mathews, Belle Fourche, S. Dak.; J. C. Thysell, Dickinson, N. Dak.; M. Pfaender, Mandan, N. Dak.; H. C. McKinstry, Hettinger, N. Dak.; W. M. Osborn, North Platte, Nebr.; W. D. Griggs, Dalhart, Tex.; C. A. Burmeister, Amarillo, Tex.; J. E. Mundell, Big Spring, Tex.; F. L. Kelso, Ardmore, S. Dak.; W. A. Peterson, Mandan, N. Dak.; J. T. Sarvis, Ardmore, S. Dak.; G. W. Morgan, Huntley, Mont.; J. H. Jacobson, Mitchell, Nebr.; H. G. Smith, Tucumcari, N. Mex.; L. N. Jensen, Woodward, Okla.; J. G. Lill, Garden City, Kans.; R. S. Towle, Edgeley, N. Dak.; A. J. Ogaard, Williston, N. Dak.; C. B. Brown, Dalhart, Tex.; L. D. Willey, Archer, Wyo.; J. B. Kuska, Colby, Kans.; and A. E. Seamans, Akron, Colo.

The following-named men have held positions on the scientific staff of the Office of Dry-Land Agriculture during the past nine years, but have resigned or have been transferred to other offices of the Department of Agriculture: Sylvester Balz, F. L. Kennard, J. E. Payne, L. E. Hazen, C. A. Jensen, H. R. Reed, W. O. Whitcomb, C. H. Plath, F. Knorr, and R. W. Edwards.

The data here reported from the stations in Kansas, Nebraska, North Dakota, and Montana have been obtained in cooperation with the agricultural experiment stations of their respective States. In South Dakota, Colorado, Texas, Oklahoma, and New Mexico the stations are operated by the United States Department of Agriculture.

Field, office, and laboratory facilities, teams, and implements have been provided by the Office of Western Irrigation Agriculture, at Huntley, Mont., Belle Fourche, S. Dak., and Mitchell, Nebr., and by the Office of Cereal Investigations at Amarillo, Tex., and Archer, Wyo. The Biophysical Laboratory has cooperated in obtaining the meteorological data reported.

NOTE.—This bulletin is intended for all who are interested in the agricultural possibilities of the Great Plains area.

87674°—Bull. 218—15——1

The study as here made shows the effect of the cropping and cultivation of the land in only the one year preceding the growth of the oats. A study of the cost of production by each of the methods under trial and the resulting profit or loss are also given.

Results are presented from an aggregate of 74 station years, involving an aggregate of 2,115 plat years. By station year is meant one year at one station; by plat year is meant one plat at one station for one year.

FIG. 1.—Sketch map of the Great Plains area, which includes parts of ten States and consists of about 400,000 square miles of territory. Its western boundary is indicated by the 5,000-foot contour. The location of each field station within the area is shown by a dot within a circle (⊙).

Such a mass of material furnishes an infinite amount of detail for study, but it is the purpose of this bulletin to consider only the broader bearings and more obvious and important phases of the work, rather than a study of the details.

This bulletin, dealing with only the one crop, does not afford a measure for judging the agricultural possibilities for other crops of any section of the region. The Office of Dry-Land Agriculture of the United States Department of Agriculture began field work in the investigation of methods of crop production in the Great Plains in 1906. The work begun at that time has been constantly added to until 20 stations were in operation in 1914. Data from only 14 of these stations are here presented; those that have records of but one or two years are not included.

The method of work adopted was that of raising the different crops both in different combinations or systems of rotation and under different methods of cultivation in systems of continuous cropping. In no case have rotations of over six years in length been used. Those of even this length have been tried only with sod crops. More of the work has been done with 3-year and 4-year rotations.

AREA INCLUDED IN THESE INVESTIGATIONS.

The area covered by these investigations is shown in figure 1 and consists of about 400,000 square miles of territory. It includes the western parts of North Dakota, South Dakota, Nebraska, Kansas, Oklahoma, and Texas, and the eastern portions of Montana, Wyoming, Colorado, and New Mexico. The fact that the determining factor in crop production is the limited rainfall is responsible for a general uniformity in conditions throughout the area. There is, however, a wide range of soil, climatic conditions, and altitude. The lowest station is Edgeley, N. Dak., with an altitude of 1,468 feet and the highest is Archer, Wyo., with an altitude of 6,012 feet. The length of the growing season for oats is naturally much the same throughout the area, but there is a variation of approximately a month to six weeks in the respective dates of seeding and harvesting oats, the southern section using the earlier dates.

CLIMATIC CONDITIONS.

The area is characterized by a varying amount of annual and seasonal precipitation, with very uncertain distribution. Years of relatively high precipitation with favorable distribution may be followed by years of relatively low precipitation with very unfavorable distribution. It may be said that the uncertainty of the distribution rather than the total amount of rainfall received is the factor that makes crop production hazardous. In connection with this work, complete climatic data have been obtained. It is not practicable, however, to give them in this publication. Table I shows the minimum, maximum, and average annual and seasonal rainfall and the seasonal evaporation at each station for the years for which the yields are here reported. By seasonal is meant the precipitation or evaporation for the period between the average time of seeding and the average time of harvesting. No attempt is made here to show any of the other climatic factors or the amount of water already in the soil at seeding time, any one of which may have an important influence on yields. The annual precipitation as here given is not the annual as determined from the complete record, but is the average annual precipitation of the years whose results are under study.

TABLE I.—*Annual and seasonal precipitation and seasonal evaporation at fourteen stations in the Great Plains area.*[1]

Station.	Altitude[2] (feet).	Precipitation[3] (inches).						Seasonal evaporation[3] (inches).		
		Annual.			Seasonal.					
		Minimum.	Maximum.	Average.	Minimum.	Maximum.	Average.	Minimum.	Maximum.	Average.
Judith Basin	4,228	14.96	23.78	18.06	6.50	10.90	8.62	19.117	26.273	21.330
Huntley	3,000	11.92	11.92	11.92	5.00	7.35	6.18	19.820	20.594	20.207
Williston	1,875	10.28	18.99	14.84	5.62	12.00	8.31	21.104	28.269	24.705
Dickinson	2,543	11.93	21.22	16.69	5.31	16.27	10.06	18.379	27.366	22.377
Edgeley	1,468	11.94	21.95	16.71	5.08	15.73	9.60	17.664	25.362	20.657
Hettinger	2,253	12.72	15.68	14.20	8.82	12.89	10.69	20.111	24.248	22.430
Belle Fourche	2,950	6.64	17.73	13.11	1.92	12.75	6.82	23.627	33.906	27.220
Scottsbluff	3,950	13.77	18.51	16.14	5.56	8.26	7.11	24.698	26.647	25.718
North Platte	3,000	11.18	23.01	18.05	4.38	11.25	7.77	25.954	35.255	30.253
Akron	4,600	14.51	22.46	18.28	5.32	9.52	7.82	25.917	32.691	28.781
Hays	2,050	15.59	27.80	21.30	3.87	12.87	9.55	29.390	41.317	32.628
Garden City	2,900	11.82	23.58	18.54	5.01	8.16	6.85	33.315	38.926	35.332
Dalhart	4,000	13.69	16.35	15.11	4.54	14.86	8.17	33.381	41.002	38.596
Amarillo	3,676	10.69	27.80	18.28	5.03	11.49	7.05	32.305	40.704	36.709

[1] The years covered are the same as for the data shown in the other tables for the several stations.

[2] The altitude given is for the field where the work was done and is based in most cases on that of the nearest town.

[3] The record of annual precipitation for 1914 is not included. The records of seasonal precipitation and evaporation for 1914 are included for all stations, the evaporation being figured from Apr. 1 to July 31. The seasonal rainfall is the measurement from Apr. 1 to July 31 for stations north of and including that at Belle Fourche. For stations south of Belle Fourche it is the amount between Mar. 1 and June 30. Evaporation measurements are made from a free water surface, in a tank sunk into the soil to almost its full depth. The water surface is kept about level with the surface of the ground.

GENERAL PLAN OF THE INVESTIGATIONS.

The same variety of oats is used on all plats at a station during any one year. The intention is to use the best variety that is available for general use. Changes are made only when seed breeding, selection, or varietal testing makes available for general use a better variety. No attempt is made to use the same variety at different stations. The rate, time, and manner of seeding are the same for all plats at a station in any one year. As compared with more humid sections, the seeding is light, the usual rate being 6 pecks per acre. All seeding is done with a drill, rows being spaced from 6 to 8 inches apart, depending upon the locality. In different places different styles of drills are used.

In the present study a table is presented for each station. The first part of such table shows the yields that have been obtained in each year by each of the different methods under which oats have been grown, considering only the variations in the one year preceding the crop. The previous crop whose stubble was treated as specified is also shown. Where more than one plat has been under the same treatment for the previous year, only the average yield of the whole number of plats so grown is given. Column 2 of the table shows the number of plats so averaged. The succeeding columns need no explanation, as they show the yields for each year as indicated and the averages of each method for the whole period of years. In the last column, where the average appears under the heading "Average," the calculation is from the left. The averages of the different methods of treatment are the averages of the whole number of plats that entered into their composition. For a rough comparison of seasons the bottom line of the first half of the table gives the averages of all plats for each year, the average of the yearly average yields appearing in the last column to the right.

As here presented the treatment of the land is specified as fall plowed, spring plowed, sod breaking, subsoiled, listed, disked, green manured, and summer tilled. Under these headings are subdivisions to show the preceding crop.

Where oats appear following wheat on either fall or spring plowed land it has been in rotations of at least 3 years in length. Where oats follow oats the system has been that of continuous cropping.

Fall plowing is done as early as practicable and to a good depth, the standard being set at 8 inches. The ground after being plowed may be worked down or left rough through the winter, as seems advisable. Spring plowing is done as early as practicable in the spring, with the exception of one plat at each station, on which oats follow oats. It is done to a good depth, about 8 inches, and given sufficient cultivation with the harrow, or disk if necessary, to form a good seed bed. On one plat which is continuously cropped to oats at each station, spring plowing is shallow (only about 4 inches) and is given a minimum of cultivation.

Sod is broken in the fall as early as hay production for the year is over.

Subsoiling is done on land continuously cropped to oats. The treatment of the plat that appears at some stations under this heading is the same as the treatment of the plat that appears under "Fall plowed," except that it is subsoiled. At the time of plowing a subsoiler is run in every other furrow to an additional depth of 6 or 8 inches, making a total depth of about 14 inches. This is usually done two years in succession and then omitted for two years.

The plat that appears at some stations under the heading "Listed," following oats, is a plat continuously cropped to oats. At the time of fall plowing this plat is furrowed out with the lister instead of being plowed. In the spring it is worked down level and the seed bed prepared without the use of the plow.

The plats on disked corn ground are all in rotation with other crops. Both 3-year and 4-year rotations comprise this series. The other crops may be winter wheat, spring wheat, barley, green manure, or potatoes. In some of the rotations summer tillage replaces one of the crops.

Where oats are grown after a green-manure crop the system is that of a 4-year rotation in which one crop is corn and the other one of the small grains.

Summer tillage is of the intensive type. The land lies fallow for a year. It is kept clear of weeds and as far as practicable a mulch is maintained on it during the time between the harvest of the preceding crop and the seeding of the oats. This involves a period in some cases as long as 21 months. In some cases it is necessary to plow the land more than once during this period, in order either to maintain a surface receptive to water and that will resist blowing or to prevent the growth of weeds. The long period of summer tillage, together with the intensive methods practiced, have made this an expensive system of production. Experiments are under way to determine the most economical method of summer tilling. Indications are that a less intensive method than that practiced in the work here reported will give practically as good returns.

The yields given in these tables begin with the second year of crop production at each station. The first year's crop is produced on land uniform in its treatment.

In cases where an entire crop has been lost by hail or other agency that could not possibly be overcome by cultivation the years are not considered in computing averages. Such failures must of course enter into the final results of agricultural endeavor. They are, however, of such uncertain occurrence that the series of years here considered is too short to permit an attempt to establish their normal frequency for any locality. This is in effect what would be done by including them in averages. It is believed that less error is introduced by recognizing their occurrence and excluding them from averages. When the loss of a crop is due to conditions that might possibly have been overcome by cultural practices a zero yield for that year is included in the calculations.

Embodying the basic data given in Tables II, III, and IV, the second part of the table for each station has been compiled. In this are brought together in summary form the yields detailed in the first part of such table. The value of the average yields thus obtained is calculated and given, together with a computation of the cost of production. The last line of the table gives the profit or loss resulting from the production of oats by the method stated. Loss is indicated by the minus sign. In this second part of each table there are two general headings: "Tillage treatment" and "Previous crop." Under the first general heading the plats are grouped entirely by treatment without considering the previous crop. Under the second heading treatment is not considered, and the grouping is entirely governed by the crop immediately preceding the oats. This really makes two tables combined in one, with subdivisions common to both.

Figure 2 shows a diagram of the dry-land rotation field at the Belle Fourche Field Station. This station being a representative one will serve to illustrate the general scheme and plan of work.

The plats here, as in all of the work, are one-tenth acre in size. Their dimensions are 2 by 8 rods. Along their larger dimension the plats are separated by bare alleys 4 feet in width. Along the ends of the plats they are separated by roads 20 feet wide.

At this station five crops are represented in a series of continuously cropped plats lettered from A to F. In this group, plats C and D are alternately cropped and summer tilled, so that each year a crop is grown on land that was summer tilled the previous year, and a plat is summer tilled for cropping the next year.

The remainder of the field is in rotations in which each plat is known by a rotation number and letter. On the field diagram the separation of rotations is indicated by heavy lines.

The movement of the crops is in the direction from Z to A and from A back to the letter that marks the other end of the rotation.

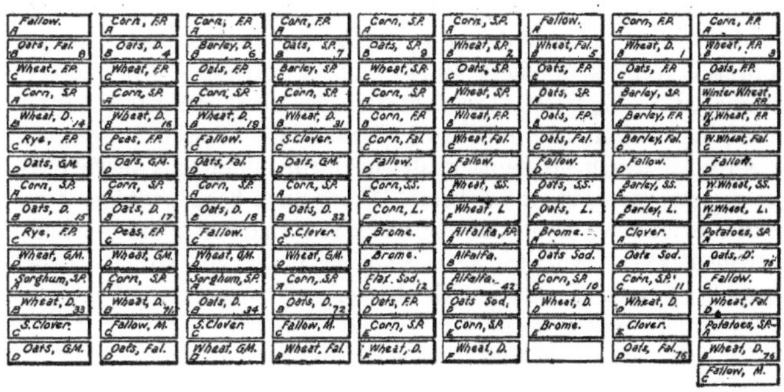

FIG. 2.—Diagram of the dry-land rotation field at the Belle Fourche Field Station. The lettering shows the cropping practiced in 1914. The explanation of abbreviations used after the name of a crop is as follows: *D.*=Disked, *Fal.*=summer tilled, *F. P.*=fall plowed, *G. M.*=green manured, *L.*=listed, *M.*=manured, *S. P.*=spring plowed, *S. S.*=subsoiled.

In figure 2 the diagram is filled out to show the cropping in 1914. The letters following the crop indicate the treatment given the ground in preparation for it, S. P. standing for spring plowed, F. P. for fall plowed, Fal. for summer tilled, G. M. for green manured, and D. for disked. The addition of the letter M. indicates the use of manure.

To illustrate: In 1914 plat A of the 4-year rotation No. 14 was in corn on spring-plowed ground, plat B was in wheat on disked corn ground, and plat C was in winter rye on fall-plowed land. This would be plowed under for green manure. Plat D was in oats where winter rye had been turned under the year before. In 1915 A will be in wheat, B in winter rye, C in oats, and D in corn.

Some of the rotations are calculated to conserve or increase the fertility of the soil, while others may perhaps deplete it. In the present stage of the work the effects of rotations as units are greatly overshadowed by the effects of the cropping and cultivation of a single year. This is due to the fact that the controllable factors are water supply, physical condition of the seed bed, and a certain recognized, if not understood, effect of the crop immediately preceding. Uniformity in these factors is largely restored by the cultivation or cropping of a single season. After a careful study of the data, it seems advisable at the present time to prepare a series of bulletins discussing in each the results relating to but one crop as determined by the treatment of the land in only the one year immediately preceding the growth of the crop.

COMPARISON OF CULTURAL METHODS.

The methods under study vary a great deal in the labor involved and in the consequent cost of production by each method. Table IV has therefore been compiled in order to show the average cost by each of the methods under study. These data have been prepared from the records of eight representative stations. An average of the records for 5½ years at each station has been used in preparing it. This is equivalent to a record of 44 years at one station. An accurate record has been kept of all the farm operations performed in the various methods under trial. These have been averaged for the eight stations. The amount of work required for some methods of treatment varies with the season and with the soil, and the expense of some operations varies with the soil. The amount of labor performed under each of the methods was neither more nor less than that which the man in charge believed to be necessary to bring about the results sought.

In computing the cost of the various operations a fixed wage of $2 a day for a man and $1 a day for a horse was adopted. This may be above or below the actual labor cost in any particular locality, but it is believed to be a fair average and one that will afford a profitable market to the farmer for his labor. The time required of men and teams to cover a given acreage in each of the several farm operations obviously varies with soils and other conditions. The average shown in Table II has been determined from the actual experience of a large number of men connected with these investigations, experience that has extended over a wide range of conditions and many years of time.

The factors included in the cost of production are calculated on an acre basis for each of the separate operations performed, beginning with the preparation of the land and ending with the harvesting and shocking of the grain. To these items are added the cost of seed at 60 cents per acre, interest and taxes on the land investment calculated at 8 per cent on a valuation of $20 per acre, and the deterioration and repairs of the binder at 15 cents per acre. No allowance is made for the deterioration of other farm equipment, as it is believed that the wages allowed for men and teams are sufficient to cover this item for the remainder of the equipment. The above-mentioned items are fixed charges per acre; that is, they do not vary greatly with the yield per acre except for the item of twine, but this variation is not sufficient to affect materially the relative total cost of production under the several methods.

Table II shows the cost per acre, based upon what is considered an average day's work for each of the farm operations involved, at the above-mentioned wage. As before stated, the type of soil and seasonal conditions will determine to a certain extent the labor required and the consequent cost per acre.

TABLE II.—*Average cost per acre*[1] *of the farm operations involved in growing oats in the Great Plains area.*

[The wage scale assumed is $2 per day for each man and $1 per day for each horse.]

Operation.	Force employed.		Day's work.	Item cost.	Cost per acre.
	Men.	Horses.			
			Acres.		
Plowing	1	4	3½		$1.71
Disking	1	4	8		.75
Harrowing	1	4	35		.17
Subsoiling	1	3	3½		1.43
Drilling	1	4	15		.40
Cultivating	1	4	16		.38
Listing	1	4	10		.60
Harvesting:					
Cutting and binding	1	4	15	$0.40	.93
Shocking	1			.13	
Twine				.25	
Binder wear and repair				.15	

[1] The cost of thrashing is not included in the cost per acre, but it is estimated at 5 cents per bushel and deducted from the price of 35 cents in the granary, thus giving a value of 30 cents per bushel in the shock.

The average farm price of oats used in these computations is based on the data given in Table III, furnished by the Bureau of Crop Estimates. The four States of Kansas, Nebraska, North Dakota, and South Dakota were selected because their extensive oat production has given them established market prices which are not greatly influenced by local conditions. As given in Table III, the average farm price of oats on December 1 for the past 10 years has been nearly 35 cents per bushel. It costs about 5 cents per bushel to take the grain from the shock, thrash it, and put it in the granary on the farm. This cost per bushel does not vary greatly with the yield and is therefore a fixed price per bushel instead of a fixed price per acre, as is the case with the other costs of production. The relative profits of producing oats under the different methods can therefore best be determined by finding the difference between the fixed cost per acre and the value per acre of the grain at the point where the fixed cost per acre ends, which, as before stated, is when the grain is in the shock. Knowing that the average farm value of oats in the granary is 35 cents per bushel, and that it costs 5 cents per bushel to take it from the shock, thrash it, and put it in the granary, it is obvious that it would be worth 30 cents per bushel in the shock. This valuation of 30 cents per bushel has therefore been used as a basis for calculating the relative crop values, costs, and profits per acre of the various methods under trial.

TABLE III.—*Average price of oats at the farm granary for 10 years in four States of the Great Plains area.*

[The quotations are given in cents per bushel. Those for the year 1914 are for the date of Nov. 1; in other years Dec. 1 is taken as the date.]

Year.	North Dakota.	South Dakota.	Nebraska.	Kansas.	Average.
1905	23	23	24	28	24½
1906	27	25	26	31	27¼
1907	40	39	37	42	39½
1908	42	41	41	45	42¼
1909	33	34	35	43	36¼
1910	37	30	28	34	32¼
1911	41	43	43	45	43¾
1912	22	25	30	35	28
1913	30	34	38	45	36¾
1914	36	38	39	43	39
Average	33	33	34	39	34¾

In conformity with the foregoing explanation, Table IV gives in detail the cost of producing oats in the shock, expressed in dollars and cents and in bushels per acre at 30 cents per bushel. These prices are used as a working basis and are not offered as being exact. It is fully realized that the price of any or all factors used in obtaining them may vary locally from the fixed price assumed.

TABLE IV.—*Cost per acre of producing oats in the shock in the Great Plains area, showing averages of data from eight stations.*

Method of preparation.	Number of operations.						Cost of preparation.	Cost per acre.				Total cost of production.	
	Plowing.	Harrowing.	Disking.	Subsoiling.	Listing.	Drilling.		Seed.	Drilling.	Harvesting.	Interest and taxes.	In dollars.	In grain, at 30 cents per bushel.
Disked corn land	......	1.3	1	......	......	......	$0.97	$0.60	$0.40	$0.93	$1.60	4.50	15.0
Listed	......	1.6	1.2	......	1	......	1.77	.60	.40	.93	1.60	5.30	17.7
Spring plowed	1	1.3	.5	......	......	......	2.31	.60	.40	.93	1.60	5.84	19.5
Fall plowed	1	2.3	.9	......	......	......	2.78	.60	.40	.93	1.60	6.31	21.0
Subsoiled	1	1.7	.9	0.5	......	......	3.39	.60	.40	.93	1.60	6.92	23.1
Summer tilled	1.5	9.2	2.6	......	......	......	6.12	.60	.40	.93	3.20	11.25	37.5
Green manured:													
With rye [1]	2	6.5	2.4	......	......	1	7.73	.60	.40	.93	3.20	12.86	42.9
With peas [2]	2	5.8	2.7	......	......	1	10.73	.60	.40	.93	3.20	15.86	52.9
Average cost of green manuring	......	......	......	......	......	......	......	......	......	......	......	14.36	47.9

[1] The cost of rye per acre for seed is estimated at $1.
[2] The cost of peas per acre for seed is estimated at $4.

RESULTS AT THE SEVERAL STATIONS.

Accompanying the discussion of each station is a very brief description of the soil, with particular reference to its depth and its water-holding capacity. Only such information is given as is necessary to understand fully the interpretation of the results.

JUDITH BASIN FIELD STATION.

The field station at Moccasin, Mont., in the Judith Basin, is located on a heavy clay soil of limestone origin. The soil is apparently very rich in available fertility. It is underlain at a depth of approximately 3 feet by a limestone gravel that is closely cemented with lime materials. The gravel subsoil, which extends to a depth of about 30 feet, is practically free from soil. While it is so closely cemented that it does not unduly drain the soil, it is not of a character that allows the storage of available water or the development of roots within it. The presence of gravel in the surface soil does not permit the taking of samples satisfactory for the study of soil moisture. Enough has been done, however, to make it certain that the supply of water that can be stored in this soil is limited. This shallowness of the soil and consequent limitation of the quantity of water that can be stored in it and recovered by the crop makes the crop dependent in large part upon the rains that fall while it is growing.

While the oat crop is not at present the most important commercial crop in the Judith Basin, good yields have been obtained at this field station and a profit realized by all methods under trial. In 1912 the crop was destroyed by a local hail storm. Yields have therefore been calculated on the basis of five years. In the experiments in crop rotation and cultivation methods, 33 plats of oats have been grown each year. This number was increased by the addition of new work in 1913, but only work started in 1908 is here reported. As here presented, the results are arranged to study only the effect of cropping and cultivation in the one year preceding the growth of oats. No attempt is made to study rotations as units.

Table V shows that while there may be great seasonal variations in yields the differences resulting from cultural conditions are generally small. With the exception of the comparatively high yield by summer tillage and the low yield on both brome-grass and alfalfa sods and following flax on brome-grass sod, the differences in yield from different preparations are too small to have meaning.

The low yields on brome-grass and alfalfa sod and following flax on brome-grass sod are due to the fact that at this station sod crops recover after breaking to such an extent as to choke out the oats. The profitableness of these crops in themselves, together with the poor results which follow their breaking, indicates that the sod crops should remain down for long periods rather than enter into short rotations.

TABLE V.—*Yields and cost of production of oats by different methods at the Judith Basin Field Station, 1909 to 1914, inclusive.*

Treatment and previous crop.	Number of plats averaged.	Yield per acre (bushels.) 1909	1910	1911	1912	1913	1914	Average.
Fall plowed:								
Wheat	6	[1] 64.9	[1] 20.5	53.0	(2)	62.8	53.0	50.8
Oats	1	66.2	20.9	51.5	(2)	65.0	49.3	50.6
Barley	1	57.8	19.3	53.7	(2)	64.4	54.0	49.8
Winter wheat	1	....	....	53.1	(2)	70.6	52.1	58.6
Flax	1	63.7	19.5	45.7	(2)	33.7	46.2	41.8
Total or average	10	63.9	20.2	52.2	....	61.1	52.0	49.9
Spring plowed:								
Wheat	1	63.1	25.3	51.5	(2)	54.5	45.3	47.9
Oats	1	75.3	24.3	52.0	(2)	64.1	44.6	52.1
Corn	2	72.4	23.1	54.5	(2)	63.1	49.2	52.5
Total or average	4	70.8	24.0	53.1	....	61.2	47.1	51.2
Sod breaking:								
Alfalfa	1	56.8	14.3	33.1	(2)	30.6	47.1	36.4
Brome-grass	2	62.5	17.8	22.5	(2)	38.6	21.5	32.6
Clover	1	72.5	22.8	37.8	(2)	50.3	50.6	46.8
Total or average	4	63.6	18.2	29.0	....	39.5	35.2	37.1
Subsoiled: Oats	1	63.7	25.3	53.0	(2)	65.0	40.6	49.5
Listed: Oats	1	72.5	22.8	53.5	(2)	63.4	37.5	49.9
Disked: Corn	6	[3] 57.3	[3] 24.4	55.6	(2)	75.1	54.2	53.3
Green manured:								
Rye	2	68.7	25.7	56.8	(2)	75.9	54.3	56.3
Peas	2	71.2	21.0	52.0	(2)	75.3	46.7	53.2
Total or average	4	69.9	23.4	54.4	....	75.6	50.5	54.8
Summer tilled	3	70.5	23.6	63.2	(2)	76.2	58.7	58.4
Average of all 33 plats	....	65.5	22.2	51.4	....	64.3	49.4	50.6

SUMMARY OF YIELDS AND DIGEST OF COST.

Yields, values, etc. (average per acre).	Tillage treatment. Fall plowed (10 plats).	Spring plowed (4 plats).	Disked (6 plats).	Listed (1 plat).	Subsoiled (1 plat).	Green manured (4 plats).	Summer tilled (3 plats).	Previous crop. Sod (4 plats).	Corn (8 plats).	Small grain (13 plats).	Flax (1 plat).
Yields of grain:											
1909 ......bushels	63.9	70.8	57.3	72.5	63.7	69.9	70.5	63.6	61.6	65.8	63.7
1910 ......do	20.2	24.0	24.4	22.8	25.3	23.4	23.6	18.2	24.0	22.0	19.5
1911 ......do	52.2	53.1	55.6	53.5	53.0	54.4	63.2	29.0	55.3	52.8	45.7
1912 ......do	(2)	(2)	(2)	(2)	(2)	(2)	(2)	(2)	(2)	(2)	(2)
1913 ......do	61.1	61.2	75.1	63.4	65.0	75.6	76.2	39.5	72.1	63.4	33.7
1914 ......do	52.0	47.1	54.2	37.5	40.6	50.5	58.7	35.2	53.0	49.3	46.2
Average	49.9	51.2	53.3	49.9	49.5	54.8	58.4	37.1	53.2	50.7	41.8
Crop value, cost, etc.:											
Value	$14.97	$15.36	$15.99	$14.97	$14.85	$16.44	$17.52	......	......	......	......
Cost	6.31	5.84	4.50	5.30	6.92	14.36	11.25	......	......	......	......
Profit	8.66	9.52	11.49	9.67	7.93	2.08	6.27	......	......	......	......

[1] Only 4 plats in 1909 and 1910. [2] Destroyed by hail. [3] Only 5 plats in 1909 and 1910.

When the cost of production is taken into consideration, as in the last part of Table V, it is seen that the less expensive methods are more profitable. This is a direct result of the lack of differences in crop values as great as the differences in cost of production. Great freedom is offered the farmer in the choice of the place he will give oats in his cropping system and in the manner in which he will prepare the land for the crop.

HUNTLEY FIELD STATION.

The field station at Huntley, Mont., is located in the valley of the Yellowstone River, just below the first bench. The soil is a heavy gumbo to a depth of about 8 feet. Underlying the soil is a considerable depth of freely drained gravel. This soil carries a large supply of available water and allows deep feeding of the crop. Consequently, it is possible to store in it a maximum quantity of water that can be recovered by the crop.

Data of only two years are available from the Huntley station. These both have been years of heavy production. The results of two years are not sufficient evidence on which to draw conclusions, but may be of value as indicators. The extreme range by different preparations in the average of the two years has been from 41.2 bushels on fall-plowed oat ground to 62.1 bushels after peas as green manure.

In both years the yield by both spring and fall plowing has been heavier on wheat stubble than on oat stubble. In both years the yield has been heavier by spring plowing than by fall plowing of either wheat or oat stubble.

As compared with similar oat stubble fall plowed, there has been a small increase in yields each year as a result of subsoiling. The average of this increase has been 4.9 bushels per acre. But a still further increase of 1.1 bushels per acre has resulted from furrowing with a lister and leaving the ground rough through the winter instead of plowing. The yields following corn have averaged heavier than those following small grain, but not as heavy as those following either summer tillage or green manure. Disking corn ground has been as good a preparation as plowing it. The highest average yields have been obtained by summer tillage and green manure.

A profit has been realized from the production of the crop by all the methods under trial. The smallest profit, $3.22 per acre, has been by the most expensive method, green manuring. The largest profit, $11.40 per acre, has been by the least expensive method, disking corn ground. Spring plowing and listing are of about equal rank, with profits of nearly $9 per acre. Fall plowing, subsoiling, and summer tillage have each given an annual profit of about $7 per acre.

TABLE VI.—*Yields and cost of production of oats by different methods at the Huntley Field Station, 1913 and 1914.*

Treatment and previous crop.	Number of plats averaged.	Yield per acre (bushels). 1913	1914	Average.
Fall plowed:				
Wheat	4	37.5	50.4	44.0
Oats	1	34.0	48.4	41.2
Barley	1	34.0	52.3	43.2
Total or average	6	36.4	50.4	43.4
Spring plowed:				
Wheat	1	42.8	55.6	49.2
Oats	1	35.3	50.6	43.0
Corn	2	44.4	60.3	52.4
Total or average	4	41.7	56.7	49.2
Sod breaking:				
Alfalfa	1	46.9	51.9	49.4
Brome-grass	1	51.9	43.7	47.8
Total or average	2	49.4	47.8	48.6
Subsoiled: Oats	1	39.3	52.8	46.1
Listed: Oats	1	45.6	48.7	47.2
Disked: Corn	8	43.7	62.2	53.0
Green manured:				
Rye [1]	2	46.2	63.9	55.1
Peas	2	64.5	59.7	62.1
Total or average	4	55.4	61.8	58.6
Summer tilled	3	60.8	57.6	59.2
Average of all 29 plats	....	45.6	56.7	51.2

SUMMARY OF YIELDS AND DIGEST OF COST.

Yields, values, etc. (average per acre).	Tillage treatment. Fall plowed (6 plats).	Spring plowed (4 plats).	Disked (8 plats).	Listed (1 plat).	Sub-soiled (1 plat).	Green manured (4 plats).	Summer tilled (3 plats).	Previous crop. Corn (10 plats).	Small grain (10 plats).	Sod (2 plats).
Yields of grain:										
1913...bushels..	36.4	41.7	43.7	45.6	39.3	55.4	60.8	43.8	38.1	49.4
1914.......do....	50.4	56.7	62.2	48.7	52.8	61.8	57.6	61.8	51.0	47.8
Average	43.4	49.2	53.0	47.2	46.1	58.6	59.2	52.8	44.6	48.6
Crop value, cost of production, etc.:										
Value	$13.02	$14.76	$15.90	$14.16	$13.83	$17.58	$17.76	....	....	....
Cost	6.31	5.84	4.50	5.30	6.92	14.36	11.25	....	....	....
Profit	6.71	8.92	11.40	8.86	6.91	3.22	6.51	....	....	....

[1] Barley was used as green manure in 1912.

WILLISTON FIELD STATION.

The experimental work at Williston, N. Dak., is conducted on a silt soil that carries a considerable supply of available water and on which the depth of feeding is limited only by the depth to which the character of the crop limits the development of roots.

TABLE VII.—*Yields and cost of production of oats by different methods at the Williston Field Station, 1910 to 1914, inclusive.*

Treatment and previous crop.	Number of plats averaged.	Yield per acre (bushels).					
		1910	1911	1912	1913	1914	Average.
Fall plowed:							
Wheat	3	1.4	8.6	57.6	36.0	74.1	35.5
Oats	1	2.2	8.1	46.9	30.3	60.6	29.6
Barley	1	2.2	8.8	61.2	28.9	87.5	37.7
Flax	1	5.0	2.8	61.9	12.2	52.8	26.9
Total or average	6	2.3	7.6	57.1	29.9	70.5	33.5
Spring plowed:							
Wheat	1	2.0	22.5	60.0	36.2	70.3	38.2
Oats	1	3.1	9.1	47.8	34.7	51.6	29.3
Corn	2	1.7	10.0	69.7	46.8	65.1	38.7
Total or average	4	2.1	12.9	61.8	41.1	63.0	36.2
Sod breaking:							
Brome-grass	1	7.8	1.6	63.1	27.5	71.6	34.3
Clover	1	9.1	5.9	66.6	40.2	85.3	41.4
Total or average	2	8.5	3.8	64.9	33.9	78.5	37.9
Disked: Corn	4	2.5	15.0	64.1	42.5	65.5	37.9
Green manure:							
Rye	1	4.1	7.5	61.9	48.0	63.7	37.0
Peas	1	3.8	9.1	57.5	45.3	89.4	41.0
Total or average	2	4.0	8.3	59.7	46.7	76.6	39.1
Summer tilled	3	5.9	16.8	77.1	39.8	79.7	43.9
Average of all 21 plats	....	3.5	11.0	63.2	37.8	71.0	37.3

SUMMARY OF YIELDS AND DIGEST OF COST.

Yields, values, etc. (average per acre).	Tillage treatment.					Previous crop.			
	Fall plowed (6 plats).	Spring plowed (4 plats).	Disked (4 plats).	Green manured (2 plats).	Summer tilled (3 plats).	Sod (2 plats).	Corn (6 plats).	Small grain (7 plats).	Flax (1 plat).
Yields of grain:									
1910 ... bushels	2.3	2.1	2.5	4.0	5.9	8.5	2.2	2.0	5.0
1911 ... do	7.6	12.9	15.0	8.3	16.8	3.8	13.3	10.6	2.8
1912 ... do	57.1	61.8	64.1	59.7	77.1	64.9	66.0	55.5	61.9
1913 ... do	29.9	41.1	42.5	46.7	39.8	33.9	43.9	34.0	12.2
1914 ... do	70.5	63.0	65.5	76.6	79.7	78.5	65.3	70.3	52.8
Average	33.5	36.2	37.9	39.1	43.9	37.9	38.1	34.5	26.9
Crop value, cost of production, etc.:									
Value	$10.05	$10.86	$11.37	$11.73	$13.17	....	....	....	....
Cost	6.31	5.84	4.50	14.36	11.25	....	....	....	....
Profit or loss	3.74	5.02	6.87	−2.63	1.92	....	....	....	....

The record of five years from Williston includes three years of heavy and two of very low production. When averaged for the five years the results do not show a wide variation in yields by different tillage methods. The yield of oats has been higher each year except 1910 by both spring and fall plowing when the crop followed wheat than when it followed oats. In every year except 1914 the yield has been higher following either wheat or oats when the land was spring plowed than when it was fall plowed.

The yields on disked corn ground have averaged higher than those on the stubble of any small grain plowed in the fall and approximately the same as on the stubble of wheat and corn plowed in the spring. The highest average yields have been produced by summer tillage. When cost of production is taken into consideration, it is seen in the last part of Table VII that the higher yields from summer tillage and green manure have been obtained at a cost proportionately greater than the increase in yields.

The only method showing production at a loss is that of green manuring. The smallest profit, $1.92 per acre, has been by summer tillage, which has given the highest yield. Disked corn ground, owing both to high yield and low cost, shows the greatest average profit, $6.87 per acre. The average profit from spring plowing has been $5.02 and from fall plowing $3.74.

DICKINSON FIELD STATION.

The soil at the field station at Dickinson, N. Dak., is somewhat lacking in uniformity. It is characterized as a sandy clay loam to a depth of approximately 5 feet. Below this depth is a lighter soil which in some cases becomes very sandy or pure sand. The soil has the capacity to retain a large supply of water and to give up a large proportion of it to the crop. This, together with the depth to which a crop may feed, makes it possible to store in this soil an exceptionally large quantity of water that can be recovered by the crop.

The results of six years are available for study from Dickinson Station. The crop in 1912 was destroyed by hail shortly before maturity and is not included in computing averages. The crop of 1914 was damaged at least 50 per cent by hail.

The average annual yields have ranged from 8.9 bushels in 1911 to 67.8 bushels in 1909. The averages for the six years by different methods of cultivation and cropping range from 29.6 bushels on fall-plowed oat ground to 49.9 bushels by summer tillage. While this is a comparatively wide range in results from different methods, it is apparent that the ability of a method to increase yields is dependent upon the season. It will be noted that in 1909, a season of heavy production, there were comparatively small differences in yield from different methods. In 1911, when the seasonal rainfall was very deficient, summer tillage and rye as green manure gave fair yields, while other methods were nearly or quite failures. During the years of average climatic conditions the differences in yields have not been so extreme, but with few exceptions summer tillage, green manuring, and disking corn ground have consistently given the best yields. The highest average, 49.9 bushels, for the five years has been by summer tillage. This is closely approached by rye as green manure with an average of 49 bushels and disked corn ground with an average of 47.5 bushels.

TABLE VIII.—*Yields and cost of production of oats by different methods at the Dickinson Field Station, 1908 to 1914, inclusive.*

Treatment and previous crop.	Number of plats averaged.	Yield per acre (bushels).							
		1908	1909	1910	1911	1912	1913	1914	Average.
Fall plowed:									
Wheat	3	37.9	63.6	32.0	2.0	(1)	60.2	17.9	35.6
Oats	1	32.8	58.4	26.0	1.6	(1)	44.4	14.4	29.6
Barley	1	44.7	61.9	27.8	1.4	(1)	61.0	19.5	36.1
Flax	1	30.0	61.9	26.8	2.2	(1)	62.2	19.2	33.7
Total or average	6	36.9	62.2	29.4	1.9	....	58.1	17.8	34.4
Spring plowed:									
Wheat	4	51.0	65.4	27.9	3.1	(1)	51.8	22.6	37.0
Oats	1	48.4	55.9	32.0	6.6	(1)	33.0	15.3	31.9
Corn	2	55.8	70.8	36.7	6.0	(1)	47.7	18.9	39.3
Total or average	7	52.0	65.6	31.0	4.4	....	48.0	20.5	36.9
Sod breaking:									
Alfalfa	1	65.6	75.3	33.7	1.1	(1)	45.3	22.8	40.6
Brome-grass	1	61.6	65.0	44.6	2.8	(1)	51.9	27.2	42.2
Clover	1	54.7	63.8	29.0	2.7	(1)	55.0	22.0	37.9
Total or average	3	60.6	68.0	35.8	2.2	....	50.7	24.0	40.2
Disked: Corn	5	65.0	75.6	40.7	12.8	(1)	64.2	26.7	47.5
Green manure:									
Rye	1	59.7	65.3	46.3	22.6	(1)	59.4	40.5	49.0
Peas	1	49.4	70.3	34.2	6.4	(1)	55.0	33.1	41.4
Sweet clover	1	65.3	69.7	28.0	8.6	(1)	57.8	21.2	41.8
Total or average	3	58.1	68.4	36.2	12.5	....	57.4	31.6	44.0
Summer tilled	3	57.7	70.1	47.2	29.8	(1)	57.1	37.4	49.9
Average of all 27 plats	....	53.3	67.8	35.4	8.9	....	55.6	24.5	40.9

SUMMARY OF YIELDS AND DIGEST OF COST.

Yields, values, etc. (average per acre).	Tillage treatment.					Sod (3 plats).	Previous crop.		
	Fall plowed (6 plats).	Spring plowed (7 plats).	Disked (5 plats).	Green manured (3 plats).	Summer tilled (3 plats).		Corn (7 plats).	Small grain (10 plats).	Flax (1 plat).
Yields of grain:									
1908 ....bushels..	36.9	52.0	65.0	58.1	57.7	60.6	62.4	44.4	30.0
1909 ....do....	62.2	65.6	75.6	68.4	70.1	68.0	74.2	62.9	61.9
1910 ....do....	29.4	31.0	40.7	36.2	47.2	35.8	39.6	29.3	26.8
1911 ....do....	1.9	4.4	12.8	12.5	29.8	2.2	10.8	2.8	2.2
1912 ....do....	(1)	(1)	(1)	(1)	(1)	(1)	(1)	(1)	(1)
1913 ....do....	58.1	48.0	64.2	57.4	57.1	50.7	59.5	52.6	62.2
1914 ....do....	17.8	20.5	26.7	31.6	37.4	24.8	24.5	19.3	19.2
Average	34.4	36.9	47.5	44.0	49.9	40.2	45.2	35.2	33.7
Crop value, cost, etc.:									
Value	$10.32	$11.07	$14.25	$13.20	$14.97	....	....	....	....
Cost	6.31	5.84	4.50	14.36	11.25	....	....	....	....
Profit or loss	4.01	5.23	9.75	−1.16	3.72	....	....	....	....

[1] Destroyed by hail.

Spring plowing has averaged a little better than fall plowing, irrespective of the kind of stubble plowed. The relative merits of the two vary from year to year, depending upon the season and the condition of the ground at plowing time. Generally, when the ground is wet at the time of fall plowing, the better results are obtained from it. On the other hand, if fall plowing is done when the ground is dry, it has not been as good as spring plowing.

When the cost of production is considered, as in the second part of Table VIII, it is seen that the high cost of green manure has caused the growth of oats by this method to be done at a loss of $1.16 per acre. The high yields and low cost of preparation of disked corn ground have combined to make it show the largest profit of any method, $9.75 per acre. Intermediate between these are spring plowing with $5.23, fall plowing with $4.01, and summer tillage with $3.72 profit per acre, respectively.

EDGELEY FIELD STATION.

The field station at Edgeley, N. Dak., is located on a soil that is derived from the decomposition of shale, which in undecomposed particles is found very near the surface. In the third foot the shale, while broken and offering fairly free passage to water, is not as yet broken down into soil. The depth of feeding of crops is practically limited to the first 2 feet. The first foot carries an unduly large supply of water available to the crop. The limited depth of soil that functions in the storage of water and in the development of the crop, however, limits the quantity of available water that can be carried in the soil to about half that carried by soils of greater depth. This makes the crop practically dependent upon rains that fall while it is growing.

Edgeley offers for study of oat production an unbroken record of eight years. Five of the eight years have been productive of heavy crops from practically all methods, while three have been years of light production from practically all methods.

The range of yields from different methods of preparation and cropping as exhibited in the average of the eight years is comparatively small. This is as might be expected from the soil on which the station is located. Its shallowness makes the crop much more dependent upon the seasonal precipitation than it is in deeper soils. It is, consequently, impossible to realize much benefit from methods of cultivation calculated to store water in the lower zone of normal crop-feeding depth.

Oats on land which was summer tilled the previous year have produced an average yield of 38.3 bushels per acre, but this is only 4.8 bushels more than the average on disked corn ground and 6.4 bushels more than the average of all crops following small grain.

TABLE IX.—*Yields and cost of production of oats by different methods at the Edgeley*[1] *Field Station, 1907 to 1914, inclusive.*

Treatment and previous crop.	Number of plats averaged.	Yield per acre (bushels).								
		1907	1908	1909	1910	1911	1912	1913	1914	Average.
Fall plowed:										
Wheat	4	28.0	25.5	59.3	10.7	2.8	61.1	34.3	51.3	34.1
Oats	1	21.4	15.3	46.8	10.3	.3	60.3	21.5	30.0	25.7
Barley	1	32.5	15.9	60.3	14.3	1.6	57.8	27.5	48.5	32.3
Flax	1	......	22.5	53.1	15.6	.6	55.0	27.5	50.3	32.1
Total or average	7	27.6	21.7	56.7	11.8	1.9	59.6	30.5	47.7	32.2
Spring plowed:										
Wheat	2	29.7	20.6	54.2	9.7	2.4	56.2	46.4	44.0	32.9
Oats	1	21.3	16.9	57.5	6.2	.5	53.8	28.4	36.9	27.7
Corn	2	15.2	20.8	59.8	7.8	7.1	73.6	40.6	33.3	32.3
Total or average	5	20.4	19.8	57.1	8.2	3.9	62.7	40.5	38.3	31.4
Sod breaking:										
Alfalfa	1	......	9.7	48.7	3.8	.2	45.3	8.7	42.2	22.7
Brome-grass	1	33.8	16.3	55.0	8.1	.6	54.4	37.1	41.3	30.8
Clover	1	......	11.3	50.3	3.1	5.0	49.1	51.5	47.8	31.2
Total or average	3	33.8	12.4	51.3	5.0	1.9	49.6	32.5	43.8	28.8
Disked: Corn	7	28.2	20.1	55.4	7.9	3.7	60.5	43.6	48.2	33.5
Green manured:										
Rye	1	37.5	24.7	61.8	9.3	10.9	75.0	40.0	48.5	38.5
Peas	1	32.5	19.4	53.8	6.5	1.7	64.4	53.7	46.9	34.9
Sweet clover	1	......	19.4	45.3	7.1	.3	61.2	35.9	50.9	31.4
Total or average	3	35.0	21.2	53.6	7.6	4.3	66.9	43.2	48.8	35.1
Summer tilled	5	33.8	19.9	59.0	11.0	9.3	70.9	54.1	48.1	38.3
Average of all 30 plats	....	27.9	19.6	56.0	9.1	4.1	61.9	40.6	46.0	33.2

SUMMARY OF YIELDS AND DIGEST OF COST.

Yields, values, etc. (average per acre).	Tillage treatment.					Previous crop.			
	Fall plowed (7 plats).	Spring plowed (5 plats).	Disked (7 plats).	Green manured (3 plats).	Summer tilled (5 plats).	Sod (3 plats).	Corn (9 plats).	Small grain (9 plats).	Flax (1 plat).
Yields of grain:									
1907.......bushels	27.6	20.4	28.2	35.0	33.8	33.8	23.0	27.0	....
1908.......do	21.7	19.8	20.1	21.2	19.9	12.4	20.3	20.8	22.5
1909.......do	56.7	57.1	55.4	53.6	59.0	51.3	56.3	56.7	33.1
1910.......do	11.8	8.2	7.9	7.6	11.0	5.0	7.9	10.3	15.6
1911.......do	1.9	3.9	3.7	4.3	9.3	1.9	4.4	2.0	.6
1912.......do	59.6	62.7	60.5	66.9	70.9	49.6	63.4	58.7	55.0
1913.......do	30.5	40.5	43.6	43.2	54.1	32.5	42.9	34.2	27.5
1914.......do	47.7	38.3	48.2	48.8	48.1	43.8	44.9	45.4	50.3
Average	32.2	31.4	33.5	35.1	38.3	28.8	32.9	31.9	32.1
Crop value, cost, etc.:									
Value	$9.66	$9.42	$10.05	$10.53	$11.49	....	....	....	....
Cost	6.31	5.84	4.50	14.36	11.25	....	....	....	....
Profit or loss	3.35	3.58	5.55	−3.83	.24	....	....	....	....

[1] Additions were made to the work at this station in the spring of 1909. The number of plats shown in the average is the number from 1909 to 1913, but it is not in all cases correct for 1907 and 1908.

The yields of oats following rye plowed under for green manure have averaged practically the same as those on summer-tilled land. The yields following peas as a green manure have not averaged quite so high, while those following sweet clover have been still lower.

The average yield on alfalfa sod has been the lowest in the series. On both brome-grass and clover sods the average yields have been practically the same as after small grains.

The yield of oats following wheat on both spring-plowed and fall-plowed land appears to be better than when following oats on land so prepared.

Little difference is to be observed in the average results following either spring or fall plowing of small-grain stubble for oats. There are differences that develop with differences in seasons, but on the whole it would appear from the evidence at hand that the time for plowing for oats at this station would be determined chiefly, if not solely, by the matter of economy and convenience in doing the work.

When the cost of preparation by the different methods under study is taken into consideration, it is seen that this cost, rather than differences in yield, is the determining factor. The greatest average profit, $5.55 per acre, has been realized from oats on disked corn ground. Oats on spring-plowed and fall-plowed land have been productive of nearly equal profits of about $2 less. The slightly increased yield by summer tillage has not been sufficient to meet the increased cost of the method and profits from it have fallen to 24 cents per acre. Green manuring has been responsible for an average loss of $3.83 per acre.

HETTINGER FIELD STATION.

The soil at the field station at Hettinger, N. Dak., is a heavy clay loam. The seasons during which the work has been carried on have been such that the results of soil-moisture study are not yet conclusive in determining the proportion of water that can be stored in the soil and recovered by a crop. It is probable, however, that the depth of feeding is not limited by any physical peculiarity of the soil and that the supply of available water that can be stored is large. It is reasonable, therefore, to expect that on this soil the maximum effect will be realized from methods of tillage calculated to store water.

The results of three years of fair production are available from the Hettinger station. Records for this length of time are not so valuable an index to methods of production as the longer records at other stations in the State. It appears evident, both from the records and from field observations, that they are complicated somewhat by soil differences. While some of these differences are recognized in their manifestations, their nature has not been satisfactorily determined. In the study as here arranged, the most difficulty is offered by the two unduplicated plats of oats following oats, one prepared by spring plowing and the other by fall plowing. Both of these appear to have a higher yielding power than is consistent with the results at other stations in the State. That this is due in some measure to soil differences has been observed in the field.

TABLE X.—*Yields and cost of production of oats by different methods at the Hettinger Field Station, 1912, 1913, and 1914.*

Treatment and previous crop.	Number of plats averaged.	Yield per acre (bushels).			
		1912	1913	1914	Average.
Fall plowed:					
Wheat	3	19.0	17.9	22.2	19.7
Oats	1	36.3	28.1	29.4	31.3
Barley	1	34.4	20.0	27.5	27.3
Flax	1	17.2	21.5	17.5	18.7
Total or average	6	24.2	20.6	23.5	22.8
Spring plowed:					
Wheat	4	14.6	34.5	41.5	30.2
Oats	1	32.8	37.6	44.4	38.3
Corn	2	25.3	40.2	31.8	32.4
Total or average	7	20.3	36.5	39.1	32.0
Sod breaking:					
Alfalfa	1	17.2	24.7	17.2	19.7
Brome-grass	1	35.3	13.5	25.0	24.6
Clover	1	10.0	13.8	26.9	16.9
Total or average	3	20.8	17.3	23.0	20.4
Disked:					
Corn	6	26.0	41.8	38.8	35.5
Potatoes	1	23.7	38.2	36.0	32.6
Total or average	7	25.6	41.3	38.4	35.1
Green manured:					
Rye	1	22.5	19.7	17.8	20.0
Peas	1	17.5	26.0	23.8	22.4
Sweet clover	1	22.5	25.6	24.4	24.2
Total or average	3	20.8	23.8	22.0	22.2
Summer tilled	5	27.3	38.3	30.8	32.1
Average of all 31 plats	....	23.5	31.7	31.4	28.9

SUMMARY OF YIELDS AND DIGEST OF COST.

Yields, values, etc. (average per acre).	Tillage treatment.					Previous crop.				
	Fall plowed (6 plats).	Spring plowed (7 plats).	Disked (7 plats).	Green manured (3 plats).	Summer tilled (5 plats).	Sod (3 plats).	Corn (8 plats).	Small grain (10 plats).	Flax (1 plat).	Potatoes (1 plat).
Yields of grain:										
1912....bushels..	24.2	20.3	25.6	20.8	27.3	20.8	25.8	21.9	17.2	23.7
1913.......do....	20.6	36.5	41.3	23.8	38.3	17.3	41.4	27.7	21.5	38.2
1914.......do....	23.5	39.1	38.4	22.0	30.8	23.0	37.0	33.4	17.5	36.0
Average	22.8	32.0	35.1	22.2	32.1	20.4	34.7	27.7	18.7	32.6
Crop value, cost, etc.:										
Value	$6.84	$9.60	$10.53	$6.66	$9.63	....	....	....	....	....
Cost	6.31	5.84	4.50	14.36	11.25	....	....	....	....	....
Profit or loss	.53	3.76	6.03	−7.70	−1.62	....	....	....	....	....

Spring plowing has given markedly better results than fall plowing in two of the three years. Disked corn ground and disked potato ground have been about equal to spring-plowed land in crop-producing power. Summer tillage has failed at this station to be productive of the increases in yields that have attended its use at the other stations in the State. In 1914 this may have been due to the fact that the fallows were allowed to become weedy in 1913.

The lowest yields have followed the breaking of sod and the use of green manure.

When methods are considered in broad groups and production is combined with cost, as in the second part of Table X, the data become more instructive. This shows that green manuring, the most expensive method, has been at the same time the least productive. Instead of providing a profit it has been a source of the greatest loss, $7.70 per acre. The disking of potato or corn ground is the least expensive preparation and has been the most productive of the general groups in bushels per acre, as well as in dollars per acre. It shows an average profit of $6.03.

Spring plowing and fall plowing both show profit, the greater profit being from the spring plowing.

Summer tillage, with its high production cost, gave only slightly greater yields and has not been able to pay for the labor and the use of the land. It is debited with an average loss of $1.62 per acre.

While the general trend of these results is reliable, it is very likely that their detail will be subject to change by the extension of the record.

BELLE FOURCHE FIELD STATION.

The field-station farm near Newell, S. Dak., on the Belle Fourche Reclamation Project, is located on a heavy gumbo clay soil. The soil is derived from decomposition of Pierre shale. From the soil at the surface there is a rapid change to broken but undecomposed shale. Near the bottom of the second foot is a comparatively impervious layer of soil. The first foot and at least a part of the second foot carry a large supply of available water. It is probable that but little use is made of either water or soil below the first 2 feet. In spite of the heavy soil and the large supply of water that can be obtained by the plant from that portion of it near the surface, the shallowness of feeding reduces the quantity of water that can be carried in the soil to about one-half of that available in deeper soils. The result of this is shown in the yields.

The results of six years are shown in Table XI. In one year production was heavy, in two years it was fair, in one it was very poor, and in 1911 the drought was so extreme that no method was able to overcome it. The preceding year had been so dry that practically no water was stored in the soil by any method.

TABLE XI.—*Yields and cost of production of oats by different methods at the Belle Fourche Field Station, 1909 to 1914, inclusive.*

Treatment and previous crop.	Number of plats averaged.	Yield per acre (bushels). 1909	1910	1911	1912	1913	1914	Average.
Fall plowed:								
Wheat	3	54.3	0	0	6.2	16.8	12.7	15.0
Oats	1	46.9	0	0	6.6	15.8	24.7	15.7
Barley	1	65.6	0	0	11.4	23.1	12.2	18.7
Flax	1	64.7	0	0	0	16.3	22.8	17.3
Total or average	6	56.7	....	....	6.1	17.6	16.3	16.1
Spring plowed:								
Wheat	1	42.5	6.9	0	9.5	16.9	15.0	15.1
Oats	1	48.8	9.2	0	11.7	17.8	13.0	16.8
Corn	2	60.5	8.3	0	7.2	20.1	23.7	20.0
Total or average	4	53.1	8.2	....	8.9	18.7	18.8	18.0
Sod breaking:								
Alfalfa	1	65.0	0	0	0	16.3	13.0	15.7
Brome-grass	1	67.7	0	0	7.0	25.9	12.0	18.8
Clover	1	63.8	*a* 8.1	0	[1] 16.7	13.1	12.2	19.0
Total or average	3	65.5	2.7	....	7.9	18.4	12.4	17.8
Subsoiled: Oats	1	60.8	0	0	7.3	16.3	20.3	17.5
Listed: Oats	1	56.7	7.2	0	8.6	18.7	21.4	18.8
Disked:								
Corn	6	58.9	7.6	0	10.9	25.6	30.6	22.3
Sorghum	1	57.3	5.2	0	10.3	18.1	21.1	18.7
Potatoes	1	51.9	9.8	0	10.6	29.7	35.9	23.0
Total or average	8	57.8	7.6	....	10.8	25.2	30.1	21.9
Green manured:								
Rye	1	69.4	9.2	0	4.8	31.3	29.5	24.0
Peas	1	76.6	11.3	0	4.7	32.8	28.1	25.6
Sweet clover	2	50.9	0	0	7.3	27.1	34.6	20.0
Total or average	4	61.9	5.1	....	6.0	29.6	31.7	22.4
Summer tilled	5	74.2	17.4	0	8.1	34.8	44.2	29.8
Average of all 32 plats	....	60.9	6.8	....	8.2	23.9	26.3	21.0

SUMMARY OF YIELDS AND DIGEST OF COST.

Yields, values, etc. (average per acre).	Tillage treatment. Fall plowed (6 plats).	Spring plowed (4 plats).	Disked (8 plats).	Listed (1 plat).	Subsoiled (1 plat).	Green manured (4 plats).	Summer tilled (5 plats).	Previous crop. Sod (3 plats).	Corn (8 plats).	Small grain (9 plats).	Flax (1 plat).	Sorghum (1 plat).	Potatoes (1 plat).
Yields of grain:													
1909......bushels..	56.7	53.1	57.8	56.7	60.8	61.9	74.2	65.5	59.3	53.8	64.7	57.3	51.9
1910......do....	0	8.2	7.6	7.2	0	5.1	17.4	2.7	7.8	2.6	0	5.2	9.8
1911......do....	0	0	0	0	0	0	0	0	0	0	0	0	0
1912......do....	6.1	8.9	10.8	8.6	7.3	6.0	8.1	7.9	10.0	8.2	0	10.3	10.6
1913......do....	17.6	18.7	25.2	18.7	16.3	29.6	34.8	18.4	24.2	17.7	16.3	18.1	29.7
1914......do....	16.3	18.8	30.1	21.4	20.3	31.7	44.2	12.4	28.9	16.1	22.8	21.1	35.9
Average	16.1	18.0	21.9	18.8	17.5	22.4	29.8	17.8	21.7	19.7	17.3	18.7	23.0
Crop value, cost, etc.:													
Value	$4.83	$5.40	$6.57	$5.64	$5.25	$6.72	$8.94	....	....	....	....	....	....
Cost	6.31	5.84	4.50	5.30	6.92	14.36	11.25	....	....	....	....	....	....
Profit or loss	−1.48	−.44	2.07	.34	−1.67	−7.64	−2.31	....	....	....	....	....	....

a There was no stand of clover before oats.

The highest yields have followed summer tillage, peas and rye as green manure, and disking potato and corn ground.

Listing has given a little higher yields than plowing similar stubble. Subsoiling is of doubtful advantage. Its average is slightly greater than the average of similar stubble plowed either in the fall or in the spring. There has been, however, no consistency in the results from year to year.

In spite of the combination of bad seasons, disked ground shows an average profit of $2.07. With the exception of one plat cropped to potatoes and one plat cropped to sorghum, the disked land was previously in corn. Listing shows a nominal profit and spring plowing a nominal loss. Both fall plowing and subsoiling show losses of about $1.50 per acre. Summer tillage has the highest yield, but the practice of this method has resulted in an average loss of $2.31 per acre. Green manure, with a yield only slightly above the average and with the highest cost of production, is debited with a loss of $7.64 per acre.

SCOTTSBLUFF FIELD STATION.

The work at Scottsbluff, Nebr., is conducted at a field station located on the North Platte Irrigation Project. The soil is a comparatively light sandy loam. At a depth varying from 5 to 8 feet there is a sharp break from sandy loam to either sand or Brulé clay. Above this point the soil offers no unusual resistance to the downward passage of water or to the development of roots. Owing to its light character, however, it is possible to store in it only a moderate supply of available water. While the evidence on this point is not yet complete, the proportion of water that can be stored in this soil is known to be somewhere intermediate between the corresponding capacities of the Belle Fourche and the North Platte soils.

The results of three years are available from the Scottsbluff station. In each of these years production was largely determined by the supply of water available to the crop both from the rainfall and from the water stored in the soil. Consequently, considerable differences in production from differences in preparation were brought out.

The highest yields each year have been produced on land summer tilled the previous year. The average yield, 38.2 bushels per acre, from this method is over twice that from fall-plowed land that had raised a crop of small grain.

The next highest yields have been those from the green-manured plats. Between peas and rye for green manure the difference is small and not consistent from year to year.

Disked corn ground stands third in average yield of oats, but it owes this position to a very high yield in one year only.

Spring plowing has, on the whole, given better results than fall plowing, although the one plat following oats on spring plowing has been the poorest in the field. This plat is plowed shallow and given little cultivation. It also has a poor location in the field and results from it are entitled to little weight.

TABLE XII.—*Yields and cost of production of oats by different methods at the Scottsbluff Field Station, 1912, 1913, and 1914.*

Treatment and previous crop.	Number of plats averaged.	Yield per acre (bushels).			
		1912	1913	1914	Average.
Fall plowed:					
Wheat	4	11.5	20.4	20.2	17.4
Oats	1	21.6	16.9	14.7	17.7
Barley	1	9.0	22.2	15.9	15.7
Flax	1	38.4	25.0	10.0	24.5
Total or average	7	16.4	20.8	17.3	18.2
Spring plowed:					
Wheat	2	25.5	25.8	14.4	21.9
Oats	1	19.4	15.0	8.4	14.3
Corn	2	33.8	20.8	13.9	22.8
Sorghum	1	35.0	39.7	14.4	29.7
Total or average	6	28.8	24.7	13.2	22.2
Sod breaking:					
Alfalfa	1	41.9	13.4	5.6	20.3
Brome-grass	2	([1])	27.6	14.4	21.0
Clover	1	([1])	20.0	17.8	18.9
Total or average	4	41.9	22.1	13.0	25.7
Subsoiled: Oats	1	27.8	17.5	15.9	20.4
Listed: Oats	1	25.3	23.1	12.8	20.4
Disked: Corn	8	43.0	19.8	16.0	26.3
Green manured:					
Rye	2	34.6	35.3	21.4	30.4
Peas	3	29.6	29.4	23.4	27.5
Total or average	5	31.6	31.8	22.6	28.7
Summer tilled	4	45.5	44.0	25.0	38.2
Average of all 36 plats	....	32.3	25.4	17.3	25.0

SUMMARY OF YIELDS AND DIGEST OF COST.

Yields, values, etc. (average per acre).	Tillage treatment.							Previous crop.			
	Fall plowed (7 plats).	Spring plowed (6 plats).	Disked (8 plats).	Listed (1 plat).	Sub-soiled (1 plat).	Green ma-nured (5 plats).	Sum-mer tilled (4 plats).	Corn (10 plats).	Small grain (11 plats).	Sod (4 plats).	Flax (1 plat).
Yields of grain:											
1912....bush..	16.4	28.8	43.0	25.3	27.8	31.6	45.5	41.1	18.2	41.9	38.4
1913....do....	20.8	24.7	19.8	23.1	17.5	31.8	44.0	20.0	20.7	22.1	25.0
1914....do....	17.3	13.2	16.0	12.8	15.9	22.6	25.0	15.6	16.1	13.0	10.0
Average....	18.2	22.2	26.3	20.4	20.4	28.7	38.2	25.6	18.3	25.7	24.5
Crop value, cost, etc.:											
Value.......	$5.46	$6.66	$7.89	$6.12	$6.12	$8.61	$11.46	......	......	......	......
Cost........	6.31	5.84	4.50	5.30	6.92	14.36	11.25	......	......	......	......
Profit or loss.....	−.85	.82	3.39	.82	−.80	−5.75	.21	......	......	......	......

[1] In 1911 brome-grass and clover did not come up, so these plats were summer tilled, and, therefore, the yields are not figured in these tables.

Subsoiling and listing show small increases over similar stubble fall plowed.

The shortness of the record and the inconsistency among the yields make it unsafe to base conclusions on such small differences.

When cost of production is considered in connection with yields it is seen that the only things that stand clearly by themselves are disked corn ground, with an average profit of $3.39 per acre, and the use of green manure, with a loss of $5.75. The other methods as grouped here show either losses or gains so small as to be subject to changes in their relative positions by a single crop.

NORTH PLATTE FIELD STATION.

The work here presented is conducted on the table-land of the North Platte Field Station. The soil is of the type generally known as loess. With the exception of the humus accumulated near the surface, it is practically uniform to great depths. The storage and use of water is unlimited by the depth of the soil or any peculiarities in it. The development of roots is limited only by the physiological character of the crops grown and the available moisture. It is a soil on which a maximum of results from tillage methods would be expected.

The North Platte Field Station presents for study the records of eight years. In three of these years the production has been good, in three it has been poor, and in two years the crop has been a failure.

Spring-plowed wheat stubble has given better results than fall plowing in five of the six years that have produced crops, but the great difference in favor of fall plowing in 1908 reduces the average gain from spring plowing to less than 2 bushels per acre.

On the plats continuously cropped to oats fall plowing has given better results than spring plowing in four of the six years, the average advantage in favor of it being more than 4 bushels per acre. The spring-plowed plat following oats is the only one in the series that is given shallow plowing.

Fall plowing oats after oats has been consistently better than after wheat, while with spring plowing the reverse has been the case. The poorest yields have been obtained following alfalfa and brome-grass. These two crops exhaust the available soil moisture and leave the following crop entirely dependent upon seasonal rainfall. Oats following them have usually been the first to suffer from drought.

Disked corn ground shows about the same average yields of oats as the crop raised after small grains.

Oats following green manure show a small increase in average yields over all other methods except that of summer tillage. Little difference is to be observed between the results following the use of peas and of rye for this purpose.

TABLE XIII.—*Yields and cost of production of oats by different methods at the North Platte Field Station, 1907 to 1914, inclusive.*

Treatment and previous crop.	Number of plats averaged.	1907	1908	1909	1910	1911	1912	1913	1914	Average.
Fall plowed:										
Wheat	4	30.9	61.0	24.4	7.3	0	9.7	0	7.9	17.7
Oats	1	36.0	68.5	24.1	11.9	0	10.6	0	14.7	20.7
Barley	1	23.1	49.1	20.0	6.6	0	14.7	0	10.0	15.4
Total or average	6	30.5	60.2	23.6	7.9	......	10.7	......	9.4	17.8
Spring plowed:										
Wheat	2	34.5	47.7	32.8	12.5	0	18.6	0	9.1	19.4
Oats	1	30.0	34.4	31.3	11.3	0	18.7	0	5.0	16.3
Corn	2	34.6	54.3	31.3	12.2	0	14.4	0	9.7	19.6
Sorghum	1	30.0	45.0	28.8	8.1	0	12.5	0	7.8	16.5
Total or average	6	33.0	47.2	31.4	11.5	......	16.2	......	8.4	18.5
Sod breaking:										
Alfalfa	1	24.0	36.8	14.4	2.5	0	12.5	0	7.2	12.2
Brome-grass	1	22.2	40.0	16.6	4.7	0	7.2	0	5.6	12.0
Total or average	2	23.1	38.4	15.5	3.6	......	9.9	......	6.4	12.1
Disked: Corn	1	40.6	53.4	22.5	11.9	0	6.6	0	7.8	17.9
Green manured:										
Rye	2	30.5	73.8	[a]32.5	16.4	0	10.3	0	10.0	21.7
Peas	2	28.5	75.8	34.8	14.6	0	13.8	0	9.7	22.2
Total or average	4	29.5	74.8	34.0	15.5	......	12.0	......	9.9	22.0
Summer tilled	4	34.3	87.1	37.3	26.2	0	19.6	0	14.9	27.4
Average of all 36 plats	....	31.4	61.8	28.4	13.1	......	13.7	......	9.8	19.8

SUMMARY OF YIELDS AND DIGEST OF COST.

Yields, values, etc. (average per acre).	Tillage treatment.					Previous crop.			
	Fall plowed (6 plats).	Spring plowed (6 plats).	Disked (1 plat).	Green manured (4 plats).	Summer tilled (4 plats).	Sod (2 plats).	Corn (3 plats).	Small grain (9 plats).	Sorghum (1 plat).
Yields of grain:									
1907...bushels	30.5	33.0	40.6	29.5	34.3	23.1	36.6	31.3	30.0
1908......do	60.2	47.2	53.4	74.8	87.1	38.4	54.0	54.6	45.0
1909......do	23.6	31.4	22.5	34.0	37.3	15.5	28.3	26.5	28.8
1910......do	7.9	11.5	11.9	15.5	26.2	3.6	12.1	9.3	8.1
1911......do	0	0	0	0	0	0	0	0	0
1912......do	10.7	16.2	6.6	12.0	19.6	9.9	11.8	13.3	12.5
1913......do	0	0	0	0	0	0	0	0	0
1914......do	9.4	8.4	7.8	9.9	14.9	6.4	9.1	8.8	7.8
Average	17.8	18.5	17.9	22.0	27.4	12.1	19.0	18.0	16.5
Crop value, cost of production, etc.:									
Value	$5.34	$5.55	$5.37	$6.60	$8.22	....	....	....	....
Cost	6.31	5.84	4.50	14.36	11.25	....	....	....	....
Profit or loss	−.97	−.29	.87	−7.76	−3.03	....	....	....	....

[a] Only 1 plat in 1909.

The heaviest yields have been those following summer tillage, exceeded only by disked corn ground in 1908. But when the cost of production is taken into consideration, as in the last part of Table XII, it is shown that the average increase in production due to summer tillage has not been sufficient to pay for its increased cost as compared with several other methods. It shows a loss of $3.03 per acre. Disked corn ground with its smaller yield shows an average profit of 87 cents per acre. Spring and fall plowing with about the same yields as disked corn ground have just about paid expenses. The use of green manure, with a high production cost and an average yield of only 22 bushels per acre, has resulted in an average loss of $7.76 per acre.

AKRON FIELD STATION, COLO.

The soil of the field-station farm at Akron, Colo., is of a clay-loam type, locally known as "tight land." It is characterized in the native vegetation by a growth of short grass. As it carries in each unit section a considerable supply of water, and as it offers no physical resistance to the development of roots, it is possible to store in it a large quantity of water available to a crop. It is a soil on which maximum results would be expected by practicing methods of tillage calculated to store water.

Of the six years offered for study from this station, two years have been productive of good crops of oats, two of light crops, and two of poor. They do not show in their average a very wide range in yields as a result of different cultural or cropping practices. The heaviest yields have followed summer tillage, which has given an average for the six years of 28.7 bushels per acre. The next highest yield, 25.3 bushels per acre, has been from spring-plowed corn ground. This has been only 1 bushel per acre more in its yield than spring-plowed wheat stubble.

Green manuring has barely maintained yields as high as those from land on which a crop of grain was harvested.

Disked land shows a strong advantage in its yields of oats in favor of corn as a preceding crop, as compared with the use of sorghum, milo, and kafir as preceding crops.

The poorest yields of oats have been obtained following alfalfa and brome-grass sods and on disked sorghum land.

Oats following wheat have been better by both spring and fall plowing than oats following oats.

The relative merits of fall and spring plowing appear to be dependent on the season, but the average of the seasons under study is slightly in favor of spring plowing.

Subsoiling, when compared with plowing at the same time without subsoiling, has been done at the expense of sharp reductions in yield.

Furrowing with a lister and leaving the ground rough through the winter has produced slightly greater average yields than plowing similar stubble either in the fall or spring.

TABLE XIV.—*Yields and cost of production of oats by different methods at the Akron Field Station, 1909 to 1914, inclusive.*

Treatment and previous crop.	Number of plats averaged.	Yield per acre (bushels).						
		1909	1910	1911	1912	1913	1914	Average.
Fall plowed:								
Wheat	3	19.3	14.1	10.5	47.7	7.6	35.5	22.5
Oats	1	14.1	8.0	15.9	46.9	.6	36.9	20.4
Barley	1	20.8	10.2	15.9	37.2	.6	39.1	20.6
Total or average	5	18.6	12.1	12.7	45.4	4.8	36.5	21.7
Spring plowed:								
Wheat	1	18.3	14.8	1.7	46.9	16.6	47.5	24.3
Oats	1	21.1	10.9	4.3	41.9	6.6	39.4	20.7
Corn	2	21.6	20.8	5.3	49.6	5.0	49.4	25.3
Total or average	4	20.6	16.8	4.2	47.0	8.3	46.4	23.9
Sod breaking:								
Alfalfa	1	8.8	2.7	0	29.4	1.9	30.6	12.2
Brome-grass	1	20.2	2.2	0	27.5	1.6	35.0	14.4
Total or average	2	14.5	2.5	0	28.5	1.8	32.8	13.4
Subsoiled: Oats	1	16.1	11.3	8.4	35.3	0	30.3	16.9
Listed: Oats	1	15.6	11.1	5.3	54.7	3.6	40.9	21.9
Disked:								
Corn	7	20.9	18.2	.4	38.5	7.3	48.5	22.3
Sorghum	1	16.1	5.0	0	25.0	1.9	37.8	14.3
Milo	2	15.7	12.2	0	41.9	7.2	40.7	19.6
Kafir	2	14.6	6.7	0	40.3	5.5	40.5	17.9
Total or average	12	18.6	14.2	.2	38.2	6.5	45.0	20.5
Green manured:								
Rye	1	21.0	20.0	2.7	38.4	5.0	44.4	21.9
Peas	1	22.0	11.9	0	38.4	1.2	38.1	18.6
Sweet clover	1	13.0	5.2	3.9	45.8	5.0	41.6	19.1
Total or average	3	18.7	12.4	2.2	40.9	3.7	41.4	19.9
Summer tilled	3	28.9	17.1	7.1	56.4	16.5	45.9	28.7
Average of all 31 plats	....	19.4	13.3	4.0	42.3	6.6	42.2	21.3

SUMMARY OF YIELDS AND DIGEST OF COST.

Yields, values, etc. (average per acre).	Tillage treatment.							Previous crop.					
	Fall plowed (5 plats).	Spring plowed (4 plats).	Disked (12 plats).	Listed (1 plat).	Subsoiled (1 plat).	Green manured (3 plats).	Summer tilled (3 plats).	Sod (2 plats).	Corn (9 plats).	Small grain (9 plats).	Milo (2 plats).	Sorghum (1 plat).	Kafir (2 plats).
Yields of grain:													
1909..bush..	18.6	20.6	18.6	15.6	16.1	18.7	28.9	14.5	21.1	18.2	15.7	16.1	14.6
1910..do....	12.1	16.8	14.2	11.1	11.3	12.4	17.1	2.5	18.7	12.1	12.2	5.0	6.7
1911..do....	12.7	4.2	.2	5.3	8.4	2.2	7.1	0	1.5	9.2	0	0	0
1912..do....	45.4	47.0	38.2	54.7	35.3	40.9	56.4	28.5	40.9	45.1	41.9	25.0	40.3
1913..do....	4.8	8.3	6.5	3.6	0	3.7	16.5	1.8	6.8	5.6	7.2	1.9	5.5
1914..do....	36.5	46.4	45.0	40.9	30.3	41.4	45.9	32.8	48.7	37.9	40.7	37.8	40.5
Average..	21.7	23.9	20.5	21.9	16.9	19.9	28.7	13.4	23.0	21.4	19.6	14.3	17.9
Crop value, cost, etc.:													
Value......	$6.51	$7.17	$6.15	$6.57	$5.07	$5.97	$8.61	......	......	......	......	......	......
Cost.......	6.81	5.84	4.50	5.30	6.92	14.36	11.25	......	......	......	......	......	......
Profit or loss....	.20	1.33	1.65	1.27	−1.85	−8.39	−2.64	......	......	......	......	......	......

When the value of the average crop is studied in connection with the cost of its production, as in the last part of Table XIV, less difference is perhaps found in the resulting profits or losses than in the yields themselves. To this statement should be excepted green manuring, which has not been productive of increases in yields at all commensurate with their cost. The use of this method has been responsible for an average loss of $8.39 per acre.

Profits and losses by all other methods come within a range of about $2 per acre. These differences are not sufficient to warrant strong recommendation of any particular method as essentially better than others. The indications of the evidence at hand are that the growth of oats will about pay for the use of land and for labor and other expenses incurred in their growth.

HAYS FIELD STATION.

The soil on which the experimental work has been conducted at the station at Hays, Kans., is a heavy silt loam. It carries a large supply of water available to a crop. Penetration to the lower depth, however, is slow. The very compact zone in the third foot offers marked resistance both to the downward passage of water and to the development of roots. While the evidence is not as complete as might be desired, it appears that the proportion of water that can be stored in this soil is somewhat above the average.

The work at Hays was started in 1906. The crop that year was raised on land uniform for all plats. The crop of 1907 was largely destroyed by the green bug (spring-grain aphis); hence, it is not included in the table. The crop of 1909 was entirely destroyed by hail and is not included in computing average yields. Its inclusion would only serve to reduce the averages, and reduce the differences obtained from cultural conditions in other years. The crop of 1911 is included in computing the averages as its failure was due to drought. Oats after wheat on both fall-plowed and spring-plowed land have been better than where oats followed oats.

Fall plowing of both wheat and oat stubble has been better for the production of oats than spring plowing of similar stubble.

The yields given for oats following sod land, both brome-grass and alfalfa, are comparatively high. They are, however, misleading and should not be given weight as a measure of the producing value of sod at this station, as there never has been in this work a heavy or well-established sod to break up.

The plat subsoiled and the one listed have both been continuously cropped to oats. They should be compared directly with the oats following oats on fall-plowed land. While there is little difference between the results of either subsoiling or listing, both have produced higher yields than plowing in either the fall or spring.

TABLE XV.—*Yields and cost of production of oats by different methods at the Hays Field Station, 1908 to 1914, inclusive.*

Treatment and previous crop.	Number of plats averaged.	Yield per acre (bushels). 1908	1909	1910	1911	1912	1913	1914	Average.
Fall plowed:									
Wheat	3	23.8	[1]	25.3	0	44.3	9.8	29.2	22.1
Oats	1	3.7	[1]	16.6	0	37.7	10.6	27.0	15.9
Barley	1	35.5	[1]	30.2	0	25.6	8.1	29.2	21.4
Total or average	5	22.1	......	24.5	......	39.2	9.6	28.7	20.7
Spring plowed:									
Wheat	1	26.0	[1]	36.6	0	19.0	6.2	22.3	18.4
Oats	1	1.3	[1]	11.3	0	35.2	3.3	20.8	12.0
Corn	2	17.2	[1]	32.0	0	36.4	11.3	23.2	20.0
Total or average	4	15.4	......	28.0	......	31.8	8.0	22.4	17.6
Sod breaking:									
Alfalfa	1	22.5	[1]	37.5	0	30.5	4.5	25.9	20.2
Brome grass	1	30.1	[1]	36.4	0	33.5	5.1	25.8	21.8
Total or average	2	26.3	......	37.0	......	32.0	4.8	25.9	21.0
Subsoiled: Oats	1	17.9	[1]	24.5	0	45.1	21.8	26.6	22.7
Listed: Oats	1	28.0	[1]	17.0	0	47.6	15.3	29.7	22.9
Disked:									
Corn	1	16.3	[1]	16.9	0	39.0	13.0	30.6	19.3
Sorghum	1	22.1	[1]	36.2	0	27.2	17.6	29.1	22.0
Total or average	2	19.2	......	26.6	......	33.1	15.3	29.9	20.7
Summer tilled	2	16.2	[1]	24.5	3.7	41.1	30.3	33.0	24.8
Average of all 17 plats	....	20.1	......	26.6	.4	37.0	12.8	27.5	20.7

SUMMARY OF YIELDS AND DIGEST OF COST.

Yields, values, etc. (average per acre).	Tillage treatment. Fall plowed (5 plats).	Spring plowed (4 plats).	Disked (2 plats).	Listed (1 plat).	Subsoiled (1 plat).	Summer tilled (2 plats).	Previous crop. Sod (2 plats).	Corn (3 plats).	Sorghum (1 plat).	Small grain (9 plats).
Yields of grain:										
1908........bushels..	22.1	15.4	19.2	28.0	17.9	16.2	26.3	16.9	22.1	20.4
1909........do....	[1]	[1]	[1]	[1]	[1]	[1]	[1]	[1]	[1]	[1]
1910........do....	24.5	28.0	26.6	17 0	24.5	24.5	37.0	26.9	36.2	23.6
1911........do....	0	0	0	0	0	3.7	0	0	0	0
1912........do....	39.2	31.8	33.1	47.6	45.1	41.1	32.0	37.3	27.2	38.1
1913........do....	9.6	8.0	15.3	15.3	21.8	30.3	4.8	11.9	17.6	10.5
1914........do....	28.7	22.4	29.9	29.7	26.6	33.0	25.9	25.7	29.1	27.0
Average	20.7	17.6	20.7	22.9	22.7	24.8	21.0	19.8	22.0	19.9
Crop value, cost of production, etc.:										
Value	$6.21	$5.28	$6.21	$6.87	$6.81	$7.44	......	......	......	......
Cost	6.31	5.84	4.50	5.30	6.92	11.25	......	......	......	......
Profit or loss	—.10	—.56	1.71	1.57	—.11	—3.81	......	......	......	......

[1] Destroyed by hail.

Corn ground, either spring plowed or disked, has not produced as good crops of oats as wheat stubble plowed in the fall. The yield from disked sorghum ground has been slightly better than from disked corn ground.

Summer tillage has a slightly higher average than any other method of preparation for oats. The increase in yield, however, over other methods is small.

Differences in average yields from different methods have been so small that the cost of production is the determining factor in profits or losses.

Disked land and listed land, owing to fair average yields and low cost of production, have shown profits.

Fall plowing, spring plowing, and subsoiling have produced crops just about sufficient to pay for their cost.

Summer tillage is debited with a loss of $3.81 per acre.

GARDEN CITY FIELD STATION.

The work at Garden City, Kans., is on a high upland. The soil is a light silt loam. With the exception of the accumulated humus near the surface, it is practically uniform to a depth of at least 15 feet. The development of roots is limited only to the depth to which water is available and by the physiological character of the crop. The light character of the soil, however, makes it possible to store in each unit of it only a comparatively small proportion of water. This is not entirely overcome by the depth of soil. The results in storing water have been determined largely by the limited quantity available for storage. In no year under any method practiced has the soil been filled with water to as great a depth as it is possible for the crop to develop roots and to use available water.

During the six years covered by the production of oats at this station, two years have been total failures, one from drought and one from hail. In 1912 and 1914 sufficient grain was produced to offer some encouragement to the growing of this crop. The production during the other two years was very light.

The chief value in presenting these records is to show that oats are not well enough adapted to prevailing conditions and yield too poorly to justify their growth on any considerable area. Under such circumstances, oats should give way to crops better adapted to this region.

The highest average yields of oats have been obtained on summer-tilled land and on listed land, which produced an average of 12.8 bushels per acre.

None of the yields have been large enough to pay for cost of production and, in general, the more expensive the method the greater the loss resulting from its practice.

TABLE XVI.—*Yields and cost of production of oats by different methods at the Garden City Field Station, 1909 to 1914, inclusive.*

Treatment and previous crop.	Number of plats averaged.	Yield per acre (bushels). 1909	1910	1911	1912	1913	1914	Average.
Fall plowed:								
Wheat	3	2.1	6.6	0	17.0	(1)	13.3	7.8
Oats	1	3.2	10.3	0	23.1	(1)	8.1	8.9
Barley	1	3.1	10.0	0	29.7	(1)	12.8	11.1
Total or average	5	2.5	8.0	....	20.8	....	12.2	8.7
Spring plowed:								
Wheat	1	1.3	7.2	0	21.9	(1)	....	7.6
Oats	1	1.0	5.3	0	8.8	(1)	2.2	3.5
Corn	2	3.1	7.4	0	22.9	(1)	....	8.4
Total or average	4	2.1	6.8	....	19.1	....	2.2	6.0
Subsoiled: Oats	1	2.6	10.0	0	15.9	(1)	17.3	9.2
Listed: Oats	1	2.2	11.6	0	27.8	(1)	22.2	12.8
Disked:								
Corn	8	1.5	9.3	0	21.8	(1)	12.2	9.0
Sorghum	1	0	7.5	0	8.8	(1)	....	4.1
Milo	2	.6	5.7	0	28.0	(1)	....	8.6
Kafir	2	1.2	5.5	0	27.1	(1)	....	8.5
Total or average	13	1.2	8.0	....	22.5	....	12.2	8.8
Green manure:								
Rye	1	1.5	12.8	0	20.2	(1)	10.5	9.0
Peas	1	.9	12.8	0	22.5	(1)	....	9.1
Total or average	2	1.2	12.8	....	21.4	....	10.5	9.2
Summer tilled	3	4.6	16.2	0	25.8	(1)	17.2	12.8
Average of all 28 plats	....	2.0	9.2	0	22.0	....	13.1	9.3

SUMMARY OF YIELDS AND DIGEST OF COST.

Yields, values, etc., (average per acre).	Tillage treatment. Fall plowed (5 plats).	Spring plowed (4 plats).	Disked (13 plats).	Listed (1 plat).	Subsoiled (1 plat).	Green manured (2 plats).	Summer tilled (3 plats).	Previous crop. Corn (10 plats).	Small grain (9 plats).	Sorghum (1 plat).	Milo (2 plats).	Kafir (2 plats).
Yields of grain:												
1909...bushels	2.5	2.1	1.2	2.2	2.6	1.2	4.6	1.8	2.2	0	0	1.2
1910......do	8.0	6.8	8.0	11.6	10.0	12.8	16.2	8.9	8.2	7.5	5.7	5.5
1911......do	0	0	0	0	0	0	0	0	0	0	0	0
1912......do	20.8	19.1	22.5	27.8	15.9	21.4	25.8	22.0	19.8	8.8	28.0	27.1
1913......do	(1)	(1)	(1)	(1)	(1)	(1)	(1)	(1)	(1)	(1)	(1)	(1)
1914......do	12.2	2.2	12.2	22.2	17.3	10.5	17.2	12.2	12.8	(2)	(2)	(2)
Average	8.7	6.0	8.8	12.8	9.2	9.2	12.8	9.0	8.6	4.1	8.6	8.5
Crop value, cost, etc.:												
Value	$2.61	$1.80	$2.64	$3.84	$2.76	$2.76	$3.84	.....	.....	.....	.....	.....
Cost	6.31	5.84	4.50	5.30	6.92	14.36	11.25	.....	.....	.....	.....	.....
Loss	-3.70	-4.04	-1.86	-1.46	-4.16	-11.60	-7.41	.....	.....	.....	.....	.....

[1] Destroyed by hail. [2] Discontinued.

DALHART FIELD STATION.

The soil at Dalhart is a sandy loam. In some respects it behaves like sand. In other respects it exhibits the characteristics of a heavy clay soil. Its water-holding capacity is comparatively limited. The crops appear, however, to be able to utilize its water to the depth of a normal development.

TABLE XVII.—*Yields and cost of production of oats by different methods at the Dalhart Field Station, 1909 to 1914, inclusive.*

Treatment and previous crop.	Number of plats averaged.	Yield per acre (bushels).						
		1909	1910	1911	1912	1913	1914	Average.
Fall plowed:								
Wheat	3	0	(1)	0	(1)	0	15.8	4.0
Oats	1	0	(1)	0	(1)	0	26.4	6.6
Barley	1	0	(1)	0	(1)	0	16.2	4.1
Total or average	5						18.0	4.5
Spring plowed:								
Wheat	1	0	(1)	0	(1)	0	13.7	3.4
Oats	1	0	(1)	0	(1)	0	14.3	3.6
Corn	2	0	(1)	0	(1)	0		0
Total or average	4						14.0	3.5
Sod breaking:								
Alfalfa	1	5.9	(1)	0	(1)	0		2.0
Brome	1	0	(1)	0	(1)	0		0
Total or average	2	3.0						1.0
Listed: Oats	1	0	(1)	0	(1)	0	23.4	5.9
Disked:								
Corn	6	0	(1)	0	(1)	0	16.7	4.2
Sorghum	1	0	(1)	0	(1)	0	15.0	3.8
Milo	2	0	(1)	0	(1)	0		0
Kafir	2	0	(1)	0	(1)	0		0
Total or average	11						15.9	4.0
Green manured:								
Rye	1	0	(1)	0	(1)	0		0
Peas	1	0	(1)	0	(1)	2.0		.7
Total or average	2					1.0		.3
Summer tilled	3	12.1	(1)		(1)	3.3	21.6	9.3
Average of all 27 plats		1.5				.4	18.0	5.0

[1] Destroyed by hail.

TABLE XVII.—*Yields and cost of production of oats by different methods at the Dalhart Field Station, 1909 to 1914, inclusive*—Continued.

SUMMARY OF YIELDS AND DIGEST OF COST.

Yields, values, etc. (average per acre).	Tillage treatment.						Previous crop.					
	Fall plowed (5 plats).	Spring plowed (4 plats.)	Disked (11 plats).	Listed (1 plat).	Green manured (2 plats).	Summer tilled (3 plats).	Corn (8 plats).	Sorghum (1 plat).	Small grain (8 plats).	Sod (2 plats).	Milo (2 plats).	Kafir (2 plats).
Yields of grain:												
1909.....bushels..	0	0	0	0	0	12.1	0	0	0	3.0	0	0
1910.......do....	(1)	(1)	(1)	(1)	(1)	(1)	(1)	(1)	(1)	(1)	(1)	(1)
1911.......do....	0	0	0	0	0	0	0	0	0	0	0	0
1912.......do....	(1)	(1)	(1)	(1)	(1)	(1)	(1)	(1)	(1)	(1)	(1)	(1)
1913.......do....	0	0	0	0	1	3.3	0	0	0	0	0	0
1914.......do....	18.0	14.0	15.9	23.4	......	21.6	16.7	15.0	17.7	......	......	......
Average........	4.5	3.5	4.0	5.9	.3	9.3	4.2	3.8	4.4	1.0	0	0
Crop value, cost of production, etc.:												
Value............	$1.35	$1.05	$1.20	$1.77	$0.09	$2.79	......	......	......	......	......	......
Cost.............	6.31	5.84	4.50	5.30	14.36	11.25	......	......	......	......	......	......
Loss...........	−4.96	−4.79	−3.30	−3.53	−14.27	−8.46	......	......	......	......	......	......

[1] Destroyed by hail.

Much the same work has been done with oats at Dalhart as at the other field stations. Determined efforts have been made for six years to grow this crop under a wide range of methods of preparation and culture, but without success. It has been variously destroyed by hail, drought, and soil blowing. The few crops that have been harvested were grown on summer-tilled land, but the yields have been so low, both actually and in comparison with other crops better adapted to the region, as to furnish no indication of their profitable production.

The low yields and high percentage of failures of oats at this station resulting from each and all of the various methods of tillage employed indicate little possibility of overcoming conditions by any cultural practices. This indication is strengthened when the time covered by these tests is considered. It can only be concluded that the combination of soil and climatic conditions existing at this station is not congenial to the production of oats.

The grain sorghums have produced good crops of feed every year at this station and have made good average grain yields. As compared with these crops oats has no place in the cropping system under conditions similar to those at this station.

AMARILLO FIELD STATION.

The soil at Amarillo, Tex., is a heavy clay silt. It is of the type locally known as "tight land" or "short-grass land." While the evidence is not as complete as could be desired, it appears that the storage of water and the development of the feeding roots of the crop are interfered with by a comparatively impervious layer of soil in the third foot. The soil above this, however, is competent to take care of all the water that it has been possible to store, even under a system of alternate cropping.

The results of six years are available from Amarillo. The year 1910 was lost by reason of an enforced change in the location of the station. In three of the six years yields have been fair and in three they have been very poor.

Only one method of preparation—summer tillage—has departed very far in its results from the general average. The average yield by this method has been 27.6 bushels per acre. The extreme range in the average of all other methods is from 13.2 bushels on spring-plowed wheat stubble to 18.4 bushels on peas as green manure and on fall plowing after barley. There is little profit in discussing differences within so narrow a range of yields.

It may be noted that fall plowing of either wheat or oat stubble has been better than spring plowing of either. Subsoiling has not been productive of yields as high as those by fall plowing similar stubble. Furrowing with a lister and leaving the ground rough through the winter has been practically as good as plowing.

Disking corn ground has given about the same results as plowing it. Disked milo and kafir ground have given markedly poorer results than corn ground.

The yields following green manure have corresponded closely to those following a harvested crop rather than to those following summer tillage.

When the cost of production is considered in connection with the value of the average crops produced by different methods, it is seen that the more expensive methods—summer tillage, subsoiling, and green manuring—have been the cause of losses ranging from $2.39 to $9.17. Fall plowing, spring plowing, and listing also show small losses. The low cost of preparation of disked land has resulted in its showing a profit of $0.24 per acre.

TABLE XVIII.—*Yields and cost of production of oats by different methods at the Amarillo Field Station, 1909 to 1914, inclusive.*

Treatment and previous crop.	Number of plats averaged.	Yield per acre (bushels).						
		1909	1910	1911	1912	1913	1914	Average.
Fall plowed:								
Wheat	3	26.7	14.3	26.4	9.7	6.8	19.0	17.2
Oats	1	32.2	0	27.5	14.1	2.5	30.9	17.9
Barley	1	31.3	0	35.6	9.1	7.2	26.9	18.4
Total or average	5	28.7	8.6	28.5	10.5	6.0	23.0	17.6
Spring plowed:								
Wheat	1	23.4	0	35.7	9.7	3.1	7.5	13.2
Oats	1	20.0	0	28.2	9.7	0	29.4	14.6
Corn	2	21.9	0	36.0	17.2	1.4	21.1	16.3
Total or average	4	21.8	....	34.0	13.5	1.5	19.8	15.1
Subsoiled: Oats	1	28.1	0	19.2	8.8	4.1	30.6	15.1
Listed: Oats	1	29.7	0	26.8	11.6	6.9	26.9	17.0
Disked:								
Corn	6	22.7	0	28.7	14.3	3.4	33.4	17.1
Milo	2	19.3	0	25.9	11.9	1.9	28.8	14.6
Kafir	2	16.5	0	26.7	8.2	1.8	26.8	13.3
Total or average	10	20.8	....	27.7	12.6	2.8	31.1	15.8
Green manure:								
Rye	1	31.9	5.0	18.0	13.8	5.6	22.2	16.1
Peas	1	27.5	8.4	25.9	15.0	6.5	26.9	18.4
Total or average	2	29.7	6.7	22.0	14.4	6.1	24.6	17.3
Summer tilled	2	32.5	24.4	36.2	17.7	17.4	37.1	27.6
Average of all 25 plats	....	24.8	4.2	28.7	12.7	4.9	27.4	17.1

SUMMARY OF YIELDS AND DIGEST OF COST.

Yields, values, etc. (average per acre).	Tillage treatment.							Previous crop.			
	Fall plowed (5 plats).	Spring plowed (4 plats).	Disked (10 plats).	Listed (1 plat).	Sub-soiled (1 plat).	Green manured (2 plats).	Summer tilled (2 plats).	Corn (8 plats).	Small grain (9 plats).	Milo (2 plats).	Kafir (2 plats).
Yields of grain:											
1908 . bush.	28.7	21.8	20.8	29.7	28.1	29.7	32.5	22.5	27.2	19.3	16.5
1909 . . . do	8.6	0	0	0	0	6.7	24.4	0	4.8	0	0
1911 . . . do	28.5	34.0	27.7	26.8	19.2	22.0	36.2	30.5	28.0	25.9	26.7
1912 . . . do	10.5	13.5	12.6	11.6	8.8	14.4	17.7	15.0	10.2	11.9	8.2
1913 . . . do	6.0	1.5	2.8	6.9	4.1	6.1	17.4	2.9	4.9	1.9	1.8
1914 . . . do	23.0	19.8	31.1	26.9	30.6	24.6	37.1	30.3	23.2	28.8	26.8
Average	17.6	15.1	15.8	17.0	15.1	17.3	27.6	16.9	16.4	14.6	13.3
Crop value, cost of production, etc.:											
Value	$5.28	$4.53	$4.74	$5.10	$4.53	$5.19	$8.28	......	......	......	......
Cost	6.31	5.84	4.50	5.30	6.92	14.36	11.25	......	......	......	......
Profit or loss	−1.03	−1.31	.24	− .20	−2.39	−9.17	−2.97	......	......	......	......

GENERAL DISCUSSION OF RESULTS.

In the preceding pages data have been presented and briefly discussed separately for each station without reference to results at other stations. In the following pages the data are considered from a more general standpoint. Table XIX will assist in this study.

In this table the average yields at the several stations are grouped under different methods of preparation. The figures here given are taken from the tables showing details for each station.

Data in regard to yields and cost of production are also assembled in such a way as to show the profit or loss in dollars and cents per acre for the average crop for each method for which it has been computed at each station.

TABLE XIX.—*Comparison of the average yields and profit or loss in the production of oats by different methods at fourteen stations in the Great Plains area.*

Statement of data.	Number of years averaged.	Methods of tillage.						
		Fall plowed.	Spring plowed.	Listed.	Sub-soiled.	Disked.	Green ma-nured.	Sum-mer tilled.
1	2	3	4	5	6	7	8	9
Yields per acre (bushels):[1]								
Judith Basin	5	49.9	51.2	49.9	49.5	53.3	54.8	58.4
Huntley	2	43.4	49.2	47.2	46.1	53.0	58.6	59.2
Williston	5	33.5	36.2	....	....	37.9	39.1	43.9
Dickinson	6	34.4	36.9	....	....	47.5	44.0	49.9
Edgeley	8	32.2	31.4	....	....	33.5	35.1	38.3
Hettinger	3	22.8	32.0	....	....	35.1	22.2	32.1
Belle Fourche	6	16.1	18.0	18.8	17.5	21.9	22.4	29.8
Scottsbluff	3	18.2	22.2	20.4	20.4	26.3	28.7	38.2
North Platte	8	17.8	18.5	....	....	17.9	22.0	27.4
Akron	6	21.7	23.9	21.9	16.9	20.5	19.9	28.7
Hays	6	20.7	17.6	22.9	22.7	20.7	....	24.8
Garden City	6	8.7	6.0	12.8	9.2	8.8	9.2	12.8
Dalhart	4	4.5	3.5	5.9	....	4.0	.3	9.3
Amarillo	6	17.6	15.1	17.0	15.1	15.8	17.3	27.6
Average[1]	5	24.4	25.8	24.1	24.7	28.3	28.7	34.3
Profit or loss (−) per acre:								
Judith Basin	5	$8.66	$9.52	$9.67	$7.93	$11.49	$2.08	$6.27
Huntley	2	6.71	8.92	8.86	6.91	11.40	3.22	6.51
Williston	5	3.74	5.02	....	....	6.87	− 2.63	1.92
Dickinson	6	4.01	5.23	....	....	9.75	− 1.16	3.72
Edgeley	8	3.35	3.58	....	....	5.55	− 3.83	.24
Hettinger	3	.53	3.76	....	....	6.03	− 7.70	−1.62
Belle Fourche	6	−1.48	− .44	.34	−1.67	2.07	− 7.64	−2.31
Scottsbluff	3	− .85	.82	.82	− .80	3.39	− 5.75	.21
North Platte	8	− .97	− .29	....	....	.87	− 7.76	−3.03
Akron	6	.20	1.33	1.27	−1.85	1.65	− 8.39	−2.64
Hays	6	− .10	− .56	1.57	− .11	1.71	....	−3.81
Garden City	5	−3.70	−4.04	−1.46	−4.16	−1.86	−11.60	−7.41
Dalhart	6	−4.96	−4.79	−3.53	....	−3.30	−14.27	−8.46
Amarillo	6	−1.03	−1.31	− .20	−2.39	.24	− 9.17	−2.97

[1] The averages of columns 3, 4, 7, and 9 only are comparable.

On the whole, seasonal conditions have produced much wider variations in yields than have been produced by differences in cultivation. Some seasons are so favorable that any and all methods give good returns at stations where oats can be successfully grown.

Other seasons have been so unfavorable at some stations that no method of cultivation has been able to produce a crop of oats. Less common than either of these are the seasons when there is just the combination of factors nearly or quite to prohibit production by some methods while allowing others to produce good crops. When the results of a series of years are averaged together, as must be done in a continuous agriculture, the wide differences obtained in exceptional years tend to be much reduced.

Perhaps the first thing that impresses one in viewing the average yields from all stations is the much better adaptation of oats to the northern than to the southern section of the Great Plains. There is an almost constant decrease in yields from the northern stations having cooler, shorter seasons to the southern stations having warmer, longer seasons. This decrease is about the same for the heavier yielding as it is for the lighter yielding methods. This proves that there is a lack of adaptation of the crop to the combination of soil and climatic conditions existing at the southern stations. The fact that all methods fail to produce even fair average yields at these stations shows that this lack of adaptation can not be overcome by cultural practices.

General averages for all of the stations mean little, because differences in yield obtained at one station may be balanced by differences in an opposite direction at another station.

The division into the two general groups of fall plowing and spring plowing is a striking example of such compensation of differences and the resulting lack of difference in the general average. With the trifling exception of a fraction of a bushel at Edgeley, spring plowing at all stations north of Hays has given higher averages than fall plowing. At Hays and the stations south of it fall plowing has been in about an equal degree better than spring plowing. The greater number of stations represented in the northern group makes the general average of averages show a small margin in favor of spring plowing. This, however, is of no binding force or value to those stations whose results show fall plowing to be the better practice for them.

At all stations north of North Platte disking has been productive of higher average yields than either fall plowing or spring plowing. At North Platte, Dalhart, and Amarillo it is between the two. At Hays it is the same as fall plowing and higher than spring plowing, and at Garden City it is higher than either. In the general average of all the stations reported it has a yield of 28.3 bushels per acre, against 25.8 bushels for spring plowing and 24.4 bushels for fall plowing. The great bulk of the land disked is corn ground, as is shown in detail in the tables for each station.

With the exception of a sharp decrease from subsoiling at Akron and a similar increase from listing at Garden City, the yields from each of these practices have not departed far from the yields of ordinary plowing. Some of the details of departure or lack of it have been discussed in dealing with separate stations where closer comparisons could be drawn with exactly similar stubble.

Green manuring averaged as a group was productive of higher yields than either fall or spring plowing or disking corn ground at 9 of the 13 stations for which results with this method are reported. At Dickinson this method was exceeded by disking corn ground. At Hettinger, Akron, and Dalhart green manuring gave poorer yields than any of the three other methods mentioned. At Amarillo this method gave yields exceeding those by fall plowing.

Of all the methods under trial, as grouped in Table XIX, summer tillage produced the highest yields at every station except Hettinger, where is was exceeded only by yields on disked corn ground. Averaged for all the stations, its increase of yield over fall plowing lacked one-tenth of a bushel of being 10 bushels per acre. The greatest departure from this general average was at Scottsbluff, where the increase was 20 bushels per acre.

Sod breaking as a preparation for oats has very generally stood at or near the bottom of the list, as is discussed in some detail under each station where it has been on trial.

As values and cost of production are here figured, it is seen in Table XIX that oats have been produced at a profit by at least one method at all stations except Garden City and Dalhart. At two stations, Judith Basin and Huntley, a profit has been realized by all methods.

Generally speaking, good yields have combined with low cost of production to make disked land which has been chiefly corn ground show the greatest profit at all stations where a profit has been realized from any method.

At all stations where it has been tried, listing either has been more profitable or has resulted in less loss than fall plowing.

Subsoiling has yielded a profit at two stations and a loss at six. It can not be said, however, that it was a profitable practice at any station, as its profits were less and its losses greater than those of fall plowing. It should be compared with fall plowing, as it is a modification of that method.

At all the ten stations north of Hays, except Belle Fourche and North Platte (where the losses were 44 cents and 29 cents, respectively), spring plowing was productive of profitable crops. At Hays the average loss from it was only 56 cents per acre. At Amarillo the loss increased to $1.31. At Garden City and Dalhart spring plowing, in common with all other methods, shows a loss.

At Akron, Colo., and at all North Dakota and Montana stations fall plowing showed a profit. At Scottsbluff the nominal profits from spring plowing were converted to nominal losses by fall plowing. At the other stations the losses by the two methods were about the same.

The cost of green manuring was so high that at only two stations, Judith Basin and Huntley, did it show a profit. At these stations the profits were smaller than those by any other method. At all other stations it either converted the profit of other methods into a loss or was productive of the greatest loss of any method. In probably only two or three cases has the loss been small enough to make it possible to change it to a profit by distributing a part of the cost to following crops.

Summer tillage as here figured shows a profit at six stations and a loss at eight. In two cases the profits are nominal, i. e., they are so small that changes in the average yields by extension of the record might change their position. In no case was the profit as here figured as great as by some other method. Except at Dalhart and Garden City, the average losses at those stations showing a loss have ranged from $1.62 to $3.81. Considering the fact shown in the details from the separate field stations, it seems that as summer tillage sometimes produced a crop when other methods failed it might have a place in the production of oats, even though somewhat greater net profits may be obtained in the average of a series of years by other methods. Sureness of production, especially of feed crops, is as important as the amount of net profit per acre, if not more important.

A reference to the companion publication on spring wheat (Bulletin 214 of the Department series) will show that the relative response of oats to summer tillage is somewhat greater than that of spring wheat.

CONCLUSIONS.

(1) The relatively poor adaptation of oats to the southern section of the Great Plains can not be overcome by cultivation.

(2) Seasonal conditions cause much wider variations in yields than can be caused by differences in cultivation.

(3) When the results of a series of years are averaged, as must be done in a continuous agriculture, the great differences which are obtained only in exceptional years tend to be much reduced.

(4) At stations north of Hays, spring plowing has been generally more productive of oats than fall plowing. At Hays and the stations south of it fall plowing has been in about an equal degree better than spring plowing.

(5) At Garden City and all stations north of North Platte, disking corn ground has been productive of higher average yields of oats

than either fall or spring plowing. At North Platte, Hays, Dalhart, and Amarillo it yielded either the same as one of them or its place was intermediate between the two.

(6) With the exception of a sharp decrease at Akron, the yields by subsoiling have not departed far from those by ordinary plowing. It has not been a profitable practice, as the profits by it have been less and the losses greater than by fall plowing, of which it is a modification and with which it should be compared.

(7) At all stations where it has been tried, listing for oats has been either more profitable or has resulted in less loss than fall plowing.

(8) Green manuring has been productive of higher yields than either fall or spring plowing, or disking corn ground, at nine of the thirteen stations from which results by it are reported. The cost of production by this method was so high that it showed a profit at only two stations.

(9) Oats following summer tillage produced the highest average yields at all stations except Hettinger, where the yield was exceeded only by that on disked corn ground. While the expense of the method has prevented its being the most profitable, the degree of insurance which it affords against failure of the feed crop might justify its practice in oat production in at least some sections of the Great Plains.

(10) Disking corn ground yielded the highest profits of any method tested at all stations except Garden City and Dalhart. At these two stations the crop was produced at a loss, but this loss was less than by any other method.

ADDITIONAL COPIES
OF THIS PUBLICATION MAY BE PROCURED FROM
THE SUPERINTENDENT OF DOCUMENTS
GOVERNMENT PRINTING OFFICE
WASHINGTON, D. C.
AT
10 CENTS PER COPY
▽

WASHINGTON : GOVERNMENT PRINTING OFFICE : 1915

UNITED STATES DEPARTMENT OF AGRICULTURE

BULLETIN No. 219

Contribution from the Bureau of Plant Industry
WM. A. TAYLOR, Chief

Washington, D. C. ▼ June 2, 1915.

CORN IN THE GREAT PLAINS AREA

RELATION OF CULTURAL METHODS TO PRODUCTION

By

E. C. CHILCOTT, Agriculturist in Charge, and J. S. COLE
and W. W. BURR, Assistants, Office of
Dry-Land Agriculture

CONTENTS

WASHINGTON
GOVERNMENT PRINTING OFFICE
1915

BULLETIN OF THE
U.S. DEPARTMENT OF AGRICULTURE

No. 219

Contribution from the Bureau of Plant Industry, Wm. A. Taylor, Chief.
June 2, 1915.

CORN IN THE GREAT PLAINS AREA: RELATION OF CULTURAL METHODS TO PRODUCTION.

By E. C. Chilcott, *Agriculturist in Charge*, and J. S. Cole and W. W. Burr, *Assistants*, *Office of Dry-Land Agriculture.*[1]

CONTENTS.

INTRODUCTION.

In planning the experimental work of the Office of Dry-Land Agriculture to study methods of crop production under dry-land conditions in the Great Plains, corn was given rather a prominent place. Experience had shown that in the production of fodder it was at least as safe a crop, and perhaps as productive, as any that could be grown in a large part of the area. Experience had also shown that

[1] All of the members of the scientific staff of the Office of Dry-Land Agriculture have contributed more or less to this paper by having charge of field investigations and by assisting in the preparation of data for records or for publication. The scientific staff as at present constituted consists of the following members, named in the order of length of service: W. W. Burr, Denver, Colo.; E. F. Chilcott, Woodward, Okla.; O. J. Grace, Akron, Colo.; J. S. Cole, Denver, Colo.; J. M. Stephens, Moccasin, Mont.; A. L. Hallsted, Hays, Kans.; O. R. Mathews, Belle Fourche, S. Dak.; J. C. Thysell, Dickinson, N. Dak.; M. Pfaender, Mandan, N. Dak.; H. C. McKinstry, Hettinger, N. Dak.; W. M. Osborn, North Platte, Nebr.; W. D. Griggs, Dalhart, Tex.; C. A. Burmeister, Amarillo, Tex.; J. E. Mundell, Big Springs, Tex.; F. L. Kelso, Ardmore, S. Dak.; W. A. Peterson, Mandan, N. Dak.; J. T. Sarvis, Ardmore, S. Dak.; G. W. Morgan, Huntley, Mont.; J. H. Jacobson, Mitchell, Nebr.; H. G. Smith, Tucumcari, N. Mex.; L. N. Jensen, Woodward, Okla.; J. G. Lill, Garden City, Kans.; R. S. Towle, Edgeley, N. Dak.; A. J. Ogaard, Williston, N. Dak.; C. B. Brown, Dalhart, Tex.; L. D. Willey, Archer, Wyo.; J. B. Kuska, Colby, Kans.; and A. E. Seamans, Akron, Colo.

The following-named men have held positions on the scientific staff of the Office of Dry-Land Agriculture during the past nine years, but have resigned or have been transferred to other offices of the Department of Agriculture: Sylvester Balz, F. L. Kennard, J. E. Payne, L. E. Hazen, C. A. Jensen, H. R. Reed, W. O. Whitcomb, C. H. Plath, F. Knorr, and R. W. Edwards.

The data here reported from the stations in Kansas, Nebraska, North Dakota, and Montana have been obtained in cooperation with the agricultural experiment stations of their respective States. In South Dakota, Colorado, Texas, Oklahoma, and New Mexico the stations are operated by the United States Department of Agriculture.

Field, office, and laboratory facilities, teams, and implements have been provided by the Office of Western Irrigation Agriculture at Huntley, Mont.; Belle Fourche, S. Dak., and Mitchell, Nebr., and by the Office of Cereal Investigations at Amarillo, Tex., and Archer, Wyo. The Biophysical Laboratory has cooperated in obtaining the meteorological data reported.

Note.—This bulletin is intended for all who are interested in the agricultural possibilities of the Great Plains area.

corn growing possessed merit as a preparation of the land for a crop of small grain. When these two factors are combined in one crop they make its growth of double importance. Corn is the only crop at present available that offers this advantage which at the same time lends itself to large acreage and a general farming system.

The grain sorghums fit equally well into a farming system that includes the production of live stock, but they are not adapted to the whole of the Great Plains, and furthermore have not in general shown an effect so beneficial as corn on the following crop.

Potatoes have approximately the same effect as corn upon most crops that may follow them, but the potato crop does not lend itself so well to growth on a large acreage.

The effect of the growth and clean cultivation of corn as compared with summer tillage and various other methods of preparation has been shown in bulletins simultaneously written on the growth of spring wheat, oats, and barley in the Great Plains area. In these publications it has been shown that the crops following corn have consistently given high yields as compared with other methods of preparing a seed bed for these crops. In many cases the highest yields of small grain have been obtained on disked corn ground. In many other cases where disked corn ground has not been productive of the highest yields, it has so nearly approached them that when the cost of preparation is considered it is found to be productive of the greatest profit. This has attached so much importance to the corn crop that it appears to be desirable to present the actual data on the production of corn in the different years at the different stations and under different methods of cultivation and preparation for the crop.

While corn in most cases has been grown in preparing for other crops and in cropping systems primarily arranged for the growth of other crops, the necessity for studying methods of producing the crop itself has not been overlooked. In general terms, corn has been grown by different methods under a system of continuous cropping. It has been grown at some stations in 2-year rotations of alternate corn and wheat and corn and oats. It has been grown in 3-year rotations where the other two crops were wheat and oats or barley and oats. It has been grown in 4-year rotations with small grains and fallow or the use of green manure. It has also been raised as the second crop from the sod in sod rotations. In some of the rotations manure has been applied before plowing the ground for corn.

Some of the rotations are calculated to conserve or increase the fertility of the soil, while others may perhaps deplete it. In the present stage of the work the effects of the rotations as units are greatly overshadowed by the effects of the cropping and cultivation for a single year. This is due to the fact that the controlling factors are water supply, physical condition of the seed bed, and a certain recognized, although not fully understood, effect of the crop immediately preceding. Uniformity in these factors is largely restored by the cultivation or cropping of a single season. After a careful study of the data, it seemed advisable to present in this bulletin the yields of corn as determined by the cropping and treatment of the land in only the one year immediately preceding the growth of the crop.

In the study that is here made only the more important and obvious results will be discussed. The tables themselves when critically studied show much more than is here mentioned. No attempt is made to study rotations as a whole. There are cumulative effects of rotations and farming systems that are not negligible, but which are not discussed here. Other studies have shown that these effects are of far less immediate importance than the effect of the preceding crop, the preparation of the seed bed, and the seasonal conditions.

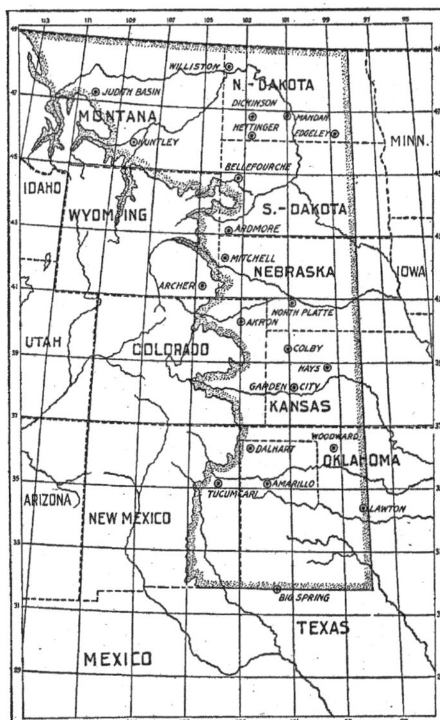

FIG. 1.—Sketch map of the Great Plains area, which includes parts of ten States and consists of about 400,000 square miles of territory. Its western boundary is indicated by the 5,000-foot contour. The location of each field station within the area is shown by a dot within a circle (⊙).

AREA COVERED BY THESE STUDIES.

The area (fig. 1) included in these investigations covers a part of ten States: Montana, North Dakota, South Dakota, Wyoming, Nebraska, Colorado, Kansas, Oklahoma, Texas, and New Mexico. It extends from the ninety-eighth meridian of longitude to the foothills of the Rocky Mountains and from the Canadian border to the thirty-second parallel of latitude.

The altitudes vary from approximately 1,400 feet in the north to 6,000 feet at Cheyenne, Wyo. The southern portion of the territory has a higher average altitude, a higher average rainfall, and a correspondingly higher rate of evaporation than the northern portion.

CLIMATIC CONDITIONS.

The climate of the Great Plains has been classified as semiarid. It may be better to say that it is changeable, varying from season to season from almost humid conditions to almost arid, with a mean annual precipitation relatively low. Years of relatively high precipitation may be followed by years of relatively low precipitation. Other climatic factors usually correspond with the rainfall. A year of relatively high rainfall will have a lower rate of evaporation, higher humidity, and lower wind velocity than will be found in the unfavorable years.

Another climatic factor of much importance in crop production in the Great Plains is the distribution of the rainfall. A relatively low rainfall, properly distributed, may produce a crop where a much higher rainfall, coming with unfavorable distribution, may result in a crop failure.

No attempt will be made in this bulletin to give a full description or record of the climatic conditions at the various stations during the time covered by these investigations.

Table I gives the maximum, minimum, and average annual and seasonal precipitation and seasonal evaporation at each station for the years for which experimental work is here reported. By seasonal is meant the period between the average time of seeding and the average time of harvesting.

TABLE I.—*Annual and seasonal precipitation and seasonal evaporation at fourteen stations in the Great Plains area.*[1]

Station.	Altitude (feet).[2]	Precipitation (inches).[3]						Seasonal evaporation (inches).[3]		
		Annual.			Seasonal.					
		Minimum.	Maximum.	Average.	Minimum.	Maximum.	Average.	Minimum.	Maximum.	Average.
Judith Basin	4,228	14.96	23.78	18.06	7.04	17.21	9.34	22.012	29.353	24.491
Huntley	3,000	11.92	11.92	11.92	5.92	6.02	5.97	23.754	24.214	23.984
Williston	1,875	10.28	18.99	14.84	4.75	14.49	9.66	20.422	26.877	24.216
Dickinson	2,543	11.93	21.22	16.69	6.85	16.28	9.79	20.673	25.745	23.919
Edgeley	1,468	11.94	21.95	16.71	7.85	14.98	10.11	18.663	24.893	21.866
Hettinger	2,253	12.72	15.68	14.20	8.92	12.47	10.36	21.539	28.239	24.639
Belle Fourche	2,950	6.64	17.73	13.11	4.08	9.78	6.90	26.472	33.750	28.794
Scottsbluff	3,950	13.77	18.51	16.14	2.53	8.52	4.69	23.804	29.381	26.081
North Platte	3,000	11.18	23.01	18.05	6.85	12.66	9.45	28.445	38.168	32.359
Akron	4,600	14.51	22.46	18.28	6.42	13.86	9.02	26.064	35.654	31.420
Hays	2,050	15.59	27.80	21.30	8.18	17.97	11.17	30.625	44.373	35.790
Garden City	2,900	11.82	23.58	18.54	2.79	14.43	8.65	34.325	43.510	38.185
Dalhart	4,000	13.69	16.35	15.11	5.09	9.85	8.01	35.459	41.748	38.988
Amarillo	3,676	10.69	27.80	18.28	6.17	11.38	9.13	33.804	42.076	36.724

[1] The years covered are the same as for the data shown in the other tables for the several stations.

[2] The altitude given is for the field where the work was done and is based in most cases on that of the nearest town.

[3] The records of annual precipitation for 1914 are not included. The records of seasonal precipitation and evaporation for 1914 are included for all stations, being figured from May 1 to Sept. 1. Evaporation measurements are made from a free water surface, in a tank sunk into the soil to almost its full depth. The water surface is kept about level with the surface of the ground.

In these investigations seasonal variations in climatic factors have been of more importance in crop production than differences in methods of tillage. This is shown by the fact that at some stations in some years climatic conditions have been such that all methods have resulted in practical failures in yields. In other years all methods have given fair returns.

Figure 2 shows the earliest and latest dates of the last killing frost in the spring, the earliest and latest dates of the first killing frost in the fall, and the average length of the frost-free period at each station. The heavy hatched horizontal bars represent the periods between the average dates of the last killing frost in the spring and the first killing frost in the fall, or the average frost-free period, the actual number of days being also shown. The solid-line curve at the left shows the earliest date at which the frost-free period has begun. The broken-

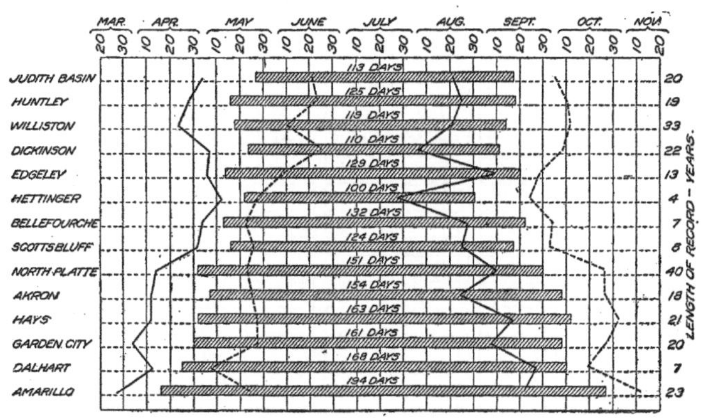

FIG. 2.—Diagram showing the average frost-free periods and the earliest and the latest dates at which the last killing frost in the spring and the first killing frost in the fall has occurred at fourteen stations in the Great Plains area.

line curve at the left represents the latest date at which the last killing frost of the spring has occurred. The solid-line curve at the right represents the earliest date and the broken-line curve at the right the latest date at which the first killing frost of the fall has occurred.

This diagram shows clearly the increase in the length of the frost-free period from the north to the south. The shortest average frost-free period is 100 days at Hettinger and the longest one 194 days at Amarillo. The length of the period free from frost is more important in the production of corn than in the production of the small grains. Young corn being easily injured by frost, planting must be delayed until there is little further danger from this source. Where the season is short the crop may be caught by frost in the fall. This necessitates the use of short-season varieties in a portion of the Great Plains. As a season of average length can not be depended on, the production of mature corn has been so uncertain at some stations as to make the crop unprofitable if grown for grain alone.

GENERAL PLAN OF THE INVESTIGATIONS.

The method of work adopted in these investigations involved the raising of different crops in various combinations or systems of rotations and under different methods of cultivation in systems of continuous cropping. Most of the work has been done with 3-year and 4-year rotations. No rotations of greater length than six years have been used. Those of this length have been tried with sod crops only.

FIG. 3.—Diagram of the dry-land rotation field at the Akron Field Station. The lettering shows the cropping practiced in 1914. The explanation of abbreviations used is as follows: *D.*=Disked, *Fal.*=summer tilled, *FP.*=fall plowed, *GM.*=green manured, *L.*=listed, *M.*=manured, *S.*=spring plowed, *SS.*=subsoiled.

PLAT AND ROTATION OUTLINES.

Figure 3 shows a diagram of the dry-land rotation field at the Akron Field Station. This is one of the oldest stations of the Office of Dry-Land Agriculture, and is a representative one that will serve to illustrate the general scheme and plan of work. The plats involved in the work at this station and at all of the stations are one-tenth of an acre in size. Their dimensions are 2 by 8 rods. Along their larger dimension the plats are separated by alleys 4 feet wide. Along the ends of the plats they are separated by roads 20 feet wide. At all of the stations five crops are represented in a series of continuously cropped plats, lettered on the diagram from A to G. In this group C and D are alternately cropped and summer tilled so that each year a crop is grown after summer tillage and a plat is summer tilled for cropping the next year. The remainder of the field is in rotations in which each plat is known by a rotation number and letter. On the field diagram the separation of rotations is indicated by heavy lines. The movement of the crops in the rotation is from Z to A, and from A back to the letter that marks the other end of the rotation.

In figure 3 the diagram is filled out to show the cropping in 1914. The letters following the crop indicate the treatment given the ground in preparation for the crop: SP. stands for spring plowed, FP. for fall plowed, Fal. for summer tilled, GM. for green manured, D. for disked, etc.

As an illustration, rotation 14 may be used: In 1914, plat A of this 4-year rotation was planted to corn on spring-plowed ground, B was in wheat on disked corn ground, and C was in winter rye after fall plowing. Plat D was in oats where winter rye had been turned under the preceding year. In 1915, A will be in wheat, B in winter rye, C in oats, and D in corn.

VARIETIES.

In these investigations no attempt was made to grow the same variety at different stations. The aim was to select a variety well adapted to the conditions of the station where it was grown. The same variety has not been grown at any station during the entire period of the investigations. When a variety was obtained that was thought to be better adapted to local conditions than the one previously grown, a change was made.

At most of the stations, early-maturing varieties have been used. In the northern part of the area the growing season is so short that only very early varieties are at all safe. Increasing altitude with its correspondingly cooler nights, or decreasing water supply, has much the same effect as increasing latitude. At Hays, North Platte, and Amarillo varieties are grown that are somewhat larger and later maturing than those grown at the other stations.

DETERMINATION OF YIELDS.

The corn is harvested either when mature or when growth is stopped by frost. It is cut with a binder and shocked in the field. The shocks stand until cured, usually about a month. They are then weighed and the sound corn, if any, is husked and weighed. Where sound corn is produced, the yield as tabulated is given in bushels in the column headed "Grain." The column headed "Stover" [1] shows the total weight when no grain is produced and the difference be-

[1] In the tables of this bulletin only the term "stover" is used, because the corn was husked whenever marketable or whenever it was produced in sufficient quantity to warrant husking. In cases where the yield of grain was not sufficient to warrant husking the term "fodder" would be more exact.

tween the weight of the grain and the total weight when corn is husked. The grain weights are converted into bushels on the basis of 70 to 75 pounds per bushel, depending upon the dryness at the time of husking.

In some cases when the crop did not dry out or cure well the weights have been arbitrarily reduced by the percentage estimated or determined to be necessary to bring them to normal air dryness. Only occasionally is it necessary to do this in the Great Plains area.

SEEDING AND STAND.

The time of planting corn at the various stations is more uniform than the time of seeding the small grains. Small grains are usually seeded as early as the season will permit in the southern as well as in the northern portion of the area. This is done because the small grain will withstand the cooler weather of the early spring and may be able to mature in advance of drought which so frequently occurs at about harvest time. Corn, on the other hand, requires warm weather and a warm soil. In the southern portion of the territory, therefore, where the growing season is longer, the usual practice is to wait for the soil to become warm, thus delaying the planting. In the northern part of the territory the season is so short that the planting can not be delayed, and the planting season is advanced to the limit of safety. This delay in the southern part and advancement in the northern part tends to equalize the time of planting throughout the territory. In the southern part of the territory the usual date of planting is May 10 to 15; in the northern part, May 25 to June 1, a difference of about two weeks.

At North Platte all the corn included in these studies was planted with a lister. At all of the other stations the corn is surface planted in rows, with the exception of one or two listed plats at each station. To insure a uniform stand, the corn is planted thicker than it is intended to grow and then thinned to the desired stand. This may in some cases interfere with differences in stand that might result from differences in seed bed, but it appears to be the only practicable way to handle the crop in experimental work where it is desired to eliminate as many variable factors as possible.

The thickness of the stand of corn that is finally established at the various stations depends upon the amount of water which past experience has shown may be expected during the growing season and upon the expectation of producing grain. At the Judith Basin Field Station the corn is thinned to a distance of 9 inches between the plants. At this station there is enough available water to maintain a thick stand, but the growing season is so short that grain is not matured. At the stations where the amount of available water is less and the growing season longer, the distance between the plants is increased until in some cases it is as much as 24 inches. It seems possible that this distance should be made still greater at some of the stations.

SEED-BED PREPARATION.

The results from different methods have been tabulated and are here presented in such a manner as to show the effect of the cropping or cultivation and preparation of the land in the one year prior to the corn planting. The tables show the effect of plowing for corn both in the spring and in the fall and after both corn and small grain, the effects of listing and of subsoiling where these have been tried, and the effect of summer tillage.

In the tables as presented, the yields reported in the columns headed "Spring plowed, after corn" are from plat A, continuously cropped to corn. This plat is shallow spring plowed and is given a minimum of cultivation.

The yields reported in the columns headed "Fall plowed, after corn" are from plats continuously cropped to corn under a system of fall plowing and cultivation for the conservation of water both in the fall and in the spring. Fall plowing is done as early as practicable. It is done to a good depth, the standard being set at 8 inches. The ground after plowing may be worked down or left rough through the winter, as seems advisable. This plat at each station is generally known in this work as continuous-corn plat B.

The yields reported after summer tillage are from two plats alternately summer tilled and cropped to corn. One of the pair is in corn and the other is summer tilled each year. These are the plats generally known as C and D in the continuous-corn series. Summer tillage is of the intensive type. The land lies fallow one year and until planting time the following year. In so far as it is practicable to do so the plat is kept free from weeds and a mulch is maintained on it during the period between the time of harvesting the preceding crop and the time of planting the corn. This period in some cases is as long as 18 months. In some cases it is necessary to plow the land more than once during this period, either to maintain a surface receptive to water and that will resist blowing or to prevent the growth of weeds. The long period of summer tillage, involving the nonproduction of a crop for one year, together with the intensive methods practiced, have made this an expensive system of treatment.

The subsoiled plat is continuously cropped to corn. It is handled the same as plat B except that at the time of plowing it is subsoiled. A depth of about 14 inches is usually reached. Where the history of the station is sufficiently long for it to have been accomplished, it has been subsoiled two years in succession. Subsoiling was then suspended for two years and then resumed. The plat is known as E in the continuous-corn series.

87563°—Bull. 219—15——2

The yields reported in the column headed "Listed" are also from land continuously cropped to corn. Where the yield reported is from one plat only, it is from a plat that receives no cultivation before planting with the lister. Where it is given as an average of two plats, one is disked and cultivated during the spring before planting. All the other yields are from corn in rotations with other crops, as designated.

No attempt is made in this bulletin to discuss the various types of soils at the different stations. The yields show that the soils at some stations offer very little, if any, response to differences in tillage methods, while other soils do respond to tillage, the response varying from year to year with the varying combinations of climatic factors. A brief discussion of the soils at the different stations is given in a bulletin simultaneously prepared (Bulletin 214 of the department series) entitled "Spring wheat in the Great Plains area: Relation of cultural methods to production."

COMPARISON OF CULTURAL METHODS.

The methods under study vary a great deal in the labor involved and in the consequent cost of production. An accurate record has been kept of all farm operations performed in pursuance of the various methods under trial. These records have been averaged for eight representative stations having the longest period of trial. It is recognized that this average does not exactly represent the requirements of any station. The amount of work required for some methods varies with the season and with the soil. While recognizing this, it seems more practicable to use a fixed basis for all the stations than to try to adjust the cost for each station separately.

Table IV gives in the columns headed "Number of operations" the average number of times each of the separate operations have been performed in growing the crop. The amount of labor performed under each of the methods was neither more nor less than that which the man in charge believed to be necessary.

In practice it is probable that much of the corn produced in the dry-farming section will be either siloed or fed in the bundle rather than shelled and sold on the market. The cost of production therefore has been computed for the corn in the shock.

In computing the costs of the various operations a fixed wage of $2 a day for a man and $1 a day for a horse was adopted. This may be above or below the actual labor cost in any particular locality, but it is believed to be a fair average and one that will afford a profitable market to the farmer for his labor. The time required for men and teams to cover a given acreage in the several farm operations obviously varies with soils and other conditions. The average shown in Table II has been determined from the actual experience of a large number of men connected with these investigations—experience that has extended over a wide range of conditions and many years of time.

The factors included in the cost of production are calculated on an acre basis for each of the separate operations performed, beginning with the preparation of the land and ending with the harvesting and shocking of the crop. To these items are added the cost of seed, at 22 cents per acre; interest and taxes on the land investment, calculated at 8 per cent on a valuation of $20 per acre; and the deterioration and repairs of the binder, at 15 cents per acre. No allowance is made for the deterioration of other farm equipment, as it is believed that the wages assigned for men and teams are sufficient to cover this item of expense.

TABLE II.—*Average cost per acre of the farm operations involved in growing corn in the Great Plains area.*

[The wage scale assumed is $2 per day for each man and $1 per day for each horse.]

Operation.	Force employed.		Day's work.	Item cost.	Cost per acre.
	Men.	Horses.			
			Acres.		
Plowing	1	4	3½		$1.71
Disking	1	4	8		.75
Harrowing	1	4	35		.17
Subsoiling	1	3	3½		1.43
Drilling	1	4	15		.40
Cultivating	1	4	16		.38
Listing	1	4	10		.60
Harvesting:					
Cutting and binding	1	3	8	$0.62½	1.50
Shocking	2			.50	
Twine				.22½	
Binder wear and repair				.15	

Table II shows the cost per acre, based upon what is considered an average day's work for each of the farm operations involved, at the above-mentioned wage. The cost of production as computed in Tables II and IV is not offered as being absolute for any locality, either in the amount of labor required or its cost. It is recognized that the labor cost will vary with individuality and conditions. The cost of twine to bind an acre of corn obviously varies with the character of the crop. The assumed land value would be too low for many sections of the Plains. The estimated cost used in the table would be low for even an average crop in sections where heavy yields are obtained. Recognizing these and other possible variations, the cost shown in the tables is used simply to give a working basis for the comparison of the results by different methods.

VALUATION OF THE CROP.

The average farm price of corn on December 1 for 10 years is given in Table III. These data were furnished by the Bureau of Crop Estimates. The four States of North Dakota, South Dakota, Nebraska, and Kansas were selected as representative of the most stable market conditions within the area included in these investigations. This table shows that the average farm price of corn on December 1 in the four States has been 51 cents per bushel for the period considered.

TABLE III.—*Average price of corn at the farm bin for 10 years in four States of the Great Plains area.*

[The quotations are given in cents per bushel. Those for the year 1914 are for the date of Nov. 1; in other years Dec. 1 is taken as the date.]

Year.	North Dakota.	South Dakota.	Nebraska.	Kansas.	Average.	Year.	North Dakota.	South Dakota.	Nebraska.	Kansas.	Average.
1905.....	36	31	32	33	33	1911.....	60	53	55	63	57¾
1906.....	39	29	29	32	32¼	1912.....	43	37	37	40	39¼
1907.....	60	46	41	44	47¾	1913.....	52	56	65	78	62¾
1908.....	60	50	51	55	54	1914.....	60	56	60	70	61½
1909.....	55	50	50	54	52¼						
1910.....	58	40	36	45	44¾	Average.	52	45	46	61	51

The value of corn fodder or stover is difficult to estimate. The average farm price of hay in North Dakota, South Dakota, Nebraska, and Kansas on December 1 for the 10 years ended 1913 has been $6.22 per ton. Very few feeding experiments are available from which to determine the relative values of corn fodder and hay. As a matter of experience and observation and from the best evidence obtainable, it is believed that corn stover of the quality produced in the dry-farming sections is worth at least two-thirds as much as hay. This is admittedly an estimate. The stover produced in the area covered by this bulletin varies widely in quality. In some cases it is either immature corn or corn that failed to produce ears. In those localities where marketable corn has been produced it is that portion of the crop remaining after the grain has been husked. For the sake of uniformity in the tables the designation "Stover" is used in all cases.

Under the heading "Total cost of production," in Table IV, the costs are computed as fixed charges per acre for the crop in the shock. Values are computed on the basis of $4 per ton for the fodder or stover and 40 cents per bushel for the corn in the shock. The average farm price of corn for the past 10 years as shown in Table III has been 51 cents per bushel in the bin. The use of the price of 40 cents in the shock allows 11 cents per bushel for husking, shelling, and putting the corn in the bin. It is believed that this is a liberal allowance.

TABLE IV.—*Comparative cost per acre of producing corn by different methods.*[1]

[Averages of data from eight stations.]

Method of preparation.	Number of operations.				Cost of preparation.	Cost per acre.					Total cost of production.		
	Plowing.	Harrowing.	Disking.	Subsoiling.		Seed.	Planting.	Cultivation.[2]	Harvesting.	Interest and taxes.	In dollars.	In fodder at $4 per ton.	In grain at 40 cents per bushel.
Listed	......	1	1	......	$0.92	$0.22	$0.60	$1.14	$1.50	$1.60	5.98	1.50	15
Spring plowed	1	1.4	.6	......	2.40	.22	.25	1.14	1.50	1.60	7.11	1.78	17.8
Fall plowed	1	1.4	1.1	......	2.78	.22	.25	1.14	1.50	1.60	7.49	1.87	18.7
Subsoiled	1	1.4	1.1	0.5	3.47	.22	.25	1.14	1.50	1.60	8.18	2.05	20.5
Summer tilled	1.4	8.3	3	......	6.05	.22	.25	1.14	1.50	3.20	12.36	3.09	30.9

[1] This cost does not include an estimate of the cost of husking and cribbing.
[2] The cost of cultivation is based on three cultivations.

RESULTS AT INDIVIDUAL STATIONS.

Tables V to XVII, inclusive, present for each station the results of different methods of seed-bed preparation for corn. Each table presents the results for a single station. Except at stations where no grain was produced, the yields of both grain and stover by each of the methods studied are given for each year. The average yield of both grain and stover is also given for the entire period of years under study. The value of each of these is computed separately and shown. In the line designated "Total value" the combined value of both grain and stover is given. In the line designated "Cost" is given for each method of tillage the cost of production as determined in accordance with the explanation already made. In the last line of the table is given the profit or loss by each method as shown by the foregoing determinations. This is not given as being absolute, but is shown as a basis for the comparison of different methods of producing the corn crop and for comparing the production of corn with other crops.

JUDITH BASIN FIELD STATION.

During the five years covered by the records of the field station at Moccasin, Mont., in the Judith Basin, good average yields of corn fodder have been produced. No marketable grain has been obtained. The season is so short, and at this altitude so much cool weather prevails, that corn does not ordinarily reach maturity. The growing of corn at this station is to be considered, therefore, from the standpoint of the production of fodder rather than of grain. Its value lies in the possibility of increasing the number of live stock kept on the farm rather than in its production as a cash market crop. The corn at this station does not grow tall and coarse. It is so short that it can be harvested with a grain binder, and it has a large proportion of leaves to the stalk, so that it makes excellent feed.

A careful study of the yields in Table V shows that the seasonal influence is much greater than the influence of tillage. This is brought out by the wide variation in average yields in different years and the much smaller variation in the yields from different methods within the same year.

Good or heavy average yields of fodder are shown by all methods, but little consistent advantage of one method over another. The lack of consistent differences in yield by various methods of tillage indicates that this soil offers little response to any particular method of seed-bed preparation for corn. This lack of response is doubtless due to the shallowness of the soil, and has been found true thus far for the spring-sown small grains, as well as for corn. Perhaps the chief thing to be noted in the yields is that corn has averaged somewhat better after corn than after small grain. Summer tillage has been productive of yields intermediate between the two.

TABLE V.—*Yields and cost of production of corn by different methods at the Judith Basin Field Station, 1909 to 1914, inclusive.*

Yields, values, etc. (average per acre).	Fall plowed.		Spring plowed.		Sub-soiled, after corn (1 plat).	Listed, after corn (1 plat).	Summer tilled (1 plat).
	After corn (1 plat).	After small grain (9 plats).	After corn (1 plat).	After small grain (16 plats).			
Yields of stover:							
1909....pounds..	11,120	10,011	10,100	8,603	11,420	11,700	11,530
1910....do....	2,900	2,385	2,760	2,626	3,650	3,260	3,300
1911....do....	7,000	6,174	7,250	5,895	4,780	6,700	3,850
1912....	(1)	(1)	(1)	(1)	(1)	(1)	(1)
1913....pounds..	4,000	3,683	5,000	4,227	5,800	4,450	6,100
1914....do....	3,700	4,122	4,900	4,500	5,000	3,800	3,500
Average....	5,744	5,275	6,002	5,193	6,130	5,982	5,656
Value....	$11.49	$10.55	$12.00	$10.39	$12.26	$11.96	$11.31
Cost....	7.49	7.49	7.11	7.11	8.18	5.98	12.36
Profit or loss....	4.00	3.06	4.89	3.28	4.08	5.98	−1.05

[1] The crop in 1912 was partially destroyed by hail. Some corn was produced, but the lack of uniformity in the yields makes it inadvisable to use the results in this table.

All methods except summer tillage have been productive of profitable crops. The greatest profit, $5.98 per acre, has been by the least expensive method—listing. The next largest profit, $4.89 per acre, has been by spring plowing after corn. Excluding summer tillage, the small difference in the net results by different methods indicates that the problem is one of utilization of the feed rather than of the method of its production.

HUNTLEY FIELD STATION.

The results of two years at Huntley, Mont., are shown in Table VI. In both years good crops of grain were produced. With the exception of subsoiling, the relative performance of different methods is quite consistent. In 1914 the subsoiled ground apparently lacked water to mature its crop. Greater differences have been manifested in the yields of grain than in those of stover.

TABLE VI.—*Yields and cost of production of corn by different methods at the Huntley Field Station in 1913 and 1914.*

Yields, values, etc. (average per acre).	Fall plowed.				Spring plowed.				Subsoiled, after corn (1 plat).		Listed, after corn (1 plat).		Summer tilled (1 plat).	
	After corn (1 plat).		After small grain (6 plats).		After corn (1 plat).		After small grain (16 plats).							
	Grain.	Stover.	Grain.	Stover.	Grain.	Stover.	Grain.	Stover.	Grain.	Stover.	Grain.	Stover.	Grain.	Stover.
Yields:	*Bu.*	*Lbs.*	*Bu.*	*Lbs.*	*Bu.*	*Lbs.*	*Bu.*	*Lbs.*	*Bu.*	*Lbs.*	*Bu.*	*Lbs.*	*Bu.*	*Lbs.*
1913	14.8	1.400	19.6	1,350	24.4	1,250	28.8	1,553	25.7	2,300	30.1	1,300	27.2	1,900
1914	13.2	1,360	19.2	1,643	19.2	1,500	22.9	1,707	13.9	1,590	22.5	1,910	25.0	1,490
Average	14.0	1,380	19.4	1,497	21.8	1,375	25.2	1,654	19.8	1,945	26.3	1,605	26.1	1,695
Value	$5.60	$2.76	$7.76	$2.99	$8.72	$2.75	$10.08	$3.31	$7.92	$3.89	$10.52	$3.21	$10.44	$3.39
Total value	$8.36		$10.75		$11.47		$13.39		$11.81		$13.73		$13.83	
Cost	7.49		7.49		7.11		7.11		8.18		5.98		12.36	
Profit	.87		3.26		4.36		6.28		3.63		7.75		1.47	

Particularly in the production of grain, spring plowing has been markedly better than fall plowing. After both fall and spring plowing the yield has been better following small grain than following corn. Subsoiling for this crop has been done only on ground continuously cropped to corn. The yield by this method in 1914 was the lowest of any except by the fall plowing of similar ground.

Slightly higher yields than by any other method have been obtained by listing on ground continuously cropped to corn. Corn following summer tillage has been productive of crops practically equal to those on listed corn ground. On the whole, there is little choice to be made from so short a record between the yields on summer-tilled land, listed corn ground, and spring-plowed grain stubble.

Profits ranging from 87 cents (by fall plowing after corn and $1.47 by summer tillage) to $6.28 (by spring plowing after small grains and $7.75 by listing after corn) have been realized. All methods except fall plowing after corn, subsoiling after corn, and summer tillage have shown a profit from the grain crop alone.

WILLISTON FIELD STATION.

The results of five years at Williston, N. Dak., are available for study and are shown in Table VII. In only two of these years has mature corn been produced. In each of these years the yield has been very good. The yields of stover in 1912 are exceptionally high—

much higher than the stand and height would indicate. It has been impossible, however, to detect any error in the computations.

TABLE VII.—*Yields and cost of production of corn by different methods at the Williston Field Station, 1910 to 1914, inclusive.*

Yields, values, etc. (average per acre).	Fall plowed.				Spring plowed.				Summer tilled (1 plat).	
	After corn (1 plat).		After small grain (4 plats).		After corn (1 plat).		After small grain (12 plats).			
	Grain.	Stover.	Grain.	Stover.	Grain.	Stover.	Grain.	Stover.	Grain.	Stover.
Yields:	*Bu.*	*Lbs.*	*Bu.*	*Lbs.*	*Bu.*	*Lbs.*	*Bu.*	*Lbs.*	*Bu.*	*Lbs.*
1910	....	1,440	....	1,770	....	1,560	....	1,617	....	4,540
1911	....	3,040	....	3,404	....	3,560	....	4,200	....	4,660
1912	....	11,600	....	18,235	....	13,500	....	16,010	....	9,420
1913	38.3	7,230	14.7	7,608	31.5	6,470	25.7	6,322	45.2	7,280
1914	38.4	4,400	49.1	4,698	43.9	3,810	44.6	4,536	42.8	3,720
Average	15.3	5,542	12.8	7,143	15.1	5,780	14.1	6,537	17.6	5,924
Value	$6.12	$11.08	$5.12	$14.29	$6.04	$11.56	$5.64	$13.07	$7.04	$11.85
Total value	$17.20		$19.41		$17.60		$18.71		$18.89	
Cost	7.49		7.49		7.11		7.11		12.36	
Profit	9.71		11.92		10.49		11.60		6.53	

There is a lack of consistent differences in the production by different methods from year to year and of any wide variation in the average results for the whole period of years. Marked responses to cultural conditions indicated in certain seasons are balanced by different reactions in other seasons. If no marked benefit attends the use of any method, greater freedom is left in the choice of methods.

With the values of grain and fodder and the comparative cost of production as here computed, the corn crop shows a profit by all methods under which it has been grown. The least profit, $6.53 per acre, has been from summer-tilled land. Greater profits have been realized from corn after small grain than from corn after corn. Only small differences are exhibited in the profits realized by fall plowing and spring plowing.

A study of other crops at this station has shown them to be more responsive than corn to differences in cultural conditions. The place of corn in the rotation should therefore be subordinated to the interest of the other crops.

The comparatively small-growing varieties of corn which are planted in this section produce a high percentage of leaves, which give a high value to the fodder. When grain is produced it makes the feed all the more valuable. The production of a large supply of good feed per acre, together with the fact shown in other studies that corn is one of the best crops to precede small grain, should give this crop an important place in the farm economy of this section.

DICKINSON FIELD STATION.

Table VIII shows the results of a study of the production of corn at Dickinson, N. Dak., for six years, exclusive of 1912, when the crop was destroyed by hail. Four of these years were productive of grain, but in the other two years fodder only was produced.

TABLE VIII.—*Yields and cost of production of corn by different methods at the Dickinson Field Station, 1908 to 1914, inclusive.*

Yields, values, etc. (average per acre).	Fall plowed.				Spring plowed.				Summer tilled (1 plat).	
	After corn (1 plat).		After small grain (4 plats).		After corn (1 plat).		After small grain (16 plats).			
	Grain.	Stover.	Grain.	Stover.	Grain.	Stover.	Grain.	Stover.	Grain.	Stover.
Yields:	*Bush.*	*Lbs.*	*Bush.*	*Lbs.*	*Bush.*	*Lbs.*	*Bush.*	*Lbs.*	*Bush.*	*Lbs.*
1908	....	1,660	....	2,247	....	2,000	....	2,787	....	1,070
1909	52.4	2,000	49.5	2,005	58.4	2,280	49.7	2,156	45.2	1,710
1910	26.1	2,220	22.8	1,790	26.2	2,280	22.2	1,948	8.4	1,220
1911	....	4,500	....	3,225	....	4,300	....	4,195	....	4,800
1912	(1)	(1)	(1)	(1)	(1)	(1)	(1)	(1)	(1)	(1)
1913	27.9	1,050	33.1	2,100	28.2	2,110	26.3	1,575	26.3	1,230
1914	12.7	1,200	18.2	1,495	15.9	1,200	20.6	1,788	7.3	900
Average	19.9	2,105	20.6	2,144	21.5	2,362	19.8	2,408	14.5	1,822
Value	$7.96	$4.21	$8.24	$4.29	$8.60	$4.72	$7.92	$4.82	$5.80	$3.64
Total value	$12.17		$12.53		$13.32		$12.74		$9.44	
Cost	7.49		7.49		7.11		7.11		12.36	
Profit or loss	4.68		5.04		6.21		5.63		−2.92	

[1] Destroyed by hail.

The point most emphasized in a comparison of the yields by different methods is the decreased production attending the growth of corn on summer-tilled land. The only year when yields by summer tillage have compared favorably with those by other methods was in 1911. This was the driest year in the series shown. Corn has not generally suffered from a lack of water at this station. No significance attaches to the small differences to be noted between the yields of corn following corn and of corn following small grains.

By all methods except summer tillage the grain crop alone has been sufficient to afford a small profit. On summer-tilled land the crop has been grown at an average loss of $2.92 when the value of both grain and stover is considered. In the average of the six years under study, spring plowing has given somewhat better returns than fall plowing. The difference is not great enough, however, to be of much practical importance.

EDGELEY FIELD STATION.

The results of eight years at Edgeley, N. Dak., are presented in Table IX. In three of these years mature grain has been produced. In two other years there were prospects for a good crop of grain, but it did not mature. In the other three years but few ears set and the yield was chiefly stover.

TABLE IX.—*Yields and cost of production of corn by different methods at the Edgeley Field Station, 1907 to 1914, inclusive.*

Yields, values, etc. (average per acre).	Fall plowed.				Spring plowed.				Summer tilled (1 plat).	
	After corn (1 plat).		After small grain (5 plats).		After corn (1 plat).		After small grain (20 plats).			
	Grain.	Stover.	Grain.	Stover.	Grain.	Stover.	Grain.	Stover.	Grain.	Stover.
Yields:	*Bush.*	*Lbs.*	*Bush.*	*Lbs.*	*Bush.*	*Lbs.*	*Bush.*	*Lbs.*	*Bush.*	*Lbs.*
1907	0	2,850	0	3,200	0	1,550	0	2,261	0	1,150
1908	0	2,300	0	2,150	0	2,250	0	1,973	0	1,500
1909	33.3	2,350	29.8	2,750	37.4	2,650	29.7	3,025	36.5	2,050
1910	0	2,100	0	1,250	0	1,650	0	1,661	0	1,850
1911	0	4,750	0	4,730	0	4,400	0	4,572	0	5,500
1912	0	6,250	0	6,040	0	7,300	0	6,382	0	6,500
1913	19.4	2,100	19.6	2,486	16.0	2,850	21.8	2,965	14.1	1,850
1914	3.6	1,610	16.5	3,004	5.1	2,380	15.9	3,117	3.9	3,010
Average	7.0	3,039	8.2	3,201	7.3	3,129	8.4	3,245	6.8	2,926
Value	$2.80	$6.07	$3.28	$6.40	$2.92	$6.26	$3.36	$6.49	$2.72	$5.85
Total value	$8.87		$9.68		$9.18		$9.85		$8.57	
Cost	7.49		7.49		7.11		7.11		12.36	
Profit or loss	1.38		2.19		2.07		2.74		−3.79	

On the whole, only small differences are exhibited in the yields from different methods of preparation for the corn crop. There is a slight advantage in favor of spring plowing over fall plowing on both corn ground and small-grain stubble. The yields of both grain and stover were somewhat better when the corn followed small grain than when it followed corn. The relative response to these sequences was the same on both fall and spring plowing.

The four preparations for corn—fall and spring plowing following corn and fall and spring plowing following small grain—rank in order of yield obtained as follows: (1) Spring plowing on small-grain stubble, (2) fall plowing on small-grain stubble, (3) spring plowing on corn ground, and (4) fall plowing on corn ground. Average profits ranging from $1.38 to $2.74 per acre have been realized by these methods. The difference exhibited in the results attending the use of these methods is not great enough to be in itself a determining factor in the choice of rotations or in the management of the farm and its work. Summer tillage as a preparation for corn has given poorer results than any other method. In only one year has it been productive of the largest crop. The average yield of both grain and stover by this method is less than by any other method under study. The value of the average corn crop on summer-tilled land has been $3.79 per acre less than the cost of its production as crop values and comparative costs are here computed.

BELLE FOURCHE FIELD STATION.

Table X presents the results of the work of six years with corn in rotations and under varying tillage methods at Belle Fourche, S. Dak. In one year, 1911, extreme drought caused a failure of all methods under trial. In three of the six years grain was produced by all methods. In the other two years all methods produced fodder, but grain was produced only upon land which was summer tilled the previous year.

TABLE X.—*Yields and cost of production of corn by different methods at the Belle Fourche Field Station, 1909 to 1914, inclusive.*

Yields, values, etc. (average per acre).	Fall plowed.				Spring plowed.				Subsoiled, after corn (1 plat).		Listed, after corn (1 plat).		Summer tilled (1 plat).	
	After corn (1 plat).		After small grain (4 plats).		After corn (1 plat).		After small grain (17 plats).							
	Grain.	Stover.	Grain.	Stover.	Grain.	Stover.	Grain.	Stover.	Grain.	Stover.	Grain.	Stover.	Grain.	Stover.
Yields:	*Bu.*	*Lbs.*	*Bu.*	*Lbs.*	*Bu.*	*Lbs.*	*Bu.*	*Lbs.*	*Bu.*	*Lbs.*	*Bu.*	*Lbs.*	*Bu.*	*Lbs.*
1909	23.5	5,310	19.4	3,365	24.4	4,560	18.3	2,891	20.8	4,000	24.8	4,575	20.8	4,860
1910	0	2,760	0	1,705	0	3,560	.1	3,014	0	3,140	0	3,800	14.8	2,500
1911	0	0	0	0	0	0	0	0	0	0	0	0	0	0
1912	29.7	3,250	21.7	2,875	26.4	2,700	20.2	2,515	26.3	3,100	27.5	2,150	28.4	2,750
1913	6.5	1,060	7.8	985	7.8	900	8.0	995	9.4	1,060	9.7	800	23.6	960
1914	0	1,350	0	1,000	0	1,150	0	1,035	0	1,450	0	1,450	14.2	2,000
Average	10.0	2,288	8.1	1,655	9.8	2,145	7.8	1,742	9.4	2,125	10.3	2,129	17.0	2,178
Value	$4.00	$4.58	$3.24	$3.31	$3.92	$4.29	$3.12	$3.48	$3.76	$4.25	$4.12	$4.26	$6.80	$4.36
Total value	$8.58		$6.55		$8.21		$6.60		$8.01		$8.38		$11.16	
Cost	7.49		7.49		7.11		7.11		8.18		5.98		12.36	
Profit or loss	1.09		−.94		1.10		−.51		−.17		2.40		−1.20	

Corn after corn produced more grain and more stover than corn after small grain. Little difference is shown in the yields by spring plowing and by fall plowing. Each of these methods has been tried after both corn and small grain.

Subsoiling was practiced on land continuously cropped to corn. It produced yields practically the same as similarly cropped land plowed either in the spring or fall without subsoiling.

Planting with the lister on land continuously cropped to corn produced yields practically the same as those from corn ground plowed and surface planted.

The highest average yield of grain has been from land summer tilled the previous year. The increase in the average comes chiefly from the grain produced in 1910 and 1914, when other methods failed, and to its increase of yield over other methods in 1913. The yield of stover from this method does not show an increase over that following the several methods by which corn is grown following corn.

Neither the average grain crop nor the average stover crop alone by any method under trial has been sufficient to pay the cost of producing it. When both are considered together, the crop shows for all methods variations ranging from a loss of $1.20 on summer-tilled land to a profit of $2.40 on listed corn ground. Both spring and fall plowing after corn show profits of more than a dollar an acre. Fall and spring plowing following small grains and subsoiling following corn all show losses of less than a dollar per acre. In general terms, the corn crop at this place has just about paid the expense of its production, including something for the use of the land. The greatest crop assurance has been by summer tillage, but the cost of the method has resulted in a small loss from its use.

SCOTTSBLUFF FIELD STATION.

Some of the results of the work for three years with corn at Scottsbluff, Nebr., are presented in Table XI. The production of both grain and fodder was good each year. The value of the grain crop alone was sufficient to realize a profit by all methods under trial.

TABLE XI.—*Yields and cost of production of corn by different methods at the Scottsbluff Field Station, in 1912, 1913, and 1914.*

Yields, values, etc. (average per acre).	Fall plowed.				Spring plowed.				Subsoiled, after corn (1 plat).		Listed, after corn (1 plat).		Summer tilled (1 plat).	
	After corn (1 plat).		After small grain (9 plats).		After corn (1 plat).		After small grain (20 plats).							
	Grain.	Stover.	Grain.	Stover.	Grain.	Stover.	Grain.	Stover.	Grain.	Stover.	Grain.	Stover.	Grain.	Stover.
Yields:	*Bu.*	*Lbs.*	*Bu.*	*Lbs.*	*Bu.*	*Lbs.*	*Bu.*	*Lbs.*	*Bu.*	*Lbs.*	*Bu.*	*Lbs.*	*Bu.*	*Lbs.*
1912	38.0	2,400	36.2	4,406	40.8	3,300	40.7	4,770	40.0	4,300	21.6	2,900	49.7	5,600
1913	32.2	1,660	26.4	2,148	27.8	1,740	31.4	2,550	26.1	1,700	38.6	1,700	35.6	2,600
1914	20.1	1,200	11.0	994	15.0	700	7.5	1,020	14.2	840	14.6	620	31.7	1,400
Average	30.1	1,753	24.5	2,516	27.9	1,913	27.5	2,770	26.8	2,280	24.9	1,740	39.0	3,200
Value	$12.04	$3.51	$9.80	$5.03	$11.16	$3.83	$11.00	$5.54	$10.72	$4.56	$9.96	$3.48	$15.60	$6.40
Total value	$15.55		$14.83		$14.99		$16.54		$15.28		$13.44		$22.00	
Cost	7.49		7.49		7.11		7.11		8.18		5.98		12.36	
Profit	8.06		7.34		7.88		9.43		7.10		7.46		9.64	

The only method of preparation that in any year produced a yield of either grain or stover greater than that from summer-tilled land was that of listing corn ground in 1913. Methods other than summer tillage do not exhibit sufficient consistent differences in yield to warrant very definite conclusions as to their comparative merits. The lack of consistency is shown in the comparative yields of both grain and stover. Some of the methods producing the best yields of grain have been among the lowest in yield of stover and vice versa.

No one of the six methods other than summer tillage maintained a position as either the best or poorest throughout the three years.

The greatest profit, $9.64 per acre, was from corn on land that was summer tilled the preceding year. A profit nearly as great, $9.43 per acre, was realized from corn by spring plowing following small grain. An average profit of $8.06 per acre was realized from corn following corn by fall plowing. Subsoiling after corn, fall plowing after small grain, listing after corn, and spring plowing after corn show profits ranging from $7.10 to $7.88 per acre.

NORTH PLATTE FIELD STATION.

The results of eight years are available for study from the field station at North Platte, Nebr. A study of Table XII shows that this station has produced four good crops of corn. In two other years the average yields were low, but good yields were produced by some methods. In the remaining two years some corn was produced but not enough to warrant husking. The average for eight years shows that there is very little choice to be made between fall and spring plowing, nor were wide differences manifested in the results by these methods in any of the years comprising the series.

TABLE XII.—*Yields and cost of production of corn by different methods at the North Platte Field Station, 1907 to 1914, inclusive.*

Yields, values, etc. (average per acre).	Fall plowed.				Spring plowed.				Summer tilled (1 plat).	
	After corn (1 plat).		After small grain (9 plats).		After corn (1 plat).		After small grain (9 plats).			
	Grain.	Stover.	Grain.	Stover.	Grain.	Stover.	Grain.	Stover.	Grain.	Stover.
Yields:	*Bush.*	*Lbs.*	*Bush.*	*Lbs.*	*Bush.*	*Lbs.*	*Bush.*	*Lbs.*	*Bush.*	*Lbs.*
1907	27.7	4,360	19.0	4,529	28.7	4,680	19.9	4,609	17.9	4,920
1908	24.6	2,660	27.4	3,143	38.6	3,250	24.0	3,463	38.2	3,530
1909	31.6	2,790	26.1	2,354	29.0	2,470	25.8	2,613	25.0	2,300
1910	6.2	2,500	2.6	1,200	8.9	2,440	5.8	1,633	21.9	3,300
1911	0	580	0	755	0	980	0	746	0	930
1912	39.9	2,330	26.1	2,165	34.1	2,340	26.0	2,734	35.1	2,340
1913	0	1,780	0	1,540	0	1,740	0	1,503	0	2,240
1914	15.5	2,060	3.9	1,458	8.5	1,600	3.2	1,156	27.9	2,130
Average	18.2	2,383	13.3	2,143	18.5	2,438	13.2	2,307	20.8	2,711
Value	$7.28	$4.77	$5.32	$4.29	$7.40	$4.88	$5.28	$4.61	$8.32	$5.42
Total value	$12.05		$9.61		$12.28		$9.89		$13.74	
Cost	7.49		7.49		7.11		7.11		12.36	
Profit	4.56		2.12		5.17		2.78		1.38	

From differences in crop sequence marked results have been obtained. Corn grown continuously on the same land has averaged about 5 bushels per acre more by both fall and spring plowing than when grown on small-grain stubble. The average increase in yield where corn follows corn as compared with corn following small grain is much greater in the grain than in the stover yields. Following sorghum there was a sharp decrease in yield. In rotations where corn followed oats on brome-grass and alfalfa sods the yield was considerably less than that obtained on similarly prepared land that had not been in sod.

Land that was summer tilled the previous year produced six good crops of grain in the eight years under study. In the other two years it did not produce sufficient grain to warrant husking. During the six years the average yield of grain was about 2 bushels more and the yield of fodder about 300 pounds more per acre by summer tillage than that produced by spring plowing corn ground, the next highest yielding method.

On spring-plowed corn ground the average value of the crop of grain alone has been more than sufficient to pay the cost of producing the crop. On fall-plowed corn ground the average value of the grain for eight years has lacked only 20 cents of paying the cost of production. All methods show a profit when a value is assigned to the stover or fodder. The profits per acre from the different methods have been as follows: Summer tillage, $1.38; fall plowing after small grain, $2.12; spring plowing after small grain, $2.78; fall plowing after corn, $4.56; and spring plowing after corn, $5.17.

AKRON FIELD STATION.

Table XIII presents the results of the work of six years in methods of production of corn at Akron, Colo. All methods have produced fodder every year. Summer-tilled land has produced a grain crop every year, its average yield for the entire period being 20.9 bushels of grain and 2,257 pounds of stover per acre. Other methods have met from one to three more or less complete failures of the grain crop. The average yield of corn after corn by both spring and fall plowing, however, has been practically the same as on summer-tilled land.

Corn after small grain was markedly poorer in yield of both grain and stover than corn following corn by either fall or spring plowing. Subsoiling the land where corn follows corn resulted in decreased yields every year as compared with fall plowing similar land without subsoiling it. Planting with the lister resulted in a still further decrease in yields.

The difference in the results following fall and spring plowing are negligible when the average of the whole series of years is considered. Fall and spring plowing of land where corn follows corn are the only methods that show a profit from the grain crop alone. When a value is assigned to the stover, all methods show profits ranging from 51 cents per acre on land which was summer tilled the previous year to $5.43 by spring plowing where corn followed corn.

TABLE XIII.—*Yields and cost of production of corn by different methods at the Akron Field Station, 1909 to 1914, inclusive.*

Yields, values, etc. (average per acre).	Fall plowed.				Spring plowed.				Sub-soiled, after corn (1 plat).		Listed, after corn (2 plats).		Summer tilled (1 plat).	
	After corn (1 plat).		After small grain (12 plats).		After corn (1 plat).		After small grain (9 plats).							
	Grain.	Stover.	Grain.	Stover.	Grain.	Stover.	Grain.	Stover.	Grain.	Stover.	Grain.	Stover.	Grain.	Stover.
Yields:	*Bu.*	*Lbs.*	*Bu.*	*Lbs.*	*Bu.*	*Lbs.*	*Bu.*	*Lbs.*	*Bu.*	*Lbs.*	*Bu.*	*Lbs.*	*Bu.*	*Lbs.*
1909	27.3	3,890	24.6	2,424	30.0	4,700	23.5	2,499	32.8	4,300	26.1	4,325	25.0	3,190
1910	18.3	1,640	7.7	1,438	21.6	1,840	10.8	1,590	12.7	1,490	15.1	1,000	21.4	1,350
1911	0	1,040	5.4	1,378	1.3	1,210	.4	776	0	1,180	1.4	1,105	12.9	1,690
1912	46.9	3,040	30.0	2,393	33.9	2,500	31.0	2,303	37.1	2,440	22.0	2,060	33.6	2,500
1913	9.9	1,840	.5	1,010	13.6	2,020	4.3	1,476	4.3	1,290	9.0	1,530	13.7	2,410
1914	17.3	2,300	9.3	1,968	15.9	2,060	12.0	1,833	13.9	1,980	9.5	1,750	18.6	2,400
Average	20.0	2,292	12.9	1,769	19.4	2,388	13.7	1,746	16.8	2,113	13.9	1,962	20.9	2,257
Value	$8.00	$4.58	$5.16	$3.54	$7.76	$4.78	$5.48	$3.49	$6.72	$4.23	$5.56	$3.92	$8.36	$4.51
Total value	$12.58		$8.70		$12.54		$8.97		$10.95		$9.48		$12.87	
Cost	7.49		7.49		7.11		7.11		8.18		5.98		12.36	
Profit	5.09		1.21		5.43		1.86		2.77		3.50		.51	

HAYS FIELD STATION.

Table XIV presents some of the results of different methods of growing corn at Hays, Kans. The data are presented for only six years. In 1911 and 1913, for which no figures are given in the table, there would have been yields of forage, but the crop while suffering from drought was destroyed by grasshoppers. The area of the plats was so small that the damage from the insects was much worse than it would have been on larger fields. The surrounding area is cropped chiefly to small grains. When these are harvested, the grasshoppers move from the stubble into the corn and sorghums.

Corn produced an average of a little over 1½ tons of fodder and 5.5 to 9.9 bushels of grain per acre. Little difference is exhibited in the yields by different methods. Such differences as are shown are not consistent from year to year. While the crop is productive of a good amount of feed each year, it appears to offer little possibility as a grain crop. With values as here assigned to the grain and forage the crop shows a small profit from all methods except summer tillage, which is charged with an average loss of 54 cents per acre. The greatest profits were by listing after corn and by spring plowing after corn. These show average annual profits of $2.69 and $2.67 per acre, respectively.

TABLE XIV.—*Yields and cost of production of corn by different methods at the Hays Field Station, 1907 to 1914, inclusive.*[1]

Yields, values, etc. (average per acre).	Fall plowed.				Spring plowed.				Subsoiled, after corn (1 plat).		Listed, after corn (1 plat).		Summer tilled (1 plat).	
	After corn (1 plat).		After small grain (4 plats).		After corn (1 plat).		After small grain (10 plats).							
	Grain.	Stover.	Grain.	Stover.	Grain.	Stover.	Grain.	Stover.	Grain.	Stover.	Grain.	Stover.	Grain.	Stover.
Yields:	*Bu.*	*Lbs.*	*Bu.*	*Lbs.*	*Bu.*	*Lbs.*	*Bu.*	*Lbs.*	*Bu.*	*Lbs.*	*Bu.*	*Lbs.*	*Bu.*	*Lbs.*
1907	12.2	6,820	4.1	6,543	13.1	6,950	4.4	5,684	13.6	6,660	7.8	6,790	9.5	6,850
1908	3.1	4,280	5.2	5,910	.9	5,520	6.4	5,133	8.8	5,065	7.4	4,200	14.8	6,965
1909	7.9	584	13.0	936	4.1	1,340	18.8	1,516	8.0	560	5.9	510	15.3	1,190
1910	6.8	2,950	6.9	2,768	11.0	2,900	6.6	2,609	7.4	3,205	6.1	2,210	8.4	2,900
1912	1.8	1,585	1.3	1,864	2.1	2,050	2.5	1,912	5.5	2,075	6.5	1,890	3.9	2,220
1914	5.5	3,135	2.7	3,050	5.2	3,245	2.4	2,888	6.4	3,350	3.6	2,960	7.4	3,450
Average	6.2	3,226	5.5	3,512	6.1	3,668	6.9	3,290	8.3	3,486	6.2	3,093	9.9	3,929
Value	$2.48	$6.45	$2.20	$7.02	$2.44	$7.34	$2.76	$6.58	$3.32	$6.97	$2.48	$6.19	$3.96	$7.86
Total value	$8.93		$9.22		$9.78		$9.34		$10.29		$8.67		$11.82	
Cost	7.49		7.49		7.11		7.11		8.18		5.98		12.36	
Profit or loss	1.44		1.73		2.67		2.23		2.11		2.69		−.54	

[1] The crops of 1911 and 1913 were so nearly destroyed by drought and insects that no yields were weighed.

GARDEN CITY FIELD STATION.

Table XV presents data on the production of corn by different methods at Garden City, Kans. Yields are presented for only four years. In both 1908 and 1910 there was a fair crop of fodder but weights were not obtained. In 1913 the crop was destroyed by a hailstorm on July 4.

TABLE XV.—*Yields and cost of production of corn by different methods at the Garden City Field Station in 1909 and 1911 to 1914, inclusive.*

Yields, values, etc. (average per acre).	Fall plowed.		Spring plowed.		Subsoiled, after corn (1 plat).	Listed, after corn (2 plats).	Summer tilled. (1 plat).
	After corn (1 plat).	After small grain (11 plats).	After corn (1 plat).	After small grain (11 plats).			
Yields of stover:							
1909 ... pounds	....	2,972	....	3,446	....	2,180	....
1910 ... do	1,400	934	1,100	1,269	750	695	4,000
1912 ... do	4,620	4,498	5,580	3,935	4,500	5,570	5,780
1913 ... do	(1)	(1)	(1)	(1)	(1)	(1)	(1)
1914[2] ... do	3,040	2,668	2,460	2,100	4,840	2,830	4,320
Average	3,020	2,768	3,047	2,688	3,363	2,819	4,700
Value	$6.04	$5.54	$6.09	$5.38	$6.73	$5.64	$9.40
Cost	7.49	7.49	7.11	7.11	8.18	5.98	12.36
Loss	−1.45	−1.95	−1.02	−1.73	−1.45	−.34	−2.96

[1] Destroyed by hail.
[2] The yield of grain was very small in 1914, and its weight was included with the stover.

No grain in sufficient quantity to husk was produced in any year by any of the methods under trial. The only material difference to be noted in the yields by different methods is the increased yield attending the growth of corn on land which was summer tilled the previous season. The method of summer tillage gave an average yield of 4,700 pounds of fodder per acre for the three years that weights were obtained. The crop produces a good amount of feed, but with the valuation and costs as here assigned it has been grown at small losses, ranging from 34 cents per acre by listing after corn to $2.96 on summer-tilled land.

DALHART FIELD STATION.

Table XVI presents data obtained in the growth of corn by different methods at Dalhart, Tex. The results of the work of six years are given. In three of the six years grain was produced by all methods.

TABLE XVI.—*Yields and cost of production of corn by different methods at the Dalhart Field Station, 1909 to 1914, inclusive.*

Yields, values, etc. (average per acre).	Fall plowed.				Spring plowed.				Listed, after corn (1 plat).		Summer tilled (1 plat).	
	After corn (1 plat).		After small grain (12 plats).		After corn (1 plat).		After small grain (7 plats).					
	Grain.	Stover.	Grain.	Stover.	Grain.	Stover.	Grain.	Stover.	Grain.	Stover.	Grain.	Stover.
Yields:	*Bu.*	*Lbs.*	*Bu.*	*Lbs.*	*Bu.*	*Lbs.*	*Bu.*	*Lbs.*	*Bu.*	*Lbs.*	*Bu.*	*Lbs.*
1909	0	1,000	0	946	0	700	0	1,014	0	2,250	0	3,400
1910	8.6	3,160	9.2	2,947	15.1	3,610	15.3	2,914	25.6	3,340	25.6	4,110
1911	0	4,000	0	2,771	0	4,000	0	2,708	12.4	2,350	2.8	3,000
1912	7.4	2,250	14.1	2,779	10.5	2,200	9.7	2,751	21.0	3,100	23.0	3,300
1913	0	2,000	0	2,405	0	2,150	0	1,037	0	1,750	0	6,150
1914	35.6	3,855	20.3	3,566	31.5	3,690	17.0	3,255	25.1	2,740	30.8	3,440
Average	8.6	2,711	7.3	2,569	9.5	2,725	7.0	2,280	14.0	2,588	13.7	3,900
Value	$3.44	$5.42	$2.92	$5.14	$3.80	$5.45	$2.80	$4.56	$5.60	$5.18	$5.48	$7.80
Total value	$8.86		$8.06		$9.25		$7.36		$10.78		$13.28	
Cost	7.49		7.49		7.11		7.11		5.98		12.36	
Profit	1.37		.57		2.14		.25		4.80		.92	

The two heaviest yielding methods were summer tillage and listing after corn. Between the grain yields by these two methods there is little difference, but in the yield of fodder the summer tillage shows a marked superiority. Between the other methods little choice is to be made, although corn appears to yield slightly heavier after corn than after small grains and slightly heavier by spring plowing than by fall plowing. The crop was produced at a profit by all methods under trial. The net profits realized range from 25 cents per acre by spring plowing after small grain to $2.14 by spring plowing after corn and $4.80 by listing after corn.

AMARILLO FIELD STATION.

Table XVII presents the results in the growth of corn during seven years by different methods at Amarillo, Tex. No data are presented for 1910, as the station was moved and only one method was on trial that year. Fodder was produced each year by all methods, but in only one year was there a creditable production of grain.

TABLE XVII.—*Yields and cost of production of corn by different methods at the Amarillo Field Station, 1907 to 1914, inclusive, except 1910.*

Yields, values, etc. (average per acre).	Fall plowed.				Spring plowed.				Subsoiled, after corn (1 plat).		Listed, after corn (2 plats).		Summer tilled (1 plat).	
	After corn (1 plat).		After small grain (11 plats).		After corn (1 plat).		After small grain (3 plats).							
	Grain.	Stover.	Grain.	Stover.	Grain.	Stover.	Grain.	Stover.	Grain.	Stover.	Grain.	Stover.	Grain.	Stover.
Yields:	*Bu.*	*Lbs.*	*Bu.*	*Lbs.*	*Bu.*	*Lbs.*	*Bu.*	*Lbs.*	*Bu.*	*Lbs.*	*Bu.*	*Lbs.*	*Bu.*	*Lbs.*
1907	1.4	3,270	2.3	2,997	3.1	3,280	2.1	3,010	1.1	3,490	2.2	2,935	5.7	3,710
1908	22.9	4,580	19.8	3,107	20.3	3,300	14.7	2,863	25.7	3,810	24.7	2,390	27.6	3,700
1909	2.7	1,310	0	1,596	.6	560	0	1,383	1.7	990	5.4	1,043	6.4	1,890
1911	9.2	2,075	8.9	2,145	8.1	1,945	9.5	1,960	7.1	1,720	7.8	1,998	9.3	2,050
1912	.7	1,680	1.7	1,848	2.6	2,160	1.1	1,829	1.0	2,080	1.7	2,015	3.3	2,840
1913	0	380	0	773	0	700	0	383	0	430	0	225	0	1,750
1914	3.6	4,140	5.1	3,641	1.1	1,500	2.8	2,733	5.1	4,850	7.0	2,870	8.0	5,320
Average	5.8	2,491	5.4	2,301	5.1	1,921	4.3	2,023	6.0	2,481	7.0	1,925	8.6	3,037
Value	$2.32	$4.98	$2.16	$4.60	$2.04	$3.84	$1.72	$4.05	$2.40	$4.96	$2.80	$3.85	$3.44	$6.07
Total value	$7.30		$6.76		$5.88		$5.77		$7.36		$6.65		$9.51	
Cost	7.49		7.49		7.11		7.11		8.18		5.98		12.36	
Profit or loss	−.19		−.73		−1.23		−1.34		−.82		.67		−2.85	

The yields by different methods show comparatively small differences. Summer tillage shows a small increase in yield of both grain and stover over all other methods of preparations. Fall plowing was a somewhat better preparation than either spring plowing or listing. Subsoiling failed to increase yields over fall plowing similar land without subsoiling. Listing shows a small profit of 67 cents per acre. All other methods show losses ranging from 19 cents per acre by fall plowing after corn to $2.85 on summer-tilled land.

GENERAL DISCUSSION OF RESULTS.

In the foregoing pages the results of growing corn by different methods of land preparation have been discussed in more or less detail for each individual station. It yet remains to take a broader view of the problem, and the relative merits of different methods will be considered for the Great Plains area as a whole. Some comparisons of station with station as representatives of different sections of country whose results are indicative of the comparative value of corn to such sections will also be made.

For this study, Table XVIII has been compiled from the data given in Tables V to XVII, inclusive. The average yields of corn by each method and the profits or losses attending the use of each method, as shown in the detail tables for the several stations, are here assembled.

TABLE XVIII.—*Comparison of the average yields and profit or loss in the production of corn by different methods at thirteen field stations in the Great Plains area.*

Statement of data.	Methods of tillage.													
	Fall plowed.				Spring plowed.				Subsoiled, after corn.		Listed, after corn.		Summer tilled.	
	After corn.		After small grain.		After corn.		After small grain.							
	Grain.	Stover.	Grain.	Stover.	Grain.	Stover.	Grain.	Stover.	Grain.	Stover.	Grain.	Stover.	Grain.	Stover.
Yields per acre:	*Bu*	*Lbs.*	*Bu.*	*Lbs.*	*Bu.*	*Lbs.*	*Bu.*	*Lbs.*	*Bu.*	*Lbs.*	*Bu.*	*Lbs.*	*Bu.*	*Lbs.*
Judith Basin	.....	5,744	.....	5,275	.....	6,002	.....	5,193	.....	6,130	.....	5,982	.....	5,656
Huntley	14.0	1,380	19.4	1,497	21.8	1,375	25.2	1,654	19.8	1,945	26.3	1,605	26.1	1,695
Williston	15.3	5,542	12.8	7,143	15.1	5,780	14.1	6,537	.....	.....	.....	.....	17.6	5,924
Dickinson	19.9	2,105	20.6	2,144	21.5	2,362	19.8	2,408	.....	.....	.....	.....	14.5	1,822
Edgeley	7.0	3,039	8.2	3,201	7.3	3,129	8.4	3,245	.....	.....	.....	.....	6.8	2,926
Belle Fourche	10.0	2,288	8.1	1,655	9.8	2,145	7.8	1,742	9.4	2,125	10.3	2,129	17.0	2,178
Scottsbluff	30.1	1,753	24.5	2,516	27.9	1,913	27.5	2,770	26.8	2,280	24.9	1,740	39.0	3,200
North Platte	18.2	2,383	13.3	2,143	18.5	2,438	13.2	2,307	.....	.....	.....	.....	20.8	2,711
Akron	20.0	2,292	12.9	1,769	19.4	2,388	13.7	1,746	16.8	2,113	13.9	1,962	20.9	2,257
Hays	6.2	3,226	5.5	3,512	6.1	3,668	6.9	3,290	8.3	3,486	6.2	3,093	9.9	3,929
Garden City	.....	3,020	.....	2,768	.....	3,047	.....	2,688	.....	3,363	.....	2,819	.....	4,700
Dalhart	8.6	2,711	7.3	2,569	9.5	2,755	7.0	2,280	.....	.....	14.0	2,588	13.7	3,900
Amarillo	5.8	2,491	5.4	2,301	5.1	1,921	4.3	2,023	6.0	2,481	7.0	1,925	8.6	3,037
Average	12.9	2,922	11.5	2,961	13.5	2,915	12.1	2,914	.....	.....	.....	.....	16.2	3,380
Profit or loss (—) per acre:														
Judith Basin	$4.00		$3.06		$4.89		$3.28		$4.08		$5.98		$—1.05	
Huntley	.87		3.26		4.36		6.28		3.63		7.75		1.47	
Williston	9.71		11.92		10.49		11.60		....		....		6.53	
Dickinson	4.68		5.04		6.21		5.63		....		....		—2.92	
Edgeley	1.38		2.19		2.07		2.74		....		....		—3.79	
Belle Fourche	1.09		— .94		1.10		— .51		— .17		2.40		—1.20	
Scottsbluff	8.06		7.34		7.88		9.43		7.10		7.46		9.64	
North Platte	4.56		2.12		5.17		2.78		....		....		1.38	
Akron	5.09		1.21		5.43		1.86		2.77		3.50		.51	
Hays	1.44		1.73		2.67		2.23		2.11		2.69		— .54	
Garden City	—1.45		—1.95		—1.02		—1.73		—1.45		— .34		—2.96	
Dalhart	1.37		.57		2.14		.25		....		4.80		.92	
Amarillo	— .19		— .73		—1.23		—1.34		— .82		.67		—2.85	

Three series of graphs (figs. 4, 5, and 6) are also presented. Figure 4, prepared from a part of the data in Table XVII, shows in graphic form the average yields of grain in bushels per acre at each station for each of the five methods studied that have been under trial at all of the stations. The Judith Basin Field Station is not shown in this figure for the reason that grain was neither produced nor expected at that station in this work. Garden City is also omitted because the grain there produced was insufficient to warrant husking.

Figure 5 is a graphic presentation of the yields of stover as shown in Table XVIII. Like figure 4, it includes only the five methods that have been under trial at all stations.

Figure 6, prepared from Table VIII, shows graphically the average relative profit or loss attending the use of each of the five methods at each of the stations.

Table XVIII, illustrated in part in figure 4, shows that during the years covered by this work creditable average yields of grain have been obtained by all methods at Huntley, Williston, Dickinson, Scottsbluff, North Platte, and Akron, and by one method at Belle Fourche and Dalhart. No grain has been produced either at the Judith Basin Field Station or at Garden City.

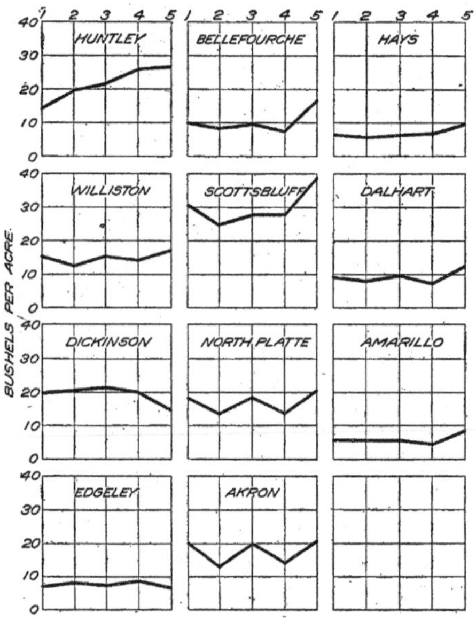

FIG. 4.—Graphs showing the average yields of corn in bushels per acre by different methods at eleven field stations in the Great Plains area. The methods of tillage are indicated by Arabic numerals at the top, as follows: *1*, Fall plowing after corn; *2*, fall plowing after small grain; *3*, spring plowing after corn; *4*, spring plowing after small grain; *5*, summer tillage. The field stations of Judith Basin and Garden City do not appear, because the corn grown at these stations produced no grain.

Little difference is shown in the average yields of grain by the different cultural methods in use at Williston, Edgeley, Hays, and Amarillo. At Dickinson, Belle Fourche, and Dalhart the only method of preparation giving yields departing far from the others has been that of summer tillage. At Dickinson summer tillage has been responsible for a decrease in yields and at Belle Fourche and Dalhart for an increase.

Between the yields following fall and spring plowing little general difference is to be noted, except that at Huntley fall plowing has been better than spring plowing, and at Scottsbluff fall plowing after corn has been better and fall plowing after small grains poorer than spring plowing after either. At some stations more difference is to be noted as a result of crop sequence than as a result of difference in time of plowing. At Huntley corn has been better after small grain than after corn. At both North Platte and Akron corn after corn by both fall and spring plowing has been markedly better than corn after small grain.

Figure 5 presents the average yields of fodder at each of the stations. The results by each of the five methods that have been under trial at all stations are shown separately.

It appears that the yields reported from the Judith Basin Field Station and from Williston are abnormally high. While the yields have generally been good at these stations, it is doubtful if they have been as much higher than those at some of the other stations, as these figures indicate. It is probable that in the years showing excessively high yields the crop has not been well dried at the time of weighing.

A very striking fact brought out by this graphic showing is the uniformity in the amount of stover or fodder produced by all methods at the stations in Montana and North Dakota. So far as the production of rough feed is concerned, there appears very little difference on which to base a choice. South of North Dakota there is a general agreement of heavier yields of stover or fodder after corn than after small grain, except that at Scottsbluff the yields are heavier after small grain than after corn.

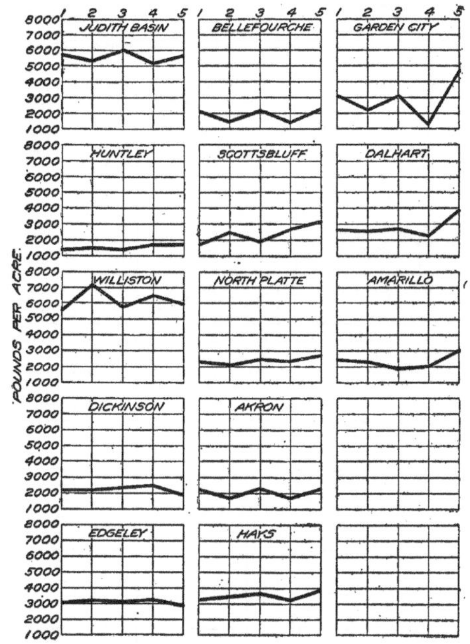

FIG. 5.—Graphs showing the average yields of corn stover in pounds per acre by different methods at thirteen field stations in the Great Plains area. The methods of tillage are indicated by Arabic numerals at the top, as follows: *1*, Fall plowing after corn; *2*, fall plowing after small grain; *3*, spring plowing after corn; *4*, spring plowing after small grain; *5*, summer tillage.

Small differences in stover yields are to be noted between the results following spring and fall plowing. On the whole, the average yields by the two methods are almost the same.

The most noticeable effect resulting from cultural practice is the very marked increase in the yield of stover resulting from growing corn on summer-tilled land at the more southern stations—Garden City, Dalhart, and Amarillo. Only small increases in yields have attended the use of this method at Scottsbluff, North Platte, and Hays.

Subsoiling has not markedly affected the yields, except that at Akron it has decreased them.

Listing has materially increased the yields at Huntley and at Dalhart. At the other stations the effect has not been marked.

The last half of Table XVIII, illustrated in part in figure 6, presents the average relative profits and losses attending the growth of corn by different methods at each of the stations. It shows corn to be relatively much less profitable at Belle Fourche, Garden City, Dalhart, and Amarillo than at the other stations.

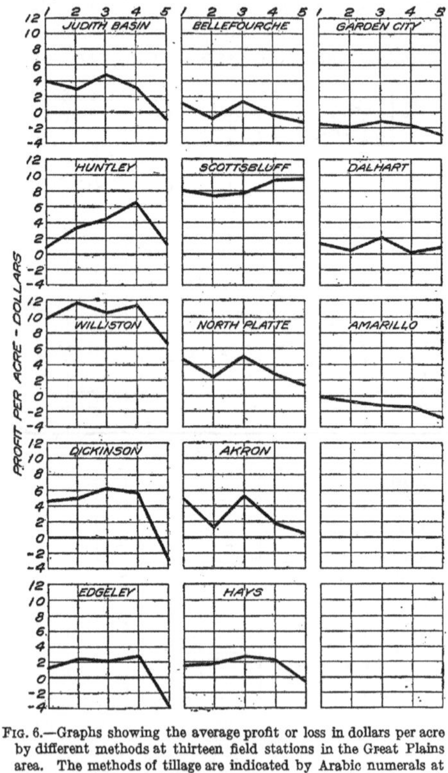

Fig. 6.—Graphs showing the average profit or loss in dollars per acre by different methods at thirteen field stations in the Great Plains area. The methods of tillage are indicated by Arabic numerals at the top, as follows: *1*, Fall plowing after corn; *2*, fall plowing after small grain; *3*, spring plowing after corn; *4*, spring plowing after small grain; *5*, summer tillage.

Scottsbluff is the only station where summer tillage as a preparation for corn has proved the most profitable method. At most of the stations this method has been the least profitable. Its use has resulted in actual loss at the stations of Judith Basin, Dickinson, Edgeley, Belle Fourche, Hays, Garden City, and Amarillo.

It is shown very clearly in figure 6 that greater profit has been realized from corn after corn than from corn after small grain at Akron and North Platte. At Huntley, corn after small grain has been more profitable.

Listing has been tried at nine stations. Except at Scottsbluff and Akron, it has been the most profitable method under trial. As has been pointed out, the relative profitableness of this method has been largely due to its low cost.

A careful reading of the data given in the table will show that corn as a grain or cash crop can not be profitably grown in large portions of the Great Plains. At only 5 of the 13 stations have the grain yields been sufficiently large to indicate a possibility of the crop being profitably produced for the grain only. At Huntley, Dickinson, Scottsbluff, North Platte, and Akron enough grain was produced by some methods to pay the cost of production and show small profits. Taken as a whole, however, the data show that, in order to realize the full profit, the corn should be considered as a feed crop. To pay the cost of production in many sections, it is necessary to utilize the roughage produced.

CONCLUSIONS.

(1) No one method of seed-bed preparation is essential to the production of corn in the Great Plains.

(2) Differences in seed-bed preparation, other than summer tillage, have not produced wide differences in grain yields, except at Huntley, Mont.

(3) Summer tillage has slightly increased the grain yield at all except three stations and has materially increased the fodder yields at the three southern stations. The increase in yields, however, has not been sufficient to make it the most profitable method at any station except Scottsbluff.

(4) At some of the stations, especially at North Platte and Akron, crop sequence is more important than seed-bed preparation in the production of corn.

(5) At 8 of the 13 stations corn as a grain crop has not been produced at a profit by any method.

(6) When a value of $4 per ton is assigned to the stover or fodder, corn has been profitably grown by some method at all but one of the stations.

(7) The response to differences in culture and crop sequence is greater in the southern and central portion of the Great Plains than it is in the northern portion.

ADDITIONAL COPIES
OF THIS PUBLICATION MAY BE PROCURED FROM
THE SUPERINTENDENT OF DOCUMENTS
GOVERNMENT PRINTING OFFICE
WASHINGTON, D. C.
AT
5 CENTS PER COPY
▽

UNITED STATES DEPARTMENT OF AGRICULTURE

BULLETIN No. 220

Contribution from the Office of Public Roads
LOGAN WALLER PAGE, Director

Washington, D. C. ▼ June 7, 1915.

ROAD MODELS

Prepared by the Office of Public Roads

CONTENTS

WASHINGTON
GOVERNMENT PRINTING OFFICE
1915

BULLETIN OF THE U.S. DEPARTMENT OF AGRICULTURE

No. 220

Contribution from the Office of Public Roads, Logan Waller Page, Director.
June 7, 1915.

ROAD MODELS.

Prepared by the Office of Public Roads.

CONTENTS.

INTRODUCTION.

The Office of Public Roads of the United States Department of Agriculture made an exhibit of road models for the first time in 1909 at the Alaska-Yukon-Pacific Exposition. The aim was to put on view such striking examples in miniature of model roads that visitors would not only appreciate the beneficent effects of improved roads but would, at the same time, be able to understand the methods of their construction.

Since the Alaska-Yukon-Pacific Exposition closed, the exhibit of the Office of Public Roads has been displayed at Omaha, Nebr., during the National Corn Exposition; at Knoxville, Tenn., during the Southern Appalachian Exposition; at Chicago, Ill., during the National Land and Irrigation Exposition; at New York City during the Travel and Vacation Exposition and the Domestic Science Exposition; at Atlantic City, N. J., during the American Road Congress; at Lethbridge, Alberta, during the International Dry-Land Congress; at Buenos Aires, Argentina, during the International Agricultural Exposition; at Turin, Italy, during the International Exposition;

NOTE.—This bulletin contains illustrations and descriptions of the models in miniature of roads, bridges, and culverts and of road machinery exhibited by the Office of Public Roads at expositions and fairs and on railroads. Methods of construction are discussed.

and at various other expositions and fairs. The models have also been displayed on road trains at all important places along the route of the Pennsylvania Railroad in the State of Pennsylvania and along the entire system of the Southern Railroad, also along the St. Louis & San Francisco Railroad, the Atlantic Coast Line, the Nashville, Chattanooga & St. Louis Railroad, and the New York Central & Hudson River Railroad. A comprehensive exhibit of these models, illustrating all standard types of construction, has been installed at the Panama-Pacific Exposition in San Francisco, Cal.

The models, as a rule, are constructed on a scale of 1 inch to the foot, so that each model is one-twelfth the size of the actual road which it represents. Modifications of the methods of construction may be necessary to meet local conditions. Advice and information relating to road construction, maintenance, or improvement in any section of the country may be obtained upon application to the Director of the Office of Public Roads.

The descriptions of the models are so arranged in this bulletin as to present the historic development of road building. The Roman road is described first, and then descriptions are given successively of the French roads, after the ideas of the Romans and of Trésaguet, the roads of MacAdam and Telford, and finally the various types of modern construction. Among the latter are models showing brick, concrete, asphalt-block, macadam, sand-clay, gravel, and earth roads. There are other models showing the processes of maintenance, resurfacing, and bituminous macadam construction by the mixing and penetration methods. One model shows the various methods of draining and strengthening unstable foundations, while another shows a typical method of treating gravel or macadam roads to make them dustless and to prevent their disintegration under automobile traffic. Two models recently added to the series illustrate, respectively, road location and roadside treatment.

ROMAN ROADS.

The Romans began building roads on a large scale more than 300 years before the Christian era. The Appian Way, one of the most celebrated of their roads, was begun in 312 B. C., by Appius Claudius Cæcus. This road led from Rome to Capua, a distance of 142 Italian miles. It was later continued to Brindisi, making the total distance 360 miles. Rome continued as a great road-building nation for about 600 years, and fragments of some of its roads still remain. The Appian Way is said to have been in good condition more than 800 years after its construction.

The Roman construction was not uniform, though always extremely massive. The general form of construction employed during the reign of Cæsar Augustus, when Roman road building seems to have reached its height, was a massive road from 16 to 30 feet wide, from 3 to 4 feet thick, and laid in 3 or 4 courses. The first course was almost invariably of large, flat, field or quarry stones laid on the earth subgrade, except in swamps, where poles, logs, brush, or even boards were used beneath the stone course. The other courses varied extremely with the available material and the period and importance of the road. Either small stones, with and without mortar, or gravel, broken brick, tiles, etc., were used for the second and third courses. The surface or wearing course consisted of well-cut, irregular, close-fitting polygonal blocks on a few of the more important roads, but more often it consisted of uncut stones, not unlike our cobblestone pavements, or of gravel, and in some cases of a mixture of sand and clay or clay and gravel.

Some of the more important roads near Rome were practically lined with temples, porticoes, and statues. On all roads inscribed milestones were placed at regular intervals.

Plate II, figure 1, shows a model of the Appian Way. This is the highest type of road constructed by the Romans.

Section A shows the contignatum pavimentum, composed of lime and sand, straw, rushes, or reeds, and sometimes laid on sills or boards.

Section B shows the statumen, or foundation, composed of two courses of flat stones laid dry or in lime mortar. The depth of this course was from 16 to 18 inches.

Section C shows the rudus, or rubble, composed of broken stone mixed with lime in the proportion of 1 part of lime to 3 parts of stone. Sometimes the material was taken from old buildings. This course was laid from 6 to 9 inches deep.

Section **D** represents the nucleus, composed of coarse gravel and lime used hot, or bricks, potsherds, or broken tile mixed with lime and covered with a thin layer of lime mortar.

Section E shows the summa crusta, or pavimentum, consisting of polygonal blocks joined with the greatest nicety. This course was about 6 inches deep and about 16 feet wide.

Section F indicates the curbs, which were 2 feet wide and 18 inches high, with mounting blocks as shown at G. These blocks also served as seats for travelers.

Section H shows a side road, the surface of which was composed of gravel flushed with mortar. The width was from 6 to 8 feet.

FRENCH ROADS.

From the viewpoint of construction, road building in France may be divided into three periods—the period of Roman influence, the period of Trésaguet, and the modern period.

FRENCH CONSTRUCTION PREVIOUS TO 1775 (ROMAN METHOD).

By the time that road building was revived in France, in the seventeenth century, the Roman methods of road building had been greatly modified, though the Roman form, especially in the foundation, was still retained. Under the ministry of Colbert (1660–1669) as controller general of finances, about 15,000 miles of stone roads were built, practically all with an undrained foundation consisting of one or more layers of large flat stones placed in the bottom of a trench-like excavation. These stones were then covered with a thick layer of more or less finely broken stone. As no systematic maintenance was attempted, the roads rutted badly, and it was only rarely that the broken stone consolidated properly. The total thickness of the roads was from 1½ to 2½ feet.

Plate II, figure 2, illustrates the type of road constructed in France previously to 1775. This type was modeled on the Roman system.

Section A shows the earth foundation, which was flat.

Section B represents the first course. This course was composed of flat stones laid by hand in two or more layers. The total width of this course was 18 feet and the depth was from 9 to 10 inches.

Section C shows the second course, a layer of small stones, which were broken in place with hand hammers.

Section D shows the finished surface. This course was composed of stones broken by hand into sizes smaller than the underlying material. It was left to be consolidated by traffic. The total thickness of the road in the center was from 18 to 20 inches and at the sides from 12 to 14 inches.

TRÉSAGUET METHOD.

About 1775 a form of construction, supplemented by continual maintenance, came into prominence in France. It had long been advocated by Pierre Marie Jérôme Trésaguet, a noted French engineer. He held that good drainage and systematic maintenance were absolutely necessary for good roads. By providing a properly crowned and drained foundation, he reduced the required thickness more than one-half and provided a better and more serviceable road. The small stones were broken more uniformly and, by a little attention after placing, soon bonded under the traffic. The resulting roads were smooth and afforded comfortable traveling.

Plate III, figure 1, illustrates the type of road constructed in France by Trésaguet from 1775 to 1830.

Section A shows the earth foundation shaped parallel to the finished surface.

Section B represents the first course, which was composed of flat stones laid on edge lengthwise across the road and beaten to an even surface. The depth of this course was about 5 inches.

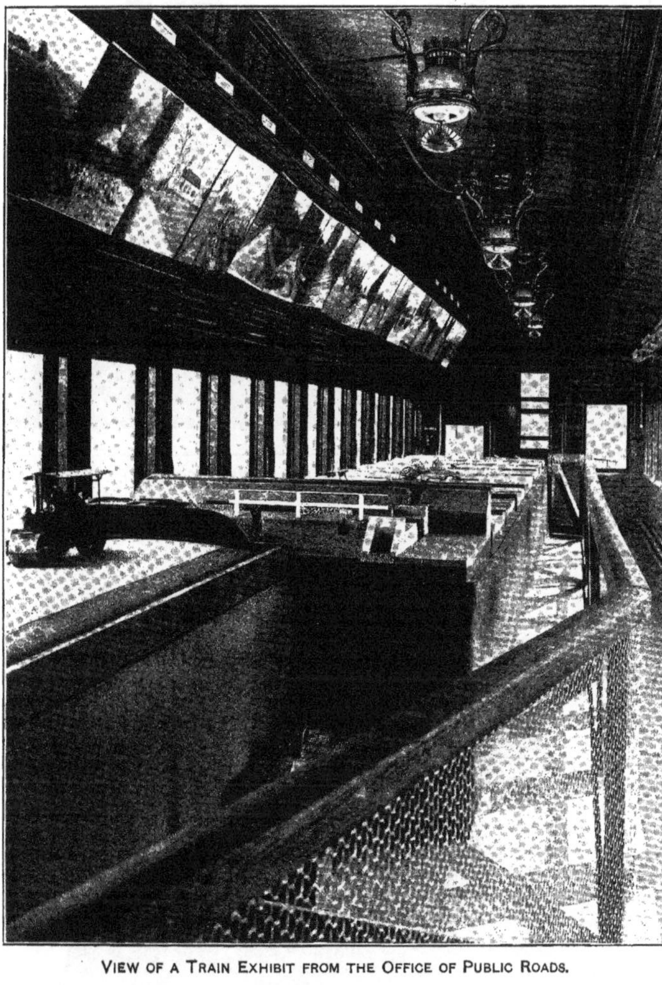

VIEW OF A TRAIN EXHIBIT FROM THE OFFICE OF PUBLIC ROADS.

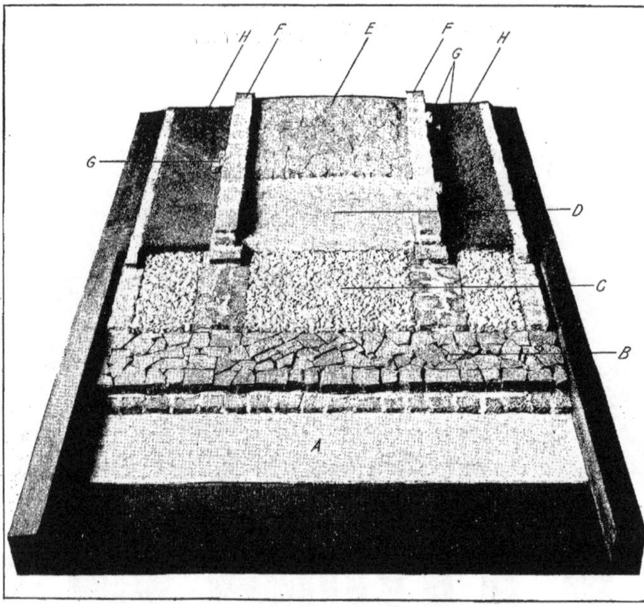

FIG. 1.—MODEL SHOWING THE APPIAN WAY (300 B. C.).

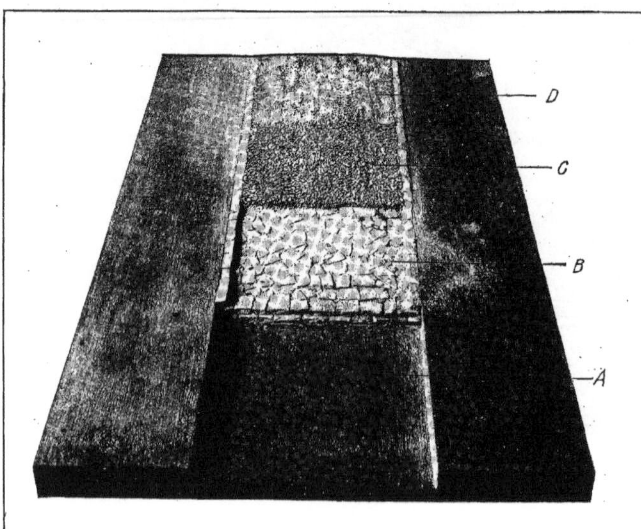

FIG. 2.—MODEL SHOWING A FRENCH ROAD BUILT BEFORE 1775 (ROMAN METHOD).

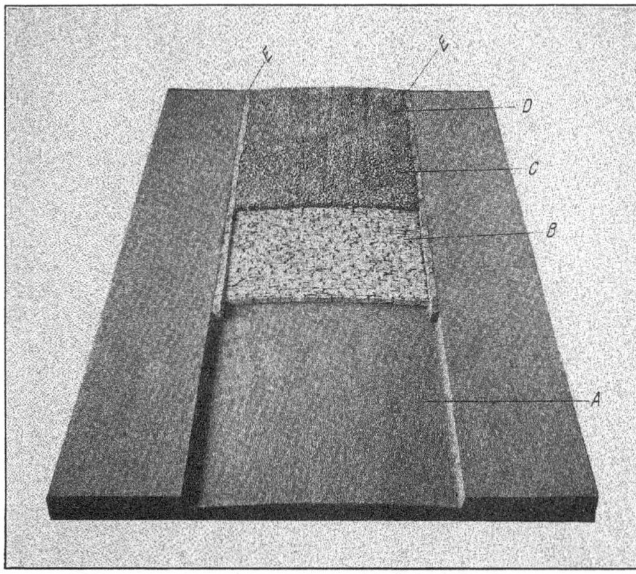

FIG. 1.—MODEL SHOWING A FRENCH ROAD OF TRÉSAGUET, BETWEEN 1775 AND 1830.

FIG. 2.—MODEL SHOWING A MACADAM ROAD OF THE TYPE BUILT BY MACADAM (1816).

FIG. 1.—MODEL SHOWING A TELFORD ROAD OF THE TYPE BUILT BY TELFORD (1820).

FIG. 2.—MODEL SHOWING LOCATION AND ALIGNMENT; OLD AND NEW ROADS.

Section C shows the second course, which was of small stones laid and beaten by hand hammers. The finished layer was composed of broken stones about the size of walnuts and was spread with a shovel.

Section **D** represents the finished road as consolidated by travel. The crown was made 6 inches, the width 18 feet, and the total thickness about 10 inches.

E shows the curbs, which were composed of rough, flat stones, set on edge. The upper edge was made flush with the road surface.

MACADAM METHOD OF CONSTRUCTION.

The macadam method of construction was introduced in England and Scotland by a Scotchman, John Loudon MacAdam (1756–1836). The chief features of MacAdam's construction were a raised, thoroughly drained, and crowned earth foundation, stone broken to a uniform size not exceeding 1½ inches, and no addition of binding material to the broken stone. MacAdam also insisted that the finished road should have a slight crown and that broken stone when spread on the road should be kept raked smooth until thoroughly consolidated by traffic. This form of construction continued practically unchanged until the introduction of the road roller, about 1870.

During the past 40 years the methods of construction and maintenance have been greatly modified, yet the term "macadam" is still applied to broken-stone roads.

At the present time the macadam road is built in courses, with the coarser stones at the bottom and the finer on top. Stone screenings or sand are used for binding. In practically every case the stone is broken by machinery.

Plate III, figure 2, illustrates a macadam road of the type constructed during the first period of macadam construction, which began about 1816.

Section A shows the earth foundation, which was always made higher than the surface of the adjacent ground so as to facilitate the escape of water from the foundation and the surface.

Section B shows the layer of hand-broken stone, with a depth of 10 inches. This stone was broken to sizes weighing about 6 ounces, and no stone was used that exceeded 1½ inches in its greatest dimension. The surface of the road was raked regularly during the process of consolidation. No rollers were used, and the stone was compacted by traffic.

Section C shows the finished road, from 16 to 18 feet wide. The crown was raised from 4 to 6 inches. MacAdam contended that the stones would lock or bond by virtue of their angularity and so make a water-tight crust, and that it was neither necessary nor desirable "to bond a road with earth, clay, chalk, or other material that would imbibe water or be affected by frost." The surface of the road was kept even and smooth by the addition of fresh material where necessary. This material was placed on the road in thin layers in damp weather in order that the new material might more readily bond and incorporate with the old.

TELFORD METHOD OF ROAD BUILDING.

This form of construction takes its name from the celebrated engineer, Thomas Telford (1757–1834), who, besides doing many other notable things, constructed 920 miles of roads in the Highlands of Scotland and also a large mileage in the mountainous sections of Wales and in the north of England. To-day the chief characteristic of the telford road is a base of fairly regular stones, about 3 by 5 by 7 inches in their smallest dimensions, placed by hand on the wider of the long narrow faces and with the greatest dimension perpendicular to the axis of the road. The blocks are then "keyed in" by filling the interstices with stone spalls, chips, or small gravel. Any projecting points are broken off. On this base is placed a wearing surface of broken stone from 4 to 7 inches deep. Originally the telford road was constructed with a flat subgrade, and a slight crown was obtained by using larger stones in the center. In present construction, however, the subgrade is given the same crown as the finished road, and stones of uniform size are used throughout. Formerly, too, the wearing surface was placed and consolidated in the same manner as the wearing surface of the old macadam road.

The telford base is used very generally in the construction of important roads in Austria-Hungary, Germany, Russia, Switzerland, and the Scandinavian countries. Some of the roads of England and Scotland which were formerly macadam are proving too weak for the present heavy traffic and are being relaid with a telford base.

Plate IV, figure 1, illustrates a telford road as constructed during the first period, which began about 1820.

Section A shows the earth foundation, from 16 to 20 feet wide, and flat.

Section B represents the telford base, composed of stones about 7 inches in depth. No stone more than 3 inches wide was placed at the top.

Section C shows the top course, about 7 inches thick at the crown. It was composed of hand-broken stone, in pieces not heavier than 6 ounces, which would pass through a circular ring not larger than 2½ inches in diameter.

Section D shows the finished road, bonded with 1 inch of gravel. The crown was made 6 inches for the road, which was surfaced to a width of 18 feet.

LOCATION AND ALIGNMENT.

When a new road is to be built, or an old road rebuilt, the profile should be established and the curves plotted by a competent engineer. The sharp curves and steep grades should be eliminated by a proper alignment or by cuts and fills. When a grade exceeds 6 feet in 100 feet, it is considered excessive for heavy traffic. A curve with less than a 200-foot radius is considered dangerous for fast traffic. Embankments, trees, and shrubs which obscure the line of sight on sharp curves should be cut back in order that rapidly moving vehicles approaching each other may be able to pass without accident.

In selecting the location for a new road, low, swampy ground or ground subject to overflow should be avoided. The road should be located on solid ground. In mountainous or hilly sections it should be located on the sidehill slopes, with southern or western exposure, where the natural drainage is good, and not in creek or river bottoms.

The road should be as straight as possible, but a good grade is preferred to straightness. Generally a road should be located around long steep inclines instead of over them. If this is impracticable then the length of the road up the incline should be increased sufficiently to obtain a good grade. Dangerous railroad grade crossings should be avoided by relocation of the road or by overhead bridges or underpasses.

Plate IV, figure 2, illustrates the relocation of an old road. To the right is shown the old earth road, with such characteristic features as steep grades, poor alignment, dangerous grade crossings, unsafe wooden bridge, and inadequate drainage. The dilapidated farm buildings and the old district schoolhouse featured on the model, with their unsightly and insanitary surroundings, are the usual accompaniment of such a road. To the left is shown the new road, located on higher ground, along sidehill slopes, with easy grades and pleasing, practical alignment. The grade crossing has been eliminated. A bridge and permanent culverts have been built and good drainage provided as well as a well constructed and maintained macadam surface. The sightly farm buildings and attractive consolidated district schoolhouse are supplied with pure water by means of windmill and reservoir.

FOUNDATION, OR SUBGRADE, AND SHOULDERS.

In the construction of all types of gravel or macadam roads it is necessary, in order to obtain the most economical results, to prepare the foundation, or subgrade, and shoulders of the road carefully. After the subgrade has been properly shaped and before any broken stone or other material is put on, it should be thoroughly rolled and compacted. Water-puddling may be resorted to in case the soil requires it. All hollows and depressions which develop during the rolling should be filled with good material. If soft or spongy places develop during the rolling, the soft or spongy material should be taken out and replaced with good material and the subgrade again rolled. This process of filling and rolling is repeated until no depressions develop and the subgrade has been brought to its proper elevation, which is as much below the established grade as the thickness of the surfacing course to be used. The shoulders ought also to be rolled in the same manner, but in places where the character of the material makes the use of a heavy roller impracticable, a lighter roller may be used. The shoulders are built at the same time as the subgrade and with it form a trench to hold the surfacing material. They may be built either by excavation or by piling up earth as the work progresses. The shoulders also serve to widen the road for the passing of vehicles. They are usually given a sharper slope than the paved portion of the road.

Plate V, figure 1, shows a model illustrating several methods of road drainage. It will be noted that the roadbed is located partly in a cut and partly on a sidehill.

Section A shows a surface ditch (*h*) at the top of the slope, a side drain (*c*) opening into a culvert (*a*) with a drop inlet (*b*), a telford base, a section of guard rail (*g*), and a shoulder drain (*d*).

The surface water falling on a large area sloping toward the road is often kept from the road and out of the road gutters, where it usually does considerable damage, by a surface ditch such as (*h*). The side ditch (*e*) is used to gather the water originating on or along a roadway and to carry it to points of outlet. As a general rule the bottom of the ditch is lower than the low point on the subgrade of the road. The size of the ditch varies with the amount of water it is necessary to accommodate. The shape of the ditch varies with climatic, soil, and topographic conditions. The side drain (*c*) is constructed to carry off the ground water which is often found in hilly sections. In the model the trench is represented to be 2½ feet deep, 12 inches wide at the bottom, and 18 inches wide at the top. On the bottom of the trench is placed tile pipe, usually 6 inches in diameter. The pipe is laid without cement, and loose stone is carefully filled around the sides and top of the pipe to the top of the trench. The side drain empties in some suitable outlet. For example, the one in this model empties in a drop inlet (*b*), which also serves as an outlet to the surface and side ditches. The drop inlet empties into a culvert (*a*), which carries the water under the road. This type of inlet prevents the bank from sliding and closing the culvert, which sometimes happens in hilly sections.

The purpose of the shoulder drain (*d*) is to permit water to escape from the subgrade during or immediately after the construction of a gravel, macadam, or other road of crushed stone. These drains are generally a little deeper than the subgrade and slope toward the side ditches, to which they carry the water. They are filled with crushed stone to a depth of 6 or 8 inches and are covered over with earth. The shoulder drains are required in clay soils and are placed at the low points in the grade as well as at frequent intervals on flat grades.

The telford base is extensively used in locations on swampy or marshy ground.

The guard rail shown in the model is desirable along steep slopes to protect travelers. The fence is painted to prolong its life. The white color enables the public to discern it at night. The posts are about 6 inches in diameter and about 7 feet long, and are set in the ground to a depth of 3½ feet. About 18 inches from the ground a plank, 2 by 6 inches, is notched into the posts. The top rail is then placed about 18 inches above the top edge of this plank. It may be either 4 by 4 inch timber, notched into the top of the post, or a plank, 2 by 6 inches, spiked to the top of the post, which has been sawed off to a slope of 3 inches.

Section B shows a V drain base with a side outlet.

The V drain base, when used in through cuts, is cheaper than the telford method with two side drains, especially in a section of country where field stone abounds. It, like the telford, is often used in wet and spongy ground. The water flows to and along the point of the V drain (*i*) until a suitable outlet can be secured. The center is usually excavated 2 feet and the sides about 16 inches below the finished grade. The material excavated is thrown to the sides, forming the shoulders. In swamp sections it is sometimes necessary to haul material for the shoulders. The V drain is then filled with stone to a depth of 18 inches at the center and 10 inches at the sides. These stones grade from 8 inches in thickness down to a few inches. The large-sized stones are placed at the bottom, while the small stones are used at the top. The surface should then be rolled and the surfacing material spread and rolled. V drains are sometimes built of brickbats, slag, or even sand, or any material that will permit the water to seep rapidly to the point of the V. This type of construction permits the use of field stone of an inferior type and assists in clearing many farm lands of an otherwise waste product.

Section C shows a center drain with laterals and cobble gutters.

The center drain with laterals, sometimes called a blind or French drain, furnishes another mode of draining the foundation of a road. As with the V drain, the water is brought to the center of the road and conducted to some suitable outlet. The model shows these drains about 2 feet deep, about 12 inches wide at the bottom, and about 18 inches wide at the top. A drain tile is placed at the bottom of the trench, which is then filled with stones from a few inches up to 8 inches in thickness.

The cobble gutters (*f*) show an effective way of carrying away surface water on steep grades. The stones vary in thickness from 8 to 12 inches and are laid on a sand or gravel base. They are well rammed and given a coat of sand, which is carefully swept in, and then the stones are rammed again. These gutters are easily cleaned and carry the water along rapidly without damage to the road by washing.

EARTH AND SAND-CLAY ROADS.

The mileage of roads in the United States is so great and the traffic on many of the country roads so light that it will be impossible and impracticable for years to come to improve more than a small percentage of the roads with a hard surface. This does not mean, however, that all other roads should be neglected. They should, as rapidly as possible, be improved to the extent warranted by their importance. The common clay roads may be greatly improved by a little judicious grading and systematic maintenance.

Frequently, especially in the South, many of the country roads may be improved, for all practical purposes, by incorporating sand or clay, as the case may require, with the surface soil of the road. Thousands of miles of sand-clay roads have already been built in the Southern States at an average cost of about $750 per mile. These roads meet the present needs of many localities as well as would a more expensive form of construction.

EARTH ROADS.

Plate V, figure 2, illustrates the construction and maintenance of an earth road.

Section A shows the old and unimproved roadbed. The surface is characteristic of altogether too many earth roads. The center is lower than the sides, which makes it impossible for the water to run toward the ditches; and even if this were possible there are no roadside ditches to carry it away. In consequence, the road is usually full of ruts and mudholes.

Section B illustrates a section of earth road under improvement, with a road machine or grader. The width of the section shown is equivalent to about 33 feet of finished surface from ditch to ditch. The use of a reversible road machine is shown in opening roadside ditches and in shaping the road surface so that it will shed water. The work of this machine is equivalent to the labor of many men, and it is done far better than possible with picks and shovels. An earth road should have a width of at least 20 feet, preferably 24 to 30 feet. If the road is narrow, wagons are likely to use the center of it and make deep ruts. The surface drainage is provided for by giving the road an average crown or slope from center to sides of 1 inch to the foot. Side ditches should be built, as shown in section B, on all earth roads except sandy sections, which are best when damp. Ditches can be made and maintained with a road machine, but care should be taken that they have a fall sufficient to carry the water along the side of the road. Through wet and swampy land it is often necessary to raise the roadbed above the general level of the country in order to secure drainage.

Section C illustrates an earth road which, though surfaced by a road machine, has rutted under heavy traffic and is being maintained by the split-log drag. In the road illustrated by sections B and C the crown or slope from the center to the sides is equivalent to 1 inch to the foot.

For continuous maintenance the split-log drag shown on the model has been devised. This miniature drag has been built to the same scale as the road model, 1 inch to the foot. The full-sized drag can be made best from a log 7 or 8 inches in diameter and from 6 to 8 feet long. The log should be carefully split, and the halves, with the flat sides vertical and facing to the front, connected by stakes. The halves, though of the same length, are joined so that one end of the rear half is from 16 to 20 inches nearer the center of the road than the corresponding end of the front half. An ordinary trace chain and a set of doubletrees are then attached in such manner that when the horses move forward the drag will be pulled along the road at an angle of about 45 degrees, with the forward end nearest the ditch in order to move the earth toward the road center.

The drag should be light enough to be lifted by one man. The best material is dry red cedar, though red elm and walnut are excellent, while box elder, soft maple, elm, or willow are superior to oak, hickory, or ash. A platform is usually placed on the cross stakes to strengthen the drag and furnish a place for the driver to stand. After a little practice a man can learn how best to shift his weight so as to make the drag cut, spread, and pack the earth properly.

Filling the ruts by dragging up one side of the road and down the other is all that should be undertaken the first time, but this should be repeated after each heavy rain. As a mile of road can be dragged in a few hours, this method of maintenance is simple and inexpensive. If the drag is used in conjunction with the road machine, fairly good earth roads can be built at a small expense. Dragging is done for 50 cents per mile in some parts of the country. At this rate a mile of earth road can be dragged once a month for $6 annually. Some remarkable results have been accomplished with the drag without the aid of the road machine. Farmers' Bulletin 597,[1] "The Road Drag and How to Use It," deals fully with this subject.

---

[1] Copies of this publication will be sent free to persons applying to the Secretary of Agriculture, Washington, D. C.

SAND-CLAY ROADS.

Plate VI, figure 1, illustrates the construction of a sand-clay road 16 feet wide and 8 inches thick when compacted. The crown, as shown, is 1 inch to the foot.

Section A represents an unimproved sand road about 33 feet wide; section B, the road slightly rounded to receive the clay; section C, the road covered with clay to a depth of 6 inches; section D, the harrowing or mixing process; and section E, the completed road. The process is as follows:

The road is first shaped, then covered with from 4 to 6 inches of clay and worked with a disk or tooth harrow until the sand and clay are thoroughly mixed, first dry and finally wet. The final mixing should be done, if possible, during rainy weather. When the mixing has been done, the surface is brought to a crown of 1 inch to the foot with the road machine or split-log drag and covered with a thin layer of sand. After two or three rains it may be found necessary to apply more sand. This method produces a smooth, cheap, and satisfactory road suitable for light traffic.

Similar results can be secured by adding sand to a clay road and providing good surface drainage. When building on a clay foundation, it is advisable to plow the clay before adding the sand in order to insure a thorough mixing.

The failure of a sand-clay road is generally due to one of two causes, the use of an unsuitable material or the combination of the sand and clay in wrong proportions. The clay should be of a quality which, while sticky, yet will mix readily with the sand and form a firm bond after the wet mixture has been shaped and dried out. Some clays, such as the "joint" clays, have so little of the plastic or sticky quality that after a rain they quickly separate from the particles of sand and make a dusty road. Where available, the sand selected should be sharp and coarse. With regard to the proportions of sand and clay, any excess of clay above the amount necessary to fill the tiny spaces between the grains of sand will result in a more or less muddy road. Farmers' Bulletin 331,[1] "Sand-clay and Burnt-clay Roads," gives full information on the subject of constructing these roads.

GRAVEL ROADS.

Plate VI, figure 2, illustrates the stages of construction for one type of gravel road. The graded width is 33 feet and the surfaced width is 16 feet. The crown is three-fourths inch per foot.

Section A represents the side ditches, shoulders, and the prepared subgrade, with the center about 10 inches higher than the bottom of the side ditch.

---

[1] Copies of this publication will be sent free to persons applying to the Secretary of Agriculture, Washington, D. C.

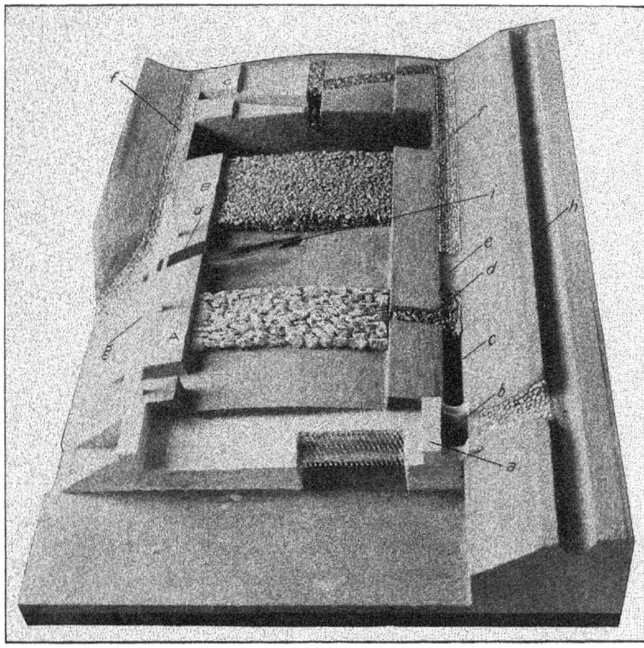

FIG. 1.—MODEL SHOWING VARIOUS METHODS OF ROAD DRAINAGE.

FIG. 2.—MODEL OF AN EARTH ROAD, SHOWING SPLIT-LOG DRAG AND ROAD GRADER IN OPERATION.

FIG. 1.—MODEL OF A SAND-CLAY ROAD.

FIG. 2.—MODEL OF A GRAVEL ROAD.

FIG. 1.—MODEL OF A WATER-BOUND MACADAM ROAD.

FIG. 2.—MODEL OF A BITUMINOUS MACADAM ROAD—PENETRATION METHOD.

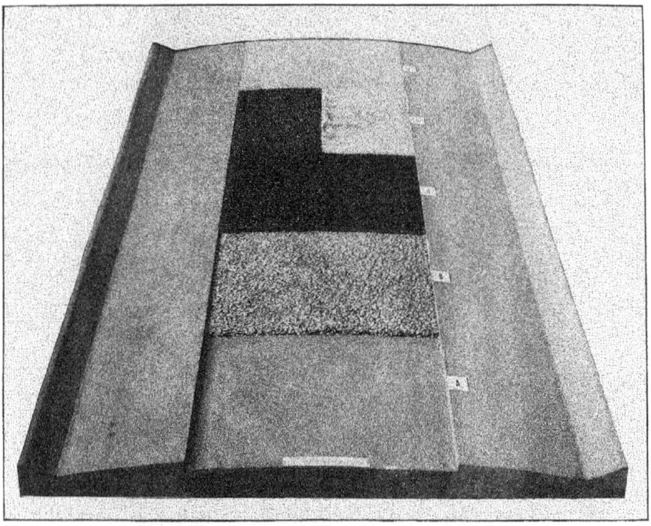

FIG. 1.—MODEL OF A BITUMINOUS MACADAM ROAD—MIXING METHOD.

FIG. 2.—MODEL SHOWING A ROCK-ASPHALT MACADAM ROAD.

Section B shows the first course of gravel spread and rolled to a thickness of about 4 inches at the center and 3 inches at the sides.

Section C represents the finished road after the second course of gravel has been spread and compacted. The second course when compacted is 2 inches in thickness at the center and 1½ inches at the sides.

Many gravels as found in nature are not suitable for use on the road, unless modified by the addition or elimination of certain materials. The products of some pits are deficient in bonding materials, such as sand or clay, and at the same time may have an excess of large pebbles. In general, the gravel should be screened and the graded material laid in courses according to the manner of macadam road construction.

MACADAM ROADS.

WATER-BOUND MACADAM ROADS.

Plate VII, figure 1, illustrates the construction of a water-bound macadam road 16 feet wide, 6 inches thick at the center, and 4 inches thick at the sides when rolled. The crown of the finished road as shown is one-half inch to the foot. The road is graded for a width of 33 feet.

Section A represents the prepared subgrade properly crowned and rolled; section B, the first course of broken stone, 4 inches thick compacted; section C, the second course, 2 inches thick compacted; and section D, the finished road.

In preparing for the construction of a road of this type, the procedure given on page 7, for foundation, or subgrade, and shoulders, should be followed. After the subgrade has been prepared, a layer of broken stone of approved size and quality for the first or bottom course should be spread evenly over it to such depth that it shall have, when rolled, the required thickness. The depth of the loose stone may be gauged by laying upon the subgrade cubical blocks of wood of the proper size, and spreading the stone evenly to conform to them.

The roller should be run along the edge of the stone backward and forward several times on each side of the road before rolling the center. If a filler is desired for the bottom course it should be clean, coarse sand, or stone screenings supplemented by the product of the crusher not otherwise used in top or bottom courses. It should be spread uniformly over the surface and then swept in and rolled dry. This process must be continued until no more will go in dry, when the surface should be sprinkled to more effectually fill the voids. Any irregularities or depressions may be made good with broken stone of the size used in the bottom course, and screenings or filler should not be used for this purpose.

The second or top course should be spread on the bottom course to such depth that it shall have, when completed, the required thickness. Blocks of wood of proper size may be used to gauge the depth of the loose stone. Care must be taken to preserve the grade and crown, also to prevent a wavy surface, and all irregularities and depressions ought to be made up with stone the size of the top-course stone. After the surface is true to line, grade, and cross-section, and rolled until the stone ceases to wave in front of the roller, it should be covered with a light coating of screenings, spread on dry, rolled, and swept in. The filler for the top course must be of top-course stone screenings in which the percentage of dust is not excessive. The spreading, sweeping, and rolling in of screenings should be continued until no more will go in dry, after which it is best to sprinkle the road until the top course is saturated. The sprinkler is then followed by the roller. More screenings should be added if necessary, and the sweeping, sprinkling, and rolling continued until a grout has been formed of the screenings, stone dust, and water that shall fill all the voids in the top course and shall form a wave before the wheels of the roller.

When the wave of grout has been produced over the whole section of the road this portion of the road should be left to dry, after which it can be opened to travel. Enough screenings should be spread on top of the macadam to leave a wearing surface about three-eighths of an inch thick.

A miniature steam roller is shown in Plate I of this bulletin. For further information on the subject of macadam roads, Farmers' Bulletin 338,[1] "Macadam Roads," may be of interest.

BITUMINOUS MACADAM ROADS.

Since the coming of the automobile, the resulting aggravation of the dust nuisance, and the consequent raveling of the water-bound macadam roads, numerous methods have been devised to secure a lasting road surface reasonably free from dust and at the same time within the financial means available for main-line country roads.

While the several methods differ greatly as to name and the details of carrying out the work, the fundamental aim of each is the same. This is to secure a smooth, waterproof, and durable surface composed of mineral aggregate, usually broken stone, bonded not only by the mechanical interlocking of the fragments, but by a bituminous material which coats the fragments and fills the interstices. Refined tars, oil asphalts, and fluxed natural asphalts are the binders more commonly employed.

[1] Copies of this publication will be sent free to persons applying to the Secretary of Agriculture, Washington, D. C.

The usual methods of construction are known as the mixing method and the penetration method. In the mixing method a more or less closely graded aggregate is mixed either by hand or machinery with the proper amount of bituminous material before placing it on the road. In the penetration method the wearing or second course of stone is laid and rolled as in ordinary macadam; but instead of applying the screenings, hot bituminous material is poured or sprayed over the stone in sufficient quantity to coat the fragments and penetrate the top course to a depth of 2 or 3 inches. In each of these forms of construction it is customary to spread a second and light application of hot bituminous material over the surface in order to fill the exposed voids completely and make the surface waterproof. A sufficient quantity of pea gravel or stone chips is then added to take up any excess of bitumen, the surface is rolled thoroughly, and the road thrown open to traffic.

PENETRATION METHOD.

Plate VII, figure 2, illustrates the construction of a bituminous macadam road according to the penetration method.

Section A represents the prepared subgrade 16 feet wide, with the crown one-half inch to the foot; section B, the first course of No. 1 stone, 4 inches in thickness when compacted after rolling. This course is partially filled with sand or stone chips when necessary to insure a solid foundation. Section C shows the second course of No. 2 stone, 2 inches in thickness when compacted after rolling; section D, the application of bituminous material at the rate of about 1½ gallons to the square yard; section E, a coating of stone chips which has been rolled; section F, seal coat of bituminous material applied at the rate of about one-half gallon per square yard; and section G, the completed surface, with clean stone chips lightly rolled.

The construction of this road, as far as the completion of the No. 1 and No. 2 courses, is the same as an ordinary macadam road. From that point it varies from the method of construction of a macadam road in that hot bituminous material is flushed into the No. 2 course before the screenings are applied.

MIXING METHOD.

Plate VIII, figure 1, illustrates the construction of a bituminous macadam road according to the mixing method.

Section A shows the prepared subgrade 16 feet wide, with the crown three-eighths inch to the foot; section B, the foundation course of No. 1 stone compacted to a depth of about 4 inches. This course is partially filled with sand or stone chips, as shown in model, when necessary to insure a solid foundation. Section C shows the wearing course before and after rolling, consisting of a properly proportioned mixture of stone and bituminous material. The stone may be the product of the crusher ranging in size from that which will be retained on a screen having circular openings one-half inch in diameter to that which will pass a screen having circular openings 1¼ inches in diameter. Stone of this size will require from 18 to 20 gallons of bituminous material per cubic yard of stone.

The wearing course is laid to a depth of 3½ inches loose, which will compact to a thickness of about 2 inches by rolling. Section D shows the application of a seal coat of hot bituminous material and clean stone chips, and section E shows the finished surface after final rolling.

SURFACE TREATMENT.

The surface treatment of an old macadam road with bituminous material is shown in Plate IX, figure 1.

Section A shows a disintegrated macadam surface; section B, the surface after sweeping; section C, the application of bituminous material at the rate of about one-half gallon per square yard; and section D, the application of pea gravel or stone chips to the treated surface, completing the treatment.

Before any application of bituminous material is made all loose material should be removed and the road surface should be free from dust, clean and dry. The bituminous material is applied either hot or cold, depending upon the consistency of the material. It may be poured by hand, or by means of a mechanical distributor, and in the former case should be thoroughly broomed into the surface, in order to secure perfect adhesion. Enough stone chips or pea gravel should then be applied to take up any excess bituminous material that may be left on the surface.

RESURFACING MACADAM ROADS.

Plate IX, figure 2, illustrates the reconstruction of a macadam road after it has become badly worn. The macadam width as shown is 16 feet, and the crown is one-half inch to the foot.

Section A represents the worn macadam surface; section B, the surface after spiking; section C, the road after it has been recrowned; section D, the application of new stone of No. 2 size, compacted to 3 inches after rolling; section E, the application of bituminous material by the penetration method at the rate of about 1½ gallons per square yard; section F, a coating of stone chips which has been rolled; section G, a seal coat of bituminous material averaging about one-half gallon per square yard; and section H, the finished surface covered with stone chips or pea gravel.

This model illustrates the usual custom of restoring a macadam road which has become badly worn and rutted, owing to excessive travel and lack of maintenance.

FIG. 1.—MODEL SHOWING REPAIR AND MAINTENANCE OF MACADAM ROADS—SURFACE TREATMENT.

FIG. 2.—MODEL SHOWING REPAIR OF A MACADAM ROAD—RESURFACING ROAD.

FIG. 1.—MODEL SHOWING CEMENT CONCRETE ROAD.

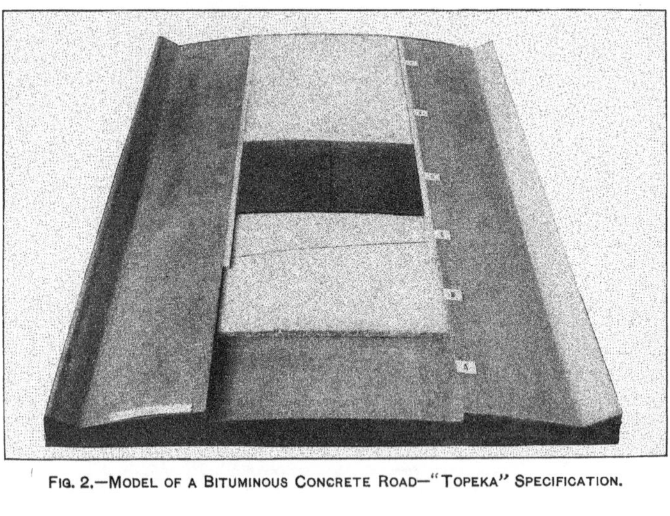

FIG. 2.—MODEL OF A BITUMINOUS CONCRETE ROAD—"TOPEKA" SPECIFICATION.

ROCK-ASPHALT MACADAM ROADS.

Plate VIII, figure 2, represents a rock-asphalt macadam road surfaced to a width of 16 feet. The macadam is compacted to a total depth of 8½ inches and the crown is made one-half inch to the foot. The rock asphalt is spread on the road at the rate of 80 pounds to the square yard.

Section A represents the prepared subgrade; section B, the first course of stone, ranging in size from 2 to 3 inches, with a depth of 3 inches when compacted; section C, the second course of stone, ranging in size from 2 to 3 inches, filled with stone chips or sand, and having a depth of 3 inches when compacted; section D, the third course of stone, ranging in size from 1½ to 2½ inches, with a depth of 2½ inches when compacted; section E, the rock asphalt, to the extent of 40 pounds per square yard, or about three-fourths inch loose, raked and rolled in to fill the voids; and section F shows the finished surface, composed of rock asphalt, spread at the rate of 40 pounds per square yard, which is equivalent to a course about three-fourths inch thick before rolling.

CEMENT CONCRETE ROADS.

Concrete roads are a comparatively new development in the effort to find a material which will successfully withstand both automobile and horse-drawn traffic. Concrete pavements were laid first in 1869 in Grenoble, France, where many streets are still paved with this material. In this country the first use of the concrete pavement was probably in Bellefontaine, Ohio, where several sections were laid in 1893 and 1894.

A large mileage of concrete roads has been built in Wayne County, Mich. These roads are built of a 1:1½:3 mixture throughout, with a minimum thickness of 7 inches. The width of the surfaced roadway varies from 9 to 24 feet. The county road officials are very well pleased with this form of construction, and are building many more miles of it.

In other instances a leaner concrete is used, and the surface protected by a cushion coat of some bituminous binder with sand, fine gravel, or screenings. This surface coating is renewed as often as may be necessary.

Plate X, figure 1, illustrates the construction of a concrete road graded to a width of 33 feet and paved to a width of 16 feet. The concrete is placed to a depth of 7 inches in the center and 4 inches at the sides. The crown of the road is three-eighths inch to the foot. Section A represents the prepared subgrade; section B the fresh concrete placed in position, mixed in the proportion of 1:1¾:3; section C, a 2-inch earth blanket, placed to minimize evaporation while curing; section D shows various types of expansion joints, namely, wood, felt, and bituminous filler; section E, the bituminous carpet coat consisting of one-third to one-half gallon of bituminous material per square yard and sufficient "torpedo" sand or stone chips to provide a satisfactory wearing surface.

BITUMINOUS CONCRETE ROADS—"TOPEKA SPECIFICATION."

Plate X, figure 2, represents a type of bituminous concrete construction. It is preferably laid over a concrete base to the depth shown, but is frequently constructed over a well-consolidated macadam or crushed-stone base.

Section A shows the subgrade; section B, the concrete foundation composed of broken stone or gravel concrete mixed in the proportion 1:3:7 and having a finished thickness of 6 inches. Section C demonstrates the manner of constructing the curbs. It also shows the joint left at the end of each day's work. Section D shows the layer of bituminous concrete before and after rolling. The composition of this concrete is commonly as follows:

	Per cent.
Bitumen soluble in carbon bisulphide	7–11
Mineral aggregate passing a 2-mesh sieve	100
Passing 2-mesh sieve and retained on 4-mesh sieve	5–10
Passing 4-mesh sieve and retained on 10-mesh sieve	8–22
Passing 10-mesh sieve and retained on 40-mesh sieve	25–55
Passing 40-mesh sieve and retained on 200-mesh sieve	18–30
Passing 200-mesh sieve	5–11

Section E shows the application of a seal coat with stone chip dressing. The amount of bituminous material applied should not exceed one-half gallon to the square yard, and the seal coat is frequently omitted when the bituminous concrete is sufficiently dense to warrant the omission.

Section F shows the finished surface.

PAVED ROADS OTHER THAN CONCRETE.

Paved roads are sometimes advisable where there is heavy traffic. The materials which have been adapted to country roads during the past years are brick, asphalt block, granite block, and a small stone block extensively used in Germany and known as "kleinpflaster."

A good paving brick laid on a sand cushion with a substantial concrete foundation makes a road well adapted to both horse-drawn and motor traffic. The first cost of such a road is generally high, but this is largely offset by its durability and low maintenance cost.

Asphalt blocks are molded from sand, broken stone, and asphalt under pressure into rectangular blocks, which are laid on a concrete foundation somewhat in the same manner as brick. The asphalt blocks are more resilient than the brick and consequently more free from noise. They have as yet not been used to any great extent on the country roads of the United States. The small sett, or "klein-pflaster," pavement of Germany is as yet almost unknown in this country. A hard, tough rock, preferably basalt or diabase, is broken by machinery into cubes 3 to 4 inches in size. These are placed on a light sand cushion, with a concrete or old macadam base as foundation. In Germany they are generally laid in an oyster shell or mosaic pattern, while in Hungary and Austria they are laid in rows at 45 degrees to the axis of the road. This pavement may be laid at a fairly low first cost, is not expensive to maintain, is neither noisy nor slippery, and is well adapted to mixed traffic.

ASPHALT-BLOCK ROADS.

Plate XI, figure 1, represents an asphalt-block road.

Section A shows the subgrade, and beginning with section B is shown the concrete curb. Section B shows the concrete base 6 inches thick, mixed in the proportion 1 : 3 : 7; section C, the cement mortar bed, one-half inch thick, composed of 1 part of slow-setting Portland cement and 4 parts of sand; section D, the asphalt block surface. The asphalt blocks are 5 inches wide, 12 inches long, and 2 inches thick. In section E the surface has been covered with sand which has been screened through a $\frac{1}{8}$-inch mesh screen. This sand carpet is used to fill the joints between the blocks, and should be allowed to remain for 30 days. The surface should then be swept clean.

BRICK ROADS.

Plate XI, figure 2, illustrates the construction of a 28-foot roadway, 14 feet of which is a brick road with 6-inch concrete curbings. There is a 3-foot earth shoulder along one edge of the brick roadway, and the remaining 11 feet form an earth road on the opposite side. The earth road has a slope toward its ditch of 1 inch to the foot. The outer 11 feet of the brick roadway has a slope of three-eighths inch to the foot, but the slope of the inner 3 feet is less, forming the crown of the road. The earth road is preferred in dry weather by many drivers of horses.

Section A illustrates the prepared subgrade for the brick roadway; section B, the concrete curbing placed along the edges of the pavement; section C, a stone base 6 inches deep, and section D, a concrete base 6 inches deep. Either of these bases may be used, although the concrete is generally preferable. This base course of the road may vary in thickness from 4 to 8 inches, according to soil conditions, but 6 inches is in most general use. Section E shows the sand cushion, about 2 inches deep; section F, the brick laid and rolled but not grouted; section G, the expansion joint between the brick and the curb; and section H illustrates the grouted brick surface ready for travel. In addition, a properly constructed mixing box is shown, in which the grout is prepared.

CULVERTS AND BRIDGES.

The first highway bridges in this country were constructed of wood and required much attention for repairs and renewals. Later, wrought and cast iron were combined with wood in what became known as combination bridges. The present general demand for structures composed of more permanent materials is due largely to the expense and inconvenience of maintaining those of wood or combined wood and iron. In many sections there is also need for stronger bridges because of the increase in weight of traffic. Steel possesses the requisite strength, but it is subject to rust and rapid deterioration if not protected with a durable covering. Portland cement concrete is quite free from objectionable qualities, and by skillfully combining steel and concrete in highway bridges it is possible to utilize the good features of each material, and at the same time overcome their disadvantages. Reinforced concrete bridges may be made strong and durable. The concrete can be cast in any shape, and the surface finished in many different ways to secure a pleasing appearance. Such bridges cost more in the beginning, but practically nothing to maintain, while those of wood, or steel not incased in concrete, require frequent painting and renewal of parts.

Culverts constructed of stone and concrete are generally superior to those made of pipe and are less liable to injury by freezing. Hard-burned bricks are suitable for culvert material in localities where they are cheap and where stone or concrete materials are not easily available. Brick culverts are not so durable as those made of stone or concrete, especially in cold climates, where freezing is likely to occur.

Plate XII, figure 1, represents a bridge of the incased I-beam type, having a span of 24 feet, height of 6 feet, and width of roadway of 20 feet. The steel I-beams are 18 inches in depth, weigh 55 pounds per linear foot, and are spaced 3 feet 3 inches apart. The concrete is held firmly to the bottoms of the beams by wires of No. 10 gauge in the form of vertical loops spaced 8 inches apart. Lettered cards are used to designate the parts, as follows:

A, 6½-inch reinforced concrete floor slab; B, ½-inch twisted steel bars, spaced 8 inches apart and resting on the I-beams; C, steel I-beams; E, wooden forms (framing 3 by 6 inches, 3 feet on centers; boards 1¼ by 8 inches); F, parapet and railing; G, wing walls (top thickness, 12 inches, bottom thickness varies with height of wall, generally not less than four-tenths of height); H, footing (course obtained by adding 1 foot to thickness of abutment wall at base,

FIG. 1.—MODEL SHOWING AN ASPHALT-BLOCK ROAD.

FIG. 2.—MODEL OF A BRICK ROAD.

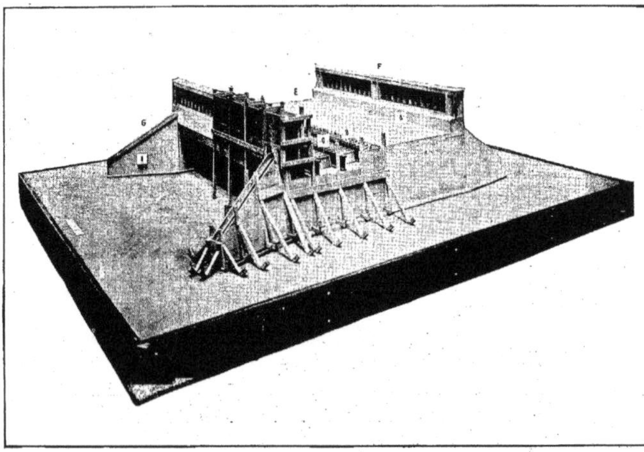

FIG. 1.—MODEL SHOWING REINFORCED CONCRETE BRIDGE—INCASED I-BEAM TYPE.

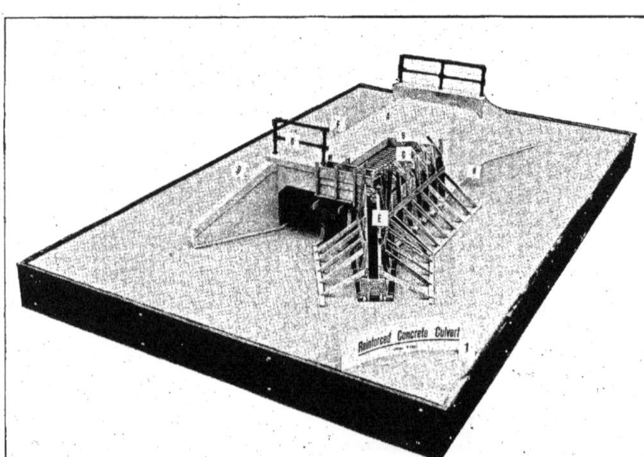

FIG. 2.—MODEL SHOWING REINFORCED CONCRETE CULVERT—SLAB TYPE.

MODEL SHOWING ROADSIDE TREATMENT.

depth made such that footing will extend to rock, hardpan, or other suitable foundation material; where rock is not found the depth is governed by character of soil and topographical features).

The concrete is made of Portland cement, clean sand, and hard broken stone or gravel, mixed in the following proportions:

Superstructure, 1:2:4 (size of stone, ¼ to 1 inch).
Abutments above footings, 1:2½:5 (size of stone, ¼ to 2½ inches).
Footings, 1:3:6 (size of stone, ¼ to 2½ inches).

Plate XII, figure 2, represents a reinforced concrete culvert having a span of 8 feet and height of 4 feet, with 24-foot width of roadway. Lettered cards are used to designate the parts, as follows:

A, reinforced concrete floor slab, 10½ inches in thickness; B, ⅝-inch twisted steel bars, 1½ inches from the underside of the floor slab, spaced 6 inches center to center and parallel to the center line of the roadway (there are also ½-inch twisted steel bars, 12 inches center to center, extending the full width of the bridge perpendicularly to the center line of the roadway); C, abutment wall (thickness at top, 13 inches; thickness at base, 1 foot 10 inches); D, wing walls (thickness at top, 10 inches; thickness at base, 1 foot 1 inch to 2 feet 3½ inches); E, forms (framing, 2 by 4 inches, 3 feet on centers; boards, 1¾ by 8 inches); F, pipe railing (2-inch galvanized-iron pipe protected by painting); G, concrete parapet (top thickness, 1 foot 6 inches); H, footing (2 feet 6 inches wide by 3 feet or more in depth, depending on foundation material).

The concrete is made of Portland cement, clean sand, and hard broken stone or gravel, mixed in the following proportions:

Superstructure, 1:2:4 (size of stone, ¼ to 1 inch).
Abutments above footings, 1:2½:5 (size of stone, ¼ to 2½ inches).
Footings, 1:3:6 (size of stone, ¼ to 2½ inches).

Any kind of surfacing or pavement may be used over these bridges.

ROADSIDE TREATMENT.

Plate XIII has been designed to emphasize various methods of roadside treatment. Well-trimmed trees furnish shade along the roads and aid in preventing the road surfaces from drying out and raveling. Neat signposts stand at the crossroads, and in place of a fence the house lawn is divided from the road by a sightly hedge. The use of the guardrail is shown, with the concrete retaining wall where the road follows the creek bank. A well-constructed concrete arch bridge is a feature of the model. The slopes of the fill extending from the bridge to the crossroad are sodded to prevent slides. Traffic on the fill is protected by double guardrails.

The schoolhouse represents a type of the modern consolidated country school. Its concrete walk to the road furnishes a good example in the use of the small culvert where the walk leads over the ditch before reaching the road. This same use of the culvert is made at the driveway entrance to the house. Architectural features of Monticello, the former home of Thomas Jefferson, were followed in the construction of this dwelling. The rustic summer house and the spring house in its cool white furnish pleasing sights across the fields, which have been cleared of undergrowth and left with only a few well-placed trees and shrubs.

ROAD MACHINERY.

Many good roads were built before the invention of road-building machinery, but modern machinery has done much to simplify the process and reduce the cost of road construction. The power-driven road roller has made possible the construction of a macadam road in a few days or weeks, where formerly traffic was required to make its way laboriously over the loose stones for months before the surface became even reasonably consolidated.

The steam road roller was invented by M. Louis Lemoine, of Bordeaux, France. The French Government granted him a patent in 1859. The first English patent was granted to Messrs. Clark and Bathe in 1863. The first steam road roller used in the United States was imported from England in 1868, and its first use was on the United States arsenal grounds in Philadelphia.

The stone crusher has greatly reduced the labor of preparing broken stone. It was the invention, in 1858, of Eli Whitney Blake, of New Haven, Conn. He was a nephew of Eli Whitney, the inventor of the cotton gin. Mr. Blake's crusher was used first in Central Park, New York City, in crushing rock for concrete. In 1859 the city of Hartford, Conn., purchased one of these crushers for use in the improvement of its streets and roads. This was the first successful application of mechanical power to breaking stone for road-building purposes.

CRUSHER PLANT.

Figure 1, represents a portable stone-crusher plant. A crusher plant is indispensable in the construction of first-class broken-stone roads, and if such work is to be done well and cheaply the plant must be complete and conveniently arranged.

Sometimes the crusher can be located so near the quarry that the rock may be sent down grade in tramcars and delivered to the mouth of the crusher by gravity, thus saving much hand labor. The crusher should be provided with an elevator for delivering the broken stone to the screen, which separates the material into proper sizes. The screen should be in three sections. The first section usually contains openings 1 inch in diameter. Through these openings the fragments of stone known as "screenings" drop into a bin corresponding to that marked A in the model. The openings of the second section of screen are 2 inches in diameter. The stones which pass through these openings into bin B are called No. 2 stone. The third or last section of screen has 3-inch openings, passing No. 1 stone into bin C. The tailings, or larger stones, will be forced through the opening at the end of the screen, from which they will drop into the tailings conveyor, to be crushed finally or eliminated from the work. The jaws of the crusher should be set so as to make as few tailings as possible. The sizes of these screen openings may vary, according to the quality of the stone. For instance, in crushing a hard stone, the openings of each section may be of slightly smaller diameter, since it is customary

FIG. 1.—Model of portable crushing plant in operation.

to crush a hard stone to somewhat smaller grades than a softer material.

When soft stones are being crushed, a dust jacket having a ¼-inch mesh may be placed over the first section to eliminate dust from the screenings. The bins A, B, and C, for receiving the various sizes of crushed rock, should be provided with slanting metal bottoms and sliding doors, so that the material may be loaded into wagons by gravity.

Two types of crusher are commonly used, one the jaw crusher, shown in figure 1, and the other the gyratory crusher. The jaw crusher is generally used for portable plants. In this machine one of the jaws moves backward and forward by means of a toggle joint and an eccentric, and the stone descends as the jaw recedes. As the jaw returns it grips the stone and crushes it. The maximum size of the product is determined by the distance between the jaw plates at the lower edge.

The essential feature of the gyratory crusher consists of a perpendicular iron shaft which revolves with an eccentric motion. Around the top of the shaft, which is conically shaped, is a hollow iron receptacle somewhat resembling an inverted bell. By the eccentric motion of the shaft the conical portion crushes the rock alternately against different sides of the inner surface of the bell.

FIG. 2.—Model of road grader.

ROAD GRADERS.

Figure 2 shows in miniature a road grader which is used in building earth roads and in preparing the subgrade for hard-surfaced roads. The frame supports an adjustable scraper blade, the front end of which may be used to plow a furrow, while the rear end pushes the earth along the surface of the blade toward the center of the road or distributes it smoothly. The blade may be set at any angle or tilted either backward or forward according to the work to be done.

It is advisable to use the grader when the ground is soft, preferably in the early summer, in order to give the loose earth time to settle and pack before the fall rains begin. If the work is done in the fall not more than 3 or 4 inches of loose earth should be put on at one working.

ADDITIONAL COPIES
OF THIS PUBLICATION MAY BE PROCURED FROM
THE SUPERINTENDENT OF DOCUMENTS
GOVERNMENT PRINTING OFFICE
WASHINGTON, D. C.
AT
15 CENTS PER COPY
▽

BULLETIN OF THE U.S. DEPARTMENT OF AGRICULTURE

No. 221

Contribution from the Bureau of Entomology, L. O. Howard, Chief.
June 16, 1915.

(PROFESSIONAL PAPER.)

THE SOUTHERN CORN LEAF-BEETLE.[1]

By E. O. G. Kelly,
Entomological Assistant, Cereal and Forage Insect Investigations.

CONTENTS.

INTRODUCTION.

The southern corn leaf-beetle (*Myochrous denticollis* Say) has become a pest of considerable importance during the last few years and has commanded the attention of entomologists on several occasions. Although the habits of this beetle are not fully known, it seems advisable to publish the known facts and suggest possible remedies.

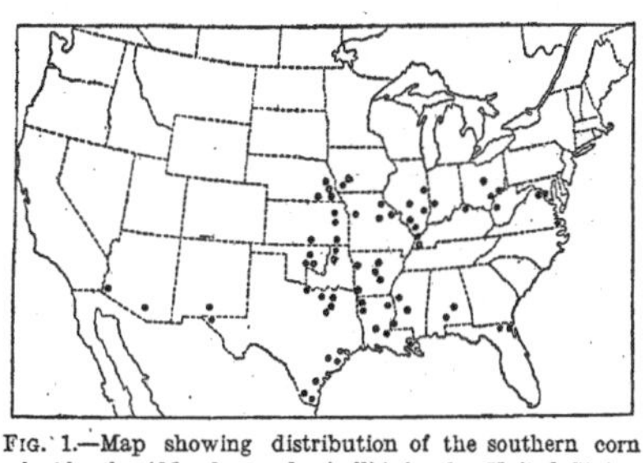

Fig. 1.—Map showing distribution of the southern corn leaf-beetle (*Myochrous denticollis*) in the United States. (Original.)

The writer's attention was first called to the destructive habits of these beetles in the summer of 1905, while investigating insects injurious to corn in southern Illinois. At that time numbers of adults were found feeding on grains of roasting ears in cornfields in the bottom lands of the Ohio River. Since being located by the Bureau of Entomology in southern Kansas the writer has watched this little beetle and as occasion offered made close investigation of its habits and life history. The occurrence of

[1] *Myochrous denticollis* Say; order Coleoptera, family Chrysomelidæ.

Note.—This bulletin is of especial interest to entomologists in the southern half of the United States.

numbers of beetles near Wellington, Kans., in 1910, and again in 1913, together with an outbreak in northern Texas in the spring of 1910, and in eastern Arkansas in 1913 and 1914, afforded material and opportunity for further extensive investigations.

Numbers of the larvæ have from time to time been found in the soil, always in close proximity to corn roots which were more or less eaten, but in no instance have they actually been observed feeding on corn roots, although especial attention has been given their feeding habits.

HISTORY.

In the Report of the Commissioner of Agriculture for 1887, Prof. F. M. Webster (Webster, 1887), then a special agent of the Division of Entomology, stated that beetles were observed in Louisiana during April in considerable numbers in fields of young corn. They were found in soil about the stems and attacking the young corn plants by gnawing the outside of the stems, without doing serious injury. His report on a later outbreak at Cheshire, Ohio, in 1900, was the first record of their having done serious damage (Webster, 1900). Since that time, however, they have been reported as having done serious injury at several points in Kansas, notably in the vicinity of Douglas, in 1905, as reported by E. S. Tucker (Tucker, 1905). The writer observed that they did considerable damage to young corn at Wellington, Kans., in 1910 and 1913, and severe damage in the neighborhood of Paris, Ark., in 1913, where several hundred acres of young corn were destroyed in early May, necessitating replanting—the second planting also suffering severely. Again, in 1914, serious damage was done in western Arkansas, but none was recorded in Kansas.

Mr. T. D. Urbahns reported slight injury to young corn in the vicinity of Plano, Tex., in April, 1909. The adults were cutting the edges of young corn leaves, leaving them quite ragged. The infested field was one which had been planted to cotton the previous year and was of the same type of soil as a heavy timbered stretch of black land adjacent.

Mr. Vernon King reported that the beetles had ruined several acres of young corn on farms near Charleston, Mo., in May, 1913, stating that the beetles were more numerous on black soil; in fact, none at all was found on light sandy soil. From one to four adults were observed on each plant and the plants were literally reduced to fragments. (See Pl. I, figs. 1 and 2.) The infested fields were those of recent clearing in bottom lands.

During April and early May, 1915, a second serious invasion of this species took place in this same locality. Mr. King having resigned, the second investigation was carried out by Mr. E. H. Gibson, who used the poisoned-bran bait with good success in destroying the beetles, applying it about the hills of corn where the beetles were at work.

Observations in both Louisiana and Ohio by Prof. Webster (Webster, 1901) and in Kansas, Texas, and Arkansas by the writer seem to indicate that the insect occurs in destructive abundance on lands that have previously been devoted to pasture or lands that have been allowed to lapse into a semiwild condition, not having been cultivated for several years.

DISTRIBUTION.

The species is widely distributed over the southern half of the United States, extending from the extreme southeastern part of Arizona to southern Texas, becoming more numerous directly north of Brownsville, thence northward to southern Iowa, and eastward to northern Illinois and central Ohio and to Washington, D. C., the most southeastern point recorded being in northern Florida. This insect has not been reported from Tennessee, North Carolina, South Carolina, or Georgia, but evidently it may occur in these States. (See map, fig. 1.)

Prof. F. M. Webster (Webster, 1901) remarks in regard to the distribution of other species—

> *Myochrous squamosus* ranges from northern Arizona and New Mexico to the Platte River in Nebraska and northwest into Montana, probably through western South Dakota and Wyoming. *Myochrous longulus*, the only remaining species to be mentioned, is known to range from southern California and Arizona northward into Colorado, where it has been reported to Dr. Le Conte, without exact locality. It not unlikely occurs also in Utah, although it has not yet been reported from there in the literature, so far as I am able to learn, but in any case overlapping the territory inhabited by *Myochrous squamosus* in northern Arizona and New Mexico, and also probably in Colorado, while the latter species borders on and possibly mingles with *Myochrous denticollis* in southwestern Arizona, eastern New Mexico, western Kansas, and extreme southeastern Nebraska.

DESCRIPTION AND LIFE-HISTORY NOTES.

The insect was described by Dr. Thomas Say in 1824 (Say, 1824) under the name of *Colaspis denticollis*, from specimens collected in Missouri. Dr. Say did not mention any food plant in connection with his description. It was first described as an insect pest to growing corn by Prof. F. M. Webster (Webster, 1901).

THE EGG.

The egg (fig. 2) is small, oval, pale yellow, and about 0.036 of an inch in length and 0.015 of an inch in diameter. The surface is smooth and slightly glistening. The female deposits her eggs in clusters of from 10 to 50 in the field, carefully placing them in small pieces of weeds, hollow straws, in crevices, in clods of dirt, but always near corn plants.

Close searching in the neighborhood of plants other than corn has failed to reveal them, although the beetles have been noted feeding on other plants at egg-laying time. In the laboratory, under artificial conditions, the eggs will hatch in from 6 to 10 days, rarely going as long as 15 days. Eggs have been observed from early April in northern Texas till the middle of May in Kansas.

THE LARVA.

The newly-hatched larvæ are nearly cylindrical, about 1 mm. long and 0.03 mm. in diameter, tapering slightly and becoming somewhat flattened toward the posterior extremity. They are pale yellow, except the first thoracic segment and head, which are creamy white. The head is a little broader than the thorax, and the body is covered with downy hairs. Within five days after the hatching the larvæ become a creamy white, which color is retained until maturity.

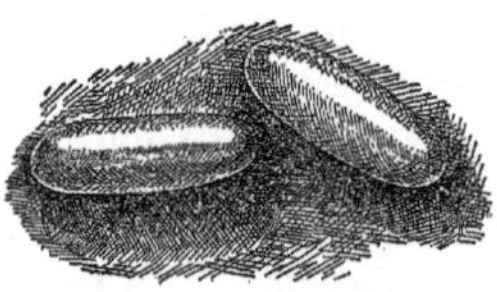

FIG. 2.—The southern corn leaf-beetle: Eggs. (Original.)

The mature larvæ (fig. 3) are 6 to 8 mm. in length and about 2 mm. in diameter. The head is slightly smaller than the thorax, the body becoming a little larger toward the anal extremity. The thoracic segments bear stout legs, and beginning with the second abdominal segment the next seven segments each bear a pair of ambulatory processes (fig. 3, *a*) which terminate in a long hair, accompanied by four shorter hairs. The anal plate (fig. 3, *b*) consists of five parts, which are very characteristic of this species and form a character which separates it from all other larvæ of the Eumolpini group.

During the last six years the writer and other members of the Bureau of Entomology have been making efforts to rear the larvæ of this species from egg to maturity, in order to determine definitely its food plant and exact life history. In the laboratory almost every form of receptacle has been used that could be devised, from a tiny vial with several kinds of food in it, fitted with blotting paper to absorb undue moisture, to flowerpots buried in the soil, which it was thought might simulate more natural conditions.

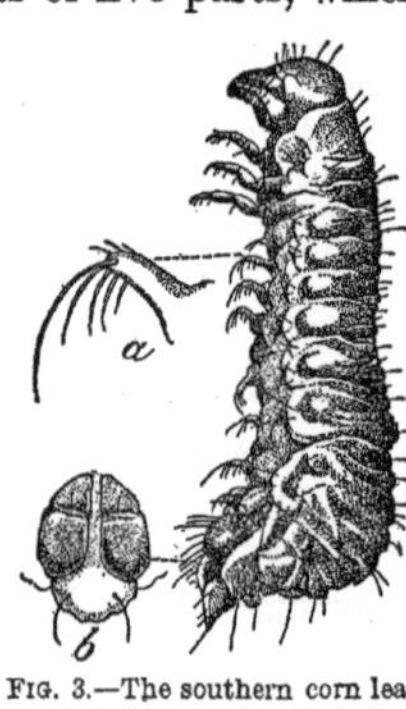

FIG. 3.—The southern corn leaf-beetle: Larva. *a*, Ambulatory process; *b*, anal plate. (Original.)

The list of growing plants involved in these experiments is as follows: Cocklebur (*Xanthium spinosum*), smartweed (*Persicaria hydropiper*), Japan clover (*Lespedeza striata*), crab grass (*Syntherisma sanguinale*), sorghum (*Sorghum vulgare*), alfalfa (*Medicago sativa*), cotton (*Gossypium* sp.), corn (*Zea mays*), wheat (*Triticum vulgare*), bluegrass (*Poa pratensis*), pigweed (*Chenopodium* sp.), and barnyard grass (*Echino-*

chloa crus-galli). Kernels of wheat and corn which had been soaked in water, pieces of decaying straws, corn pith, and toadstools were also tried, with negative results.

A few larvæ, fed on a combination of decaying corn pith and growing cornroots, failed to mature, probably for other reasons than lack of proper food, but were sufficiently large for use in identifying those collected in the field.

Numerous searches have been made in cornfields, wheat fields, grass, and fields grown up with weeds, and the larvæ have not yet been found feeding on plants other than corn. Larvæ have been found in the soil in cornfields where cocklebur and corn plants were growing together, and where corn was growing alone, but in no other situation.

The first larvæ found in the field were observed by Mr. T. H. Parks and the writer at Wellington, Kans., on July 20, 1910, in small round earthen cells from 4 to 6 inches deep, with a tiny burrow leading toward the cornroots, which had been more or less eaten. The larvæ hastily retreated to safety and feigned death when disturbed. By way of further determining this habit, a larva was allowed to crawl on the surface of the soil, when on suddenly jarring the soil several inches from it it hastily retreated and "folded up." Although a diligent search was made for feeding larvæ during the following days of July and up until the middle of August, none was found, though numbers of larvæ were unearthed.

The field in which the larvæ were first found is the dark waxy second bottom land which becomes very gummy and sticky during wet weather and very hard during dry weather. The outbreaks and damage reported by Prof. Webster, Mr. Tucker, and Mr. King and those observed by the writer in Kansas, Texas, and Arkansas have all been on soil of this character. In sandy or light soils very few larvæ or pupæ have been found and correspondingly few injured cornroots have been observed.

From the laboratory notes made at Brownsville, Tex., latitude 26°, by Mr. R. A. Vickery, it appears that the larval period probably extends from about April 1 to about June 15, while the writer's observations at Plano, Tex., latitude 33°, and at Paris, Ark., latitude 35°, show that the larval period ranges from April 15 to July 1, and at Wellington, Kans., latitude 37°, from May 1 to July 15.

In the bottom lands of the Arkansas River, near Paris, Ark., the larvæ had pupated and practically all the adults had issued by July 22, 1914, indicating that they began pupating as early as July 1. In the vicinity of Wellington, Kans., the larvæ began to pupate about the middle of July, pupæ being found as early as July 20 and as late as August 14. The period for maturing the pupa seems to be about 15 days, although no exact data have been obtained.

THE PUPA.

The first pupæ (fig. 4) to be found were in earthen cells in the soil near corn plants at depths of from 4 to 6 inches. The finding of pupæ which were nearly mature at this time, some of which changed to adults by the next morning, indicated that the larvæ had finished feeding and were in their pupal cells.

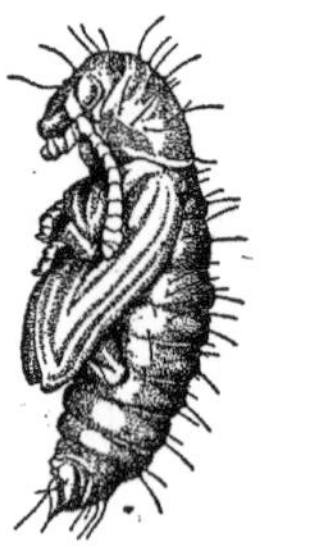

FIG. 4.—The southern corn leaf-beetle: Pupa. (Original.)

The pupa is white until within one day of maturity, when it begins to darken.

In dorsal view the head is bent ventrad; the bristles on the head are prominent and irregularly placed in a double row on the median dorsal line; there is a single row of setæ above the plural suture; the eighth abdominal segment has a semicircular row of setæ and the anal segment is supplied with a stout, curved spine; each abdominal segment bears several stout setæ on the dorsum. In lateral view the body is longer than wide, tapering from the fifth abdominal segment; the antennæ are directed dorsad around the femora of the two front pairs of legs, thence backward with the tips lying near the claws of the middle legs and on top of them; the elytra and wings are rather short, thick, tapering toward the tip, and folded over the posterior legs, the tarsi of which reach the eighth segment. In ventral view the head is as long as the thorax, directed forward, with the front lying between the tarsi of the front pair of legs; the elytra and the tarsi nearly meet ventrally, forming a deep ventral groove. The pupa is 5 to 6 mm. long and from 3 to 3.5 mm. wide.

THE ADULT.

FIG. 5.—The southern corn leaf-beetle: Adult. (Original.)

To the average farmer the beetles (fig. 5) can be recognized as small, dark brownish beetles, more or less covered with bits of soil. They are about three-sixteenths of an inch long and about one-third as wide. They have the habit of dropping from their food plant to the ground and hiding when disturbed, and owing to this habit they are very rarely seen. Quite often farmers have noticed seriously damaged young corn, the plants being literally in fragments, and have been unable to locate the cause on account of this habit of the beetles of dropping to the ground and hiding. It is sometimes difficult even for trained entomologists to locate them.

Dr. Thomas Say (Say, 1824) described the adult as follows:

Body black, slightly bronzed, covered with dense, robust cinereous hairs; antennæ dull rufous at base; thorax with three equal, equidistant teeth on the lateral edge; elytra, lateral edge minutely dentated; tip simple; anterior tibiæ and posterior thighs one-toothed. Length, nearly one-fifth of an inch.

The beetle seems to prefer to feed early in the morning, late in the evening, or at night, or on cloudy days; very rarely it feeds during the heat of the day, and at this time of the day it is generally found under clods of dirt or down beneath the leaves of the plants.

HIBERNATION.

The adult beetles issue from pupal cells about the middle of July in central Arkansas and the 1st of August in southern Kansas, emergence extending over a period of about one month. They do considerable feeding on the kernels of unripe ears of corn and buds of cocklebur before entering hibernation, which begins early in the fall. They have been observed by Mr. W. R. McConnell hibernating under piles of corn husks, in fodder shocks, in cornfields, and also in clumps of *Andropogon scoparius*, *Andropogon virginicus*, and *Cyperus rotundus*. Mr. A. H. Rosenfeld (Rosenfeld, 1911) found one adult hibernating in Spanish moss (*Tillandsia usneoides*).

Adults were found in hibernation in the fall of 1913 throughout bottom-land cornfields near Paris, Ark., these being the same fields that had been devastated the previous spring. In a large cotton field adjacent to one of these cornfields beetles were found in large numbers under piles of rubbish, in the open unpicked cotton bolls, and a large number were found lying on the ground beneath a large pile of recently picked cotton.

While investigating the hibernation of this insect in central Arkansas the writer's attention was called to a cotton gin from the dirt spout of which the beetles were being shaken from cotton which was then being brought in from the fields for ginning. A double handful of living beetles were thus collected in a short time. The manager of the cotton gin informed the writer that he had been noticing these beetles since early fall and that they were more numerous in late November. This cotton gin was located in the Arkansas River bottoms and only such cotton as was grown in the immediate vicinity was ginned.

After leaving this locality, the writer visited a gin located near the edge of the foothills, where both hill-land cotton and bottom-land cotton were being ginned. The bottom-land cotton produced a few beetles, but the upland cotton was apparently free from them. In the town of Paris, two large cotton gins were visited and searched for this beetle, but owing to the fact that most of the cotton they were receiving at this time was from the hill land, none of the beetles could be found. However, in the pile of rubbish and dirt at the side of the gin which had been thrown from the dirt auger several fragments of dead beetles were found. The manager of this gin could not give any information regarding the occurrence of the beetles. He had noticed, however, some large brown cases which occurred rather numerously early in the fall, probably the pupal cases of the cotton leaf-worm (*Alabama argillacea* Hübn.).

CROPS DAMAGED.

Corn is the only cultivated crop that has been known to be attacked in sufficient numbers to cause serious damage. The beetles, upon first emerging from hibernation in the early spring, attack very young cocklebur and early volunteer corn, the crop not having been planted at that time.

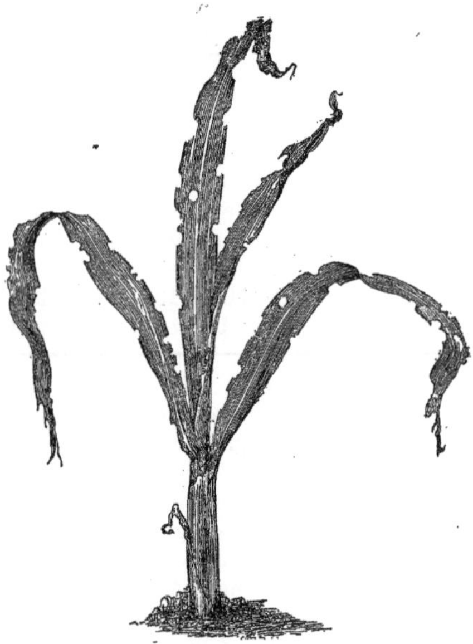

FIG. 6.—Young corn plant showing work of adult of the southern corn leaf-beetle. (Original.)

Besides corn, the beetles have been observed by the writer to attack the young leaves and growing shoots of cocklebur, smartweed, Japan clover, and crab grass. Mr. Vickery has observed them feeding on sorghum and alfalfa—on the latter plant, however, only in rearing cages in the laboratory. Mr. W. R. McConnell has found them feeding on sorghum in the field and also on *Alopecurus geniculatus*. Some of the agents of the branch of Southern Field Crop Insect Investigations have observed them feeding on the cotton plant.

The ragged appearance of the corn plant (fig. 6) is indicative of their presence, especially the notched edges of the leaves, and where the beetles appear in sufficient numbers to devastate a field these notches become so numerous that the plant dies. (Pl. II.) The early planting seems to be the one most seriously affected, although the second planting on the farm of a Mr. Baskins and on other farms near Paris, Ark., was about 50 per cent damaged in 1913, the

FIG. 1.—CORNFIELD DEVASTATED BY ADULTS OF THE SOUTHERN CORN LEAF-BEETLE. (FROM WEBSTER.)

FIG. 2.—CORNER OF SAME FIELD AFTER SECOND PLANTING. (FROM WEBSTER.)

WORK OF THE SOUTHERN CORN LEAF-BEETLE (MYOCHROUS DENTICOLLIS).

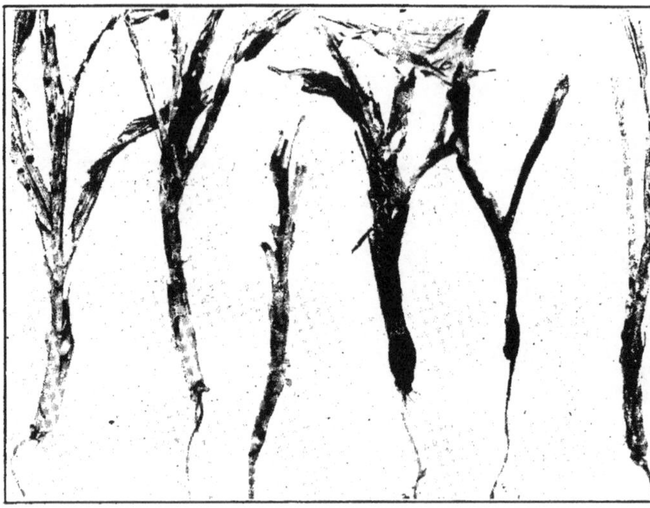

FIG. 1.—YOUNG CORN PLANTS KILLED BY ADULTS OF THE SOUTHERN CORN LEAF-BEETLE. (ORIGINAL.)

FIG. 2.—CORN PLANT COMPLETELY DESTROYED BY THE SOUTHERN CORN LEAF-BEETLE. (ORIGINAL.)

WORK OF THE SOUTHERN CORN LEAF-BEETLE.

first planting having been entirely destroyed. The devastation of 1914 was very severe but not so heavy as in 1913.

Considerable search on cotton and wheat growing in the vicinity of infested cornfields near Paris, Ark., developed no damage to these crops.

DISSEMINATION.

The beetles have powerful wings and have been observed in fields long distances from where they originated. Especially was this true in one instance, during the fall of 1910, where it was positively known that they developed in certain bottom-land fields, later migrating 2 miles to a field of late upland corn, where great numbers of them were found feeding upon the belated ears. In this last-mentioned field the farmer planted wheat and in the operation the drill raked up piles of the corn leaves, among which great numbers of the beetles hibernated during the following winter. Counts made the following spring, before they left hibernating quarters, indicated that about 80 per cent of these beetles survived the winter. A lot of the dead beetles were kept for parasites, but no parasites developed. From these hibernating quarters beetles emerged in this same field in late March, after the weather had become warm. They were noticed flying in a northerly direction, though just where they went could not be determined.

It does not seem to the writer that an outbreak of this insect is brought about by the growing of any particular crop on a certain field, but it would appear that an outbreak is very likely to follow where a field has been allowed to lie idle, especially so if allowed to grow cocklebur and volunteer corn for a year or more and to become very weedy and foul, thus affording hibernating quarters.

The fact that adults have been found hibernating in grasslands, in which situation larvæ have never been found, indicates that they do not necessarily hibernate in the field in which they breed, and furthermore that they do fly away from their breeding grounds.

REMEDIES.

A great number of beetles have been taken at lights, which would indicate that a powerful light trap situated in the vicinity of the infested field might materially reduce them. In the early fall, when they are flying in search of hibernating quarters, it is possible that the light trap would catch large numbers.

Judging from the conditions of fields in which they have been observed hibernating in large numbers, the cleaning up of all rubbish in the cornfields early in the fall, especially in fields for very late corn, would prove an effective remedy as a protection for the succeeding crop. The fact that large numbers were observed in the vicinity of cotton gins would suggest that the managers of cotton gins might use their rubbish and trash for boiler fuel and thus destroy a great number of the beetles.

Ordinarily the beetles attack a field of corn when it is very young and destroy it before the farmer becomes aware of their presence. No remedy has been found that can be recommended in combating them after they enter the cornfield. If the crop is so badly damaged as to be worthless it can be replanted with safety from damage by this insect about one month after the regular planting time. Within a few days after they have killed out the first planting they will leave the field, thus making it safe to replant.

From all the writer has been able to observe or learn the beetles leave their hibernating quarters in early spring, depositing their eggs about young corn plants as soon as these are available for their purpose. It would also appear that the season of oviposition is prolonged and that it is these overwintering beetles that feed upon and destroy the corn plants while thus engaged. This would lead to the somewhat anomalous assumption that the parent beetle under stress of hunger destroys the food plant of the larvæ, which if true would account for the very erratic occurrence of the outbreaks of this pest.

As an additional suggestion, the fact that the beetles appear and disappear with considerable regularity from south to north, taken together with the fact that corn planted three or four weeks after the usual planting season has escaped attack of the beetle, would indicate that something might be gained by delaying corn planting in localities where beetles have been injurious the previous year.

Mr. E. H. Gibson, in his experimental work with this species in the vicinity of Charleston, Mo., during late April and early May, 1915, reports having found that, after repeated trials under varying conditions, carried out with check experiments, the beetles can be readily destroyed by a poisoned-bran bait, consisting of 25 pounds of wheat bran, 1 pound of Paris green, 1 gallon of low-grade molasses, and the juices of 3 oranges, with enough water to bring the mixture to a stiff dough. The best success in the use of this poisoned bait was obtained when applied in the late afternoon. It would seem that this measure might be an extremely practical one if applied to the restricted areas from which the beetles frequently spread, the bait being scattered lightly on the ground among the plants where the beetles are at work.

LITERATURE CITED.

POPENOE, E. A. A list of Kansas Coleoptera. *In* Trans. Kans. Acad. Sci., v. 5, p. 21–40, 1877.

ROSENFELD, A. H. Insects and spiders in Spanish moss. *In* Jour. Econ. Ent., v. 4, no. 4, p. 398–409, August, 1911.

SAY, THOMAS. Descriptions of coleopterous insects collected in the late expedition to the Rocky Mountains. *In* Jour. Phila. Acad. Nat. Sci., v. 3, p. 403–462, 1824. (Say's Complete Writings, v. 2, N. Y., 1859., p. 215.)
Colaspis denticollis, p. 448.

TUCKER, E. S. Some insect pests to be treated by fall plowing. The southern corn-leaf beetle. (*Myochrous denticollis*, Say.) *In* Kans. Farmer, v. 43, no. 44, p. 1112, Nov. 2, 1905.

TUCKER, E. S. Random notes on entomological field work. *In* Canad. Ent., v. 43, no. 1, p. 22–32, January, 1911.
Myochrous denticollis, p. 27.

WEBSTER, F. M. Report on the season's observations and especially upon corn insects. *In* Rpt. U. S. Comr. Agr. for 1887, p. 147–154.
Myochrous denticollis, p. 150.

WEBSTER, F. M. Insects of the year in Ohio. U. S. Dept. Agr., Div. Ent., Bul. 26, new ser.; p. 84–90, 1900.
Myochrous denticollis, p. 87.

WEBSTER, F. M. The southern corn-leaf beetle; a new insect pest of growing corn. *In* Jour. N. Y. Ent. Soc., v. 9, no. 3, p. 127–132, pl. VII–IX, September, 1901.

ADDITIONAL COPIES
OF THIS PUBLICATION MAY BE PROCURED FROM
THE SUPERINTENDENT OF DOCUMENTS
GOVERNMENT PRINTING OFFICE
WASHINGTON, D. C.
AT
5 CENTS PER COPY
▽

UNITED STATES DEPARTMENT OF AGRICULTURE

BULLETIN No. 222

Contribution from the Bureau of Plant Industry
WM. A. TAYLOR, Chief

Washington, D. C. | May 24, 1915

BARLEY IN THE GREAT PLAINS AREA

RELATION OF CULTURAL METHODS TO PRODUCTION

By

E. C. CHILCOTT, Agriculturist in Charge, and J. S. COLE and W. W. BURR, Assistants, Office of Dry-Land Agriculture

CONTENTS

WASHINGTON
GOVERNMENT PRINTING OFFICE
1915

BULLETIN OF THE U.S. DEPARTMENT OF AGRICULTURE

No. 222

Contribution from the Bureau of Plant Industry, Wm. A. Taylor, Chief.
May 24, 1915.

BARLEY IN THE GREAT PLAINS AREA: RELATION OF CULTURAL METHODS TO PRODUCTION.

By E. C. Chilcott, *Agriculturist in Charge*, and J. S. Cole and W. W. Burr, *Assistants, Office of Dry-Land Agriculture.*[1]

CONTENTS.

INTRODUCTION.

In this bulletin are given the data obtained from different methods of seed-bed preparation for barley and a study of the cost of production under each of the various methods. Investigations have been

[1] All of the members of the scientific staff of the Office of Dry-Land Agriculture have contributed more or less to this paper by having charge of field investigations and by assisting in the preparation of data for records or for publication. The scientific staff as at present constituted consists of the following members, named in the order of length of service: W. W. Burr, Denver, Colo.; E. F. Chilcott, Woodward, Okla.; O. J. Grace, Akron, Colo.; J. S. Cole, Denver, Colo.; J. M. Stephens, Moccasin, Mont.; A. L. Hallsted, Hays, Kans.; O. R. Mathews, Belle Fourche, S. Dak.; J. C. Thysell, Dickinson, N. Dak.; M. Pfaender, Mandan, N. Dak.; H. C. McKinstry, Hettinger, N. Dak.; W. M. Osborn, North Platte, Nebr.; W. D. Griggs, Dalhart, Tex.; C. A. Burmeister, Amarillo, Tex.; J. E. Mundell, Big Spring, Tex.; F. L. Kelso, Ardmore, S. Dak.; W. A. Peterson, Mandan, N. Dak.; J. T. Sarvis, Ardmore, S. Dak.; G. W. Morgan, Huntley, Mont.; J. H. Jacobson, Mitchell, Nebr.; H. G. Smith, Tucumcari, N. Mex.; L. N. Jensen, Woodward, Okla.; J. G. Lill, Garden City, Kans.; R. S. Towle, Edgeley, N. Dak.; A. J. Ogaard, Williston, N. Dak.; C. B. Brown, Dalhart, Tex.; L. D. Willey, Archer, Wyo.; J. B. Kuska, Colby, Kans.; and A. E. Seamans, Akron, Colo.

The following-named men have held positions on the scientific staff of the Office of Dry-Land Agriculture during the past nine years, but have resigned or have been transferred to other offices of the Department of Agriculture: Sylvester Balz, F. L. Kennard, J. E. Payne, L. E. Hazen, C. A. Jensen, H. R. Reed, W. O. Whitcomb, C. H. Plath, F. Knorr, and R. W. Edwards.

The data here reported from the stations in Kansas, Nebraska, North Dakota, and Montana have been obtained in cooperation with the agricultural experiment stations of their respective States. In South Dakota, Colorado, Texas, Oklahoma, and New Mexico the stations are operated by the United States Department of Agriculture.

Field, office, and laboratory facilities, teams, and implements have been provided by the Office of Western Irrigation Agriculture, at Huntley, Mont., Belle Fourche, S. Dak., and Mitchell, Nebr., and by the Office of Cereal Investigations at Amarillo, Tex., and Archer, Wyo. The Biophysical Laboratory has cooperated in obtaining the meteorological data reported.

Note.—This bulletin is intended for all who are interested in the agricultural possibilities of the Great Plains area.

87710°—Bull. 222—15——1

conducted at fourteen different stations in the Great Plains area. Barley has been grown to a minor extent in the rotations at all stations, although it has not been considered as important a crop as either wheat or oats.

At some of the stations the work has been continuous for eight years; at other stations it has been but recently started. The results of the first year's work at any station are not used, as the land is uniform in preparation for all plats. From the stations having the longer records the results are the most valuable, since they include a greater range of climatic conditions. Where a short record is given it can show only the effect of the different tillage methods under the particular combinations of climatic factors obtaining during that time. The crop on any series of plats having the same methods of tillage may behave quite differently under the combinations of climatic factors that may occur in succeeding years. The relative position assumed by the various methods in the first year's results may or may not be changed from that arrangement by subsequent work. It is certain, however, that the range of difference between the methods will vary with changing climatic factors. Wide differences in yields between methods that may be shown in a short record will tend to be narrowed as the length of the record is increased.

The method of work adopted was that of raising the standard crops of each station both in rotations and by different methods of preparation under systems of continuous cropping. In no case have rotations requiring more than six years been used. Those of even this length have been tried only when sod of tame-grass crops is included. More of the work has been done with 3-year and 4-year rotations.

In this bulletin are shown only the crop immediately preceding and the tillage involved in preparing the seed bed for barley. In the present stage of development of the work the effect of the immediately preceding crop and of the method of handling its stubble in preparing the seed bed greatly overshadows the effects of the rotations considered as units. Some of the rotations are calculated to conserve or to accumulate fertility and organic matter in the soil, while others may perhaps deplete it, but on the naturally fertile soils of the Plains such results are not strongly shown in the first years of treatment. The controllable factors that exert the greatest influence on production are the water supply, the physical condition of the seed bed, and a recognized, if not understood, effect of the immediately preceding crop. The crop of a single year brings the land back to so near uniformity in these factors that their probable residual effect is not great enough with the work in hand to introduce serious error into the study here made.

This bulletin, which deals with only one crop, does not afford any criterion by which to judge the agricultural possibilities of any section of the region for other crops. The fact that the combination of soil and climatic conditions in certain sections is not favorable to the production of barley does not signify that such conditions will prove unfavorable to other crops.

IMPORTANCE OF BARLEY AS A GRAIN CROP.

In some sections of the region barley has not been considered strictly as a market crop, but rather as a feed crop. In certain parts of the Northwest it has been grown quite extensively as a market crop. The price is usually determined by the quality of the barley from a brewing standpoint, the demand being for a product that is uniform, well matured, and of good color. Certain sections of the dry-land regions afford opportunity to grow barley of good quality, especially in those years when conditions are favorable for the production of a good, plump berry. The dry weather, with the absence of dews, gives good conditions under which to harvest the crop without injury to quality or color. In the main, however, barley has been grown in the Great Plains as feed rather than as a market crop.

Barley has the advantage of requiring on the average a shorter growing season than either oats or wheat, and is, therefore, exposed for a shorter length of time to the unfavorable climatic conditions likely to occur. When seeded at approximately the same time as oats, it will ripen with or before the earliest oats. The variety of barley which is grown determines somewhat the length of the growing season, but the foregoing applies to the average barleys. Earliness of maturity may be of considerable importance in enabling a crop to escape drought.

AREA INCLUDED IN THESE INVESTIGATIONS.

The area included in these investigations covers a part of 10 States, viz, Montana, North Dakota, South Dakota, Wyoming, Nebraska, Colorado, Kansas, Oklahoma, Texas, and New Mexico. It extends from the ninety-eighth meridian of longitude to the foothills of the Rocky Mountains and from the Canadian border to the thirty-second parallel.

The altitude varies from approximately 1,400 feet in the northeastern part of the area to 6,000 feet at Cheyenne, Wyo. These represent the highest and the lowest altitudes. The southern portion of the territory has a higher average altitude and higher average rainfall and a correspondingly higher rate of evaporation than the northern portion. The average annual precipitation at the various stations varies from about 15 to 21 inches.

Figure 1 shows the location of the various field stations within the area which, as outlined, is bounded on the west by the 5,000-foot contour and does not include Archer, Wyo.

CLIMATIC CONDITIONS.

The climate of the Great Plains has been classified as semiarid. It may be better to say that it is changeable, varying from season to season from almost humid to almost arid, with a relatively low mean annual precipitation. Years of relatively high precipitation may be followed by years of relatively low precipitation. Other climatic factors usually correspond to the rainfall. A year of relatively high rainfall will have a lower rate of evaporation and higher relative humidity than will be found in the unfavorable years.

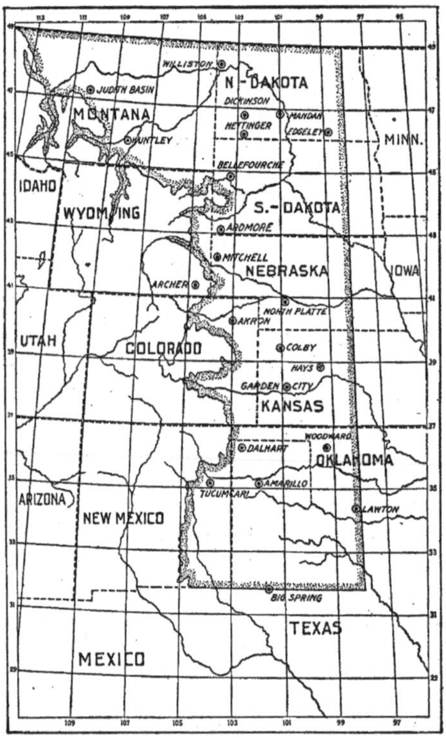

FIG. 1.—Sketch map of the Great Plains area, which includes parts of ten States and consists of about 400,000 square miles of territory. Its western boundary is indicated by the 5,000-foot contour. The location of each field station within the area is shown by a dot within a circle (⊙).

Another climatic factor of much importance in crop production on the Plains is the distribution of the rainfall, which within certain limits is more important than the total amount. A relatively low rainfall properly distributed may produce a crop where a much higher rainfall coming with unfavorable distribution may result in a crop failure, each starting with the same amount of available water in the soil. A vast difference in crop yields usually results from a soil that starts out in the spring with a small amount of stored moisture and one that is well supplied with moisture.

Space in this bulletin will not allow a full description or record of the climatic conditions at the various stations during the time covered by these investigations. These records are published by the United States Weather Bureau.

Seasonal variation in climatic factors is probably more important than difference in methods of tillage. This is shown by the fact that in some years climatic conditions at some stations are such that all methods result in failures. In other years all methods may give fair returns. At some stations the greatest actual increases in yield as a result of tillage methods is usually obtained under the most favorable climatic conditions. In Table I are given the maximum, minimum, and average annual and seasonal precipitation and seasonal evaporation. By seasonal is meant the time between the average seeding and the average harvesting dates. No attempt is made to show other climatic factors, though all are important.

TABLE I.—*Annual and seasonal precipitation and seasonal evaporation at fourteen stations in the Great Plains area.*[1]

Station.	Altitude (feet).[2]	Precipitation (inches).[3]						Seasonal evaporation (inches).[3]		
		Annual.			Seasonal.					
		Minimum.	Maximum.	Average.	Minimum.	Maximum.	Average.	Minimum.	Maximum.	Average.
Judith Basin	4,228	14.96	23.78	18.06	6.50	10.90	8.62	19.117	26.273	21.330
Huntley	3,000	11.92	11.92	11.92	5.00	7.35	6.18	19.820	20.594	20.207
Williston	1,875	10.28	18.99	14.84	5.62	12.00	8.31	21.104	28.269	24.705
Dickinson	2,543	11.93	21.22	16.69	5.31	16.27	10.06	18.379	27.366	22.377
Edgeley	1,468	11.94	21.95	16.71	5.08	15.73	9.60	17.664	25.362	20.657
Hettinger	2,253	12.72	15.68	14.20	8.82	12.89	10.69	20.111	24.248	22.430
Belle Fourche	2,950	6.64	17.73	13.11	1.92	12.75	6.82	23.627	33.906	27.220
Scottsbluff	3,950	13.77	18.51	16.14	5.56	8.26	7.11	24.698	26.647	25.718
North Platte	3,000	11.18	23.01	18.05	4.38	11.25	7.77	25.954	36.255	30.253
Akron	4,600	14.51	22.46	18.28	5.32	9.52	7.82	25.917	32.691	28.781
Hays	2,050	15.59	27.80	21.30	3.87	12.87	9.55	29.390	41.317	32.628
Garden City	2,900	11.82	23.58	18.54	5.01	8.16	6.85	33.315	38.926	35.332
Dalhart	4,000	13.69	16.35	15.11	4.54	14.86	8.17	33.381	41.002	38.596
Amarillo	3,676	10.69	27.80	18.28	5.03	11.49	7.05	32.305	40.704	36.709

[1] The years covered are the same as for the data shown in the other tables for each station.

[2] The altitude given is for the field where the work was done and is based in most cases on that of the nearest town.

[3] The record of annual precipitation for 1914 is not included. The records of seasonal precipitation and evaporation for 1914 are included for all stations, the evaporation being figured from Apr. 1 to July 31. The seasonal rainfall is the amount from Apr. 1 to July 31 for stations north of and including that at Belle Fourche. For stations south of Belle Fourche it is the amount between Mar. 1 and June 30. Evaporation measurements are made from a free water surface, in a tank sunk into the soil to almost its full depth. The water surface is kept about level with the surface of the ground.

GENERAL PLAN OF THE INVESTIGATIONS.

In the work at the various stations barley has been grown under a number of different tillage methods, but has not occupied as many plats as the other crops.

The same variety of barley has been grown on all the plats seeded to that crop at the same station during the same year. The aim has been to grow a variety adapted to the local conditions at the station where it has been grown. Different varieties have been grown at different stations. At some stations a 6-rowed barley has been used, some stations have used a 2-rowed barley, and some have used a hull-less variety. It is possible that in some cases the variety grown may not have been the very best obtainable for that section, but by using the same variety in all of the methods under study uniformity in this factor has been obtained.

Uniformity in rate, time, and manner of seeding has been observed on all plats at the same station. There is naturally some variation between the different stations. Differences in climatic conditions have been recognized in differences in the rate of seeding, but at the same stations it has been uniform. The usual rate of seeding has been 6 pecks of hulled barley and 3 pecks of hull-less. Both the 6-rowed and the 2-rowed barleys are hulled varieties.

There is considerable variation in the time of seeding for the different field stations throughout the area, it being about a month earlier in the southern than in the northern portion. At some of the stations the time of seeding is about the same as that of wheat and oats. At others it is a little later. All seeding has been done with a drill. Some stations, on account of the type of soil, have used the press drill in order to firm the soil around the seed. At other stations a drill without a press attachment has been used.

For a comparative study of the effect of environment and for securing data on production, certain parts of the work are made uniform at all stations. This results in the attempted growth of barley and other crops in sections to which they are not adapted and in their growth at certain stations by methods not adapted to the conditions obtaining there.

Considering the fact that no two stations can have exactly the same combination of soil and climatic factors and that the combination resulting from any two seasons is not the same, it is evident that the consequent effects of the different tillage methods will not be the same. Therefore, the results obtained from different methods at each station are given separately.

In this bulletin a table divided into two parts is presented for each station. The first part shows the yields that have been obtained each year by each of the different methods under which barley has been grown, considering only the treatment during the one year immediately preceding the crop. Where more than one plat has been grown under the same treatment for the previous year, only the average yield of the whole number of plats so grown is given. Column 2 shows the number of plats so averaged. In the presentation of yields, the column headed "Treatment and previous crop" indicates the method of preparation, whether fall plowed, spring plowed, listed, subsoiled, disked, green manured, or summer tilled. Some of these are again subdivided, to show the previous crop. In the last column, where the average appears under the heading "Average," the calculation is from the left. For a rough comparison of seasons, the bottom line of the first half of the table gives the averages of all plats for each year, the average of the yearly average yields appearing in the last column to the right.

In the second part of the table for each station the yields are brought together to show the average yields by years for each method and the average yield for the entire period for each method. The computations of cost and profit are founded on the basic data shown in Tables II, III, and IV. The value of the average yields by each method is calculated. The last line of the table gives the average profit or loss resulting from the production of barley by the method stated at the head of the column. Loss is indicated by the minus sign. This study deals with only the one crop and does not take into consideration the relative profitableness of other crops or of all crops, considered as a whole, in the farming system.

Throughout the tables, where barley follows barley under any treatment, it is in a system of continuous cropping to barley by the method indicated.

The methods of operation have been similar at all stations. Fall plowing is done as early as practicable after harvest. It is done to a good depth, the standard being set at 8 inches. Ground may be either worked down or left rough over winter. Where barley follows barley after spring plowing, the stubble is undisturbed until spring, when it is plowed shallow, usually to a depth of 4 inches, and given a minimum of cultivation, which usually consists of one or two harrowings. In those cases where an additional plat appears under the heading "Spring plowed," it is plowed deep instead of shallow.

Under the subhead "Listed" there is shown at some stations the yield from one plat continuously cropped to barley. Instead of plowing this plat, it is furrowed out with a lister at the time of fall plowing. It is cultivated down level by seeding time.

Under the subhead "Subsoiled" there is shown at the stations where it has been tried the results of a plat continuously cropped to barley. At the time of plowing, a subsoil plow is run in the bottom of the furrow, usually loosening the soil to a total depth of about 14 inches. The variation from this depth is hardly more than 2 inches either way. In general, subsoiling has been done for two years in succession and omitted for two years.

Under the subhead "Disked" are given the yields obtained on corn stubble prepared by disking. The corn is harvested in the fall with a corn binder and no tillage given the plat until spring. Then it is disked to put it in condition for seeding.

Under the subhead "Green manured" are given the yields of barley following the plowing under of rye or peas, as specified. This treatment is in a 4-year rotation in which one of the other crops consists of corn and one of small grain.

At each station at least one plat of barley is grown on summer-tilled land. The method of summer tillage practiced has been of the intensive type. The ground is fall plowed, and clean cultivation is continued through the next year and until the barley is seeded in the second spring. In some cases it is necessary to replow during the summer, when the land is fallow. At other stations summer-tilled plats are plowed but once. Experiments not here reported are under way to ascertain the best method of fallowing. Indications are that equally good results can be obtained with a less intensive method than has been practiced.

FIG. 2.—Diagram of the dry-land rotation field at the Amarillo Field Station. The lettering shows the cropping practiced in 1914. The explanation of the abbreviations used after the name of a crop is as follows: *D.*=Disked, *Fal.*=summer tilled, *F. P.*=fall plowed, *G. M.*=green manured, *L.*=listed, *M.*=manured, *S. P.*=spring plowed, *S. S.*=subsoiled.

The yields given in these tables begin with the second year of crop production at each station. All crops are produced the first year on land under uniform treatment. In some cases an entire crop has been lost by hail. These years are not considered in computing averages, as the crops under all methods alike were destroyed.

Figure 2 shows dia a-gram of the dry-land rotation field at the Amarillo Field Station. This station, being a representative one, will serve to illustrate the general scheme and plan of work. The plats here, as in all the work, are one-tenth acre in size. Their dimensions are 2 by 8 rods. Along their larger dimension the plats are separated by bare alleys 4 feet in width. Along the ends of the plats they are separated by roads 20 feet wide. At this station five crops are represented in a series of continuously cropped plats lettered from A to F or G. In this group plats C and D are alternately cropped and summer tilled, so that each year a crop is grown on land that was summer tilled the previous year and a plat is summer tilled for cropping the next year.

The remainder of the field is in rotations in which each plat is known by a rotation number and letter. On the field diagram the separation of the rotations is indicated by heavy lines.

The movement of the crops in the rotation is in the direction from Z to A and from A back to the letter that marks the other end of the rotation.

In figure 2 the diagram is filled out to show the cropping in 1914. The letters following the crop indicate the treatment given the ground in preparation for it, S. P. standing for spring plowed, F. P. for fall plowed, Fal. for summer tilled, G. M. for green manured, S. S. for subsoiled, L. for listed, and D. for disked. To illustrate: In 1914 plat A of the 4-year rotation No. 91 was in corn on fall-plowed ground, plat B was in oats on disked corn ground, and plat C was in peas on fall-plowed land. This would be plowed under for green manure. Plat D was in winter wheat where peas had been turned under the year before. In 1915, A will be in oats, B in peas, C in winter wheat, and D in corn.

COMPARISON OF CULTURAL METHODS ON THE BASIS OF COST.

The methods under study vary a great deal in the labor involved and in the consequent cost of preparation. Table IV has therefore been compiled in order to show the average cost by the methods under study as determined from the data of eight of the stations having the most trustworthy records. An average of the records for 5½ years at each station has been used in compiling this table. This is equivalent to a record of 44 years at one station. An accurate record has been kept of all the farm operations performed under the various methods under trial. These have been averaged for the eight stations. The amount of work required for some methods of treatment varies with the season and with the soil, and the expense of some operations varies with the soil. The amount of labor performed under each of the methods was neither more nor less than that which the man in charge believed to be necessary to bring about the results sought.

In computing the costs of the various operations a fixed wage of $2 a day for a man and $1 a day for a horse was adopted. This may be above or below the actual labor cost in any particular locality, but it is believed to be a fair average and one that will afford a profitable market to the farmer for his labor. The time required for men and teams to cover a given acreage in each of the several farm operations obviously varies with soils and other conditions. The average shown in Table II has been determined from the actual experience of a large number of men connected with these investigations, which experience has extended over a wide range of conditions and many years of time.

The factors included in the cost of production are calculated on an acre basis for each of the separate operations performed, beginning with the preparation of the land and ending with the harvesting and shocking of the grain. To these items are added the cost of seed at 75 cents per acre, interest and taxes on the land investment calculated at 8 per cent on a valuation of $20 per acre, and the deterioration and repair of the binder at 15 cents per acre. No allowance is made for the deterioration of other farm equipment, as it is believed that the wages allowed for men and teams are sufficient to cover this item for the remainder of the equipment. The above-mentioned items are fixed charges per acre; that is, they do not vary greatly with the yield per acre except for the item of twine, but this variation is not sufficient to materially affect the relative total cost of production under the several methods.

Table II shows the cost per acre based upon what is considered an average day's work for each of the farm operations involved at the above-mentioned wage. As before stated, the type of soil and seasonal conditions will determine to a certain extent the labor required and the consequent cost per acre. The cost of production as computed in Tables II and IV is not offered as being absolute for any locality, either in the amount of labor required or its cost, but is given as a working basis for the comparison of the results by different methods of preparation.

TABLE II.—*Average cost per acre*[1] *of the farm operations involved in growing barley in the Great Plains area.*

[The wage scale assumed is $2 per day for each man and $1 per day for each horse.]

Operation.	Force employed.		Day's work.	Item cost.	Cost per acre.
	Men.	Horses.			
			Acres.		
Plowing	1	4	3½		$1.71
Disking	1	4	8		.75
Harrowing	1	4	35		.17
Subsoiling	1	3	3½		1.43
Drilling	1	4	15		.40
Cultivating	1	4	16		.38
Listing	1	4	10		.60
Harvesting:					
Cutting and binding	1	4	15	$0.40	.93
Shocking	1			.13	
Twine				.25	
Binder wear and repair				.15	

[1] The cost of thrashing is not included in the cost per acre, but it is estimated at 6 cents per bushel and deducted from the price of 47 cents in the granary, thus giving a value of 41 cents per bushel in the shock.

The average farm price of barley used in these computations is based on the data given in Table III, furnished by the Bureau of Crop Estimates. The four States of North Dakota, South Dakota, Nebraska, and Kansas were selected because their extensive grain production has given them established market prices which are not greatly influenced by local conditions.

TABLE III.—*Average price of barley at the farm granary for ten years in four States of the Great Plains area.*

[The quotations are given in cents per bushel. Those for the year 1914 are for the date of Nov. 1; in other years Dec. 1 is taken as the date.]

Year.	North Dakota.	South Dakota.	Nebraska.	Kansas.	Average.	Year.	North Dakota.	South Dakota.	Nebraska.	Kansas.	Average.
1905	30	29	31	32	30½	1911	85	88	60	60	73¼
1906	33	32	31	33	32¼	1912	35	42	42	40	39¾
1907	58	61	50	54	55¾	1913	40	46	49	55	47¾
1908	46	47	46	54	48¼	1914	42	49	42	44	44¼
1909	43	45	43	53	46						
1910	55	57	45	45	50½	Average.	47	50	44	47	47

Table III shows that the average farm price of barley on December 1 for the past 10 years has been 47 cents per bushel. It costs about 6 cents per bushel to take the grain from the shock, thrash it, and put it in the granary on the farm. This cost per bushel does not vary greatly with the yield, and is therefore a fixed price per bushel instead of a fixed price per acre, as is the case with the other costs of production.

The relative profits of producing barley under the different methods can therefore be best determined by finding the difference between the fixed cost per acre and the value per acre of the grain at the point where the fixed cost per acre ends, which, as before stated, is when the grain is in the shock. Knowing that the average farm value of barley in the granary is 47 cents per bushel, and that it costs 6 cents per bushel to take it from the shock, thrash it, and put it in the granary it is obvious that it would be worth 41 cents per bushel in the shock. This valuation of 41 cents per bushel has therefore been used as a basis for calculating the relative crop values, costs, and profits per acre by the various methods under trial.

TABLE IV.—*Cost per acre of producing barley in the shock in the Great Plains area, showing averages of data from eight stations.*

Method of preparation.	Number of operations.						Cost of preparation.	Cost per acre.				Total cost of production.	
	Plowing.	Harrowing.	Disking.	Subsoiling.	Listing.	Drilling.		Seed.	Drilling.	Harvesting.	Interest and taxes.	In dollars.	In grain at 41 cents per bushel.
Disked corn land	......	1.3	1	......	......	......	$0.97	$0.75	$0.40	$0.93	$1.60	4.65	11.3
Listed	......	1.6	1.2	......	1	......	1.77	.75	.40	.93	1.60	5.45	13.3
Spring plowed	1	1.3	.5	......	......	......	2.31	.75	.40	.93	1.60	5.99	14.6
Fall plowed	1	2.3	.9	......	......	......	2.78	.75	.40	.93	1.60	6.46	15.8
Subsoiled	1	1.7	.9	0.5	......	......	3.39	.75	.40	.93	1.60	7.07	17.2
Summer tilled	1.5	9.2	2.6	......	......	......	6.12	.75	.40	.93	3.20	11.40	27.8
Green manured:													
With rye [1]	2	6.5	2.4	......	......	1	7.73	.75	.40	.93	3.20	13.01	31.7
With peas [2]	2	5.8	2.7	......	......	1	10.73	.75	.40	.93	3.20	16.01	39.0
Average cost of green manuring	......	......	......	......	......	......	......	......	......	......	......	14.51	35.4

[1] The cost of rye per acre for seed is estimated at $1. [2] The cost of peas per acre for seed is estimated at $4.

In conformity with the foregoing explanation, Table IV gives in detail the cost of producing barley in the shock, expressed in dollars and cents and in bushels per acre at 41 cents per bushel in the shock.

RESULTS AT THE SEVERAL STATIONS.

No attempt will be made in this bulletin to discuss the various types of soils found at the several stations.[1] It will be noted in the tables that follow that the soils at some of the stations have given but little response to differences in tillage methods under any climatic conditions thus far obtaining. The soils at some other stations do respond to tillage. Differences in yields are obtained from different methods of tillage. The amount of variation in yields changes from year to year with the changing combination of climatic conditions.

JUDITH BASIN FIELD STATION, MONT.

The results of five years are presented from the field station at Moccasin, Mont., in the Judith Basin. The crop in the sixth year was destroyed by hail before maturity and is not used in calculating the averages. Four of the years have been productive of heavy yields, but in the other year the yields were light.

Barley, like the other spring-sown grain crops at this station, does not exhibit marked differences in yield as a result of different preparations for the crop. In 1913 both fall and spring plowed barley land show a marked drop in yields. In 1914 the same thing is noted on the spring-plowed barley plat. This was due to injury from gophers rather than to the difference in seed-bed preparation. This damage with the consequent shortage of yield, unduly augments the average differences.

The uniformity of results obtained shows that the method of seed-bed preparation is not an important factor in the production of spring-sown crops at this place. The farmer should concern himself with the problem of getting the work done at the most convenient time and in the most economical manner.

The lack of wide variation in yield is explained by the shallowness of the soil on the station farm. The water that falls either in rain or snow between the time of harvest of one crop and the commencement of rapid growth of the next, during the years under study, was sufficient to supply the proportion of water that the soil can retain within reach of the crop. Water accumulated in the soil by the special methods of cultivation in excess of this proportion was lost by penetrating beyond recovery by the plant, and no increase in yield was realized from it.

[1] For a brief discussion of the different soil types, see U. S. Dept. of Agriculture Bul. 214, entitled "Spring wheat in the Great Plains area: Relation of cultural methods to production."

TABLE V.—*Yields and cost of production of barley by different methods at the Judith Basin Field Station, 1909 to 1914, inclusive.*

Treatment and previous crop.	Number of plats averaged.	Yield per acre (bushels).						
		1909	1910	1911	1912	1913	1914	Average.
Fall plowed: Barley	1	43.3	12.5	24.1	(1)	21.9	18.0	24.0
Spring plowed:								
Barley	1	45.2	10.0	(2)	(1)	21.9	11.6	22.5
Oats	1	39.1	11.6	23.9	(1)	31.7	21.2	25.9
Total or average	2	42.2	10.8	23.9	(1)	26.8	16.4	24.0
Listed: Barley	1	47.9	12.5	30.4	(1)	32.5	21.8	29.0
Subsoiled: Barley	1	48.3	15.0	32.6	(1)	32.9	23.5	30.5
Disked: Corn	1	42.7	16.6	29.7	(1)	34.6	21.6	29.0
Summer tilled	1	49.4	15.8	27.5	(1)	32.7	25.8	30.2
Average of all 7 plats	....	45.1	13.4	28.0	(1)	29.7	20.5	27.3

SUMMARY OF YIELDS AND DIGEST OF COST.

Yields, values, etc. (average per acre).	Tillage treatment.						Previous crop.	
	Fall plowed (1 plat).	Spring plowed (2 plats).	Disked (1 plat).	Listed (1 plat).	Subsoiled (1 plat).	Summer tilled (1 plat).	Small grain (5 plats).	Corn (1 plat).
Yields of grain:								
1909 .... bushels	43.3	42.2	42.7	47.9	48.3	49.4	44.8	42.7
1910 .... do	12.5	10.8	16.6	12.5	15.0	15.8	12.3	16.6
1911 .... do	24.1	23.9	29.7	30.4	32.6	27.5	27.8	29.7
1912 .... do	(1)	(1)	(1)	(1)	(1)	(1)	(1)	(1)
1913 .... do	21.9	26.8	34.6	32.5	32.9	32.7	28.2	34.6
1914 .... do	18.0	16.4	21.6	21.8	23.5	25.8	19.2	21.6
Average	24.0	24.0	29.0	29.0	30.5	30.2	26.5	29.0
Crop value, cost of production, etc.:								
Value	$9.84	$9.84	$11.89	$11.89	$12.51	$12.38	....	....
Cost	6.46	5.99	4.65	5.45	7.07	11.40	....	....
Profit	3.38	3.85	7.24	6.44	5.44	.98	....	....

[1] Destroyed by hail. [2] The yield from this plat is omitted, owing to an error in time of seeding.

The cost of production and the value of the crop as here computed show a profit by all methods under trial. The profits range from 98 cents by summer tillage to $7.24 on disked corn ground.

HUNTLEY FIELD STATION.

The records of only two years of yields under four different methods of treatment are available for study from Huntley, Mont. In 1913 there was little difference between spring-plowed oat stubble and disked corn ground as a preparation for barley. In 1914 disked corn ground was markedly the better of the two. The heaviest yields each year were obtained from land on which peas were plowed under for green manure. In 1914 there was a marked increase in the yield on ground on which rye was plowed under. In preparation for 1913, barley was plowed under instead of rye, with the result that there was a sharp decrease in yield.

A profit was realized from all the methods under trial. The largest profit, $9.50 per acre, was on disked corn ground. Spring plowing shows a profit of $6.15 per acre, while the average profit from green manure was $3.45.

TABLE VI.—*Yields and cost of production of barley by different methods at the Huntley Field Station, 1913 and 1914.*

Treatment and previous crop.	Number of plats averaged.	Yield per acre (bushels). 1913	1914	Average.
Spring plowed: Oats	1	24.5	34.6	29.6
Disked: Corn	4	23.2	45.7	34.5
Green manured:				
Rye	1	19.6	55.6	37.6
Peas	1	36.3	63.6	50.0
Total or average	2	28.0	59.6	43.8
Average of all 7 plats		24.7	48.1	36.4

SUMMARY OF YIELDS AND DIGEST OF COST.

Yields (average per acre).	Tillage treatment. Spring plowed (1 plat).	Disked (4 plats).	Green manured (2 plats).	Previous crop. Small grain (1 plat).	Corn (4 plats).	Values, etc. (average per acre).	Tillage treatment. Spring plowed (1 plat).	Disked (4 plats).	Green manured (2 plats)
Yields of grain:						Crop value, cost, etc.:			
1913........bushels..	24.5	23.2	28.0	24.5	23.2	Value...	$12.14	$14.15	$17.96
1914............do....	34.6	45.7	59.6	34.6	45.7	Cost.....	5.99	4.65	14.51
Average.............	29.6	34.5	43.8	29.6	34.5	Profit.	6.15	9.50	3.45

WILLISTON FIELD STATION.

The results of five years are available from Williston, N. Dak. In two of these years the yields were heavy, one year they were fair, and two years they were very poor.

Between the fall and spring plowing of barley stubble, there is little difference to be noted, except in 1912, when fall plowing was much the better. Between barley and oat stubble plowed in the spring, the only year that showed a significant difference was 1914, when the advantage was with the oat stubble. The crop on summer tillage was every year better than that following either oats or barley. For three years summer tillage yielded heavier than disked corn ground and for two years the reverse was the case. The high yield together with low cost combined to make disked corn ground show the greatest profit, $6.63 per acre. The higher cost of summer tillage reduced the profit from it to 41 cents per acre. Both fall and spring plowing show small profits.

TABLE VII.—*Yields and cost of production of barley by different methods at the Williston Field Station, 1910 to 1914, inclusive.*

Treatment and previous crop.	Number of plats averaged.	Yield per acre (bushels).					
		1910	1911	1912	1913	1914	Average.
Fall plowed: Barley	1	0.6	3.3	46.1	14.8	17.4	22.0
Spring plowed: Barley	1	.8	5.8	31.7	14.4	21.4	14.8
Oats	1	.2	4.6	30.0	15.6	36.7	17.4
Total or average	2	.5	5.2	30.9	15.0	29.1	16.1
Disked: Corn	1	.4	4.2	50.8	28.6	53.5	27.5
Summer tilled	1	5.2	12.7	54.4	21.9	49.7	28.8
Average of all 5 plats	....	1.4	6.1	42.6	19.1	36.7	21.2

SUMMARY OF YIELDS AND DIGEST OF COST.

Yields, values, etc. (average per acre).	Tillage treatment.				Previous crop.	
	Fall plowed (1 plat).	Spring plowed (2 plats).	Disked (1 plat).	Summer tilled (1 plat).	Small grain (3 plats).	Corn (1 plat).
Yields of grain:						
1910 bushels	0.6	0.5	0.4	5.2	0.5	0.4
1911 do	3.3	5.2	4.2	12.7	4.6	4.2
1912 do	46.1	30.9	50.8	54.4	35.9	50.8
1913 do	14.8	15.0	28.6	21.9	14.9	28.6
1914 do	22.0	29.1	53.5	49.7	26.7	53.5
Average	17.4	16.1	27.5	28.8	16.5	27.5
Crop value, cost of production, etc.:						
Value	$7.13	$6.60	$11.28	$11.81	....	....
Cost	6.46	5.99	4.65	11.40	....	....
Profit	.67	.61	6.63	.41	....	....

DICKINSON FIELD STATION.

The results of six years are available from Dickinson, N. Dak. The crop of 1912 was destroyed by hail before maturity, and as failure from this cause could not be overcome by cultural methods it is not included in determining the average. Five of the years studied produced good crops of barley. In the remaining year the average yield was small, but the variation between the results from different methods of preparation was wide.

The results attendant upon the fall and spring plowing of barley stubble and of growing barley on either spring-plowed oat stubble or barley stubble have been largely dependent upon the season. The seasonal differences have equalized each other until, when the results of the five years are averaged, little choice is to be made between them. Summer tillage increased the crop an average of about 7 bushels, bringing it up to 32.5 bushels per acre. Disked corn ground, however, brought the average yield up to 37.4 bushels per acre and gave a higher yield than summer tillage five years out of six.

Having at the same time the highest yield and the lowest cost of production, disked corn ground shows much the highest profit of any method under trial. The average profit from it was $10.68 per acre. Both spring and fall plowing show profits of about $4 per acre. The cost of summer tillage reduced the profits from it to $1.93 per acre.

TABLE VIII.—*Yields and cost of production of barley by different methods at the Dickinson Field Station, 1908 to 1914, inclusive.*

Treatment and previous crop.	Number of plats averaged.	Yield per acre (bushels).							
		1908	1909	1910	1911	1912	1913	1914	Average.
Fallplowed: Barley	1	24.0	39.0	31.1	1.2	(1)	34.8	20.2	25.1
Spring plowed:									
Barley	1	33.5	39.8	28.3	9.6	(1)	19.2	25.0	25.9
Oats	1	34.4	49.2	19.8	2.4	(1)	20.2	13.3	23.2
Total or average	2	34.0	44.5	24.1	6.0	....	19.7	19.2	24.6
Disked: Corn	1	45.6	53.8	28.6	12.3	(1)	44.8	39.1	37.4
Summer tilled	1	30.0	50.0	24.0	19.1	(1)	36.9	35.2	32.5
Average of all 5 plats	....	33.5	46.4	26.4	8.9	(1)	31.2	26.6	28.8

SUMMARY OF YIELDS AND DIGEST OF COST.

Yields, values, etc. (average per acre).	Tillage treatment.				Previous crop.	
	Fall plowed (1 plat).	Spring plowed (2 plats).	Disked (1 plat).	Summer tilled (1 plat).	Small grain (3 plats).	Corn (1 plat).
Yields of grain:						
1908 ... bushels	24.0	34.0	45.6	30.0	30.6	45.6
1909 ... do	39.0	44.5	53.8	50.0	42.7	53.8
1910 ... do	31.1	24.1	28.6	24.0	26.4	28.6
1911 ... do	1.2	6.0	12.3	19.1	4.4	12.3
1912 ... do	(1)	(1)	(1)	(1)	(1)	(1)
1913 ... do	34.8	19.7	44.8	36.9	24.7	44.8
1914 ... do	20.2	19.2	39.1	35.2	19.5	39.1
Average	25.1	24.6	37.4	32.5	24.7	37.4
Crop value, cost of production, etc.:						
Value	$10.29	$10.09	$15.33	$13.33	....	....
Cost	6.46	5.99	4.65	11.40	....	....
Profit	3.83	4.10	10.68	1.93	....	....

[1] Destroyed by hail.

EDGELEY FIELD STATION.

The results of eight years of uninterrupted work are presented from Edgeley, N. Dak. In five of these years the yields were good, in one year they were light, and in two years the crops were practically failures from all methods under trial. No method showed any merit in overcoming the drought of these extreme years at this station. In five of the years under study the highest yield was obtained on disked corn ground. The maximum yield by this method was 37.1 bushels per acre, while the average for the eight years was 23.4 bushels per acre.

The next highest average yield, 20 bushels per acre, was by summer tillage. The average from spring-plowed oat land was 19.7 bushels per acre. The advantage of either fall or spring plowing barley stubble varied within narrow limits, but in the average of the series of years no choice is to be made between the two. This indication that the time of plowing is not an important factor allows greater latitude in planning the work of the farm. The plan should be to get the work done early and thus avoid as far as possible the augmentation of work at seeding time. This is of especial importance in the northern portion of the Great Plains, where the seeding season is necessarily short.

The only method under trial that did not produce barley at a profit is summer tillage. This shows an average loss of $3.20 per acre. The greatest profit, $4.94, was realized from disked corn ground. Fall and spring plowing both show small profits.

TABLE IX.—*Yield and cost of production of barley by different methods at the Edgeley Field Station, 1907 to 1914, inclusive.*

Treatment and previous crop.	Number of plats averaged.	Yield per acre (bushels).								
		1907	1908	1909	1910	1911	1912	1913	1914	Average.
Fall plowed: Barley	1	9.4	24.2	24.7	1.6	0.1	26.5	20.2	26.9	16.7
Spring plowed:										
Barley	1	10.2	25.0	27.0	1.2	......	24.2	17.9	32.3	17.2
Oats	1	10.6	26.0	32.7	1.4	.1	34.0	18.9	33.6	19.7
Total or average	2	10.4	25.5	29.9	1.3	.1	29.1	18.4	33.0	18.5
Disked: Corn	1	18.3	31.9	33.1	2.9	.4	30.2	37.1	33.1	23.4
Summer tilled	1	16.0	24.2	28.3	2.2	.8	32.3	26.8	29.4	20.0
Average of all 5 plats	....	12.9	26.3	29.2	1.9	.3	29.4	24.2	31.1	19.4

SUMMARY OF YIELDS AND DIGEST OF COST.

Yields, values, etc. (average per acre).	Tillage treatment.				Previous crop.	
	Fall plowed (1 plat).	Spring plowed (2 plats).	Disked (1 plat).	Summer tilled (1 plat).	Small grain (3 plats).	Corn (1 plat).
Yields of grain:						
1907 .... bushels	9.4	10.4	18.3	16.0	10.1	18.3
1908 .... do	24.2	25.5	31.9	24.2	25.1	31.9
1909 .... do	24.7	29.9	33.1	28.3	28.1	33.1
1910 .... do	1.6	1.3	2.9	2.2	1.4	2.9
1911 .... do	.1	.1	.4	.8	.1	.4
1912 .... do	26.5	29.1	30.2	32.3	28.2	30.2
1913 .... do	20.2	18.4	37.1	26.8	19.0	37.1
1914 .... do	26.9	33.0	33.1	29.4	30.9	33.1
Average	16.7	18.5	23.4	20.0	17.9	23.4
Crop value, cost of production, etc.:						
Value	$6.85	$7.59	$9.59	$8.20	....	....
Cost	6.46	5.99	4.65	11.40	....	....
Profit or loss	.39	1.60	4.94	−3.20	....	....

HETTINGER FIELD STATION.

Results for three years have been obtained at Hettinger, N. Dak. All were years of good barley yields. The highest yields were obtained each year by summer tillage and the lowest, with one exception, on disked corn ground. The average yield from summer tillage was more than twice that from the disked land. Following small grain, a decided advantage attended spring-plowed barley stubble. The crops in this group yielded better than on disked corn ground, but not as good as by summer tillage.

TABLE X.—*Yields and cost of production of barley by different methods at the Hettinger Field Station, 1912, 1913, and 1914.*

Treatment and previous crop.	Yield per acre (bushels).				
	Number of plats averaged.	1912	1913	1914	Average.
Fall plowed: Barley	1	23.5	27.1	9.2	19.9
Spring plowed:					
Barley	1	26.3	39.6	16.3	27.4
Oats	1	22.9	28.0	20.0	23.6
Total or average	2	24.6	33.8	18.2	25.5
Disked: Corn	1	13.5	21.0	10.2	14.9
Summer tilled	1	37.8	38.8	18.7	31.8
Average of all 5 plats		24.8	30.9	14.9	23.5

SUMMARY OF YIELDS AND DIGEST OF COST.

Yields, values, etc. (average per acre).	Tillage treatment.				Previous crop.	
	Fall-plowed (1 plat).	Spring-plowed (2 plats).	Disked (1 plat).	Summer-tilled (1 plat).	Small grain (3 plats).	Corn (1 plat).
Yields of grain:						
1912 bushels	23.5	24.6	13.5	37.8	24.2	13.5
1913 do	27.1	33.8	21.0	38.8	31.6	21.0
1914 do	9.2	18.2	10.2	18.7	15.2	10.2
Average	19.9	25.5	14.9	31.8	23.7	14.9
Crop value, cost of production, etc.:						
Value	$8.16	$10.46	$6.11	$13.04		
Cost	6.46	5.99	4.65	11.40		
Profit	1.70	4.47	1.46	1.64		

The relative position assumed by the various methods may be due in part to the distribution of the rainfall for the two years, 1911 and 1912, and may be changed with subsequent work. In both 1911 and 1912 a heavy rainfall came in August and September. The corn, which was still growing, used this water, while a portion of it was accumulated in the small-grain plats, where the grain was already harvested, and in the summer-tilled plats. The corn plats were therefore short of available water when the barley was seeded and consequently gave lower yields. Weeds were also a factor in decreasing the yields on disked corn ground.

A profit was realized from all methods under trial. Between fall plowing, disking, and summer tillage there was little difference. Spring plowing shows a considerably larger average profit than any of the other methods.

BELLE FOURCHE FIELD STATION.

The results of six years at Belle Fourche, S. Dak., are available for study. In only one year was the yield heavy. Three of those years gave light yields from most methods; in one year the crop was a total failure from all methods, and in the other year only one method gave any yield and that was light.

TABLE XI.—*Yields and cost of production of barley by different methods at the Belle Fourche Field Station, 1909 to 1914, inclusive.*

Treatment and previous crop.	Number of plats averaged.	Yield per acre (bushels).						
		1909	1910	1911	1912	1913	1914	Average.
Fall plowed: Barley	1	25.0	4.8	0	0	8.9	7.1	7.6
Spring plowed:								
Barley	1	23.8	4.4	0	5.2	17.0	5.2	9.3
Oats	1	28.1	3.6	0	0	6.8	5.8	7.4
Total or average	2	26.0	4.0	....	2.6	11.9	5.5	8.3
Listed: Barley	1	30.2	0	0	0	7.8	8.1	7.7
Subsoiled: Barley	1	33.8	0	0	0	7.8	6.3	8.0
Disked: Corn	1	47.1	5.0	0	0	8.9	12.2	12.2
Summer tilled	1	37.3	3.0	0	0	13.4	21.7	12.6
Average of all 7 plats	....	32.2	3.0	....	.7	10.1	9.5	9.3

SUMMARY OF YIELDS AND DIGEST OF COST.

Yields, values, etc. (average per acre).	Tillage treatment.						Previous crop.	
	Fall plowed (1 plat).	Spring plowed (2 plats)	Disked (1 plat).	Listed (1 plat).	Sub-soiled (1 plat).	Summer tilled (1 plat).	Small grain (5 plats)	Corn (1 plat).
Yields of grain:								
1909 .... bushels	25.0	26.0	47.1	30.2	33.8	37.3	28.2	47.1
1910 .... do	4.8	4.0	5.0	0	0	3.0	2.6	5.0
1911 .... do	0	0	0	0	0	0	0	0
1912 .... do	0	2.6	0	0	0	0	1.0	0
1913 .... do	8.9	11.9	8.9	7.8	7.8	13.4	9.7	8.9
1914 .... do	7.1	5.5	12.2	8.1	6.3	21.7	6.5	12.2
Average	7.6	8.3	12.2	7.7	8.0	12.6	8.0	12.2
Crop value, cost of production, etc.:								
Value	$3.12	$3.40	$5.00	$3.16	$3.28	$5.17	....	....
Cost	6.46	5.99	4.65	5.45	7.07	11.40	....	....
Profit or loss	−3.34	−2.59	.35	−2.29	−3.79	−6.23		

In the year of heavy yields and in the following year of very light yields the best production was on disked corn ground. In 1912 the only yield secured was from spring-plowed barley stubble. The same plat also gave the highest yield in 1913. It is probable that in both cases these results were due to the fact that the crop on this plat made a poor start and had a thinner stand, which helped it in withstanding the drought of the summer.

Subsoiling, as compared with fall-plowing done at the same time, appears to have been effective in increasing the crop in the year of good yield, but not in overcoming drought in other years. The same observation applies to furrowing with the lister instead of plowing.

In the average results from the whole period of years, summer tillage and disking corn ground stand by themselves. On the basis of yield there is little or no choice to be made between the two. But when the cost of production is figured in connection with the value of the crop it is seen that by all methods except the use of disked corn ground the crop has been produced at a loss. The low cost of production by the disking method enables it to show a nominal average profit of 35 cents per acre.

SCOTTSBLUFF FIELD STATION.

The results of only two years with barley are available for study from Scottsbluff, Nebr. The crop of 1913 was lost through a fault in the seed that made it necessary to reseed. The reseeded crop grew and maintained the continuity of the work in the effect upon the ground for the following crop, but was too late to mature before growth was checked by the hot weather of midsummer. Production in one year was good and in the other it was poor.

TABLE XII.—*Yields and cost of production of barley by different methods at the Scottsbluff Field Station, 1912 and 1914.*

Treatment and previous crop.	Number of plats averaged.	Yield per acre (bushels).[1]		
		1912	1914	Average.
Fall plowed: Barley	1	23.5	4.4	14.0
Spring plowed:				
Barley	1	21.3	6.0	13.7
Oats	1	22.5	11.8	17.2
Total or average	2	21.9	8.9	15.4
Disked: Corn	1	31.3	5.8	18.6
Listed: Barley	1	23.8	5.0	14.4
Subsoiled: Barley	1	24.8	5.2	15.0
Summer tilled	1	39.6	15.6	27.6
Average of all 7 plats		26.7	7.7	17.2

[1] The crop of 1913 was a failure, due to poor seed.

TABLE XII.—*Yields and cost of production of barley by different methods at the Scottsbluff Field Station, 1912 and 1914*—Continued.

SUMMARY OF YIELDS AND DIGEST OF COST.

Yields, values, etc. (average per acre).	Tillage treatment.						Previous crop.	
	Fall plowed (1 plat).	Spring plowed (2 plats)	Disked (1 plat).	Listed (1 plat).	Sub-soiled (1 plat).	Summer tilled (1 plat).	Small grain (5 plats)	Corn (1 plat).
Yields of grain:								
1912....bushels..	23.5	21.9	31.3	23.8	24.8	39.6	23.2	31.3
1913 [1]....do....	......	......	......	......	......	......	......	......
1914....do....	4.4	8.9	5.8	5.0	5.2	15.6	6.5	5.8
Average....	14.0	15.4	18.6	14.4	15.0	27.6	14.9	18.6
Crop value, cost of production, etc.:								
Value....	$5.74	$6.31	$7.63	$5.90	$6.15	$11.32	......	......
Cost....	6.46	5.99	4.65	5.45	7.07	11.40	......	......
Profit or loss....	−.72	.32	2.98	.45	−.92	−.08	......	......

[1] The crop of 1913 was a failure, due to poor seed.

The highest yield in both years was from summer tillage. The average yield from this method is 9 bushels per acre greater than the average on disked corn ground, the next highest yielding method under trial. Between other methods there is little difference in yields, although in 1914 the spring-plowed oat ground appeared to have a decided advantage. Spring plowing, disking, and listing all show small profits, the greatest being from disking. Fall plowing, subsoiling, and summer tillage all show small losses.

NORTH PLATTE FIELD STATION.

In the eight years under study at North Platte, Nebr., there have been two heavy crops of barley, three light crops, two poor crops, and one failure from drought and grasshoppers.

In the average of the whole series of years a small advantage appears in favor of fall plowing. There have been large differences in individual years of the series. The greatest difference in any one year has been in favor of fall plowing, but in the greater number of years there has been a smaller difference in favor of spring plowing. The greatest difference in favor of spring plowing over fall plowing was in 1909. Germination was much slower on the spring-plowed than on either fall-plowed or summer-tilled land, owing to the fact that the seed bed was not in as good shape. A late freeze caught the crop on the fall-plowed and summer-tilled land at a tender stage, while the crop on the spring-plowed plats, being slower, escaped almost entirely. The difference in yield between spring and fall plowing in that year was therefore due to a difference in stand.

The one plat on disked-corn ground has been low in yield, its average being below that of barley following small grain. There is some evidence to support the belief that the location of the rotation containing this plat is such that it is normally a little lower in yield than the rest of the field.

The only method under trial that exhibits power to markedly increase the yield over other methods is summer tillage. This power has not been manifested every year, but in some years it has been very marked. The average yield for eight years by this method has been 26.7 bushels per acre as against 16.3 bushels where the crop followed small grain. This increase in yield has been just about equal to the increased cost of growing the crop under this method. All methods show either a profit or a loss of less than $1 per acre.

TABLE XIII.—*Yields and cost of production of barley by different methods at the North Platte Field Station, 1907 to 1914, inclusive.*

Treatment and previous crop.	Number of plats averaged.	Yield per acre (bushels).								
		1907	1908	1909	1910	1911	1912	1913	1914	Average.
Fall plowed: Barley	1	40.0	43.3	10.4	12.5	0	14.6	5.0	11.0	17.1
Spring plowed:										
Barley	1	39.0	19.6	21.5	13.8	0	20.8	6.5	5.3	15.8
Oats	1	40.2	22.3	18.6	16.0	0	20.0	6.3	3.6	15.9
Total or average	2	39.6	21.0	20.1	14.9	......	20.4	6.4	4.5	15.9
Disked: Corn	1	30.6	24.9	21.5	7.9	0	12.3	5.0	5.2	13.4
Summer tilled	1	39.0	67.7	23.8	26.0	0	20.0	16.5	20.8	26.7
Average of all 5 plats	....	37.8	35.6	19.2	15.2	......	17.5	7.9	9.2	17.8

SUMMARY OF YIELDS AND DIGEST OF COST.

Yields, values, etc. (average per acre).	Tillage treatment.				Previous crop.	
	Fall-plowed (1 plat).	Spring-plowed (2 plats).	Disked (1 plat).	Summer-tilled (1 plat).	Small grain (3 plats).	Corn (1 plat).
Yields of grain:						
1907 ... bushels	40.0	39.6	30.6	39.0	39.7	30.6
1908 ... do	43.3	21.0	24.9	67.7	28.4	24.9
1909 ... do	10.4	20.1	21.5	23.8	16.8	21.5
1910 ... do	12.5	14.9	7.9	26.0	14.1	7.9
1911 ... do	0	0	0	0	0	0
1912 ... do	14.6	20.4	12.3	20.0	18.5	12.3
1913 ... do	5.0	6.4	5.0	16.5	5.9	5.0
1914 ... do	11.0	4.5	5.2	20.8	6.6	5.2
Average	17.1	15.9	13.4	26.7	16.3	13.4
Crop value, cost of production, etc.:						
Value	$7.01	$6.52	$5.49	$10.95	....	....
Cost	6.46	5.99	4.65	11.40	....	....
Profit or loss	.55	.53	.84	— .55	....	....

AKRON FIELD STATION.

The results at Akron, Colo., secured by fall plowing barley stubble, furrowing with a lister instead of plowing, spring plowing barley stubble, spring plowing oat stubble, and disking corn ground in preparation for barley, have been dependent upon the season. Some seasons have favored one method and other seasons other methods, but on the whole little choice is to be made from the average of the six years under study. Subsoiling as compared with fall plowing without subsoiling has been done at a distinct loss each year except the first.

Summer tillage has increased the average yield from 17.6 bushels following a small-grain crop to 24.8 bushels per acre. Subsoiling and summer tillage show small losses of $1.33 and $1.23 per acre. Other methods show profits ranging from $1.17 on fall-plowed land to $2.89 on disked corn ground.

TABLE XIV.—*Yields and cost of production of barley by different methods at the Akron Field Station, 1909 to 1914, inclusive.*

Treatment and previous crop.	Number of plats averaged.	Yield per acre (bushels).						
		1909	1910	1911	1912	1913	1914	Average.
Fall plowed: Barley	1	16.8	10.5	16.3	27.9	3.1	36.7	18.6
Spring plowed:								
Barley	1	19.7	13.1	8.7	28.8	4.6	32.1	17.8
Oats	1	22.2	10.2	2.5	35.2	7.9	40.2	19.7
Total or average	2	21.0	11.7	5.6	32.0	6.3	36.2	18.8
Listed: Barley	1	19.2	12.6	4.6	36.0	4.4	30.8	17.9
Subsoiled: Barley	1	19.8	6.9	5.2	22.5	1.5	27.9	14.0
Disked: Corn	3	18.7	12.9	1.7	28.9	6.4	42.0	18.4
Summer tilled	1	24.6	16.0	12.6	40.2	16.3	46.2	24.8
Average of all 9 plats	....	19.8	12.0	6.1	30.8	6.3	37.8	18.8

SUMMARY OF YIELDS AND DIGEST OF COST.

Yields, values, etc. (average per acre).	Tillage treatment.						Previous crop.	
	Fall plowed (1 plat).	Spring plowed (2 plats).	Disked (3 plats).	Listed (1 plat).	Subsoiled (1 plat).	Summer tilled (1 plat).	Small grain (5 plats).	Corn (3 plats).
Yields of grain:								
1909 bushels	16.8	21.0	18.7	19.2	19.8	24.6	19.5	18.7
1910 do	10.5	11.7	12.9	12.6	6.9	16.0	10.7	12.9
1911 do	16.3	5.6	1.7	4.6	5.2	12.6	7.5	1.7
1912 do	27.9	32.0	28.9	36.0	22.5	40.2	30.1	28.9
1913 do	3.1	6.3	6.4	4.4	1.5	16.3	4.3	6.4
1914 do	36.7	36.2	42.0	30.8	27.9	46.2	33.5	42.0
Average	18.6	18.8	18.4	17.9	14.0	24.8	17.6	18.4
Crop value, cost of production, etc.:								
Value	$7.63	$7.71	$7.54	$7.34	$5.74	$10.17	....	....
Cost	6.46	5.99	4.65	5.45	7.07	11.40	....	....
Profit or loss	1.17	1.72	2.89	1.89	−1.33	−1.23	....	....

HAYS FIELD STATION.

In the results for seven years presented for study from Hays, Kans., one crop has been lost by hail. With the exception of 3.4 bushels per acre produced by summer tillage, one crop has been lost by drought. In two years the average yield was heavy, in two it was light, and in one it was fair. In the matter of productive and nonproductive years, the record for barley at this station is the same as that of oats. The year when the crop was destroyed by hail is not included in computing the averages.

TABLE XV.—*Yields and cost of production of barley by different methods at the Hays Field Station, 1908 to 1914, inclusive.*

Treatment and previous crop.	Number of plats averaged.	Yield per acre (bushels).							
		1908	1909	1910	1911	1912	1913	1914	Average.
Fall plowed: Barley	1	12.4	(1)	19.7	0	28.8	4.0	16.7	13.6
Spring plowed:									
Barley	1	5.8	(1)	12.5	0	22.4	2.6	9.9	8.9
Oats	1	9.2	(1)	15.0	0	29.8	17.0	9.4	13.4
Total or average	2	7.5	......	13.8	......	26.1	9.8	9.7	11.2
Listed: Barley	1	10.1	(1)	19.7	0	31.8	2.1	12.6	12.7
Subsoiled: Barley	1	14.8	(1)	19.3	0	33.8	4.6	15.2	14.6
Disked	6	11.0	(1)	28.3	0	25.1	3.5	16.4	14.1
Green manured:									
Rye	1	21.5	(1)	32.3	0	16.9	12.9	15.3	16.5
Peas	1	5.0	(1)	34.1	0	17.7	14.0	16.2	14.5
Total or average	2	13.3	......	33.2	......	17.3	13.5	15.8	15.5
Summer tilled	1	18.9	(1)	18.4	3.4	36.2	20.9	18.0	19.3
Average of all 14 plats	....	11.7	......	24.3	.2	26.3	7.1	15.1	14.1

SUMMARY OF YIELDS AND DIGEST OF COST.

Yields, values, etc. (average per acre).	Tillage treatment.							Previous crop.		
	Fall plowed (1 plat).	Spring plowed (2 plats).	Disked (6 plats).	Listed (1 plat).	Subsoiled (1 plat).	Green manured (2 plats).	Summer tilled (1 plat).	Small grain (5 plats).	Corn. (4 plats).	Kafir. (2 plats).
Yields of grain:										
1908.....bush..	12.4	7.5	11.0	10.1	14.8	13.3	18.9	10.5	11.3	10.4
1909.....do....	(1)	(1)	(1)	(1)	(1)	(1)	(1)	(1)	(1)	(1)
1910.....do....	19.7	13.8	28.3	19.7	19.3	33.2	18.4	17.2	26.6	31.6
1911.....do....	0	0	0	0	0	0	3.4	0	0	0
1912.....do....	28.8	26.1	25.1	31.8	33.8	17.3	36.2	29.3	26.1	23.0
1913.....do....	4.0	9.8	3.5	2.1	4.6	13.5	20.9	6.1	3.1	4.4
1914.....do....	16.7	9.7	16.4	12.6	15.2	15.8	18.0	12.8	15.6	18.2
Average	13.6	11.2	14.1	12.7	14.6	15.5	19.3	12.7	13.8	14.6
Crop value, cost of production, etc.:										
Value	$5.58	$4.59	$5.78	$5.21	$5.99	$6.36	$7.91	......	......	......
Cost	6.46	5.99	4.65	5.45	7.07	14.51	11.40	......	......	......
Profit or loss.	− .88	−1.40	1.13	− .24	−1.08	−8.15	−3.49	......	......	......

1 Destroyed by hail.

The results range from an average yield of 8.9 bushels per acre on spring-plowed barley land to 19.3 bushels per acre on summer-tilled land. Green manure is in second place, with average yields of 15.5 bushels per acre. In all but the first year, peas plowed under produced slightly larger crops than winter rye similarly treated. There has been a gain of 1 bushel per acre from subsoiling over fall plowing not subsoiled. Furrowing over winter with a lister produced practically the same as fall plowing. Fall-plowed barley stubble gave better results than spring-plowed barley stubble. Spring-plowed oat stubble produced practically the same as fall-plowed barley stubble. Disked corn ground produced slightly better yields than the average of the crops following small grains on fall or spring plowing.

The main positive result shown in the table of yields is an increase of about 6 bushels an acre as the result of summer tillage, or a somewhat lesser increase as a result of modifying the summer tillage by plowing under a crop of green manure.

The only method that produced barley at a profit was that of disking corn ground. This shows a profit of $1.13 per acre. All other methods show losses which range from 24 cents on listed ground to $3.49 on summer-tilled land and $8.15 on green-manured land.

GARDEN CITY FIELD STATION.

During the work of six years with barley under study at Garden City, Kans., one crop has been lost by drought and one by hail. In the other four years, yields have been obtained.

The highest average yield, 11 bushels per acre, has been obtained from summer tillage. Next to this in point of average yield is disked corn ground. Subsoiling has given the same average yields as fall plowing done at the same time without subsoiling. Marked advantage in two years appears to have been derived from furrowing with a lister and leaving the land rough through the winter instead of plowing.

On the whole the average yields are so low and there are so many inconsistencies in the behavior of the different methods from year to year that the results are chiefly valuable as indicators rather than as definite guides to practice. It appears that there is sound reason for the consensus of opinion as evidenced by farm practice which gives little place to spring-sown barley in the territory served by this station.

The crop has been produced at a loss by all the methods under trial. The losses range from $1 per acre on disked corn ground to $6.89 on summer-tilled land.

TABLE XVI.—*Yields and cost of production of barley by different methods at the Garden City Field Station, 1909 to 1914, inclusive.*

Treatment and previous crop.	Number of plats averaged.	Yield per acre (bushels).						Average.
		1909	1910	1911	1912	1913	1914	
Fall plowed: Barley	1	4.8	5.4	0	9.0	(1)	15.2	6.9
Spring plowed:								
Barley	1	2.4	1.0	0	6.9	(1)	3.9	2.8
Oats	1	5.7	2.3	0	17.0	(1)	3.5	5.7
Total or average	2	4.1	1.7		12.0		3.7	4.3
Listed: Barley	1	3.2	5.0	0	14.5	(1)	18.8	8.3
Subsoiled: Barley	1	3.7	5.2	0	8.5	(1)	17.3	6.9
Disked: Corn	3	4.8	5.4	0	15.8	(1)	18.5	8.9
Summer tilled	1	10.0	13.5	0	13.1	(1)	18.5	11.0
Average of all 9 plats		4.6	5.4		12.9		15.7	7.7

SUMMARY OF YIELDS AND DIGEST OF COST.

Yields, values, etc. (average per acre).	Tillage treatment.						Previous crop.	
	Fall plowed (1 plat).	Spring plowed (2 plats).	Disked (3 plats).	Listed (1 plat).	Sub-soiled (1 plat).	Summer tilled (1 plat).	Small grain (5 plats).	Corn (3 plats).
Yields of grain:								
1909 bushels	4.8	4.1	4.8	3.2	3.7	10.0	4.0	4.8
1910 do	5.4	1.7	5.4	5.0	5.2	13.5	3.8	5.4
1911 do	0	0	0	0	0	0	0	0
1912 do	9.0	12.0	15.8	14.5	8.5	13.1	11.2	15.8
1913[1] do	(1)	(1)	(1)	(1)	(1)	(1)	(1)	(1)
1914 do	15.2	3.7	18.5	18.8	17.3	18.5	11.7	18.5
Average	6.9	4.3	8.9	8.3	6.9	11.0	6.1	8.9
Crop value, cost of production, etc.:								
Value of crop	$2.83	$1.76	$3.65	$3.40	$2.83	$4.51		
Cost of production	6.46	5.99	4.65	5.45	7.07	11.40		
Loss	−3.63	−4.23	−1.00	−2.05	−4.24	−6.89		

[1] Destroyed by hail.

DALHART FIELD STATION.

Persistent attempts have been made for six years to grow barley at the station at Dalhart, Tex. The crop has been lost in the different years by hail, drought, and soil blowing.

In only two years have any yields been obtained. If this record is indicative of average conditions, as it is believed to be, it would show that spring-sown barley has no place in the farm practice of this section.

TABLE XVII.—*Yields and cost of production of barley by different methods at the Dalhart Field Station, 1909 to 1914, inclusive.*

Treatment and previous crop.	Number of plats averaged.	Yield per acre (bushels).						Average.
		1909	1910	1911	1912	1913	1914	
Fall plowed: Barley	1	0	(1)	0	(1)	0	15.6	3.9
Spring plowed:								
Barley	1	0	(1)	0	(1)	0	7.7	1.9
Oats	1	0	(1)	0	(1)	0	....	....
Total or average	2	....	....	....	....	....	7.7	1.9
Listed: Barley	1	0	(1)	0	(1)	0	17.6	4.4
Disked: Corn	3	0	(1)	0	(1)	0	6.4	1.6
Summer tilled	1	7.5	(1)	0	(1)	0	18.1	6.4
Average of all 8 plats	....	1.3	....	....	....	....	13.1	3.6

SUMMARY OF YIELDS AND DIGEST OF COST.

Yields, values, etc. (average per acre).	Tillage treatment.					Previous crop.	
	Fall plowed (1 plat).	Spring plowed (2 plats).	Disked (3 plats).	Listed (1 plat).	Summer tilled (1 plat).	Small grain (4 plats).	Corn (3 plats).
Yields of grain:							
1909 .... bushels	0	0	0	0	7.5	0	0
1910 .... do	(1)	(1)	(1)	(1)	(1)	(1)	(1)
1911 .... do	0	0	0	0	0	0	0
1912 .... do	(1)	(1)	(1)	(1)	(1)	(1)	(1)
1913 .... do	0	0	0	0	0	0	0
1914 .... do	15.6	7.7	6.4	17.6	18.1	13.6	6.4
Average	3.9	1.9	1.6	4.4	6.4	3.4	1.6
Crop value, cost of production, etc.:							
Value	$1.60	$0.78	$0.66	$1.80	$2.62	....	....
Cost	6.46	5.99	4.65	5.45	11.40	....	....
Loss	−4.86	−5.21	−3.99	−3.65	−8.78	....	....

[1] Destroyed by hail.

AMARILLO FIELD STATION.

The results with barley at Amarillo, Tex., have been tabulated for six years; 1910 is not included, owing to the necessity of changing the location of the farm. The crop of that year was the first from prairie sod and was raised on land uniform in its preparation for all plats. While there was some growth of straw, a crop of grain did not mature. Three of the six years under study were productive of much better average yields than the other three. During two years the crop was practically a failure by all methods. In the remaining year one method, summer tillage, gave a yield of 17.5 bushels per acre, while most of the other methods were failures. On the average, there appears to have been no increase in yields from subsoiling, from listing instead of plowing, or from raising the barley on disked corn ground.

The only method that has consistently shown increases sufficient to attract attention is summer tillage. Under this method barley has given an average yield for six years of 12.6 bushels per acre, with a maximum yield in any one year of 19.6 bushels per acre. On the whole, barley does not seem to offer more promise for this section than any other of the spring-sown small grains.

A loss by all methods under trial has attended the growth of the crop. These losses range from $1.94 on disked corn ground to $6.23 on summer-tilled land.

TABLE XVIII.—*Yields and cost of production of barley by different methods at the Amarillo*[1] *Field Station for 1908, 1909, and 1911 to 1914, inclusive.*

Treatment and previous crop.	Number of plats averaged.	Yield per acre (bushels).						
		1909	1910	1911	1912	1913	1914	Average.
Fall plowed: Barley	1	13.2	5.8	11.7	1.7	0	16.7	8.2
Spring plowed:								
Barley	1	7.9	0	12.2	2.7	0	21.0	7.3
Oats	1	8.1	0	12.3	1.1	0	2.7	4.0
Average	2	8.0	0	12.3	1.9	0	11.9	5.7
Listed: Barley	1	10.8	0	11.4	1.5	0	13.1	6.1
Subsoiled: Barley	1	11.9	0	10.3	1.5	0	17.1	6.8
Disked: Corn	1	7.5	0	11.8	1.7	0	18.8	6.6
Summer tilled	1	15.2	17.5	15.0	4.2	4.2	19.6	12.6
Average of all 7 plats	....	10.7	3.3	12.1	2.1	.6	15.6	7.4

SUMMARY OF YIELDS AND DIGEST OF COST.

Yields, values, etc. (average per acre).	Tillage treatment.						Previous crop.	
	Fall-plowed (1 plat).	Spring-plowed (2 plats).	Disked (1 plat).	Listed (1 plat).	Sub-soiled (1 plat).	Summer-tilled (1 plat).	Small grain (5 plats).	Corn (1 plat).
Yields of grain:								
1908 .... bushels	13.2	8.0	7.5	10.8	11.9	15.2	10.4	7.5
1909 .... do	5.8	0	0	0	0	17.5	1.2	0
1911 .... do	11.7	12.3	11.8	11.4	10.3	15.0	11.6	11.8
1912 .... do	1.7	1.9	1.7	1.5	1.5	4.2	1.7	1.7
1913 .... do	0	0	0	0	0	4.2	0	0
1914 .... do	16.7	11.9	18.8	13.1	17.1	19.6	14.1	18.8
Average	8.2	5.7	6.6	6.1	6.8	12.6	6.5	6.6
Crop value, cost of production, etc.:								
Value	$3.36	$2.34	$2.71	$2.50	$2.79	$5.17	....	....
Cost	6.46	5.99	4.65	5.45	7.07	11.40	....	....
Loss	−3.10	−3.65	−1.94	−2.95	−4.28	−6.23	....	....

[1] The location of the station was changed in 1910, and the records for that year were not used.

GENERAL DISCUSSION OF RESULTS.

In the preceding pages the data have been presented and discussed for each station separately. In the following pages some of the more important phases are discussed from a more general standpoint.

To facilitate this study, Table XIX has been prepared, bringing together for each station the average yields as grouped for this study under different methods of preparation, and also assembling the data from the tables of yields and cost of production in such a way as to show the profit or loss in dollars and cents per acre for the average crop by each method for which it has been computed at each station.

Table XIX shows that the yields at Belle Fourche, Garden City, Dalhart, and Amarillo have been markedly lower than at the 10 other stations. While some methods have increased the yields at these stations, they have not brought them up to a point that offers much encouragement for the growth of barley. The only profit shown from any method under study at these stations is one of 35 cents per acre from disked corn ground at Belle Fourche. This nominal profit has resulted from the low cost of production rather than from the amount of yield. The indications are that the combination of soil and climatic conditions at these stations is not favorable to the growth of barley, nor can the unfavorable conditions be overcome by cultural practices.

TABLE XIX.—*Comparison of the average yields and profit or loss in the production of barley by different methods of tillage at fourteen stations in the Great Plains area.*

Statement of data.	Number of years averaged.	Methods of tillage.						
		Fall plowed.	Spring plowed.	Listed.	Sub-soiled.	Disked.	Green manured.	Summer tilled.
Yields per acre (bushels):								
Judith Basin	5	24.0	24.0	29.0	30.5	29.0		30.2
Huntley	2		29.6			34.5	43.8	
Williston	5	17.4	16.1			27.5		28.8
Dickinson	6	25.1	24.6			37.4		32.5
Edgeley	8	16.7	18.5			23.4		20.0
Hettinger	3	19.9	25.5			14.9		31.8
Belle Fourche	6	7.6	8.3	7.7	8.0	12.2		12.6
Scottsbluff	2	14.0	15.4	14.4	15.0	18.6		27.6
North Platte	8	17.1	15.9			13.4		26.7
Akron	6	18.6	18.8	17.9	14.0	18.4		24.8
Hays	6	13.6	11.2	12.7	14.6	14.1	15.5	19.3
Garden City	5	6.9	4.3	8.3	6.9	8.9		11.0
Dalhart	4	3.9	1.9	4.4		1.6		6.4
Amarillo	6	8.2	5.7	6.1	6.8	6.6		12.6
Profit or loss (—) per acre:								
Judith Basin	5	$3.38	$3.85	$6.44	$5.44	$7.24		$0.98
Huntley	3		6.15			9.50	$3.45	
Williston	5	.67	.61			6.63		.41
Dickinson	6	3.83	4.10			10.68		1.93
Edgeley	8	.39	1.60			4.94		—3.20
Hettinger	3	1.70	4.47			1.46		1.64
Belle Fourche	6	—3.34	—2.59	—2.29	—3.79	.35		—6.23
Scottsbluff	2	— .72	.32	.45	— .92	2.98		— .08
North Platte	8	.55	.53			.84		— .55
Akron	6	1.17	1.72	1.89	—1.33	2.89		—1.23
Hays	6	— .88	—1.40	— .24	—1.08	1.13	—8.15	—3.49
Garden City	5	—3.63	—4.23	—2.05	—4.24	—1.00		—6.89
Dalhart	4	—4.86	—5.21	—3.65		—3.99		—8.78
Amarillo	6	—3.10	—3.65	—2.95	—4.28	—1.94		—6.23

Table XIX also shows that at 10 of the 14 stations under study disked corn ground has been productive of higher yields of barley than either the fall or spring plowing of stubble. At Hettinger and North Platte it has been clearly exceeded by both. At Akron it has been exceeded by both, but the differences among the three are only fractions of a bushel. At Amarillo disked corn land has been between fall-plowed and spring-plowed stubble in yield Its low cost of production has made it the most profitable method under trial at all stations except Hettinger. It has been productive of a profit at all stations except Garden City, Dalhart, and Amarillo. This study, dealing with but one crop, does not consider the relative profitableness of other crops in the farming system.

It should be borne in mind that at all stations disking corn ground as a preparation for all small grain crops has been done upon corn land kept free from weeds. If weeds were allowed to develop in the corn, similar results should not be expected. To the extent that the weeds developed or were unhindered in their growth, just so far would the corn ground approach a grain stubble in the condition of the seed bed. If the weeds matured seed, further damage by their growth might be done to the succeeding crop.

Preparing the ground with a lister instead of a plow has been practiced at eight stations. At only one station, Judith Basin, were the yields very materially different from those on fall-plowed land. But, as has been pointed out, the yields on fall-plowed land at that station were lowered somewhat by damage done by gophers. At the other stations, though it did not in all cases give higher yields than plowing, it showed, owing to a lower cost of preparation, slightly more profit where profits are shown and less loss where losses are shown than plowing.

The difference between spring and fall plowing is largely one of season. In the average of the 13 stations at which both were under trial there is practically no difference. At only three stations is there a difference of over 2 bushels per acre. At the four more southern stations the advantage has been with fall plowing. This is the only consistent territorial difference to be noted in the comparison of these two methods, but production at these four stations and at Belle Fourche has resulted in a loss by both methods. Spring plowing shows a profit at all other stations, and fall plowing shows a profit at all others except Scottsbluff.

Subsoiling in preparation for the barley crop has been practiced at seven stations. At only two of these has the consequent yield departed far from that on fall-plowed land. At the Judith Basin station there has been a marked gain and at Akron a marked decrease. In the average of the seven stations the yield from this method has been only 0.4 of a bushel more than from fall plowing. The cost of the method has been such that it has paid a profit at only the Judith Basin station.

The highest average yields at eleven of the fourteen stations have been by summer tillage. At the Judith Basin station subsoiled land has yielded a fraction of a bushel higher. At Dickinson and Edgeley the yields on disked corn ground have been appreciably higher than on summer tilled-land. While the averages of all the stations are not strictly comparable, summer tillage has increased the yield over the fall plowing and the spring plowing of cropped land nearly one-half. The average increase over disked corn ground has not been nearly so great.

These increases in yields have not been in proportion to the increased cost of the method. In no case has summer tillage been the most profitable method under trial. As values and costs are here figured, this method shows a profit at only four stations, Judith Basin, Williston, Dickinson, and Hettinger. At Scottsbluff, North Platte, and Hays the losses have been small. At the other seven stations they have been sufficiently great to discourage hope of changing them to profits by the extension of the record or by an adjustment of value or cost.

Green manuring for barley has been tried at only two stations, Huntley and Hays. At Huntley, where it was in comparison with only spring-plowed land and disked corn ground, it gave the highest average yield. This average is the highest resulting from any method at any station. The record, however, is for only two years. At Hays its yield has been greater than that on land from which a crop was harvested, but not as high as that on summer-tilled ground.

On the whole, differences in climatic conditions of different seasons have produced much wider variations in yields than have resulted from differences in cultivation. Some seasons have a combination of climatic factors so adverse as to produce failures by all methods of tillage at some stations. Other seasons have conditions so favorable that any and all methods of tillage produce good crops. Still other seasons prohibit production by some methods, but allow it with others. The greater the number of years averaged the more nearly will the final figure represent average seasonal conditions. This longer average will also tend to reduce the wide differences that may result between methods during some seasons especially favorable to some particular method. No method so far tried, however, has been able to overcome the extremely unfavorable conditions which sometimes exist.

CONCLUSIONS.

(1) Differences in the climatic conditions of different seasons have caused much wider variations in yields than have resulted from differences in cultivation.

(2) Yields at Belle Fourche, Garden City, Dalhart, and Amarillo have been markedly lower than those obtained at the other field

stations. The only profit shown at any of these stations is 35 cents an acre on disked corn ground at Belle Fourche.

(3) The highest average yields at eleven of the fourteen stations have been by summer tillage. On the average, it increased the yields nearly one-half over those produced on land cropped in the preceding year. On account of its cost it has not been the most profitable method of production.

(4) At ten of the fourteen stations under study disked corn ground produced higher yields than from either the fall plowing or the spring plowing of barley stubble. It has been the most profitable method under trial at all the stations except Hettinger.

(5) The relative advantage of either fall or spring plowing is largely dependent upon the season. In the general average of the thirteen stations at which each method has been tried there is practically no difference. At only three stations has there been an average difference of over 2 bushels per acre between the two methods. At the four more southern stations fall plowing has been better than spring plowing.

(6) At the seven stations where subsoiling for barley has been tried it has produced an average of only 0.4 of a bushel more than fall plowing. At only two stations has there been a marked difference in the results of the two methods. At one of these, subsoiling has been responsible for an increase and at the other for a decrease in yield.

(7) At eight stations listing instead of plowing has been tried. While the resulting yields have not been materially different from those on fall-plowed land, the lower cost of listing has made it the more profitable method.

ADDITIONAL COPIES
OF THIS PUBLICATION MAY BE PROCURED FROM
THE SUPERINTENDENT OF DOCUMENTS
GOVERNMENT PRINTING OFFICE
WASHINGTON, D. C.
AT
5 CENTS PER COPY
▽

UNITED STATES DEPARTMENT OF AGRICULTURE

BULLETIN No. 223

Contribution from the Bureau of Plant Industry
WM. A. TAYLOR, Chief

BOTANICAL CHARACTERS OF THE LEAVES OF THE DATE PALM USED IN DISTINGUISHING CULTIVATED VARIETIES

By

SILAS C. MASON, Arboriculturist, Crop Physiology and Breeding Investigations

CONTENTS

WASHINGTON
GOVERNMENT PRINTING OFFICE
1915

BULLETIN OF THE
U.S. DEPARTMENT OF AGRICULTURE

No. 223

Contribution from the Bureau of Plant Industry, Wm. A. Taylor, Chief.
June 23, 1915.

(PROFESSIONAL PAPER.)

BOTANICAL CHARACTERS OF THE LEAVES OF THE DATE PALM USED IN DISTINGUISHING CULTIVATED VARIETIES.

By Silas C. Mason,
Arboriculturist, Crop Physiology and Breeding Investigations.

CONTENTS.

INTRODUCTION.

At the present time most students of the date rely largely, if not wholly, on the fruiting characters for means of distinguishing the numerous varieties.

While it is recognized that in the Old World date-growing countries the natives distinguish almost intuitively the different varieties of dates by the tree habit and leaf characters, but little attention has been given to these points by European and American students of the date and no attempt has been made to systematize these characters.

The date trees certainly possess such characters, and the varietal distinctions are as constant in the trunk and leaf as they are in the fruits.

From the beginning of the study of the imported date trees in the American gardens there has been felt the need of a method of comparing and describing the different trees in the absence of their fruit and independently of their fruit characters.

This becomes of importance in assisting date work along two very distinct lines—the identification and comparison of varieties, either imported or originating in this country, and the study of seedlings originating from the cross-pollination of different varieties.

Note.—This bulletin is of interest to date growers, especially in the Southwestern States.

87664°—Bull. 223—15——1

To enable the observer to make such foliage comparisons in a precise and systematic manner, capable of tabulation for future reference, is the most important use to which this study of date-foliage characters can be put.

Most of the workers in the date gardens of the Department of Agriculture soon learn to recognize the more prominent varieties by such obvious characters as a slender or a heavy trunk; leaves with broad or narrow rib bases, erect and rigid in growth or more or less spreading, feathery, and graceful. Less elementary characters are recognized, but not formulated, which would distinguish two varieties which might agree in the more fundamental points. There are differences in the broad outlines of the leaf blade as a whole and differences in the blade, as to whether it is smooth and nearly flat or whether from varying angles of the pinnæ it appears on the defensive with bayonet-like points thrust out in all directions, as if to resist assault.

Most persons who become familiar with date trees will distinguish between trees of varieties which possess many characters in common if they are side by side for comparison; fewer will be able to keep the resemblances and differences in mind if the compared trees are on opposite sides of the garden, and a still smaller number will be able to keep varietal characters clearly in mind in going from one locality to another.

The object of this study has been to determine just what varietal characters in date trees consist in; then to apply names and formulate these so that they may be used in classifying and determining varieties, much as floral and foliage characters are used by the systematic botanist.

Perhaps of all cultivated plants the date palm is the most mechanical or geometrical in its external structure. The cylindrical, columnar trunk has the overlapping leaf bases, like inverted tiles, arranged in broad right or left spirals. The rachis, or rib, is long, smooth, and rodlike, and its expansion toward the base is along symmetrically molded surfaces.

The leaflets, or pinnæ, are in symmetrical ranks from either side of the rib, and each individual has its polished sword-shaped blade folded lengthwise with the precision of machine work. In the unopened leaf the pinnæ are placed with the compactness of the ribs of a fan; and in expanding each assumes within certain limits a definite angle with the rachis peculiar to its class.

Having such features to deal with, the writer feels that no further explanation is needed for the very mechanical way in which the subject of date-tree characters is treated. It is the only method by which the subject can be approached.

THE DATE TREE.

Date trees have no true branches, but during their earlier years, and under some conditions up to a considerable age, buds are pushed in the axils of the leaves and later develop into suckers or offshoots. These, if left undisturbed, may form trunks and tops of their own and grow to a size second only to the parent tree and identical with it in leaf and fruit characters. When these offshoots are removed at a proper size and planted by themselves they afford the only means we have of propagating the parent variety true to type. (See Pl. I.)

The flower stalks of the date are produced from the axils of the leaves in similar positions to those in which the offshoots are produced.

While many genera of palms have either perfect or monœcious flowers, all species of the genus Phoenix are diœcious, the male and female flowers being borne on separate trees. In rare instances both pistillate and staminate flowers are produced on the same spike.[1]

In noticing a date tree closely, one finds only a central columnar trunk, from the one bud at the top of which new leaves are pushing out, while around its sides the older leaves clasp the stem with their broad-sheathed bases. If the tree has reached some age and the trunk has gained a few feet in height, the older lower leaves will probably have been cut away, leaving a foot or more of their bases arranged in orderly position around the trunk in the manner of reversed tiles. Closely wedged in between these are dozens of sheets of very tough, coarse-matted fiber, called "leef" by the Arabs, the remnants of the leaf sheaths. (Pl. II.) The real trunk of the date tree is inside of these and is greatly strengthened and protected by them. It is strengthened and supported by the wrapping of their tough fibers against the leverage of the desert winds, which exert a powerful pressure upon the broad top. It is protected from bruising and battering or the gnawing of grazing animals, and insulated alike against the intense heat or the sudden freezing weather of the winter months, which may descend upon even a date-growing desert.[2]

LEAF CHARACTERS OF THE DATE.

Upon a casual examination of a date leaf the most obvious feature is the long flexible blade, which may vary in length from 3 or 4 feet in a young plant to 9, 12, or even 16 feet in a tree of mature age. (Pl. III.)

[1] As the various species of this genus hybridize readily with one another, the so-called date palms grown in many nurseries and sold for ornamental planting in California and Florida are often crossed to such an extent that the true *dactylifera* characters, as found in the trees obtained from the Sahara, are difficult to recognize, and the application of the rules laid down in this bulletin to such would lead to confusion.

[2] Date trees in Arizona and California subject for a few hours to a temperature of 15° or 18° F. may have the outer leaves killed, or at 12° F. all exposed leaves may be killed and the protected bud or growing point of the tree remain uninjured, so that new leaves are pushed from the center when spring opens.

The axis of this blade is a stout polished rib, technically called the rachis, which may be several inches broad where the leaf is attached to the trunk, but tapers to a slender tip of less than a quarter of an inch. (See Plate I.) As the leaves are placed on the trunk the face of the leaf, which is inward or toward the center of the tree, may be called the ventral surface. The reverse of this, away from the tree, is the dorsal surface. The right and left sides will be designated with the leaf in a vertical position and with the observer facing the trunk.

If an entire old leaf is cut away at its attachment to the trunk it will be found that the thick, wedge-shaped base shows torn and ragged margins, or perhaps a bit of matted fiber still clinging to it, where the fibrous sheath has been torn away. At the line of attachment sheets of this fiber encircle the tree. If a date palm be dissected, cutting away leaf after leaf till we get toward the bud, we find leaves with their original structure entire and the margins of the wide base of the rib thinning out to a continuous mat of brown fibers, which forms a complete sheath encircling all the younger growth. As the area of active growth is approached, near the center this sheath will be yellowish white, soft, and succulent, not more than 2 or 3 inches in diameter, and 8 inches or a foot in length. In a large tree the sheath may be 20 inches or more in length. On the opposite side from the rachis the margin of the sheath has an upward expansion into a broad lingua, or tongue, with coarsely incised margins and a blunt-pointed or an acuminate apex, which sometimes protrudes several inches against the inclosed leaves and which varies in a manner somewhat characteristic of different varieties. The diagonal arrangement of the fibers allows the sheath to expand a good deal, but the continual pushing upward of new leaves from within and the expansion of the trunk finally rupture it or tear it loose from the sides of the rib. Its lower margin remains attached to the trunk, so that this wrapping of old sheath fiber may persist for many years. In rare instances, the variety Lagoo, for example, the sheath has ear-shaped or auriculate expansions at the upper margin of its attachment to the rachis. Figure 1 shows a typical date leaf with the various parts.

An entire leaf comprises the upper expanded portion, properly called the blade, which includes the length from the first spines to the top, and the lower portion, representing the petiole, including the broad, wedge-shaped base of the rachis and the sheath. The blade is divided into the spine area and the pinnæ area, the exact separation of which sometimes can be only approximated. Varieties differ greatly in the proportion of the leaf blade occupied by the spines, which may range from 18 or 20 per cent to 45 per cent of the entire blade length.

A 9-YEAR-OLD DATE TREE IN THE COOPERATIVE DATE GARDEN, TEMPE, ARIZ.

A large number of offshoots, shown both at the base of the trunk and on its sides, are trimmed up and ready for removal.

A 20-YEAR-OLD MALE DATE PALM IN THE MECCA COOPERATIVE DATE GARDEN, MECCA, CAL.

COOPERATIVE DATE GARDEN AT TEMPE, ARIZ.

View looking west from the roof of the office building. The trees are shown 10 years after planting

A HAYANY DATE TREE, 10 YEARS OLD, AT THE TEMPE COOPERATIVE DATE GARDEN.

This tree shows a number of offshoots on the trunk, 3 or 4 feet from the ground; also graceful foliage and long, flexible "ribbon" pinnæ.

The broad outlines of the blade vary considerably with different varieties and are determined by the length of the pinnæ in different parts of the blade and the angles which they form with the rachis and plane. To illustrate: If in a given leaf the pinnæ at the middle of the blade are 16 inches long and placed at right angles, or 90°, with the rachis and lie in the plane of the blade; that is, so that the leaf is flat, the leaf will be 32 inches broad, not counting the breadth of the rachis fig. 2, *A*, *bb*). Let the same length of pinnæ be placed inclined only 45° from the rachis and still in the plane of the blade, then the blade will be but 22⅝ inches broad (fig. 2, *A*, *cc*). But let the pinnæ, instead of lying flat (fig. 2, *B*, *b*) diverge 45° from the plane of the blade, as well as 45° from the rachis (fig. 2, *B*, *c*), then the leaf blade becomes a V-shaped trough only 16 inches broad, or half the breadth of the blade with the pinnæ flat and at right angles.

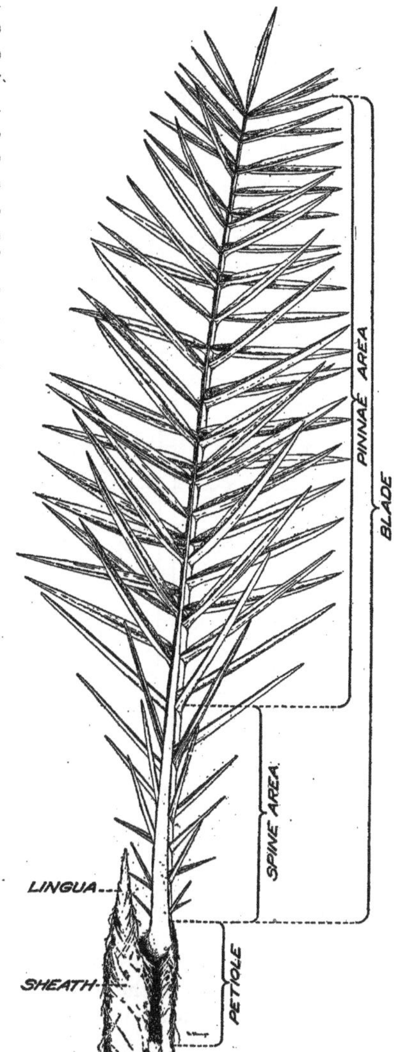

FIG. 1.—A typical date leaf, showing its various parts.

THE RACHIS.

A close inspection of the rachis of the date leaf shows that it is irregularly four-sided; the inner or ventral surface is usually strongly arched or at the first spines is made up of two ogee curves turned together. The back or dorsal surface is moderately or often strongly rounded at the base, slightly rounded or rarely flattened toward the top. The sides or lateral faces are flat or somewhat concave, and their inner margins, at first slightly converging, as they approach the top are drawn so near together as to give a triangular cross section to the rib.

The characteristic form or habit of tree tops of each date variety, due to the curves of the leaf blades, is largely determined by the flexibility of the rachis. This is governed in part by the degree of firmness and elasticity of the fiber of the rachis, but more by the way in which the diameter diminishes along the different faces.

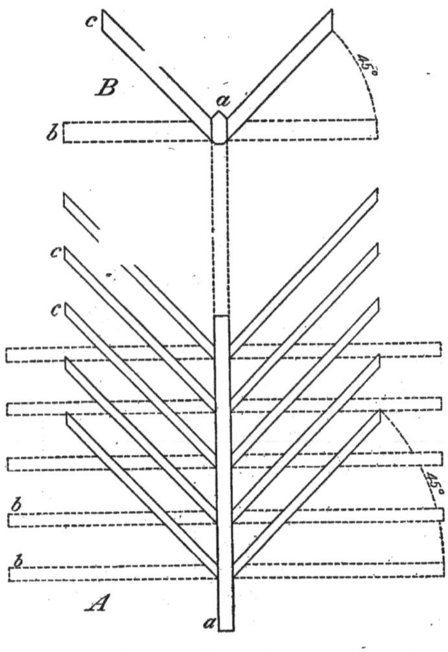

FIG. 2.—Diagram showing how the size of the date leaf is affected by the angles which the pinnæ form with the rachis. *A* represents the leaf as lying flat, the dotted lines (*b b*) showing the breadth the leaf would have with the pinnæ at 90° of axial divergence, the solid lines (*c c*) showing the breadth of the leaf with pinnæ diverging 45° from the axis. *B* represents a cross-section view of the leaf, *b* showing the pinnæ lying in the blade plane, or flat, but with an axial divergence of 45°; *c* shows the same pinnæ also diverging 45° from the blade plane.

The feathery grace of the Areshti variety is due to the leaves maintaining considerable rigidity in the lower portion, but with the rachis diminishing to a delicate and slender flexibility at the apex. The broad, open top and loose, lazy curves of the Rhars leaves are due to a rather rapid diminishing in the diameter of the rachis a short distance above the base, yet maintaining too much size in the apical portion to give grace or airiness. In the Thoory and other varieties of that class the thick, strong rachis holds its size and rigidity well up in the blade, curving only when forced out by the growth of the inner leaves. Such trees have a stiff and uncompromising aspect through the entire top.

The relative size and form of the rachis in different portions of the blade are so characteristic in the different varieties and such important factors in determining the form assumed by the tree top that it has been thought worth while to make outline tracings of the cross sections of the rachis of leaves of the different varieties, four series of which are reproduced with the descriptions of the respective varieties as text figures in this bulletin. (See figs. 11, 13, 14, and 15.) The first section is in all cases made just below the lowest spines; that is, at the base of what has been defined as the blade of the leaf, the others 1 or 2 feet apart to the apex or near it.

THE PINNÆ.

The organs commonly called leaflets, or properly pinnæ, of the date leaf, including those suppressed as spines, number from 50 or 60 to 130 on each side of the rachis. The two sides of the leaf are fairly symmetrical as to the length of the pinnæ blades and the angles at which they are placed with the rachis, but not quite symmetrical in numbers, there sometimes being a difference of four or five pinnæ on opposite sides of the leaf. While the occurrence of pinnæ in pairs is not infrequent, it appears to be largely accidental, and with the general irregularity of their positions they can not be regarded as being paired and opposite in position in the sense in which the members of many compound leaves are so recorded.

The pinnæ are borne on the lateral faces of the rachis, with normally a single pinna at the apex. In Plates I and IV the terminal pinnæ show very plainly on a number of leaves.

On the lower part of the blade the leaflike pinnæ are replaced by stiff acute spines, from 1 inch to 7 or 8 inches in length. These are really modified pinnæ, as is clearly shown by the channel in one side corresponding to the fold of the pinnæ blade; also by their mode of attachment and arrangement in groups. The larger spines pass by gradations into stiff spinelike forms, which will be called spike pinnæ. Above these there are in some varieties extra long, narrow forms, so thin and weak as to be pendulous, which will be referred to in descriptions as ribbon pinnæ. In Plate IV the long, pendulous ribbon pinnæ can be noticed on the lower portion of several leaves.

Each pinna consists of a green, leathery, sword-shaped or ensiform blade, folded lengthwise, and a cushiony expansion or callus, called the pulvinus, by which it is attached to the rachis.

In a few varieties the lower pinnæ and some spines do not immediately broaden beyond the pulvinus into the thin blade, but have a short, solid, necklike portion, elliptical in cross section, for which the name collum (Latin for "neck") is proposed.

Toward the upper end of the leaf in certain varieties the folds of the pinnæ blade are somewhat unequal, the lower or proximal fold being a little broader than the upper one. Instead of being inserted directly into the rachis it is attached along the side, running downward (decurrent) along the lateral face for an inch or two. With the fold of the blade slightly broader than the face of the rib, a free wing results, and a series of these with corresponding wings from the opposite side of the rachis may form a narrow channel along the middle of the inner face of the leaf. When such wings and channels are conspicuous they constitute good varietal characters and also are of some importance in affording harbors for scale insects, particularly *Phoenicococcus marlatti*.

When the new leaves issue from the center of the crown, three, making a complete circle of the stem, usually follow in close succession and are crowded into the form of an irregular cylinder. This gives to each emerging leaf the form of a third of a cylinder with an acuminate apex, the pinnæ being folded as compactly as the ribs of a fan upward against the rachis. With the expansion of the rachis the pinnæ diverge and the cushiony pulvinus at the base of each, at first scarcely noticeable, rapidly expands, pushing the pinna to its characteristic angle and holding it there securely.

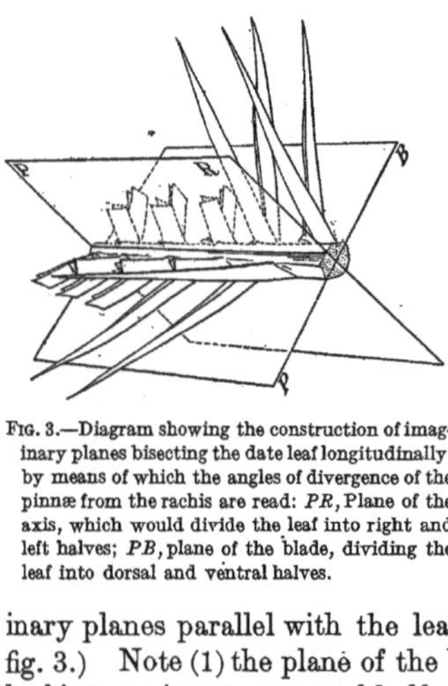

FIG. 3.—Diagram showing the construction of imaginary planes bisecting the date leaf longitudinally, by means of which the angles of divergence of the pinnæ from the rachis are read: *PR*, Plane of the axis, which would divide the leaf into right and left halves; *PB*, plane of the blade, dividing the leaf into dorsal and ventral halves.

ANGLES OF PINNÆ WITH THE RACHIS.

The difference in appearance of the leaves of varieties of dates is largely due to the different angles at which the pinnæ diverge from the rachis. At first sight these are confusing and are best understood by constructing two imaginary planes parallel with the leaf and vertical to each other. (See fig. 3.) Note (1) the plane of the blade (*PB*), which would divide the leaf into an inner or ventral half and an outer or dorsal half, and (2) the plane of the rachis (*PR*) at a right angle to the first and dividing the leaf into right and left halves.

If all pinnæ lay in the first plane there would be only two ranks, a right and a left rank, and the blade would be broad and flat, its outlines determined by the length and axial angles of the pinnæ. If the pinnæ were inserted vertically or at 90° to the second plane, they would project from either side like the teeth of a double comb.

Actually but few pinnæ in *Phoenix dactylifera* lie in either position, but the exact position of any pinna may be recorded with precision by determining its angle with each of these two planes.

It is not to be supposed that date leaves are so perfectly laid off along geometric lines that we have but to read a set of angles, refer to a table, and say with confidence, "this is Thoory," or "this is Hayany." But it is true that certain ranges of angles are found only in certain varieties, and, along with other characters, are important factors in identification.

PINNÆ CLASSES.

A third character in the insertion of the pinnæ remains. In all species of the genus Phoenix the folded pinnæ are attached to the rachis, with the margins and channel inward, or toward the ventral face of the leaf, and in some species, as *Phoenix canariensis*, they are quite uniformly attached with the channel directly inward, or at right angles with the blade plane.

In the date palm, while all the pinnæ face generally inward, or ventrally, only a portion of them face directly inward or at right angles to the blade plane. An important class of them are placed facing obliquely forward or upward, and about an equal number face obliquely backward or downward, thus giving three distinct classes of pinnæ as to position.

Those with the fold facing directly inward, or attached at right angles with the rib, will be called introrse,[1] using a botanical term meaning "directed inward."

A second class includes pinnæ with the channel directed obliquely upward, or toward the apex of the leaf, and for these the term antrorse,[2] meaning "directed upward or higher," will be used.

In a third class the pinnæ have the channel directed more or less obliquely, downward, or toward the base of the leaf, and the term retrorse,[3] meaning "directed back or downward," will be applied to these.

PINNÆ GROUPS.

Studying the pinnæ along the side of a leaf, we soon notice that these classes of pinnæ are not placed at random, but that there is a regularity in their succession. In other words, the pinnæ along the respective sides of the rachis are arranged in groups of two, three, four, or, rarely, five, a group of two being the most common. These groups fall into regular and irregular classes. The regular groups, which constitute the normal or regular form of arrangement, consist of a lower or proximal antrorse pinna and an upper or distal retrorse pinna, between which may occur one, two, or, rarely, three introrse pinnæ. Figure 4 shows the ventral surface and left side of a section of a rachis with the pinnæ cut to about an inch long. There are

[1] "Introrse, *intror'sus* (Mod. Lat.), turned inward, toward the axis."

[2] "Antrorse, *antror'sus* (antero-, before, *versus*, turned toward), directed upward, opposed to retrorse."

[3] "Retrorse, *retror'sum* (Lat.), directed backward or downward." (Jackson, A Glossary of Botanical Terms.)

four paired groups in succession, each of an antrorse pinna (*a*) and a retrorse pinna (*r*).

Figure 5, *A*, shows a ventral view of a section of a leaf, on the left side (*L*) of which, from below upward, is a triple group (*a*, *i*, *r*) and a paired group (*a*, *r*). On the opposite side (*R*) is a paired group below and a triple group above.

In figure 5, *B*, the right-hand side of a section cut well toward the top of the leaf shows a triple group below and a quadruple group above. It should be noted that the antrorse and retrorse pinnæ are not placed as obliquely as in those near the base of the blade.

In figure 5, *C*, the left-hand side of a section in about the middle of the blade shows a group of five pinnæ (*a*, *i*, *i*, *i*, *r*). This group is found in comparatively few varieties and only in small numbers.

Thus, there are four kinds of these regular groups. Noting them by the initial letters of the component pinnæ, they are, first, the

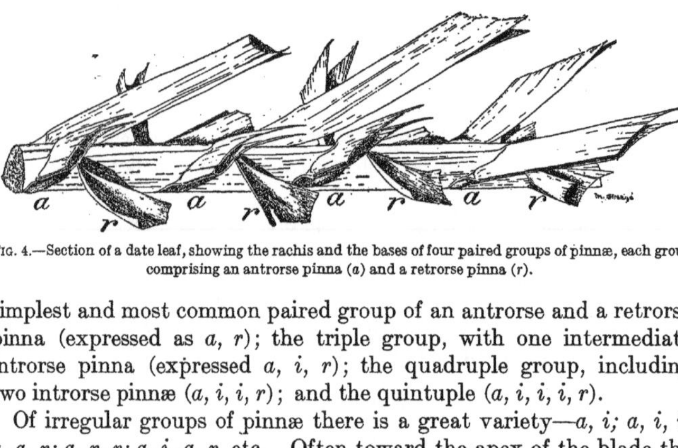

FIG. 4.—Section of a date leaf, showing the rachis and the bases of four paired groups of pinnæ, each group comprising an antrorse pinna (*a*) and a retrorse pinna (*r*).

simplest and most common paired group of an antrorse and a retrorse pinna (expressed as *a*, *r*); the triple group, with one intermediate introrse pinna (expressed *a*, *i*, *r*); the quadruple group, including two introrse pinnæ (*a*, *i*, *i*, *r*); and the quintuple (*a*, *i*, *i*, *i*, *r*).

Of irregular groups of pinnæ there is a great variety—*a*, *i*; *a*, *i*, *i*; *a*, *a*, *r*; *a*, *r*, *r*; *a*, *i*, *a*, *r*, etc. Often toward the apex of the blade the groups become obscured and the classes not well defined, merging into introrse pinnæ. In some varieties there is, especially toward the apex of the blade, a decided uniformity in leaflet insertion, the antrorse and retrorse pinnæ nearly disappear, and the groups are not well defined.

Figure 5, *D*, shows the left side of a section from a leaf of Areshti, cut near the top. Here no definite grouping could be made. The first, fourth, fifth, and seventh show a slightly oblique retrorse position, but such an area would be recorded as "indefinite."

In these the blade has nearly a plane surface, the pinnæ falling most nearly into two ranks. Where the grouping is most pronounced, six distinct ranks of pinnæ can be discerned, three on either side of the rachis. This is best noted by looking from the apex down the trough, or valley, of the blade, the rib being on a level with the eye. The 6-ranked leaves have a ragged and aggressive appearance, and with their formidable thorns and acute pinna tips are most completely armed against predatory animals.

Examining the pinnæ of the three classes—antrorse, introrse, and retrorse—we find that each has its well-defined relative position of

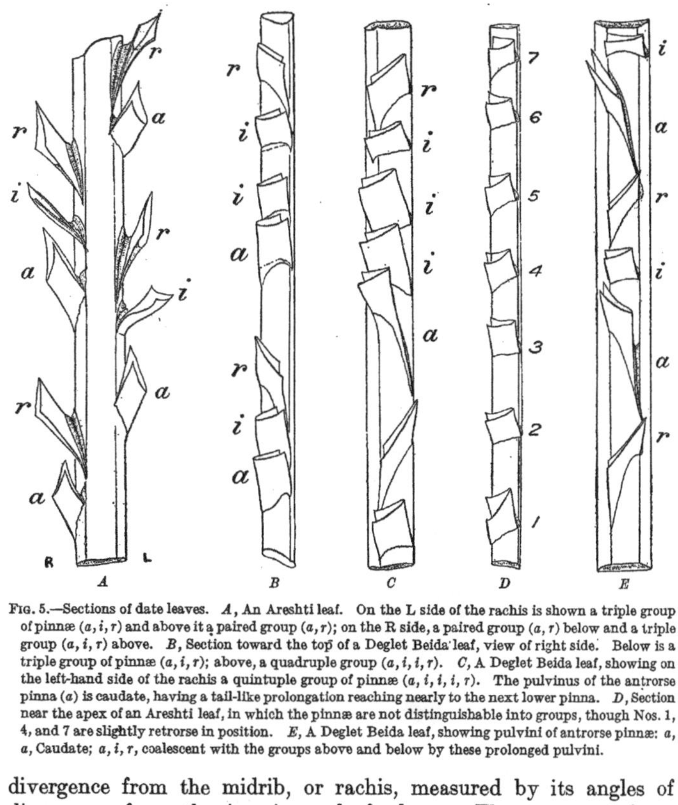

FIG. 5.—Sections of date leaves. *A*, An Areshti leaf. On the L side of the rachis is shown a triple group of pinnæ (*a, i, r*) and above it a paired group (*a, r*); on the R side, a paired group (*a, r*) below and a triple group (*a, i, r*) above. *B*, Section toward the top of a Deglet Beida leaf, view of right side. Below is a triple group of pinnæ (*a, i, r*); above, a quadruple group (*a, i, i, r*). *C*, A Deglet Beida leaf, showing on the left-hand side of the rachis a quintuple group of pinnæ (*a, i, i, i, r*). The pulvinus of the antrorse pinna (*a*) is caudate, having a tail-like prolongation reaching nearly to the next lower pinna. *D*, Section near the apex of an Areshti leaf, in which the pinnæ are not distinguishable into groups, though Nos. 1, 4, and 7 are slightly retrorse in position. *E*, A Deglet Beida leaf, showing pulvini of antrorse pinnæ: *a, a*, Caudate; *a, i, r*, coalescent with the groups above and below by these prolonged pulvini.

divergence from the midrib, or rachis, measured by its angles of divergence from the imaginary leaf planes. The antrorse pinnæ diverge least from the plane of the rachis, pointing strongly forward, and their two ranks most nearly approach each other, thus forming the greatest angle with the plane of the blade. The introrse pinnæ are placed most nearly at right angles with the plane of the rachis, or rib, and more nearly to the plane of the blade than the antrorse.

The retrorse pinnæ generally point far forward, their divergence from the plane of the rachis being slightly greater than that of the antrorse pinnæ. They may lie nearly in the plane of the blade, but they usually form angles back of that plane which must be measured dorsally.

Toward the base of the blade the groups may irregularly coincide on opposite sides of the rachis, giving the pinnæ a tufted appearance

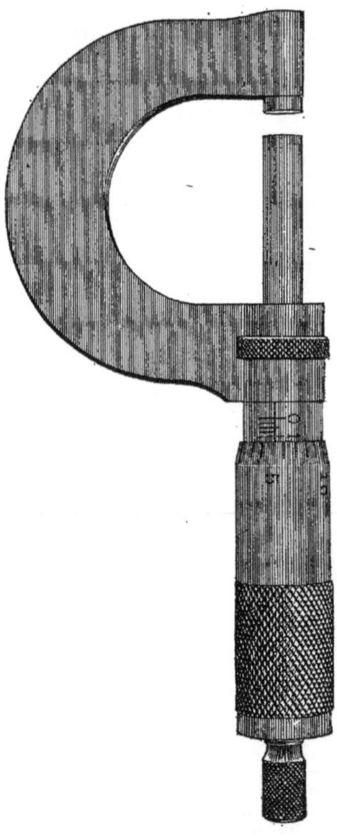

FIG. 6.—Micrometer, reading to 0.001 of an inch, for determining the comparative thickness of pinnæ of date leaves of different varieties.

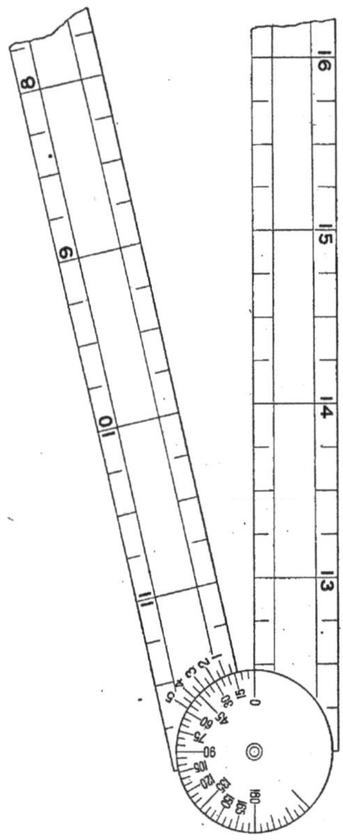

FIG. 7.—Combination 2-foot rule and protractor with vernier for determining the angles at which date-leaf pinnæ diverge from the rachis.

and leaving naked spaces of several inches between them. In other examples the groups may be coalescent through the caudate pulvini, or they may be so crowded that the pinnæ overlap like the slats in a window blind.

Figure 5, *E*, shows on the left side of a section a triple group in the middle, but coalescent with the groups above and below by the caudate pulvini of the antrorse pinnæ.

THICKNESS OF THE PINNÆ BLADE.

The pinnæ in different varieties vary considerably in texture as well as in actual thickness of the blade. Some are decidedly harsh to the touch, while those of the other extreme have a smooth, almost silky feel. Relative differences in thickness of the blades would be detected by the careful observer by comparison, but by the use of a machinist's micrometer this thickness can be made a matter of record. These instruments are graduated to read to 0.001 of an inch or to 0.01 of a millimeter and should have the improved locking device and safety ratchet for regulating the pressure.[1] (Fig. 6.) For uniformity the measurement should be made at about the broadest part of the pinna blade and near the middle of one of the folds. A number of the more familiar varieties have pinnæ that range from 0.012 of an inch (0.3048 mm.) to 0.020 of an inch (0.5080 mm.) in thickness. Others are distinguished by the greater thickness of the blade, as Thoory, with pinnæ from 0.023 of an inch (0.5842 mm.) to 0.026 of an inch (0.6604 mm.) or more in thickness.

USE OF THE FIELD PROTRACTOR.

For the measurement of the angles formed by the pinnæ with the rachis, or rib, a protractor with rather long arms is essential. As one of the necessary capacity made with the fine graduations called for in engineering is both cumbrous and expensive, a single-jointed, 2-foot metal rule, with 5-degree graduations on the hinge circle [2] and vernier reading to degrees and half degrees on the limb, has been found to be a very convenient instrument, giving the angles with sufficient precision and being instantly available for measurements in feet and inches. (See fig. 7.)

FORMS FOR THE OBSERVER'S USE.

For the field recording of characters the writer has devised a ruled and printed form, a reduced imprint of which is shown as form A.

---

[1] These instruments are furnished by tool makers in this country for the use of mechanics engaged in fine work, graduated in fractions of an inch or decimal equivalents. They may also be obtained by special order graduated in hundredths of a millimeter.

[2] The hinge circle is graduated five-eighths of the way around into spaces of 5 degrees each and figured 15°, 30°, 45°, etc., from the zero point at the inner angle when the rule is closed. Any angle a multiple of 5 degrees can accordingly be read with accuracy on this hinge circle, but for the degrees between these marks the aid of the vernier on the movable arm is needed. As will be seen when this rule is closed, a 45-degree space on the arm is graduated into 10 parts, so that one of them is equivalent to 4½ degrees, or one-half degree less than the 5-degree spaces on the circle. Every second space or the equivalent 1 degree of difference is numbered 1 to 5 in order, the 5-line degree coinciding with the 45-degree line on the circle. Now, if the rule be opened a very little, till the first vernier line marking 4½ degrees coincides with the line of the first 5 degrees on the circle, the arm has moved the difference between these, or one-half degree. Open till the second pair of marks coincides, and twice 4½, or 9, degrees of space have been moved to coincide with twice 5, or 10, degrees on the other side, a movement gaining 1 degree. So we may open to 2°, 3°, 4°, etc. In the same way starting on any even 5-degree mark, as 45°, we may open one-half degree, 1 degree, 2 degrees more. Hence, to read any angle that has been taken, read first on the hinge circle to the last full 5-degree mark inside of the angle, then add to this the degrees or half degrees to the coinciding line on the vernier. In figure 7 the rule is opened to an angle of 12½°, 10 degrees being read on the hinge circle and 2½ degrees on the vernier.

The heading provides for entering the tree to be studied, locality, garden, row and tree numbers, and date, below which the sheet is ruled in horizontal lines for noting the angles of the different classes of pinnæ: *A* (antrorse), *I* (introrse), *R* (retrorse). Above the lines, *ax* indicates that the axial divergences of the pinnæ—that is, the angles by which they diverge to the right or left from the rachis—are to be recorded.

Below the lines, P indicates the angles of divergence from the plane that would be formed by a perfectly flat blade. Below these a line provides for the record of the "Length of pinnæ" above the line and the corresponding breadths below, the breadth being noted at the broadest part, the pinnæ blade being unfolded and spread flat.

FORM A.—*Date variety,* ...., *S. P. I. No.* ...., *row* .., *tree* .., ... *garden.*

[Notes taken ...., 191... Angles of pinnæ with planes of rachis. Distance in feet from base of blade.]

		1	2	3	4	5	6	7	8	9	10	11	12
Antrorse, ax													
P													
Introrse, ax													
P													
Retrorse, ax													
P													
Length of pinnæ													
Breadth "													

Groups..

....

Remarks..

....

The vertical ruling in form A provides spaces for entries for each foot of blade length from below the first spines to the apex.

For some leaves exceeding a length of 12 feet, the record has to be carried to the ruled spaces below.

The length of the spine area and the total blade length are indicated at the same time. An average leaf being selected, it is thought that one or two characteristic readings to each foot of length from base to apex, usually along one side of the blade only, will record the characters effectively, and that two or three leaves each from as many trees will indicate the leaf characters of a given variety. For varieties of paramount importance, such as Deglet Noor, Thoory, Hayany, and a few more, of course a greater number of records are desirable.

GROUP AND CLASS RECORD.

Following the above comes the record of the classes and groups of pinnæ, made continuously from base to apex along one side of the blade. The lower thorns, usually crowded, when not distinguishable as to class or groups are indicated by a corresponding number of straight marks, then the groups are recorded by the component initial letters written together; for instance, *ar, ar, ar* would indicate three successive groups, each composed of one antrorse and one retrorse pinna.

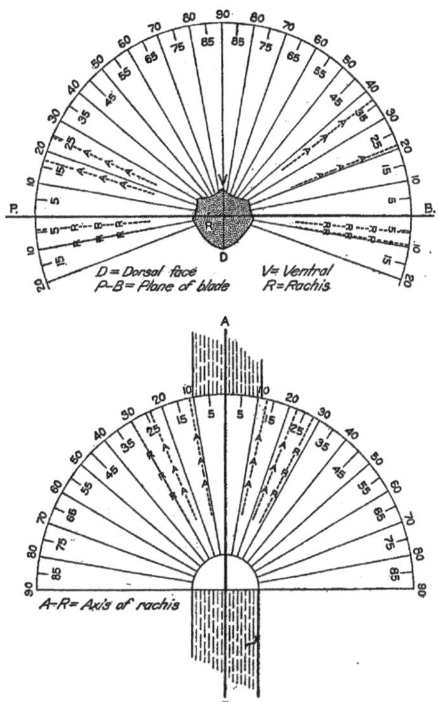

FIG. 8.—Diagrams showing the characteristic divergence of the pinnæ of a Deglet Noor date leaf, at 2 to 3 feet from the base of the leaf, recorded on form B. The upper diagram shows the divergence from the blade plane; the lower, the divergence from the apex: *A*, Antrorse pinnæ; *I*, introrse; *R*, retrorse.

ANGLE RECORD OF THE PINNÆ.

In order to accomplish the graphic representation of the various angles formed by the pinnæ with the axis and plane of the blade, a diagram has been prepared (form B)[1] representing a semicircular protractor as it might be applied for the reading of the angles recorded on form A.

The first illustration of the use of form B (fig. 8) shows the protractor scale as though laid flat upon the leaf, the zero line *AR* drawn through its center being parallel with the axis of the blade and zero toward the apex, the divergence of the right and left ranks of pinnæ would be indicated at 10°, 25°, 45°, etc.

In the second illustration of the use of form B (fig. 9) the protractor is placed as though cross-sectioning the rachis, the zero line *PB* coinciding with the plane of the blade and the line of 90° bisecting the

[1] Form B, reduced in size, is shown in figures 8, 9, and 10.

rachis into two equal parts, right and left. The ventral face of the rib is shown at *V*, the dorsal at *D*.

It will be noticed that in the illustrations of the use of form B (figs. 8–10), the protractor circle is carried 20 degrees beyond the zero plane toward the dorsal face of the rachis. This is for recording the position of the retrorse class of pinnæ, which, while sometimes forming angles of a few degrees toward the inner or ventral side, as a rule lie either at zero or inclined 5°, 10°, or even 20° dorsally.

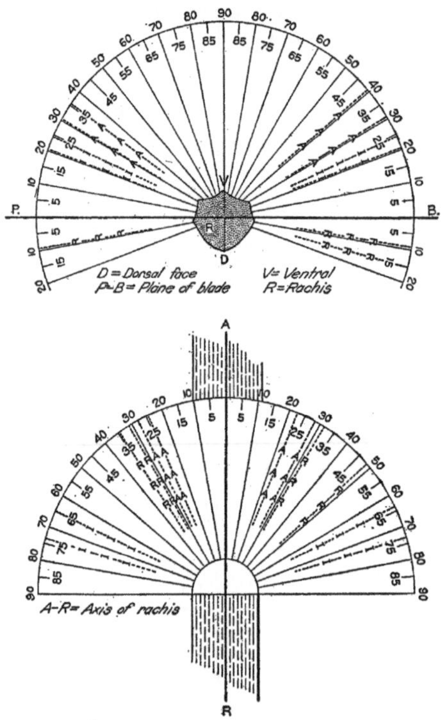

FIG. 9.—Diagrams showing the characteristic divergence of the pinnæ of a Deglet Noor date leaf, at 5 to 6 feet from the base of the leaf, recorded on form B. The upper diagram shows the divergence from the blade plane; the lower, the divergence from the apex: *A*, Antrorse pinnæ; *I*, introrse; *R*, retrorse.

APPLICATION OF THE SYSTEM TO THE DEGLET NOOR VARIETY AND ITS SEEDLINGS.

As the Deglet Noor is the most prominent variety of date yet introduced, a more extensive study of its foliage characters has been made than of any other variety. The following are some of the most striking points brought out:

The average of eight examples of Deglet Noor leaves gives the spine area as 35.5 per cent of the blade length.

For the same trees the average proportion of pinnæ of the different classes, including spines where the class is evident, to the total number on the blade, is as follows: Antrorse, 38.1 per cent; introrse, 19.4 per cent; retrorse, 34.1 per cent; uncertain, 8.4 per cent. The paired groups of pinnæ exceed all the others together.

A larger number of observations of this variety may establish a somewhat different set of ratios, but these must serve for a working basis till such can be procured.

As showing the application of such study of the leaves of a given variety and its value in selecting plants for breeding purposes, a comparison will be made of some of the Deglet Noor seedlings with the average for that variety, or what may be called a standardized tree.

Two sets of readings were taken from the Deglet Noor fruiting seedling raised by Mr. James Reed, at Thermal, Cal. In both of these the data are well within the range of variation of the eight true Deglet Noor records, and the average of the two is curiously near to the average of the Deglet Noor. The pinnæ are more closely crowded than in any of the Deglet Noor records, and the percentage of introrse pinnæ is above the average, but within the range.

The proportion of paired, triple, and quadruple groups of pinnæ is remarkably near the average. The fruit of this presumably half-blood Deglet Noor seedling has not been distinguishable from that of the standard imported Deglet Noor varieties. No other Deglet Noor seedling has been found so closely duplicating the Deglet Noor in fruit.

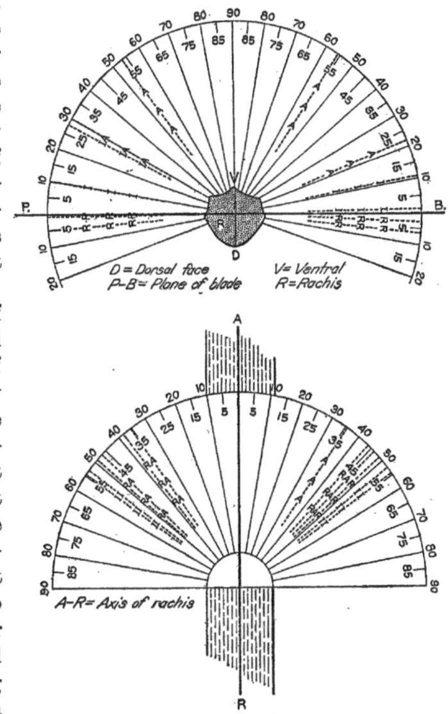

FIG. 10.—Diagrams showing the characteristic divergence of the pinnæ of a Deglet Noor date leaf, at 8 to 9 feet from the base of the leaf, recorded on form B. The upper diagram shows the divergence from the blade plane; the lower, the divergence from the apex: *A*, Antrorse pinnæ; *I*, introrse; R, retrorse.

Of others that have fruited, showing decided Deglet Noor characters in color, flavor, or texture of the fruit, none has been found with the same close approximation to Deglet Noor foliage. In a slender-fruited seedling, for example, raised by the California Date Co., at Heber, Cal., the fruit has the Deglet Noor flavor and texture in a high degree. The form of this fruit is long and slender, entirely distinct from the Deglet Noor. Referring to Table I, showing the point characters, this variety, as compared with the Deglet Noor, has the spine area shorter than any of the true Deglet Noor measurements, while the pinnæ are more crowded and have lower percentages of antrorse and retrorse pinnæ and higher percentages of introrse and undetermined pinnæ.

There are also a lower percentage of double groups of pinnæ and higher percentages of triple and quadruple groups than have been noted in any true Deglet Noor. On the whole it is considerably outside the recorded range of variation for the Deglet Noor variety, though nearer the type than the average of supposed half bloods.

It seems to be a good working hypothesis that there is a close correlation between the leaf and fruit characters of the date tree. If this be true, we should look for male trees having the leaf characters within the range of Deglet Noor variation to give us trees most capable of transmitting Deglet Noor qualities where used as pollinators. Failing in this quest, we must use those coming the nearest to such character.

So far, no male trees have been found among the Deglet Noor seedlings which correspond to the best Reed seedling in being nearly true to foliage type. Mr. Reed's seedling male trees Nos. 1 and 2 are trees of a strong Deglet Noor character, but fall considerably short of the type. However, they have been used as pollinators, and many seeds of Deglet Noor fruit of such pollinations have been sown, but none are old enough to have proved themselves.

TABLE I.—*Comparison of the average leaf characters of four important varieties of date palms.*

Average leaf characters.	Deglet Noor.	Deglet Noor, Reed's seedling.	Deglet Noor, slender-fruited seedling.	Hayany.	Menakher.	Thoory.
Blade length..........inches..	126	116	110	122	144	126
Spine area:						
Length............do....	43	38	24	23	32	32
Percentage of blade length	35.5	33	22	18	22	25.6
Total number of pinnæ on one side of rachis..........	91	98	96	96	122	69
Distribution:						
Antrorse................	32	35	30	31	27	25
Percentage of total.......	35+	36−	31+	32+	22+	36+
Introrse................	20	24	26	19	58	16
Percentage of total.....	22−	24+	27+	20−	47−	23+
Retrorse................	30	32	29	33	35	21
Percentage of total.....	33−	33−	30+	34+	29−	31−
Undetermined...........	9	7	11	13	2	7
Percentage of total.....	10−	7+	12−	14−	2−	10+
Number of groups of pinnæ:						
In groups of two.........	20	22	11	27	12	15
Percentage of total.....	61−	67−	40.7+	77+	32+	60
In groups of three........	9	8	8	7	19	8
Percentage of total.....	27+	24+	29.6	20	52	32
In groups of four.........	4	3	8	1	6	2
Percentage of total.....	12+	9+	29.6	3	16+	8
Thickness of pinnæ:						
Inches..................	0.016–0.022	0.016–0.018	....	0.017–0.020	0.017–0.022	0.022–0.030
Millimeters...............	.4064–.5588	.4064–.4727	....	.4318–.5080	.4318–.5588	.5588–.7620

In the analysis of these characters (Table I) the Deglet Noor has the highest percentage of spine area to total blade length and Hayany the lowest. Menakher stands out from the group in having nearly half of its pinnæ of the introrse class, while Hayany has the lowest percentage of any in that class. While Deglet Noor, Hayany, and Thoory have a majority of their pinnæ groups of the paired class, Hayany leads in that respect in having but a fraction short of four-fifths of its pinnæ groups in the paired class. Menakher, on the other hand, has a majority of its groups of the triple class.

The descriptions of four date varieties which follow are given as showing the application of this system of leaf study to the dates in cultivation. Among the many varieties being tested in the gardens of the Department of Agriculture these four take first rank in their respective classes and present such a wide range in leaf characters as to illustrate very clearly the principles involved.

DESCRIPTION OF THE DEGLET NOOR VARIETY.

The trees of the Deglet Noor variety have slender trunks and make a rather rapid height growth, the leaves being 9 to 11 feet long, erect spreading, forming a rather narrow vase-shaped top, becoming broader with age. The leaf base is narrow, diminishing to a firm, gradually tapering rib, which has a slight, graceful flexibility at the apical portion. It is strongly rounded dorsally, well arched ventrally, with the lateral faces of more than average breadth (fig. 11).

The spine area averages about 35 per cent of the blade length, the spines firm, with stout bases, rather long, acuminate, acutely pointed, crowded below, more scattered in the upper portion of the area, and decidedly appressed. They pass to narrow spikelike pinnæ, 12 to 18 inches in length, and the longest pinnæ, 24 to 27 inches, are reached at about the middle of the blade while but 1 inch to 1⅛ inches broad. The greatest breadth of the pinnæ, 1⅜ to 1½ inches, is usually at about 6 to 7 feet from the base, where the pinnæ are 20 to 24 inches long. They diminish steadily to 10 or 15, or rarely 18 inches, in length and seven-eighths of an inch to 1 inch in breadth at the apex of the leaf. The pinnæ throughout are acuminate in form and acutely pointed, varying in thickness of the blade from 0.016 of an inch (0.4064 mm.) to 0.022 of an inch (0.5588 mm.), from 0.017 of an inch (0.1318 mm.) to 0.020 of an inch (0.5080 mm.) being the most common, the texture being firm and rather harsh than soft. The blades are closely folded, and toward the apex of the leaf the proximal fold is slightly wider than the distal and decurrent along the rachis. The pulvini toward the base of the blade are heavy, sometimes strongly caudate, but the groups are seldom coalescent.

The paired groups of pinnæ are in the majority, often comprising 60 to 70 per cent of the whole number, while there are about 22 to 30 per cent of the triple groups, and a few are quadruple.

The antrorse pinnæ comprise from 34 to 42 per cent of the whole number, the retrorse class furnishing from 31 to 36 per cent, while of

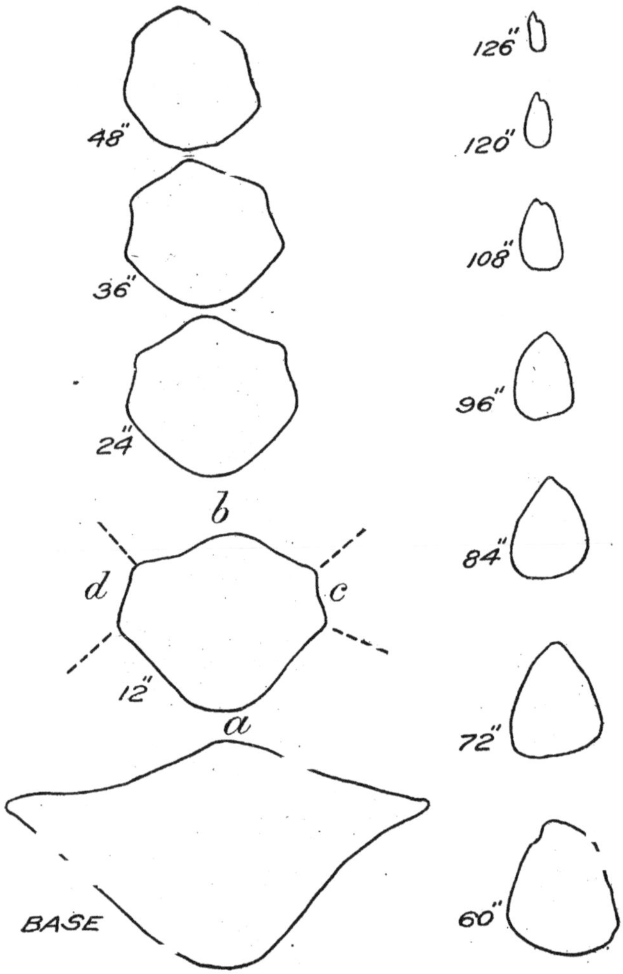

FIG. 11.—Cross sections of the rachis of a Deglet Noor date leaf, showing outlines at different distances from base to apex.

the introrse pinnæ there are but 15 to 25 per cent. Unclassified basal spines make up the balance.

In divergence from the rachis, the antrorse spines are usually rather closely appressed, a divergence of only 5° is noted in some, and other spines may diverge 25° or 30° from the axis. In some leaves the entire rank of antrorse pinnæ to the apex may not diverge more than 25° to 28°, but usually there is a spread through the middle of the blade of 35° to 42° interspersed with others of only 20° to 23°. In divergence from the plane of the blade, the antrorse class among the spines shows a good deal of variety, some basal ones diverging sharply, the majority only from 12° or 15° to 20° to 30° or more. From the middle of the blade to the apex their divergence is from 20° to 30° or rarely 40°, 45°, or more.

The introrse class, seldom found among the spines in this variety, shows strong axial angles of 40° to 50° and up to 72°, while from the blade plane their divergence ranges from zero to 15°, 20°, or 25°, a few forming angles of 35°, 40°, or even more.

In the retrorse class a few spines may stand out strongly from the rachis, but the majority are rather appressed. The retrorse pinnæ as a rule spread more than do the antrorse class at the same distances out on the blade, ranging from 24° to 40°, 45°, or 48°.

Measured from the blade plane this class has a distinct position, some being placed at zero or at 5° ventrally, but the great number incline backward from the plane, forming dorsal angles of 5° or 10°.

For a comparison of Deglet Noor seedlings of various grades with the pure variety, the above percentages and records of angles will be found to afford the means for making very close distinctions. This is important, from the fact that thus far comparisons seem to show a strong correlation between leaf and fruit characters, the seedlings bearing the nearest typical Deglet Noor fruit showing Deglet Noor leaf characters in greatest detail. By analogy, it is presumed that there will be a similar correlation between the leaf characters of male seedling trees of a given variety and their capacity for transmitting the characters of that variety when used as pollinators.

Putting the above dry array of figures into concrete form shows that the Deglet Noor has a suit of leaves thoroughly well armed at all angles of approach, especially the lower portion of the blade, with acute spines and sharply tipped pinnæ. The protection of the tender emerging leaves, but especially of the emerging flower stalks, is well provided for. In cultural practice the operator in our country is accustomed to clip off with stout shears the most of the spines, in order to give him access to the flower heads for pollination.

The fruiting stalks, or sobata, of the Deglet Noor are one of its most characteristic features. (Fig. 12.) They are, with the strands, or shamrokh, which bear the fruit, pale lemon colored in contrast with the orange-yellow or orange stalks of most varieties. They are unusually long, from 3 up to 4 or 5 feet, and 1¼ to 1½ inches broad on mature trees. The fruiting head, or portion bearing the strands, is short, the strands numerous, often 18 to 24 inches, or occasionally 27 to 30 inches long, sometimes forked. The proximal naked portion of the strand (one-third to one-half of the length) is sharply and irregularly quadrangular in cross section, the fruiting portion irregularly oval, with short zigzag angles. From 20 to 30 fruits are sometimes set on a single strand. With the growth of the fruit in weight, the stalk curves downward, till the entire load often hangs suspended nearly vertically.

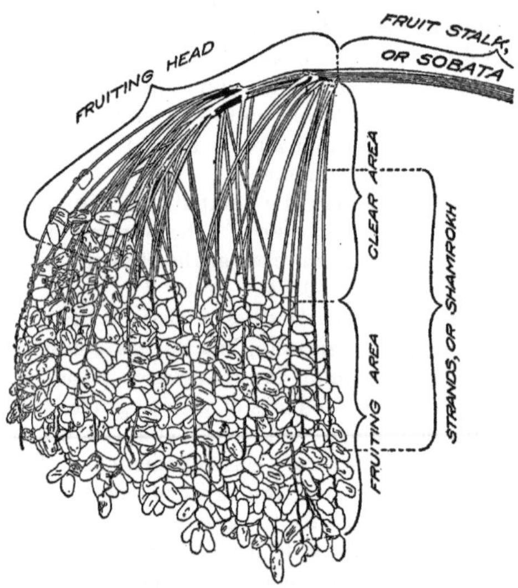

FIG. 12.—A bunch of dates of the Deglet Noor variety, showing the fruit stalk, or sobata; the fruiting head, or portion on which the strands are borne; and the strands, or shamrokh, comprising the clear area and the fruiting area.

DESCRIPTION OF THE HAYANY VARIETY.

(Birket el Ḥaggi, Birket el Ḥajji,[1] Birket el Hadji.)

The trees of the Hayany variety have rather slender trunks and moderate outcurve of leaves, forming a broadly vase-shaped top.

The leaf bases are rather coarse, broadly wedge shaped, narrowing abruptly to a wedge-shaped petiole. The rachis is of medium size, well rounded dorsally, and the lateral faces rather broad, the size diminishing gradually, but there is a decided grace and flexibility toward

[1] Several trees of this variety were received by the Office of Foreign Seed and Plant Introduction under the name of "Birket el Haggi" from Mr. Em. C. Zervudachi, of Alexandria, Egypt, in 1901, and listed under S. P. I. No. 7635. Upon fruiting they proved to be identical with "Hayany," S. P. I. No. 6438, secured by Mr. Fairchild earlier in the same year. Hayany is the correct name of the variety, which is the most numerous and most popular date of Lower Egypt. The name "Birket el Haggi" is only mentioned among Egyptian dates by Delchevalerie, who erroneously mistook the locality designation for the real name of the variety.

On the writer's visit to the Birket el Hagg district in September, 1913, he found that the people knew of no date named "Birket el Haggi," but that they had thousands of "Hayany" trees, the fruit of which was among the earliest to reach the Cairo and Alexandria markets, and so took the locality name, as "Chautauqua grapes" or "Riverside oranges" do in our country. Popenoe, "Date Growing in the Old and New World," adopts the form "Birket el Hajji," in conformity with classic Arabic pronunciation, though "Birket el Hagg" is the correct transliteration of the name of the pool and village accepted by all Egyptians and is on most of their maps.

the apex of the leaf (fig. 13). The spine area is unusually short, about 18 to 25 per cent of the blade length, and the spines are rather long, slender and acute; where considerably shaded they are inclined to be weak and soft. The spines merge into narrow spike pinnæ, followed by ribbon pinnæ 24 to 30 inches long and one-half to five-eighths of an inch wide, which are frequently pendulous, but soon give place through the middle of the blade to those of normal form, 18 to 24 inches long and 1 inch to $1\frac{1}{4}$ inches up to $1\frac{1}{2}$ or 2 inches wide with narrow attenuate tips, gradually diminishing to about 10 or 12 inches long at the apex. The pulvini are but moderately developed and creamy in color.

The lower 10 or 15 pinnæ on either side have a solid neck, which will be called the collum, from one-half inch to 2 inches in length, just above the pulvinus, from which the pinnæ expand into the folded blade of normal form. These are most strongly developed on the retrorse class of pinnæ. This character, while slightly developed in a few other Egyptian varieties, is almost an identifying character for this variety. The pinnæ blades are smooth and rather soft, not rigidly acute at the apex, but inclined to split up. The axial divergence of the pinnæ is, for the antrorse class, only about 20° to 35° near the base, becoming 45° or 50° toward the apex. The introrse and retrorse classes diverge more strongly, in some leaves to 60° or 65°. In divergence from the plane of the blade the antrorse pinnæ

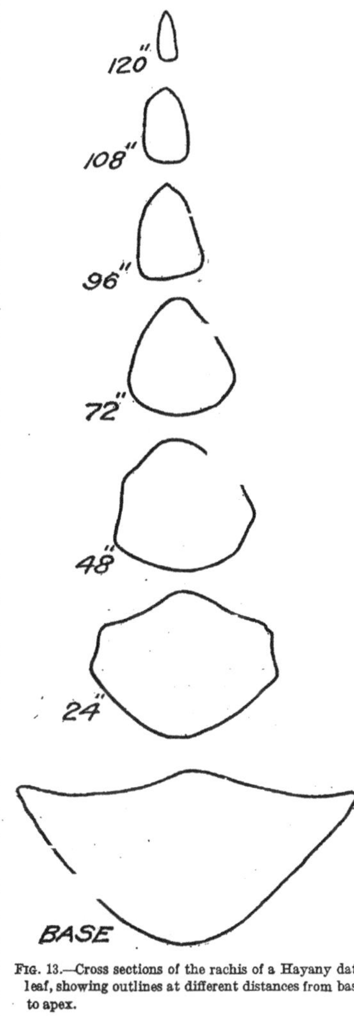

FIG. 13.—Cross sections of the rachis of a Hayany date leaf, showing outlines at different distances from base to apex.

form ranks which diverge 30° or 40° to 55° or 60°, while the introrse and retrorse pinnæ lie within 10° of the planes or diverge a little dorsally.

At Tempe, in a heavy adobe soil with an excess of subterranean moisture, this variety has been prolific in offshoots and sets them well up on the trunk, one tree as early as 1909 having six offshoots at a height of 4 to 4½ feet.

The fruit stalks are orange yellow, about 2½ or 3 feet long, 1¾ to 2 inches broad, the fruit head compact and heavy, and the strands, or shamrokh, of medium length and rather coarse.

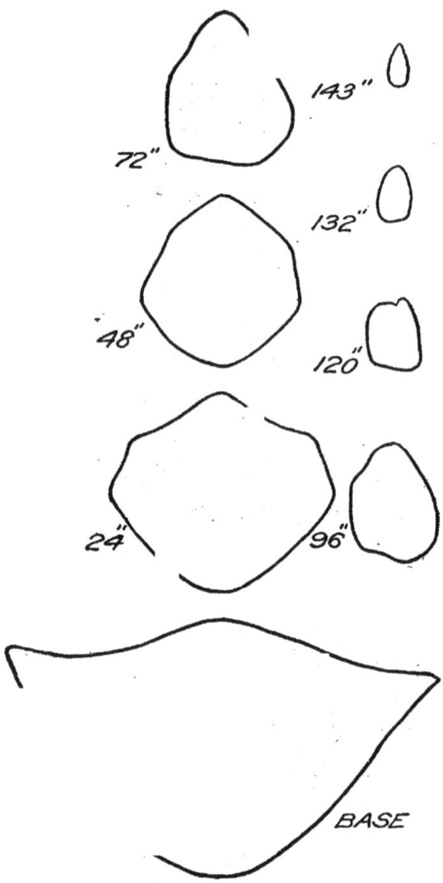

FIG. 14.—Cross sections of the rachis of a Menakher date leaf, showing outlines at different distances from base to apex.

DESCRIPTION OF THE MENAKHER VARIETY.

The trees of the Menakher variety are of beautiful and striking appearance. The growth is vigorous, though not as rank as some other varieties, and the height growth of the trunk has been rather slow.

The foliage is a dark rich green, with abundant glaucous bloom. The leaves are 9 to 12 feet long, curving outward rather stiffly below, but with an increasing flexibility toward the apex, which gives a long and beautiful sweep. The leaf bases are 7 to 9 inches broad, heavy, narrowing gradually to a stout, strongly rounded rib, which tapers slowly to a moderately slender apex (fig. 14).

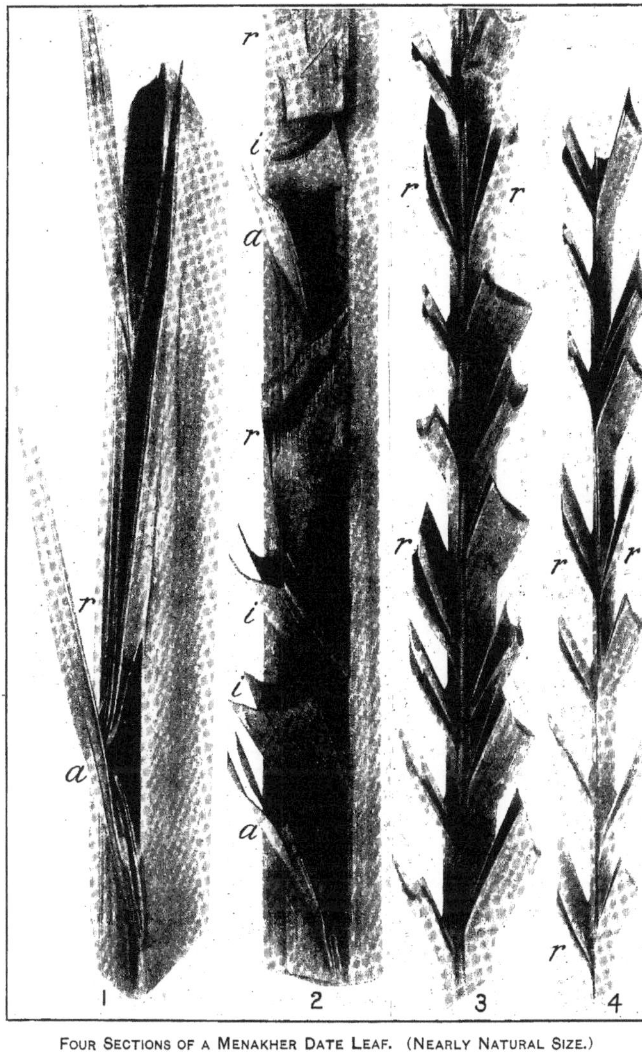

FOUR SECTIONS OF A MENAKHER DATE LEAF. (NEARLY NATURAL SIZE.)

FIG. 1.—A leaf section near the base, showing a paired group, *a, r*, of very acute spines. FIG. 2.—A section at 8 feet, showing a quadruple group, *a, i, i, r*, below and a triple group, *a, i, r*, above. FIGS. 3 and 4.—Sections at 10 and 12 feet, showing some well-defined retrorse pinnæ, *r, r*. The others will class as introrse, and no regular groups can be determined.

The spine area is from 20 to 25 per cent or more, rarely 33 to 36 per cent of the blade length. The closely set spines are short or of medium length, strong, but acute, closely appressed, passing to narrow spike pinnæ 20 to 24 inches long. The regular pinnæ at 5 to 6 feet from the leaf base are 17 to 24 inches long, $1\frac{1}{4}$ to $1\frac{3}{4}$ inches broad, decreasing in length rather gradually to about 9 to 12 inches long at the apex. (Pl. V.)

The pinnæ blades are 0.017 of an inch (0.4318 mm.) to 0.022 of an inch (0.5588 mm.) thick, firm in texture but not harsh, broadest near the base, tapering evenly to a rather acuminate acute apex. In the upper portion of the leaf the proximal fold of the pinnæ blade is decidedly broader than the distal, decurrent along the rachis, but the prominence of the ventral arch of the rachis leaves the channel formed by opposite wing margins rather open until near the top of the blade.

The pulvini are moderately heavy, frequently slenderly caudate, and there are many coalescent groups in the lower portion of the blade. The paired groups of pinnæ are considerably outnumbered by the triple and quadruple groups. The introrse pinnæ usually comprise from 40 to 48 per cent of the entire number on the blade, but sometimes yield to a high number of the retrorse class.

The slight axial divergence of all classes of pinnæ and the rather even and moderate divergence from the blade plane give to this variety a smooth, even leaf, which, with its dark, rich color, is very attractive.

The antrorse spines have but 10° to 15° of axial divergence, the lower antrorse pinnæ 15° to 20°, spreading to 30° toward the tip of the leaf.

The antrorse pinnæ diverge axially about 45° through the middle of the blade and 30° at the apex. Both these classes form angles with the blade plane of 20° to 30° or 36° in the outer 2 feet.

The axial angles of the retrorse pinnæ are a little greater than in the first-named classes, the lower pinnæ 20° to 28° or 30°, the rest of the blade 30°. These spines diverge about 15° dorsally, the pinnæ 5° dorsally, or all the upper portion at zero. In a few instances the retrorse spines and lower pinnæ have a dorsal divergence of 30° to 33°.

The fruit stalks are heavy, 3 to 4 feet long, the fruiting head 12 to 15 inches long, with numerous strong strands 12 to 18 inches in length, making a heavy, compact bunch of fruit.

But two genuine trees of the Menakher variety were finally preserved of the importation made by Mr. T. H. Kearney in 1905. One of these is at the Cooperative Date Garden at Tempe, Ariz. The other is at Mecca, Cal. The Tempe tree has made the slower growth, though it is a healthy and vigorous-looking tree. In November, 1912, its terminal bud was only 3 feet from the ground, while that of the Mecca tree was 7 feet high, with a trunk diameter of 2 feet. Whether the greater heat at Mecca or the difference in the soil is the cause of this difference in growth is not easy to say. The Tempe garden is located in a strip of land having a heavy adobe soil and so high a percentage of alkali that ordinary grain and forage crops can not be grown upon it. By the underflow of ground water from irrigated districts above, the water table has not been below 4 feet for a number of years and stands near the surface in the winter months.

The conditions at the Mecca garden are in strongest contrast with these. The soil is a fine sand, the bed of the old Salton fresh-water lake, having a considerable percentage of calcareous material in the form of partially decayed small fresh-water shells, and underlain with a few shallow strata of blue clay or silt. The only organic matter has been supplied by cover crops and the liberal application of stable manure around the roots of individual trees.

There is but a slight trace of alkali, and irrigation with very pure water from an artesian well has been abundant. While too positive conclusions should not be drawn from the behavior of a single tree in each locality, a similar slowness of growth has been noted in several trees of Thoory at Tempe, as contrasted with a very vigorous and rapid growth of that variety at Mecca and Indio. At the same time a number of varieties, such as Deglet Noor, Rhars, Itima, and Tadala, under Tempe conditions have made a rather better growth than in the sandy soil and greater heat of Mecca.

The presumption is strong that the Menakher variety finds both the temperature and the sandy soil, with the absence of the alkali of the Mecca garden, the more congenial. In fruiting, both trees have been slow to develop fruit of normal quality, but have improved from year to year. At Tempe, however, it hardly seems likely that this variety has heat enough to perfect its fruit. While a good crop was set in 1912, it was found still immature on November 10. Some fruits were coloring properly on one side and had ripened a portion of the flesh, which was of excellent flavor, but the most of them were tough and "cottony," and a good sample box could not have been collected. At Mecca a good deal of fruit developed sufficiently to be finished by "slow maturation" into a very excellent product. The rarity of this variety in Tunis and the consequent scarcity of offshoots that may be purchased will probably prevent its assuming commercial importance in the Salton Basin for many years to come.

Yet, considering the past year's performance of the Mecca tree, the writer feels that the Menakher should be regarded as promising to become one of the great commercial dates of the Salton Basin when it can be propagated in sufficient numbers.

DESCRIPTION OF THE THOORY VARIETY.

The trees of the Thoory variety are of very robust growth, with short heavy trunks. The long, heavy, rather yellowish green leaves are stiffly erect or spreading in an angular manner by bending near the base. The leaf bases are 5 to 8 inches broad, diminishing gradually

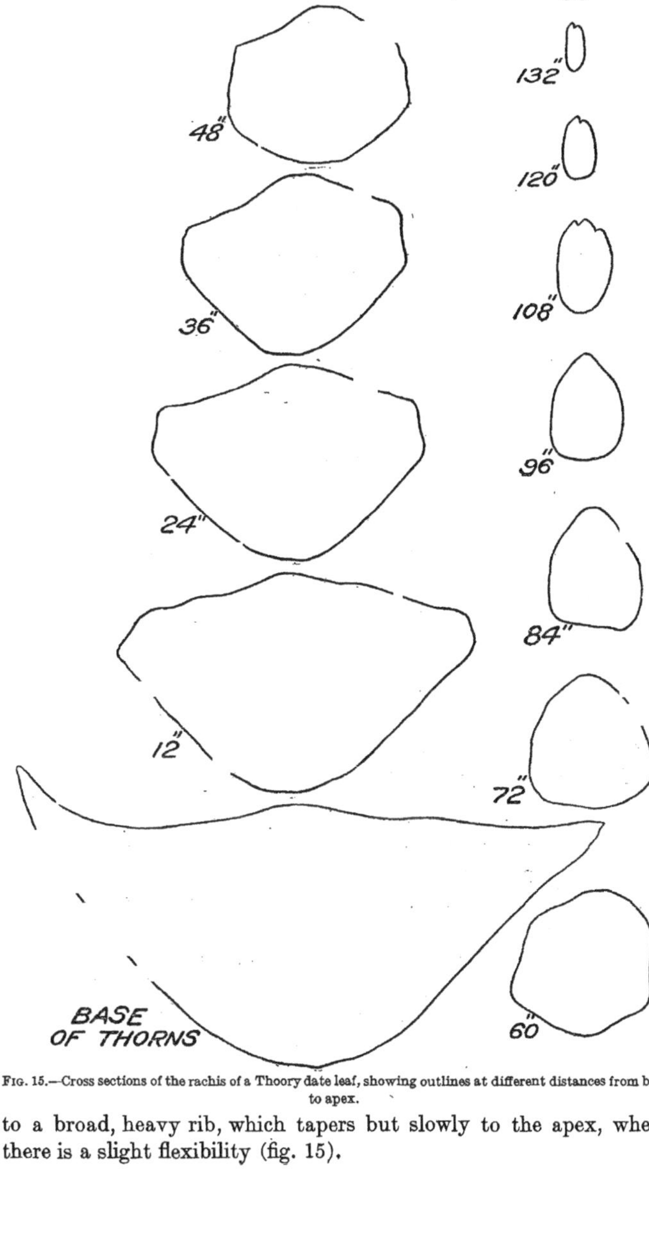

FIG. 15.—Cross sections of the rachis of a Thoory date leaf, showing outlines at different distances from base to apex.

to a broad, heavy rib, which tapers but slowly to the apex, where there is a slight flexibility (fig. 15).

The spine area is short, 15 to 30 per cent of the blade length, the sparsely set spines rather short, slender, acute, passing to a few stout spike pinnæ, 18 to 21 inches or, rarely, 25 inches long at 3 to 5 feet from the base. These are followed by pinnæ 18 to 23 inches long, diminishing slowly toward the apex, still 15 to 18 inches long at 8 or 9 feet, and the last apical ones dropping to 12 or 13 inches.

The pinnæ blades are coarse, harsh, and acute, 1½ to 2 inches broad through the greater portion of the leaf and 1¼ to 1½ inches at the apex. They are 0.018 of an inch (0.4572 mm.) to 0.024 of an inch (0.6096 mm.), occasionally 0.030 of an inch (0.7620 mm.) in thickness. The pulvini are heavy, often short caudate, and coalescent groups are common. The average space for each pinna on the rachis is broad (1.64 inches to 2.18 inches are recorded); the spines are close together at the base, but wide apart above, while the pinnæ range from 2 inches apart in the middle of the blade to 1¼ inches, or as close as 1 inch in the apical portions, but from their unusual breadth and small angles of divergence they appear crowded and overlapping.

The paired groups of pinnæ are in a decided majority, the triple groups average about half as many, and there are a few quadruple groups. The antrorse pinnæ diverge from the rachis by rather slight angles, the basal spines 25° or 30°, those above but 5° to 15°, the pinnæ from 10° to 12°, 15°, or 19°, with a small number at 25° to 32°. They form blade-plane angles of 10° to 15° for some of the spines and lower pinnæ to 22°, 25°, 32°, to 39° and 40° at 6 to 9 feet, with 30° to 35° near the apex.

An examination of leaves with the stiff, acute, antrorse pinnæ placed at these angles will convince one that their defensive efficiency is about perfect.

The introrse pinnæ, relatively of minor importance in this variety, have an axial divergence of 40° to 72°, some of them being at zero with the blade plane, others diverging 10°, 20°, to 30°, or 63°. The retrorse pinnæ diverge from the rachis from 25° or 30° through 35° and 48° to a few at 55° or 57°. These angles, combined with their dorsal divergence of 5° to 10° from the blade plane, give these two rather ragged ranks a very effective position for defense.

The fruit stalks are strong, 1½ to 2 inches in diameter and 2 to 4 feet long; the strands are coarse, 12 to 24 inches long; the color a bright orange.

The fruit of this variety, which affords one of the best examples of the dry-date class, is produced in heavy crops, the few trees in bearing showing a tendency to bear in alternate years.

UNITED STATES DEPARTMENT OF AGRICULTURE

BULLETIN No. 224

Contribution from the Bureau of Chemistry
CARL L. ALSBERG, Chief

Washington, D. C. PROFESSIONAL PAPER April 28, 1916

A STUDY OF THE PREPARATION OF FROZEN AND DRIED EGGS IN THE PRODUCING SECTION

By

M. E. PENNINGTON, Chief, Food Research Laboratory, M. K. JENKINS, Assistant Bacteriologist, and W. A. STOCKING, formerly Bacteriological Expert, assisted by S. H. ROSS, E. Q. ST. JOHN, NORMAN HENDRICKSON, and W. B. HICKS, of the Food Research Laboratory and the Omaha Food and Drug Inspection Laboratory

CONTENTS

WASHINGTON
GOVERNMENT PRINTING OFFICE
1916

UNITED STATES DEPARTMENT OF AGRICULTURE

BULLETIN No. 224

Contribution from the Bureau of Chemistry
CARL L. ALSBERG, Chief

Washington, D. C. PROFESSIONAL PAPER April 28, 1916

A STUDY OF THE PREPARATION OF FROZEN AND DRIED EGGS IN THE PRODUCING SECTION.

By M. E. PENNINGTON, *Chief, Food Research Laboratory*, M. K. JENKINS, *Assistant Bacteriologist*, and W. A. STOCKING, formerly *Bacteriological Expert*, assisted by S. H. ROSS, E. Q. ST. JOHN, NORMAN HENDRICKSON, and W. B. HICKS of the Food Research Laboratory and the Omaha Food and Drug Inspection Laboratory.[1]

CONTENTS.

INTRODUCTION.

The origin of the investigation of the preparation of frozen and dried eggs has been set forth in Circular 98 [2] of the Bureau of Chemistry. The need, from an economic viewpoint as well as that of wholesomeness, for the conservation of certain eggs out of their shells is also discussed in the circular cited. In the pursuance of the plan of work therein outlined, a study has been made of the various types of eggs going to the egg-breaking establishments in the egg-producing section. The results of this part of the investigation are given in Bulletin 51 of the Department of Agriculture.

The next step in logical sequence would be a study of the conditions prevailing in egg-breaking houses and the quality of the product sent into commerce. In the preliminary survey of the problem, as given in Circular 98, and the general observations made to determine methods of procedure and points of attack, a policy of co-operative work with the industry was outlined. These tentative plans were ultimately followed, and the information gained by uniting the observation and experimentation in the packing house with the analytical data of the laboratory is collected in the present publication.

The body of the bulletin gives a general statement of the work done and the findings which should be of interest to the general egg industry, but more particularly to manufacturers of frozen and dried products and bakers who use these products. In the appendix are given details of the investigation of use to those who have the actual management of egg-breaking plants and to chemists and bacteriologists engaged in food investigations.

[1] The assistance of J. M. Johnson and H. W. Houghton in the making of the chemical analyses during the active season of 1911 is hereby acknowledged.

[2] Practical Suggestions for the Preparation of Frozen and Dried Eggs, M. E. Pennington, Food Research Laboratory, Bureau of Chemistry, U. S. Department of Agriculture.

A part of the problem facing the investigators was the conservation of eggs in the form of a wholesome, good-quality foodstuff. Waste due to spoilage begins on the farm and increases with every step on the complicated road to the consumer. The sooner, therefore, eggs unsuited for marketing in the shell can be removed from the shell and rendered stable the more of them can be saved and the better, as a rule, will be the quality of the product. It is scarcely possible that a system of handling and distributing eggs ever will reach such perfection that the consuming centers will fail to receive some eggs not marketable in the shell. Large centers will receive so many such that it is eminently desirable that those good for food purposes be saved. But, from the economic point of view, the industry should be primarily a producing-region industry, that the expense of deterioration, transportation, and handling in the market be saved. Of first importance, therefore, is the study of breakage conditions in the producing country.

This report is based on observations made in establishments scattered between northwestern Iowa and central Kansas. The work began in the spring of 1911 and was maintained during the egg-breaking season; that is, until early September. It was continued, also, throughout the season of 1912 in the same territory.

Through the cooperation of the industry it was possible to visit and become intimately acquainted with the routine methods of many establishments, although the experimental work could be carried on with comparatively few, because of the distance between the houses and the laboratory and the size of the force of investigators required. During the season of 1911 five separate plants were studied in detail, and in 1912 three were kept under observation.

An effort was made to keep the various establishments coöperating in touch with the results obtained that improvement in the quality of the product might follow quickly upon the heels of knowledge gained. So promptly did the industry avail itself of these suggestions that the houses were constantly changing the material used, the apparatus, and the methods of work. There was, therefore, a continued tendency toward better environment and product, and each visit brought to light new phases to be studied rather than existing conditions to be confirmed by repeated observations. This rapid application of information tended to mar the scientific continuity of laboratory results, but since the object of the work was better frozen and dried eggs for the people the progressive spirit of the cooperators was encouraged, not hindered.

As the principles of cleanliness of apparatus, grading of eggs, discipline of breakers, and other fundamentals of a product of standard quality were unfolded the scope of the work broadened to take in the new problems presented. The industry found it desirable to plan the construction of breaking rooms, wash rooms, candling and receiving rooms, the application of mechanical refrigeration to the work in hand, etc., with the departmental investigators, that the principles of good handling might be fulfilled. Such activities opened a field of work in the study of sanitary surroundings for the preparation of easily infected and readily perishable products. The construction of suitable quarters for such work, therefore, forms an important part of this report.

It is highly desirable when investigating perishable commodities that they be traced from the point of origin to the point of consumption. To do this for frozen and dried eggs involves a study of the effect of long holding—since these products are almost invariably kept to tide over the season of egg scarcity—and their routine usage by the baker while in course of preparation for his products. It will be seen, therefore, that a distinct and important link in the history of the frozen or dried eggs going to the ultimate consumer must be sought outside of the packing house. Such a study in cooperation with the bakers is under way, and will be reported in due time. This report, however, deals with the industry in the packing houses of the West only.

REVIEW OF THE EGG-BREAKING HOUSES AS SEEN IN 1911.

The establishments discussed in the following pages were fair representatives of the best types of egg-breaking plants in existence in the Middle West. The management in every case was more than eager to prepare a good product and tried earnestly to use to advantage all the information then available. A survey of the field of work showed, however, that the principles of such cleanliness as is needed were not known in the industry. The equipment was not adapted to the work to be done, making for neither quality of product nor speed of operation. The rooms were so constructed that more than housewifely cleanliness was impossible, and that was attained only by an undue expenditure of time and labor. The grading by the breakers was in almost all cases a hit-or-miss operation; where a system of grading had been installed it was faulty because of a lack of knowledge of the character of the individual eggs. Such a state of affairs gave a product irregular in quality, which was not only a detriment to the baker but often resulted in the waste of good eggs as well as a utilization of bad eggs. Back of the faulty grading in the breaking room there was a universal lack of care in the candling room. Many bad eggs that should have been thrown aside by the candler were sent to the breaker, complicating her work, soiling the apparatus and, ultimately, finding their way, to a certain extent, to the food product, because her ideas of economy would not permit her to discard a large percentage of eggs, and therefore, unconsciously, she lowered her standard for food eggs.

Grading eggs, either before the candle or out of the shell, requires close attention, yet there was almost unrestricted talking, laughing, or whistling in both candling and breaking rooms. It was not possible to check the work of the individual candlers or breakers, since identities were promptly lost. Such a condition made for carelessness, as a lack of responsibility always does.

The speed of candling or breaking is a factor which must be considered from two viewpoints. If the workman soldiers or is unnecessarily slow, the cost of the work performed is unnecessarily high; on the other hand, if he works too rapidly he is sure to misgrade or do dirty work. It was, therefore, necessary to make a study of speed that both the quality of the product and the cost of production might be put on a more definite basis.

The investigation at the close of the season of 1911 had resolved itself into the following problems: (1) The construction of suitable rooms for the housing of the industry and of suitable equipment to insure cleanliness; (2) the grading of the eggs by candlers and breakers; (3) the keeping of the product after preparation and its behavior in the bakery; (4) the establishment of a system based on scientific observations by which an employee should do a full day's work that will result in a product of definite and uniform quality. The work of the season of 1912 endeavored to solve these questions. The story of the work along the lines indicated follows.

PLAN FOR THE EXPERIMENTAL WORK OF 1912.

The experiments and observations made in the six houses during the season of 1911 showed that certain forms of construction and equipment and certain methods of operation are necessary for the preparation of clean, wholesome frozen and desiccated eggs. In order to make practical application of this information, arrangements were made to work cooperatively with the management of three of the houses while remodeling their construction and equipment, making observations, and assisting in the organization of methods of operation.

Since the laboratory studies during the season of 1911 represented the product prepared under old conditions, bacteriological and chemical samples were taken in D, E, and F houses which were under observation during 1912. The bacteriological and chemical examinations of the samples were made, as in 1911, in the Omaha Food and Drug Inspection Laboratory. The results of the laboratory studies were applied practically, when possible, to improve the quality of the commercial product and to learn which eggs should be conserved for food purposes and which should not.

REMODELING OF CONSTRUCTION AND EQUIPMENT.

The plans for remodeling the construction and the equipment of the three houses were founded on the following general principles:

1. In order to prevent deterioration of eggs after receipt, the holding room, candling room, and breaking room should be insulated and refrigerated. A temperature of 30° F. to 32° F. should be maintained in the first, 50° F. to 55° F. in the second, and 60° F. to 65° F. in the third. The chilling of the candling and breaking rooms is to prevent the sweating of the eggs after they are removed from the chill room. Since the candlers and breakers spend the entire working day in the candling and breaking rooms, it is necessary that both be ventilated. The breaking room and wash room should be built with nonabsorbent walls and floor and should have an abundant supply of natural light. The washroom should be separate from the breaking room and should have a floor sloping toward a drain.

2. The most important piece of equipment in the candling room is the egg candle. It should be supplied with a strong, white light and with openings from three-fourths to one and one-fourth inches in diameter.

3. The apparatus in the breaking room should be of metal, or of a material permitting of absolute cleanliness. The table should have metal legs and a nonabsorbent top, such as monel metal, zinc, galvanized iron, or glass. The breaking trays should be made of a metal which will not rust. The tray should be constructed with a removable breaking knife, with a support for the cups, so that they will not set in the drip collecting from the knife and so that they will not set directly under the knife. The cups should be transparent, not opaque. The egg mixers, preferably, should be surrounded with brine and so constructed that they will permit of steam sterilization for 20 minutes.

4. The wash room should be supplied with hot and cold water and equipped with sinks and sterilizers.

ORGANIZATION OF METHODS OF OPERATION.

The reorganization of the methods of operation included the work of the candling room, breaking room, and wash room.

1. A plan was made to elaborate a system of overinspection in the candling room, to check the work of individual candlers, to recover good eggs thrown out in rejects, and to keep bad eggs which can be detected by the candle from being passed as good.
2. The organization of the work in the breaking room included rules for the proper manipulation of the egg during breaking, for methods of grading, for changing apparatus after breaking a bad egg, for behavior of breaker, and for cleaning the room and its equipment.
3. A routine was established in the wash room whereby the thorough washing and sterilization of all apparatus coming in contact with food egg was insured. Particular attention was given to the arrangement of the equipment of the room to save time and labor.

COORDINATION OF FIELD AND LABORATORY WORK.

From 40 to 50 laboratory samples were taken each week of the various types of eggs occurring throughout the egg-breaking season and of the commercial product during the different stages of its preparation. In some cases large subsamples were taken for later study in bakeries.

The routine bacteriological examination included the determination of the total number of organisms present, the total number of organisms producing gas in lactose bile, and, in some cases, the isolation and identification of members of the *Bacillus coli* group; the routine chemical analyses involved the determination of moisture and the amount of ammoniacal nitrogen by the Folin method. For further details of technic see pages 74 to 77 in U. S. Department of Agriculture Bulletin 51.

Regular visits of five to six days' duration, beginning on April 22 and ending on September 17, 1912, were made on successive weeks to D, E, and F houses. The observations made in the packing house on the quality of the breaking stock, on the efficiency of the grading in the candling and breaking rooms, and on the sanitary precautions enforced in the breaking room and wash room were correlated from time to time with the laboratory data. This information was then utilized as a basis for new or continued work on succeeding visits to the three houses.

PUBLICATION OF RESULTS OF THE INVESTIGATION.

The data obtained from the compilation of the descriptions and laboratory findings of the samples prepared from the various types of eggs occurring throughout the egg-breaking season have been published in Bulletin 51 of the U. S. Department of Agriculture. Upon these data are based the principles of the grading of the eggs used by the breakers and the determination of their fitness or unfitness for human food.

The details of the practical application of the principles of construction and equipment, the observations in the packing house, the organization of candling room, breaking room, and wash room, and the laboratory findings in samples of the commercial product are correlated, discussed, and summarized in the following pages of this report.

The results of the study of samples taken in the field and followed through the bakery, together with a detailed description of equipment, with illustrations, and a discussion of scientific management as applied to the preparation of canned eggs will be given in later publications.

GENERAL STATEMENT OF THE INVESTIGATION AND THE RESULTS.

The frozen-egg industry, hardly 15 years old, is permanent, because it has developed as the direct result of an economic need. Many eggs, such as cracked, small, dirty, shrunken, and slightly heated eggs, commercially termed seconds, reach the first concentrating center in a wholesome condition, but if shipped in the shell to a distant consuming center they would markedly decompose and be entirely unfit for food purposes. The new industry believed that cracked eggs and seconds could be conserved by freezing out of the shell, and the baker thereby supplied with wholesome eggs at a reasonable price during the whole year.

As was to be expected, the new industry had to face many problems. The general public had its usual prejudice against any food coming from cold storage. The industry was ignorant of the general principles of bacterial cleanliness in the commercial preparation of a perishable foodstuff. Unprincipled persons, thinking they could conceal inferiority of low-grade eggs by freezing them en masse, brought the industry into disrepute. Food officials were groping in the dark in their efforts to protect the public against decomposed eggs. These contending forces were fast making the investment of money in the preparation of frozen and dried eggs a hazardous business proposition.

It was at this time that the Department of Agriculture began its study of the problem. Science had not entered the door of the frozen-egg industry as it had done in allied enterprises—for example, dairying. The investigators had before them the task of laying the groundwork for the scientific preparation of an extremely perishable product.

EVOLUTION IN CONSTRUCTION, EQUIPMENT, AND OPERATIONS.

When this investigation was begun the breaking room in D house was the most modern, and that of E house the most old-fashioned. The former was the only one of five houses under observation in 1911 to have refrigeration in this department. In fact, to this house must be given the credit of being the first to build a model egg-breaking room. It was built entirely of concrete, and the walls were white enameled. The windows were insulated and always closed; therefore, they were fly and dust proof, a condition not found in unchilled rooms. Persons entering the model room were astonished at the whiteness and the abundance of light. In truth, the room had been patterned after a hospital operating room. The practical success of this experiment is shown by the fact that E house built a similar room, but with a capacity about five times as great, for the season of 1912. The egg-breaking room of E house before and after remodeling is shown in Plates IV, V, and VI. The appearance of the breaking room of D and F houses is shown in Plates VII and VIII, figure 2. A freezer with brine-pipe shelves to hold the eggs during freezing is illustrated in Plate XIII, figure 1.

The equipment and the methods followed in the breaking room were for the most part crude. It was in this quarter that a large part of the efforts of the investigators was first centered.

The device used for cracking and holding the eggs during grading was one of the first pieces of apparatus to be attacked. Laboratory studies showed that for the sake of cleanliness the edge on which the eggs were broken should be adjustable and should not be located directly over the cups into which the eggs were dropped; that these containers should be supported by a wire screen or other device to prevent their becoming soiled with drippings of egg; and, thirdly, that glass cups with a capacity of two to three eggs should be used to prevent waste and to facilitate grading. A discussion of these findings with the managements of D, E, and F houses resulted in each perfecting an egg-breaking outfit conforming to the above specifications. F house, however, used metal instead of glass cups. F house also developed a mechanical method for the separation of white and yolk. These changes were begun in 1911 and completed for the season of 1912. Illustrations of breaking outfits of the old type are shown in figures 5 and 7 and also in Plate IX, figure 2. The newly devised egg-breaking trays are shown in Plate IX, figure 3; Plate X, figures 1 and 2; and also figure 6.

The method of cleaning utensils was practically revolutionized as a result of the experiments of the investigators. The washing departments, except in D house, were generally located in a corner of the breaking room. The washing was done in a hit-and-miss fashion. Bacteriological tests showed that even though the utensils were apparently clean to the senses they were excellent seed beds for the bacterial contamination of the product (see Plate I, figures 1 and 2; Plate II, figure 1; and Plate III, figures 1, 2, and 3). That this was the case was shown also by the fact that the bacteria in the product increased as it passed from one container to another in its routine handling in the breaking and drying room. Experiments showed that the only sure method of rendering the utensils bacterially clean was to steam them for 15 to 20 minutes at a temperature of 210° to 212° F. The efficiency of this operation was proved by the fact that the product handled in sterilized utensils contained markedly fewer organisms, other conditions being equal, than did that prepared in containers cleansed by the usual commercial method.

Since these experiments showed that the thorough cleansing and sterilization of utensils afforded a direct means of lowering the numbers of bacteria in the product, and thereby enhancing its stability, the cooperating members of the industry did not require a second bidding to build sanitary well-equipped wash rooms outside of the breaking rooms. In fact, the new wash rooms of E and F houses in 1912 were models of efficiency (see Plates XI and XII).

It was found, also, that the fingers of the breakers, especially after breaking "sweaty," dirty, or bad eggs, were a fertile source of contamination. Actual contact of eggshell and fingers could not be eliminated, neither could a slight wetting of the tips of the thumbs and forefingers with egg be avoided. But both these objectionable practices could be reduced to a minimum by care and skill. Shell contamination was lessened because the cool air of the chilled breaking rooms prevented the formation of water by condensation. D house and E house in 1912, because of adequate refrigeration, were not troubled with wet-shelled eggs. As would be expected, dirty eggs through contact with the girls' fingers furnished more bacteria to the product, other conditions being equal, than did clean eggs. It was also observed that the breaking of eggs with hands constantly wet with egg not only made the skin tender and oftentimes painfully sore, but also increased the number of bacteria in the product. This condition parallels that obnoxious practice in the dairy industry of milking with wet hands. The handling of the egg with the tips of the fingers, thereby preventing the rest of the hand from becoming wet, and the frequent drying of the ends of the fingers with tissue paper, not only made it possible for the girls to keep their hands in good condition, but also presented a practical means of lessening contamination. The bacteria furnished to the fingers by the outside of the egg were few compared with those derived from the contents of an infected egg, such as a sour egg or egg with a green white. Bacterial examination showed that the thorough washing and drying of hands after breaking a bad egg was the only means of avoiding this contamination. These findings are illustrated in Plate I, figure 4; Plate II, figures 2 and 3; and Plate III, figure 4.

A very common practice was the use of rags, always unsightly, interchangeably for wiping utensils, hands, and the floor. The bacterial examination of water wrung from such cloths revealed hundreds of millions of organisms. These agents, instead of cleaning, spread the dirt. The improvement in the manipulation of the egg, the devising of an outfit suitable for breaking eggs, and the introduction of tissue paper and paper towels for drying hands, practically abolished the use of cloths except for cleaning the tables. These few cloths could readily be laundered, or sterilized, after each day's work, so that they could be kept sweet and clean. These changes eliminated a number of the sources of contamination of the product and did much to improve the appearance of the breaking room as well.

The introduction of pails in place of shipping cases to convey the eggs from the candling to the breaking rooms eliminated considerable dust and litter. The devising of a tray for the holding of leaking eggs made it possible to carry them to the breaking room in a clean condition (see Plate VIII, figure 1; Plate IX, figure 1; and Plate XIII, figure 2.)

As can readily be seen from this discussion, the laboratory findings practically revolutionized the apparatus used and the routine followed in the breaking room. Instead of the haphazard collection of odd pieces of china, glass, and tin, there were evolved machines accurately adapted to the work to be done; and the careless, inconsequent methods of cracking and emptying the shells were replaced by a standardized, definite routine, making for both quality and efficiency.

GRADING THE BREAKING STOCK BY CANDLING.

The classes of eggs principally used for breaking were seconds, cracked, and dirty eggs. It is to be expected that eggs sold for breaking stock would contain a higher percentage of loss than would eggs sold as current receipts, and such, by actual observation, was found to be the case. Comparative data collected in D house showed, as illustrated in Table 1, that from eggs purchased especially for breaking 6.6 per cent of bad eggs were rejected in July and 10.6 per cent in August, whereas from its current receipts only 3.5 per cent were discarded in July and only 3.1 per cent in August.

TABLE 1.—*Condensed candling reports of D house.*

I. CURRENT RECEIPTS.

Month.	Total receipts.	Firsts, seconds, checks.		Bad eggs.	
	Dozen.	*Dozen.*	*Per cent.*	*Dozen.*	*Per cent.*
June	85,083$\frac{3}{4}$	83,730$\frac{7}{12}$	98.4	1,353$\frac{1}{6}$	1.6
July	53,109$\frac{5}{12}$	51,265$\frac{5}{6}$	96.5	1,843$\frac{7}{12}$	3.5
August	72,040$\frac{2}{3}$	69,781$\frac{1}{3}$	96.9	2,259$\frac{1}{3}$	3.1
Total	210,133$\frac{5}{6}$	204,777$\frac{3}{4}$	97.4	5,456$\frac{1}{12}$	2.6

II. EGGS SHIPPED TO D HOUSE FOR BREAKING PURPOSES.

Month.	Total. receipts.	Seconds and checks, good eggs.		Bad eggs.	
	Dozen.	*Dozen.*	*Per cent.*	*Dozen.*	*Per cent.*
July	27,024$\frac{1}{3}$	25,230	93.4	1,794$\frac{1}{3}$	6.6
August	27,948$\frac{1}{4}$	24,953$\frac{3}{4}$	89.3	2,994$\frac{1}{2}$	10.6
Total	54,972$\frac{7}{12}$	50,183$\frac{3}{4}$	91.3	4,788$\frac{5}{6}$	8.7

In order to give farmers, hucksters, grocers, etc., an inducement to improve the quality of the eggs they sell, and in order to put the buying of eggs on the same basis as the buying of other commodities, all the cooperating houses after June 1 purchased all of their eggs on a quality basis.

Instructions in the cooperating houses were to the effect that only eggs with whole yolks, excluding "blood rings" and those having blood clots or mold, should be graded by the candle as fit for food purposes. In the spring, but more especially later in the season, it was observed that the grading of eggs by the candle as ordinarily practiced was far from accurate. Bad eggs were passed as good eggs, and vice versa. The correction of these errors to save food eggs and to prevent objectionable eggs going to the breaking room and there contaminating and spoiling good eggs was of sufficient importance to warrant careful consideration by both the industry and the investigators. The detailed results of this investigation will be presented in another publication. The practical application of the findings may be summarized as follows:

The keynote of accurate grading is a knowledge of the quality of eggs and good management. First, there must be a foreman in each candling room who is not only an expert candler but also a good executive. Second, each case or pail of eggs should be tagged with the number of the individual candler that he may have a sense of responsibility and that the accuracy of his candling may be determined. Third, the candlers should be instructed to place all eggs difficult to grade with the rejects or in a container by themselves in order to reduce the number of bad eggs going to the breaking room. Fourth, the foreman of the breaking room should be on the alert to detect bad eggs which are present in breaking stock due to errors in candling and to report the same to the candling room. Fifth, all doubtful eggs should be recandled by an expert to recover those which are good. E and F houses operated their candling room according to this system with excellent results.

GRADING IN THE BREAKING ROOM.

If good organization was important in the candling room, it was even more so in the breaking room; here the product (good eggs being furnished) gained or lost in quality, depending upon the mode of handling. Here, also, the cost of preparation increased or decreased with the efficiency of the working force. First in importance was the foreman, for upon him should rest the responsibility of the work of the breaking force and the condition of the ultimate product. He should be able to command the respect of his subordinates, be conversant with the fundamental principles of bacterial cleanliness, and be familiar with the different types of eggs occurring in breaking stock.

Owing to the decided changes made in equipment and methods, the routine work in the breaking room in 1912 was quite different from that of 1911. The duties of the foreman the second season included the enforcement of the following: Clean manipulation of the egg during breaking, the proper method of grading, the changing of apparatus and the cleaning of hands after breaking a bad egg, the correct speed for breaking, the thorough washing and sterilization of utensils, and the maintenance of discipline in the breaking force.

Since the presence of one infected egg would contribute myriads of bacteria to the liquid product, the study of the grading of eggs out of the shell became a very important part of the work. As has been stated, the candling of eggs is a very efficient means of eliminating bad eggs from breaking stock, but it is by no means accurate. It is also generally understood by those familiar with eggs before the candle and out of the shell that there are some types of objectionable eggs, such as musty or sour eggs, which can only be detected when broken. The laboratory findings on composite samples of eggs graded to definite types and broken under clean commercial conditions showed, as given in Bulletin 51 of the U. S. Department of Agriculture, the following facts:

The majority of the samples of white rots, eggs with yolk lightly adherent to the shell, and all of the samples of sour eggs, black rots, eggs with green albumens, eggs with yolk heavily adherent to the shell, and all other eggs with bad odors, were infested with bacteria. *B. coli* were present in most of these eggs and constituted the predominating organism in sour eggs.

The eggs with yolk lightly adherent to the shell were slightly lower in quality than the regular breaking stock eggs, whereas the sour eggs, white rots, eggs with green whites, and eggs with yolk heavily adherent to the shell showed considerably more deterioration. Eggs with bloody whites, or eggs with blood rings, should not be used. The cause of the musty egg, the odor of which increases on heating, thereby creating disaster in the bakery, has not been determined.

The candler aimed to eliminate all of these types of egg from breaking stock except sour and musty eggs and eggs with green whites. As a matter of fact, blood rings, white rots, and eggs with yolk lightly stuck to shell were frequently miscandled. Cracked eggs with moldy shells were not always detected by the candlers.

This condition of affairs made it necessary that the breakers be able to recognize all kinds of bad eggs, for upon them rested the final responsibility of eliminating bad eggs from the finished product. It was, therefore, incumbent upon the foreman to select well-qualified girls. If a breaker, for instance, did not have a delicate sense of smell she would not be able to detect incipient forms of musty eggs, sour eggs, etc.; or, if she were not quick of perception, she would not recognize eggs with light green whites, etc. The importance of accurate grading is emphasized by the fact that one musty egg would spoil over 30 pounds of liquid egg, worth at least $5. If, on the other hand, she threw away eggs fit for food purposes, she incurred a financial loss to the company.

The preservation of strict order among the breakers was a matter of importance. If a girl, for instance, gossiped with her neighbor, she not only broke fewer eggs but her grading suffered. If she chewed gum she blunted her sense of smell. In order to encourage good steady work and at the same time give the girls a rest from the continuous breaking of eggs, which involves constant attention and the repeated use of the same muscles, they were given, in addition to the noon hour, a recess of about 15 minutes in the middle of each half day. They were allowed to go out of the room, move about, and to converse freely. Such relaxation enabled the girls to do more and better work.

SPEED OF BREAKING.

After the routine of 1912 had become well established observations were made of the time required to take the necessary steps to break and grade an egg and also of the average number of eggs broken per minute, and during longer intervals of time. The results may be summarized as follows:

The speed of breaking depends upon the breaker, the quality of the eggs, and the character and arrangement of the equipment. The split-second timer showed that the successive motions made by the best breakers were as rythmic as those of a machine. The number of eggs broken per minute averaged from 12 to 16, or from 12 to 16 cases of 30 dozen eggs each per working-day of 10 hours. These figures refer to the breaking of eggs without separating into white and yolk. The breakers at E house were the swiftest, those of F house slightly slower, and those at D house the slowest.

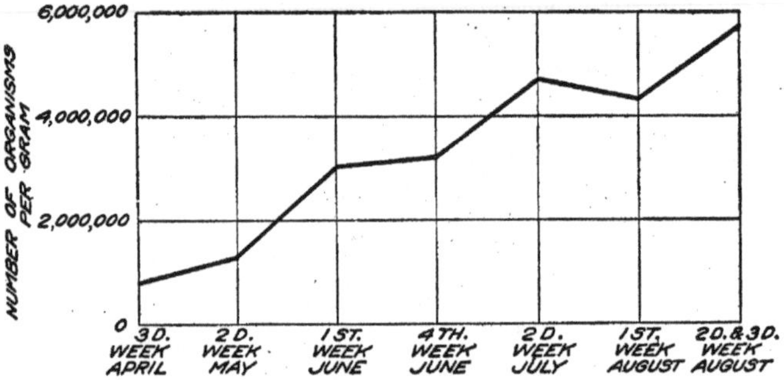

FIG. 1.—Diagram showing the seasonal variation in the bacterial content of the commercial product of E house in 1912.

In E house the pails of eggs, the breaking outfit, the chute for the shells, and the container for the liquid product were so arranged that the motions required to break an egg were minimized and were all in one direction. In F house half of the force worked left-handedly because the egg supply was contained in egg cases. The case would be right-handed for one girl and left-handed for the girl working opposite. It took longer to remove eggs from cases, particularly if they were in fillers, than it did from pails. In D house the breakers dropped the shells into a container on the floor at the side instead of into a hopper directly in front. The former was slower. These small differences mean but a few tenths of a second for each egg broken, but aggregate minutes and hours when the whole working-day is taken into consideration. Other factors being eliminated, it was found that a girl working from left to right could break over 40 dozen more eggs per day than if she worked in the opposite direction.

It was also observed that the arm could empty cups more quickly than the nose could notify the brain of the odor of the contents. For example, a breaker may be surprised to find that she has put a "light must" or a "beginning sour" into the container for good eggs before her mind has apprised her of the character of the egg. For this reason a limit should be set to the number of eggs broken in a given time. Though the girls were not paid according to the quantity of work accomplished, there was an inherent tendency for some to break very rapidly. The supervisor should make it as much of a point to slacken the pace of these workers as to hurry those who are slow. With the present equipment and methods a girl should not break more than 16 eggs per minute, and if the breaking stock contains many bad eggs the limit should be reduced to 12.

SEASONAL VARIATION IN QUALITY OF PRODUCT.

The practical man is familiar with the seasonal variation in the quality of the egg supply. His knowledge is more often confined to the differences in the condition of the eggs in the shell than to that of the frozen and dried products. Since the latter, in the houses under observation, were prepared from eggs which were graded by the senses as fit for food purposes, this is to be expected since small differences in quality can only be detected by careful laboratory procedures.

In order to determine what part weather conditions played in the ultimate product, samples were taken systematically in two houses during the season of 1912.

TABLE 2.—*Seasonal variation in bacterial content of commercial samples of mixed egg. (D house, 1912.)*

Period of sampling.	Number of samples.	Average number of bacteria per gram.	Ammoniacal nitrogen (Folin method).		Average atmospheric temperature prevailing 15 days before sampling.	Rainfall during the 15 days previous to sampling.
			Wet basis.	Dry basis.		
			Per cent.	*Per cent.*	*°F.*	*Inches.*
May 27 to 29	4	640,000	....	....	79	0.05
June 1 to 15	11	660,000	0.0018	0.0061	83	.42
June 17 to 27	4	570,000	.0020	.0067	74	2.78
July 1 to 12	5	650,000	.0022	.0072	83	.12
July 16 to 31	10	1,400,000	.0022	.0070	93	.80
Aug. 10 to 13	3	1,500,000	.0020	.0065	87	2.88
Aug. 19 to 23	7	1,700,000	.0021	.0068	87	3.97

These studies show that there is a tendency for the bacterial count and the amount of ammoniacal nitrogen to increase as the egg-breaking season progresses (see Tables 2 and E-IV, appendix, and figure 1).

CLASSES OF EGGS PRESENTING SPECIAL PROBLEMS.

LEAKING EGGS.

Eggs with shell and inner membranes broken are termed "leakers" by the trade. There are all gradations, from the egg which has lost very little of its contents to the egg which has practically nothing left in its shell but the yolk.

During periods of the year when receipts are low and the number of leakers consequently few, they are commonly sold in the shell to near-by consumers and employees of the packing house. In the season of heavy receipts, when there are more leakers than can be used locally, they are either thrown out with the rots or broken out and frozen. The second method of disposal is the one concerned in this investigation.

Formerly if the leakers were to be conserved for food purposes, the candlers sorted these eggs from receipts as they worked and either broke them immediately into a container near by or placed them in pans or pails to be opened in another room. Neither method was satisfactory. If the eggs were opened in a dark candling room they could only be graded in the shell, which was insufficient. Then, too, it was impossible to break eggs under sanitary conditions in a candling room. On the other hand, if the leakers were placed in pails, the damage to the shell was increased, and a large part of the contents ran over the shells and collected around the eggs in the bottom of the pail, thereby making it impossible to prepare a clean product from leakers handled in this manner.

TRAY METHOD OF HANDLING LEAKERS.

To avoid these difficulties a tray method of handling leakers was devised. The tray was made of galvanized iron and consisted of a drip pan upon which was placed a plate with perforations for holding the leaking eggs. (Pl. XIII, fig. 2.) The openings were round and about 1⅝ inches in diameter, or hexagonal with sides about six-tenths of an inch in length. The plate was kept in position by means of solder in the corners of the drip pan, or by projections soldered on the sides about 1 inch from the bottom. The trays were 1 to 2 inches high, with perpendicular or beveled sides, and 1 foot square or 1 foot wide by 2 feet long, the former having a capacity of 3 dozen eggs, the latter 6 dozen. The smaller size was much more convenient because it took up less space in the candling room.

After a leaking egg was candled it was placed, damaged end up, in one of the holes of the tray. When filled the tray was carried to the breaking room, where the eggs were broken and graded. The breaking and grading of these eggs was delegated to a few expert girls, because it was impossible to grade leakers as closely by the candle or to break them in as cleanly a manner as cracked or sound eggs. The leaking eggs were opened with the thumb and the two first fingers of each hand, and in many instances without using a breaking knife. Precaution was taken to keep the leaking end of the egg down while the egg was being opened so that the contents would drop into the cup instead of running over the shell and wetting the fingers of the breaker. The same principles used in the grading of the regular breaking stock were used for leakers, except that the grading of soft eggs was done much more closely.

During the first part of the season bacteriological and chemical tests were made of six small samples of leaking eggs collected in the candling room and opened and graded carefully in the breaking room. The results are given in Table 3. These results compared favorably with those obtained from contemporaneous samples of eggs broken from cracked and whole eggs, and warranted further investigation of leaking eggs to determine whether they could safely be conserved for food purposes.

TABLE 3.—*Experimental samples of leaking eggs, opened in the breaking room (D house, 1912).*

Sample No.	Source.	Date of collection.	Bacteria per gram on plain agar incubated at—		Gas-producing bacteria per gram in lactose bile.	Ammoniacal nitrogen (Folin method).		Moisture.	Number of eggs in sample.
			20° C.	37° C.		Wet basis.	Dry basis.		
						Per cent.	*Per cent.*	*Per cent.*	
4273	D-1	May 8	2,100	1,300	10,000	0.0015	0.0053	71.91	13
4274	D-1	do	16,500	4,200	0	.0013	.0045	70.83	13
4275	D-1	do	45,000	34,500	10,000				6
4284	D-1	do	37,000	5,000	100	.0019	.0067	71.53	12
4286	D-1	do	100,000	62,000	10	.0013	.0046	71.85	12

Laboratory tests of three samples of leaking eggs broken in the candling room at F house during May showed a variation of from 1,600,000 to 25,000,000 per gram in the bacterial count, and of 10,000 to 100,000 per gram in the number of presumptive *B. coli*. (Table 4.) Sample No. 4370, representing 150 pounds of leakers, broken in the candling room of F house during the latter part of May, showed the high count of 25,000,000 organisms per gram, but a low amount of ammoniacal nitrogen, namely, 0.0020 per cent on the fresh basis and of 0.0067 per cent on the dry basis. These results indicate that most of the eggs in the product were sound, but that there were some highly contaminated eggs in the mass. Their presence was probably due to the impossibility of eliminating infected eggs when opening leakers in a candling room. Results of samples taken about a month later, but handled by the tray method, gave as shown in Table F–X (appendix) bacterial counts varying from 23,500 to 1,700,000 per gram and the number of presumptive *B. coli* between 10 and 10,000 per gram. These results indicated, therefore, that the minimum count of the samples of leaking eggs opened in the candling room was, approximately, the same as the maximum count of those opened in the breaking room; and that the presumptive number of *B. coli* was also, in most cases, higher in eggs handled by the old method.

TABLE 4.—*Commercial samples of leaking eggs broken in the candling room (F house, 1912).*

Sample No.	Source.	Date of collection.	Bacteria per gram on plain agar incubated at—		Gas-producing bacteria per gram in lactose bile.	Liquefying organisms per gram.	Ammoniacal nitrogen (Folin method).		Moisture.	Weight of sample.
			20° C.	37° C.			Wet basis.	Dry basis.		
							Per ct.	*Per ct.*	*Per ct.*	*Lbs.*
4214.......	F-1	May 1	4,300,000	2,100,000	10,000	1,400,000	0.0017	0.0054	69.74	420
4224.......	F-1	May 2	3,800,000	1,800,000	100,000	430,000	.0016	.0054	70.35	....
4243.......	F-1	May 3	1,600,000	950,000	10,000	650,000	.0017	.0062	72.55	....
4370.......	F-2	May 23	25,000,000	6,300,000	100,000	12,000,000	.0020	.0067	70.09	150

GRADING LEAKING EGGS.

An analysis of the kind and number of rejects found on breaking 350 dozen candled leakers handled by the tray method, showed that 5.2 per cent consisted of deteriorated eggs, which could have been detected by careful candling had the eggs been whole or merely cracked, and 4.4 per cent of infected eggs which could have been eliminated out of the shell. The percentage and kinds of eggs making up the 5.2 per cent of deteriorated eggs ordinarily detected in candling were as follows:

	Per cent.		Per cent.
White rots....................................	57.8	Eggs with blood rings........................	6.9
Eggs with moldy shells.......................	17.8	Eggs with yolk nearly mixed with white....	5.9
Eggs with adherent yolk.....................	7.8	Rotten eggs..................................	3.6

Following are the percentage and kinds of eggs making up the 4.4 per cent of infected eggs which could only be detected out of the shell:

	Per cent.		Per cent.
Sour eggs....................................	40.1	Eggs with a moldy odor.....................	3.7
Soft eggs.....................................	30.4	Eggs with an abnormal odor (not bad)......	2.1
Eggs with a green white.....................	20.8	Eggs with a bad odor.........................	2.6

From these results it is seen that of the badly deteriorated eggs occurring among leakers, white and sour rots, eggs with moldy shells and soft eggs were the most frequent.

Since a portion of the contents of leaking eggs has been lost, it would be expected that a smaller amount of liquid egg would be obtained from these eggs as compared with that from cracked or whole eggs. That this is the case is shown by the fact that an average of 27.7 pounds of liquid egg were obtained from eight different lots of 30 dozen leaking eggs, as compared with an average of 34 pounds from a large number of cases of cracked and whole eggs.

LABORATORY RESULTS ON LEAKERS HANDLED COMMERCIALLY BY THE TRAY METHOD.

Fifty-three samples were taken of leaking eggs handled on trays and opened in the breaking room; 17 were obtained at D house, 16 at E house, and 20 at F house. The laboratory findings are given in detail in Tables D-IV, E-VII, and F-X, respectively (appendix, pp. 99, 77, and 89), and are summarized in Table 5.

TABLE 5.—*Summary of laboratory results on leaking eggs, tray method of handling, 1912.*

I. BACTERIOLOGICAL DATA.

House.	Number of samples.	Number of organisms per gram.			Gas-producing bacteria per gram in lactose bile.	
		Minimum.	Maximum.	Average.	Minimum.	Maximum.
D....................................	17	500	3,700,000	470,000	0	100,000
E....................................	16	200,000	6,000,000	2,800,000	0	100,000
F....................................	20	23,500	4,500,000	910,000	0	1,000,000

TABLE 5.—*Summary of laboratory results on leaking eggs, tray method of handling, 1912*—Continued.

II. CHEMICAL DATA.

House.	Number of samples.	Percentage of ammoniacal nitrogen.						Percentage of moisture.		
		Wet basis.			Dry basis.					
		Minimum.	Maximum.	Average.	Minimum.	Maximum.	Average.	Minimum.	Maximum.	Average.
D	13	0.0013	0.0022	0.0017	0.0047	0.0076	0.0058	69.07	72.83	71.18
E	11	.0020	.0028	.0023	.0066	.0079	.0074	64.12	70.60	68.16
F	13	.0015	.0028	.0020	.0049	.0080	.0065	65.59	71.42	69.33

The bacterial counts and the percentages of ammoniacal nitrogen of samples of good quality leaking eggs handled by the tray method, broken in a cleanly manner and graded carefully, were no greater than those found in synchronous samples of seconds, dirty, or cracked eggs.

Samples with high bacterial counts and, in some cases, with high percentages of ammoniacal nitrogen are grouped in Table 6. In most instances these results could be traced to poor grading during breaking or to low-grade receipts from which the leaking eggs were sorted.

TABLE 6.—*Commercial samples of low quality, leaking eggs, tray method, 1912.*

Sample No.	Source.	Date of collection.	Bacteria per gram on plain agar incubated at—		Gas-producing bacteria per gram in lactose bile.	Liquefying organisms per gram.	Ammoniacal nitrogen (Folin method).		Moisture.	Size of sample.	Number of discards.
			20° C.	37° C.			Wet basis.	Dry basis.			
							Per ct.	*Per ct.*	*Per ct.*	*Doz.*	
4503	F-3	June 11	4,900,000	3,300,000	10,000	1,800,000	0.0022	0.0074	70.13	6	4
4526	F-3	June 12	19,000,000	15,000,000	100,000	800,000	.0021	.0068	69.18	6	......
4737	E-5	July 13	36,000,000	3,000,000	10,000	....	.0029	.0105	72.43	24	53
4858	D-5	July 29	14,000,000	19,000,000	10,000	....	.0019	.0064	70.43	6	16
4859	D-5	...do	20,000,000	67,000,000	100,000	....	.0019	.0065	70.58	6	9

The amount of moisture averaged 71.18 per cent in the 13 samples of leaking eggs taken at D house, 68.16 per cent in the 11 samples taken at E house, and 69.33 per cent in the 15 taken at F house. These figures were lower than those found when cracked or whole eggs were examined, due to the fact that some of the white, which contains considerably more water than the yolk, had been lost.

SOFT EGGS.

Eggs which are not separable into white and yolk are termed soft eggs in this report. This egg is illustrated in Plate XIV. It may have a whole yolk before the candle, but may be ruptured during the process of breaking.

Thirteen samples of soft eggs were taken, in which there was observed a considerable variation in both the bacterial content and the amount of ammoniacal nitrogen. For example, 53.8 per cent of the samples contained less than 5,000,000 bacteria per gram, and 46.2 per cent, between 6,100,000 and 80,000,000 per gram. (See Table F-VIII, Appendix.)

The samples with counts under 5,000,000 contained an average of 0.0021 per cent of ammoniacal nitrogen on the wet basis and 0.0074 per cent on the water-free basis; those with counts over 5,000,000 showed an average of 0.0026 per cent on the wet basis and of 0.0086 per cent on the water-free basis. The average amount of loosely-bound nitrogen in the samples of soft egg, with counts under 5,000,000 per gram, is practically the same as that found in samples of whole egg which could be separated into white and yolk.

It is evident from these results that a large percentage of soft eggs contain comparatively few organisms and a comparatively small amount of loosely bound nitrogen, and also that others are markedly infected and deteriorated. It is quite probable that infected soft eggs are incipient forms of sour eggs, white rots, etc., which have not yet acquired their identifying characteristics.

SECOND-GRADE FROZEN EGGS.

The second-grade product was prepared from eggs showing incipient deterioration by the senses and from drippings from the breaking knife. By far the greatest number of the samples of these eggs showed, as given in Table F–V (Appendix, p. 84), decided infection and marked deterioration. The average bacterial count was 35,000,000 per gram; and the average amount of ammoniacal nitrogen, 0.108 per cent on the dry basis. These results are considerably higher than those found in any of the first-grade products (see Tables 11 and 12).

Samples were taken of some of the component eggs of the second-grade product. The results are correlated in Table F–XII (Appendix, p. 92). Both the incipient sour eggs and the eggs with white beginning to turn green contained millions of bacteria and a comparatively large amount of ammoniacal nitrogen. These data show very plainly that it is impossible to detect by the senses sour eggs or eggs with green whites until the bacteria have developed in sufficient numbers to cause a partial decomposition of the egg material. Cracked eggs with moldy shells, even though the appearance and odor of their contents were normal, frequently contained many organisms. The amount of ammoniacal nitrogen was, however, not excessive.

The bacterial count of nine samples of drippings from breaking knives and trays varied from 10,000 to 13,000,000. There were between 100 and 100,000 *B. coli* per gram in the different samples. This drip contributed fewer organisms to the second-grade product than did the eggs showing incipient deterioration by the senses.

The wide variation of 71.79 to 84.60 per cent of moisture was due to the difference in the amount of drippings or white present.

These results show very conclusively that incipient forms of sour eggs, eggs with green whites, etc., are not only heavily infected but are distinctly decomposed. The laboratory studies of the second-grade product coincide with the decision of the senses as applied to the eggs constituting it, namely, that it is unfit for food purposes.

TANNERS' EGGS.

Tanners' eggs are prepared from the discards from the candling and breaking room minus the eggs with a bad odor, or, in other words, all eggs admittedly unfit for food except those with a repugnant odor. The latter are not included because they would be disagreeable for the tanners to handle. The eggs regularly graded for tanners' purposes are as follows:

Candling-room discards.—White rots, eggs with moldy shells, eggs with adherent yolks, eggs with blood rings, and eggs with yolk nearly mixed with white, etc.

Breaking-room discards.—Sour eggs, eggs with green whites, eggs with a moldy odor, other eggs with abnormal odors, and good eggs, when bad eggs are broken in a cup with them, etc.

Many of these eggs are illustrated in Bulletin 51 of the U. S. Department of Agriculture; others are shown in this report in Plates XV and XVI.

In Table 7 are given the laboratory findings in samples of tanners' eggs, four of which were prepared from eggs discarded in the candling room and six from eggs rejected in the breaking room. It will be noted that every sample is heavily infected with organisms and that with few exceptions those prepared in the breaking room were about twice as heavily infected as those made from eggs discarded during candling. This difference would have been still greater had no good eggs been present in the former.

The number of bacteria in tanners' eggs varied from 31,000,000 to 150,000,000, being markedly greater than the average count found in the samples of first-grade eggs. The minimum figure, however, is not far from the average bacterial content of the second-grade product, i. e., 35,000,000.

The amount of chemical decomposition was also greater in the tanners' grade prepared from eggs rejected in the breaking room than in that made from the bad eggs found on candling. The average amount of ammoniacal nitrogen found in the former was 0.0099 per cent on the dry basis and in the latter 0.0160 per cent.

TABLE 7.—*Commercial samples of tanners' egg.*

Sample No.	Source.	Size and description of sample.	Date of collection 1912.	Bacteria per gram on plain agar incubated at—		Gas-producing bacteria per gram in lactose bile.	Liquefying organisms per gram.	Ammoniacal nitrogen (Folin method).		Moisture.
				20° C.	37° C.			Wet basis.	Dry basis.	
		I.								
		Commercial discards, minus rots with bad odor, from candling room:						*Per cent.*	*Per cent.*	*Per cent.*
4528	F-3	Churn	June 12	45,000,000	33,000,000	1,000,000	2,300,000	0.0025	0.0087	71.34
41014	D-6	15 dozen; mostly large old blood rings and eggs with broken-down yolks previously adherent to shell	Aug. 19	46,000,000	33,000,000	1,000,000	....	.0034	.0119	71.38
41035	D-6	7 pounds; mostly large broken-down blood rings	Aug. 21	31,000,000	11,000,000	100,000	....	.0021	.0074	71.64
41068	E-7	15 dozen	Aug. 27	65,000,000	73,000,000	1,000,000	....	.0033	.0115	71.40
		II.								
		Commercial discards from breaking-room:								
4195	E-1	15 pounds	Apr. 26	100,000,000	17,000,000	1,000,000	....	.0069	.0219	68.53
4220	F-1	30 pounds	May 2	46,000,000	12,000,000	1,000,000	11,000,000	....	....	....
4348	E-2	12 pounds	May 17	130,000,000	24,000,000	1,000,000	....	.0041	.0146	71.89
4555	D-3	30 pounds	June 17	110,000,000	56,000,000	1,000,000	20,000,000	.0047	.0156	69.82
4561	D-3	35 pounds	...do....	150,000,000	68,000,000	10,000,000	60,000,000	.0055	.0157	65.06
4569	D-3	70 pounds	June 18	39,000,000	20,000,000	1,000,000	6,000,000	.0039	.0124	68.73

COMPARATIVE STUDY IN TWO HOUSES ON EGGS BEFORE AND AFTER DESICCATION.

The belt system used in E and F houses differed in some respects. In E house the hot air entered the ducts in which the belts circulated through several flues and was expelled through two others. In F house there was one inlet and one outlet for the hot air. By the arrangement of the air ducts in E house the supply of air coming in contact with the drying egg was replenished before it had become saturated with moisture. The temperature of the intake air in E house varied from 135° F. to 160° F. for whole egg, and in F house it was 160° F. for yolk and 140° F. for mixed egg. The temperature of the outgoing air was about 10° lower in E house and about 30° lower in F house than the incoming air. E house desiccated about 150 pounds of whole egg in one hour and F house about 80 pounds.

The belts of E house were considerably longer than those of F house; consequently they were supported on the lower side by rollers. The portion of the egg on the belt coming in contact with these rollers did not dry as quickly as the films of eggs on the exposed sections of the belt. As a result, sticky masses, commercially termed "wet lumps," were mixed with the flaky egg scraped from the belts. The imperfectly dried portions, however, represented but a small amount of the final product. They were screened and subjected to further drying. The average moisture content of the dried product immediately after being removed from the belts was at E house 8.82 for the whole egg. E house did not subject the dried egg to secondary drying. F house, however, exposed the product to a temperature of 100° F. for about five hours. The percentage of moisture then averaged 6.13 for the mixed egg and 5.04 for the yolks, as against 11.24 per cent for mixed egg and 11.21 per cent for yolk when the dried egg was removed from the belts.

BACTERIAL CONTENT.

Eighteen comparative examinations were made of the product in E house before and after desiccation. The results given in Table E-V (Appendix, p. 74) show in practically every case (if the count of the dried product be divided by 3 to make it comparable with the liquid egg) that there is a reduction in the number of bacteria during the process of desiccation.

The lowest count found in samples of the flaky dried egg, as shown in Table E-III (Appendix, p. 70), was 65,000 per gram and the highest 20,000,000. The average count for the 48 samples was 3,600,000. The number of *B. coli* varied from 0 to 1,000,000 per gram. Only 6, or 12.5 per cent, contained 1,000,000. (Table E-VIII, Appendix, p. 78.)

The bacterial content of the samples of "wet lumps" averaged 6,900,000 and varied from 1,100,000 to 18,000,000 per gram. Corresponding samples of flaky egg contained between 430,000 and 12,000,000 organisms per gram (Table E-II). Comparative results, given in Table E-II (Appendix, p. 68), indicate that in some instances there is a multiplication of organisms in wet lumps during the process of desiccation. There was practically no difference in the bacterial content of wet lumps before and after secondary drying.

In the spring of the year there was practically no increase in the number of bacteria during drying. In the summer, however, there was appreciable multiplication during desiccation (see Table F-I, Appendix, p. 80). This is undoubtedly due to the warmer weather and the greater amount of water in the air during the summer.

It is probable that an increase in the air supply to the belts and an increase and rearrangement of the inlet and outlet ducts would facilitate desiccation and prevent multiplication of bacteria without diminishing the solubility of the dried product.

AMMONIACAL NITROGEN.

The amount of ammoniacal nitrogen found in the desiccated products of E and F houses is not comparable with the amount present in liquid egg before drying. For example, the parallel tests given in Table E-V (Appendix, p. 74) showed that the percentage of ammoniacal nitrogen calculated on the dry basis varied from 0.0073 to 0.0093 in the liquid egg and from 0.0009 to 0.0016 in the corresponding product after desiccation. Similar variations can be seen in Table F-VI (Appendix, p. 76). These results indicate that a portion of the ammoniacal nitrogen was volatilized during desiccation.

The amount of ammoniacal nitrogen volatilized from the product during desiccation is not constant, according to the above tables. For instance, samples 41079 and 41085 listed in Table E-V contained 0.0093 per cent of loosely bound nitrogen in the liquid form, but after desiccation one contained 0.0009 per cent and the other 0.0015 per cent. Since, therefore, the amount of loosely bound nitrogen lost from eggs during drying is variable, it is not possible to judge the quality of the liquid egg from the quantity found in dried egg, or vice versa.

A comparison of the amount of ammoniacal nitrogen and the bacterial content of dried whole egg, dried mixed egg, and dried yolks shows, as can be observed in Tables E–V, F–II, and F–IV, a tendency to greater quantities of ammoniacal nitrogen when the product is heavily infected with bacteria, but the relation between the two is far from being as definite or as conclusive as when the tests are applied to liquid egg.

COMPARISON OF THE LIQUID PRODUCT FROM THREE HOUSES IN 1912.

There was but slight variation found in the amount of ammoniacal nitrogen in the commercial liquid products prepared by the cooperating houses in which the mode of preparation was the same. The average bacterial contents of the liquid products of D and F houses, which derived their breaking stock mostly from their current receipts, were nearly the same. The number of bacteria in the liquid egg of E house was greater than for the other two houses. The latter purchased its breaking stock from other houses; consequently it was somewhat older at the time of breaking than that of the other two houses. The data summarizing the findings for the three houses are given in Tables 8, 9, 10, E–VIII (Appendix), and F–XI (Appendix).

TABLE 8.—*Summary of laboratory results on commercial samples taken in D house during 1912.*

I. CHEMICAL RESULTS.

Description of sample.	Number.	Percentage of ammoniacal nitrogen.						Percentage of moisture.		
		Wet basis.			Dry basis.					
		Average.	Minimum.	Maximum.	Average.	Minimum.	Maximum.	Average.	Minimum.	Maximum.
Whites	7	0.0004	0.0002	0.0006	0.0028	0.0016	0.0046	87.27	86.96	87.90
Yolks	13	.0029	.0024	.0037	.0070	.0054	.0083	57.79	53.64	64.06
Mixed egg	34	.0020	.0014	.0025	.0067	.0046	.0082	69.46	68.33	71.43

II. BACTERIOLOGICAL RESULTS.

Organisms per gram.	Whites.		Yolks.		Mixed egg.	
	Number of samples.	Per cent.	Number of samples.	Per cent.	Number of samples.	Per cent.
0 to 10,000 inclusive	3	13.6	3	15.0	1	2.2
10,001 to 50,000 inclusive	4	18.2	3	15.0	....	....
50,001 to 100,000 inclusive	3	13.6	3	15.0	....	....
100,001 to 500,000 inclusive	8	36.3	3	15.0	14	30.4
500,001 to 1,000,000 inclusive	3	13.6	5	25.0	15	32.6
1,000,001 to 5,000,000 inclusive	1	4.5	3	15.0	16	34.8
Total	22	....	20	....	46	....
Average	280,000		480,000		1,000,000	
Minimum	100		200		5,100	
Maximum	1,500,000		2,100,000		3,300,000	

Number of organisms per gram producing gas in lactose bile.	Whites.		Yolks.		Mixed egg.	
	Number of samples.	Per cent.	Number of samples.	Per cent.	Number of samples.	Per cent.
Less than 10	4	19.0	2	11.1	....	....
10	2	9.5	1	5.6	....	....
100	3	14.3	4	22.2	3	6.5
1,000	6	28.6	5	27.7	11	23.9
10,000	4	19.0	2	11.1	15	32.6
100,000	2	9.5	2	11.1	15	32.6
1,000,000	....	....	2	11.1	2	4.3
Total	21	....	18	....	46	....

TABLE 9.—*Summary of laboratory results on commercial samples taken in E house during 1912.*

I. CHEMICAL RESULTS.

Description of sample.	Table No.	Number of samples.	Percentage of ammoniacal nitrogen.						Percentage of moisture.		
			Wet basis.			Dry basis.					
			Average.	Minimum.	Maximum.	Average.	Minimum.	Maximum.	Average.	Minimum.	Maximum.
Whites	E-VI	3	0.0005	0.0005	0.0006	0.0044	0.0040	0.0049	87.84	87.55	88.31
Yolks	E-VI	4	.0035	.0029	.0039	.0083	.0072	.0092	58.37	57.72	59.56
Whole eggs	E-IV	32	.0021	.0016	.0024	.0075	.0054	.0087	72.33	70.23	74.17

II. BACTERIOLOGICAL RESULTS.

Description of sample.	Table No.	Number of samples.	Per cent of samples with counts over 5,000,000 per gram.	Number of organisms per gram.		
				Average.	Minimum.	Maximum.
Liquid eggs:						
Whites	E-VI	7	0	730,000	1,000	1,800,000
Yolks	E-VI	6	0	630,000	5,500	1,300,000
Whole eggs	E-IV	38	26.3	3,100,000	700,000	11,000,000
Desiccated whole eggs:						
Flaky eggs	E-III	48	20.8	3,600,000	65,000	20,000,000
Wet lumps	E-II	26	50.0	6,900,000	1,100,000	18,000,000

TABLE 10.—*Summary of laboratory results on commercial samples taken in F house during 1912.*

I. CHEMICAL RESULTS.

Description of sample.	Table No.	Number of samples.	Percentage of ammoniacal nitrogen.						Percentage of moisture.		
			Wet basis.			Dry basis.					
			Average.	Minimum.	Maximum.	Average.	Minimum.	Maximum.	Average.	Minimum.	Maximum.
Whites	21	3	0.0004	0.0002	0.0006	0.0031	0.0016	0.0046	87.13	87.01	87.36
Yolks	{21, F-VII}	6	.0038	.0034	.0045	.0086	.0075	.0103	55.87	53.74	57.25
Whole eggs	F-IX	5	.0020	.0019	.0021	.0070	.0067	.0071	72.34	71.62	73.29
Sugared yolks	F-VII	7	.0030	.0028	.0033	.0062	.0058	.0067	51.12	49.89	53.07
Mixed eggs	F-III	10	.0023	.0017	.0027	.0071	.0053	.0082	68.06	67.00	70.81
Soft eggs	F-VIII	11	.0023	.0018	.0031	.0080	.0066	.0098	71.24	67.04	72.99
Second-grade eggs	F-V	14	.0023	.0008	.0040	.0108	.0052	.0182	78.20	71.79	84.60

II. BACTERIOLOGICAL RESULTS.

Description of sample.	Table No.	Number of samples.	Per cent of samples with count over 5,000,000 per gram.	Number of organisms per gram.		
				Average.	Minimum.	Maximum.
Liquid eggs:						
Whites	21	10	10.0	[1] 220,000	1,000	7,500,000
Yolks	{21, F-VII}	28	10.71	[2] 550,000	6,800	7,500,000
Whole eggs	F-IX	9	0	1,300,000	340,000	3,500,000
Mixed eggs	F-III	12	8.33	1,700,000	470,000	6,800,000
Soft eggs	F-VIII	13	46.1	20,000,000	130,000	80,000,000
Second-grade frozen eggs	F-V	14	92.8	35,000,000	4,200,000	92,000,000
Desiccated eggs:						
Yolks	F-II	15	66.6	41,000,000	71,000	110,000,000
Mixed eggs	F-IV	32	59.4	29,000,000	160,000	200,000,000

[1] Two samples with exceptionally high counts not included in this average.
[2] Three samples with exceptionally high counts not included in this average.

GENERAL SUMMARY OF LABORATORY RESULTS ON COMMERCIAL SAMPLES, 1912.

The bacteriological and chemical findings of the data obtained from commercial samples of liquid egg taken in D, E, and F houses during 1912 are summarized in Tables 11 and 12 and shown graphically in figures 2, 3, and 4.

The average number of bacteria per gram in the whites was 350,000, in the yolks 530,000, and in the whole and mixed eggs 1,800,000. The average amount of ammoniacal nitrogen on the dry basis was 0.0031 per cent in the whites, 0.0076 per cent in the yolks, and 0.0074 per cent in the whole eggs.

A comparison of these results shows that the average count of the whites is about half that of the yolks, and that the latter contained approximately one-third as many bacteria as the whole and mixed eggs. The antiseptic action of the white may explain its lower bacterial content as compared with that of the yolks, whole eggs, and mixed eggs. It may be that the presence of soft eggs in the whole and mixed eggs offers also an explanation of their higher bacterial content.

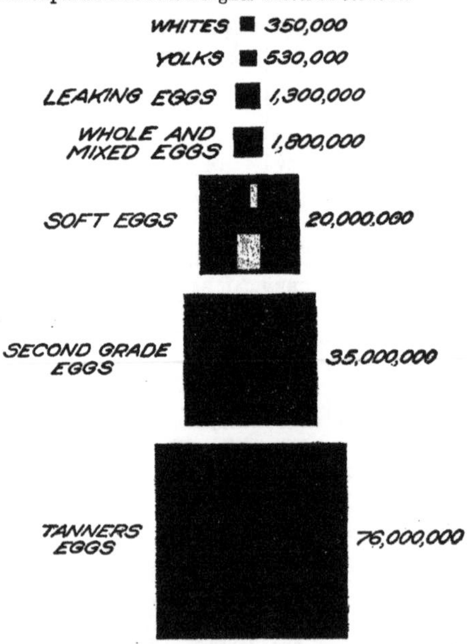

FIG. 2.—Diagram showing average number of organisms per gram in commercial samples taken in D, E, and F houses in 1912.

It is interesting to note that the average count of the product prepared from leaking eggs is not far different from that of the whole and mixed eggs. The average count of the former was 1,300,000 and of the latter 1,800,000.[1] The amount of chemical decomposition was no greater in the leaking eggs than in the whole and mixed egg.

The product prepared from soft eggs graded as fit for food purposes contained decidedly more bacteria than the whole or mixed egg, but the amounts of ammoniacal nitrogen in the two were not so very far apart. The average number of organisms in the soft eggs numbered 20,000,000 per gram, as compared with 1,800,000 in the whole and mixed egg, whereas the percentage of loosely bound nitrogen averaged 0.0080 on the dry basis in the former and 0.0074 in the latter. The bacteria in the soft eggs were not present in sufficient numbers or for a sufficient length of time to effect a decomposition of the egg material.

On the other hand, the second-grade frozen egg prepared from "beginning sours," eggs with light-green whites, etc., and the tanners' egg were not only heavily in-

[1] Weighted average of bacterial content of whole and mixed eggs given in Table 11.

fected but were decomposed. The average number of bacteria in the former was 35,000,000 per gram and in the latter 76,000,000. The amount of ammoniacal nitrogen was 0.0108 per cent on the dry basis in the second-grade egg and 0.0133 in the tanners' egg. These comparative data, together with the practical observations of the eggs used in the former product, show very conclusively that second-grade canned or dried eggs are unfit for food purposes.

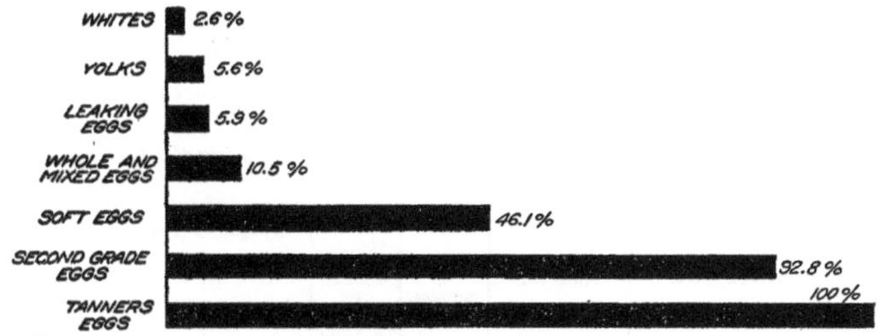

FIG. 3.—Diagram showing percentage of commercial samples with counts over 5,000,000 per gram (samples taken in D, E, and F houses during 1912).

As the houses under observation during 1912 were three of the largest producers of canned and dried eggs in the United States, it is instructive to compare the quality of their output as indicated by its bacterial content with that offered for sale for food during the two years previous to the investigation. Stiles and Bates found in a study of 312 samples of frozen egg collected from different sources during the years of 1909 to 1911, inclusive, that 58.3 per cent contained over 10,000,000 bacteria per gram. Of 216 samples of liquid egg obtained from the cooperating houses during this investigation in 1912, only 1.4 per cent were found to contain over 10,000,000 per gram.[1]

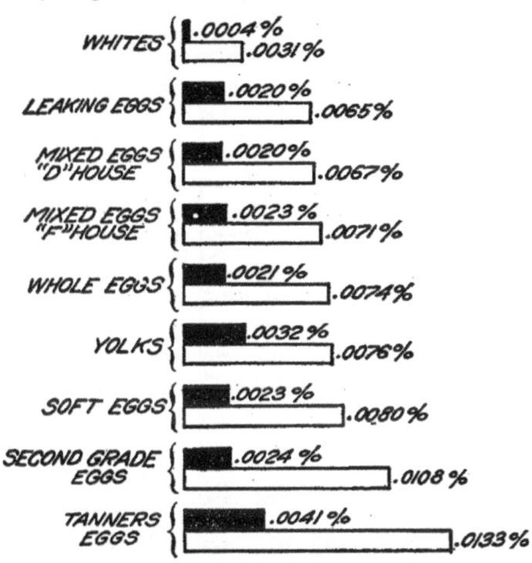

FIG. 4.—Diagram showing average percentage of ammoniacal nitrogen in commercial samples taken in D, E, and F houses during 1912.

The maximum count in the three houses in 1912 was 11,000,000 per gram, while the maximum found by Stiles and Bates was 1,180,000,000.

The difference in the bacterial contents of the samples of dried egg was equally as marked. Stiles and Bates found that 83.3 per cent of the samples purchased on the open market contained over 10,000,000 per gram. Only 6.3 per cent of 48 samples

[1] Stiles and Bates, Bureau of Chemistry, United States Department of Agriculture, Bulletin No. 158, p. 29.

taken in E house contained over this number, while in F house 55.3 per cent of the samples were in excess of 10,000,000.

The maximum number per gram found in the samples of dried eggs taken in 1912 was 20,000,000 for E house and 200,000,000 for F house, and in the samples collected between 1909 and 1911 by Stiles and Bates, 2,100,000,000. It is known in the case of F house that the raw material was of good quality and that the bacteria increased during desiccation.

The samples studied by Stiles and Bates represented not only frozen and dried egg prepared from good eggs by the best methods known at the time, but also products made from unfit raw material.

These comparative data speak well for the quality of the product prepared by the new methods in the three houses under investigation.

TABLE 11.—*General summary of bacterial counts on commercial samples taken in D, E, and F houses during 1912.*

Description of sample.	Table No.	Number of samples.	Per cent of samples with counts over 5,000,000 per gram.	Number of organisms per gram.		
				Average.	Minimum.	Maximum.
Liquid eggs:						
Whites	D-III, 17, E-VI, 21.	39	2.6	[1] 350,000	100	7,500,000
Yolks	D-III, E-VI, 21, F-VII.	54	5.56	[2] 530,000	200	7,500,000
Whole eggs	E-IV, F-IX	47	21.28	2,700,000	340,000	11,000,000
Mixed egg from D house	D-II	46	0	1,000,000	5,100	3,300,000
Mixed egg from F house	F-III	12	8.33	1,700,000	470,000	6,800,000
Leaking eggs	D-IV, E-VII, F-X.	53	5.88	1,300,000	500	6,000,000
Soft eggs	F-VIII	13	46.14	20,000,000	130,000	80,000,000
Second-grade eggs	F-V	14	92.8	35,000,000	4,200,000	92,000,000
Tanners' egg	7	10	100.0	76,000,000	31,000,000	150,000,000

[1] One sample with an exceptionally high count not included in this average.
[2] Three samples with exceptionally high counts not included in this average.

TABLE 12.—*General summary of chemical results on commercial samples taken in D, E, and F houses during 1912.*

Description of sample.	Table No.	Number of samples.	Percentage of ammoniacal nitrogen.						Percentage of moisture.		
			Wet basis.			Dry basis.					
			Average.	Minimum.	Maximum.	Average.	Minimum.	Maximum.	Average.	Minimum.	Maximum.
Whites	D-III, 17, E-VI, 21.	13	0.0004	0.0002	0.0006	0.0031	0.0016	0.0049	87.37	86.96	88.31
Yolks	D-III, 17, E-VI, 21.	23	.0032	.0024	.0045	.0076	.0054	.0103	57.88	53.64	64.06
Sugared yolks	F-VII	7	.0030	.0028	.0033	.0062	.0058	.0067	51.12	49.89	53.07
Whole eggs	E-IV, F-IX	43	.0021	.0016	.0024	.0074	.0054	.0087	72.33	70.23	74.17
Mixed egg from D house.	D-II	34	.0020	.0014	.0025	.0067	.0046	.0082	68.88	68.33	71.43
Mixed egg from F house.	F-III	10	.0023	.0017	.0027	.0071	.0053	.0082	68.06	67.00	70.81
Leaking eggs	D-IV, E-VII, F-X.	37	.0020	.0013	.0028	.0065	.0047	.0080	69.63	64.12	72.83
Soft eggs	F-VIII	11	.0023	.0018	.0031	.0080	.0066	.0098	71.24	67.04	72.99
Second-grade eggs and drippings.	F-V	14	.0024	.0008	.0040	.0108	.0052	.0182	78.20	71.79	84.60
Tanners' egg	7	9	.0041	.0021	.0069	.0133	.0074	.0219	69.98	65.06	71.89

CONCLUSIONS.

1. Eggs commonly used for breaking stock by reputable firms are small and oversized eggs, dirty and cracked eggs, and shrunken eggs.

2. In order to check deterioration, the eggs should be held in chilled surroundings before and during the process of candling, breaking, and mixing preparatory to freezing or drying.

3. All eggs, even during the spring months, should be candled previous to breaking.

4. In order to insure well-candled eggs going to the breaking room, the system of candling should be such that the work of the individual candlers is checked.

5. In order to prevent waste, the eggs difficult to grade should be set aside by the regular candlers to be recandled by an expert.

6. All eggs used in the preparation of frozen and dried eggs should be graded out of the shell as well as by the candle, because certain heavily infected eggs, such as sour eggs and eggs with green whites, can only be detected when broken.

7. In order to insure a good product, bacterial cleanliness and careful grading must be obtained during the process of preparation.

8. The fingers of the breakers should be kept dry and clean.

9. In order to prevent waste and to insure good grading, not more than three eggs should be broken into a cup before emptying.

10. Good eggs should not be saved when a bad egg has been broken into a cup with them.

11. White and yolk are contaminated less by the mechanical than the shell method of separation. Only clean eggs should be separated by the latter process.

12. The percentage of "rots" rejected on candling and the organisms in the liquid egg saved increases as the season advances.

13. Canned eggs with the majority of samples having counts of less than 5,000,000 bacteria per gram, and with 100,000 *B. coli* or less can be prepared in the producing section from regular breaking stock, provided strict cleanliness and careful grading have been observed. The ammoniacal nitrogen will very seldom be over 0.0024 on the wet basis or 0.0087 on the dry basis.

14. A second-grade frozen product prepared from eggs showing incipient decomposition to the senses, such as "beginning sours" and eggs with green whites, are not only heavily infected but chemically decomposed. These eggs are unfit for food purposes.

15. Only two grades of canned eggs should be prepared when grading eggs out of the shell, namely, food egg and tanners' egg.

16. Leaking eggs handled on special trays between candling and breaking room and graded carefully are as fit for breaking as regular breaking stock.

17. Tanners' egg contains markedly larger numbers of bacteria and larger amounts of ammoniacal nitrogen than does food egg.

18. The control of the supply of air to drying belts to prevent saturation from the liquid egg is an important factor in preventing multiplication of bacteria in the product during the process of desiccation.

19. The amount of ammoniacal nitrogen in desiccated egg is not a reliable index to the quality of the raw material from which it is prepared, because this substance is volatilized unevenly during the process of desiccation.

20. The following eggs should be discarded during grading: Black, white, mixed and sour rots, eggs with green whites, eggs with stuck yolks, musty eggs, moldy eggs, "blood rings," eggs containing diffuse blood, and eggs with abnormal odor.

GLOSSARY.

"Seconds" are small and oversized eggs, dirty eggs, and shrunken eggs.

"Leakers" are eggs with shell and inner membranes broken.

A "blood ring" is a fertile egg in which the embryo has developed sufficiently to show blood.

A soft egg is an egg the yolk of which appears whole before the candle, but breaks when opened.

A "strong-odor" egg is an egg which has an eggy odor.

An "off" egg is an egg which has a slightly abnormal odor.

A "beginning sour" is an egg showing the first signs of the odor characteristic of sour eggs.

"Mixed egg" is a product prepared by adding yolks to whole egg.

"Drip" is the liquid egg, mostly white, which collects in the bottom of the breaking tray while eggs are being broken.

Second-grade egg is a product prepared from "drip" and incipient forms of deteriorated eggs, such as "beginning sours," eggs with light-green whites, etc.

"Tanners' egg" is a product made from the rejects of the candling and breaking rooms, minus eggs with a bad odor. It is used, as the name implies, for tanning leather.

"Flaky egg," as opposed to "wet lumps," is the more thoroughly dried portion of egg coming from the drying belts.

A "churn" is a device for breaking yolks and for mixing yolk and whole egg

APPENDIX.

DETAILS OF EXPERIMENTS IN EACH COOPERATING HOUSE, 1911 AND 1912.

CONDITIONS OBSERVED IN B HOUSE IN 1911.

THE BREAKING ROOM.

In B house a small room, about 12 by 12 feet, constructed entirely of concrete, screened, and on the fourth floor of a modern creamery, was set aside for egg breaking. It was not refrigerated. It was clean.

The table used in this house is shown in figure 5. It was covered with zinc, had a shelf at the side to support the egg case, and a hole in the middle of the table through which the shells were thrown into a bucket below. At the back of the table, to the left of the breaker, stood a pail of water. This was used to wash the saucer and the hands of the breaker after a bad egg. The saucer was not dried, consequently it carried water to the shelf on which it rested, keeping the latter continually sloppy, and occasionally drops fell into the containers below. One saucer only was provided, hence it was in constant use. This type of breaking outfit was seen in a number of establishments.

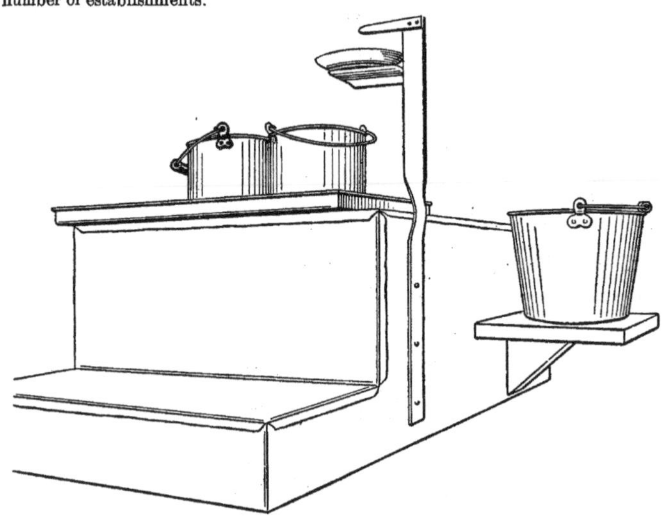

FIG. 5.—Table and breaking outfit (B house, 1911).

The eggs in this house were separated by the shell method when whites and yolks were desired; whole eggs went into the saucer. In the shell-separating method—that is, the usual housewifely fashion of tipping the egg back and forth until the white is drained off—the white ran into a saucer, the yolk was dumped into a small yolk bucket, and the white from the saucer into its bucket. The whites were collected in containers of various sizes, according to the wishes of the trade, and stored at one side of the room from the beginning of the work in the morning until noontime, when it was removed to the freezer; and again, from the beginning of the afternoon until the close of the day, when a second trip was made to the freezer.

The yolks were put into a 40-quart milk can. This at noontime and again at night was emptied into a large straight-sided can provided with an ordinary creamery faucet. The yolk was poured into this churn through a large mesh wire sieve to remove scraps of eggshell. It was then stirred with a paddle in the churn until the yolks were thoroughly broken and mixed, or the whites and yolks of the whole eggs made into a uniform liquid. The containers were then placed below the faucet of the churn and the egg run into them. The churn was washed at noontime after it was used and again at night.

The eggs were chilled before breaking, but their long wait after removal from the shell in this hot room effectually undid the good which previous chilling does to a perishable product.

Sources of Bacterial Contamination.

In order to determine the bacterial cleanliness of this method and equipment, each obvious factor was tested by laboratory methods for the amount of contamination.

Plate I, figure 1, represents the number of colonies which developed on a 4-inch petri plate from one drop of water taken from the saucer after throwing away a bad egg and washing in running hot water. It is obvious, from the large number of colonies developing, that this method of cleaning the receiver is not sufficient to remove the organisms furnished by the undesirable egg. Plate I, figure 2, shows the number of bacteria in one drop of water which had collected on the shelf holding the wet saucer. Here, again, is a rich source of bacterial contamination of the final product. As one would expect, there are many more organisms in this drop of drip than were obtained from the saucer itself.

The picture of the breaking equipment shows a shallow metal tray that was placed under the egg pails for the sake of cleanliness. This tray gradually collected drippings of water from the saucer and its shelf and of egg which ran down the sides of the pails when their contents were emptied into the milk can; consequently, there were even more organisms in the liquid that accumulated in the tray than there were on either the saucer or the shelf, and when the pails were emptied this liquid sometimes dropped into the final receiver. One drop of it was examined with the result shown in Plate I, figure 3. The organisms as they developed on a 4-inch petri plate were so numerous that it was impossible to distinguish them as individual colonies. Each step of this process added more and more bacteria to the product, though as carried out it was even cleaner than the usual kitchen methods. The breaker had no means of detecting either the source or the amount of the infection that his routine caused.

The bacteria on finger tips wet with egg are shown in Plate I, figure 4. To obtain this preparation, the breaker touched her five wet finger tips against the bottom of a dry, sterile petri plate. Agar was then poured in, shaken to distribute the organisms evenly, and incubation allowed to proceed. The results indicate that the hands of the egg breaker are also a source of infection which, if possible, must be overcome.

Comparison of the Commercial Product with Experimental Samples.

This house did not buy eggs especially for breaking, but used breaking stock sorted from their current receipts. The supply of eggs going to the breaker while the house was under observation was of exceptionally good quality. The bacterial count and chemical analysis of eight samples, including whole egg, yolks and whites, are given in Table 13, Part I. The odor and appearance of all the samples were excellent. The amount of loosely bound nitrogen is low, indicating that, in the shell at least, the eggs were of good quality. But the number of bacteria in the final product shows a wide variation, which can not, apparently, be attributed to the eggs. The minimum count for egg white is less than 1,000, and the maximum is 6,500,000 per gram; the minimum for yolks is 2,000,000 and the maximum is 4,800,000 per gram. The number of presumptive *B. coli* varied from 100 to 100,000 per gram.

An effort was made to eliminate the sources of contamination already described by modifying the equipment and more effectually cleaning the apparatus soiled by eggs that were discarded. Instead of the apparatus in use in this house, there was substituted the breaking outfit pictured and described on page 11 of Circular 98, Bureau of Chemistry, United States Department of Agriculture. Trays holding pails for liquid egg were discarded. Tissue paper was provided on which to dry finger tips. Pails and cans, such as were commonly used, were retained; but all were washed in water at 160° F. and held in that water for five minutes or steamed.

TABLE 13.—*Experimental and commercial samples of whites, yolks, and whole egg.* (*B house, 1911.*)

Sample No.	Description of sample.	Date of collection.	Bacteria per gram on plain agar incubated at— 20° C.	Bacteria per gram on plain agar incubated at— 37° C.	Gas-producing bacteria per gram in lactose bile.	Liquefying organisms per gram.	Ammoniacal nitrogen (Folin method). Wet basis.	Ammoniacal nitrogen (Folin method). Dry basis.	Moisture.	Ether extract.
	I.									
	Commercial samples:						*Per cent.*	*Per cent.*	*Per cent.*	*Per cent.*
436	Whites, from 8-pound pail	Aug. 3	190,000	92,000	10,000	10,000	0.0004			
437	Yolks, from 40-quart can two-thirds full, contents not well mixed	do	4,800,000	4,000,000	10,000		.0029	0.0067	56.86	24.93
438	Whites, from 25-pound pail	do	530,000	420,000	10,000	1,000	.0005			
439	Whole egg, afternoon's leakers broken at end of day	do	3,000,000	2,500,000	1,000		.0013			
441	Whites, from pail	Aug. 4	(1)	(1)	100		.0005			
442	Whites, from pail just filled	do	2,700,000	2,300,000	10,000	1,000	.0005			
443	Yolks, in 40-quart can from Nos. 441 and 442	do	2,000,000	1,200,000	100,000	130,000	.0032	.0071	54.95	26.73
444	Whites, from pail just filled	do	6,500,000	4,100,000	100,000	130,000	.0007			
	II.									
	Experimental samples broken into sterilized apparatus:									
449	Whites of 40 cracks	Aug. 5	(1)	(1)	(1)		.0007			
450	Yolks of above	do	(1)	(1)	(1)		.0034	.0079	56.85	25.44
452	Water drips from Nos. 449 and 450	do	3,000	1,800						
453	Whites, same eggs as Nos. 449 and 450	do	(1)	(1)	100		.0007			
454	Yolks of above	do	(1)	(1)	(1)		.0039	.0087	55.13	26.70
	Commercial sample:									
455	Yolks, from same eggs as Nos. 449, 450, 453, and 454	do	4,300,000	3,500,000	100,000		.0033			
	III.									
	Experimental samples broken into apparatus washed in water at 160° F.:									
463	Whites	do	23,500	19,000	100					
456	Yolks of sample No. 463	do	260,000	180,000	(1)	20,000	.0032			
457	Whites	do	52,000	42,000	(1)		.0008			
458	Yolks of sample No. 457	do	350,000	350,000		25,000	.0033			
462	Drip	do	22,500	11,500	(1)	9,500				
	Commercial samples:									
459	Whites, from pail	do	260,000	270,000	10	200,000	.0007			
460	Yolks, from pail	do	4,100,000	4,200,000	100,000	50,000	.0037	.0087	57.56	25.04
461	Yolks, from 40-quart can	do	1,000,000	820,000	100	20,000	.0031	.0079	60.8	23.10

[1] Less than 1,000.

There were a sufficient number of knives and sherbet cups to permit each soiled piece to be sterilized for fifteen minutes before being again put into service. The apparatus was considered soiled as soon as it had come into contact with an egg that had to be discarded. Current breaking stock furnished the eggs. The results of the laboratory examination of the experimentally prepared product are shown in Part II of Table 13. In order to comprehend their true significance, the bacterial findings obtained must be compared with those found in commercial sample No. 455. The eggs used in these two series were not only from the same lot but from the same cases, the experimental samples coming from one side and the commercial samples being taken from the other, in the routine fashion of the house. Their similarity is further confirmed by the chemical analyses, which are practically identical. The number of bacteria in the experimental samples are uniformly less than 1,000 per gram, and the organisms of the *coli* group are greatly reduced in number, not exceeding 100 per gram, while the corresponding figures for the commercial sample are 4,300,000 bacteria and 100,000 *B. coli.*

Part III of Table 13 gives the results obtained when the equipment was washed and held in hot water at 160° F. before use. When contaminated by a bad egg it was not used again until it had been washed and sterilized. The finger tips were kept dry as before. The number of bacteria per gram is, practically speaking, reduced to a negligible quantity, and the presumptive *coli* organisms are also practically excluded. To emphasize what such cleanliness means the counts should be compared with the commercial samples Nos. 459–461. Here again the bacteria per gram ran over 4,000,000 in the case of the yolks, and the *B. coli* ran as high as 100,000. These eggs, as before, were from the opposite half of the cases furnishing the experimental samples. Such a demonstration, confirmed by many others, showed that the best of eggs, if handled in dirty utensils, would give a product containing many bacteria.

CONDITIONS OBSERVED IN C HOUSE IN 1911.

The equipment used in C house in the preparation of the egg for freezing was also of interest, because it varied in character for almost every breaker. The fancies of the individual girls were more apt to determine the kind of utensils used than any experienced judgment concerning fitness for the work to be done. Sometimes 20 girls were employed, but there was no discipline. The forewoman was the social associate of the girls, and many were the interruptions while town doings were discussed. The whole atmosphere of the breaking room was one of easy-going self satisfaction.

The Breaking Room and Equipment.

The egg-breaking room was long and narrow. Two windows on the outer side wall were screened, as was also the door. The floor was of wood for rather more than half its length, the balance being of concrete and slightly lower in level.

A long table made of wood and covered with zinc stretched from end to end of the room. At this table, facing the light, the girls sat. About 18 inches above the table and running along the wall and across the windows was a galvanized-iron gutter about 5 inches in diameter and about 2 inches deep. Over this were water faucets so placed that they could be reached without the girls leaving their seats, and in this stream of cold water the girls rinsed fingers and utensils. About half way down the room, breaking the table line, was a wooden trough supplied with hot and cold water and used for the general cleaning and washing.

At the two ends of the room were large galvanized-iron cans, supplied with stirrers and creamery faucets and called churns. In these the eggs were mixed before being put into their final carriers.

The girls were using heavy walled glass tumblers, tin cups, agateware cups, sherbet glasses, and ordinary china teacups, depending entirely upon the preference of the worker and the receptacle available. Each girl had a small tray—tin, agate, or black japanned ware—on which she placed the egg receptacles. She also had a group of agateware buckets, holding about 3 quarts each, into which she emptied her smaller receivers. These buckets were dumped into the churns, or, in the case of egg white, directly into 30-pound pails, in which they were frozen. When the study of C house was made it was putting out egg white, egg yolk (sugared and unsugared), and a first, second, and third grade of whole egg. The third grade was known as "tanners'," and was not for food purposes.

ROUTINE OF EGG BREAKING.

All the eggs coming to the breaking room were candled, but the candlers were apt to put in doubtful eggs for the breakers to grade, rather than take the time and trouble to decide in the candling room whether they were or were not fit for food. All the eggs were chilled, but the breaking room was not, hence there was a profuse sweating of shells during much of the egg-breaking season.

The girls removed the fillers and flats, layer by layer, as they reached them, and took several eggs at one time, holding them in the right hand, and pushing up one at a time for shell cracking and emptying. Of course, dirty eggs, sweating also, immediately resulted in badly soiled hands. The eggs were cracked on the edge of a cup, glass, or whatever type of receptacle the breaker happened to have. Generally, it was not suited to cracking an egg because it mashed and splintered the shells instead of making a clean cut. Having cracked the shell, the girl was supposed to hold it over the glass and determine, by the appearance of the egg at the crack, whether it could or could not be separated into white and yolk, or to which grade of egg it belonged. If it could be separated, the white was drained off, housewife fashion, into one receptacle, and the yolk dropped into another. If the egg was too "soft" to separate, but odorless, it went into first-grade whole eggs. If it was a little "off," or "strong," or a "beginning sour," it went into second-grade whole eggs. The tanners' egg was composed of white rots, which were not too malodorous, musty eggs, moldy eggs, eggs with a bloody white, and blood-ring eggs.

The forewoman gave some instructions regarding the grading of eggs by appearance, odor, taste, etc. In practice, every girl graded according to her own sweet will. Hence, the output of the different breakers was very uneven. In the long run, judging by observation, about as many firsts went into seconds as there were seconds put into firsts.

When some of the egg yolk, during the process of separation, ran into the tumbler of egg white, it was fished out by means of a spoon, or, more commonly, by a piece of egg shell. If an objectionable yolk got into the yolk cup, or some of a bad egg into a food-egg grade, the entire contents of the receptacle was supposed to go into the bucket indicated by the character of the egg last entering. In practice, however, the breaker used a spoon or an egg shell to take out as much of the objectionable egg as she could see and quite disregarded its presence when grading. The remnants left were a fine source of contamination and foci for bacterial troubles later on. The girls in C house used cups and tumblers large enough to hold from 6 to 10 eggs. Many times it was the last egg required to fill the vessel that was off grade. The instinctive desire on the part of the breaker to procure as much high-grade product for her employer as possible, and her reluctance to swell the amount in her tanners' bucket, will override all instructions forbidding the removal of objectionable eggs as just described. The only way to overcome the habit is to have the first receiver so small that it cannot accommodate more than two or three eggs.

CLEANLINESS.

The problem of cleanliness assumed a different aspect in C house, because of the running cold water to which every girl had easy access. Laboratory methods were called in to determine the efficacy of frequent rinsing in cold water with the supplementary cleaning in hot water twice a day in removing the bacteria of the objectionable egg, or other dirt, from hands and utensils.

At noontime, after the usual cleaning in hot water, a number of the cups, tumblers, etc., were tested for bacterial contamination. In every case, abundant evidence of insufficient cleansing was observed. Plate II, figure 1, shows the growth resulting when the edge of a tumbler was just touched against a sterile agar film on a petri plate.

To gain some idea of the number of organisms adhering to the vessels, a drop of water from each of a number of tumblers was plated as is customary when colonies are to be counted. A glass which had received yolks gave an average of 630 organisms to the drop; one that had been used for whites gave 570; the glass that had received the tanners' egg gave 5,900 per drop. That the pails into which the eggs were first emptied were prolific carriers of organisms was also proved. Plating in this case gave 2,600,000 per cc, equivalent to 20 drops. That more bacteria would adhere to the agateware pails than to china or glass cups was to be expected, because of the greater roughness of the former.

It was desirable, also, to determine to what extent the fingers of these girls passed on the bacteria of rejected eggs to those that had but few. Plate II, figure 2, shows the number of colonies which developed when a sterile petri plate was touched with the tips of five fingers that had just been washed because they were wet with egg—but not with objectionable egg. For comparison with this, Plate II, figure 3, is given. Here we have the result of breaking a tanners' egg. Even though the hands were washed in running cold water, the mere touch of finger tips gave so many colonies that they were innumerable.

The lessons here are quite plain. First, ordinary washing of either hands or utensils is not sufficient to keep them, bacterially, fit for egg breaking; and, second, when bad eggs, unfit for food, are broken the removal of the hordes of bacteria which they carry becomes an extremely difficult task.

Comparison of the Commercial Product with Experimental Samples.

A number of samples of the product of C house were taken during the months of July and August, 1911. The bacterial content of the whites were, on the whole, the lowest; yolk was considerably higher, and the whole egg the highest. The greater number of the routine samples of whole egg were of the second grade. (See Table C–I, Appendix, p. 64.) It will also be seen that some of the so-called second-grade egg is of quite as good, if not better, quality than the first grade—a result which was to be expected from the loose methods of grading.

The glass cups, adjustable knives, and wire-screened tray, described on page 11 of Circular 98, were taken to C house in order to determine the character of the eggs used as indicated by cleanly methods of handling. A supply of live steam in a near-by creamery was utilized to sterilize the apparatus. Part I of Table 14 shows the results obtained from eggs with cracked shells, when sterilized apparatus was used, and, under "Commercial samples" are shown similar eggs broken in very cleanly fashion in the apparatus belonging to the house. The second-grade, commercial, whole egg is decidedly richer in organisms than is the first-grade whole egg (9,200,000 in one case and 4,900,000 in the other), but because the number of samples is so small but little stress can be laid on the findings. The higher bacterial count for the first-grade whole egg of the experimental samples is probably due to the fact that soft eggs without bad odor but which would not separate were used—an interesting side light on the results of errors in grading. Considering the whites and yolks only, the count of the commercial samples varied from 310,000 per gram in the white to 1,600,000 in the yolk, as compared with 810,000 and 770,000 in the experimental series. When the experiment was repeated, using seconds with sound shells instead of cracked eggs, all the bacterial counts were decidedly lower.

TABLE 14.—*Experimental and commercial samples of whites, yolks, and whole egg (C house, 1911).*[1]

Sample No.	Description of sample.	Date of collection.	Bacteria per gram on plain agar incubated at— 20° C.	Bacteria per gram on plain agar incubated at— 37° C.	Gas-producing bacteria per gram in lactose bile.	Liquefying organisms per gram.	Ammoniacal nitrogen (Folin method). Wet basis.	Ammoniacal nitrogen (Folin method). Dry basis.	Moisture.	Ether extract.
	I.									
	Experimental samples broken into apparatus steamed 15 minutes (cracked eggs):									
	First grade—						*Per cent.*	*Per cent.*	*Per cent.*	*Per cent.*
578	Whites	Aug. 22	810,000	710,000	100		0.0002			
579	Yolks	do	770,000	480,000	1,000	350,000	.0026			
576	Whole egg	do	1,200,000	1,200,000	(2)		.0015			
	Second grade—									
577	Whole egg	do	8,500	13,000	1,000		.0017			
	Tanners' grade—									
581	Whole egg	do	64,000,000	55,000,000	1,000,000	28,000,000	.0015	0.0062	74.03	10.64
	Commercial samples:									
	First grade—									
573	Whites	do	310,000	400,000	10,000	200,000	.0002			
574	Yolks	do	1,600,000	1,400,000	1,000,000	210,000	.0028			
580	Whole egg	do	4,900,000	4,900,000	100,000	260,000	.0018			
	Second grade—									
575	Whole egg	Aug. 8	9,200,000	8,500,000	100,000,000	1,000,000	.0020			
	II.									
	Experimental samples broken into apparatus steamed 15 minutes (seconds—whole shells):									
	First grade—									
602	Whites, 15 dozen	Aug. 22	6,000	2,000	100		.0002			
603	Yolks, 15 dozen	do	27,500	22,500	100		.0024			
605	Whole egg, 15 dozen	do		15,500	1,000					
	Second grade—									
604	Whole egg, 15 dozen	Aug. 8	6,300,000	6,000,000	1,000,000	2,400,000				

[1] Apparatus: Sherbet cups, 2-quart agateware buckets, new breaking tray, glass rod to mix, 30-pound cans for permanent containers.
[2] 0 in 1:10,000.

CONDITIONS OBSERVED IN E HOUSE DURING TWO CONSECUTIVE YEARS.

Season of 1911.

This firm erected a building a few years ago especially to put up evaporated eggs. Refrigeration was installed, but the business soon outgrew the supply. However, the eggs were put into the chill room as soon as received, and usually they were candled 24 hours later.

THE BREAKING ROOM.

The room in which the eggs were broken was about 75 feet long, 27 feet wide, and 11 feet high, and was on the second floor. It opened at one end into a room where the finished product was being put into packages and at the other into a small room where the liquid egg was held in a creamery tank, cooled by a brine-chilled stirring machine until it was needed to replenish the supply going to the drying belts. The temperature in the drying room was often 110° F. or more. Wood partitions separated the drying from the breaking room; hence it was impossible to keep the latter cool.

The outer wall of the breaking room was brick; the partition walls were of wood. A row of windows, high up, were always wide open for light and air. The ceiling was high, and with open beams. The floors had calked seams, such as are used in meat-packing houses. The breaking room is pictured in Plate IV.

At one end of the room was a long sink with hot and cold water, where all the utensils were washed. Tables extended along each side of the room. These were covered with zinc and supported the cases of eggs and individual breaking equipment. The eggs were broken on an apparatus (Pl. IX, fig. 2) consisting of a wedge-shaped knife supported on a half-inch iron pipe which was screwed by a flange to the table top. A funnel-shaped metal collar surrounded the knife and discharged the leakage from the eggs into the shell tubs. This collar was added late in the season and served to keep tables and floors far cleaner than they had previously been. There was still, however, a great waste of egg from leakage.

The girls broke from 13 to 24 eggs a minute. As it is impossible to grade at this rate, good eggs were sometimes discarded and bad eggs were sometimes used.

The number of bad eggs going to the breakers was unnecessarily increased because the candling was not accurate. The candlers simply "flashed" eggs in front of the light and threw them, pell-mell, into the cases, so that a large number of eggs with sound shells were made into cracked eggs and those with cracked shells were wrecked. The extra work and unnecessary loss that such poor candling entailed in the breaking room was shown, for example, by one breaker who found 9 bad eggs in one case. These she threw away and with them 24 good ones. She also made nine trips the entire length of the room, to get clean pans, since instructions were to take a pan to be washed after it had received a tanners' egg.

The liquid egg was collected in buckets. Those, in turn, were emptied into a large churn through a wire screen. Rubber hose led from the churn to the long creamery tank before mentioned. This hose was dirty and could not be cleaned. It was replaced by sanitary piping, which permitted of sterilization in every part, just as soon as the actual condition of the rubber hose was made known to the management.

From the tanks the egg was led by a gate valve into buckets; the buckets were carried to galvanized-iron tanks which supplied the feeding trough of drying machines of the belt type. The belt was constructed in the usual way. The temperature was about 160° F., and the time required was from one to one and one-half hours for one run. Flaky egg was the result. It was put up generally in barrels, or in small tin cans, for household use. Two grades were made—one for food purposes, the other for tanning leather.

SOURCES OF BACTERIAL CONTAMINATION.

Observation would indicate that the method of cleaning utensils in use in E house failed to cleanse, bacteriologically speaking. The facts that the laboratory revealed are indicated in Plate III, figures 1, 2, and 3. The importance of the findings in relation to the bacterial content of the product is emphasized by the fact that the tests were made at noontime, when an especially thorough washing was given to insure cleanliness during the afternoon.

The breakers paid no attention to cleanliness of hands, so far as the egg itself was concerned. Their hands were constantly wet with good egg, and bad and dirty shells were handled regardlessly.

Touching the tips of such fingers very lightly against a petri plate containing agar showed that their hands were far from clean, as is seen in Plate III, figure 4. The growth on the plate itself was shown the girls and was a revelation to them.

The lack of knowledge of the fundamentals of bacterial cleanliness is perfectly apparent from the efforts of the management to conduct their business in a cleanly fashion. The other appliances coming in contact with the liquid egg were just as ill suited, bacteriologically speaking, to the work they had to do, yet every effort was being made, so far as the knowledge of those in charge went, to throw away bad eggs and to put out only a high-class product.

COMPARISON OF COMMERCIAL PRODUCT WITH EXPERIMENTAL SAMPLES.

Table 15 gives the laboratory findings on the liquid egg prepared under the conditions just described. The minimum number of organisms obtained was 3,300,000 per gram; the maximum was 23,000,000. The number of gas producers in lactose bile medium ran from 100,000 to at least 1,000,000. In many cases these results are too low, because dilutions were not made in sufficient number to estimate higher counts. The loosely bound nitrogen, calculated on the fresh material, was from 0.0020 to 0.0030 per cent.

All these samples were intended for human food. The tanners' egg which was being made is shown in samples Nos. 327 and 484. There is a noteworthy leap upward in both bacterial content and loosely bound nitrogen.

This series of examinations in Table 15 does more than give the condition of the final product in that it illustrates to a certain extent how the organisms increased as the egg went from one container to another. The first of each of the paired examinations represents egg which had been in contact with the hands of the breaker, the knife blade, the little agateware pan, and the agateware bucket. The second sample represents the same egg after it had been strained, thoroughly churned to mix white and yolk, and allowed to pass through the rubber hose for storage in the large tank.

Part II of Table 15 traces the liquid egg from the storage tank to the drying belt and gives the final outcome after all the manipulations. During the drying process the water content of the liquid egg is reduced to one-third or less of its original amount. Likewise the number of organisms is reduced, though not in such marked proportion. It must be remembered that bakers dissolve this dried egg in water; hence, on the liquid basis it would have only about one-third as many organisms per gram as are shown on the dry basis. The lowest bacterial count for the dried egg was found to be 3,700,000, the highest 17,000,000, with an average of 9,200,000 per gram. The loosely bound nitrogen in the dried product is considerably less than in the liquid egg. Undoubtedly some of this form of nitrogen is driven off by the heat and aeration in the process of drying; therefore this substance can not be taken as an index of quality on the same basis as in the liquid product.

In order to determine the effect of breaking the same eggs that were being used in E house, in what might be termed an approximately bacterially clean fashion, the experiments reported in Table 16 were made. The apparatus used for this purpose was that described on page 27. It was cleaned by washing in running water, then heated in a steam box for 20 minutes. The technique of breaking was as given on page 23 for B house. The results are given as samples Nos. 485 and 486 in Table 16, cracked and dirty eggs. Samples Nos. 489 and 503 were from the same lots of eggs, but were broken by one of the women in the regular fashion. The difference in bacterial content is astonishing (11,000,000 in the commercial product as compared with less than 1,000 bacteria in the experimental samples in the case of dirty eggs), but the loosely bound nitrogen is practically the same, indicating about the same amount of aging in the shell.

Sample No. 488 (clean eggs) was broken by the same operator who prepared the other experimental samples, but in this case the usual equipment of the house was used and the work was done as nearly as possible as the regular breakers did it. It may be compared with sample No. 487, which was taken from the same lot of eggs and was the work of an egg breaker employed in E house. It will be seen that like equipment and methods produced like results, whether the operator was an egg breaker or a bacteriologist.

TABLE 15.—*Commercial samples of liquid and dried eggs (E house, 1911).*

Sample No.	Description of samples.	Date of collection.	Bacteria per gram on plain agar incubated at—		Gas-producing bacteria per gram in lactose bile.	Liquefying organisms per gram (000 omitted).	Ammoniacal nitrogen (Folin method).		Moisture.	Ether extract.
			20° C.	37° C.			Wet basis.	Dry basis.		
	I.									
							Per cent.	*Per cent.*	*Per cent.*	*Per cent.*
	Liquid whole egg before drying:									
298	From 3 pails before going to first tank	July 20	7,600,000	6,000,000	100,000	220	0.0026	......	......	......
299	From hose entering large tank	do	11,000,000	9,900,000	100,000	200	.0026	......	......	......
300	From 3 pails	......	......	......	100,000+	......	.0025	......	......	......
301	From hose entering large tank	July 20	5,300,000	4,600,000	100,000+	150	.0025	......	......	......
302	From 3 pails	do	2,600,000	3,300,000	100,000+	80	.0023	......	......	......
303	From hose entering large tank	do	7,700,000	6,200,000	100,000+	120	.0020	......	......	......
477	Liquid egg from 3 pails before straining	Aug. 7	......	9,400,000	1,000,000	170	.0025	......	......	......
478	No. 477, from hose entering large tank	do	15,000,000	14,000,000	1,000,000+	350	.0026	......	......	......
479	From 3 pails before straining	do	7,300,000	6,500,000	1,000,000	95	.0028	......	......	......
480	No. 479, from hose entering large tank	do	12,000,000	11,000,000	100,000+	50	.0022	......	......	......
501	From 3 pails before straining	Aug. 8	9,100,000	8,200,000	1,000,000	......	.0028	......	......	......
502	No. 501, from hose going to large tank	do	13,000,000	7,800,000	1,000,000+	......	.0030	......	......	......
504	From 3 pails before straining	Aug. 9	12,000,000	7,700,000	1,000,000+	......	.0029	......	......	......
505	Do	do	16,000,000	12,000,000	100,000+	......	.0029	......	......	......
506	From hose entering large tank	do	23,000,000	12,000,000	1,000,000+	......	.0025	......	......	......
	II.									
	Whole eggs before and after drying:									
304	From 6 pails from large tank going to reservoir of belt No. 4	July 20	8,600,000	7,200,000	100,000+	900	.0023	......	......	......
325	Dried egg from belt No. 4 (11 a. m.)	do	7,100,000	3,500,000	1,000,000	250	.0022	0.0024	7.40	37.12
326	Dried egg from belt No. 4 (3 p. m.)	do	8,800,000	3,500,000	1, 00+	2,700	.0014	.0015	6.50	37.69
305	From 6 pails from large tank going to reservoir of belt No. 2	do	13,000,000	8,300,000	100, 00+	......	.0021	......	......	......
323	Dried egg from belt No. 2	do	5,900,000	5,000,000	1,000,000	450	.0016	.0017	7.83	36.77
481	From tank for belt No. 2	do	12,000,000	11,000,000	1,000, 00+	700	.0022	......	......	......
490	Dried egg from belt No. 2	do	8,900,000	7,800,000	1,000,000	......	......	......	6.24	37.45
482	From tank for belt No. 4	do	14,000,000	13,000,000	1,000,000+	3,500	.0023	......	......	......
491	Dried egg from belt No. 4	do	12,000,000	6,000,000	1,000, 00+	700	.0013	.0014	6.94	37.57
483	From tank for belt No. 1	do	14,000,000	8,000,000	1,000, 00+	3,000	.0022	......	......	......
493	Dried egg from belt No. 1	do	17,000,000	15,000,000	1,000, 00+	3,500	.0025	.0028	9.23	36.34
	III.									
	Dried whole egg:									
322	From belt No. 1	July 20	11,000,000	11,000,000	1,000,000+	270	.0017	.0018	7.68	36.66
324	From belt No. 3	do	3,700,000	3,100,000	100,000+	290	.0016	.0017	8.50	36.42
492	From belt No. 5	Aug. 8	10,000,000	5,800,000	1,000,000	4,000	.0018	.0020	7.09	37.23
494	1 year old	do	7,600,000	3,500,000	10,000+	100	......	......	......	......

TABLE 15.—*Commercial samples of liquid and dried eggs (E house, 1911)*—Continued.

Sample No.	Description of samples.	Date of collection.	Bacteria per gram on plain agar incubated at—		Gas-producing bacteria per gram in lactose bile.	Liquefying organisms per gram (000 omitted).	Ammoniacal nitrogen (Folin method).		Moisture.	Ether extract.
			20° C.	37° C.			Wet basis.	Dry basis.		
	IV.									
	Tanners' egg:									
	Liquid egg—						*Per cent.*	*Per cent.*	*Per cent.*	*Per cent.*
306	From supply tank on way to belt No. 5	July 20	110,000,000	220,000,000	100,000+	....	0.0057	0.0091	....	....
484	Spots and leakers	Aug. 7	....	150,000,000	1,000,000+	5,000	.0043	.0117	....	....
	Dried egg—									
327	From belt No. 5	July 20	84,000,000	4,600,000	1,000,000+	4,000	....	....	....	31.50

TABLE 16.—*Experimental and commercial samples of whole egg (E house, 1911).*

Sample No.	Description of sample.	Date of collection.	Bacteria per gram on plain agar at—		Gas-producing bacteria per gram in lactose bile.	Liquefying organisms per gram.	Ammoniacal nitrogen (Folin method, wet basis).
			20° C.	37° C.			
	Experimental samples of whole egg:						*Per cent.*
485	Cracked eggs	Aug. 8	42,000	25,000	1,000	....	0.0028
486	Dirty eggs	do	(1)	(1)	1,000	....	.0028
	Commercial samples:						
487	Clean eggs	do	5,700,000	4,100,000	1,000	600,000	.0030
488	Clean eggs	do	5,400,000	5,100,000	....	50,000	.0026
489	Dirty eggs	do	11,000,000	7,800,000	(1)	300,000	.0026
503	Commerical breaking stock	do	8,600,000	6,100,000	1,000,000	300,000	.0028

[1] Less than 1,000.

Season of 1912, After Remodeling.

This plant was practically rebuilt so far as the space used for candling, breaking, and storage of eggs was concerned. All the rooms involved in handling the eggs from their receipt until they went to the drying machine were refrigerated.

The increased supply of refrigeration was used to chill all incoming eggs at least 24 hours before candling; to keep the candling room at about 55° F.; to maintain a temperature of 60° F. in the breaking room; to keep the liquid egg at a temperature below 40° F. while holding it to supply the drying machines; and, finally, to freeze the liquid egg, if it was to go into commerce hard frozen.

CONSTRUCTION.

Breaking room.—The construction of the breaking room was materially changed. It was insulated with 2 inches of cork and was of reinforced concrete construction except the ceiling, which consisted of two layers of tongued-and-grooved 3-inch boards. The windows were closed with four panes of glass for insulation, with a prism glass on the outside to evenly distribute the light. The walls and ceiling were finished with white waterproof enamel. The wash room was separate from the breaking room, and a vestibule protected the latter from atmospheric temperatures. The creamery tank was in the opposite end of the breaking room and was not partitioned off. Brine pipes fastened to the ceiling and an incoming supply of chilled air furnished the necessary refrigeration and ventilation. The general appearance of the room is shown in Plates V and VI.

Wash room.—The room in which the cleansing and sterilizing of the egg-breaking apparatus was performed was also of cement construction, well lighted and with floor drains. (Pl. XI, fig. 1.)

Freezer.—The freezer was constructed with brine-pipe racks on which the cans of liquid egg were set. These racks, through which the brine circulated, greatly expedited the freezing of the egg. (Pl. XIII, fig. 1.)

Candling room.—The candles, which had two holes, were remodeled so that the oval openings against which the eggs rested were of such a size and the edges so beveled that the egg entirely closed the space. A tungsten electric bulb was placed behind each hole. As the eggs were graded they were placed in galvanized-iron buckets holding 12 dozen each. In the bottom of each bucket was a woven-wire screen supported by a 1-inch galvanized-iron rim. The eggs rested on this screen, which served as a cushion, so lessening breakage and offering a protection from the leakage which might collect in the bottom of the pail. The outfit of one candler is shown in Plate IX, figure 1.

When filled, the buckets were transported to the breaking room on a mechanical carrier, consisting of two endless belts connected by crossbars on which the buckets hung by loose hooks, so that they were always upright. This arrangement obviated the necessity of taking trucks into the breaking room.

EQUIPMENT.

Breaking room.—The tables used in the breaking room were covered with zinc and were supported on legs of galvanized-iron pipe. (Pls. V and VI and Pl. IX, fig. 3.) No wood was exposed. Four holes, about 5 inches in diameter, were placed at equal distances along the middle of the table. Into these holes galvanized-iron funnels were fitted, and served to conduct the shells into the galvanized-iron tubs which were set below them on the floor. One such funnel was used by two breakers. On the end of the table a frame, constructed of galvanized-iron pipe, was used to support the trays which held the sterilized cups and breaking knives. Under this tray, on the table itself, was a second tray used to collect the soiled apparatus. (Pl. V.)

The breaking outfit consisted of a rectangular cast-iron base into which were soldered two uprights, one of which terminated in a ring to hold the cup, the other in a flat plate with two buttons for holding the breaking knife. This knife was about 4 inches long and about 1 inch wide. A white enameled pan rested on the base to catch the liquid egg which dropped off the breaking knife. The cup used was of annealed glass with a smooth surface inside and out and held four eggs. The construction, in detail, of this breaking equipment is shown in figure 6. The eggs were emptied from the shells into the cups, which were, in turn, emptied into a 12-quart enameled pail.

A galvanized-iron box for holding the tissue paper used for drying fingers is shown in Plate IX, figure 3. These boxes were hung on the pails containing the shell eggs.

Wash room.—The wash room (Pl. XI, fig. 1) was equipped with metal throughout. It contained two round-bottomed sinks, two sterilizers, and gas-pipe shelves to hold pails, trays, etc., after sterilization. The sinks were supplied with an abundance of hot and cold water.

The sterilizers were built of galvanized iron in two compartments, and had shelves formed of perforated pipes which supplied the steam. A flue from the top of the box was connected with a damper and a fan in order to remove the steam quickly after the sterilization was finished. A thermometer, especially constructed for such work, was a necessary part of the apparatus. One sterilizer was used for cups exclusively and was supplied with wire-bottomed trays which rested on the steam pipes and were made to fit the space. The other sterilizer was used for buckets, shell tubs, and other bulky equipment. An auxiliary wash room with a sink and a sterilizer was a part of the drying-room equipment.

CONDITIONS PREVAILING EVERY THIRD WEEK FROM APRIL TO SEPTEMBER.

Visit No. 1 (April 22 to 27).

There were seven visits of one week each made to E house during the season of 1912. At the time of the first visit the refrigerating machinery was not in operation, but the temperature in the candling room and the breaking room was from 60° F. to 65° F., due to the cool weather. Steam was plentiful and the sterilizers and wash room were in operation. The breaking room had the equipment already described, with the exception of the new breaking outfit. A makeshift was used while waiting until the new forms of apparatus arrived. It was sloppy; therefore, the girls were forced to use cloths to wipe tables, cups, hands, and, sometimes, the floor. These rags were always wet and always unsightly. A bacterial examination of the water squeezed from 12 of them showed that they were carrying germs to the number of 150,000,000 to each cubic centimeter. Until the improved apparatus was obtained it was decided to substitute clean pieces of cheesecloth for the indiscriminate rags and to wash and sterilize them twice daily. The breakers were provided with clean white gowns and caps. Each girl was given a clean towel every morning.

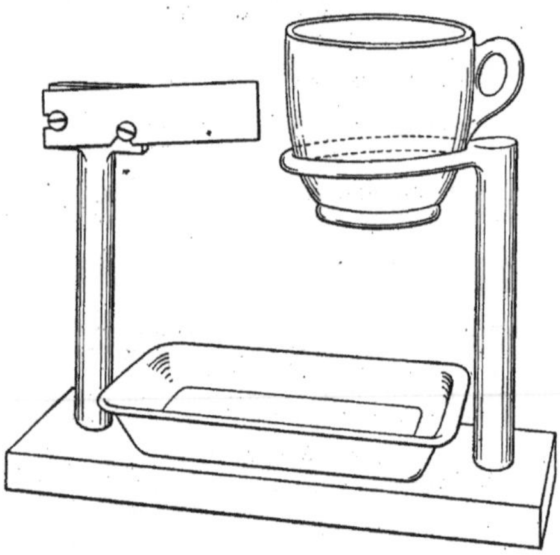

FIG. 6.—Egg-breaking outfit (E house, 1912).

All apparatus which came in contact with the egg was sterilized after washing, and laboratory tests showed that it was free from bacteria, with the exception of the troughs and brushes used to feed and spread the egg on the drying belt. This difficulty was partially corrected by lengthening the period of steaming, and plans were made to obtain a duplicate set of these devices to permit of sterilizing after each run.

The supply of eggs.—During this period the egg supply of this house consisted of dirty and cracked eggs sorted by other firms from lots going into storage. It was the custom in this house to candle all incoming stock, regardless of the season. The candlers found a sufficiently large number of incubator rots to warrant this extra grading before submitting the eggs to the breakers. At this season the eggs were purchased on the "case-count" basis.

Breaking-room routine.—There were employed at this time 15 girls, with an average output of 14 cases per girl per day of 10 hours. Very few of these girls had been egg breakers. It was deemed best to instruct from the start rather than to remodel objectionable fixed habits. A foreman accustomed to ruling girls, but ignorant of the business of egg breaking, was in charge.

The girls were drilled in the essentials of bacterial cleanliness as well as in the grading of the eggs. They were instructed to wash their hands after a bad egg and to dry them before returning to work. While working, fingers were to be kept dry by means of tissue paper. The aim, however, was so to handle the eggs that the fingers did not become wet. Inexperienced or inefficient breakers always have wet hands. The instructions regarding clean, dry hands were illustrated by making finger prints on agar plates. The bacterial growth resulting was especially useful in showing the breakers the persistence of the organisms characterizing green white eggs, which were plentiful at this time. The routine of cracking, turning, opening, and draining the shells was that described when discussing D house in 1912 (p. 58).

Eggs at this time cost 18 cents per dozen. It was necessary, therefore, to prevent waste as far as possible. Constant supervision enforced the regulation to turn the eggs upward quickly after cutting to prevent leakage, and to hold the two halves of the shell long enough to drain thoroughly. Another form of waste was due to the fact that 4 eggs were put into the cup before emptying; therefore 3 good eggs were sometimes lost because of 1 bad one. The management feared that too much time would be lost if the girls emptied the cups after each 3 eggs instead of 4. Observations made with a split second timer showed that it required 26 seconds longer to open a dozen eggs when breaking 3 instead of 4 eggs to a cup before emptying. By interpolation, this difference amounts, on a case basis, to only 1.3 minutes. This extra time was considered negligible when compared with the number of good eggs saved if the cup was emptied when it contained 3 eggs.

Other observations made amply confirm the foregoing statement. For example, during one-half day, there came to the breaking room 195 bad eggs. These were mixed by the breakers, when breaking 4 eggs to the cup, with 301 good eggs, which were, of course, discarded. At 18 cents a dozen this loss, during one-half day, amounted to $4.50. It would seem desirable, to prevent waste and contamination as well as to insure good grading, to work toward means by which each egg shall be handled separately.

TABLE 17.—*Contamination of good eggs with green-white eggs (E house, 1912). (Commercially prepared in packing house by breaking 4 eggs per cup and endeavoring to "pour off" the bad egg.)*

Sample No.	Visit.	Date of collection.	Bacteria per gram on plain agar incubated at—		Gas-producing bacteria per gram in lactose bile.	Liquefying organisms per gram.	Size of sample.
			20° C.	37° C.			
4166	E 1	Apr. 22	26,000,000	750,000	10,000	....	2 quarts.
4271	D 1	May 7	1,200,000	500,000	10,000	0 in 10,000	4 eggs.
4280	D 1	May 8	4,200,000	39,000	10	530,000	Do.
4305	E 2	May 13	35,000,000	22,000,000	1,000,000	4,700,000	8 eggs.
4319	E 2	May 14	14,000,000	15,000,000	10,000	15,000,000	
4327	E 2	May 15	7,800,000	500,000	100	5,500,000	5 eggs.
4341	E 2	May 17	9,700,000	1,300,000	0 in 10,000	6,100,000	7 eggs.

It is not possible to separate the undesirable from the desirable egg by pouring out of the cup the visible undesirable egg. This fact is illustrated by experiments grouped in Table 17. When an egg with a green white was received in a cup already holding one or more good eggs, the green-white egg was poured off and the eggs remaining were collected and examined. The bacterial findings, as given in Table 17, show that the bacteria from the green eggs contaminated the good eggs, the extent of which is brought out by comparing the counts of the commercial product of the house made at the same time as the experiments under consideration. It was against the rules of the breaking room to use any liquid egg out of the shell which had been in contact with a bad egg. The bacterial variation in the regular product was from 140,000 to 1,500,000 per gram; the lowest finding for the good eggs in contact with a green-white egg was 1,200,000, and the maximum was 35,000,000. This principle holds true for any highly infected egg in contact with a good egg, and effectually disposes of the habit of pouring out the visible portions of the bad egg and using the rest.

The product.—Two series of experiments were made on different days, tracing the egg step by step from the first pail to the final dried product. The results of these experiments, as listed in Table E-I (Appendix, p. 66), under visit No. 1, showed that the sources of contamination existing in 1911 had been eliminated except in one instance—namely, the brushes used to spread the egg on the drying belt. Even here the total count did not rise, but there was an appreciable increase in the number of *B. coli*. There is a discrepancy in the number of bacteria reported in this sequence of samples. This is due, probably, to the fact that they were taken at the outset of the work before the routine of taking and handling samples was established. Too much reliance can not, therefore, be placed on them, but they do serve to show a trend which is later confirmed when the same criticisms of technic can not be made.

The eight samples of liquid whole egg to determine progressive contamination had a variation in bacterial count ranging from 140,000 organisms per gram to 1,500,000 and in the number of *B. coli* from 0 to 10,000.

The final dried products of the two series of experiments had, as listed in Table E-I (Appendix, p. 66), under samples Nos. 4177 and 4191, a count of 1,300,000 in the first case and 430,000 per gram in the second. The number of *B. coli* in sample No. 4177, before and after drying, was 1,000 per gram; in No. 4191, 10,000 per gram before drying and none afterwards. They had probably been killed by heat during desiccation. Three other samples of dried egg taken during this period had bacterial contents similar to specimen No. 4177.

Immediately after the desiccated egg was scraped from the belt it was sifted to break up the flakes and to separate out the wet lumps. (See p. 15.) To insure thorough drying, the screened egg was placed in a bin at a temperature of 100° F. for a few hours. Determination of moisture in the flaky egg before and after this secondary drying showed practically no change in the water content.

The wet lumps were rubbed through a sieve with the hands or by means of a grooved block of wood about 4 inches square and placed in a bin at about 100° F. for final drying. The wet lumps sifted from the same run as the dried egg described under No. 4191 had, as shown in Table E-II (Appendix, p. 68), 14,000,000 bacteria per gram and a moisture content of 18 per cent, both of which are distinctly higher than the corresponding flaky portion. Other samples of wet lumps taken before and after sifting, and after secondary drying, had bacterial counts of 2,400,000, 2,100,000, and 3,300,000 per gram respectively. The moisture content was reduced from 17.40 to 6.94 per cent by secondary drying.

Visit No. 2 (May 13 to 18).

The refrigerating had not been completed, and the new breaking outfits had not arrived. Since the former visit an extra set of brushes had been made for each drying belt, so that it was possible to have them changed between runs. They were always steamed for an hour instead of 20 minutes. An extra set of feeding troughs were in the process of making. Duplicate parts of the mixing device had been purchased so that one set could be washed and sterilized while the other was in operation.

The breaking stock of this period consisted of about 235 cases of cracked eggs per day. Grading the eggs before the candle was being done well. The work in the breaking room was also good when the number of untrained girls and the makeshift apparatus are taken into consideration.

It was customary for the girls to break enough eggs in the afternoon to cover the belts during the first run in the morning. The weather was so warm that there was bacterial multiplication in the liquid product while being held overnight without refrigeration, as may be seen from the bacterial contents of the corresponding dried products, given in Table 18.

TABLE 18.—*Effect of lack of refrigeration of liquid stock upon bacterial content of dried product (E house, 1912).*

Sample No.	Visit.	Date of collection.	Bacteria per gram on plain agar incubated at— 20° C.	Bacteria per gram on plain agar incubated at— 37° C.	Gas-producing bacteria per gram in lactose bile.	Liquefying organisms per gram.
COMMERCIAL SAMPLES OF DRIED EGG PREPARED FROM LIQUID EGG HELD AT ROOM TEMPERATURE OVER NIGHT.						
4295	2	May 1	9,200,000	5,000,000	100,000	300,000
4296	2	May 3	15,000,000	11,000,000	10,000	0 in 10,000
4431	3	May 21	5,300,000	1,300,000	10,000	20,000
4432	3	May 23	7,100,000	1,400,000	10,000	20,000
COMMERCIAL SAMPLES OF DRIED EGG PREPARED FROM LIQUID EGG IMMEDIATELY AFTER BREAKING.						
4297	2	May 6	1,100,000	900,000	10,000	70,000
4298	2	May 8	900,000	550,000	10,000	0 in 10,000

Six samples of desiccated egg taken on this visit showed from 65,000 to 13,000,000 organisms to the gram, as tabulated in Table E–III and E–V (Appendix, pp. 70 and 74), under visit No. 2.

A study of the dried product of four different runs showed, as expressed in Table E–II (Appendix, p. 68), under visit No. 2, that the wet lumps in every case had a higher bacterial content than the flaky egg. In some samples this difference was negligible; in others it was marked. The moisture content of the wet lumps varied from 16.46 to 21.68 per cent.

TABLE 19.—*Commercial samples of liquid and dried tanners' egg (E house, 1912).*

Sample No.	Description of sample.	Date of sampling.	Visit.	Bacteria per gram on plain agar incubated at—		Gas-producing bacteria per gram in lactose bile.	Liquefying organisms per gram.	Ammoniacal nitrogen (Folin method).		Moisture.
				20° C.	37° C.			Wet basis.	Dry basis.	
								P. ct.	*P. ct.*	*P. ct.*
4195	Liquid egg.....	Apr. 26	1	100,000,000	17,000,000	1,000,000+	....	0.0069	0.0219	68.53
4323	Dried egg......	May 14	2	20,000,000	4,700,000	100,000+	1,200,000	.0024	.0025	5.54
4347	.....do.........	May 17	2	48,000,000	4,800,000	10,000+	2,600,000	.0020	.0021	6.90
4348	Liquid egg.....	...do....	2	130,000,000	24,000,000	1,000,000+	....	.0041	.0146	71.89

During this visit two samples of liquid and two of dried tanners' egg were taken. The laboratory results given in Table 19 showed, as would be expected, an excessive number of bacteria and large quantities of ammoniacal nitrogen.

Visit No. 3 (June 1 to 5).

The third trip to this house was made when most of the new equipment for the season was in operation. The extra set of supply troughs to the drying belts had been made; two creamery tanks, with a capacity of 800 gallons each, were installed; the new breaking outfits were in use; and, most important of all, there was a plentiful supply of refrigeration, so that the eggs could be kept cold from time of receipt until the liquid was spread on the drying belts.

Each tank had a continuously revolving brine coil, which served to keep the egg at a temperature just above freezing until it was drawn off to be dried. These creamery tanks were especially constructed in that the lids were perforated to permit of the steam hose being inserted, and the joints were tight enough and strong enough to hold the steam. A temperature of 210° F. was readily maintained for one-half hour. Of course, the cold brine was emptied from the pipes before the steam was admitted.

With the accession of refrigeration the receipts had been doubled, so that the drying room was in operation day and night. The force had been increased so that all the eggs were candled and broken during the day. The egg supply consisted of "dirties" and "checks," about half and half.

The work of the candlers was fair; the work in the breaking room, however, was very unsatisfactory because the forewoman was not enforcing the routine decided upon. The girls, for instance, were only occasionally washing hands and changing knives after bad eggs. Their manipulation of the new breaking outfit was an example of how poorly a good piece of apparatus can be used. They gave the eggs too hard a blow on the breaking knife and then did not turn the crack upward, consequently a large amount of white leaked from the egg into the drip tray.

Because of the large number of eggs with incipient odors and because of the large percentage of bad eggs in the breaking stock, the girls were continuously in need of assistance in deciding on doubtful eggs. On account of the unreliability of the girls and the importance of careful grading, it was absolutely necessary that a well-qualified person should have charge of the breaking room.

During this period 31 samples of the commercial product were obtained—five from the large storage tanks in the breaking room and the balance in the drying room before and after desiccation.

The five samples taken from these tanks had about double the number of bacteria found in similar specimens taken on visit No. 2. The number of bacteria in the present samples is shown in Table E–IV (Appendix, p. 72). There was also a slight increase in the amount of ammoniacal nitrogen.

The laboratory results showed no marked changes in the dried product when compared with those obtained during the previous experimental period.

Visit No. 4 (June 24 to 28).

The egg supply consisted of one half checks and the other half a mixture of seconds and dirty eggs.

The management had not succeeded in obtaining a forewoman to replace the one who left during visit No. 3. An attempt was made to promote a conscientious girl from the ranks, but the breakers absolutely refused to recognize one of their number as their head. The position required a good disciplinarian as well as one who could appreciate and enforce the principles of bacterial cleanliness as applied to the preparation of food on a large scale.

The supply of eggs was not sufficient to keep the girls at work the whole day. They received the same daily wage whether they worked all or part of a day, consequently there was a concerted effort to break the eggs in as short a time as possible. This undue haste led to unclean work and to careless grading.

The low quality of the work during this week, as well as the untidy appearance of the breaking room, showed what can be expected when a number of irresponsible girls are allowed to work without direct and strict supervision.

The work of the candlers was superior to that of the breakers. The foreman, shortly before this visit, was directed to recandle daily the rejects from the different candlers. The finding of only six edible eggs on breaking one-half case of rejects after secondary candling indicated that the work was being done very efficiently.

From a chemical and bacteriological viewpoint the quality of the liquid and dried product was practically the same as found on the last visit. A few samples of desiccated egg, however, contained more organisms than had been noted heretofore. The wet lumps showed no greater infection than the flaky egg.

Visit No. 5 (July 19 to 24).

The conditions in the breaking room were greatly improved because the superintendent had been able to give some attention to the breakers. The egg supply had not increased, consequently he was able to reduce the breaking force to a number sufficient to complete the work by the regular closing time. He dismissed the more inefficient girls and particularly those who had been promoters of disorderly work. This culling resulted in an altogether different spirit in the breaking force, for each of the remaining girls was not only anxious to do good work but was also desirous of retaining her position.

With this change in the attitude of the breakers it was a comparatively simple matter to get them to manipulate the egg properly, to break at a sufficiently low speed to permit careful grading, and to make the necessary changes in apparatus after opening an infected egg.

As a consummation to the improved conditions, the superintendent succeeded on July 16, 1913, in getting a forewoman whom the girls immediately and cheerfully recognized as their superior. The young woman was trained along sanitary lines, consequently she could appreciate the principles of bacterial cleanliness which were being applied here to the preparation of frozen and dried eggs. By instruction and observation she quickly learned to recognize the various kinds of eggs occurring in breaking stock, and was soon competent to supervise grading as well as clean handling of eggs. Gum chewing was prohibited among the girls, since with such a highly flavored substance in the mouth, eggs with incipient odors would not be detected.

She also stopped conversation between breakers because it was necessary for best results that a girl give her entire attention to her task. As a compensation for steady work the forewoman gave the girls a five-minute recess in the middle of each half day. The increased efficiency of the breaking force under the new régime more than balanced the time utilized by the intermission.

On one of the first days of the visit two of the breaking girls were given the position of pages. Their duties were to transport the trays of clean apparatus from the wash room to the breaking room, to carry the same back when dirty, and to look after the general appearance of the breaking room. Formerly the breakers stopped their work to do these errands. Inasmuch as this work kept the pages busy, this change in the organization did not add to the operating expenses, but greatly facilitated the work of the breakers.

A few changes in equipment had been made since the last visit. For instance, new racks had been made to hold the breaking knives from the time they were washed until they were used in the breaking room. Another change was the placing of a clockface with movable hands on each sterilizer door. After filling a sterilizer with apparatus, the operator noted the time of day and placed the hands of the clockface at the hour and minute when the supply of steam should be cut off. This mechanism enabled the operator to know definitely that each portion of apparatus was sterilized for 25 minutes.

The egg supply consisted of current receipts as well as checks, dirties, and seconds. The general candling of the receipts was fair, but the recandling of the discards was not accurate. The latter duty had been assigned to one of the regular candlers because the foreman was now checking the work of individuals candling to select good eggs to go to the breaking room. He recandled pails of eggs selected at random, and when he found an undue number of deteriorated eggs he notified the original candler. Under this system of overinspection the girls developed more care in grading.

Quantitative determinations given in Table E–IV (Appendix), under visit No. 5, showed that samples of the regular breaking stock contained 46.9 per cent more bacteria and 10 per cent more ammoniacal nitrogen than did similar samples obtained on the previous visit. Similarly, Table E–III shows that the desiccated product contained more organisms than did the samples taken on the preceding visit. The larger amount of bacteria in the liquid egg probably accounts for this increase. The increase in the bacterial content was no doubt due to the hot weather which prevailed during the first half of July.

The data on the commercial product, as recorded in Table E–IV (Appendix), prepared from current receipts, showed the same amount of loosely bound nitrogen as did the eggs discussed before, but the number of bacteria was about one-third less. The latter difference may, perhaps, be explained by fewer infected eggs in current receipts as compared with the seconds, dirty, and cracked eggs of the regular breaking stock.

Visit No. 6 (August 5 to 9).

The egg supply consisted of the same classes of eggs as on the previous visit, but there were fewer current receipts.

The general candling was good, and the recandling of the discards was improved. The breakers were doing good work under the direction of the new forewoman. In fact, the management of the breaking room was better than it had been at any time during the season.

As the firm was putting up an order of dried yolk, about one-third of the breaking force was separating eggs into white and yolk. The separation was effected by a trough separator of the gravity type. This device was effective for spring eggs, but was not very efficient for the soft eggs which occurred at this period. The girls, consequently, were continuously removing broken yolk from the apparatus, and with the best of manipulation they could not prevent portions of yolk getting into the white.

Bacteriological and chemical examinations of whole egg before and after drying proved the breaking stock to be of practically the same quality as on the preceding visit. The weather was cooler during the latter half than it was during the first part of July, consequently there was no greater deterioration in the egg supply.

Table E–VI (Appendix p. 76) gives the results of 13 samples of white and yolk separated by the device already described. The maximum number of bacteria found was 1,800,000; the minimum 1,000. It is of interest in this connection to note that the counts in every case are lower than those in synchronous samples of whole egg taken from the large storage tanks. It is probable that the soft eggs which enter the latter product offer an explanation of its higher bacterial content.

Samples were taken of the product broken each day during the interval between visits No. 5 and No. 6. During this interval the management purchased 1,153 cases of firsts which had been deluged with water while a fire was being extinguished in the building in which they were stored. A chemical examination of the eggs proved them to be comparatively fresh and to contain no more water than is ordinarily found in breaking stock. The eggs were broken in three days' time, but the last portion was not finished until four days after receipt because a Sunday intervened between the last two days. The forewoman stated that the grading was simple on the first and second days, but was very perplexing on the last day, because many of the eggs had become musty. The mustiness of these eggs pervaded the atmosphere of the breaking room to such an extent that it was almost impossible to detect any other odor. The changes observed in these eggs indicate that the wetting of shells plays a part in the production of musty eggs.

It is interesting to observe the increase in the number of bacteria in the product broken each day. The count on the first day was 1,600,000; on the second, 2,400,000; and on the fourth, 5,100,000 per gram. The *B. coli* numbered 10,000 in the liquid egg broken on Friday and Saturday and 100,000 in the product obtained on Monday. The amount of ammoniacal nitrogen found in the eggs was practically the same on the fourth day as on the second. The bacteria, therefore, had not multiplied sufficiently to break down the protein material of the egg.

The management held the regular receipts, including the checks, until all the wet eggs were broken. Two samples taken of the liquid product made from cracked eggs kept in a chill room four days had a count of 4,500,000 in one case and 5,400,000 in the other, as compared with 1,100,000 and 1,600,000 in eggs broken immediately on receipt. These results show the deleterious effect of holding warm-weather checks, even if they are kept in cool surroundings.

Visit No. 7 (August 19 to 24).

The seventh and last trip to this house was made during the last week the plant was in operation.

The breaking stock consisted of the same classes of eggs as are discussed under the sixth visit, with the exception of some dirty eggs which had been in storage since the middle of April. The low quality of the receipts was shown by the fact that over 20 per cent was rejected by candling. Since it was impossible to purchase a sufficient supply of eggs to fill the orders for the desiccated product, the firm was melting frozen stock prepared earlier in the season and mixing it with the liquid egg direct from the breakers.

With the decrease in receipts the candling, breaking, and drying forces were reduced. It now required only eight girls to break the egg supply.

During the interval between this and the previous trip daily samples were taken from the large storage tanks. These samples were obtained before the management began mixing frozen and liquid egg, hence they are comparable with previous samples from the large tanks. Table E–IV (Appendix), visit No. 7, shows that the average count of samples taken on the sixth visit was 4,300,000 per gram; of the specimens obtained on the present trip, 5,700,000. A similar increase in the amount of loosely bound nitrogen was also observed. These results also show the low quality of the receipts.

Five samples of the liquid mixture, composed of frozen and shell eggs, gave, as expressed in Table E–V (Appendix), under visit No. 7, counts varying from 6,400,000 to 19,000,000 per gram. The amount of ammoniacal nitrogen determined was greater than was ordinarily found in food egg. From a bacteriological and chemical viewpoint these samples showed more deterioration than any previous series of specimens taken from the food product prepared by this house. The deleterious effect of rehandling the frozen eggs, together with the low quality of the shell-egg stock, is the probable explanation of this low-quality product. Since the laboratory results of these samples are not comparable with those of the general output, they will not be included in the general averages.

CONDITIONS OBSERVED IN F HOUSE DURING TWO CONSECUTIVE YEARS.

SEASON OF 1911.

CONSTRUCTION, EQUIPMENT, AND ROUTINE.

The building in which this egg-breaking plant is established is built of brick and is several stories in height. The room in which the eggs are broken was located in a corner of the second floor and faced two streets. It had three windows on one side and one on the other. In cool weather—which was but seldom—these windows were kept closed. They were screened against flies. A supply of air, which was washed but not chilled, was fanned into this room, but it was not considered adequate for ventilation. At one end of the room a raised concrete platform held a sink with hot and cold water and a small steam table; along one side of the room was another concrete platform holding churns for the mixing of the egg. The remainder of the room, which was occupied by the egg breakers, was floored with hard maple. The walls and ceiling were plaster, white enameled. Two doors, one at each end of a side wall, served for entrance and exit. The temperature of the room seldom rose above 80° F.

The 40 girls employed worked at five zinc-covered tables. One girl at each table presided over the other seven and was responsible to the foreman. White caps and half-sleeve gowns were worn, completely covering all garments.

Early in the season the eggs were emptied from the shells into white-enameled cups, three of which were set in a white-enameled pie plate. The shells were cut on a small piece of steel clamped across one cup. This apparatus is pictured in figure 7. Yolks, whites, whole firsts, whole seconds, and tanners' grades were made. The drippings from the eggs collected in the plates and were objectionable. A suggestion to the manager resulted in the placing of metal racks in the pie plates, thus lifting the bottom of the cups out of the drip.

The liquid egg was collected in agateware buckets holding 20 pounds. From these it was transferred to the churns and then drawn by a gate valve into the 30-pound cans, which served as the final containers.

It was the custom of the girls in this house to use rags of various sorts for wiping fingers, cups, tables, and the floor indiscriminately. The utensils were washed in hot water, but frequently the girls, in an excess of zeal, would wipe a comparatively clean piece of apparatus on a wet bacteria-laden rag, thereby very largely undoing the good done by washing. Fingers were constantly wet.

The supply of incoming eggs in the shell was chilled before candling. Frequently there was an interval of several days between the candling and the breaking of the eggs. Even though the eggs were kept under refrigeration, it was found better to break immediately after candling (see p. 40).

The work of the candlers was fair; but too many eggs that should have been stopped in the candling room found their way to the breakers. This resulted, as it always does, in lax grading and carelessness in changing apparatus after breaking a bad egg.

The general principles of bacterial cleanliness to be striven for in the egg breaking were discussed with the management, and it was decided to try several breaking outfits and systems of operation, using the table of eight girls as a unit. From these experiments there evolved a new breaking outfit. This consisted of metal racks supported on a traylike base and having an adjustable knife, which could readily be removed after a bad egg had been cracked on it. Glass sherbet cups received the eggs. A mechanical separator of white and yolk, which could be attached to the knife, was also devised. Until this invention the shell method of separating had been used.

The table was also modified in that four holes, each about 5 inches in diameter, were cut in a row down the middle. Below these were set the shell cans and into them were fitted galvanized-iron funnels, that the shells might be more accurately and easily guided into the cans below.

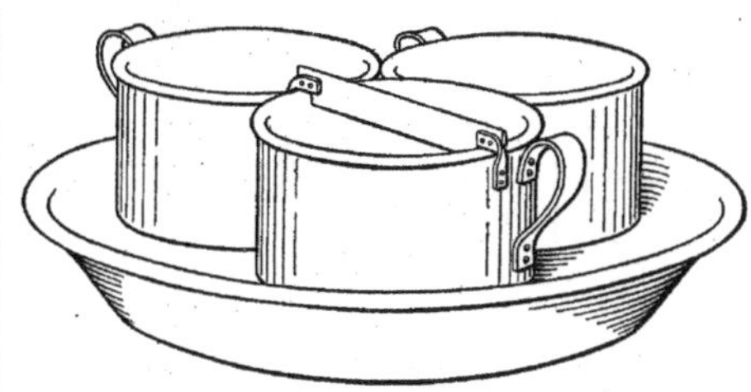

FIG. 7.—Outfit used for egg breaking before remodeling.

Tissue paper was provided for drying fingers, and the rags were abolished. A little steam sterilizer was also rigged up for experimental purposes only.

When the girls had become somewhat accustomed to the new forms of apparatus, some laboratory examinations were made of the output prepared under the old and the new conditions. The comparative results are given in Table 20.

EXPERIMENTAL AND COMMERCIAL SAMPLES.

A mixture of summer firsts and seconds when broken under the cleanly conditions just described and when the apparatus and containers were steam sterilized gave the results for white and yolk shown in Table 20, Part I, experiments Nos. 519 and 518. The total number of bacteria is low and *B. coli* were not found in a 1 to 100 dilution. A repetition of this test, using seconds only and the old type of breaking outfit, gave equally as good results, as is shown in experiments Nos. 526 to 528, inclusive.

Cracked eggs, which had been candled the day before, were also broken on the new tray and with sterilized apparatus. The findings on these eggs are recorded in experiments Nos. 520 to 525, inclusive. It will be observed that grading became necessary in this experiment. From the two cases broken, the routine grading practice of this house yielded 1½ pounds of a second-grade liquid egg, and between 2 and 3 pounds of tanners' egg. The latter included the drip which collected in the breaking trays. The number of bacteria in white and yolk from these checked eggs were not very numerous, though higher than in the sound eggs of similar grade. The whole egg contained some that had soft yolks, and the second-grade whole egg consisted almost exclusively of eggs of this variety, with some that were beginning to sour. The very high bacterial content of the second-grade whole egg again indicates that a study of grading was needed to supplement that of cleanliness. The bacteria in the tanners' egg were reduced in number by the amount of drip which entered it. The drip from clean trays and cups is very different, bacterially, from that collecting on rough and unsterilized apparatus.

TABLE 20.—*Experimental and commercial samples of whites, yolks, and whole egg (F house, 1911).*

EFFECT OF STERILIZATION OF UTENSILS UPON FINAL PRODUCT.

Sample No.	Description of sample.	Date of collection.	Bacteria per gram on plain agar incubated at—		Gas-producing bacteria per gram in lactose bile.	Liquefying organisms per gram.	Ammoniacal nitrogen (Folin method).		Moisture.
			20° C.	37° C.			Wet basis.	Dry basis.	
	I.								
	Eggs broken in apparatus steamed 15 minutes:								
	Firsts and seconds—						*Per cent.*	*Per cent.*	*Per cent.*
519	Whites, 60 dozen	Aug. 12	120,000	(1)	(1)	....	....	....	....
518	Yolks of No. 519	...do....	41,000	(1)	(1)	....	....	....	....
	Seconds—								
526	Whites	...do....	69,000	(1)	(1)	....	....	....	....
527	Yolks of No. 526	...do....	(1)	(1)	(1)	....	....	....	....
528	Whole egg	...do....	37,000	(1)	(1)	....	....	....	....
	Cracked eggs—								
520	Whites	...do....	660,000	250,000	1,000	....	0.0004	....	....
521	Yolks of No. 520	...do....	450,000	390,000	10,000	....	.0037	....	....
523	Whole egg	...do....	1,000,000	520,000	10,000	....	.0026	....	....
524	Second-grade whole egg, 1½ pounds	...do....	[2] 100,000	370,000,000	100,000	....	.0047	....	....
525	Tanner's egg, 2 to 3 pounds	...do....	58,000,000	70,000,000	1,000,000	....	....	....	....
	Seconds, clean shelled—								
538	Whites	Aug. 14	(1)	(1)	100	Present.	....	....	....
539	Yolks of No. 538	...do....	(1)	(1)	100	....	.0040	....	....
540	Whole egg	...do....	1,400,000	1,300,000	(1)	....	.0022	....	....
543	Do.	Aug. 15	(1)	(1)	(1)	....	.0021	....	....
544	Tanner's egg	...do....	81,000,000	64,000,000	100	1,500,000	....	....	....
	Dirty eggs—								
545	Whole egg	...do....	450,000	390,000	10,000	Present.	.0022	....	....
546	Tanner's egg	...do....	320,000,000	480,000,000	100,000	Present.	....	....	....
	II.								
	Eggs broken in apparatus cleaned according to commercial routine:								
	Cracked eggs (same lot of eggs as Nos. 520 to 525, inclusive)—								
534	Whites	Aug. 14	61,000,000	67,000,000	1,000,000	Present.	.0006	....	....
535	Yolks	...do....	4,000,000	2,800,000	1,000,000	Present.	.0038	....	....
536	Whole egg	...do....	1,100,000	580,000	100,000	Present.	.0022	....	....
	Dirty eggs—								
547	Whole egg	Aug. 15	8,700,000	8,400,000	1,000,000	....	.0022	....	....

	III.								
	Desiccated egg during the process of preparation:								
	Cracked eggs—								
530	Liquid whole egg from churn	Aug. 14	2,600,000	2,300,000	10,000	Present.	.0022		
531	Liquid whole egg from supply tank to belt	do	4,400,000	4,000,000	100,000	Present.	.0020		
532	Desiccated egg	do	27,000,000	22,000,000	1,000,000	Present.	.0015		
	Clean seconds—								
541	Liquid whole egg from pails	Aug. 15	1,400,000	1,300,000	100,000	250,000	.0025	0.0063	60.55
542	Liquid whole egg from churn	do	2,400,000	1,300,000	10,000		.0020		
551	Liquid whole egg from supply tank to belt	do	19,000,000	18,000,000	1,000,000	2,500,000			
550	Desiccated egg	do	33,000,000	26,000,000	100,000		.0011	.0012	11.96

[1] Less than 1,000.

[2] Innumerable in a dilution of 1 to 100,000.

Clean seconds, after clean breaking and collecting, gave the products listed under Nos. 538 to 540, inclusive, and again in experiment No. 543. Again the yolks and whites showed less than 1,000 bacteria per gram. From lot 543 was obtained the sample of tanners' egg, given in experiment No. 544. A count of 81,000,000 bacteria is accounted for by the fact that the egg was composed chiefly of green-white eggs, sour eggs, and the drip from the trays.

The foregoing findings are encouraging in that they correlate bacterial findings with cleanliness and grading. To confirm this indication, similar eggs were broken with the old apparatus cleaned by water alone and using the old methods of procedure. Under such conditions, checked eggs from the same lot as those used in experiments Nos. 520 to 525 were broken and prepared as white and yolk as well as whole egg. The number of bacteria in these samples varied from 67,000,000 to 1,100,000, a sharp contrast to the experimental product just discussed. The ammoniacal nitrogen is practically identical with that obtained previously. These eggs were traced through the operation of churning and drying, with the results shown in samples Nos. 530 to 532, inclusive, the counts running between 2,600,000 and 4,400,000 on the liquid egg and reaching 27,000,000 for the dried product. The count on sample No. 532, however, the dried product, must be divided by 3 to make it comparable with the liquid egg. It will be observed that every step in the process caused an increase in the number of organisms. Checked eggs commonly run higher in bacteria than do eggs with sound shells of comparable grade. It was, therefore, decided to break some sound, clean eggs by the old methods for comparative purposes. The findings are given as samples Nos. 541 to 550, inclusive, and show a maximum bacterial content of 33,000,000. This series traces the whole egg from the first collecting pails to the dried product. The initial count of the liquid egg, namely, 1,400,000, is comparable with that given for No. 530.

Dirty eggs were also to be studied as checks and seconds had been. To this end samples Nos. 545, 546, and 547 were prepared. The clean routine gave a count of 450,000 per gram, with 10,000 *B. coli*, whereas the old methods of breaking dirty eggs gave 8,700,000 total count and 1,000,000 *B. coli*. These eggs had unusually filthy shells and were a severe test of cleanliness of handling.

Such preliminary experiments serve to confirm and extend the findings for houses B, C, and E, as seen during 1911.

SEASON OF 1912.

CHANGES IN CONSTRUCTION AND EQUIPMENT.

The breaking room of F house was not reconstructed in strict accordance with the experimental requirements of this investigation because the management was planning to remodel the entire establishment in the near future. Some important changes, however, were made in the breaking equipment, and a separate wash room was built so that all utensils could be washed outside the breaking room. Plate VII and Plate VIII, figure 1, picture the latter with the equipment in 1912.

The egg supply was conveyed to the breaking room in the usual shipping cases. Fillers were omitted, if the eggs were not cracked. These containers, and particularly the ones used for checks, carried more dirt into the room than was taken in by any other means. The galvanized-iron buckets shown in two of the pictures were used experimentally for cracked eggs.

The breaking outfit used during the latter part of 1911 had been improved. (Pl. VIII, fig. 1; Pl. X, fig. 1.) The tray was made of iron, heavily plated with tin. The eggs were broken on a piece of spun brass inserted in one portion of a tool-steel breaking knife. The whole was tinned. It was notched at each end to fit over set screws in the two uprights. The breaking cups were made of spun brass plated with aluminum. They were supported and held in place by small pieces of spun brass soldered to the bottom of the pan. These, also, were tinned.

The pictures show the position of the cups in the tray. The one under the breaking portion of the knife caught the drip from the eggs while they were bring cracked; the second underneath the separator was used for whites and the one next for yolks. The fourth, located at one side of the drip cup, was used for soft eggs. If the eggs were not separated the fourth cup was not used. On the lower side of the tray at each corner were soldered pieces of metal which served to anchor the outfit to the breaking stand. The latter was made of spun brass plated with tin.

From a viewpoint of convenience of manipulation and ease of cleaning, the breaking outfit was very efficient. One defect, however, was the substitution of metal for glass cups. The former, on account of being opaque, interfered with grading incipient forms of deteriorated eggs such as "beginning greens." This difficulty was minimized, however, when the eggs were separated into white and yolk, because a very fair view of each egg was obtained during the process of mechanical separation. Inasmuch as by far the greater part of the commercial product of this house was prepared from separated stock, this imperfection in the breaking apparatus was not as much of a detriment to the product as a whole as would be the case if used when whole egg constituted the principal output.

After the eggs were broken they were poured from the cups into new 30-pound cans, which, after one-half day's service, were cleaned and used for final containers of frozen egg. The tables supporting the breaking outfit and the containers of the shell eggs and liquid egg were the same, with a few modifications, as used during the season of 1911. A fair idea of the construction of the tables and the arrangement of the apparatus on them can be ascertained from the pictures. The stools were of sanitary construction. Particular attention had been given to the height of breaking stands, tables, and stools, in order to make them comfortable and convenient for the breakers.

Three new sanitary washbowls installed in the center of the room (Pl. VII) were used mostly for rinsing yolk from separators; a fourth (Pl. XI, fig. 2), located under the wash-room window, was used for washing hands.

Linen towels about six inches square were used both for wiping hands after washing and for drying fingers during egg breaking. A towel was used only once, then laundered. A supply was kept on racks suspended above each table and on a shelf over the washbowl under the window.

For the assistance of persons contemplating the purchase of egg-breaking equipment the following inventory is given of the number of pieces of small apparatus used by the 52 girls of this breaking room during the season of 1912:

Breaking knives	134	Egg separators	97
Cups	379	Aluminum spoons	57
Trays	61	Finger towels	4,320

From these data the number of utensils necessary for a room with a smaller or larger working capacity can be calculated.

The wash room was 12 feet square; the walls were plastered and covered with enamel, and the floor was made of cement. The latter sloped toward a drain located at one side of the room. The washing equipment was unique; it consisted of a round-bottomed sink, two revolving brushes, two rinsing devices, a steam jet, a dairy sterilizer, a chute for transferring clean cans to the breaking room, and a sliding window for passing apparatus back and forth between the wash room and breaking room. (Pl. XI, fig. 2; Pl. XII, figs. 1, 2.) The equipment was so arranged that it saved time and labor.

The sink was supplied with an abundance of hot and cold water and was furnished with a perforated draining rack. A pan beneath the latter conveyed the drippings back to the sink.

The two mechanical brushes were driven at a speed of about 300 revolutions per minute by a one-quarter horsepower motor supplied with reducing belts. One of the brushes originally designed for cleaning milk bottles was used to wash breaking cups; the other was specially constructed by bolting ordinary scrubbing brushes to an aluminum center and was used for scrubbing 30-pound cans that were smeared with egg.

The device pictured in the extreme right end of the sink consisted of a nozzle and a percussion valve connected with a water pipe. When the nozzle was pressed down the valve opened and water sprayed out. This mechanism was used for rinsing cups.

The conical-shaped fixture at the left of the can brush was supplied with both a water and a steam jet and was used for rinsing and steaming large utensils.

Routine of Handling Product.

As soon as the preliminary container was full the eggs were transferred promptly to cool surroundings. The whites were weighed into either 10 or 30 pound cans and immediately conveyed to a freezer. The yolks and whole egg were poured into the mixing churns and cooled to a temperature just above freezing. If the liquid was to be frozen it was weighed into 30-pound cans and taken to a freezer; if the egg was to be desiccated it was drawn off into 40-quart milk cans and taken to the drying room. The product, however, was kept in a chill room if any time intervened between cooling and desiccation. The desiccation of the liquid egg has already been discussed in detail on page 15.

CONDITIONS PREVAILING EVERY THIRD WEEK FROM MAY UNTIL SEPTEMBER.

Visit No. 1 (first week in May).

Organization of wash room.—The new washing equipment having just been installed, experiments were made to determine the quickest and most effective methods of cleansing the various utensils used in the breaking room. As a result of these experiments and observations working directions were prepared, which may be summarized as follows:

1. Rinse new cans in running water and steam in the dairy sterilizer for at least 10 minutes. If the cans show visible signs of uncleanness, such as dust, scrub before rinsing.
2. Wash all utensils coming in contact with food egg in clean, lukewarm water containing soap powder. Use the revolving brushes for cleaning the breaking cups and 30-pound cans. Rinse the cups on the mechanical rinser. Wash the other apparatus with ordinary scrubbing brushes and rinse in running water from the faucet. Sterilize all the apparatus for at least 20 minutes.
3. Keep the brushes sweet by frequent sterilization.
4. Exercise particular care in scrubbing and rinsing the mixing churns. Run steam through a steam hose into each churn for five minutes.
5. At noon wash spoons, knives, cups, and breaking trays; rinse and sterilize all but the last. Wipe off tables. Put new sterilized cans on them in place of those used to receive the broken eggs during the morning.
6. At night cleanse all apparatus, sterilize the pieces coming in contact with food egg, and perform the other necessary cleaning, such as scrubbing floors, washing walls, etc.

Bacteriological examinations showed that the churns, after being carefully washed with warm water containing soda, rinsed thoroughly, and steamed for five minutes, were practically sterile. The churns were so constructed that the brine could not be drawn from the cooling coils. On account of the expansion of the cold liquid it was impossible to steam the churn longer than five minutes at one time. Because of the importance of the cleansing previous to steaming this work was delegated to a picked crew of girls.

Experiments similar to those carried on in the new wash room were undertaken in the workroom in which utensils from the egg-drying room were cleansed. The washing equipment for this work was located on a drained cement floor and consisted of a steam jet and a sink supplied with hot and cold water. All apparatus was being thoroughly washed, but not rinsed; the larger pieces were being heated for a few seconds over the steam jet. The pieces of hose used to convey the liquid egg from the supply tanks to the troughs feeding the belts were scrubbed on the inside with a specially devised brush, rinsed and steamed.

Laboratory tests of condensation water from apparatus washed and steamed as described showed about 200 bacteria per cubic centimeter. An examination of sterile water passed a few times through a cleansed hose also disclosed several hundred organisms to the cubic centimeter.

Inasmuch as the heating of apparatus over a steam jet was inconvenient, time consuming, and did not insure sterilization, a box sterilizer was planned, so that the small utensils from the drying room and the milk cans used to transfer the liquid egg from the breaking room could be sterilized for 20 minutes. The supply tanks to the belts were too large to put in the sterilizer. Consequently, they were sterilized by passing steam into them from a hose. A rinsing jet was also installed in the sink. These additions to the washing equipment greatly simplified the work of this department.

The efficient operation of the two wash rooms insured thorough cleansing of all utensils coming in contact with liquid food egg.

Breaking stock.—The breaking stock of this house consisted of small, dirty, and cracked eggs sorted by inspection from the current receipts of this house, its several branch houses, and a few neighboring packers who did not have facilities for egg breaking. The firm did not pay for leakers and moldy eggs occurring in "checks" from the latter source.

The breaking stock of this period consisted chiefly of cracked eggs, because a large percentage of the small and dirty eggs were being shipped in the shell. The firm began candling checks on April 12, 1912, and current receipts on May 6, 1912.

Organization of breaking room.—The foreman of the breaking room was eminently qualified for his position on account of his training and executive ability. He had been in charge of this breaking room from the time of its establishment, and previous to that time he had supervised a candling room. Consequently, he was familiar with the various classes of eggs occurring throughout the season.

At this time there were about six tables in use, each having a capacity of eight girls. Inasmuch as the successful operation of this room required constant detailed supervision, one girl at each table was made responsible for the work of the other seven, as in 1911. The foreman gave his orders to the table chief rather than to each individual girl. With such an organization it was possible for the management to inaugurate changes and to make rules for routine and be assured that they would be enforced.

The product.—The management was preparing frozen whites, frozen tanners' egg, dried yolks, and a dried mixture compounded from one part yolk and two parts whole egg. The latter product was termed in this investigation "mixed egg."

Two series of experiments showed, as illustrated in Table F-I (Appendix, p. 80), that the liquid egg was not contaminated as it passed from the cans on the breaking tables through various containers to the drying room.

The mixed egg sampled for these observations was broken from cracked eggs. The bacterial content varied from 800,000 to 1,300,000 per gram in the different samples. The lowest number of *B. coli* observed was 1,000 and the highest 100,000 per gram.

The percentage of ammoniacal nitrogen found in two samples of mixed egg was 0.0017 on the wet basis. In five samples of whole egg used in the preparation of this product, the amount of this constituent varied from 0.0014 to 0.0017 per cent. These nitrogen determinations prove, therefore, that the classes of spring eggs used in the preparation of mixed egg were, commercially speaking, fresh.

Two samples of desiccated product prepared from the two lots of mixed egg, taken in connection with the study of outside contamination, contained 650,000 bacteria per gram in one case and 1,000,000 in the other. These counts, when divided by 3 to make them comparable with liquid egg, indicate that bacteria were killed during desiccation. The moisture content averaged 11.85 per cent in these two samples taken directly from the belts and 4.32 per cent after secondary drying. The bacteria in the two products were not materially affected by the latter process.

Two samples of desiccated yolk, as given in Table F-II, visit 1 (Appendix, p. 81), showed the widely divergent counts of 71,000 and 17,000,000 per gram. The latter count was probably caused by multiplication of bacteria during desiccation because the highest number discovered in 19 samples of liquid-food egg was not over 1,300,000 per gram. Later samples also justify this supposition.

Samples of white, yolk and tanners' egg obtained from cracked eggs by four girls using the same receiving cans gave the results shown in Table 21, visit 1, which indicate that the eggs were of good quality; that they were graded carefully and that the technic of breaking was clean. Since the white and yolk were obtained from only two cases of eggs, the counts can not be taken as an indication of the bacterial content of the general output. This statement is verified by the differences in the number of bacteria in various lots of breaking-stock eggs opened under the same conditions as the samples just discussed. For example, counts of 600, 500,000, and 600,000 were obtained from three different cases of checks, and 300 and 600,000 from two lots of seconds.

Visit No. 2 (May 20 to 24).

The breaking stock consisted of one-half small and dirty eggs and the other half checks. All receipts were now being candled, consequently the breaking stock was practically free from deteriorated eggs with the exception of those which could be detected only when out of the shell.

After the new box sterilizer was installed for steaming utensils from the drying room, there was practically no contamination of the product from improperly cleansed utensils. The bacteria in the liquid-food eggs were, therefore, due to the organisms occurring originally in the shell eggs and to contamination during breaking. The problem henceforth was to determine to what extent the bacteria from these two sources could be eliminated.

Since the previous visit the management had changed the system of grading. Eggs showing no signs of deterioration were used in a first-grade product in the form of either whole eggs, whites, or yolks. Soft eggs, not separable into white and yolk, were used in the whole eggs and graded as firsts. A typical soft egg is also pictured in Plate XIV. The commercial mixture was made from yolks and whole eggs. A second-grade food article was prepared from drip and incipient forms of sour, moldy, green-white eggs and all eggs of a doubtful quality. The third grade, or tanners' egg, was made of the rejects from the candling and breaking room, minus eggs with a strongly objectionable odor, such as musty eggs. Since good eggs have to be discarded when a bad egg is broken in a cup with them, a large number of good eggs were also present in the tanners' stock.

TABLE 21.—*Comparative data showing the efficiency of the grading of breaking stock (F house, 1912).*

Sample No.	Description and size of sample.	Date of collection.	Bacteria per gram on plain agar incubated at—		Gas-producing bacteria per gram in lactose bile.	Liquefying organisms per gram.	Ammoniacal nitrogen (Folin method).		Moisture.
			20° C.	37° C.			Wet basis.	Dry basis.	
	Visit No. 1.								
	Cracked eggs:						*Per cent.*	*Per cent.*	*Per cent.*
4218	Whites, 30 pounds	May 2	36,500	1,400	100	0 in 100	0.0002	0.0016	87.36
4219	Yolks, 30 pounds	...do...	6,800	700	100	0 in 100	......	......	......
4220	Tanners' egg	...do...	46,000,000	12,000,000	1,000,000	11,000,000	......	......	......
	Visit No. 2.								
	Seconds:								
4366	Whites, 30 pounds	May 21	4,200,000	1,100,000	1,000	1,500,000	......	......	......
4367	Yolks, 30 pounds	...do...	1,600,000	230,000	100	310,000	......	......	......
4368	Soft eggs, 10 pounds	...do...	35,000,000	10,000,000	100	2,500,000	.0024	.0084	71.54
4369	Second-grade eggs, 3 pounds	...do...	27,000,000	1,900,000	10,000	18,000,000	.0040	.0182	78,07
	Visit No. 3.								
	Regular breaking stock:								
4495	Whites, 10 pounds	June 10	1,000	500	100	0 in 1,000	.0004	.0031	87.04
4496	Yolks, 10 pounds	...do...	7,000	4,500	10	5,000	.0040	.0093	56.96
4497	Soft eggs, 3 pounds	...do...	390,000	320,000	100,000	14,000	.0020	.0071	71.91
4498	Second-grade eggs, 10 pounds	...do...	4,200,000	2,400,000	100,000	50,000	.0014	.0068	79.35
	Seconds:								
4499	Whites, 30 pounds	June 11	110,000	150,000	100	100,000	......	......	......
4500	Yolks, 30 pounds	...do...	110,000	140,000	100,000	70,000	......	......	......
4501	Second-grade eggs, 25 pounds	...do...	22,000,000	12,000,000	1,000,000	6,500,000	.0022	.0079	72.27
4509	Whites, 30 pounds	...do...	460,000	180,000	10	0 in 10,000	.0006	.0046	87.01
4510	Yolks, 30 pounds	...do...	1,500,000	750,000	100	0 in 10,000	.0045	.0103	56.35
4511	Soft eggs, 30 pounds	...do...	14,000,000	4,300,000	10,000	......	.0029	.0098	70.49
4512	Second-grade eggs, 10 pounds	...do...	59,000,000	38,000,000	1,000,000	5,500,000	.0026	.0130	80.02
	Visit No. 4.								
	Regular breaking stock:								
4656	Whites, 25 pounds	July 2	29,000	1,500	10	20,000	......	......	......
4657	Yolks, 25 pounds	...do...	5,300,000	1,000,000	10,000	10,000	......	......	......
4658	Soft eggs	...do...	130,000	13,000	1,000	190,000	.0021	.0075	71.95
4659	Second-grade eggs, 10 pounds	...do...	6,800,000	10,000,000	100,000	5,000,000	.0008	.0052	84.60

	Visit No. 5.								
	Regular breaking stock:								
4793	Whites, 18 pounds	July 22	7,500,000	5,400,000	0				
4794	Yolks, 10 pounds	do	7,200,000	5,200,000	10		.0035	.0080	56.33
4795	Soft eggs, 22 pounds	do	3,600,000	3,000,000	1,000		.0025	.0083	70.02
4796	Second-grade eggs, 3 pounds	do	7,300,000	5,500,000	10,000		.0026	.0097	73.20
4806	Whites, 10 pounds	do	200,000	220,000	10				
4807	Yolks, 12 pounds	do	41,000	31,500	10		.0037	.0080	53.74
4808	Soft eggs, 25 pounds	do	(1)	63,000,000	10,000		.0031	.0094	67.04
4809	Second-grade eggs, 10 pounds	do	92,000,000	72,000,000	10,000		.0021	.0111	81.02
	Visit No. 6.								
	Firsts:								
4952	Whites, 28 pounds	Aug. 12	850,000	550,000	1,000				
4953	Yolks, 25 pounds	do	850,000	700,000	1,000		.0034	.0075	54.60
4955	Soft eggs, 5 pounds	do	1,700,000	1,400,000	100,000		.0020	.0072	72.39
4954	Second-grade eggs, 15 pounds	do	84,000,000	79,000,000	100,000		.0022	.0078	71.79
	Seconds:								
4977	Whites, 20 pounds	Aug. 14	40,000	40,000	100				
4978	Yolks, 20 pounds	do	130,000	130,000	0		.0037	.0087	57.25

1 Innumerable in 100,000.

Three consecutive samples of "mixed egg" taken from the hose, from the drying belts, and after secondary desiccation, contained 6,800,000, 10,000,000, and 21,000,000 bacteria per gram, respectively. The ammoniacal nitrogen in the liquid egg was also high for spring eggs. These results were the exception, for a second sample, liquid "mixed egg," had a low percentage of ammoniacal nitrogen and showed 470,000 bacteria per gram. Additional specimens of the desiccated product contained not more than 800,000 in four cases and 3,100,000 in a fifth. The results cited are charted in Tables F–I, F–III, and F–IV under visit No. 2. (Appendix, pp. 80, 82, and 83.)

Four samples taken from cans on the breaking tables gave interesting results, as shown in Table 21. The whites and yolks had a higher bacterial content than is ordinarily found in spring eggs. The counts of the soft and second-grade eggs were 35,000,000 and 27,000,000, respectively, whereas the amount of ammoniacal nitrogen, as calculated on the dry basis, was 0.0084 and 0.0182 per cent, respectively. It will be noticed that, although there were more bacteria in the soft eggs, they did not show as much chemical change as the second-grade product. This can, perhaps, be explained on the ground that even sterile eggs show an appreciable increase in loosely bound nitrogen after long keeping, due, in all probability, to enzyme action.

Three other samples of the second-grade eggs proved to be heavily infected (27, 47, and 58 million bacteria per gram), as illustrated in Table F–V (Appendix, p. 84) under visit No. 2. Since the water content of this grade of eggs varies with the amount of drip, or albumen contained in it, the chemical results must be calculated on the dry basis before conclusions can be drawn. The percentage of ammoniacal nitrogen in these three samples, thus figured, was practically identical with that found in tanners' egg (0.0111 to 0.0182 per cent). Additional samples of this grade of egg were taken on the next visit.

Visit No. 3 (June 10 to 15).

The firm began purchasing its receipts on a quality basis on June 1, 1912, consequently shrunken eggs were included in the breaking stock as well as small, cracked, and dirty eggs. The checks constituted 40 per cent of the eggs broken.

The candlers were doing painstaking work as usual; the girls, as a whole, were breaking the eggs in a remarkably clean manner. The breakers had been instructed to change all apparatus after eggs put into the second-grade product. This precaution was necessary in order to prevent contamination of the No. 1 product, since samples of the second grade taken on the last visit proved to be heavily infected.

Three series of samples taken at random from the different grades at one breaking table proved, as illustrated in Table 21, that in all but one case whites, yolks, and whole eggs graded as firsts had a low bacterial content. The one exception was sample No. 4511, prepared from eggs not separable into white and yolk. This specimen showed 14,000,000 bacteria per gram and 0.0029 per cent ammoniacal nitrogen on the wet basis. These results are higher than those ordinarily found in food egg and indicate the presence of eggs which should have been put into the second-grade product. The latter, as given in Table F–V (Appendix, p. 84) and Table 21, showed deterioration, both bacteriologically and chemically, as would be expected from the low quality of the eggs used. These results, with the exception of sample No. 4511, indicate that the grading in the breaking room was being done fairly well.

Samples taken from component parts of the second-grade product gave the following results: 47,000 and 1,900,000 bacteria per gram in two lots of drip; 210,000,000 in whites and 26,000,000 in yolks of eggs with light-green albumens; and 440,000,000 in "beginning sour" eggs. The latter contained an amount of ammoniacal nitrogen comparable with that found in tanners' egg. These data amply explain the cause of the low quality of the second-grade eggs.

Two samples representing 400 pounds of commercial liquid yolks had less than 500,000 organisms to the gram. An examination of similar yolks, before and after secondary drying, showed the astoundingly high counts of 110,000,000 and 95,000,000, respectively. A third sample had a similar bacterial content. A laboratory examination of mixed egg from the churn disclosed 1,000,000 organisms to the gram; the same test applied to nine samples of dried mixed egg proved that 44.4 per cent of the counts were 39,000,000 or over. These results point conclusively to multiplication of bacteria during the process of desiccation.

Visit No. 4 (July 1 to 6).

Owing to a shortage in receipts, the firm was breaking firsts in addition to the regular breaking stock. The latter now consisted of 22.1 per cent firsts, 41.5 per cent seconds, and 36.3 per cent checks.

The firm had elaborated the system of checking the work of individual workers so that the errors of candling were reduced to a minimum. Not only were good eggs saved, but bad eggs, detectable by the candle, were practically eliminated from the shell eggs used for food purposes.

The girls were doing exemplary work. The fact that laboratory results proved that portions of the No. 1 product contained eggs which properly belonged in the No. 2 liquid eggs, or perhaps tanners' grade, was not to their discredit, because of the practical impossibility of making three grades of eggs.

A sixth series of samples taken from the grading tables showed irregular results. The whites contained 29,000 bacteria, as compared with 5,300,000 in the yolks. The soft eggs, however, had only 130,000, which number proved that these eggs were being graded carefully. The sample of second-grade eggs showed considerably less infection and less decomposition than usual; the bacterial content was 10,000,000 per gram, and the percentage of ammoniacal nitrogen was 0.0052 on the dry basis. The chemical analysis also proved that this product contained 84 per cent of drip, or albumen. The latter always gives a low percentage of ammoniacal nitrogen and, in many cases, low bacterial counts. Three samples of drip taken during this interval gave the variable counts of 10,000, 240,000, and 13,000,000 per gram.

In order to determine the cause of the high counts observed in the dried product prepared on the previous visit, seven samples of mixed egg before drying were taken. The laboratory examination gave, as shown in Table F–III, a minimum number of 700,000 and a maximum of 3,700,000 per gram. In no case was the percentage of ammoniacal nitrogen excessive. It would appear from these results that the bacterial content of the liquid stock did not account for the large numbers found in the desiccated product. Six samples of dried yolks and 11 of desiccated mixed egg gave, as shown in Tables F–II and F–IV (Appendix, pp. 81 and 83), in all but three cases, counts varying from 14,000,000 to 200,000,000 per gram.

Three series of samples taken of the product before and after drying showed, in two cases, as given in Table F–VI (Appendix, p. 85), under visit No. 4, a considerable multiplication of bacteria in the eggs during desiccation, the counts increasing from about 1,000,000 to 36,000,000 and 50,000,000 per gram. There was no apparent increase while the egg was subjected to the process of secondary drying.

The foregoing data indicate that the high counts found in some of the samples of the final dried product were due to the development of bacteria in the liquid egg during desiccation. The preparation of dried eggs was discontinued shortly after this visit, hence the study of the conditions leading to the increased number of organisms during desiccation could not be continued in this plant.

Visit No. 5 (July 22 to 27).

The fifth visit to this house was made during the week beginning July 22, 1912. The breaking stock was composed of about one-half firsts and one-half a mixture of seconds and checks.

There was a large number of badly deteriorated eggs in receipts, due to the hot July weather. The candlers, with few exceptions, were doing good work. The breakers were handling the eggs in a clean manner and, to all appearances, were grading the eggs properly.

Two series of samples representing egg as it left the breakers, as recorded in Table 21, gave the usual variable results. The counts of the white and yolk in the first series were higher than was found in any two similar samples taken during the season of 1912, over 7,000,000 per gram. The fact that the laboratory found no *B. coli* in the whites and only 10 in the yolks indicates that the technic of breaking was clean. The large number of bacteria may, perhaps, be accounted for by the low quality of July receipts. The soft eggs contained half as many and the second grade practically the same number of organisms as were found in whites and yolks. The percentage of ammoniacal nitrogen was slightly higher in the second-grade product than in the soft eggs. A second series of samples gave results very different from those just described. The whites and yolks contained comparatively few organisms, but the soft eggs and the second-grade product, on the other hand, had 63,000,000 and 92,000,000, respectively. The amount of protein decomposition in the two latter samples was large, as would be expected from the high counts above. The two series of samples taken on the same day, but from different tables, illustrate well the irregularity of the grading. The girls were conscientious, experienced egg breakers. The results, therefore, show very strikingly the practical impossibility of commercially making two uniform grades of food egg.

Table F–VII (Appendix, p. 86) gives the laboratory results of nine samples of sugared yolks taken from the mixing churns. Some of the lots were broken from firsts, others from seconds, and still others from a mixture of firsts, seconds, and cracked eggs. The lowest count was 34,000 from firsts and the highest 2,400,000 from checks.

Intermediate numbers of bacteria were obtained from the yolks broken from a mixture of the different classes of eggs. The chemical analysis in all cases indicated but a small amount of protein decomposition.

Six samples of soft egg from the mixing churns and buckets contained, as shown in Table F-VIII (Appendix, p. 87), large numbers of organisms in three cases and a comparatively low number in the others. The percentage of loosely bound nitrogen in these samples varied with the bacterial count; two samples, for instance, containing 950,000 and 63,000,000 organisms per gram, had 0.0018 and 0.0031 per cent ammoniacal nitrogen, respectively, on the wet basis. The latter amount is not ordinarily found in food eggs.

In order to study the various classes of eggs making up breaking stock, lots of 15 dozen each were broken in a clean manner by expert graders. The counts were less than 25,000 in two portions of firsts, under 110,000 in two lots of seconds, and 2,200,000 in one sample of checks. The amount of ammoniacal nitrogen in all of the samples was in accordance with that found in good food eggs. It would be expected that the counts would be low in the firsts, somewhat higher in the seconds, and still greater in the hot-weather checks. Since all receipts become lower in quality as the season advances, the July firsts are not comparable with April firsts. For this reason the percentage of ammoniacal nitrogen is lower in April than in July eggs.

Visit No. 6 (August 12 to 17).

The sixth trip to this plant was made during the week beginning August 12, 1912, when, owing to the lateness of the season, the receipts had decreased considerably. The management was now breaking 51.9 per cent firsts, 27.9 per cent seconds, and 20.2 per cent checks. On account of the extreme warm weather the egg supply contained a large percentage of low-grade eggs, among which were many blood rings and eggs with broken yolks.

The vitelline membranes were so weak that it was a difficult matter to separate the eggs into white and yolk, consequently the larger proportion were canned in the form of whole eggs.

The bacteriological and chemical results of four samples taken from the breaking tables proved, as shown in Table 21, that the grading was done accurately. The counts of whites, yolks, and soft eggs were reasonably low and that of the second-grade product very high.

The bacterial content of four samples of sugared yolk was low except in one case (Table F-VII). Since a large percentage of the output now consisted of whole eggs, several samples were taken of this product after it was mixed in the churns. Table F-IX (Appendix, p. 88) shows that the count was not unusually high in any case and that the percentage of ammoniacal nitrogen was in accordance with the amount found in good breaking stock.

A laboratory study was made of nine samples of liquid egg broken from three different classes of eggs making up the breaking stock. The eggs were broken in the packing house in a clean manner and graded carefully. From a bacteriological and chemical viewpoint the quality of the liquid product was very good, with the exception of two samples of cracked eggs and seconds (Nos. 4904 and 4908). The data substantiating this conclusion are correlated in Table 22.

TABLE 22.—*Different classes of eggs used for breaking stock (F house, 1912, visit No. 6).*

Sample No.	Description of sample.	Date of collection.	Bacteria per gram on plain agar incubated at—		Gas-producing bacteria per gram in lactose bile.	Ammoniacal nitrogen (Folin method).		Moisture.
			20° C.	37° C.		Wet basis.	Dry basis.	
						Per. ct.	*Per. ct.*	*Per. ct.*
4904	Seconds, 30 dozen	Aug. 5	5,000,000	5,100,000	100,000			71.41
4905	....do	...do	600,000	600,000	1,000			70.98
4908	Cracked eggs, 30 dozen	...do	4,300,000	4,200,000	1,000,000	0.0021	0.0064	67.33
4909	....do	...do	850,000	800,000	10			71.60
4912	Current receipts, 30 dozen	...do	7,000	6,500	1,000	.0016	.0060	73.32
4915	Current receipts, 12 dozen	Aug. 6	240,000	240,000	100	.0016	.0057	72.05
4916	....do	...do	17,500	0 at 1,000	10			
4944		Aug. 8	400,000	36,500	100			
4936		Aug. 7	450,000	420,000	10	.0015	.0053	71.62

CONDITIONS OBSERVED IN D HOUSE DURING TWO CONSECUTIVE YEARS.

Season of 1911.

CONSTRUCTION, EQUIPMENT, AND ROUTINE.

D house installed during the winter of 1910–11 a breaking room, which at this time was the only one of its kind in the country. (Pl. VIII, fig. 2.) The room was 22 by 28 feet. It was insulated with cork on the two outer walls and shavings on the two inner walls. The five windows in the room were insulated with five glasses and four air spaces, the outer pane being of prism glass. The entire room was of concrete construction, the floor being covered with nonabsorbent paint, the walls and ceilings with white enamel. The temperature varied from 60° F. to 65° F. The door of the room opened into a passageway which was divided off at one end for a wash room. The sink was equipped with steam table as well as hot and cold water, and wire racks for draining apparatus.

The breaking tables (Pl. VIII, fig. 2) consisted of gas-pipe frames with slate tops. Resting firmly on these were galvanized iron stands, also with slate tops, holding the small breaking trays at a proper height for convenient work. (Pl. X, fig. 2.) The breaking pans were tin, about 1 foot square and about 3 inches deep. A groove at the top of the pan held a tin-bound piece of one-half-inch mesh wire cloth. Across this wire cloth, and separated by two tin uprights about 3 inches high, was stretched tightly another piece of heavy tin, thereby dividing the top of the tray into two halves. On this piece of tin, which was sharp, the eggs were broken. Sherbet cups were used to receive the eggs. The whites and yolks were separated by the shell method.

The liquid egg was collected in cream pails holding 30 pounds. These, when filled, were emptied into a galvanized churn with a capacity of 200 pounds and mixed by hand with a perforated metal dasher. The mixture was drawn off by means of a creamery faucet into 25-pound tin cans and immediately transferred to the freezer. Only one grade of food egg, and no tanners', was prepared.

At first all cans and utensils were washed and steamed for one minute or less on the steam table whenever changed. Near the end of the season a creamery sterilizer was provided, then all utensils were steamed for 15 minutes at 212° F. The girls wore uniforms and caps. Paper towels were used for drying fingers. All the eggs were chilled before candling in a refrigerated room. The supply of eggs from the candling to the breaking room was practically continuous, hence there was no time for deterioration between candling and breaking. About 15 filled buckets stood overnight to supply the breakers early in the morning. No egg cases were taken into this room, but galvanized buckets holding 12 dozen eggs each were substituted, because they were far more cleanly. The whites and yolks were separated by the shell method.

The force consisted of one foreman, five to ten breaking girls, one or two women to wash apparatus, one messenger boy, and two candlers. Approximately 26,000 pounds of frozen eggs were prepared in a week.

COMPARISON OF COMMERCIAL AND EXPERIMENTAL SAMPLES.

Table D–I (Appendix, p. 94) gives the laboratory results on 38 samples of white, yolk, and mixed egg prepared under the conditions just described. Twenty-four of the number, or 63.2 per cent, had a bacterial count below 1,000,000 per gram and the rest were under 5,000,000. The quantitative tests for *B. coli* never showed over 100,000 per gram, and in many cases the number was considerably lower. The small amount of ammoniacal nitrogen found in the different samples showed that the eggs entering the product were of good quality. The laboratory findings confirmed the impressions gained by the observation of the routine in use, namely, that the management was handling the egg according to the best methods known at that time.

Table 23 gives five series of experiments showing the difference in bacterial contamination of eggs broken commercially from clean seconds as compared with the product obtained in the same manner from dirty eggs. All of the eggs used were of about the same freshness as shown by the uniform quantity of loosely bound nitrogen in the different samples. Variation in quality, therefore, could have no influence in these tests on the bacterial counts. The results in four out of five cases show that the organisms were present in much larger numbers in the product from the dirty eggs, although all the counts were fairly low. The *B. coli* in the majority of the tests were also more plentiful in the liquid from the dirty eggs.

TABLE 23.—*Clean eggs compared with dirty eggs (D House, 1911).*

Sample No.	Description of samples.	Date of collection.	Bacteria per gram on plain agar incubated at—		Gas-producing bacteria per gram in lactose bile.	Liquefying organisms per gram.	Ammoniacal nitrogen (Folin method, wet basis).
			20° C.	37° C.			
	Whole egg:	1911.					*Per cent.*
243	Clean shells	July 12	29,500	100,000	10	....	0.0017
244	Dirty shells	...do....	19,000	67,000	10	2,000	.0017
234	Clean shells	July 11	4,900	3,600	1,000	....	.0017
235	Dirty shells	...do....	190,000	140,000	100	....	.0017
353	Clean shells	July 24	(1)	68,000	100	....	.0018
354	Dirty shells	...do....	1,700,000	2,100,000	100,000	....	.0016
373	Clean shells	July 25	10,500	(1)	0	10,000	.0019
374	Dirty shells	...do....	960,000	810,000	10,000	210,000	.0016
385	Clean shells	July 26	77,000	240,000	1,000	....	.0018
386	Dirty shells	...do....	4,700,000	3,000,000	1,000,000	....	.0020

[1] Sterile at 1,000.

The same differences in bacterial count were observed in the drip collecting in the bottom of the tray after breaking clean and dirty eggs. These results are given in Table 24.

TABLE 24.—*Drip in breaking tray from clean and dirty eggs (D House, 1911).*

Number.	Description of samples.	Date of collection.	Bacteria per gram on plain agar incubated at room temperature.	Gas-producing bacteria per gram in lactose bile.
	I.			
375	Clean eggs	July 25, 1911	24,500	....
376	.....do	.....do.......	32,500	....
387	.....do	July 26, 1911	95,000	1,000
388	.....do	.....do.......	81,000	10,000
	II.			
377	Dirty eggs	July 25, 1911	450,000	....
378	.....do	.....do.......	410,000	....
389	.....do	July 26, 1911	1,600,000	100,000
390	.....do	.....do.......	600,000	1,000

A SPECIAL STUDY APPLYING INFORMATION OBTAINED DURING THE SUMMER OF 1911 TO A WELL-EQUIPPED HOUSE.

The construction of the room in D house was excellent and the equipment good. Cleanliness could be maintained and the work people were flexible. It seemed desirable, therefore, to put into practical operation in this house the information on the handling of frozen eggs that had been gathered during the course of investigations in 1911. The first week of September, 1911, was chosen for this series of experiments. The weather in that section of the country had been very hot and humid, and the deterioration of the egg supply had hastened accordingly. It was the season also for the tall weeds to fall, hence many stolen nests were discovered and their contents sent to market. These factors combined to give a supply of eggs that were very difficult to grade, and the loss in both the candling and breaking rooms was heavy.

The candlers and breakers have an inherent tendency to keep the records of losses as low as possible, thinking that they are benefiting their employer thereby, hence the candler will pass eggs that should be discarded, and the breaker, after throwing away a certain number, will begin to save eggs that she would not have used had their number been fewer. This condition prevailed in D house at the time of the experiments and was caused by the sudden influx of low-grade eggs. It was necessary, therefore, to supervise the work of the candlers and the grading of the breakers as well as to instill the fundamentals of bacterial cleanliness into the people cleaning the apparatus.

A dairy sterilizer had been installed and it was found that 20 minutes at 210° F. was sufficient to render cups, cans, and breaking knives sterile. All apparatus coming in contact with the egg was, therefore, subjected to this treatment. The churn in which the eggs were mixed and the pails in which the liquid egg was collected were sterilized at noon and again at night to be in readiness for the work of the next morning.

It was observed that many of the eggs had very weak yolks and some had cloudy whites, but the greatest number of rejects were broken-down blood rings. These eggs were difficult to grade and were in such large proportion that the breakers became lax in grading, as stated before. Utensils were clean, but the hands of the breakers were wet and their manipulation of the egg was not exact.

The samples in the first section of Table 25 were taken when the conditions just described prevailed. The ammoniacal nitrogen was not high and the bacterial count varied from 650,000 per gram in the white to 2,300,000 in the yolk. It seemed desirable, however, to investigate the influence on the bacterial count of more careful grading in the breaking room. Samples Nos. 652 to 654, inclusive, show that care in this quarter alone is not enough if there is poor grading in the candling room, as the counts still varied from 220,000 in the white to 1,800,000 in the mixed egg. Three girls were then instructed to handle the eggs in the usual fashion, but to be exceedingly careful to eliminate every doubtful egg and to replace soiled with clean apparatus whenever an egg was discarded—a precaution which had sometimes been neglected because of the number of discards. The work of each of these girls was tested separately. The number of bacteria in the product prepared by them was low, as is evidenced in samples Nos. 661 to 666, inclusive, the counts exceeding 1,000 per gram in only two cases, and these not exceeding 310,000.

Later in the same day the supply of eggs coming from the candling room was plentifully sprinkled with undesirable eggs—stuck spots, broken yolks, disintegrated blood rings, etc. With such a supply two of the girls were instructed to handle the eggs as accurately as possible, cracking sharply, turning quickly to prevent leakage, emptying shells neatly, and keeping fingers clean and dry by means of tissue paper. The results are given in samples Nos. 668 to 671, inclusive. The counts are high; in fact, that of 18,000,000 in the white is far beyond any other count in the whole series and can not be explained by any observed condition. With a better class of eggs, though the work of the candlers was still unsatisfactory, samples of yolk, white, and mixed egg, handled in as cleanly a manner as the girls were capable of, gave the results shown by samples Nos. 672 to 674, inclusive, the mixed egg running up to 1,700,000 bacteria per gram.

Closer attention to grading in the breaking room resulted in the elimination from the output of the house of many eggs that were considered "doubtful." They were collected in a clean pail and examined. Samples Nos. 656, 679, 680, and 681 show that the number of bacteria was, in all but sample No. 680, decidedly above that usually observed, varying from 1,600,000 to 19,000,000. The loosely bound nitrogen was not high. The eggs going to make up these samples had soft yolks, disintegrated and bleached blood rings, milky whites, yolks so heavily settled that they were almost adherent, and almost all of them showed evidences of having had wet shells. The hot, humid weather, and eggs from stolen nests would seem sufficient reasons to account for the presence of these deteriorated eggs and their number.

Improvement on the part of the candlers was now demanded. Their first efforts, supplemented by careful grading and handling in the breaking room, were encouraging, as indicated by samples Nos. 675 to 678, inclusive, where the output of only one breaker contained enough organisms to be worthy of consideration, that is, 2,200,000 per gram, the others varying from less than 1,000 to 64,000.

Still more exactness on the part of the candlers, as well as better receipts, and the same care, with the better work that practice in the cleanly way of holding the egg gave to the breakers, yielded the output samples in the series Nos. 682 to 690. The total number of organisms was reduced to less than 1,000 per gram, except in two specimens; the organisms of the *coli* group were almost eliminated. The breakers worked steadily and rapidly. With the better grading in the candling room the loss of time, due to changing soiled for clean apparatus, washing hands, etc., was saved, and the judgment of the breaker when accepting an egg as satisfactory was more trustworthy.

TABLE 25.—*Experimental breaking and grading (D house, 1911).*

Sample No.	Source and description of sample.	Date of collection.	Bacteria per gram on plain agar incubated at— 20° C.	Bacteria per gram on plain agar incubated at— 37° C.	Gas-producing bacteria per gram in lactose bile.	Liquefying organisms per gram.	Ammoniacal nitrogen (Folin method). Wet basis.	Ammoniacal nitrogen (Folin method). Dry basis.	Moisture.	Ether extract.
	DOUBTFUL GRADING IN BOTH CANDLING AND BREAKING ROOM.									
	Seconds:						*Per cent.*	*Per cent.*	*Per cent.*	*Per cent.*
649	Whites	Sept. 6	650,000	280,000	10,000	130,000	0.0002			
650	Yolks of No. 649	...do...	2,300,000	2,000,000	1,000	190,000	.0020	0.0047	57.82	21.30
651	Mixed egg (very low-grade seconds)	...do...	1,100,000	1,200,000	100,000	140,000	.0015			
659	Mixed egg from churn	Sept. 7	1,600,000	1,600,000	100,000		.0016			
660	Yolks	...do...	1,100,000	1,100,000	100,000	120,000	.0031	.0075	58.86	20.79
	GOOD GRADING IN BREAKING ROOM BUT POOR GRADING IN CANDLING ROOM.									
	Seconds (some cracked, some dirty):									
652	Mixed egg	Sept. 6	1,800,000	1,500,000	100,000	110,000	.0016			
653	Do	...do...	1,800,000	1,600,000	100,000	300,000	.0015			
654	Whites of No. 653	...do...	220,000	250,000	1,000	0				
	Regular breaking, ordinary candling:									
	Breaker No. 1—									
661	Yolks	Sept. 7	(1)	(1)	1,000		.0023			22.24
662	Whites	...do...	(1)	(1)	(1)					
	Breaker No. 2—									
663	Yolks	...do...	30,000	26,000	100	0	.0026	.0063	58.93	21.11
664	Whites	...do...	310,000	270,000	(1)					
	Breaker No. 3—									
665	Yolks	...do...	(1)	(1)	(1)		.0018	.0044	58.77	21.09
666	Whites	...do...	(1)	(1)	(1)					
	Careful breaking, ordinary candling:									
	Breaker No. 2—									
668	Yolks	...do...	3,500,000	4,200,000	10,000		.0029	.0070	58.34	21.25
669	Whites	...do...	3,200,000	2,800,000	100,000+					
	Breaker No. 1—									
670	Yolks	...do...	3,600,000	4,000,000	1,000	750,000	.0024	.0055	56.66	22.50
671	Whites	...do...	18,000,000	17,700,000	100,000	6,200,000				
	Clean breaking:									
672	Yolks	Sept. 8	56,000	55,000	10,000		.0024	.0058	58.79	22.88
673	Mixed egg	...do...	1,700,000	1,700,000	10,000	110,000	.0015			
674	Whites	...do...	20,000	15,500	10,000		.0003			

	GOOD GRADING IN BREAKING ROOM AND IMPROVED GRADING IN CANDLING ROOM.									
	Clean breaking:									
	Breaker No. 2—									
675	Mixed egg	Sept. 8	38,500	43,500	10,000		.0012			
	Breaker No. 1—									
676	Mixed egg	do	2,200,000	2,300,000	(2)	830,000	.0019			
	Breaker No. 3—									
677	Mixed egg	do	(1)	(1)	10,000		.0014			
	Breaker No. 4									
678	Mixed egg	do	64,000	45,500	10,000	0	.0014			
	VERY GOOD GRADING IN BOTH CANDLING AND BREAKING ROOM.									
	Clean breaking—seconds, cracked and dirty eggs:									
	Regular breaking—									
682	Yolks of seconds	Sept. 9	73,000	140,000	1,000		.0021			
683	Whites	do	(1)	(1)	100		.0001			
	Breaker No. 3—									
684	Whites	do	1,200	(3)	(3)	(3)	0	.0004		
685	Yolks	do	(1)	(1)	(1)		.0024	.0058	58.72	22.72
	Breaker No. 2—									
686	Yolks	do	(1)	(1)	(1)		.0032	.0078	58.75	23.22
687	Whites	do	(1)	(1)	(1)		.0001			
688	Mixed egg	do	130,000	76,000	100	40,000				
	Breaker No. 4—									
689	Whites	do	(1)	(1)	(1)		.0001			
690	Yolks	do	(1)	(1)	(1)		.0028	.0065	57.04	24.48
655	Doubtful eggs	Sept. 6		2,800,000	100,000		.0019			
656	Do	do	19,000,000	23,000,000	1,000,000		.0016			
679	Do	Sept. 8	7,400,000	4,600,000	100,000		.0020			
680	Do	Sept. 9	1,600,000	970,000	1,000,000					
681	Do	do	10,000,000	11,000,000	1,000,000		.0020			

(1) Less than 1,000. (2) Less than 10,000. (3) Less than 100.

Season of 1912.

CHANGES IN CONSTRUCTION AND EQUIPMENT.

The construction and equipment of D house needed but little further alteration to bring it into accord with the information gained during the previous season. One of the most important additions in equipment made during the season of 1912 was the installation in the breaking room of a sanitary washbowl with running water. This convenience saved considerable time, because formerly whenever a girl broke an infected egg she had to go outside of the room to wash her hands.

In the season of 1912 the passageway outside the breaking room was converted into an anteroom opening into the breaking room on one side and into a newly constructed freezer on the other. The wash room, which formerly occupied this passage, was transferred to a large storeroom into which the third door of the anteroom opened. The fourth door of the anteroom led to a toilet room for the breakers.

The new freezer was well insulated, the walls and ceiling were enameled white, and the floor was made of hard maple. Along two sides of the room were brine-pipe racks on which the 30-pound cans of liquid egg were set while freezing. One side of this room is pictured in Plate XIII, figure 1. The proximity of this freezer to the breaking room greatly facilitated the disposal of the eggs after they were broken.

CONDITIONS PREVAILING EVERY THIRD WEEK FROM APRIL TO SEPTEMBER.

Visit No. 1 (May 6 to 11).

At this time the breaking stock consisted of small, cracked, and dirty eggs sorted from the current receipts of this house and other houses within convenient shipping distance.

On the first day of the visit the eggs were not being candled. It was observed that the girls in the breaking room were annoyed by the frequency of the bad eggs which could have been eliminated by candling. The management on the next day began candling the eggs bought from other houses for breaking purposes. This change in routine, however, only partially corrected the trouble in the breaking room, because the work of the candlers was inefficient and because the current receipts of D house were not graded before going to the breakers.

Most of the egg breakers had worked the previous season, consequently they had received the benefit of the week's training in September, 1911, when they were taught the principles of bacterial cleanliness as applied to the handling of a food product and as far as possible the essential points to be observed in the grading of eggs out of the shell. These instructions were codified and a written copy given each girl to be followed by her in her work during the ensuing season. Their observance had considerable influence on the cleanliness of the product. In substance the rules were as follows:

1. Hands and uniform must be kept clean.
2. Do not use any apparatus coming in contact with food egg unless it has previously been both washed and sterilized.
3. *Breaking the eggs.*—Grasp the egg with the thumb, first and second fingers of the right hand. Give the egg a quick blow on the sharp part of the knife with sufficient force to make an even cut just through the shell and its membrane. Quickly turn the crack upward so there will be no leakage from the egg while it is being transferred from the knife to the cup. With the first and second fingers on the ends of the egg, use the tips of the thumbs to pull the two halves of the shell apart. To empty the shell turn each half directly upside down so that they do not touch each other and drain for the length of time to count one, two, three. Do not let the cups touch the knife.
4. *When separating white from yolk*, have three cups on the tray. Put two on the side which gets the best light, far enough back to be able to crack the eggs on the knife well beyond the cups. Put the other cup on the other side of the tray behind the breaking place on the knife. Put the white into the first cup, the yolk into the second. The other cup on the opposite side is for soft or doubtful eggs. Never separate dirty eggs by the shell method.
5. *Drying fingers.*—Only the tips of the fingers should touch the eggs. They should be dried frequently on tissue paper.
6. Use two cups and, unless bad eggs are prevalent, put two and no more into each cup before emptying.
7. *Smell* and look at every cup of eggs carefully before emptying.
8. *When emptying cups*, pour out eggs, then touch edge of cup against inside of can at least 2 inches below the rim. Do not, therefore, fill cans too full.
9. *Eggs to be discarded.*—Musty, moldy, and sour eggs, eggs with a bloody or green white, mixed rots, eggs with a stuck yolk, white rots, and eggs with a bad odor.

10. *Cleaning after a bad egg.*—Remove all pieces of apparatus with which the egg has come in contact and wash hands before getting clean equipment. For instance, if the infected egg has reached the cup, a recently sterilized knife and cup will be required, or, if the egg spattered on the tray, the entire outfit will have to be replaced. When a bad egg is present in the cup with good ones, all must be thrown away. Spooning or pouring out what can be seen of a bad egg is not allowed.

11. Have cups, knives, trays, churn, and collecting buckets washed and sterilized at noon and again at night.

12. Never break eggs while the room is being swept or for one hour afterwards.

The girls, eight in number, were apt, intelligent, and desirous of learning the underlying principles involved in the preparation of clean, wholesome canned eggs. Their work at this time was good except in one detail—they were not washing hands after every discarded egg, an excusable omission, because they had to go through two doors to get to running water. This inconvenience was obviated when the sanitary washbowl was installed.

A few minor pieces had been added to the list of breaking equipment. For example, screens for the bottom of the egg pails; racks for the handling of the cups in and out of the sterilizer, etc.; and two removable shelves under each breaking stand, one for clean cups and knives and the other for the same when dirty.

The sanitary conditions in the breaking room were excellent. Laboratory tests showed that all the utensils, after sterilizing according to the regular routine, were sterile and that the air was practically free from bacteria. The latter was controlled by fumigating the room once a week with formaldehyde and potassium permanganate.

This house began to break eggs about April 10. On April 17 three samples from checked eggs were taken. Their bacterial examination showed, as given in Tables D-II and D-III (Appendix, pp. 96 and 98), under this date, the exceptionally low count of 5,100, 100, and 200 organisms per gram for mixed egg, white, and yolk, respectively; and no *B. coli* in the sample of white and only 100 in the other two samples. The amount of ammoniacal nitrogen for the three specimens was identical with that of fresh eggs. On account of prompt handling and cool weather the cracked eggs had not deteriorated previous to breaking.

Similar samples obtained for the most part from cracked eggs were procured during the regular visit in the early part of May when the output per day was one-third more than it was at the time of the preliminary visit. The laboratory results still showed a comparatively low bacterial content, as indicated in Tables D-II and D-III under visit No. 1, but there is observed an increase as compared with the count of the previous samples. The white contained 13,500, the yolk 64,000, and the mixed egg 170,000 organisms per gram. The *B. coli* in each of these specimens numbered 1,000 per gram. There was also slightly more loosely bound nitrogen in the eggs at this period.

The differences in the number of bacteria and the ammoniacal nitrogen in the two lots of samples are almost negligible from a practical viewpoint. They are, however, readily detected by laboratory methods, and are probably due to an increased rate of deterioration in the cracked eggs because of warmer weather.

Visit No. 2 (May 27 to 31).

The second series of observations in this house was made when practically all the additions and changes in equipment had been installed. The sanitary washbowl and the remodeled breaking tray were in operation.

Plate X, figure 2, shows a girl at work with the remodeled apparatus. On her right in a galvanized-iron pail is her egg supply; at her left on the table is the 25-pound cream pail for the liquid egg, and on the floor the can for the shells; in front of her on the breaking stand is the breaking tray. Underneath the stand can be observed the shelves for holding the supply of apparatus. Over the girl's head is suspended a package of tissue paper (not shown in picture) for drying fingers.

The new breaking tray, about 1 foot square and 2 inches deep, consists of a copper pan for the drip, a wire screen for supporting the cups, and a breaking knife of boiler steel, the different parts being arranged as pictured in Plate X, figure 2. The pan is tinned on the inside. The ends of the blade are so beveled that they fit into V-shaped openings in the two uprights on the screen. One end of the upper side of the knife is sharpened for about 3 inches. An egg can be broken on this edge without splintering the shell and with very little leakage from the crack while the egg is being transferred from the knife to the cup.

This firm began buying its eggs on a "quality basis" on the 1st of June. The lots coming in during the earlier part of the day were taken to the candling room, which was now under refrigeration and immediately graded; those received late in the afternoon were kept over night in a chill room at about 32° F. and candled the next day

All of the eggs, however, would have been chilled 24 hours before they were graded but for the fact that many of the vendors insisted on payment on the date of the sale.

The present system of buying insured the grading of all eggs going to the breaking room. The breaking stock now included shrunken eggs candled out of receipts as well as small and cracked eggs. On account of the dry weather there were not many dirty eggs at this time. There were but few badly deteriorated eggs in the supply, consequently the work in the breaking room was not materially affected by the kind of work done in the candling room.

The maximum daily output of canned eggs at this time was practically the same as the first week in May. The weather had not yet become sufficiently warm to produce many seconds; therefore, the supply of eggs for breaking purposes was chiefly small, dirty, and cracked eggs.

In two experiments in which both the white and the yolk of the egg were examined, the bacterial count, as given in Table D-III, visit No. 2, (Appendix, p. 98), was not higher than similar samples taken in April and early May. The third pair of samples had in the white 1,500,000 and in the yolk 950,000, a considerably higher count than has been observed heretofore. The *B. coli* also had increased decidedly. The higher count in these samples may be due to the fact that clean and dirty eggs were sent together to the breaking room. The girls who were separating by the shell method were instructed not to break dirty eggs, but they, of necessity, had to handle them and, therefore, fingers were soiled. The fact that there were more bacteria in the white than in the yolk lends color to this inference. Previously, when the dirty eggs were more plentiful, the candlers sorted them into lots by themselves and they were broken for mixed egg.

Three samples of mixed egg from seconds, as recorded in Table D-II, under visit No. 2, (Appendix, p. 96), had a minimum bacterial content of 320,000, a maximum of 950,000 organisms per gram, and a range in the number of *B. coli* from 1,000 to 10,000. These counts are considerably higher than any found in previous samples; the amount of loosely bound nitrogen had also slightly increased.

Twelve samples of mixed eggs taken each working day during the interval between the second and third visit (see Table D-II, under dates May 29 to June 15, inclusive), showed no material increase in the bacterial content and no change in the ammoniacal nitrogen. In fact, many of the counts were lower. Six of the samples contained less than 400,000 bacteria per gram; the number in the other six was not over 2,200,000. The maximum count of this series of experiments was higher than has been found in samples taken at an earlier date, but the average was about the same.

Visit No. 3 (June 17 to 22).

The third visit was made between the dates June 17 and 22, inclusive, when, owing to prolonged cool weather and a shortage in the egg supply, there were few seconds to be used for breaking. The number of girls in the breaking room had been reduced from eight to four, and often they worked for only part of a day. The eggs were of good quality, so the grading was comparatively simple. A tanners' grade was being made of the discards in the breaking room. The preparation of this grade, however, was soon abandoned.

At this time there were obtained eight samples of food egg, of which five were whites and three yolks. The laboratory examination showed that neither the bacterial count nor the amount of ammoniacal nitrogen had increased when compared with the results obtained from similar samples taken previously.

Three samples were also taken of the tanners' eggs, which, as would be expected, were heavily infected with bacteria, the number aggregating, in some cases, more than 100,000,000 per gram. The high amount of ammoniacal nitrogen, about treble that found in the food eggs at this time, indicated to what degree the material had deteriorated. These results are given in Table 26.

TABLE 26.—*Commercial samples of tanners' liquid egg—Discards from breaking room (D house, 1912).*

Sample No.	Visit.	Date of collection.	Bacteria per gram on plain agar incubated at—		Gas-producing bacteria per gram in lactose bile.	Liquefying organisms per gram.	Ammoniacal nitrogen (Folin method).		Moisture.	Size of sample.
			20° C.	37° C.			Wet basis.	Dry basis.		
							Per ct.	*Per ct.*	*Per ct.*	*Lbs.*
4555	3	June 17	110,000,000	56,000,000	1,000,000	20,000,000	0.0047	0.0156	69.82	30
4561	3	...do....	150,000,000	68,000,000	10,000,000	60,000,000	.0055	.0157	65.06	35
4569	3	June 18	39,000,000	20,000,000	1,000,000	6,000,000	.0039	.0124	68.73	70

Some experiments were conducted during this week to check the cleanliness of the routine of the breaking room. For this investigation four samples of eggs in the shell were procured—one of clean seconds, one of cracked eggs, and two of dirty eggs. The samples, consisting of 12 dozen eggs each, were divided equally into two portions. One was broken commercially in the packing house, and the other was opened aseptically in the laboratory. These comparative experiments, listed in Table 27, not only indicate the superior quality of the breaking stock at this season, but also show how closely the aseptic methods of the laboratory can be approximated under commercial conditions.

TABLE 27.—*Comparative samples of eggs opened commercially and aseptically (D house, 1912).*

[Samples collected June 19, 1912.]

Sample No.	Description and size of sample.	Bacteria per gram on plain agar incubated at—		Gas-producing bacteria per gram in lactose bile.	Liquefying organisms per gram.	Ammoniacal nitrogen (Folin method).		Moisture.	Number of discards.	Method of opening.
		20° C.	37° C.			Wet basis.	Dry basis.			
	Visit No. 3.					*Per ct.*	*Per ct.*	*Per ct.*		
4572	Cracked, 6 dozen	140,000	75,000	0	....	0.0019	0.0071	73.22	2	Commercial.
4573	.....do..........	200	350	0	....	.0018	.0065	72.09	1	Aseptic.
4585	Leakers of No. 4573, 1½ dozen.	200	100	0	....	.0019	.0068	72.03	0	Commercial.
4578	Clean seconds, 6 dozen.	600	300	0	0 in 1,000	.0016	.0059	73.00	0	Do.
4579	.....do..........	0	0	0	0 in 1,000	.0017	.0061	72.13	2	Aseptic.
4576	Dirty, 6 dozen...	400	400	10	0 in 1,000	.0017	.0065	73.85	0	Commercial.
4577	.....do..........	200	50	0	0 in 1,000	.0017	.0061	72.29	0	Aseptic.
4581	.....do..........	13,000	3,000	1,000	2,000	.0017	.0063	72.87	0	Commercial.
4582	.....do..........	150	0	0	0 in 1,000	.0017	.0061	72.02	......	Aseptic.

Visit No. 4 (July 9 to 12).

During the interval between the third and fourth visits the weather had been warm, with the result that the percentage of seconds in receipts increased and many of the fertile eggs contained hatch spots or blood rings. A typical heated egg is pictured in Plate II, U. S. Department of Agriculture Bulletin No. 51. On account of inefficient candling many blood rings found their way to the breaking room, thereby increasing the difficulties of grading as well as necessitating frequent changes of apparatus. This poor work led one to suspect that the candlers might be just as careless in throwing away edible eggs as they were in not eliminating the bad eggs. That this suspicion was well founded is shown by the fact that when two cases of discards from the candling room were broken one contained 9.7 per cent food eggs and the other the astonishingly high percentage of 29.4 per cent. This was too great a loss to be passed unnoticed, therefore the candling foreman was instructed to recandle daily the eggs discarded by the different candlers. This work was a part of the candling room routine for the remainder of the season.

Up to the present time the girls had worked practically without supervision and according to the instructions given them at the beginning of the season. Now, in order to train new girls and on account of the increased difficulty in grading, one of the cleanest and most experienced egg breakers was given charge of the room. Her duties were as follows:

1. Enforce instructions to breakers.
2. Supervise washing and sterilizing of apparatus and supply of same to breaking room.
3. If a breaker is dirty, disobedient, unable to grade, or inefficient, consult with the management regarding her discharge.
4. If candling is not satisfactory, report to the management.
5. Decide on doubtful eggs.
6. Supervise cleaning of breaking room, toilet room, hallway, and wash room.

Samples taken during this visit and also those taken by an employee of the plant during the investigator's absence showed practically no change in the bacterial count or the amount of ammoniacal nitrogen of the commercial product. Previous work on hatch-spot eggs proved them to be nearly sterile when opened aseptically and to contain low quantities of ammoniacal nitrogen. Therefore one would not expect that the presence of a large percentage of these eggs in the breaking stock would materially affect either its bacterial content or its chemical composition.

Visit No. 5 (July 29 to August 2).

The fifth series of observations was made when, owing to a prolonged period of hot weather, there was an increased supply of eggs for breaking. Many of the eggs were distinctly lower in quality than the breaking stock previously used. The regular candling room was not large enough to handle all the eggs, therefore an auxiliary candling room was established in one corner of a storeroom. Not being refrigerated, it was very hot. To take care of the extra supply of eggs, new candlers were required. From this fact, together with the increased difficulty in grading such low quality eggs, it could be predicted that large numbers of bad eggs would not be detected and would therefore gain access to the breaking room.

An observation made in the breaking room showed that 41 bad eggs, or 9.5 per cent, were found in a total of 36 dozen. These should all have been eliminated by the candlers. An analysis of the 41 eggs showed that they consisted of 2 eggs containing mold spots, 6 blood rings, 13 white rots, and 20 eggs with an adherent yolk.

The effect of so many bad eggs in the breaking-room stock is shown by the fact that the product broken from the lot of 36 dozen eggs contained 20,000,000 organisms per gram.

An investigation in the candling room showed that the trouble was chiefly ignorance on the part of the new candlers. By working with them for a short time and pointing out which eggs should be saved and which discarded the number of bad eggs in the breaking stock was promptly reduced.

In order to put a check on the work of individual candlers, each man was instructed to place a tag bearing his name on every bucket of eggs candled by him. Under this system the work of an individual candler could be traced into the breaking room. Under this regulation the men worked more cautiously, and as long as this system was in use the work in the candling room was greatly improved.

The girls in the breaking room, now 14 in number, were doing efficient work under the supervision of the new forewoman. The organization previously described, including a forewoman, had been in operation about two weeks. During this time the increased efficiency in the breaking room was equivalent to the wages of the forewoman.

Up to this time one-half of the girls had their egg supply on the left instead of on the right side; observations with a split-second stop watch showed that 1.8 seconds were lost for every four eggs broken when a girl reached for her eggs with her left rather than with her right hand.

Estimating these results on the basis of a 10-hour day, a girl reaching to the right for the eggs could break 1.4 more cases a day than she could when working toward the left. In accordance with these results, all the apparatus on the breaking table was rearranged so that no extra motions were made from the time the egg was removed from the pail until it reached its final container.

The majority of the commercial samples taken during the latter part of July contained not only more bacteria but also more loosely bound nitrogen than did any previous series of samples. For instance, the five specimens of mixed eggs collected during the investigator's absence and the five collected during visit No. 5 had, as given in Table D-II, visit No. 5 (Appendix), an average count of 1,400,000 organisms per gram as compared with 650,000 in the samples taken during the first half of the month. The white and yolk samples showed an even greater increase in bacteria.

During this visit there was received one shipment of 72 cases of checks which showed a combined loss in the candling and breaking room of 14.6 per cent. The bacterial findings given in Table 28 showed that the product from these eggs had a materially higher bacterial content than the regular product. Many of the eggs were moldy. They were obtained from a shipper who had gradually sorted them out of his receipts as unsuited for shipping and had therefore sold them to an egg-breaking establishment.

TABLE 28.—*Commercial samples of low quality, cracked eggs (D house, 1912.)*

Sample No.	Description and size of sample.	Date of collection.	Bacteria per gram on plain agar incubated at—		Gas-producing bacteria per gram in lactose bile.	Ammoniacal nitrogen. (Folin method).		Moisture.
			20° C.	37° C.		Wet basis.	Dry basis.	
	Visit No. 5.					*Per ct.*	*Per ct.*	*Per ct.*
4855	Cracked eggs, 125 pounds....	July 29	6,000,000	5,500,000	100,000	0.0023	0.0075	69.19
4856	.....do..........	...do.....	4,800,000	4,000,000	100,000	....	....	....
4886	Cracked eggs, 100 pounds....	Aug. 1	5,400,000	4,300,000	100,000	.0017	.0062	72.69

A second shipment of checked eggs, which had been in commerce, as was the other shipment cited, but obtained from a different shipper, gave similar results. The product was of lower quality than the average output of this house; hence the purchase of such eggs was promptly discontinued.

Visit No. 6 (August 19 to 24).

The sixth and last visit was made when, owing to the lateness of the egg-laying season, the receipts were very light.

The candlers had become careless because the tag system of checking had been abolished when the force was decreased. The work of the breakers, however, was as good as during the last visit, because the organization and routine of the breaking room was not changed even though the number of girls had been reduced.

The quality of the breaking stock had not improved, consequently the counts of samples procured on the fifth and sixth visits were practically the same; the average count of the 10 samples of mixed egg taken the latter half of July was 1,400,000 per gram; of the same number of samples collected during the visit under discussion, it was 1,700,000 organisms per gram (Table D-II, Appendix, p. 96).

During this visit a gravity type trough separator for whites and yolks was tried. This device did not prove mechanically successful for separating warm-weather eggs. Samples of white and yolk separated by the trough method, both during its experimental stage and after its perfection, gave the counts listed in Table 29. If the results under visits 2 and 5 be compared with the counts for similar periods in Table D-III (Appendix, p. 98), which gives whites and yolks separated by the shell method, it will be observed that in all cases there are fewer bacteria in the samples separated by the trough method. This is particularly true of the number of *B. coli.*

TABLE 29.—*Commercial samples of whites and yolks—Trough method of separation (D house, 1912).*

Sample No.	Description and size of sample.	Date of collection.	Bacteria per gram on plain agar incubated at—		Gas-producing bacteria per gram in lactose bile.	Ammoniacal nitrogen (Folin method).		Moisture.
			20° C.	37° C.		Wet basis.	Dry basis.	
	Visit No. 2.							
						Per ct.	*Per ct.*	*Per ct.*
4403	Whites, seconds, 15 pounds	May 27	[1] 1,600	150	[1] 0	0.0004	0.0031	87.10
4404	Yolks of No. 4403, 15 pounds	...do	[1] 1,200	400	[1] 10	.0033	.0072	54.15
	Visit No. 5.							
4861	Whites, seconds and cracked eggs, 20 pounds	July 29	[2] 320,000	190,000	[2] 1,000	......	......	......
4862	Yolks of No. 4861, 20 pounds	...do	[2] 100,000	150,000	[2] 1,000	.0030	.0068	56.05
4868	Whites, seconds, 13 pounds	July 30	[2] 360,000	330,000	[2] 1,000	......	......	......
4869	Yolks of No. 4868, 11 pounds	...do	[2] 110,000	90,000	[2] 0 in 100	.0037	.0083	55.42
	Visit No. 6.							
41005	Whites, seconds, 25 pounds	Aug. 19	27,000	22,000	1,000	......	......	......
41006	Yolks of No. 41005, 15 pounds	...do	300,000	180,000	1,000	.0029	.0067	56.66
41011	Whites, seconds, 18 pounds	...do	600,000	650,000	0	.0003	.0023	86.96
41012	Yolks of No. 41011, 13 pounds	...do	650,000	600,000	0	.0030	.0065	53.64
41026	Whites, seconds and cracked eggs, 30 pounds	Aug. 20	490,000	360,000	1,000	......	......	......
41027	Yolks of No. 41026, 30 pounds	...do	800,000	650,000	10,000	.0027	.0075	64.06

[1] Comparable figures obtained by the shell method of separation (Table D III, p. 98, Appendix) vary from 15,000 to 950,000 bacteria in the yolks and from 60,000 to 1,500,000 in the whites, *B. coli* varying from 100 to 10,000.

[2] Comparable figures from the same source show a maximum bacterial content of 650,000 for the whites, 2,100,000 for the yolks, and from 100 to 1,000,000 *B. coli*—a pronounced superiority of the trough-separated product.

By the shell method the egg, during the shifting of the yolk from one half shell to the other, is sure to come in contact with the fingers of the breaker and the outside of the shells, both of which, as foregoing statements have proved, are serious sources of contamination. By the trough method the egg, on the other hand, comes in contact with practically nothing except the cup and separator, both of which can be kept clean by frequent sterilizing.

TABULATED RESULTS.

TABLE C-I.—*Commercial samples of whites, yolks, and whole eggs, 1911.*

Sample No.	Description of sample.	Date of collection.	Bacteria per gram on plain agar incubated at— 20° C.	Bacteria per gram on plain agar incubated at— 37° C.	Gas-producing bacteria per gram in lactose bile.	Liquefying organisms per gram.	Ammoniacal nitrogen (Folin method). Wet basis.	Ammoniacal nitrogen (Folin method). Dry basis.	Moisture.	Ether extract.
							Per cent.	*Per cent.*	*Per cent.*	*Per cent.*
	Whites:									
187	From 17 pound pail	July 6	240,000	380,000	10,000	2,000	0.0005	0.0037	86.64	
189	From 3 pails at end of morning's breaking	..do....	85,000	55,000	10,000	5,500				
404	From pail ready for freezer	July 31	160,000	120,000	0 in 1:1,000	4,000	.0005			
407	Do	..do....	120,000	58,000	10,000	0	.0006			
409	Do	..do....	110,000	65,000	100,000	0	.0005			
411	Do	Aug. 1	1,500,000	1,200,000	1,000		.0005			
413	Do	..do....	1,200,000	430,000	1,000	500,000	.0004			
416	Do	..do....	23,000	18,000	1,000	0	.0003			
563	Do	Aug. 21	31,000	17,000	10,000		.0004			
566	Do	..do....	44,500	36,000	1,000		.0002			
573	Cracked eggs	Aug. 22	330,000	350,000	10,000	200,000	.0002			
594	Seconds from pail ready for freezer	..do....	90,000	67,000	1,000	10,000	.0002			
	Yolks:									
184	From churn	July 6	270,000	230,000	[1] 10,000	100,000	.0039	.0090	56.48	24.66
185	Sugared yolk from churn	..do....	150,000	200,000	[1] 10,000	40,000	.0037	.0073	49.26	23.01
188	From churn	..do....	630,000	820,000	[1] 1,000	120,000	.0032	.0074	56.74	22.85
402	Sugared yolks from churn	July 31	1,200,000	940,000	1,000	160,000	.0035	.0073	51.85	22.37
406	Do	..do....	1,900,000	900,000	100,000	120,000	.0034	.0072	52.90	21.09
408	Do	Aug. 2	120,000	490,000	10,000	200,000	.0034	.0071	52.21	22.17
410	Do	July 31	460,000	410,000	10,000	30,000	.0036	.0075	52.31	22.35
414	Do	Aug. 1	250,000	230,000	1,000	20,000	.0034	.0071	51.81	23.23
415	Do	..do....	420,000	450,000	10,000	10,000	.0035	.0073	52.33	23.47
564	Do	Aug. 21	320,000	310,000	10,000	200,000	.0028	.0058	51.90	20.76
567	Do	..do....	300,000	270,000	10,000	0	.0029	.0061	52.07	21.07
574	Do	Aug. 22	1,400,000	1,600,000	1,000,000	210,000	.0028	.0060	53.08	22.41
595	Do	Aug. 23	8,000,000	3,700,000	100,000	1,500,000	.0020	.0074	72.95	10.89
	Whole eggs from churn:									
412	First grade	Aug. 2	1,900,000	1,900,000	10,000		.0024			
580	Better than a second but not a first grade	Aug. 22	4,500,000	4,900,000	[1] 100,000	260,000	.0018			
186	Second grade	July 6	3,300,000	9,500,000	10,000		.0022	.0085	74.16	9.60
403	Do	July 31	12,000,000	11,000,000	[1] 1,000,000	500,000	.0023			
405	Do	..do....	5,700,000	2,600,000	1,000,000	130,000	.0024			
417	Do	Aug. 2	8,100,000	5,700,000	[1] 100,000	400,000	.0020			
565	Do	Aug. 1	6,100,000	6,600,000	[1] 100,000		.0018			
568	Do	Aug. 21	790,000	800,000	1,000		.0019			

[1] Number of gas-producing bacteria not determined beyond this number.

TABLE E-I.—*Successive commercial samples of liquid and dried eggs, 1912.*

Sample No.	Description of sample.	Date of collection.	Bacteria per gram on plain agar incubated at—		Gas-producing bacteria per gram in lactose bile.	Liquefying organisms per gram.	Ammoniacal nitrogen (Folin method).		Moisture.
			20° C.	37° C.			Wet basis.	Dry basis.	
	Visit No. 1.						*Per cent.*	*Per cent.*	*Per cent.*
4169	Liquid egg from mixer	Apr. 22	700,000	150,000	1,000				
4170	Liquid egg from storage tank	do	430,000	120,000	1,000				
4171	Liquid egg from supply tank to belt No. 3	do	290,000	120,000	1,000				
4177	Dried egg from belt No. 3	do	800,000	1,300,000	1,000	40,000			9.04
4185	Liquid egg from 17 pails	Apr. 25	950,000	20,500	100	30,000			
4186	Liquid egg from mixer	do	900,000	90,000	0	0 in 10,000			68.01
4187	Liquid egg from storage tank	do	140,000	160,000	100	0 in 10,000			
4188	Liquid egg from supply tank to belt No. 5	do	1,500,000	96,000	100	500,000			
4189	Liquid egg after brushes	do	850,000	42,500	10,000	0 in 10,000			
4191	Dried egg after belt No. 5	do	430,000	91,000	0	110,000			7.13
4192	Wet lumps after belt No. 5	do	14,000,000	17,000,000	1,000				18.00
	Visit No. 2.								
4300	Liquid egg from storage tank	May 13	1,500,000	700,000	100,000	450,000	0.0016	0.0054	70.29
4301	Liquid egg from supply tank to belt	do	1,400,000	1,000,000	10,000	400,000			
4302	Liquid egg after brushes	do	1,400,000	1,100,000	100,000	77,000			
4312	Dried egg from belt	do	1,400,000	1,100,000	1,000,000	200,000	.0006	.0007	7.78
4350	Liquid egg from mixer	May 17	1,000,000	120,000	10,00	150,000	.0016	.0058	72.64
4351	Liquid egg from supply tank to belt No. 5	do	1,000,000	220,000	100,00	140,000			
4354	Liquid egg after brushes	do	850,000	180,000	10,00	170,000			
4352	Liquid egg from supply tank to belt No. 4	do	900,000	310,000	1,000,00	160,000			
4359	Dried egg from belt No. 4	do	3,400,000	2,600,000	100,00	2,700,000	.0012	.0013	9.62
4360	Dried egg from belt No. 3	do	900,000	850,000	1,000,000	110,000	.0009	.0010	10.78
	Visit No. 3.								
4439	Liquid egg from supply tank belt No. 1	June 1	3,800,000	1,300,000	100,000	330,000			
4447	Dried egg from belt No. 1	do	4,200,000	1,600,000	100,000	100,000			
4448	Wet lumps from belt No. 1	do	15,000,000	11,000,000	1,000,000	1,200,000			
4440	Liquid egg from supply tank to belt No. 2	do	3,100,000	1,200,000	100,000	350,000			
4449	Dried egg from belt No. 2	do	1,600,000	600,000	100,000	100,000			
4450	Wet lumps from belt No. 2	do	12,000,000	5,900,000	100,000	210,000			

4441	Liquid egg from supply tank to belt No. 3	do	3,300,000	1,700,000	100,000	220,000			
4442	Liquid egg after brushes	do	3,900,000	1,900,000	1,000,000	3,000,000			
4451	Dried egg from belt No. 3	do	4,200,000	1,700,000	100,000	200,000	.0008	.0009	9.89
4452	Wet lumps from belt No. 3	do	3,800,000	1,800,000	100,000	130,000	.0028	.0036	21.48
4443	Liquid egg from supply tank to belt No. 4	do	3,100,000	1,300,000	1,000,000	310,000			
4453	Dried egg from belt No. 4	do	1,300,000	750,000	100,000	150,000	.0008	.0009	9.07
4454	Wet lumps from belt No. 4	do	3,600,000	1,100,000	100,000	300,000	.0011	.0013	17.36
4445	Liquid egg from supply tank to belt No. 5	do	4,000,000	1,400,000	100,000	280,000			
4446	Liquid egg after brushes	do	2,100,000	900,000	100,000	190,000			
4455	Dried egg from belt No. 5	do	1,200,000	900,000	100,000	120,000			
	Visit No. 4.								
4592	Liquid egg from supply tank to belt No. 5	June 24	4,000,000	850,000	100,000	1,000,000	.0020	.0073	72.65
4593	Dried egg from belt No. 5	do	3,400,000	1,100,000	100,000	100,000	.0013	.0014	8.64
4594	Wet lumps from belt No. 5	do	3,900,000	850,000	100,000	1,000,000			
4610	Liquid egg from supply tank to belt No. 5	June 25	1,500,000	260,000	100,000				
	Visit No. 5.								
4738	From pails—2 hours' break	July 15	3,400,000	1,600,000	100,000				
4739	Storage tank	do	4,000,000	1,800,000	100,000		.0021	.0081	74.17
4740	Five supply tanks	do	7,400,000	5,300,000	100,000				
4742	Dried egg from four belts	do	9,300,000	4,200,000	1,000,000				11.30
4743	Wet lumps from four belts	do	11,000,000	7,500,000	1,000,000				21.00
	Visit No. 6.								
4922	Liquid egg from supply tank to belt No. 5	Aug. 6	5,100,000	3,400,000	100,000		.0020	.0073	72.55
4925	Dried egg from belt No. 5	do	5,000,000	2,800,000	1,000,000		.0010	.0011	9.15
4926	Wet lumps from belt No. 5	do	5,000,000	4,800,000	1,000,000				
	Visit No. 7.								
41061	Liquid egg from supply tank to belt No. 5	Aug. 26	19,000,000	5,500,000	100,000		.0031	.0112	72.38
41063	Dried egg from belt No. 5	do	5,800,000	2,100,000	100,000				8.80
41064	Wet lumps from belt No. 5	do	8,200,000	4,100,000	1,000,000				

TABLE E-II.—*Commercial samples of dried egg compared with wet lumps from belt, 1912.*

[See table E-VIII for summary.]

Sample No.	Description of sample.	Date of collection.	Bacteria per gram on plain agar incubated at— 20° C.	Bacteria per gram on plain agar incubated at— 37° C.	Gas-producing bacteria per gram in lactose bile.	Liquefying organisms per gram.	Ammoniacal nitrogen (Folin method). Wet basis.	Ammoniacal nitrogen (Folin method). Dry basis.	Moisture.
	Visit No. 1.						*Per cent.*	*Per cent.*	*Per cent.*
4191	Dried egg from belt No. 5	Apr. 25	430,000	91,000		110,000	0.0006	0.0007	7.13
4192	Wet lmps from belt No. 5	..do	14,000,000	17,000,000	1,000		.0024	.0029	18.00
	Visit No. 2.								
4309	Dried egg	May 13	1,300,000	950,000	10,000	80,000	.0009	.0010	10.84
4308	Wet lmps	..do	9,200,000	10,000,000	100,000	340,000	.0010	.0013	20.54
4315	Dried egg, 93.5 pounds	May 14	850,000	1,300,000	10,000	110,000	.0004	.0004	7.40
4316	Wet lmps, 20 pounds	..do	1,900,000	2,800,000	100,000	190,000	.0014	.0017	18.79
4325	Dried egg, 96 pounds	May 15	2,000,000	800,000	1,000	190,000	.0007	.0008	10.53
4326	Wet l ups, 6.5 pounds	..do	2,900,000	1,100,000	10,000	650,000	.0007	.0008	16.46
4335	Wet lumps	May 16	6,300,000	5,100,000	1,000,000	250,000			
4355	Dried egg	May 17	800,000	700,000	10,000	16,000	.0008	.0009	9.20
4356	Wet lumps	..do	6,900,000	6,100,000	1,000,000		.0018	.0023	21.68
	Visit No. 3.								
4447	Dried egg	June 1	4,200,000	1,600,000	100,000	100,000			
4448	Wet lmps	..do	15,000,000	11,000,000	1,000,000	1,200,000			
4449	Dried egg from belt No. 2	..do	1,600,000	600,000	100,000	100,000			
4450	Wet lumps from belt No. 2	..do	12,000,000	5,900,000	100,000	210,000			
4451	Dried egg from belt No. 3	..do	4,200,000	1,700,000	100,000	200,000	.0008	.0009	9.89
4452	Wet lmps from blt No. 3	..do	3,800,000	1,800,000	100,000	130,000	.0028	.0036	21.48
4453	Dried egg from belt No. 4	..do	1,300,000	750,000	100,000	150,000	.0008	.0009	9.07
4454	Wet lmps from belt No. 4	..do	3,600,000	1,100,000	100,000	300,000	.0011	.0013	17.36
4472	Dried egg fom blt No. 2	June 3	2,300,000	800,000	10,000				
4473	Wet lmps from belt No. 2	..do	2,700,000	850,000	1,000,000		.0013	.0017	22.01

4474	Dried egg from belt No. 3	do	2,600,000	900,000	1,000,000		.0007	.0008	6.76
4475	Wet lumps from belt No. 3	do	2,100,000	800,000	100,000		.0014	.0018	23.23
4480	do	June 5	4,100,000	2,100,000	100,000		.0011	.0014	20.56
4481	do	do	6,400,000	4,700,000	100,000		.0008	.0009	8.68
	Visit No. 4.								
4593	Dried egg from belt No. 5, approximately 100 pounds	June 24	3,400,000	1,100,000	100,000	100,000	.0013	.0014	8.64
4594	Wet lumps from belt No. 5, a few pounds	do	3,900,000	850,000	100,000	1,000,000			
4614	Dried egg from belt No. 4	June 25	880,000	210,000	1,000		.0015	.0016	7.18
4615	Wet lumps from belt No. 4, a few pounds	do	1,100,000	330,000	10,000				
4618	Dried egg from belt No. 5	June 27	12,000,000	8,400,000	10,000	200,000	.0017	.0019	8.94
4619	Wet lumps from belt No. 5, approximately 7 pounds	do	18,000,000	16,000,000	10,000		.0053	.0067	21.21
	Visit No. 5.								
4731	Dried egg	July 13	4,100,000	2,300,000	1,000,000		.0010	.0011	8.06
4732	Wet lumps	do	9,400,000	6,300,000	1,000,000		.0013	.0016	18.30
4742	Dried egg from 4 belts	do	9,300,000	4,200,000	1,000,000				11.30
4743	Wet lumps from 4 belts	do	11,000,000	7,500,000	1,000,000				21.00
4750	Dried egg from 5 belts	July 16	2,200,000	700,000	100,000		.0016	.0018	8.86
4751	Wet lumps from 5 belts	do	3,400,000	2,000,000	100,000		.0014	.0018	22.90
4788	Dried egg from belt No. 5	July 19					.0016	.0017	8.36
4789	Wet lumps from belt No. 5	do							16.24
	Visit No. 6.								
4925	Dried egg from belt No. 5	Aug. 6	5,000,000	2,800,000	1,000,000		.0010	.0011	9.15
4926	Wet lumps from belt No. 5	do	5,000,000	4,800,000	1,000,000				
4948	do	Aug. 8	4,500,000	1,800,000	1,000,000				8.20
4929	Dried egg	Aug. 7	3,900,000	3,400,000	100,000		.0006	.0006	6.75
4930	Wet lumps	do	5,100,000	8,400,000	1,000,000				19.00
	Visit No. 7.								
41063	Dried egg from belt No. 5	Aug. 26	5,800,000	2,100,000	100,000				8.80
41064	Wet lumps from belt No. 5	do	8,200,000	4,100,000	1,000,000				
41066	Wet lumps	Aug. 27	4,700,000	2,400,000	100,000		.0015	.0016	6.89
41077	do	Aug. 28	14,000,000	14,000,000	10,000		.0010	.0011	6.34

TABLE E-III.—*Commercial samples of desiccated egg from belt, 1912.*

[Flaky dried egg—summarized in Table E-VIII.]

Sample No.	Description of sample.	Date of collection.	Bacteria per gram on plain agar incubated at—		Gas-producing bacteria per gram in lactose bile.	Liquefying organisms per gram.	Ammoniacal nitrogen (Folin method).		Moisture.
			20° C.	37° C.			Wet basis.	Dry basis.	
	Visit No. 1.						*Per cent.*	*Per cent.*	*Per cent.*
4177	From belt No. 3	Apr. 22	800,000	1,300,000	1,000	10,000	0.0002	0.0002	9.04
4191	From belt No. 5	Apr. 25	430,000	91,000	0	110,000	.0006	.0007	7.13
4196	do	Apr. 26	1,400,000	160,000	10,000		.0008	.0009	9.70
	Visit No. 2.								
4294	From belt No. 5	Apr. 29	65,000	35,000	1,000	10,000			
4297	Third run	May 6	1,100,000	900,000	10,000	70,000			
4298	First run	May 8	900,000	550,000	10,000	10,000			
4309		May 13	1,300,000	950,000	10,000	80,000	.0009	.0010	10.84
4312	Last run	do	1,400,000	1,100,000	1,000,000	200,000	.0006	.0007	7.78
4315		May 14	850,000	1,300,000	10,000	110,000	.0004	.0004	7.40
4325	From belt No. 4	May 15	2,000,000	800,000	1,000	190,000	.0007	.0008	10.53
4355		May 17	800,000	700,000	10,000	16,000	.0008	.0009	9.20
4359	From belt No. 4; not drying well	do	3,400,000	2,600,000	100,000	2,200,000	.0012	.0013	9.62
4360	From belt No. 3	do	900,000	850,000	1,000	110,000	.0009	.0010	10.78
	Visit No. 3.								
4434	First run	May 26	4,000,000	1,100,000	1,000	200,000			
4433	First run; refrigeration installed on this date	May 27	1,200,000	550,000	1,000	18,000			
4437		May 29	600,000	260,000	1,000	20,000			
4447	From belt No. 1	June 1	4,200,000	1,600,000	100,000	100,000			
4449	From belt No. 2	do	1,600,000	600,000	100,000	100,000			
4451	From belt No. 3	do	4,200,000	1,700,000	100,000	200,000	.0008	.0009	9.89
4453	From belt No. 4	do	1,300,000	750,000	100,000	150,000	.0008	.0009	9.07
4455	From belt No. 5	do	1,200,000	900,000	100,000	120,000			
4472	From belt No. 2	June 3	2,300,000	800,000	10,000				
4474	From belt No. 3	do	2,600,000	900,000	1,000,000		.0007	.0008	6.76
	Visit No. 4.								
4600	From belt No. 3	June 11	550,000	150,000	100,000	110,000			
4601	From belt No. 5; No. 4602 after standing in bin 2 days	June 17	6,000,000	5,400,000	1,000	130,000			
4602		June 15	5,700,000	5,200,000	100,000	100,000			
4603	From belt No. 2	June 17	1,300,000	330,000	10,000	400,000			
4604	From belt No. 4	June 20	1,400,000	250,000	100,000	300,000			
4605	From belt No. 3	June 22	3,400,000	2,000,000	1,000	100,000			

4614	From belt No. 4	June 25	880,000	210,000	1,000	...	.0015	.0016	7.18
4618	From belt No. 5	June 27	12,000,000	8,400,000	10,000	200,000	.0017	.0019	894
4623	...	..do....	7,500,000	7,500,000	1,000	40,000	.0018	.0019	6.44
4593	...	June 24	3,400,000	1,100,000	100,000	100,000	.0013	.0014	8.64
	Visit No. 5.								
4722	...	July 13	20,000,000	14,000,000	1,000,000	...	.0008	.0009	10.30
4728	From belt No. 5	July 12	9,400,000	7,000,000	100,000	...	...	...	...
4731	...	July 13	4,100,000	2,300,000	1,000,000	...	.0010	.0011	8.06
4742	From 4 belts	July 15	9,300,000	4,200,000	1,000,000	...	...	...	11.30
4749	....do	July 16	4,400,000	3,000,000	10,000	...	.0015	.0016	8.84
1750	From 5 belts	..do....	2,200,000	700,000	100,000	...	.0016	.0018	8.86
4788	....do	July 19	...	...	...	...	.0016	.0017	8.36
	Visit No. 6.								
4925	From belt No. 5	Aug. 6	5,000,000	2,800,000	1,000,000	...	.0010	.0011	9.15
4929	From bin	Aug. 7	3,900,000	3,400,000	100,000	...	.0006	.0006	6.75
4933	...	Aug. 8	2,300,000	1,900,000	100,000	...	.0006	.0006	7.43
	Visit No. 7.								
41063	From belt No. 5	Aug. 26	5,800,000	2,100,000	100,000	...	...	...	8.80
41065	...	Aug. 27	1,100,000	600,000	D0,000	...	.0015	.0016	8.78
41073	From belt No. 5	Aug. 28	12,000,000	2,100,000	10,000	...	.0017	.0019	10.06
41083	From belt No. 3	Aug. 29	4,200,000	3,100,000	10,000	...	.0015	.0016	8.82
41084	...	..do....	5,700,000	2,500,000	100,000	...	.0014	.0015	8.10
41085	From belt No. 5	..do....	4,800,000	2,300,000	10,000	...	.0008	.0009	9.84

TABLE E-IV.—*Commercial samples of liquid whole egg from storage tanks, 1912.*

Sample No.	Date of collection of sample.	Date of examination of sample.	Bacteria per gram at— 20° C.	Bacteria per gram at— 37° C.	Gas-producing bacteria per gram in lactose bile.	Liquefying organisms per gram.	Ammonical nitrogen (Folin method). Wet basis.	Ammonical nitrogen (Folin method). Dry basis.	Moisture.
							Per cent.	Per cent.	Per cent.
	Third week in April (visit No. 1).								
4169	Apr. 22	May 2	700,000	145,000	1,000				
4186	Apr. 25	May 1	900,000	90,000	0	0 in 10,000			
	Average		800,000	120,000					
	Second week in May (visit No. 2).								
4300	May 13	May 15	1,500,000	700,000	100,000	450,000	.0016	.0054	70.29
4350	May 17	May 22	1,000,000	120,000	10,000	150,000	.0016	.0058	72.64
	Average		1,300,000	410,000			.0016	.0056	
	First week in June (visit No. 3).								
[1] 4438	June 1	June 5	2,900,000	1,000,000	100,000	280,000	.0018	.0065	72.29
4463	June 3 (a. m.)	June 7	3,100,000	1,000,000	100,000	50,000	.0016	.0058	72.56
[2] 4464	June 3 (p. m.)	do	4,100,000	2,600,000	100,000	250,000			
4470	June 4 (a. m.)	do	3,200,000	1,200,000		310,000	.0017	.0061	72.09
[3] 4478	June 4 (p. m.)	June 11	2,300,000	1,200,000	10,000		.0019	.0070	72.73
	Average		3,100,000	1,400,000			.0018	.0064	
	Fourth week in June (visit No. 4).								
4589	June 24 (a. m.)	June 26	3,300,000	830,000	100,000	100,000	.0019	.0064	70.23
[4] 4599	June 24 (p. m.)	June 27	4,300,000	800,000	10,000		.0019	.0069	72.43
4607	June 25 (a. m.)	do	2,500,000	570,000	1,000	1,000,000	.0022	.0079	72.23
4612	June 25 (p. m.)	do	2,700,000	1,900,000	0				
4622	June 27	June 28	3,400,000	660,000	10,000	100,000	.0020	.0074	72.90
4636	June 28 (p. m.)	June 29	2,800,000	900,000	100,000	100,000	.0022	.0080	72.64
	Average		3,200,000	940,000			.0020	.0073	
	Second week in July (visit No. 5)—Regular breaking stock.								
4721	July 13 (a. m.)	July 16	4,600,000	2,400,000	1,000,000		.0022	.0079	72.08
4736	July 13 (p. m.)	do	5,500,000	1,700,000	10,000		.0024	.0087	72.48
[5] 4739	July 15 (a. m.)	July 17	4,000,000	1,800,000	100,000		.0021	.0081	74.17
	Average		4,700,000	2,000,000			.0022	.0082	

	Second week in July (visit No. 5)—Current receipts.								
[6] 4762	July 16 (p. m.)	July 18	1,400,000	800,000	100,000		.0022	.0079	72.32
[7] 4767	July 17 (a. m.)	July 19	1,900,000	650,000	100,000		.0020	.0073	72.54
4774	July 17 (p. m.)	do	1,500,000	550,000	100,000		.0024	.0084	71.55
[6] 4787	July 19	July 22					.0024	.0086	72.18
	Average		1,600,000	680,000			.0023	.0081	
	First week in August (visit No. 6).								
[8] 4906	Aug. 5 (a. m.)	Aug. 7	5,200,000	3,600,000	100,000				72.04
[2] 4913	Aug. 5 (p. m.)	do	3,500,000	3,900,000	100,000		.0021	.0076	72.29
4914	Aug. 6 (p. m.; held in tank 7 hours)	do	4,500,000	4,200,000	100,000				
[2] 4923	Aug. 6 (p. m.)	Aug. 8	3,200,000	2,500,000	100,000		.0020	.0073	72.49
[9] 4927	Aug. 7 (a. m.)	Aug. 9	4,100,000	3,300,000	100,000		.0020	.0079	72.35
[2] 4932	Aug. 7	do	5,100,000	5,000,000	1,000,000				
	Average		4,300,000	3,800,000			.0020	.0078	72.29
	Second and third weeks in August (visit No. 7).								
[2] 4939	Aug. 8 (p. m.)[10]		5,400,000	3,500,000	100,000		.0023	.0084	72.57
4049	Aug. 9 (p. m.)		4,600,000	5,000,000	100,000		.0021	.0077	72.58
4050	Aug. 11 (p. m.)		4,300,000	2,300,000	100,000		.0022	.0080	72.34
4051	Aug. 12 (p. m.)		2,600,000	1,200,000	10,000		.0020	.0073	72.60
4052	Aug. 13 (p. m.)		6,400,000	2,700,000	1,000,000		.0024	.0086	72.03
4053	Aug. 14 (p. m.)		5,800,000	3,000,000	1,000,000		.0024	.0084	72.63
4054	Aug. 15 (p. m.)		5,200,000	3,000,000	100,000		.0020	.0071	71.77
4055	Aug. 16 (p. m.)		7,000,000	3,000,000	100,000		.0020	.0072	72.25
4056	Aug. 17 (p. m.)		3,400,000	1,500,000	100,000		.0022	.0080	72.40
4057	Aug. 19 (p. m.)		11,000,000	5,400,000	100,000		.0023	.0085	73.00
4058	Aug. 20 (p. m.)		7,400,000	2,300,000	10,000		.0021	.0078	73.09
	Average		5,700,000	2,900,000	247,000		.0022	.0079	72.48

[1] Temperature of sample, 46° F.
[2] Temperature of sample, 40° F.
[3] Temperature of sample, 42° F.
[4] Temperature of sample, 56° F.
[5] Temperature of sample, 48° F.
[6] Temperature of sample, 38° F.
[7] Temperature of sample, 44° F.
[8] Temperature of sample, 34° F.
[9] Temperature of sample, 35° F.
[10] The sample taken Aug. 8 was collected during the sixth visit. Samples taken between this date and Aug. 19, the first day of the seventh visit, were collected by an employee of E[illegible], and are included with the analyses of samples taken during the seventh visit.

TABLE E-V.—*Comparative commercial samples of egg before and after desiccation, 1912.*

Sample No.	Description of sample.	Date of collection.	Bacteria per gram on plain agar incubated at—		Gas-producing bacteria per gram in lactose bile.	Liquefying organisms per gram.	Ammoniacal nitrogen (Folin method).		Moisture.
			20° C.	37° C.			Wet basis.	Dry basis.	
							Per cent.	*Per cent.*	*Per cent.*
	Visit No. 1.								
4171	Liquid egg from tank No. 3	Apr. 22	290,000	120,000	1,000	400,000			
4177	Dry egg from belt No. 3	do	800,000	1,300,000	1,000	40,000	0.0002	0.0002	9.04
4189	Liquid egg from tank No. 5	Apr. 25	850,000	42,500	10,000	0 in 10,000			
4191	Dry egg from belt No. 5	do	430,000	91,000		110,000	.0006	.0007	7.13
	Visit No. 2.								
4301	Liquid egg	May 13	1,400,000	1,000,000	10,000	400,000			
4312	Dry egg	do	1,400,000	1,100,000	1,000,000	200,000	.0006	.0007	7.78
4351	Liquid egg from tank No. 5	May 17	1,000,000	220,000	100,000	140,000			
4358	Dry egg from belt No. 5	do	13,000,000	11,000,000	100,000	3,700,000	.0010	.0011	9.10
4352	Liquid egg from tank No. 4	do	900,000	310,000	1,000,000	160,000			
4359	Dry egg from belt No. 4	do	3,400,000	2,600,000	100,000	2,700,000	.0012	.0013	9.62
	Visit No. 3.								
4439	Liquid egg from tank No. 1	June 1	3,800,000	1,300,000	100,000	330,000			
4447	Dry egg from belt No. 1	do	4,200,000	1,600,000	100,000	100,000			
4440	Liquid egg from tank No. 2	do	3,100,000	1,200,000	100,000	350,000			
4449	Dry egg from belt No. 2	do	1,600,000	600,000	100,000	100,000			
4441	Liquid egg from tank No. 3	do	3,300,000	1,700,000	100,000	220,000			
4451	Dry egg from belt No. 3	do	4,200,000	1,700,000	100,000	200,000	.0008	.0009	9.89
4443	Liquid egg from tank No. 4	do	3,100,000	1,300,000	1,000,000	310,000			
4453	Dry egg from belt No. 4	do	1,300,000	750,000	100,000	150,000	.0008	.0009	9.07
4445	Liquid egg from tank No. 5	do	4,000,000	1,400,000	100,000	280,000			
4455	Dry egg from belt No. 5	do	1,200,000	900,000	100,000	120,000			
	Visit No. 4.								
4592	Liquid egg from tank No. 5	June 24	4,000,000	850,000	100,000	1,000,000	.0020	.0073	72.66
4593	Dry egg from belt No. 5	do	3,400,000	1,100,000	100,000	100,000	.0013	.0014	8.64

	Visit No. 5.								
4740	Liquid egg from all 5 tanks	July 15	7,400,000	5,300,000	100,000				
4742	Dry egg from all 5 belts	do	9,300,000	4,200,000	1,000,000				11.30
	Visit No. 6.								
4922	Liquid egg from tank No. 5	Aug. 6	5,100,000	3,400,000	100,000		.0020	.0073	72.55
4925	Dry egg from belt No. 5	do	5,000,000	2,800,000	1,000,000		.0010	.0011	9.15
	Visit No. 7.								
41061	Liquid egg from tank No. 5	Aug. 26	19,000,000	5,500,000	100,000		.0031	.0112	72.38
41063	Dry egg from belt No. 5	do	5,800,000	2,100,000	100,000				8.80
41072	Liquid egg from tank No. 5	Aug. 28	6,400,000	2,200,000	100,000				72.67
41073	Dry egg from belt No. 5	do	12,000,000	2,100,000	10,000		.0017	.0019	10.06
41078	Liquid egg from tank No. 3	Aug. 29	8,200,000	2,900,000	1,000,000		.0025	.0089	71.98
41083	Dry egg from belt No. 3	do	4,200,000	3,100,000	10,000		.0015	.0016	8.82
41079	Liquid egg from tank No. 4	do	11,000,000	3,100,000	100,000		.0026	.0093	2.00
41084	Dry egg from belt No. 4	do	5,700,000	2,500,000	100,000		.0014	.0015	8.10
41080	Liquid egg from tank No. 5	do	8,400,000	3,500,000	100,000		.0026	.0093	2.07
41085	Dry egg from belt No. 5	do	4,800,000	2,300,000	10,000		.0008	.0009	9.84

TABLE E-VI.—*Commercial samples of whites and yolks—Trough method of separation, 1912.*

Sample No.	Description and size of sample.	Date of collection.	Bacteria per gram on plain agar incubated at—		Gas-producing bacteria per gram in lactose bile.	Ammoniacal nitrogen (Folin method).		Moisture.
			20° C.	37° C.		Wet basis.	Dry basis.	
	Visit No. 4.					*Per cent.*	*Per cent.*	*Per cent.*
4608	Whites, 24 dozen	June 25	1,000	0 in 1,000	0	0.0006	0.0049	87.68
4609	Yolks of No. 4608, 24 dozen	...do....	5,500	500	0	.0029	.0072	59.56
4626	Whites, 10 pounds	June 27	750,000	1,000	0	....	....	....
4627	Yolks of No. 4626, 15 pounds	...do....	1,300,000	1,000	0	....	....	....
	Visit No. 5.							
4723	Whites, 90 pounds	July 13	1,800,000	600,000	10,000	.0005	.0040	87.55
4747	Whites, 20 pounds	July 16	1,000,000	850,000	100,000	....	....	....
4748	Yolks of No. 4747, 20 pounds	...do....	1,100,000	1,300,000	10,000	....	....	....
4771	Whites, 19 pounds	July 17	34,000	13,000	1,000	....	....	....
4772	Yolks, 19 pounds	...do....	30,000	18,500	1,000	.0039	.0092	57.72
	Visit No. 6.							
4920	Whites, 270 pounds	Aug. 6	300,000	330,000	10,000	.0005	.0043	88.31
4921	Yolks of No. 4920, 270 pounds	...do....	900,000	700,000	10,000	.0034	.0081	58.02
4937	Whites, 150 pounds	Aug. 8	1,200,000	600,000	10,000	....	....	....
4938	Yolks of No. 4937, 150 pounds	...do....	430,000	250,000	10,000	.0036	.0086	58.16

TABLE E-VII.—*Commercial samples of leaking eggs—Handled by the tray method, 1912.*

Sample No.	Size of sample.	Date of collection.	Bacteria per gram on plain agar incubated at— 20° C.	Bacteria per gram on plain agar incubated at— 37° C.	Gas-producing bacteria per gram in lactose bile.	Liquefying organisms per gram.	Ammoniacal nitrogen (Folin method). Wet basis.	Ammoniacal nitrogen (Folin method). Dry basis.	Moisture.	Number of eggs discarded.
	Visit No. 4.						*Per cent.*	*Per cent.*	*Per cent.*	
4591	6 dozen	June 24	1,300,000	550,000	10	140,000	0.0022	0.0073	69.78	2
4595	5 dozen	..do	2,700,000	900,000	100	50,000				3
4606	5 dozen	June 25	410,000	4,200	0		.0023	.0076	69.68	4
4613	5 dozen	..do	3,500,000	480,000	10,000					1
4625	5 dozen	..do	1,800,000	1,200,000	1,000	10,000				7
4628	5 dozen	June 28	200,000	44,500	10,000		.0020	.0068	70.60	3
	Visit No. 5.									
4730	18 dozen	July 13	3,500,000	2,000,000	1,000		.0023	.0073	68.63	
4741	25 pounds	July 15	6,000,000	5,100,000	100,000					
4744	30 dozen	..do	800,000	500,000	100,000					
4745	24 dozen	..do	4,300,000	3,400,000	10,000					[1] 3
4756	24 pounds	July 16	2,300,000	550,000	10,000		.0024	.0078	69.21	[1] 3
4763	30 dozen	..do	5,600,000	650,000	100,000		.0022	.0066	66.86	[1] 5
4764	18 dozen	July 17	500,000	59,000	100		.0023	.0074	68.86	[1] 3.2
4770	30 dozen	..do	3,200,000	650,000	1,000		.0028	.0079	64.53	35
4779	30 dozen	July 19					.0024	.0078	69.05	36
	Visit No. 6.									
4924	30 dozen	Aug. 6	5,400,000	5,900,000	10,000		.0025	.0070	64.12	[1] 4½
4943	25 pounds, pail three-fourths full	Aug. 8	2,500,000	1,000,000	1,000		.0024	.0076	68.42	

[1] Pounds.

TABLE E-VIII.—*Summary of bacteriological results on commercial samples of liquid and dried eggs, 1912.*

NUMBER OF ORGANISMS PER GRAM.

Description of sample.	50,001 to 100,000		100,001 to 500,000		500,001 to 1,000,000		1,000,001 to 5,000,000		5,000,001 to 10,000,000		10,000,001 and over.		Total number of samples
	No.[1]	Per cent.	No.[1]	Per cent.	No.[1]	Per cent.	No.[1]	Per cent.	No.[1]	Per cent.	No.[1]	Per cent.	
I.													
Samples taken during three different stages of the preparation of desiccated eggs:													
Liquid egg from storage tanks (Table E-IV)					2	5.26	26	68.42	9	23.67	1	2.63	38
Liquid egg from supply tanks to drying belts (Table E-V)			1	5.55	3	16.66	7	38.88	5	27.77	2	11.11	18
Flaky dried egg directly from drying belts (Table E-III)	1	2.08	1	2.08	6	12.50	30	62.50	7	14.58	3	6.25	48
Wet lumps directly from drying belts (Table E-II)							13	50.00	7	26.92	6	23.07	26
II.													
Comparative samples of whole egg before and after desiccation:													
Liquid egg from supply tank to belt (Table E-V)			1	5.55	3	16.66	7	38.88	5	27.77	2	11.11	18
Flaky dried egg directly from drying belt (Table E-V)			1	5.55			12	66.66	3	16.66	2	11.11	18
III.													
Comparative samples of flaky dried egg and wet lumps:													
Flaky dried egg directly from drying belt (Table E-III)			1	5.00	2	10.00	14	70.00	2	10.00	1	5.00	20
Wet lumps directly from drying belt (Table E-II)							10	50.00	5	25.00	5	25.00	20
Total													206

NUMBER OF GAS-PRODUCING ORGANISMS PER GRAM IN LACTOSE BILE.

Description of sample.	0		1,000		10,000		100,000		1,000,000		Total number of samples.
	No.[1]	Per cent.	No.[1]	Per cent.	No.[1]	Per cent.	No.[1]	Per cent.	No.[1]	Per cent.	
IV.											
Samples taken during three different stages of the preparation of desiccated eggs:											
Liquid egg from storage tanks (Table E–IV)	2	5.4	2	5.4	7	18.91	22	59.45	4	10.81	37
Liquid egg from supply tanks to drying belts (Table E–V)			1	5.55	2	11.11	12	66.66	3	16.66	18
Flaky dried egg from drying belts (Table E–III)	1	2.08	11	22.91	13	27.08	17	35.41	6	12.50	48
Wet lumps from drying belts (Table E–II)			1	3.85	4	15.38	11	42.30	10	38.50	26
V.											
Comparative samples of whole egg before and after desiccation:											
Liquid egg from supply tank to belt (Table E–V)			1	5.88	1	5.88	12	70.58	3	17.64	17
Flaky dried egg from belt (Table E–V)			1	5.88	3	17.64	10	58.82	3	17.64	17
VI.											
Comparative samples of flaky dried egg and wet lumps:											
Flaky dried egg directly from belt (Table E–III)			2	10.52	5	26.31	8	42.10	4	21.05	19
Wet lumps directly from belt (Table E–II)					3	15.79	8	42.10	8	42.10	19
Total											201

[1] Number of samples.

TABLE F-I.—*Successive commercial samples of mixed egg, 1912.*

Sample No.	Description of sample (broken from cracked eggs).	Date of collection.	Bacteria per gram on plain agar incubated at—		Gas-producing bacteria per gram in lactose bile.	Liquefying organisms per gram.	Ammoniacal nitrogen (Folin method).		Moisture.
			20° C.	37° C.			Wet basis.	Dry basis.	
	Visit No. 1.						*Per cent.*	*Per cent.*	*Per cent.*
4207	Liquid egg from buckets	May 1	1,000,000	750,000	10,000	280,000			
4208	Liquid egg from churn	..do	800,000	500,000	100,000	240,000	0.0017	0.0053	68.89
4209	Liquid egg from three creamery cans	..do	950,000	700,000	10,000	200,000			
4210	Liquid egg from hose	..do	1,100,000	800,000	100,000	130,000			
4211	Liquid egg from feeding trough	..do	850,000	410,000	10,000	300,000			
4212	Dried egg from belt	..do	650,000	600,000	10,000	130,000	.0008	.0010	11.25
4213	Dried egg after second drying	..do	800,000	440,000	10,000	80,000	.0007	.0007	3.74
4225	Liquid egg from churn	May 3	1,000,000	370,000	100,000	110,000	.0017	.0057	70.81
4226	Liquid egg from creamery cans	..do	1,100,000	480,000	100,000	150,000			
4227	Liquid egg from supply tank	..do	900,000	350,000	1,000	250,000			
4228	Liquid egg from hose	..do	900,000	290,000	10,000	190,000			
4229	Liquid egg from feeding trough	..do	1,300,000	600,000	10,000	110,000			
4230	Dried egg from belt	..do	1,000,000	340,000	100,000	190,000	.0012	.0014	12.46
4231	Dried egg after second drying	..do	850,000	480,000	1,000	160,000	.0012	.0013	4.89
	Visit No. 2.								
4379	Liquid egg from hose	May 23	6,800,000	1,300,000	100,000	2,000,000	.0024	.0073	67.22
4380	Dried egg from belt	..do	10,000,000	10,000,000	100,000	80,000	.0013	.0015	11.03
4381	Dried egg after second drying	..do	21,000,000	20,000,000	100,000	38,000			9.21
	Visit No. 4.								
4651	Liquid egg from supply tank	July 1	3,700,000	2,200,000	100,000	200,000	.0026	.0080	67.50
4652	Dried egg from belt	..do	4,000,000	2,300,000	100,000	500,000	.0024	.0027	9.92
4653	Dried egg after second drying	..do	14,000,000	14,000,000	100,000	10,000			4.65
4661	Liquid egg from supply tank	July 2	1,100,000	330,000	10,000	0 in 100,000	.0024	.0075	68.14
4662	Dried egg from belt	..do	36,000,000	29,000,000	10,000	0 in 10,000	.0021	.0024	10.99
4663	Dried egg after second drying	..do	22,000,000	22,000,000	10,000	0 in 10,000			
4664	Wet lumps	..do	60,000,000	62,000,000	10,000				
4665	Liquid egg from supply tank	..do	1,200,000	230,000	1,000	0 in 10,000	.0027	.0082	67.00
4666	Dried egg from belt	..do	50,000,000	51,000,000	10,000	250,000	.0031	.0035	11.85
4667	Dried egg after second drying	..do	35,000,000	28,000,000	100,000	0 in 100,000			

TABLE F-II.—*Commercial samples of dried yolk before and after secondary drying, 1912.*

Sample No.	No. of visit.	Date of collection.	Bacteria per gram on plain agar incubated at—		Gas-producing bacteria per gram in lactose bile.	Liquefying organisms per gram.	Ammoniacal nitrogen (Folin method).		Moisture.
			20° C.	37° C.			Wet basis.	Dry basis.	
BEFORE SECONDARY DRYING.									
							Per cent.	*Per cent.*	*Per cent.*
4232 [1]...	1	May 3	71,000	28,500	100	0 in 100,000	0.0017	0.0018	9.02
4248....	1	May 4	17,000,000	18,000,000	10,000	100,000	....	....	....
4372....	2	May 6	130,000	51,000	10,000	12,000	....	....	....
4515 [2]...	3	June 11	110,000,000	160,000,000	100,000	0 in 10,000	.0083	.0096	13.40
4644....	4	June 22	80,000,000	89,000,000	1,000	0 in 100,000	....	....	....
AFTER SECONDARY DRYING.									
4483....	3	May 29	1,800,000	2,000,000	10,000	25,000	....	....	....
4492....	3	June 10	77,000,000	78,000,000	100,000	8,000	.0056	.0059	5.07
4493....	3	...do....	49,000,000	44,000,000	100,000	10,000	.0052	.0055	6.25
4518 [3]...	3	June 12	95,000,000	68,000,000	10,000	0 in 10,000	....	....	3.88
4641....	4	June 17	3,200,000	3,000,000	100,000	0 in 10,000	....	....	....
4643....	4	June 19	33,000,000	36,000,000	100,000	0 in 100,000	....	....	....
4645....	4	June 24	2,100,000	1,900,000	100,000	0 in 100,000	....	....	....
4646....	4	June 26	39,000,000	33,000,000	10,000	0 in 100,000	....	....	....
4648....	4	June 27	86,000,000	60,000,000	100,000	200,000	....	....	....
4997 [4]...	6	Aug. 16	29,000,000	24,000,000	1,000	....	.0052	.0055	4.96

[1] Previous run to Nos. 4225 to 4231. [2] Same egg as No. 4518. [3] Same egg as No. 4515. [4] Dried yolk.

TABLE F-III.—*Commercial samples of mixed egg, 1912.*

Sample No.	Description of sample.	Date of collection.	Bacteria per gram on plain agar incubated at—		Gas-producing bacteria per gram in lactose bile.	Liquefying organisms per gram.	Ammoniacal nitrogen (Folin method).		Moisture.
			20° C.	37° C.			Wet basis.	Dry basis.	
	Visit No. 1.						*Per cent.*	*Per cent.*	*Per cent.*
4208	Cracked eggs from churn	May 1	800,000	500,000	100,000	240,000	0.0017	0.0053	68.89
4225	do	May 3	1,000,000	370,000	100,000	110,000	.0017	.0057	70.81
	Visit No. 2.								
4379	From hose of supply tank	May 23	6,800,000	1,300,000	100,000	2,000,000	.0024	.0073	67.22
4385	Mostly seconds from churn	do	470,000	220,000	100,000	60,000	.0019	.0060	68.23
	Visit No. 3.								
4502	Mostly seconds from churn	June 11	1,000,000	420,000	10,000	300,000			
	Visit No. 4.								
4651	From supply tank	July 1	3,700,000	2,200,000	100,000	200,000	.0026	.0080	67.50
4661	do	July 2	1,100,000	330,000	10,000	0 in 100,000	.0024	.0075	68.14
4671	From churn	do	700,000	400,000	100,000	0 in 100,000	.0022	.0069	67.96
4665	From supply tank	do	1,200,000	230,000	1,000	0 in 10,000	.0027	.0082	67.00
4654	do	July 1	1,300,000	650,000	100,000	100,000			
4673	From churn	July 3	1,400,000	410,000	10,000	0 in 100,000	.0026	.0079	67.29
4674	do	do	1,300,000	450,000	10,000	0 in 100,000	.0025	.0077	67.58

TABLE F-IV.—*Commercial samples of mixed egg before and after secondary drying, 1912.*

SAMPLES TAKEN FROM BELT.

Sample No.	Number of visit.	Date of collection.	Bacteria per gram on plain agar incubated at— 20° C.	Bacteria per gram on plain agar incubated at— 37° C.	Gas-producing bacteria per gram in lactose bile.	Liquefying organisms per gram.	Ammoniacal nitrogen (Folin method). Wet basis.	Ammoniacal nitrogen (Folin method). Dry basis.	Moisture.
							Per cent.	*Per cent.*	*Per cent.*
4212	1	May 1	650,000	600,000	10,000	130,000	0.0008	0.0010	11.25
4230	1	May 3	1,000,000	340,000	100,000	190,000	.0012	.0014	12.46
4373	2	May 9	430,000	100,000	1,000	15,000	....	....	....
4374	2	May 10	800,000	700,000	10,000	16,000	....	....	....
4375	2	May 13	160,000	85,000	10,000	40,000	....	....	....
4376	2	May 15	3,100,000	2,900,000	1,000	25,000	....	....	....
4377	2	May 17	320,000	150,000	1,000	35,000	....	....	....
4380	2	May 23	10,000,000	10,000,000	100,000	80,000	.0013	.0015	11.03
1482	3	May 27	1,300,000	1,400,000	1,000,000	0 in 100	....	....	....
4491	3	June 10	3,200,000	3,400,000	100,000	100,000	.0008	.0009	11.60
45	3	June 11	53,000,000	58,000,000	100,000	400,000	.0021	.0024	10.84
1642	4	June 18	200,000,000	190,000,000	100,000	100,000	....	....	....
4652	4	July 1	4,000,000	2,300,000	100,000	500,000	.0024	.0027	9.92
62	4	July 2	36,000,000	29,000,000	10,000	0 in 10,000	.0021	.0024	10.99
66	4	...do....	50,000,000	51,000,000	10,000	250,000	.0031	.0035	11.85
SAMPLES TAKEN AFTER SECONDARY DRYING.									
1213	1	May 1	800,000	440,000	10,000	80,000	0.0007	0.0007	3.74
431	1	May 3	850,000	480,000	1,000	160,000	.0012	.0013	4.89
4381	2	May 23	21,000,000	20,000,000	100,000	38,000	....	....	9.21
1484	3	May 31	7,400,000	5,900,000	1,000,000	10,000	....	....	....
1485	3	June 3	4,400,000	5,200,000	10,000	12,000	....	....	....
86	3	June 5	42,000,000	45,000,000	10,000	8,000	....	....	....
1487	3	June 7	5,400,000	3,000,000	1,000,000	20,000	....	....	....
1494	3	June 10	59,000,000	59,000,000	1,000,000	22,000	.0003	.0003	8.20
4519	3	June 12	39,000,000	34,000,000	100,000	200,000	....	....	5.26
46	4	June 25	86,000,000	77,000,000	1,000,000	300,000	....	....	....
49	4	June 28	23,000,000	21,000,000	100,000	1,000,000	....	....	....
50	4	June 29	84,000,000	77,000,000	100,000	100,000	....	....	....
58	4	July 1	14,000,000	14,000,000	1000	10,000	....	....	4.65
68	4	July 2	22,000,000	22,000,000	10,000	0 in 10,000	....	....	....
65	4	...do....	35,000,000	28,000,000	100,000	0 in 100,000	....	....	....
86	4	July 3	36,000,000	34,000,000	100,000	1,000,000	.0021	.0023	6.96
1998	6	Aug. 16	70,000	9000	1000	....	.0022	....	....

TABLE F-V.—*Commercial samples of second-grade frozen egg, 1912.*

Sample No.	Size and description of sample.	Date of collection.	Bacteria per gram on plain agar incubated at—		Gas-producing bacteria per gram in lactose bile.	Liquefying organisms per gram.	Ammoniacal nitrogen (Folin method).		Moisture.
			20° C.	37° C.			Wet basis.	Dry basis.	
	Visit No. 2.						*Per cent.*	*Per cent.*	*Per cent.*
4365	400 pounds from churn	May 21	58,000,000	21,000,000	1,000,000	+in 100,000	0.0025	0.0111	77.56
4369	3 pounds from can	..do	27,000,000	1,900,000	10,000	18,000,000	.0040	.0182	78.07
4383	15 pounds from can	May 23	47,000,000	18,000,000	1,000,000	15,000,000	.0031	.0133	76.69
	Visit No. 3.								
4498	10 pounds from bucket	June 10	4,200,000	2,400,000	100,000	50,000	.0014	.0068	79.35
4501	25 pounds (seconds) from bucket	June 11	22,000,000	12,000,000	1,000,000	6,500,000	.0022	.0079	72.27
4512	10 pounds (seconds) from bucket	..do	59,000,000	38,000,000	1,000,000	5,500,000	.0026	.0130	80.02
4527	400 pounds from churn	June 12	11,000,000	8,600,000	1,000,000	1,400,000	....	....	....
	Visit No. 4.								
4659	From bucket	July 2	6,800,000	10,000,000	100,000	5,000,000	.0008	.0052	84.60
4675	400 pounds from churn	July 3	33,000,000	17,000,000	10,000,000	10,000,000	.0025	.0124	79.86
	Visit No. 5.								
4796	3 pounds from bucket	July 22	7,300,000	5,500,000	10,000	....	.0026	.0097	73.20
4800	400 pounds from churn	..do	....	....	10,000	....	.0023	.0110	79.06
4809	10 pounds from bucket	..do	92,000,000	72,000,000	10,000	....	.0021	.0111	81.02
4826	90 pounds from churn	July 23	11,000,000,	11,000,000	100,000	....	.0019	.0099	80.81
	Visit No. 6.								
4954	15 pounds from bucket	Aug. 12	84,000,000	79,000,000	100,000	....	.0022	.0078	71.79
4970	400 pounds from churn	Aug. 13	32,000,000	31,000,000	1,000,000	....	.0028	.0144	80.60

TABLE F-VI.—*Commercial samples of mixed egg before and after drying on belt, 1912.*

Sample No.	Description of sample.	Date of collection.	Bacteria per gram on plain agar incubated at—		Gas-producing bacteria per gram in lactose bile.	Liquefying organisms per gram.	Ammoniacal nitrogen (Folin method).		Moisture.
			20° C.	37° C.			Wet basis.	Dry basis.	
	Visit No. 1.						*Per cent.*	*Per cent.*	*Per cent.*
4208	Liquid egg	May 1	800,000	500,000	100,000	240,000	0.0017	0.0053	68.89
4212	Dried egg	...do	600,000	600,000	10,000	130,000	.0008	.0010	11.25
4225	Liquid egg	May 3	1,000,000	370,000	100,000	110,000	.0017	.0057	70.81
4230	Dried egg	...do	1,000,000	340,000	100,000	190,000	.0012	.0014	12.46
	Visit No. 2.								
4379	Liquid egg	May 23	6,800,000	1,300,000	100,000	2,000,000	.0024	.0073	67.22
4380	Dried egg	...do	10,000,000	10,000,000	100,000	80,000	.0013	.0015	11.03
	Visit No. 4.								
4651	Liquid egg	July 1	3,700,000	2,200,000	100,000	200,000	.0026	.0080	67.50
4652	Dried egg	...do	4,000,000	2,300,000	100,000	500,000	.0024	.0027	9.92
4661	Liquid egg	July 2	1,100,000	330,000	10,000	0 in 100,000	.0024	.0075	68.14
4662	Dried egg	...do	36,000,000	29,000,000	10,000	0 in 10,000	.0021	.0024	10.99
4665	Liquid egg	...do	1,200,000	230,000	1,000	0 in 10,000	.0027	.0082	67.00
4666	Dried egg	...do	50,000,000	51,000,000	10,000	250,000	.0031	.0035	11.85

TABLE F-VII.—*Commercial samples of yolks from churn, mechanical method of separation, 1912.*

Sample No.	Description and size of sample.	Date of collection.	Bacteria per gram on plain agar incubated at—		Number of gas-producing bacteria per gram in lactose bile.	Liquefying organisms per gram.	Ammoniacal nitrogen (Folin method).		Moisture.
			20° C.	37° C.			Wet basis.	Dry basis.	
	WITHOUT ADDED SUGAR.						*Per cent.*	*Per cent.*	*Per cent.*
	Visit No. 1:								
4246	Seconds and cracked eggs, 400 pounds	May 4	160,000	76,000	1,000	30,000			
	Visit No. 3:								
4506	Seconds and cracked eggs, 400 pounds	June 11	370,000	170,000	1,000	50,000			
4513	Seconds, 400 pounds	...do....	210,000	200,000	1,000	40,000			
	Visit No. 5:								
4830	Cracked eggs, 400 pounds	July 24	1,800,000	1,600,000	10,000				
	WITH 10 PER CENT ADDED SUGAR.								
	Visit No. 4:								
4676	400 pounds	July 13	290,000	210,000	100,000	1,000,000			
	Visit No. 5:								
4797	Firsts, seconds, and cracked eggs, 200 pounds	July 22	550,000	390,000	10,000		0.0031	0.0063	50.41
4804	400 pounds	...do....	500,000	350,000	0		.0033	.0067	50.38
4811	Do	...do....	200,000	160,000	10,000				
4821	Firsts, 400 pounds	July 23	150,000	130,000	10,000		.0029	.0058	50.30
4822	Do	...do....	34,000	41,000	1,000		.0029	.0058	49.89
4825	Firsts and [illegible]ds, 400 pounds	...do....	70,000	64,000	1,000				
4828	Cracked eggs, 400 pounds	July 24	2,400,000	2,100,000	100,000		.0029	.0060	51.74
4832	Firsts and cracked eggs, 400 pounds	...do....	1,000,000	700,000	100,000				
4839	Firsts and cracked eggs	July 25	420,000	480,000	10,000				
	Visit No. 6:								
4959	Firsts, 400 pounds	Aug. 12	480,000	440,000	10,000		.0031	.0065	52.06
4969	Firsts and seconds, 400 pounds	Aug. 13	460,000	340,000	1,000				
4973	Firsts, seconds, and cracked eggs, 400 pounds	Aug. 14	350,000	350,000	10,000		.0028	.0060	53.07
4968	Firsts and [illegible]ds, 400 pounds	Aug. 13	7,500,000	440,000	10,000				

TABLE F-VIII.—*Commercial samples of soft egg, 1912.*

Sample No.	Description and size of sample.	Date of collection.	Bacteria per gram on plain agar incubated at—		Gas-producing bacteria per gram in lactose bile.	Liquefying organisms per gram.	Ammoniacal nitrogen (Folin method).		Moisture.
			20° C.	37° C.			Wet basis.	Dry basis.	
	Visit No. 2.						*Per cent.*	*Per cent.*	*Per cent.*
4368		May 21	35,000,000	10,000,000	100	2,500,000	0.0024	0.0084	71.54
	Visit No. 3.								
4497	From bucket, 3 pounds	June 10	390,000	320,000	100,000	14,000	.0020	.0071	71.91
4511	From bucket, 30 pounds	June 11	14,000,000	4,300,000	10,000		.0029	.0098	70.49
4523	From bucket, 15 pounds	June 12	5,900,000	6,100,000	1,000,000	330,000	.0021	.0070	69.94
4531	From bucket	June 13	250,000	190,000	10,000	10,000			
	Visit No. 4.								
4658	From bucket	July 2	130,000	13,000	1,000	190,000	.0021	.0075	71.95
	Visit No. 5.								
4795	From bucket, 22 pounds	July 22	3,600,000	3,000,000	1,000		.0025	.0083	70.02
4798	From churn	do	11,000,000	55,000,000	100,000		.0023	.0085	72.99
4808	From bucket, 25 pounds	do	(1)	63,000,000	10,000		.0031	.0094	67.04
4810	From churn, 200 pounds	do	80,000,000	76,000,000	1,000,000				
4819	Firsts from churn, 200 pounds	July 23	950,000	850,000	100,000		.0018	.0066	72.76
4834	Firsts, seconds, and cracked, 400 pounds eggs from churn	July 24	4,900,000	3,000,000	100,000		.0020	.0071	71.96
	Visit No. 6.								
4961	Firsts and seconds from churn, 400 pounds	Aug. 12	2,100,000	2,000,000	100,000		.0021	.0078	72.99

[1] Innumerable in 100,000.

TABLE F-IX.—*Commercial samples of whole egg from churn, 1912.*

Sample No.	Description and size of sample.	Date of collection.	Bacteria per gram on plain agar incubated at—		Gas-producing bacteria per gram in lactose bile.	Ammoniacal nitrogen (Folin method).		Moisture.
			20° C.	37° C.		Wet basis.	Dry basis.	
	Visit No. 5.					*Per cent.*	*Per cent.*	*Per cent.*
4846	Firsts and seconds, 360 pounds	July 25	1,200,000	850,000	10,000			
	Visit No. 6.							
4956	Firsts and seconds, 400 pounds	Aug. 12	2,300,000	1,500,000	100,000	0.0019	0.0067	71.62
4962	Firsts	..do..	550,000	500,000	10,000	.0020	.0071	71.67
4980	Firsts and seconds, 400 pounds	Aug. 14	500,000	450,000	1,000	.0019	.0071	73.29
4984	Firsts, seconds, and cracked eggs, 400 pounds	Aug. 15	1,900,000	1,300,000	100,000			
4986	Firsts, 400 pounds	..do..	3,500,000	1,800,000	10,000			
4989	..do..	..do..	340,000	200,000	10			
4991	..do..	..do..	1,000,000	550,000	10,000	.0021	.0070	72.30
4996	Seconds and cracked eggs, 400 pounds	Aug. 16	700,000	460,000	10,000	.0019	.0070	72.80

TABLE F-X.—*Commercial samples of leaking eggs—Handled by the tray method, F house, 1912.*

Sample No.	Size and description of sample.	Date of collection.	Bacteria per gram on plain agar incubated at—		Gas-producing bacteria per gram in lactose bile.	Liquefying organisms per gram.	Ammoniacal nitrogen (Folin method).		Moisture.	Eggs discarded.
			20° C.	37° C.			Wet basis.	Dry basis.		
	Visit No. 3.									
	Whole egg:						*Per cent.*	*Per cent.*	*Per cent.*	
4488	6 dozen	June 10	950,000	750,000	1,000	0 in 100,000	0.0017	0.0059	70.92	....
4490	Do	do	110,000	74,000	1,000	250,000	.0015	.0049	71.42	1
4507	Do	June 11	23,500	4,000	10	4,000	....	....	....	0
4508	Do	do	49,500	54,000	1,000	25,000	.0019	.0064	70.31	....
4520	Do	June 12	54,000	40,000	100	0 in 1,000	.0019	.0063	69.68	0
4524	Do	do	1,700,000	2,000,000	10,000	4,000	.0020	.0063	68.34	1
4525	Do	do	1,400,000	420,000	1,000	25,000	.0017	.0059	71.26	....
	White and yolk separated:									
4514	6 dozen whites	June 11	52,000	33,000	10	2,000	.0004	.0033	88.08	....
4517	6 dozen yolks of No. 4514	do	250,000	120,000	100	0 in 1,000	.0029	.0062	54.62	....
	Visit No. 4.									
	Whole egg:									
4655	6 dozen	July 1	430,000	360,000	1,000	60,000	....	....	....	4
4670	Do	July 2	53,000	54,000	0	50,000	.0021	.0067	68.81	3
4681	Do	July 3	77,000	12,000	1,000	10,000	....	....	....	A few.
4682	Do	do	1,300,000	1,200,000	1,000,000	20,000	....	....	....	1
	Visit No. 5.									
	Whole egg:									
4792	30 dozen	July 22	900,000	550,000	1,000	....	....	....	....	26
4820	24 dozen	July 23	2,900,000	2,800,000	10,000	....	.0027	.0078	65.59	42
	Visit No. 6.									
	Whole egg:									
4958	6 dozen	Aug. 12	....	4,500,000	10,000	....	.0025	.0080	68.62	....
4974	Do	Aug. 14	650,000	700,000	10,000	....	.0018	.0058	68.76	....
4979	12 dozen	do	240,000	140,000	1,000	....	.0020	.0065	69.16	....
4990	15 dozen	Aug. 15	1,100,000	800,000	1,000	....	.0021	.0068	69.25	10
4995	6 dozen	Aug. 16	1,500,000	1,000,000	100	....	.0023	.0075	69.17	10

TABLE F-XI.—*Detailed summary of bacteriological results on commercial samples taken before and after drying, 1912.*

TOTAL NUMBER OF ORGANISMS PER GRAM.

Description of samples.	101 to 1,001		1,001 to 10,000		10,001 to 50,000		50,001 to 100,000		100,001 to 500,000		500,001 to 1,000,000		1,000,001 to 5,000,000		5,000,001 to 10,000,000		10,000,001 to 50,000,000		50,000,001 to 100,000,000		100,000,001 to 500,000,000		Total number of samples.
	Number.[1]	Per cent.	Number.[1]	Per cent.	Number.[1]	Per cent.	Number.[1]	Per cent.	Number.[1]	Per cent.	Number.[1]	Per cent.	Number.[1]	Per cent.	Number.[1]	Per cent.	Number.[1]	Per cent.	Number.[1]	Per cent.	Number.[1]	Per cent.	
Liquid egg:																							
White from grading table (Table 21)	1	10.0			3	30.0			3	30.0	1	10.0	1	10.0	1	10.0							10
Yolk from grading table (Table 21)			2	20.0	1	10.0			2	20.0	1	10.0	2	20.0	2	20.0							10
Yolk from mixing churn (Table F-VII)					1	5.55	1	5.55	11	61.11	2	11.11	2	11.11	1	5.55							18
Whole egg (Table F-IX)									2	22.22	3	33.33	4	44.44									9
Mixed egg (Table F-III)									1	8.33	4	33.33	6	50.0	1	8.33							12
Soft egg (Table F-VIII)									3	23.07	1	7.69	3	23.07	1	7.69	2	15.38	3	23.07			13
Second-grade egg (Table F-V)													1	7.14	2	14.28	7	49.98	4	28.57			14
Desiccated egg:																							
Yolks (Table F-II)							1	6.66	1	6.66			3	20.0			5	33.33	4	26.66	1	6.66	15
Mixed egg (Table F-IV)									3	9.38	5	15.62	5	15.62	3	9.38	10	31.24	5	15.62	1	3.12	32
Comparative samples of mixed egg before and after desiccation:																							
Liquid (Table F-VI)											2	33.33	3	50.0	1	16.66							6
Dry (Table F-VI)											2	33.33	1	16.66	1	16.66	2	33.33					6
Total																							145

NUMBER OF GAS-PRODUCING ORGANISMS PER GRAM IN LACTOSE BILE.

Description of samples.	Less than 10.		10		100		1,000		10,000		100,000		1,000,000		10,000,000		Total number of samples.
	Number.[1]	Per cent.	Number.[1]	Per cent.	Number.[1]	Per cent.	Number.[1]	Per cent.	Number.[1]	Per cent.	Number.[1]	Per cent.	Number.[1]	Per cent.	Number.[1]	Per cent.	
Commercial samples of liquid egg:																	
Whites (Table 21)	1	10.0	3	30.0	4	40.0	2	20.0									10
Yolks (Table 21)	1	10.0	3	30.0	3	30.0	1	10.0	1	10.0	1	10.0					10
Yolks from churn (Table F-VII)	1	5.55					6	33.33	8	44.44	3	16.66					18
Whole egg (Table F-IX)			1	11.1			1	11.1	5	55.55	2	22.22					9
Mixed egg (Table F-III)							1	8.33	4	33.33	7	58.33					12
Soft egg (Table F-VIII)					1	7.69	2	15.38	3	23.07	5	38.45	2	15.38			13
Second-grade egg (Table F-V)									4	26.66	4	26.66	6	40.00	1	6.66	15
Commercial samples of desiccated egg:																	
Yolks (Table F-II)					1	6.66	2	13.33	5	33.33	7	46.66					15
Mixed egg (Table F-IV)							4	12.5	10	31.25	12	37.5	6	18.75			32
Comparative samples of mixed egg before and after desiccation:																	
Liquid (Table F-VI)							1	16.66	1	16.66	4	66.66					6
Dry (Table F-VI)									3	50.00	3	50.00					6
Total																	146

[1] Number of samples.

TABLE F-XII.—*Component parts of second-grade frozen egg.*

Sample No.	Size and description of sample.	Source.	Date of collection.	Bacteria per gram on plain agar incubated at— 20° C.	37° C.	Gas-producing bacteria per gram in lactose bile.	Brown colonies in Aesculin agar.	Liquefying organisms per gram.	Ammoniacal nitrogen (Folin method). Wet basis.	Dry basis.	Moisture.
	I.								*Per cent.*	*Per cent.*	*Per cent.*
	Eggs with faintly sour odor:										
4427	2 eggs, white and yolk intact	D-2	May 28	430,000,000	430,000,000	10,000,000+	+				
4460	White and yolk intact	E-3	June 1	89,000,000	73,000,000	1,000,000+	+	4,400,000	0.0038	0.0141	73.00
4530	5 eggs, soft yolks	F-3	June 13	380,000,000	440,000,000	10,000	+		.0052	.0194	73.19
4815	5 pounds	F-5	July 23	140,000,000	97,000,000	1,000,000+	+		.0032	.0113	71.57
4816	Do	F-5	...do	160,000,000	130,000,000	10,000,000+	+		.0030	.0122	75.48
4836	2¼ pounds	F-5	...do	130,000,000	120,000,000	1,000,000+	0		.0046	.0151	69.52
	II.										
	Eggs with light-green whites, odorless:										
	Mixed eggs—										
4817	5 pounds	F-5	July 23	49,000,000	23,000,000	10,000	+		.0027	.0094	71.27
4818	Do	F-5	...do	61,000,000	55,000,000	100,000	+		.0051	.0181	71.86
4420	7 eggs	D-2	May 28	320,000,000	100,000,000	1,000,000	+	3,000,000	.0040	.0136	70.70
	White and yolk separated—										
4396	7 whites	D-2	May 27	100,000,000	55,000,000	100,000	+	20,000,000	.0007	.0050	86.04
4397	Yolks of No. 4396	D-2	...do	2,700,000	1,800,000	10,000	+	650,000	.0047	.0104	56.84
4504	4 whites	F-3	June 11	210,000,000	210,000,000	100	0	30,000,000			
4505	Yolks of No. 4504	F-3	...do	26,000,000	4,700,000	0	0	+ in 100,000			
	III.										
	Cracked eggs with moldy shells:										
4217	8 eggs, odor and taste good	F-1	May 2	1,200,000	1,300,000	10	+	230,000	.0019	.0062	69.31
4241	12 eggs, odor and taste good	F-1	May 3	2,700,000	1,700,000	10	0	15,000	.0013	.0043	68.26
4398	3 eggs, odor good	D-2	May 27	4,000,000	3,100,000	100	+	0 in 1,000	.0019	.0058	67.17
4583	4 eggs, odor good	D-3	June 20	8,600,000	5,400,000	100	+	40,000	.0021	.0070	70.18
4596	Odor good	E-4	June 24	12,000,000	5,900,000	0		0	.0025	.0088	71.76
41022	6 eggs, odor good	D-6	Aug. 20	160,000	140,000	1,000			.0019	.0064	70.23
41036	11 pounds, eggs with moldy shells	D-6	Aug. 21	22,000,000	13,000,000	100,000			.0023	.0078	70.39

	IV.										
	Dripping from breaking knife and tray:										
	From cup after breaking knife—										
4521	From 6 cups	F-3	June 12	47,000	32,500	100	+	0 in 10,000	....	....	....
4522	From 7 cups	F-3	...do....	1,900,000	220,000	1,000	+	0 in 100,000	....	....	....
4660	From 6 cups	F-4	July 2	10,000	5,000	0 in 100	0	0 in 10,000	....	....	....
4668	From 7 cups	F-4	July 3	13,000,000	1,100,000	100,000	+	....	....	....	....
4679	From 10 cups	F-4	...do....	240,000	56,000	10,000	0	23,000	....	....	....
1799	From several cups	F-5	July 22	2,300,000	2,200,000	100,000	0	....	....	....	....
1987	5 pounds, after breaking No. 1 eggs	F-6	Aug. 15	420,000	480,000	10,000	....	....	.0005	.0040	87.58
	From breaking tray—										
4429	8 [illegible]es, from 1 tray	D-2	May 28	440,000	350,000	100,000	+	0 in 1,000	....	....	....
4714	From 5 trays	D-4	July 11	2,400,000	1,400,000	10,000	0	....	....	....	....
866	From 1 tray after breaking dirty eggs	D-5	July 30	2,400,000	2,000,000	100,000	....	....	....	....	....

TABLE D-I.—*Commercial samples of whites, yolks, aud mixed egg, shell method of separation, 1911.*

[Discussion, p. 53.]

Sample No.	Description of sample.	Date of collection.	Bacteria per gram on plain agar incubated at —		Gas-producing bacteria per gram.	Liquefying organisms per gram in lactose bile.	Ammoniacal nitrogen (Folin method).		Moisture.	Ether extract.
			20° C.	37° C.			Wet basis.	Dry basis.		
							Per cent.	*Per cent.*	*Per cent.*	*Per cent.*
	Whites—Shell method of separation:									
228	From 25-pound pail—early morning	July 11	700	700	10	0	0.0005			
233	Do	do	1,900	1,200	10		.0004			
237	Do	July 12	99,000	270,000	100,000	1,000	.0004			
240	Do	do	49,000	120,000	10,000	7,000	.0004			
347	Do	July 24	4,800,000	4,100,000	100,000	1,500,000	.0002			
367	Do	July 25	200,000	Sterile at 1,000.	100		.0003			
370	Do	do	42,000	47,500	1,000		.0004			
379	Do	July 26	200,000	190,000	10,000	65,000	.0007			
382	Do	do	76,000	59,000	10,000		.0006			
	Yolks—Shell method of separation:									
153	Ready for freezer	June 28	220,000	340,000	10,000	12,000	.0032			
159	From churn	do	140,000	3,000,000	10,000	20,000				
229	Do	July 11	22,000	13,000	1,000		.0031	0.0074	58.06	23.49
232	Do	do	100,000	65,000	100,000		.0027	.0074	63.38	18.88
238	Do	July 12	490,000	2,000,000	100,000	50,000	.0031	.0076	59.10	22.69
242	Do	do	3,600	47,000	10,000	0	.0033	.0080	58.60	23.44
348	Do	July 24	4,300,000	4,300,000	100	80,000	.0031	.0076	59.42	22.71
351	Do	do	510,000	440,000	10,000	1,000	.0031	.0076	59.12	22.78
368	Do	July 25	130,000	52,000	1,000		.0032	.0075	57.24	24.85
371	Do	do	1,100,000	840,000	100,000		.0031	.0072	56.68	23.24
380	Do	July 26	500,000	480,000	1,000	130,000	.0032	.0077	58.42	24.21
383	Do	do	490,000	620,000	100,000	100,000	.0032	.0079	59.61	22.98
509	Do	Aug. 10	2,900,000	2,800,000	10,000	210,000	.0029	.0071	59.01	22.56
513	Do	do	710,000	520,000	10,000	35,000	.0024	.0061	60.83	21.01
	Mixed egg:									
154	Kept about 2 hours at 65° F. before freezing	June 29	630,000	1,400,000	10,000	6,000	.0020	.0065	69.42	13.82
161	From churn	do	940,000	1,700,000	10, 00	32,000				
227	Do	July 11	130,000	720,000	100,000		.0018			
231	Do	do	14,400	7,700	10,000		.0021			
236	Do	July 12	600,000	970,000	100,000	79,000	.0019			

241	From churn	do	44,500	740,000	10,000		.0024			
349	Do	July 24	2,500,000	2,800,000	100,000	90,000	.0022			
352	Do	do	3,100,000	3,200,000	100,000	65,000	.0022			
369	Do	July 25	1,700,000	1,200,000	100,000	120,000	.0018			
372	Do	do	620,000	600,000	100,000		.0018			
381	Do	July 26	1,000,000	1,100,000	100,000	55,000	.0021			
384	Do	do	1,500,000	980,000		160,000	.0022			
508	Do	Aug. 10	820,000	560,000	100,000	0	.0020			
510	Do	do	1,200,000	810,000	10,000		.0020			

TABLE D-II.—*Commercial samples of mixed egg from churn, 1912.*

Sample No.	Description and size of sample.	Date of collection.	Bacteria per gram on plain agar incubated at— 20° C.	Bacteria per gram on plain agar incubated at— 37° C.	Gas-producing bacteria per gram in lactose bile.	Liquefying organisms per gram.	Ammoniacal nitrogen (Folin method). Wet basis.	Ammoniacal nitrogen (Folin method). Dry basis.	Moisture.
	Visit No. 1.						*Per cent.*	*Per cent.*	*Per cent.*
4161	Clean, cracked, and dirty eggs, 125 pounds	Apr. 17	5,100	400	100		0.0014	0.0046	69.28
4265	Cracked eggs and a few small and dirty eggs	May 7	170,000	8,100	1,000	70,000			
	Visit No. 2.								
4418	Seconds mixed with a few dirty and cracked eggs, 200 pounds	May 27	320,000	230,000	1,000	0 in 1,000			
4419	200 pounds	May 28	340,000	220,000	1,000	4,000	.0020	.0066	69.84
4425	do	do	950,000	340,000	10,000	0 in 1,000			
	Visit No. 3.								
4541	Seconds, 125 pounds	May 29	950,000	600,000	100,000	100,000			
4543	Seconds and cracked eggs, 125 pounds	June 1	600,000	380,000	100,000	15,000	.0018	.0063	71.43
4544	do	June 3	2,200,000	1,500,000	100,000	150,000	.0019	.0062	69.26
4545	Seconds, 125 pounds	June 4	1,700,000	1,100,000	1,000,000	300,000	.0019	.0061	69.04
4546	Seconds and cracked eggs, 125 pounds	June 5	650,000	500,000	10,000	120,000	.0017	.0058	70.56
4548	Cracked and dirty eggs, 125 pounds	June 7	170,000	120,000	1,000	0 in 1,000			
4565	Seconds, 125 pounds	June 8	240,000	140,000	100,000	20,000			
4568	Seconds (same lot as No. 4565), 125 pounds	do	390,000	250,000	1,000	0 in 1,000			
4549	Seconds and cracked eggs, 125 pounds	June 10	160,000	120,000	1,000	4,000			
4551	do	June 11	340,000	180,000	10,000	4,000			
4562	do	June 13	700,000	500,000	10,000	30,000			
4550	do	June 15	120,000	70,000	1,000	6,000	.0019	.0062	69.54
4554	do	June 17	800,000	490,000	100,000	120,000	.0018	.0059	69.35
	Visit No. 4.								
4683	Seconds and cracked eggs, 125 pounds	June 22	650,000	550,000	10,000	0 in 10,000	.0022	.0075	70.56
4684	Seconds, 125 pounds	June 25	550,000	480,000	10,000	0 in 10,000	.0021	.0070	70.02
4685	Seconds and cracked eggs, 125 pounds	June 27	260,000	130,000	10,000	0 in 10,000	.0019	.0064	70.22
4686	do	July 1	1,100,000	850,000	100,000	25,000	.0025	.0082	69.42
4687	125 pounds	July 3	150,000	100,000	100	10,000	.0021	.0071	70.22
4695	Seconds, 125 pounds	July 9	550,000	310,000	100		.0021	.0072	70.65
4704		July 10	800,000	650,000	1,000		.0017	.0056	69.41

	Visit No. 5.								
4848	Seconds and cracked eggs, 125 pounds	July 12	650,000	500,000	10,000		.0024	.0077	68.72
4850	....do	July 16	550,000	550,000	1,000		.0024	.0078	69.24
4851	....do	July 19	1,300,000	1,100,000	10,000		.0023	.0076	69.72
4852	....do	July 22	1,100,000	950,000	100,000		.0023	.0073	68.38
4853	....do	July 23	330,000	280,000	1,000		.0022	.0071	68.88
4863	Seconds, 125 pounds	July 29	1,900,000	1,300,000	10,000		.0021	.0066	68.33
4864	....do	July 30	1,200,000	950,000	100,000		.0022	.0072	69.63
4872	Seconds and a few cracked eggs	...do...	2,200,000	1,800,000	100,000				
4875	Seconds and cracked eggs, 125 pounds	July 31	3,300, 00	2,700, 00	100,000		.0019	.0060	68.53
4879	Seconds, cracked, and leaking eggs, 125 pounds	...do...	1,800,000	2,000,000	100,000		.0020	.0063	68.39
4885	Seconds and a few cracked eggs, 125 pounds	...do...	650,000	600,000	1,000,000		.0021	.0067	68.77
	Visit No. 6.								
41007	Seconds, 125 pounds	Aug. 10	2,800,000	1,600,000	100,000		.0021	.0067	68.66
41009		Aug. 12	500,000	490,000	10,000		.0018	.0059	69.50
41008	Cracked eggs, 125 pounds	Aug. 13	1,100,000	750,000	10,000		.0021	.0069	69.61
41003	Seconds and cracked eggs, 140 pounds	Aug. 19	3,100,000	1,500,000	10,000		.0024	.0077	68.90
41013	Seconds, 125 pounds	...do...	800,000	550,000	10,000		.0018	.0062	70.85
41015	Seconds (same lot as No. 41013), 125 pounds	...do...	460,000	290,000	1,000		.0018	.0059	69.37
41028	Seconds and cracked eggs, 125 pounds	Aug. 21	1,400,000	850,000	100,000		.0019	.0062	69.46
41034	....do	...do...	600,000	440,000	10,000				
41042	Cracked eggs, 125 pounds	Aug. 23	2,900,000	1,700,000	100,000		.0024	.0078	69.40
41045	....do	...do...	2,900,000	1,800,000	100,000		.0022	.0070	68.73

TABLE D-III.—*Commercial samples of whites and yolks—Shell method of separation, 1912.*

Sample No.	Description and size of sample.	Date of collection.	Bacteria per gram on plain agar incubated at—		Gas-producing bacteria per gram in lactose bile.	Liquefying organisms per gram.	Ammoniacal nitrogen (Folin method).		Moisture.
			20° C.	37° C.			Wet basis.	Dry basis.	
	Visit No. 1.						*Per cent.*	*Per cent.*	*Per cent.*
4162	Whites, cracked and small eggs, 25 pounds	Apr. 17	100	0	0		0.0002	0.0016	87.90
4163	Yolks of No. 4162	do	50	200	100		.0024	.0054	55.63
4282	Whites, cracked eggs, 25 pounds	May 8	13,500	15,000	1,000	0 in 10,000			
4283	Yolks of No. 4282, 25 pounds	do	25,000	64,000	1,000	0 in 10,000			
	Visit No. 2.								
4407	Whites, seconds, 15 pounds	May 27	1,500,000	700,000	100,000	5,000			
4408	Yolks of No. 4407	do	950,000	490,000	10,000	15,000			
4416	Whites, seconds, 25 pounds	do	60,000	20,000	100				
4417	Yolks of No. 4416	do	15,000	5,000		0 in 1,000			
4423	Whites, seconds, 10 pounds	May 28	1,000	1,000	10	0 in 1,000	.0003	.0023	87.14
4424	Yolks of No. 4423, 25 pounds	do	4,000	2,700	1,000	0 in 1,000	.0030	.0070	57.45
	Visit No. 3.								
4552	Whites, 15 pounds	June 17	430,000	300,000	10,000	30,000	.0002	.0016	87.32
4553	Yolks of No. 4552, 15 pounds	do	500,000	390,000	100,000	130,000	.0025	.0058	56.97
4563	Whites, seconds and cracked eggs, 15 pounds	June 18	97,000	110,000	10	0 in 10,000			
4564	Yolks of No. 4566, 20 pounds	do	87,000	78,000	0	0 in 10,000			
4566	Whites, seconds and cracked eggs, 20 pounds	do	13,500	12,000	1,000	0 in 10,000			
4567	Yolks of No. 4566, 20 pounds	do	15,500	17,500	100	0 in 10,000			
4542	Whites	June 1	600,000	23,000	10,000	0 in 1,000			
4547	Whites, seconds and cracked eggs, 25 pounds	June 6	18,500	15,500	10,000	0 in 1,000			
	Visit No. 4.								
4688	Whites, seconds, 75 pounds	July 9	170,000	21,500	100		.0006	.0046	87.10
4689	Yolks of No. 4689	do	650,000	250,000	1,000		.0031	.0083	62.86
4705	Whites, clean and dirty seconds, 20 pounds	July 10	65,000	22,000			.0005	.0040	87.39
4706	Yolks of No. 4705, 25 pounds	do	63,000	40,000	100		.0029	.0067	56.53
4718	Whites, cracked and dirty eggs, 20 pounds	July 11	160,000	65,000	0				
4719	Yolks of No. 4718	do	650,000	480,000	100				
	Visit No. 5.								
4870	Whites, seconds, 45 pounds	July 30	650,000	550,000	100,000				
4871	Yolks of No. 4870 and other eggs, 125 pounds	do	1,200,000	850,000	1,000,000		.0032	.0079	59.69
4876	Whites, mostly clean seconds, 84 pounds	July 31	370,000	240,000	10,000				
4880	Yolks of No. 4876, 40 pounds	do	1,400,000	1,300,000	100,000		.0025	.0066	62.13
4881	Whites, mostly seconds, 40 pounds	do	250,000	300,000	100				
4882	Yolks of No. 4882, 40 pounds	do	2,100,000	1,600,000	1,000,000				

TABLE D-IV.—*Commercial samples of leaking eggs—Handled by the tray method, 1912.*

(Discussion, p. 11.)

Sample No.	Size of sample.	Date of collection.	Bacteria per gram on plain agar incubated at—		Gas-producing bacteria per gram in lactose bile.	Liquefying organisms per gram.	Ammoniacal nitrogen (Folin method).		Moisture.	Eggs discarded.
			20° C.	37° C.			Wet basis.	Dry basis.		
	Visit No. 3.						*Per cent.*	*Per cent.*	*Per cent.*	
4559	6 dozen	June 17	75,000	59,000	10,000	0 in 10,000	0.0015	0.0053	71.55	
4560	4 dozen	...do...	17,500	7,500	1,000	0 in 1,000	.0013	.0047	72.50	
4570	3 dozen	June 18	500	0	0		.0016	.0059	72.83	2
4574	...do	June 19	5,300	2,400	10		.0018	.0064	71.76	4
4584	3½ dozen	June 20	320,000	170,000	10,000	10,000	.0014	.0050	72.06	2
	Visit No. 4.									
4690	4 dozen	July 9	750,000	550,000	100,000		.0015	.0053	71.43	3
4692	3 dozen	...do...	150,000	1,600	10					1
4703	8 dozen	July 10	15,500	7,400	0		.0017	.0059	71.19	4
4707	9 dozen	...do...	2,100,000	1,200,000	100		.0016	.0054	70.53	
4709	3 dozen	...do...	1,200	400	0		.0022	.0076	71.07	
4713	...do	July 11	3,700,000	1,400,000	1,000					3
4716	...do	...do...	54,000	18,500	100					2
	Visit No. 5.									
4867	18 dozen	July 30	230,000	150,000	1,000		.0021	.0068	69.32	18
4874	9 dozen	July 31	370,000	310,000	100,000		.0017	.0059	71.07	8
41010	6 dozen	Aug. 19	140,000	80,000	1,000		.0019	.0058	69.07	7
41030	3 dozen	Aug. 21	37,000	28,000	100					3
41038	6½ dozen	Aug. 22	61,000	31,500	0		.0017	.0059	70.99	6

ADDITIONAL COPIES
OF THIS PUBLICATION MAY BE PROCURED FROM
THE SUPERINTENDENT OF DOCUMENTS
GOVERNMENT PRINTING OFFICE
WASHINGTON, D. C.
AT
30 CENTS PER COPY
▽

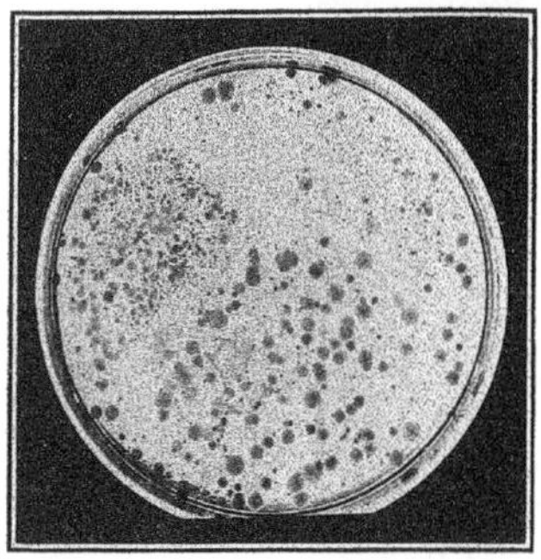

FIG. 1.—ONE DROP OF WATER FROM A SAUCER WASHED IN RUNNING WATER AFTER RECEIVING A BAD EGG. (REPRINT FROM CIRCULAR 98, BUREAU OF CHEMISTRY.)

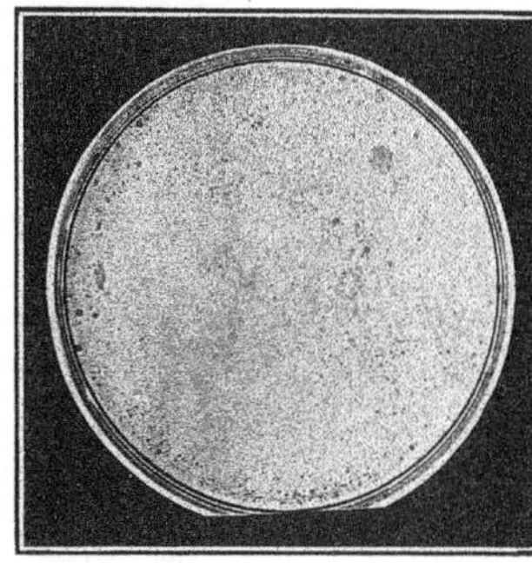

FIG. 2.—ONE DROP OF WATER FROM SAUCER SHELF. (REPRINT FROM CIRCULAR 98, BUREAU OF CHEMISTRY.)

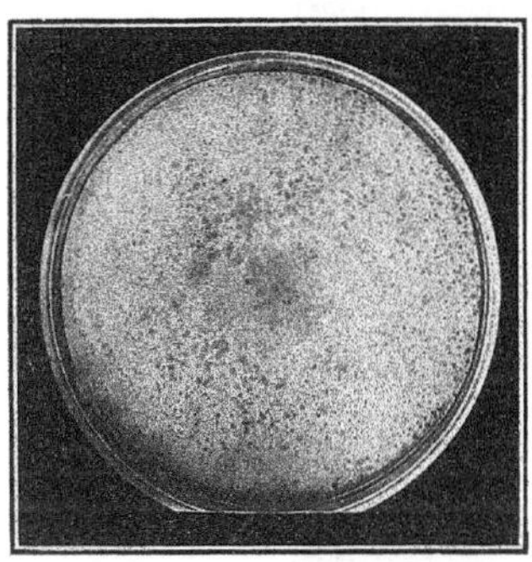

FIG. 3.—ONE DROP OF "DRIP" FROM TRAY (B HOUSE).

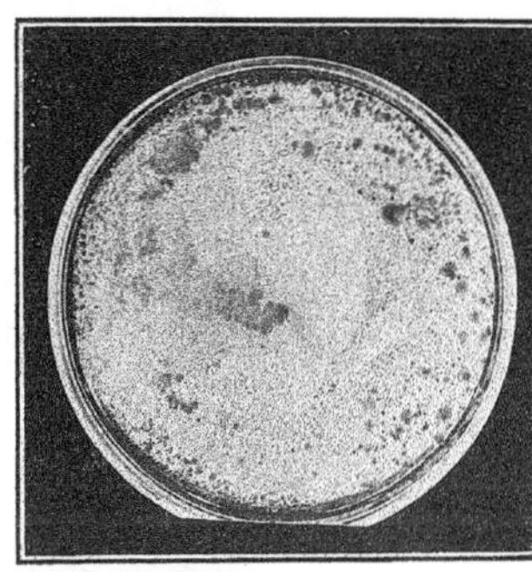

FIG. 4.—FINGER TIPS OF BREAKER (B HOUSE).

B HOUSE.

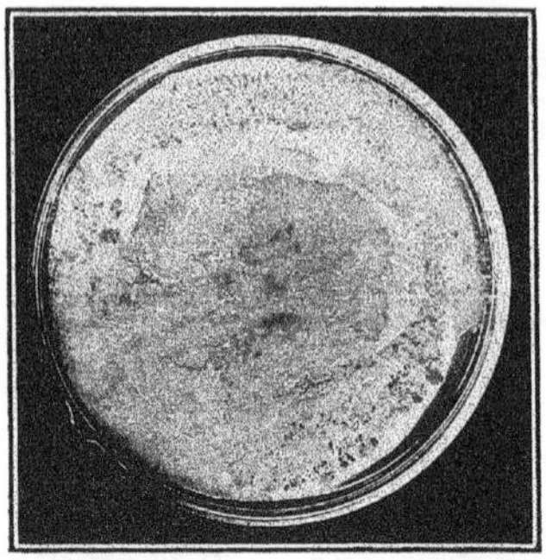

FIG. 1.—EDGE OF WASHED TUMBLER (C HOUSE).

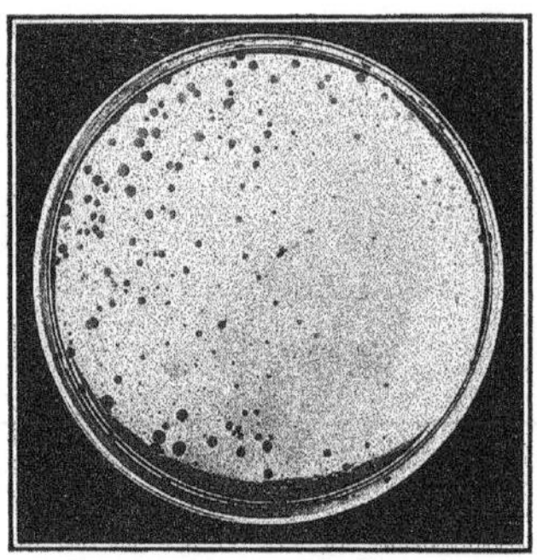

FIG. 2.—FINGER TIPS OF BREAKER (C HOUSE).

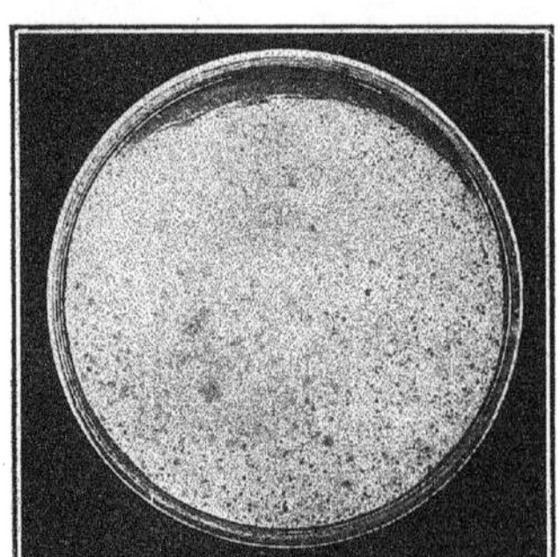

FIG. 3.—WASHED FINGER TIPS AFTER CRUSHING TANNERS' EGG.

C HOUSE.

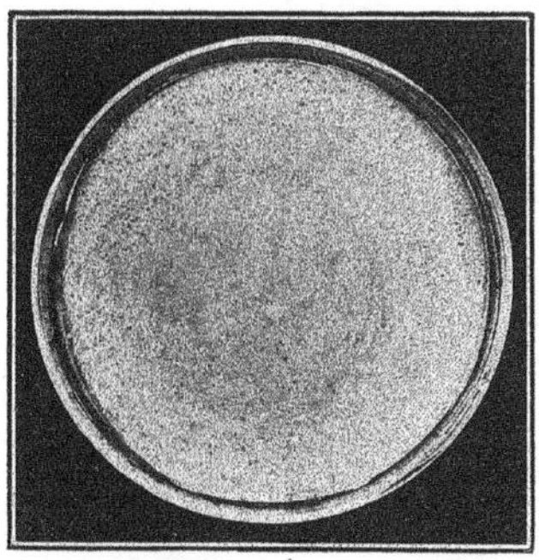

FIG. 1.—ONE DROP OF WATER FROM A WASHED PAIL (E HOUSE).

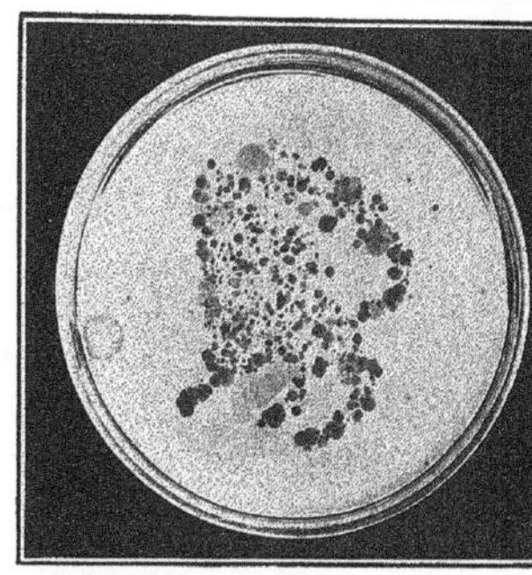

FIG. 2.—ONE DROP OF WATER FROM A CLEAN PAN (E HOUSE).

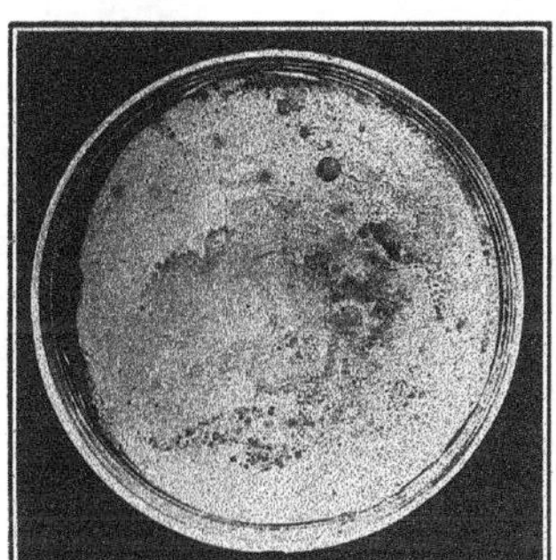

FIG. 3.—ONE DROP OF WATER FROM SINK (E HOUSE).

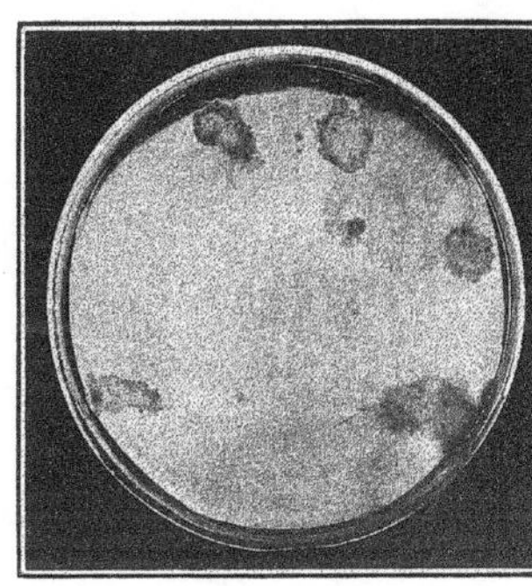

FIG. 4.—FINGER TIPS OF BREAKER (E HOUSE).

E HOUSE.

BREAKING ROOM BEFORE REMODELING (E HOUSE, 1911).

BREAKING ROOM WITH EQUIPMENT AFTER REMODELING (E HOUSE, 1912).

EGG-BREAKING ROOM IN OPERATION AFTER REMODELING (E HOUSE, 1912).

EGG-BREAKING ROOM IN OPERATION (F HOUSE, 1912).

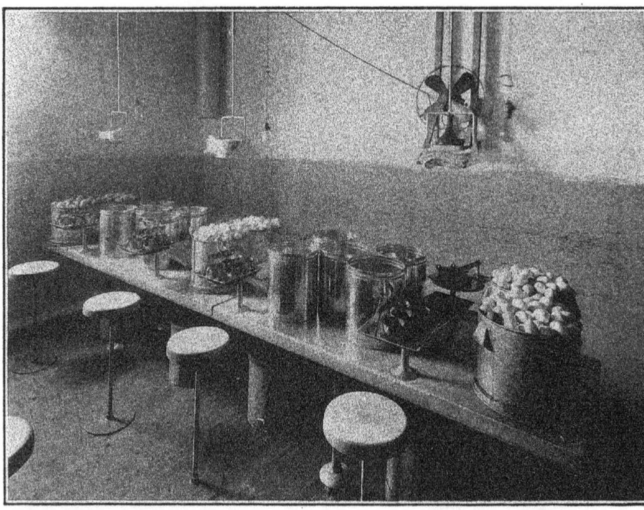

FIG. 1.—EGG-BREAKING EQUIPMENT ON TABLE (F HOUSE, 1912).

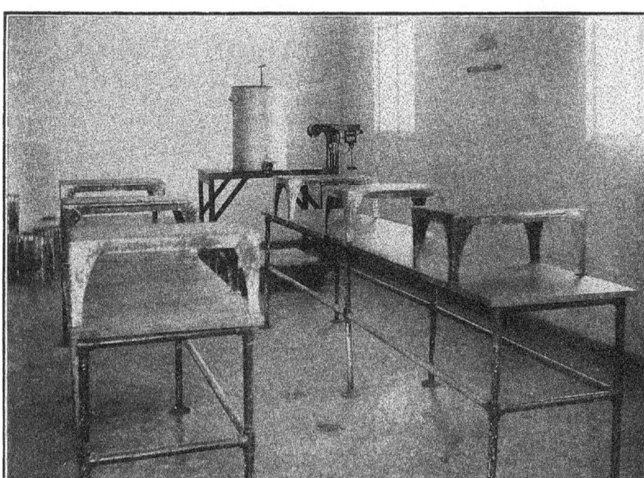

FIG. 2.—VIEW OF EGG-BREAKING ROOM SHOWING TABLES AND CHURN (D HOUSE, 1911 AND 1912).

FIG. 1.—EQUIPMENT USED BY ONE CANDLER (E HOUSE, 1912).

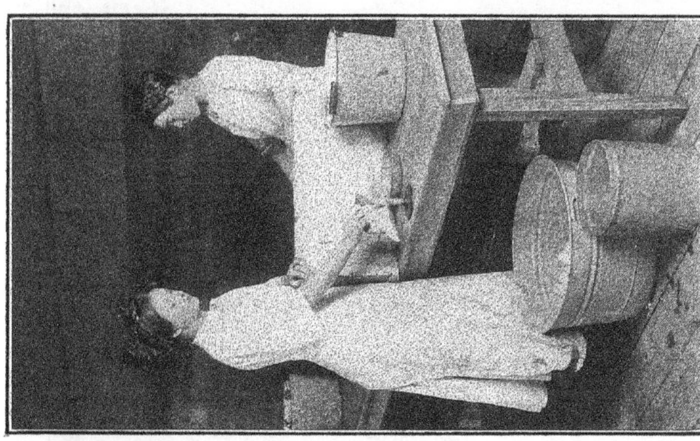

FIG. 2.—OUTFIT USED FOR EGG BREAKING BEFORE REMODELING (E HOUSE, 1911).

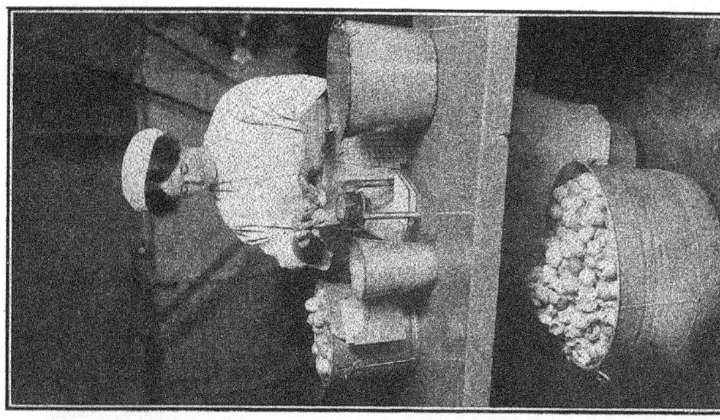

FIG. 3.—OUTFIT USED FOR EGG BREAKING AFTER REMODELING (E HOUSE, 1912).

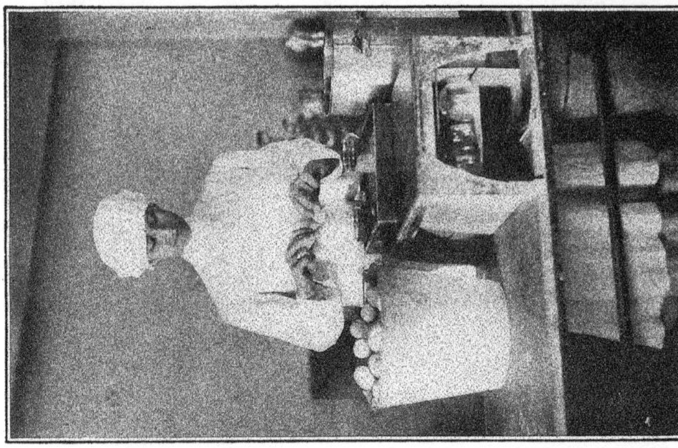

FIG. 2.—OUTFIT USED FOR BREAKING EGGS (D HOUSE, 1912).

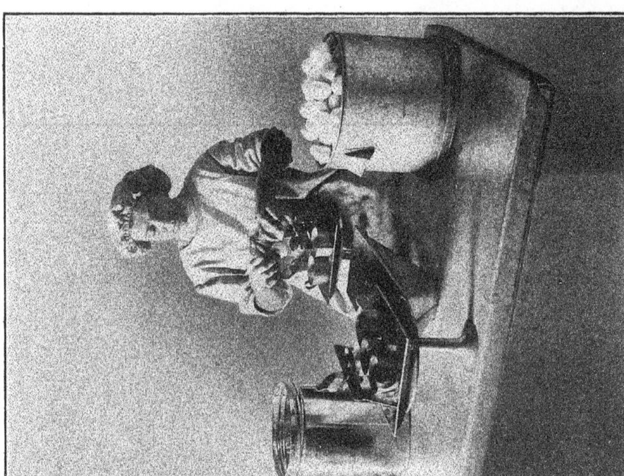

FIG. 1.—OUTFIT USED FOR BREAKING EGGS (F HOUSE, 1912).

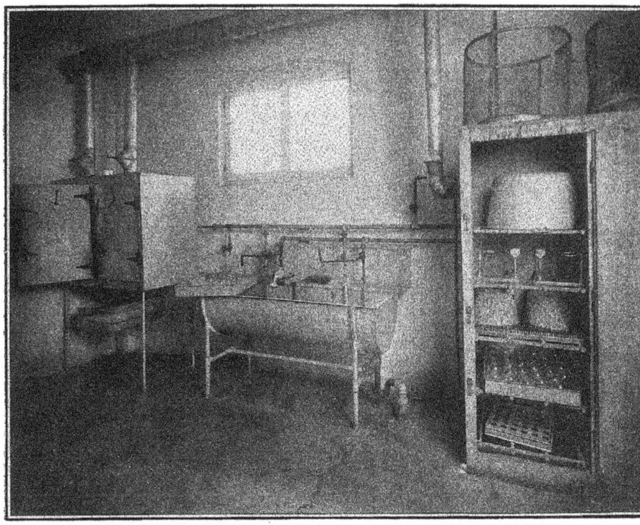

FIG. 1.—WASHING AND STERILIZING ROOM (E HOUSE, 1912).

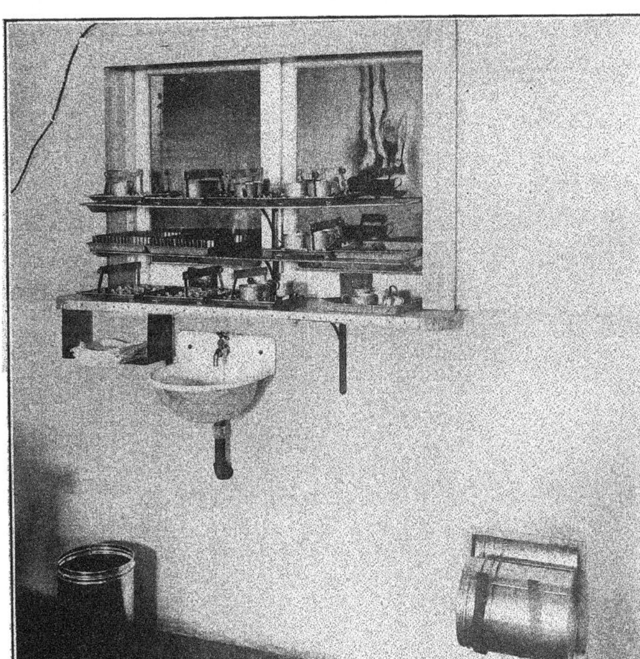

BREAKING ROOM AND

FIG. 1.—VIEW OF STERILIZING ROOM SHOWING STERILIZER, CAN CHUTE, AND WINDOW FOR TRANSFERRING APPARATUS (F HOUSE, 1912).

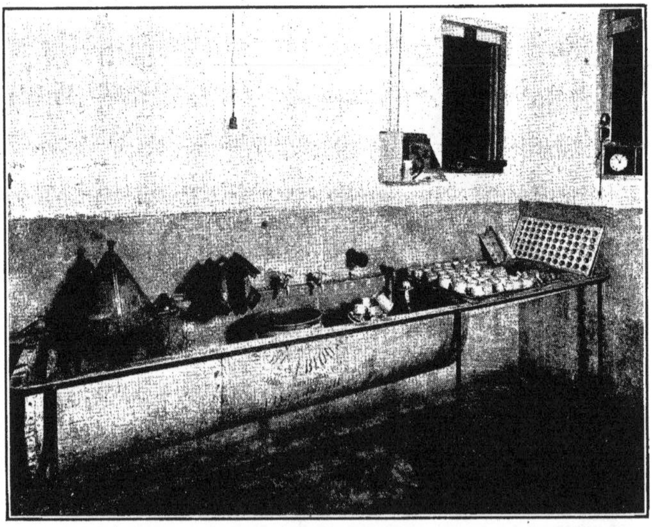

FIG. 2.—VIEW OF STERILIZING ROOM SHOWING SINK, DRAIN RACK, AND MOTOR-DRIVEN BRUSHES (F HOUSE, 1912).

FIG. 1.—FREEZER FOR CANNED EGGS (D HOUSE, 1912).

FIG. 2.—TRAY FOR LEAKING EGGS.

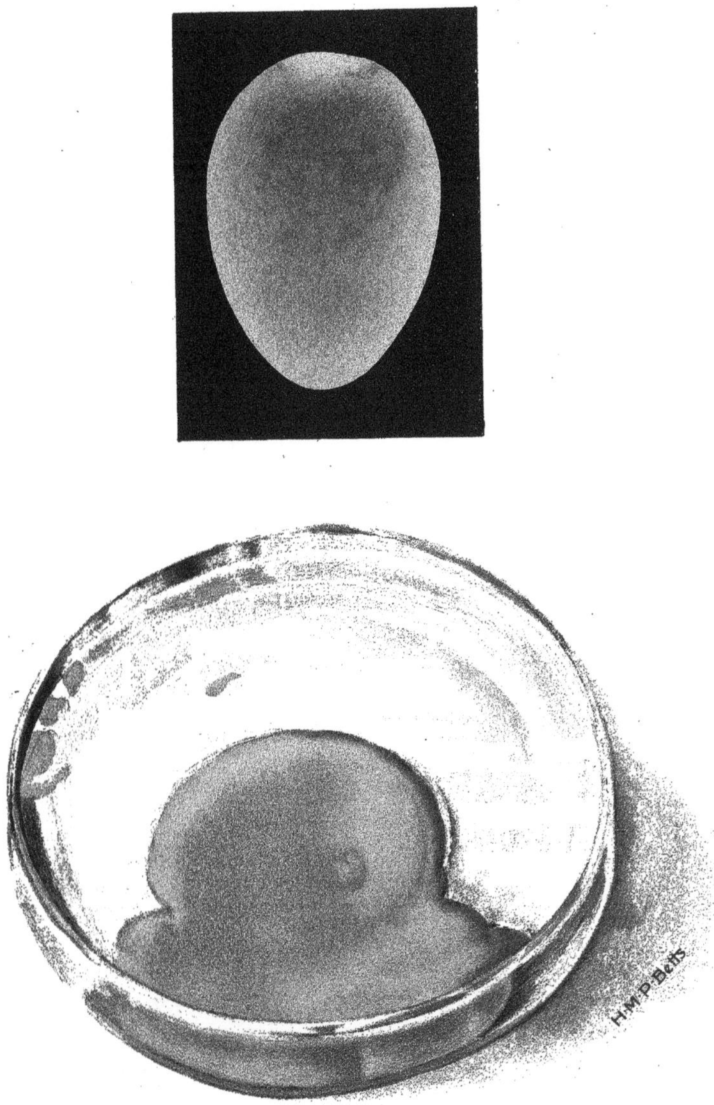

EGG WITH SOFT YOLK BEFORE THE CANDLE AND OUT OF THE SHELL

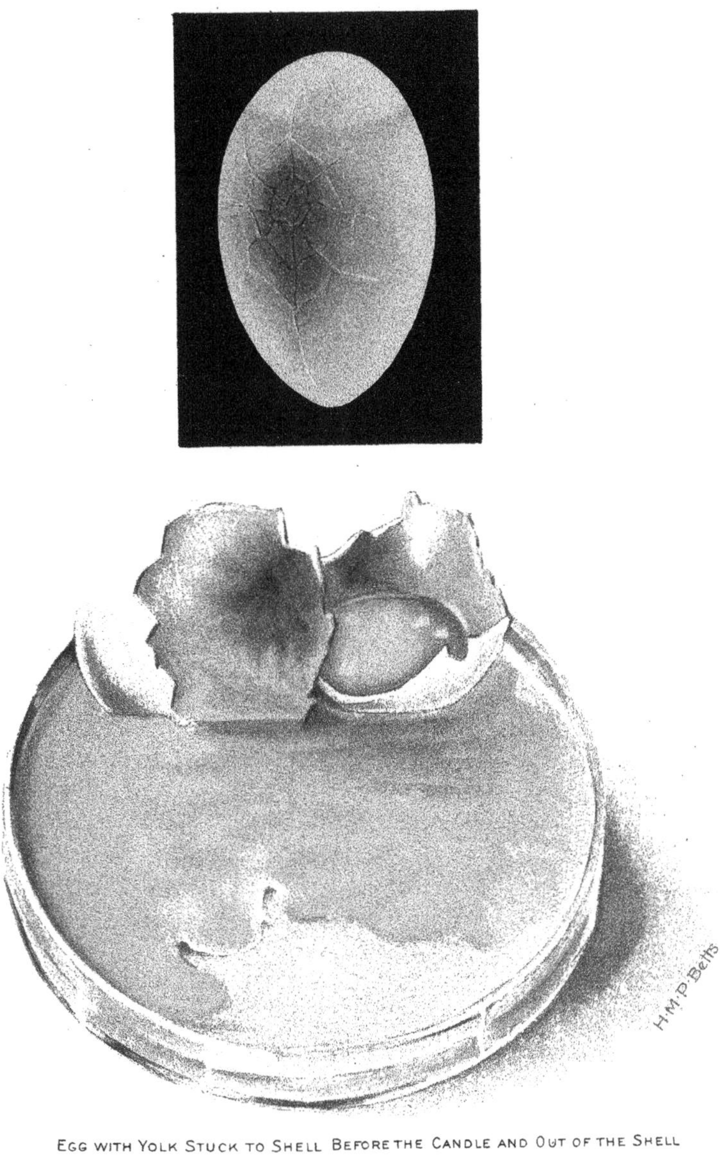

EGG WITH YOLK STUCK TO SHELL BEFORE THE CANDLE AND OUT OF THE SHELL

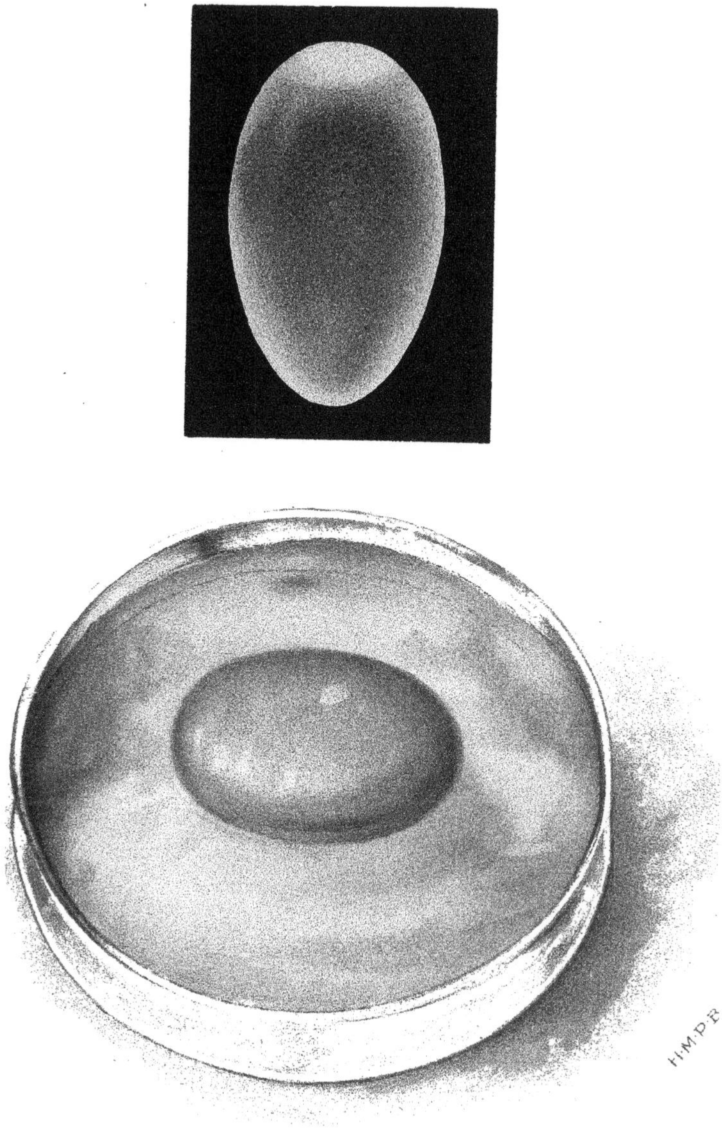

EGG SHOWING MIXED ROT BEFORE THE CANDLE AND OUT OF THE SHELL

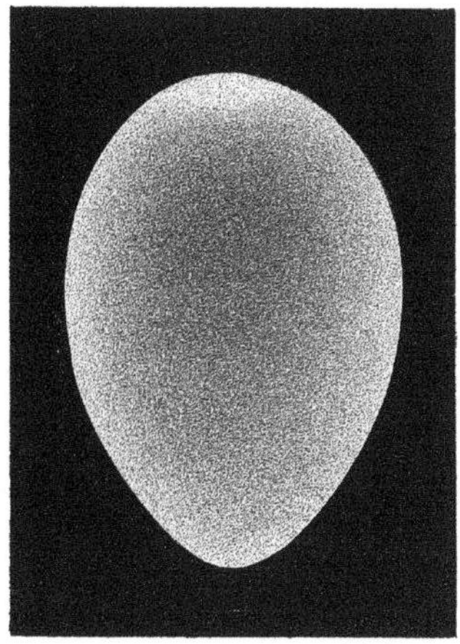

A FRESH EGG BEFORE THE CANDLE AND OUT OF THE SHELL

A SYSTEM OF ACCOUNTING FOR COOPERATIVE FRUIT ASSOCIATIONS

By

G. A. NAHSTOLL, Assistant in Cooperative Organization Accounting
and W. H. KERR, Investigator in Market Business Practice

CONTENTS

WASHINGTON
GOVERNMENT PRINTING OFFICE
1915

BULLETIN OF THE
U.S. DEPARTMENT OF AGRICULTURE
No. 225

Contribution from the Office of Markets and Rural Organization,
Charles J. Brand, Chief. May 7, 1915.

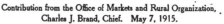

A SYSTEM OF ACCOUNTING FOR COOPERATIVE FRUIT ASSOCIATIONS.

By G. A. Nahstoll, *Assistant in Cooperative Organization Accounting*, and
W. H. Kerr, *Investigator in Market Business Practice*.

CONTENTS.

INTRODUCTION.

There are already several hundred cooperative organizations in the United States handling deciduous fruits and produce. New associations or exchanges are formed from time to time as the farmers in the various localities begin to realize the benefits to be derived from the cooperative handling and marketing of their products. Many of these organizations flourish for a short time, but each year witnesses the dissolution of a number of them. These failures frequently can be attributed either directly or indirectly to the lack of a proper system of accounting and the subsequent verification of the accounting record by means of a thorough audit.

The system outlined in this bulletin has been devised to meet the requirements of the smaller organizations handling deciduous fruits and produce on a commission basis, and it is hoped that the assistance given will lead to the adoption of simple, concise, and comprehensive methods of keeping records of sales and reporting the proceeds of such sales to the growers. A special system has been prepared for the requirements of the potato exchanges which buy outright from the grower or pool on a basis of the day's sales.

While the system here given is sufficiently flexible to admit of a great deal of expansion, it will not cover the varied needs of the larger associations of the West and Northwest, where the cooperative handling and marketing of fruit has been much more highly developed. In a later bulletin the department intends to publish a discussion of

Note.—This bulletin should be of interest to all cooperative fruit associations throughout the country.

the many accounting problems of the larger organizations and to submit forms to cover their needs.

Two methods of handling the records of settlements with the growers are shown in this bulletin. The first method, which does not provide for individual ledger accounts with the growers, has been tried out in the offices of the Delaware Produce Exchange at Dover, Del., and the second method, which provides for the use of such accounts, has been used in the offices of the Virginia Fruit Growers (Inc.), of Staunton, Va. The reasons for the change in this particular are set forth fully in the text.

OBJECT.

There are a number of different systems now in use in cooperative organizations marketing deciduous fruits and produce, but while these serve as records of the transactions, no provision is made for a proper filing of the papers supporting the figures appearing in the records. Inasmuch as the organization acts in the capacity of an agent for the growers, the accounting system should be so arranged that the history of each lot of fruit or produce delivered can be easily and quickly traced from the time it is turned over to the organization for shipment until the returns are paid to each grower.

A system providing for the filing together of all papers pertaining to the same shipment in a separate folder or envelope, where they will be readily accessible for reference, will be found to be much more satisfactory than one in which the necessary data supporting the figures which appear on the books must be procured from a number of different files. The best system of accounts for any business is the one that secures the information desired with the least effort. The aim has been, therefore, to devise the least involved system which will secure the information essential to successful management with absolute accuracy and promptness.

Wide divergence in accounting needs will be found among the various cooperative marketing organizations. This is particularly true of the various types of organizations handling deciduous fruits and produce. It has been the aim in this bulletin to give a system of accounts which will fill the needs of the smaller cooperative organizations, acting primarily as sales agencies.

MEMORANDUM RECORDS.

In the marketing of perishable products it is often found necessary to divert shipments in transit from one consignee to another in the same market or from one market to another, or a car may be forwarded as a "tramp;" that is, it may be billed out subject to the shipper's order and routed in such a manner that it can be diverted easily to one of several markets, wherever it is most probable that a sale will be made. Owing to the perishable nature of the product, deterioration may set in, and an allowance may have to be made before the consignee is willing to accept the shipment. Demurrage, switching, and extra icing charges may accrue in transit, and these must be deducted from the selling price. Fluctuations in market conditions may change the selling price even after the shipment has gone forward. Again, cars may be sent out to commission houses to be handled on consignment, while others may be sent to the auctions in the various cities. In these cases the net proceeds derived from any particular shipment will not be known until the account of sales has been received. To take care of all these contingencies, a system of accounts devised for a cooperative organization which markets deciduous fruits and produce must be very flexible, and the record of sales must be kept in memorandum form until the transaction is consummated.

Many of the systems now in use are built around a form generally known as the sales book. In this book each sale is journalized, a column being provided for charges to customers' accounts on one side, and on the other side a column for credits to the growers' accounts, for commission and for brokerage due, the journal entry being:

Dr.	Purchaser	$700.00	
Cr.	To Growers		$650.75
	Commission		34.25
	Broker		15.00

The charges to the accounts of the purchasers are posted in detail during the month, but the growers' accounts and the commission account are not credited with the net proceeds until payment is received for the shipments. In order to establish the equality of the two sides of the trial balance at the end of the month, the unpaid items would have to be taken into consideration. Or the posting to the ledger is carried out as follows:

Dr.	Purchaser	$700.00	
Cr.	To Fruit		$700.00
Dr.	Fruit	$700.00	
Cr.	To Growers		665.00
	Commission		35.00

These entries make a trial balance possible at the end of the first month, but to obtain a balance at the end of the second month all items recorded during the previous month but paid during the second necessarily would have to be taken into account in order to obtain a balance.

These systems are found, therefore, to be entirely too rigid for use in the handling of highly perishable products where provision must be made for so many contingencies. The changes on the sales book are made necessarily by interlineations, and in some instances these entries are so confusing as to be impossible of translation. Since it is difficult to obtain a trial balance at the end of each month, as a rule no balance is attempted until the close of the season, when very often it is found to be out of the question to secure a balance. As the difference between the two sides of a trial balance may be made up of several compensating errors, this procedure necessarily must be condemned.

To make this system flexible enough to take care of all such contingencies, the sales book has been discarded and an envelope system substituted therefor. The record up to the time of the receipt of the remittance is held in the envelope in memorandum form. No accounts receivable or customers' accounts are kept, thus doing away with the many adjusting and cross entries on account of allowances and changes in consignees.

Objection may be raised to the omission of accounts receivable from the ledger and the carrying of the charges in the form of memoranda. This method, however, would seem to be preferred on account of its simplicity. The time elapsing between the date of shipment and the date on which remittance is received is short and the number of shipments unpaid at any time is relatively small, all of which makes it an easy matter to locate any envelope in the unpaid file when desired. By the use of the envelopes, the file of unpaid cars is kept constantly before the office manager, whereas if ledger accounts are kept, the old balances might be unnoticed until the end of the month.

FIRST METHOD.

For organizations which do not handle growers' supplies at all or only in very limited quantities, the first method, under which no ledger accounts with individual growers are kept, is recommended. As explained under "Account Sales" (p. 14), the duplicates of the accounts sales rendered to the growers are filed in folders bearing the names of the growers at the top, and from this file any information in regard to payments made to growers can be obtained, thus eliminating the necessity of posting all these items.

The plan of this method reduced to journal entries is as follows:

Cash	$700.00	
To Fruit		$700.00

This entry is made when cash is entered on the Cash Receipts form and extended in the Fruit column.

The next step is:

Fruit	$68.25	
To Commission		$33.25
Broker		10.00
Icing, etc		25.00

This entry is made in the journal and credits the amount of commission due the exchange, the amount of brokerage due the broker, and the amount of initial icing due the ice company to the respective accounts.

The final entry is:

Fruit	$631.75	
To Cash		$631.75

This is made when checks are drawn to the growers for the amount of the net proceeds.

Should a balance exist in the ledger on account of supplies bought, and should it be desired to deduct this amount from the account sales, another journal entry is made to cover the transfer; viz:

Fruit	$20.00	
To Grower		$20.00

for the amount of the debit balance shown on the particular growers' account.

The plan of the second method is given on page 23.

BOOKS AND SPECIAL FORMS.

The following books and special forms are used in this system: The receipt, manifest, bulletin, invoice, car envelope, account sales, journal, cash receipts, cash disbursements, stub check book, and ledger. Each of these is described at length under separate headings.

THE RECEIPT.

Upon delivery of fruit by the grower it is inspected and a receipt (Form 1) is made out by the inspector or agent. This shows the name of the shipping station, date, car initials and number, grower's name, quantity, grade and kind of fruit or produce, results of inspection, and inspector's or agent's name. It is made in duplicate; the original is sent to the office and the duplicate is handed to the grower for his record. At the office the receipts are checked against the manifests to see that all the deliveries are accounted for properly.[1]

FORM 1.

THE RECEIPT.

Frankford sta. *June 8,* 1914

P R R car No. *105539*

Received for shipment of

T. C. Lunford

20 cr. XXXX Gandys

THE EUREKA PRODUCE EXCHANGE, INC.;[2]

By *H. L. SMITH,* Agent.

No. 5.

[1] The crops handled by the exchange in which this system was tried out were strawberries, cantaloupes, early pears, summer apples, and sweet potatoes in car lots. As these crops follow each other without overlapping, this simple form of receipt served the purpose better than a highly involved form.

[2] This name is a fictitious one and used for illustrative purposes only.

THE MANIFEST.

The manifest (Form 2) is written up by the agent as the car is loaded, and shows the name of the station where loaded, date, car initials and number, growers' names and addresses, and contents, segregated as to grades. It serves primarily as a manifest of the contents of the car, but later the distribution of the returns received for the shipment is made on this form, and the account sales are written up from it. The total of the amounts to be distributed to the growers, less the commission, must equal the "amount due growers," as shown on the car envelope (Form 5).

The receipts, manifest, and original and triplicate bills of lading are sent to the office by the agent. When disposition has been made of the car, the name and address of the consignee is placed on the manifest and the shipment or envelope number is also inserted at the top of the sheet.

FORM 2.

THE MANIFEST.

THE EUREKA PRODUCE EXCHANGE, INC.

Aurora, Del.

Shipt. No. *49.*

Frankford Station, *June 8,* *1914*

P R R Car No. *105539* Consignee, *H. C. Cannon & Co., Pittsburgh, Pa.*

Contents: *250 cr. Strawberries.*

Shipper.	P. O. address.	Grade.			Variety.	Net.
		xxxx	xxx	xx		
T. C. Lunford	Frankford	20			Gandy	58.00
W. H. Hinckley	Omar		8		"	21.60
B. D. Melton	Frankford			15	Parson	22.50
J. A. Barnett	Dagsboro	7			"	12.60
F. A. Long	Roxana		11		"	18.92
F. A. Long	"		1		Gandy	2.70
L. S. Munsey	Frankford		2		"	5.40
M. F. Walton	"		9		"	24.30
R. A. Winton	Omar	43			"	124.70
"	"	3			Parson	5.40
Amos Bolt	Frankford	10			Climax	18.00
F. A. Hunter	"	16			Gandy	46.40
Mrs. Helen Wise	"	10			Helen Davis	23.00
R. G. Canton	"	81			Gandy	234.90
R. G. Canton	"		14		Parson	24.08
	Total	190	45	15		642.50

THE BULLETIN.

The bulletin (Form 3) is a record of orders received and sales made, and is kept by the sales manager. As soon as a car is loaded, the sales manager is advised by telephone and is given the car number, contents, and whatever other information is desired. This advice is placed on the bulletin, and, after the sale has been confirmed, forwarding instructions are given. After a car has reached its detination and has been accepted by the consignee that portion of the bulletin pertaining to the shipment is detached and filed in the car envelope.

This form acts as a register of orders received and also as a convenient memorandum of shipments previous to the receipt of the manifests, receipts, and bills of lading which are mailed to the office by the agents and which consequently do not reach the office until the following day.

FORM 3.

THE BULLETIN.

Date, *June 8, '14*.

Purchaser.	Station.	Package. Price.	Remarks.
H. C. Cannon & Co.	*Frankford.*	*190* XXXX @	*All bright red stock, well packed.*
Pittsburg, Pa.	Car Number.	*45* XXX @	
Route, *Penna.*	*P. R. R. 105539.*	*15* XX @	
Broker,	Date Draft.	@	
		Amount.....$	
Purchaser.	**Station.**	**Package. Price.**	**Remarks.**
Lawrence Com. Co.	*Dover.*	*179* XXXX @	
Scranton, Pa.	Car Number.	*31* XXX @	
Route,	*L. V. 42639.*	*9* XX @	
Broker,	Date Draft.	@	
		Amount.....$	
Purchaser.	**Station.**	**Package. Price.**	**Remarks.**
	Delmar.	*102* XXXX @	
	Car Number.	*85* XXX @	
Route,	*P. R. R. 102030.*	*53* XX @	
Broker,	Date Draft.	@	
		Amount.....$	

THE INVOICE.

When the original receipts, manifest, and bills of lading reach the office, an invoice (Form 4) is made out in duplicate, the original is sent to the customer, and the duplicate retained for filing. In case a draft is made to cover the shipment the invoice is made in triplicate and a copy is attached to the draft.

FORM 4.

THE INVOICE.

THE EUREKA PRODUCE EXCHANGE, INC.,

PRODUCER'S AGENCY FOR

BERRIES, POTATOES, APPLES, PEARS, PEACHES, GRAPES, MELONS, CANTALOUPES, ETC.

Terms: Strictly cash. All goods sold f. o. b. our shipping points.

GENERAL OFFICES,
Aurora, Del., June 8, 1914.

Sold to H. C. CANNON & Co.,
Pittsburg, Pa.

180 Crates Strawberries (Gandy) @ $2.85	$513.00
70 " " @ $1.85	129.50
Refrigeration	25.00
	667.50

Car, P. R. R. 105539.
Routed Penna.

THE CAR ENVELOPE.

All papers relating to the same shipment are filed in a car envelope (Form 5). This includes the original growers' receipts, duplicate invoice, triplicate bill of lading, manifest, portion of bulletin, copies of telegrams and correspondence, and all papers and data relating to the shipment. On the envelope are shown the name of the shipping station, date, shipment number, car initials and number, date of invoice, name of consignee, destination, routing, diversion, second destination, new routing, amount of refrigeration (initial icing, where charges do not follow the car) and date on which paid, contents, broker's name, date of draft, amount of draft, or amount of invoice (if on open account), and remarks. It bears on its face a full record of the shipment and contains all papers supporting these figures.

The envelope is placed in the "unpaid file" until remittance is received, when it is taken from this file and the amount of the remittance, date, and cash-book page is shown thereon under "credits."[1] Entry is then made in the cash book showing the name of the remitter, shipment and car number, and the amount of the remittance, which is extended in the fruit column. The entry recording the receipt of cash is the initial record of the shipment entering the books of account, the envelope and papers contained serving as a memorandum record up to this time.

After this the envelope is stamped "Paid," and the amounts of commission, brokerage, icing, etc., are entered thereon under "debits." The difference between the amount received and the charges against the shipment is the "balance due growers," which is also shown under "debits."

---

[1] The use of the words "debit" and "credit" in this connection is arbitrary. The returns received from the shipments are called credits and the charges against these receipts are called debits, the balance representing the amount standing to the growers' credit.

A journal entry is next passed as follows:

Dr. Fruit.
Cr. Commission.
Icing (credit party furnishing initial ice).
Brokerage (credit broker).

Letters of remittance, account sales from commission houses, requests for allowances and correspondence relating thereto are all filed in the envelope. This envelope is a very satisfactory record to place before a grower in case he desires further information regarding one of his shipments, and is also a complete and comprehensive record for the auditor.

FORM 5.

THE CAR ENVELOPE.

Station *Frankford* Date *June 8, 1914*
Shipment No. *49*
Car Initial *P R R* No. *105539*
Bill Sent *6/8/14*
Consignee *H. C. Cannon & Co.,*
Destination *Pittsburgh, Pa.*
Routing *Penna.*
Diverted to
Destination
Routing
Refrigeration *25.00* Paid
Contents *160 XXXX 20 XXX Gandys*
10 XXXX 25 XXX 15 XX Parson
10 XXXX Climax 10 XXXX Helen Davis
Sold by
Date Draft Amt. Invoice
Amt. Draft *667.50*
Remarks *Excellent stock*

PAID JUNE 25, 1914.

Date Paid.	C. B.	Credits.		Jnl.	Debits.
6/25	*24*	*667.50*	Commission	*15*	*32.12*
			Brokerage		
			Icing	15	25
			Due growers		*610.38*
Total		*667.50*	Total		*667.50*

THE JOURNAL.

An eight-column journal (Form 6) has been provided with the following captions:

DEBIT.	CREDIT.
Sundries.	Sundries.
Fruit.	Merchandise.
Merchandise.	Commission.
Fruit P. & L.	Fruit P. & L.

The debit and credit Sundries columns are for all items other than those for which columns have been provided.

The Fruit column on the debit side and the Commission column on the credit side of the journal were introduced to accommodate the journal entries covering charges for commission, icing, and brokerage as shown in the explanation of the car envelope. All items chargeable to Fruit account are extended in the Fruit column; items of commission to be credited to Commission account in the Commission column and items of icing and brokerage in the credit Sundries column. The advantage of the method of collecting these items in columns and posting the total to the ledger, over that of posting them in detail direct from the car envelope, is obvious.

All transactions involving the purchase and sale of merchandise are journalized, the debit Merchandise column being used for purchases and the credit Merchandise column for sales.

The debit and credit columns, Fruit P. & L. (Fruit Profit and Loss), were introduced for the specific purpose of taking care of the profits or losses sustained on fruit which is bought outright by the association.[1]

[1] Owing to certain local conditions and customs, the Exchange in which this system was tried out buys some of the crops outright from the growers, while the others are handled on a commission basis. It may also happen that some cars will contain both fruit bought and fruit to be handled on commission. By opening this account to hold all items of profit and loss, the Fruit account is kept clear of these elements, and the equilibrium of the two sides of the Fruit account will show that returns have been made in full to the growers for all proceeds received for their shipments. A credit balance appearing on Fruit account at the end of a month would indicate money received but for which no payments as yet had been made to the shippers. This method also shows the profit made or loss sustained on each shipment bought outright. Except where such a condition exists—that is, where the exchange handles shipments on some other than a regular commission basis and an element of profit or loss arises—these columns will be found superfluous.

FORM 6.

JOURNAL.

Dr. Cr.

Fruit P. & L.	Merchandise.	Fruit.	Sundries.	L. F.	June 25, 1914.	L. F.	Sundries.	Merchandise.	Commission.	Fruit P. & L.
1	2	3	4				5	6	7	8
10.00	400.00	300.00	345.50		Amount brought forward.		425.50	320.00	296.00	14.00
		57.12			Fruit car P.R.R. $\frac{49}{108839}$					
					Commission......				32.12	
					Eastern Ice Co....		25.00			
					26					
		24.00			Fruit car L.V. $\frac{41}{23460}$					
					Commission......				24.00	
					27					
			10.00		Bills Rec.					
					A. B. Dicks.......		10.00			
					Note at 6% due in 60 days for 1913 account.					
					28					
		19.00			Fruit car P.R.R. $\frac{39}{108897}$					
					Commission...........				19.00	
10.00	400.00	400.12	355.50		Sundries...............		460.50	320.00	371.12	14.00
			400.12		Fruit.					
					Commission...........		371.12			
			400.00		Merchandise...........		320.00			
			10.00		Fruit P. & L..........		14.00			
			1,165.62				1,165.62			

1. *Fruit P. & L.* Debit Fruit Profit and Loss account at the end of month with the total of this column.
2. *Merchandise.* Debit Merchandise Purchases account with the total of this column.
3. *Fruit.* Debit Fruit account with the total of this column.
4, 5. *Sundries.* Items appearing in these columns are posted individually during the month to the debit or credit of the respective accounts.
6. *Merchandise.* Credit Merchandise Sales account with the total of this column.
7. *Commission.* Credit Commission account with the total of this column.
8. *Fruit P. & L.* Credit Fruit Profit and Loss account with the total of this column.

THE RECORD OF CASH.

Separate forms have been provided for the recording of cash receipts and cash disbursements, as the ruling of the two forms is different and in some months more of one form may be used than of the other. This would be the case particularly if the stub check book should be discarded, the cash disbursement sheets used as a check register, and all checks registered thereon, instead of being written up on the check stubs and then entered in the cash book. Owing to the comparatively small number of checks issued during the slack season, the use of the stub check book seems preferable to the other method. The method used in this system is further explained under "Cash Disbursements," page 12.

Since the functions of the cash book are to record in detail the receipts and disbursements of cash and to show at any time the balance of cash on hand, the forms have been so devised as to lessen as far as possible the work of posting, at the same time analyzing the receipts and expenditures and disclosing the balance of cash on hand.

All receipts are deposited daily, and all disbursements are made by check. When it is necessary to carry on hand a petty cash fund this should be done on the Imprest System described in U. S. Department of Agriculture Bulletin 178, "Cooperative Organization Business Methods."

Cash receipts.—The form of cash receipts (Form 7) corresponds to the left-hand side of the ordinary cash book. Columns have been provided for Sundries, Fruit, and Merchandise. All remittances received on account of shipments of fruit are extended in the Fruit column. Merchandise cash sales are extended in the Merchandise column.

A column for deposits has been provided in order to show the amount of the daily deposits, so that they can be checked against the entries appearing in the bank pass book.

FORM 7.

CASH RECEIPTS.

Date.	Name.	Items.	L. F.	Sundries. 1	Fruit. 2	Merchandise. 3	Bank deposits. 4
		Amount brought forward.		480.00	3,005.35	60.00	3,545.35
1914. June 25	H. C. Cannon & Co.	Car 49 P. R. R. 105539			667.50		
	A. B. Jones	On account		60.00			
	Cruxton Produce Co.	Car 53 LS&MS 40693			745.00		
	Cash Sales					3.00	1,475.50
26	Bills Receivable	A. L. Long		41.00			
30	L. D. Jones	Invoice 4/10		20.00			61.00
				601.00	4,417.85	63.00	5,081.85
		Fruit		4,417.85			
		Merchandise		63.00			
				5,081.85			5,081.85

1. *Sundries.* Items appearing in this column are posted in detail during the month to the credit of the respective accounts.
2. *Fruit.* Credit Fruit account with total of this column.
3. *Merchandise.* Credit Merchandise Sales account with total of this column representing cash sales of merchandise.
4. *Deposits.* The total of this column, less balance carried forward from preceding month, must equal the total of the three columns, Sundries, Fruit, and Merchandise. This shows that all amounts received have been deposited in the bank, and a comparison can easily be made between the amounts as shown to have been deposited in the bank book and the amounts which should have been deposited according to the cash book, thus providing another check on the cash.

Cash disbursements.—The cash disbursements form (Form 8) corresponds to the right-hand side of the ordinary cash book. Two sets of checks are used. The first Check Number column and the Fruit column are used for the recording of all checks issued to the growers in payment of the net proceeds of fruit shipped. The second Check Number column and the Sundries column are used for all other items. Two more columns have been provided which may be used for other accounts which may have a number of charges during the month, such as Expense. The only difference in the two sets of checks lies in numbering the growers' checks beginning with "1" and the general checks with, say, "20001," but few of which will be required.[1] The checks (Form 10) are all bound in the usual commercial form of stub check book with three checks to the sheet.

FORM 10.

No. 4007 JUNE 25, 1914. T. C. LUNFORD, Car 49 PRR 105539 Charge acc't of Fruit. $58.00	 58.00	Do not detach. For payment as memo. below. Statement, June 25.. $58.00 Less..............% Proper indorsement is receipt for the above amount.	THE EUREKA PRODUCE EXCHANGE, INC. No. 4007. AURORA, DELAWARE, *June 25, 1914.* Pay to the order of T. C. Lunford. $58.00 Fifty-eight and no/100............dollars THE EUREKA PRODUCE EXCHANGE, INC. To the FARMERS NATIONAL BANK, *Aurora, Del.* A. K. MELTON, *Treasurer.*

As explained under "Account Sales" (p. 14), the checks are written up from the accounts sales and the entry is made on the cash book in total instead of in detail, thus:

Date.	Names.	Explanation.	Check Nos.	Fruit.
	Growers Statements.	Car FGE 129	2066	
		22240	to 2078	405 00

All checks drawn in the second check book are entered in detail on the cash disbursement sheet.

The balance brought forward from the preceding month is entered in the Deposit column.

The balance in bank at any time is the difference between the Deposit column on the cash receipts side and the total of the Fruit and the Sundries columns on the cash disbursements side.[2]

Reconciliation of the bank account should be made at the end of each month, the list of outstanding checks being written on the cash disbursement sheet, or an adding-machine list pasted thereon so that it will not be lost.

[1] It is often desired by the Directorate and in many instances specified by the by-laws that certain distinctions be made between checks covering payments to growers and those covering expenses and other items. Two sets of checks were used by the Exchange in which this system was tried out, so that there would be no interruption of the work should it be desired while drawing a large number of checks in favor of growers to draw a check for some other purpose.

[2] If it is desired to carry on the ledger an account with cash, showing the monthly receipts and disbursements, this can be easily done. The total of the Sundries, Fruit, and Merchandise columns on the cash receipt's side will represent the total receipts, and the total of the Fruit and Sundries columns on the cash disbursement's side, the total disbursements.

FORM 8.

CASH DISBURSEMENTS.

Date.	Name.	Items.	L. F.	Check No.	Fruit. 1	Check No.	Sundries. 2
1914.		Brought forward..	......	....	2,840.58		326.42
June 25	Fruit Statements.......	Car PRR [illegible]........		4007 to 4018	610.38		
26	S. B. Larkin & Co......	Invoice 5/28............				20043	76.80
27	A. B. Dickson..........	Cartage.................				4	3.00
28	Fruit Statements.......	Car L. V. [illegible]........		4019 to 4022	416.30		
29	Eastern Ice Co.........	Icing PRR [illegible].......				5	25.00
30	Buston & Co............	O/c on car T&H [illegible].... Fruit P & L...........				6	5.30
30	Fruit Statements.......	Car PRR [illegible]........		4023 to 4031	326.40		
		Fruit..................			4,193.66		436.52
		Sundries...............			436.52		
					4,630.18		
		Cash balance...........			451.67		
					5,081.85		

1. *Fruit.* Debit Fruit account with the total of this column.
2. *Sundries.* Items appearing in this column are posted in detail to the debit of the respective accounts.

THE ACCOUNT SALES.

Each car lot is usually made up of the combined deliveries of several growers. In order to keep a full and complete record of the distribution of the proceeds among the shippers, the extensions are made on the manifest where a column has been provided for that purpose. The amount received for the shipment less charges, such as brokerage, icing, etc. (except commission), represents the proceeds received by the association. In writing up the account sales, it is desirable to show to the grower the amount received for the shipment and the deduction made by the association for its commission. For convenience in writing them up, therefore, the extensions are made on the above basis instead of on a basis of actual net to be paid the grower.

The account sales (Form 9) are written up in duplicate from the manifests after the extensions have been made. When these are completed, the gross amounts, commission and net amounts are totaled in order to prove the work and to establish the agreement of the total of the net amounts due growers, as shown by the account sales, with the balance due growers appearing on the envelope. Checks are then written for the net amounts shown on the account sales, and these are totaled in order to prove the accuracy of the work. This total is also used for the entry on the cash book as explained under "Cash Disbursements," page 13. The original account sales are mailed out with the checks, and the duplicates are filed in a vertical correspondence file containing a separate folder for each grower. These folders are arranged in alphabetical order.

FORM 9.

ACCOUNT OF SALE.

THE EUREKA PRODUCE EXCHANGE, INC.

AURORA, DEL., *June 25, 1914.*

Sold for account of

T. C. LUNFORD, Frankford, Del.

Frankford Station. Check No. 4007.

Date shipped.	No. packages.	Grade.	Description.	Price.	Amount.
6/8	20	XXXX	Gandys	$2.90	$58.00
			Commission		2.90
			Net proceeds		55.10

LEDGER.

No special ruling is required for the ledger leaves, but the usual stock form is used. The advantages of loose-leaf ledgers over the bound are obvious, and, judging from the manner in which they have superseded the bound books in the business world, it seems hardly necessary to enumerate these advantages here.

It seems fitting, however, to sound a note of warning regarding the misuse of the loose-leaf ledger. Under the loose-leaf system a separate leaf is required for each account. The cost of the leaf is so small that there is no reason why an individual leaf should not be given to each customer, no matter what the size of the account may be. To try to economize by using each side of the sheet for a different account or by placing several accounts on one sheet serves only to defeat in a large measure the advantages to be gained by the use of the loose-leaf ledger.

OPENING THE BOOKS.

In opening the books to be kept by the double-entry method for a newly formed organization, the only asset invested is cash received from stock subscription or membership fees, and there are generally no liabilities. An entry in detail is made in the cash book showing the names of the members and the amounts paid in. The total of these amounts is credited to the Capital Stock account. The balance of the Capital Stock account at all times should represent the par value of shares fully paid up.

If payment for the stock is not made in full, but on the installment plan, it becomes necessary to open two more accounts in the ledger: Stock Subscription and Subscribed Stock. The Stock Subscription account is debited with the amount of subscriptions for capital stock sold on the installment plan and is credited with all amounts received as partial payment on such subscriptions. The debit balance appearing on the account represents the amount due and unpaid on subscriptions for stock sold in this way. In making the first entry, the Stock Subscription account is debited for the amount of stock subscribed to be paid on the installment plan, and the Subscribed Stock account is credited for this amount. The credit balance appearing on this account represents the total amount of stock subscribed but not fully paid for. As fast as the subscriptions are fully paid up, entries are made debiting the Subscribed Stock account and crediting the Capital Stock account.

This information is here inserted merely to show the correct method of recording the sale of stock to be paid for in installments, and not as a plan of financing the organization. This method of procedure and also that of charging the amount of the stock to the growers' accounts to be deducted from the net proceeds obtained for fruit shipped, may work well in some instances, but is usually productive of dissatisfaction on the part of those who have met their obligations faithfully because those who have contributed but a portion of the amount subscribed claim and enjoy full rights and benefits.

All future entries are records of actual transactions, and the proper accounts are opened in the ledger as required.

In changing from a set of single-entry books to a double-entry, or reopening a set of double-entry books preparatory to installing this system, the financial position of the exchange should be determined by making up a statement of assets and liabilities, showing on one side the assets and on the other side the liabilities and capital invested. This statement should be made up in the following form:

ASSETS.

Cash in bank	$1,000.00		
Cash on hand	500.00		
		$1,500.00	
Bills receivable		500.00	
Accounts receivable		500.00	
Merchandise inventory		1,950.00	
Office furniture and fixtures		800.00	
Buildings		5,000.00	
Real estate		2,000.00	

LIABILITIES AND CAPITAL.

Accounts payable			$1,500.00
Bills payable			2,000.00
Capital stock			8,500.00
Balance (profit)			250.00
		12,250.00	12,250.00

The excess of assets over liabilities and capital will be shown in the statement on the credit side under the caption "Surplus." The excess of liabilities and capital over the assets, however, indicates the reverse of the above condition; namely, that a deficit exists. This amount will be shown in the statement on the debit side under the caption "Deficit."[1]

The statement of assets and liabilities is transferred to the journal and forms the opening entry displaying the financial position of the business—that is, the assets, liabilities, and capital.

WHAT ACCOUNTS TO KEEP.

The following accounts are usually needed in an organization of this kind. Further nominal accounts may be found necessary and can be opened as desired, but in the main the list here given will be found sufficiently comprehensive to cover all needs.

Capital stock.—The credit balance appearing on this account measures the amount of stock fully paid up, for which certificates of stock are issued and outstanding.

Land.—The debit balance appearing on this account measures the cost of the land owned by the organization.

Building.—The debit balance appearing on this account measures the cost of the building. If the organization owns more than one building, it will be found preferable to carry a separate account with each building.

Office equipment—The debit balance on this account measures the cost of all office furniture and equipment on hand. This includes all the heavier articles, but does not include the smaller, such as ink wells, pencils, daters, etc., which have to be renewed frequently. These should be charged to expense direct, under the distribution of office supplies.

Fixtures.—The debit balance on this account measures the cost of warehouse and platform fixtures on hand, such as shelving, counter scales, and trucks.

Cash.—Many bookkeepers do not carry a cash account in the ledger, but in taking a trial balance refer back to the cash book for the balance of cash on hand. Others transfer the balance as per cash book to the cash account in the ledger, ruling this account off arbitrarily at the end of the month. It is often desirable to show at a glance the total receipts and total disbursements for each month in order to make comparisons. The cash account in the ledger is there-

[1] Deficit is not an asset and should it be necessary to display this fact on a statement for distribution among the members, this item either should be shown in red ink on the credit side of the statement in the same position as Surplus, or it should be deducted from Capital Stock in order to show the impairment of capital. It would be shown in the above statement on the asset side, as this statement is the basis of the opening entry made in the journal.

fore debited with the balance as shown by the cash book when the account is being started, is debited with the total receipts at the end of the month, and is credited with the total disbursements. The balance of the account will therefore agree with the balance as shown by the cash book at the end of the month.

Bills receivable.—The debit balance on this account represents the face value of the notes received from others.

Bills payable.—The credit balance on this account represents the total of notes due to others.

Accounts receivable.—As explained in "Memorandum Records" (p. 2), no accounts receivable are carried on the ledger with the parties to whom the shipments of fruit are made. The car envelopes, like other financial records of the business, should be guarded carefully against loss by theft or fire and should be placed in the vault or safe at night, at least until returns for the shipments have been made to the growers, after which time they can be filed in document files.

It sometimes happens that a number of cars of fruit will be stored with a wholesaler, to be sold as needed by the trade at prevailing market prices. Payments for sales made in this manner are usually made on the basis of the lots of fruit sold instead of individual cars, in which case it might be found advisable to open an account on the ledger in the name of the wholesaler and to charge up the invoices covering the shipments. This is done by journal entry, debiting the customer's account and crediting the Fruit account. The part payments are then credited to the customer's account as they are received.

In the smaller exchanges growers' supplies are sold in but limited quantities, and usually on a basis of thirty days' credit. Ledger accounts, therefore, need be kept only with the growers purchasing supplies on credit.

Information as to credits to a particular grower for fruit sold for him can be taken from the account sales filed in the folder under his name, as described under the heading "The Account Sales," page 14. The copies of the account sales also show the number of the check sent to the grower in case it is desired to trace the payment further. As a rule, there will be but few instances where it will be found necessary to deduct a debit balance appearing on a grower's account from the account sales to be rendered to him. Should this be necessary, a journal entry is passed, charging fruit and crediting the grower's account for the amount, which is then subtracted from the account sales and a check written for the balance.

Accounts payable.—Individual accounts should be kept with creditors, the credit balance appearing on the account measuring the amount due each creditor.

Inventory.—The debit balance appearing on this account measures the cost of goods on hand at the beginning of the fiscal year.

Merchandise.—The Merchandise account is divided into two accounts: Merchandise Purchases and Merchandise Sales.

Merchandise purchases.—This account is debited with the cost of the merchandise and freight on the same. It is credited with the cost of goods returned by the organization. The debit balance appearing on this account represents the cost of merchandise purchased.

Merchandise sales.—This account is credited with the total sales and is debited with the total amount of goods returned by customers. The credit balance of the account measures the total net sales.

Trading account.—This account is a subdivision of the profit and loss account and is used only when the books are being closed. It shows how the gross profit on sales is arrived at. The use of this account is more fully explained under the heading "Closing the Books" (page 20).

Fruit.—An account is opened under the captions of "Fruit" or "Produce," according to the product handled. This account is credited with the remittances received for the shipments and charged with the gross amounts paid to the growers—that is, the net plus commission. The two sides of this account should balance at the end of the season, showing that full returns have been made to the growers.

Fruit profit and loss.—An account under the caption "Fruit Profit and Loss," or "Produce Profit and Loss" is carried only when a portion of the products are bought outright from the growers instead of all being handled on a strictly commission basis. This is explained in detail under the description of the journal (page 10). This account measures the profit made or loss sustained on products bought from the growers.

Commission.—The credit balance appearing on this account will be the amount of the commission earned.

Expense.[1]—To this account are debited all disbursements on account of expense. The account can be further subdivided into salaries, rent, insurance, etc., but in a small business it is perhaps just as practical to have the one expense account showing the distribution of the various items in the explanation column on the ledger. At the end of the year, the account is analyzed and a statement made up showing the distribution of the items under various subheadings. If a large amount of office supplies and stamps is carried over at the end of the year, it should be taken into consideration in order to arrive at the true profit or loss.

[1] A method for segregating expense items by means of an expense distribution book is explained in U. S. Department of Agriculture Bulletin No. 178—"Cooperative Organization Business Methods." This will be found a much shorter and preferable method for the larger organizations than the one here given.

Interest and discount.—This account is debited with interest paid on notes payable and credited with interest received on notes receivable. It is debited with cash discounts allowed and credited with cash discounts received.

Reserve for depreciation.—Provision for setting up a reserve for depreciation on buildings, office equipment, and fixtures is made by charging the Profit and Loss account and crediting the proper reserve accounts under the caption of "Reserve for Depreciation of Buildings," etc. This is more fully explained in U. S. Department of Agriculture Bulletin No. 178, "Cooperative Organization Business Methods."

Reserve for bad debts.—At the close of the year, a certain amount is set aside out of the profits to cover the estimated loss on bad accounts. The balances of the accounts found to be uncollectible are then charged to this account. The credit balance on this account measures the available amount reserved from profits to offset losses from bad accounts and should not be shown on the balance sheet on the credit side as a liability but should appear on the asset side as a deduction from the total amount due from customers.

Profit and loss.—This account is debited at the close of the year with the balance of all expense accounts and other nominal accounts—that is, accounts containing profit and loss elements—showing a debit balance. It is credited with the gross profit from the trading account and with the balances of any nominal accounts showing credit balances. The credit balance resulting on this account represents the net profit from operations during the year and should be transferred to the Surplus account. If a debit balance results, it is a deficit and should be charged against the balance appearing on the Surplus account. If no surplus has been created, the deficit should be charged to Deficit account.

Surplus.—This account is credited at the close of the year with the net profit as shown by the Profit and Loss account. It is debited with the amount of dividend declared, at which time the Dividend account is credited. The credit balance of the account then represents the undivided profits.

Dividend.—This account is credited when dividends are declared by the board of directors and the Surplus account is debited. The account is then debited with the total of the dividend paid.

CLOSING THE BOOKS.

An inventory of merchandise on hand is made at the end of the year. This is a schedule or list of the goods on hand, with values extended at cost prices. After all extensions have been made, these are totaled. The extensions and additions should then be verified so as to establish the accuracy of the work. If a Merchandise account has been kept, the amount of the inventory is carried into the accounts by the following entry:

Inventory.......... $1,000.00
To Merchandise.......... $1,000.00

The balance then appearing on the Merchandise account—that is, the total of sales and inventory at the end of the year, less the total of purchases and inventory at the beginning of the year—represents the gross profit on merchandise, or if there is a debit balance on the account, it represents the gross loss on merchandise. If a profit has been made on the Merchandise account, the balance is transferred to the Profit and Loss account by a journal entry as follows:

Merchandise............ $500.00
To Profit and Loss......... $500.00

If a loss was sustained the entry is:

Profit and Loss......... $500.00
To Merchandise............ $500.00

After the entry is made which carries the balance on the Merchandise account to the Profit and Loss account, the Merchandise account will appear as follows:

MERCHANDISE ACCOUNT.

Purchases	$5,500.00	Sales	$5,000.00
Profit and Loss	500.00	Inventory	1,000.00
	6,000.00		6,000.00

After the books are closed, another journal entry is made charging the Merchandise account for the next year with the amount of the inventory and crediting that account.

The above method is given for the reason that in some organizations the amount of merchandise handled is so small that, in the opinion of the bookkeepers operating the books, the additional work entailed in separating merchandise purchases and sales would hardly be warranted.

Instead of keeping a Merchandise account it would be much better to keep two accounts: Merchandise Purchases and Merchandise Sales. The amount of the inventory is allowed to stand in the Inventory account throughout the year and another account—the Trading Account—is raised at the time of closing the books. By the use of these accounts, the Inventory account would show the amount of goods on hand at the beginning of the fiscal year; the Purchases account, the cost of goods purchased; and the Sales account, the sales for the year.

In closing the books, the Inventory account would be credited and the Trading Account debited for the amount of the inventory carried over from the previous period; the Purchases account credited and the Trading Account debited for the total purchases; the Sales account debited and the Trading Account credited for total sales.

To bring the new inventory into the accounts the Inventory account is debited and the Trading Account credited for goods on hand at the close of the period. A credit balance appearing on the Trading Account would then measure the gross profit from merchandise and a debit balance would measure the gross loss. This balance is transferred to the Profit and Loss account by a journal entry. When these entries have been made, the Trading Account will appear as follows:

TRADING ACCOUNT.

Inventory as at beginning of year	$3,000.00	Sales	$15,000.00
Purchases	13,000.00	Inventory as at close of year	2,000.00
Profit and Loss	1,000.00		
	17,000.00		17,000.00

While apparently there is little difference between the Trading Account and the Merchandise account as previously shown, it will be understood that the purchases and sales are shown in the copy of the Merchandise account in total for illustrative purposes only, and they do not appear in this form in actual operation. The Trading Account, however, shows in total the component elements which make up the gross profit on sales, so that it can be viewed as a whole.

To close the nominal accounts, that is, the accounts containing profit and loss elements, into the Profit and Loss account, two journal entries are made: The first for all expense accounts and other nominal accounts showing debit balances, and the second for all nominal accounts showing credit balances. The first of the entries is as follows:

Profit and Loss	$4,300.00	
To Expense		$4,000.00
Interest		200.00
Reserve for depreciation of building		100.00

The second entry is as follows:

Fruit Profit and Loss.	$300.00	
Commission	5,000.00	
To Profit and Loss		$5,300.00

When all entries are posted to the Profit and Loss account this account will appear as follows:

PROFIT AND LOSS ACCOUNT.

Expense	$4,000.00	Fruit Profit and Loss	$300.00
Interest	200.00	Commission	5,000.00
Reserve for depreciation of building	100.00		
Balance, net profit	1,000.00		
	5,300.00		5,300.00
		Balance	1,000.00

The balance of $1,000 is then credited to the Surplus account. All closing entries should be made through the journal and not arbitrarily on the face of the ledger. It will be found advisable to list all items of profit and loss on the Profit and Loss account instead of showing these in total according to the journal entry. This will preclude the necessity of turning back to the journal each time it is desired to know the details of the items appearing in the Profit and Loss account.

After all closing entries have been made, a post-closing trial balance should be taken to test the accuracy of the work. This schedule will be found valuable in preparing the balance sheet. A full explanation of the preparation of the annual statement will be found in U. S. Department of Agriculture Bulletin No. 178, "Cooperative Organization Business Methods."

SECOND METHOD.

It will be seen that the method first given does not provide for any growers' accounts except for the sale of supplies. The second method contemplates the opening of ledger accounts for all growers. These present a complete record of the transactions with each individual grower. This method should be used in organizations where the supply business has been fully developed, and charges should be made at frequent intervals throughout the year to the growers' accounts.

After the remittance covering the shipment has been received and credited on the cash book and it is desired to make payment to the growers, the distribution of the proceeds is made on the manifest as in the previous method shown. The account sales are written up, and a journal entry is made as follows:

Fruit	$600.00	
To growers		$536.75
commission		28.25
broker		10.00
icing		25.00

If each car is made up of the combined shipments of but two or three growers, the name of each grower should be shown in the above entry with the amount of the credit opposite. If, however, the cars are made up of the shipments of many growers, the total credited to the growers' accounts should be shown in the journal entry, and the posting of the individual items should be made from the account sales to the ledger accounts. Should it be necessary to look up the details of this entry, the car number will give the reference to the information desired. Duplicate copies of the account sales are filed in folders under the growers' names, as explained under the first method.

CASH DISBURSEMENTS.

Another form of cash disbursements sheet (Form 8a) is here given, showing the ruling when but one set of checks is used. This form can be used as a check register, all checks being entered direct thereon without first being written up in the stub check book. The checks are numbered and put up in pads instead of in the usual stub check-book form, and, as the numbers follow consecutively on the register, each numbered check must be accounted for.

FORM 8A.

CASH DISBURSEMENTS.

Date.	Name.	Items.	Check No.	Amount of check.	L. F.	Growers' accounts.	Sundries.
		Amount brought forward.	....	3,540.22	......	3,200.22	340.00
1914. June 25	T. C. Lunford..........	Fr. Sta't. PRR [illegible]	4,007	58.00			
	W. H. Hinckley........	" "	8	60.00			
	B. D. Milton...........	" "	9	43.62			
	J. A. Barnett..........	" "	10	243.80		405.42	
26	A. L. Thomas..........	Expense—Cartage.......	11	3.10			3.10
27	Marion Seed Co.........	On Account............	12	100.00			100.00
30	N. K. Nelson...........	Frt. Sta't. LV [illegible]	13	36.80			
	A. L. Watson..........	" "	14	1.50			
	Mrs. B. Oliver..........	" "	15	10.62			
	J. P. Foss..............	" "	16	3.56			
	Arthur Burton.........	" "	17	80.90		133.38	
	Pay Roll...............	for month—Salaries.....	18 to 21	375.00			375.00
				4,557.12	......	3,739.02	818.10
		Cash balance...........	....	342.00			
				4,899.12			

EXPRESS SHIPMENTS.

Small shipments by express, consisting of goods sent out on consignment, are handled in the same manner as carload shipments, but a separate file is provided for filing the envelopes. Instead of using a different form of envelope for the consignments, the regular form of car envelopes can be used and the words "express consignment" stamped on the face of the envelope so that the two files may be distinguished easily.

TRIAL BALANCE.

A trial balance should be taken off the books monthly. This tests the correctness of the postings and demonstrates the agreement of the two sides of the ledger. It also gives the manager and the board of directors a view of the balances appearing on the ledger accounts, which information will be found very valuable in the conduct of the business. To obtain the same information from the ledger without the aid of such a schedule, the manager would be obliged to page through the ledger, and this method would not afford the comparisons with previous months that the monthly trial balances would furnish. A further discussion of this subject and the necessity therefor will be found in U. S. Department of Agriculture Bulletin No. 178, "Cooperative Organization Business Methods."

BINDERS.

Of the three forms—journal, cash receipts, and cash disbursements—that of the journal is the largest, measuring 16 (binding side) by 14 inches. The other two forms measure 16 by 13 inches and 16 by 13¼ inches, respectively. All of these forms therefore fit in a 16 by 14 inch stock form of binder. There are many different makes of sectional post binders on the market, both end and top locking, the price of these ranging from $3 to $9, according to the binding. Sectional post transfer binders in full canvas without the lock but with knurled nuts to fasten the binder cost from $2 to $4. These binders are made with three-eighths inch, also five-sixteenths inch posts, which are 11⅝ inches from center to center.

CONCLUSION.

Cooperative organizations desiring to install this system can procure printers' copies of the accounting forms upon request to the Chief of the Office of Markets and Rural Organization. The office will be glad to give whatever information is desired for the installation and operation of the system. In fact, it is desired to make this branch of the work as specifically helpful as possible in solving the many accounting problems of cooperative and farmers' organizations marketing agricultural products, and to aid in introducing the most modern methods of accounting, auditing, financing, and business practices. In this way it is hoped that help will be given to these organizations which will bring them to their highest efficiency in the marketing and distribution of farm products.

All correspondence should be addressed to the Chief, Office of Markets and Rural Organization, U. S. Department of Agriculture.

ADDITIONAL COPIES
OF THIS PUBLICATION MAY BE PROCURED FROM
THE SUPERINTENDENT OF DOCUMENTS
GOVERNMENT PRINTING OFFICE
WASHINGTON, D. C.
AT
5 CENTS PER COPY
▽

Lightning Source UK Ltd.
Milton Keynes UK
UKHW041335130219
336936UK00022B/199/P

9 780266 979845